THE USAGI YOJIMBO SAGA

D1501294

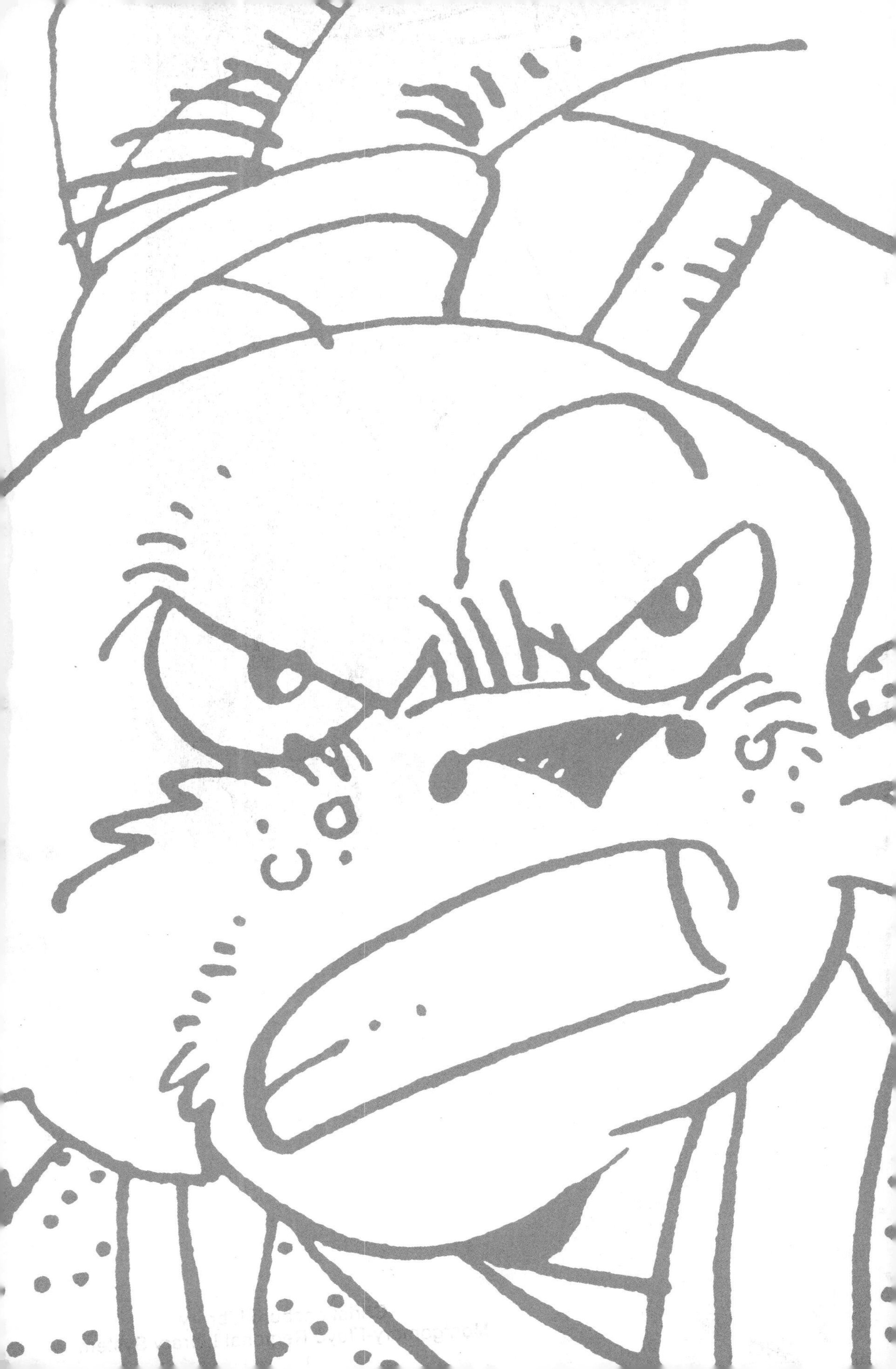

THE USAGI YOJIMBO™ SAGA

BOOK 2

Created, written,
and illustrated by

STAN SAKAI

"Return to Adachi Plain" inked by
SERGIO ARAGONÉS

"Green Persimmon" colored by
TOM LUTH

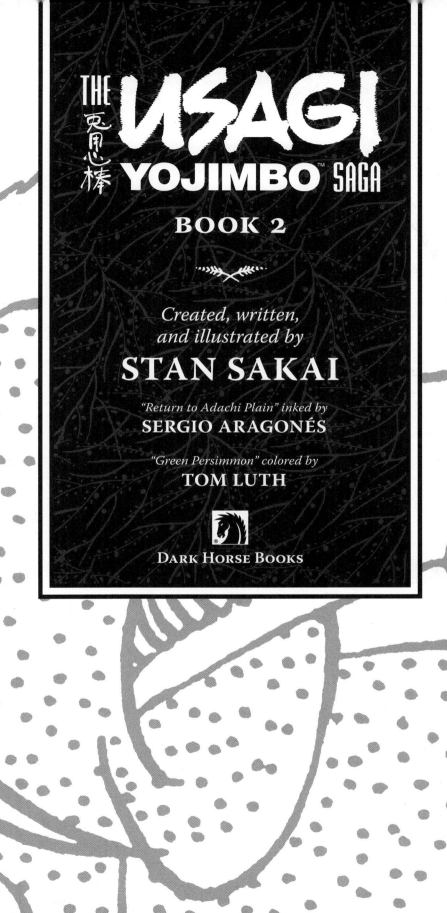

DARK HORSE BOOKS

Publisher
MIKE RICHARDSON

Series Editors
JAMIE S. RICH
and **DIANA SCHUTZ**

Collection Editor
BRENDAN WRIGHT

Assistant Editor
IAN TUCKER

Design and Digital Production
CARY GRAZZINI

THE USAGI YOJIMBO™ SAGA Book 2

This volume collects issues #7–#30 of the Dark Horse comic book series *Usagi Yojimbo Volume Three* and the Dark Horse comic book *Usagi Yojimbo Color Special* #4, along with stories from *The Art of Usagi Yojimbo* #1, published by Radio Comix, and the limited hardcover edition of *Usagi Yojimbo* Book 7: *Gen's Story*, published by Fantagraphics.

Visit the Usagi Yojimbo Dojo website:
UsagiYojimbo.com

Published by Dark Horse Books
A division of Dark Horse Comics LLC
10956 SE Main Street
Milwaukie, OR 97222
DarkHorse.com

To find a comics shop in your area, visit comicshoplocator.com
International Licensing: (503) 905-2377

Library of Congress Cataloging-in-Publication Data

Sakai, Stan, author, illustrator.
 [Graphic novels. Selections.]
 The Usagi Yojimbo saga. Book 2 / created, written, and illustrated by Stan Sakai ; Green Persimmon colors by Tom Luth. -- Limited hardcover edition.
     pages cm
 Summary: "The rabbit ronin has his first encounters with the Lord of Owls and Inspector Ishida, and in the series' longest story to date, nearly the entire cast becomes caught up in a scheme to recover the legendary Grass Cutting Sword"-- Provided by publisher.
 ISBN 978-1-61655-610-5 (pbk.) -- ISBN 978-1-61655-672-3 (limited hardcover edition)
 1. Graphic novels. [1. Graphic novels. 2. Samurai--Fiction.] I. Title.

 PZ7.7.S138Usd 2015
 741.5'973--dc23

                    2014022138

First edition: February 2015
ISBN 978-1-61655-610-5

Limited edition: February 2015
ISBN 978-1-61655-672-3

10 9 8 7 6 5 4

PRINTED IN CHINA

This one is for
Darryl and Doreen Komo,
with much aloha.

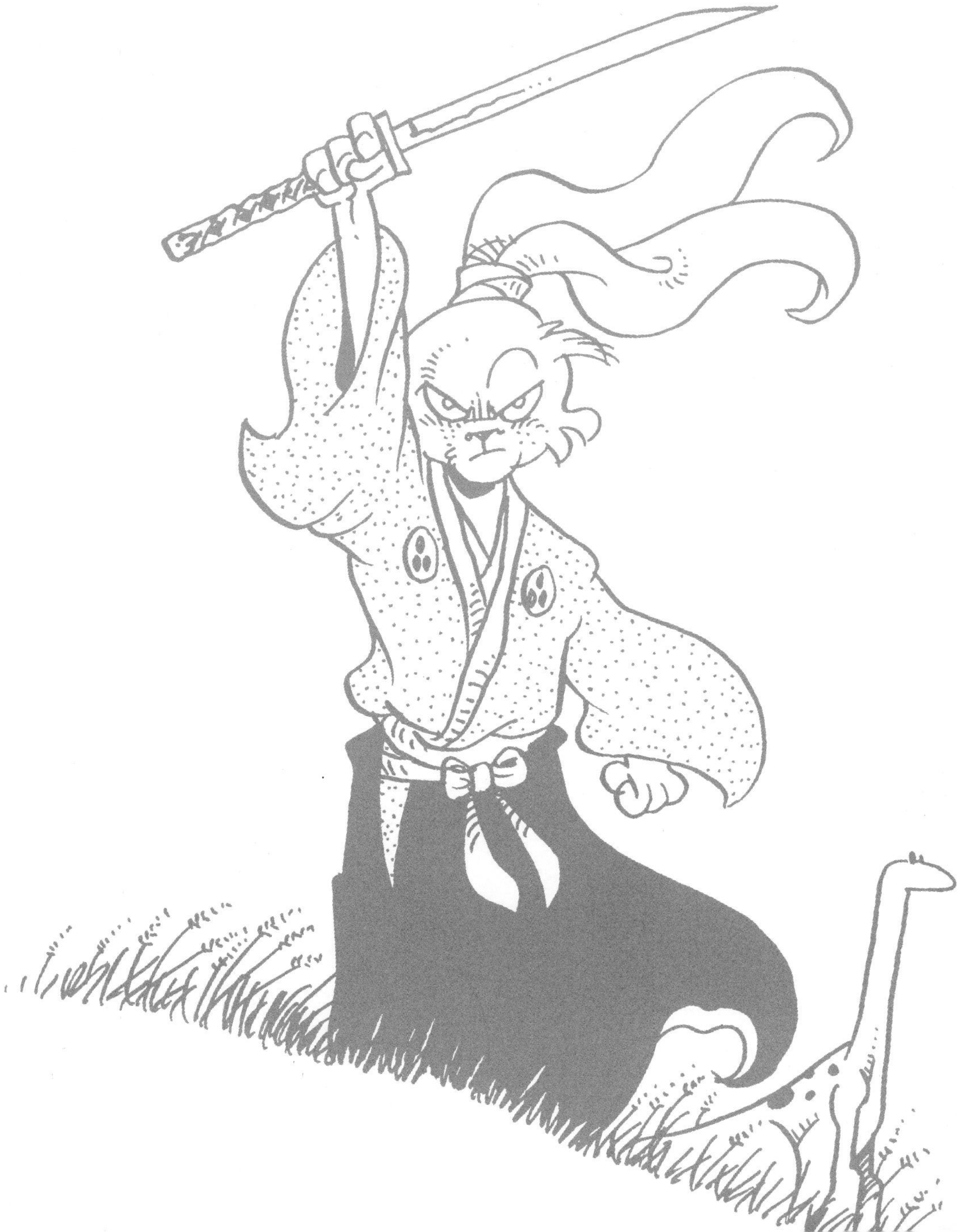

SEASONS

GRASSCUTTER

$\cdots \!\!\!\gg\!\!\!\!\times\!\!\!\!\ll\!\!\!\cdots$

GREY SHADOWS

After the death of Lord Mifune in the battle of Adachi Plain, retainer **MIYAMOTO USAGI** chose the warrior's pilgrimage, becoming a wandering *ronin* in search of peace. Practicing the warrior code of *bushido*, Usagi avoids conflict whenever possible, but when called upon, his bravery and fighting prowess are unsurpassed.

Trained in her father's Falling Rain school of swordsmanship, **TOMOE AME** serves as personal bodyguard and chief adviser to the young Lord Noriyuki of the Geishu clan. Tomoe is perhaps Usagi's equal as a fighter, with their duels to date ending in ties.

A descendant of samurai nobility, **MURAKAMI "GEN" GENNOSUKE** fell into poverty while his family pursued a vendetta and, vowing never to be poor again, turned to bounty hunting. Gen never fails to stick Usagi with the check for a meal or an inn and swears to be concerned only for himself, but his soft side sometimes briefly emerges.

Facing an arranged marriage, **INAZUMA** instead eloped with her beloved, Hisashi. When Hisashi was murdered over a gambling debt, Inazuma took revenge against his killer, an employee of Boss Bakuchi. With a bounty placed on her head by Bakuchi, she runs a floating dice game to make ends meet.

Upon the death of her brother Shingen, **KASHIRA CHIZU** became leader of the Neko ninja, a clan serving the dark lord Hikiji but often pursuing its own agendas. Though Chizu is a skilled leader, several clan members resent being commanded by a woman and seek to remove her.

If a samurai's weapon is his soul, all one needs to know about **JEI** is that his blade is solid black. Despite claiming to be an emissary of the gods sent to wipe out evil on earth, Jei appears indiscriminate in his killing and has specifically targeted Usagi for death.

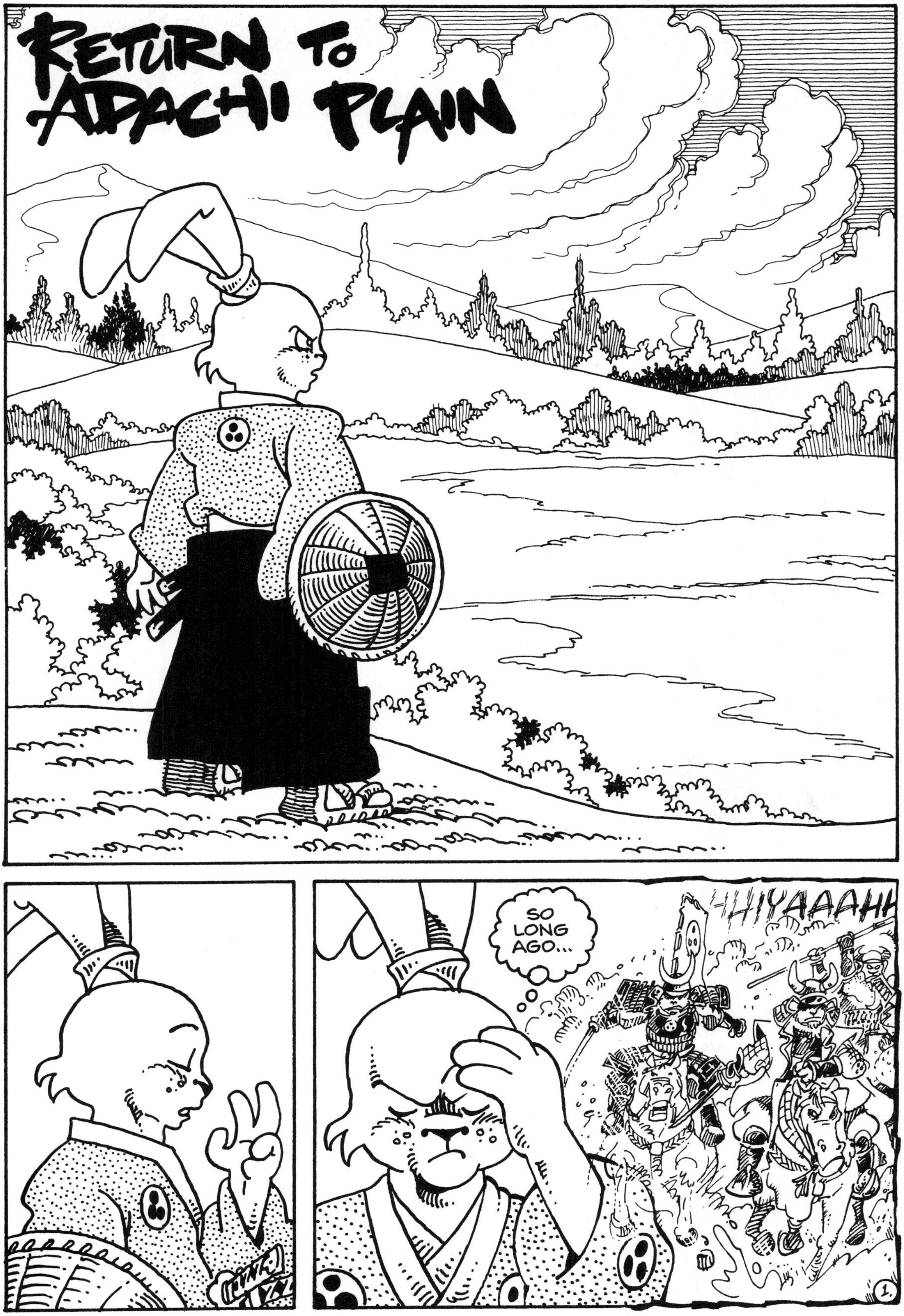
RETURN TO ADACHI PLAIN
SO LONG AGO...
HIYAAAHH

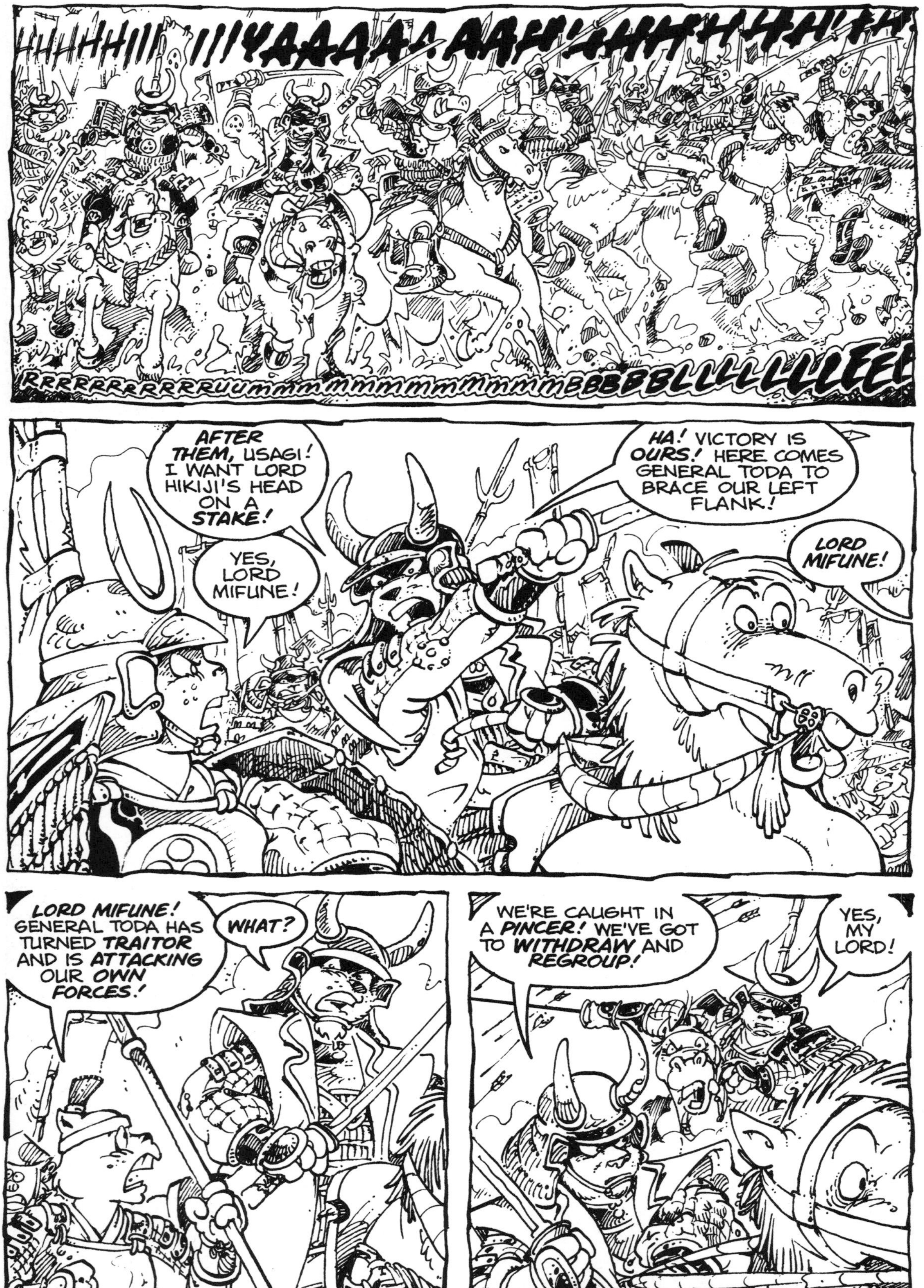
AFTER THEM, USAGI! I WANT LORD HIKIJI'S HEAD ON A STAKE!
YES, LORD MIFUNE!
HA! VICTORY IS OURS! HERE COMES GENERAL TODA TO BRACE OUR LEFT FLANK!
LORD MIFUNE!
LORD MIFUNE! GENERAL TODA HAS TURNED TRAITOR AND IS ATTACKING OUR OWN FORCES!
WHAT?
WE'RE CAUGHT IN A PINCER! WE'VE GOT TO WITHDRAW AND REGROUP!
YES, MY LORD!

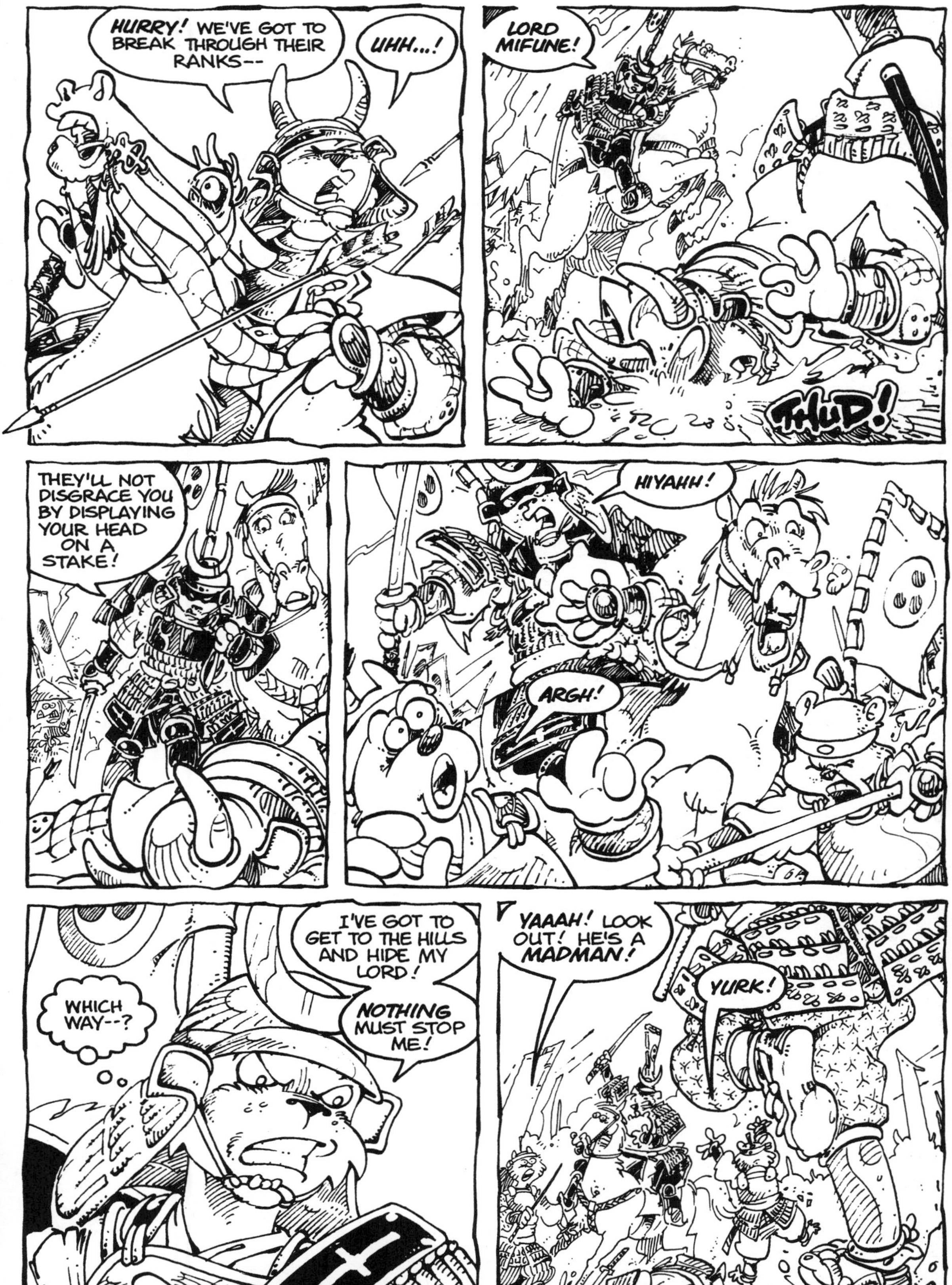
HURRY! WE'VE GOT TO BREAK THROUGH THEIR RANKS--
UHH...!
LORD MIFUNE!
THUD!
THEY'LL NOT DISGRACE YOU BY DISPLAYING YOUR HEAD ON A STAKE!
HIYAHH!
ARGH!
WHICH WAY--?
I'VE GOT TO GET TO THE HILLS AND HIDE MY LORD!
NOTHING MUST STOP ME!
YAAAH! LOOK OUT! HE'S A MADMAN!
YURK!

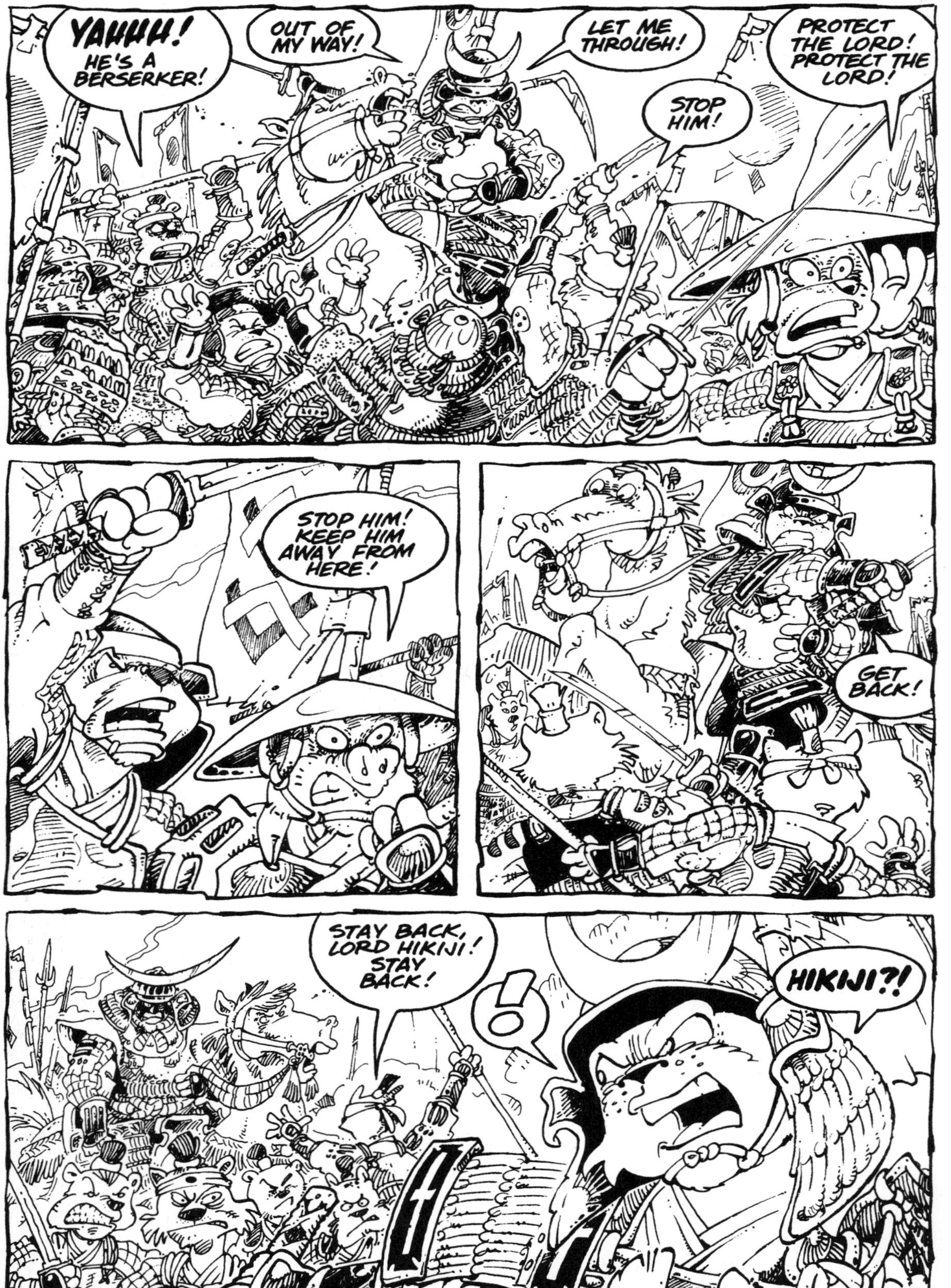
YAHHH! HE'S A BERSERKER!
OUT OF MY WAY!
LET ME THROUGH!
STOP HIM!
PROTECT THE LORD! PROTECT THE LORD!
STOP HIM! KEEP HIM AWAY FROM HERE!
GET BACK!
STAY BACK, LORD HIKIJI! STAY BACK!
!
HIKIJI?!
4.

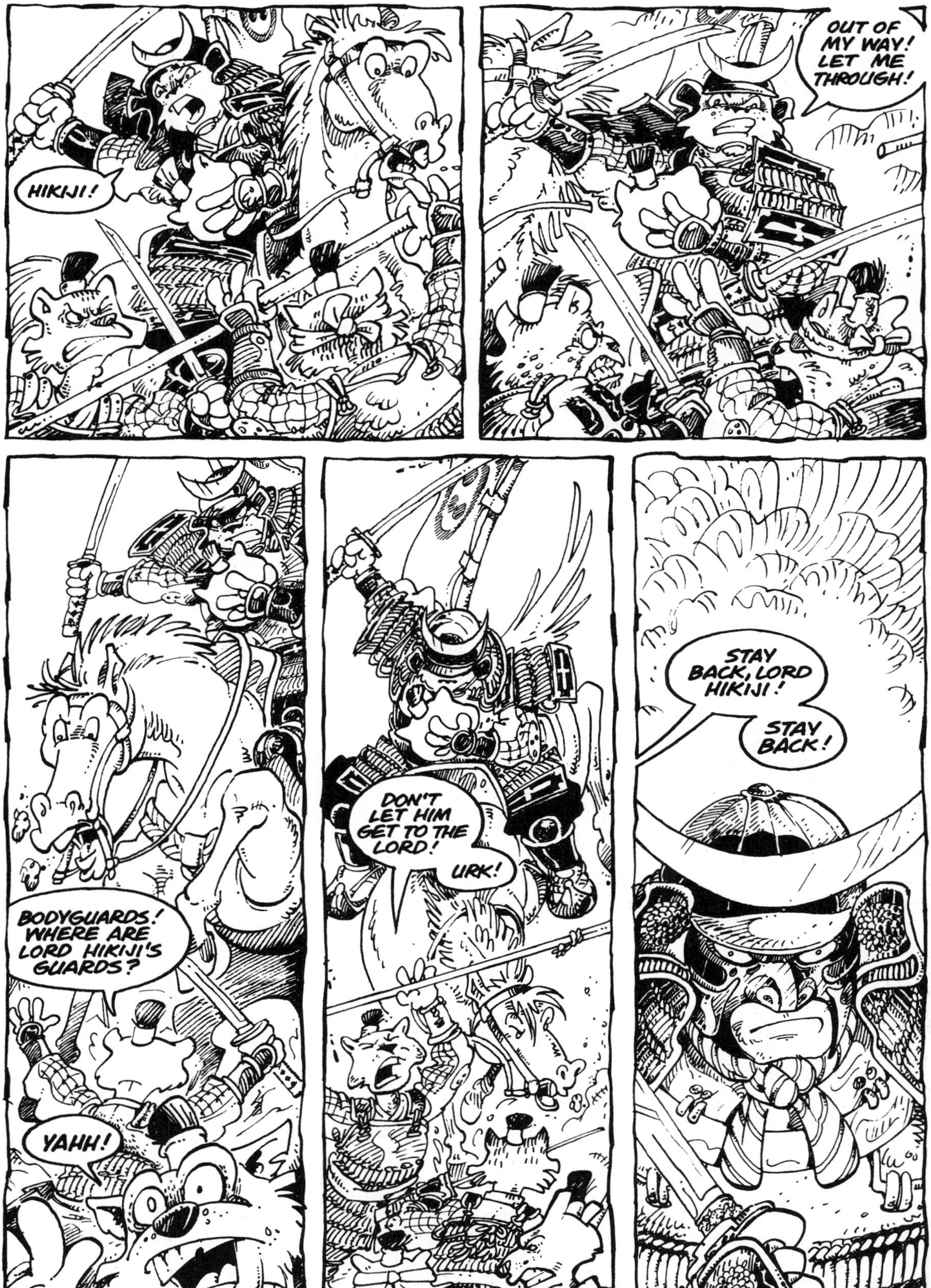
HIKIJI!
OUT OF MY WAY! LET ME THROUGH!
BODYGUARDS! WHERE ARE LORD HIKIJI'S GUARDS?
YAHH!
DON'T LET HIM GET TO THE LORD!
URK!
STAY BACK, LORD HIKIJI!
STAY BACK!

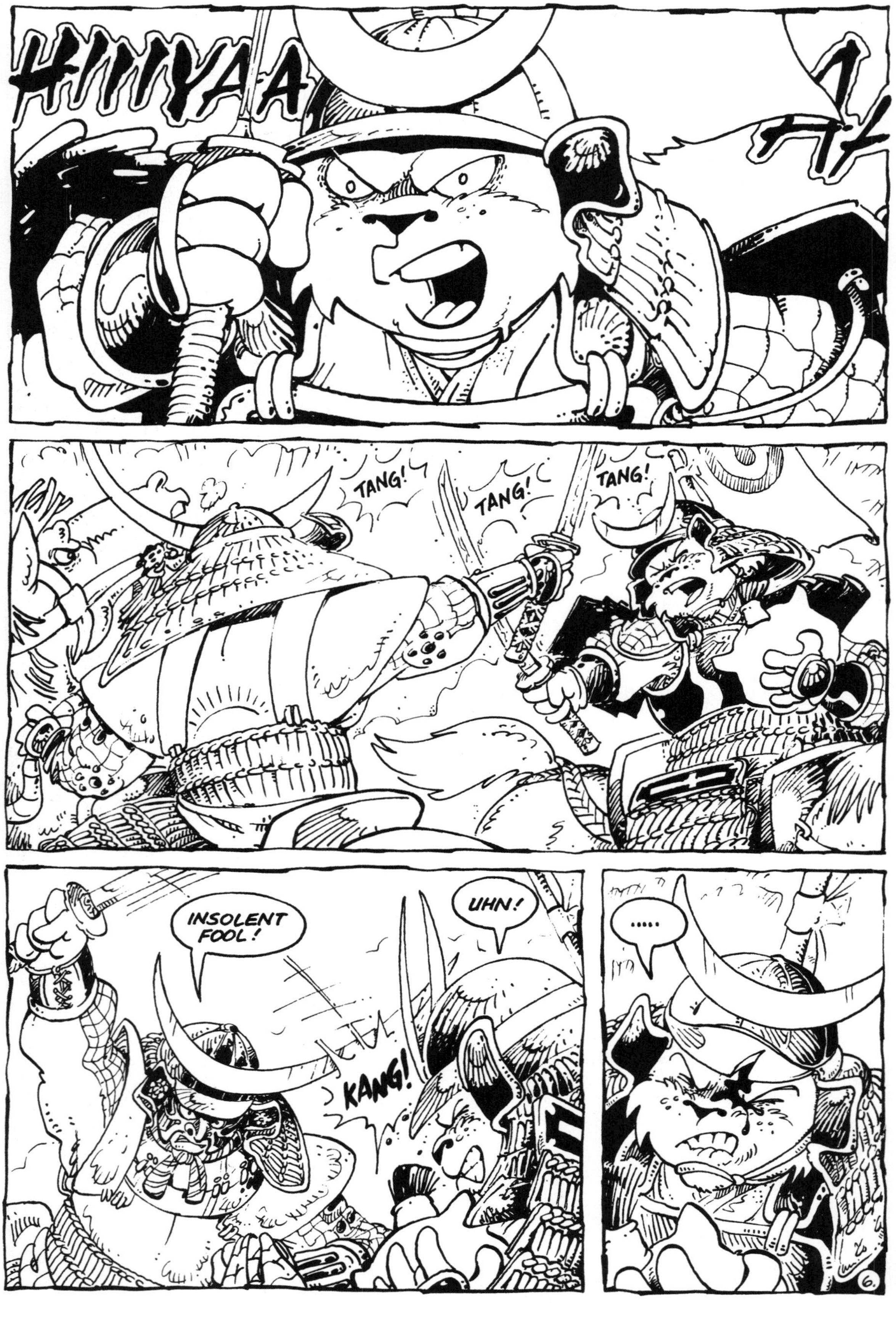
HIIYAAA
TANG!
TANG!
TANG!
INSOLENT FOOL!
UHN!
KANG!
......

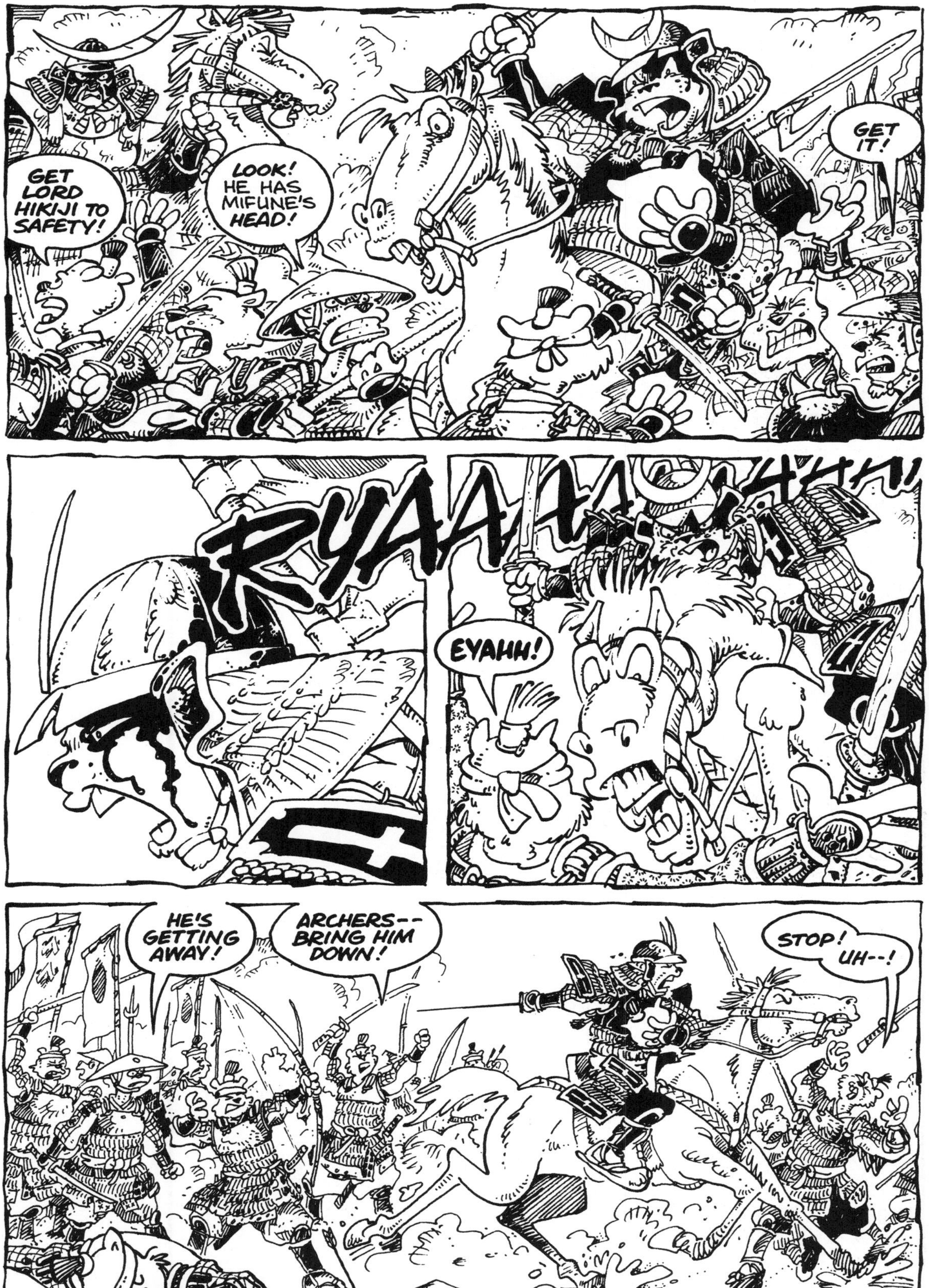
GET LORD HIKIJI TO SAFETY!
LOOK! HE HAS MIFUNE'S HEAD!
GET IT!
RYAAAAAAAAHH!
EYAHH!
HE'S GETTING AWAY!
ARCHERS-- BRING HIM DOWN!
STOP! UH--!
7.

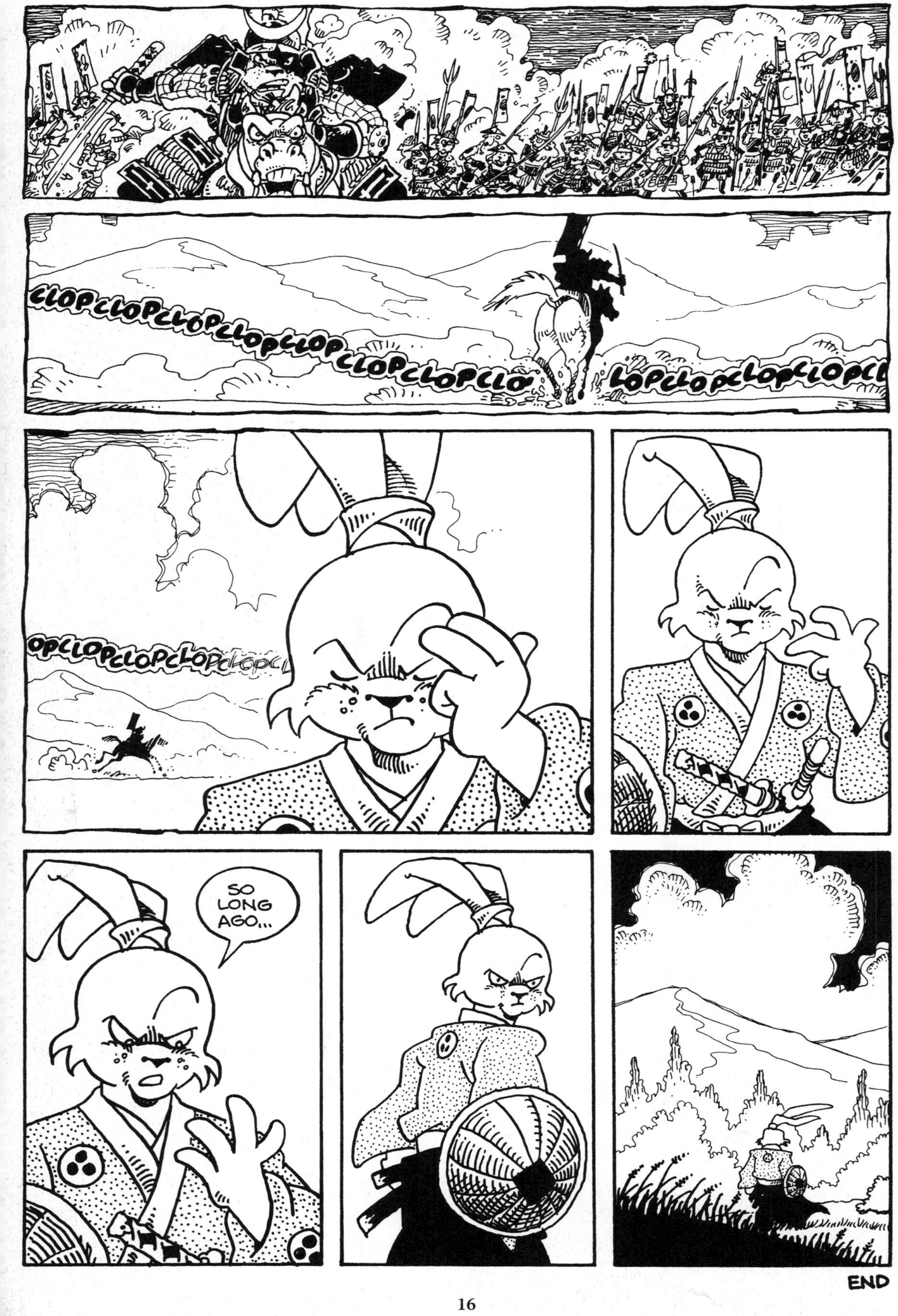
CLOPCLOPCLOPCLOPCLOPCLOPCLOPCLOPCLO
LOPCLOPCLOPCLOPCL
OPCLOPCLOPCLOPCLOPCLOPCL
SO LONG AGO...

END

SEASONS

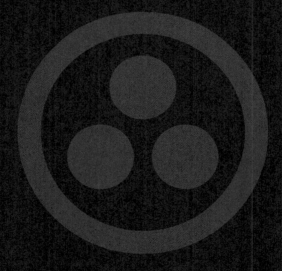

IF YOU MET STAN SAKAI before seeing his work, you would never guess that this soft-spoken, congenial man lived a good part of his life in the world of the samurai. I've met Stan a number of times at different functions over the years and always enjoyed his and his wife Sharon's company. I knew he was a cartoonist, of course—but I'd never really looked into his work, until now. Wow.

Always in a hurry, I often pick up a book of illustrations, leaf through it, and put it down, thinking that I'll come back to it for a more thorough look when I have time. When at long last I opened up a book by Stan Sakai, I made time on the spot and read it from cover to cover. Thanks to his generosity, I have since read more!

Not only are his stories engaging, action packed, and well crafted, but his drawing is so superb that it is something most of us can only aspire to. If I had to describe his style of drawing, I'd say it was somewhere between Bill Watterson and Will Eisner—which is a pretty fine place to be! Still, Stan's work is uniquely his own, which tells me that his skill for life drawing and draftsmanship comes from somewhere within.

Miyamoto Usagi, the wandering samurai, is Stan's other self. The characters Usagi encounters on his travels are also alive and complete. In a cartoonist's mind, people, places, and situations exist in a sort of dreamlike reality into which we are easily pulled whenever we wish to go there. We can hear their voices, see through their eyes, and go with them—guided partly by them and partly by our own forces through situations and storylines that almost write themselves.

Because the colorful life of Usagi, the rabbit samurai, is so much a part of Stan Sakai's life, it was a surprise for me to learn that Stan's knowledge of Japan and its history was through family and private research only. It was my great fortune to be invited with Stan and Sharon to visit Tokyo on a cultural exchange and to experience with them for the first time the beautiful and powerful culture that is Japan.

Buildings and passageways and hillsides and temples that Stan had drawn from photographs and from the magic of his imagination were there for us to see and to touch. I was impressed by his knowledge of the language and by Stan and Sharon's very deep spiritual connection to everything around us.

It was a privilege to hear them talk about their families, foods, and traditions. We were there with them in the land of Miyamoto Usagi—and I wondered how this adventure would influence Stan's future storylines!

Since then, I've seen his work a little differently, too. I've looked at the buildings and the scenery and the costumes he draws with even more respect—knowing the research that has gone into them. I know that his stories would be considered some of the best of Japanese manga and that he would be one of the most recognizable creative talents in Japan, had he begun his career there.

Stan Sakai is a genuinely modest man. He writes and draws for the love of his craft, and it shows. It has been my great pleasure to write this introduction because it has given me the opportunity to say congratulations, Stan. I admire you. I enjoy your work. Most of all, I have learned from it, and that, I think, is the best compliment one cartoonist can give to another.

Sincerely,
LYNN JOHNSTON, 1998

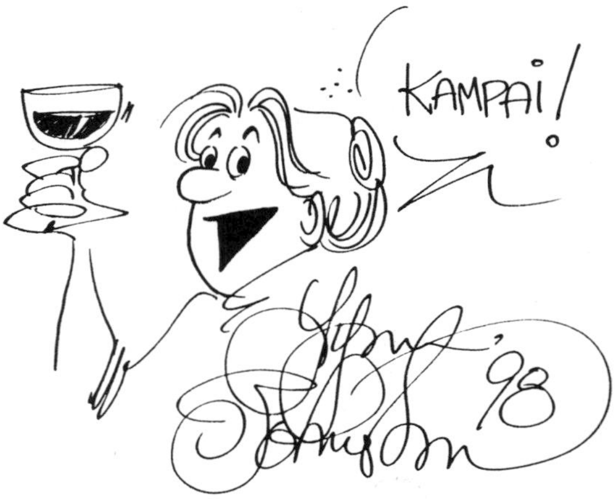
KAMPAI!
'98

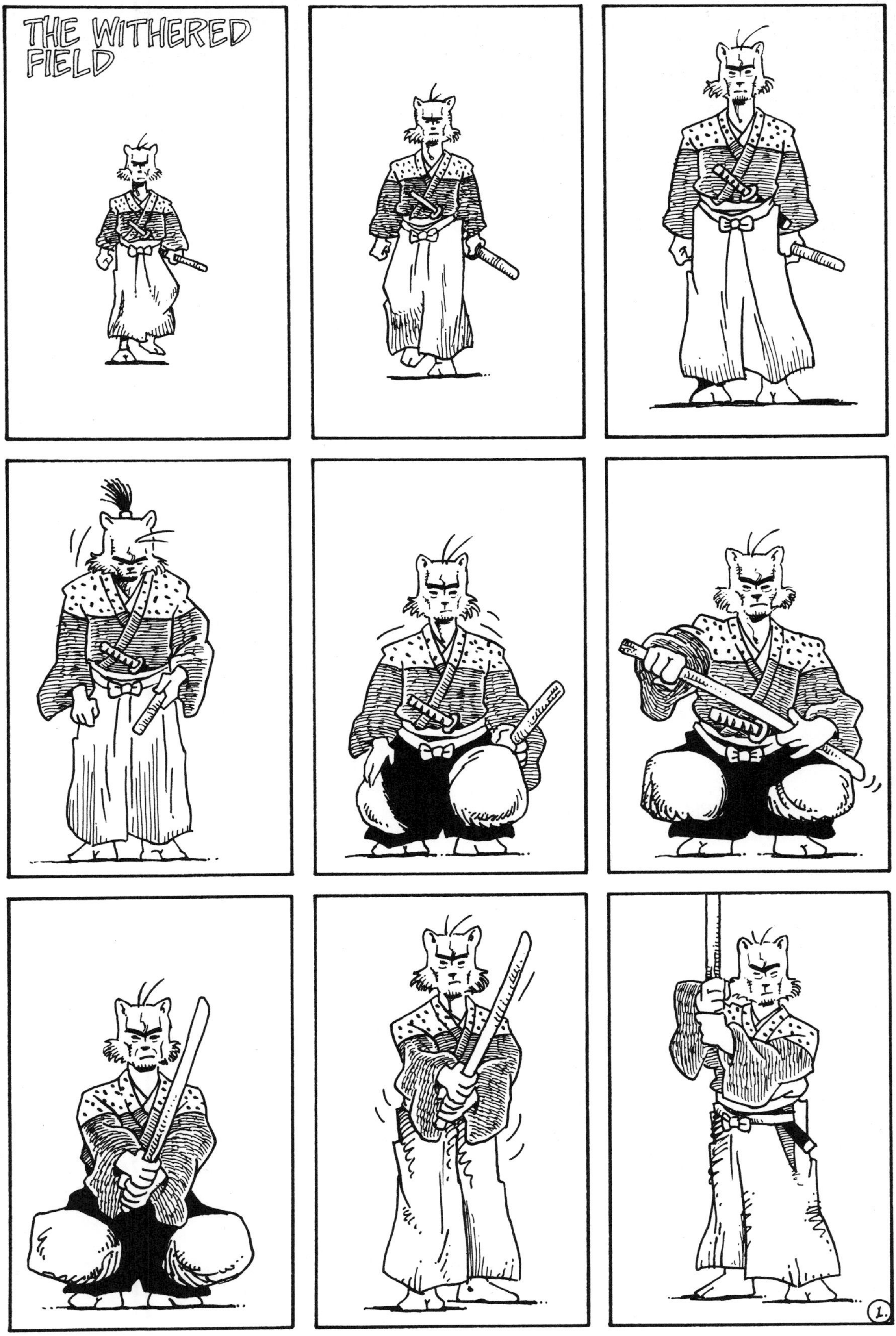
THE WITHERED FIELD
1.

HE'S DONE THIS **MANY** TIMES BEFORE.

HIS *REISHIKI* (PRE-FIGHT ETIQUETTE) IS IMPECCABLE.

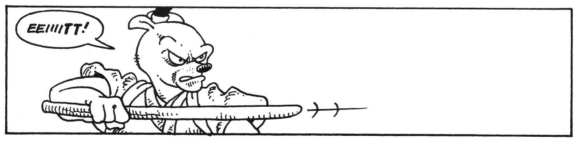

EEIIIITT!

KIIIIIII!

NGGG...

THE OUTCOME IS SO OBVIOUS.

ZZZZ

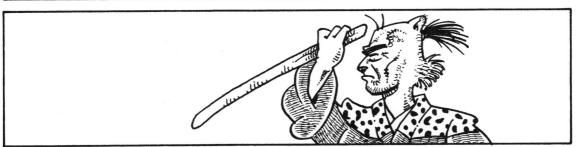

HIYAAAA!

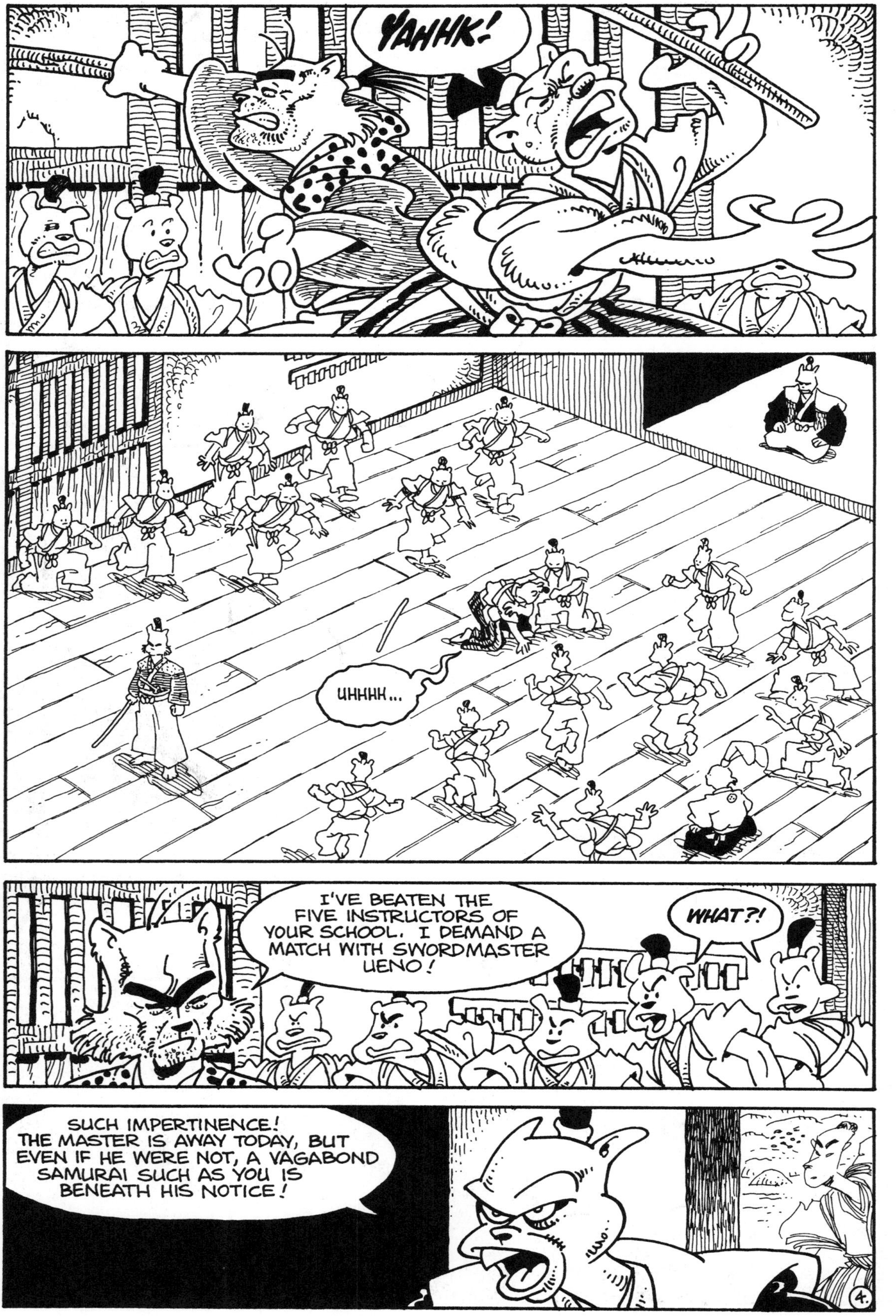
YAHHK!
UHHHH...
I'VE BEATEN THE FIVE INSTRUCTORS OF YOUR SCHOOL. I DEMAND A MATCH WITH SWORDMASTER UENO!
WHAT?!
SUCH IMPERTINENCE! THE MASTER IS AWAY TODAY, BUT EVEN IF HE WERE NOT, A VAGABOND SAMURAI SUCH AS YOU IS BENEATH HIS NOTICE!
4.

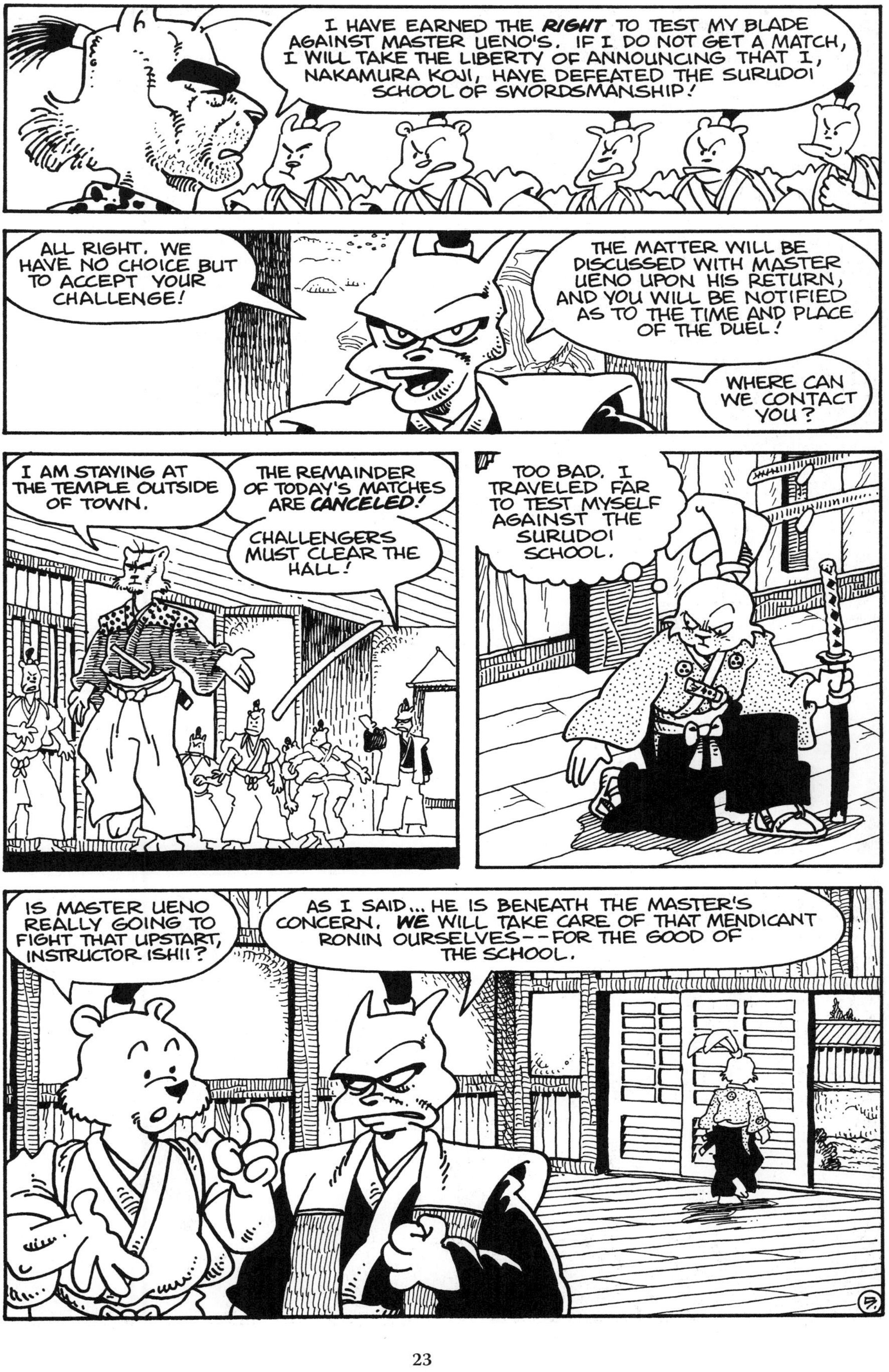
I HAVE EARNED THE RIGHT TO TEST MY BLADE AGAINST MASTER UENO'S. IF I DO NOT GET A MATCH, I WILL TAKE THE LIBERTY OF ANNOUNCING THAT I, NAKAMURA KOJI, HAVE DEFEATED THE SURUDOI SCHOOL OF SWORDSMANSHIP!
ALL RIGHT. WE HAVE NO CHOICE BUT TO ACCEPT YOUR CHALLENGE!
THE MATTER WILL BE DISCUSSED WITH MASTER UENO UPON HIS RETURN, AND YOU WILL BE NOTIFIED AS TO THE TIME AND PLACE OF THE DUEL!
WHERE CAN WE CONTACT YOU?
I AM STAYING AT THE TEMPLE OUTSIDE OF TOWN.
THE REMAINDER OF TODAY'S MATCHES ARE CANCELED!
CHALLENGERS MUST CLEAR THE HALL!
TOO BAD. I TRAVELED FAR TO TEST MYSELF AGAINST THE SURUDOI SCHOOL.
IS MASTER UENO REALLY GOING TO FIGHT THAT UPSTART, INSTRUCTOR ISHII?
AS I SAID... HE IS BENEATH THE MASTER'S CONCERN. WE WILL TAKE CARE OF THAT MENDICANT RONIN OURSELVES--FOR THE GOOD OF THE SCHOOL.

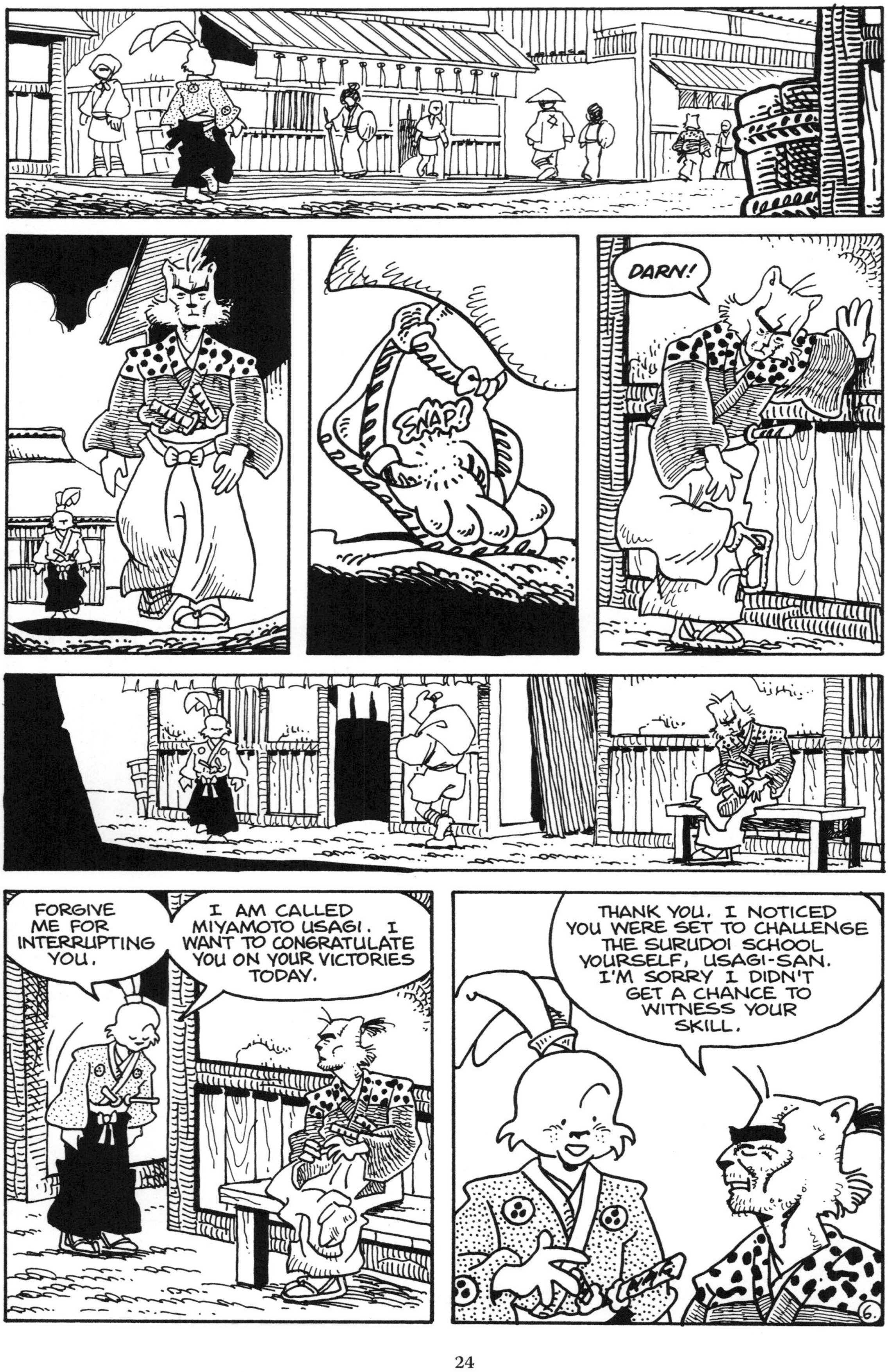
SNAP!
DARN!
FORGIVE ME FOR INTERRUPTING YOU.
I AM CALLED MIYAMOTO USAGI. I WANT TO CONGRATULATE YOU ON YOUR VICTORIES TODAY.
THANK YOU. I NOTICED YOU WERE SET TO CHALLENGE THE SURUDOI SCHOOL YOURSELF, USAGI-SAN. I'M SORRY I DIDN'T GET A CHANCE TO WITNESS YOUR SKILL.
6.

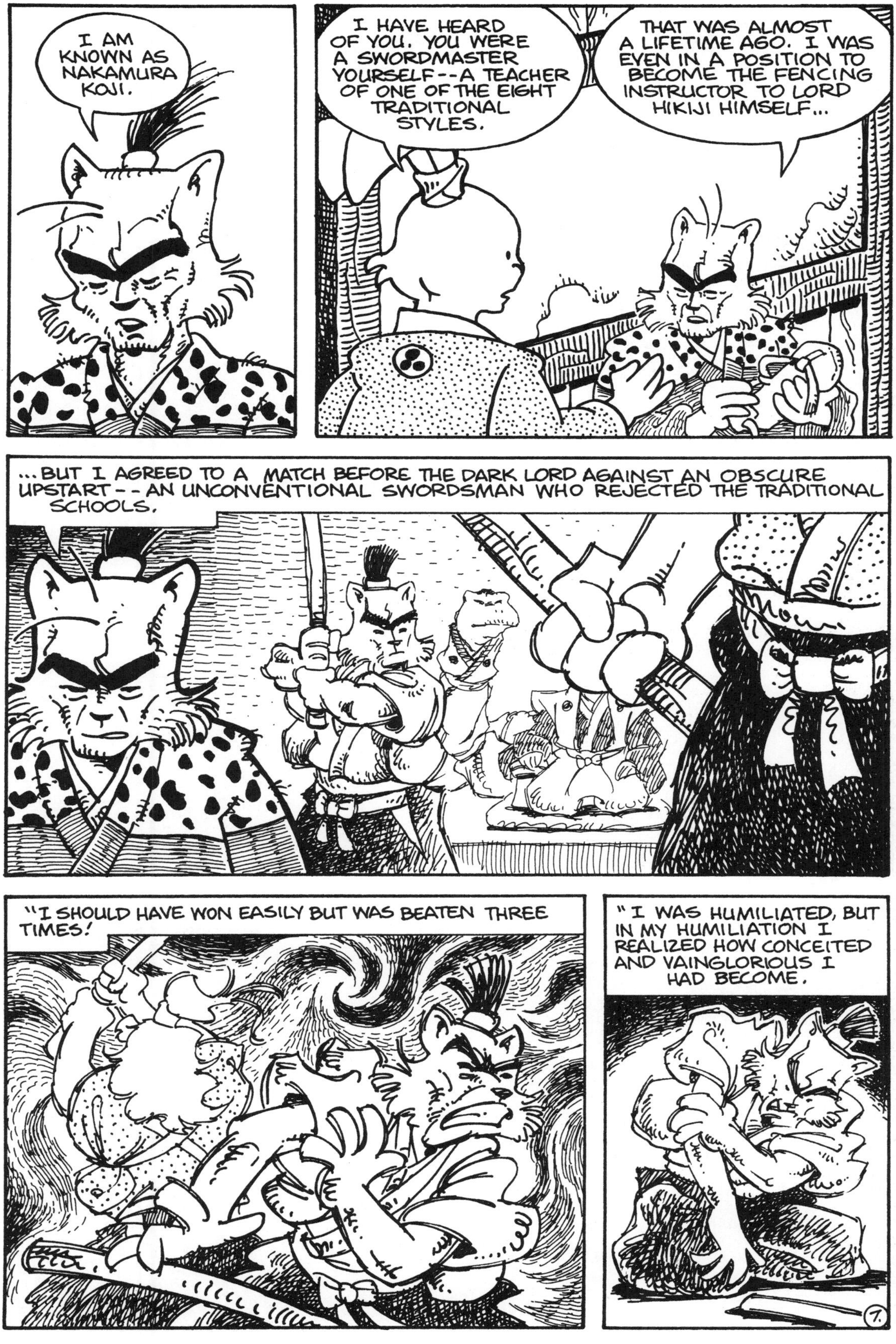
I AM KNOWN AS NAKAMURA KOJI.
I HAVE HEARD OF YOU. YOU WERE A SWORDMASTER YOURSELF--A TEACHER OF ONE OF THE EIGHT TRADITIONAL STYLES.
THAT WAS ALMOST A LIFETIME AGO. I WAS EVEN IN A POSITION TO BECOME THE FENCING INSTRUCTOR TO LORD HIKIJI HIMSELF...
...BUT I AGREED TO A MATCH BEFORE THE DARK LORD AGAINST AN OBSCURE UPSTART--AN UNCONVENTIONAL SWORDSMAN WHO REJECTED THE TRADITIONAL SCHOOLS.
"I SHOULD HAVE WON EASILY BUT WAS BEATEN THREE TIMES!
"I WAS HUMILIATED, BUT IN MY HUMILIATION I REALIZED HOW CONCEITED AND VAINGLORIOUS I HAD BECOME.
7.

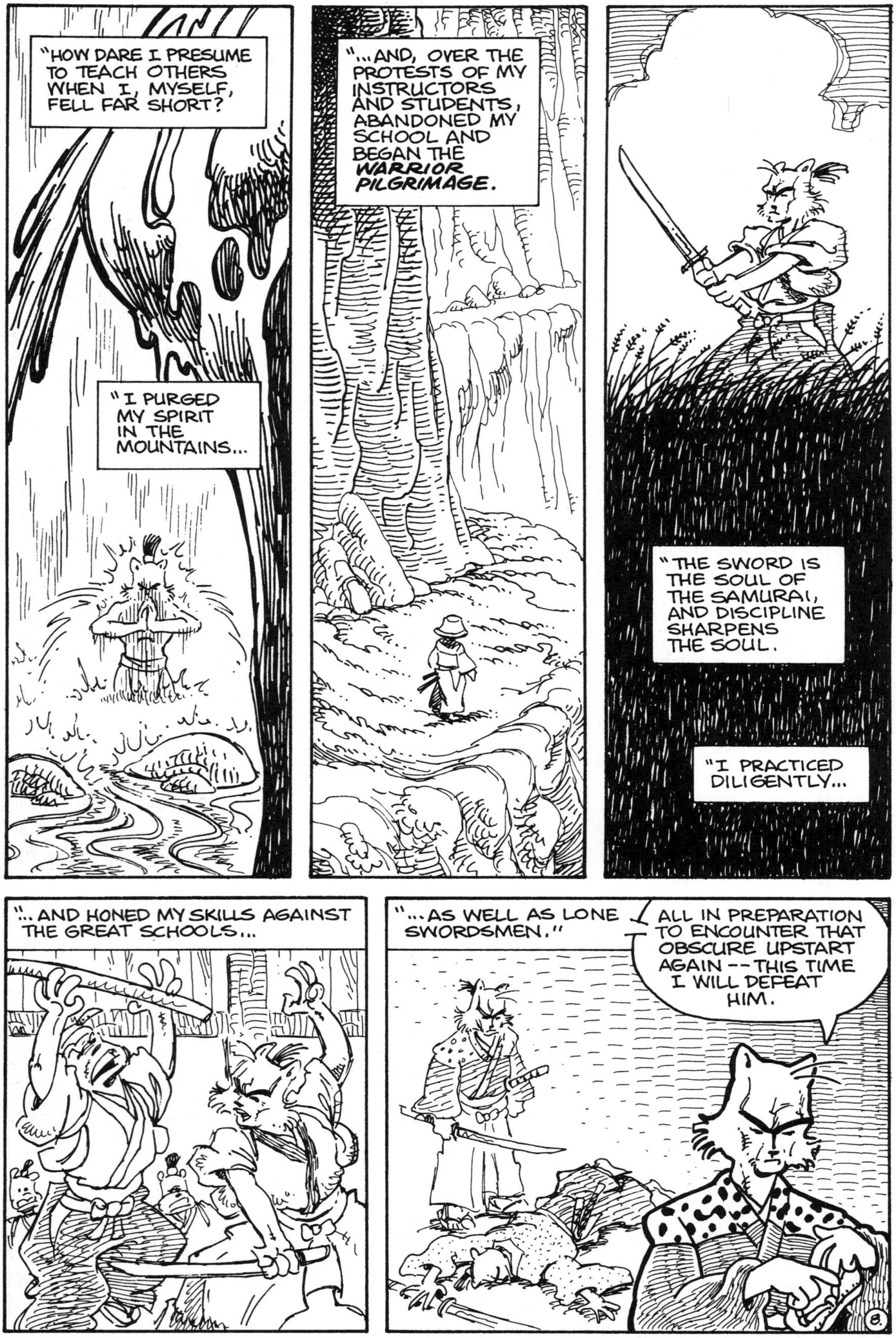
"HOW DARE I PRESUME TO TEACH OTHERS WHEN I, MYSELF, FELL FAR SHORT?
"I PURGED MY SPIRIT IN THE MOUNTAINS...
"...AND, OVER THE PROTESTS OF MY INSTRUCTORS AND STUDENTS, ABANDONED MY SCHOOL AND BEGAN THE ***WARRIOR PILGRIMAGE***.
"THE SWORD IS THE SOUL OF THE SAMURAI, AND DISCIPLINE SHARPENS THE SOUL.
"I PRACTICED DILIGENTLY...
"...AND HONED MY SKILLS AGAINST THE GREAT SCHOOLS...
"...AS WELL AS LONE SWORDSMEN."
ALL IN PREPARATION TO ENCOUNTER THAT OBSCURE UPSTART AGAIN -- THIS TIME I WILL DEFEAT HIM.
8.

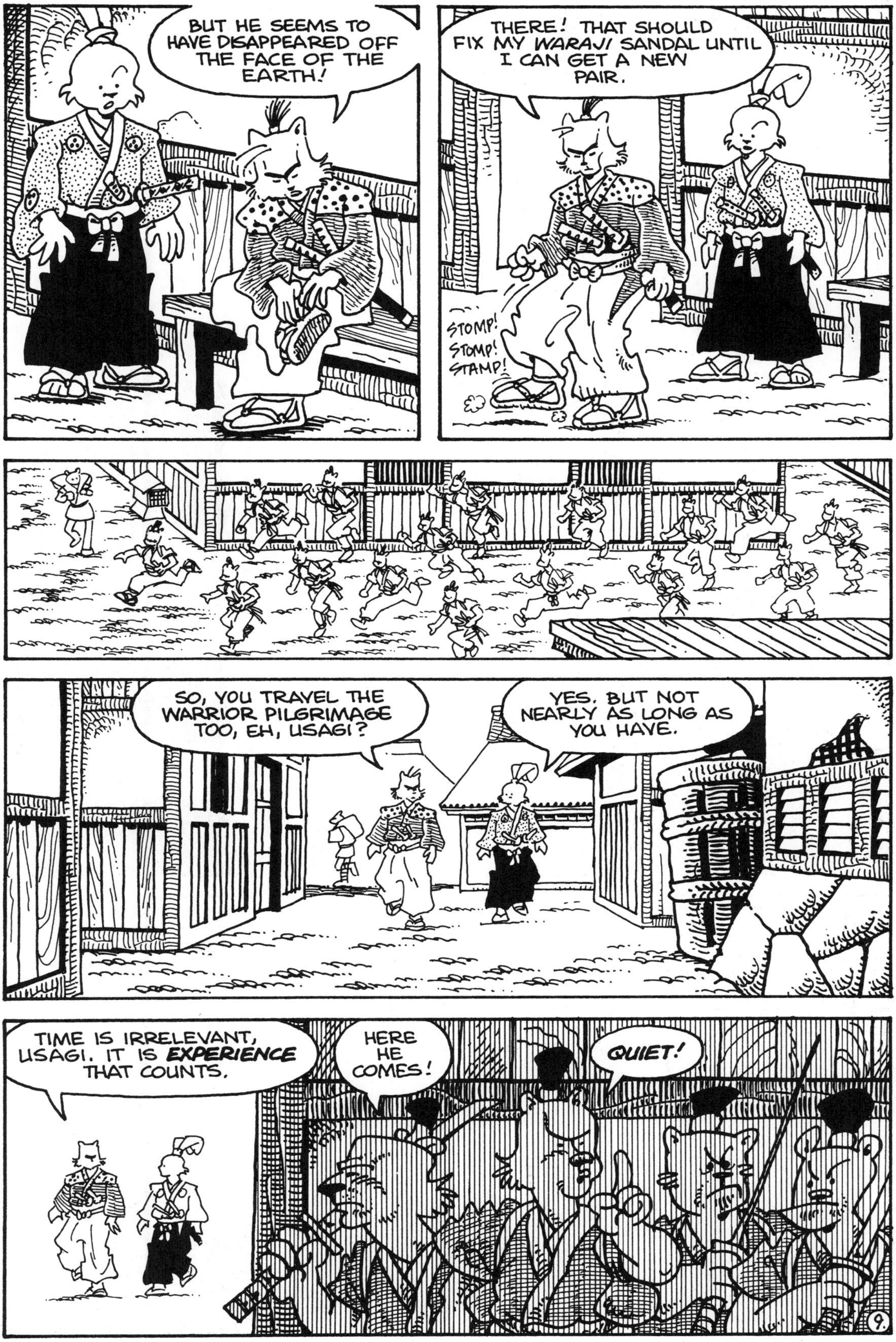
BUT HE SEEMS TO HAVE DISAPPEARED OFF THE FACE OF THE EARTH!
THERE! THAT SHOULD FIX MY WARAJI SANDAL UNTIL I CAN GET A NEW PAIR.
STOMP! STOMP! STAMP!
SO, YOU TRAVEL THE WARRIOR PILGRIMAGE TOO, EH, USAGI?
YES. BUT NOT NEARLY AS LONG AS YOU HAVE.
TIME IS IRRELEVANT, USAGI. IT IS EXPERIENCE THAT COUNTS.
HERE HE COMES!
QUIET!
9.

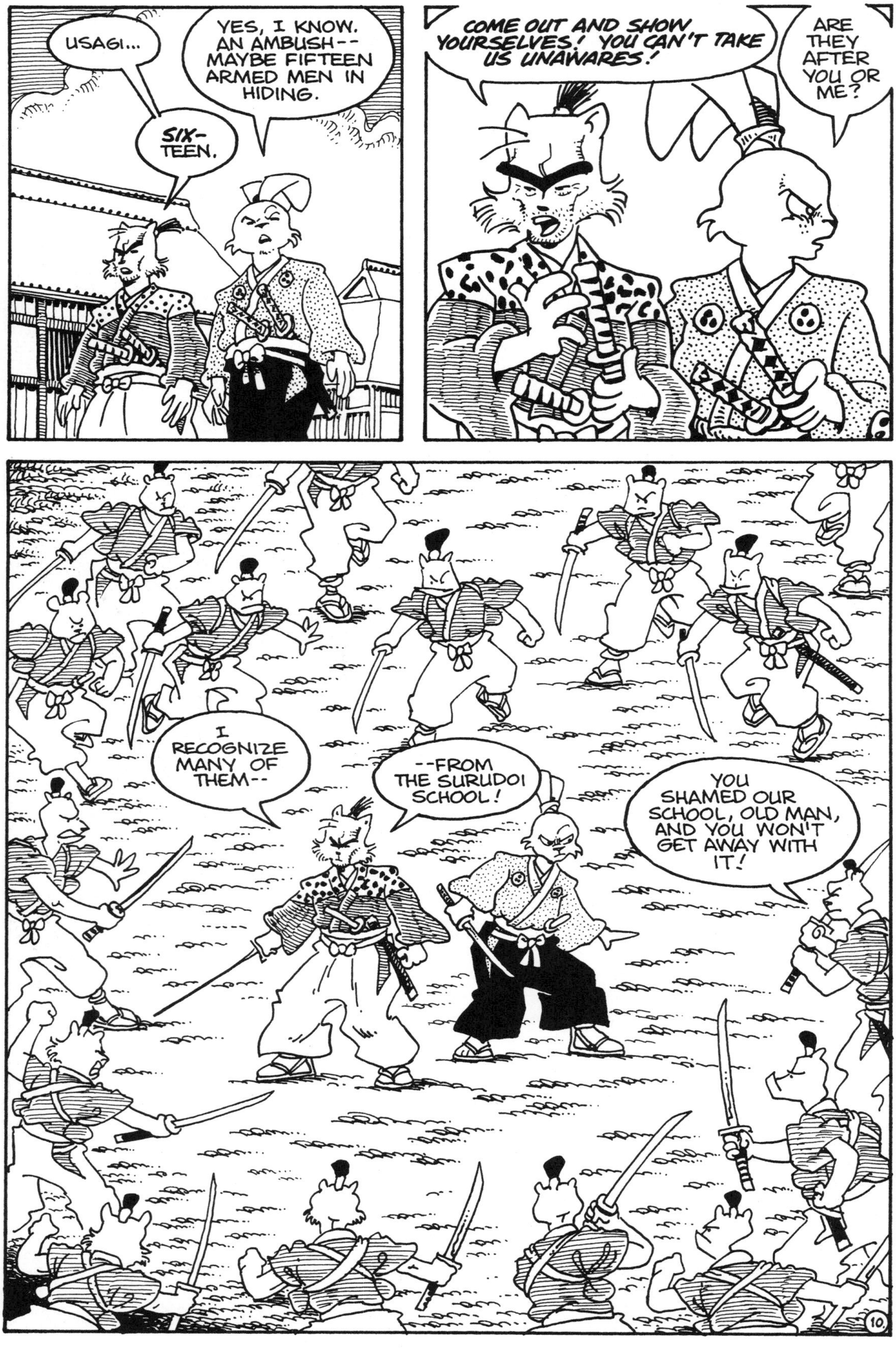
USAGI...
YES, I KNOW. AN AMBUSH-- MAYBE FIFTEEN ARMED MEN IN HIDING.
SIX-TEEN.
COME OUT AND SHOW YOURSELVES! YOU CAN'T TAKE US UNAWARES!
ARE THEY AFTER YOU OR ME?
I RECOGNIZE MANY OF THEM--
--FROM THE SURUDOI SCHOOL!
YOU SHAMED OUR SCHOOL, OLD MAN, AND YOU WON'T GET AWAY WITH IT!
10

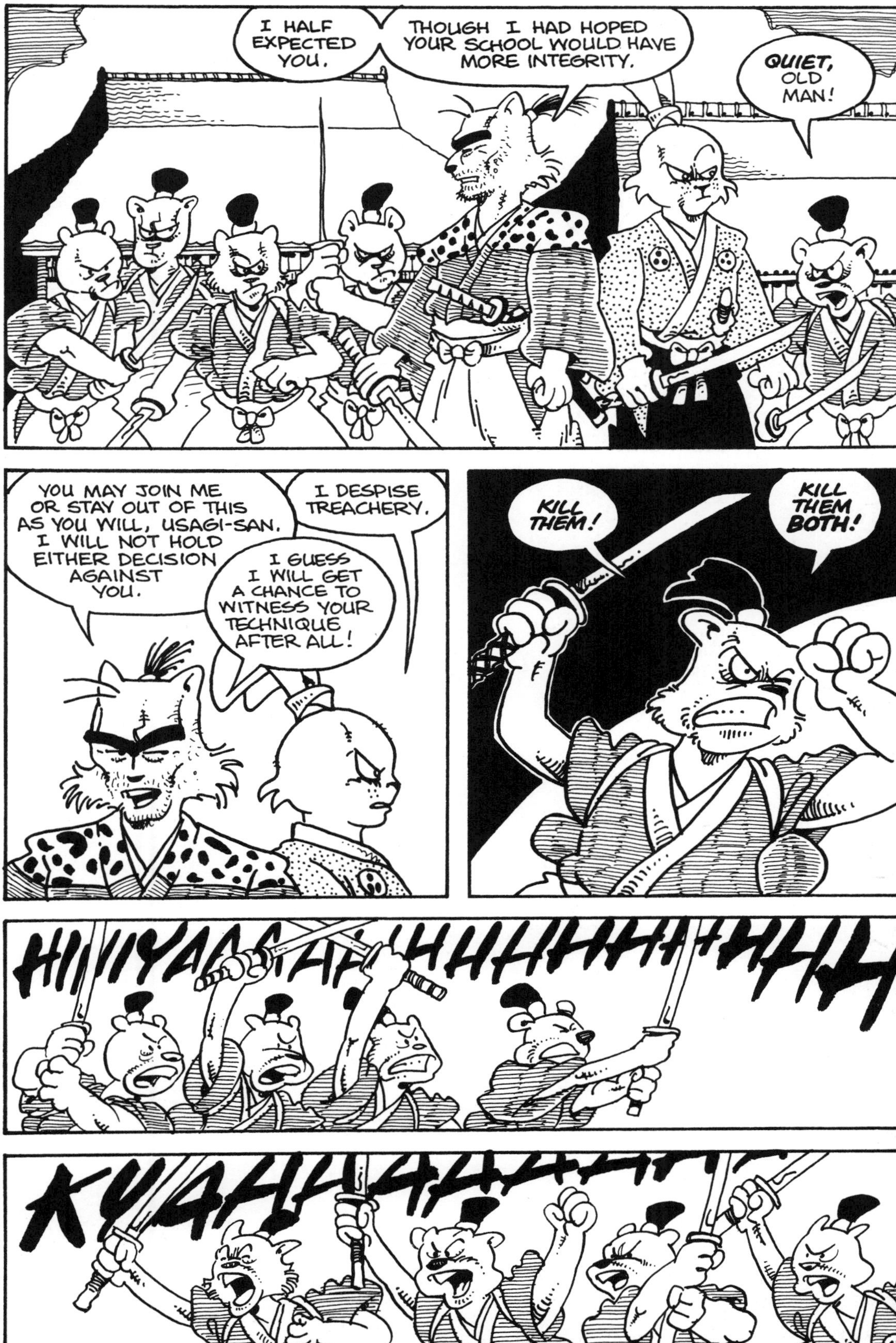
I HALF EXPECTED YOU.
THOUGH I HAD HOPED YOUR SCHOOL WOULD HAVE MORE INTEGRITY.
QUIET, OLD MAN!
YOU MAY JOIN ME OR STAY OUT OF THIS AS YOU WILL, USAGI-SAN. I WILL NOT HOLD EITHER DECISION AGAINST YOU.
I DESPISE TREACHERY.
I GUESS I WILL GET A CHANCE TO WITNESS YOUR TECHNIQUE AFTER ALL!
KILL THEM!
KILL THEM BOTH!
HIIIYAAAAHHHHHHHHHHHH
KYAHHAAAAAAAA
11.

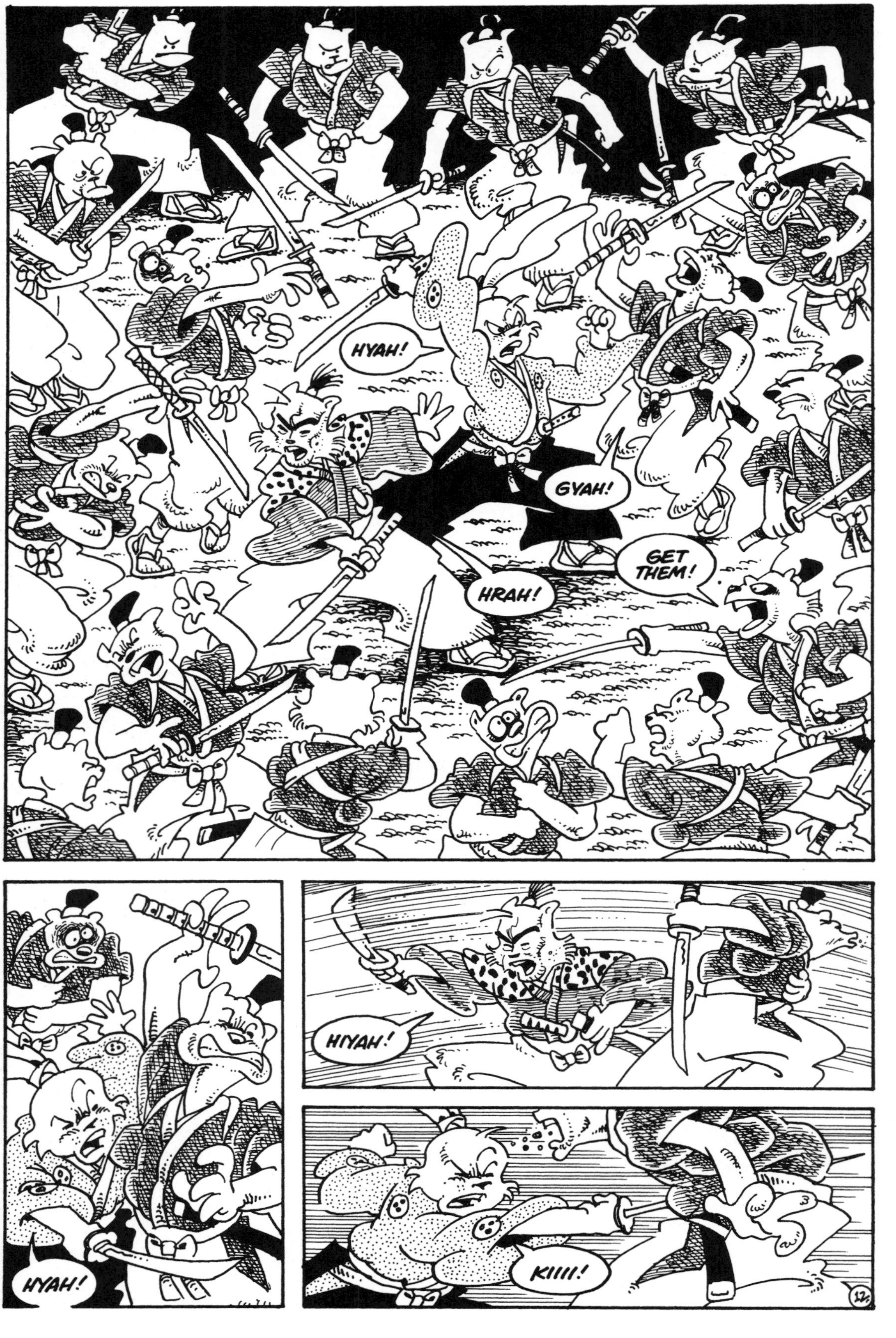
HYAH!
GYAH!
GET THEM!
HRAH!
HYAH!
HIYAH!
KIIII!
12

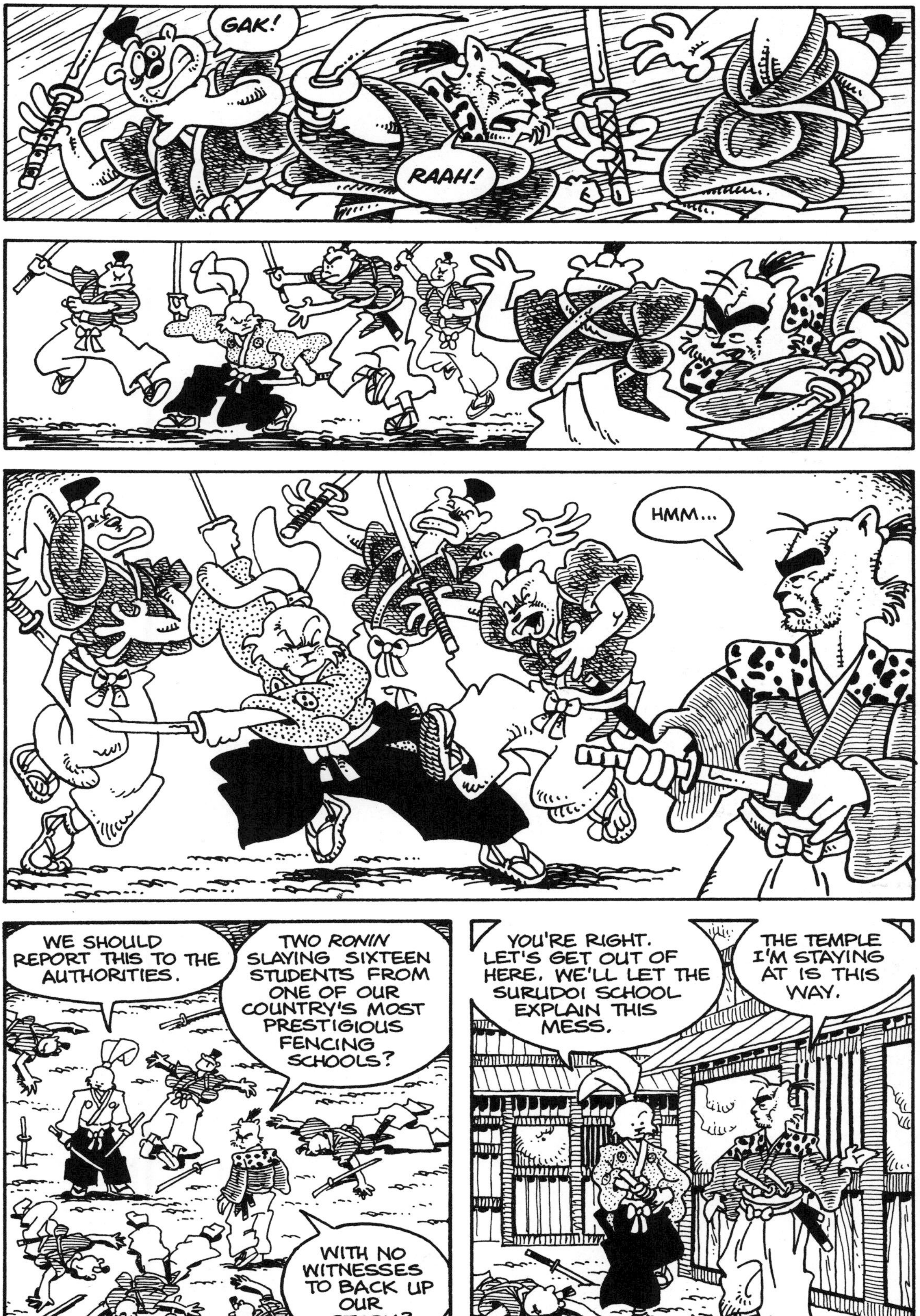
GAK!
RAAH!
HMM...
WE SHOULD REPORT THIS TO THE AUTHORITIES.
TWO *RONIN* SLAYING SIXTEEN STUDENTS FROM ONE OF OUR COUNTRY'S MOST PRESTIGIOUS FENCING SCHOOLS?
WITH NO WITNESSES TO BACK UP OUR STORY?
YOU'RE RIGHT. LET'S GET OUT OF HERE. WE'LL LET THE SURUDOI SCHOOL EXPLAIN THIS MESS.
THE TEMPLE I'M STAYING AT IS THIS WAY.
13.

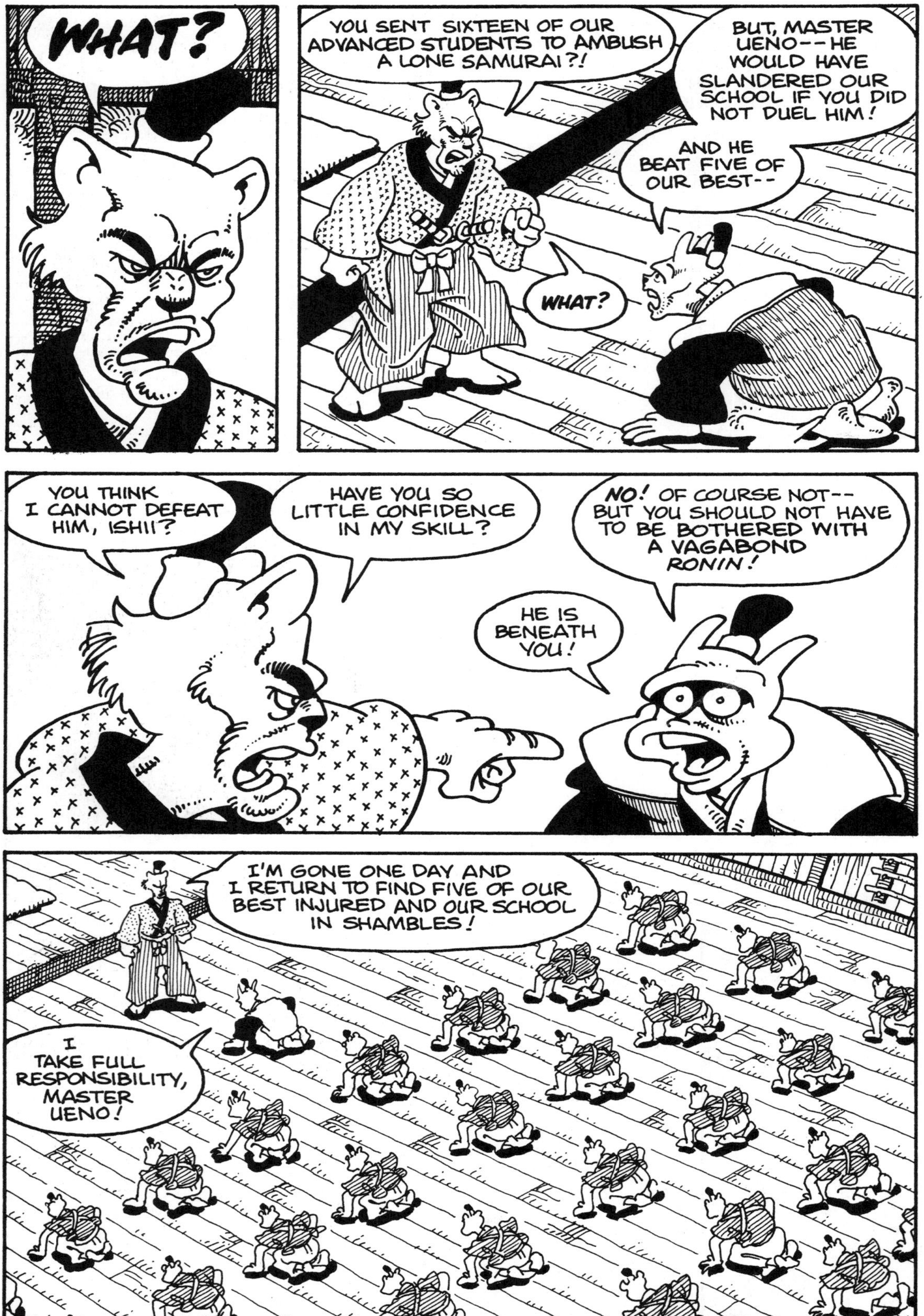
WHAT?
YOU SENT SIXTEEN OF OUR ADVANCED STUDENTS TO AMBUSH A LONE SAMURAI?!
BUT, MASTER UENO-- HE WOULD HAVE SLANDERED OUR SCHOOL IF YOU DID NOT DUEL HIM!
AND HE BEAT FIVE OF OUR BEST--
WHAT?
YOU THINK I CANNOT DEFEAT HIM, ISHII?
HAVE YOU SO LITTLE CONFIDENCE IN MY SKILL?
NO! OF COURSE NOT-- BUT YOU SHOULD NOT HAVE TO BE BOTHERED WITH A VAGABOND RONIN!
HE IS BENEATH YOU!
I'M GONE ONE DAY AND I RETURN TO FIND FIVE OF OUR BEST INJURED AND OUR SCHOOL IN SHAMBLES!
I TAKE FULL RESPONSIBILITY, MASTER UENO!
14.

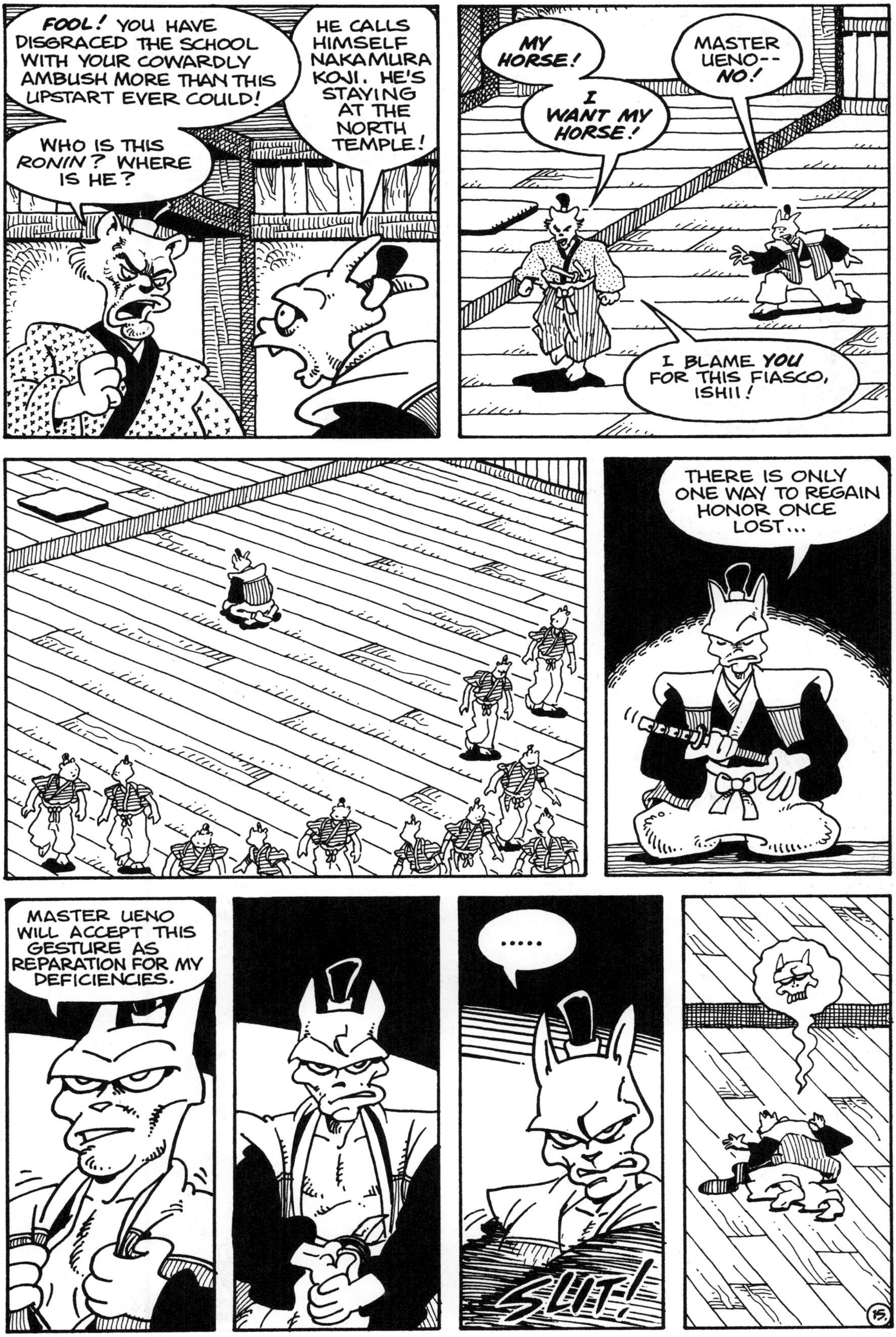
FOOL! YOU HAVE DISGRACED THE SCHOOL WITH YOUR COWARDLY AMBUSH MORE THAN THIS UPSTART EVER COULD!
WHO IS THIS RONIN? WHERE IS HE?
HE CALLS HIMSELF NAKAMURA KOJI. HE'S STAYING AT THE NORTH TEMPLE!
MY HORSE!
I WANT MY HORSE!
MASTER UENO-- NO!
I BLAME YOU FOR THIS FIASCO, ISHII!
THERE IS ONLY ONE WAY TO REGAIN HONOR ONCE LOST...
MASTER UENO WILL ACCEPT THIS GESTURE AS REPARATION FOR MY DEFICIENCIES.
.....
SLIT!
15.

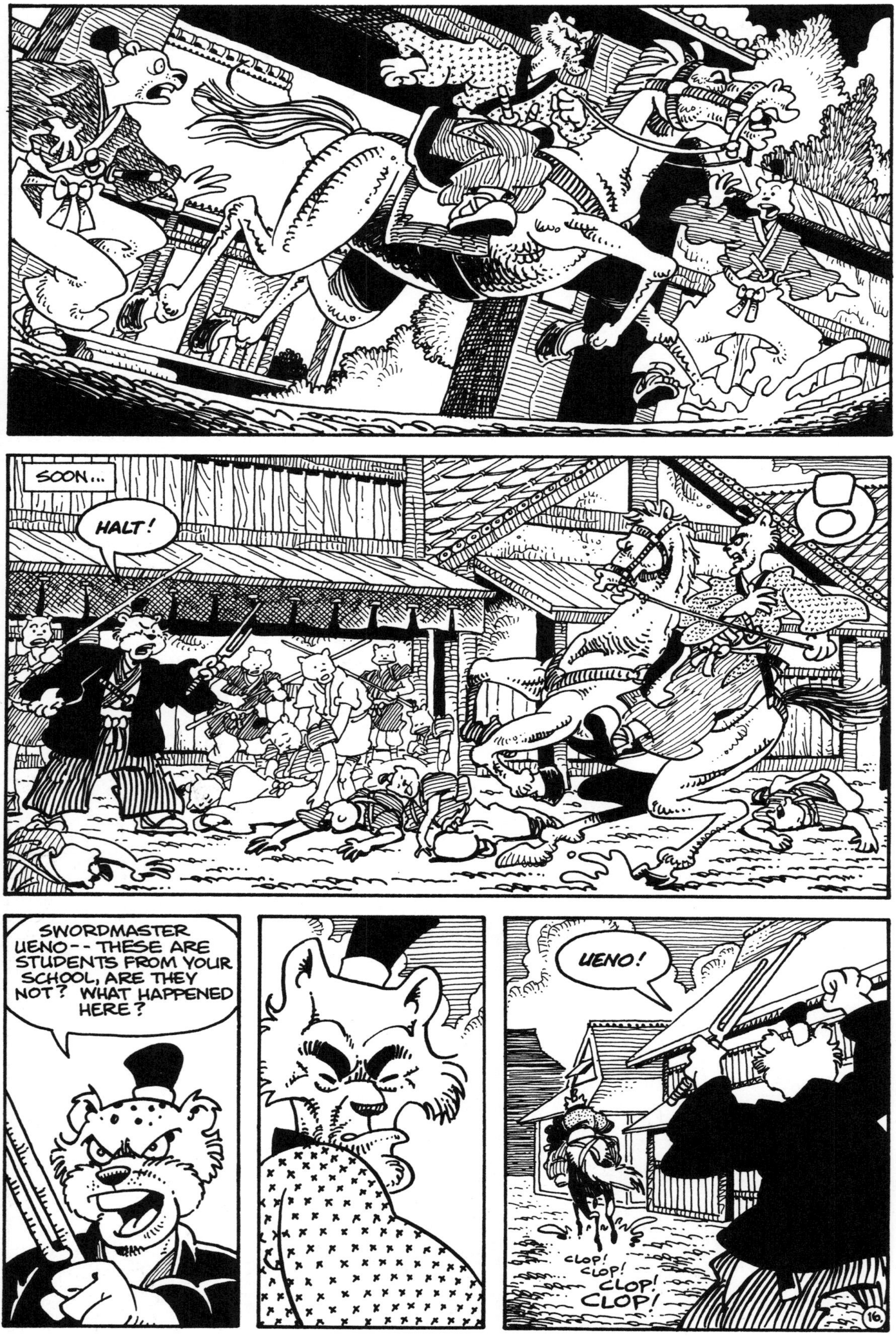
SOON...
HALT!
SWORDMASTER UENO-- THESE ARE STUDENTS FROM YOUR SCHOOL, ARE THEY NOT? WHAT HAPPENED HERE?
UENO!
CLOP! CLOP! CLOP! CLOP!
16.

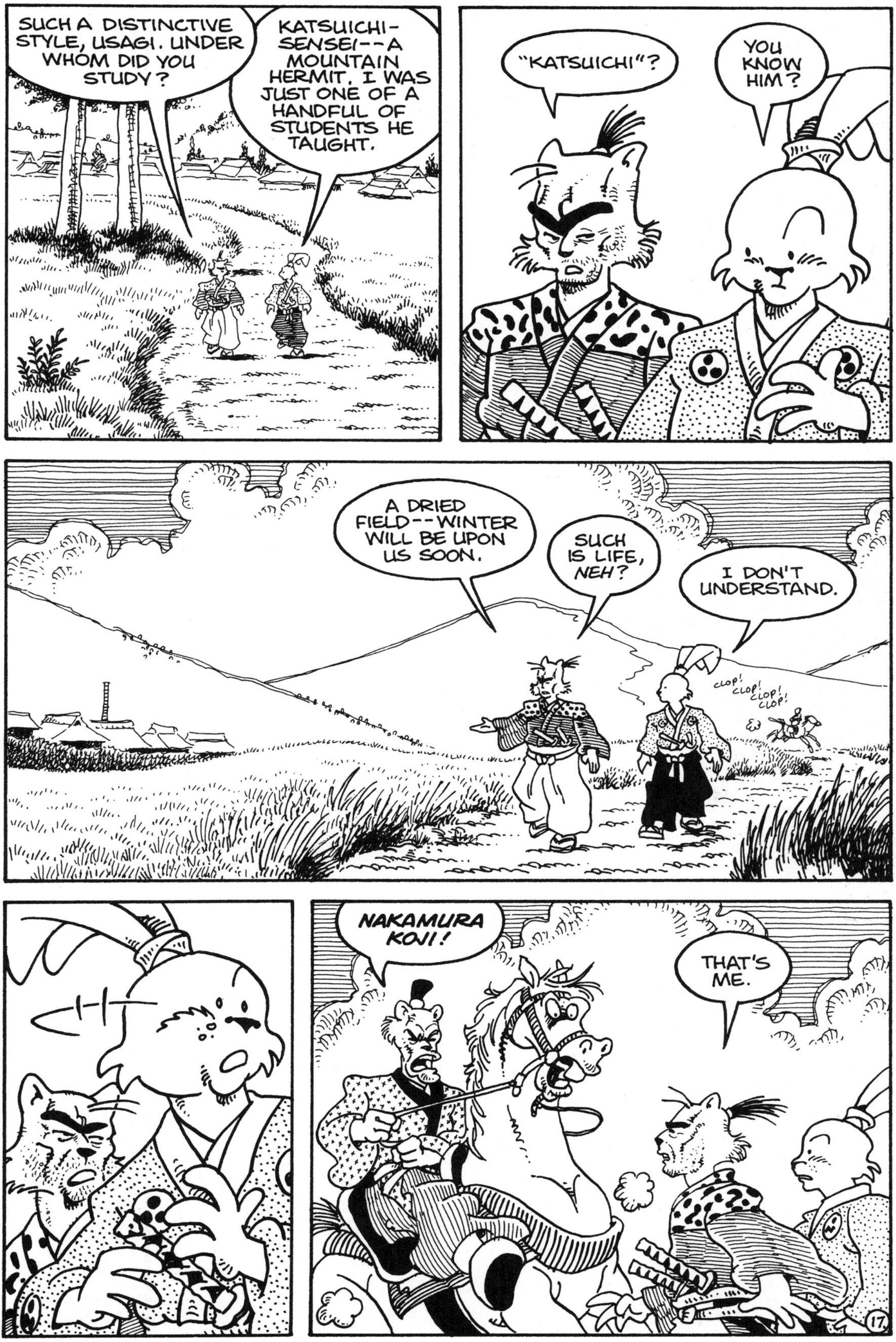
SUCH A DISTINCTIVE STYLE, USAGI. UNDER WHOM DID YOU STUDY?
KATSUICHI-SENSEI--A MOUNTAIN HERMIT. I WAS JUST ONE OF A HANDFUL OF STUDENTS HE TAUGHT.
"KATSUICHI"?
YOU KNOW HIM?
A DRIED FIELD--WINTER WILL BE UPON US SOON.
SUCH IS LIFE, NEH?
I DON'T UNDERSTAND.
CLOP! CLOP! CLOP! CLOP!
NAKAMURA KOJI!
THAT'S ME.
17

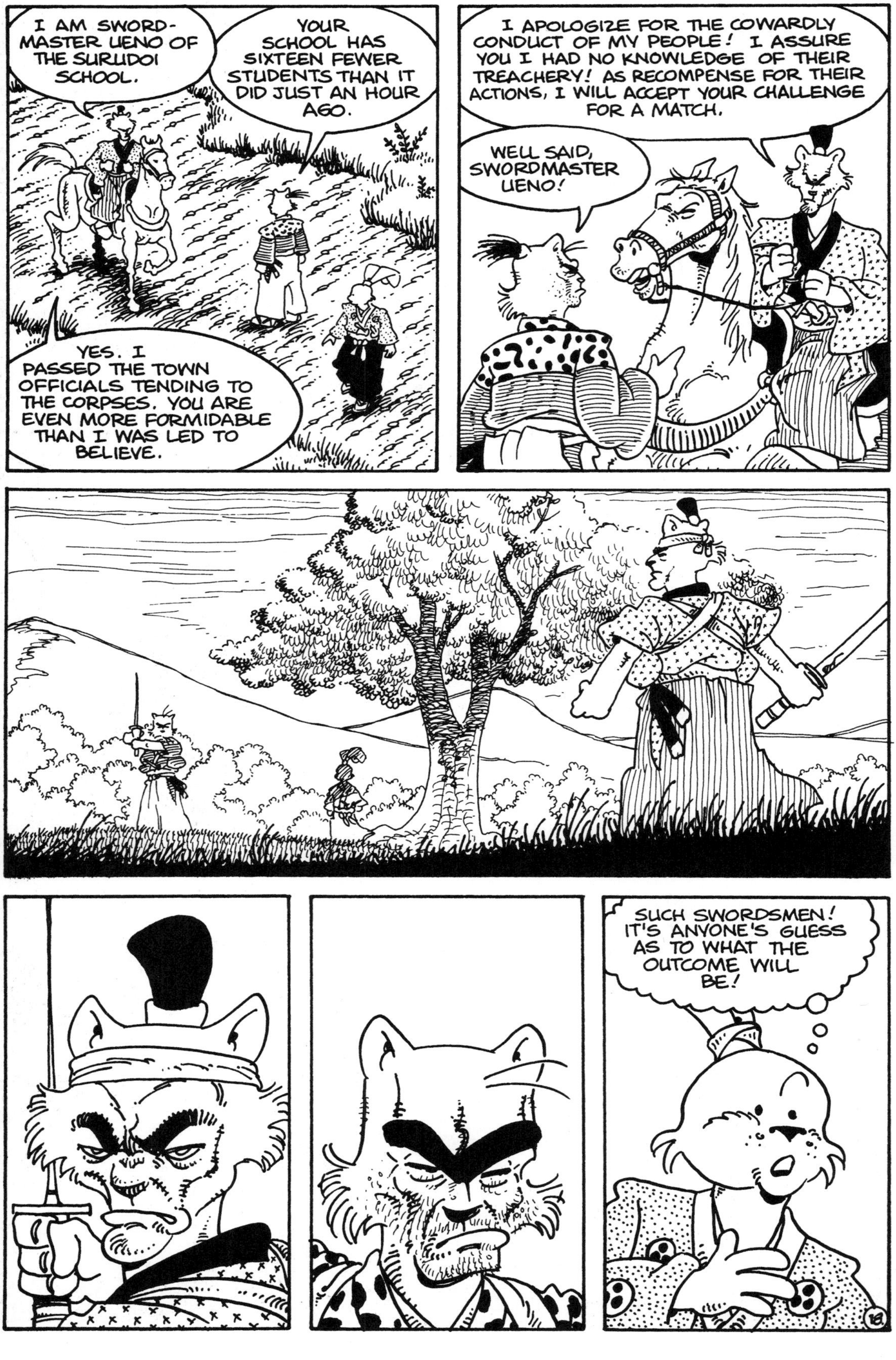
I AM SWORD-MASTER UENO OF THE SURUDOI SCHOOL.
YOUR SCHOOL HAS SIXTEEN FEWER STUDENTS THAN IT DID JUST AN HOUR AGO.
YES. I PASSED THE TOWN OFFICIALS TENDING TO THE CORPSES. YOU ARE EVEN MORE FORMIDABLE THAN I WAS LED TO BELIEVE.
I APOLOGIZE FOR THE COWARDLY CONDUCT OF MY PEOPLE! I ASSURE YOU I HAD NO KNOWLEDGE OF THEIR TREACHERY! AS RECOMPENSE FOR THEIR ACTIONS, I WILL ACCEPT YOUR CHALLENGE FOR A MATCH.
WELL SAID, SWORDMASTER UENO!
SUCH SWORDSMEN! IT'S ANYONE'S GUESS AS TO WHAT THE OUTCOME WILL BE!
18

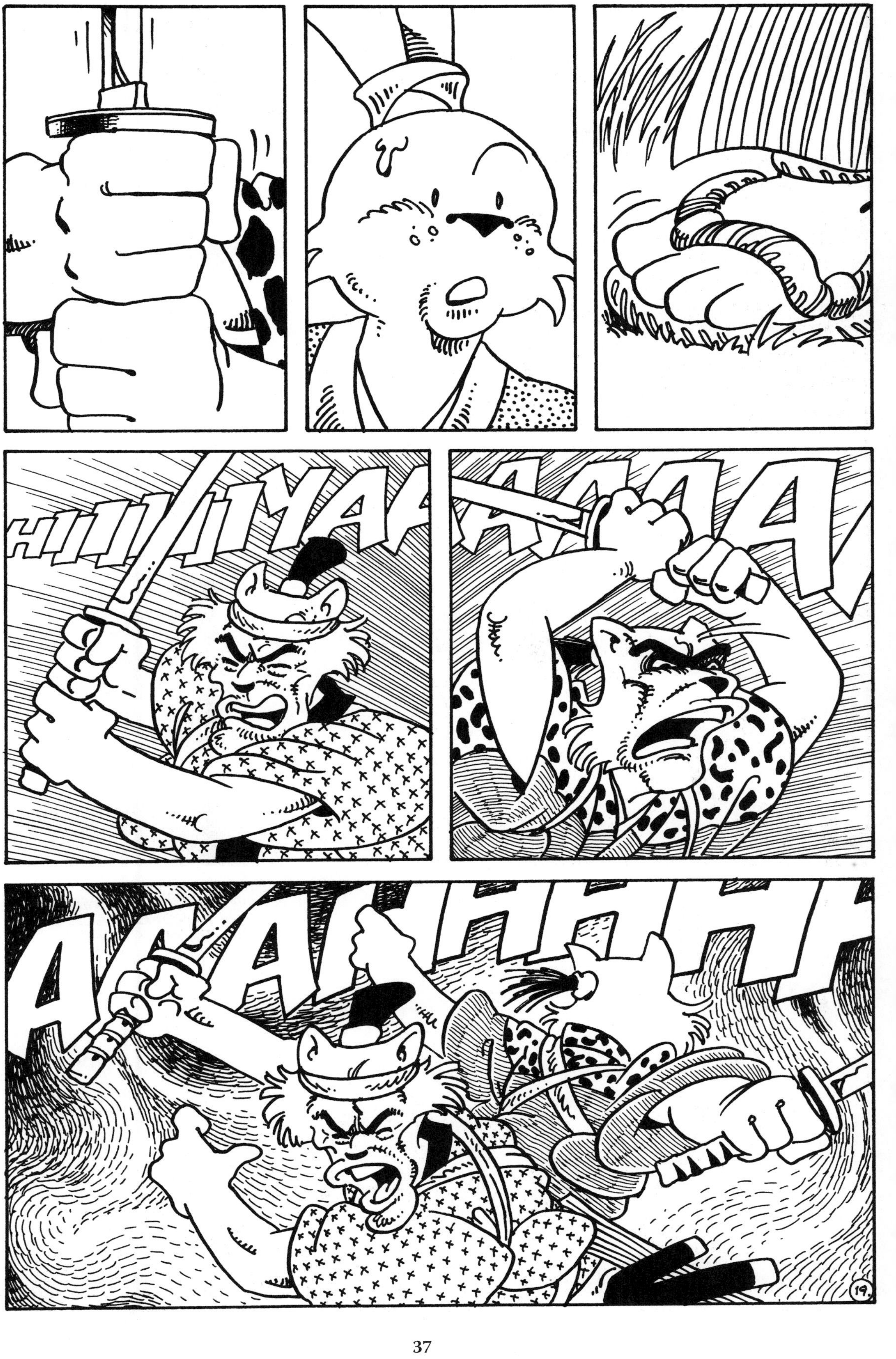
HIIIIIYAA
AAAAA
AAAHHHHH
19

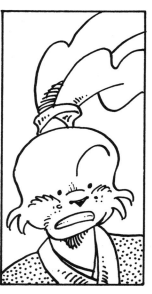

I HAVE NEVER BEFORE WITNESSED SUCH SKILL!

I HAVE ONE MORE MATCH TONIGHT...

...WITH YOU!

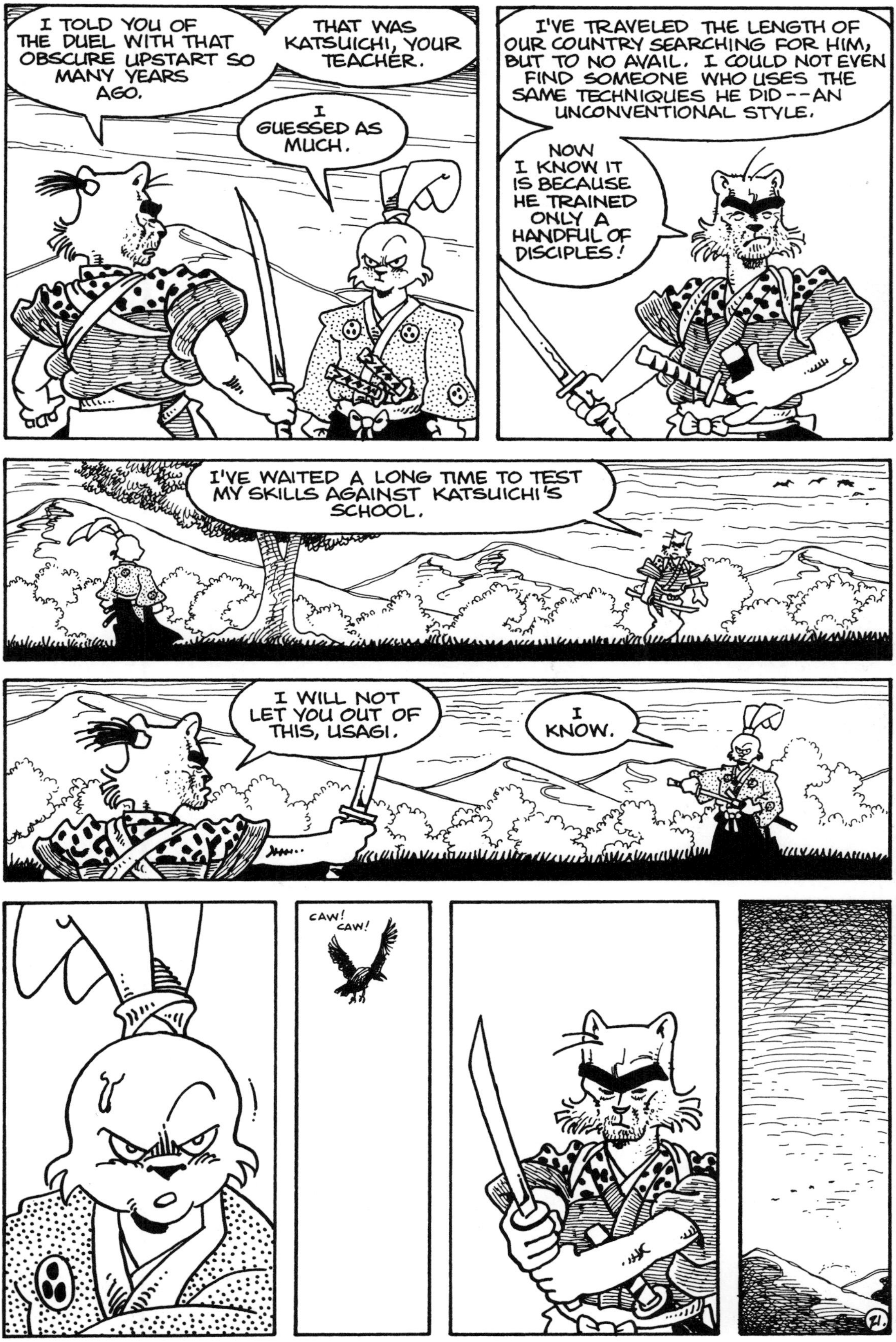

I TOLD YOU OF THE DUEL WITH THAT OBSCURE UPSTART SO MANY YEARS AGO.
THAT WAS KATSUICHI, YOUR TEACHER.
I GUESSED AS MUCH.
I'VE TRAVELED THE LENGTH OF OUR COUNTRY SEARCHING FOR HIM, BUT TO NO AVAIL. I COULD NOT EVEN FIND SOMEONE WHO USES THE SAME TECHNIQUES HE DID--AN UNCONVENTIONAL STYLE.
NOW I KNOW IT IS BECAUSE HE TRAINED ONLY A HANDFUL OF DISCIPLES!
I'VE WAITED A LONG TIME TO TEST MY SKILLS AGAINST KATSUICHI'S SCHOOL.
I WILL NOT LET YOU OUT OF THIS, USAGI.
I KNOW.
CAW! CAW!

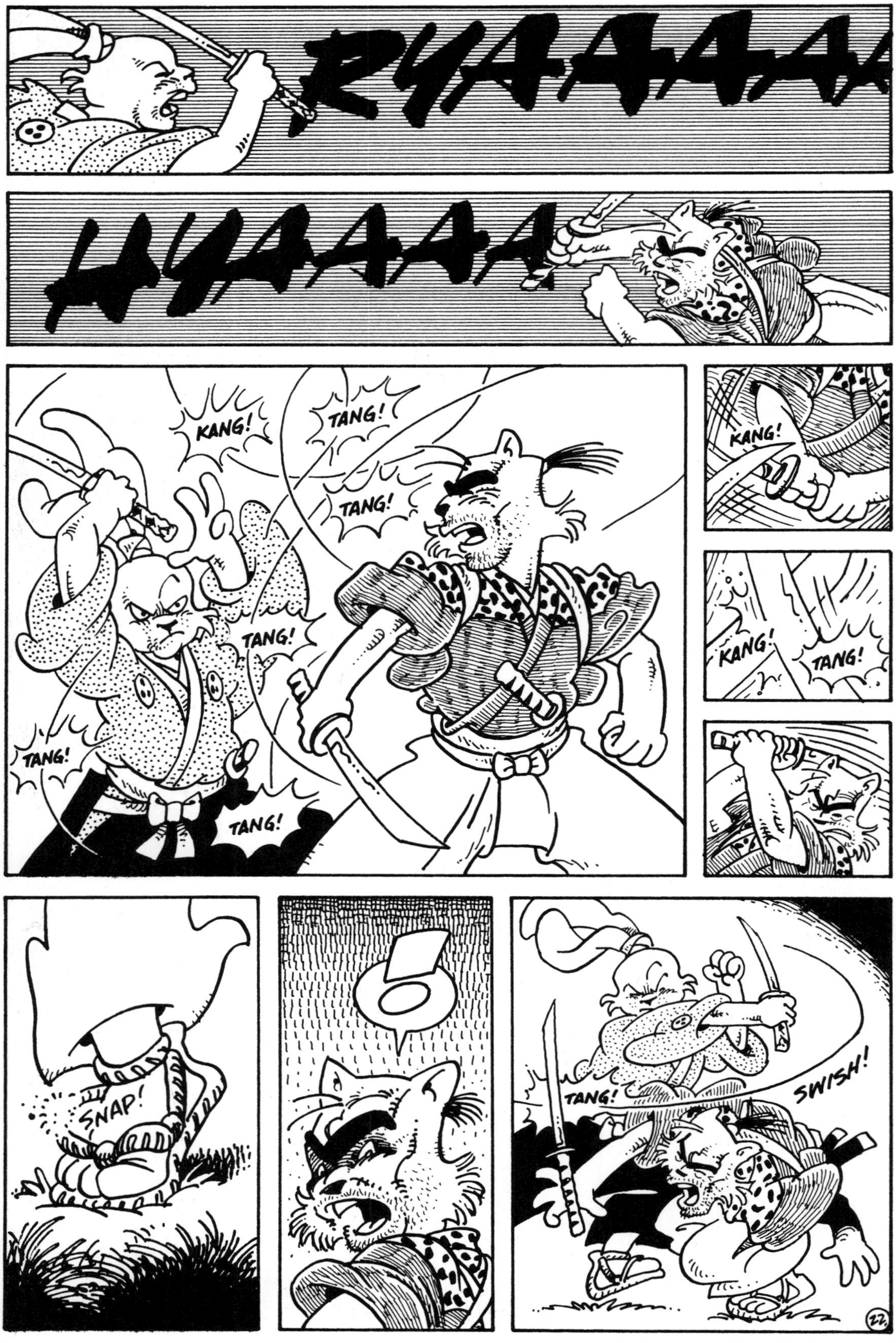
RYAAAAA
HYAAAA
KANG!
TANG!
TANG!
TANG!
TANG!
TANG!
KANG!
KANG!
TANG!
SNAP!
TANG!
SWISH!
22

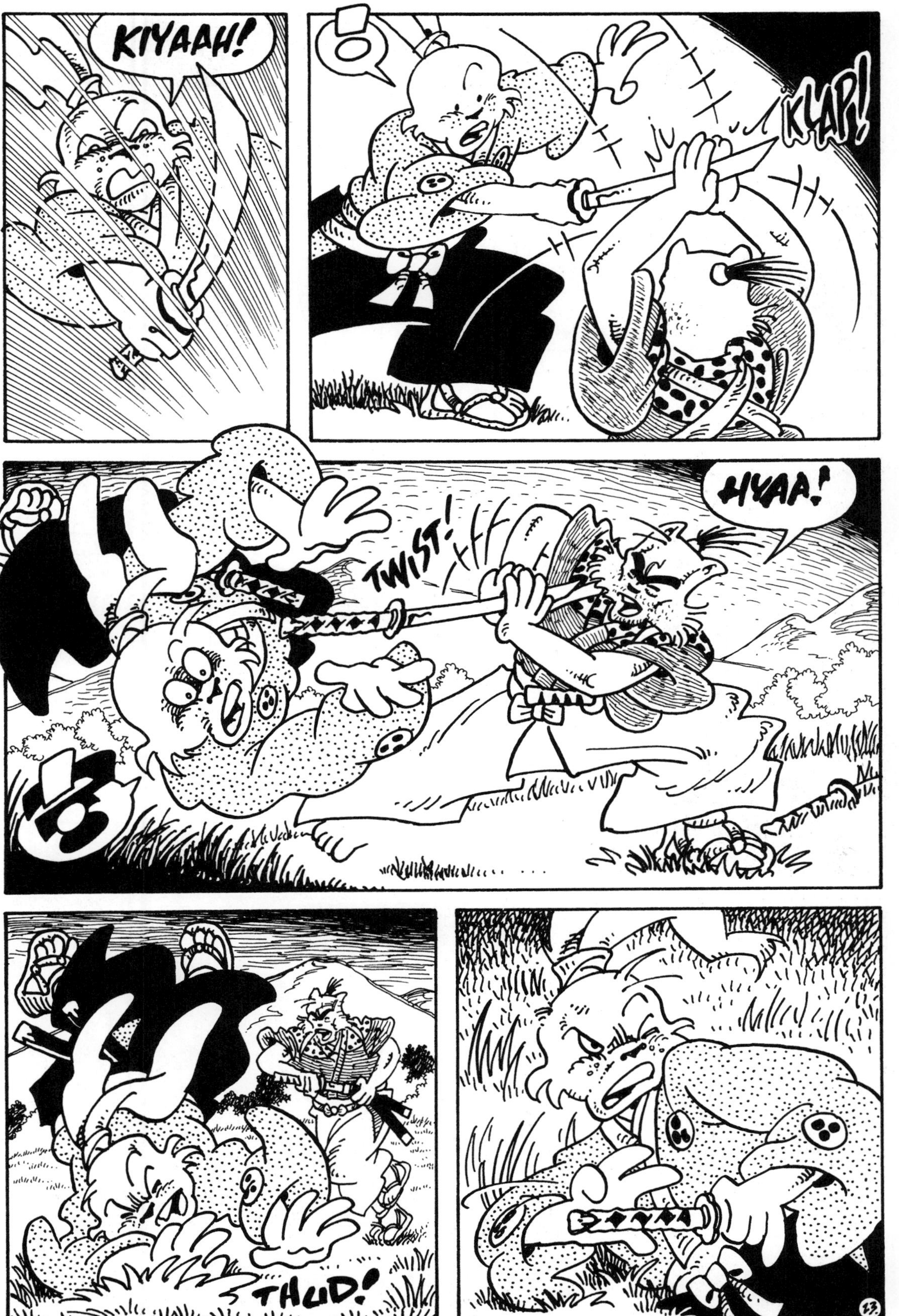
KIYAAH!
!
KLAP!
HYAA!
TWIST!
THUD!
23.

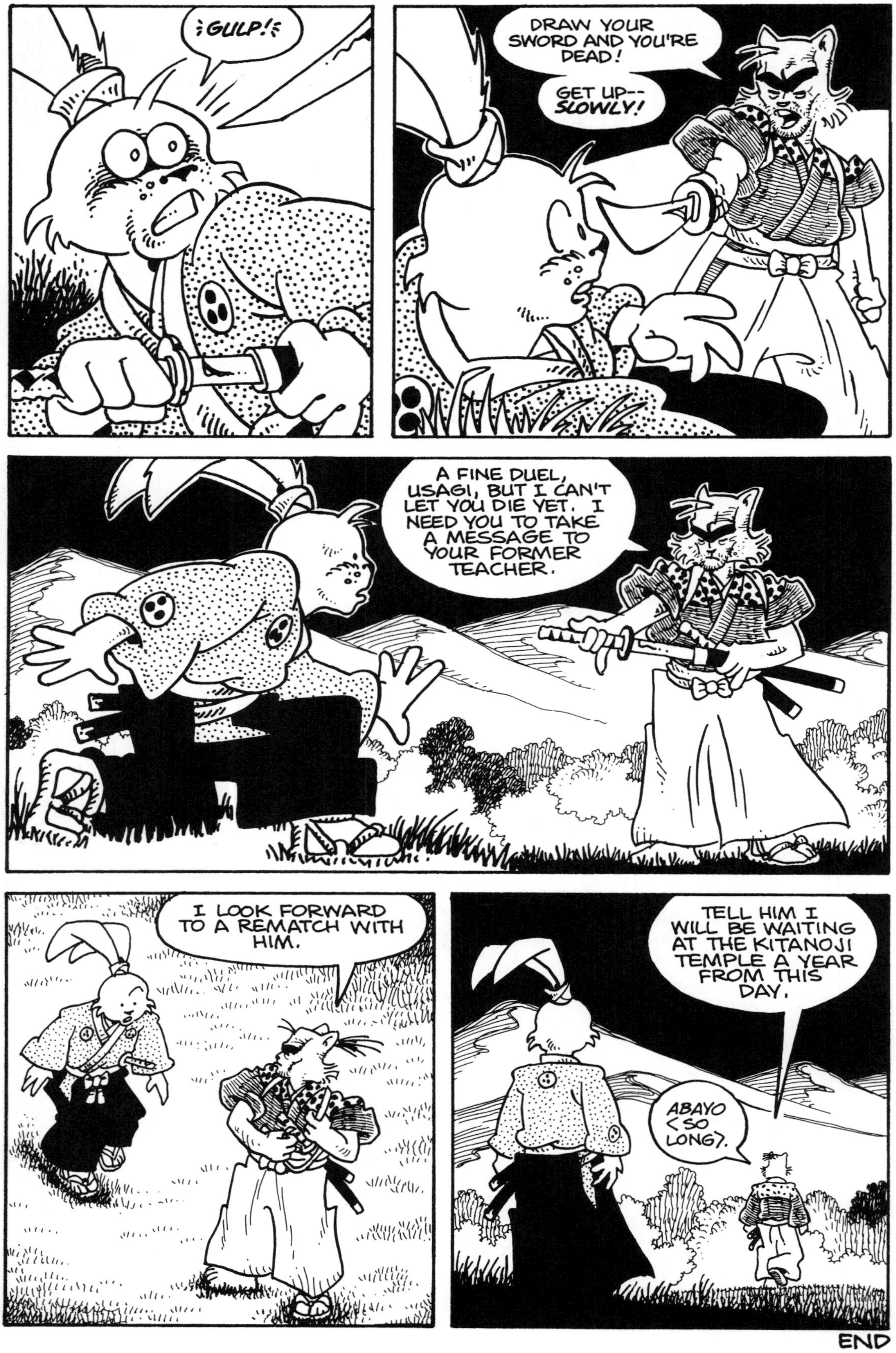

GULP!
DRAW YOUR SWORD AND YOU'RE DEAD!
GET UP-- SLOWLY!
A FINE DUEL, USAGI, BUT I CAN'T LET YOU DIE YET. I NEED YOU TO TAKE A MESSAGE TO YOUR FORMER TEACHER.
I LOOK FORWARD TO A REMATCH WITH HIM.
TELL HIM I WILL BE WAITING AT THE KITANOJI TEMPLE A YEAR FROM THIS DAY.
ABAYO <SO LONG>.
END

A Promise in the Snow

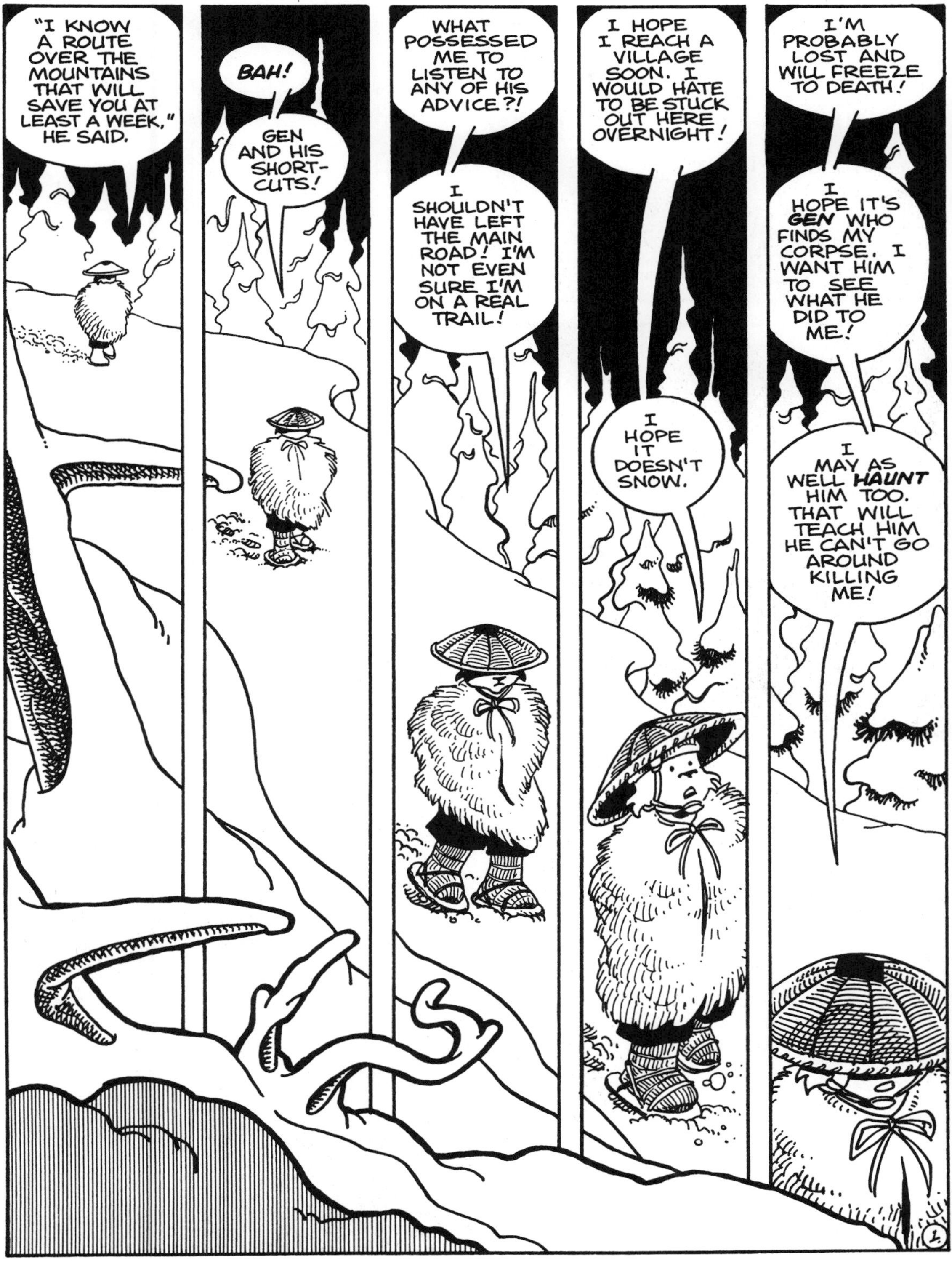
"I KNOW A ROUTE OVER THE MOUNTAINS THAT WILL SAVE YOU AT LEAST A WEEK," HE SAID.
BAH!
GEN AND HIS SHORT-CUTS!
WHAT POSSESSED ME TO LISTEN TO ANY OF HIS ADVICE?!
I SHOULDN'T HAVE LEFT THE MAIN ROAD! I'M NOT EVEN SURE I'M ON A REAL TRAIL!
I HOPE I REACH A VILLAGE SOON. I WOULD HATE TO BE STUCK OUT HERE OVERNIGHT!
I HOPE IT DOESN'T SNOW.
I'M PROBABLY LOST AND WILL FREEZE TO DEATH!
I HOPE IT'S GEN WHO FINDS MY CORPSE. I WANT HIM TO SEE WHAT HE DID TO ME!
I MAY AS WELL HAUNT HIM TOO. THAT WILL TEACH HIM HE CAN'T GO AROUND KILLING ME!

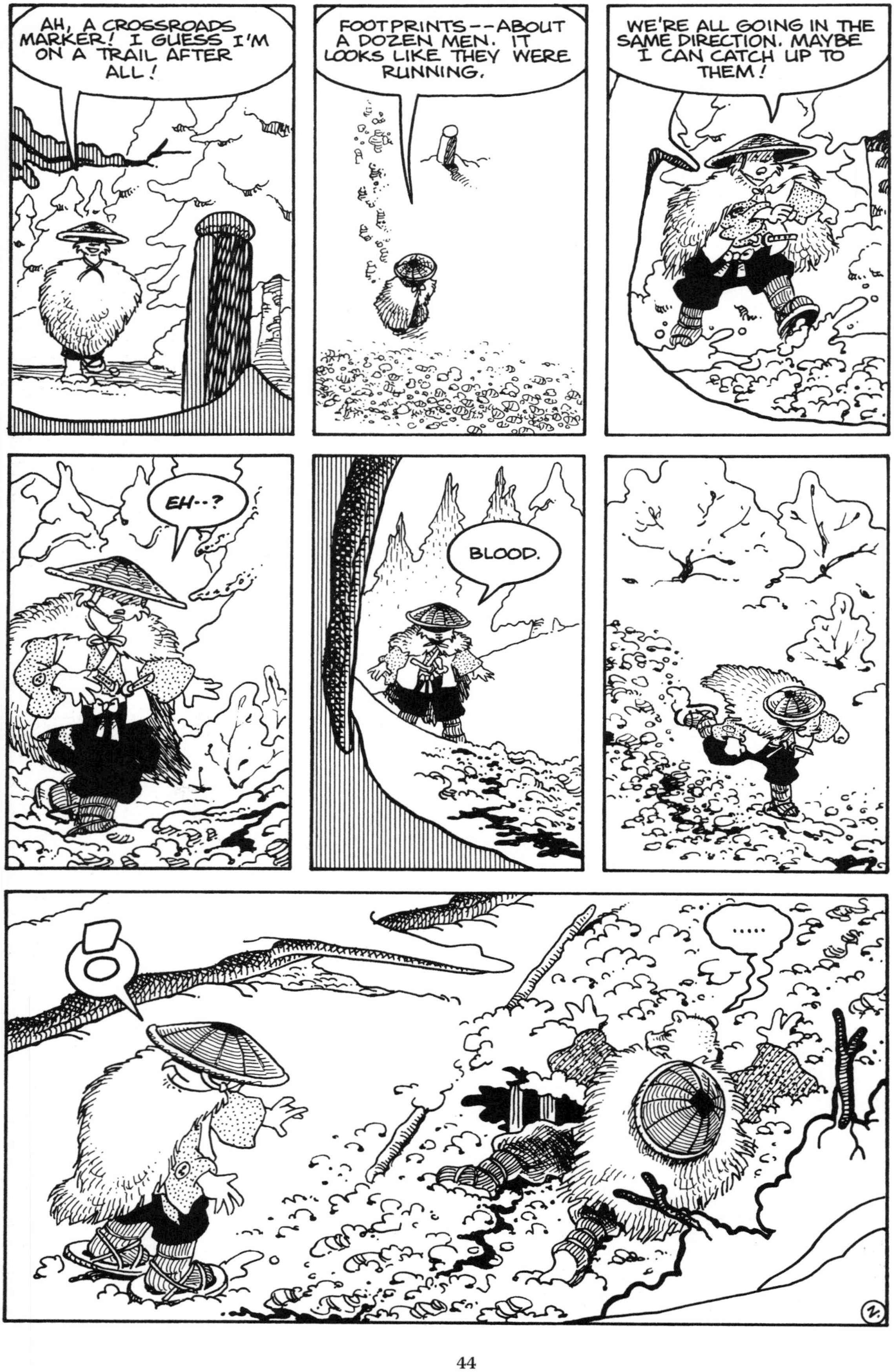
AH, A CROSSROADS MARKER! I GUESS I'M ON A TRAIL AFTER ALL!
FOOTPRINTS--ABOUT A DOZEN MEN. IT LOOKS LIKE THEY WERE RUNNING.
WE'RE ALL GOING IN THE SAME DIRECTION. MAYBE I CAN CATCH UP TO THEM!
EH--?
BLOOD.
.....
2.

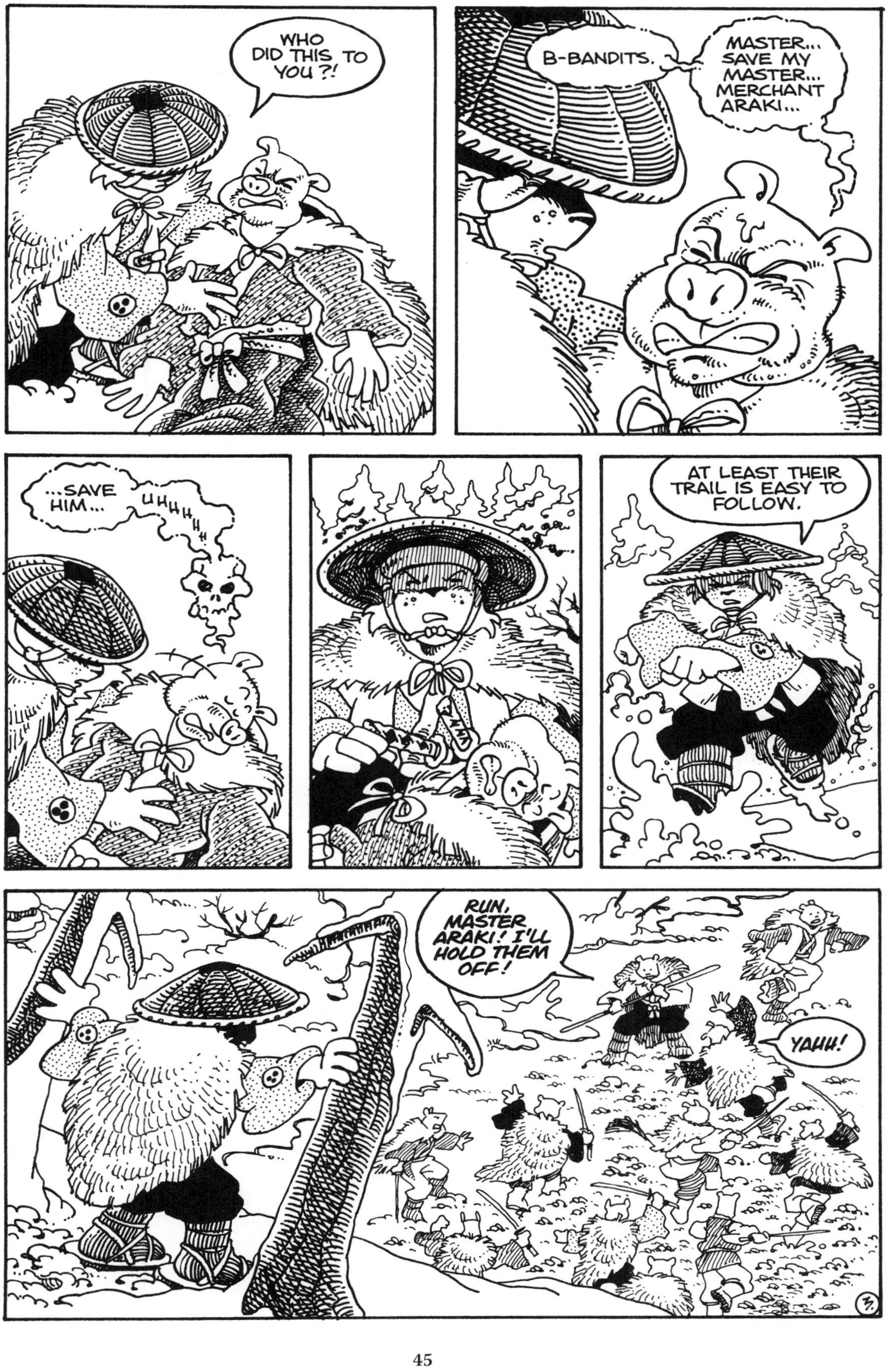
WHO DID THIS TO YOU?!
B-BANDITS.
MASTER... SAVE MY MASTER... MERCHANT ARAKI...
...SAVE HIM...
UHHHHH
AT LEAST THEIR TRAIL IS EASY TO FOLLOW.
RUN, MASTER ARAKI! I'LL HOLD THEM OFF!
YAHH!

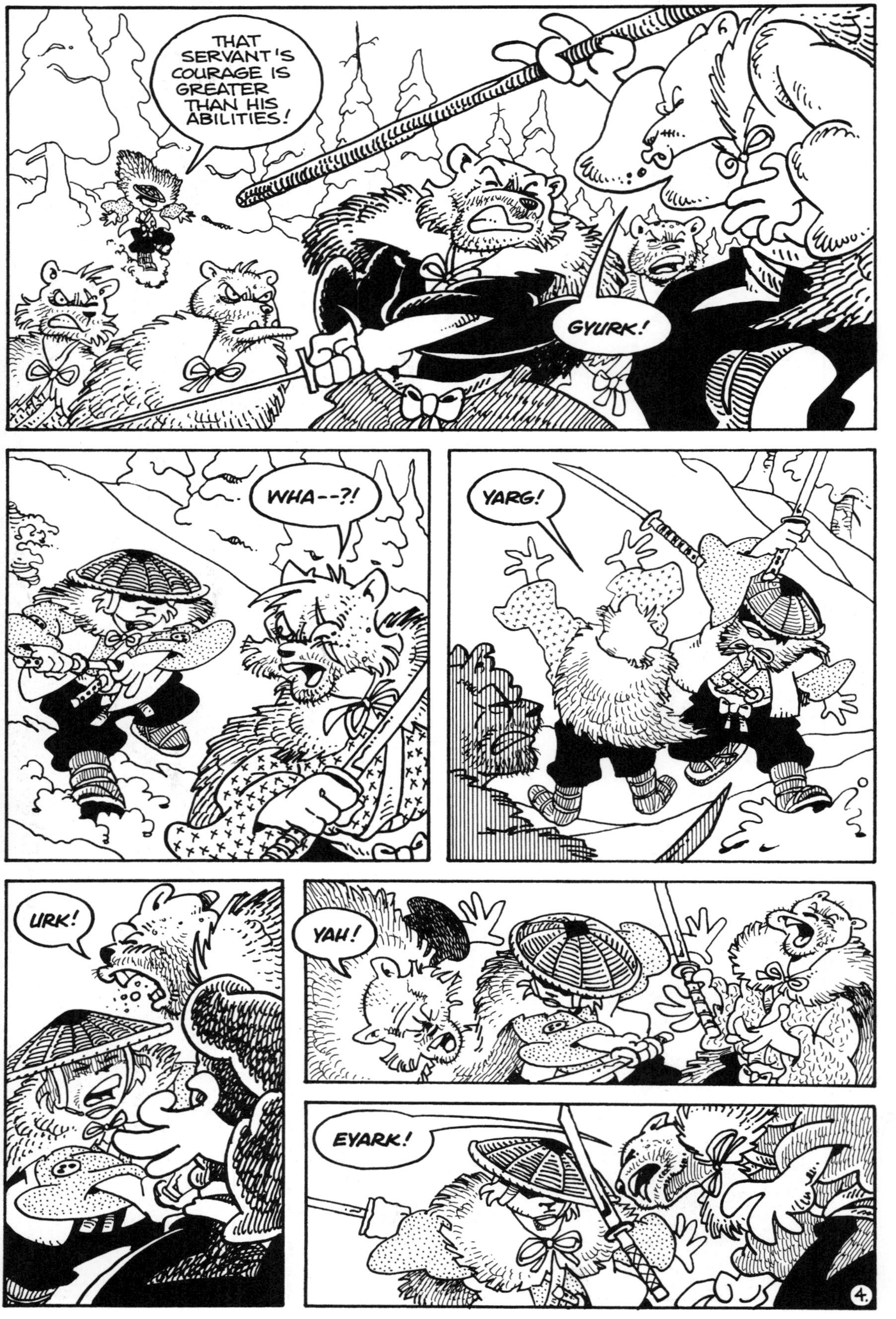
THAT SERVANT'S COURAGE IS GREATER THAN HIS ABILITIES!
GYURK!
WHA--?!
YARG!
URK!
YAH!
EYARK!
4.

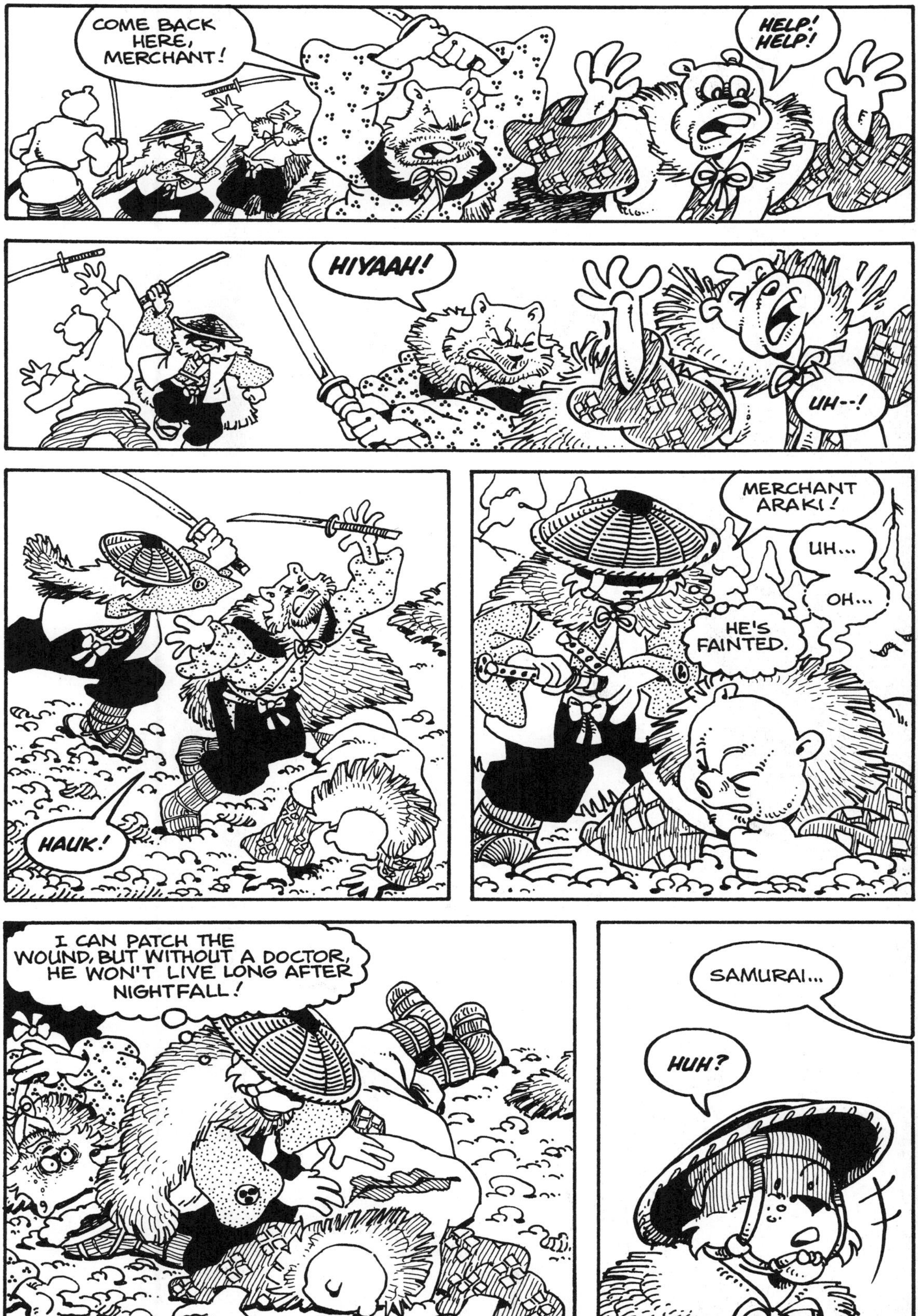
COME BACK HERE, MERCHANT!
HELP! HELP!
HIYAAH!
UH--!
HAUK!
MERCHANT ARAKI!
UH...
OH...
HE'S FAINTED.
I CAN PATCH THE WOUND, BUT WITHOUT A DOCTOR, HE WON'T LIVE LONG AFTER NIGHTFALL!
SAMURAI...
HUH?
5.

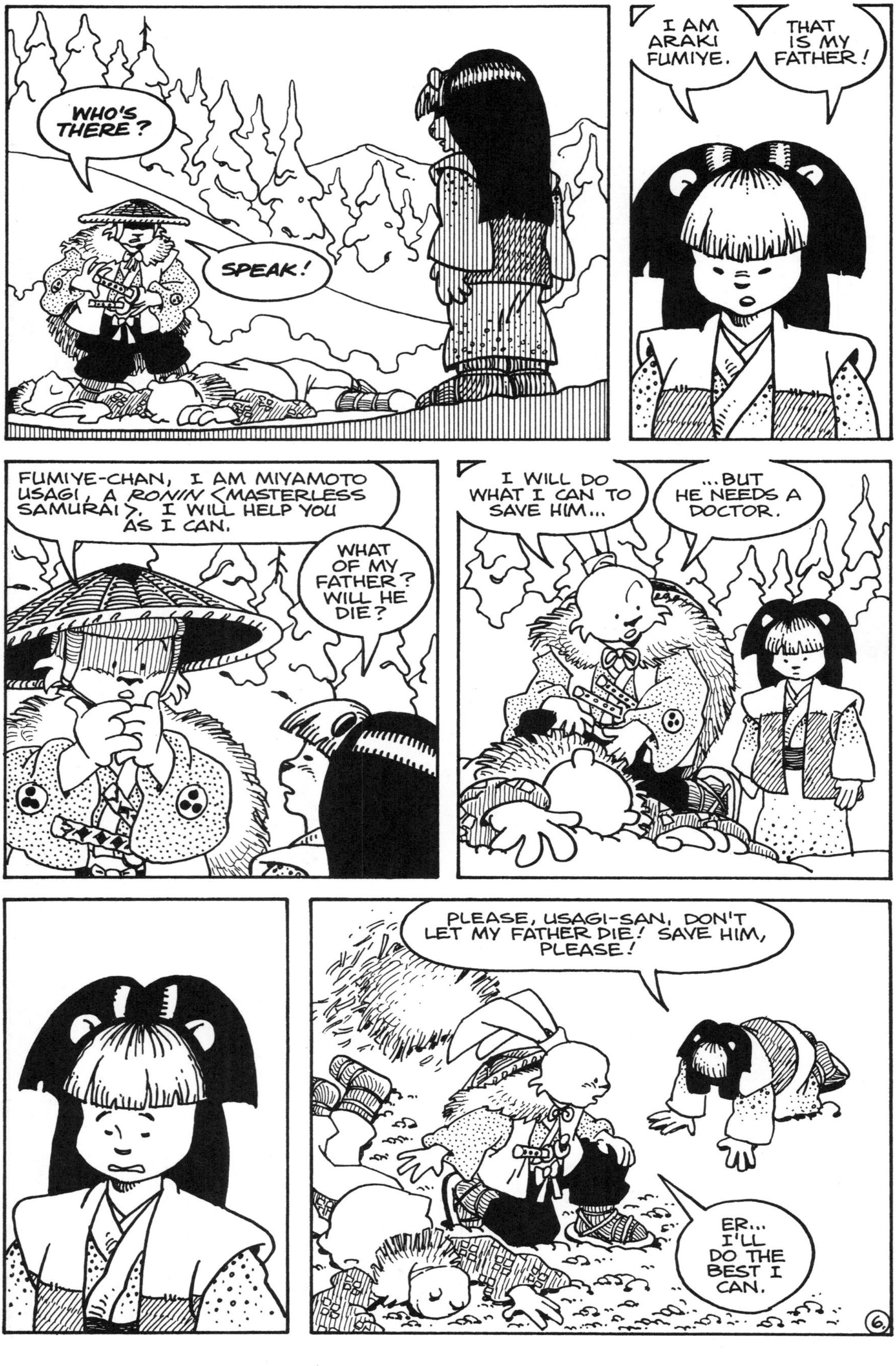
WHO'S THERE?
SPEAK!
I AM ARAKI FUMIYE.
THAT IS MY FATHER!
FUMIYE-CHAN, I AM MIYAMOTO USAGI, A *RONIN* <MASTERLESS SAMURAI>. I WILL HELP YOU AS I CAN.
WHAT OF MY FATHER? WILL HE DIE?
I WILL DO WHAT I CAN TO SAVE HIM...
...BUT HE NEEDS A DOCTOR.
PLEASE, USAGI-SAN, DON'T LET MY FATHER DIE! SAVE HIM, PLEASE!
ER... I'LL DO THE BEST I CAN.
6

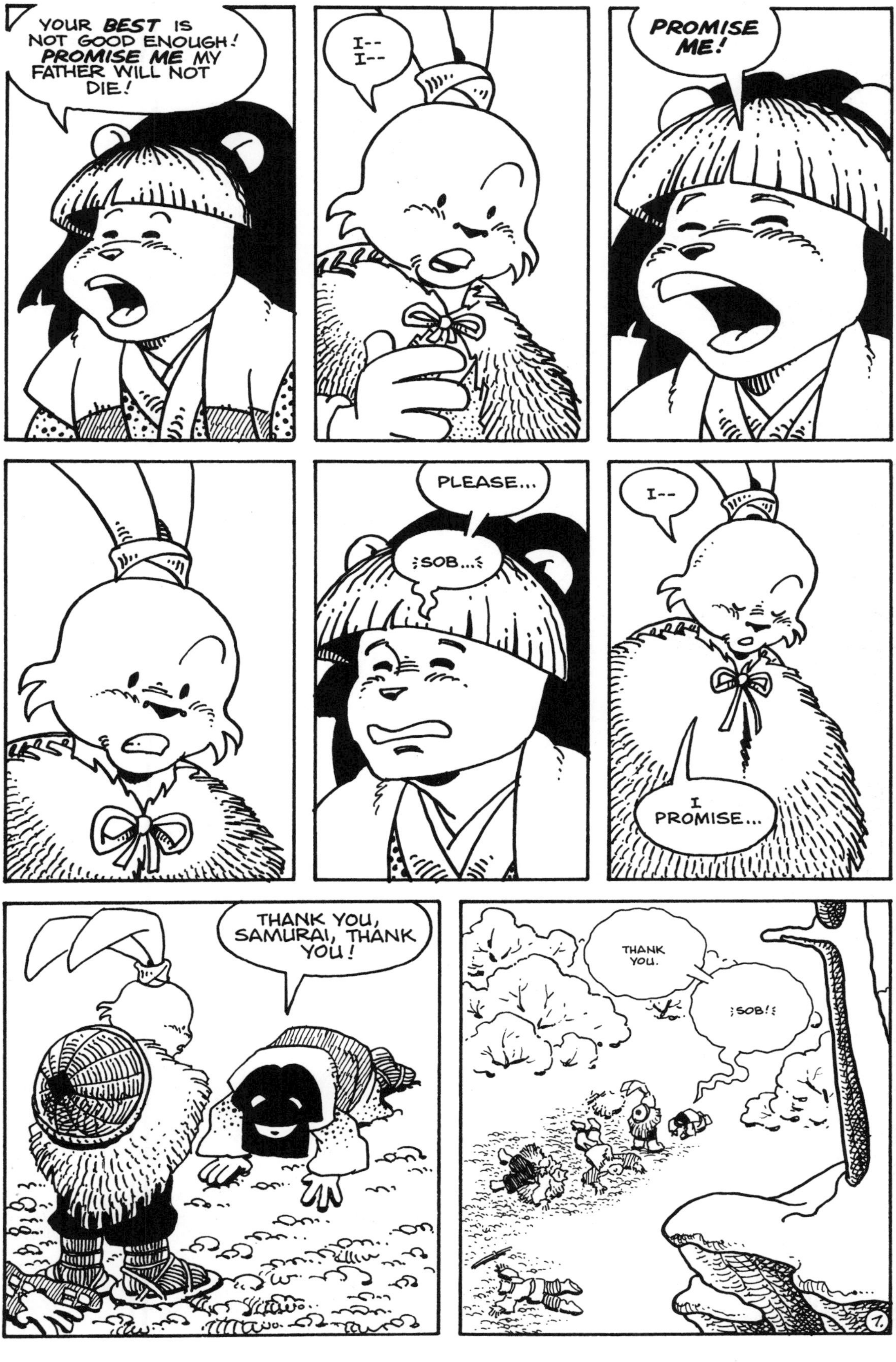
YOUR BEST IS NOT GOOD ENOUGH! PROMISE ME MY FATHER WILL NOT DIE!
I-- I--
PROMISE ME!
PLEASE...
SOB...
I--
I PROMISE...
THANK YOU, SAMURAI, THANK YOU!
THANK YOU.
SOB!
7.

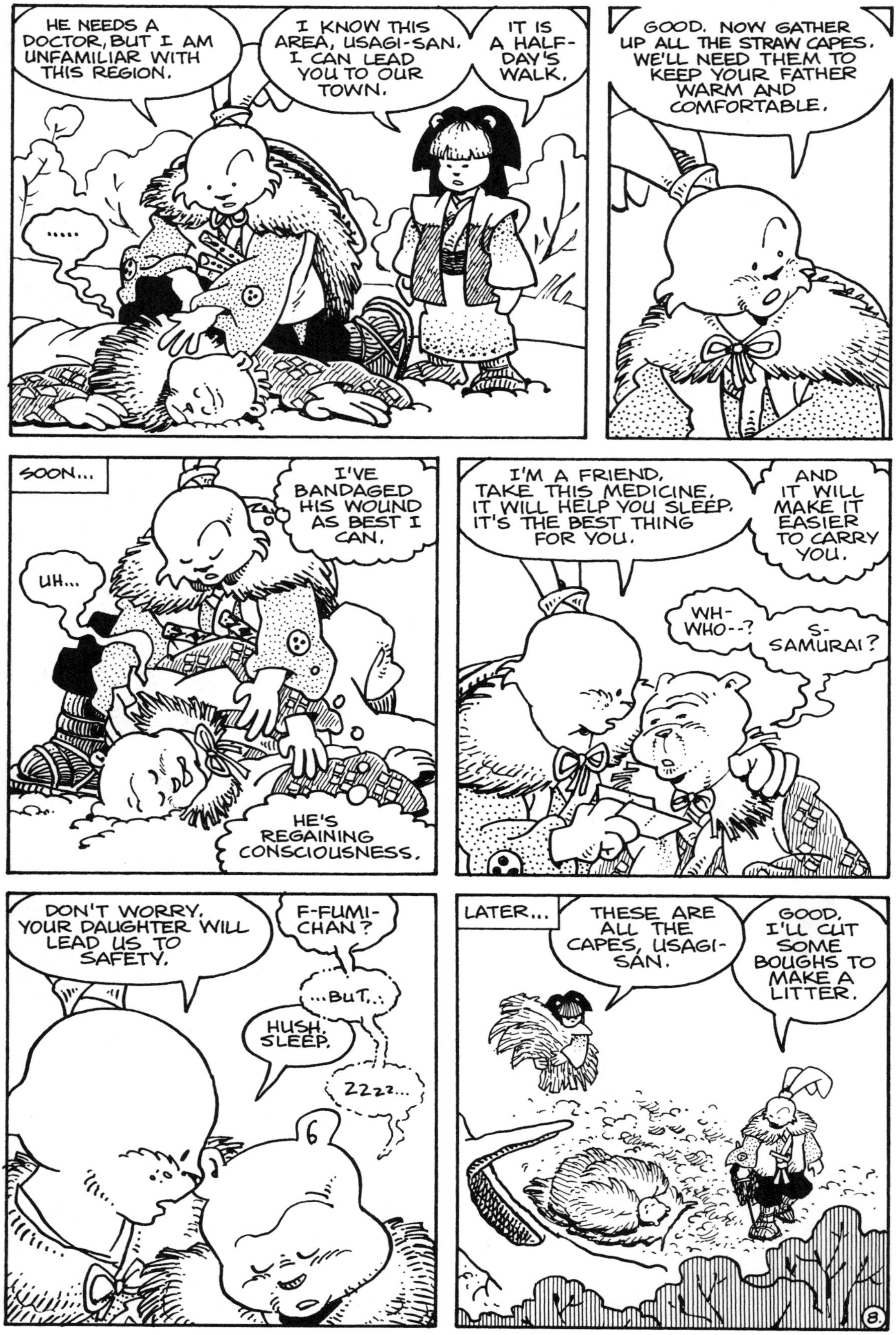
HE NEEDS A DOCTOR, BUT I AM UNFAMILIAR WITH THIS REGION.
I KNOW THIS AREA, USAGI-SAN. I CAN LEAD YOU TO OUR TOWN.
IT IS A HALF-DAY'S WALK.
.....
GOOD. NOW GATHER UP ALL THE STRAW CAPES. WE'LL NEED THEM TO KEEP YOUR FATHER WARM AND COMFORTABLE.
SOON...
I'VE BANDAGED HIS WOUND AS BEST I CAN.
UH...
HE'S REGAINING CONSCIOUSNESS.
I'M A FRIEND. TAKE THIS MEDICINE. IT WILL HELP YOU SLEEP. IT'S THE BEST THING FOR YOU.
AND IT WILL MAKE IT EASIER TO CARRY YOU.
WH-WHO--?
S-SAMURAI?
DON'T WORRY. YOUR DAUGHTER WILL LEAD US TO SAFETY.
F-FUMI-CHAN?
...BUT...
HUSH. SLEEP.
ZZzz...
LATER...
THESE ARE ALL THE CAPES, USAGI-SAN.
GOOD. I'LL CUT SOME BOUGHS TO MAKE A LITTER.
8.

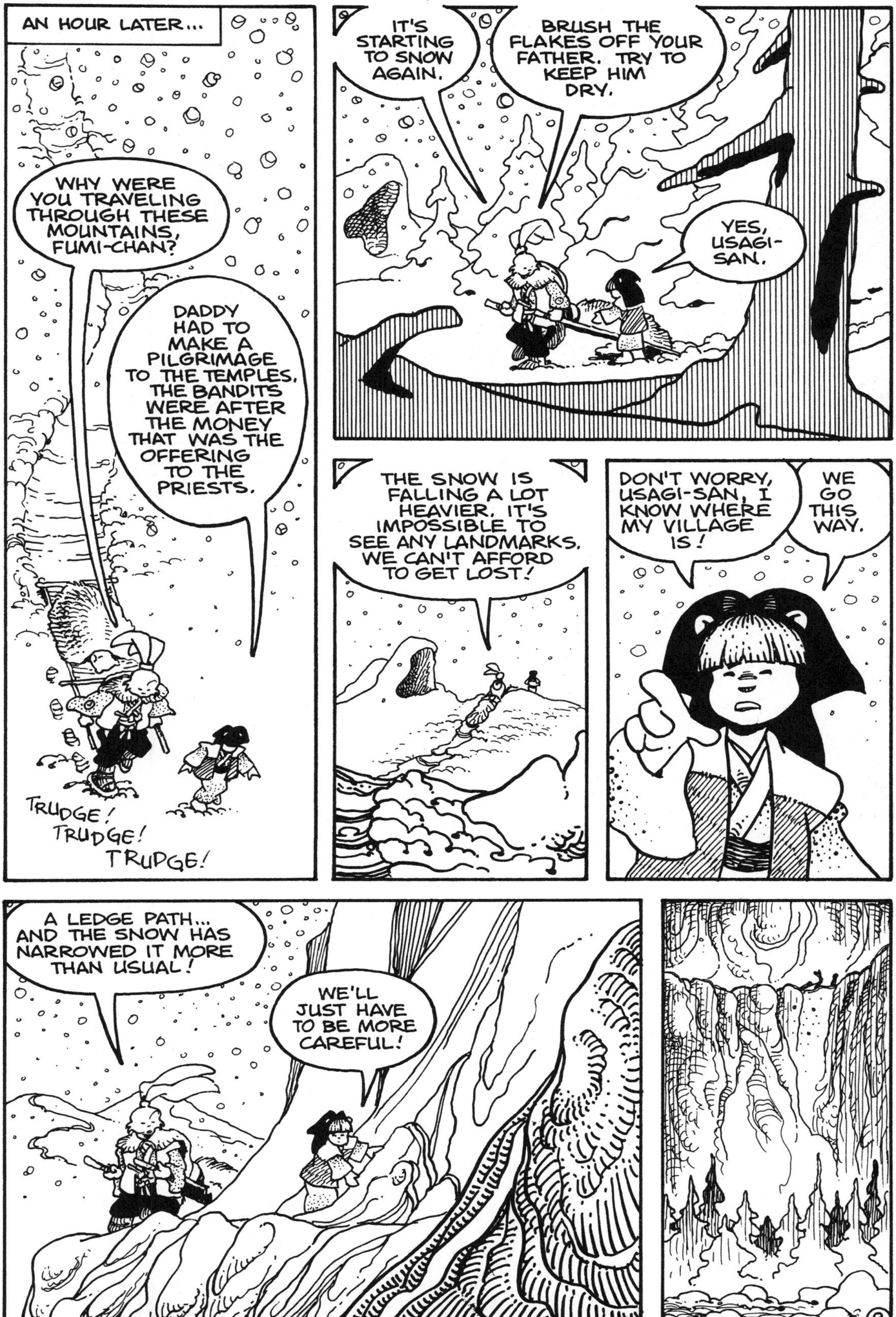
AN HOUR LATER...
WHY WERE YOU TRAVELING THROUGH THESE MOUNTAINS, FUMI-CHAN?
DADDY HAD TO MAKE A PILGRIMAGE TO THE TEMPLES. THE BANDITS WERE AFTER THE MONEY THAT WAS THE OFFERING TO THE PRIESTS.
TRUDGE! TRUDGE! TRUDGE!
IT'S STARTING TO SNOW AGAIN.
BRUSH THE FLAKES OFF YOUR FATHER. TRY TO KEEP HIM DRY.
YES, USAGI-SAN.
THE SNOW IS FALLING A LOT HEAVIER. IT'S IMPOSSIBLE TO SEE ANY LANDMARKS. WE CAN'T AFFORD TO GET LOST!
DON'T WORRY, USAGI-SAN, I KNOW WHERE MY VILLAGE IS!
WE GO THIS WAY.
A LEDGE PATH... AND THE SNOW HAS NARROWED IT MORE THAN USUAL!
WE'LL JUST HAVE TO BE MORE CAREFUL!
9.

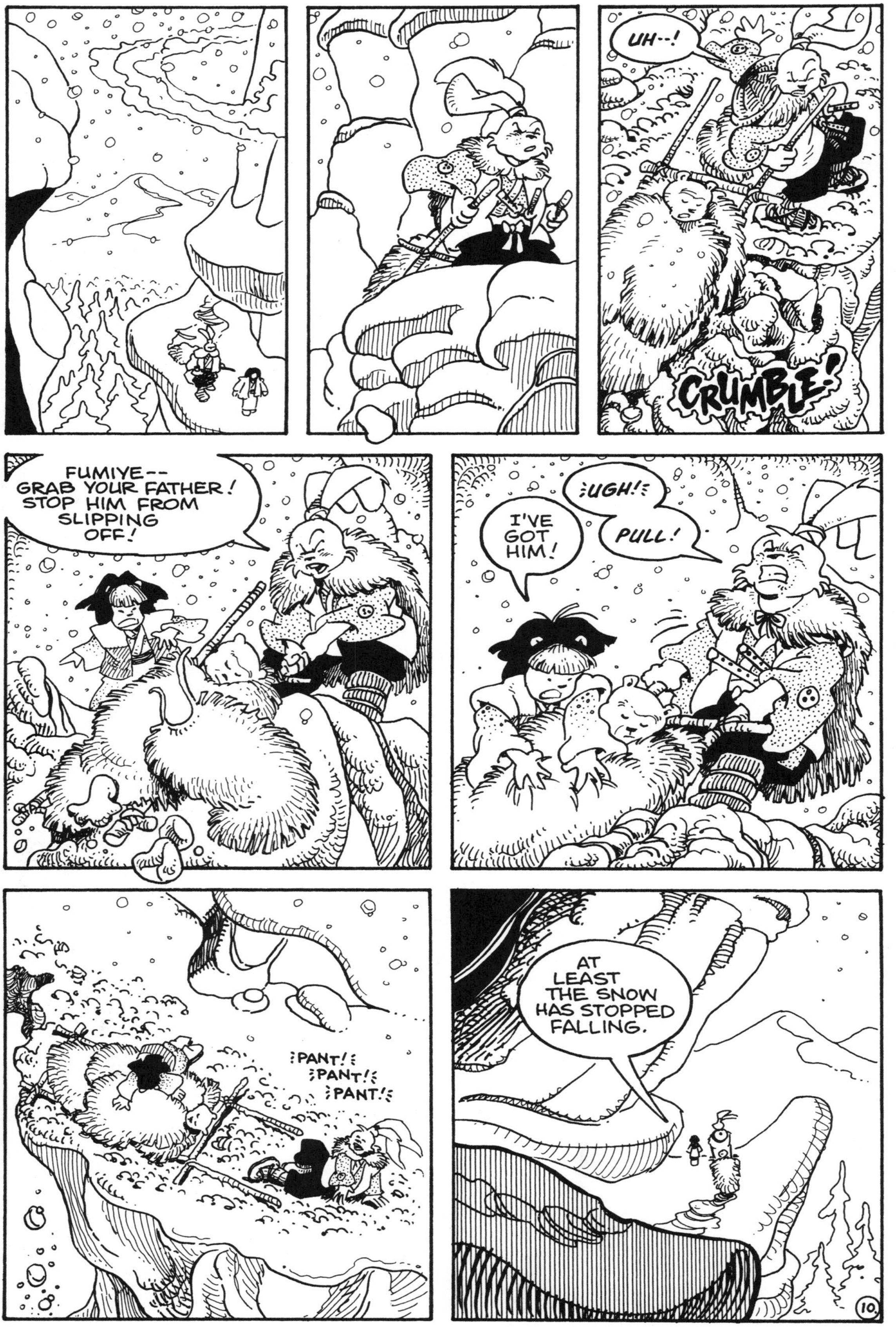

UH--!
CRUMBLE!
FUMIYE-- GRAB YOUR FATHER! STOP HIM FROM SLIPPING OFF!
I'VE GOT HIM!
UGH!
PULL!
PANT! PANT! PANT!
AT LEAST THE SNOW HAS STOPPED FALLING.
10

AFTER ANOTHER HOUR...

ARRRRRRRRRRROOOOOOOOOOO

HUH!

WHAT IS IT, USAGI-SAN?

RUN, FUMI!

WE CAN'T GET CAUGHT OUT IN THE OPEN!

RROOOOO OOO

CAUGHT BY WHOM?

AR

HURRY! SAVE YOUR BREATH FOR RUNNING!

AR ROOOO OOOOOOOO

53

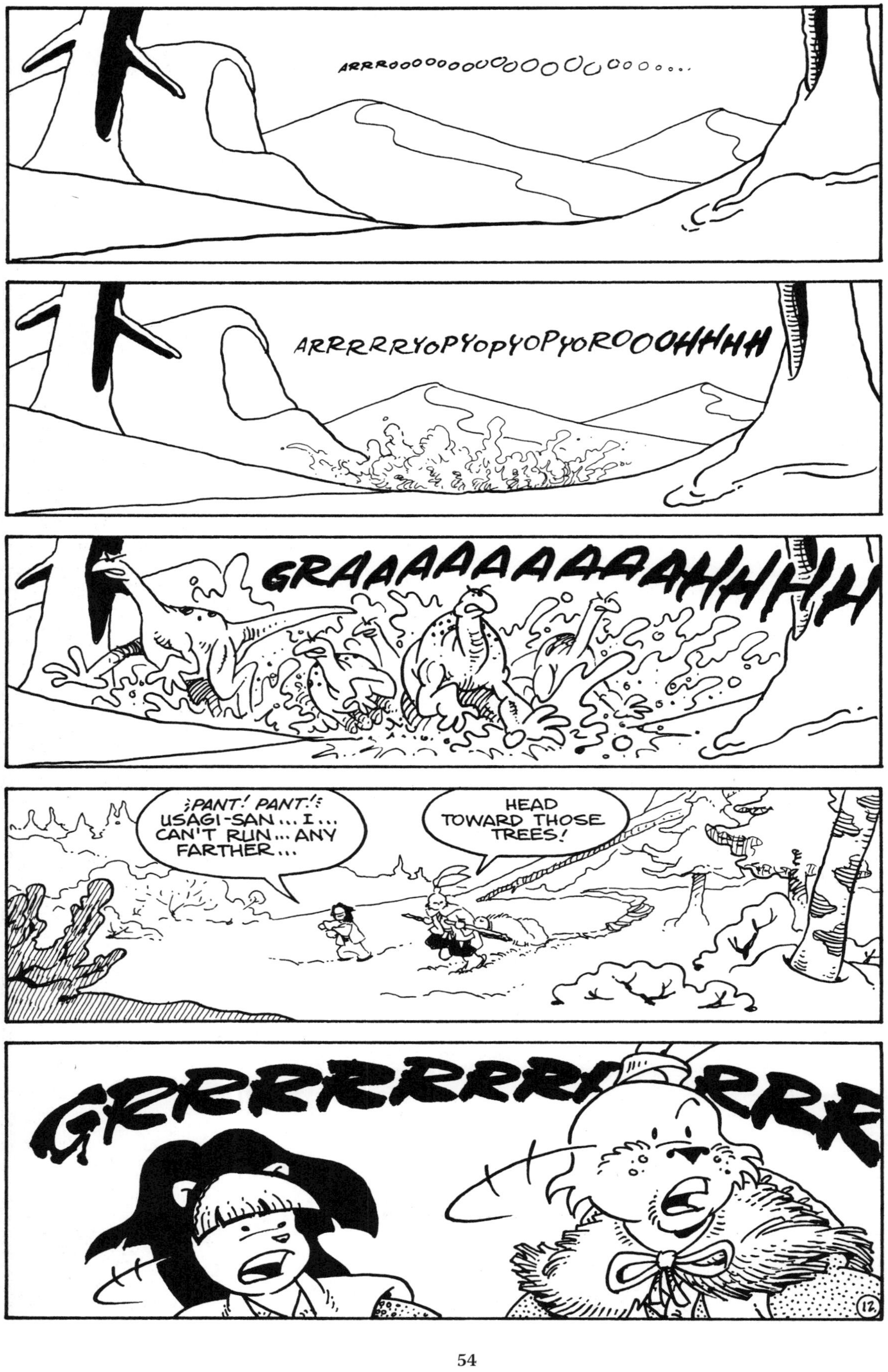
ARRROOOOOOOOOOOOOOOOOOO....
ARRRRRYOPYOPYOPYOROOOHHHH
GRAAAAAAAAAAHHHHH
PANT! PANT! USAGI-SAN... I... CAN'T RUN... ANY FARTHER...
HEAD TOWARD THOSE TREES!
GRRRRRRRRRRRRR
12

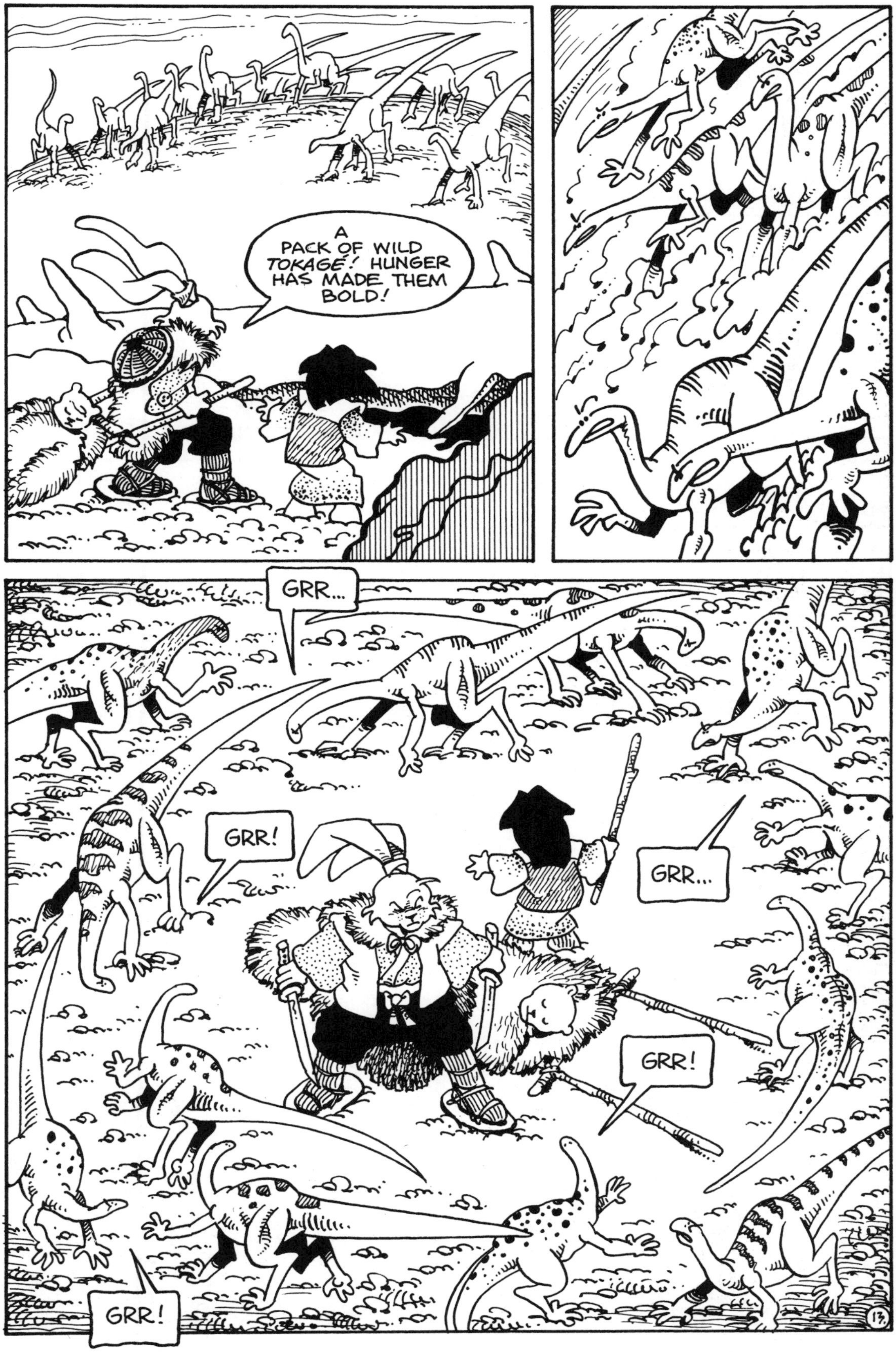
A PACK OF WILD TOKAGE! HUNGER HAS MADE THEM BOLD!
GRR...
GRR!
GRR...
GRR!
GRR!
13

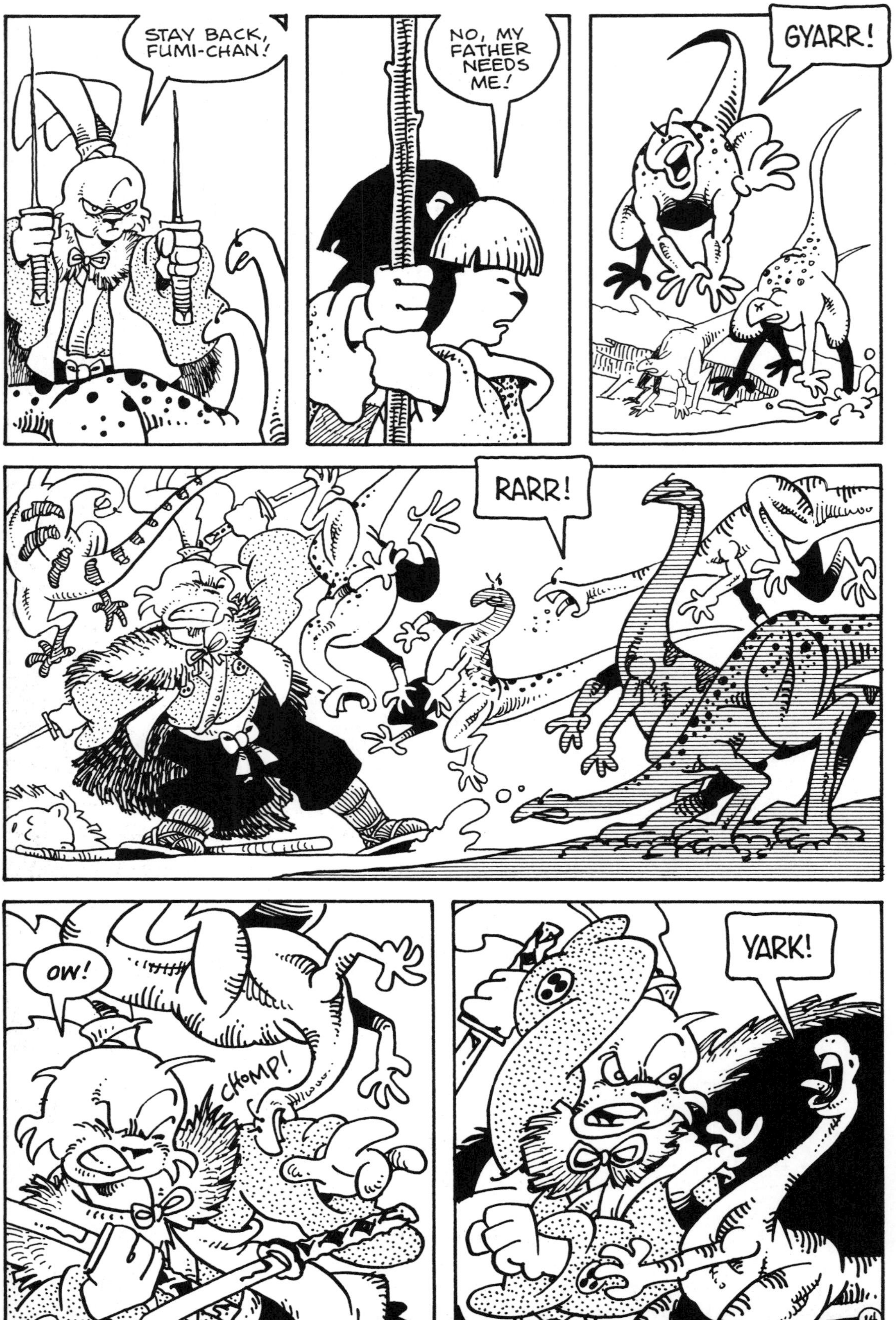
STAY BACK, FUMI-CHAN!
NO, MY FATHER NEEDS ME!
GYARR!
RARR!
OW!
CHOMP!
YARK!
14.

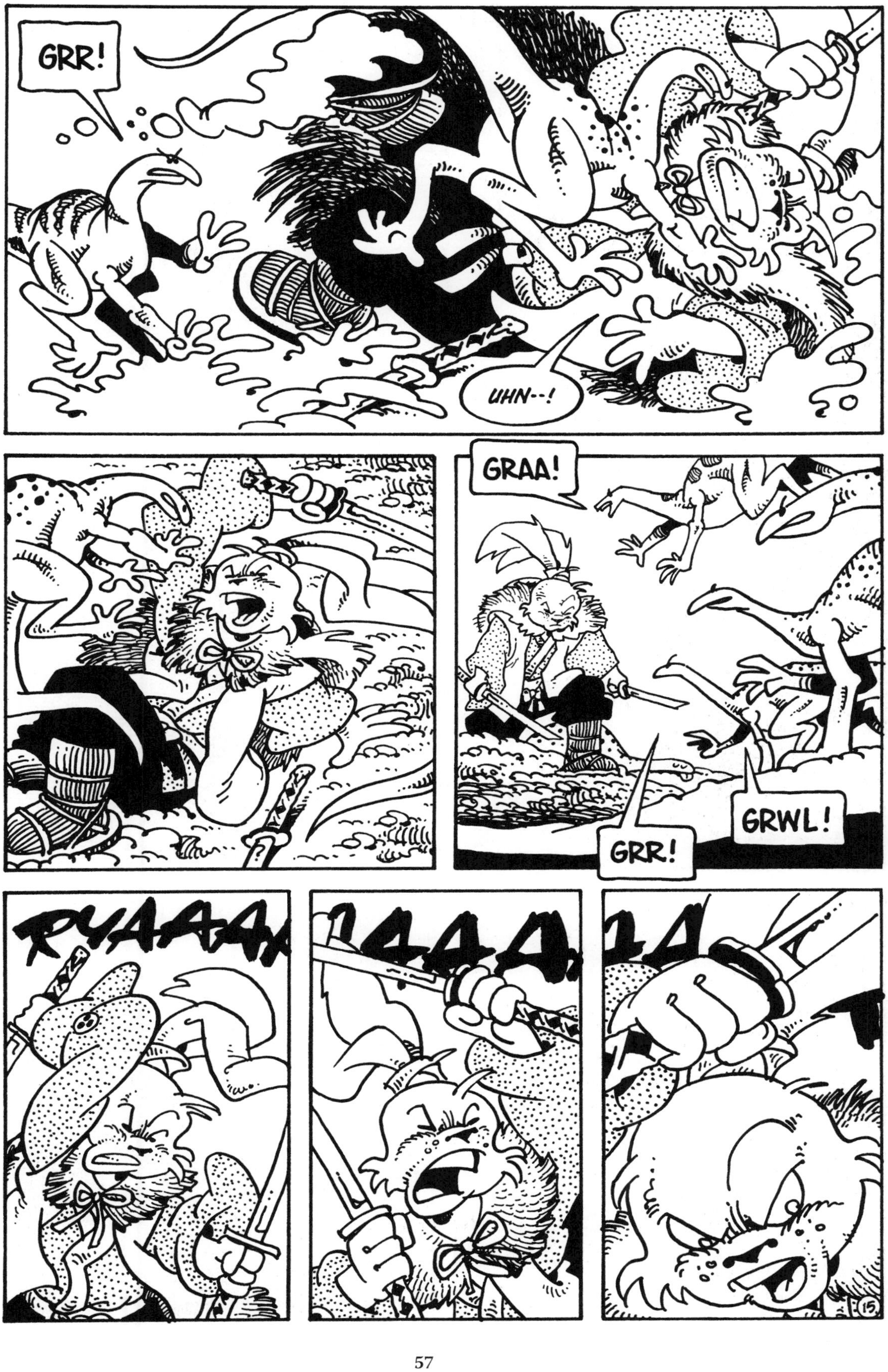
GRR!
UHN--!
GRAA!
GRR!
GRWL!
RYAAAAAAAAAAAA
15

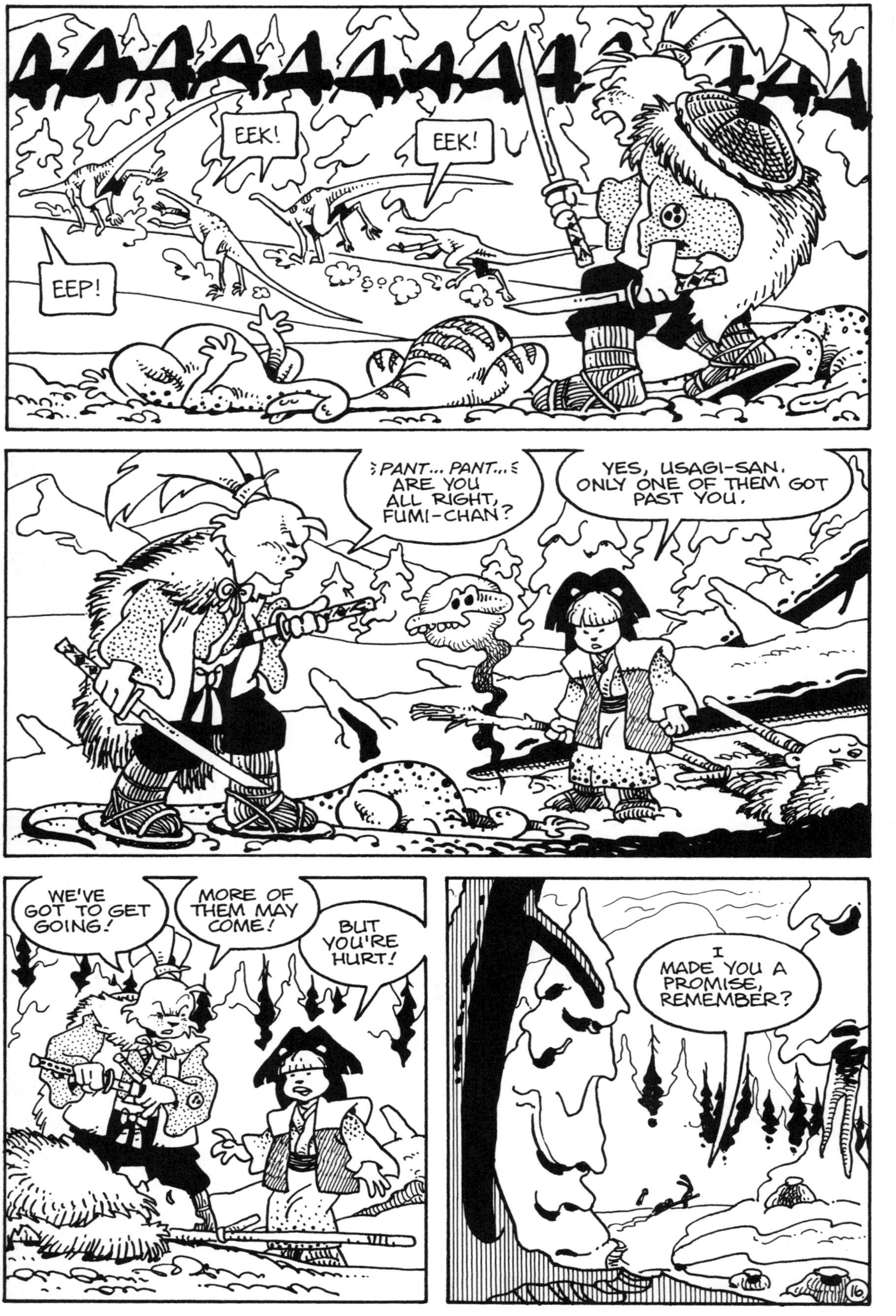

EEK!
EEK!
EEP!
PANT... PANT... ARE YOU ALL RIGHT, FUMI-CHAN?
YES, USAGI-SAN. ONLY ONE OF THEM GOT PAST YOU.
WE'VE GOT TO GET GOING!
MORE OF THEM MAY COME!
BUT YOU'RE HURT!
I MADE YOU A PROMISE, REMEMBER?
16

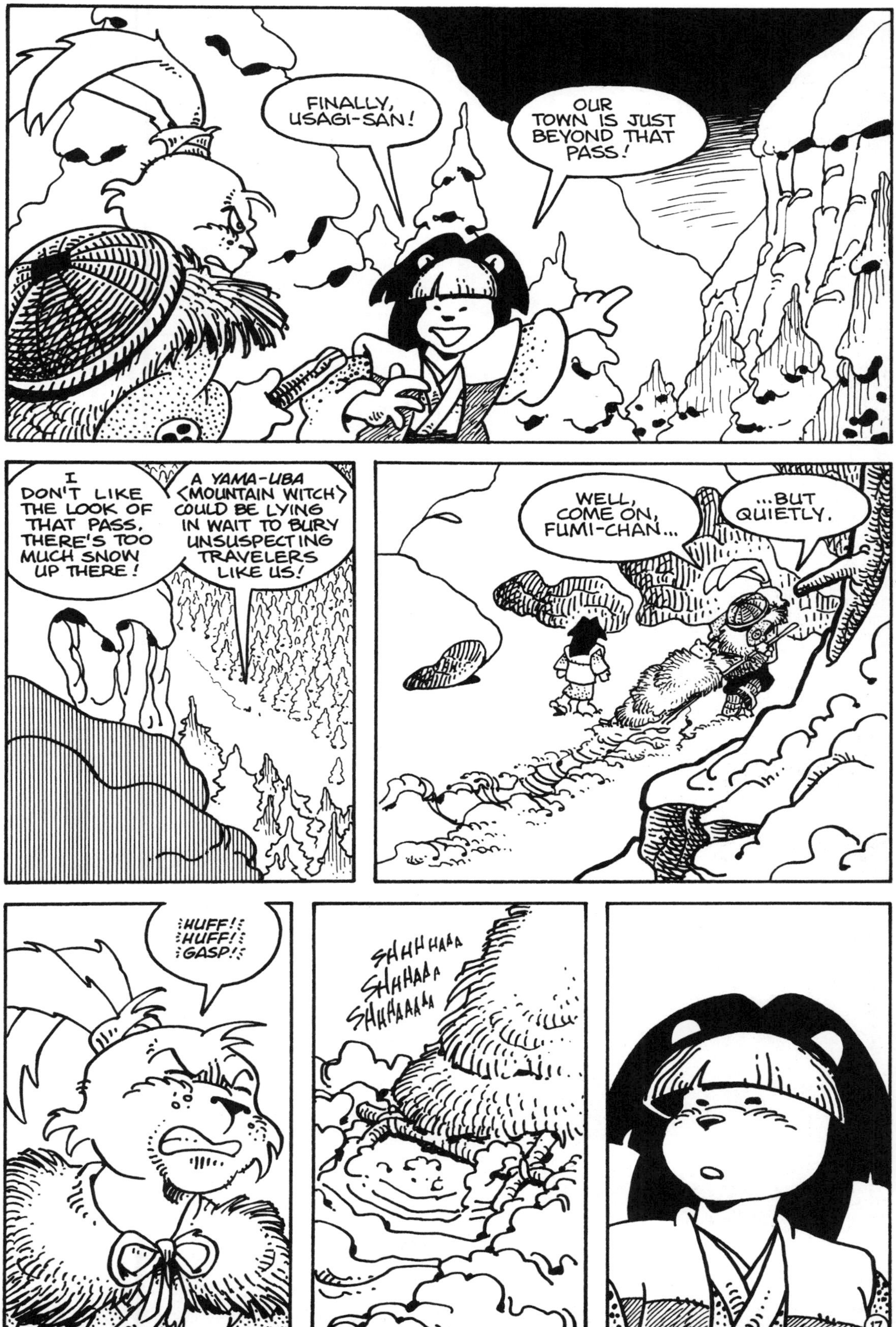
FINALLY, USAGI-SAN!
OUR TOWN IS JUST BEYOND THAT PASS!
I DON'T LIKE THE LOOK OF THAT PASS. THERE'S TOO MUCH SNOW UP THERE!
A YAMA-UBA <MOUNTAIN WITCH> COULD BE LYING IN WAIT TO BURY UNSUSPECTING TRAVELERS LIKE US!
WELL, COME ON, FUMI-CHAN...
...BUT QUIETLY.
HUFF! HUFF! GASP!
SHHHHAAA
SHHHAAA
SHHHAAAA
17

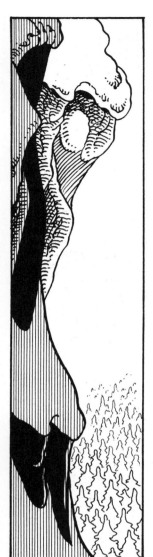

CLUMP!

CRK!

CRK!

SHOOOOOOOOOOK

JUST A LITTLE MORE AND WE'LL BE THROUGH THIS PASS.

CRUNCH!

CRUNCH!

.....ccccccccGGGGGGGGGGGGGGGGGGGGGGGGGGGGGGGGuuuuURR

.....

18.

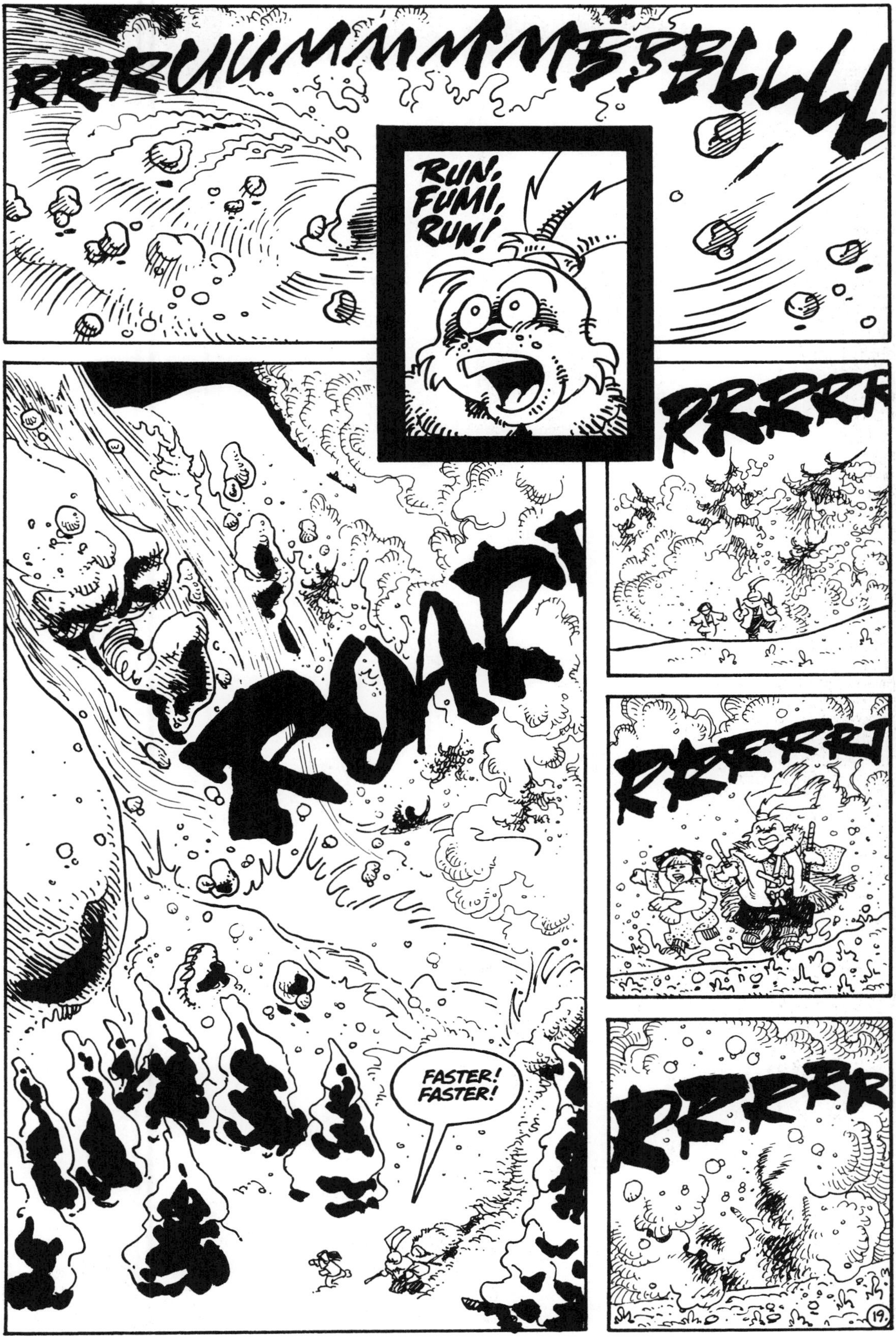
RRRUUMMMMMBBBLLL
RUN, FUMI, RUN!
ROAR
FASTER! FASTER!
RRRRRR
RRRRRR
RRRRRR
19.

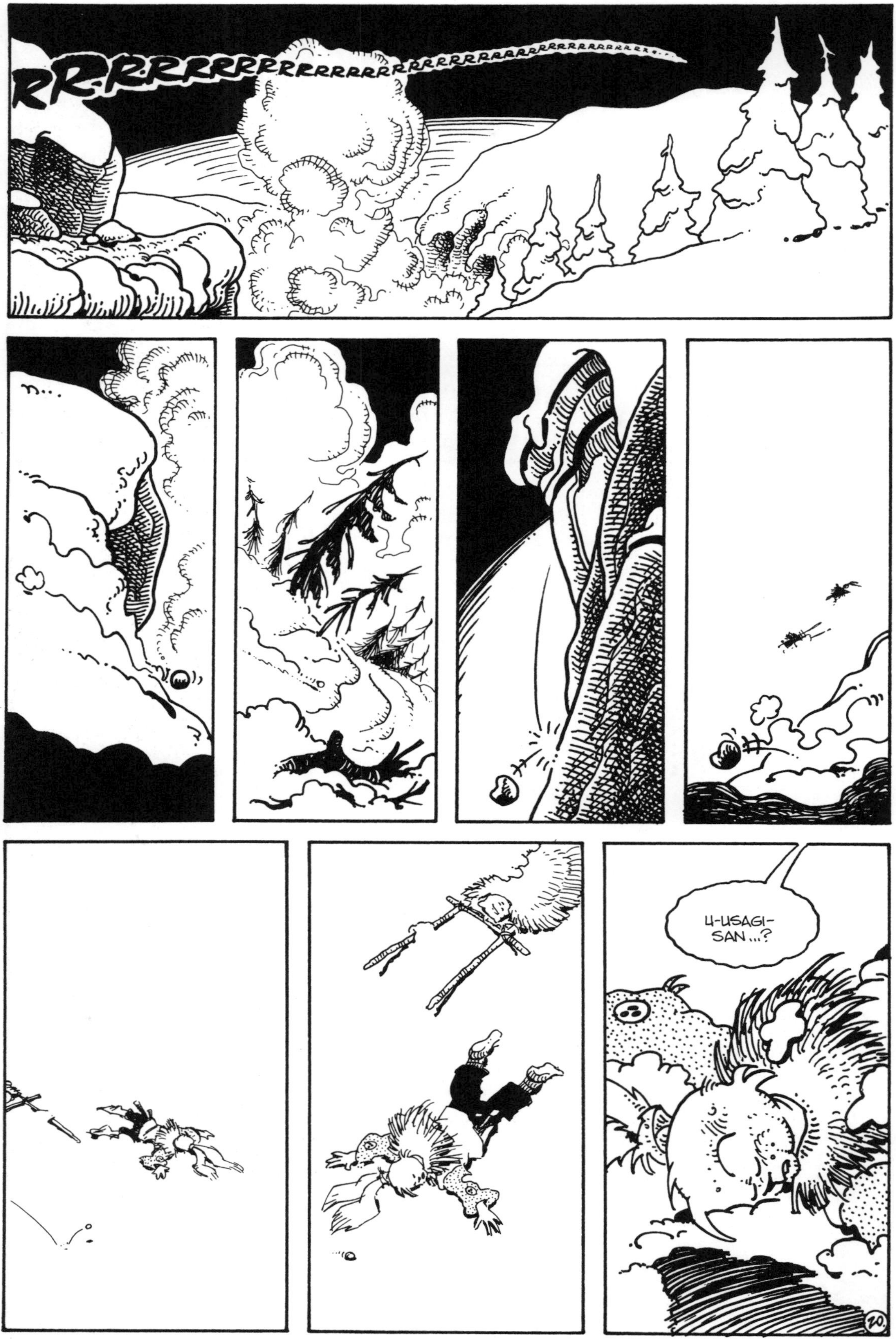
RR-R-RRRRRRRRRrrrrrrrrrrrrrrrrrrrrrrrrrrrrrrrrrrrrrrr...
U-USAGI-SAN...?

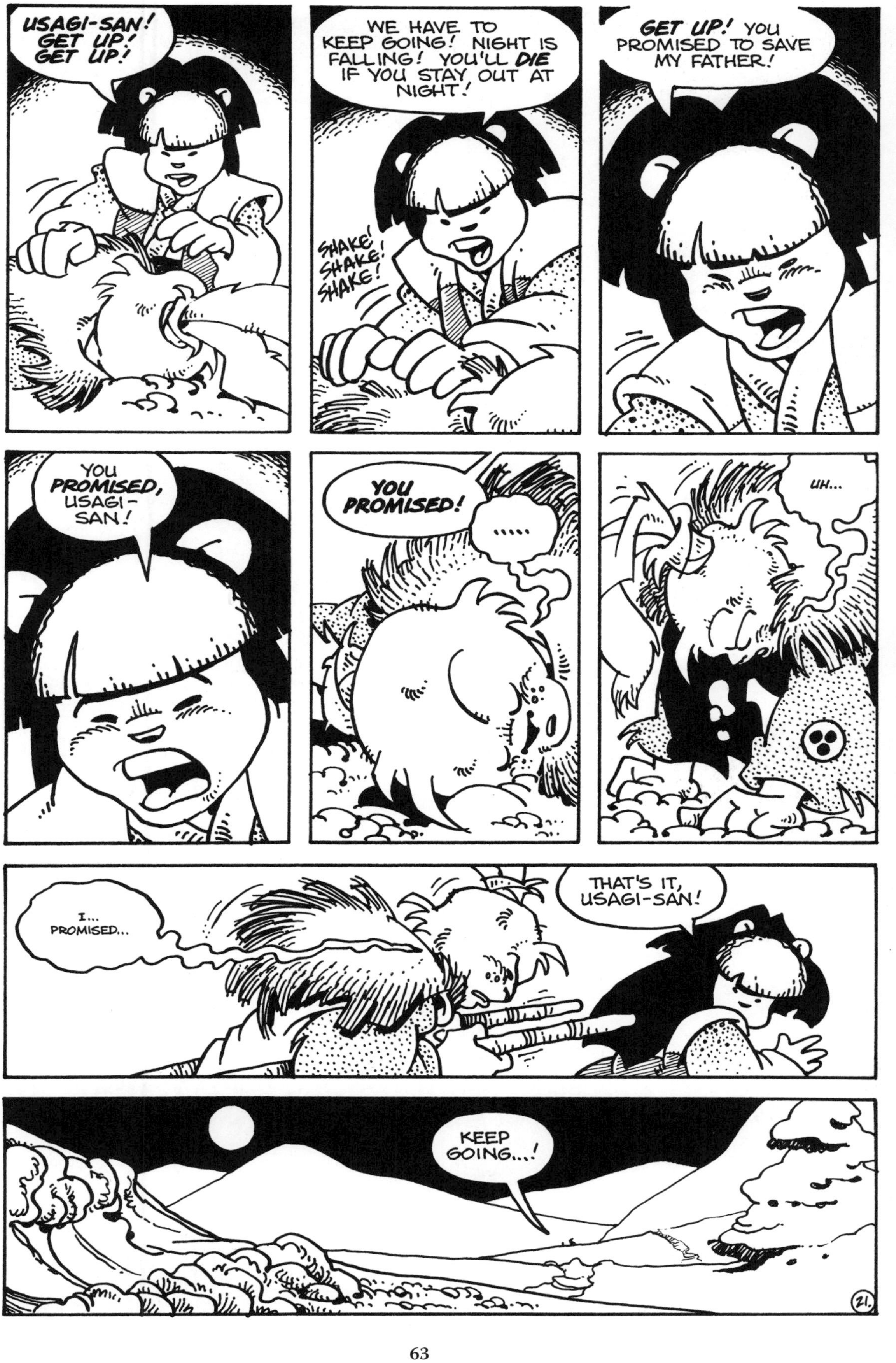
USAGI-SAN! GET UP! GET UP!
WE HAVE TO KEEP GOING! NIGHT IS FALLING! YOU'LL DIE IF YOU STAY OUT AT NIGHT!
SHAKE! SHAKE! SHAKE!
GET UP! YOU PROMISED TO SAVE MY FATHER!
YOU PROMISED, USAGI-SAN!
YOU PROMISED!
.....
UH...
I... PROMISED...
THAT'S IT, USAGI-SAN!
KEEP GOING...!
21.

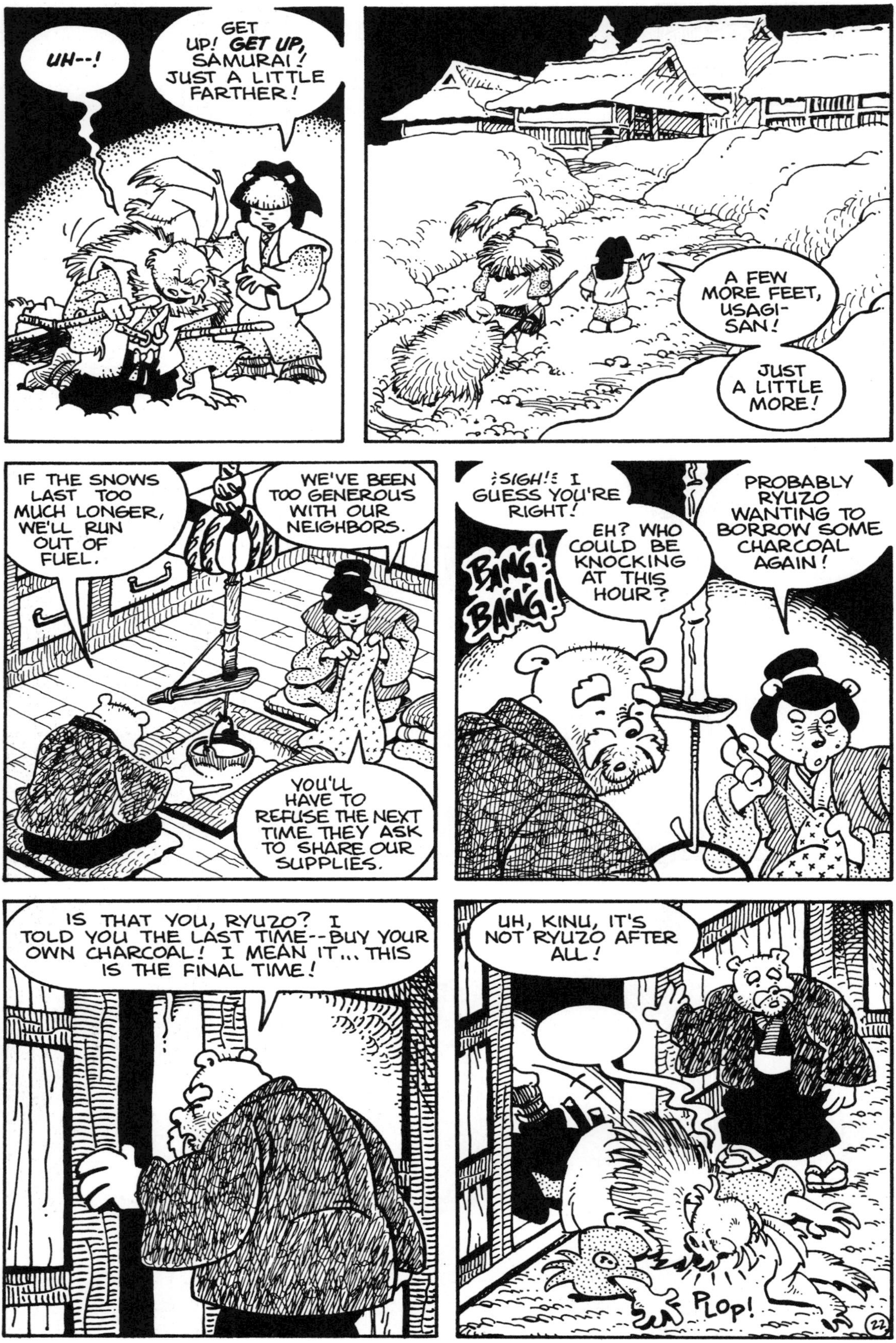
UH--!
GET UP! GET UP, SAMURAI! JUST A LITTLE FARTHER!
A FEW MORE FEET, USAGI-SAN!
JUST A LITTLE MORE!
IF THE SNOWS LAST TOO MUCH LONGER, WE'LL RUN OUT OF FUEL.
WE'VE BEEN TOO GENEROUS WITH OUR NEIGHBORS.
YOU'LL HAVE TO REFUSE THE NEXT TIME THEY ASK TO SHARE OUR SUPPLIES.
SIGH! I GUESS YOU'RE RIGHT!
BANG! BANG!
EH? WHO COULD BE KNOCKING AT THIS HOUR?
PROBABLY RYUZO WANTING TO BORROW SOME CHARCOAL AGAIN!
IS THAT YOU, RYUZO? I TOLD YOU THE LAST TIME--BUY YOUR OWN CHARCOAL! I MEAN IT... THIS IS THE FINAL TIME!
UH, KINU, IT'S NOT RYUZO AFTER ALL!
PLOP!
22

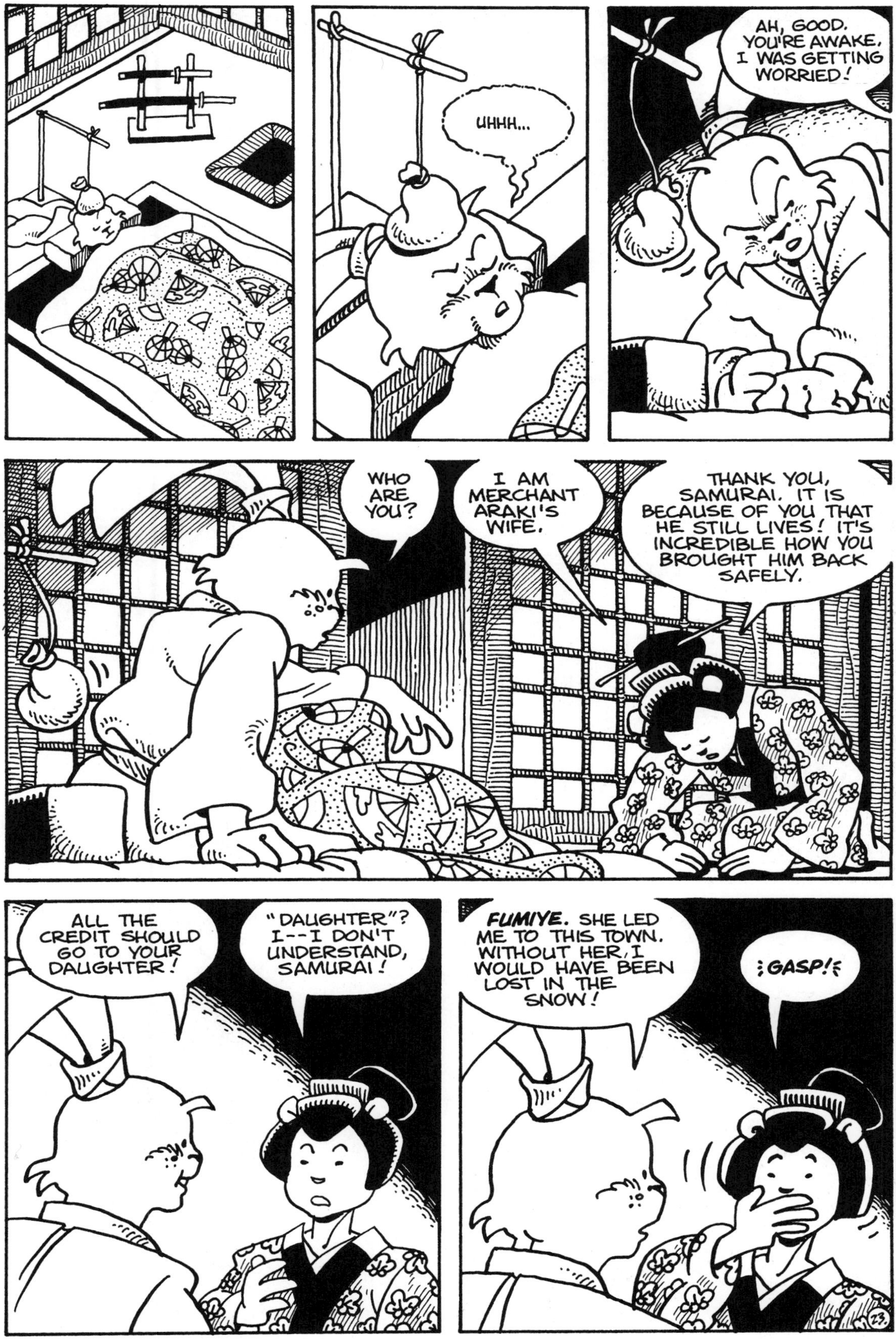
UHHH...
AH, GOOD. YOU'RE AWAKE. I WAS GETTING WORRIED!
WHO ARE YOU?
I AM MERCHANT ARAKI'S WIFE.
THANK YOU, SAMURAI. IT IS BECAUSE OF YOU THAT HE STILL LIVES! IT'S INCREDIBLE HOW YOU BROUGHT HIM BACK SAFELY.
ALL THE CREDIT SHOULD GO TO YOUR DAUGHTER!
"DAUGHTER"? I--I DON'T UNDERSTAND, SAMURAI!
FUMIYE. SHE LED ME TO THIS TOWN. WITHOUT HER, I WOULD HAVE BEEN LOST IN THE SNOW!
GASP!
23.

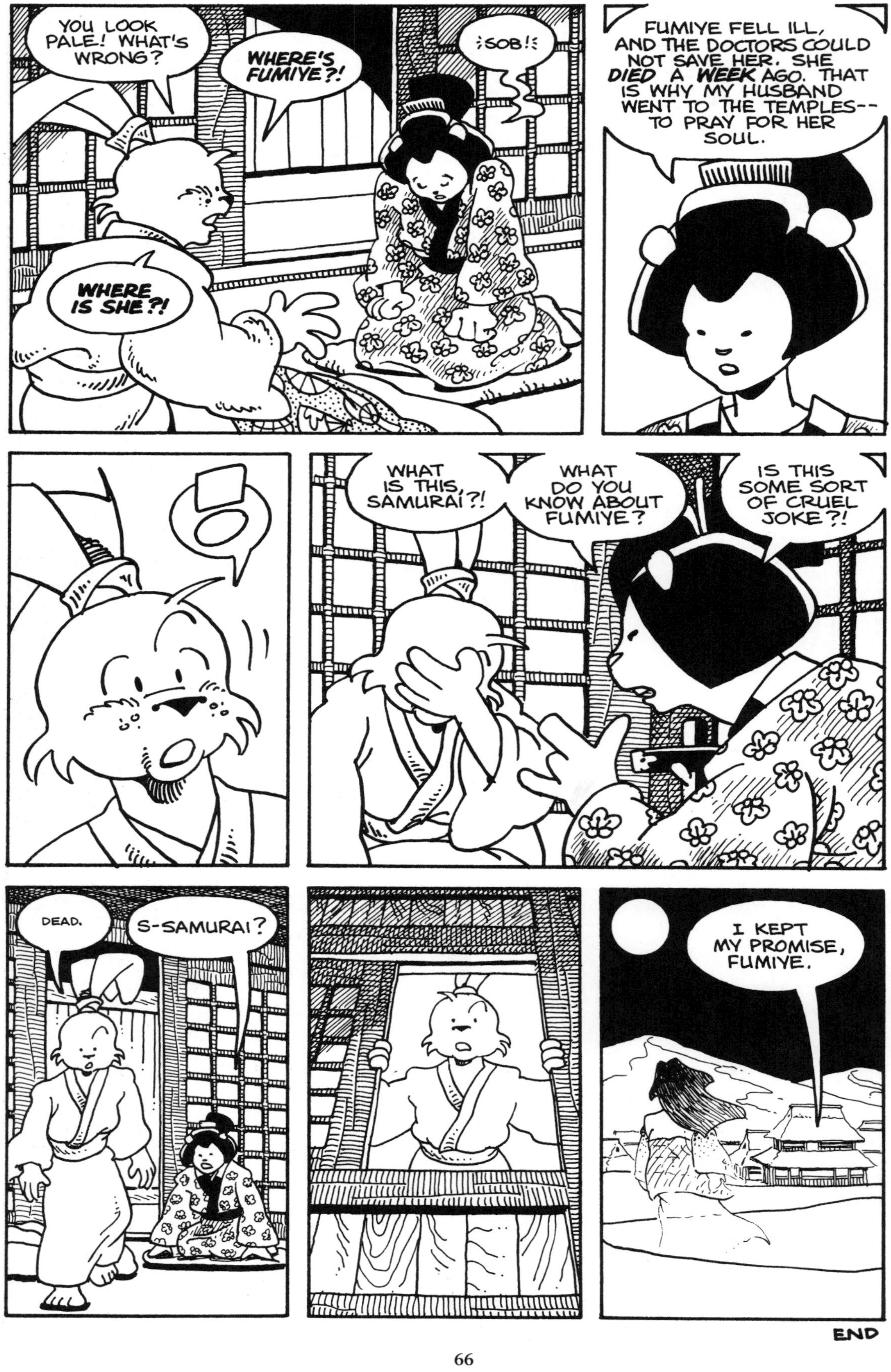
YOU LOOK PALE! WHAT'S WRONG?
WHERE'S FUMIYE?!
SOB!
WHERE IS SHE?!
FUMIYE FELL ILL, AND THE DOCTORS COULD NOT SAVE HER. SHE DIED A WEEK AGO. THAT IS WHY MY HUSBAND WENT TO THE TEMPLES-- TO PRAY FOR HER SOUL.
WHAT IS THIS, SAMURAI?!
WHAT DO YOU KNOW ABOUT FUMIYE?
IS THIS SOME SORT OF CRUEL JOKE?!
DEAD.
S-SAMURAI?
I KEPT MY PROMISE, FUMIYE.
END

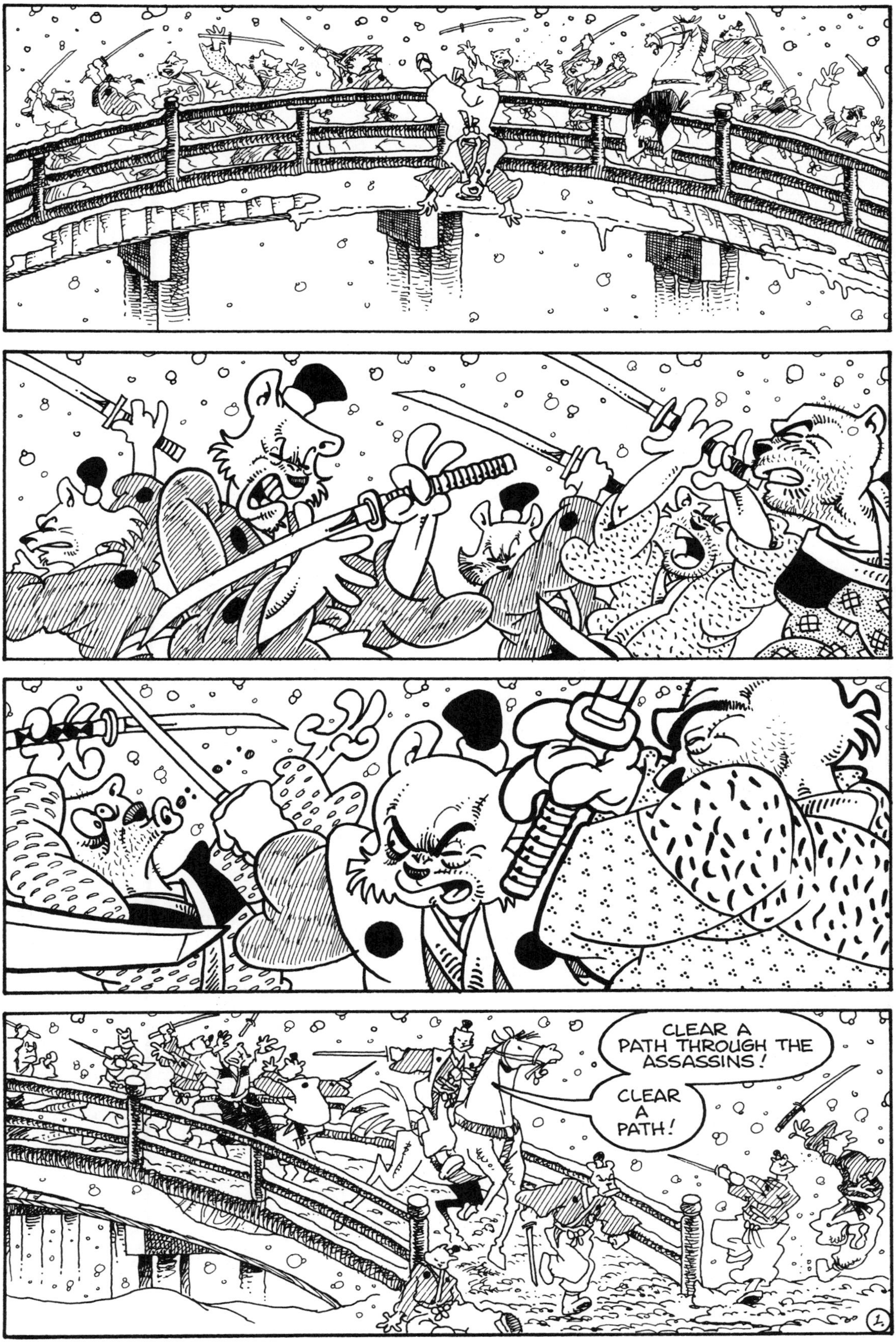
CLEAR A PATH THROUGH THE ASSASSINS!
CLEAR A PATH!
2

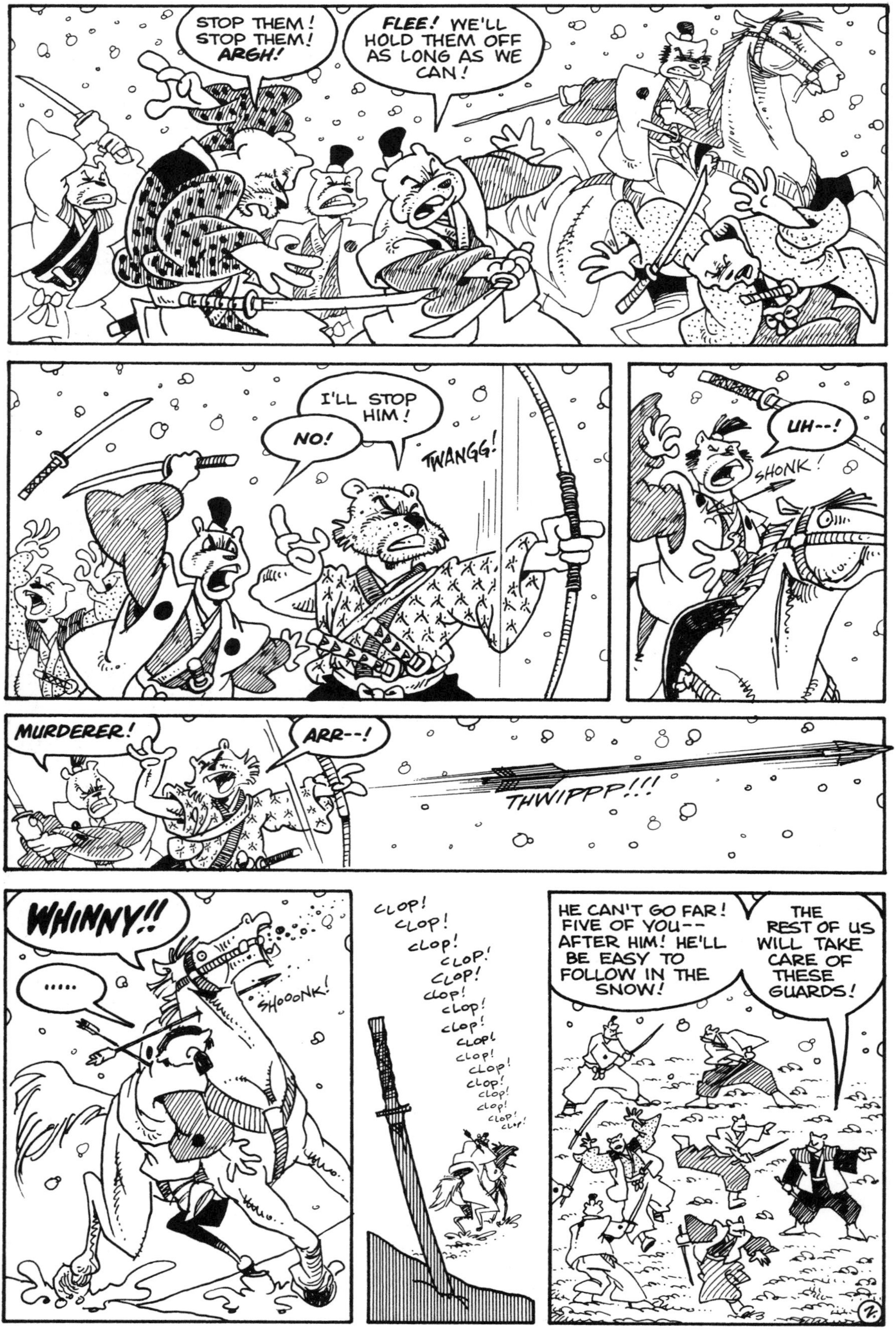
STOP THEM! STOP THEM! ARGH!
FLEE! WE'LL HOLD THEM OFF AS LONG AS WE CAN!
I'LL STOP HIM!
NO!
TWANGG!
UH--!
SHONK!
MURDERER!
ARR--!
THWIPPP!!!
WHINNY!!
.....
SHOOONK!
CLOP! CLOP! CLOP! CLOP! CLOP! CLOP! CLOP! CLOP! CLOP! CLOP! CLOP! CLOP! CLOP! CLOP! CLOP! CLOP!
HE CAN'T GO FAR! FIVE OF YOU-- AFTER HIM! HE'LL BE EASY TO FOLLOW IN THE SNOW!
THE REST OF US WILL TAKE CARE OF THESE GUARDS!
2.

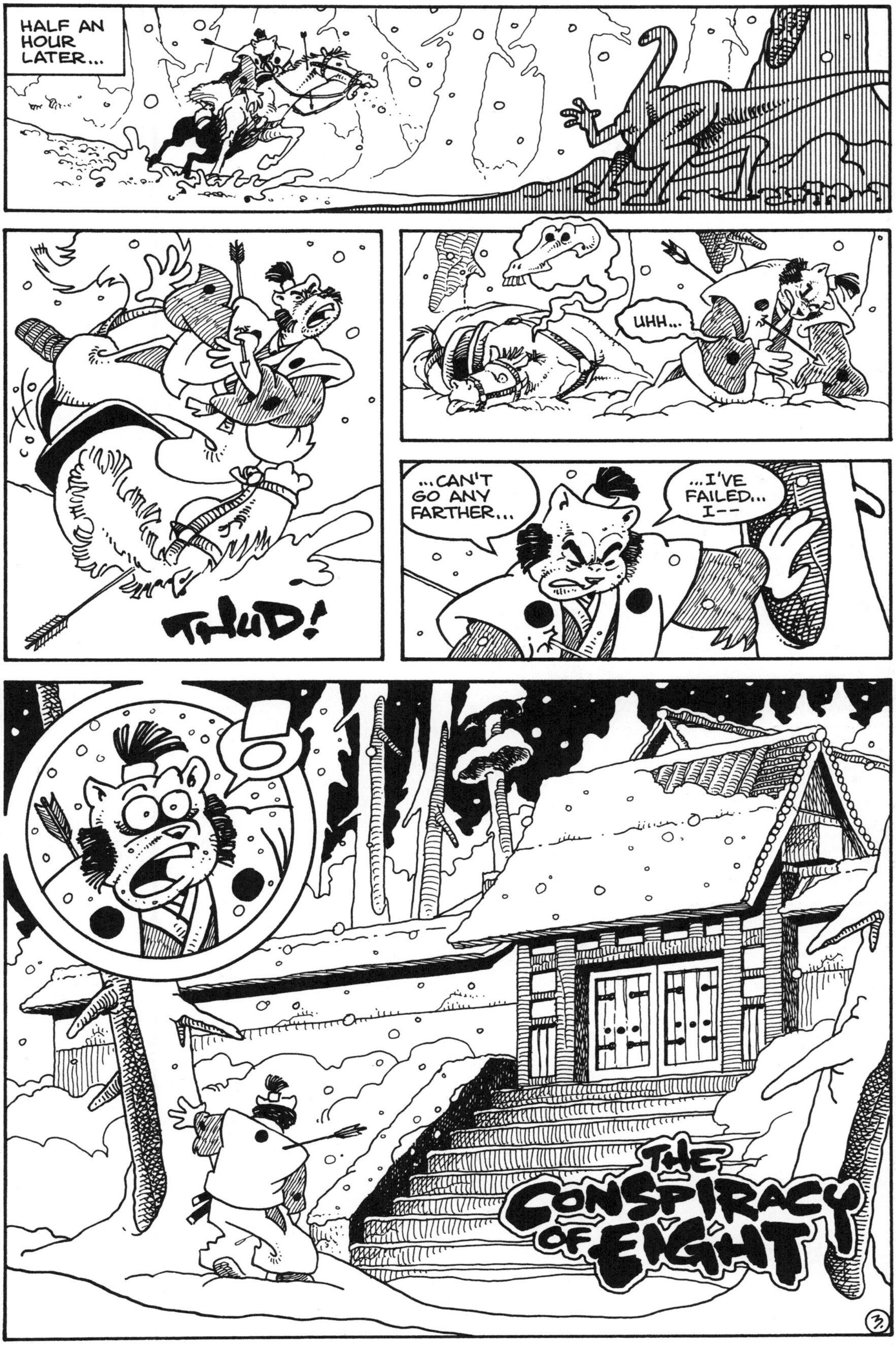
HALF AN HOUR LATER...
THUD!
UHH...
...CAN'T GO ANY FARTHER...
...I'VE FAILED... I--
!
THE CONSPIRACY OF EIGHT
3

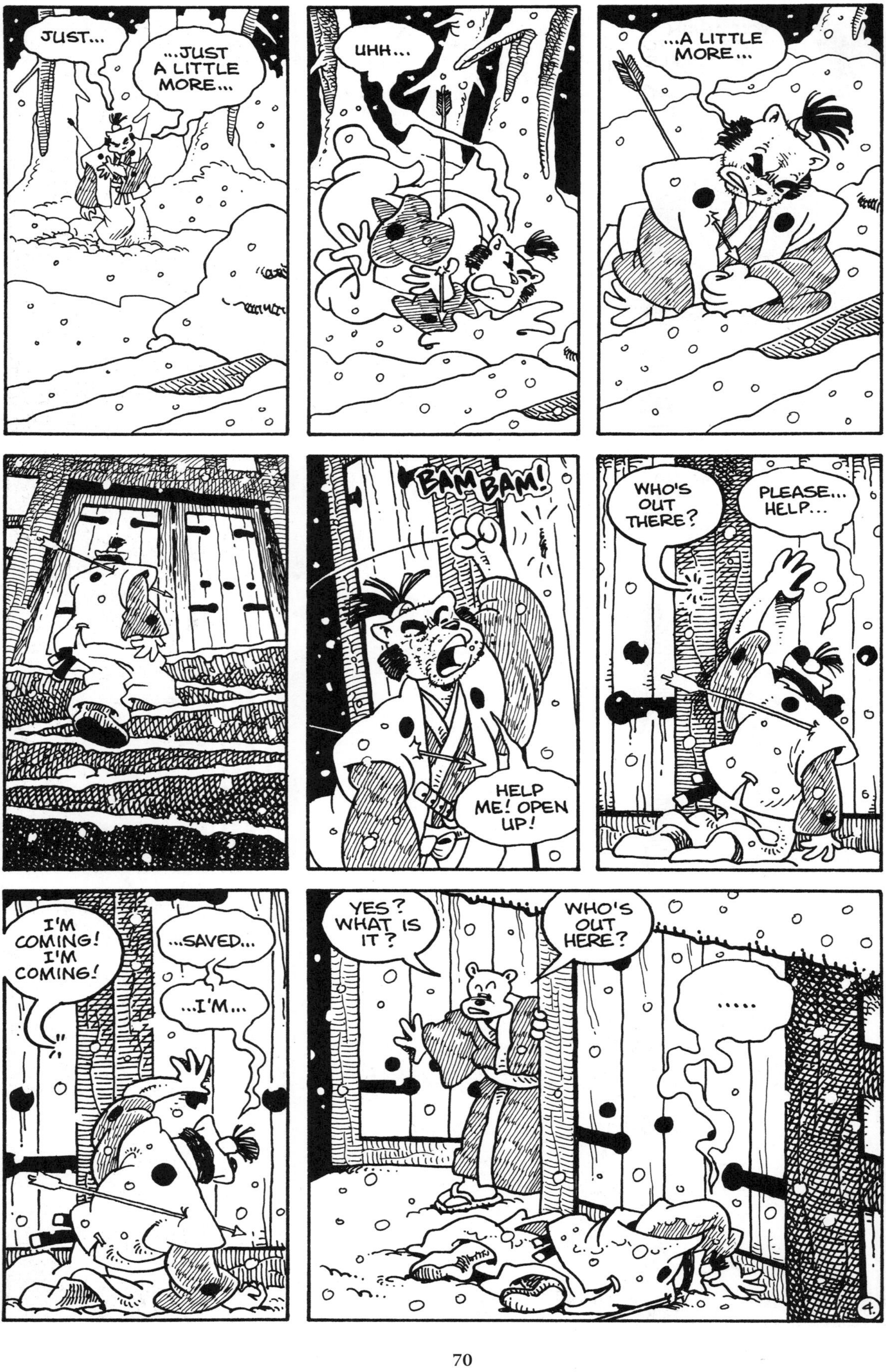
JUST...
...JUST A LITTLE MORE...
UHH...
...A LITTLE MORE...
BAM BAM!
HELP ME! OPEN UP!
WHO'S OUT THERE?
PLEASE... HELP...
I'M COMING! I'M COMING!
...SAVED...
...I'M...
YES? WHAT IS IT?
WHO'S OUT HERE?
.....
4.

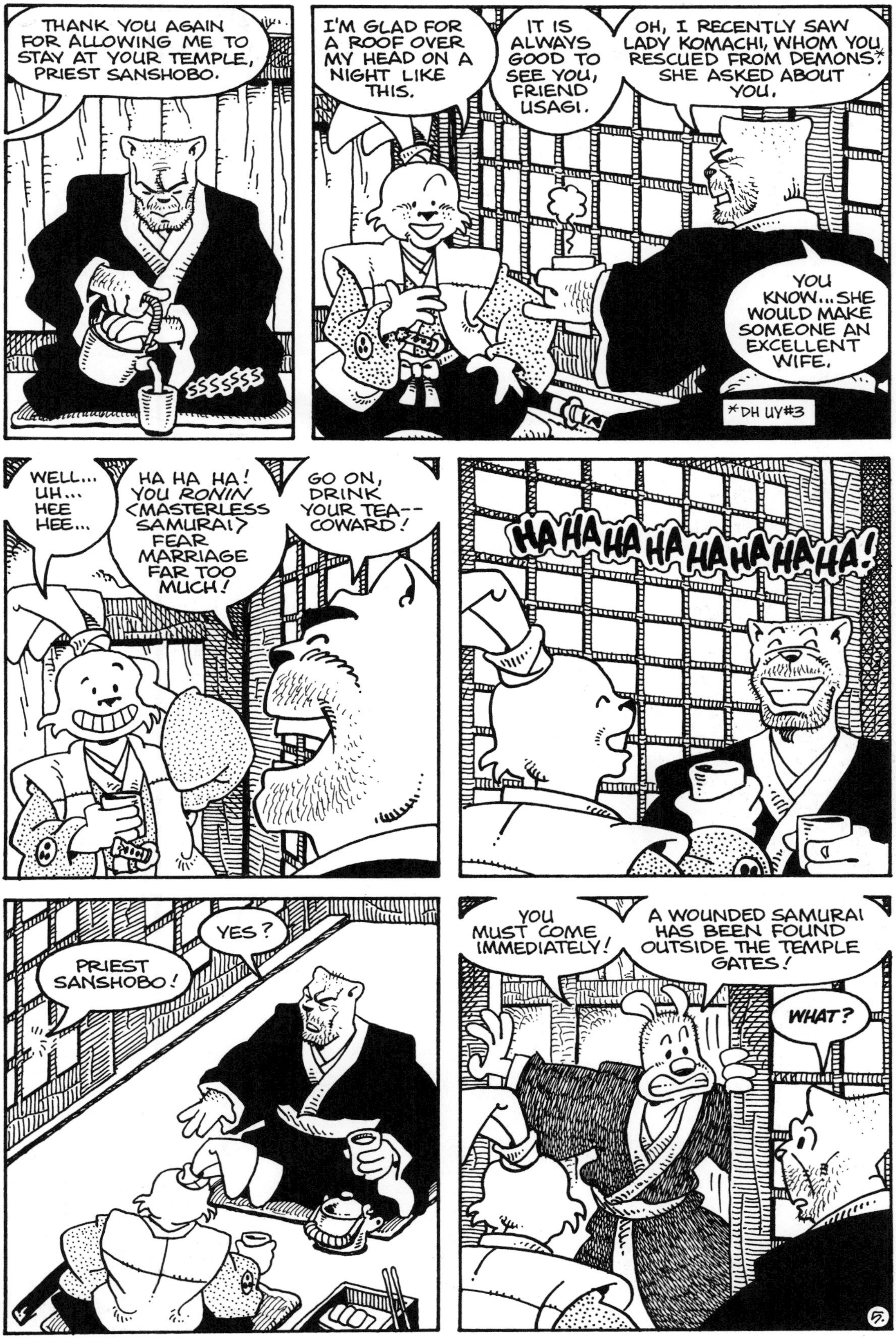
THANK YOU AGAIN FOR ALLOWING ME TO STAY AT YOUR TEMPLE, PRIEST SANSHOBO.
SSSSSSS
I'M GLAD FOR A ROOF OVER MY HEAD ON A NIGHT LIKE THIS.
IT IS ALWAYS GOOD TO SEE YOU, FRIEND USAGI.
OH, I RECENTLY SAW LADY KOMACHI, WHOM YOU RESCUED FROM DEMONS.* SHE ASKED ABOUT YOU.
YOU KNOW...SHE WOULD MAKE SOMEONE AN EXCELLENT WIFE.
*DH UY#3
WELL... UH... HEE HEE...
HA HA HA! YOU *RONIN* <MASTERLESS SAMURAI> FEAR MARRIAGE FAR TOO MUCH!
GO ON, DRINK YOUR TEA--COWARD!
HA HA HA HA HA HA HA HA HA!
PRIEST SANSHOBO!
YES?
YOU MUST COME IMMEDIATELY!
A WOUNDED SAMURAI HAS BEEN FOUND OUTSIDE THE TEMPLE GATES!
WHAT?
5.

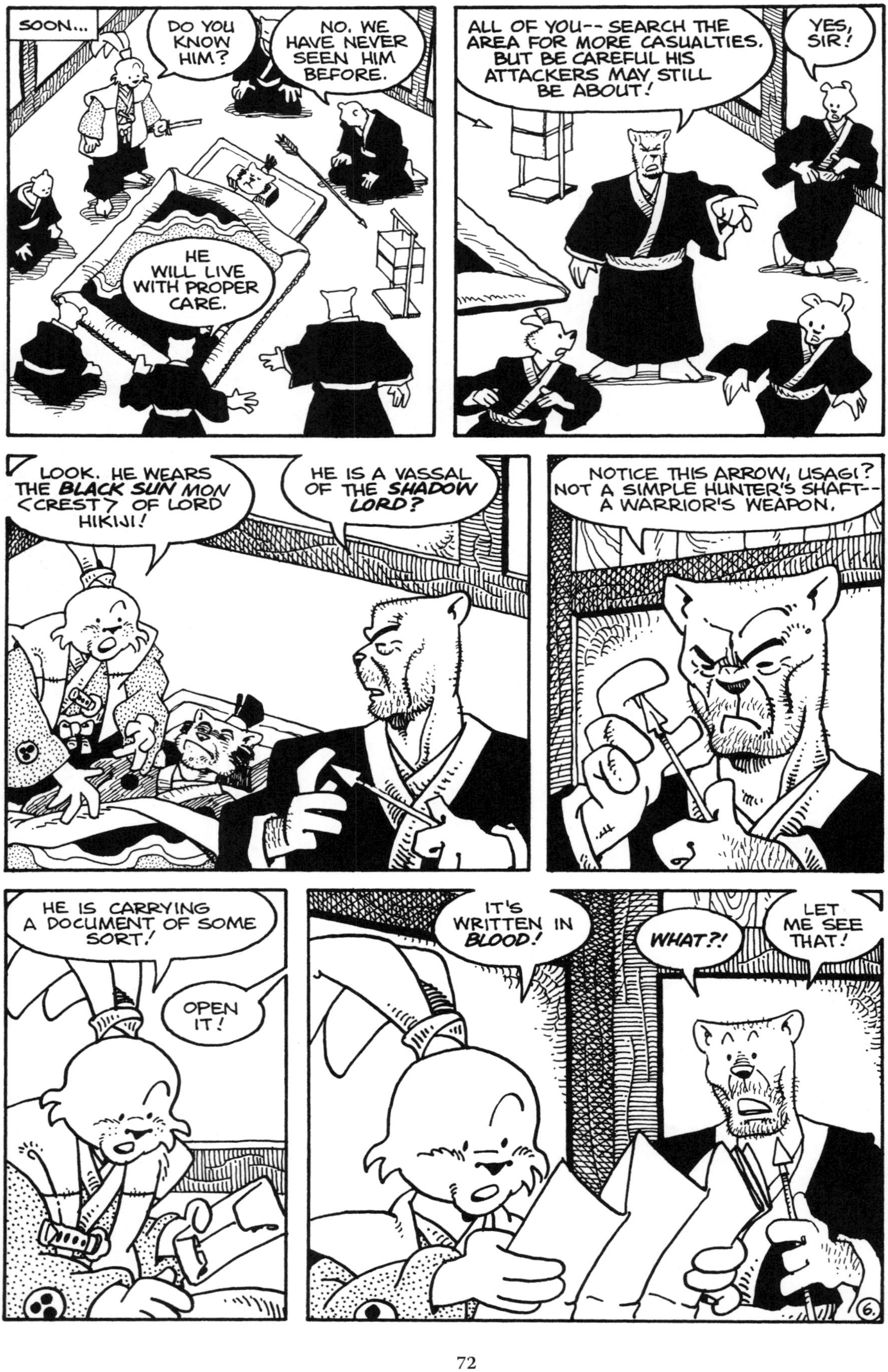

SOON...
DO YOU KNOW HIM?
NO. WE HAVE NEVER SEEN HIM BEFORE.
HE WILL LIVE WITH PROPER CARE.
ALL OF YOU-- SEARCH THE AREA FOR MORE CASUALTIES. BUT BE CAREFUL HIS ATTACKERS MAY STILL BE ABOUT!
YES, SIR!
LOOK. HE WEARS THE **BLACK SUN** MON <CREST> OF LORD HIKIJI!
HE IS A VASSAL OF THE **SHADOW LORD?**
NOTICE THIS ARROW, USAGI? NOT A SIMPLE HUNTER'S SHAFT-- A WARRIOR'S WEAPON.
HE IS CARRYING A DOCUMENT OF SOME SORT!
OPEN IT!
IT'S WRITTEN IN **BLOOD!**
WHAT?!
LET ME SEE THAT!
6.

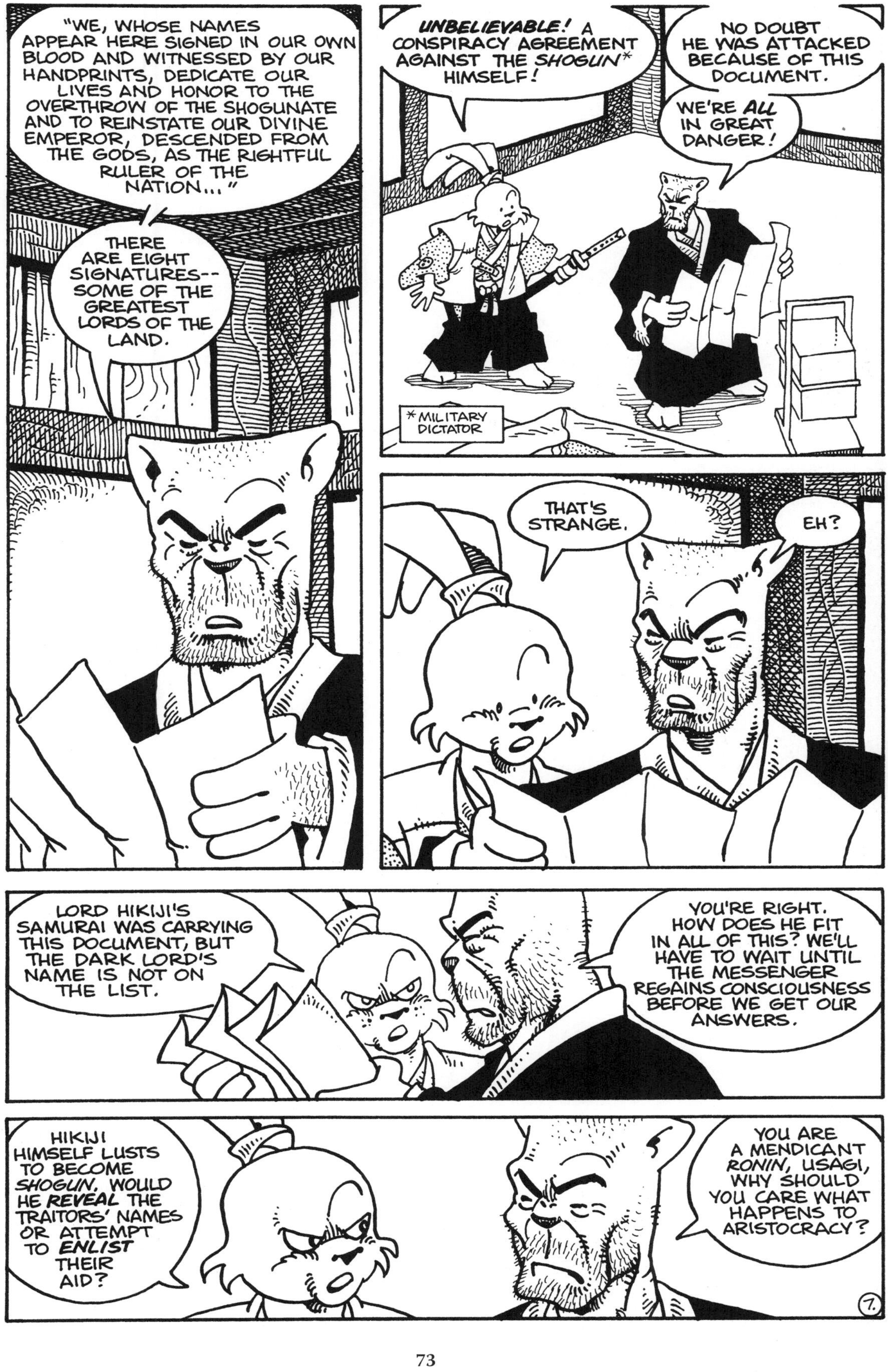
"WE, WHOSE NAMES APPEAR HERE SIGNED IN OUR OWN BLOOD AND WITNESSED BY OUR HANDPRINTS, DEDICATE OUR LIVES AND HONOR TO THE OVERTHROW OF THE SHOGUNATE AND TO REINSTATE OUR DIVINE EMPEROR, DESCENDED FROM THE GODS, AS THE RIGHTFUL RULER OF THE NATION..."
THERE ARE EIGHT SIGNATURES-- SOME OF THE GREATEST LORDS OF THE LAND.
UNBELIEVABLE! A CONSPIRACY AGREEMENT AGAINST THE *SHOGUN** HIMSELF!
NO DOUBT HE WAS ATTACKED BECAUSE OF THIS DOCUMENT.
WE'RE *ALL* IN GREAT DANGER!
*MILITARY DICTATOR
THAT'S STRANGE.
EH?
LORD HIKIJI'S SAMURAI WAS CARRYING THIS DOCUMENT, BUT THE DARK LORD'S NAME IS NOT ON THE LIST.
YOU'RE RIGHT. HOW DOES HE FIT IN ALL OF THIS? WE'LL HAVE TO WAIT UNTIL THE MESSENGER REGAINS CONSCIOUSNESS BEFORE WE GET OUR ANSWERS.
HIKIJI HIMSELF LUSTS TO BECOME *SHOGUN*, WOULD HE *REVEAL* THE TRAITORS' NAMES OR ATTEMPT TO *ENLIST* THEIR AID?
YOU ARE A MENDICANT *RONIN*, USAGI, WHY SHOULD YOU CARE WHAT HAPPENS TO ARISTOCRACY?
7.

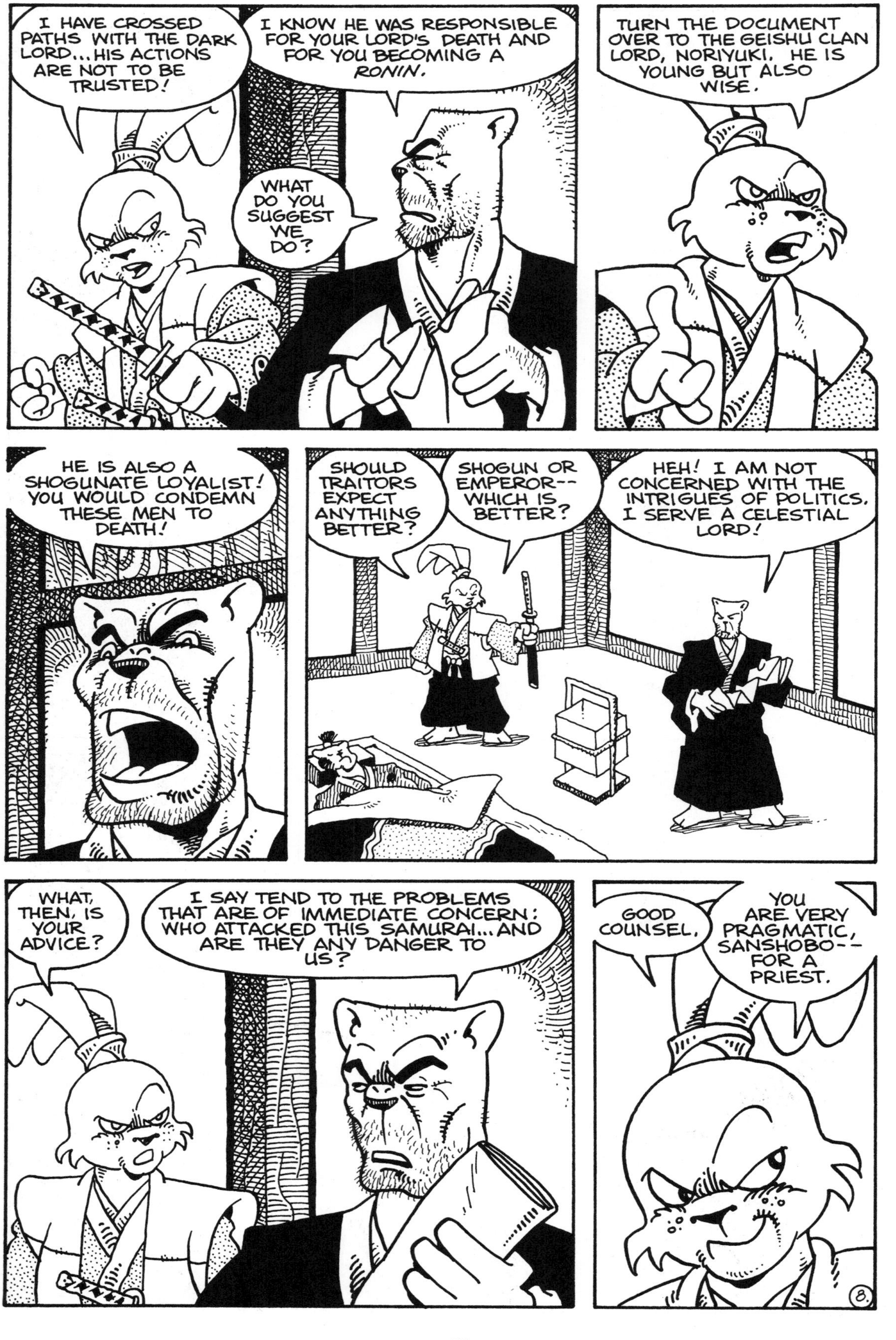
I HAVE CROSSED PATHS WITH THE DARK LORD... HIS ACTIONS ARE NOT TO BE TRUSTED!
I KNOW HE WAS RESPONSIBLE FOR YOUR LORD'S DEATH AND FOR YOU BECOMING A *RONIN*.
WHAT DO YOU SUGGEST WE DO?
TURN THE DOCUMENT OVER TO THE GEISHU CLAN LORD, NORIYUKI. HE IS YOUNG BUT ALSO WISE.
HE IS ALSO A SHOGUNATE LOYALIST! YOU WOULD CONDEMN THESE MEN TO DEATH!
SHOULD TRAITORS EXPECT ANYTHING BETTER?
SHOGUN OR EMPEROR-- WHICH IS BETTER?
HEH! I AM NOT CONCERNED WITH THE INTRIGUES OF POLITICS. I SERVE A CELESTIAL LORD!
WHAT, THEN, IS YOUR ADVICE?
I SAY TEND TO THE PROBLEMS THAT ARE OF IMMEDIATE CONCERN: WHO ATTACKED THIS SAMURAI... AND ARE THEY ANY DANGER TO US?
GOOD COUNSEL.
YOU ARE VERY PRAGMATIC, SANSHOBO-- FOR A PRIEST.
8.

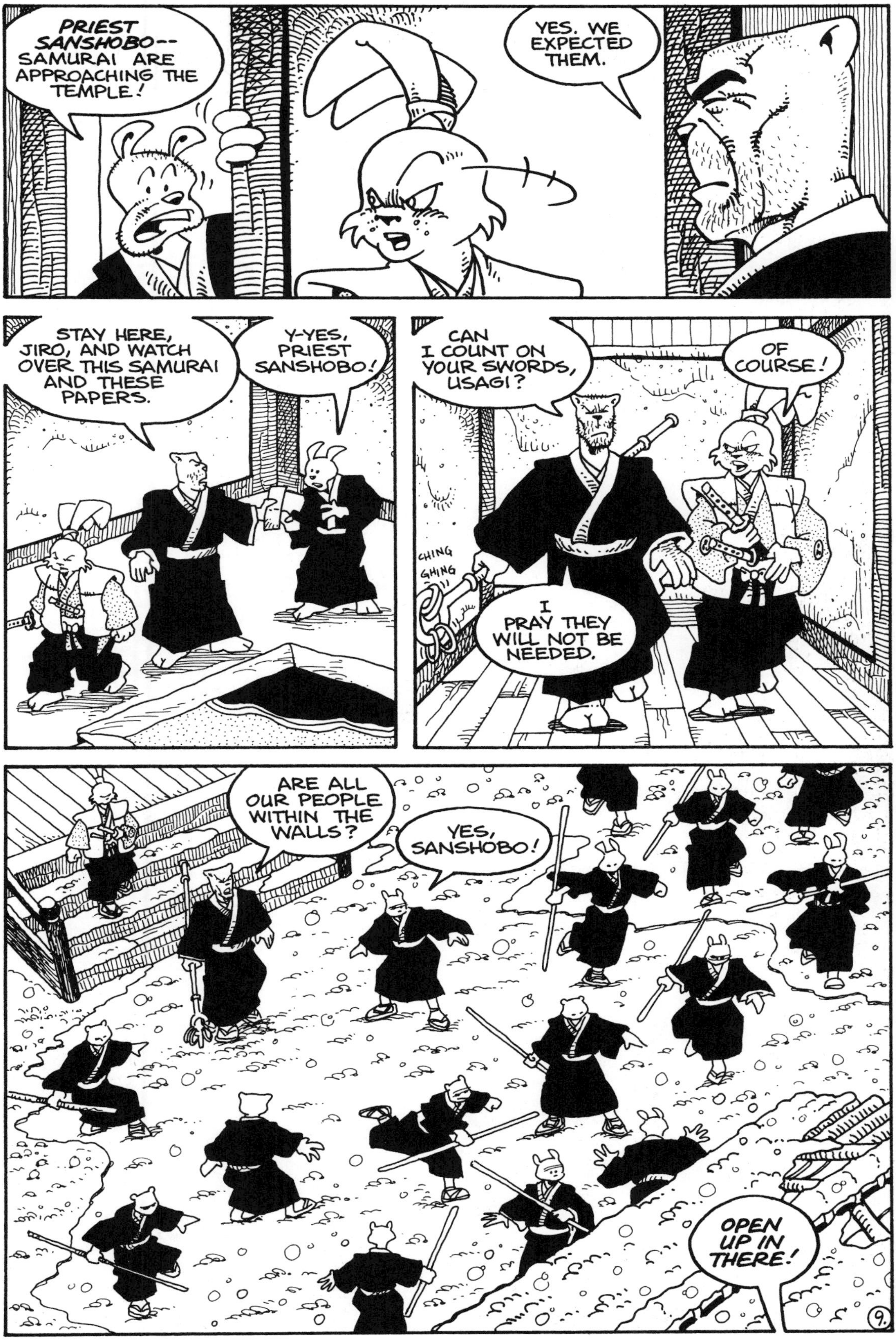
PRIEST SANSHOBO-- SAMURAI ARE APPROACHING THE TEMPLE!
YES. WE EXPECTED THEM.
STAY HERE, JIRO, AND WATCH OVER THIS SAMURAI AND THESE PAPERS.
Y-YES, PRIEST SANSHOBO!
CAN I COUNT ON YOUR SWORDS, USAGI?
OF COURSE!
CHING
CHING
I PRAY THEY WILL NOT BE NEEDED.
ARE ALL OUR PEOPLE WITHIN THE WALLS?
YES, SANSHOBO!
OPEN UP IN THERE!
9.

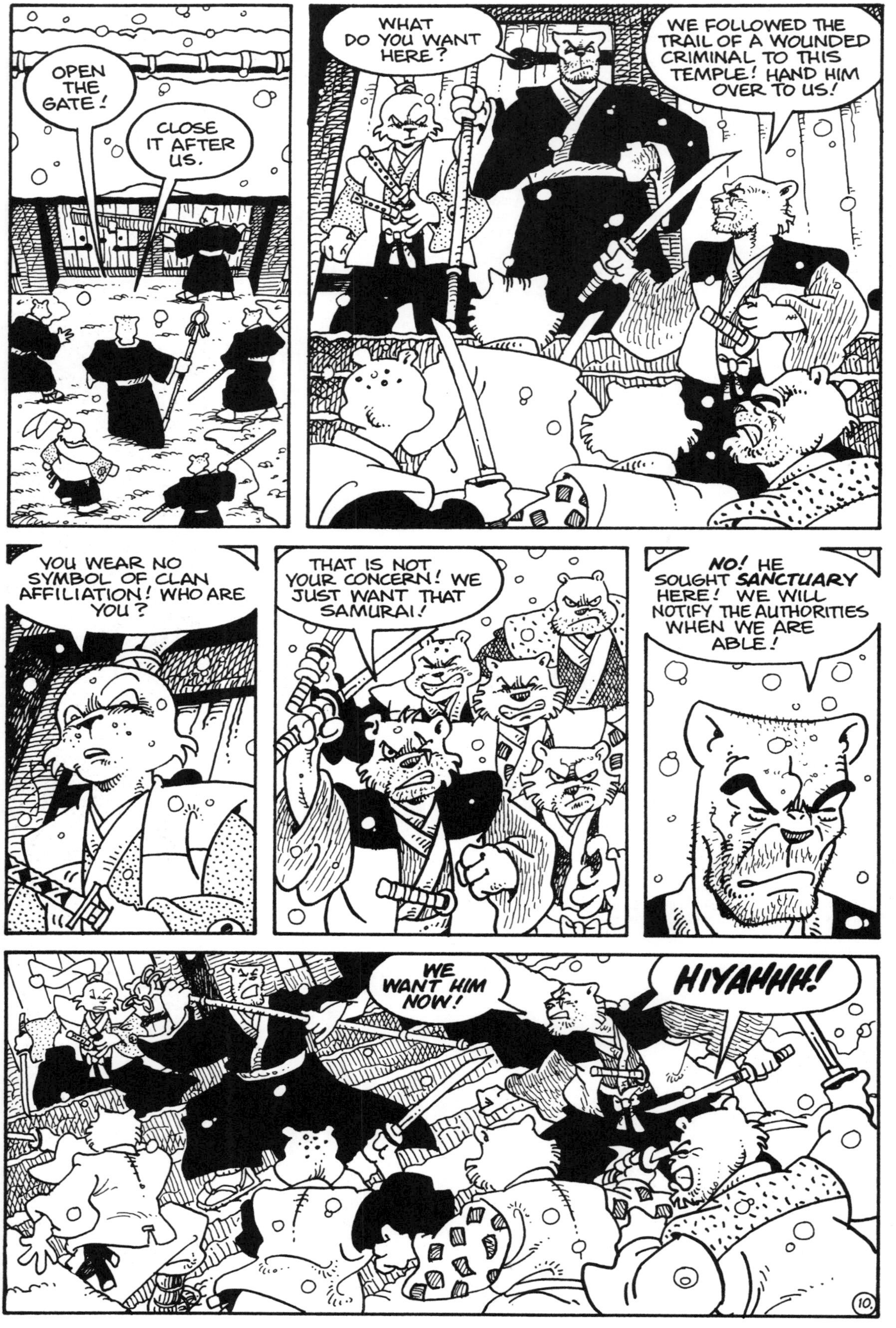
OPEN THE GATE!
CLOSE IT AFTER US.
WHAT DO YOU WANT HERE?
WE FOLLOWED THE TRAIL OF A WOUNDED CRIMINAL TO THIS TEMPLE! HAND HIM OVER TO US!
YOU WEAR NO SYMBOL OF CLAN AFFILIATION! WHO ARE YOU?
THAT IS NOT YOUR CONCERN! WE JUST WANT THAT SAMURAI!
NO! HE SOUGHT SANCTUARY HERE! WE WILL NOTIFY THE AUTHORITIES WHEN WE ARE ABLE!
WE WANT HIM NOW!
HIYAHHH!
10.

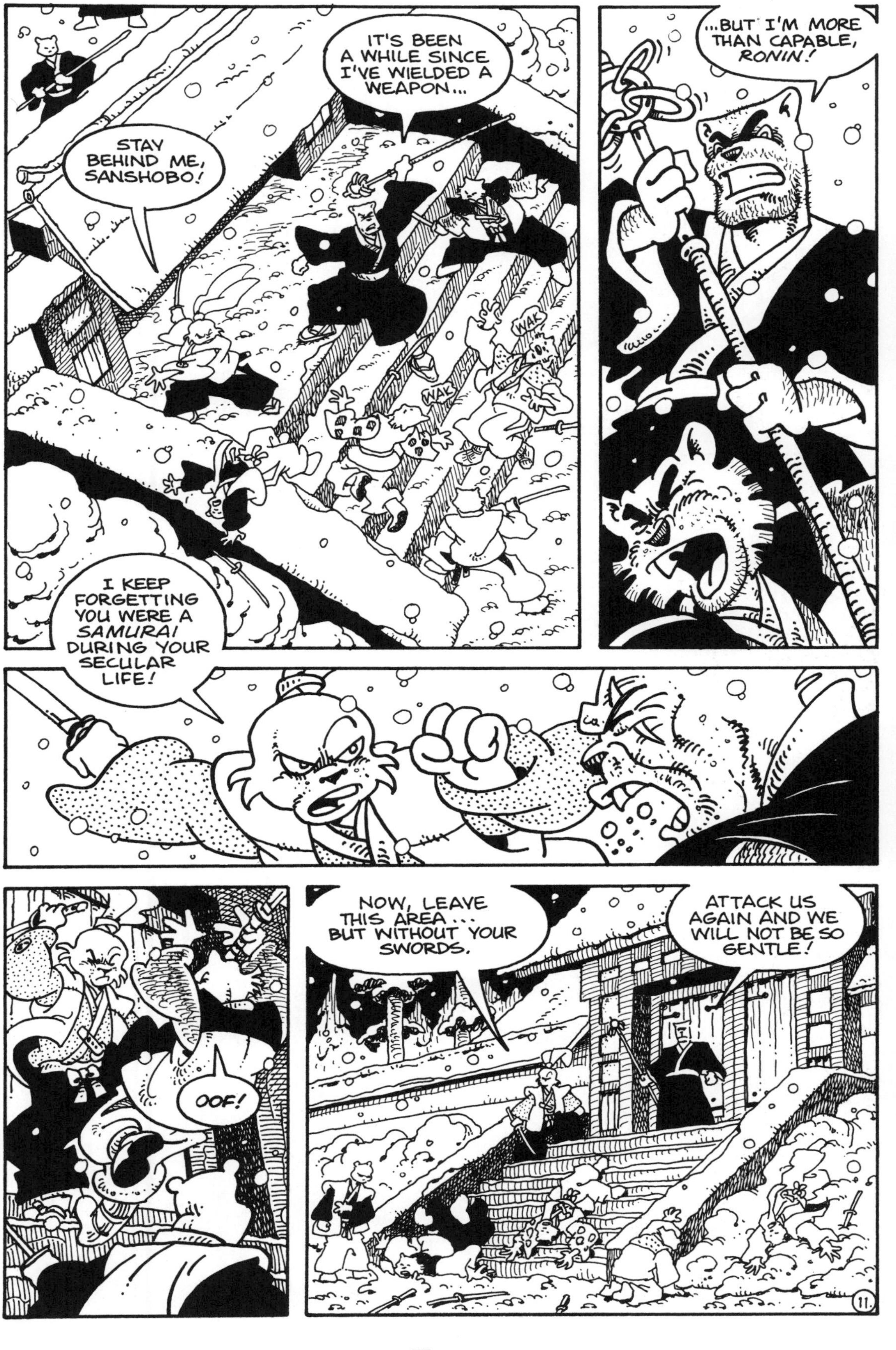
IT'S BEEN A WHILE SINCE I'VE WIELDED A WEAPON...
STAY BEHIND ME, SANSHOBO!
WAK
WAK
I KEEP FORGETTING YOU WERE A SAMURAI DURING YOUR SECULAR LIFE!
...BUT I'M MORE THAN CAPABLE, RONIN!
OOF!
NOW, LEAVE THIS AREA... BUT WITHOUT YOUR SWORDS.
ATTACK US AGAIN AND WE WILL NOT BE SO GENTLE!
11.

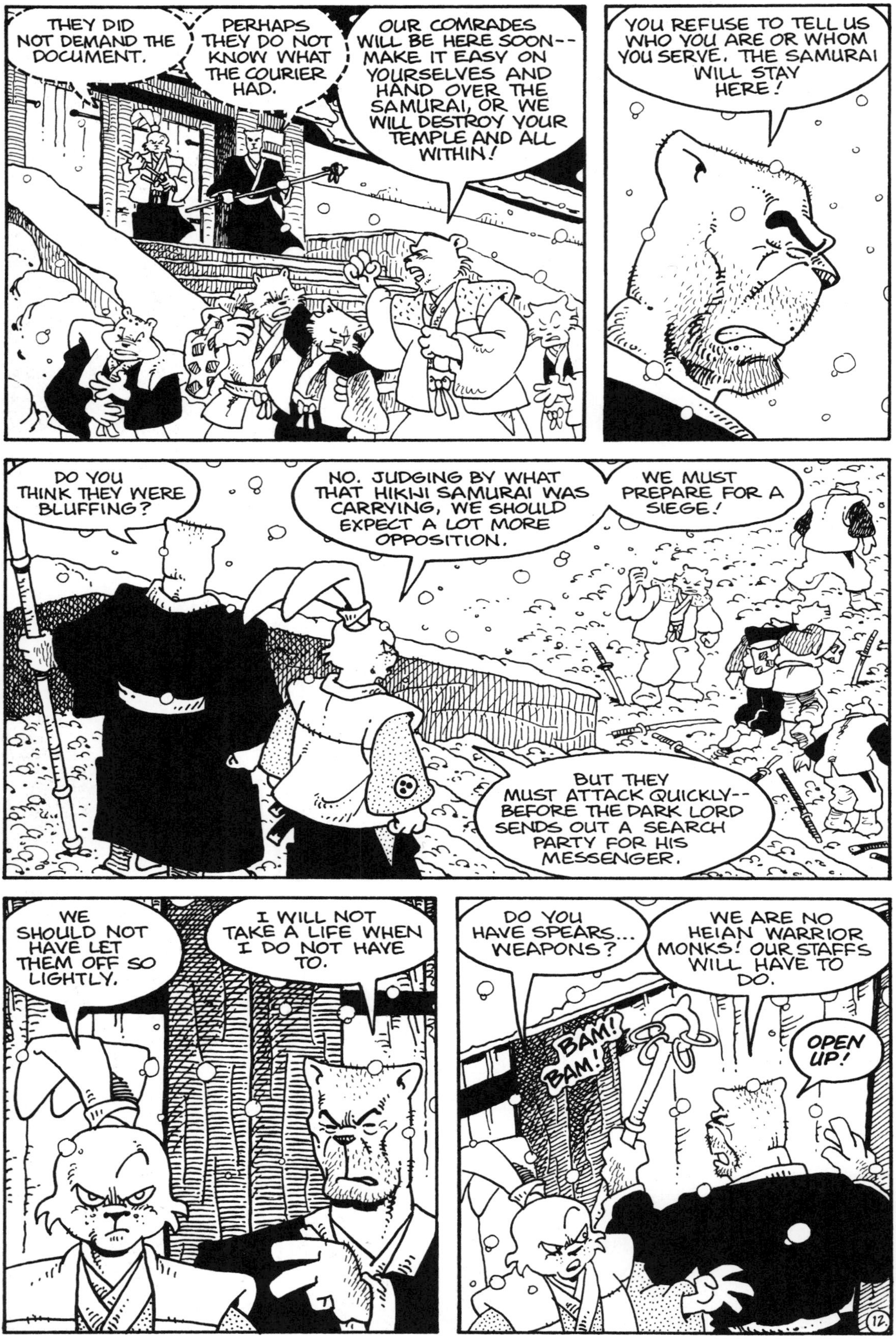
THEY DID NOT DEMAND THE DOCUMENT.
PERHAPS THEY DO NOT KNOW WHAT THE COURIER HAD.
OUR COMRADES WILL BE HERE SOON-- MAKE IT EASY ON YOURSELVES AND HAND OVER THE SAMURAI, OR WE WILL DESTROY YOUR TEMPLE AND ALL WITHIN!
YOU REFUSE TO TELL US WHO YOU ARE OR WHOM YOU SERVE. THE SAMURAI WILL STAY HERE!
DO YOU THINK THEY WERE BLUFFING?
NO. JUDGING BY WHAT THAT HIKIJI SAMURAI WAS CARRYING, WE SHOULD EXPECT A LOT MORE OPPOSITION.
WE MUST PREPARE FOR A SIEGE!
BUT THEY MUST ATTACK QUICKLY-- BEFORE THE DARK LORD SENDS OUT A SEARCH PARTY FOR HIS MESSENGER.
WE SHOULD NOT HAVE LET THEM OFF SO LIGHTLY.
I WILL NOT TAKE A LIFE WHEN I DO NOT HAVE TO.
DO YOU HAVE SPEARS... WEAPONS?
WE ARE NO HEIAN WARRIOR MONKS! OUR STAFFS WILL HAVE TO DO.
BAM! BAM!
OPEN UP!
12

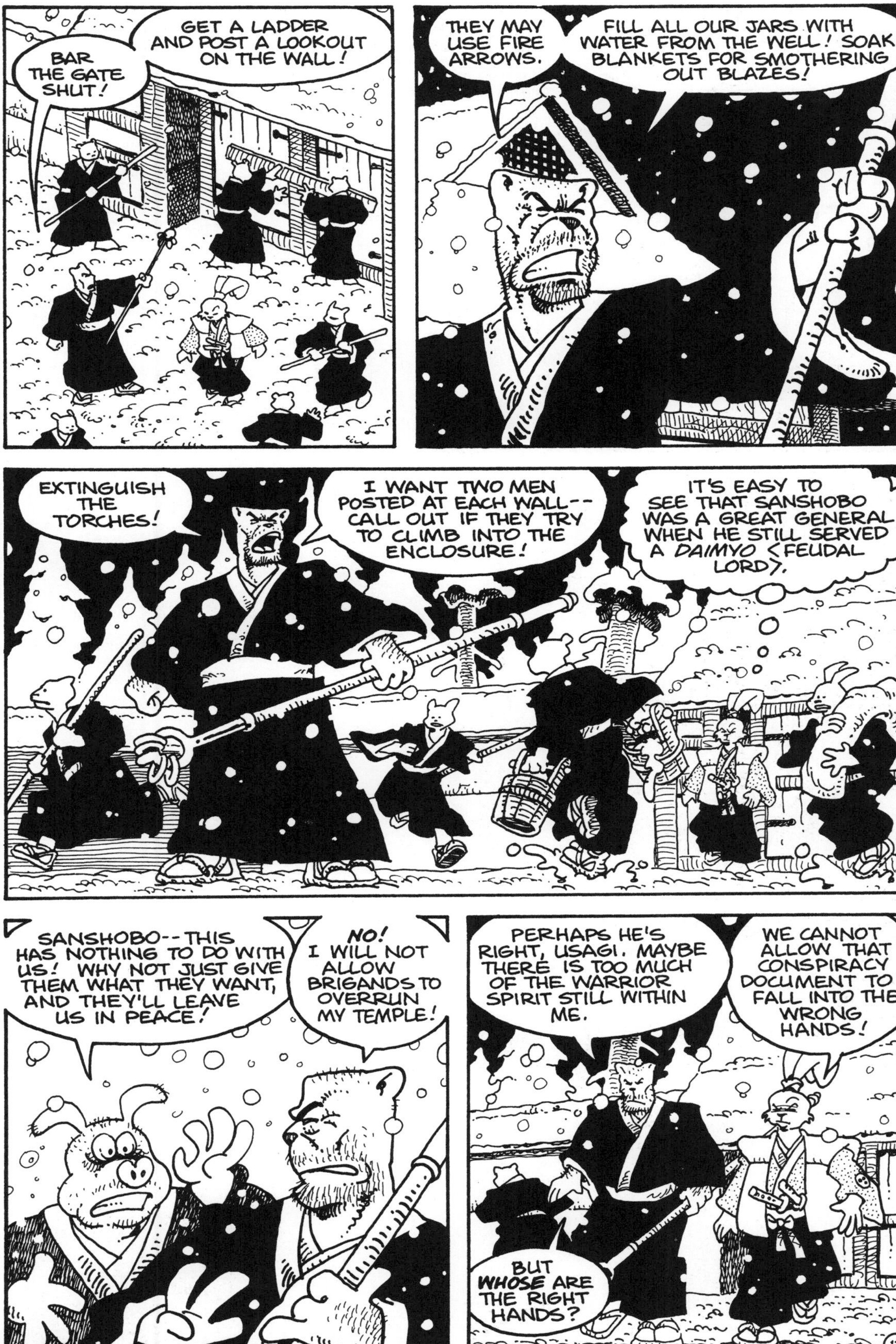
BAR THE GATE SHUT!
GET A LADDER AND POST A LOOKOUT ON THE WALL!
THEY MAY USE FIRE ARROWS.
FILL ALL OUR JARS WITH WATER FROM THE WELL! SOAK BLANKETS FOR SMOTHERING OUT BLAZES!
EXTINGUISH THE TORCHES!
I WANT TWO MEN POSTED AT EACH WALL-- CALL OUT IF THEY TRY TO CLIMB INTO THE ENCLOSURE!
IT'S EASY TO SEE THAT SANSHOBO WAS A GREAT GENERAL WHEN HE STILL SERVED A *DAIMYO* <FEUDAL LORD>.
SANSHOBO-- THIS HAS NOTHING TO DO WITH US! WHY NOT JUST GIVE THEM WHAT THEY WANT, AND THEY'LL LEAVE US IN PEACE!
NO! I WILL NOT ALLOW BRIGANDS TO OVERRUN MY TEMPLE!
PERHAPS HE'S RIGHT, USAGI. MAYBE THERE IS TOO MUCH OF THE WARRIOR SPIRIT STILL WITHIN ME.
WE CANNOT ALLOW THAT CONSPIRACY DOCUMENT TO FALL INTO THE WRONG HANDS!
BUT *WHOSE* ARE THE RIGHT HANDS?
13

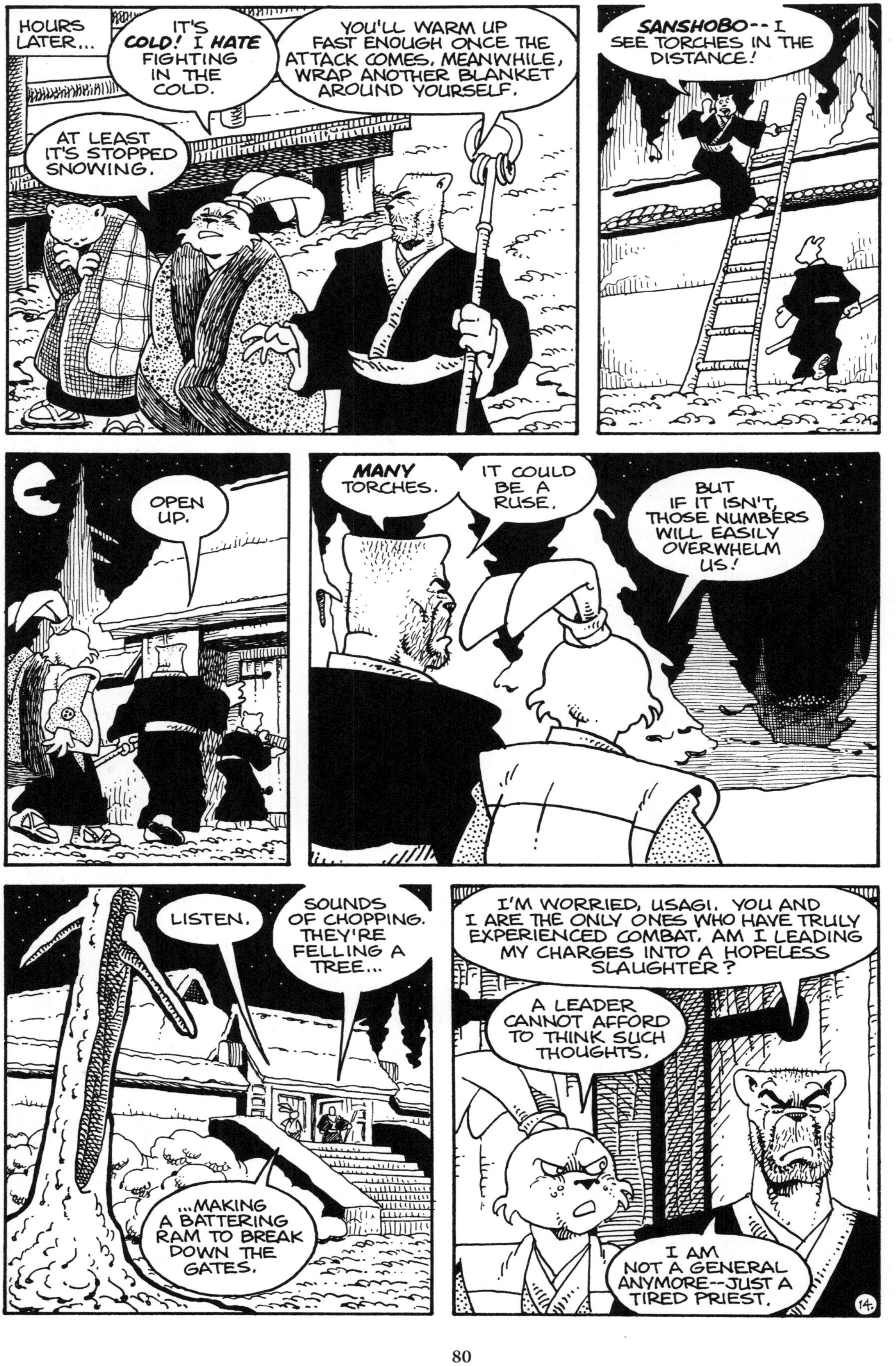
HOURS LATER...
IT'S **COLD!** I **HATE** FIGHTING IN THE COLD.
YOU'LL WARM UP FAST ENOUGH ONCE THE ATTACK COMES. MEANWHILE, WRAP ANOTHER BLANKET AROUND YOURSELF.
AT LEAST IT'S STOPPED SNOWING.
SANSHOBO--I SEE TORCHES IN THE DISTANCE!
OPEN UP.
MANY TORCHES.
IT COULD BE A RUSE.
BUT IF IT ISN'T, THOSE NUMBERS WILL EASILY OVERWHELM US!
LISTEN.
SOUNDS OF CHOPPING. THEY'RE FELLING A TREE...
...MAKING A BATTERING RAM TO BREAK DOWN THE GATES.
I'M WORRIED, USAGI. YOU AND I ARE THE ONLY ONES WHO HAVE TRULY EXPERIENCED COMBAT. AM I LEADING MY CHARGES INTO A HOPELESS SLAUGHTER?
A LEADER CANNOT AFFORD TO THINK SUCH THOUGHTS.
I AM NOT A GENERAL ANYMORE--JUST A TIRED PRIEST.
14.

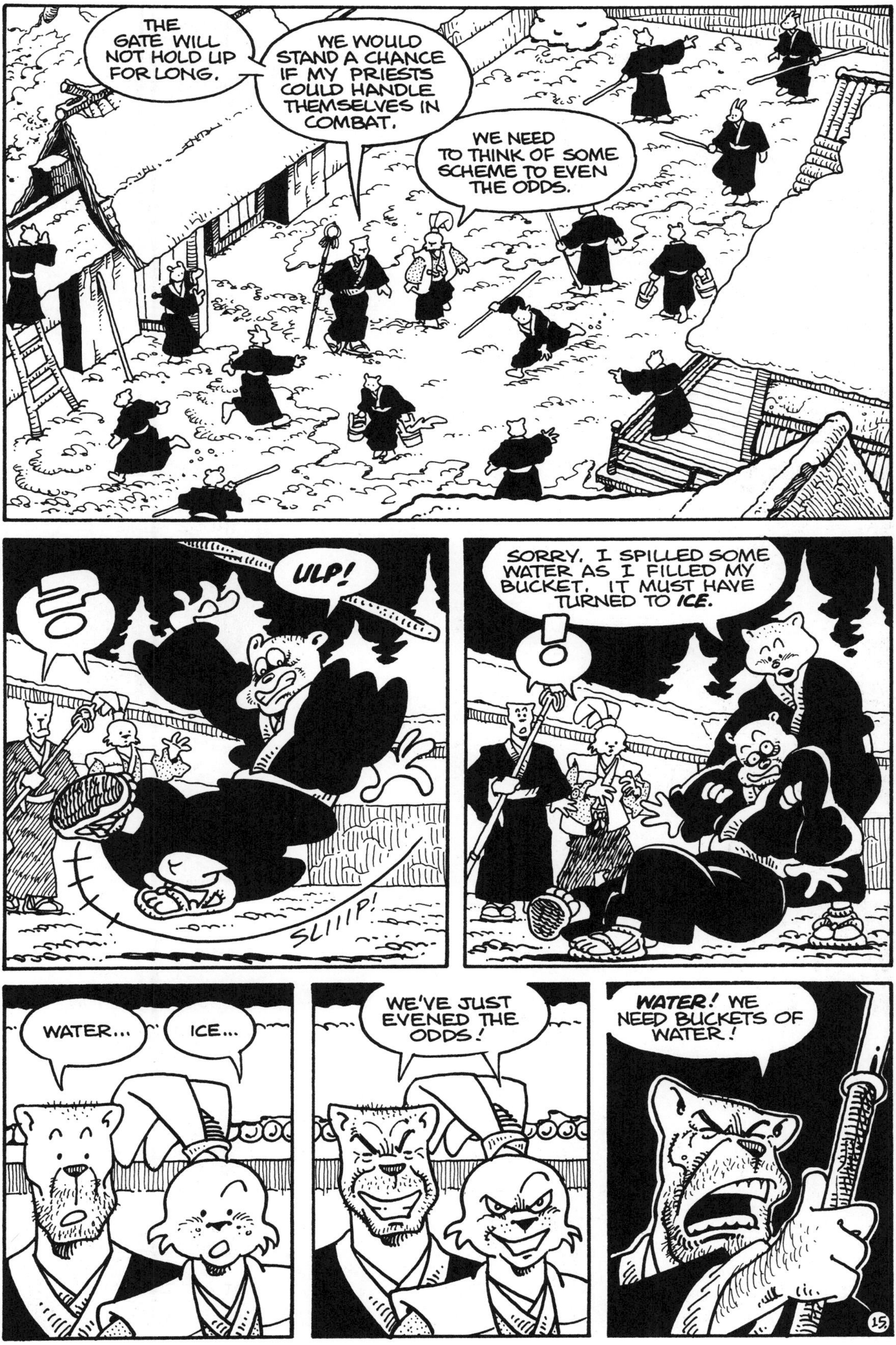
THE GATE WILL NOT HOLD UP FOR LONG.
WE WOULD STAND A CHANCE IF MY PRIESTS COULD HANDLE THEMSELVES IN COMBAT.
WE NEED TO THINK OF SOME SCHEME TO EVEN THE ODDS.
ULP!
SLIIIP!
!
SORRY, I SPILLED SOME WATER AS I FILLED MY BUCKET. IT MUST HAVE TURNED TO ICE.
WATER...
ICE...
WE'VE JUST EVENED THE ODDS!
WATER! WE NEED BUCKETS OF WATER!
15.

HERE THEY COME!

FIRE SQUAD-- TAKE CARE OF THE BLAZE!

USAGI-- ARE YOU READY?

WE'RE ALL IN POSITION!

HIYAAAAAAAAAAAAAAAAAAAAAA

AAAAAAHH!

STRIKE QUICKLY-- THE FIRES WILL NOT DISTRACT THEM FOR LONG!

SLAY THEM ALL!

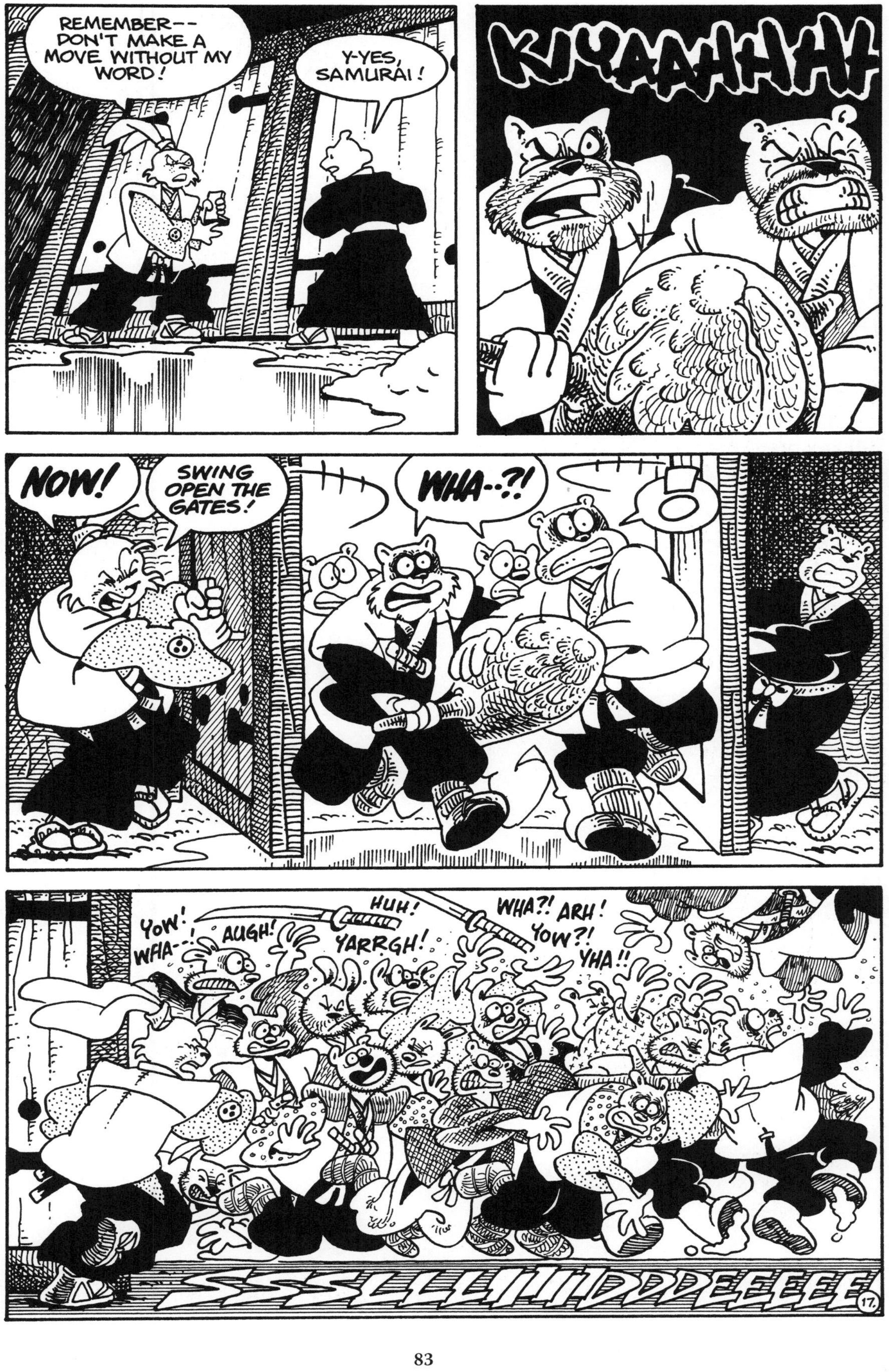
REMEMBER-- DON'T MAKE A MOVE WITHOUT MY WORD!
Y-YES, SAMURAI!
KIYAAHHHH!
NOW!
SWING OPEN THE GATES!
WHA--?!
YOW!
WHA--!
AUGH!
HUH!
YARRGH!
WHA?!
ARH!
YOW?!
YHA!!
SSSLLLIIIIDDDEEEEE
17.

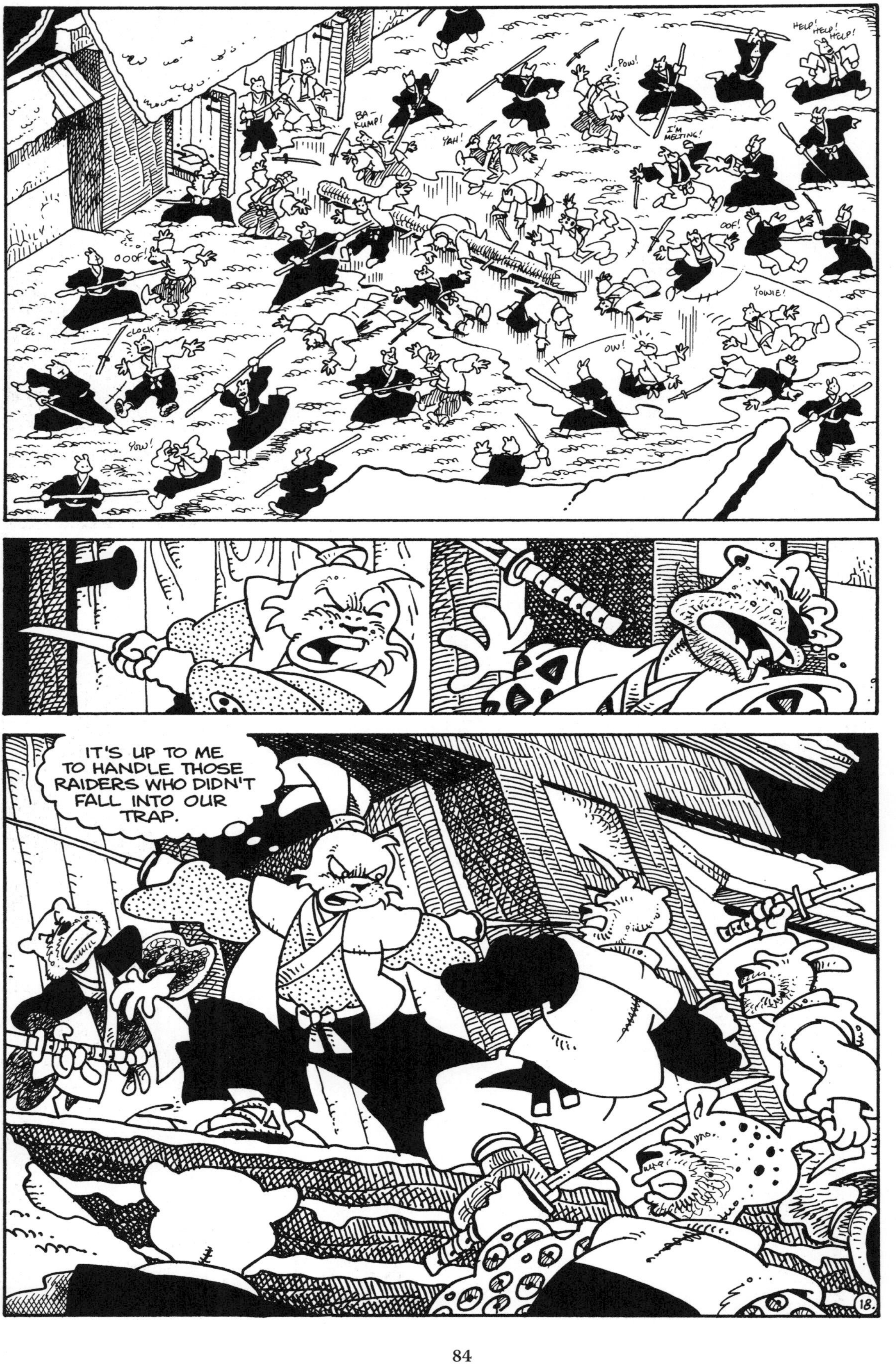
BA-KUMP!
YAH!
POW!
I'M MELTING!
HELP! HELP! HELP!
OOF!
OOF!
YOWIE!
CLOCK!
OW!
YOW!
IT'S UP TO ME TO HANDLE THOSE RAIDERS WHO DIDN'T FALL INTO OUR TRAP.
18.

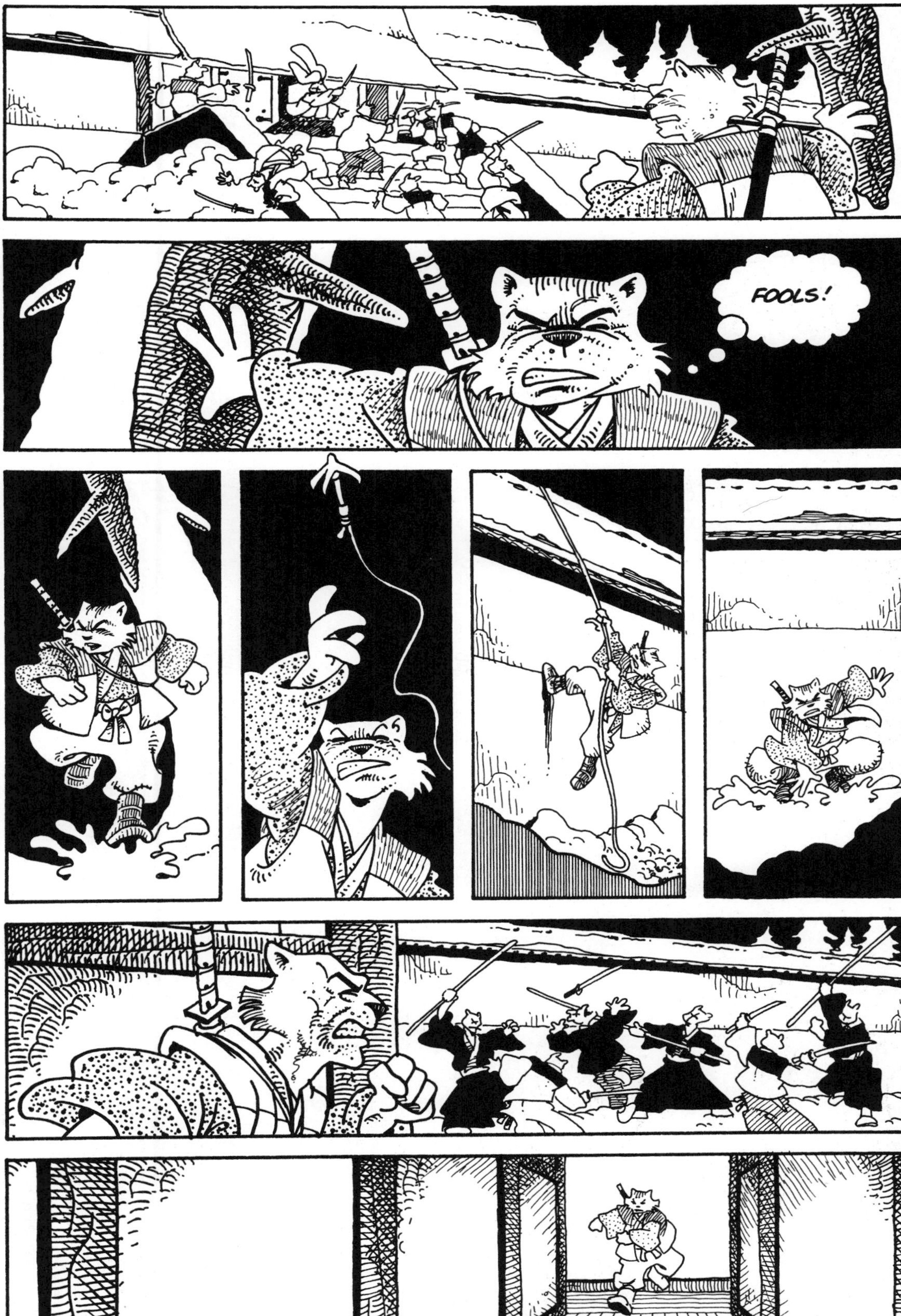
FOOLS!
19.

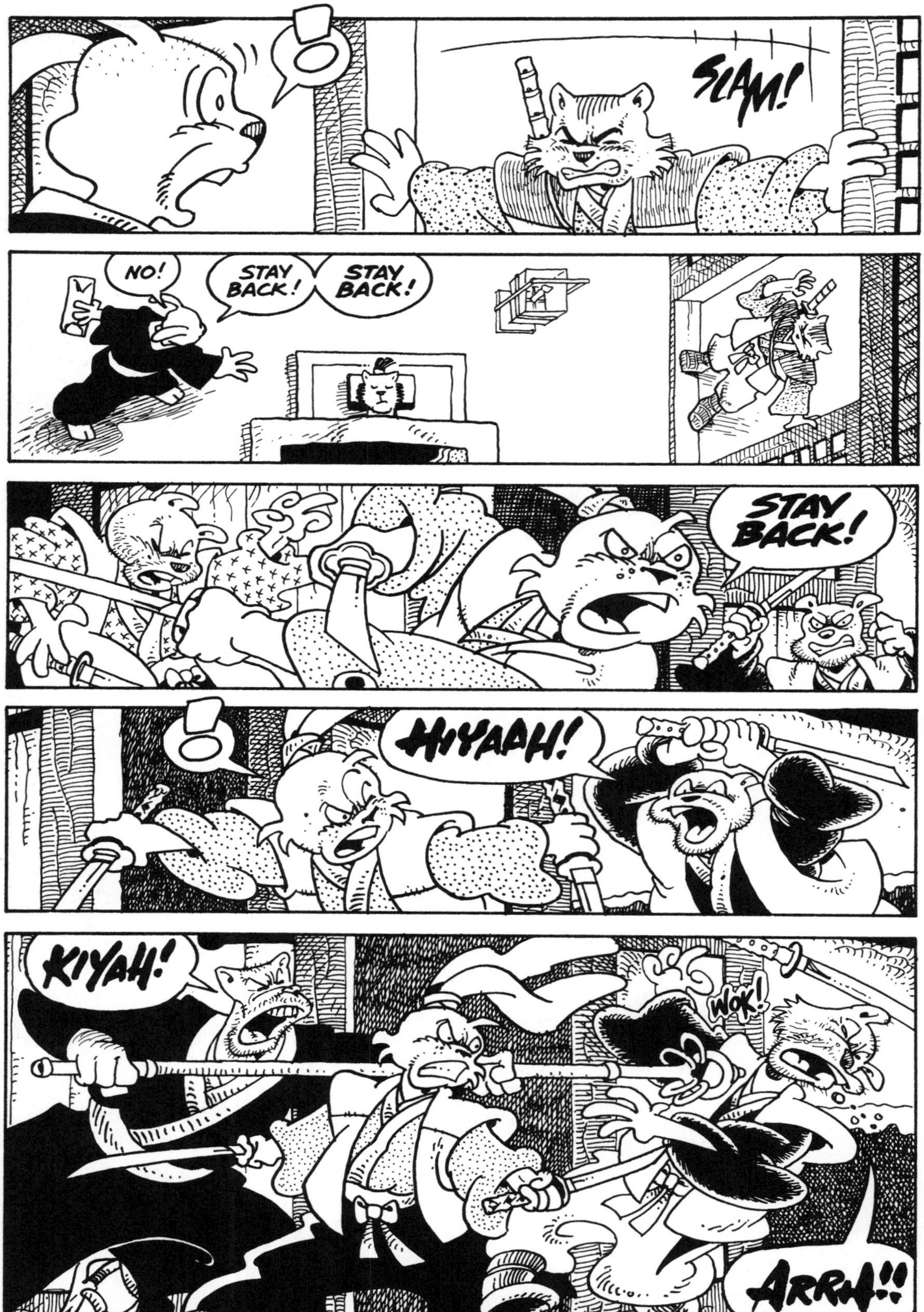
SLAM!
NO!
STAY BACK!
STAY BACK!
STAY BACK!
HIYAAH!
KIYAH!
WOK!
ARRH!!
20.

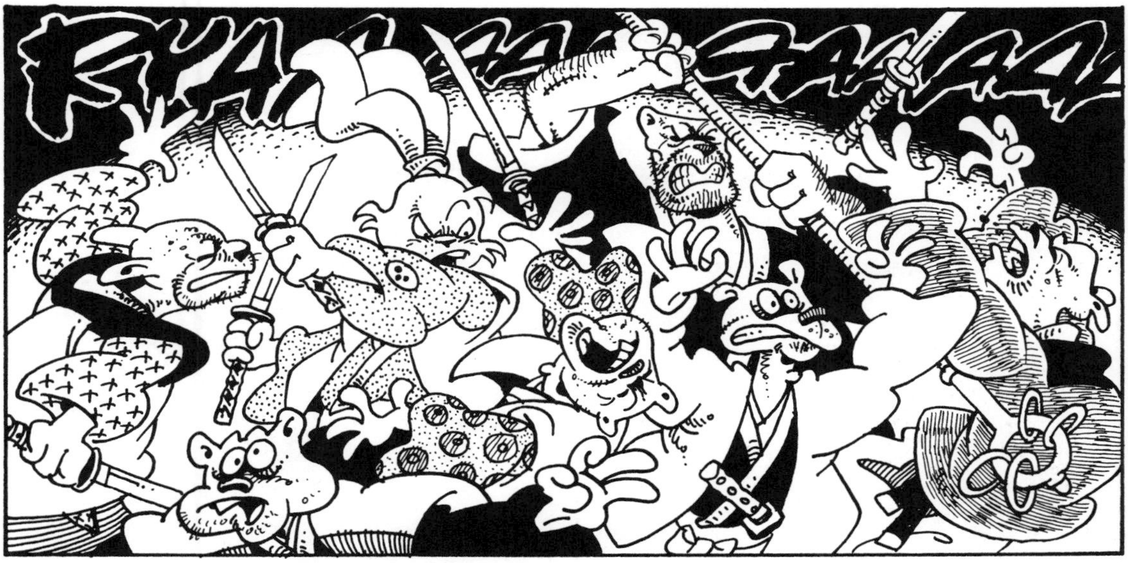

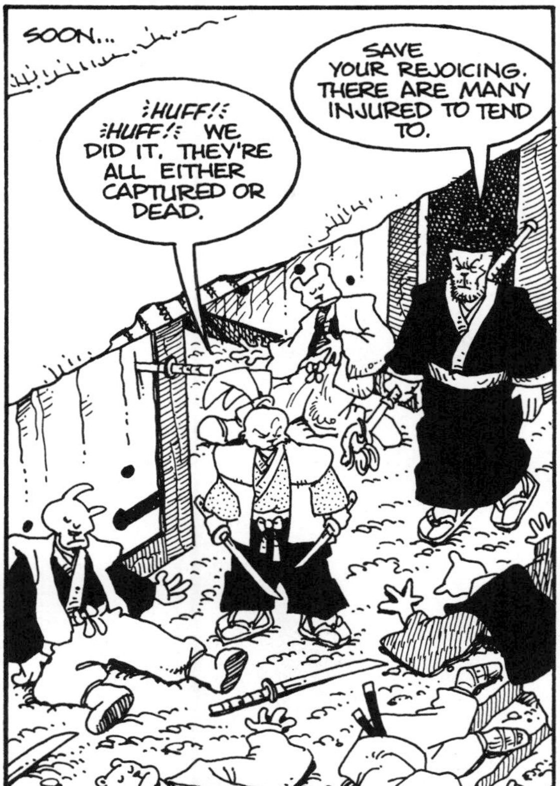

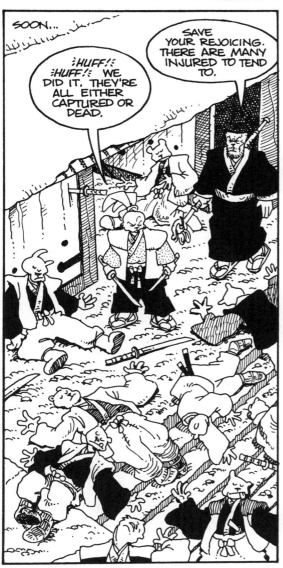

SOON...
HUFF! HUFF! WE DID IT. THEY'RE ALL EITHER CAPTURED OR DEAD.
SAVE YOUR REJOICING. THERE ARE MANY INJURED TO TEND TO.

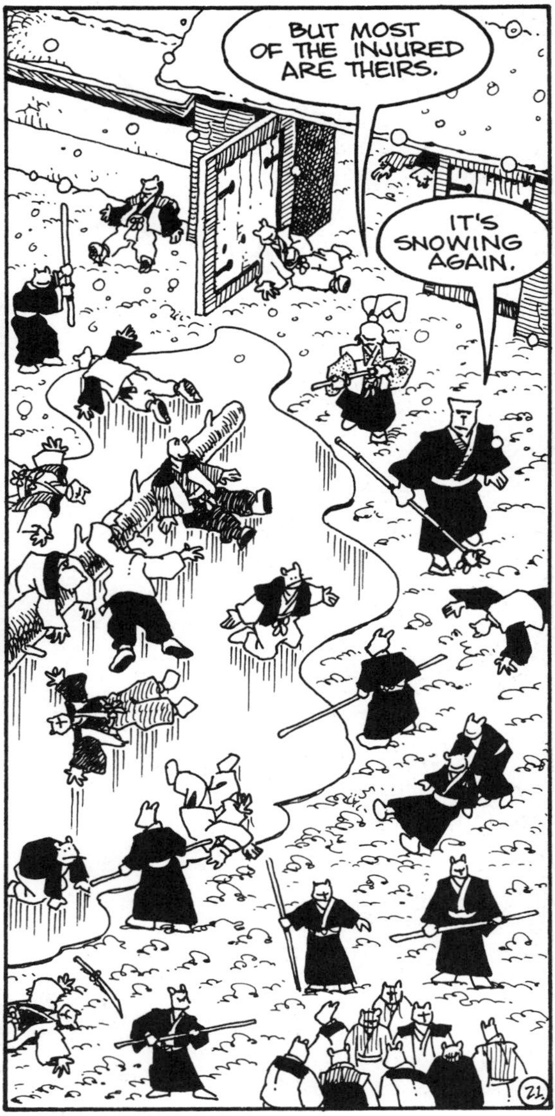

BUT MOST OF THE INJURED ARE THEIRS.
IT'S SNOWING AGAIN.

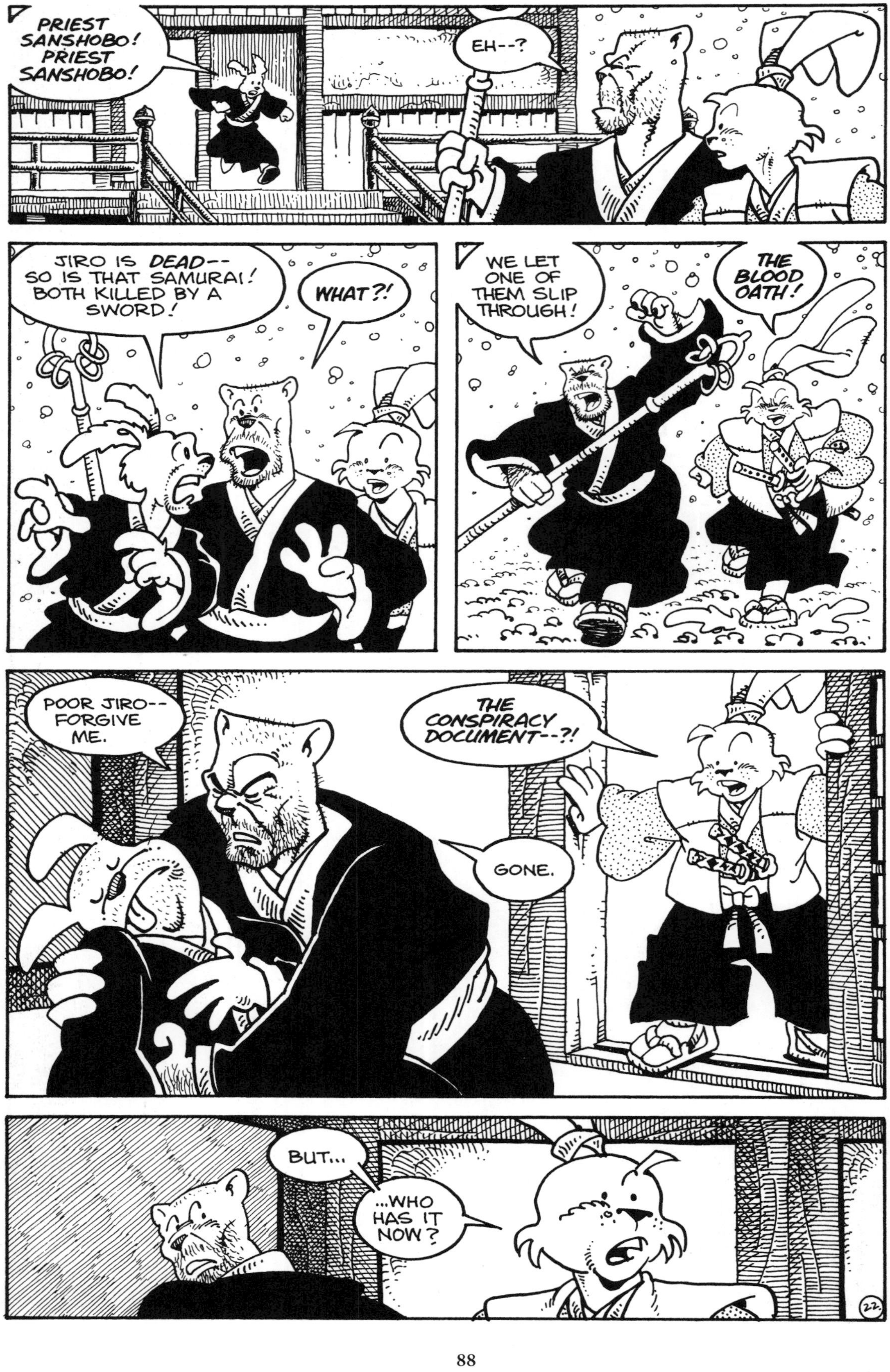
PRIEST SANSHOBO! PRIEST SANSHOBO!
EH--?
JIRO IS DEAD-- SO IS THAT SAMURAI! BOTH KILLED BY A SWORD!
WHAT?!
WE LET ONE OF THEM SLIP THROUGH!
THE BLOOD OATH!
POOR JIRO-- FORGIVE ME.
THE CONSPIRACY DOCUMENT--?!
GONE.
BUT...
...WHO HAS IT NOW?
22

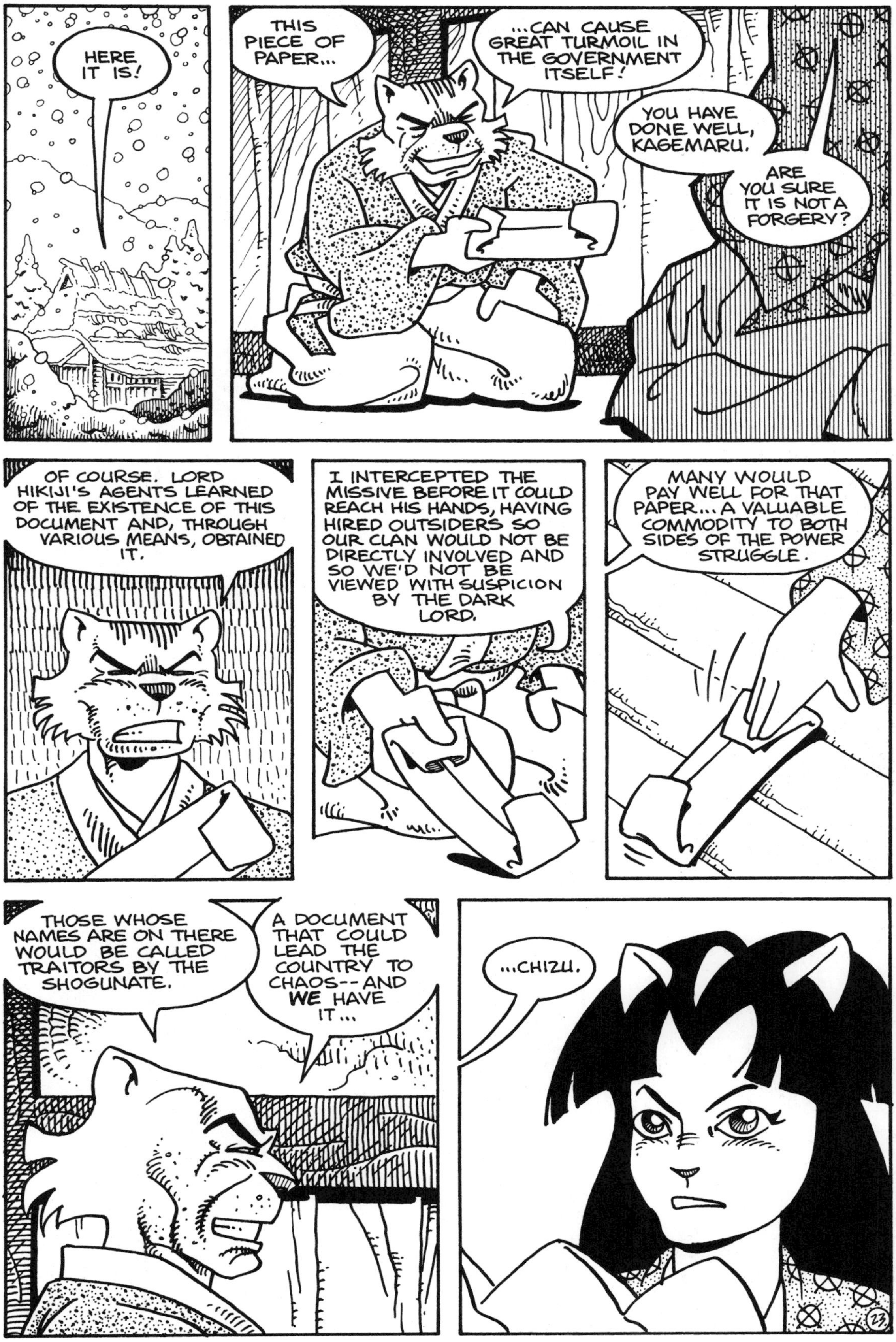
HERE IT IS!
THIS PIECE OF PAPER...
...CAN CAUSE GREAT TURMOIL IN THE GOVERNMENT ITSELF!
YOU HAVE DONE WELL, KAGEMARU.
ARE YOU SURE IT IS NOT A FORGERY?
OF COURSE. LORD HIKIJI'S AGENTS LEARNED OF THE EXISTENCE OF THIS DOCUMENT AND, THROUGH VARIOUS MEANS, OBTAINED IT.
I INTERCEPTED THE MISSIVE BEFORE IT COULD REACH HIS HANDS, HAVING HIRED OUTSIDERS SO OUR CLAN WOULD NOT BE DIRECTLY INVOLVED AND SO WE'D NOT BE VIEWED WITH SUSPICION BY THE DARK LORD.
MANY WOULD PAY WELL FOR THAT PAPER... A VALUABLE COMMODITY TO BOTH SIDES OF THE POWER STRUGGLE.
THOSE WHOSE NAMES ARE ON THERE WOULD BE CALLED TRAITORS BY THE SHOGUNATE.
A DOCUMENT THAT COULD LEAD THE COUNTRY TO CHAOS--AND **WE** HAVE IT...
...CHIZU.
23

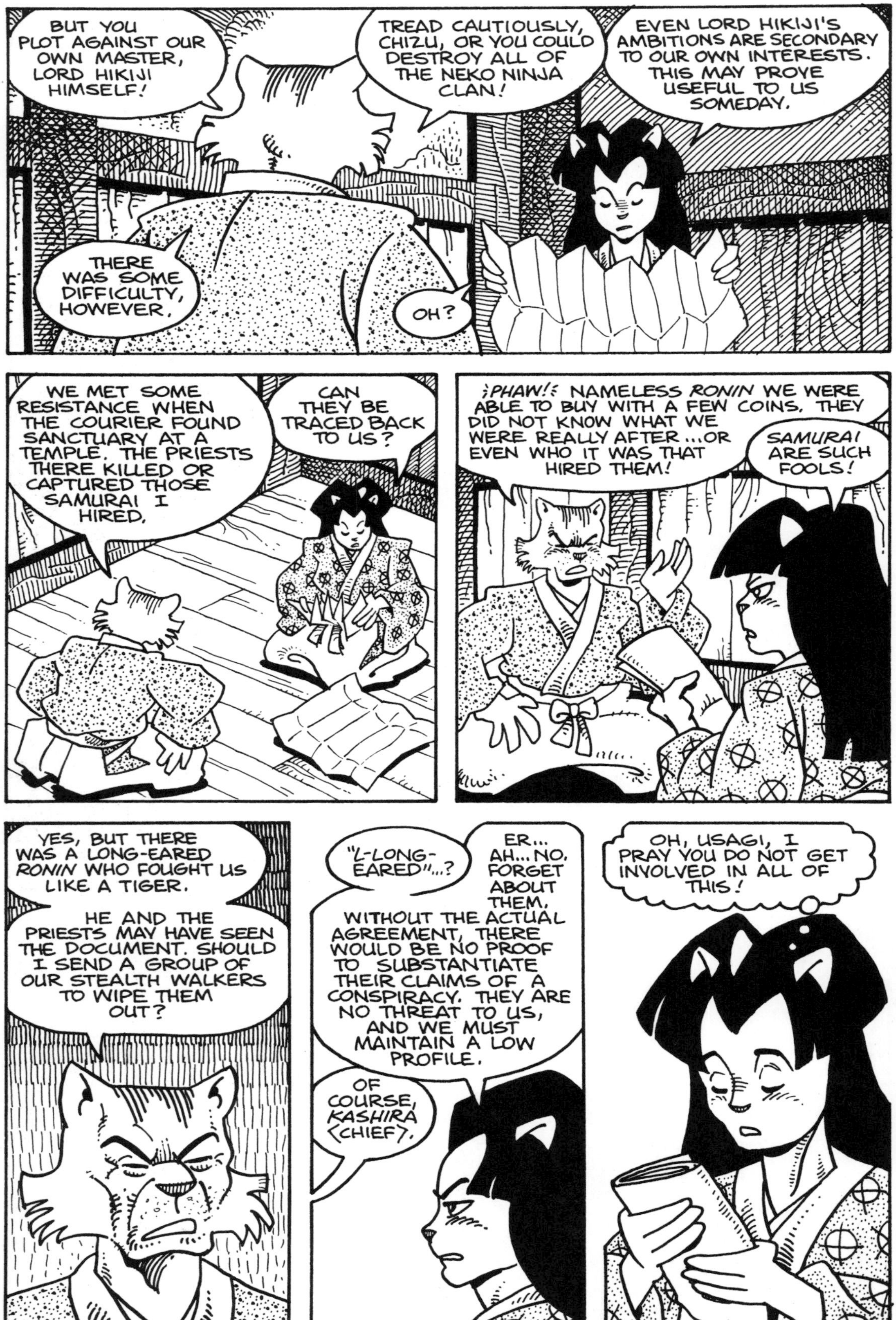
BUT YOU PLOT AGAINST OUR OWN MASTER, LORD HIKIJI HIMSELF!
TREAD CAUTIOUSLY, CHIZU, OR YOU COULD DESTROY ALL OF THE NEKO NINJA CLAN!
EVEN LORD HIKIJI'S AMBITIONS ARE SECONDARY TO OUR OWN INTERESTS. THIS MAY PROVE USEFUL TO US SOMEDAY.
THERE WAS SOME DIFFICULTY, HOWEVER.
OH?
WE MET SOME RESISTANCE WHEN THE COURIER FOUND SANCTUARY AT A TEMPLE. THE PRIESTS THERE KILLED OR CAPTURED THOSE SAMURAI I HIRED.
CAN THEY BE TRACED BACK TO US?
¡PHAW!¡ NAMELESS *RONIN* WE WERE ABLE TO BUY WITH A FEW COINS. THEY DID NOT KNOW WHAT WE WERE REALLY AFTER ...OR EVEN WHO IT WAS THAT HIRED THEM!
SAMURAI ARE SUCH FOOLS!
YES, BUT THERE WAS A LONG-EARED *RONIN* WHO FOUGHT US LIKE A TIGER.
HE AND THE PRIESTS MAY HAVE SEEN THE DOCUMENT. SHOULD I SEND A GROUP OF OUR STEALTH WALKERS TO WIPE THEM OUT?
"L-LONG-EARED"...?
ER... AH... NO. FORGET ABOUT THEM. WITHOUT THE ACTUAL AGREEMENT, THERE WOULD BE NO PROOF TO SUBSTANTIATE THEIR CLAIMS OF A CONSPIRACY. THEY ARE NO THREAT TO US, AND WE MUST MAINTAIN A LOW PROFILE.
OF COURSE, *KASHIRA* <CHIEF>.
OH, USAGI, I PRAY YOU DO NOT GET INVOLVED IN ALL OF THIS!
END

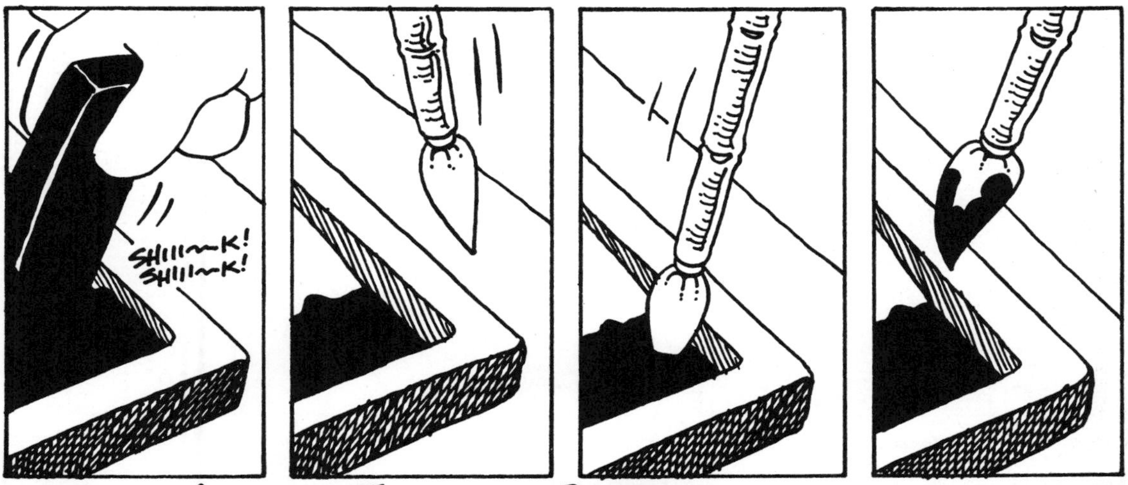
SHIII~K!
SHIII~K!

Snakes and Blossoms

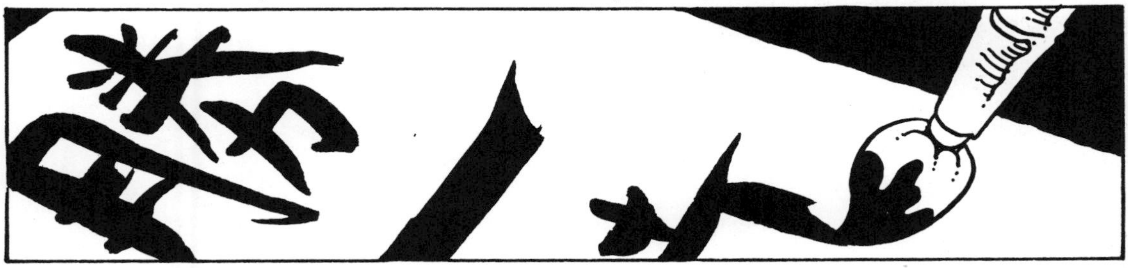

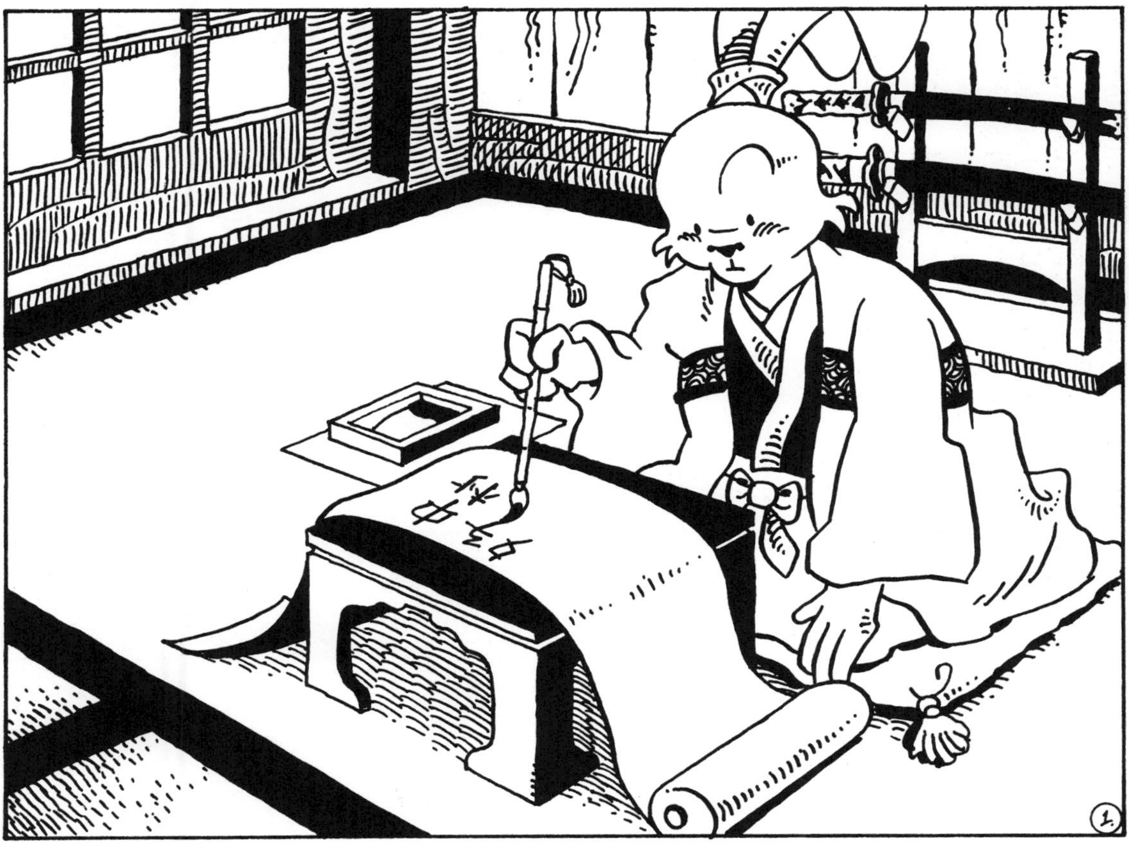

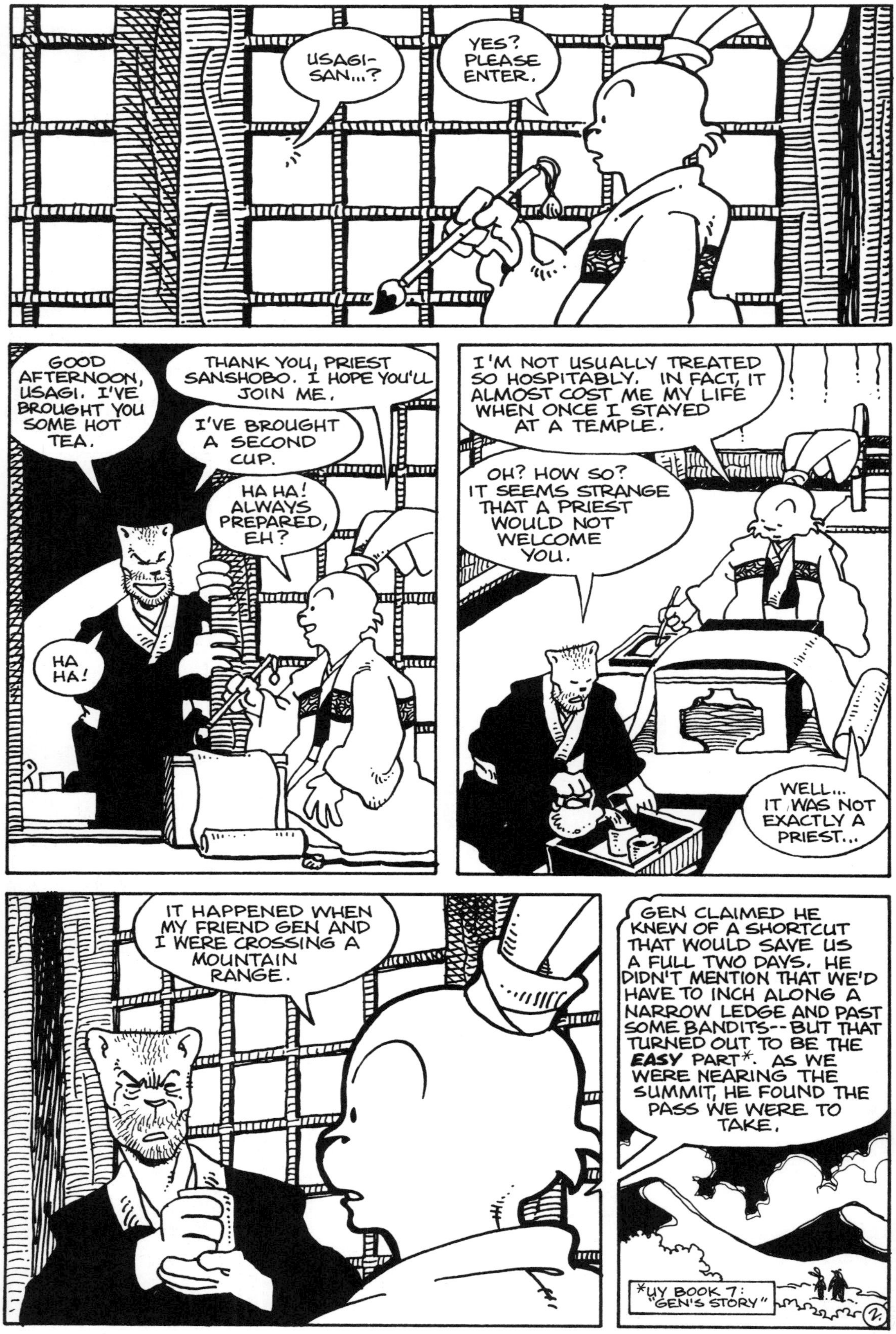
USAGI-SAN...?
YES? PLEASE ENTER.
GOOD AFTERNOON, USAGI. I'VE BROUGHT YOU SOME HOT TEA.
THANK YOU, PRIEST SANSHOBO. I HOPE YOU'LL JOIN ME.
I'VE BROUGHT A SECOND CUP.
HA HA! ALWAYS PREPARED, EH?
HA HA!
I'M NOT USUALLY TREATED SO HOSPITABLY. IN FACT, IT ALMOST COST ME MY LIFE WHEN ONCE I STAYED AT A TEMPLE.
OH? HOW SO? IT SEEMS STRANGE THAT A PRIEST WOULD NOT WELCOME YOU.
WELL... IT WAS NOT EXACTLY A PRIEST...
IT HAPPENED WHEN MY FRIEND GEN AND I WERE CROSSING A MOUNTAIN RANGE.
GEN CLAIMED HE KNEW OF A SHORTCUT THAT WOULD SAVE US A FULL TWO DAYS. HE DIDN'T MENTION THAT WE'D HAVE TO INCH ALONG A NARROW LEDGE AND PAST SOME BANDITS--BUT THAT TURNED OUT TO BE THE *EASY* PART*. AS WE WERE NEARING THE SUMMIT, HE FOUND THE PASS WE WERE TO TAKE.
*UY BOOK 7: "GEN'S STORY"
2.

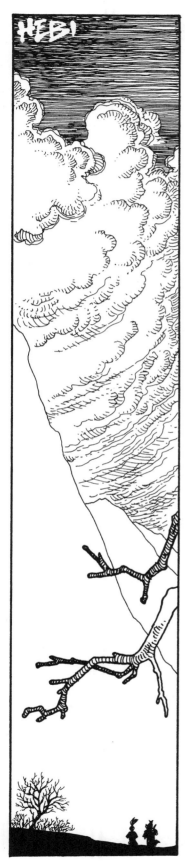

HEBI!

I DON'T LIKE THE LOOK OF THOSE CLOUDS, GEN.

WHERE IS THIS SHORT-CUT OF YOURS?

THERE! THROUGH THAT PASS, WE SHOULD REACH A TEMPLE SOON.

WE'LL SPEND THE NIGHT THERE.

SSSS.....

HIIIIIIIIII!

LOOK OUT, EARS!

OOF!

WAP!

CLICK!

UH!

HIIYAHH!!

CHOP

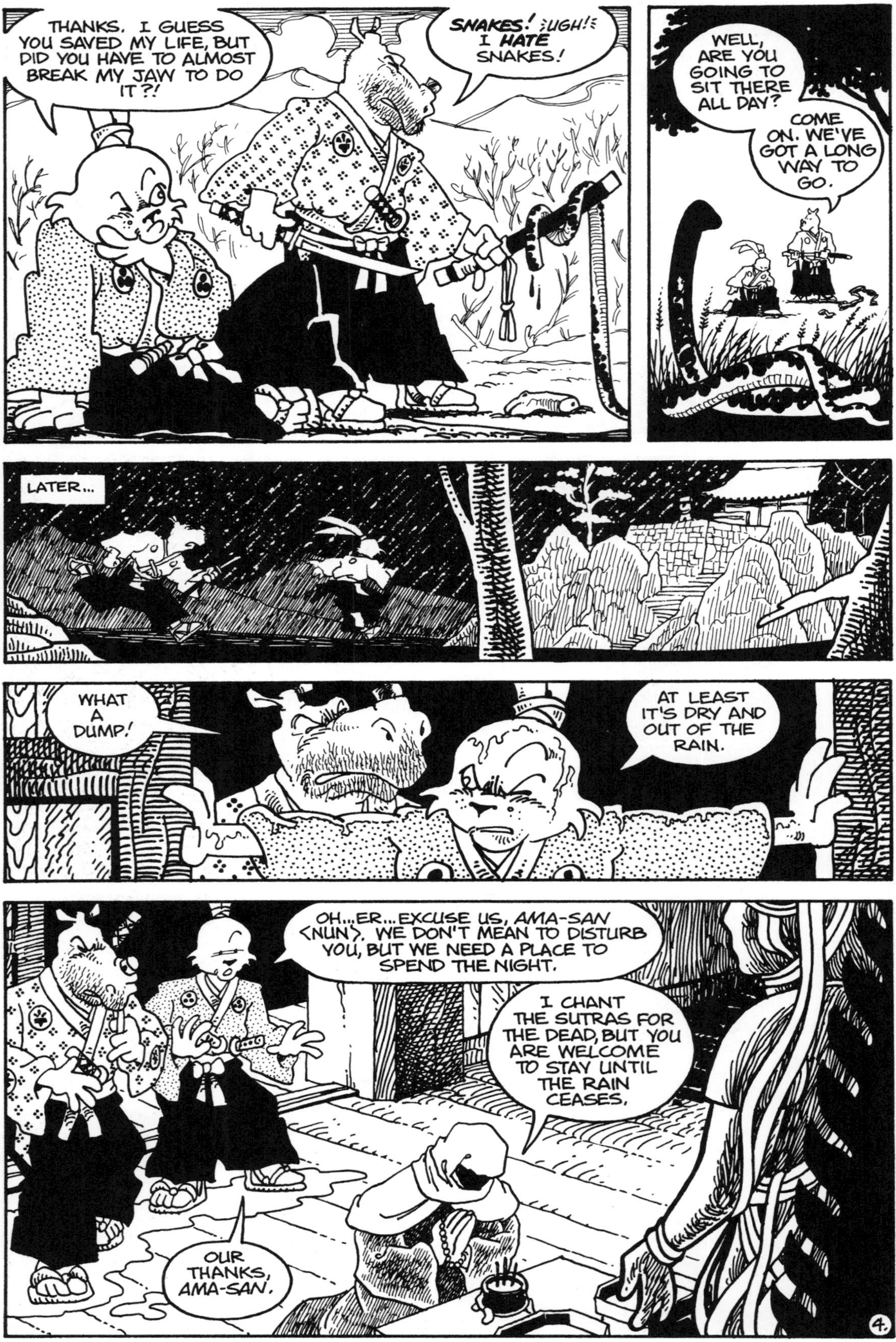
THANKS. I GUESS YOU SAVED MY LIFE, BUT DID YOU HAVE TO ALMOST BREAK MY JAW TO DO IT?!
SNAKES! UGH! I HATE SNAKES!
WELL, ARE YOU GOING TO SIT THERE ALL DAY?
COME ON. WE'VE GOT A LONG WAY TO GO.
LATER...
WHAT A DUMP!
AT LEAST IT'S DRY AND OUT OF THE RAIN.
OH...ER...EXCUSE US, AMA-SAN <NUN>. WE DON'T MEAN TO DISTURB YOU, BUT WE NEED A PLACE TO SPEND THE NIGHT.
I CHANT THE SUTRAS FOR THE DEAD, BUT YOU ARE WELCOME TO STAY UNTIL THE RAIN CEASES.
OUR THANKS, AMA-SAN.
4.

DON'T SNORE TOO LOUDLY, YOU'LL DISTURB THE AMA'S PRAYERS.

SNORE? ME? NEVER!

SOON...

≶ZNORE!≶
≶ZNORF!≶
≶ZNORK!≶

OH, WELL.

≶ZNORK!≶
≶ZNORK!≶

ZZZ...

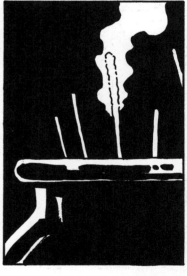

≶ZNORF!≶
≶ZNORK!≶
≶ZNO--!≶

IT'S ABOUT TIME HE STOPPED SNORING!

.....

EH--?

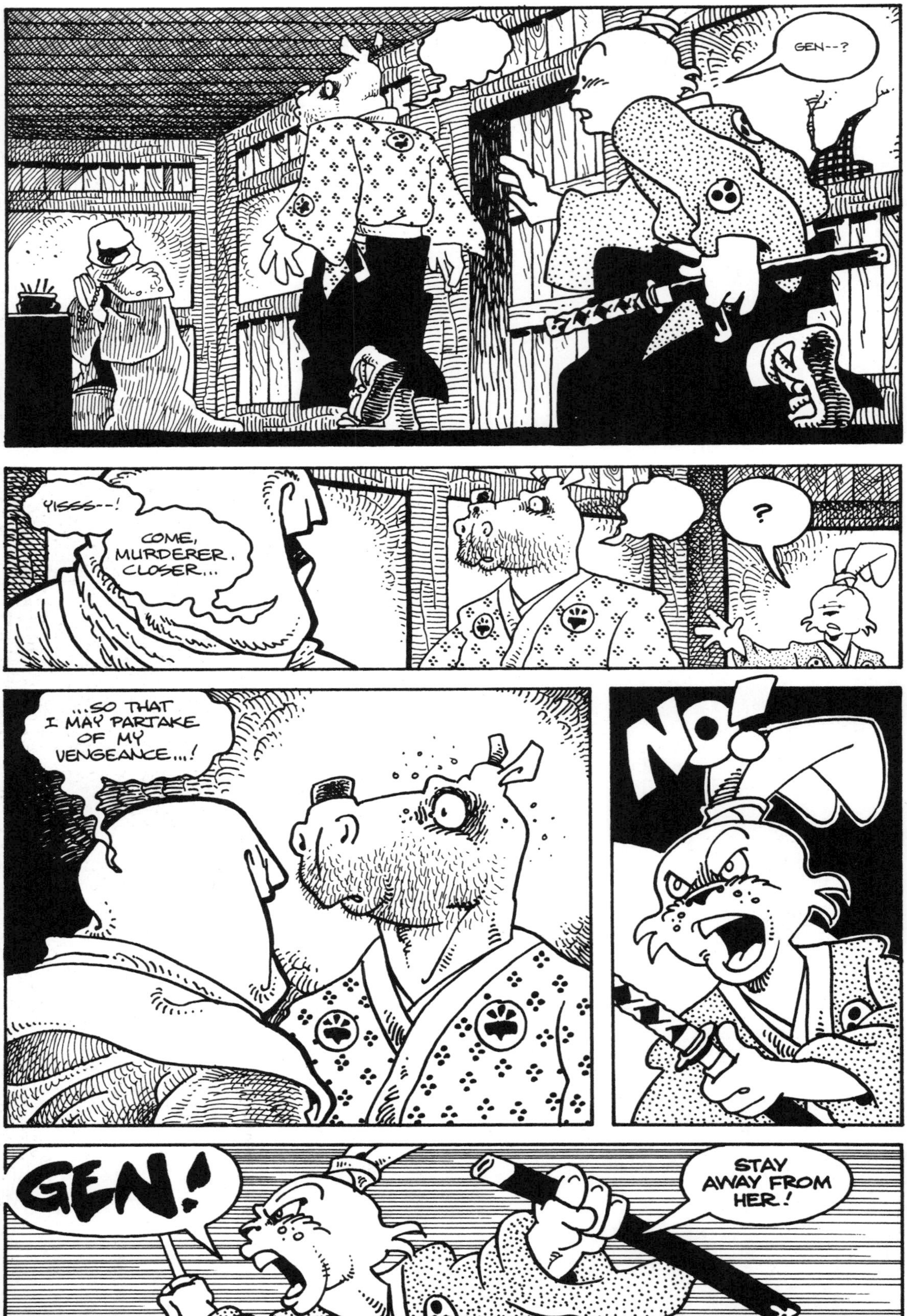
GEN--?
YISSS--!
COME, MURDERER. CLOSER...
?
...SO THAT I MAY PARTAKE OF MY VENGEANCE...!
NO!
GEN!
STAY AWAY FROM HER!
6.

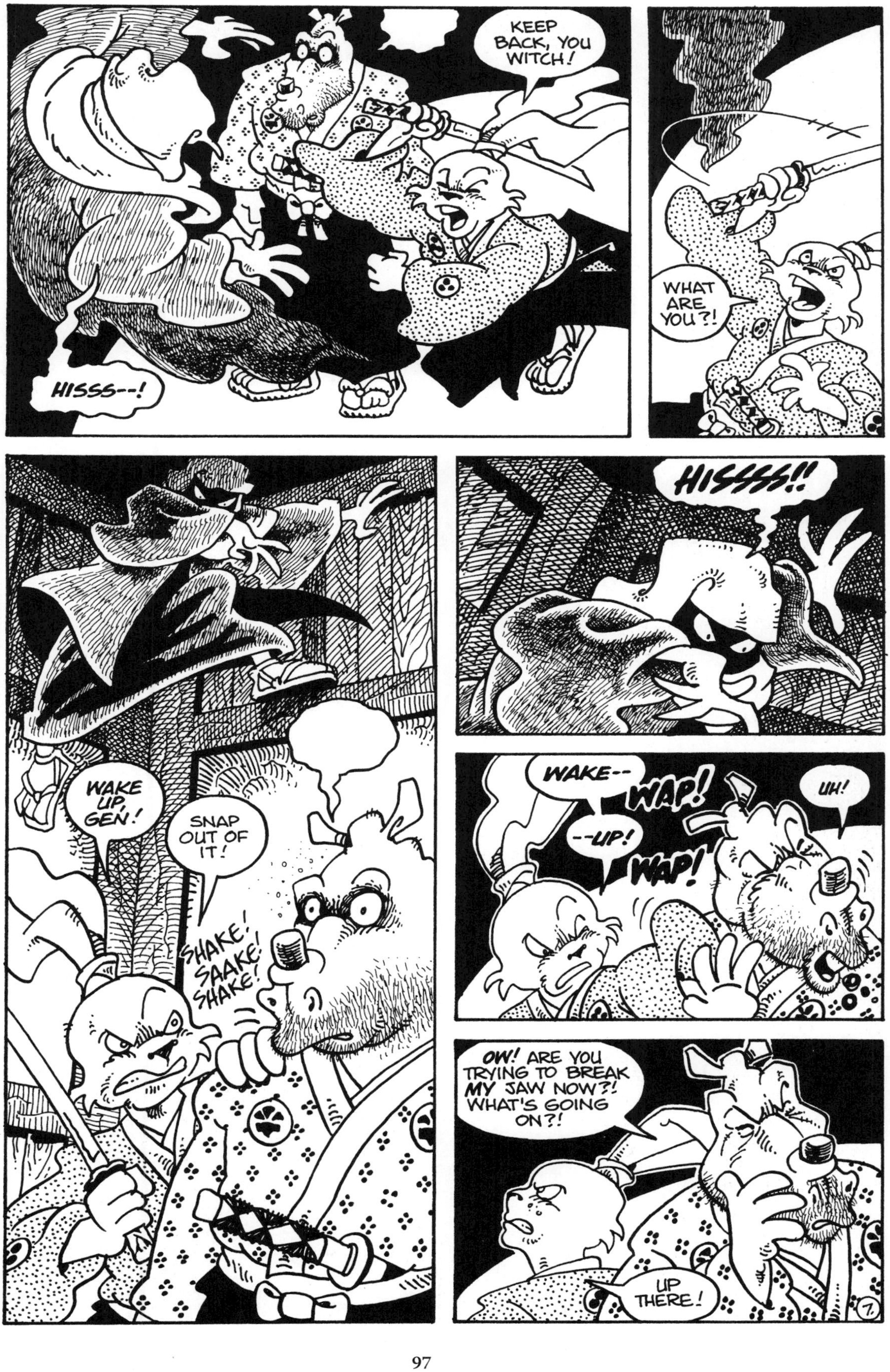
KEEP BACK, YOU WITCH!
HISSS--!
WHAT ARE YOU?!
WAKE UP, GEN!
SNAP OUT OF IT!
SHAKE! SAAKE! SHAKE!
HISSSS!!
WAKE--
WAP!
--UP!
WAP!
UH!
OW! ARE YOU TRYING TO BREAK MY JAW NOW?! WHAT'S GOING ON?!
UP THERE!
7.

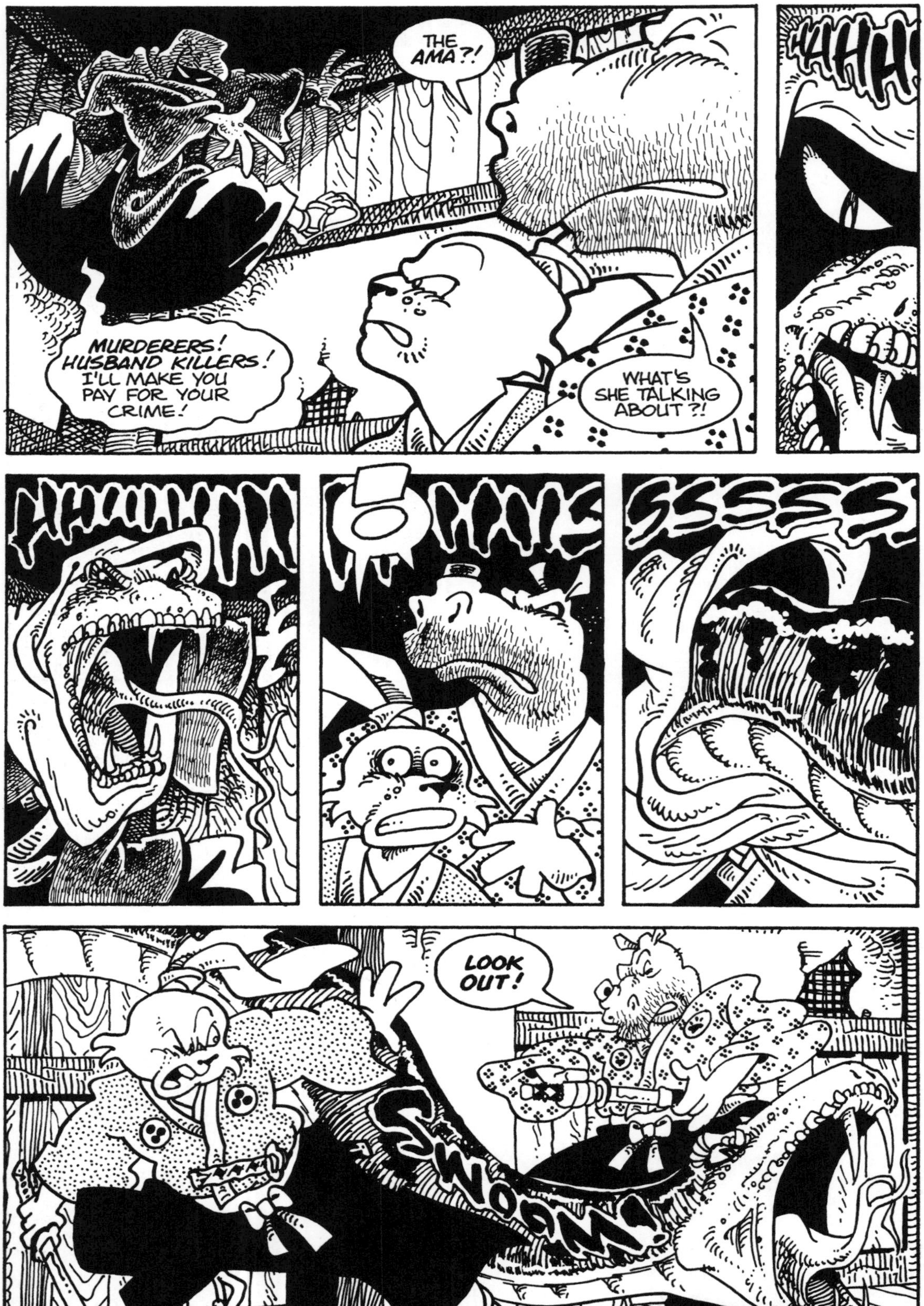
THE AMA?!
MURDERERS! HUSBAND KILLERS! I'LL MAKE YOU PAY FOR YOUR CRIME!
WHAT'S SHE TALKING ABOUT?!
LOOK OUT!
SWOOM!

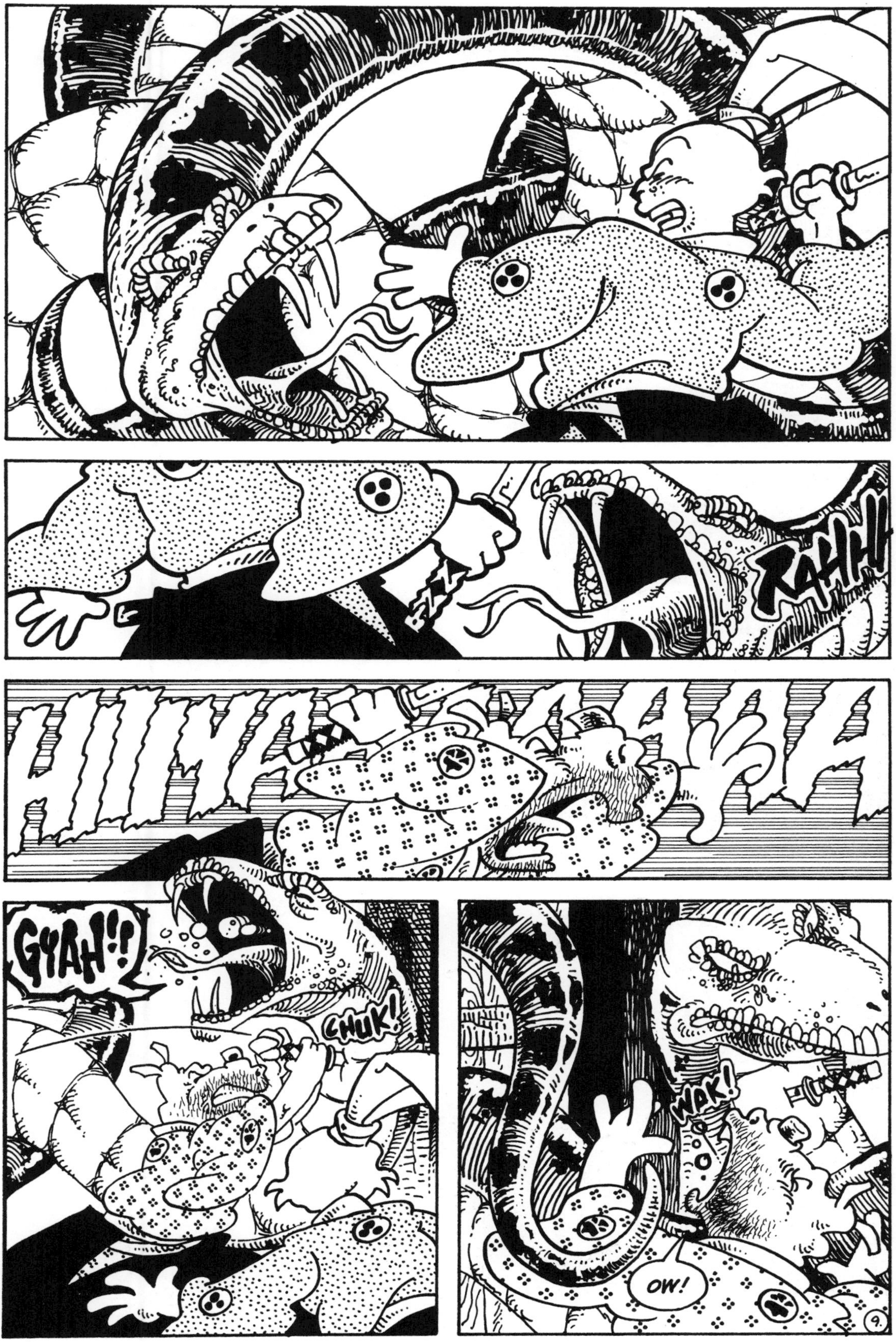
RAHHH
HIIYAAAAA
GYAH!!
CHUK!
WAK!
OW!

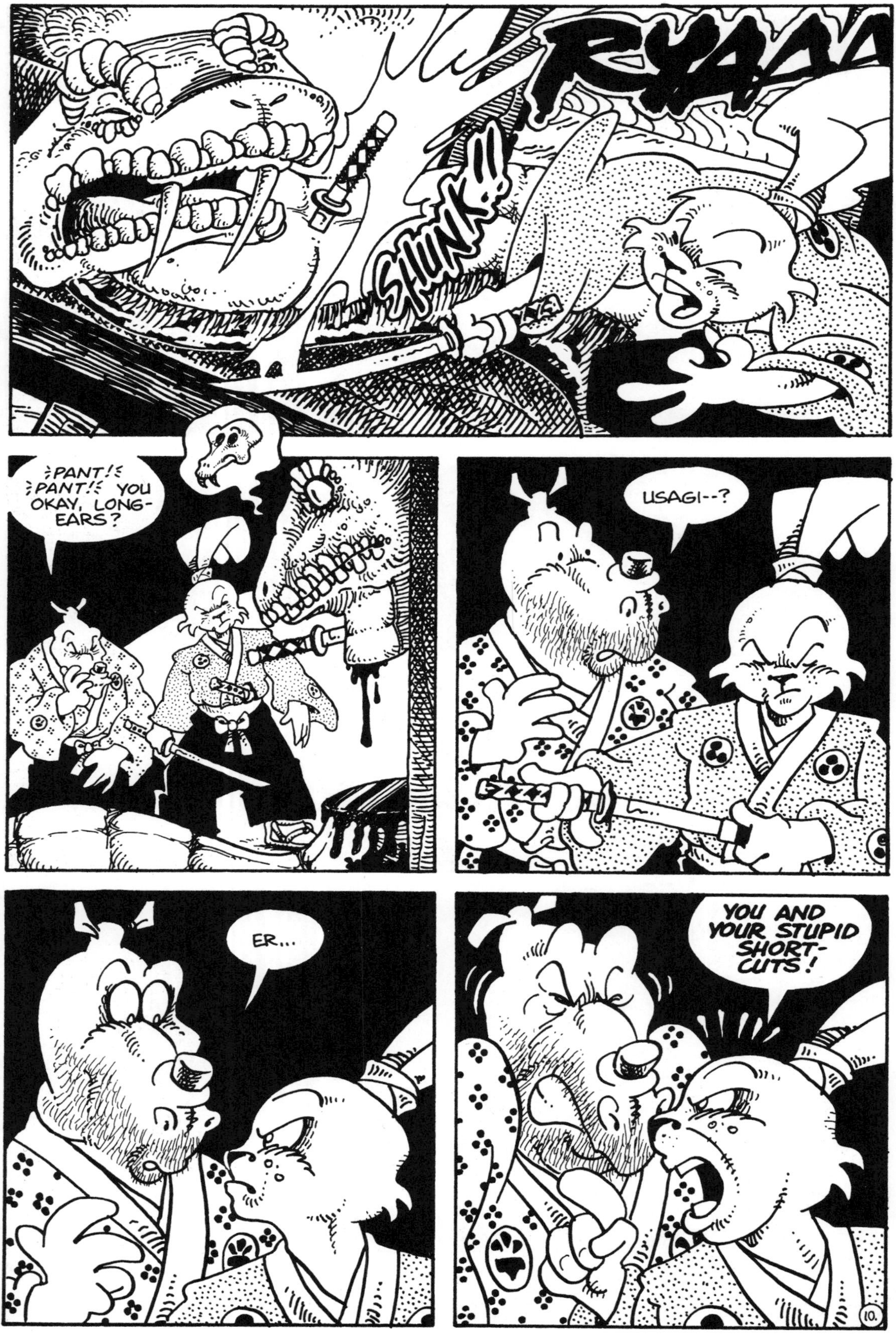
RYAA
SHUNK!!
PANT! PANT! YOU OKAY, LONG-EARS?
USAGI--?
ER...
YOU AND YOUR STUPID SHORT-CUTS!
10.

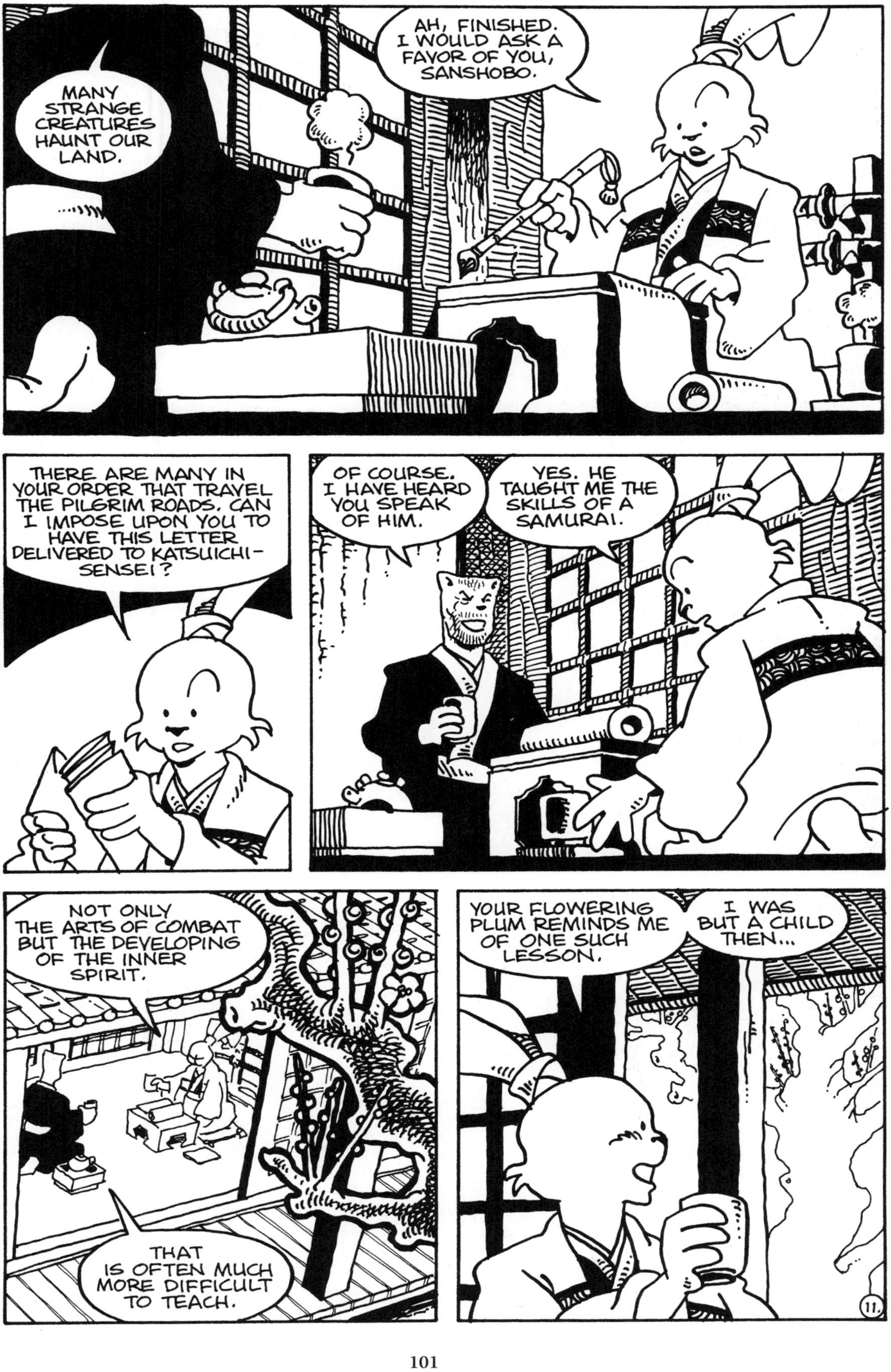
MANY STRANGE CREATURES HAUNT OUR LAND.
AH, FINISHED. I WOULD ASK A FAVOR OF YOU, SANSHOBO.
THERE ARE MANY IN YOUR ORDER THAT TRAVEL THE PILGRIM ROADS. CAN I IMPOSE UPON YOU TO HAVE THIS LETTER DELIVERED TO KATSUICHI-SENSEI?
OF COURSE. I HAVE HEARD YOU SPEAK OF HIM.
YES. HE TAUGHT ME THE SKILLS OF A SAMURAI.
NOT ONLY THE ARTS OF COMBAT BUT THE DEVELOPING OF THE INNER SPIRIT.
THAT IS OFTEN MUCH MORE DIFFICULT TO TEACH.
YOUR FLOWERING PLUM REMINDS ME OF ONE SUCH LESSON.
I WAS BUT A CHILD THEN...
11.

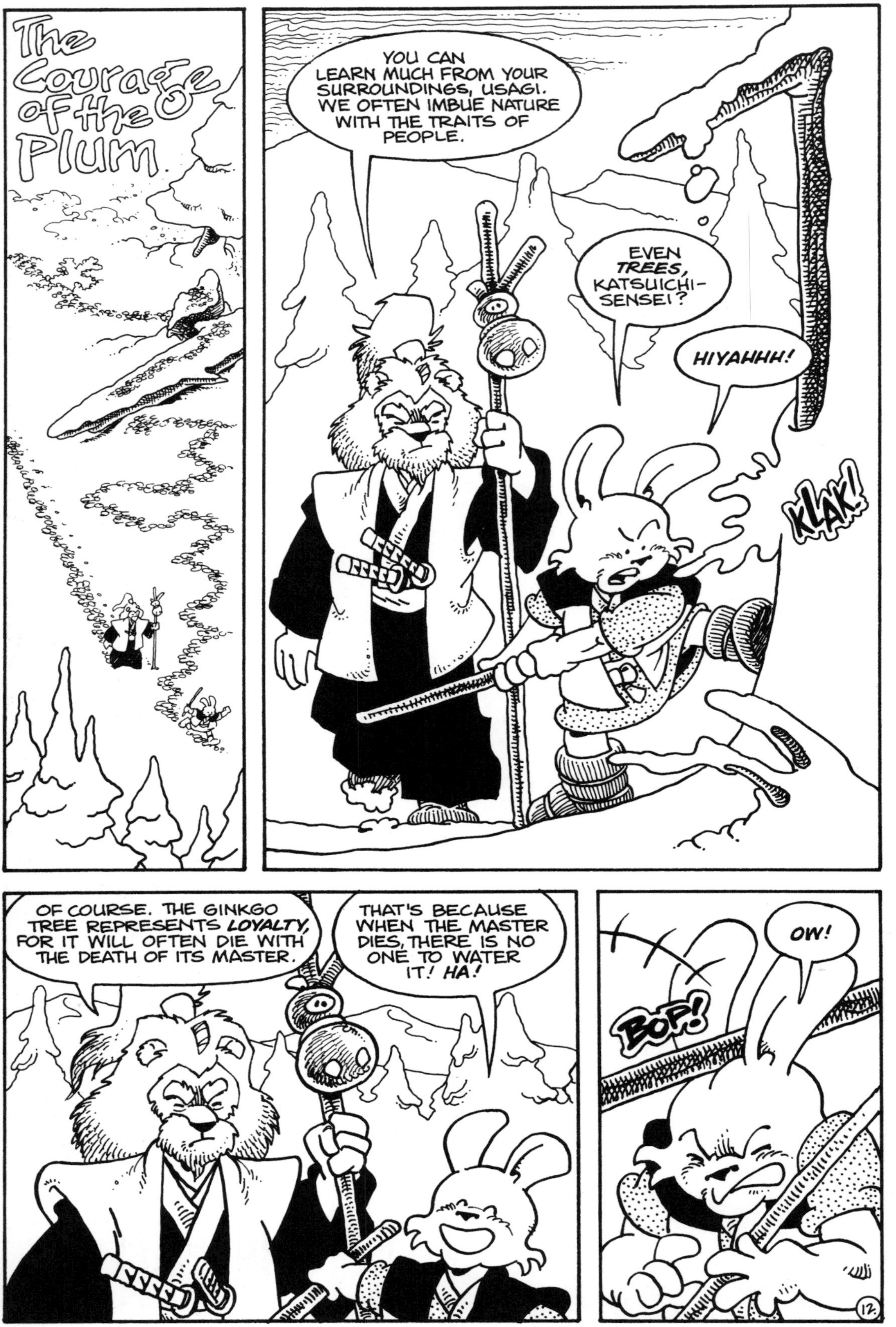
The Courage of the Plum
YOU CAN LEARN MUCH FROM YOUR SURROUNDINGS, USAGI. WE OFTEN IMBUE NATURE WITH THE TRAITS OF PEOPLE.
EVEN TREES, KATSUICHI-SENSEI?
HIYAHHH!
KLAK!
OF COURSE. THE GINKGO TREE REPRESENTS LOYALTY, FOR IT WILL OFTEN DIE WITH THE DEATH OF ITS MASTER.
THAT'S BECAUSE WHEN THE MASTER DIES, THERE IS NO ONE TO WATER IT! HA!
OW!
BOP!
12.

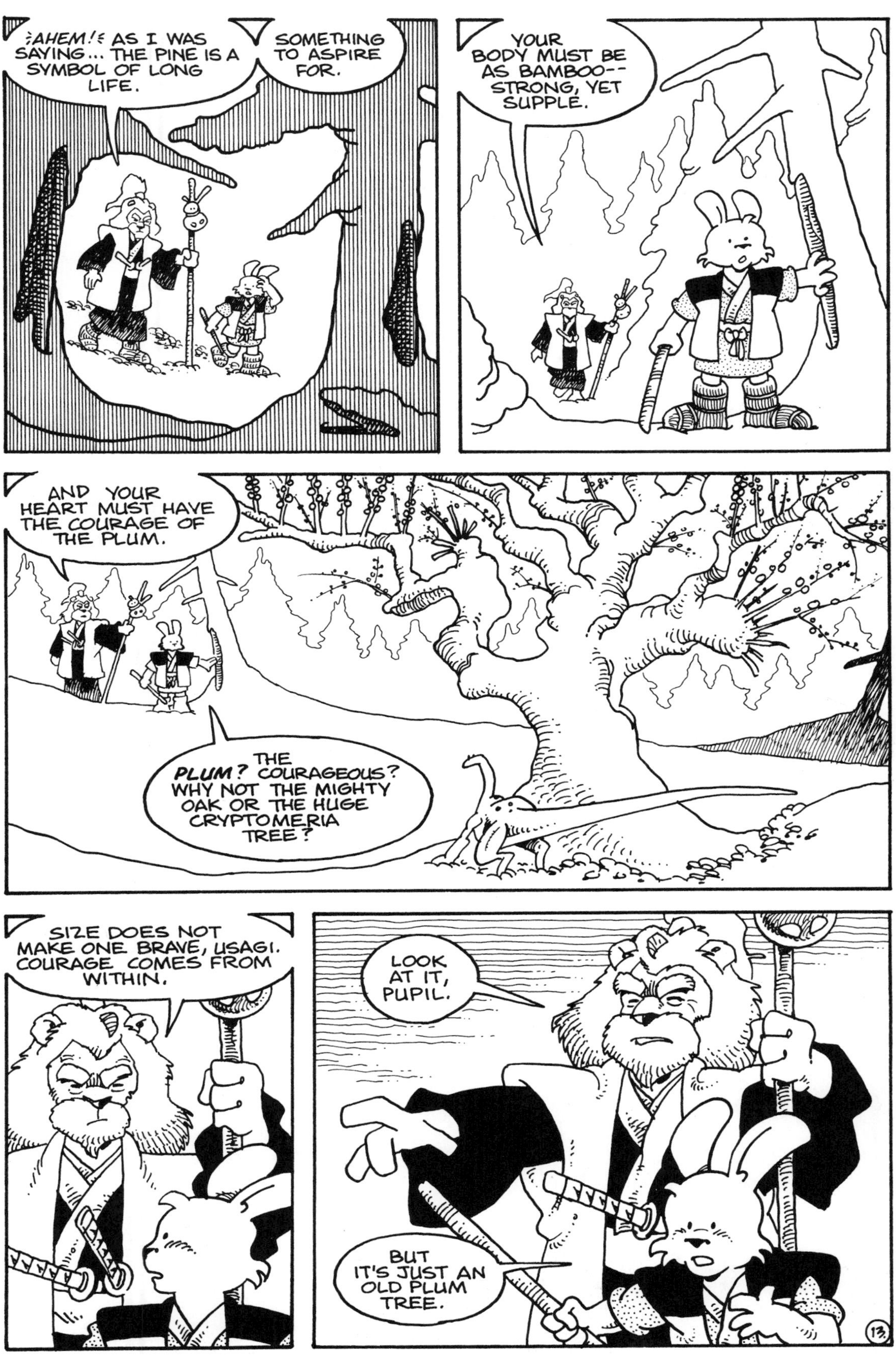
AHEM! AS I WAS SAYING... THE PINE IS A SYMBOL OF LONG LIFE.
SOMETHING TO ASPIRE FOR.
YOUR BODY MUST BE AS BAMBOO-- STRONG, YET SUPPLE.
AND YOUR HEART MUST HAVE THE COURAGE OF THE PLUM.
THE ***PLUM?*** COURAGEOUS? WHY NOT THE MIGHTY OAK OR THE HUGE CRYPTOMERIA TREE?
SIZE DOES NOT MAKE ONE BRAVE, USAGI. COURAGE COMES FROM WITHIN.
LOOK AT IT, PUPIL.
BUT IT'S JUST AN OLD PLUM TREE.
13

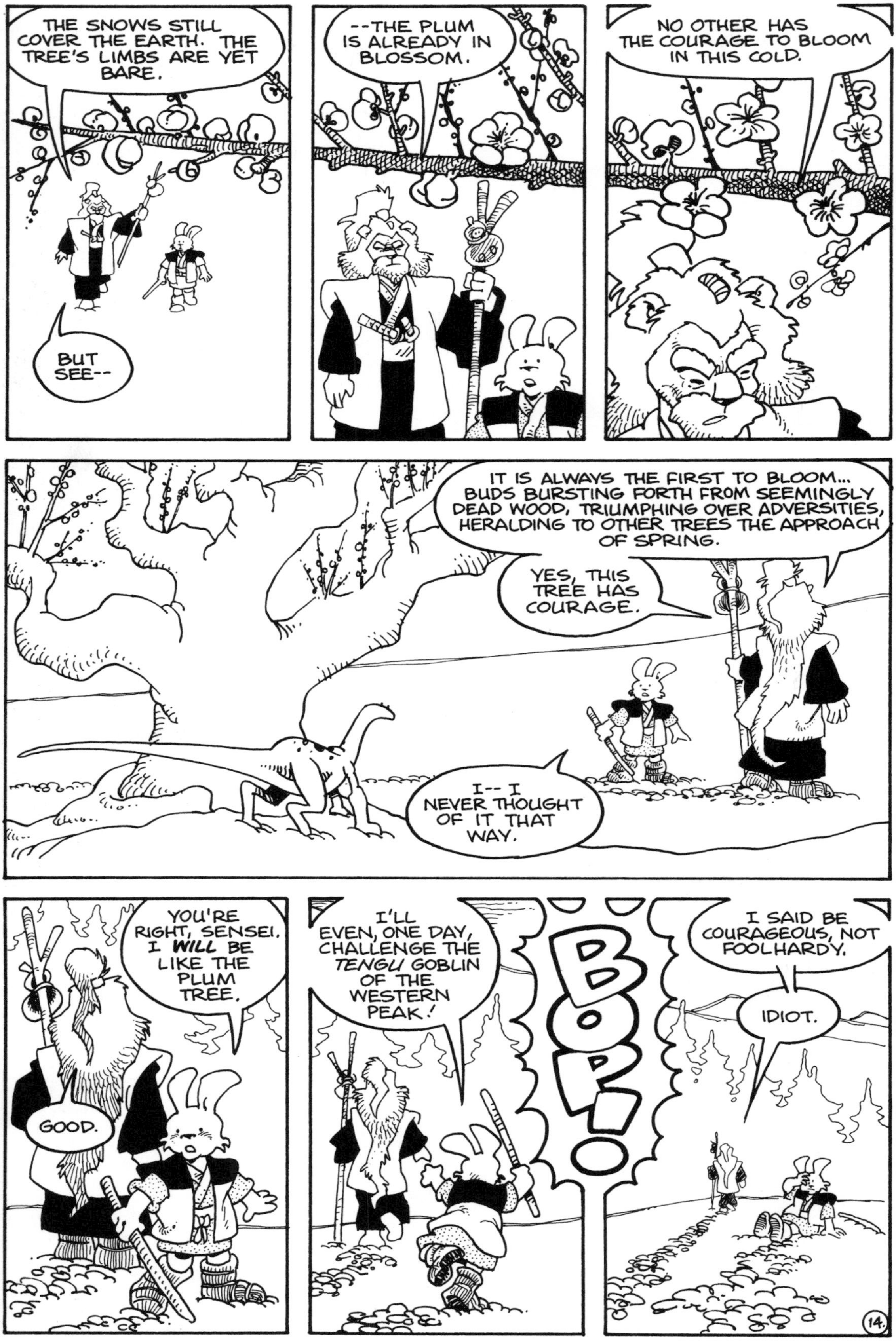
THE SNOWS STILL COVER THE EARTH. THE TREE'S LIMBS ARE YET BARE.
BUT SEE--
--THE PLUM IS ALREADY IN BLOSSOM.
NO OTHER HAS THE COURAGE TO BLOOM IN THIS COLD.
IT IS ALWAYS THE FIRST TO BLOOM... BUDS BURSTING FORTH FROM SEEMINGLY DEAD WOOD, TRIUMPHING OVER ADVERSITIES, HERALDING TO OTHER TREES THE APPROACH OF SPRING.
YES, THIS TREE HAS COURAGE.
I-- I NEVER THOUGHT OF IT THAT WAY.
YOU'RE RIGHT, SENSEI. I **WILL** BE LIKE THE PLUM TREE.
GOOD.
I'LL EVEN, ONE DAY, CHALLENGE THE *TENGU* GOBLIN OF THE WESTERN PEAK!
BOP!
I SAID BE COURAGEOUS, NOT FOOLHARDY.
IDIOT.
14.

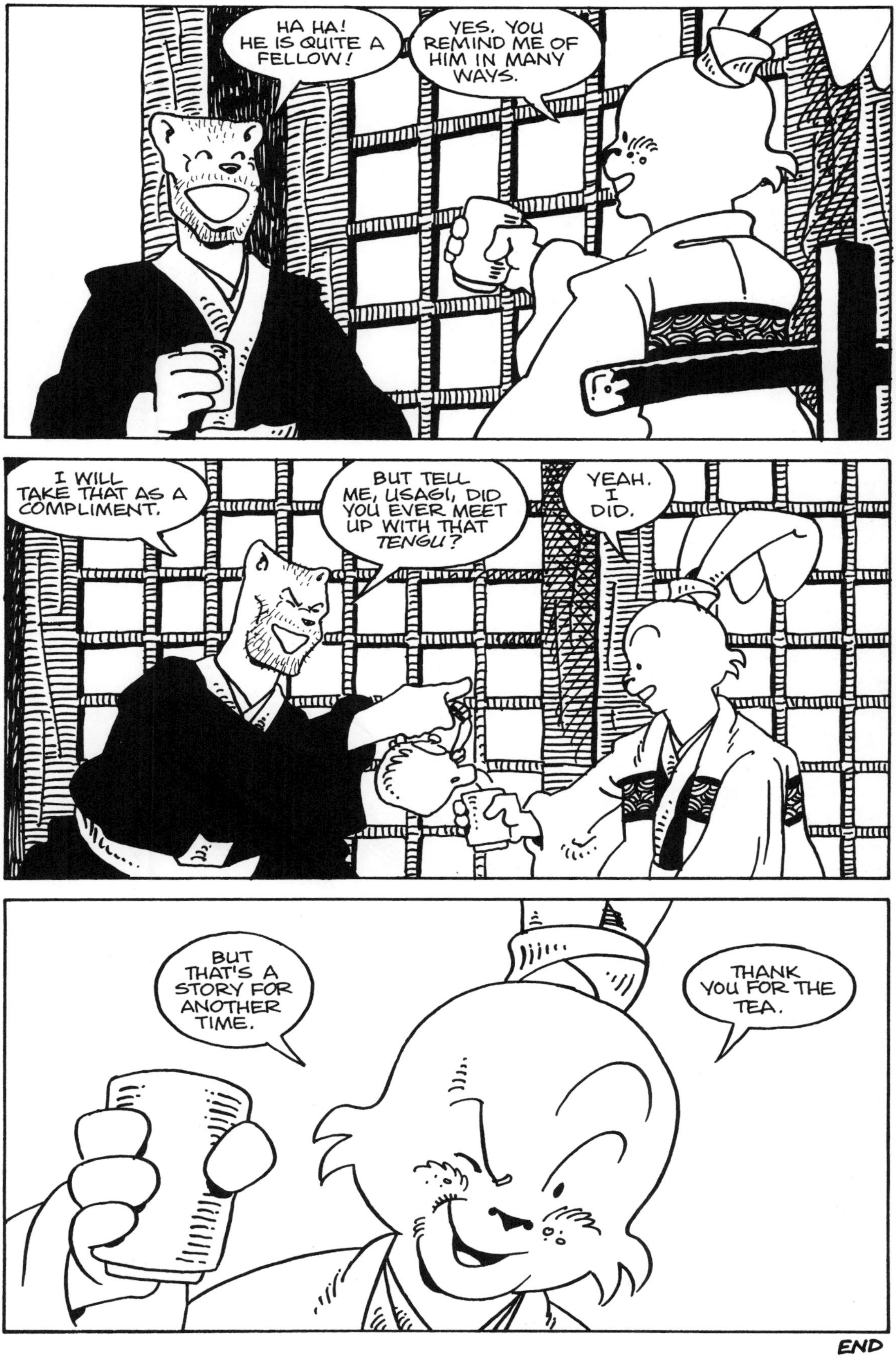
HA HA! HE IS QUITE A FELLOW!
YES. YOU REMIND ME OF HIM IN MANY WAYS.
I WILL TAKE THAT AS A COMPLIMENT.
BUT TELL ME, USAGI, DID YOU EVER MEET UP WITH THAT *TENGU*?
YEAH. I DID.
BUT THAT'S A STORY FOR ANOTHER TIME.
THANK YOU FOR THE TEA.
END

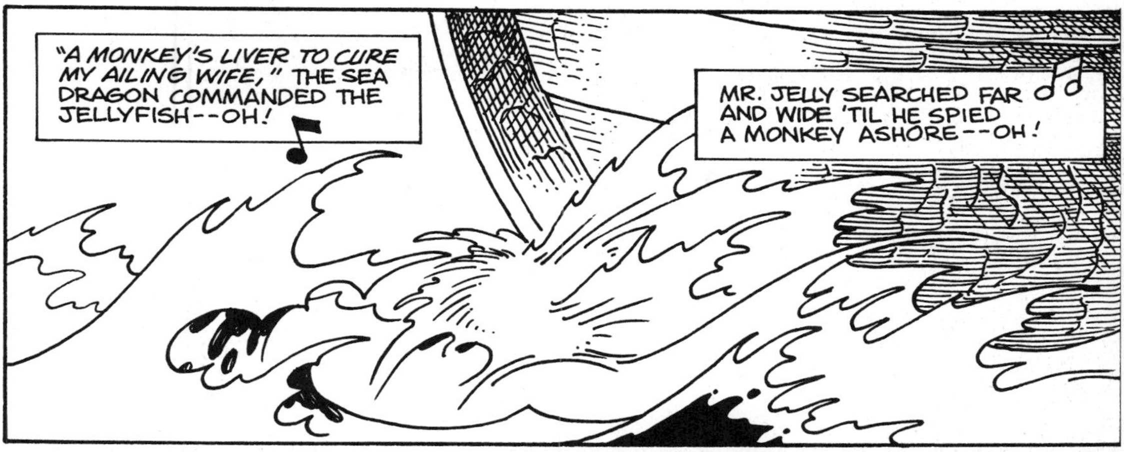
"A MONKEY'S LIVER TO CURE MY AILING WIFE," THE SEA DRAGON COMMANDED THE JELLYFISH--OH!
MR. JELLY SEARCHED FAR AND WIDE 'TIL HE SPIED A MONKEY ASHORE--OH!

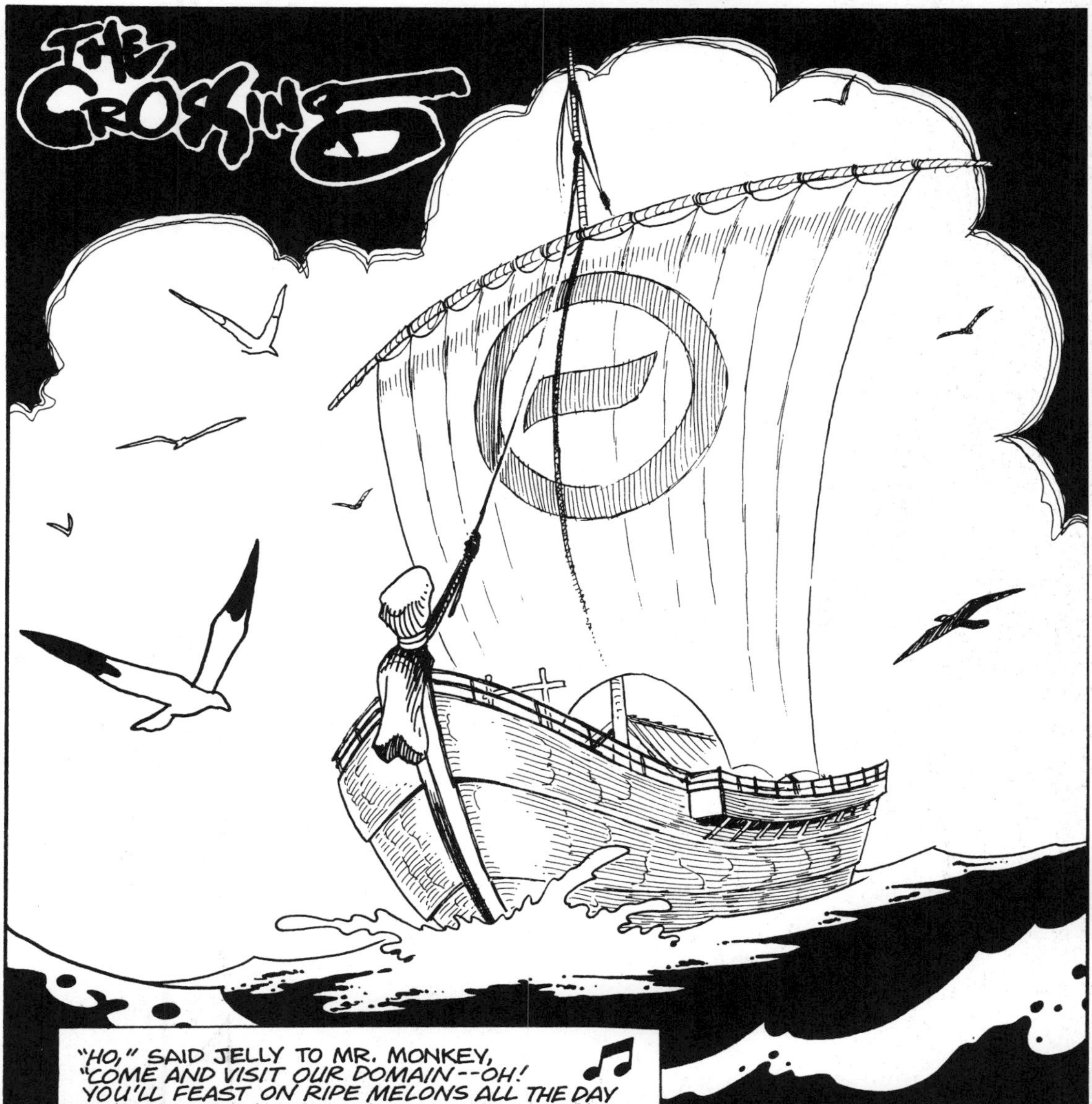
THE CROSSING
"HO," SAID JELLY TO MR. MONKEY, "COME AND VISIT OUR DOMAIN--OH! YOU'LL FEAST ON RIPE MELONS ALL THE DAY AND SLEEP IN A BIG, SILKEN BED--OH!"
1.

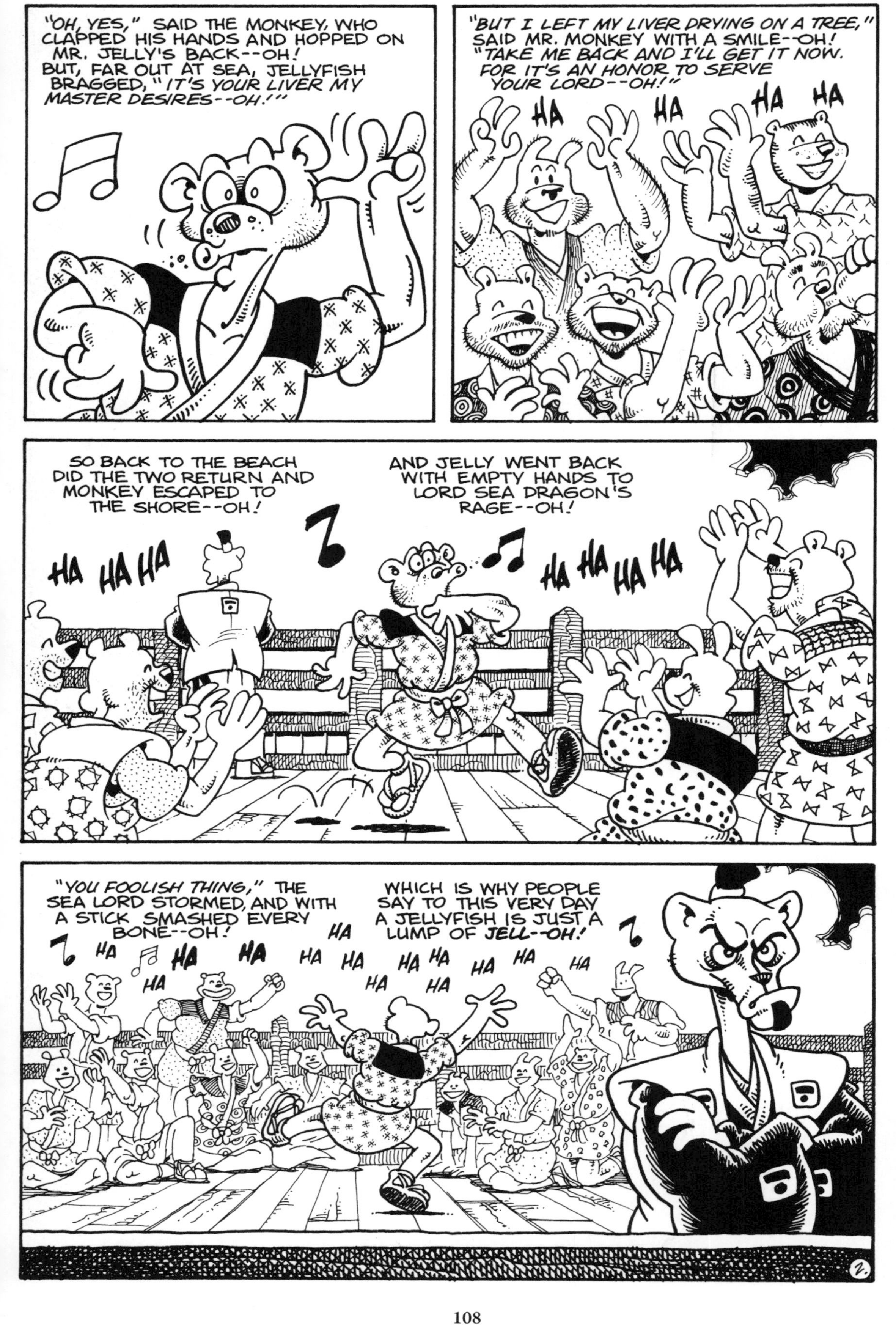
"OH, YES," SAID THE MONKEY, WHO CLAPPED HIS HANDS AND HOPPED ON MR. JELLY'S BACK--OH! BUT, FAR OUT AT SEA, JELLYFISH BRAGGED, "IT'S YOUR LIVER MY MASTER DESIRES--OH!"
"BUT I LEFT MY LIVER DRYING ON A TREE," SAID MR. MONKEY WITH A SMILE--OH! "TAKE ME BACK AND I'LL GET IT NOW. FOR IT'S AN HONOR TO SERVE YOUR LORD--OH!"
HA HA HA HA
SO BACK TO THE BEACH DID THE TWO RETURN AND MONKEY ESCAPED TO THE SHORE--OH!
AND JELLY WENT BACK WITH EMPTY HANDS TO LORD SEA DRAGON'S RAGE--OH!
HA HA HA
HA HA HA HA
"YOU FOOLISH THING," THE SEA LORD STORMED, AND WITH A STICK SMASHED EVERY BONE--OH!
WHICH IS WHY PEOPLE SAY TO THIS VERY DAY A JELLYFISH IS JUST A LUMP OF JELL--OH!
HA HA HA HA HA HA HA HA HA HA HA HA HA HA HA
2.

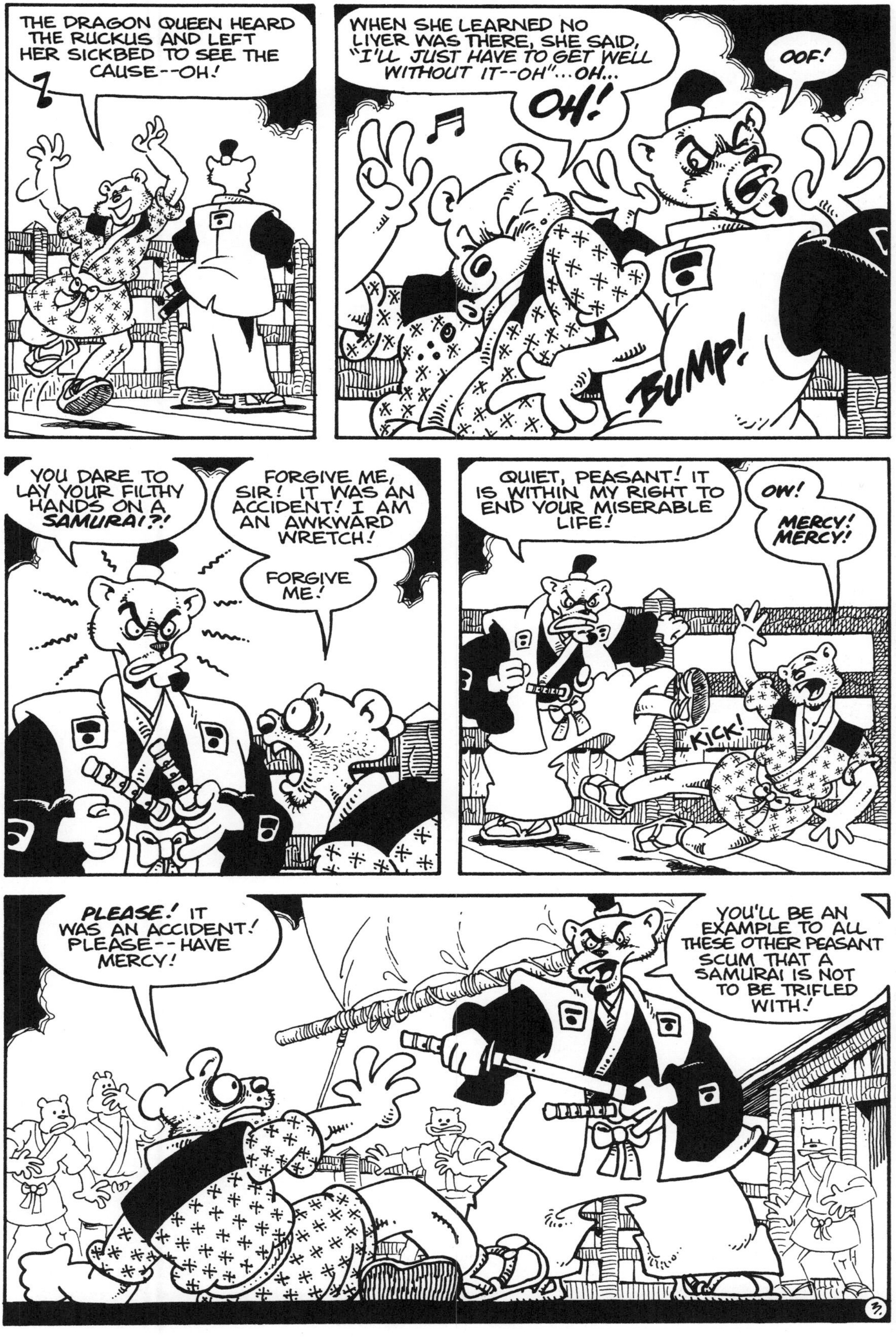
THE DRAGON QUEEN HEARD THE RUCKUS AND LEFT HER SICKBED TO SEE THE CAUSE--OH!
WHEN SHE LEARNED NO LIVER WAS THERE, SHE SAID, "I'LL JUST HAVE TO GET WELL WITHOUT IT--OH"...OH...
OH!
OOF!
BUMP!
YOU DARE TO LAY YOUR FILTHY HANDS ON A SAMURAI?!
FORGIVE ME, SIR! IT WAS AN ACCIDENT! I AM AN AWKWARD WRETCH!
FORGIVE ME!
QUIET, PEASANT! IT IS WITHIN MY RIGHT TO END YOUR MISERABLE LIFE!
OW!
MERCY! MERCY!
KICK!
PLEASE! IT WAS AN ACCIDENT! PLEASE--HAVE MERCY!
YOU'LL BE AN EXAMPLE TO ALL THESE OTHER PEASANT SCUM THAT A SAMURAI IS NOT TO BE TRIFLED WITH!
3.

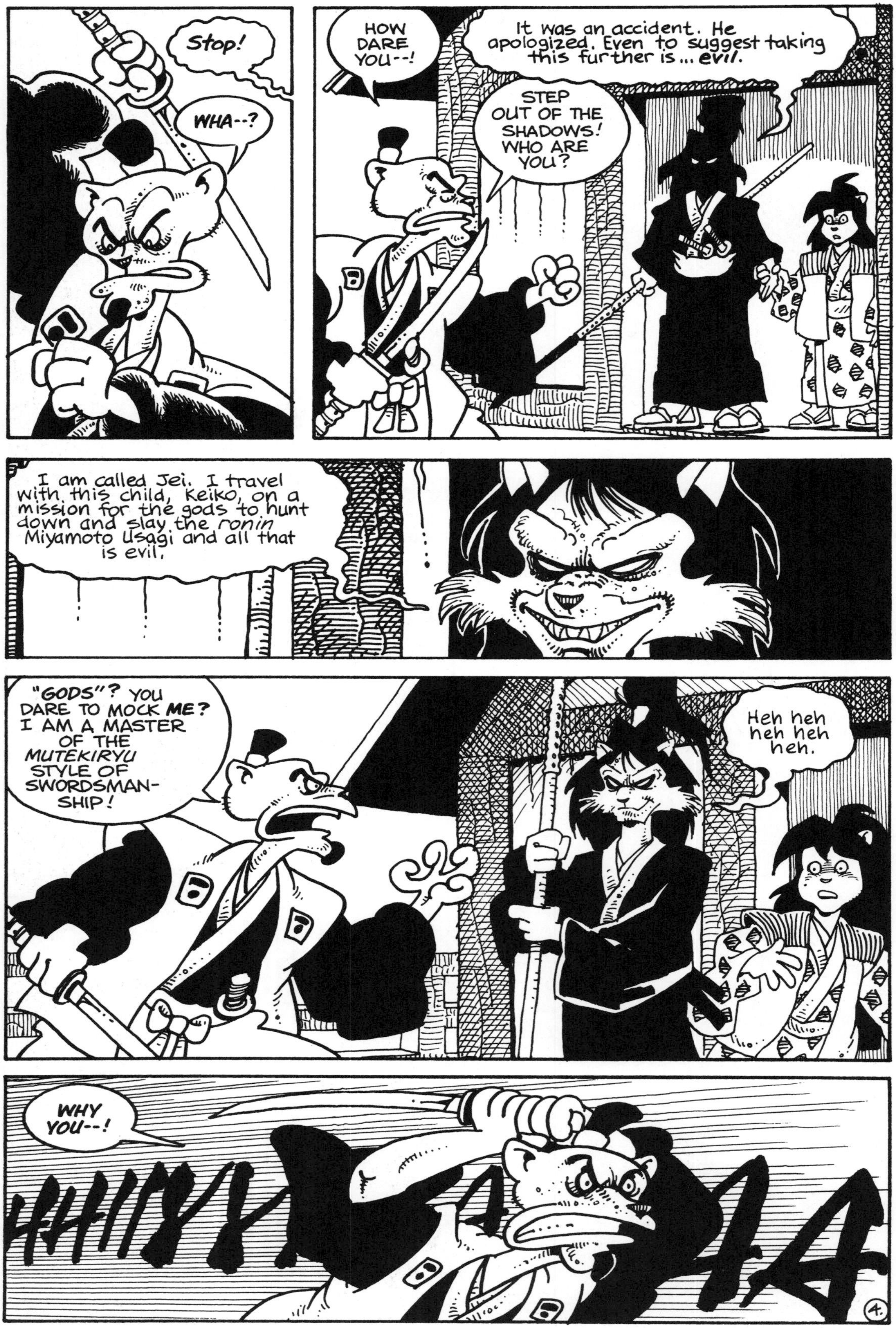
Stop!
WHA--?
HOW DARE YOU--!
It was an accident. He apologized. Even to suggest taking this further is... evil.
STEP OUT OF THE SHADOWS! WHO ARE YOU?
I am called Jei. I travel with this child, Keiko, on a mission for the gods to hunt down and slay the ronin Miyamoto Usagi and all that is evil.
"GODS"? YOU DARE TO MOCK ME? I AM A MASTER OF THE MUTEKIRYU STYLE OF SWORDSMANSHIP!
Heh heh heh heh heh.
WHY YOU--!
4.

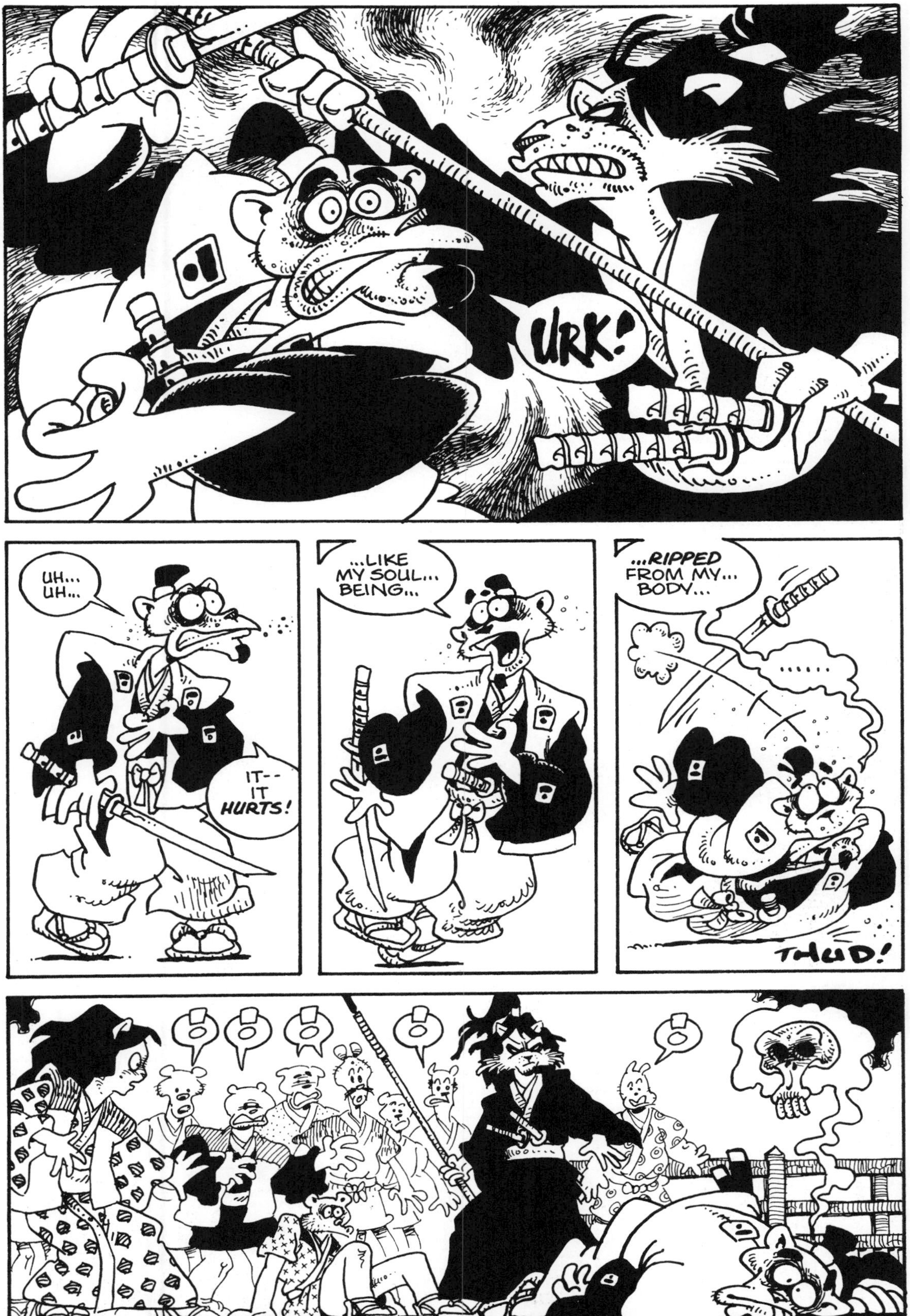
URK!
UH... UH...
IT-- IT HURTS!
...LIKE MY SOUL... BEING...
...RIPPED FROM MY... BODY...
......
THUD!
7

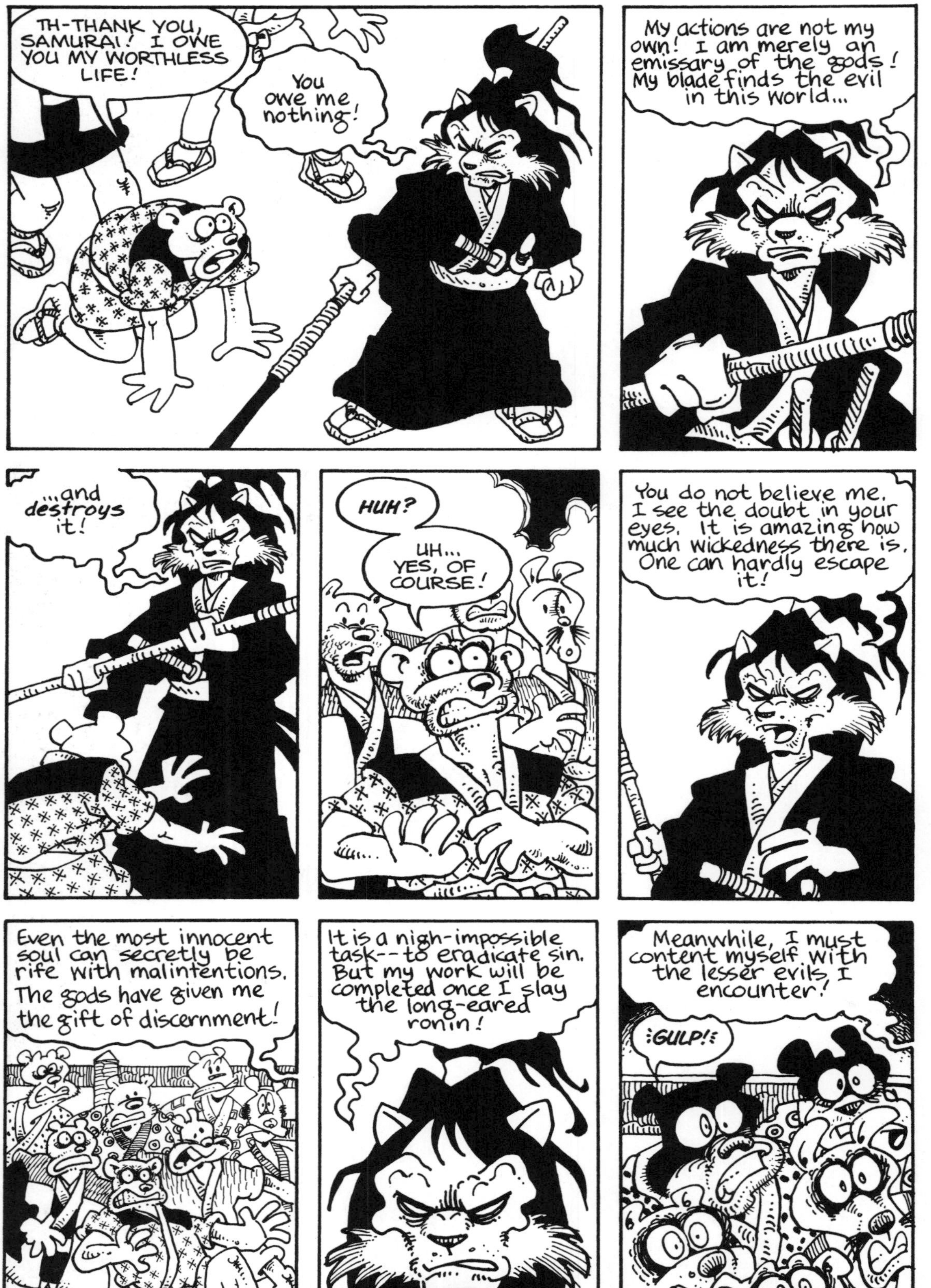
TH-THANK YOU, SAMURAI! I OWE YOU MY WORTHLESS LIFE!
You owe me nothing!
My actions are not my own! I am merely an emissary of the gods! My blade finds the evil in this world...
...and destroys it!
HUH?
UH... YES, OF COURSE!
You do not believe me. I see the doubt in your eyes. It is amazing how much wickedness there is. One can hardly escape it!
Even the most innocent soul can secretly be rife with malintentions. The gods have given me the gift of discernment!
It is a nigh-impossible task--to eradicate sin. But my work will be completed once I slay the long-eared ronin!
Meanwhile, I must content myself with the lesser evils, I encounter!
GULP!
6.

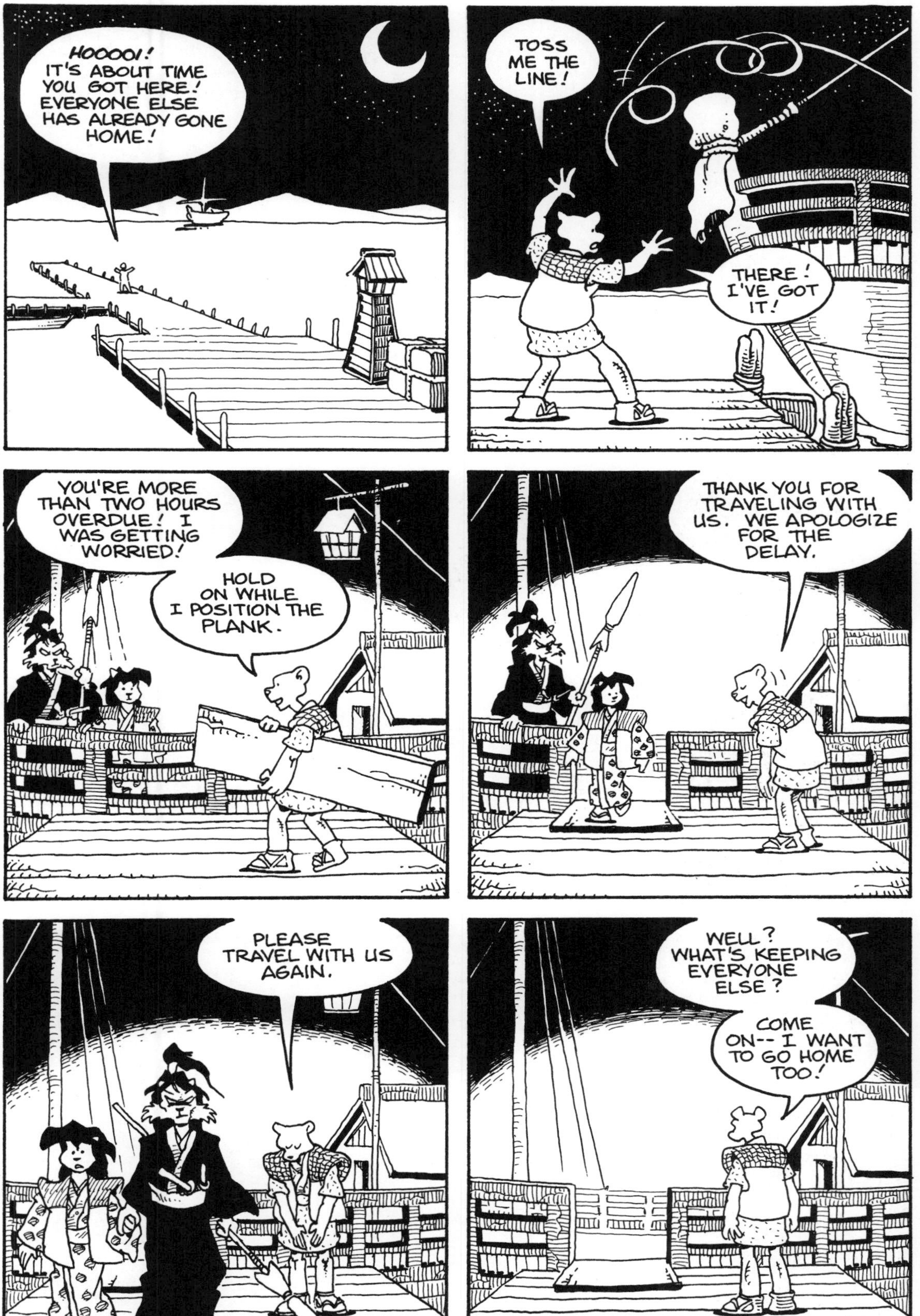
HOOOOI! IT'S ABOUT TIME YOU GOT HERE! EVERYONE ELSE HAS ALREADY GONE HOME!
TOSS ME THE LINE!
THERE! I'VE GOT IT!
YOU'RE MORE THAN TWO HOURS OVERDUE! I WAS GETTING WORRIED!
HOLD ON WHILE I POSITION THE PLANK.
THANK YOU FOR TRAVELING WITH US. WE APOLOGIZE FOR THE DELAY.
PLEASE TRAVEL WITH US AGAIN.
WELL? WHAT'S KEEPING EVERYONE ELSE?
COME ON-- I WANT TO GO HOME TOO!
7.

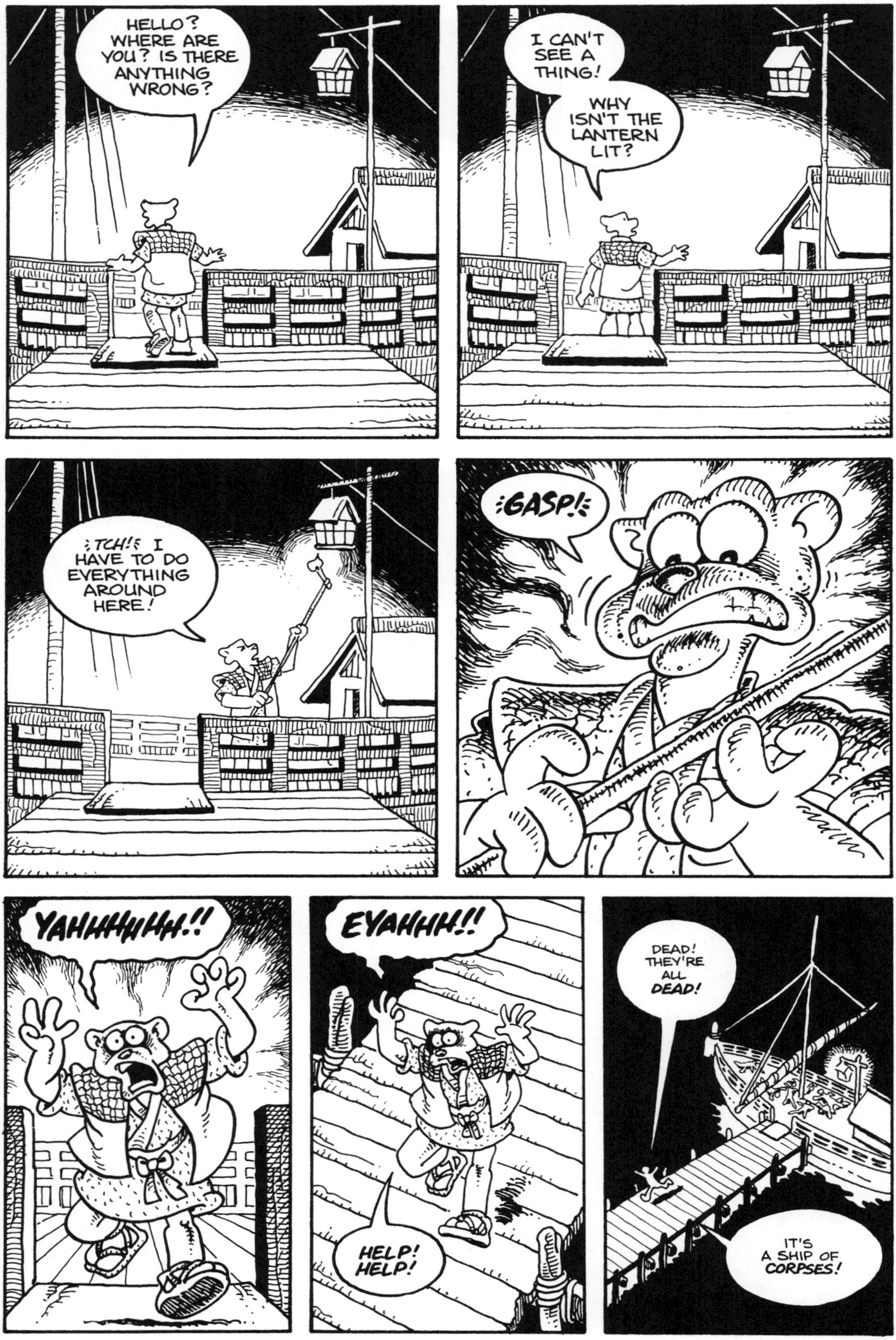
HELLO? WHERE ARE YOU? IS THERE ANYTHING WRONG?
I CAN'T SEE A THING!
WHY ISN'T THE LANTERN LIT?
TCH! I HAVE TO DO EVERYTHING AROUND HERE!
GASP!
YAHHHHHH!!
EYAHHH!!
HELP! HELP!
DEAD! THEY'RE ALL DEAD!
IT'S A SHIP OF CORPSES!
END

THE CLOSE OF THE 16TH CENTURY WAS KNOWN AS THE ***AGE OF WARS***, AS WARLORDS FOUGHT ONE ANOTHER FOR LAND AND POWER.

REBELLIONS WERE NOT UNCOMMON, AND SO IT WAS IN THE GEISHU PROVINCE AS LORD ARAKI CHALLENGED HIS LORD MATAICHI FOR CONTROL OF THE LANDS. ARAKI'S ARMY WAS LED BY GENERAL IKEDA, HERO OF A HUNDRED BATTLES. IKEDA WAS A WARRIOR AND A BRILLIANT TACTICIAN, BUT EVEN HE DID NOT REALIZE WHAT IT TRULY MEANT TO HAVE...

THE PATIENCE OF THE SPIDER

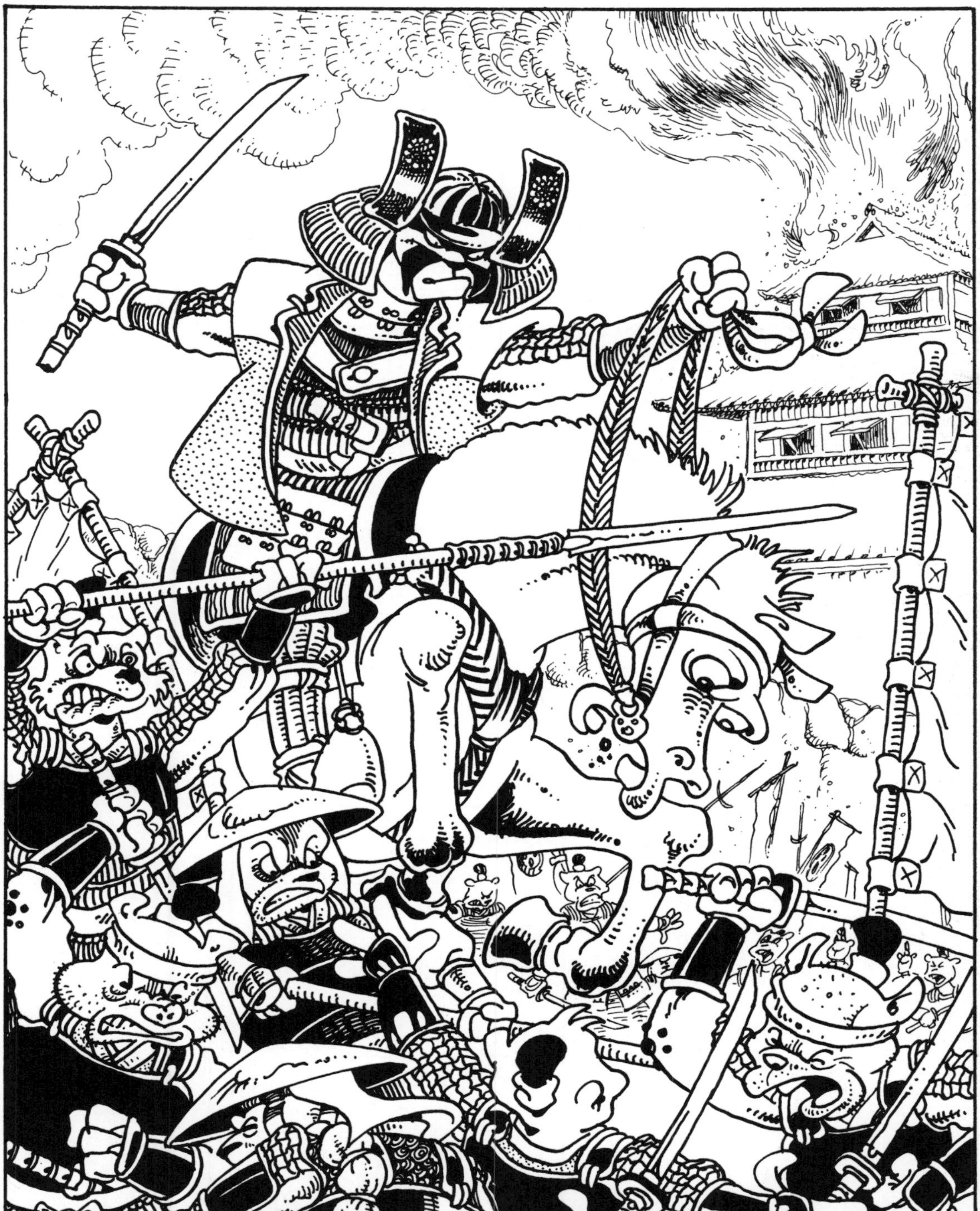

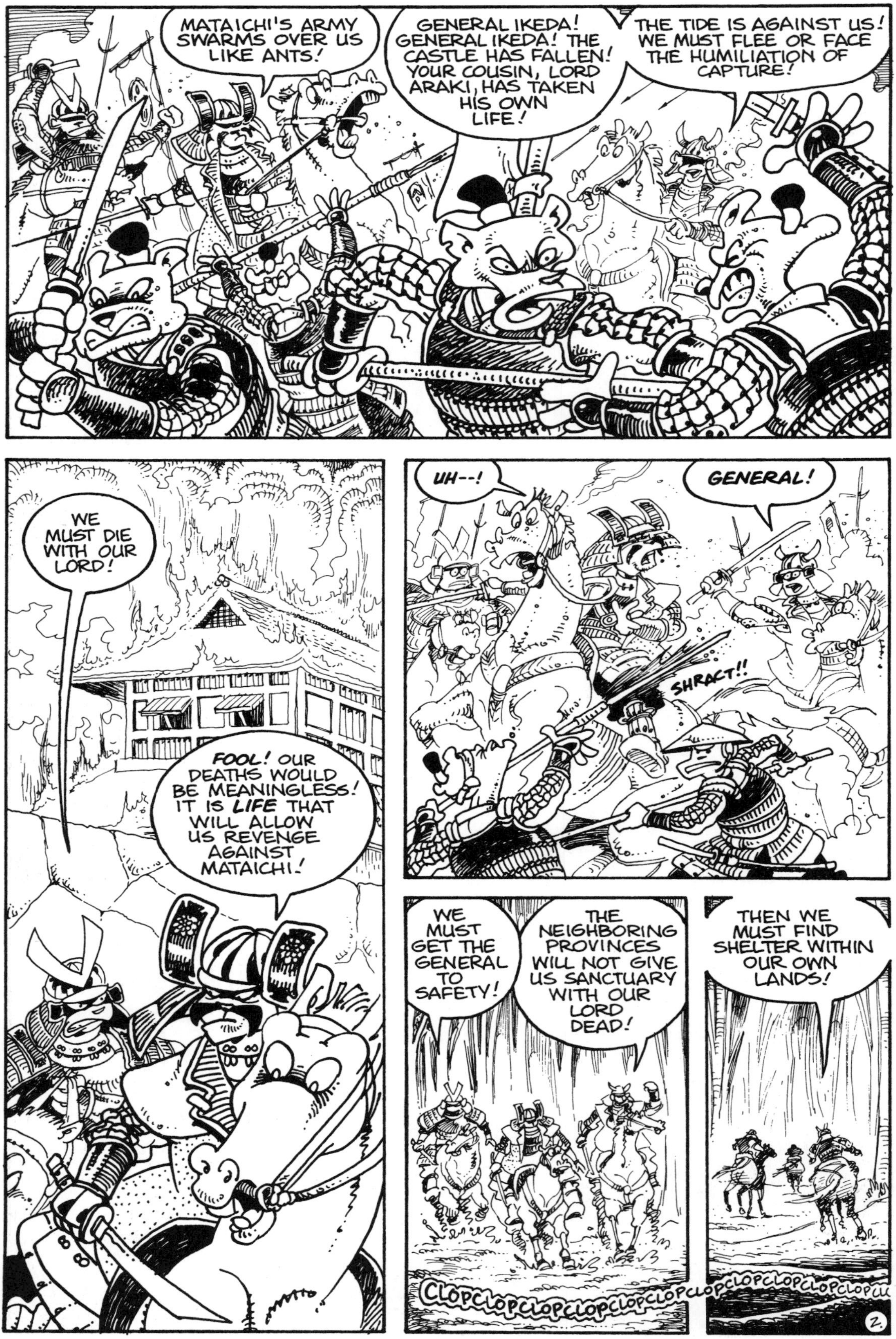
MATAICHI'S ARMY SWARMS OVER US LIKE ANTS!
GENERAL IKEDA! GENERAL IKEDA! THE CASTLE HAS FALLEN! YOUR COUSIN, LORD ARAKI, HAS TAKEN HIS OWN LIFE!
THE TIDE IS AGAINST US! WE MUST FLEE OR FACE THE HUMILIATION OF CAPTURE!
WE MUST DIE WITH OUR LORD!
FOOL! OUR DEATHS WOULD BE MEANINGLESS! IT IS LIFE THAT WILL ALLOW US REVENGE AGAINST MATAICHI!
UH--!
GENERAL!
SHRACT!!
WE MUST GET THE GENERAL TO SAFETY!
THE NEIGHBORING PROVINCES WILL NOT GIVE US SANCTUARY WITH OUR LORD DEAD!
CLOPCLOPCLOPCLOPCLOPCLOPCLOPCLOPCLOPCLOPCLOPCLU
THEN WE MUST FIND SHELTER WITHIN OUR OWN LANDS!
2.

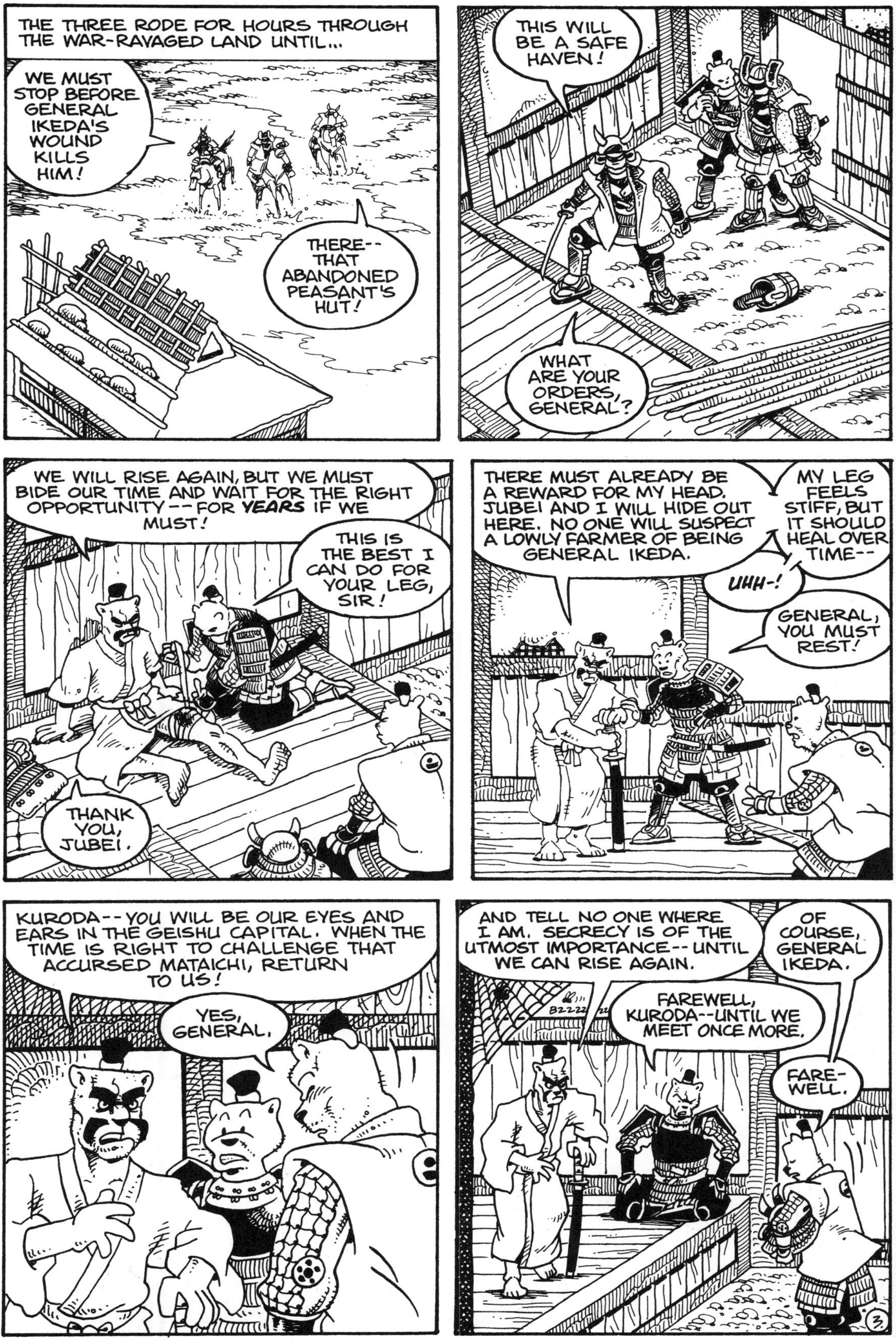
THE THREE RODE FOR HOURS THROUGH THE WAR-RAVAGED LAND UNTIL...
WE MUST STOP BEFORE GENERAL IKEDA'S WOUND KILLS HIM!
THERE--THAT ABANDONED PEASANT'S HUT!
THIS WILL BE A SAFE HAVEN!
WHAT ARE YOUR ORDERS, GENERAL?
WE WILL RISE AGAIN, BUT WE MUST BIDE OUR TIME AND WAIT FOR THE RIGHT OPPORTUNITY--FOR YEARS IF WE MUST!
THIS IS THE BEST I CAN DO FOR YOUR LEG, SIR!
THANK YOU, JUBEI.
THERE MUST ALREADY BE A REWARD FOR MY HEAD. JUBEI AND I WILL HIDE OUT HERE. NO ONE WILL SUSPECT A LOWLY FARMER OF BEING GENERAL IKEDA.
MY LEG FEELS STIFF, BUT IT SHOULD HEAL OVER TIME--
UHH-!
GENERAL, YOU MUST REST!
KURODA--YOU WILL BE OUR EYES AND EARS IN THE GEISHU CAPITAL. WHEN THE TIME IS RIGHT TO CHALLENGE THAT ACCURSED MATAICHI, RETURN TO US!
YES, GENERAL.
AND TELL NO ONE WHERE I AM. SECRECY IS OF THE UTMOST IMPORTANCE--UNTIL WE CAN RISE AGAIN.
OF COURSE, GENERAL IKEDA.
BZZZZ
FAREWELL, KURODA--UNTIL WE MEET ONCE MORE.
FAREWELL.
3

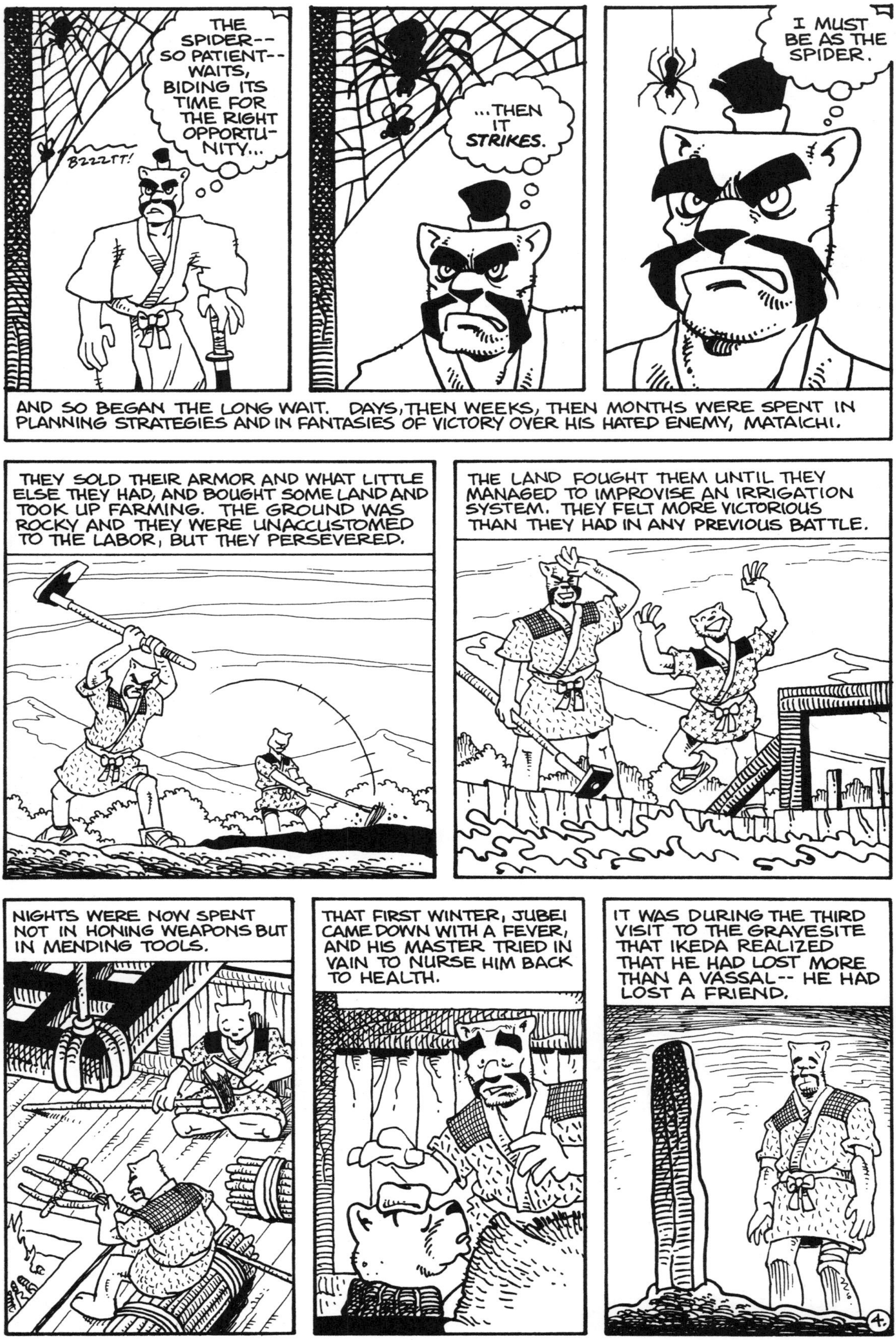
THE SPIDER-- SO PATIENT-- WAITS, BIDING ITS TIME FOR THE RIGHT OPPORTUNITY...
BZZZTT!
...THEN IT STRIKES.
I MUST BE AS THE SPIDER.
AND SO BEGAN THE LONG WAIT. DAYS, THEN WEEKS, THEN MONTHS WERE SPENT IN PLANNING STRATEGIES AND IN FANTASIES OF VICTORY OVER HIS HATED ENEMY, MATAICHI.
THEY SOLD THEIR ARMOR AND WHAT LITTLE ELSE THEY HAD, AND BOUGHT SOME LAND AND TOOK UP FARMING. THE GROUND WAS ROCKY AND THEY WERE UNACCUSTOMED TO THE LABOR, BUT THEY PERSEVERED.
THE LAND FOUGHT THEM UNTIL THEY MANAGED TO IMPROVISE AN IRRIGATION SYSTEM. THEY FELT MORE VICTORIOUS THAN THEY HAD IN ANY PREVIOUS BATTLE.
NIGHTS WERE NOW SPENT NOT IN HONING WEAPONS BUT IN MENDING TOOLS.
THAT FIRST WINTER, JUBEI CAME DOWN WITH A FEVER, AND HIS MASTER TRIED IN VAIN TO NURSE HIM BACK TO HEALTH.
IT WAS DURING THE THIRD VISIT TO THE GRAVESITE THAT IKEDA REALIZED THAT HE HAD LOST MORE THAN A VASSAL-- HE HAD LOST A FRIEND.
4.

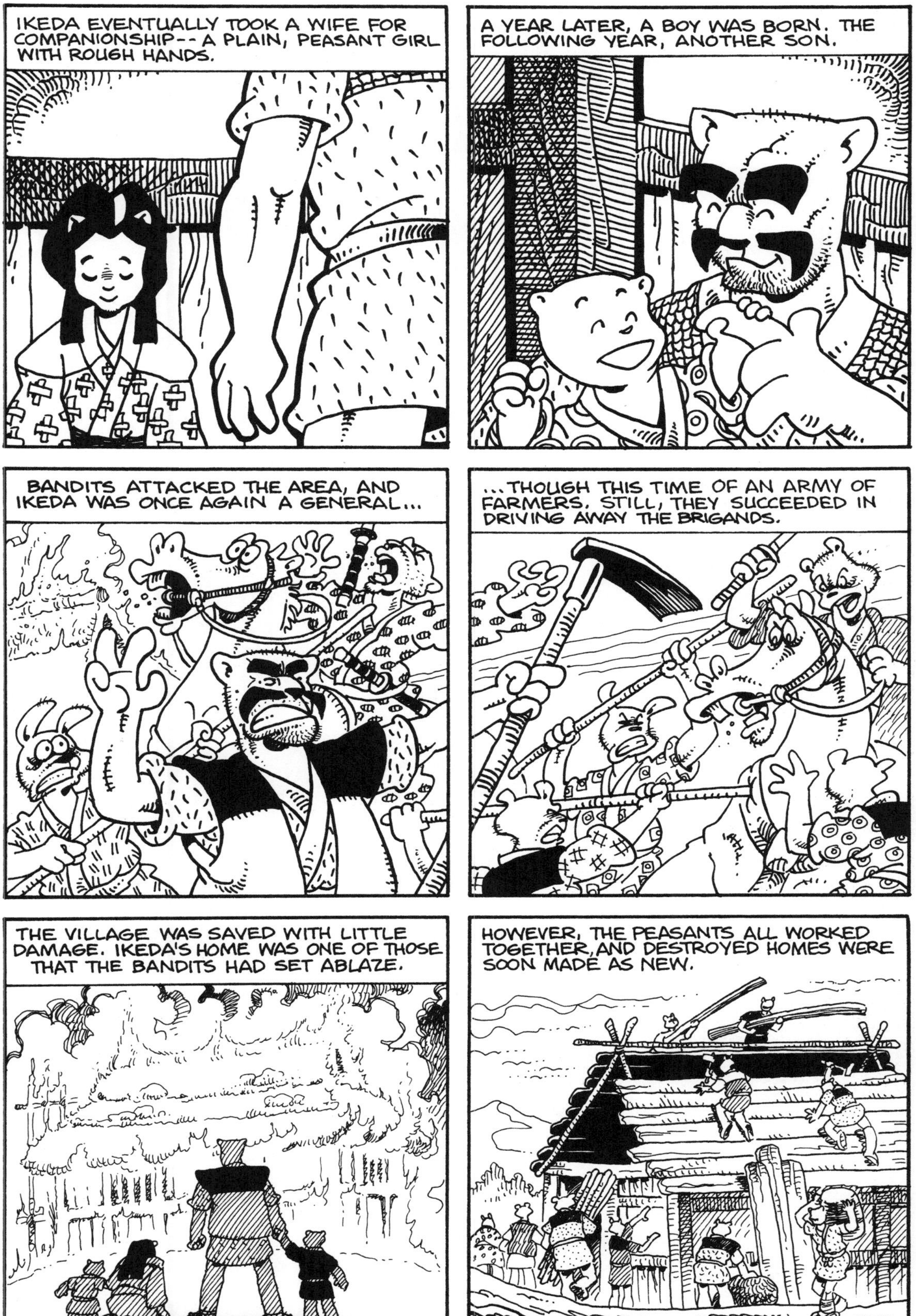
IKEDA EVENTUALLY TOOK A WIFE FOR COMPANIONSHIP-- A PLAIN, PEASANT GIRL WITH ROUGH HANDS.
A YEAR LATER, A BOY WAS BORN. THE FOLLOWING YEAR, ANOTHER SON.
BANDITS ATTACKED THE AREA, AND IKEDA WAS ONCE AGAIN A GENERAL...
...THOUGH THIS TIME OF AN ARMY OF FARMERS. STILL, THEY SUCCEEDED IN DRIVING AWAY THE BRIGANDS.
THE VILLAGE WAS SAVED WITH LITTLE DAMAGE. IKEDA'S HOME WAS ONE OF THOSE THAT THE BANDITS HAD SET ABLAZE.
HOWEVER, THE PEASANTS ALL WORKED TOGETHER, AND DESTROYED HOMES WERE SOON MADE AS NEW.
7

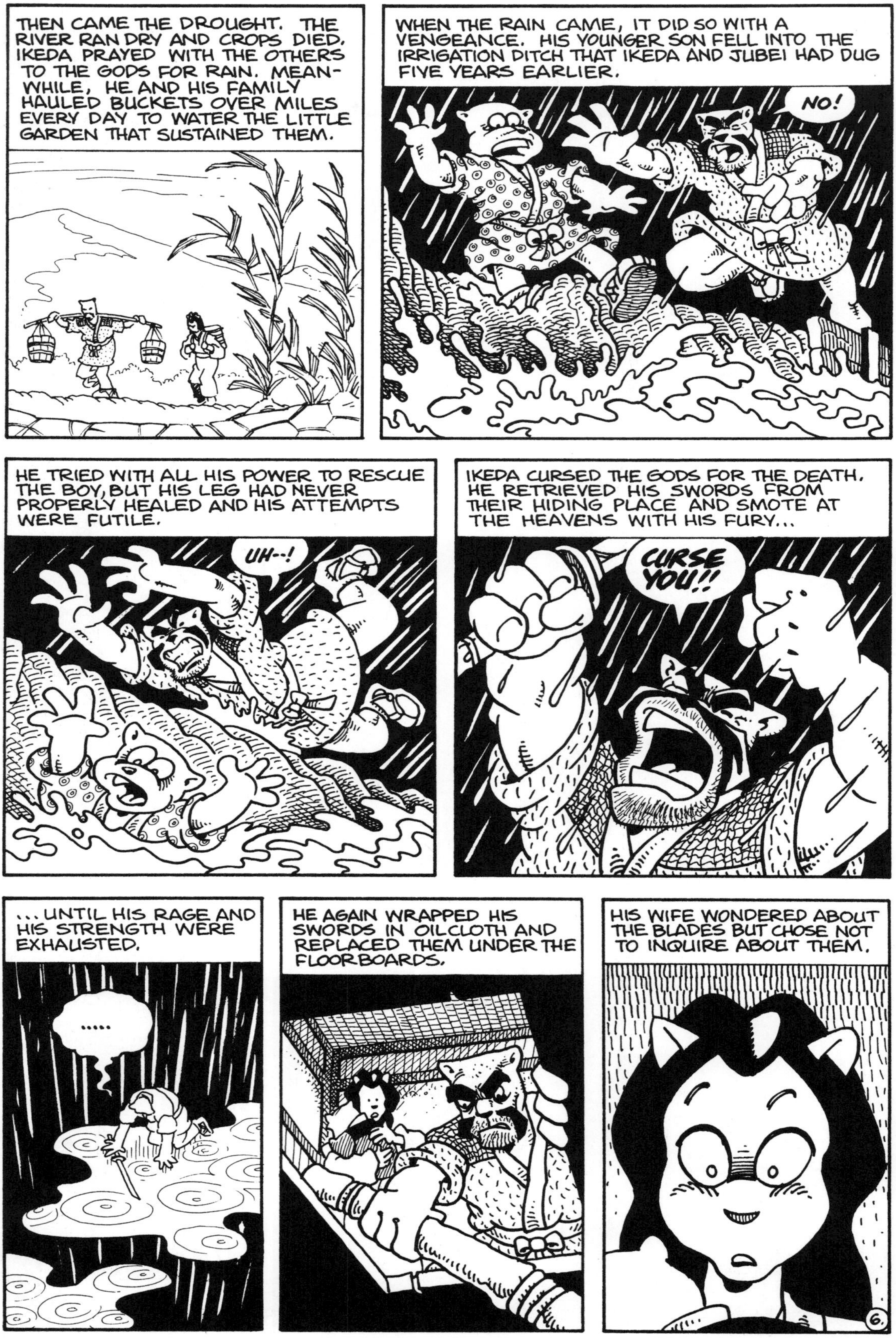
THEN CAME THE DROUGHT. THE RIVER RAN DRY AND CROPS DIED. IKEDA PRAYED WITH THE OTHERS TO THE GODS FOR RAIN. MEANWHILE, HE AND HIS FAMILY HAULED BUCKETS OVER MILES EVERY DAY TO WATER THE LITTLE GARDEN THAT SUSTAINED THEM.
WHEN THE RAIN CAME, IT DID SO WITH A VENGEANCE. HIS YOUNGER SON FELL INTO THE IRRIGATION DITCH THAT IKEDA AND JUBEI HAD DUG FIVE YEARS EARLIER.
NO!
HE TRIED WITH ALL HIS POWER TO RESCUE THE BOY, BUT HIS LEG HAD NEVER PROPERLY HEALED AND HIS ATTEMPTS WERE FUTILE.
UH--!
IKEDA CURSED THE GODS FOR THE DEATH. HE RETRIEVED HIS SWORDS FROM THEIR HIDING PLACE AND SMOTE AT THE HEAVENS WITH HIS FURY...
CURSE YOU!!
...UNTIL HIS RAGE AND HIS STRENGTH WERE EXHAUSTED.
......
HE AGAIN WRAPPED HIS SWORDS IN OILCLOTH AND REPLACED THEM UNDER THE FLOORBOARDS.
HIS WIFE WONDERED ABOUT THE BLADES BUT CHOSE NOT TO INQUIRE ABOUT THEM.
6.

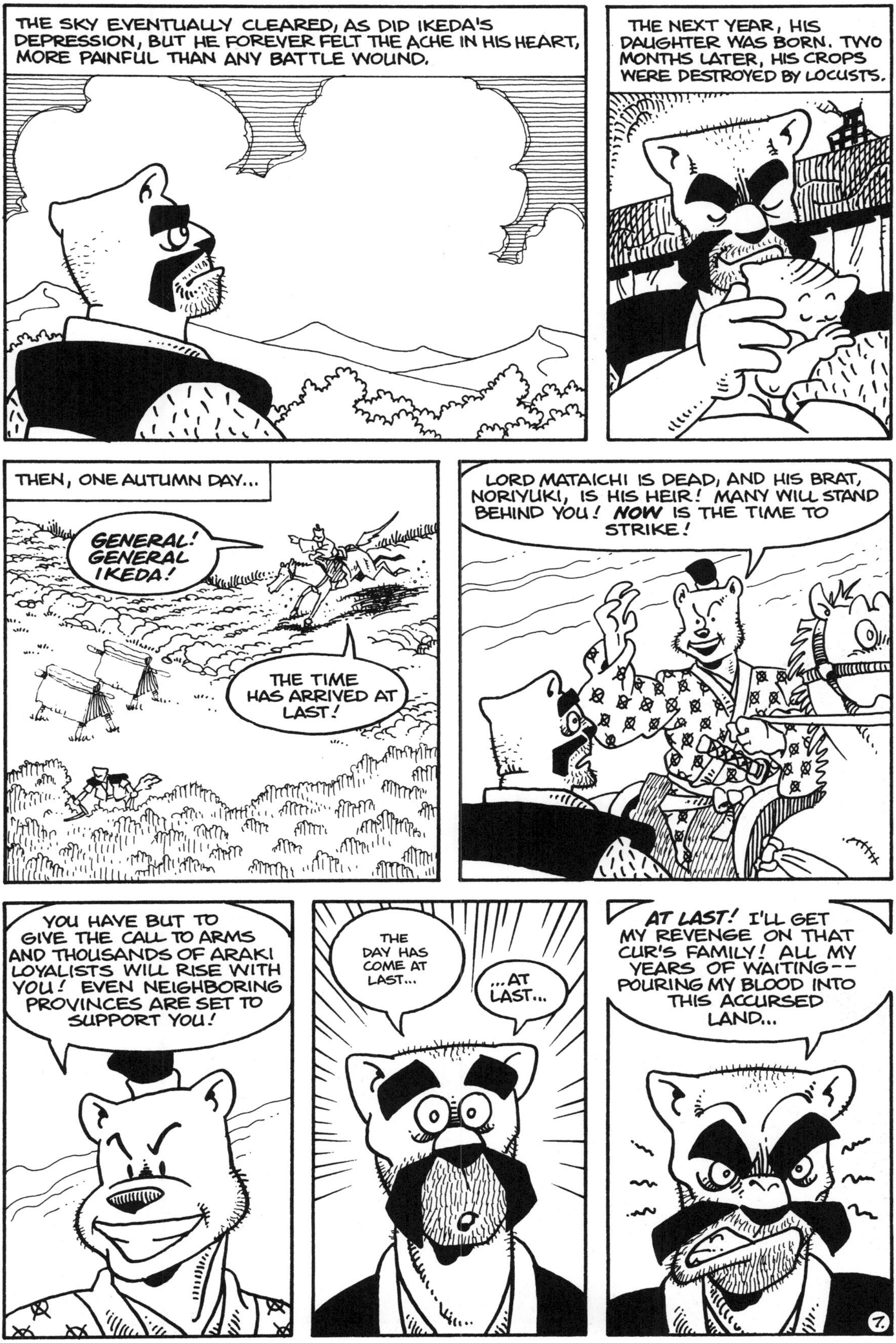
THE SKY EVENTUALLY CLEARED, AS DID IKEDA'S DEPRESSION, BUT HE FOREVER FELT THE ACHE IN HIS HEART, MORE PAINFUL THAN ANY BATTLE WOUND.
THE NEXT YEAR, HIS DAUGHTER WAS BORN. TWO MONTHS LATER, HIS CROPS WERE DESTROYED BY LOCUSTS.
THEN, ONE AUTUMN DAY...
GENERAL! GENERAL IKEDA!
THE TIME HAS ARRIVED AT LAST!
LORD MATAICHI IS DEAD, AND HIS BRAT, NORIYUKI, IS HIS HEIR! MANY WILL STAND BEHIND YOU! NOW IS THE TIME TO STRIKE!
YOU HAVE BUT TO GIVE THE CALL TO ARMS AND THOUSANDS OF ARAKI LOYALISTS WILL RISE WITH YOU! EVEN NEIGHBORING PROVINCES ARE SET TO SUPPORT YOU!
THE DAY HAS COME AT LAST...
...AT LAST...
AT LAST! I'LL GET MY REVENGE ON THAT CUR'S FAMILY! ALL MY YEARS OF WAITING-- POURING MY BLOOD INTO THIS ACCURSED LAND...
7.

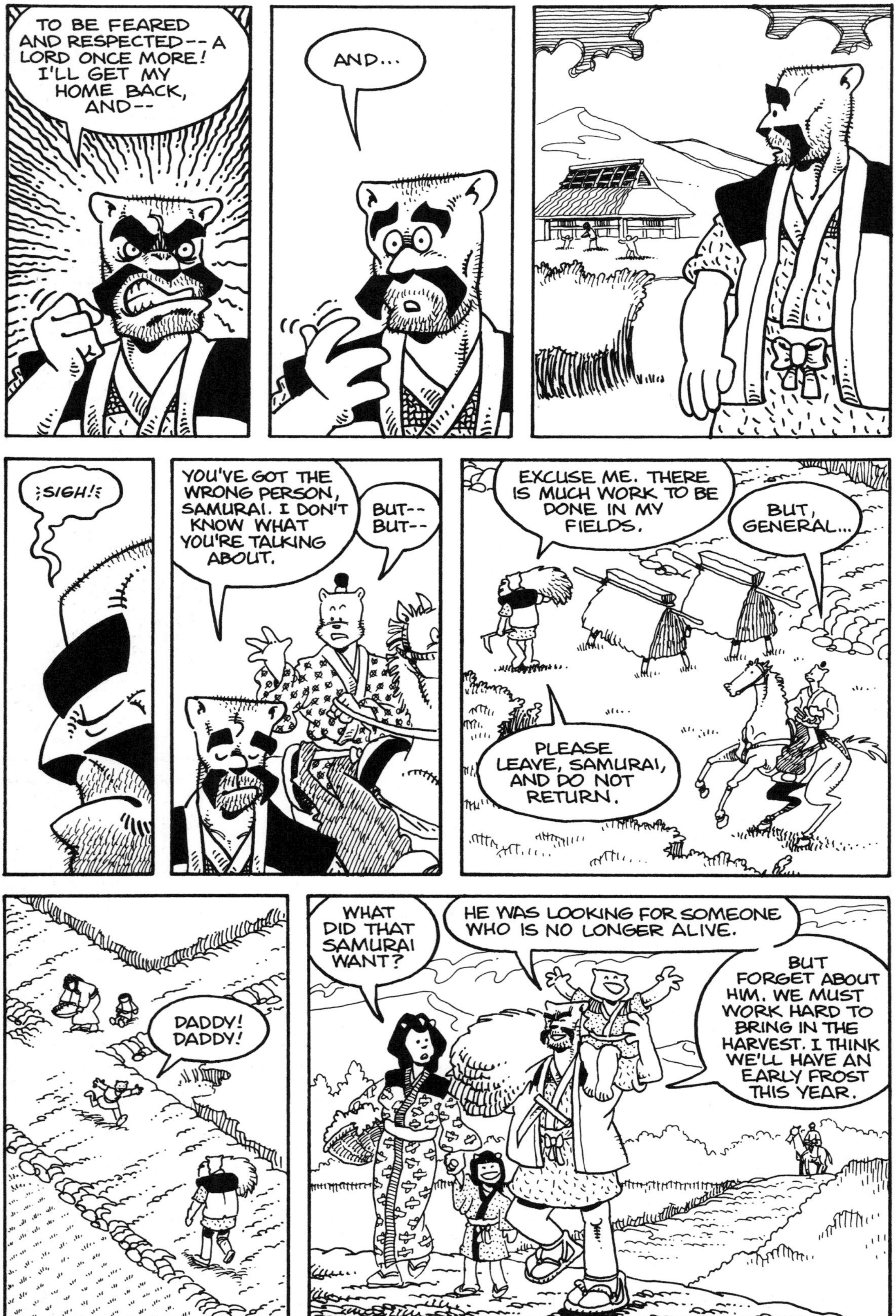
TO BE FEARED AND RESPECTED-- A LORD ONCE MORE! I'LL GET MY HOME BACK, AND--
AND...
SIGH!
YOU'VE GOT THE WRONG PERSON, SAMURAI. I DON'T KNOW WHAT YOU'RE TALKING ABOUT.
BUT-- BUT--
EXCUSE ME. THERE IS MUCH WORK TO BE DONE IN MY FIELDS.
BUT, GENERAL...
PLEASE LEAVE, SAMURAI, AND DO NOT RETURN.
DADDY! DADDY!
WHAT DID THAT SAMURAI WANT?
HE WAS LOOKING FOR SOMEONE WHO IS NO LONGER ALIVE.
BUT FORGET ABOUT HIM. WE MUST WORK HARD TO BRING IN THE HARVEST. I THINK WE'LL HAVE AN EARLY FROST THIS YEAR.
END

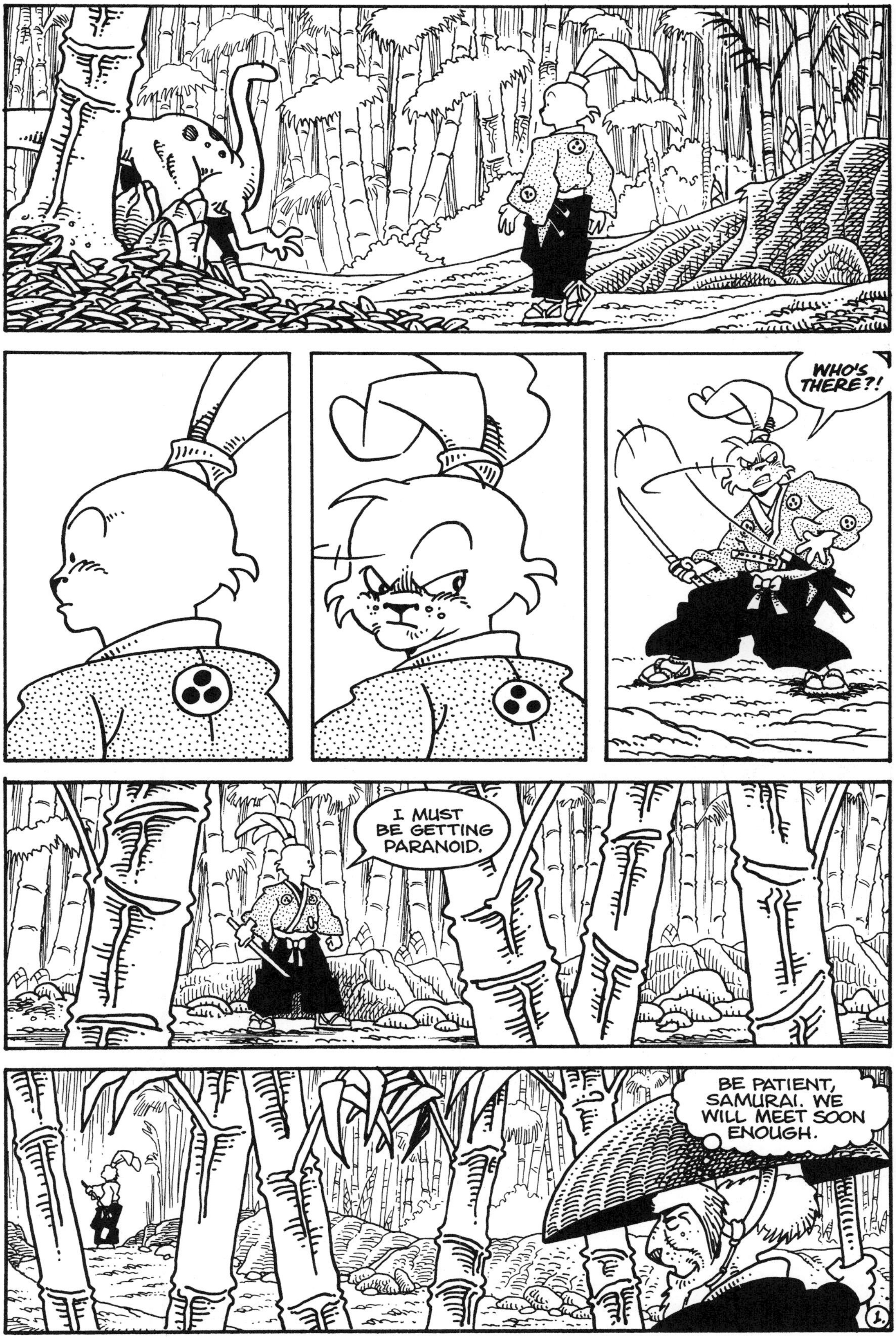
WHO'S THERE?!
I MUST BE GETTING PARANOID.
BE PATIENT, SAMURAI. WE WILL MEET SOON ENOUGH.
1.

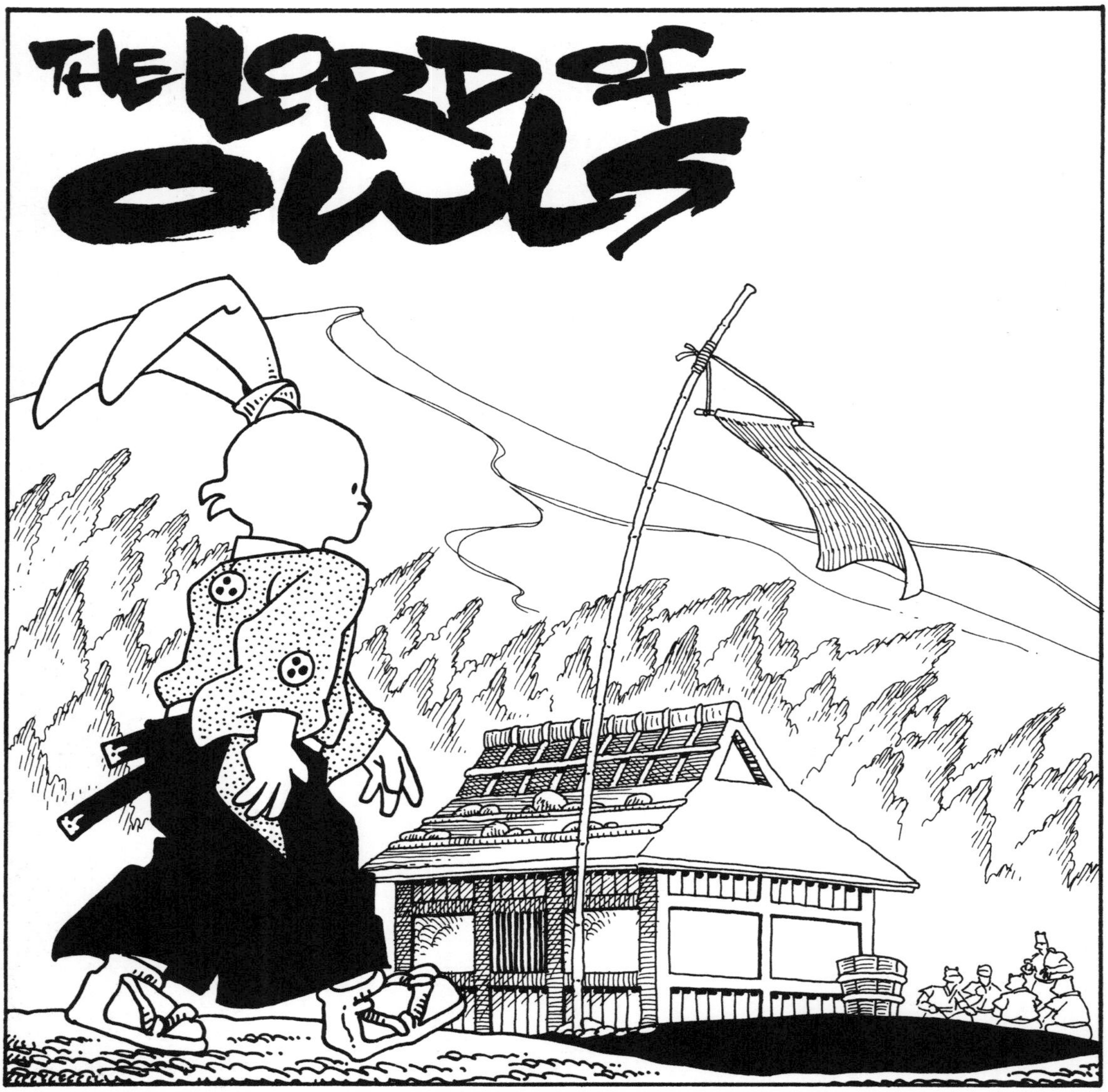
THE LORD OF OWLS

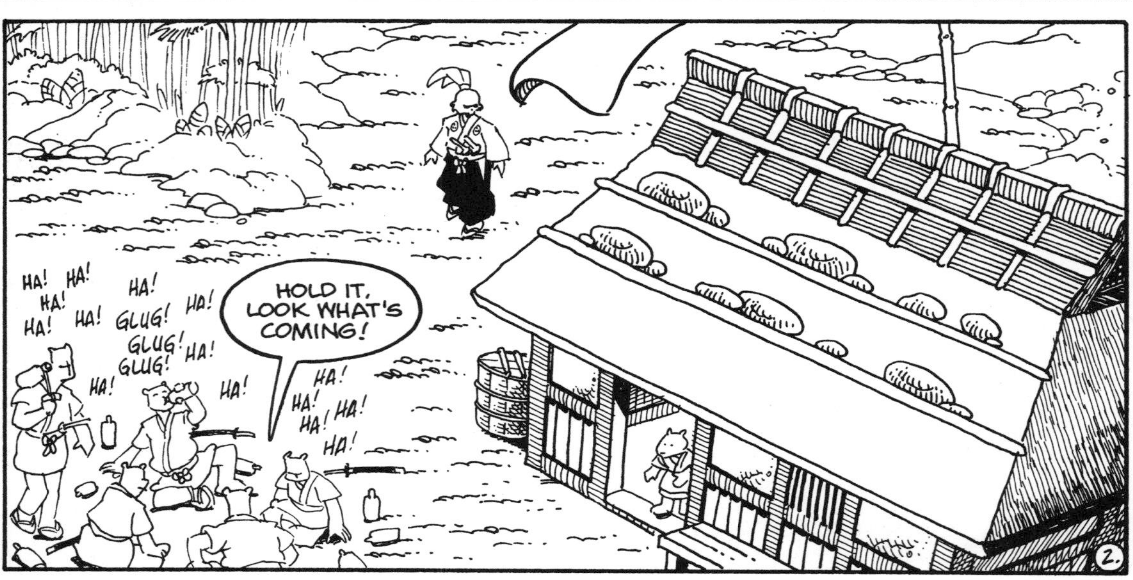
HA! HA!
HA!
HA! HA! GLUG! HA!
HA!
GLUG! HA!
GLUG!
HA! HA!
HOLD IT, LOOK WHAT'S COMING!
HA!
HA!
HA! HA!
HA!
2.

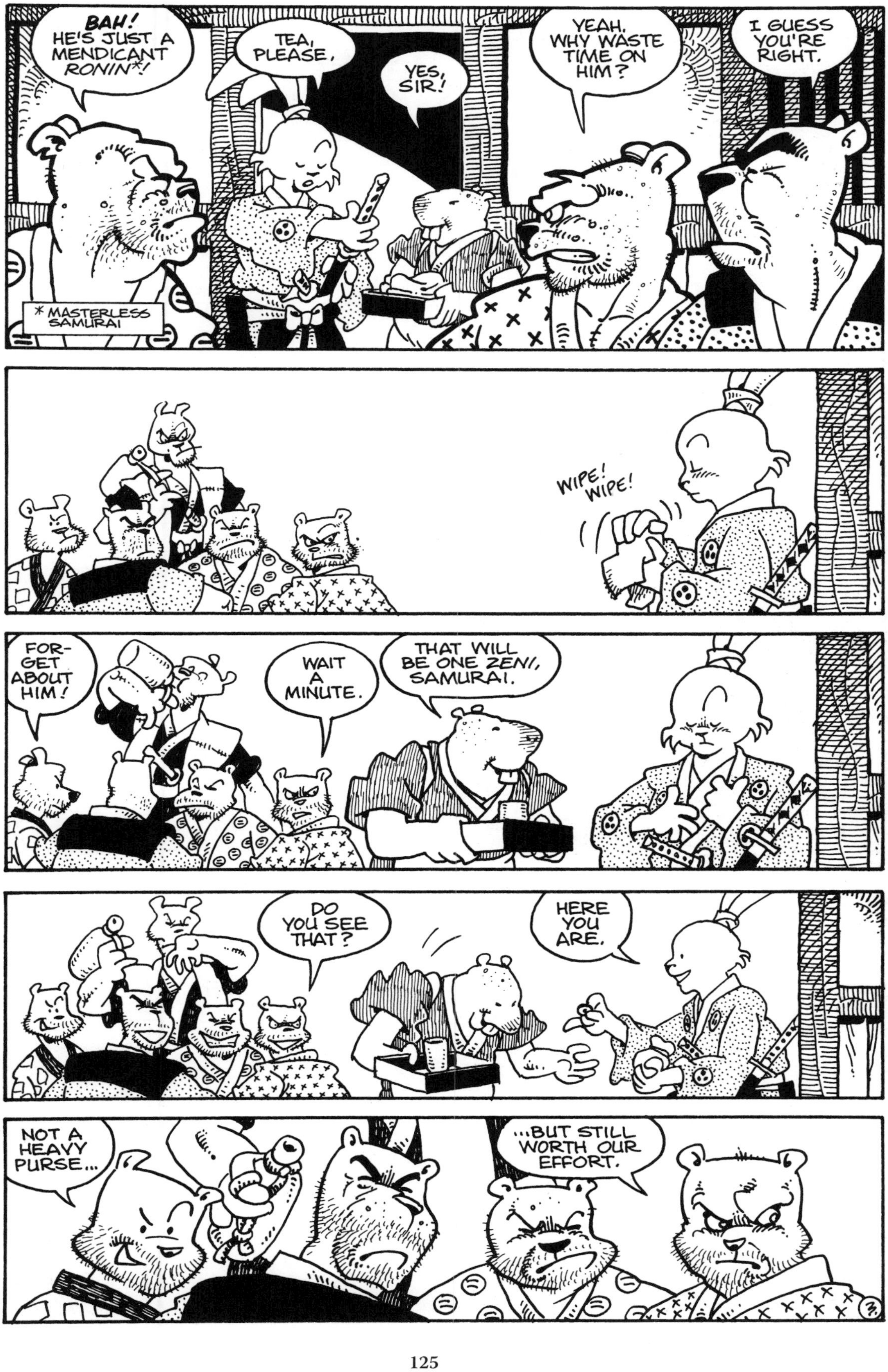
BAH! HE'S JUST A MENDICANT RONIN*!
*MASTERLESS SAMURAI
TEA, PLEASE.
YES, SIR!
YEAH. WHY WASTE TIME ON HIM?
I GUESS YOU'RE RIGHT.
WIPE! WIPE!
FOR-GET ABOUT HIM!
WAIT A MINUTE.
THAT WILL BE ONE ZENI, SAMURAI.
DO YOU SEE THAT?
HERE YOU ARE.
NOT A HEAVY PURSE...
...BUT STILL WORTH OUR EFFORT.

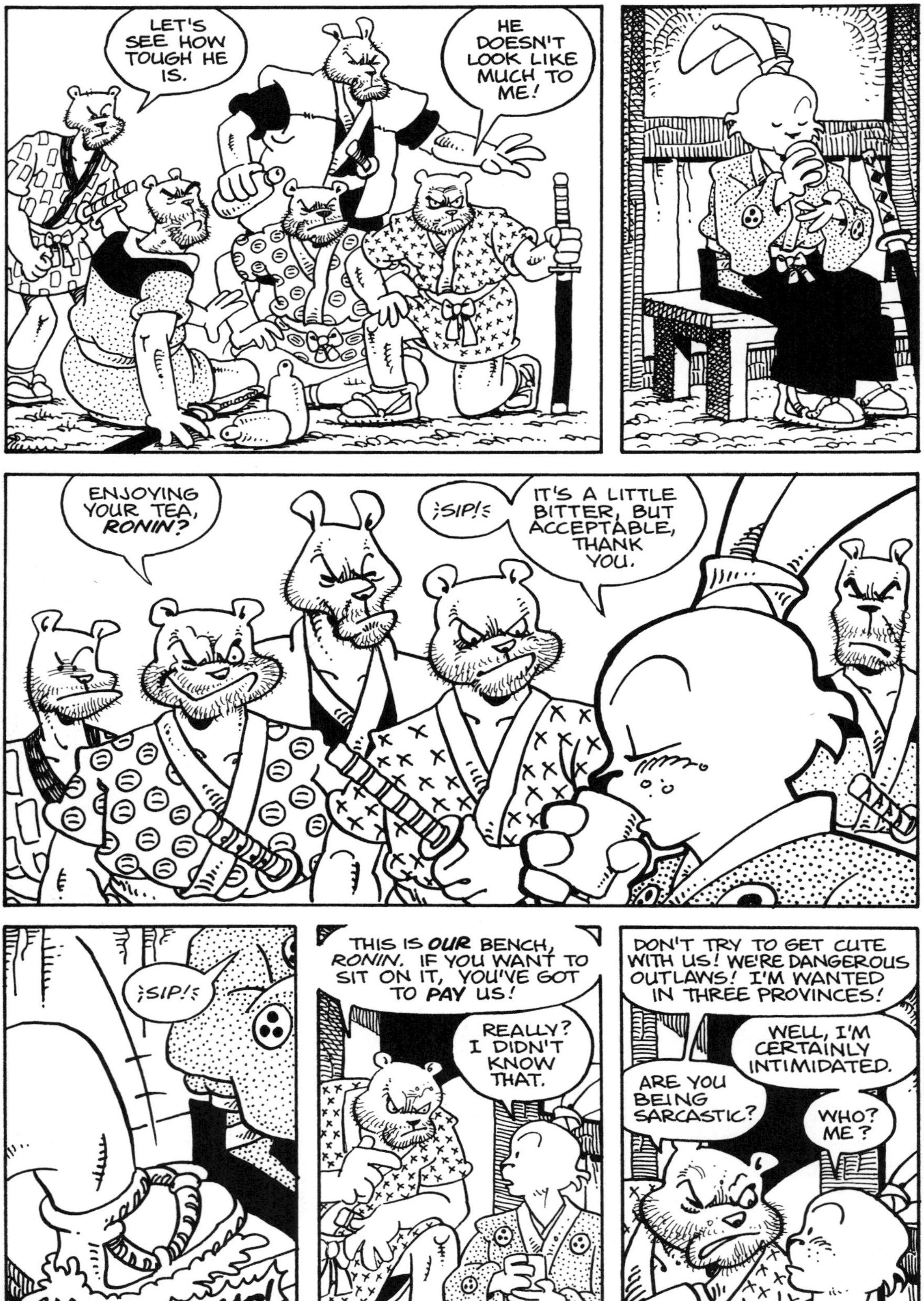
LET'S SEE HOW TOUGH HE IS.
HE DOESN'T LOOK LIKE MUCH TO ME!
ENJOYING YOUR TEA, *RONIN?*
¡SIP!
IT'S A LITTLE BITTER, BUT ACCEPTABLE, THANK YOU.
¡SIP!
STOMP!
THIS IS *OUR* BENCH, *RONIN*. IF YOU WANT TO SIT ON IT, YOU'VE GOT TO *PAY* US!
REALLY? I DIDN'T KNOW THAT.
DON'T TRY TO GET CUTE WITH US! WE'RE DANGEROUS OUTLAWS! I'M WANTED IN THREE PROVINCES!
WELL, I'M CERTAINLY INTIMIDATED.
ARE YOU BEING SARCASTIC?
WHO? ME?
4

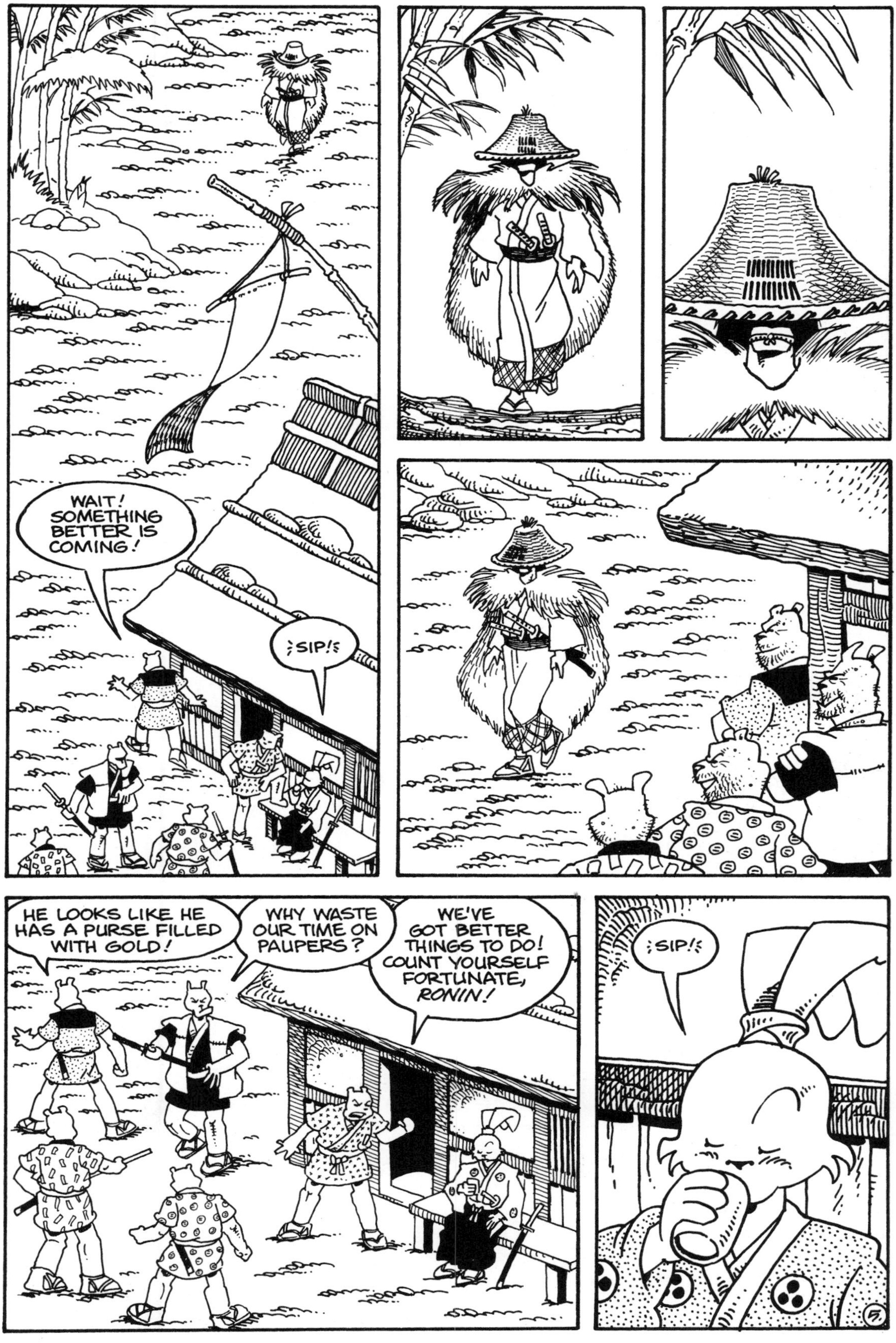

WAIT! SOMETHING BETTER IS COMING!
SIP!
HE LOOKS LIKE HE HAS A PURSE FILLED WITH GOLD!
WHY WASTE OUR TIME ON PAUPERS?
WE'VE GOT BETTER THINGS TO DO! COUNT YOURSELF FORTUNATE, *RONIN*!
SIP!

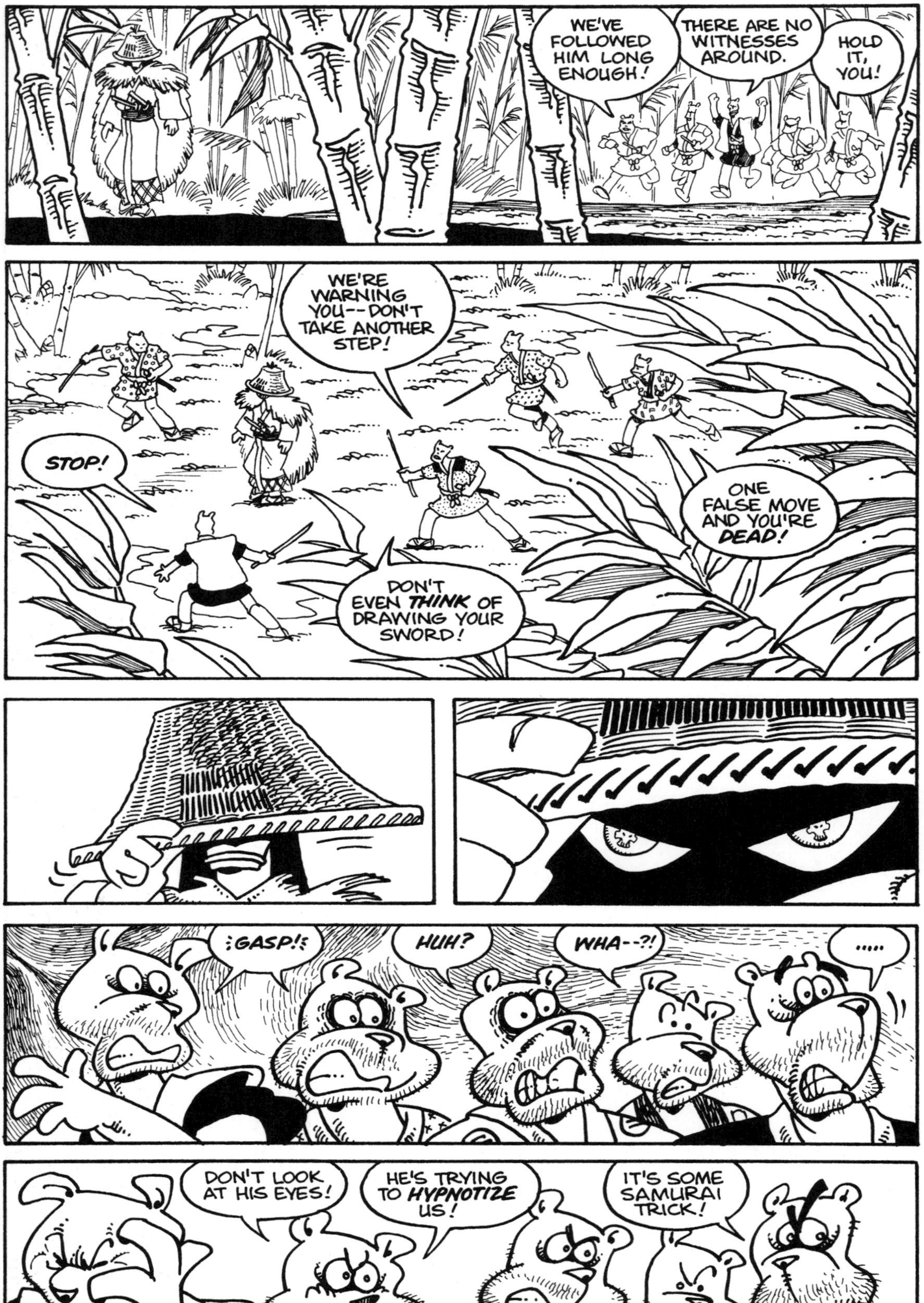
WE'VE FOLLOWED HIM LONG ENOUGH!
THERE ARE NO WITNESSES AROUND.
HOLD IT, YOU!
WE'RE WARNING YOU--DON'T TAKE ANOTHER STEP!
STOP!
ONE FALSE MOVE AND YOU'RE DEAD!
DON'T EVEN THINK OF DRAWING YOUR SWORD!
GASP!
HUH?
WHA--?!
.....
DON'T LOOK AT HIS EYES!
HE'S TRYING TO HYPNOTIZE US!
IT'S SOME SAMURAI TRICK!
6.

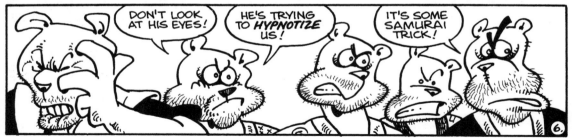

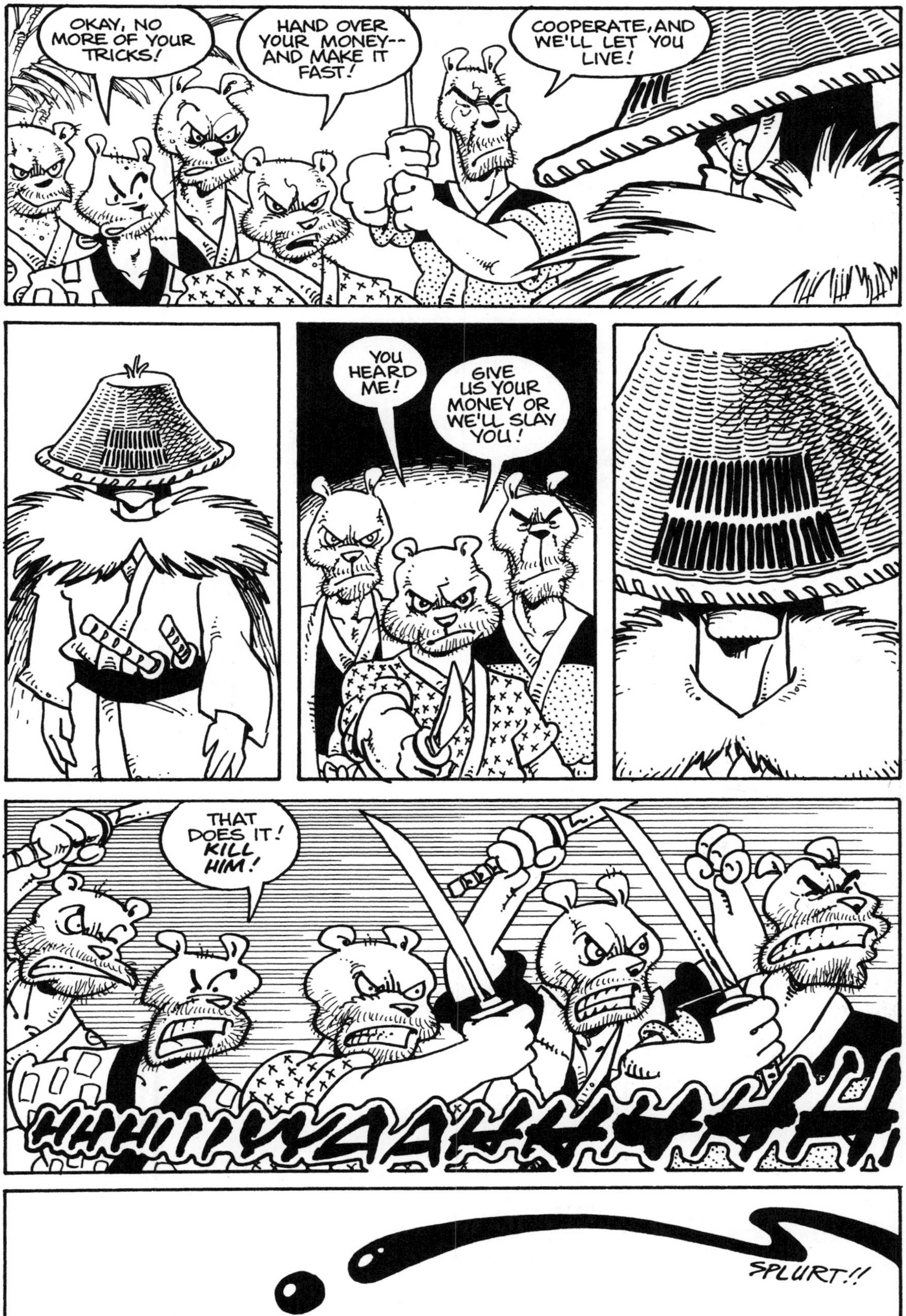
OKAY, NO MORE OF YOUR TRICKS!
HAND OVER YOUR MONEY-- AND MAKE IT FAST!
COOPERATE, AND WE'LL LET YOU LIVE!
YOU HEARD ME!
GIVE US YOUR MONEY OR WE'LL SLAY YOU!
THAT DOES IT! KILL HIM!
HHHIIIYAAAHHHHHH
SPLURT!!
7.

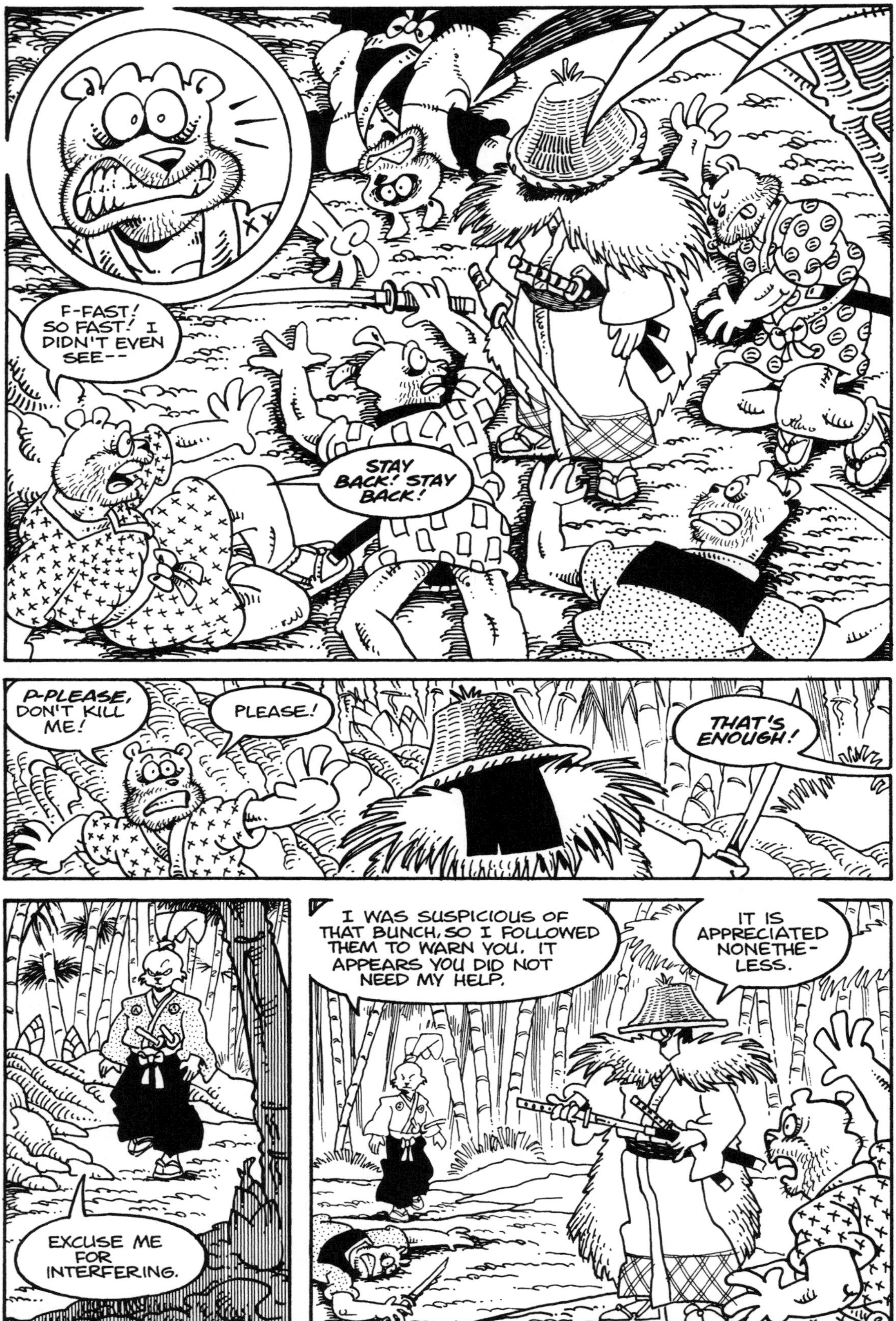
F-FAST! SO FAST! I DIDN'T EVEN SEE--
STAY BACK! STAY BACK!
P-PLEASE, DON'T KILL ME!
PLEASE!
THAT'S ENOUGH!
EXCUSE ME FOR INTERFERING.
I WAS SUSPICIOUS OF THAT BUNCH, SO I FOLLOWED THEM TO WARN YOU. IT APPEARS YOU DID NOT NEED MY HELP.
IT IS APPRECIATED NONETHE-LESS.
8

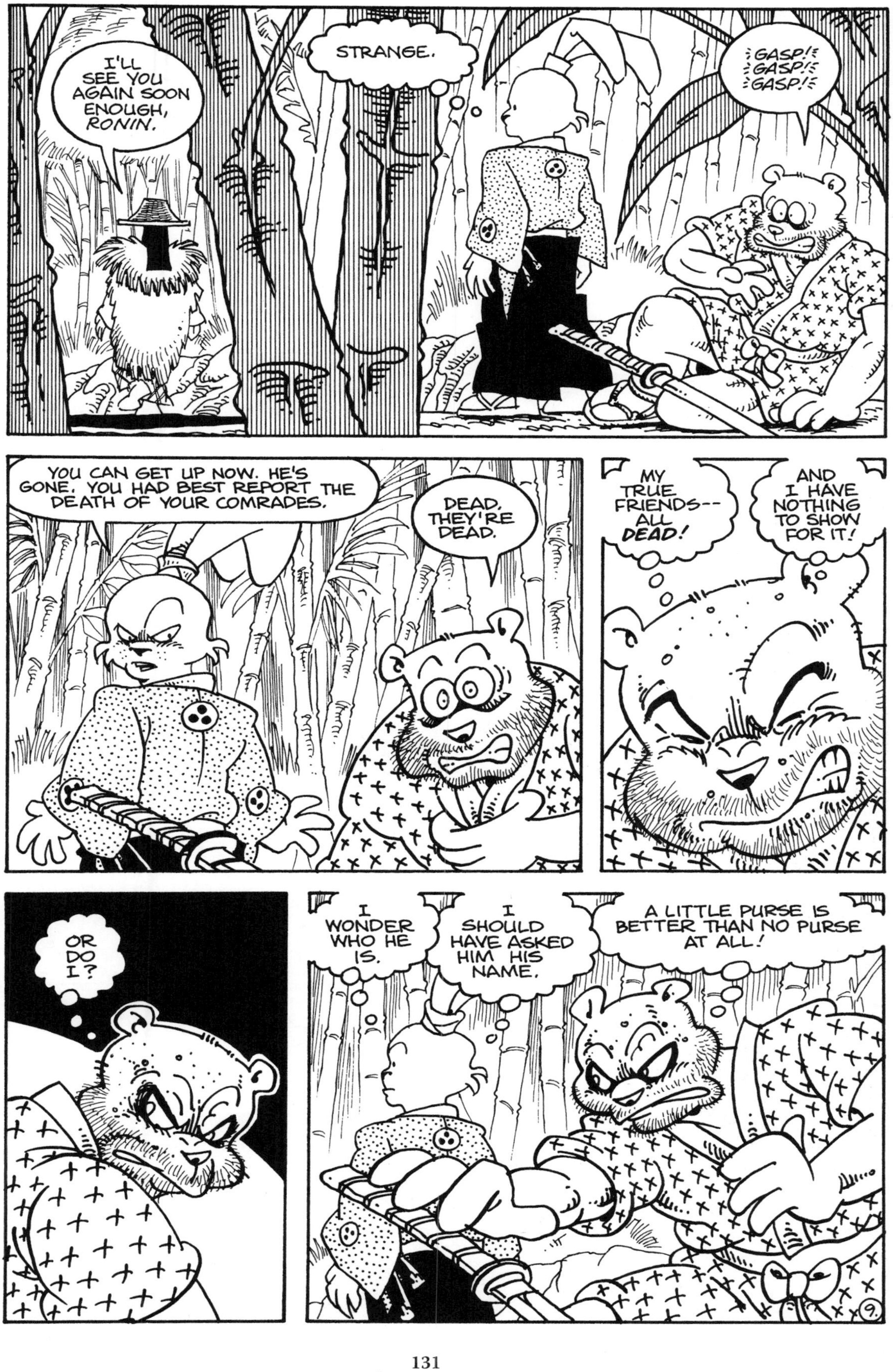
I'LL SEE YOU AGAIN SOON ENOUGH, RONIN.
STRANGE.
GASP! GASP! GASP!
YOU CAN GET UP NOW. HE'S GONE. YOU HAD BEST REPORT THE DEATH OF YOUR COMRADES.
DEAD. THEY'RE DEAD.
MY TRUE FRIENDS-- ALL DEAD!
AND I HAVE NOTHING TO SHOW FOR IT!
OR DO I?
I WONDER WHO HE IS.
I SHOULD HAVE ASKED HIM HIS NAME.
A LITTLE PURSE IS BETTER THAN NO PURSE AT ALL!
9.

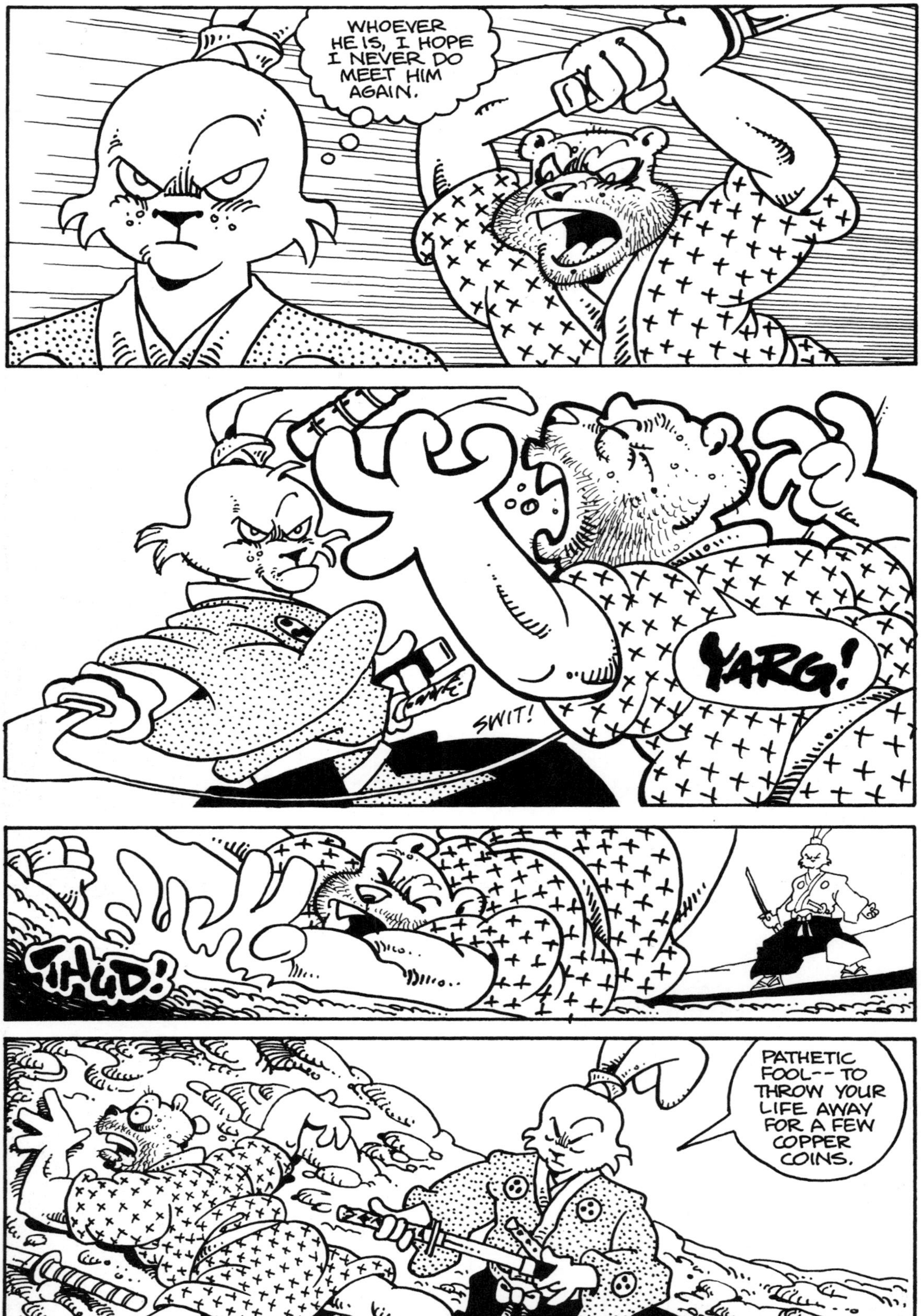
WHOEVER HE IS, I HOPE I NEVER DO MEET HIM AGAIN.
YARG!
SWIT!
THUD!
PATHETIC FOOL-- TO THROW YOUR LIFE AWAY FOR A FEW COPPER COINS.
10

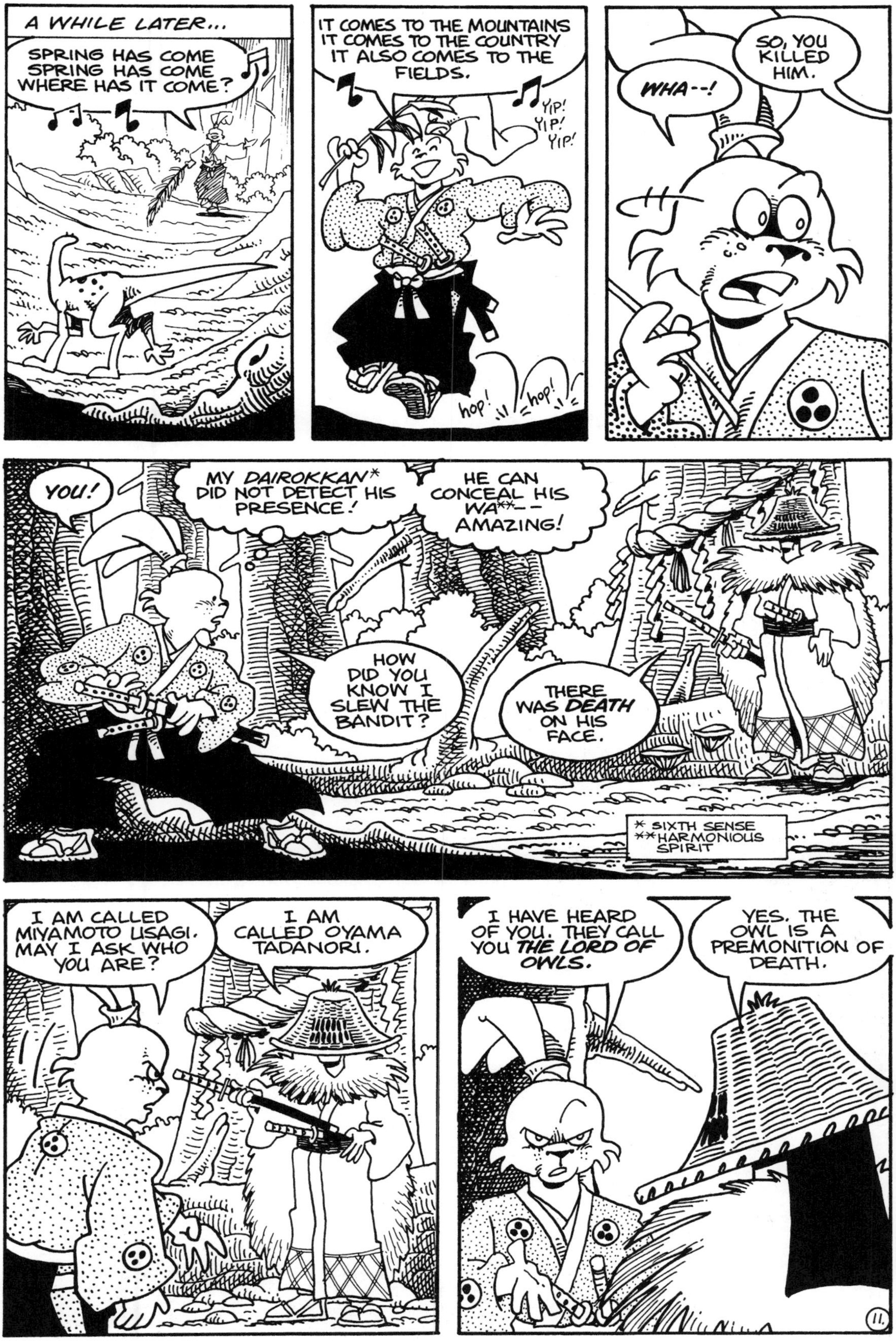
A WHILE LATER...
SPRING HAS COME SPRING HAS COME WHERE HAS IT COME?
IT COMES TO THE MOUNTAINS IT COMES TO THE COUNTRY IT ALSO COMES TO THE FIELDS.
YIP! YIP! YIP!
hop! hop!
WHA--!
SO, YOU KILLED HIM.
YOU!
MY DAIROKKAN* DID NOT DETECT HIS PRESENCE!
HE CAN CONCEAL HIS WA**--AMAZING!
HOW DID YOU KNOW I SLEW THE BANDIT?
THERE WAS DEATH ON HIS FACE.
* SIXTH SENSE
** HARMONIOUS SPIRIT
I AM CALLED MIYAMOTO USAGI. MAY I ASK WHO YOU ARE?
I AM CALLED OYAMA TADANORI.
I HAVE HEARD OF YOU. THEY CALL YOU THE LORD OF OWLS.
YES. THE OWL IS A PREMONITION OF DEATH.
11.

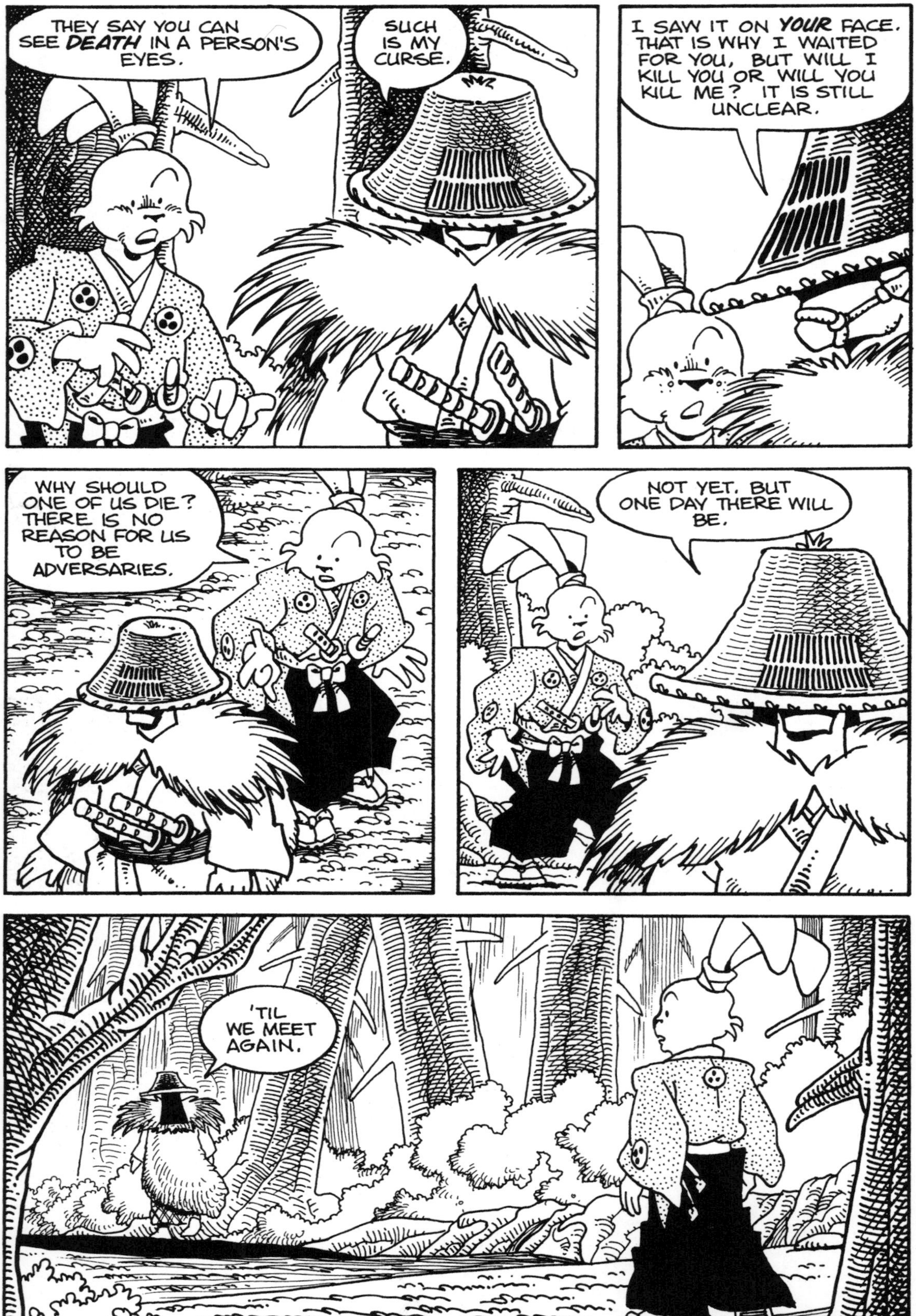
THEY SAY YOU CAN SEE DEATH IN A PERSON'S EYES.
SUCH IS MY CURSE.
I SAW IT ON YOUR FACE. THAT IS WHY I WAITED FOR YOU, BUT WILL I KILL YOU OR WILL YOU KILL ME? IT IS STILL UNCLEAR.
WHY SHOULD ONE OF US DIE? THERE IS NO REASON FOR US TO BE ADVERSARIES.
NOT YET. BUT ONE DAY THERE WILL BE.
'TIL WE MEET AGAIN.
END

THE FIRST TENET

JORENJI TEMPLE, OUTSIDE THE CITY OF EDO.

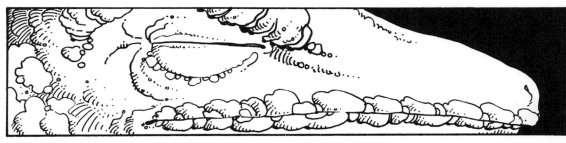

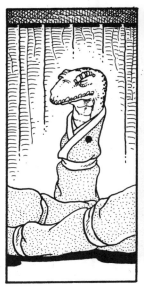

HE'S IN MEDITATION. WHAT A SIMPLE MATTER IT WOULD BE TO SLAY HIM!

THE FOOL!

I KNOW YOU'RE THERE, KAGEMARU. DON'T EVEN THINK OF TREACHERY! NOW, WHAT IS SO IMPORTANT THAT YOU HAD TO REQUEST THIS CLANDESTINE MEETING?

I'M SURE THIS MISSIVE WILL INTEREST YOU, LORD HEBI.

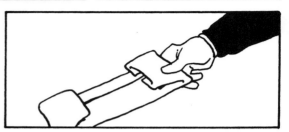

THIS IS THE CONSPIRACY AGREEMENT AGAINST THE *SHOGUN** THAT WAS STOLEN FROM OUR LORD HIKIJI'S COURIER!

*MILITARY DICTATOR

KAGEMARU-- YOU THIEF AND TRAITOR!

NO! IT WAS CHIZU! SHE IS BEHIND THE THEFT!

¡GASP!¡ CHOKE!

CHIZU?! THE LEADER OF THE NEKO NINJA?!

YES! YES!

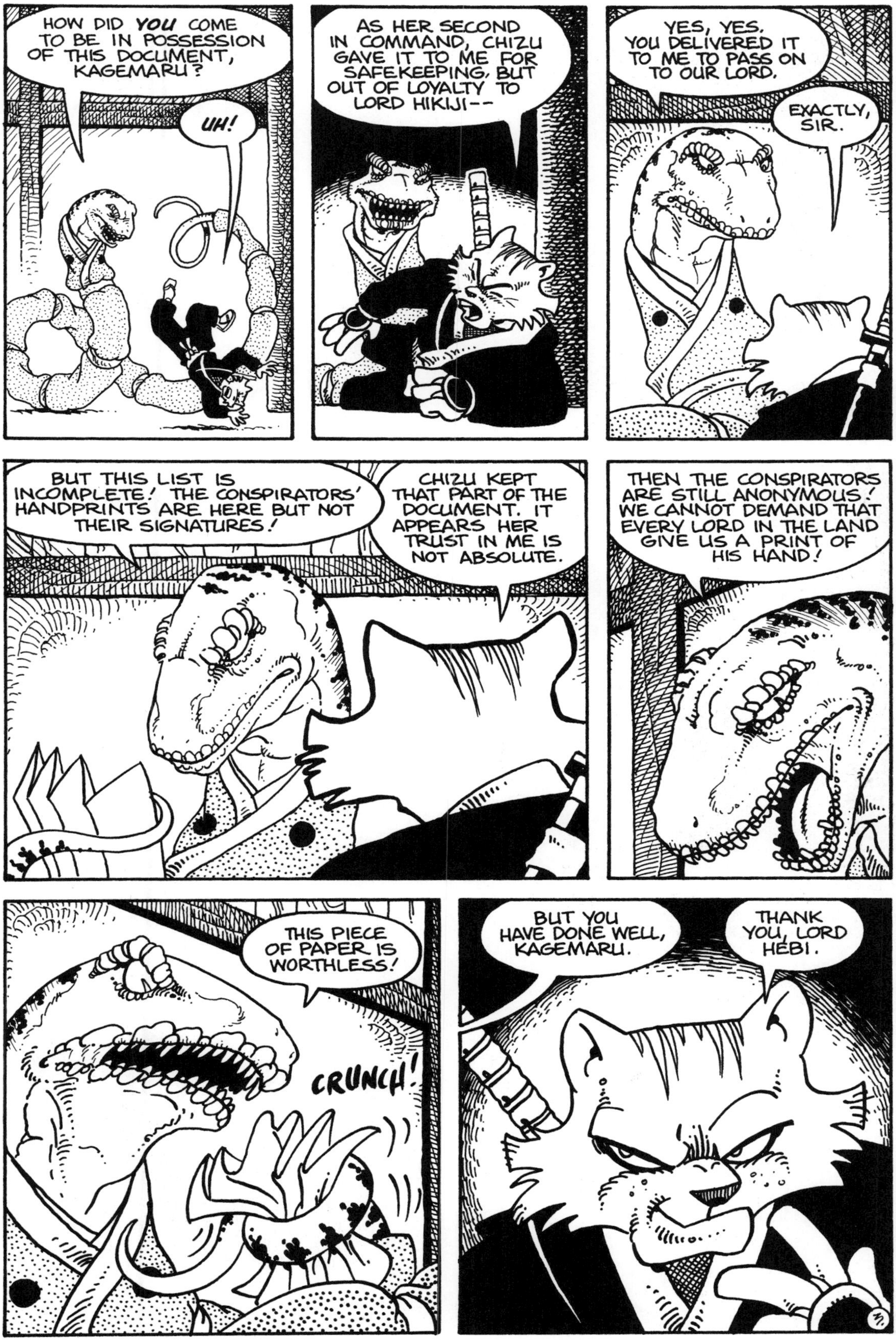
HOW DID *YOU* COME TO BE IN POSSESSION OF THIS DOCUMENT, KAGEMARU?
UH!
AS HER SECOND IN COMMAND, CHIZU GAVE IT TO ME FOR SAFEKEEPING, BUT OUT OF LOYALTY TO LORD HIKIJI--
YES, YES. YOU DELIVERED IT TO ME TO PASS ON TO OUR LORD.
EXACTLY, SIR.
BUT THIS LIST IS INCOMPLETE! THE CONSPIRATORS' HANDPRINTS ARE HERE BUT NOT THEIR SIGNATURES!
CHIZU KEPT THAT PART OF THE DOCUMENT. IT APPEARS HER TRUST IN ME IS NOT ABSOLUTE.
THEN THE CONSPIRATORS ARE STILL ANONYMOUS! WE CANNOT DEMAND THAT EVERY LORD IN THE LAND GIVE US A PRINT OF HIS HAND!
THIS PIECE OF PAPER IS WORTHLESS!
CRUNCH!
BUT YOU HAVE DONE WELL, KAGEMARU.
THANK YOU, LORD HEBI.

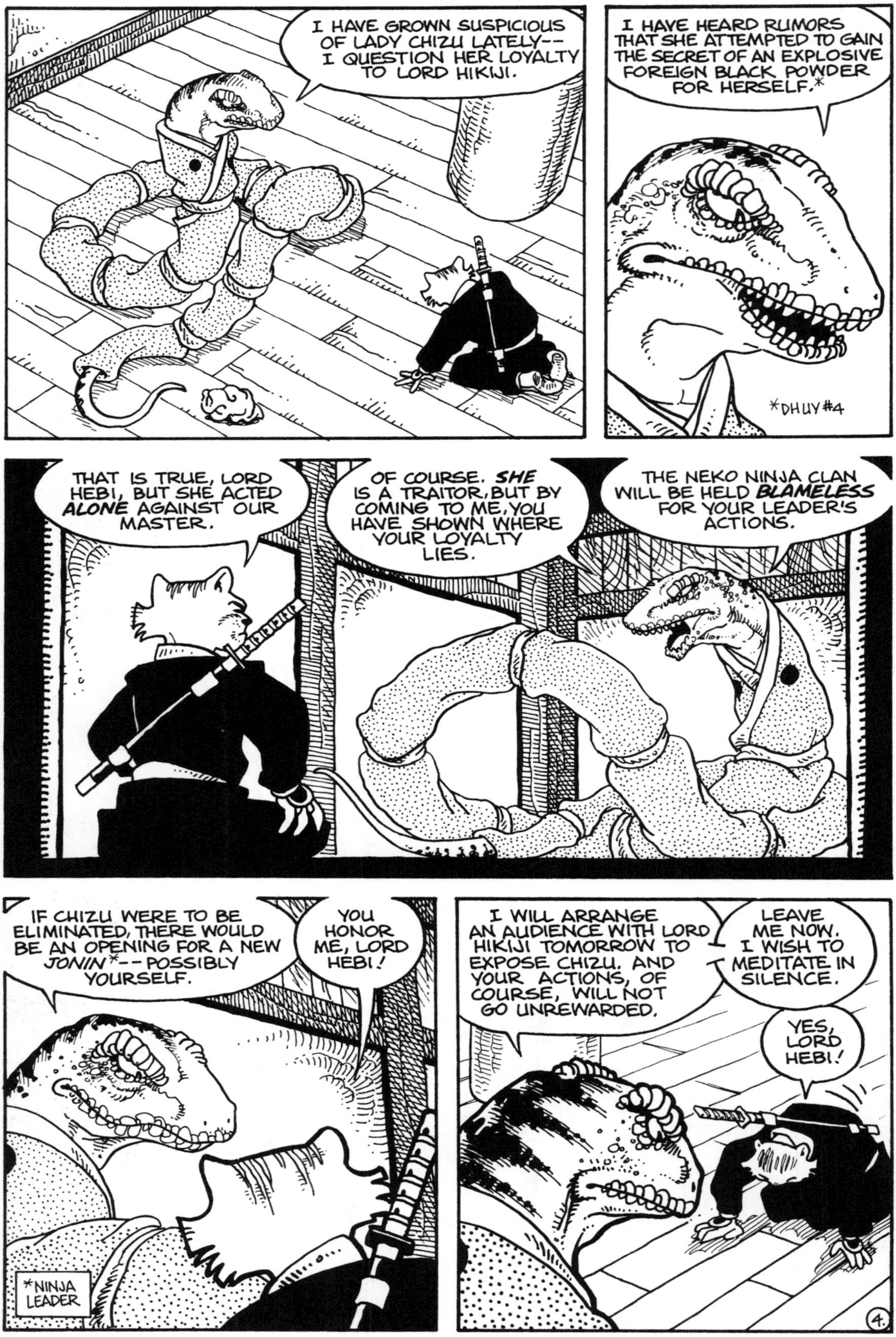
I HAVE GROWN SUSPICIOUS OF LADY CHIZU LATELY-- I QUESTION HER LOYALTY TO LORD HIKIJI.
I HAVE HEARD RUMORS THAT SHE ATTEMPTED TO GAIN THE SECRET OF AN EXPLOSIVE FOREIGN BLACK POWDER FOR HERSELF.*
*DHUY #4
THAT IS TRUE, LORD HEBI, BUT SHE ACTED ALONE AGAINST OUR MASTER.
OF COURSE. SHE IS A TRAITOR, BUT BY COMING TO ME, YOU HAVE SHOWN WHERE YOUR LOYALTY LIES.
THE NEKO NINJA CLAN WILL BE HELD BLAMELESS FOR YOUR LEADER'S ACTIONS.
IF CHIZU WERE TO BE ELIMINATED, THERE WOULD BE AN OPENING FOR A NEW JONIN*-- POSSIBLY YOURSELF.
YOU HONOR ME, LORD HEBI!
*NINJA LEADER
I WILL ARRANGE AN AUDIENCE WITH LORD HIKIJI TOMORROW TO EXPOSE CHIZU. AND YOUR ACTIONS, OF COURSE, WILL NOT GO UNREWARDED.
LEAVE ME NOW. I WISH TO MEDITATE IN SILENCE.
YES, LORD HEBI!
4.

"DECEIT IS THE FIRST TENET OF THE NINJA." CAN I AFFORD TO TRUST YOU, KAGEMARU?

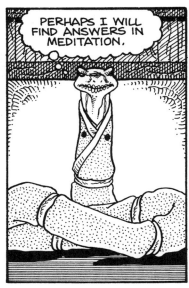

PERHAPS I WILL FIND ANSWERS IN MEDITATION.

THAT COLD-BLOODED FOOL!

DID HE REALLY IMAGINE THAT I WOULD HAND OVER THE ENTIRE DOCUMENT? THE CONSPIRATORS' NAMES ARE IN A SAFE PLACE.

I MAY NEED THEM IN THE FUTURE.

WHA--?!!

PERHAPS I IMAGINED IT.

I THOUGHT I HEARD THE FLAPPING OF WINGS.

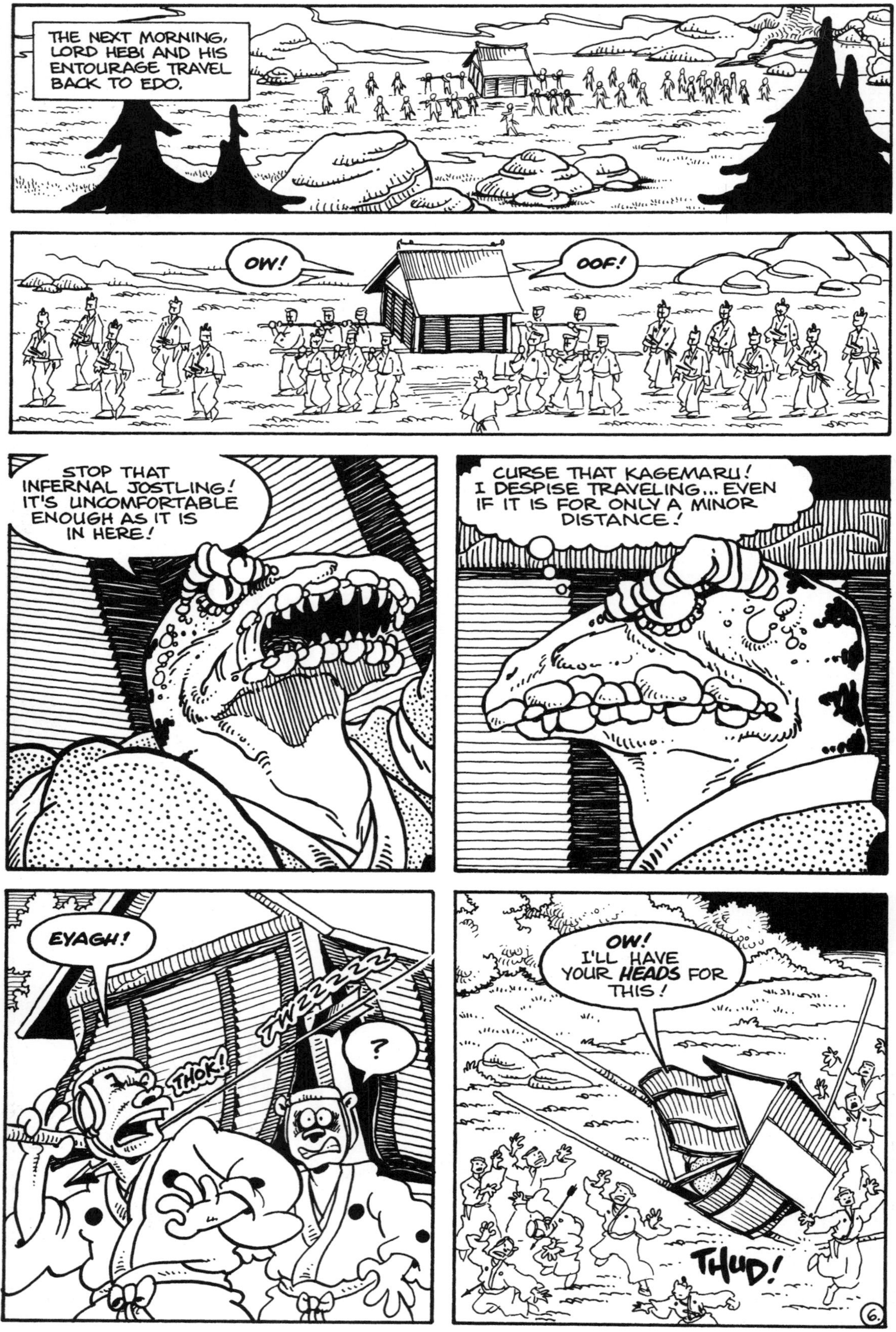
THE NEXT MORNING, LORD HEBI AND HIS ENTOURAGE TRAVEL BACK TO EDO.
OW!
OOF!
STOP THAT INFERNAL JOSTLING! IT'S UNCOMFORTABLE ENOUGH AS IT IS IN HERE!
CURSE THAT KAGEMARU! I DESPISE TRAVELING... EVEN IF IT IS FOR ONLY A MINOR DISTANCE!
EYAGH!
TWZZZZZZ
THOK!
?
OW! I'LL HAVE YOUR **HEADS** FOR THIS!
THUD!
6.

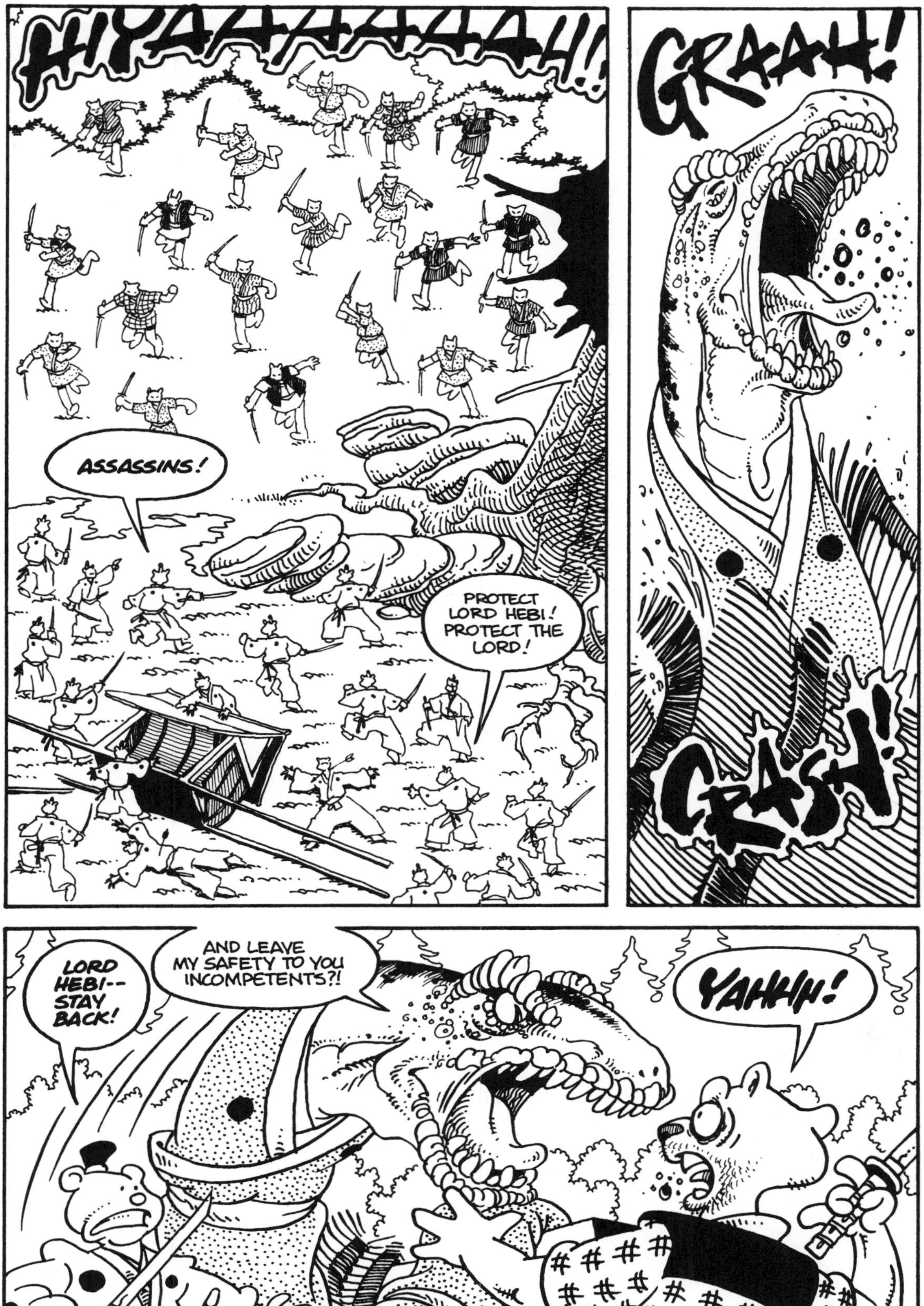
HIYAAAAAAAH!!
ASSASSINS!
PROTECT LORD HEBI! PROTECT THE LORD!
GRAAH!
CRASH!
LORD HEBI-- STAY BACK!
AND LEAVE MY SAFETY TO YOU INCOMPETENTS?!
YAHHH!
7.

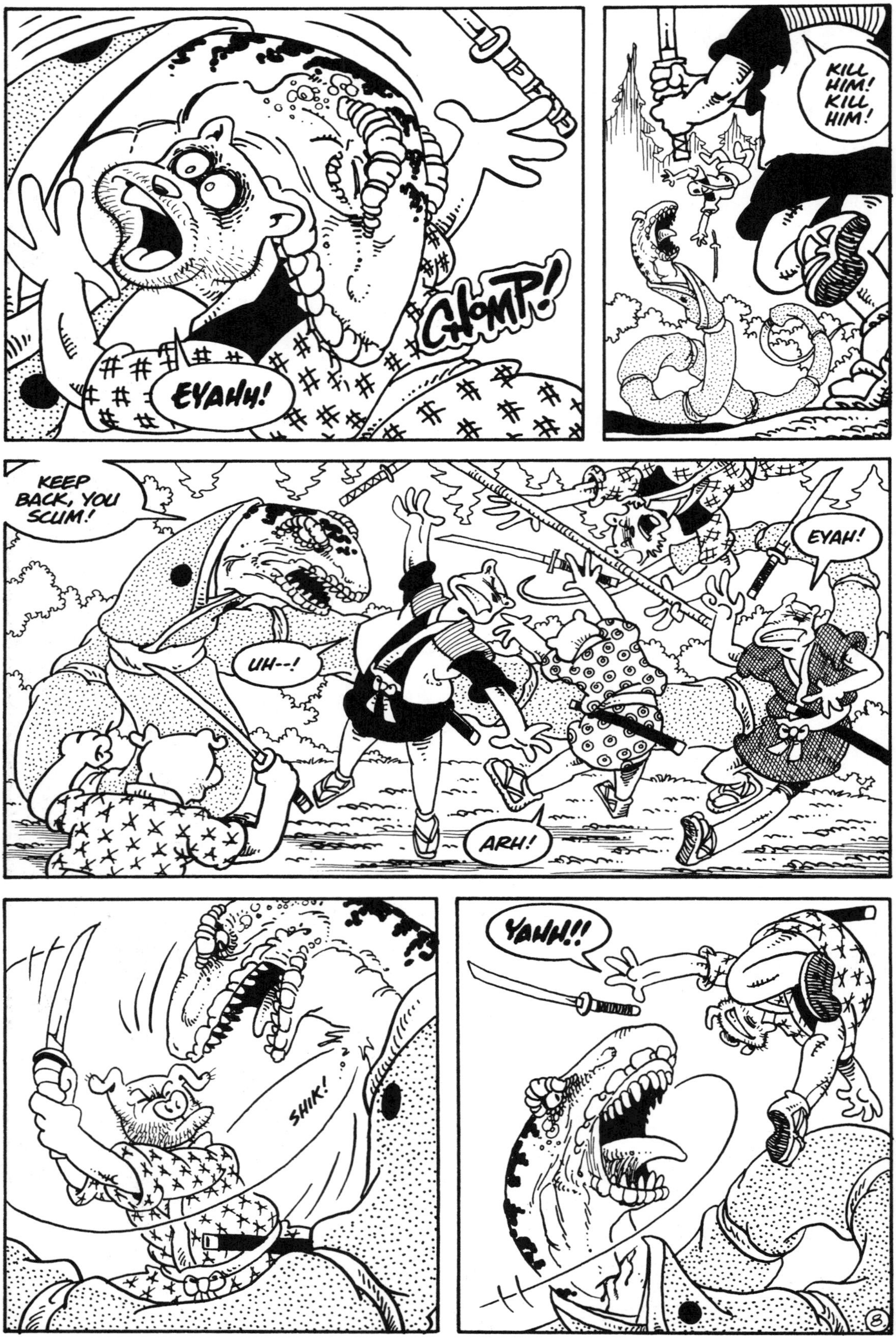
CHOMP!
EYAHH!
KILL HIM! KILL HIM!
KEEP BACK, YOU SCUM!
EYAH!
UH--!
ARH!
SHIK!
YAHH!!
8

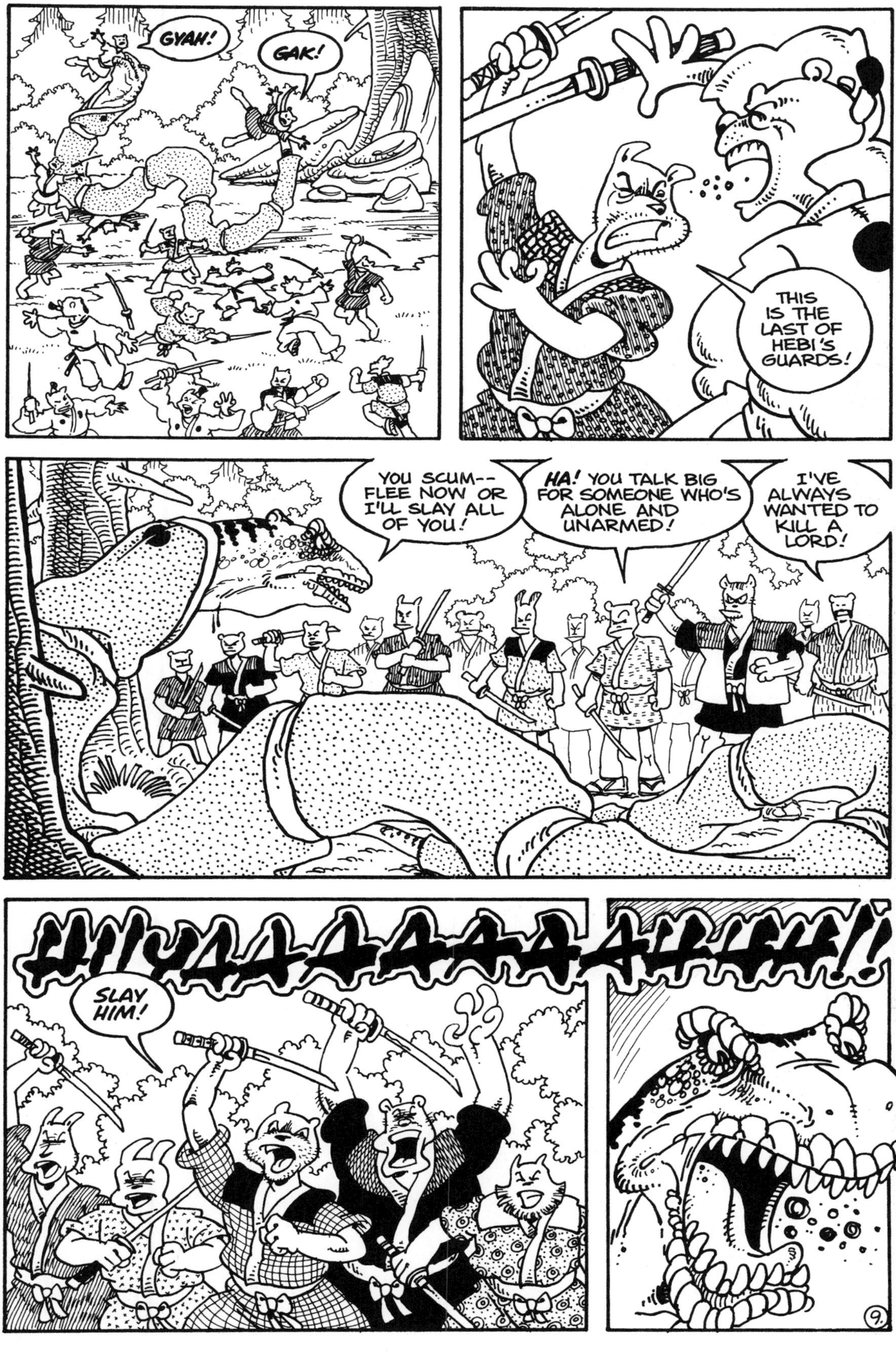
GYAH!
GAK!
THIS IS THE LAST OF HEBI'S GUARDS!
YOU SCUM-- FLEE NOW OR I'LL SLAY ALL OF YOU!
HA! YOU TALK BIG FOR SOMEONE WHO'S ALONE AND UNARMED!
I'VE ALWAYS WANTED TO KILL A LORD!
HIYAAAAAAAAAAHHH!!
SLAY HIM!
9.

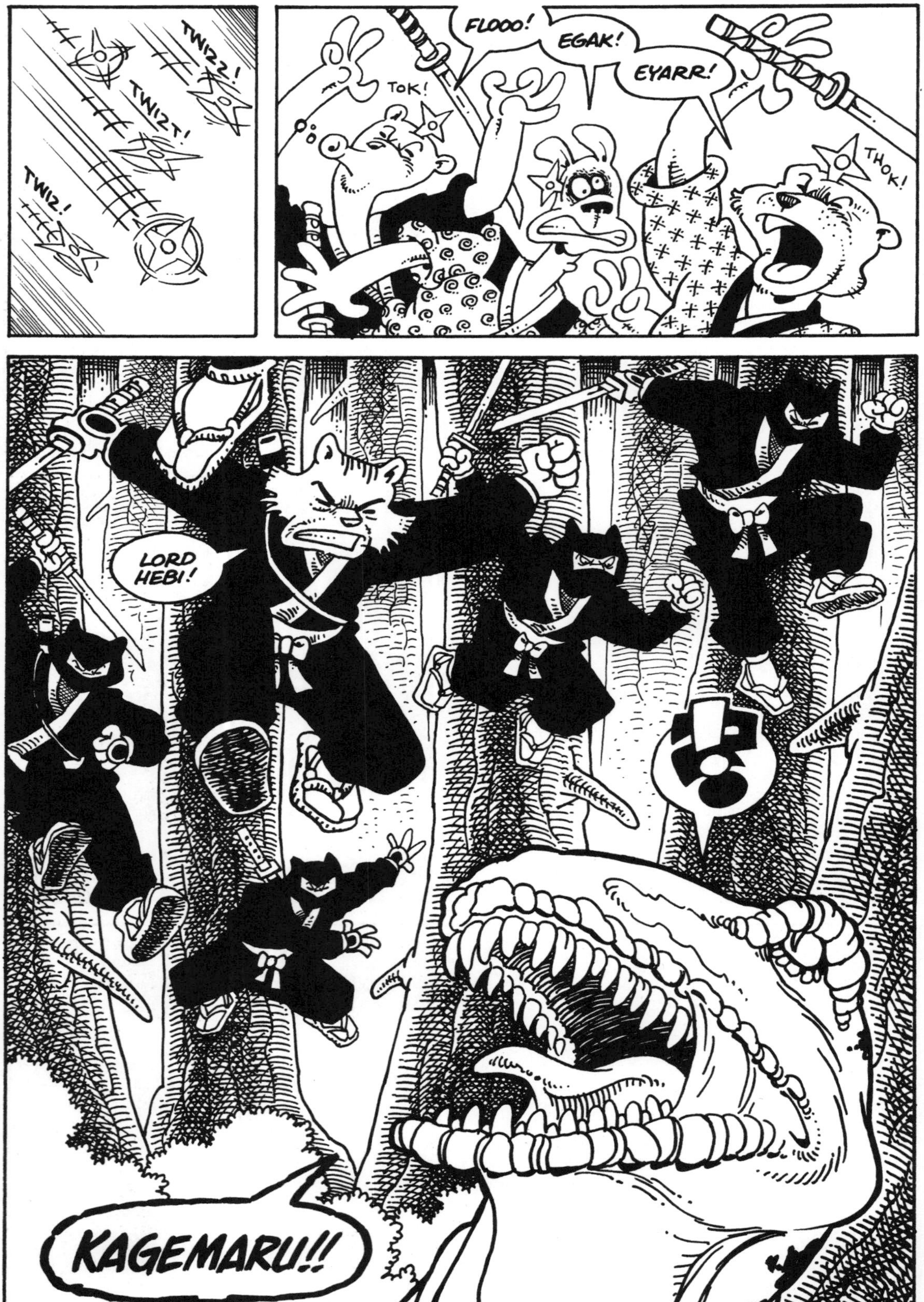
TWIZZ!
TWIZT!
TWIZ!
FLOOO!
TOK!
EGAK!
EYARR!
THOK!
LORD HEBI!
!
KAGEMARU!!
10.

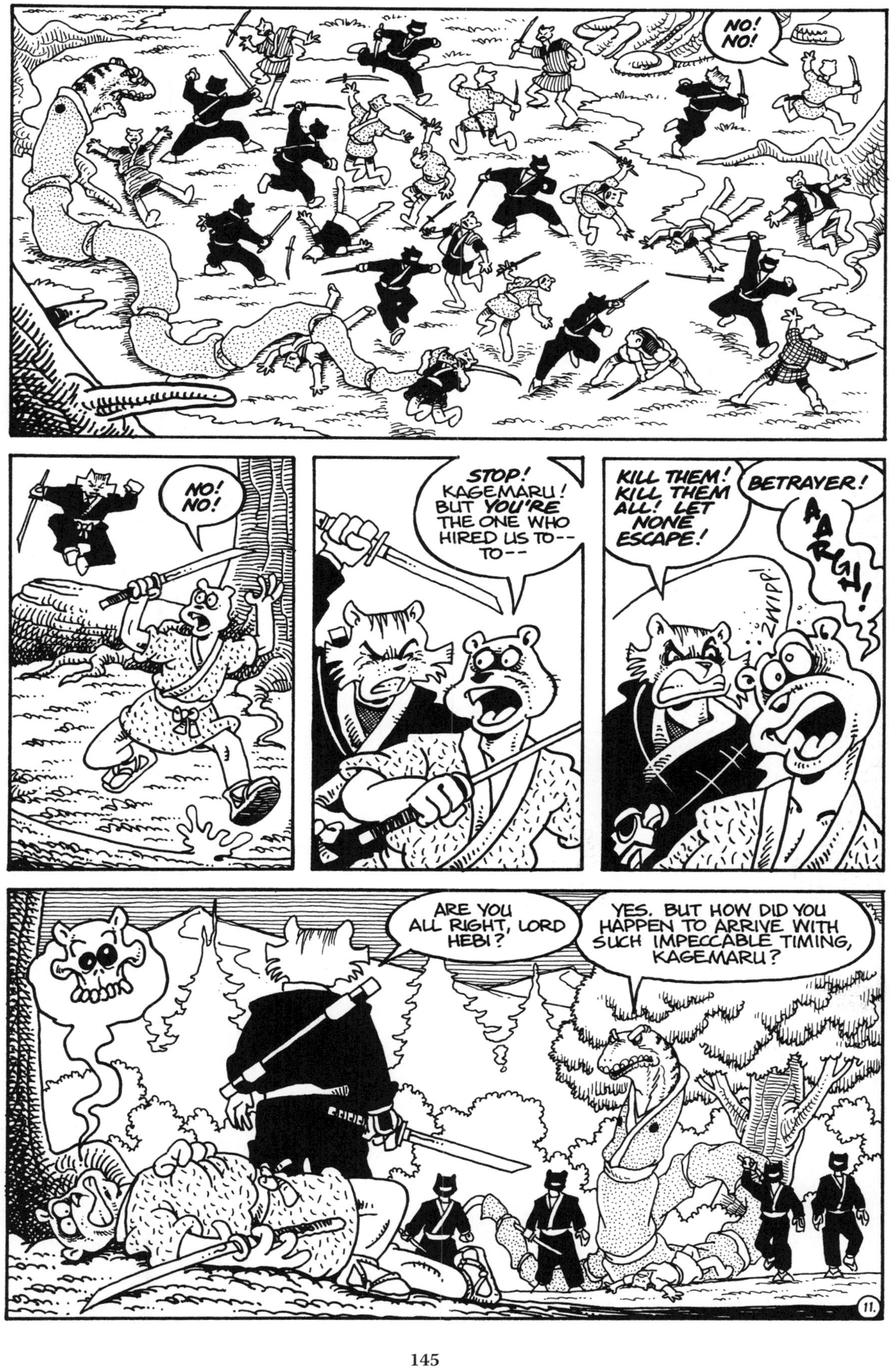

NO! NO!
NO! NO!
STOP! KAGEMARU! BUT YOU'RE THE ONE WHO HIRED US TO-- TO--
KILL THEM! KILL THEM ALL! LET NONE ESCAPE!
BETRAYER!
ZWIPP!
AARGH!
ARE YOU ALL RIGHT, LORD HEBI?
YES. BUT HOW DID YOU HAPPEN TO ARRIVE WITH SUCH IMPECCABLE TIMING, KAGEMARU?
11.

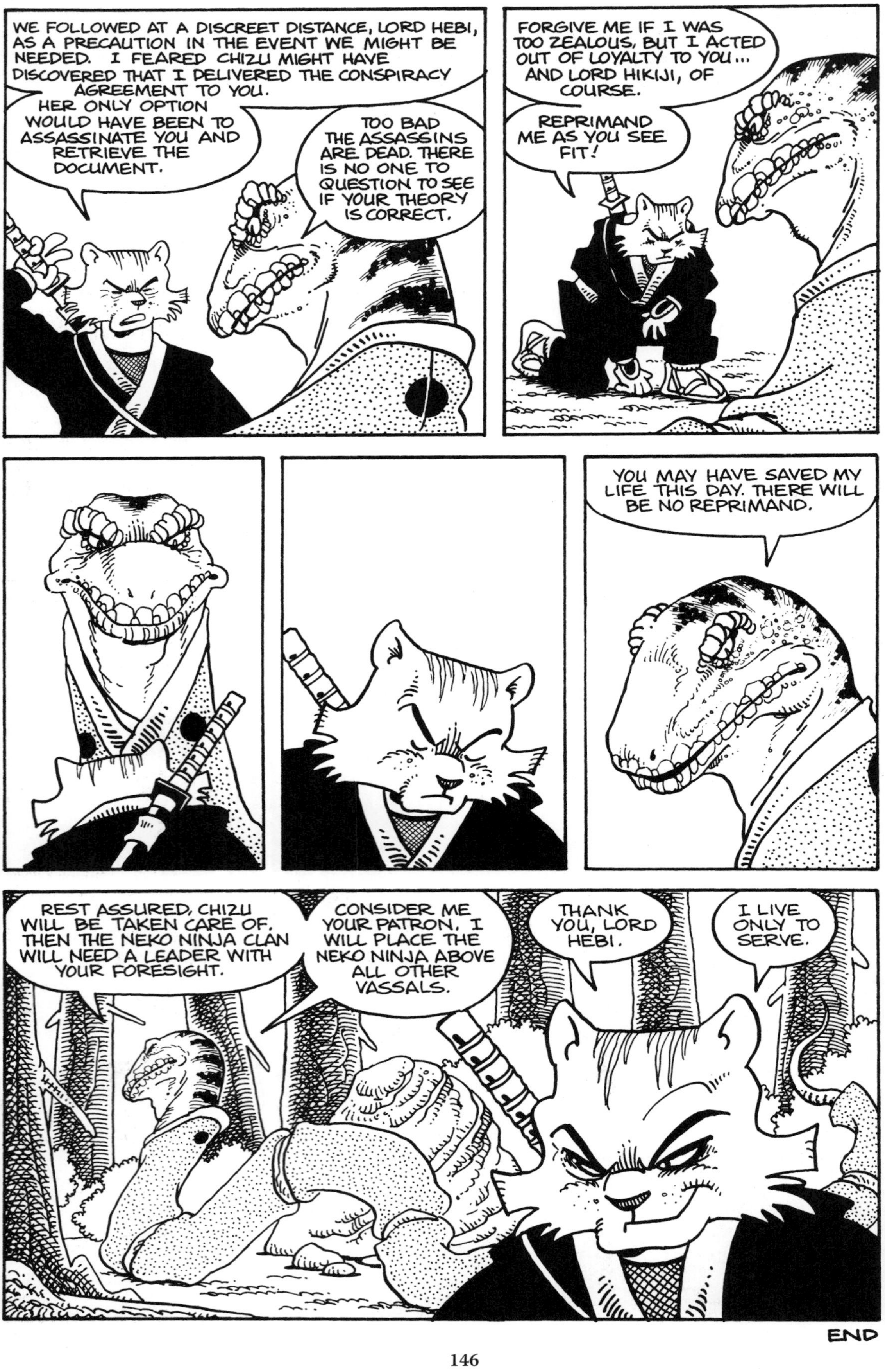
WE FOLLOWED AT A DISCREET DISTANCE, LORD HEBI, AS A PRECAUTION IN THE EVENT WE MIGHT BE NEEDED. I FEARED CHIZU MIGHT HAVE DISCOVERED THAT I DELIVERED THE CONSPIRACY AGREEMENT TO YOU.
HER ONLY OPTION WOULD HAVE BEEN TO ASSASSINATE YOU AND RETRIEVE THE DOCUMENT.
TOO BAD THE ASSASSINS ARE DEAD. THERE IS NO ONE TO QUESTION TO SEE IF YOUR THEORY IS CORRECT.
FORGIVE ME IF I WAS TOO ZEALOUS, BUT I ACTED OUT OF LOYALTY TO YOU... AND LORD HIKIJI, OF COURSE.
REPRIMAND ME AS YOU SEE FIT!
YOU MAY HAVE SAVED MY LIFE THIS DAY. THERE WILL BE NO REPRIMAND.
REST ASSURED, CHIZU WILL BE TAKEN CARE OF. THEN THE NEKO NINJA CLAN WILL NEED A LEADER WITH YOUR FORESIGHT.
CONSIDER ME YOUR PATRON. I WILL PLACE THE NEKO NINJA ABOVE ALL OTHER VASSALS.
THANK YOU, LORD HEBI.
I LIVE ONLY TO SERVE.

END

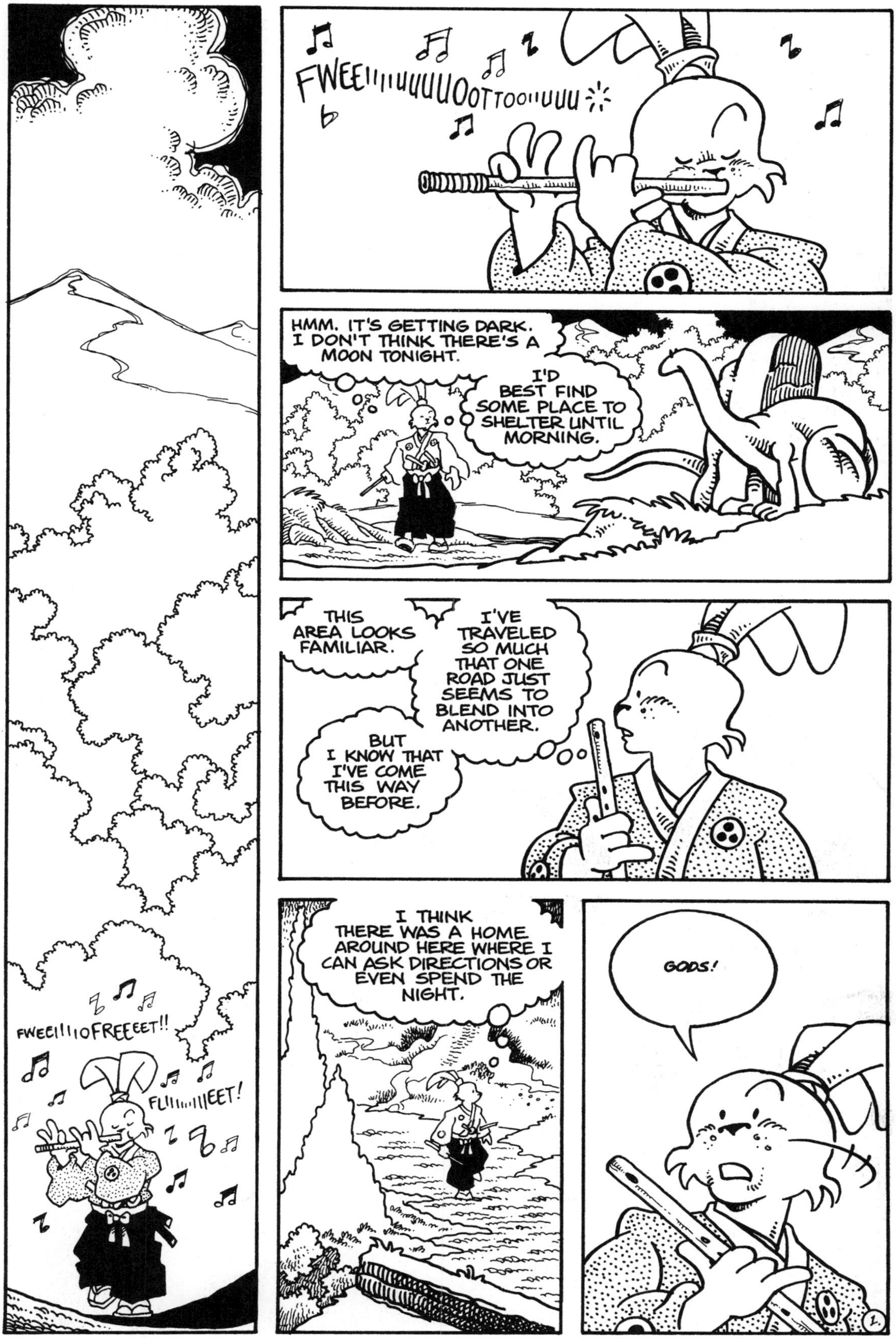
FWEEI!!!OFREEEEET!!
FLI!!!!!EET!
FWEEI!!!UUUUOOTTOO!!UUU
HMM. IT'S GETTING DARK. I DON'T THINK THERE'S A MOON TONIGHT.
I'D BEST FIND SOME PLACE TO SHELTER UNTIL MORNING.
THIS AREA LOOKS FAMILIAR.
I'VE TRAVELED SO MUCH THAT ONE ROAD JUST SEEMS TO BLEND INTO ANOTHER.
BUT I KNOW THAT I'VE COME THIS WAY BEFORE.
I THINK THERE WAS A HOME AROUND HERE WHERE I CAN ASK DIRECTIONS OR EVEN SPEND THE NIGHT.
GODS!

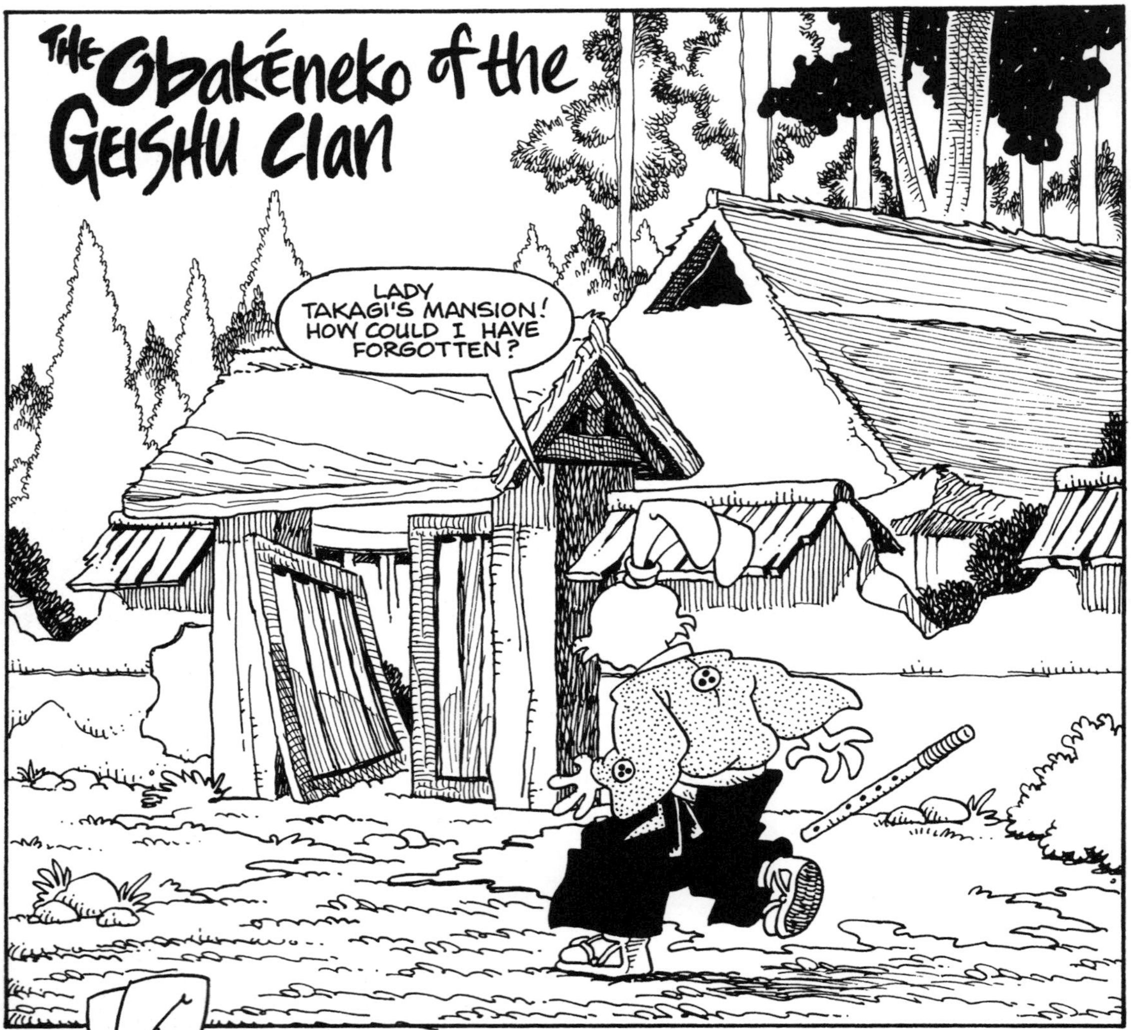
THE Obakéneko of the Geishu Clan
LADY TAKAGI'S MANSION! HOW COULD I HAVE FORGOTTEN?

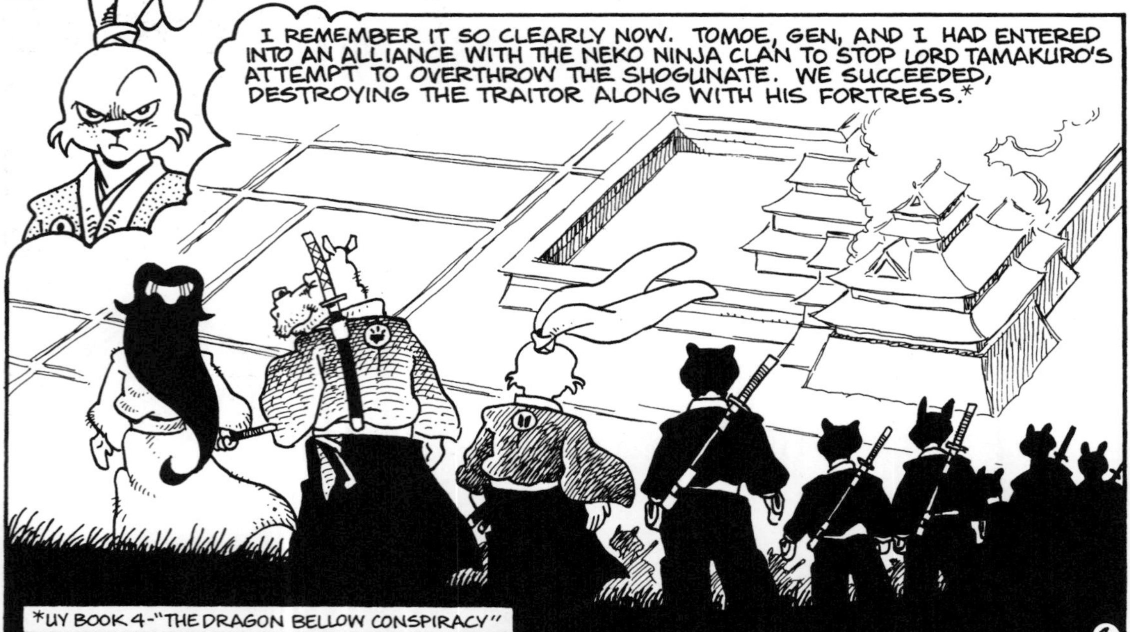
I REMEMBER IT SO CLEARLY NOW. TOMOE, GEN, AND I HAD ENTERED INTO AN ALLIANCE WITH THE NEKO NINJA CLAN TO STOP LORD TAMAKURO'S ATTEMPT TO OVERTHROW THE SHOGUNATE. WE SUCCEEDED, DESTROYING THE TRAITOR ALONG WITH HIS FORTRESS.*
*UY BOOK 4-"THE DRAGON BELLOW CONSPIRACY"
2.

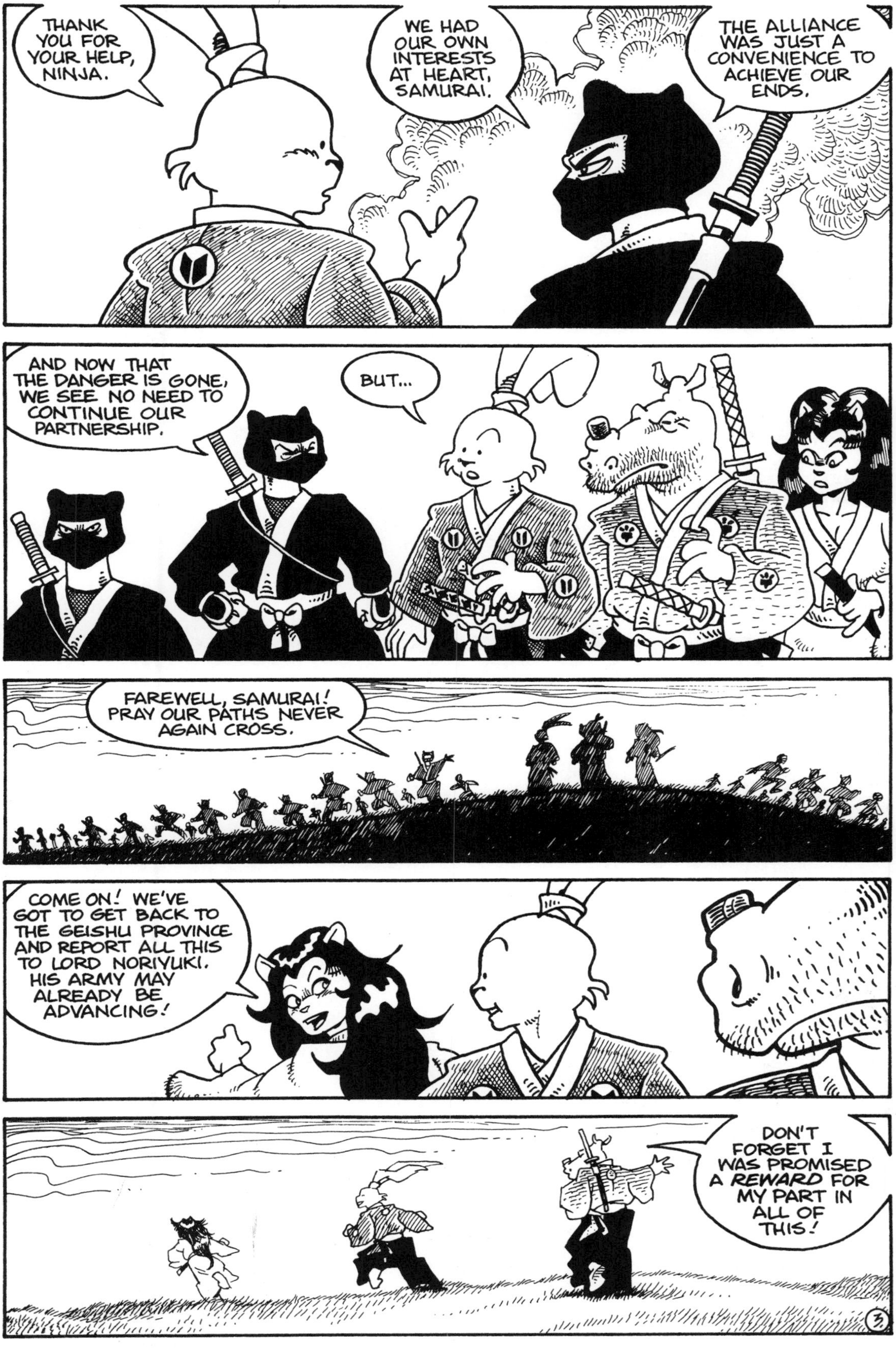
THANK YOU FOR YOUR HELP, NINJA.
WE HAD OUR OWN INTERESTS AT HEART, SAMURAI.
THE ALLIANCE WAS JUST A CONVENIENCE TO ACHIEVE OUR ENDS.
AND NOW THAT THE DANGER IS GONE, WE SEE NO NEED TO CONTINUE OUR PARTNERSHIP.
BUT...
FAREWELL, SAMURAI! PRAY OUR PATHS NEVER AGAIN CROSS.
COME ON! WE'VE GOT TO GET BACK TO THE GEISHU PROVINCE AND REPORT ALL THIS TO LORD NORIYUKI. HIS ARMY MAY ALREADY BE ADVANCING!
DON'T FORGET I WAS PROMISED A ***REWARD*** FOR MY PART IN ALL OF THIS!
3

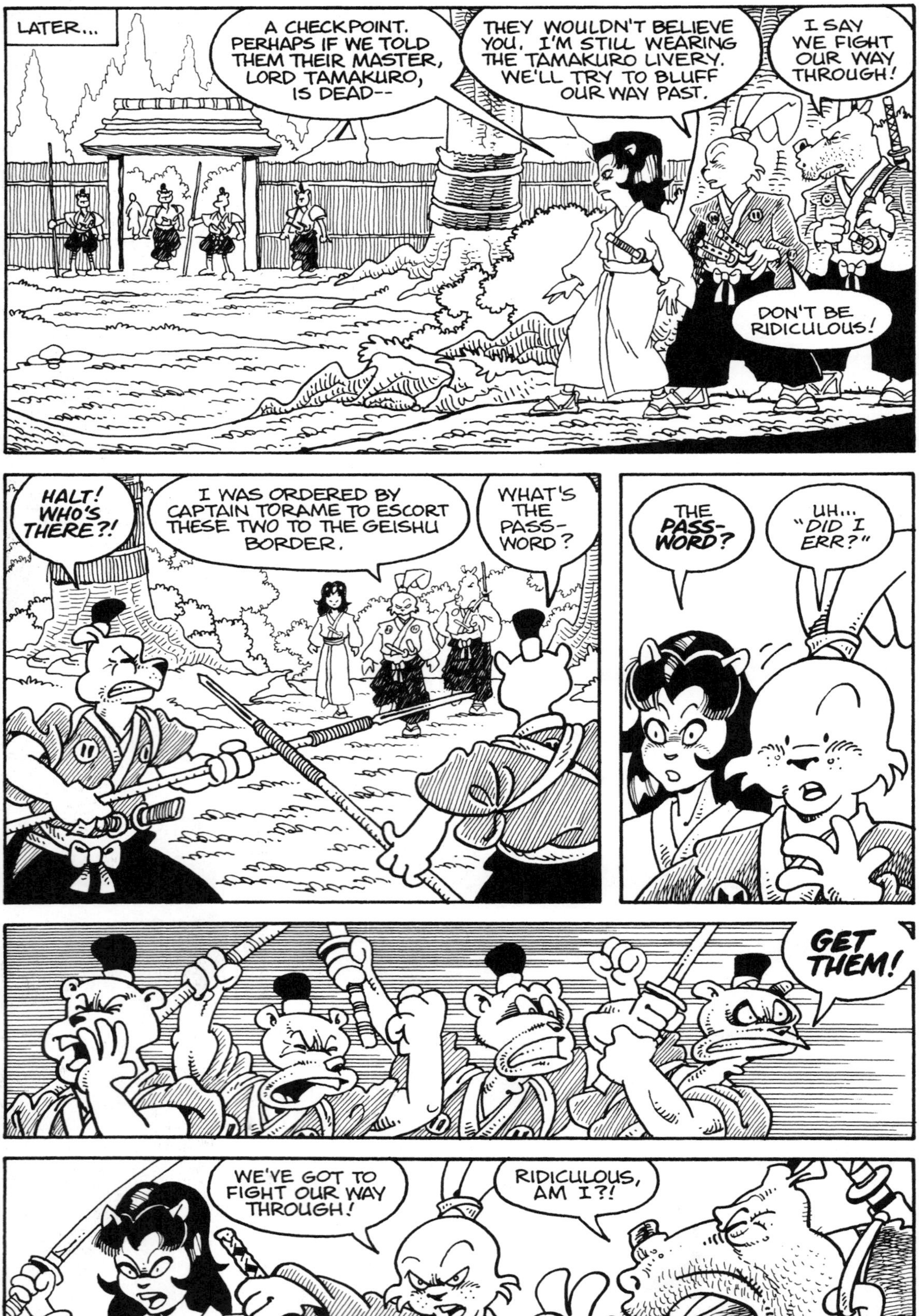
LATER...
A CHECKPOINT. PERHAPS IF WE TOLD THEM THEIR MASTER, LORD TAMAKURO, IS DEAD--
THEY WOULDN'T BELIEVE YOU. I'M STILL WEARING THE TAMAKURO LIVERY. WE'LL TRY TO BLUFF OUR WAY PAST.
I SAY WE FIGHT OUR WAY THROUGH!
DON'T BE RIDICULOUS!
HALT! WHO'S THERE?!
I WAS ORDERED BY CAPTAIN TORAME TO ESCORT THESE TWO TO THE GEISHU BORDER.
WHAT'S THE PASS-WORD?
THE PASS-WORD?
UH... "DID I ERR?"
GET THEM!
WE'VE GOT TO FIGHT OUR WAY THROUGH!
RIDICULOUS, AM I?!
4.

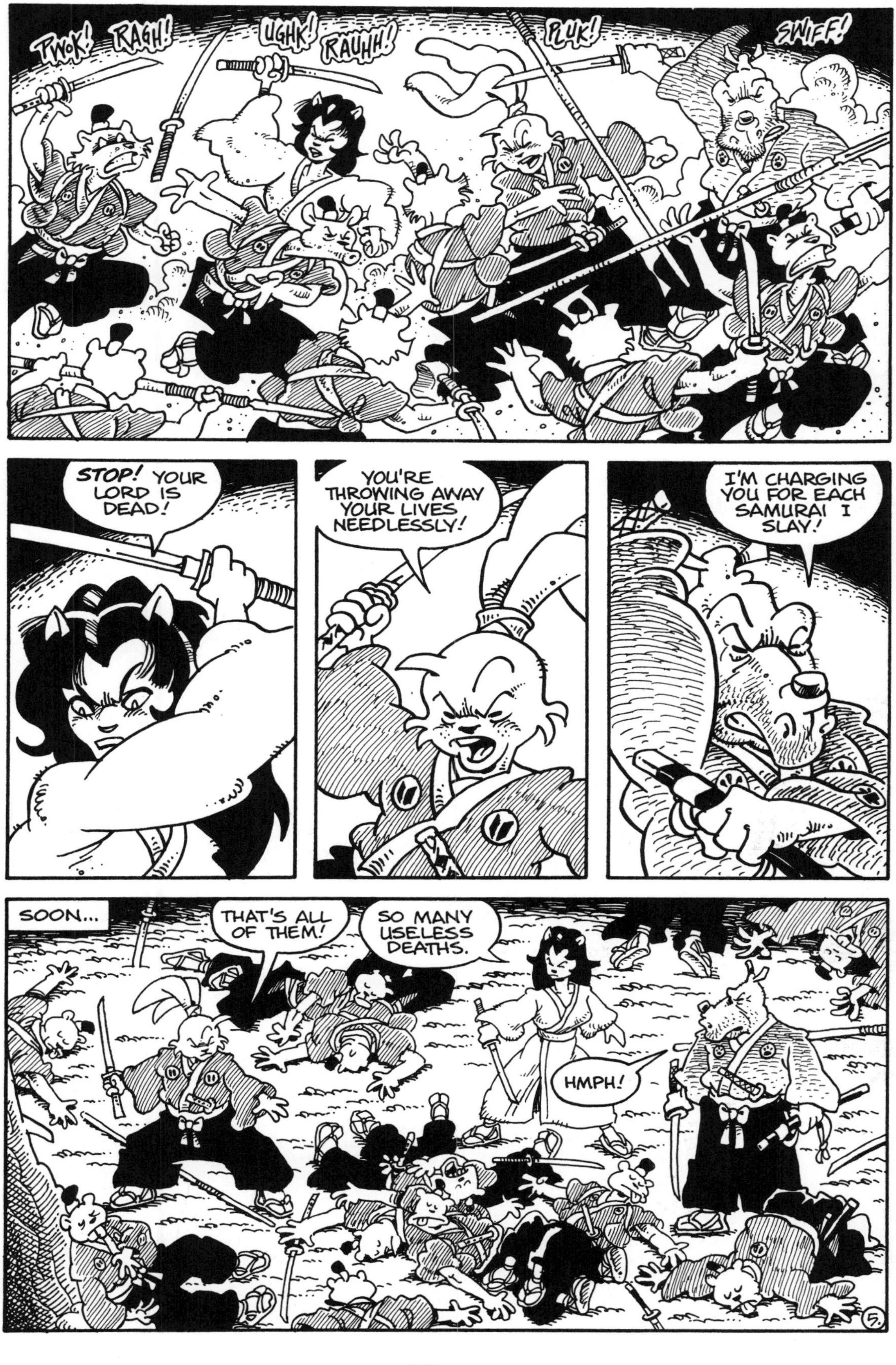
PWOK!
RAGH!
UGHK!
RAUHH!
PLUK!
SWIFF!
STOP! YOUR LORD IS DEAD!
YOU'RE THROWING AWAY YOUR LIVES NEEDLESSLY!
I'M CHARGING YOU FOR EACH SAMURAI I SLAY!
SOON...
THAT'S ALL OF THEM!
SO MANY USELESS DEATHS.
HMPH!
5.

¡GRAAK!

EH--?

BEWAARE...

WHA--!

USAGI--
WHAT IS IT?
ARE YOU
HURT?

D-DID
YOU HEAR
HIM?!

I HEARD
NOTHING!

HE'S
STONE-
COLD
DEAD.

YOU
MUST HAVE
IMAGINED IT,
USAGI.

LET'S GO.
WE'LL SOON BE
IN GEISHU
TERRITORY.

I'M
RIGHT
BEHIND
YOU.

ARE
YOU COMING,
LONG-
EARS?

ER...
YEAH. I'M
COMING.

6.

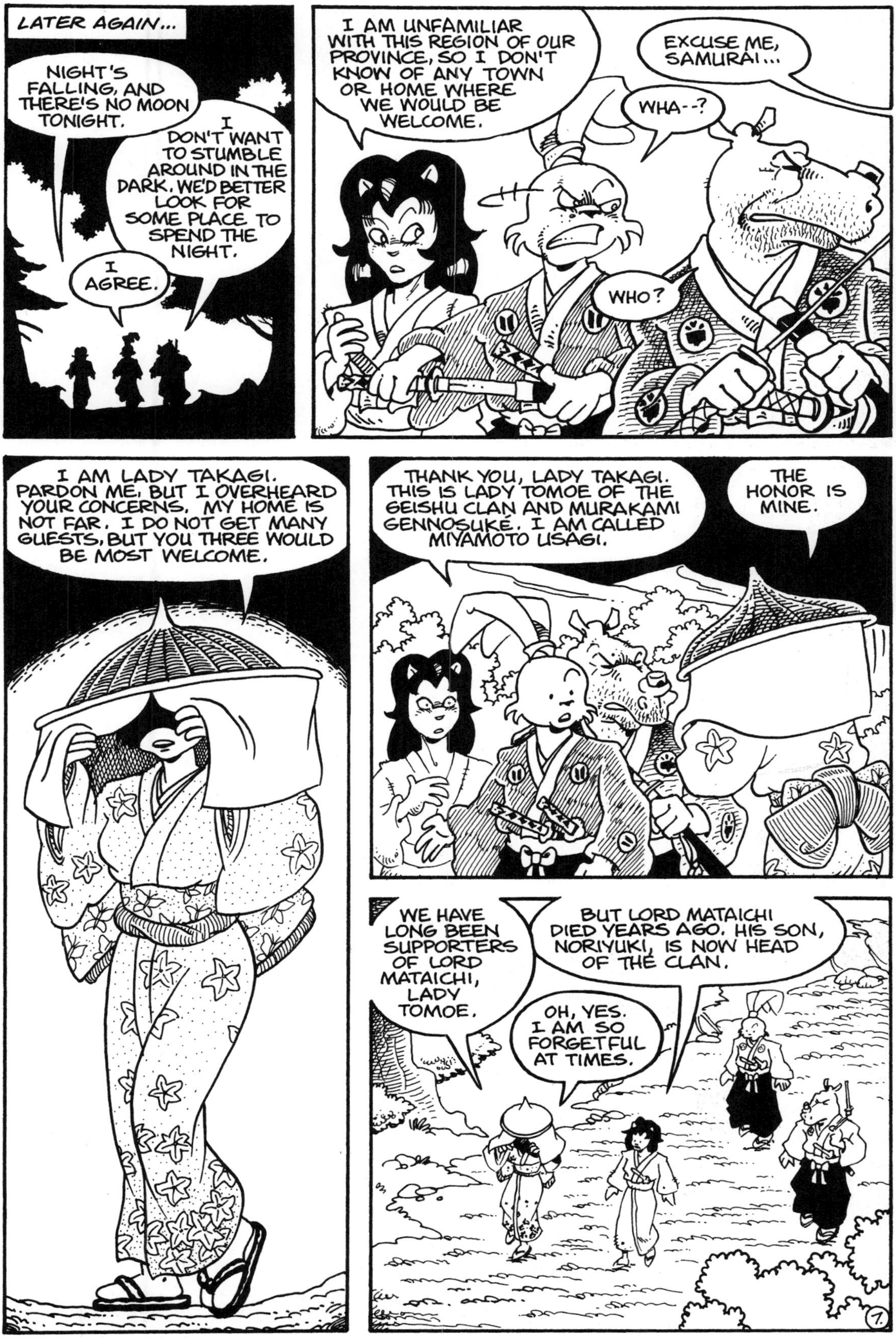
LATER AGAIN...
NIGHT'S FALLING, AND THERE'S NO MOON TONIGHT.
I DON'T WANT TO STUMBLE AROUND IN THE DARK. WE'D BETTER LOOK FOR SOME PLACE TO SPEND THE NIGHT.
I AGREE.
I AM UNFAMILIAR WITH THIS REGION OF OUR PROVINCE, SO I DON'T KNOW OF ANY TOWN OR HOME WHERE WE WOULD BE WELCOME.
EXCUSE ME, SAMURAI...
WHA--?
WHO?
I AM LADY TAKAGI. PARDON ME, BUT I OVERHEARD YOUR CONCERNS. MY HOME IS NOT FAR. I DO NOT GET MANY GUESTS, BUT YOU THREE WOULD BE MOST WELCOME.
THANK YOU, LADY TAKAGI. THIS IS LADY TOMOE OF THE GEISHU CLAN AND MURAKAMI GENNOSUKÉ. I AM CALLED MIYAMOTO USAGI.
THE HONOR IS MINE.
WE HAVE LONG BEEN SUPPORTERS OF LORD MATAICHI, LADY TOMOE.
BUT LORD MATAICHI DIED YEARS AGO. HIS SON, NORIYUKI, IS NOW HEAD OF THE CLAN.
OH, YES. I AM SO FORGETFUL AT TIMES.
7.

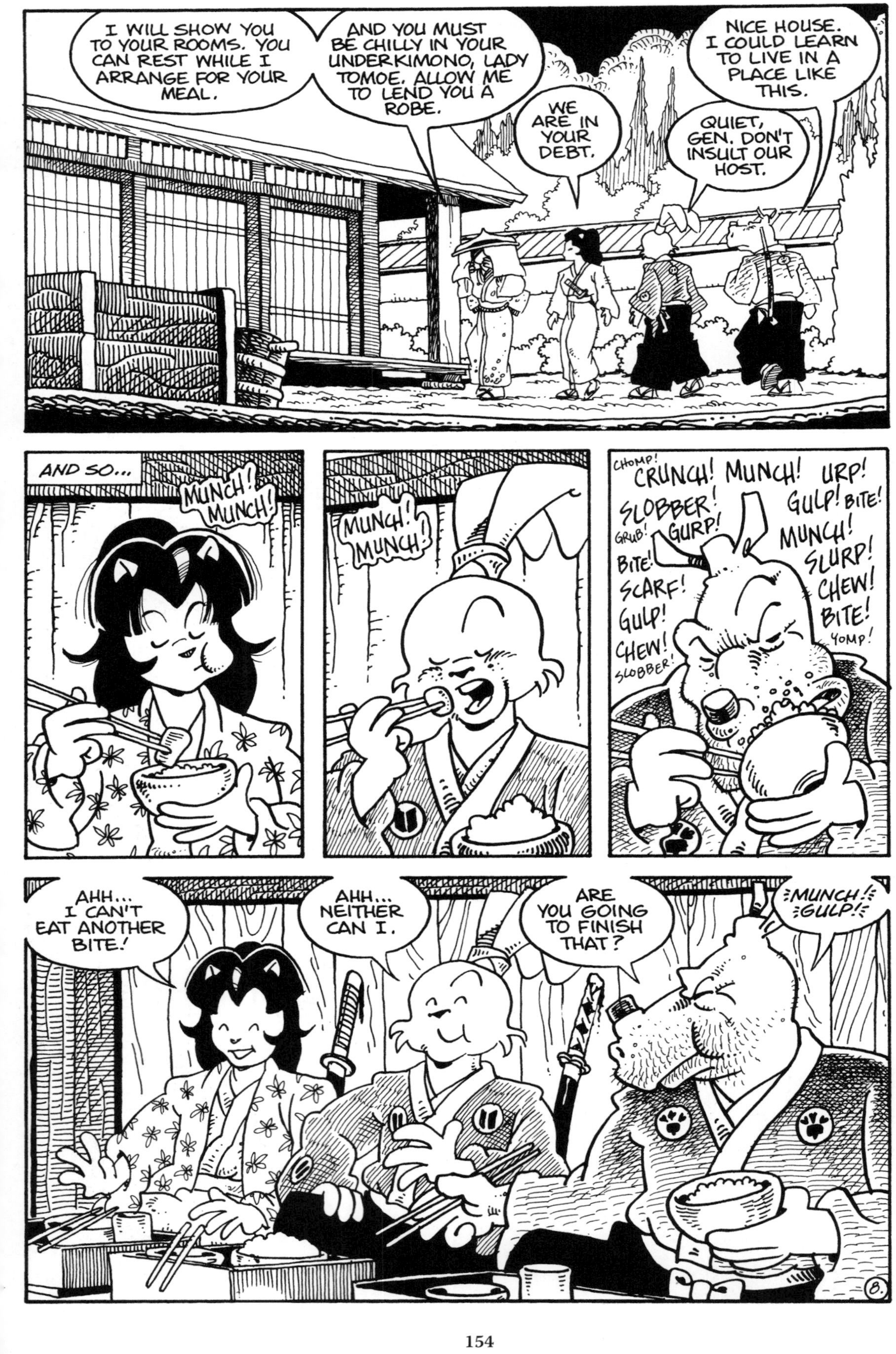
I WILL SHOW YOU TO YOUR ROOMS. YOU CAN REST WHILE I ARRANGE FOR YOUR MEAL.
AND YOU MUST BE CHILLY IN YOUR UNDERKIMONO, LADY TOMOE. ALLOW ME TO LEND YOU A ROBE.
WE ARE IN YOUR DEBT.
NICE HOUSE. I COULD LEARN TO LIVE IN A PLACE LIKE THIS.
QUIET, GEN. DON'T INSULT OUR HOST.
AND SO...
MUNCH! MUNCH!
MUNCH! MUNCH!
CHOMP! CRUNCH! MUNCH! URP!
SLOBBER! GURP! GULP! BITE!
GRUB! MUNCH!
BITE! SLURP!
SCARF! CHEW!
GULP! BITE!
CHEW! YOMP!
SLOBBER!
AHH... I CAN'T EAT ANOTHER BITE!
AHH... NEITHER CAN I.
ARE YOU GOING TO FINISH THAT?
MUNCH! GULP!
8.

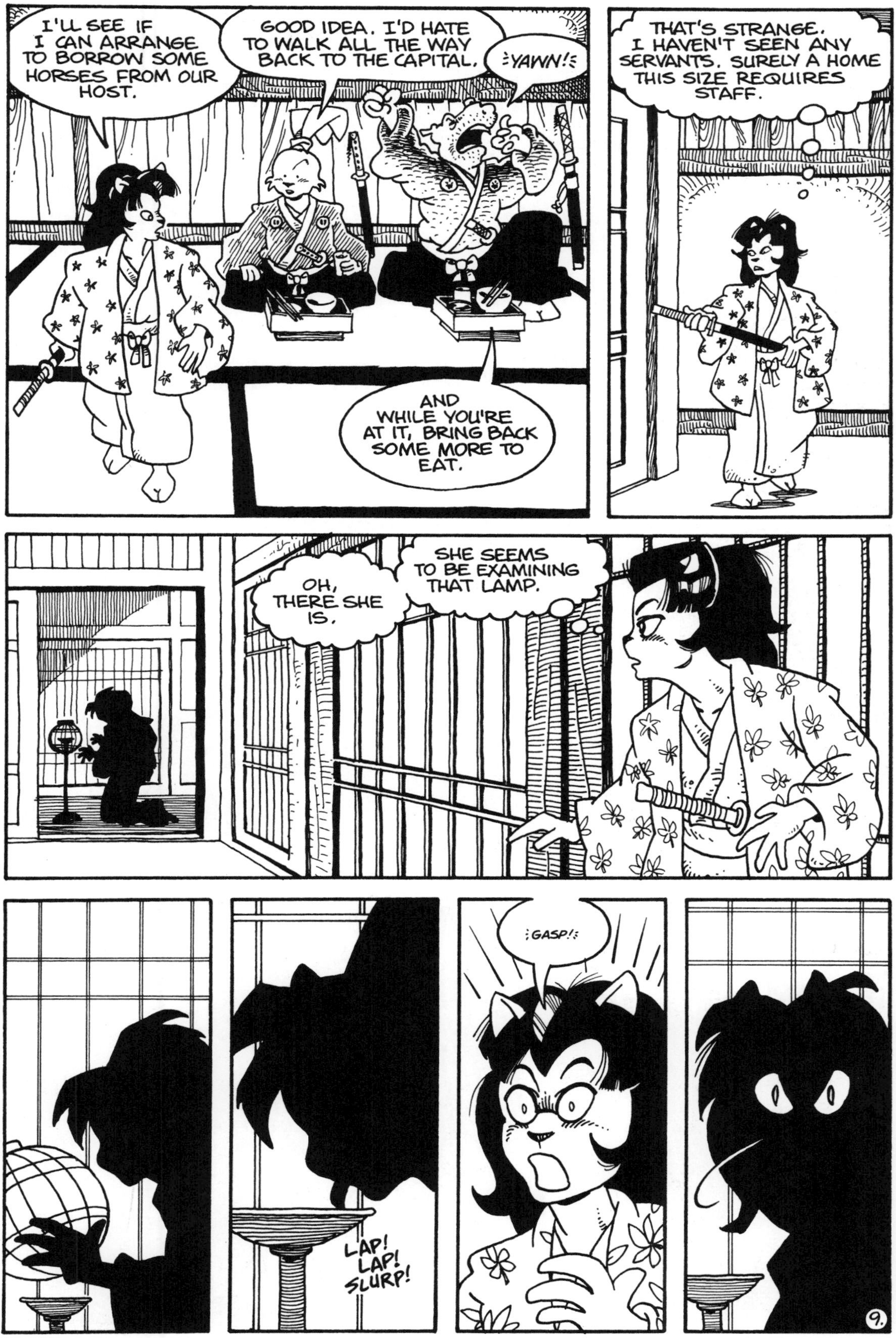
I'LL SEE IF I CAN ARRANGE TO BORROW SOME HORSES FROM OUR HOST.
GOOD IDEA. I'D HATE TO WALK ALL THE WAY BACK TO THE CAPITAL.
YAWN!
AND WHILE YOU'RE AT IT, BRING BACK SOME MORE TO EAT.
THAT'S STRANGE. I HAVEN'T SEEN ANY SERVANTS. SURELY A HOME THIS SIZE REQUIRES STAFF.
OH, THERE SHE IS.
SHE SEEMS TO BE EXAMINING THAT LAMP.
LAP! LAP! SLURP!
GASP!
9.

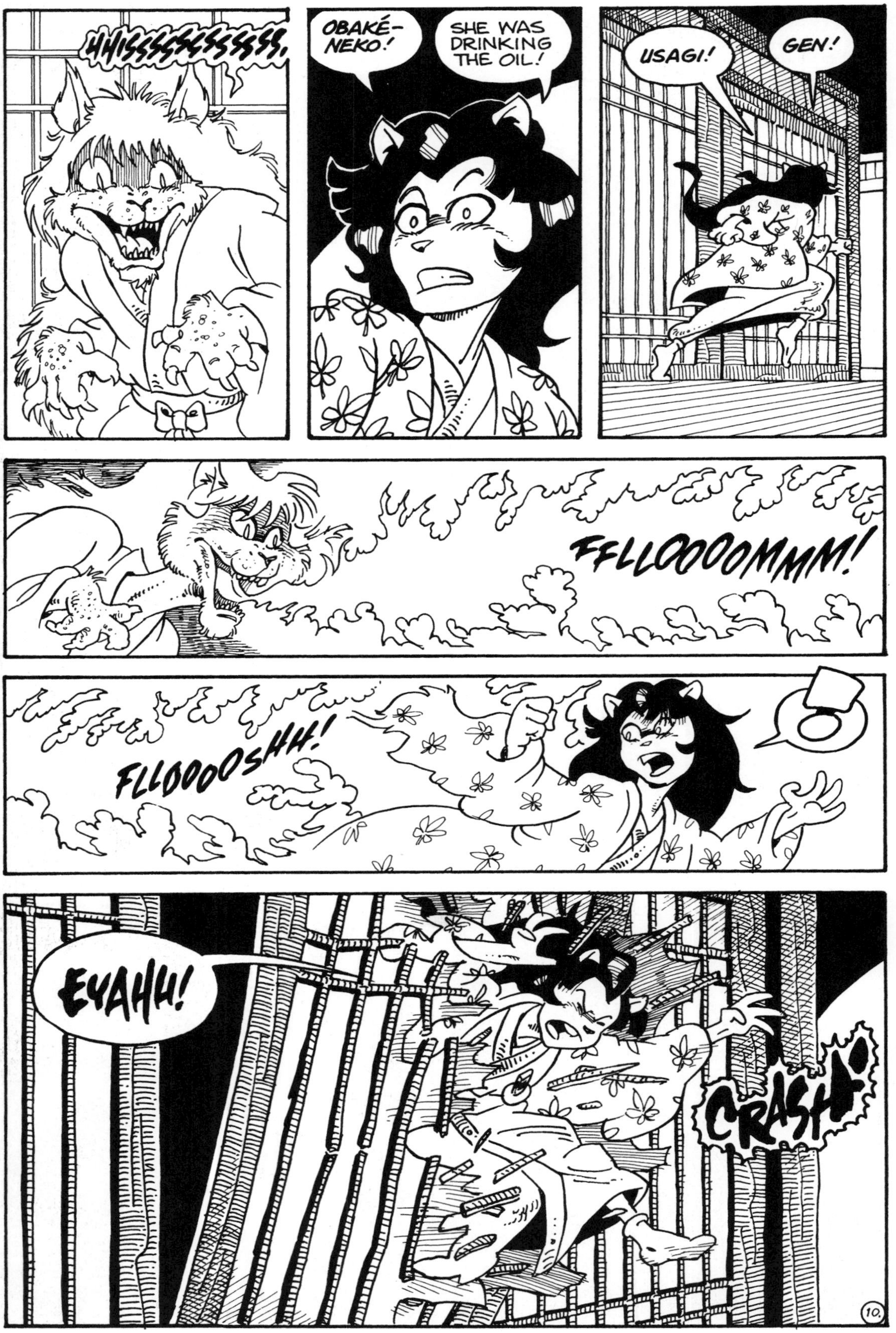

HHISSSSSSSSSSSS,
OBAKÉ-NEKO!
SHE WAS DRINKING THE OIL!
USAGI!
GEN!
FFLLOOOOMMM!
FLLOOOOSHH!
EYAHH!
CRASH!
10.

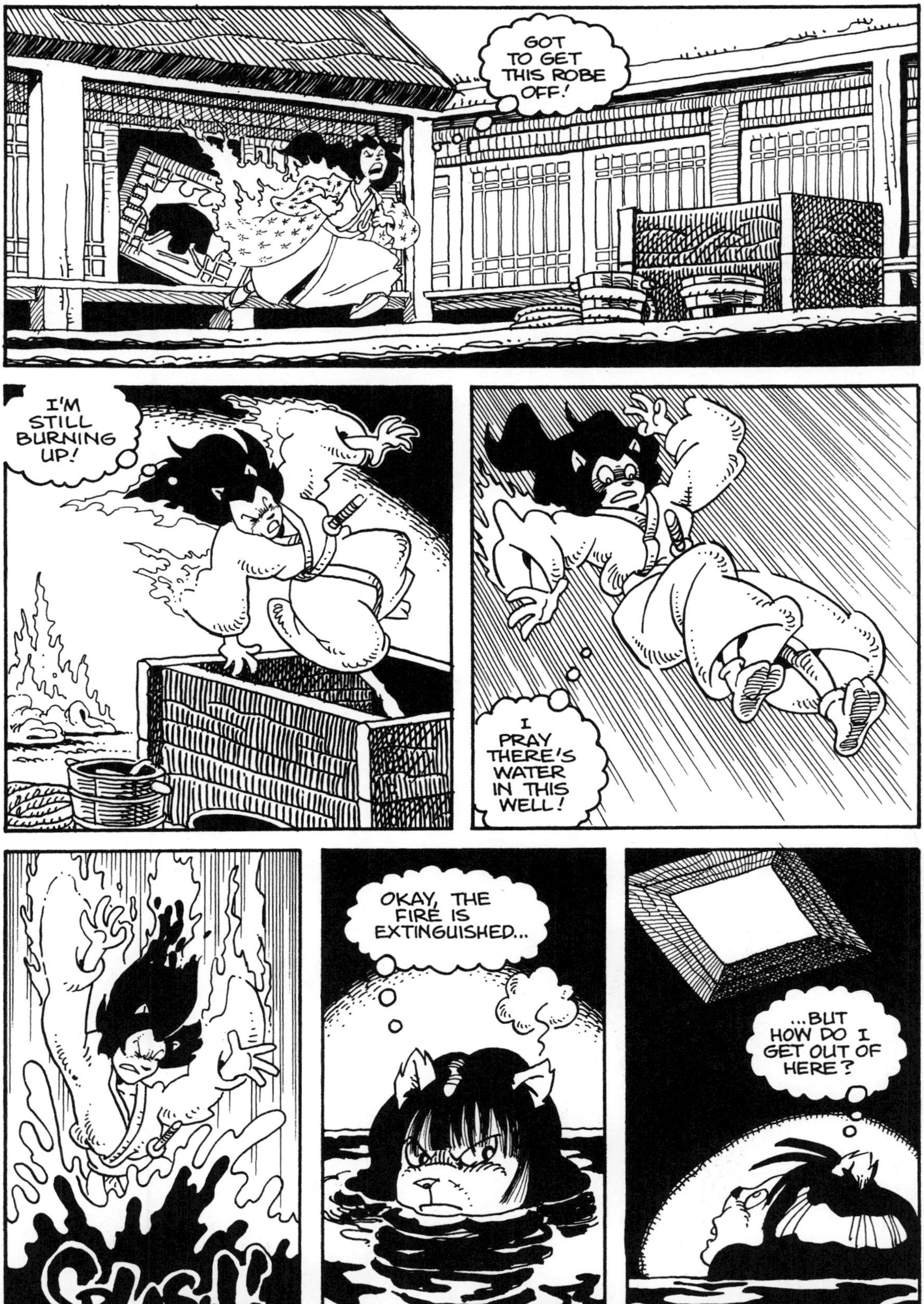

GOT TO GET THIS ROBE OFF!
I'M STILL BURNING UP!
I PRAY THERE'S WATER IN THIS WELL!
SPLASH!
OKAY, THE FIRE IS EXTINGUISHED...
...BUT HOW DO I GET OUT OF HERE?
11.

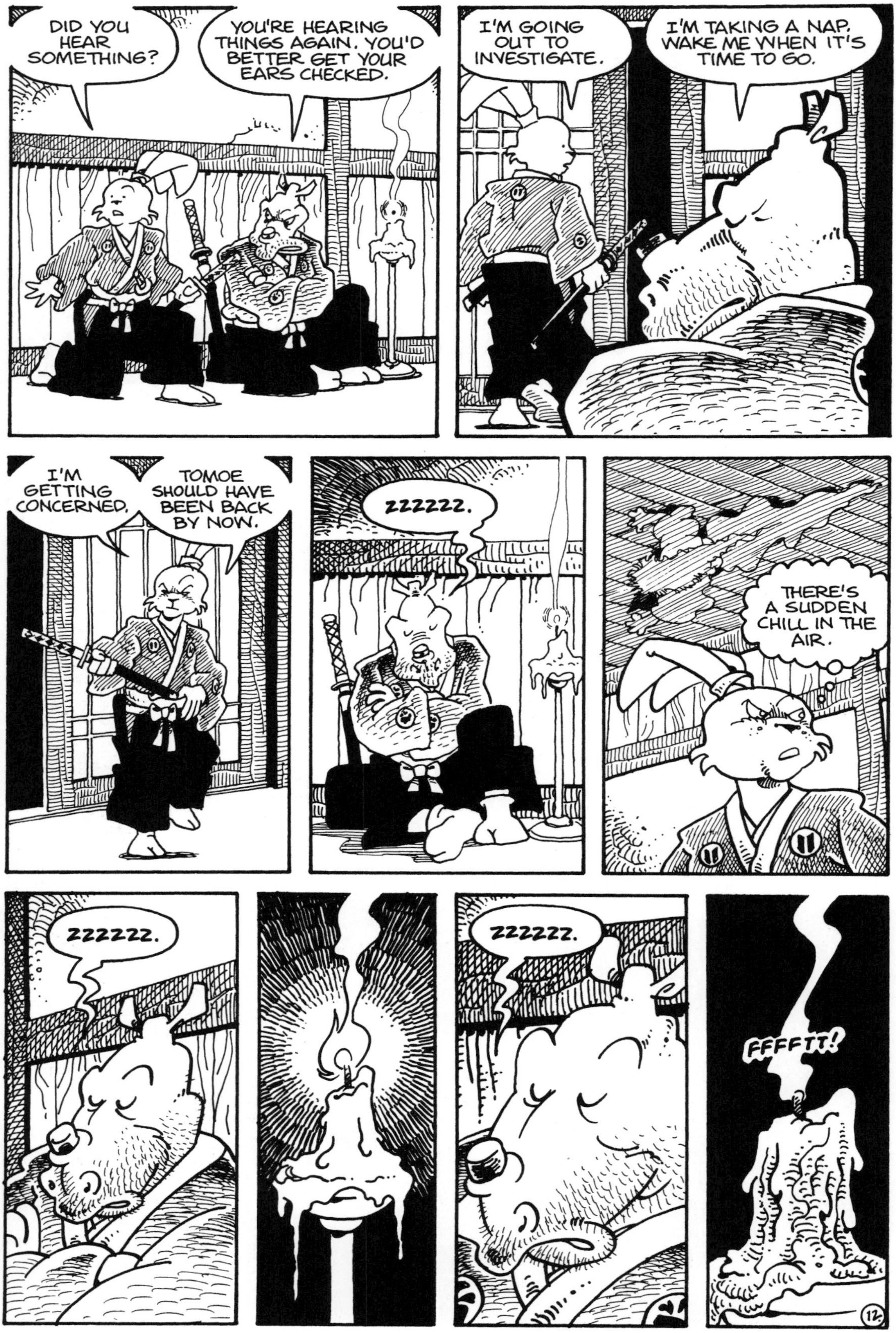
DID YOU HEAR SOMETHING?
YOU'RE HEARING THINGS AGAIN. YOU'D BETTER GET YOUR EARS CHECKED.
I'M GOING OUT TO INVESTIGATE.
I'M TAKING A NAP. WAKE ME WHEN IT'S TIME TO GO.
I'M GETTING CONCERNED.
TOMOE SHOULD HAVE BEEN BACK BY NOW.
ZZZZZZ.
THERE'S A SUDDEN CHILL IN THE AIR.
ZZZZZZ.
ZZZZZZ.
FFFFTT!
12

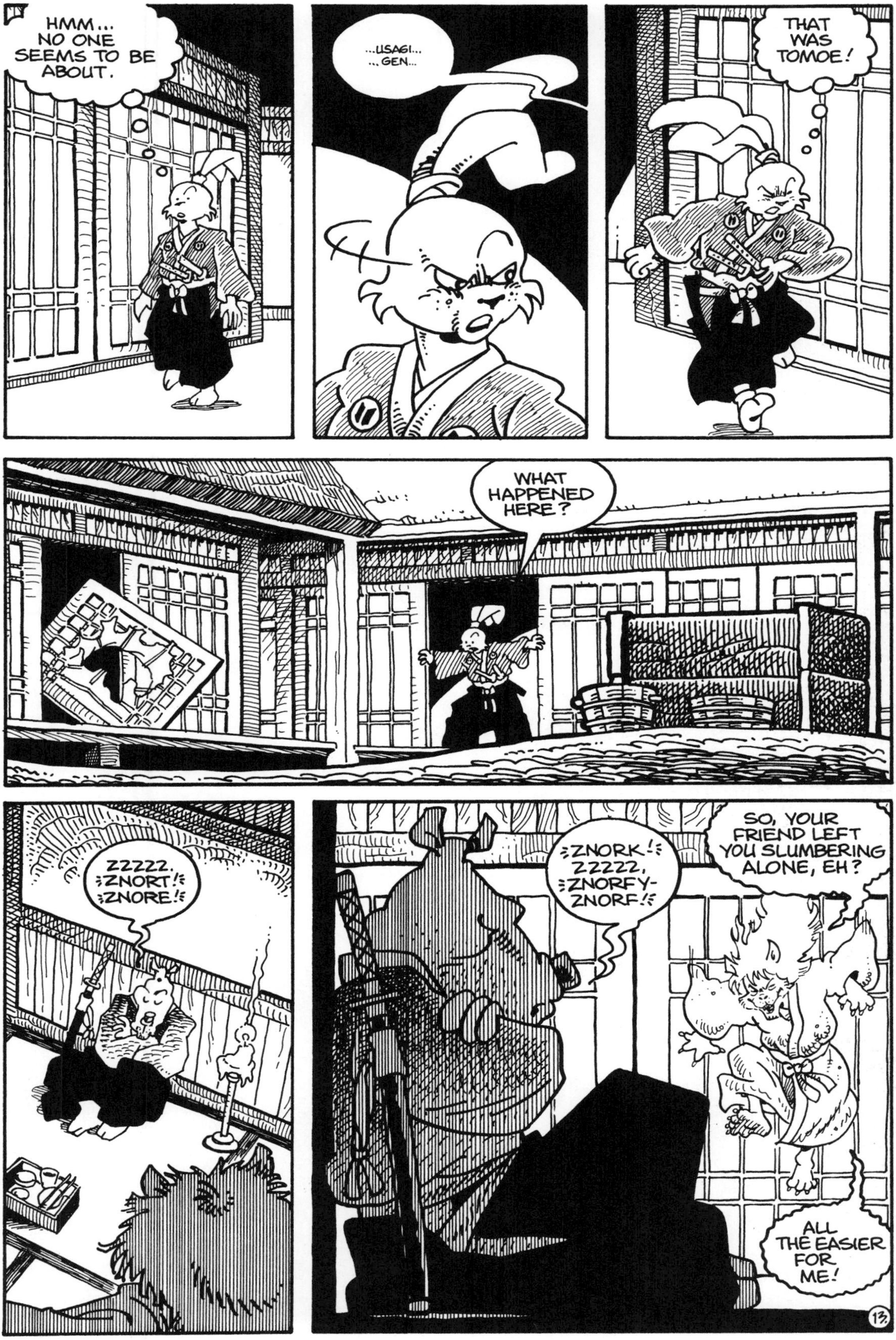
HMM... NO ONE SEEMS TO BE ABOUT.
...USAGI... ...GEN...
THAT WAS TOMOE!
WHAT HAPPENED HERE?
ZZZZZ. ZNORT! ZNORE!
ZNORK! ZZZZZ, ZNORFY-ZNORF!
SO, YOUR FRIEND LEFT YOU SLUMBERING ALONE, EH?
ALL THE EASIER FOR ME!
13

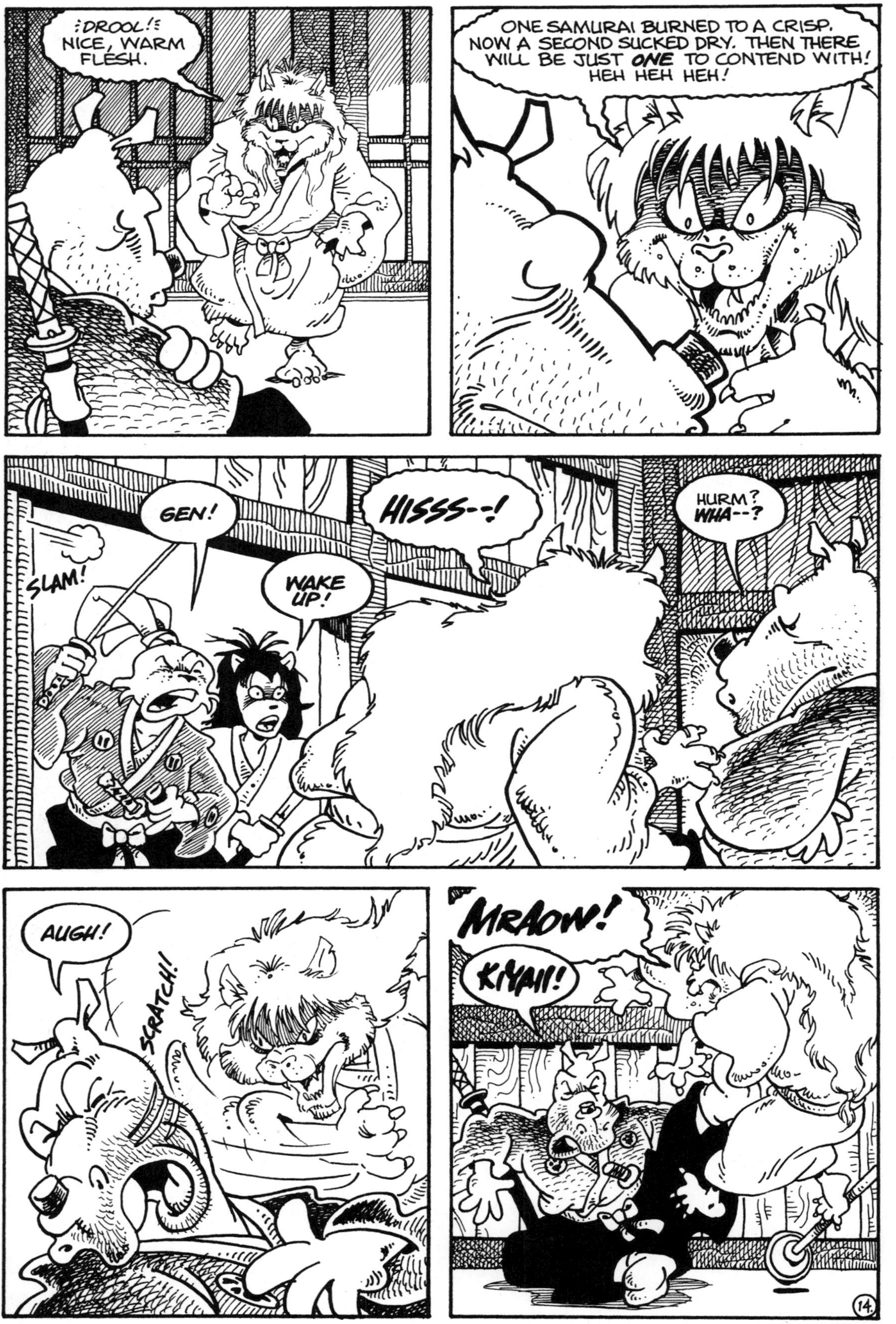

⁝DROOL!⁝ NICE, WARM FLESH.
ONE SAMURAI BURNED TO A CRISP. NOW A SECOND SUCKED DRY. THEN THERE WILL BE JUST ONE TO CONTEND WITH! HEH HEH HEH!
SLAM!
GEN!
WAKE UP!
HISSS--!
HURM? WHA--?
AUGH!
SCRATCH!
MRAOW!
KIYAII!
14.

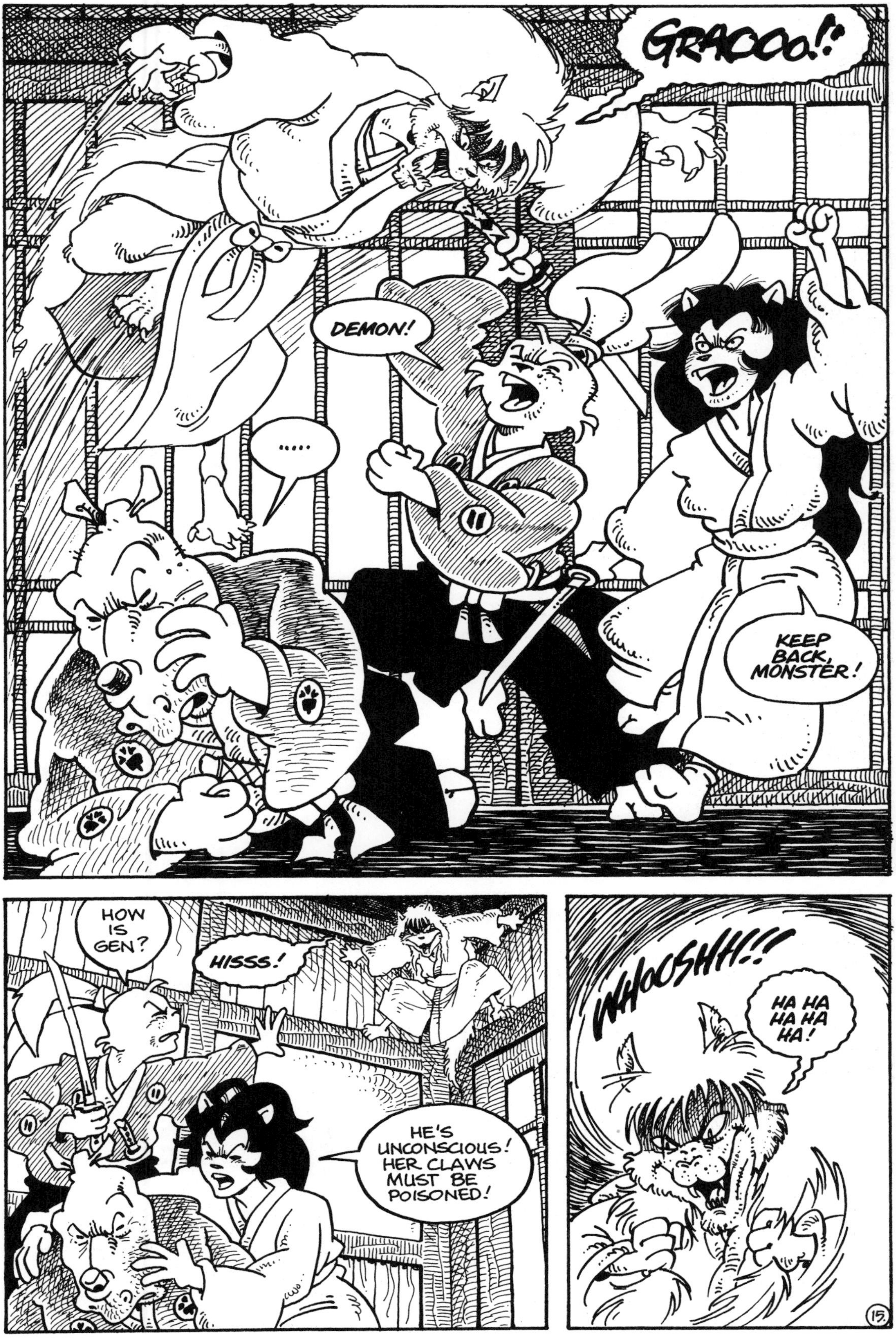
GRAOOO!!
DEMON!
.....
KEEP BACK, MONSTER!
HOW IS GEN?
HISSS!
HE'S UNCONSCIOUS! HER CLAWS MUST BE POISONED!
WHOOSHH!!
HA HA HA HA HA!
15.

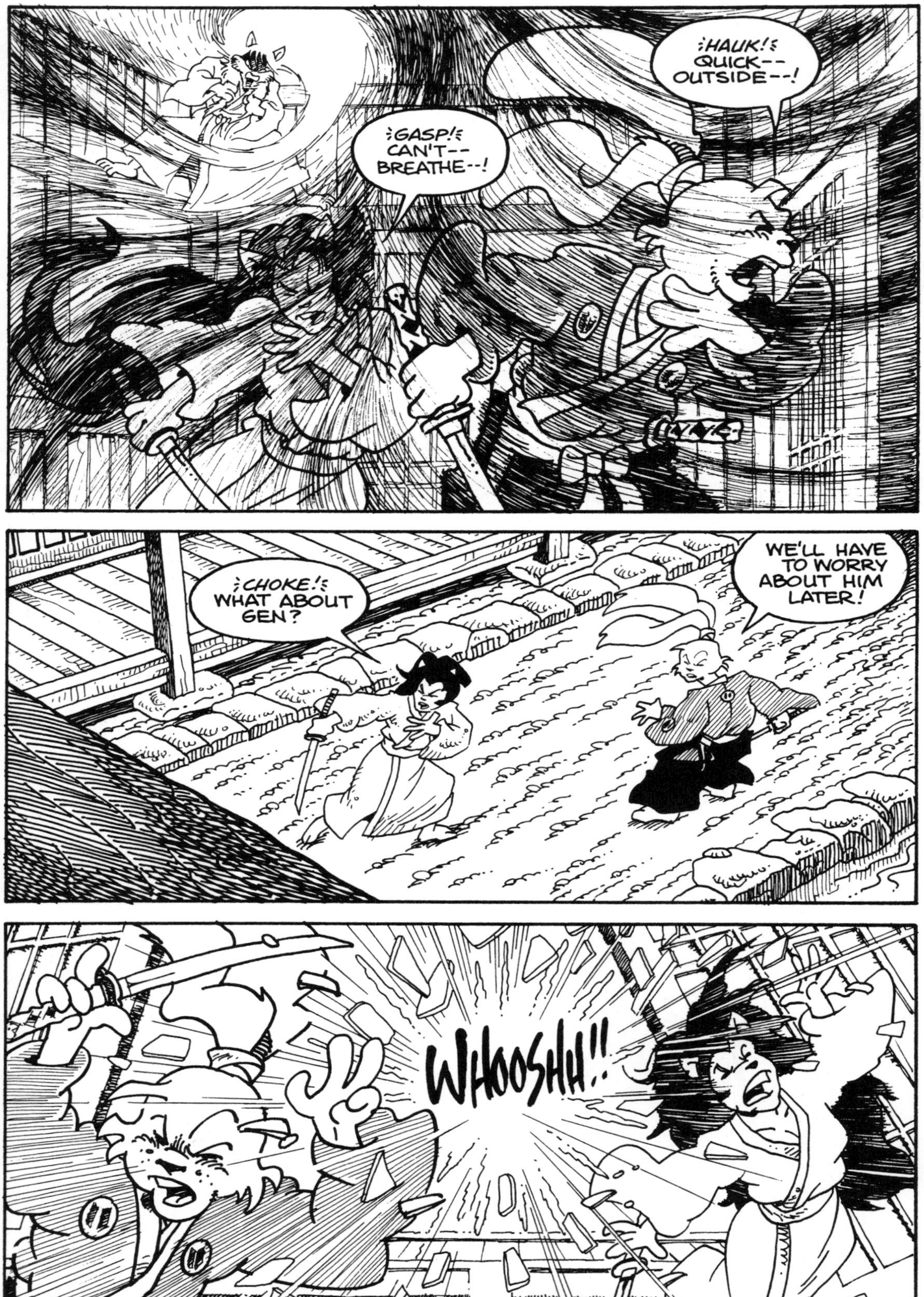
¡GASP!¡ CAN'T-- BREATHE--!
¡HAUK!¡ QUICK-- OUTSIDE--!
¡CHOKE!¡ WHAT ABOUT GEN?
WE'LL HAVE TO WORRY ABOUT HIM LATER!
WHOOSHH!!
16.

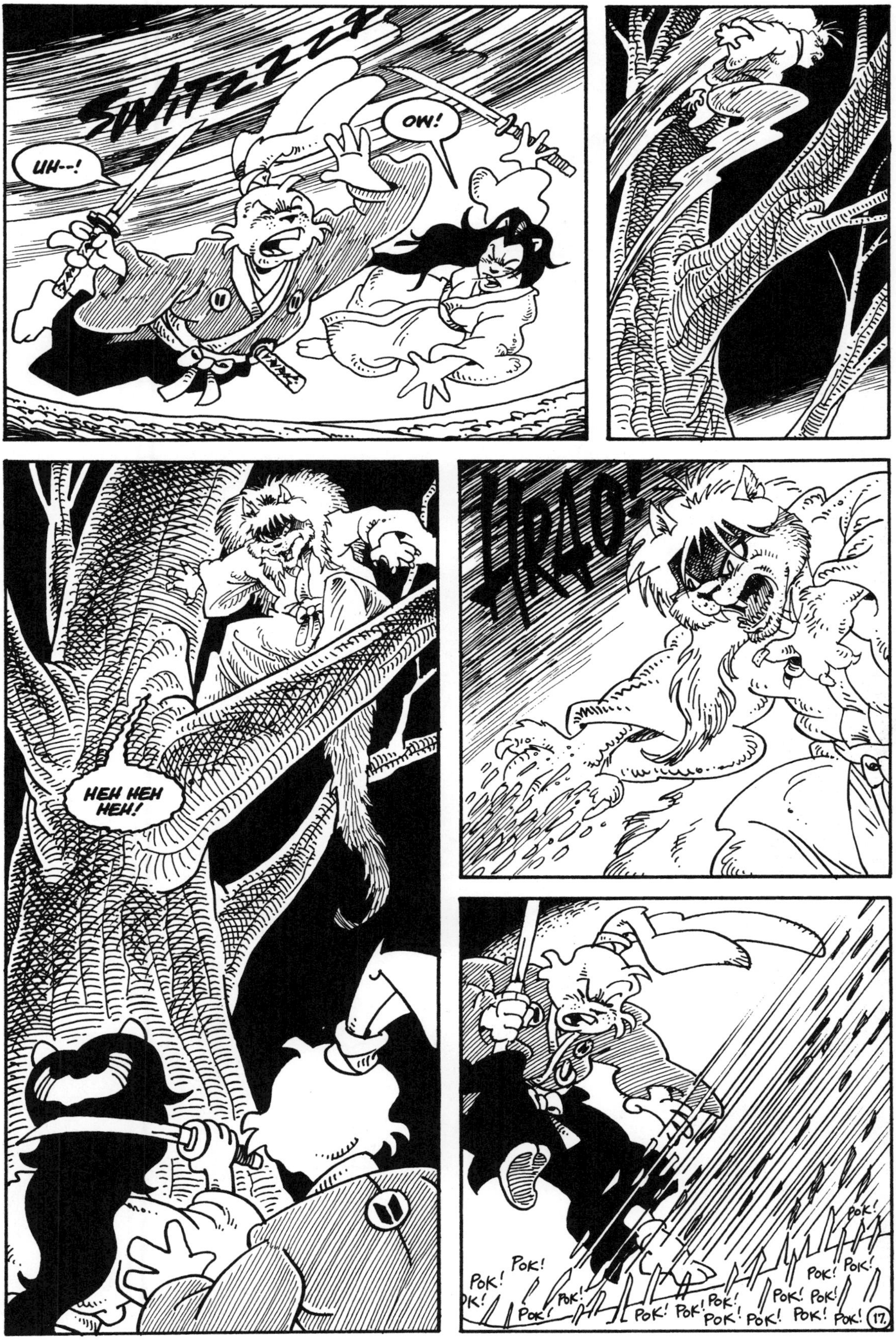
SWITZZZZZ
UH--!
OW!
HEH HEH HEH!
HRAO!
POK! POK! POK! POK! POK! POK! POK! POK! POK! POK! POK! POK! POK! POK! POK! POK!
17.

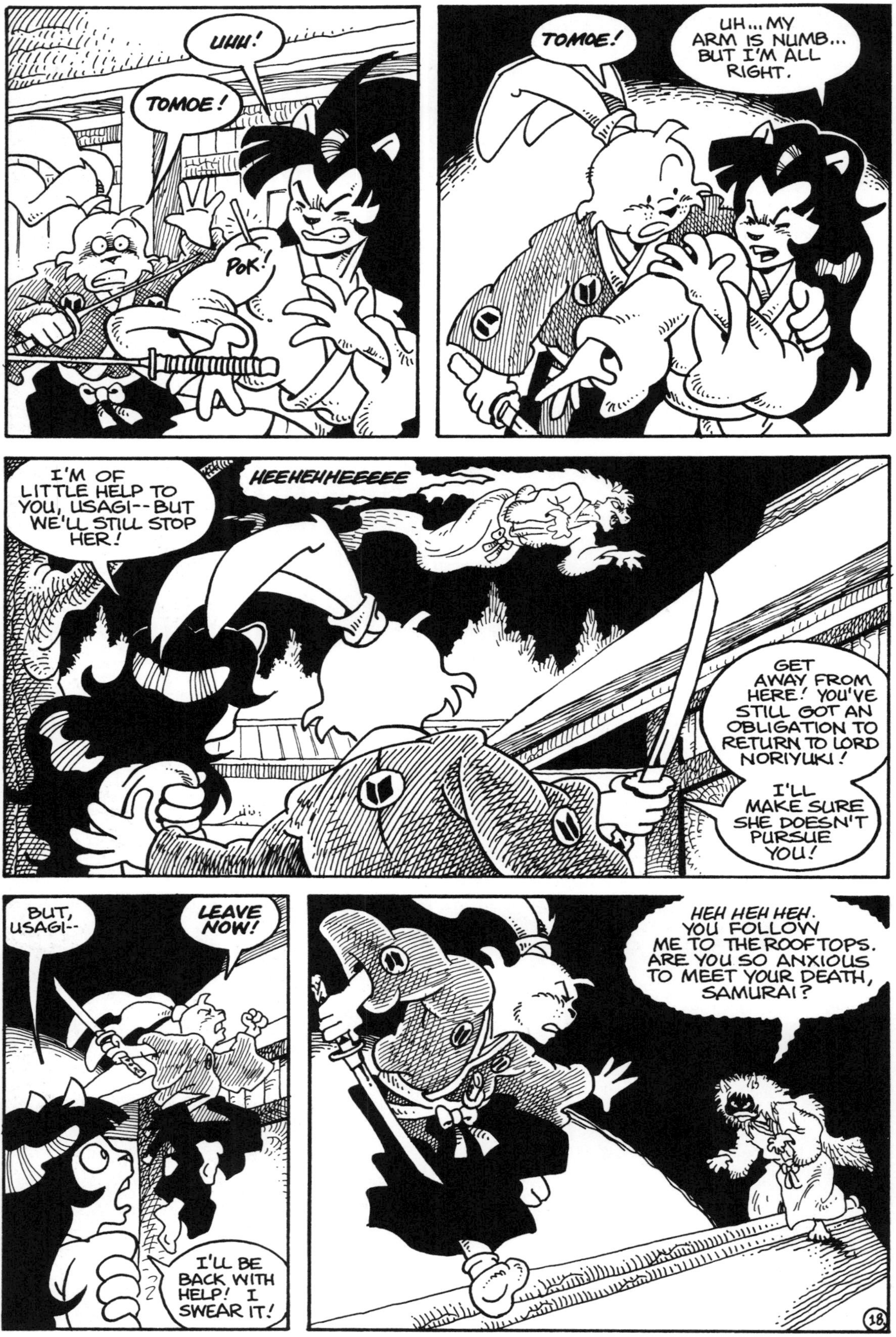
UHH!
TOMOE!
POK!
TOMOE!
UH... MY ARM IS NUMB... BUT I'M ALL RIGHT.
I'M OF LITTLE HELP TO YOU, USAGI-- BUT WE'LL STILL STOP HER!
HEEHEHHEEEEE
GET AWAY FROM HERE! YOU'VE STILL GOT AN OBLIGATION TO RETURN TO LORD NORIYUKI!
I'LL MAKE SURE SHE DOESN'T PURSUE YOU!
BUT, USAGI--
LEAVE NOW!
I'LL BE BACK WITH HELP! I SWEAR IT!
HEH HEH HEH. YOU FOLLOW ME TO THE ROOFTOPS. ARE YOU SO ANXIOUS TO MEET YOUR DEATH, SAMURAI?
18

GAZE INTO MY EYES, SAMURAI...

...MY EYES...

...MY EYES...

.....

NO!

CURSE YOU, SAMURAI!

UHN--!

HRAAH!!

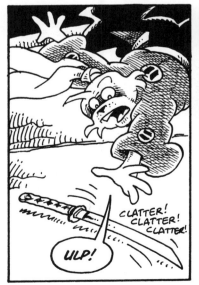

CLATTER! CLATTER! CLATTER!

ULP!

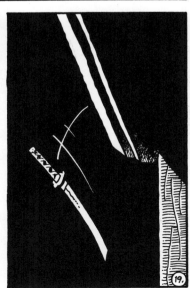

165

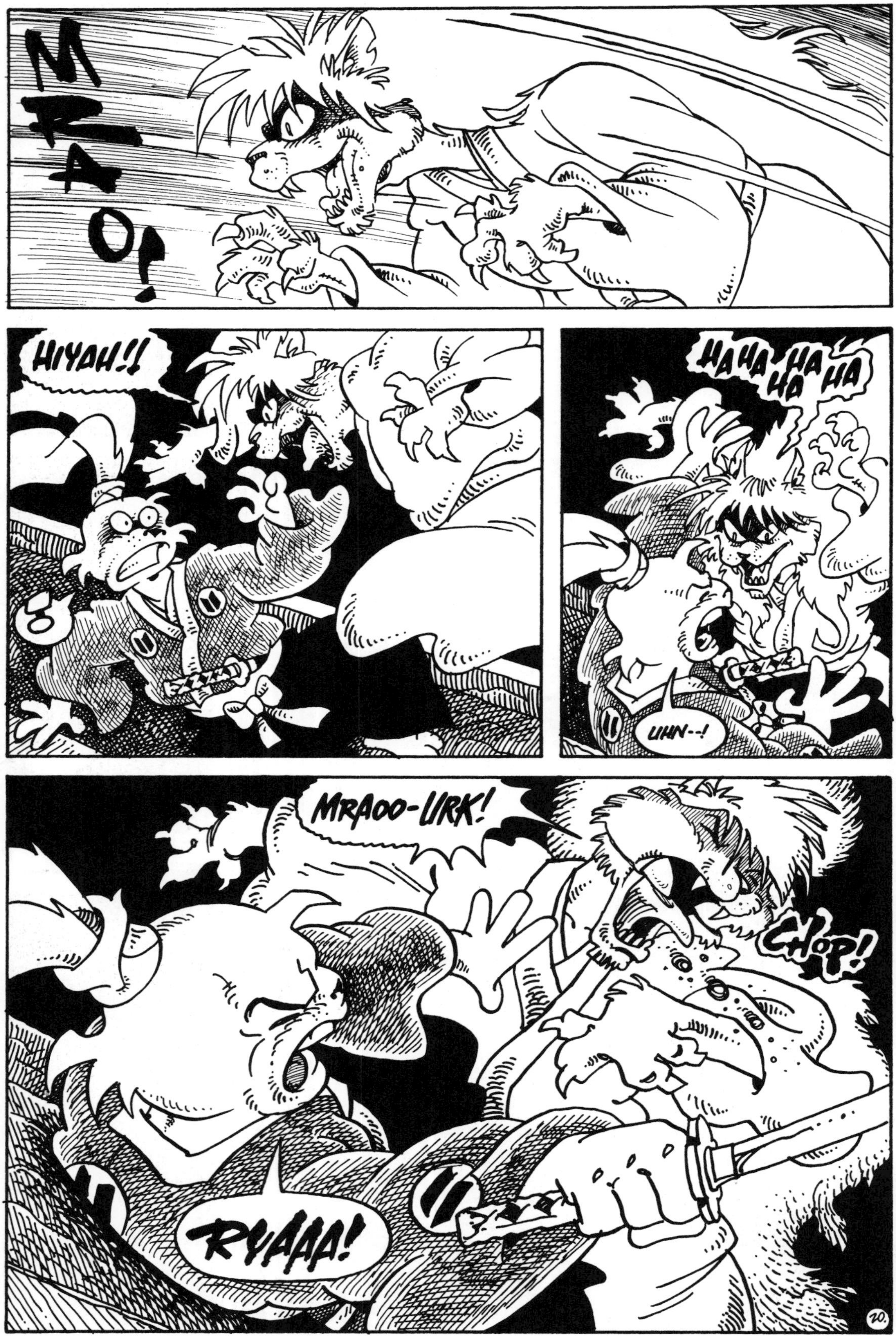
MRAO!
HIYAH!!
HA HA HA HA HA HA
UHN--!
MRAOO-URK!
CHOP!
RYAAA!
20.

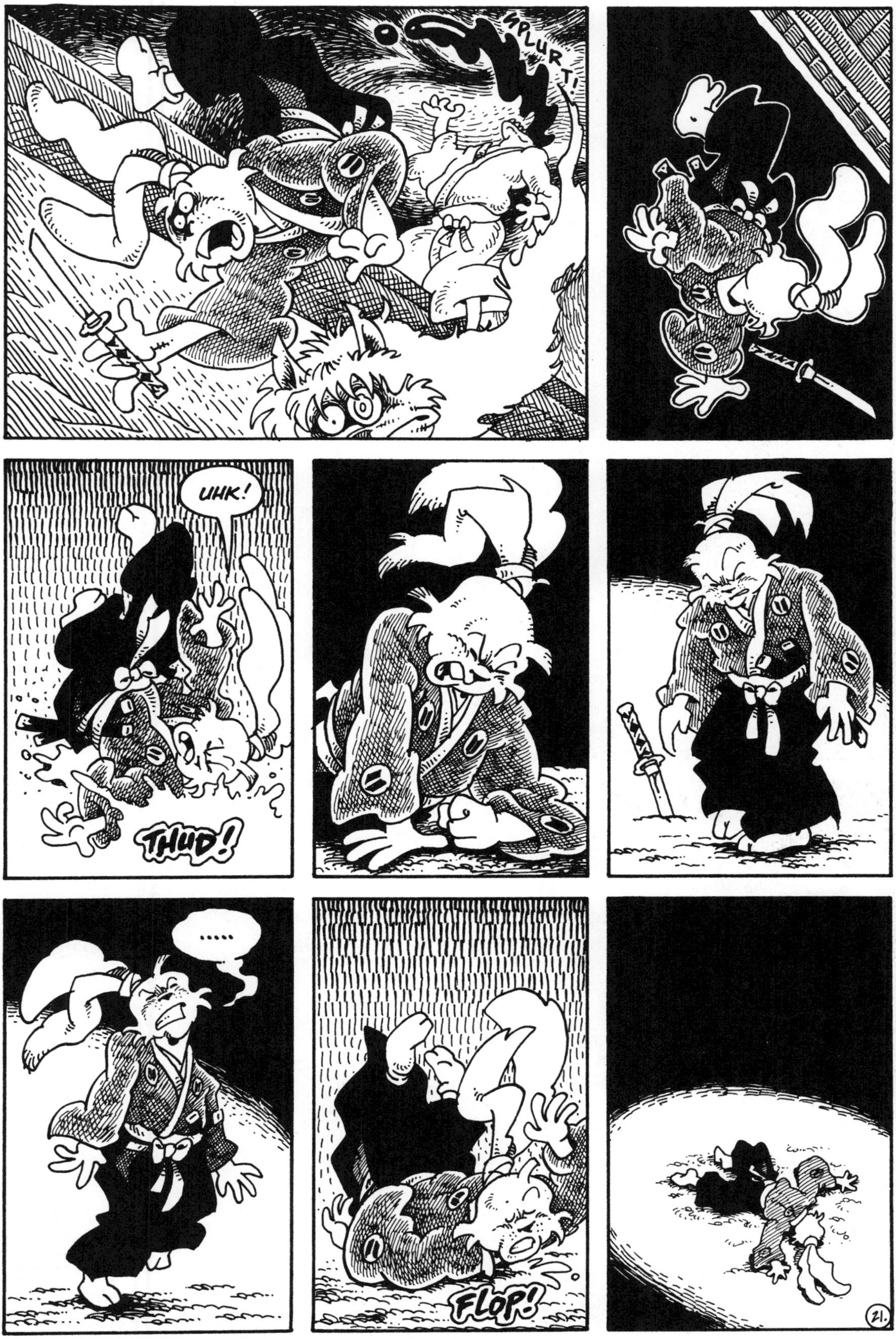
SPLURT!
UHK!
THUD!
......
FLOP!
21.

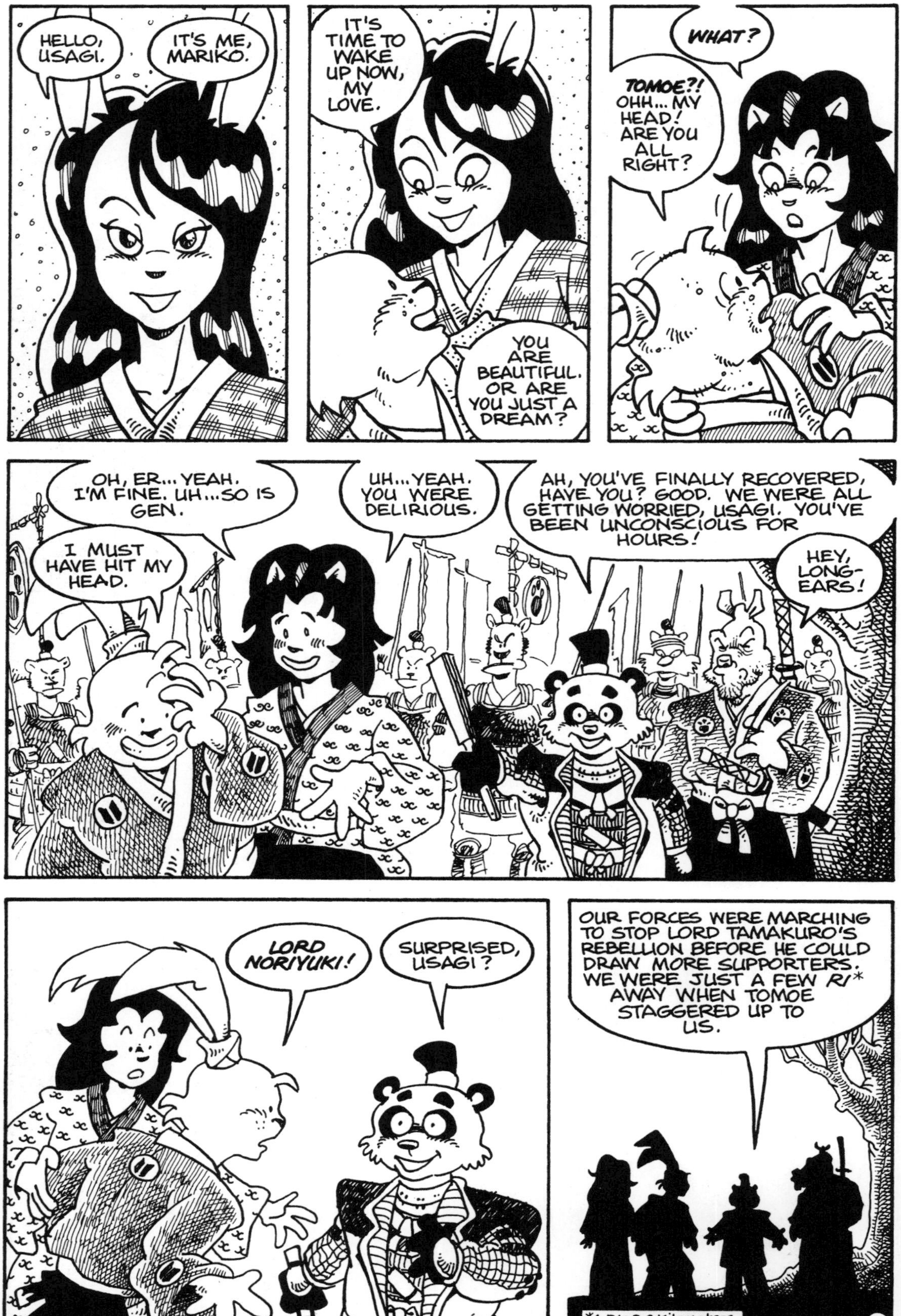
HELLO, USAGI.
IT'S ME, MARIKO.
IT'S TIME TO WAKE UP NOW, MY LOVE.
YOU ARE BEAUTIFUL. OR ARE YOU JUST A DREAM?
WHAT?
TOMOE?! OHH... MY HEAD! ARE YOU ALL RIGHT?
OH, ER... YEAH. I'M FINE. UH... SO IS GEN.
I MUST HAVE HIT MY HEAD.
UH... YEAH. YOU WERE DELIRIOUS.
AH, YOU'VE FINALLY RECOVERED, HAVE YOU? GOOD. WE WERE ALL GETTING WORRIED, USAGI. YOU'VE BEEN UNCONSCIOUS FOR HOURS!
HEY, LONG-EARS!
LORD NORIYUKI!
SURPRISED, USAGI?
OUR FORCES WERE MARCHING TO STOP LORD TAMAKURO'S REBELLION BEFORE HE COULD DRAW MORE SUPPORTERS. WE WERE JUST A FEW RI* AWAY WHEN TOMOE STAGGERED UP TO US.
*1 RI = 3.9 Kilometers
22.

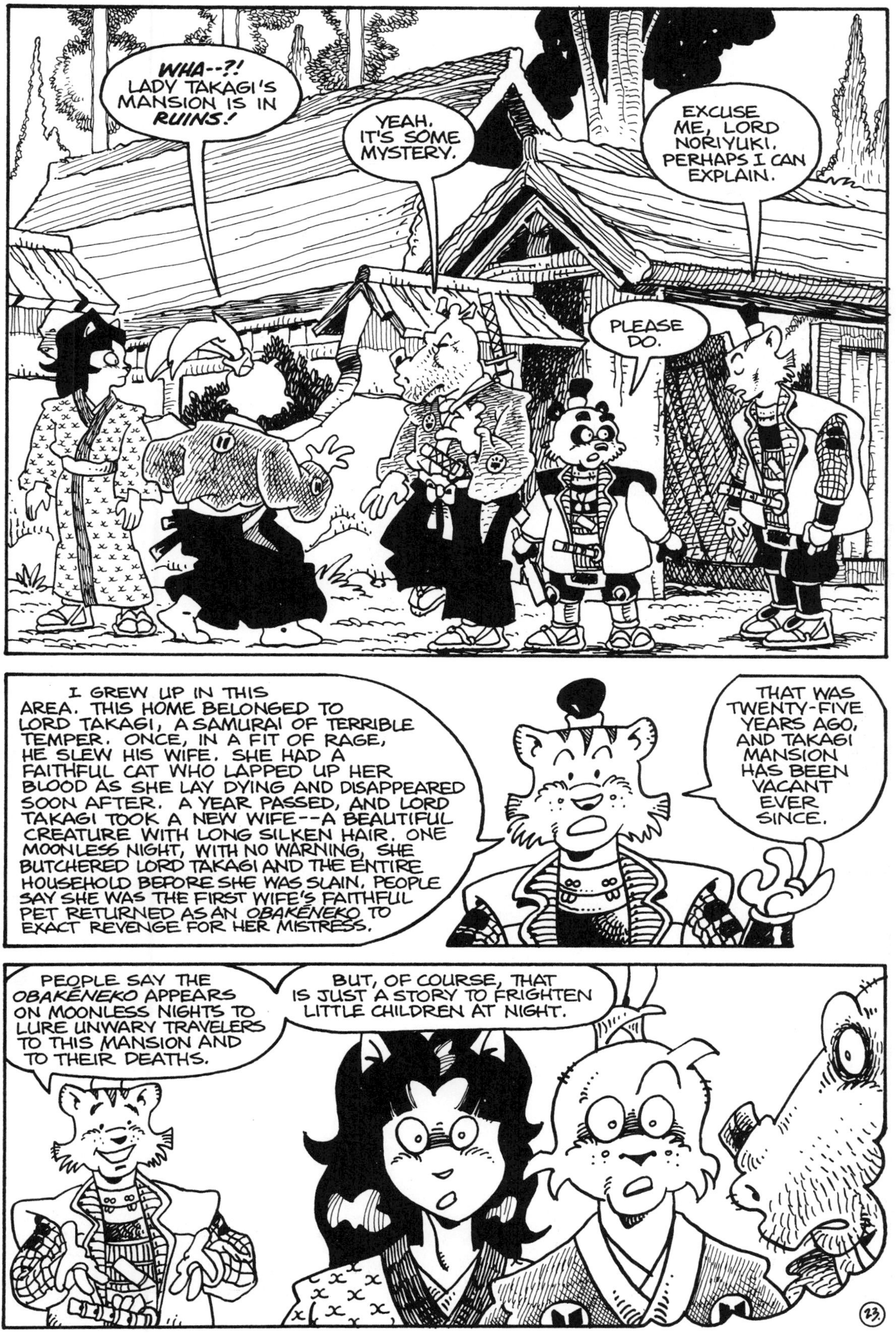

WHA--?! LADY TAKAGI'S MANSION IS IN *RUINS!*
YEAH. IT'S SOME MYSTERY.
EXCUSE ME, LORD NORIYUKI. PERHAPS I CAN EXPLAIN.
PLEASE DO.
I GREW UP IN THIS AREA. THIS HOME BELONGED TO LORD TAKAGI, A SAMURAI OF TERRIBLE TEMPER. ONCE, IN A FIT OF RAGE, HE SLEW HIS WIFE. SHE HAD A FAITHFUL CAT WHO LAPPED UP HER BLOOD AS SHE LAY DYING AND DISAPPEARED SOON AFTER. A YEAR PASSED, AND LORD TAKAGI TOOK A NEW WIFE--A BEAUTIFUL CREATURE WITH LONG SILKEN HAIR. ONE MOONLESS NIGHT, WITH NO WARNING, SHE BUTCHERED LORD TAKAGI AND THE ENTIRE HOUSEHOLD BEFORE SHE WAS SLAIN. PEOPLE SAY SHE WAS THE FIRST WIFE'S FAITHFUL PET RETURNED AS AN *OBAKÉNEKO* TO EXACT REVENGE FOR HER MISTRESS.
THAT WAS TWENTY-FIVE YEARS AGO, AND TAKAGI MANSION HAS BEEN VACANT EVER SINCE.
PEOPLE SAY THE *OBAKÉNEKO* APPEARS ON MOONLESS NIGHTS TO LURE UNWARY TRAVELERS TO THIS MANSION AND TO THEIR DEATHS.
BUT, OF COURSE, THAT IS JUST A STORY TO FRIGHTEN LITTLE CHILDREN AT NIGHT.
23.

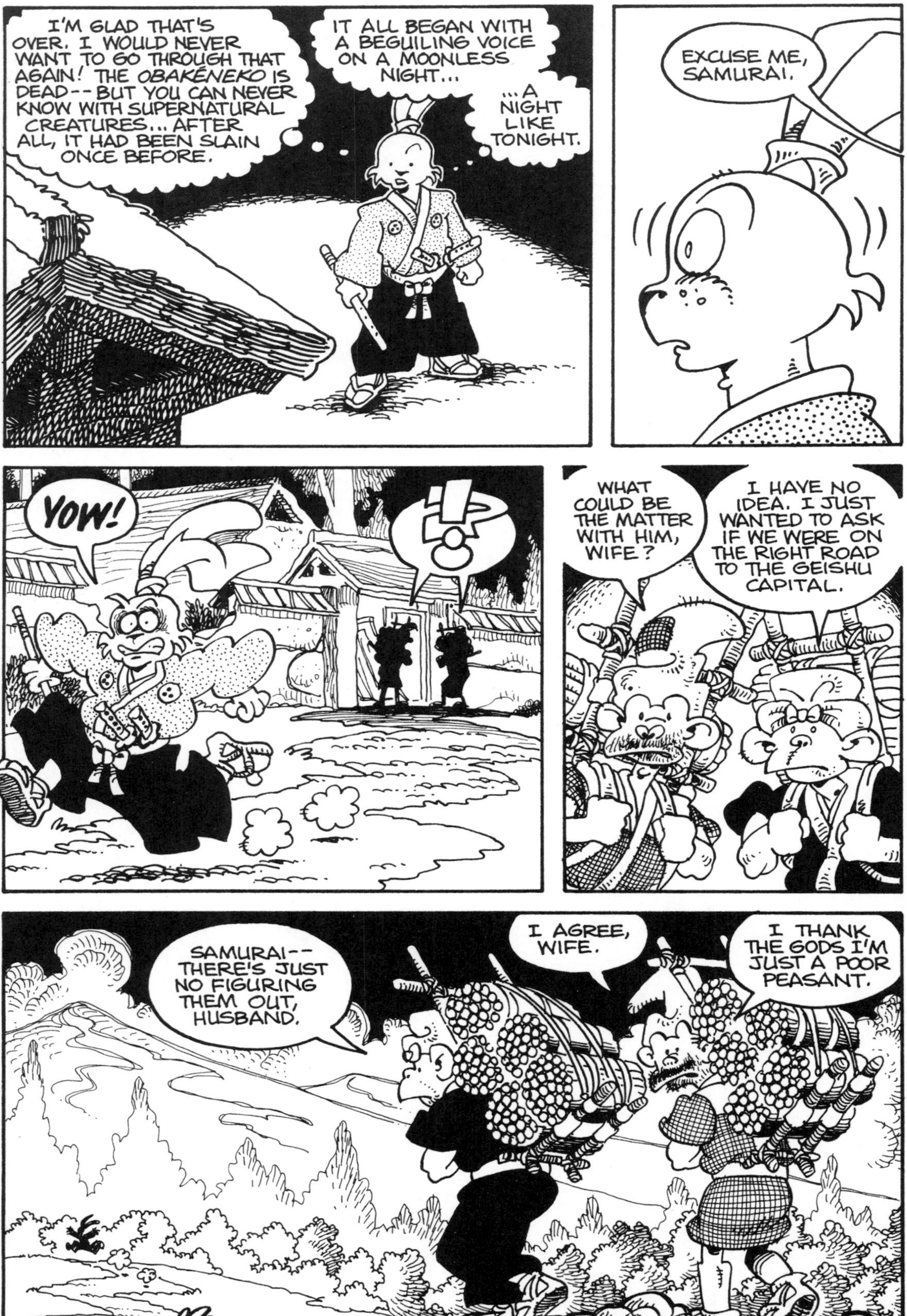
I'M GLAD THAT'S OVER. I WOULD NEVER WANT TO GO THROUGH THAT AGAIN! THE *OBAKÉNEKO* IS DEAD-- BUT YOU CAN NEVER KNOW WITH SUPERNATURAL CREATURES... AFTER ALL, IT HAD BEEN SLAIN ONCE BEFORE.
IT ALL BEGAN WITH A BEGUILING VOICE ON A MOONLESS NIGHT...
...A NIGHT LIKE TONIGHT.
EXCUSE ME, SAMURAI.
YOW!
!?
WHAT COULD BE THE MATTER WITH HIM, WIFE?
I HAVE NO IDEA. I JUST WANTED TO ASK IF WE WERE ON THE RIGHT ROAD TO THE GEISHU CAPITAL.
SAMURAI-- THERE'S JUST NO FIGURING THEM OUT, HUSBAND.
I AGREE, WIFE.
I THANK THE GODS I'M JUST A POOR PEASANT.
END

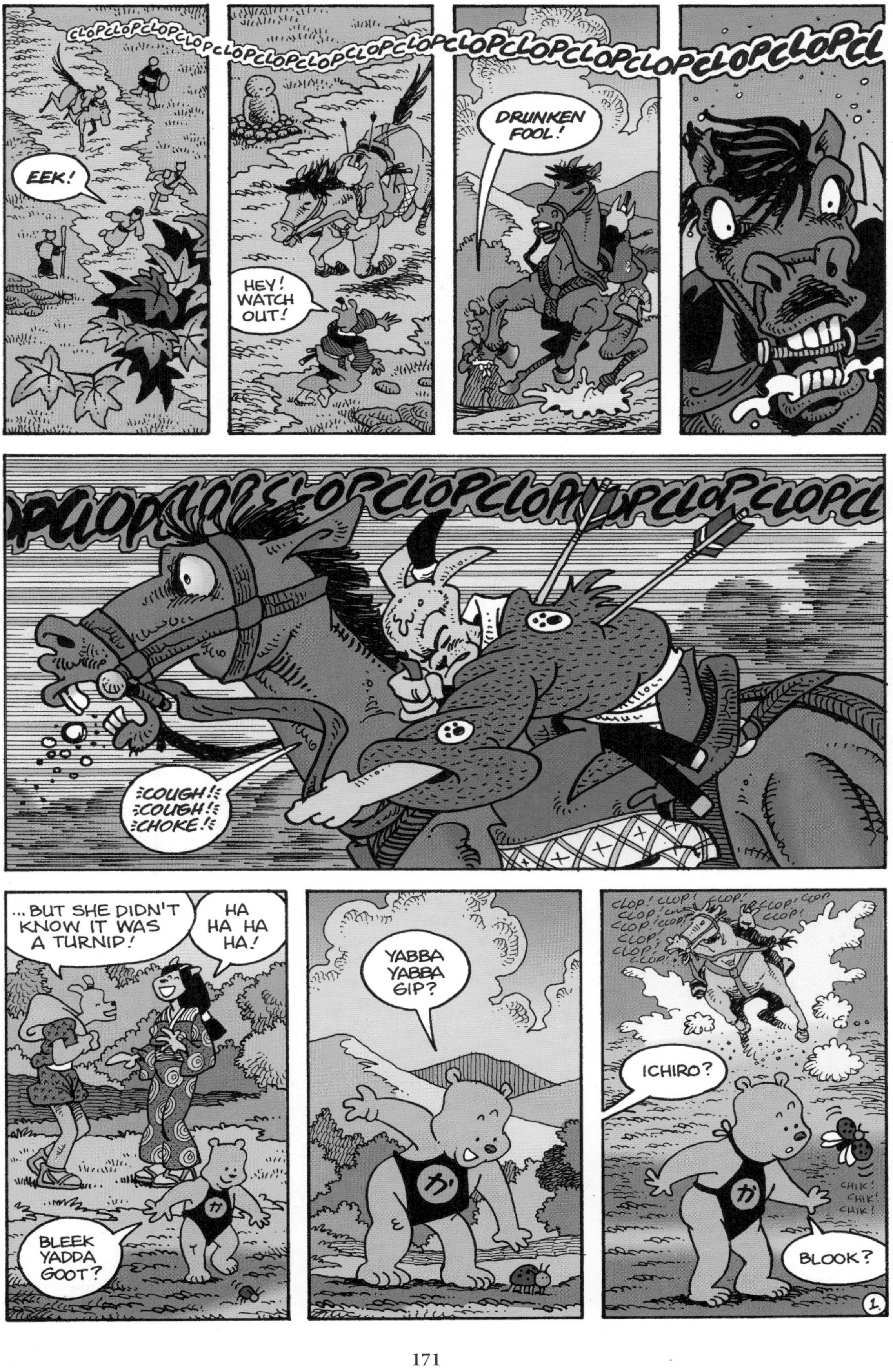
CLOPCLOPCLOPCLOPCLOPCLOPCLOPCLOPCLOPCLOPCLOPCLOPCLOPCL
EEK!
HEY! WATCH OUT!
DRUNKEN FOOL!
COUGH! COUGH! CHOKE!
...BUT SHE DIDN'T KNOW IT WAS A TURNIP!
HA HA HA HA!
BLEEK YADDA GOOT?
YABBA YABBA GIP?
CLOP! CLOP! CLOP! CLOP! CLOP! CLOP! CLOP! CLOP! CLOP!
ICHIRO?
CHIK! CHIK! CHIK!
BLOOK?
1.

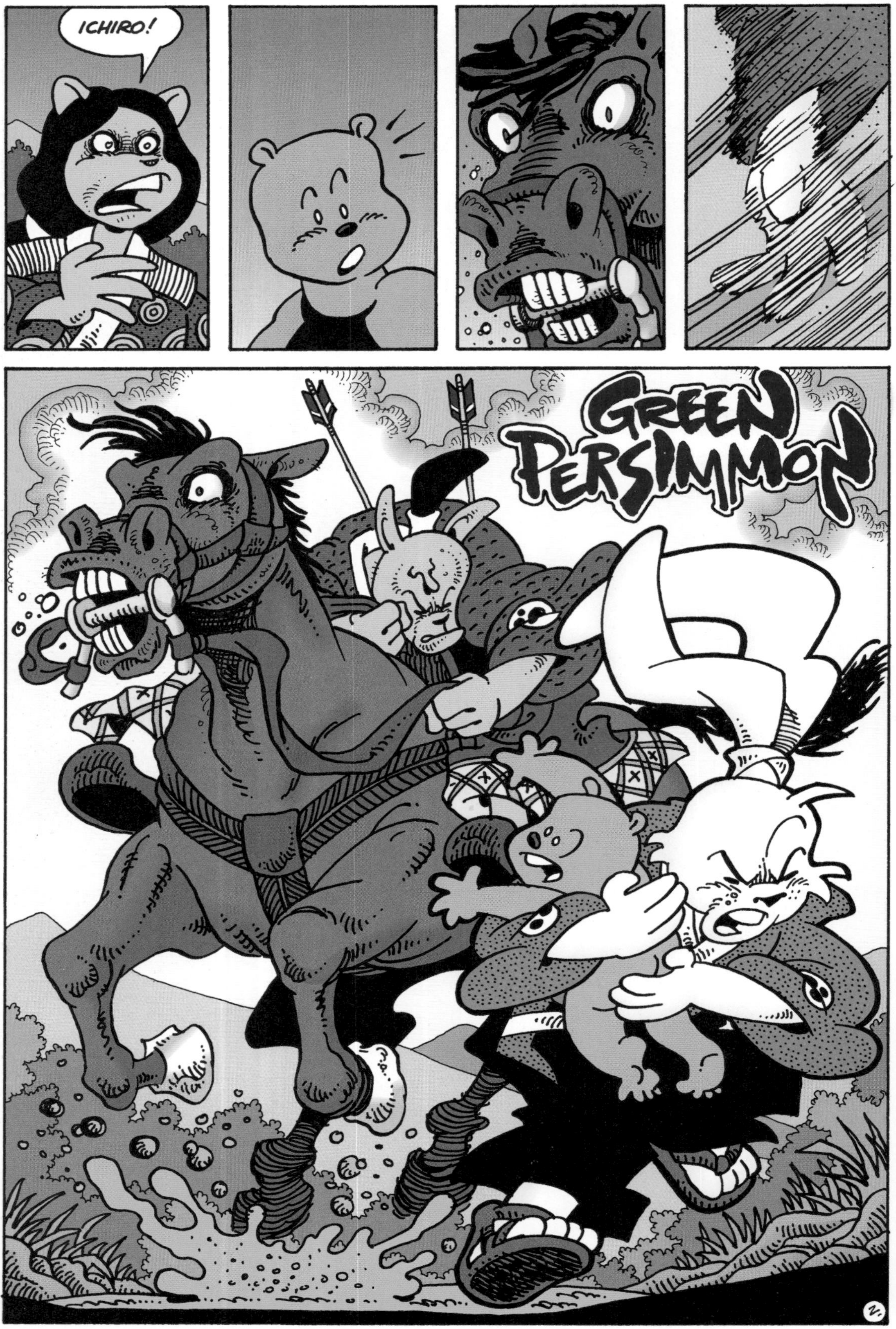
ICHIRO!
GREEN PERSIMMON
2.

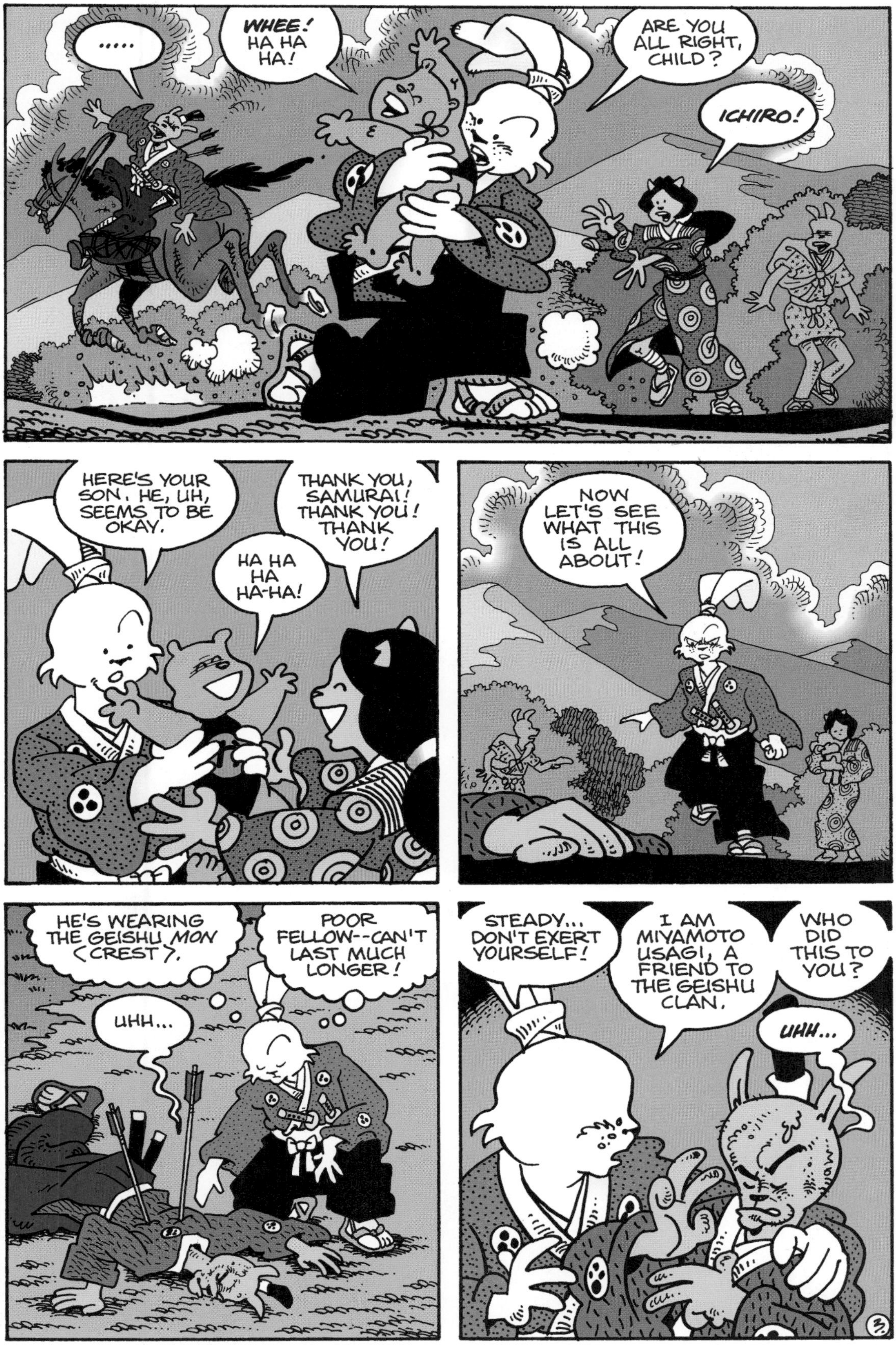

.....
WHEE! HA HA HA!
ARE YOU ALL RIGHT, CHILD?
ICHIRO!
HERE'S YOUR SON. HE, UH, SEEMS TO BE OKAY.
HA HA HA HA-HA!
THANK YOU, SAMURAI! THANK YOU! THANK YOU!
NOW LET'S SEE WHAT THIS IS ALL ABOUT!
HE'S WEARING THE GEISHU MON (CREST).
POOR FELLOW--CAN'T LAST MUCH LONGER!
UHH...
STEADY... DON'T EXERT YOURSELF!
I AM MIYAMOTO USAGI, A FRIEND TO THE GEISHU CLAN.
WHO DID THIS TO YOU?
UHH...
3

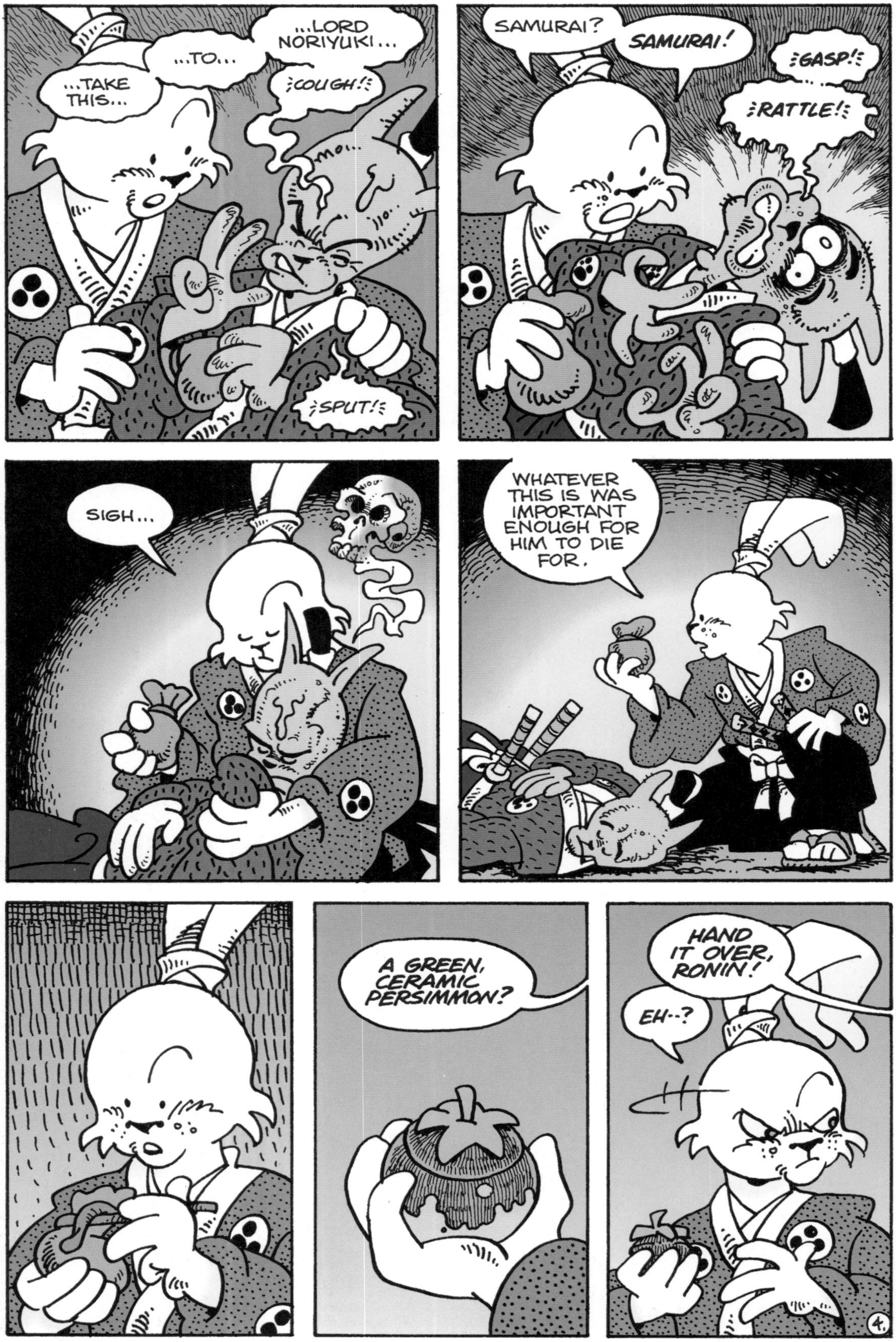
...TAKE THIS...
...TO...
...LORD NORIYUKI...
COUGH!
SPUT!
SAMURAI?
SAMURAI!
GASP!
RATTLE!
SIGH...
WHATEVER THIS IS WAS IMPORTANT ENOUGH FOR HIM TO DIE FOR.
A GREEN, CERAMIC PERSIMMON?
HAND IT OVER, RONIN!
EH--?
4.

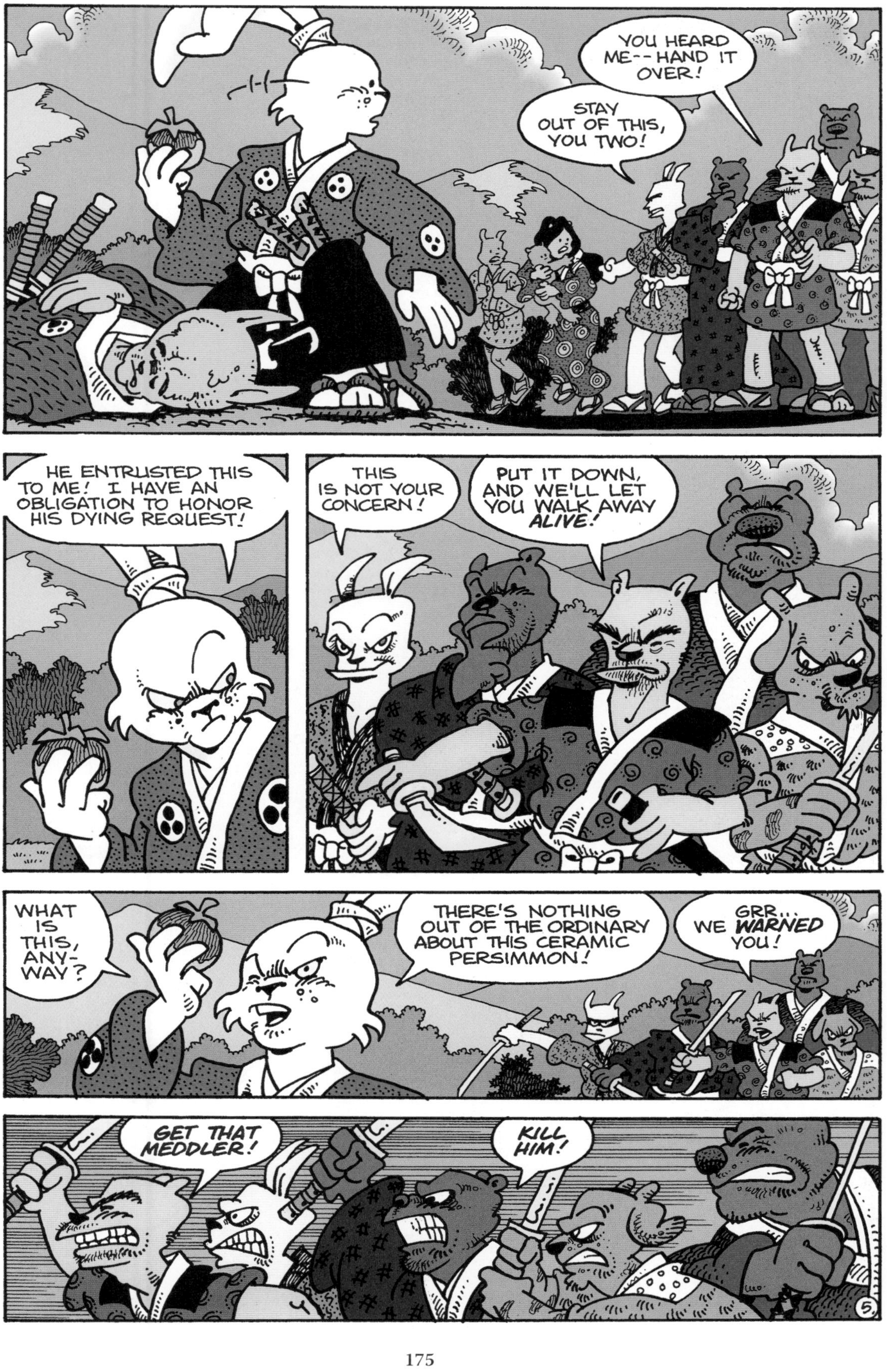
STAY OUT OF THIS, YOU TWO!
YOU HEARD ME--HAND IT OVER!
HE ENTRUSTED THIS TO ME! I HAVE AN OBLIGATION TO HONOR HIS DYING REQUEST!
THIS IS NOT YOUR CONCERN!
PUT IT DOWN, AND WE'LL LET YOU WALK AWAY ALIVE!
WHAT IS THIS, ANYWAY?
THERE'S NOTHING OUT OF THE ORDINARY ABOUT THIS CERAMIC PERSIMMON!
GRR... WE WARNED YOU!
GET THAT MEDDLER!
KILL HIM!
5

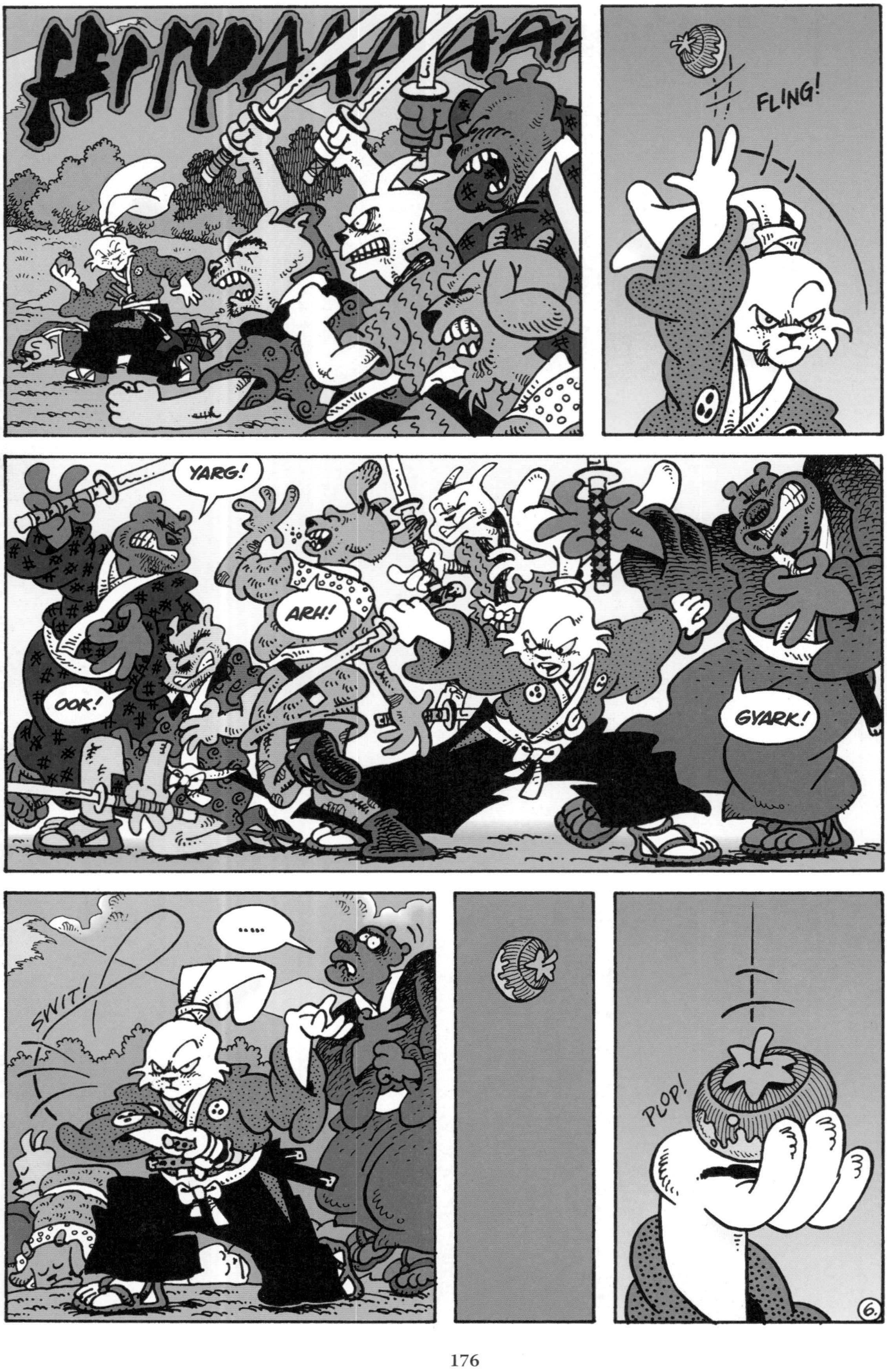
HIIYAAAAA
FLING!
YARG!
ARH!
OOK!
GYARK!
SWIT!
.....
PLOP!
6.

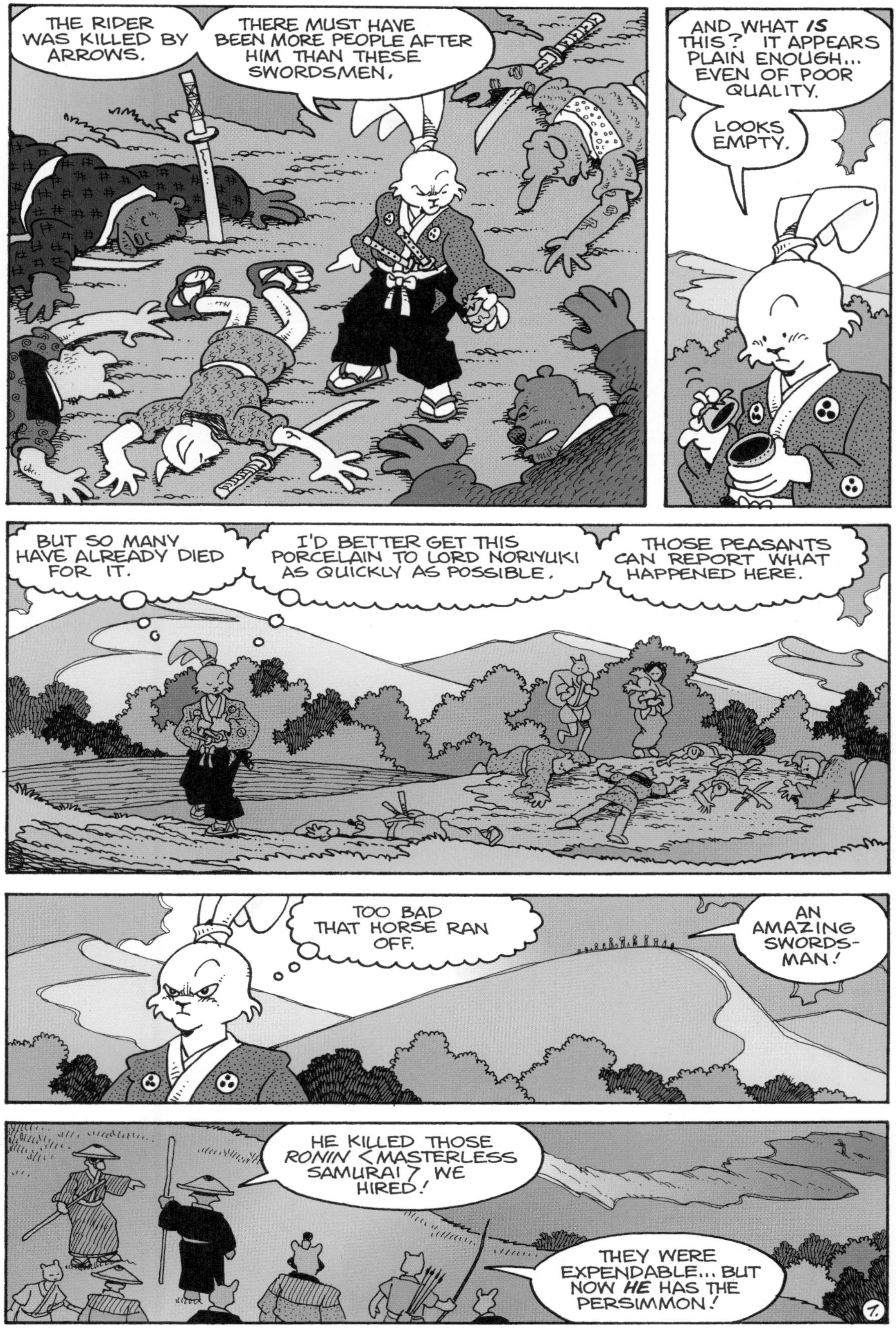
THE RIDER WAS KILLED BY ARROWS.
THERE MUST HAVE BEEN MORE PEOPLE AFTER HIM THAN THESE SWORDSMEN.
AND WHAT *IS* THIS? IT APPEARS PLAIN ENOUGH... EVEN OF POOR QUALITY.
LOOKS EMPTY.
BUT SO MANY HAVE ALREADY DIED FOR IT.
I'D BETTER GET THIS PORCELAIN TO LORD NORIYUKI AS QUICKLY AS POSSIBLE.
THOSE PEASANTS CAN REPORT WHAT HAPPENED HERE.
TOO BAD THAT HORSE RAN OFF.
AN AMAZING SWORDS-MAN!
HE KILLED THOSE *RONIN* <MASTERLESS SAMURAI> WE HIRED!
THEY WERE EXPENDABLE... BUT NOW *HE* HAS THE PERSIMMON!
7.

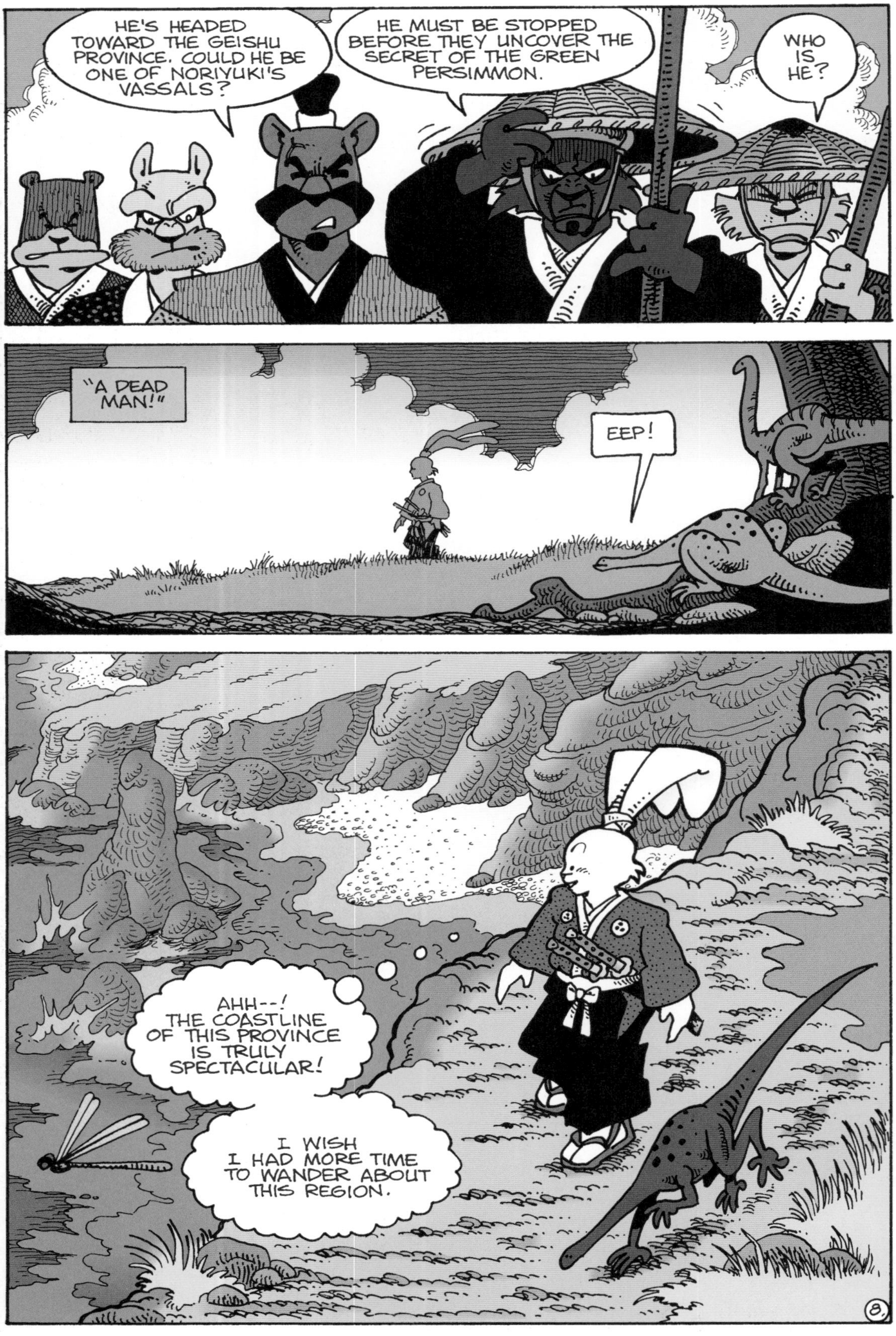
HE'S HEADED TOWARD THE GEISHU PROVINCE. COULD HE BE ONE OF NORIYUKI'S VASSALS?
HE MUST BE STOPPED BEFORE THEY UNCOVER THE SECRET OF THE GREEN PERSIMMON.
WHO IS HE?
"A DEAD MAN!"
EEP!
AHH--! THE COASTLINE OF THIS PROVINCE IS TRULY SPECTACULAR!
I WISH I HAD MORE TIME TO WANDER ABOUT THIS REGION.
8.

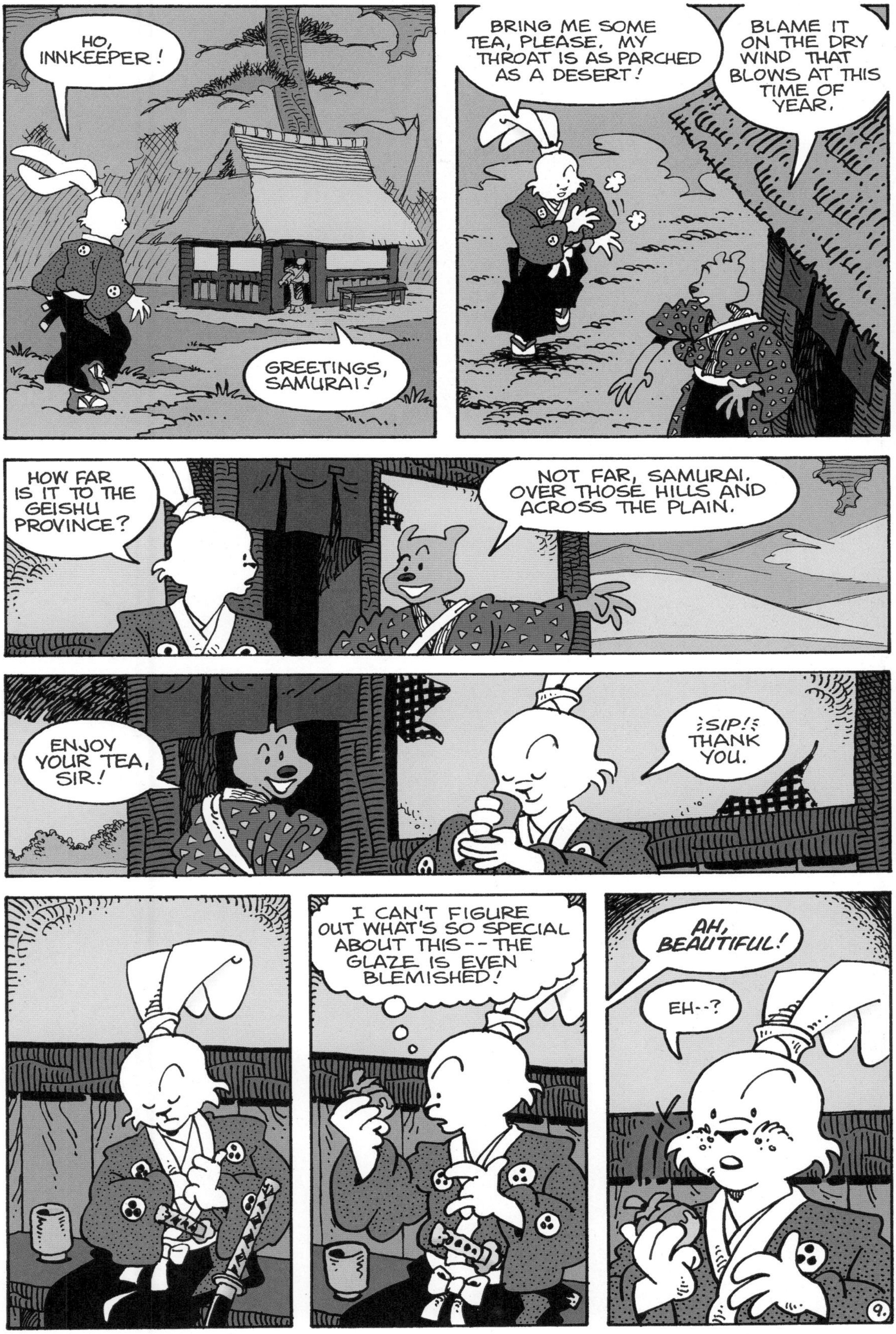
HO, INNKEEPER!
GREETINGS, SAMURAI!
BRING ME SOME TEA, PLEASE. MY THROAT IS AS PARCHED AS A DESERT!
BLAME IT ON THE DRY WIND THAT BLOWS AT THIS TIME OF YEAR.
HOW FAR IS IT TO THE GEISHU PROVINCE?
NOT FAR, SAMURAI. OVER THOSE HILLS AND ACROSS THE PLAIN.
ENJOY YOUR TEA, SIR!
SIP! THANK YOU.
I CAN'T FIGURE OUT WHAT'S SO SPECIAL ABOUT THIS-- THE GLAZE IS EVEN BLEMISHED!
AH, BEAUTIFUL!
EH--?
9.

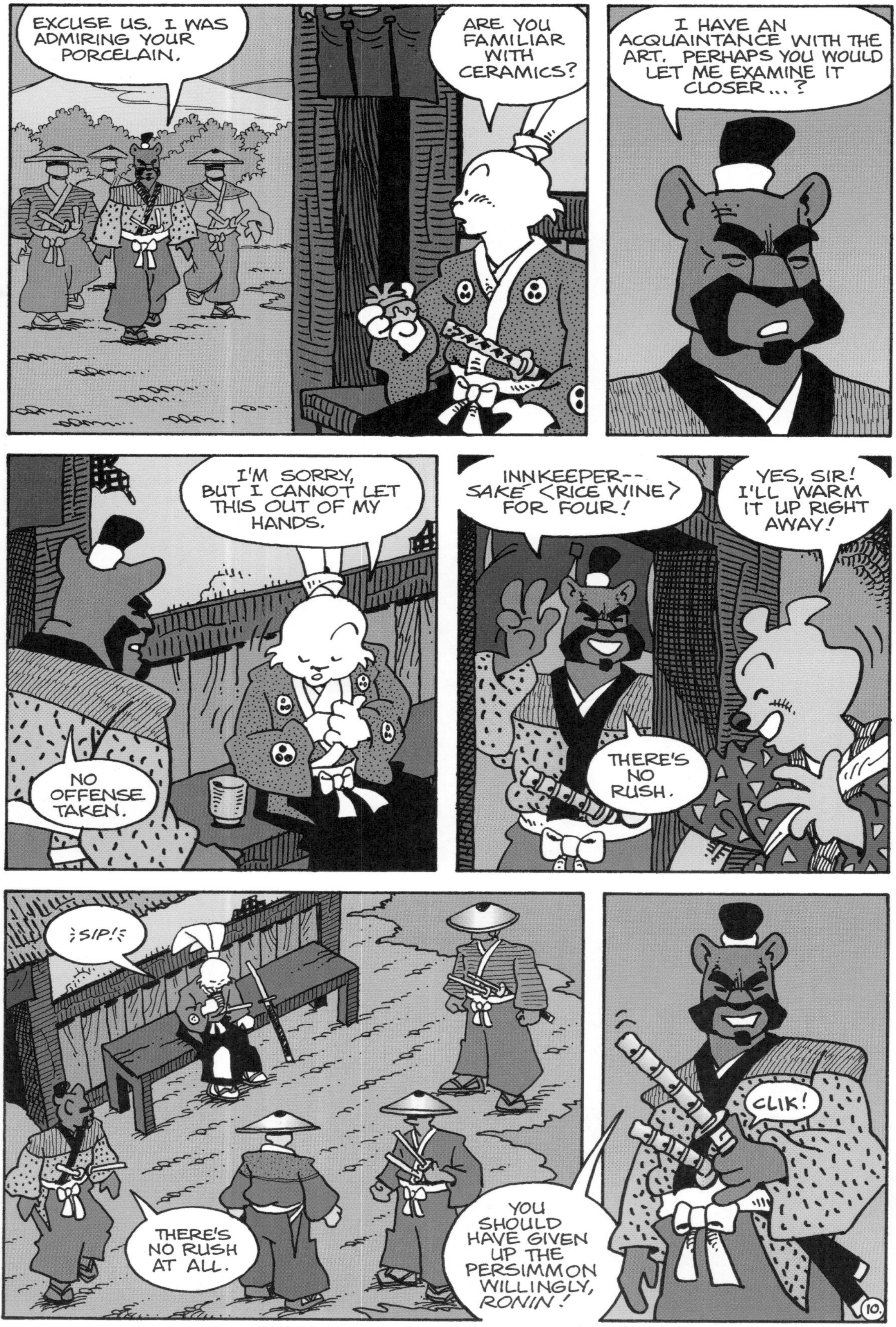
EXCUSE US. I WAS ADMIRING YOUR PORCELAIN.
ARE YOU FAMILIAR WITH CERAMICS?
I HAVE AN ACQUAINTANCE WITH THE ART. PERHAPS YOU WOULD LET ME EXAMINE IT CLOSER...?
I'M SORRY, BUT I CANNOT LET THIS OUT OF MY HANDS.
NO OFFENSE TAKEN.
INNKEEPER-- SAKÉ <RICE WINE> FOR FOUR!
YES, SIR! I'LL WARM IT UP RIGHT AWAY!
THERE'S NO RUSH.
SIP!
THERE'S NO RUSH AT ALL.
YOU SHOULD HAVE GIVEN UP THE PERSIMMON WILLINGLY, RONIN!
CLIK!
10.

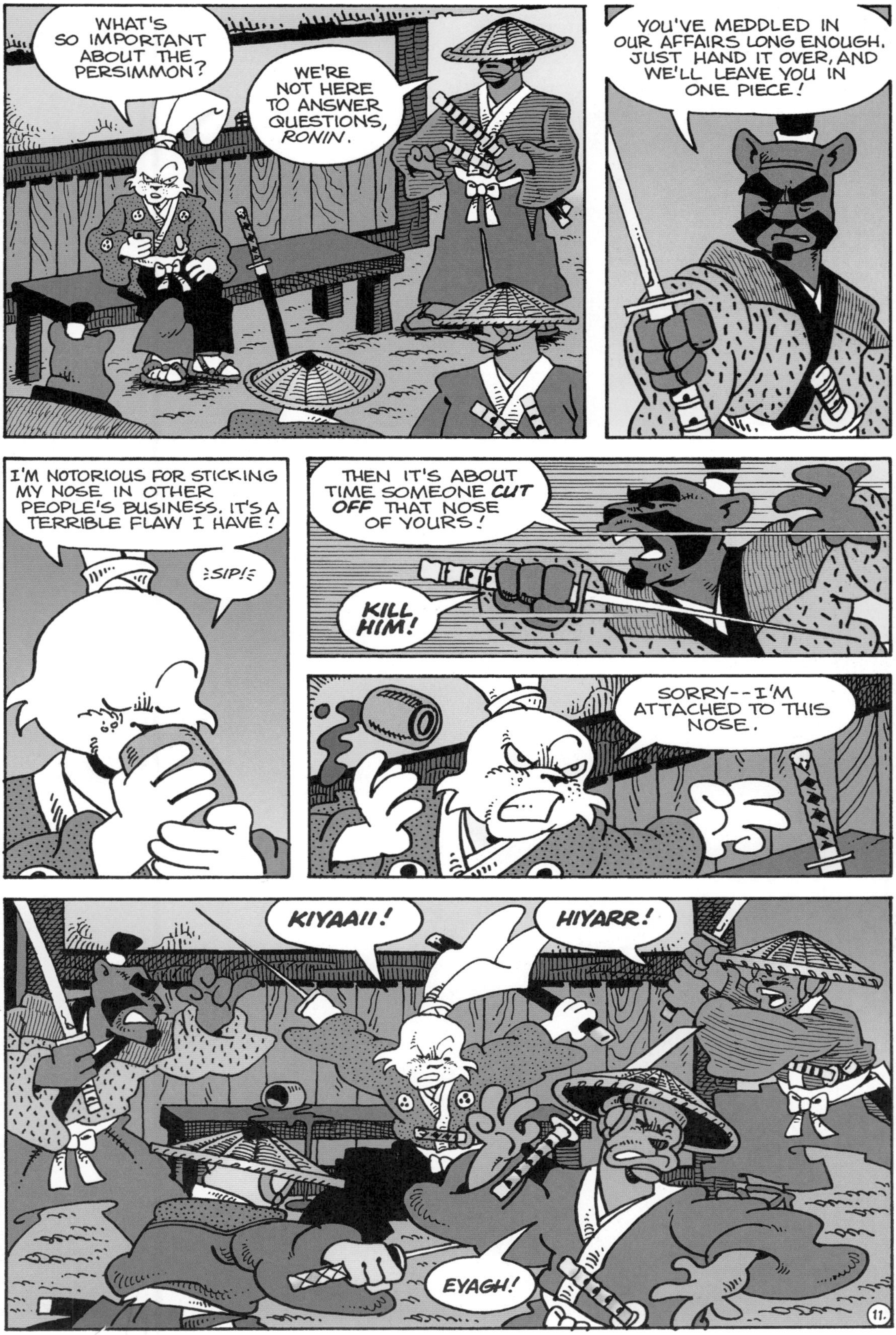
WHAT'S SO IMPORTANT ABOUT THE PERSIMMON?
WE'RE NOT HERE TO ANSWER QUESTIONS, RONIN.
YOU'VE MEDDLED IN OUR AFFAIRS LONG ENOUGH. JUST HAND IT OVER, AND WE'LL LEAVE YOU IN ONE PIECE!
I'M NOTORIOUS FOR STICKING MY NOSE IN OTHER PEOPLE'S BUSINESS. IT'S A TERRIBLE FLAW I HAVE!
SIP!
THEN IT'S ABOUT TIME SOMEONE CUT OFF THAT NOSE OF YOURS!
KILL HIM!
SORRY--I'M ATTACHED TO THIS NOSE.
KIYAAII!
HIYARR!
EYAGH!
11.

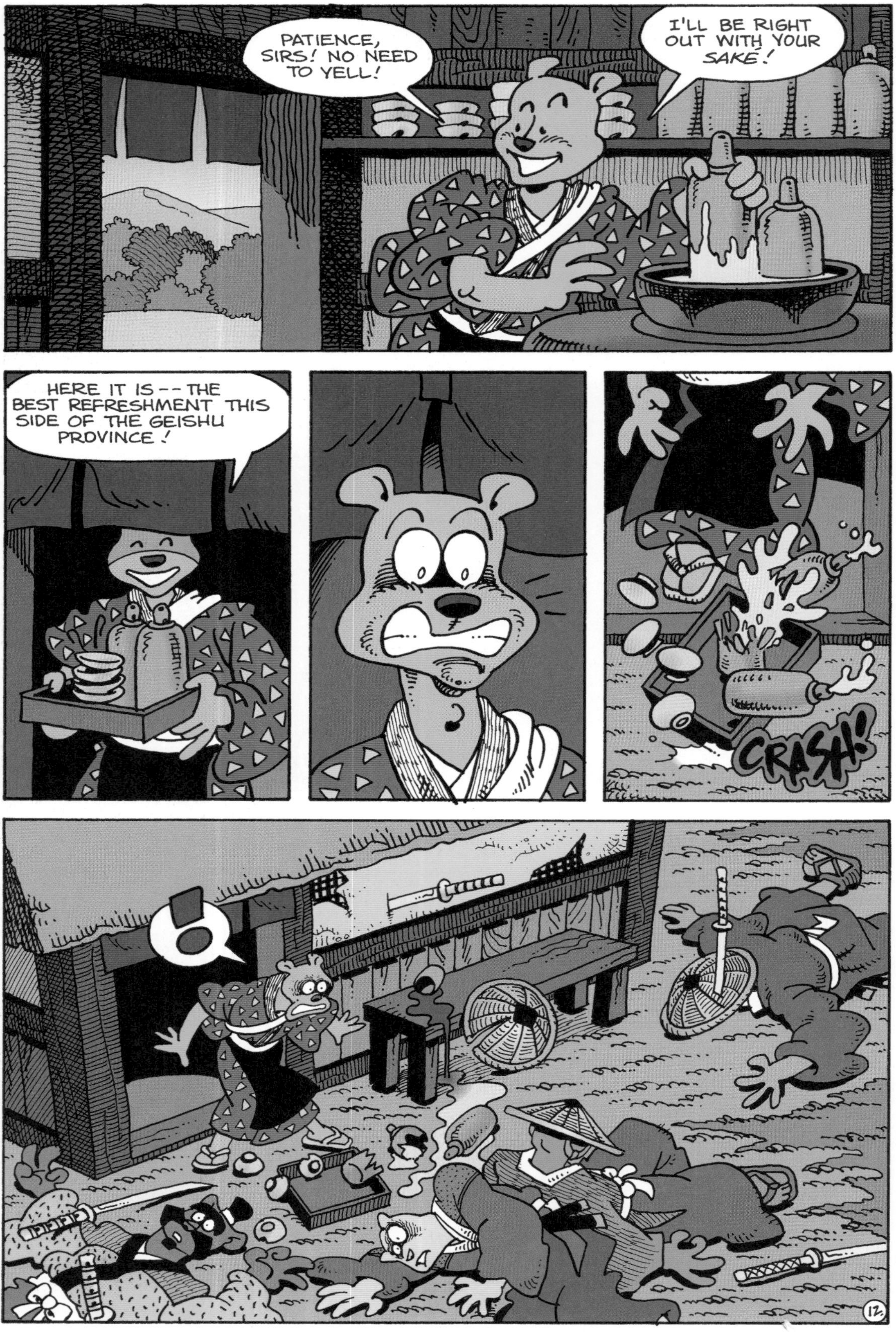
PATIENCE, SIRS! NO NEED TO YELL!
I'LL BE RIGHT OUT WITH YOUR SAKÉ!
HERE IT IS -- THE BEST REFRESHMENT THIS SIDE OF THE GEISHU PROVINCE!
CRASH!
!
12

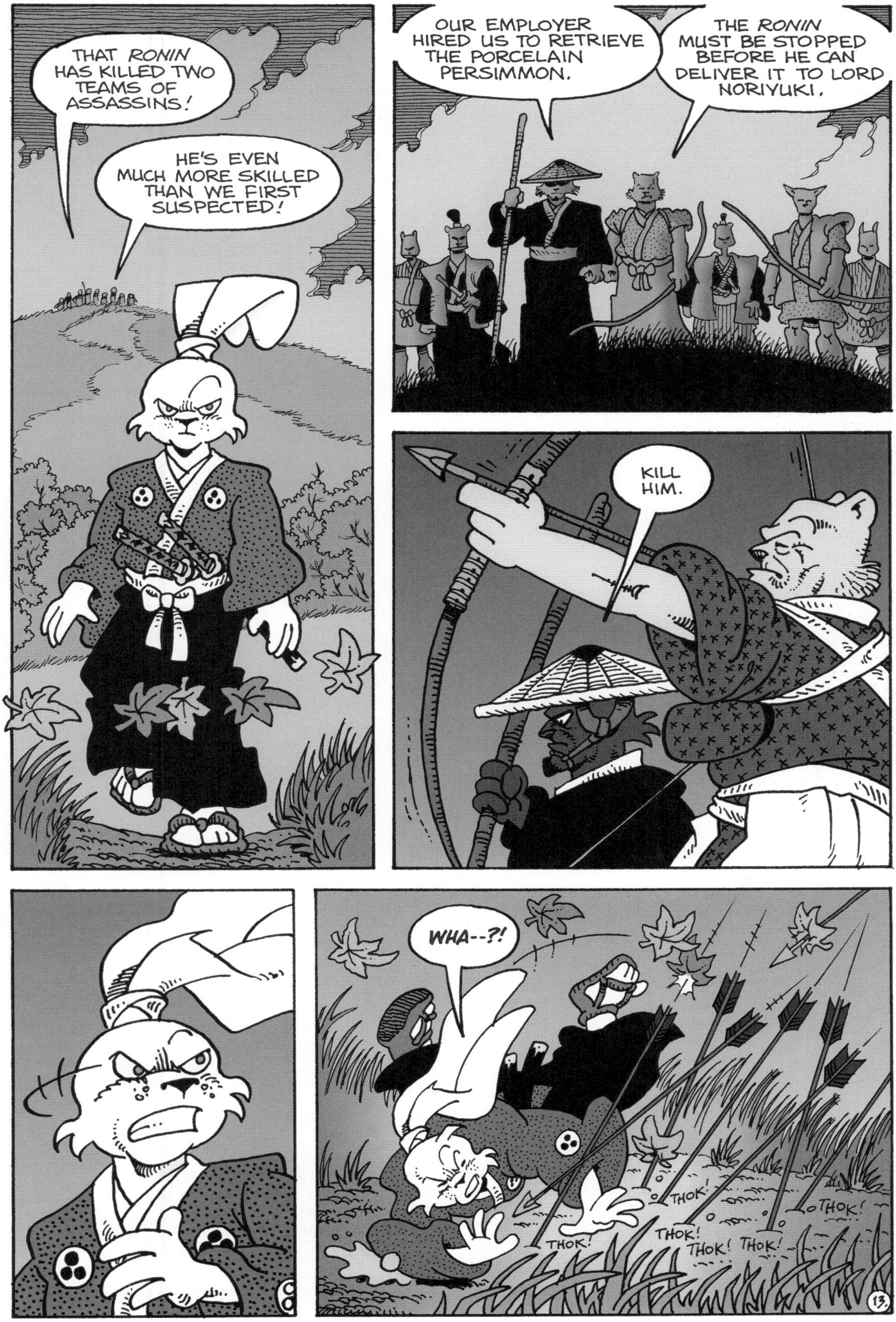
THAT *RONIN* HAS KILLED TWO TEAMS OF ASSASSINS!
HE'S EVEN MUCH MORE SKILLED THAN WE FIRST SUSPECTED!
OUR EMPLOYER HIRED US TO RETRIEVE THE PORCELAIN PERSIMMON.
THE *RONIN* MUST BE STOPPED BEFORE HE CAN DELIVER IT TO LORD NORIYUKI.
KILL HIM.
WHA--?!
THOK!
THOK!
THOK!
THOK!
THOK!
THOK!
13

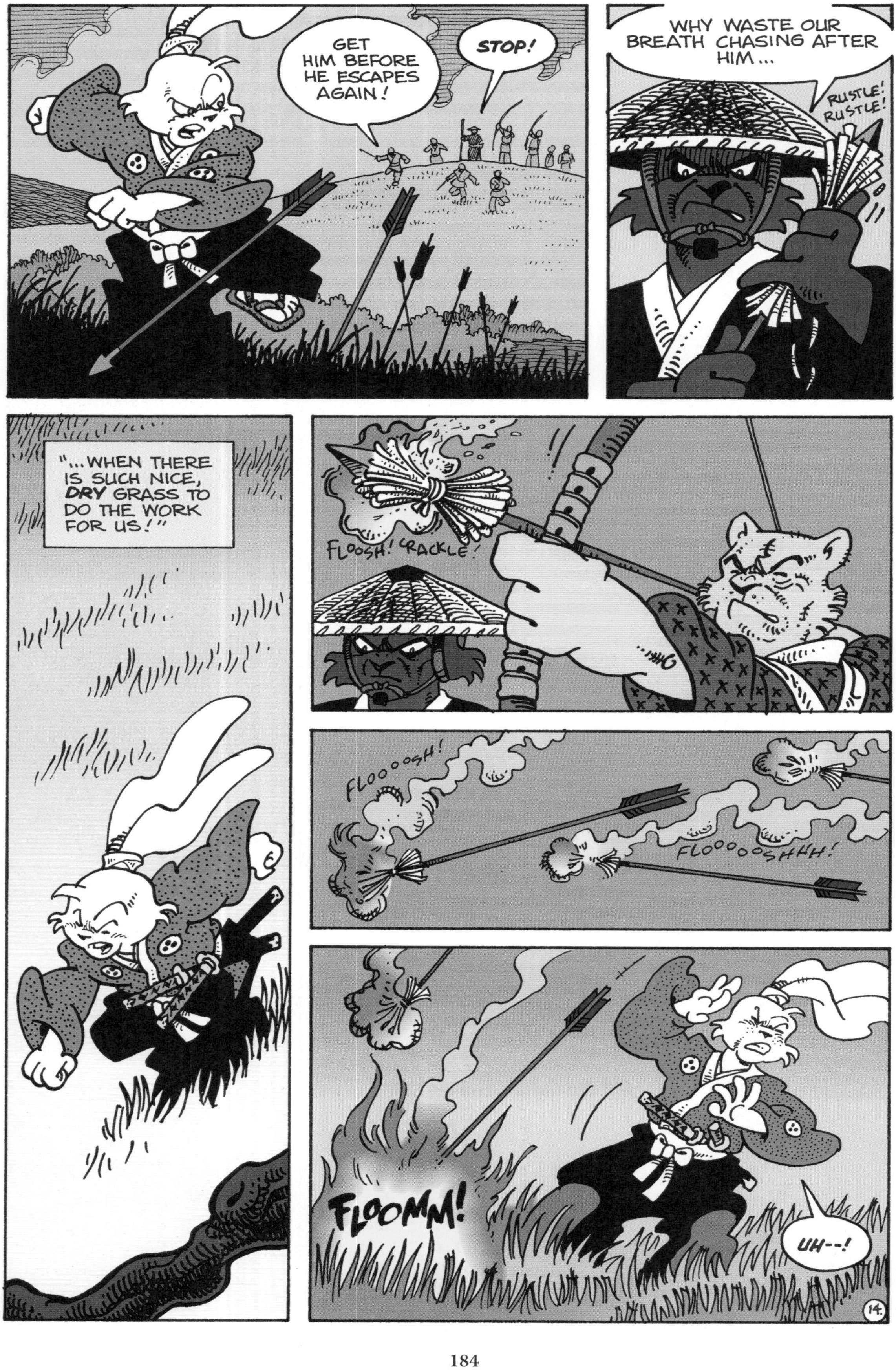
GET HIM BEFORE HE ESCAPES AGAIN!
STOP!
WHY WASTE OUR BREATH CHASING AFTER HIM...
RUSTLE! RUSTLE!
"...WHEN THERE IS SUCH NICE, DRY GRASS TO DO THE WORK FOR US!"
FLOOSH! CRACKLE!
FLOOOOSH!
FLOOOOOSHHH!
FLOOMM!
UH--!
14.

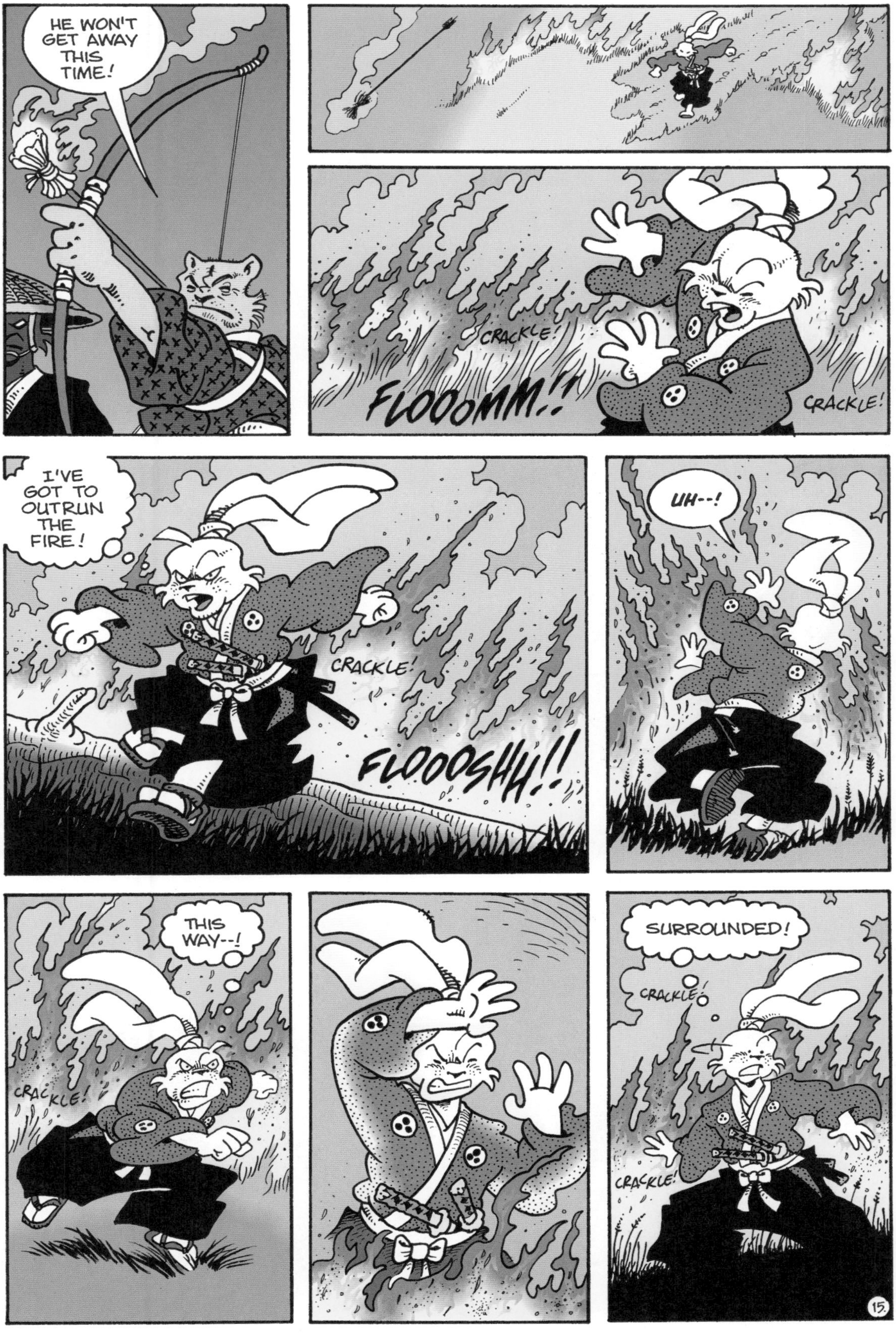
HE WON'T GET AWAY THIS TIME!
CRACKLE!
FLOOOMM!!
CRACKLE!
I'VE GOT TO OUTRUN THE FIRE!
CRACKLE!
FLOOOSHH!!
UH--!
CRACKLE!
THIS WAY--!
CRACKLE!
SURROUNDED!
CRACKLE!
CRACKLE!
15.

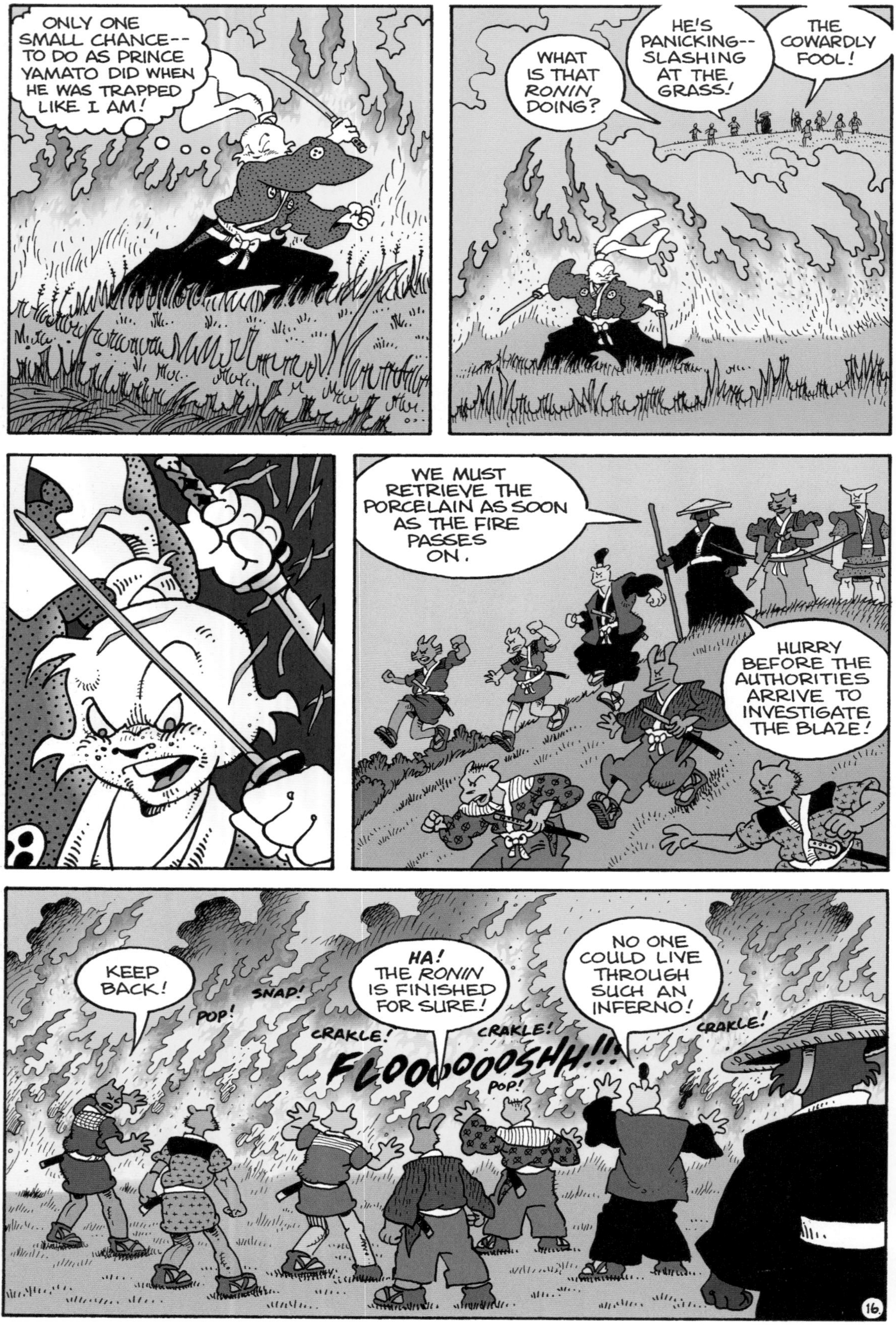
ONLY ONE SMALL CHANCE-- TO DO AS PRINCE YAMATO DID WHEN HE WAS TRAPPED LIKE I AM!
WHAT IS THAT RONIN DOING?
HE'S PANICKING-- SLASHING AT THE GRASS!
THE COWARDLY FOOL!
WE MUST RETRIEVE THE PORCELAIN AS SOON AS THE FIRE PASSES ON.
HURRY BEFORE THE AUTHORITIES ARRIVE TO INVESTIGATE THE BLAZE!
KEEP BACK!
POP!
SNAP!
CRAKLE!
HA! THE RONIN IS FINISHED FOR SURE!
CRAKLE!
FLOOOOOOOSHH!!!
POP!
NO ONE COULD LIVE THROUGH SUCH AN INFERNO!
CRAKLE!
16.

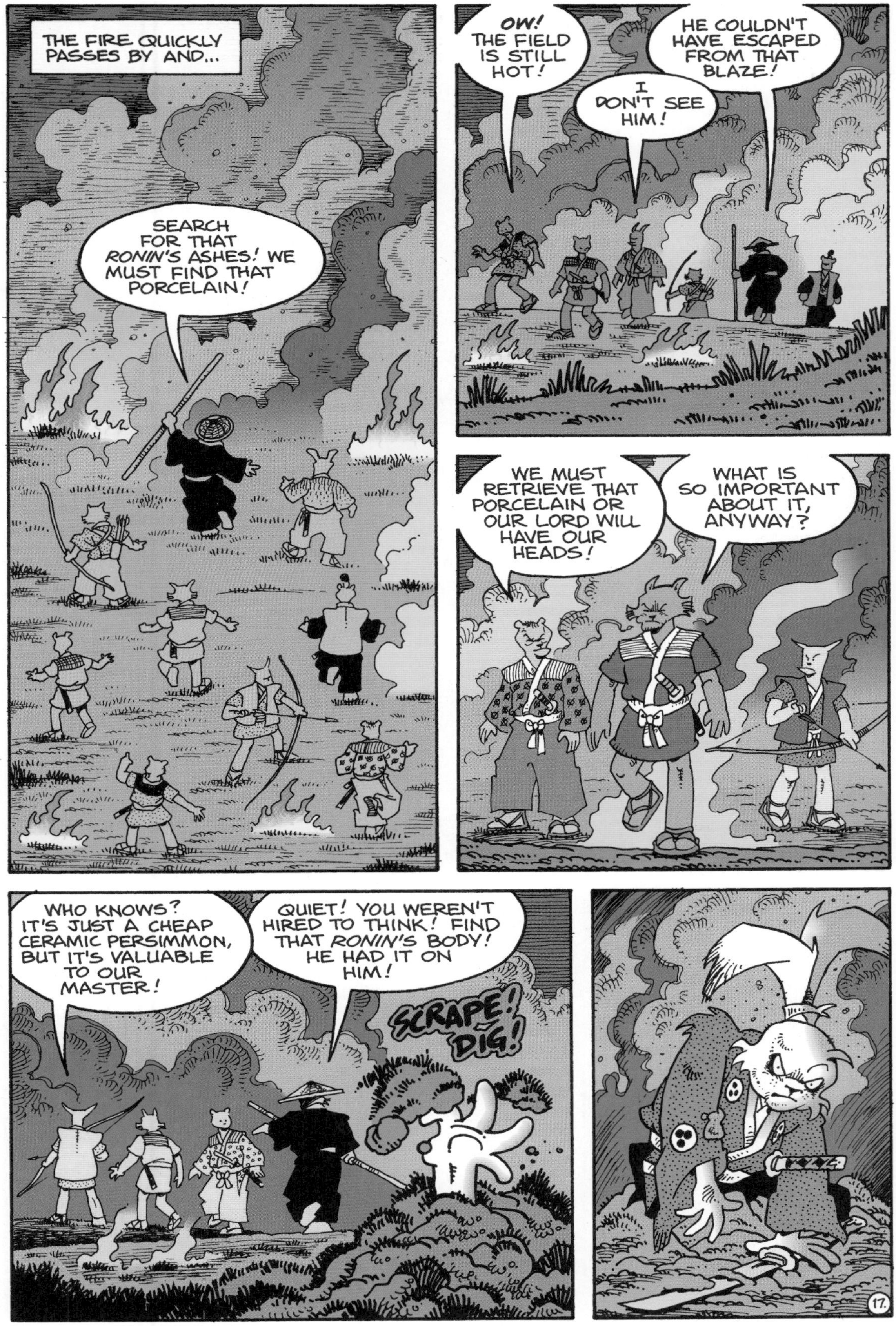
THE FIRE QUICKLY PASSES BY AND...
SEARCH FOR THAT *RONIN'S* ASHES! WE MUST FIND THAT PORCELAIN!
OW! THE FIELD IS STILL HOT!
I DON'T SEE HIM!
HE COULDN'T HAVE ESCAPED FROM THAT BLAZE!
WE MUST RETRIEVE THAT PORCELAIN OR OUR LORD WILL HAVE OUR HEADS!
WHAT IS SO IMPORTANT ABOUT IT, ANYWAY?
WHO KNOWS? IT'S JUST A CHEAP CERAMIC PERSIMMON, BUT IT'S VALUABLE TO OUR MASTER!
QUIET! YOU WEREN'T HIRED TO THINK! FIND THAT *RONIN'S* BODY! HE HAD IT ON HIM!
SCRAPE! DIG!
17.

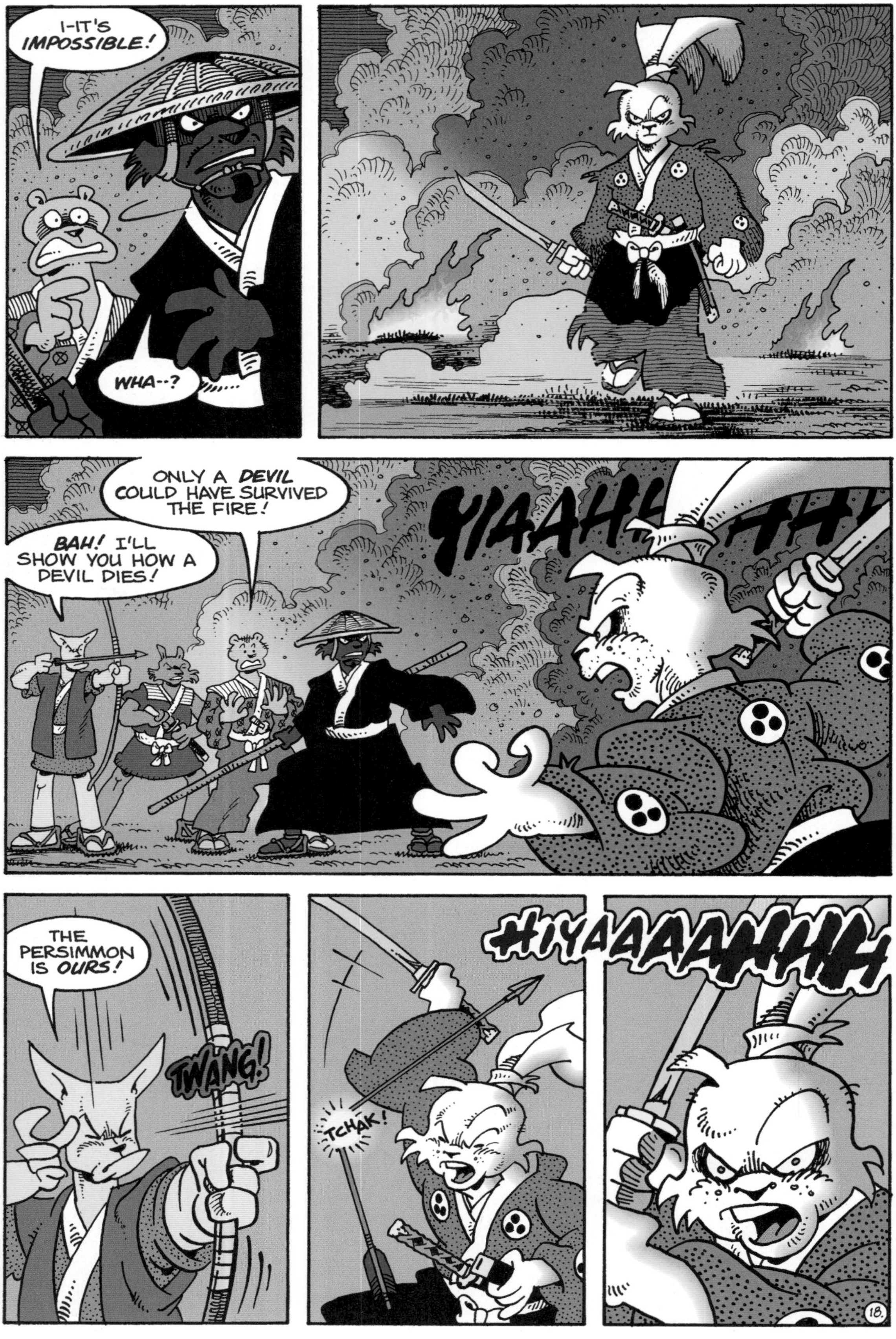
I-IT'S *IMPOSSIBLE!*
WHA--?
ONLY A *DEVIL* COULD HAVE SURVIVED THE FIRE!
BAH! I'LL SHOW YOU HOW A DEVIL DIES!
YIAAHHHHH!
THE PERSIMMON IS *OURS!*
TWANG!
TCHAK!
HIYAAAAAHHH
18.

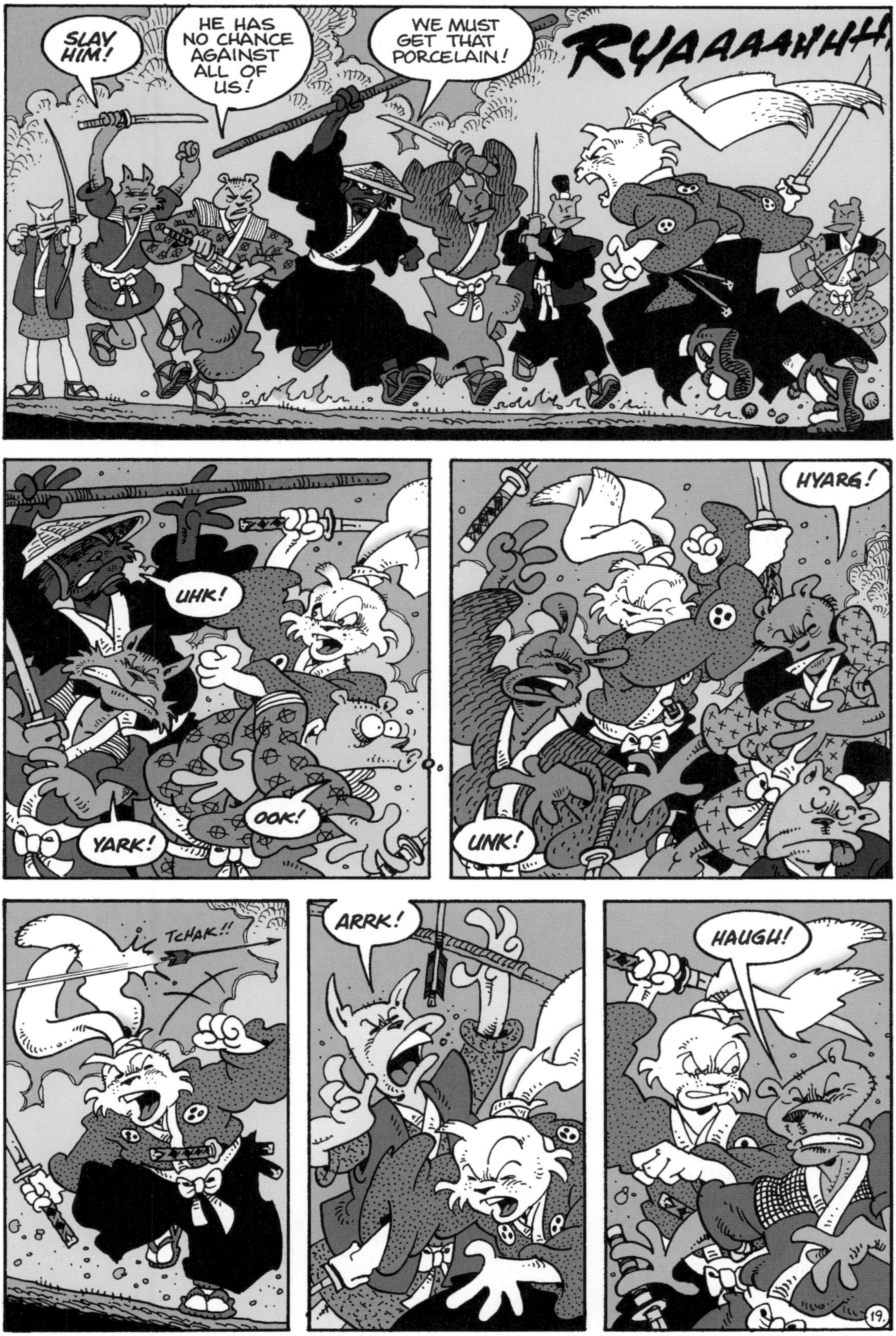
SLAY HIM!
HE HAS NO CHANCE AGAINST ALL OF US!
WE MUST GET THAT PORCELAIN!
RYAAAAAHH!
UHK!
YARK!
OOK!
HYARG!
UNK!
TCHAK!!
ARRK!
HAUGH!
19.

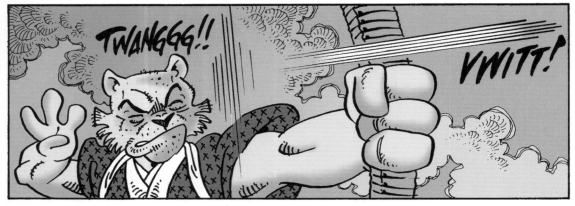

TWANGGG!! VWITT!

VWITTT!!

ARGH!

THOK!

YOU KILLED ALL MY COMRADES, RONIN! BUT I'LL AVENGE THEIR DEATHS!

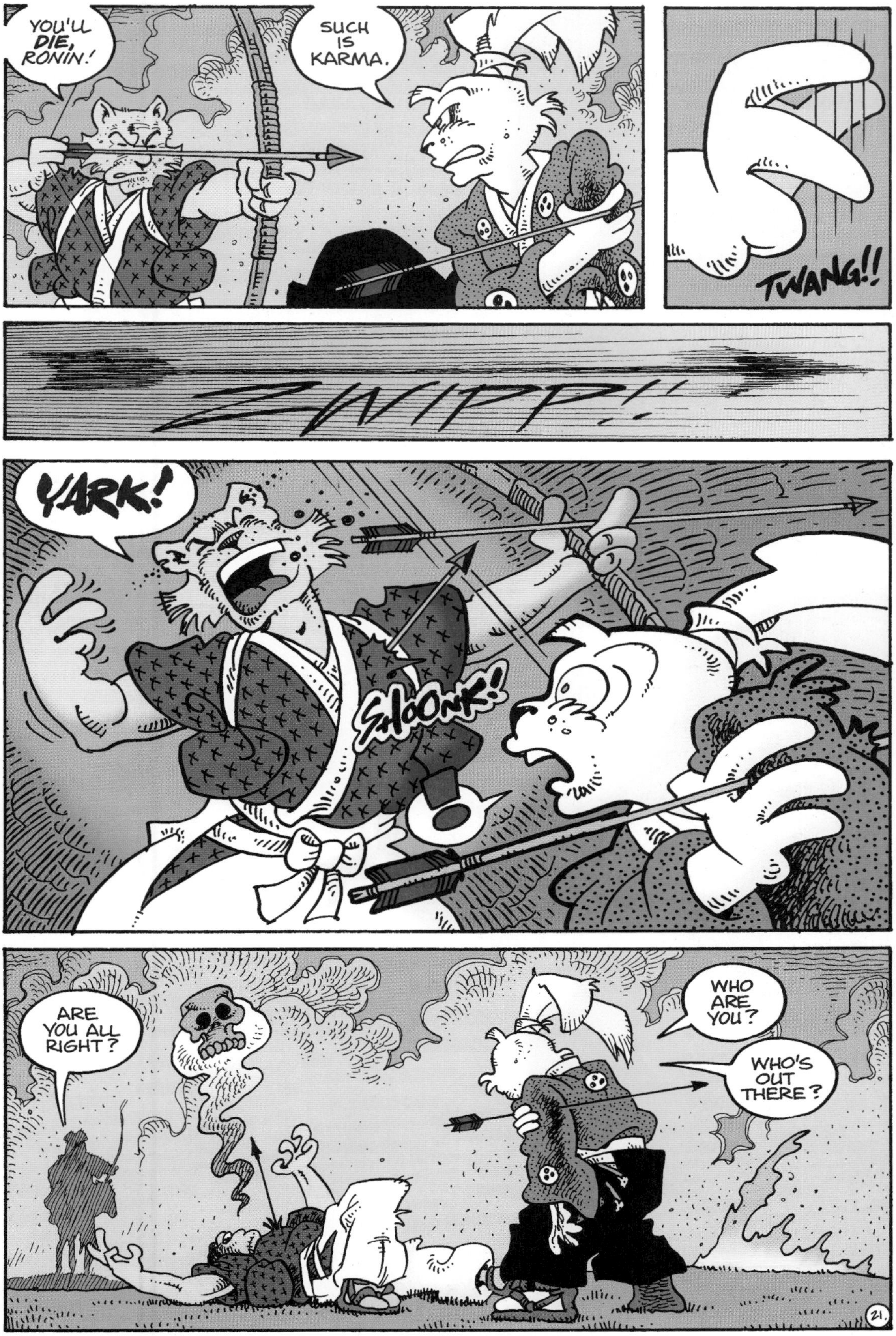
YOU'LL DIE, RONIN!
SUCH IS KARMA.
TWANG!!
ZWIPP!!
YARK!
SHOONK!
ARE YOU ALL RIGHT?
WHO ARE YOU?
WHO'S OUT THERE?
21.

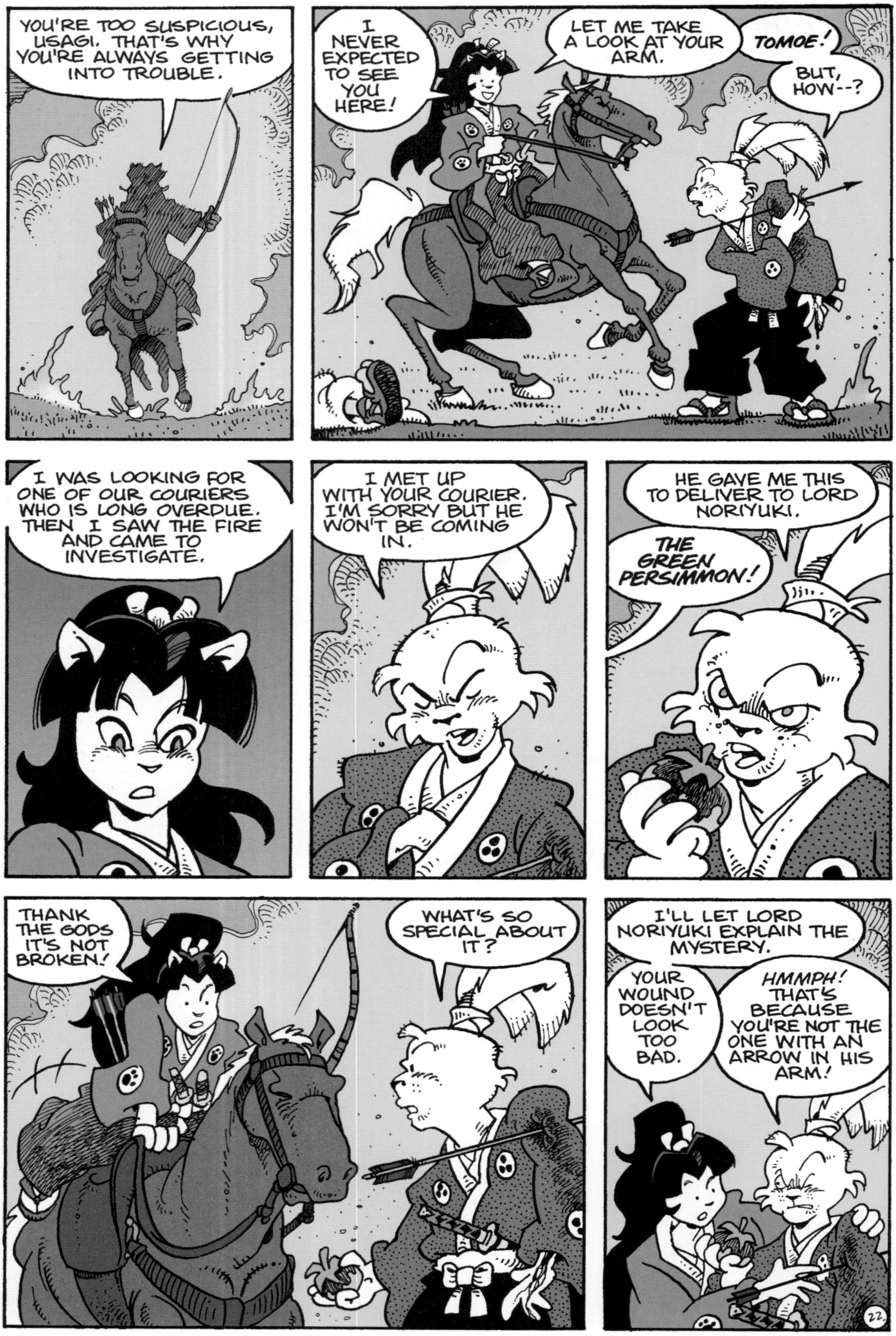
YOU'RE TOO SUSPICIOUS, USAGI. THAT'S WHY YOU'RE ALWAYS GETTING INTO TROUBLE.
I NEVER EXPECTED TO SEE YOU HERE!
LET ME TAKE A LOOK AT YOUR ARM.
TOMOE!
BUT, HOW--?
I WAS LOOKING FOR ONE OF OUR COURIERS WHO IS LONG OVERDUE. THEN I SAW THE FIRE AND CAME TO INVESTIGATE.
I MET UP WITH YOUR COURIER. I'M SORRY BUT HE WON'T BE COMING IN.
HE GAVE ME THIS TO DELIVER TO LORD NORIYUKI.
THE GREEN PERSIMMON!
THANK THE GODS IT'S NOT BROKEN!
WHAT'S SO SPECIAL ABOUT IT?
I'LL LET LORD NORIYUKI EXPLAIN THE MYSTERY.
YOUR WOUND DOESN'T LOOK TOO BAD.
HMMPH! THAT'S BECAUSE YOU'RE NOT THE ONE WITH AN ARROW IN HIS ARM!
22.

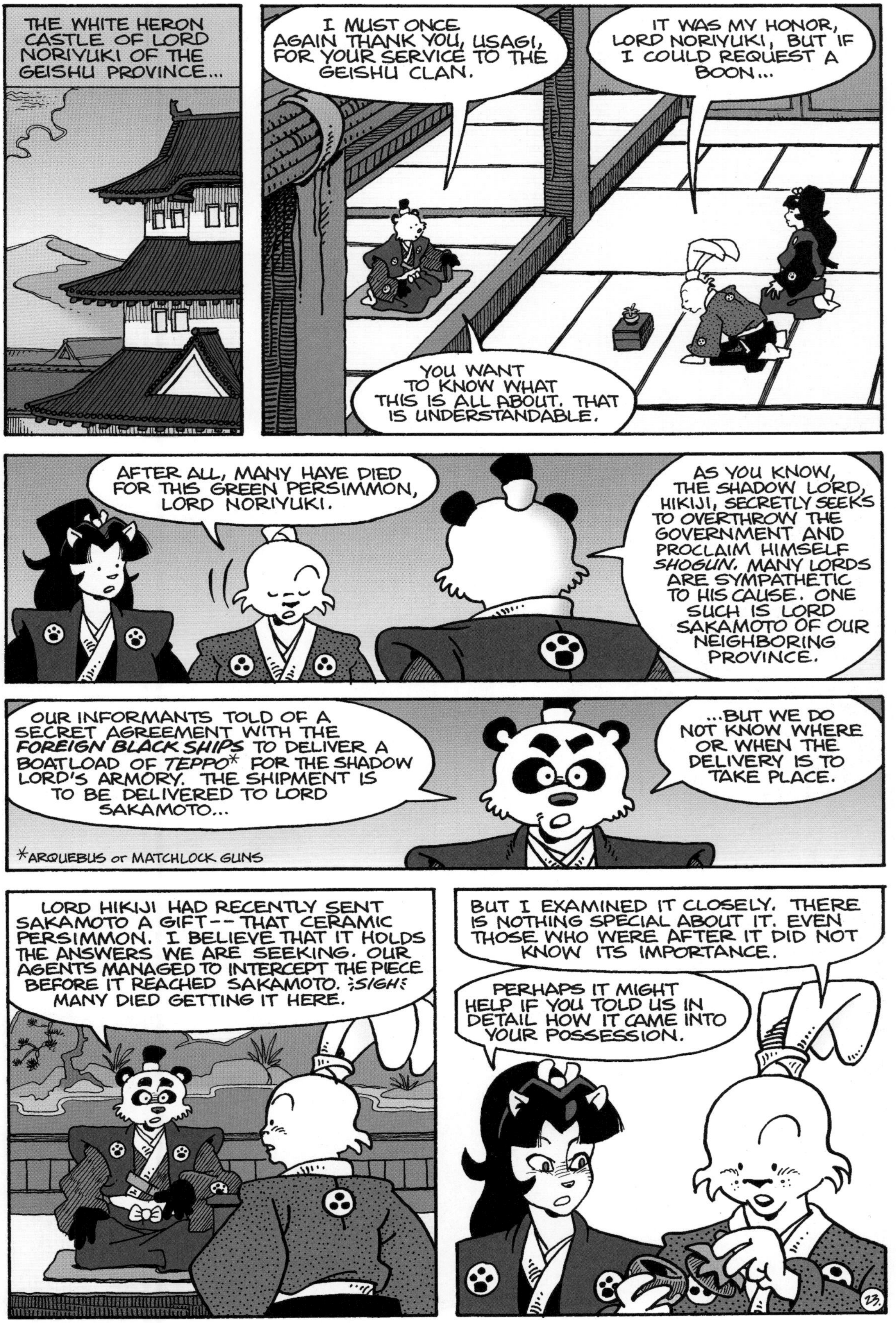
THE WHITE HERON CASTLE OF LORD NORIYUKI OF THE GEISHU PROVINCE...
I MUST ONCE AGAIN THANK YOU, USAGI, FOR YOUR SERVICE TO THE GEISHU CLAN.
IT WAS MY HONOR, LORD NORIYUKI, BUT IF I COULD REQUEST A BOON...
YOU WANT TO KNOW WHAT THIS IS ALL ABOUT. THAT IS UNDERSTANDABLE.
AFTER ALL, MANY HAVE DIED FOR THIS GREEN PERSIMMON, LORD NORIYUKI.
AS YOU KNOW, THE SHADOW LORD, HIKIJI, SECRETLY SEEKS TO OVERTHROW THE GOVERNMENT AND PROCLAIM HIMSELF *SHOGUN*. MANY LORDS ARE SYMPATHETIC TO HIS CAUSE. ONE SUCH IS LORD SAKAMOTO OF OUR NEIGHBORING PROVINCE.
OUR INFORMANTS TOLD OF A SECRET AGREEMENT WITH THE ***FOREIGN BLACK SHIPS*** TO DELIVER A BOATLOAD OF *TEPPO** FOR THE SHADOW LORD'S ARMORY. THE SHIPMENT IS TO BE DELIVERED TO LORD SAKAMOTO...
...BUT WE DO NOT KNOW WHERE OR WHEN THE DELIVERY IS TO TAKE PLACE.
*ARQUEBUS OR MATCHLOCK GUNS
LORD HIKIJI HAD RECENTLY SENT SAKAMOTO A GIFT-- THAT CERAMIC PERSIMMON. I BELIEVE THAT IT HOLDS THE ANSWERS WE ARE SEEKING. OUR AGENTS MANAGED TO INTERCEPT THE PIECE BEFORE IT REACHED SAKAMOTO. *SIGH* MANY DIED GETTING IT HERE.
BUT I EXAMINED IT CLOSELY. THERE IS NOTHING SPECIAL ABOUT IT. EVEN THOSE WHO WERE AFTER IT DID NOT KNOW ITS IMPORTANCE.
PERHAPS IT MIGHT HELP IF YOU TOLD US IN DETAIL HOW IT CAME INTO YOUR POSSESSION.
23.

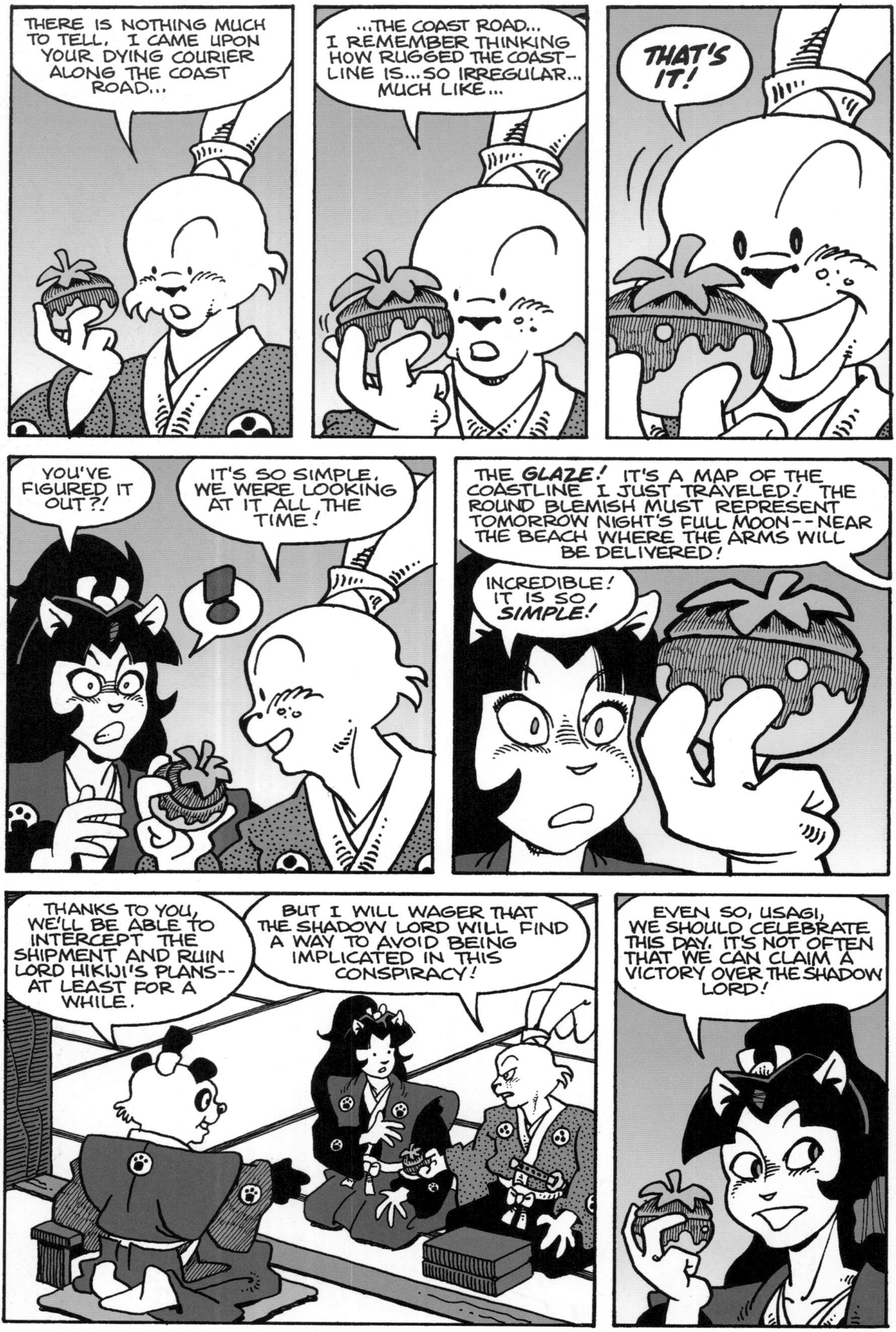
THERE IS NOTHING MUCH TO TELL, I CAME UPON YOUR DYING COURIER ALONG THE COAST ROAD...
...THE COAST ROAD... I REMEMBER THINKING HOW RUGGED THE COAST-LINE IS...SO IRREGULAR... MUCH LIKE...
THAT'S IT!
YOU'VE FIGURED IT OUT?!
IT'S SO SIMPLE. WE WERE LOOKING AT IT ALL THE TIME!
THE GLAZE! IT'S A MAP OF THE COASTLINE I JUST TRAVELED! THE ROUND BLEMISH MUST REPRESENT TOMORROW NIGHT'S FULL MOON--NEAR THE BEACH WHERE THE ARMS WILL BE DELIVERED!
INCREDIBLE! IT IS SO SIMPLE!
THANKS TO YOU, WE'LL BE ABLE TO INTERCEPT THE SHIPMENT AND RUIN LORD HIKIJI'S PLANS--AT LEAST FOR A WHILE.
BUT I WILL WAGER THAT THE SHADOW LORD WILL FIND A WAY TO AVOID BEING IMPLICATED IN THIS CONSPIRACY!
EVEN SO, USAGI, WE SHOULD CELEBRATE THIS DAY. IT'S NOT OFTEN THAT WE CAN CLAIM A VICTORY OVER THE SHADOW LORD!
END

GRASSCUTTER

WHILE I HAVE KNOWN about Stan Sakai's work for some time, I came upon *Usagi Yojimbo* only recently. This is because my attention over the years has been centered on what I regarded as the expansion of the medium as literature, and I look for those works that seem to be "pushing the envelope." From time to time I make a "discovery" such as *Bone* or encourage what I believe is a promising new self-published work. More often my attention is centered on trends, a focus that seemed so necessary during my years of teaching.

While I have always been a staunch apostle of the internationalization of our medium, I confess that I really assumed the form emanated from American comics. Oh, yes, as a student I studied early Japanese prints like the narrative work of Hiroshige, and I used a Japanese brush myself for a long time. I have admired modern Japanese graphic storytelling. But I believed it to be insular and even untranslatable. I never anticipated an integration such as that demonstrated by *Usagi*.

In the autumn of 1994 I was shepherded through Japan by Fred Schodt, a leading American scholar and expert on Japanese comics, in the company of a group of American artists and writers. I was stunned by what I found. I saw a booming industry, an enormous readership, and a pervasive social presence of the medium beyond any of my fondest dreams for the medium to which I've devoted my life. There are obvious cultural reasons for this, but the fact remains that manga, or *komikkusu* as the Japanese also call it, is a very singular form of the art of using sequentially arranged images and text to narrate a story or dramatize an idea. As in America, manga occupies a place somewhere between films, literature, and "fine" art. The range of an American comic's subject matter, however, is limited mostly to the interests of young males. They are the bestsellers, and the outer margins are left to the foraging of those who address children, women, and adult men. In Japan, comic books occupy nearly the same public acceptance as novels and films. The medium has a legitimacy not yet attained anywhere else. But perhaps the most significant characteristic of manga is the range of readership and subject matter. There are *komikkusu* specifically addressed to expectant mothers, little children, preteens, boys, girls, adults, and seniors both male and female. Many are centered on sports and games.

However enviable is this lateral coverage, the fact remains that Japanese publishers make little effort to reach beyond what is "commercial." The art is designed to shock, titillate, or emulate animation. Style and surface technique dominate art and content. Like the American superhero and horror comics, their plots are generally simple.

As far as I could see, Japanese comics are reluctant to introduce the stories or ideas of other cultures. Save for a surface fascination with American names and certain Western physical characteristics, it is hard to find manga that undertake subjects with realistic problems of the human condition. Works by other nationals that introduce foreign cultures, such as those that appear in European and American comic books, is rarely seen.

Yet for all of that, Japanese comics have an undeniable fascination and have succeeded in invading the American and European markets. There is little doubt that they deliver exciting graphics. The trouble is that they have provided us with very little insight into Japanese life, culture, or history, such as in the work of Tezuka or the classic *Gen*.

So, it was with this prejudice that I began to read the *Usagi Yojimbo* books Stan Sakai sent me. My first reaction was dismissive. I shrugged at his use of anthropomorphic characters as a way of avoiding the demands of realistic art, which made Frank Miller's *Ronin* so compelling. Gradually, however, as the story absorbed me I changed my opinion. I felt I was somehow *reading komikkusu* in *Japanese*! Stan's animal-people faces allow the reader to imagine and insert "real" faces out of their own memory. After I finished several stories, the accomplishment was obvious. I was transported into the fascinating world of Japanese folklore.

This is an important event in the progress of this medium because Stan Sakai has successfully brought to American comics a collection of Japanese fables well told in the American style. He has a good control of sequential art, and his compositions have the ability to create powerful understatements.

Usagi Yojimbo is an enduring work. *Bravo.*

WILL EISNER

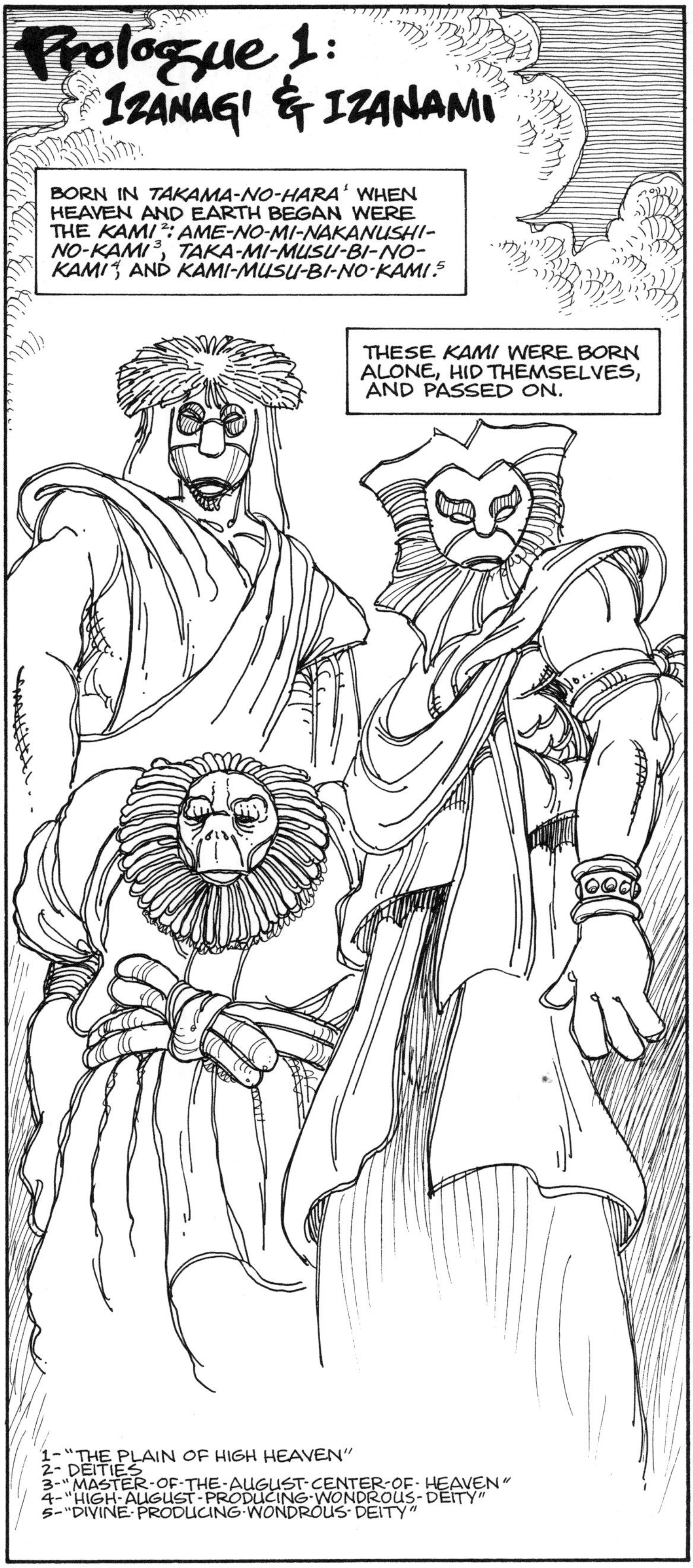
Prologue 1: Izanagi & Izanami
BORN IN TAKAMA-NO-HARA[1] WHEN HEAVEN AND EARTH BEGAN WERE THE KAMI[2]: AME-NO-MI-NAKANUSHI-NO-KAMI[3], TAKA-MI-MUSU-BI-NO-KAMI[4], AND KAMI-MUSU-BI-NO-KAMI.[5]
THESE KAMI WERE BORN ALONE, HID THEMSELVES, AND PASSED ON.
1- "THE PLAIN OF HIGH HEAVEN"
2- DEITIES
3- "MASTER-OF-THE-AUGUST-CENTER-OF-HEAVEN"
4- "HIGH-AUGUST-PRODUCING-WONDROUS-DEITY"
5- "DIVINE-PRODUCING-WONDROUS-DEITY"

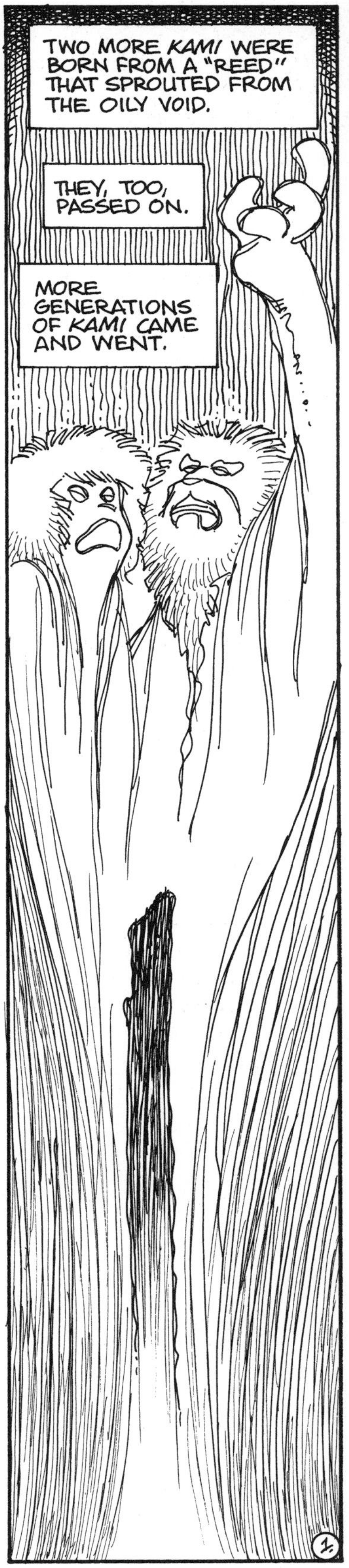
TWO MORE KAMI WERE BORN FROM A "REED" THAT SPROUTED FROM THE OILY VOID.
THEY, TOO, PASSED ON.
MORE GENERATIONS OF KAMI CAME AND WENT.
1

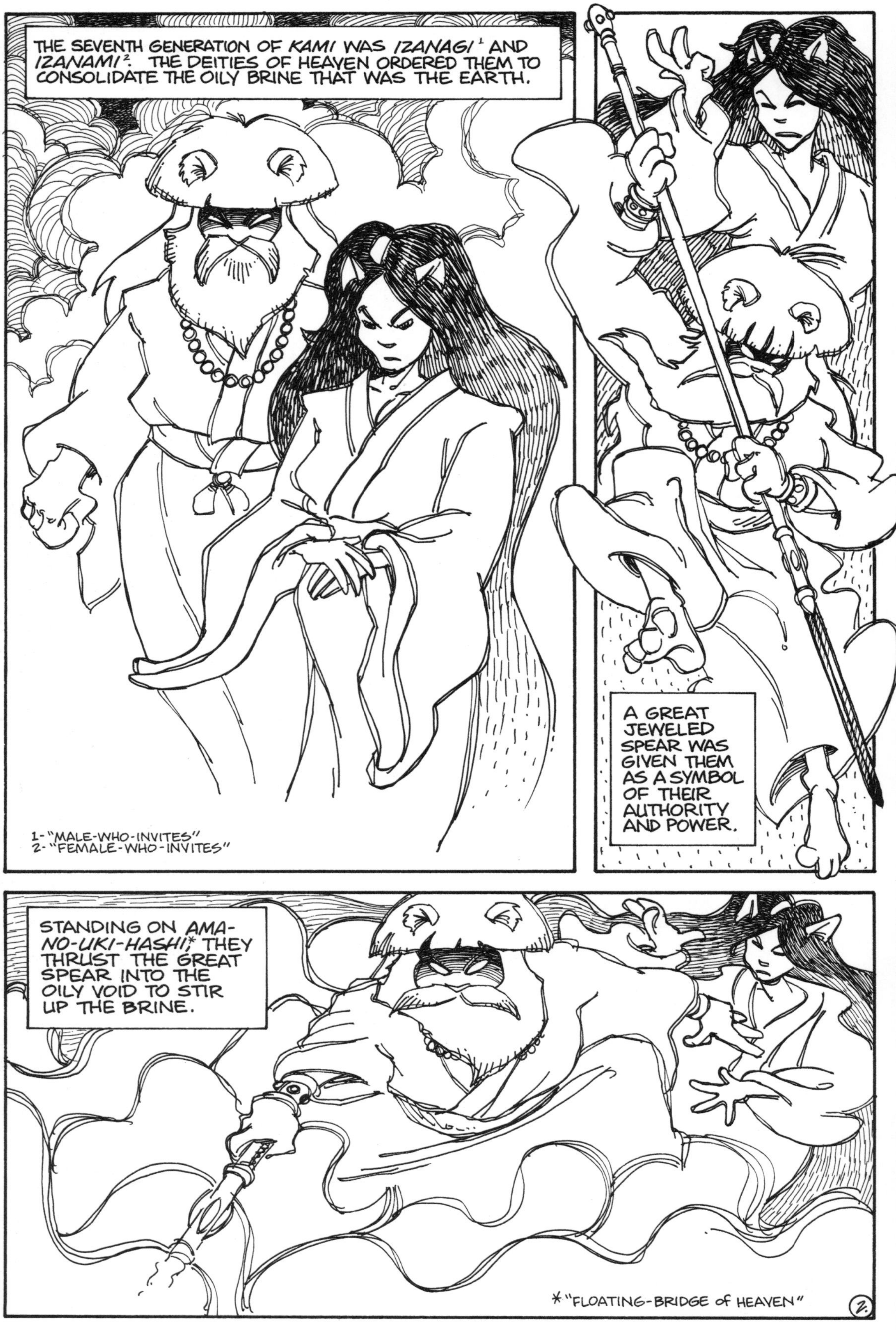
THE SEVENTH GENERATION OF KAMI WAS IZANAGI¹ AND IZANAMI². THE DEITIES OF HEAVEN ORDERED THEM TO CONSOLIDATE THE OILY BRINE THAT WAS THE EARTH.
1- "MALE-WHO-INVITES"
2- "FEMALE-WHO-INVITES"
A GREAT JEWELED SPEAR WAS GIVEN THEM AS A SYMBOL OF THEIR AUTHORITY AND POWER.
STANDING ON AMA-NO-UKI-HASHI,* THEY THRUST THE GREAT SPEAR INTO THE OILY VOID TO STIR UP THE BRINE.
* "FLOATING-BRIDGE OF HEAVEN"
2.

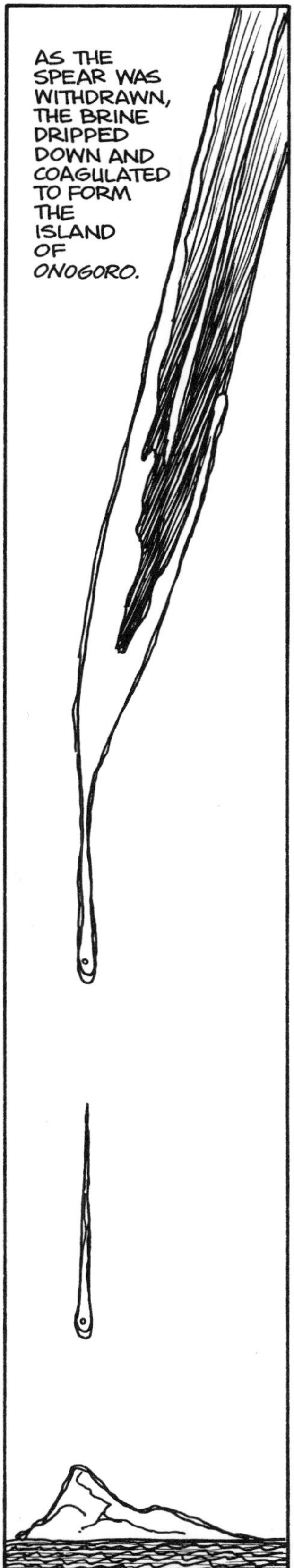
AS THE SPEAR WAS WITHDRAWN, THE BRINE DRIPPED DOWN AND COAGULATED TO FORM THE ISLAND OF *ONOGORO*.
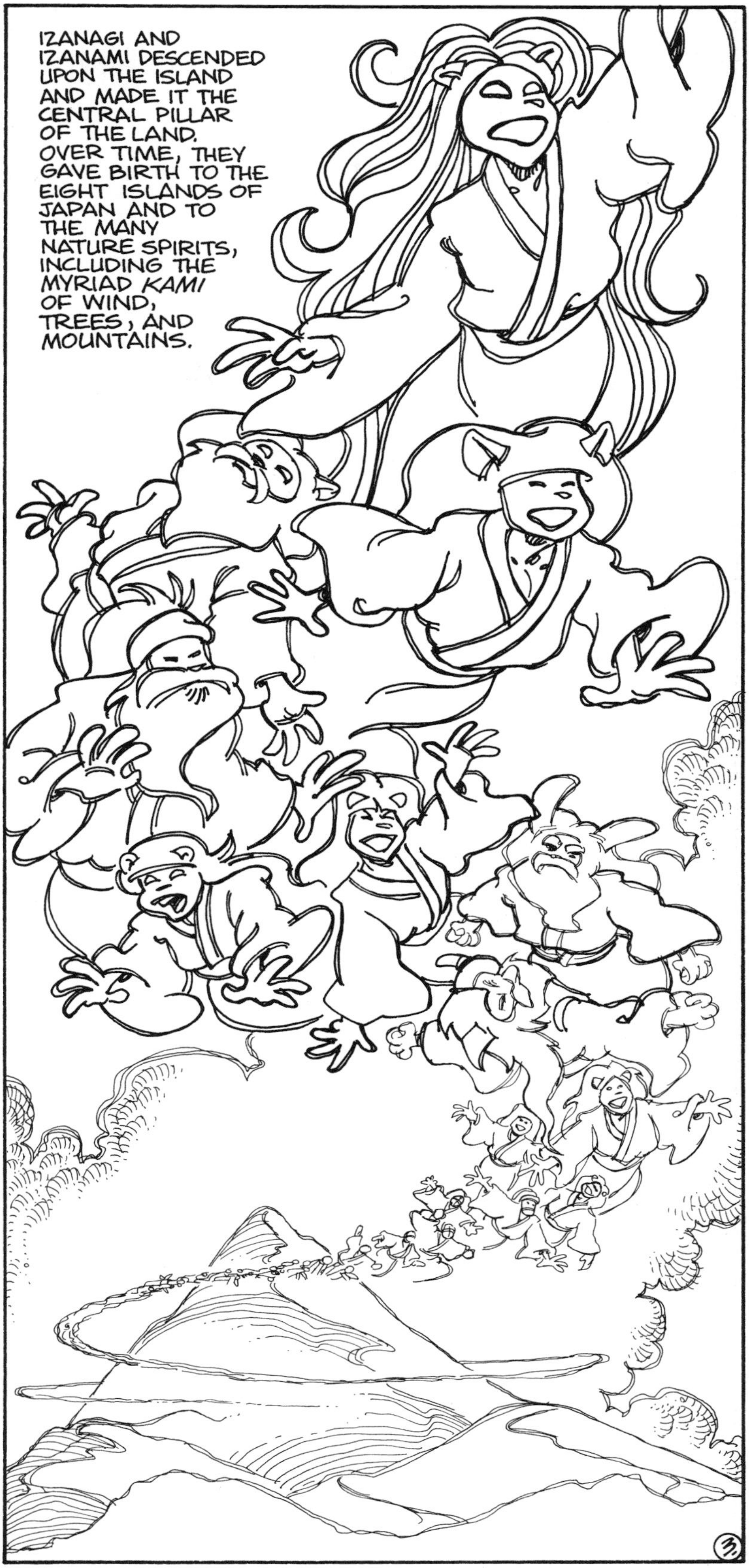
IZANAGI AND IZANAMI DESCENDED UPON THE ISLAND AND MADE IT THE CENTRAL PILLAR OF THE LAND. OVER TIME, THEY GAVE BIRTH TO THE EIGHT ISLANDS OF JAPAN AND TO THE MANY NATURE SPIRITS, INCLUDING THE MYRIAD *KAMI* OF WIND, TREES, AND MOUNTAINS.
3

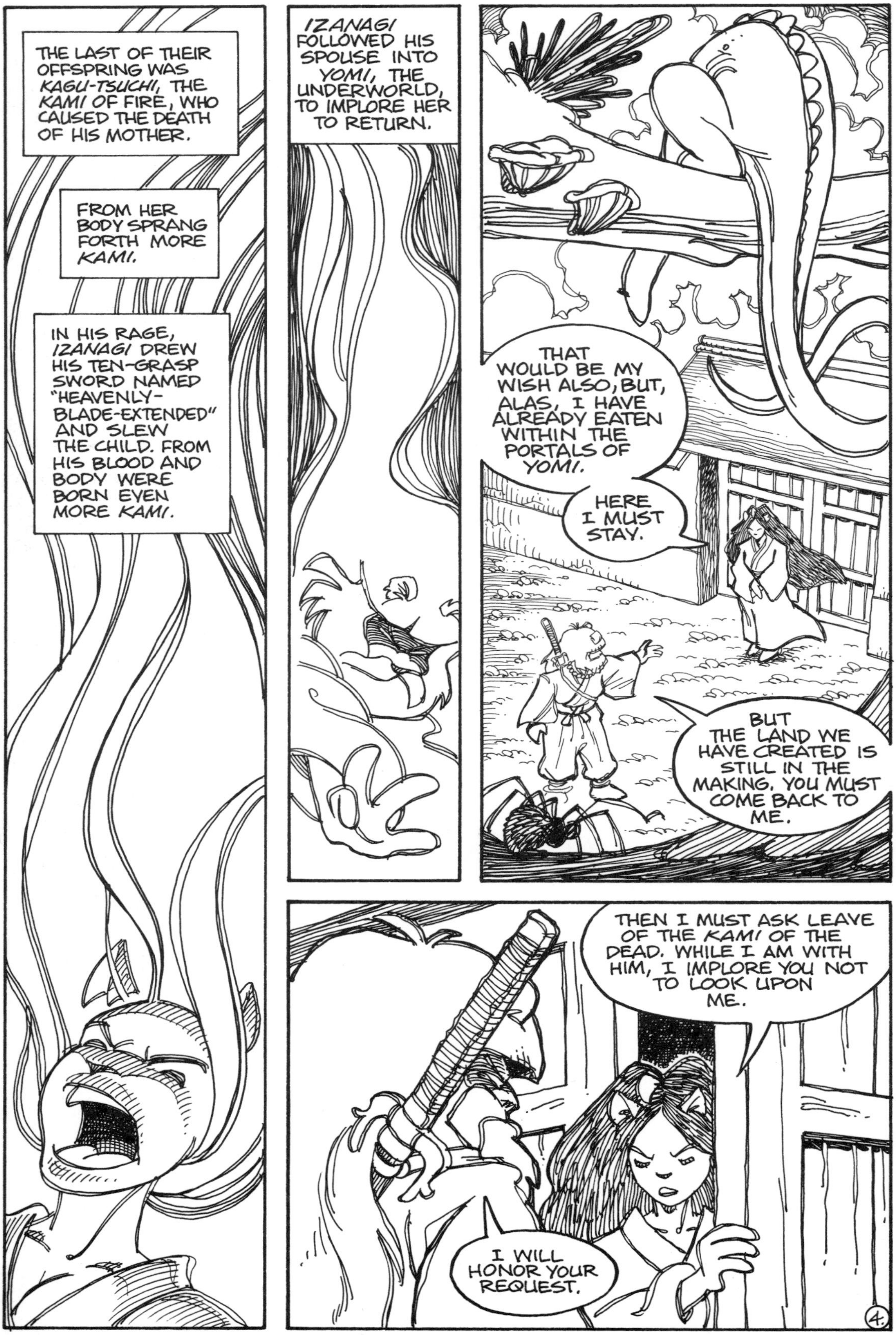
THE LAST OF THEIR OFFSPRING WAS *KAGU-TSUCHI*, THE *KAMI* OF FIRE, WHO CAUSED THE DEATH OF HIS MOTHER.
FROM HER BODY SPRANG FORTH MORE *KAMI*.
IN HIS RAGE, *IZANAGI* DREW HIS TEN-GRASP SWORD NAMED "HEAVENLY-BLADE-EXTENDED" AND SLEW THE CHILD. FROM HIS BLOOD AND BODY WERE BORN EVEN MORE *KAMI*.
IZANAGI FOLLOWED HIS SPOUSE INTO *YOMI*, THE UNDERWORLD, TO IMPLORE HER TO RETURN.
THAT WOULD BE MY WISH ALSO, BUT, ALAS, I HAVE ALREADY EATEN WITHIN THE PORTALS OF *YOMI*.
HERE I MUST STAY.
BUT THE LAND WE HAVE CREATED IS STILL IN THE MAKING. YOU MUST COME BACK TO ME.
THEN I MUST ASK LEAVE OF THE *KAMI* OF THE DEAD. WHILE I AM WITH HIM, I IMPLORE YOU NOT TO LOOK UPON ME.
I WILL HONOR YOUR REQUEST.
4.

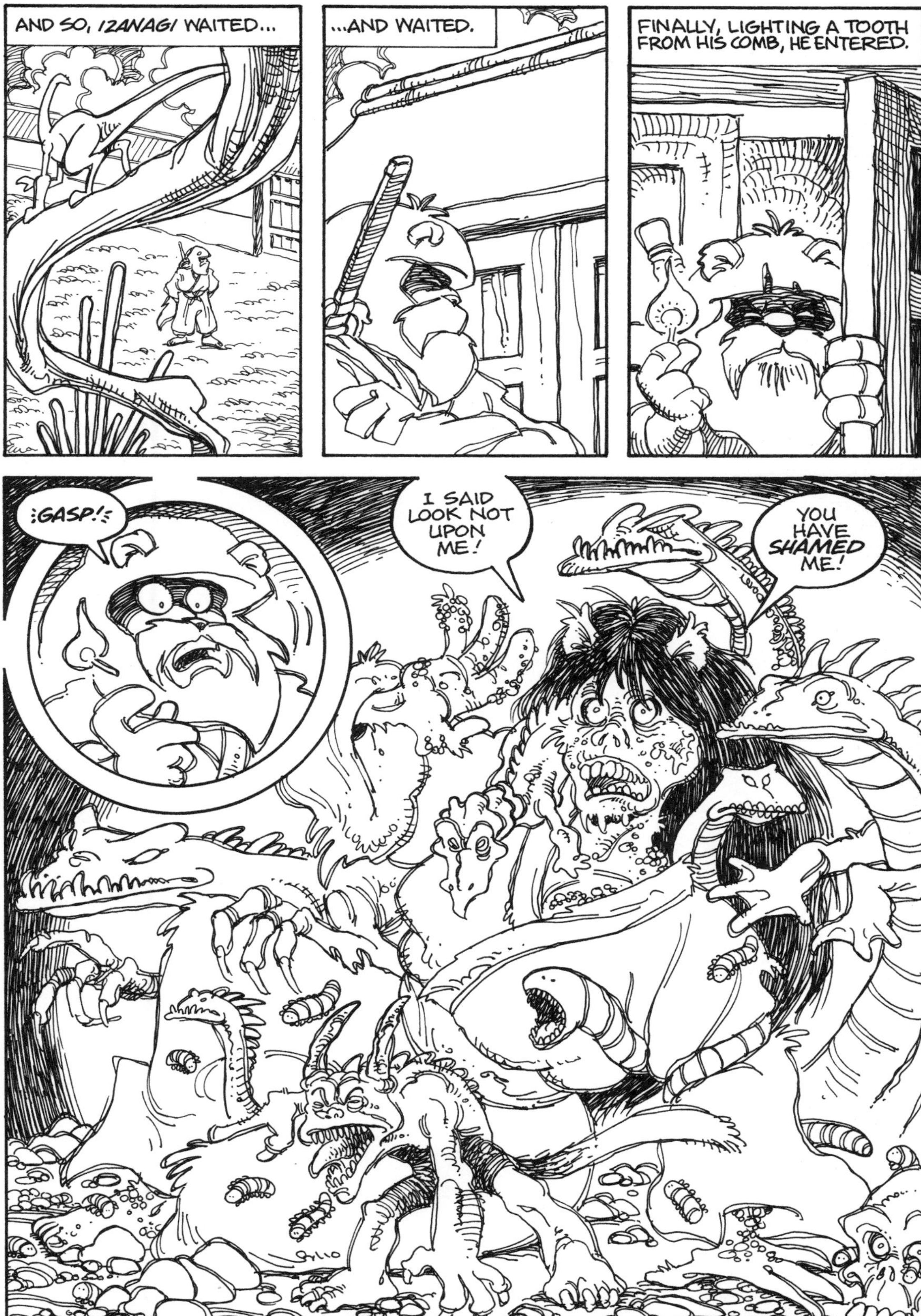
AND SO, IZANAGI WAITED...
...AND WAITED.
FINALLY, LIGHTING A TOOTH FROM HIS COMB, HE ENTERED.
GASP!
I SAID LOOK NOT UPON ME!
YOU HAVE SHAMED ME!

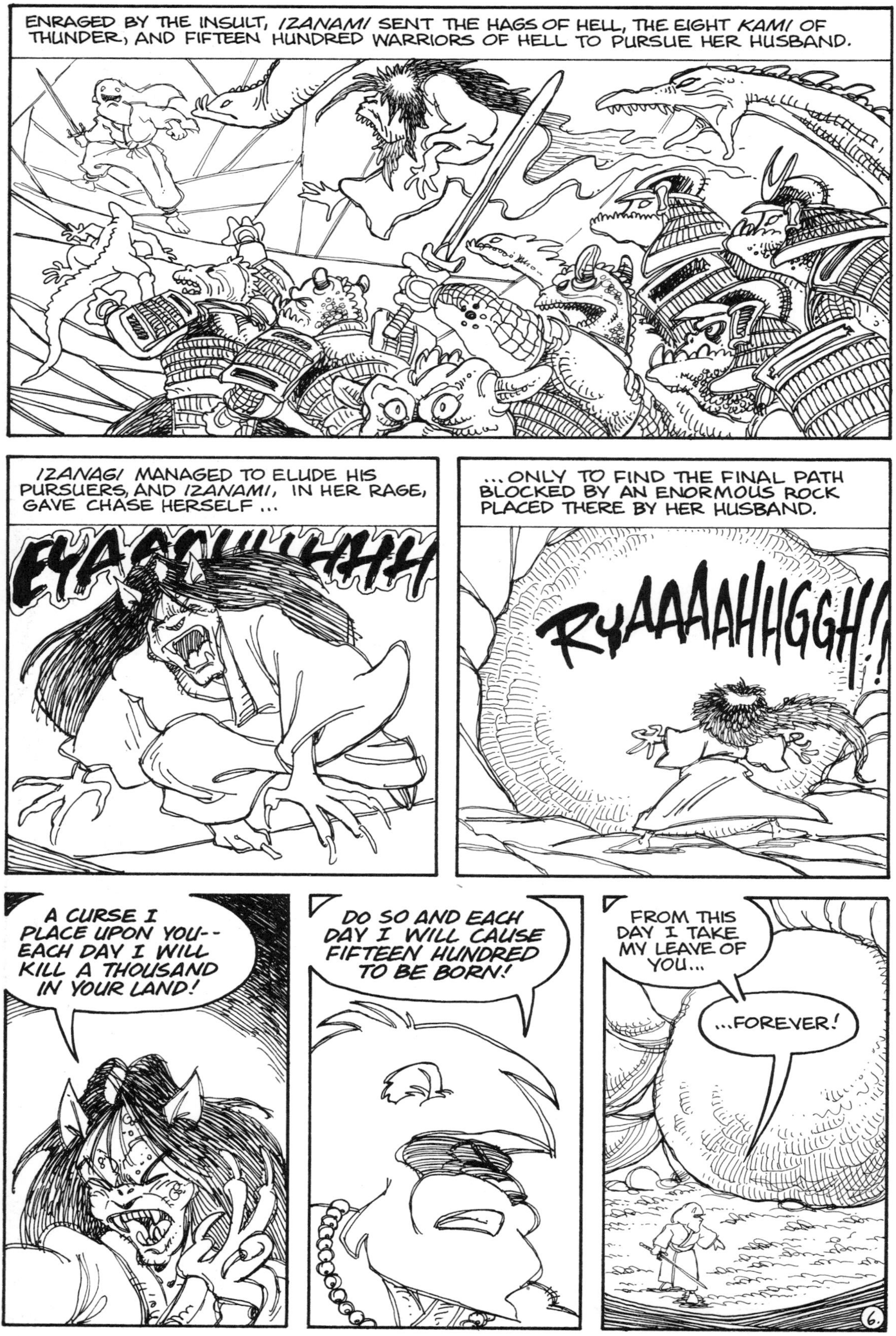
ENRAGED BY THE INSULT, *IZANAMI* SENT THE HAGS OF HELL, THE EIGHT *KAMI* OF THUNDER, AND FIFTEEN HUNDRED WARRIORS OF HELL TO PURSUE HER HUSBAND.
IZANAGI MANAGED TO ELUDE HIS PURSUERS, AND *IZANAMI*, IN HER RAGE, GAVE CHASE HERSELF ...
...ONLY TO FIND THE FINAL PATH BLOCKED BY AN ENORMOUS ROCK PLACED THERE BY HER HUSBAND.
RYAAAAHHGGH!!
A CURSE I PLACE UPON YOU-- EACH DAY I WILL KILL A THOUSAND IN YOUR LAND!
DO SO AND EACH DAY I WILL CAUSE FIFTEEN HUNDRED TO BE BORN!
FROM THIS DAY I TAKE MY LEAVE OF YOU...
...FOREVER!
6.

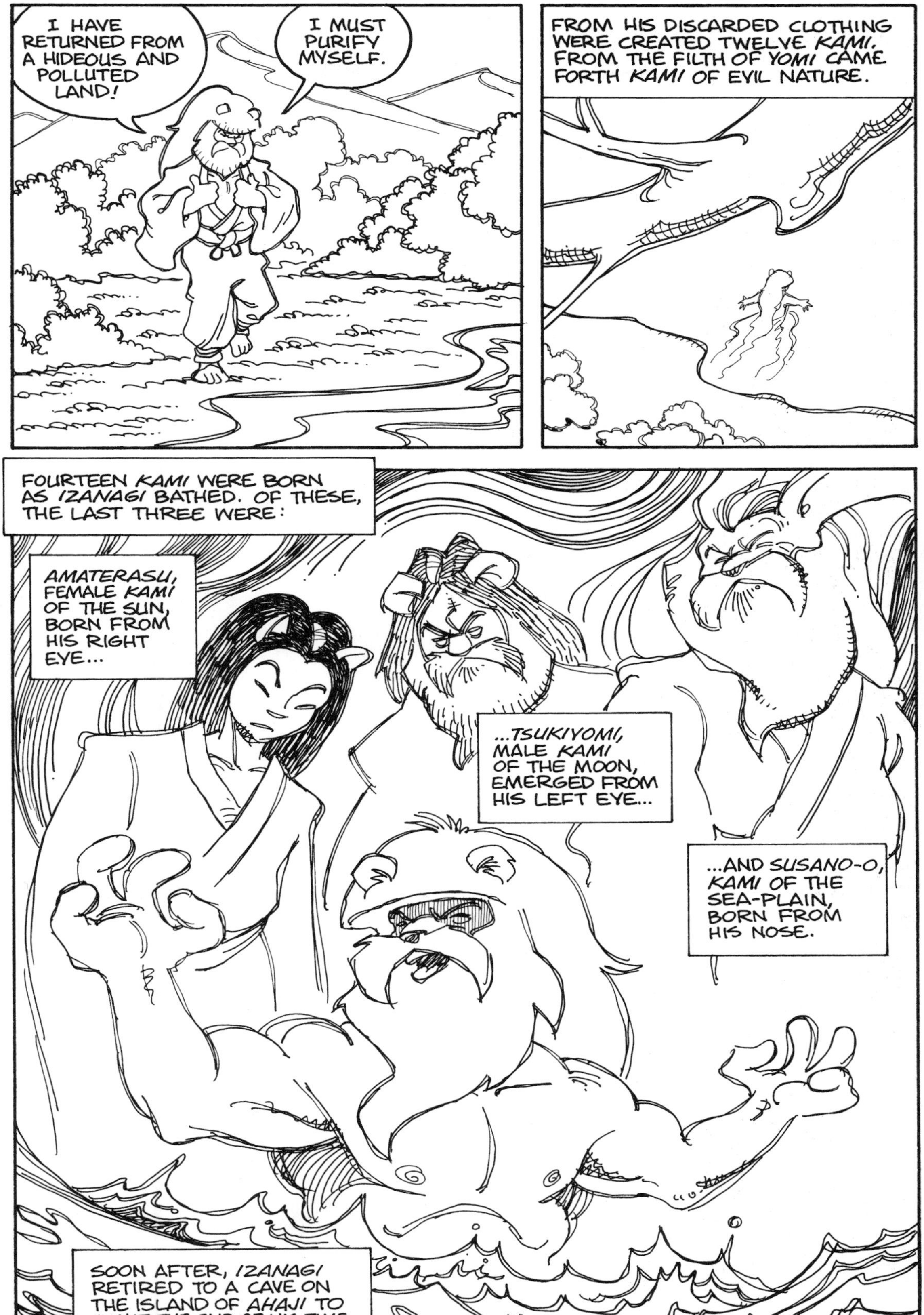
I HAVE RETURNED FROM A HIDEOUS AND POLLUTED LAND!
I MUST PURIFY MYSELF.
FROM HIS DISCARDED CLOTHING WERE CREATED TWELVE *KAMI*. FROM THE FILTH OF *YOMI* CAME FORTH *KAMI* OF EVIL NATURE.
FOURTEEN *KAMI* WERE BORN AS *IZANAGI* BATHED. OF THESE, THE LAST THREE WERE:
AMATERASU, FEMALE *KAMI* OF THE SUN, BORN FROM HIS RIGHT EYE...
...*TSUKIYOMI*, MALE *KAMI* OF THE MOON, EMERGED FROM HIS LEFT EYE...
...AND *SUSANO-O*, *KAMI* OF THE SEA-PLAIN, BORN FROM HIS NOSE.
SOON AFTER, *IZANAGI* RETIRED TO A CAVE ON THE ISLAND OF *AHAJI* TO AWAIT THE END OF HIS TIME.

END of PROLOGUE 1

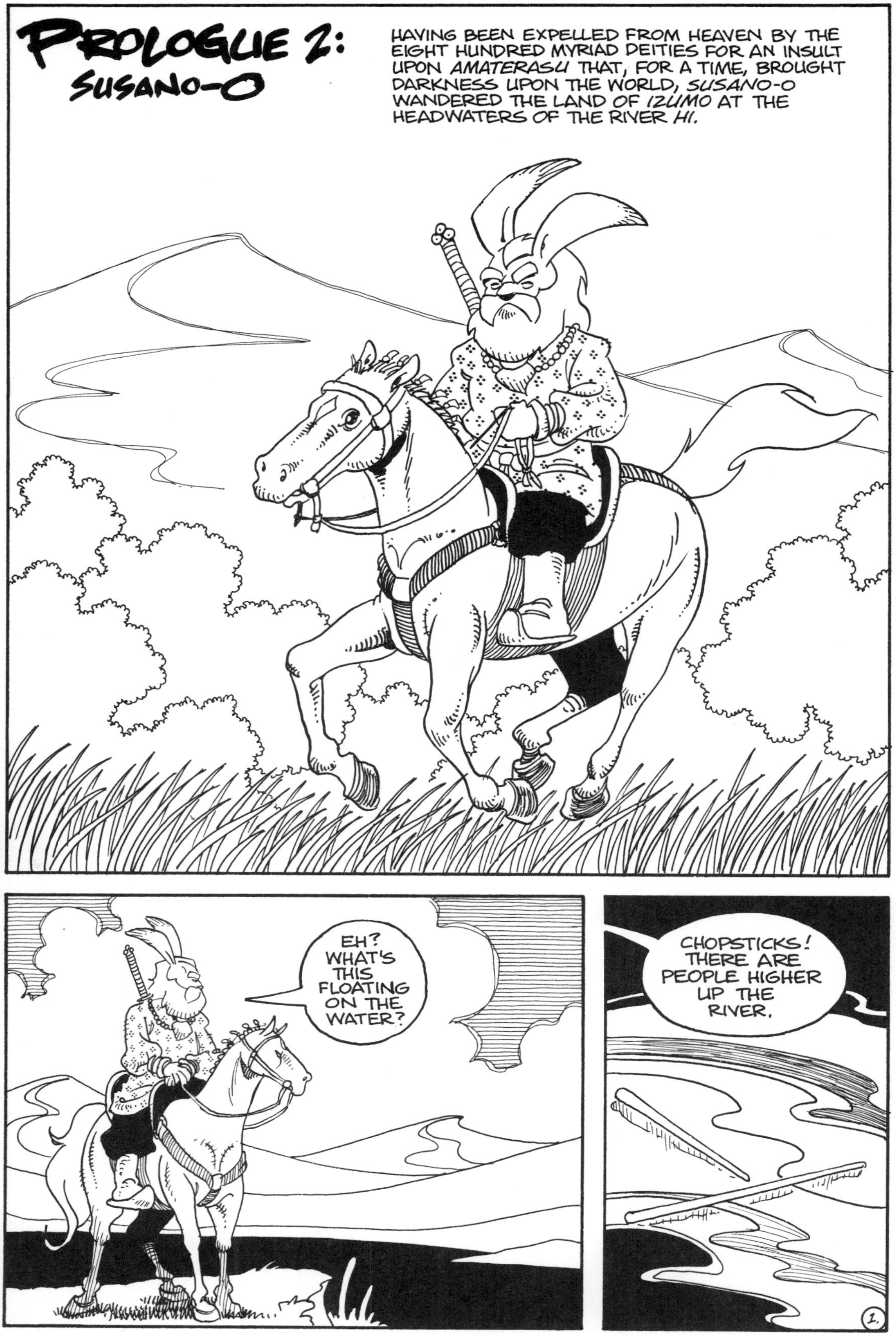
PROLOGUE 2:
SUSANO-O
HAVING BEEN EXPELLED FROM HEAVEN BY THE EIGHT HUNDRED MYRIAD DEITIES FOR AN INSULT UPON AMATERASU THAT, FOR A TIME, BROUGHT DARKNESS UPON THE WORLD, SUSANO-O WANDERED THE LAND OF IZUMO AT THE HEADWATERS OF THE RIVER HI.
EH? WHAT'S THIS FLOATING ON THE WATER?
CHOPSTICKS! THERE ARE PEOPLE HIGHER UP THE RIVER.
1.

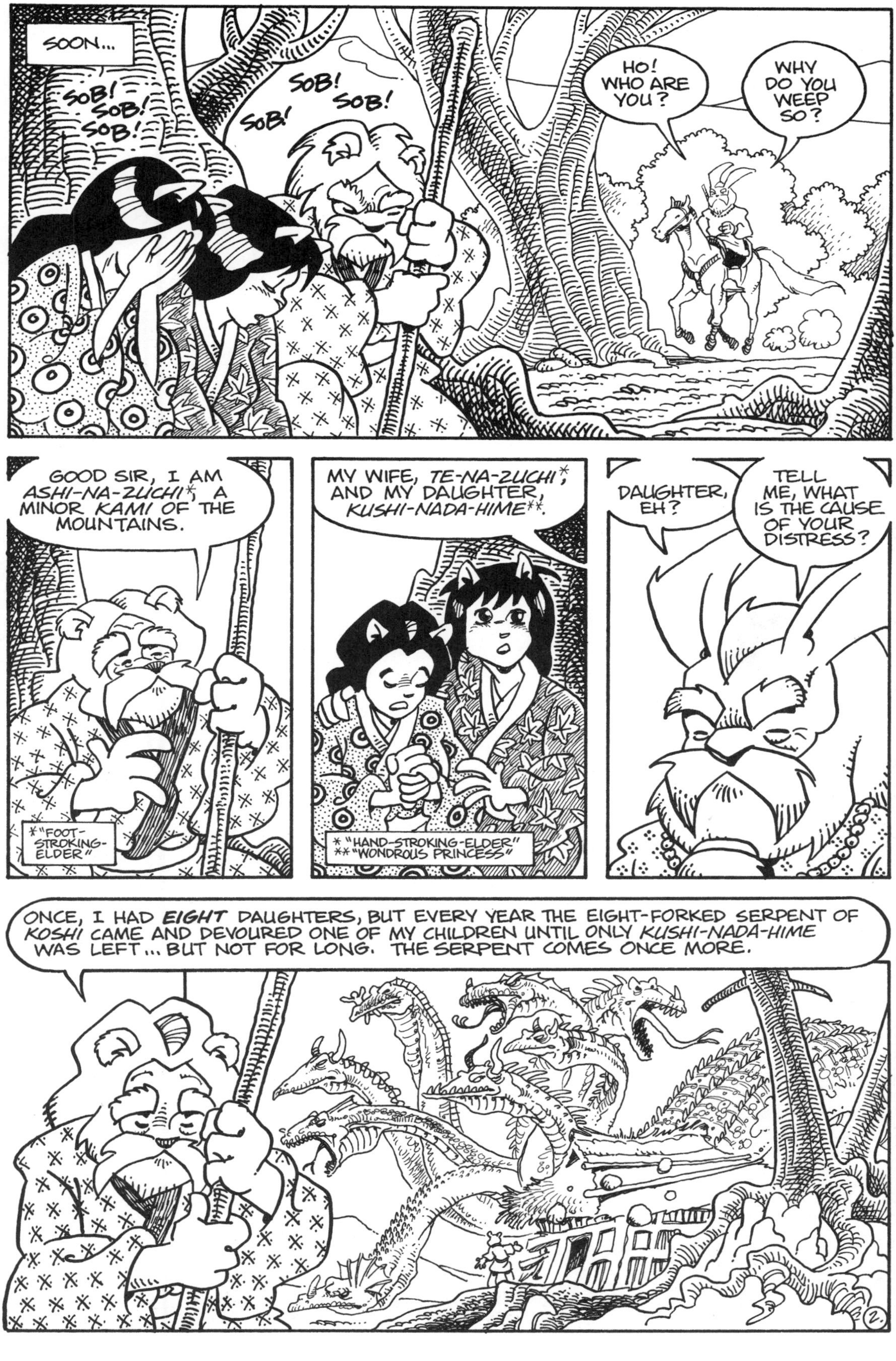
SOON...
SOB! SOB! SOB!
SOB! SOB! SOB!
HO! WHO ARE YOU?
WHY DO YOU WEEP SO?
GOOD SIR, I AM ASHI-NA-ZUCHI*, A MINOR KAMI OF THE MOUNTAINS.
*"FOOT-STROKING-ELDER"
MY WIFE, TE-NA-ZUCHI*, AND MY DAUGHTER, KUSHI-NADA-HIME**.
*"HAND-STROKING-ELDER"
**"WONDROUS PRINCESS"
DAUGHTER, EH?
TELL ME, WHAT IS THE CAUSE OF YOUR DISTRESS?
ONCE, I HAD EIGHT DAUGHTERS, BUT EVERY YEAR THE EIGHT-FORKED SERPENT OF KOSHI CAME AND DEVOURED ONE OF MY CHILDREN UNTIL ONLY KUSHI-NADA-HIME WAS LEFT... BUT NOT FOR LONG. THE SERPENT COMES ONCE MORE.
2.

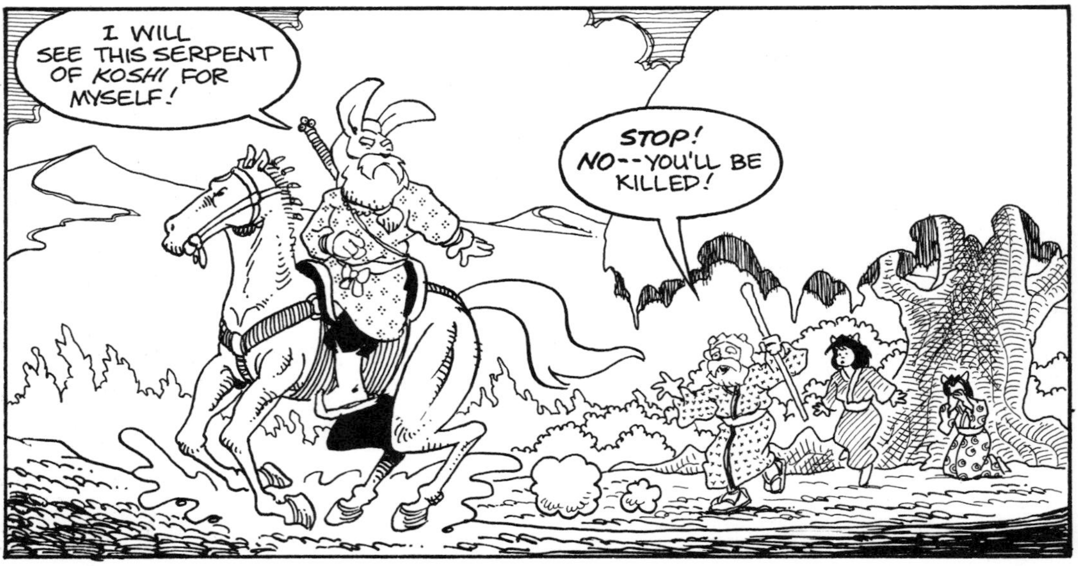
I WILL SEE THIS SERPENT OF KOSHI FOR MYSELF!
STOP! NO--YOU'LL BE KILLED!

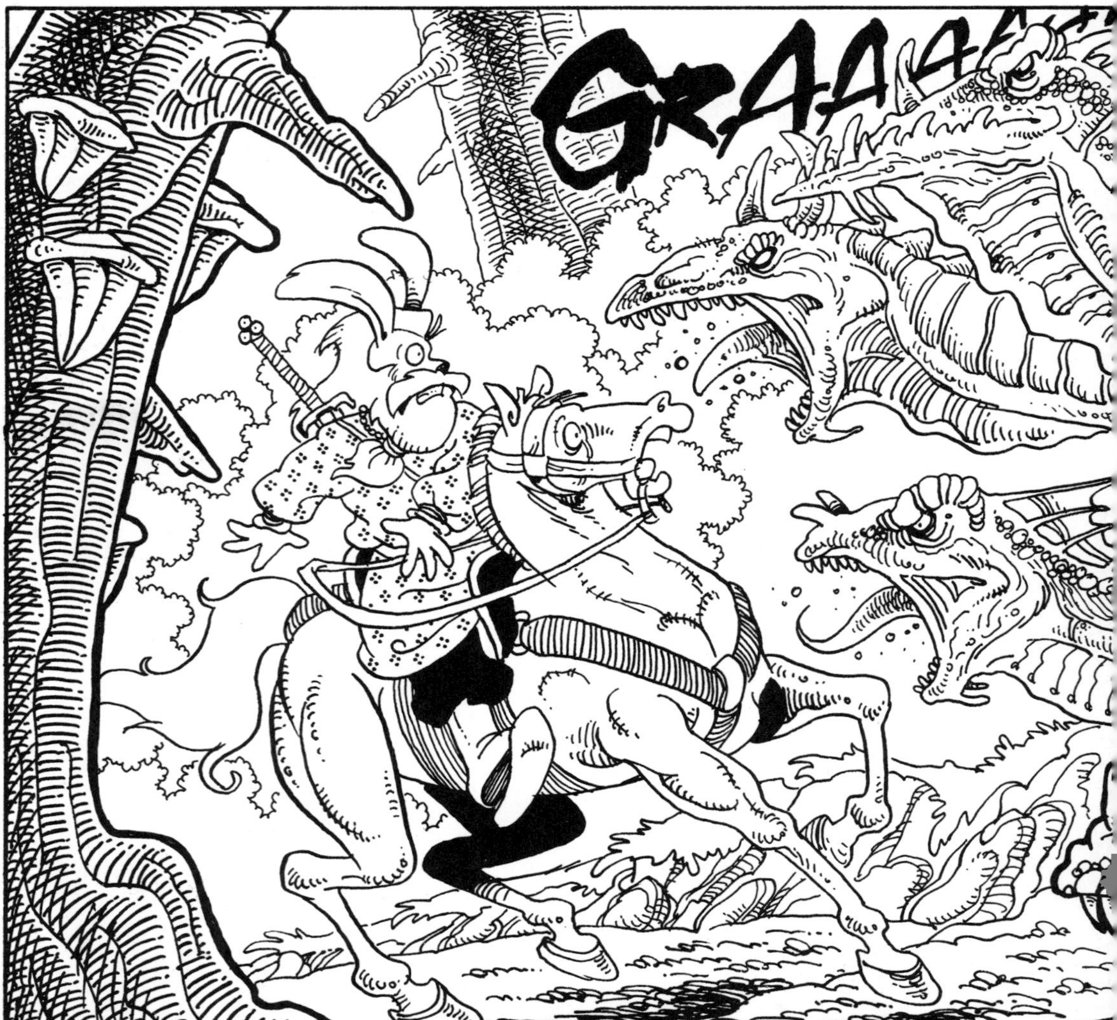
GRAAA

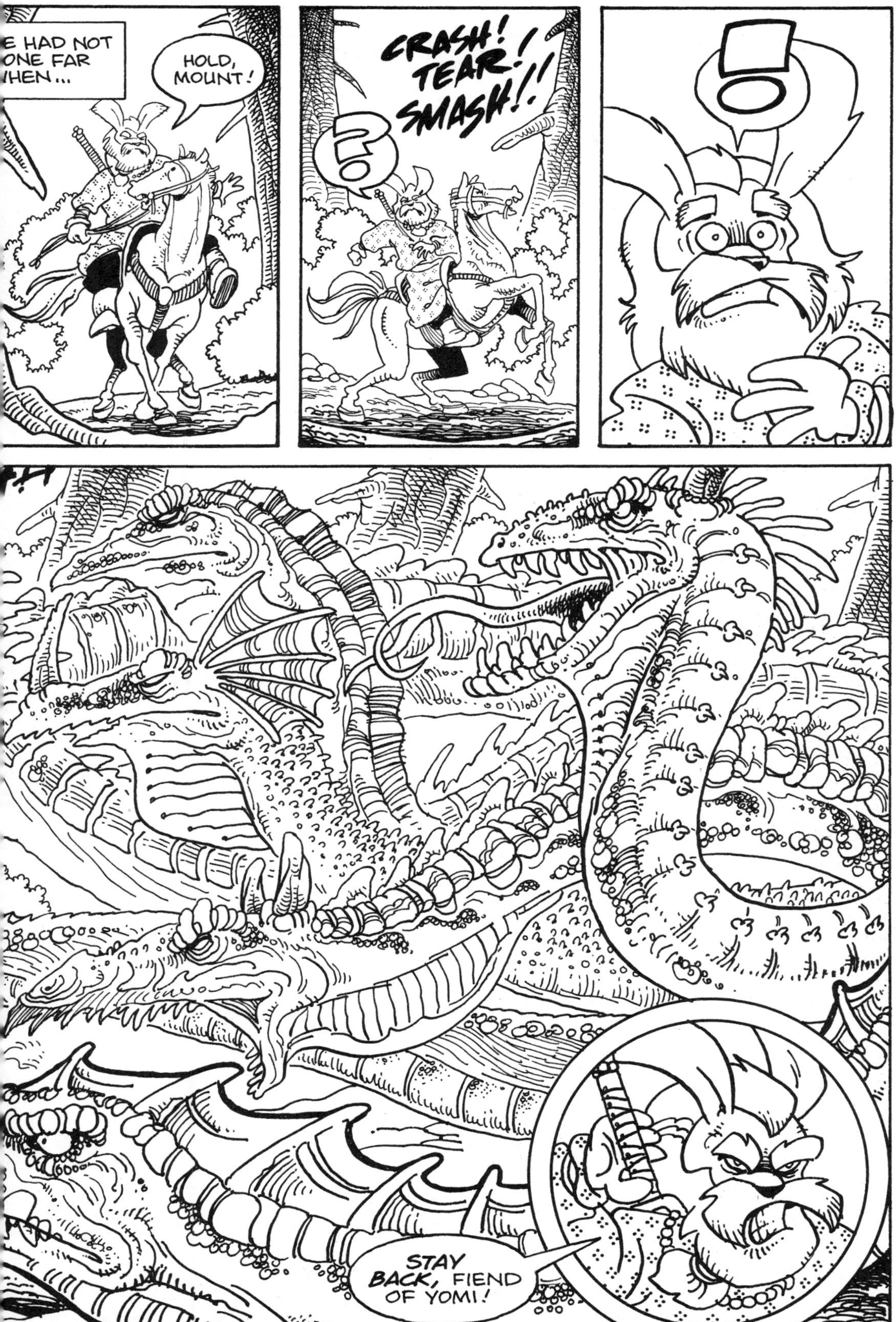
E HAD NOT
ONE FAR
WHEN...
HOLD, MOUNT!
CRASH! TEAR! SMASH!!
?!
!?
STAY BACK, FIEND OF YOMI!
4.

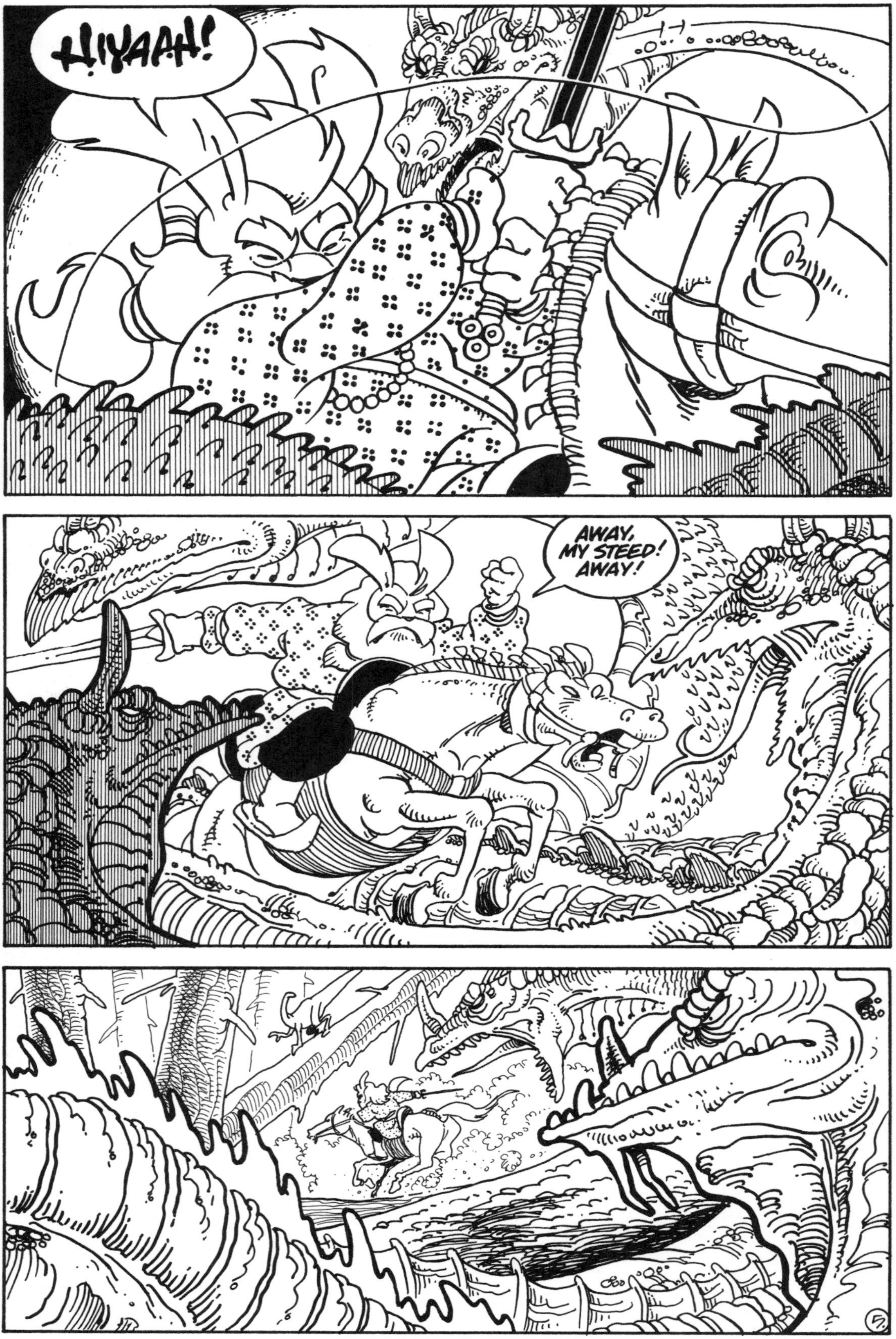
HIYAAH!
AWAY, MY STEED! AWAY!
5

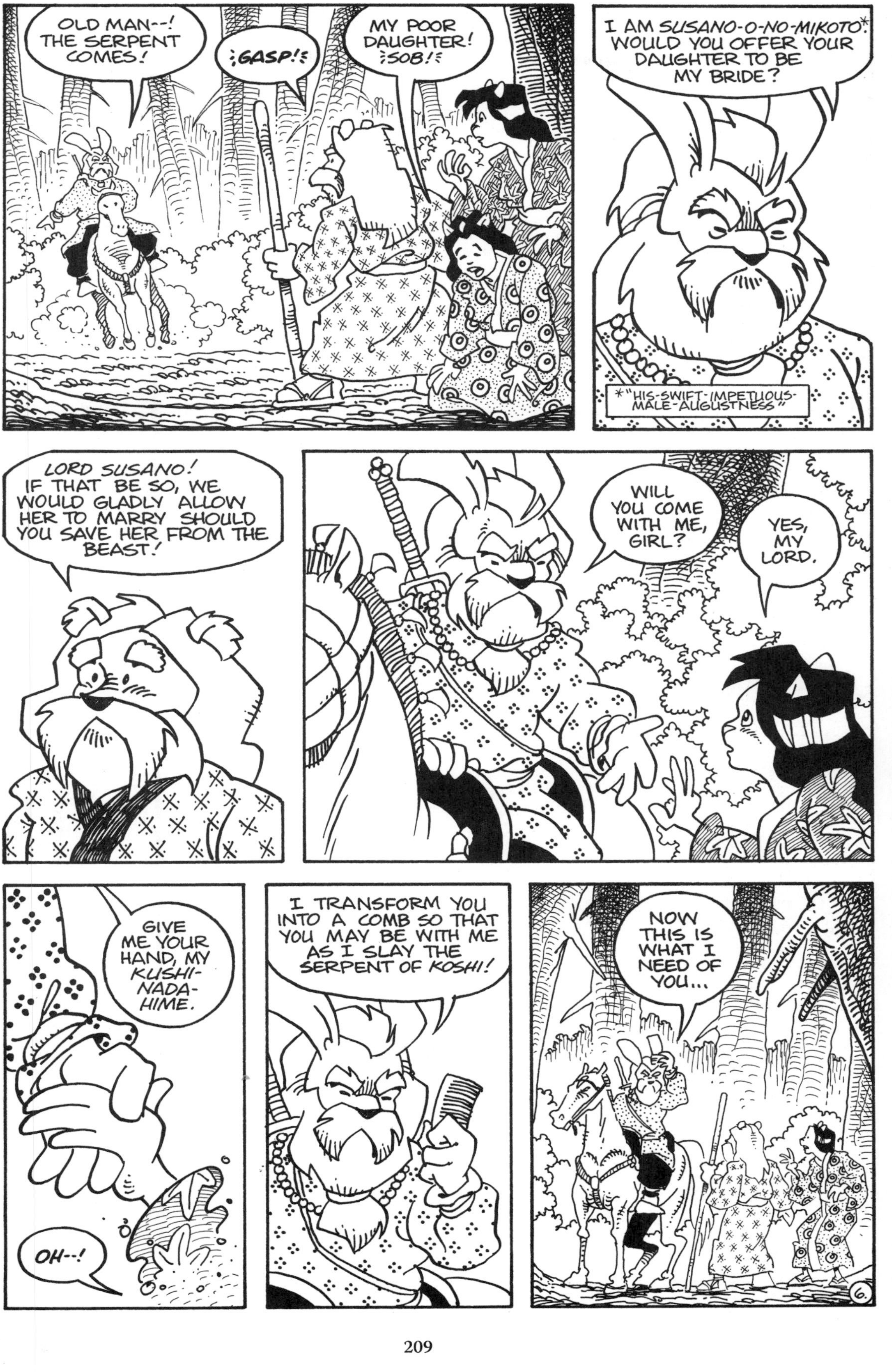
OLD MAN--! THE SERPENT COMES!
GASP!
MY POOR DAUGHTER! SOB!
I AM SUSANO-O-NO-MIKOTO* WOULD YOU OFFER YOUR DAUGHTER TO BE MY BRIDE?
*"HIS-SWIFT-IMPETUOUS-MALE-AUGUSTNESS"
LORD SUSANO! IF THAT BE SO, WE WOULD GLADLY ALLOW HER TO MARRY SHOULD YOU SAVE HER FROM THE BEAST!
WILL YOU COME WITH ME, GIRL?
YES, MY LORD.
GIVE ME YOUR HAND, MY KUSHI-NADA-HIME.
OH--!
I TRANSFORM YOU INTO A COMB SO THAT YOU MAY BE WITH ME AS I SLAY THE SERPENT OF KOSHI!
NOW THIS IS WHAT I NEED OF YOU...
6.

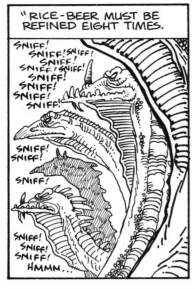

"RICE-BEER MUST BE REFINED EIGHT TIMES.

SNIFF!
SNIFF! SNIFF!
SNIFF!
SNIFF! SNIFF!
SNIFF!
SNIFF!
SNIFF!

SNIFF!
SNIFF!

SNIFF!

SNIFF!
SNIFF!
SNIFF!
HMMM...

"THEN BUILD A FENCE WITH EIGHT GATES.

SNIFF!
SNIFF!
SNIFF!
SNIFF!

SNIFF!

SNIFF!

SNIFF!

"BEYOND EACH GATE, BUILD A PLATFORM.

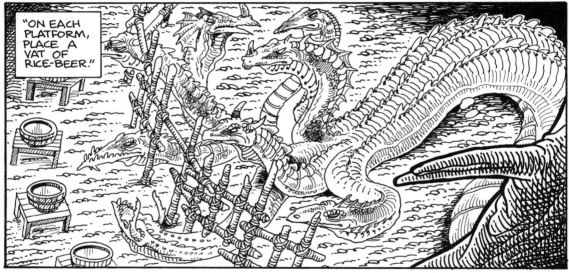

"ON EACH PLATFORM, PLACE A VAT OF RICE-BEER."

SLURP! SLURP!

AHHH... BELCH!

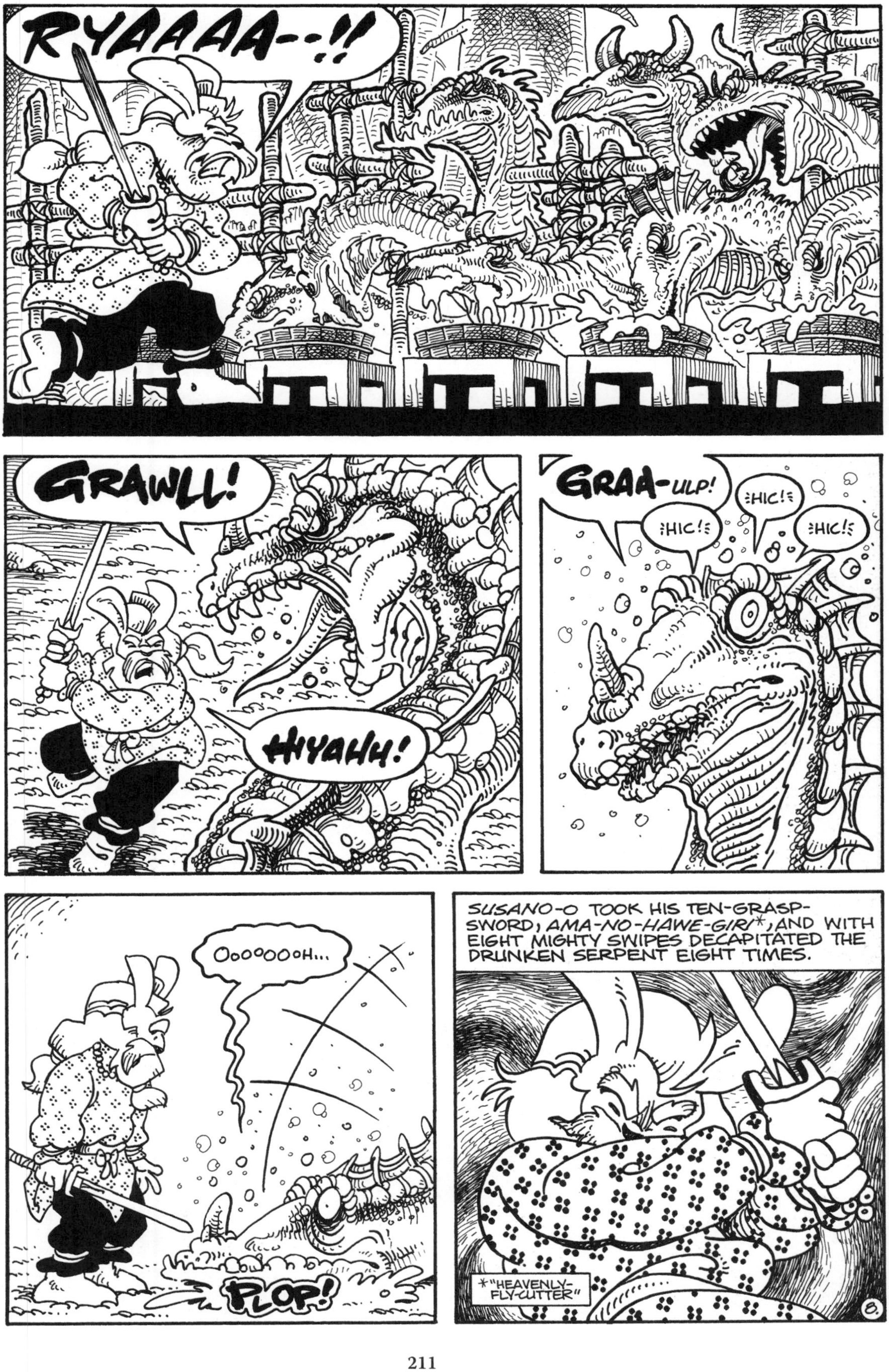
RYAAAA--!!
GRAWLL!
HIYAHH!
GRAA-ULP!
HIC!
HIC!
HIC!
OOOOOOOH...
PLOP!
SUSANO-O TOOK HIS TEN-GRASP-SWORD, AMA-NO-HAWE-GIRI*, AND WITH EIGHT MIGHTY SWIPES DECAPITATED THE DRUNKEN SERPENT EIGHT TIMES.
*"HEAVENLY-FLY-CUTTER"
8.

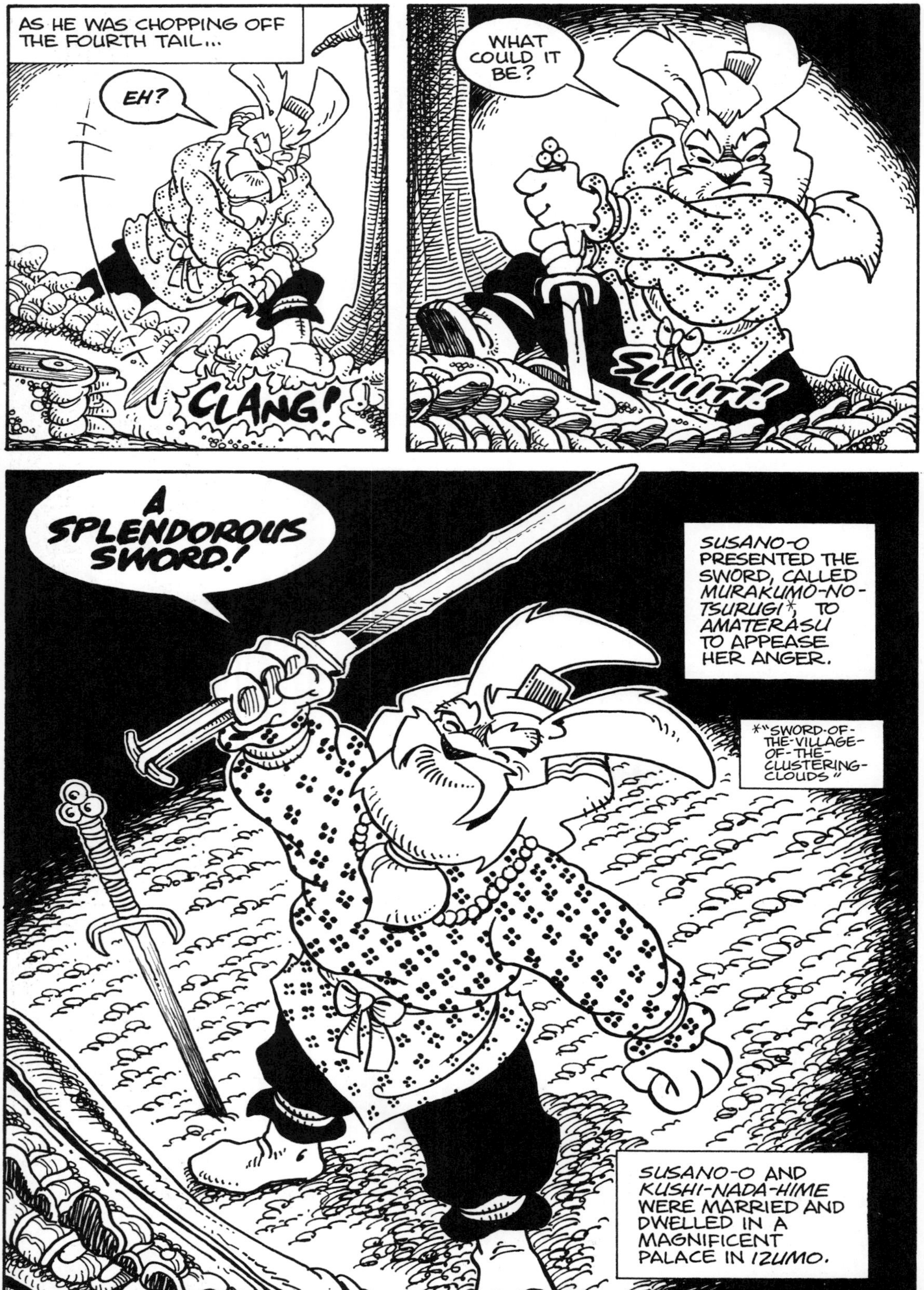
AS HE WAS CHOPPING OFF THE FOURTH TAIL...
EH?
CLANG!
WHAT COULD IT BE?
SLIIIITT!
A SPLENDOROUS SWORD!
SUSANO-O PRESENTED THE SWORD, CALLED MURAKUMO-NO-TSURUGI*, TO AMATERASU TO APPEASE HER ANGER.
*"SWORD-OF-THE-VILLAGE-OF-THE-CLUSTERING-CLOUDS"
SUSANO-O AND KUSHI-NADA-HIME WERE MARRIED AND DWELLED IN A MAGNIFICENT PALACE IN IZUMO.

END of PROLOGUE 2

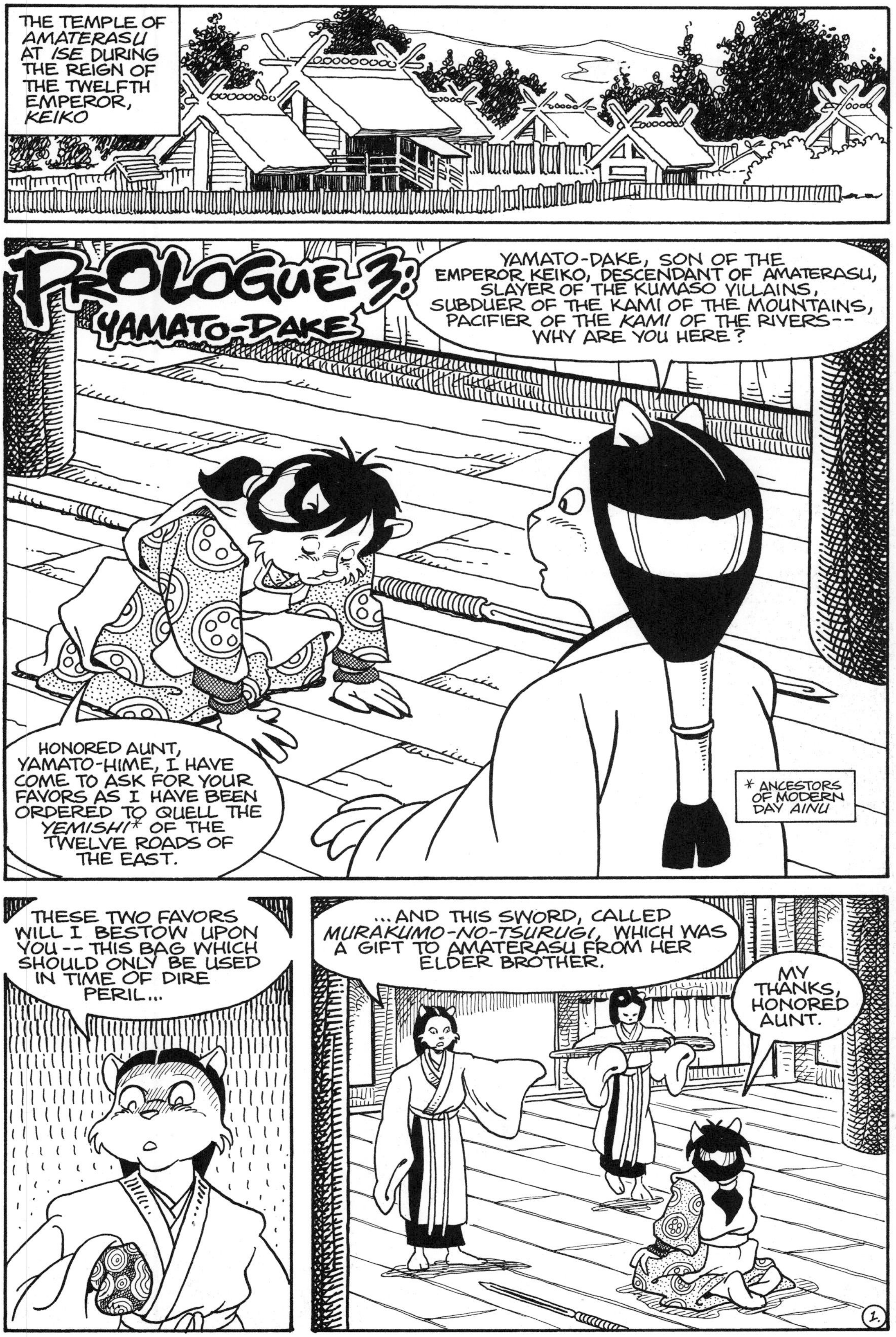
THE TEMPLE OF AMATERASU AT ISE DURING THE REIGN OF THE TWELFTH EMPEROR, KEIKO
PROLOGUE 3: YAMATO-DAKE
YAMATO-DAKE, SON OF THE EMPEROR KEIKO, DESCENDANT OF AMATERASU, SLAYER OF THE KUMASO VILLAINS, SUBDUER OF THE KAMI OF THE MOUNTAINS, PACIFIER OF THE KAMI OF THE RIVERS-- WHY ARE YOU HERE?
HONORED AUNT, YAMATO-HIME, I HAVE COME TO ASK FOR YOUR FAVORS AS I HAVE BEEN ORDERED TO QUELL THE YEMISHI* OF THE TWELVE ROADS OF THE EAST.
* ANCESTORS OF MODERN DAY AINU
THESE TWO FAVORS WILL I BESTOW UPON YOU -- THIS BAG WHICH SHOULD ONLY BE USED IN TIME OF DIRE PERIL...
...AND THIS SWORD, CALLED MURAKUMO-NO-TSURUGI, WHICH WAS A GIFT TO AMATERASU FROM HER ELDER BROTHER.
MY THANKS, HONORED AUNT.
1.

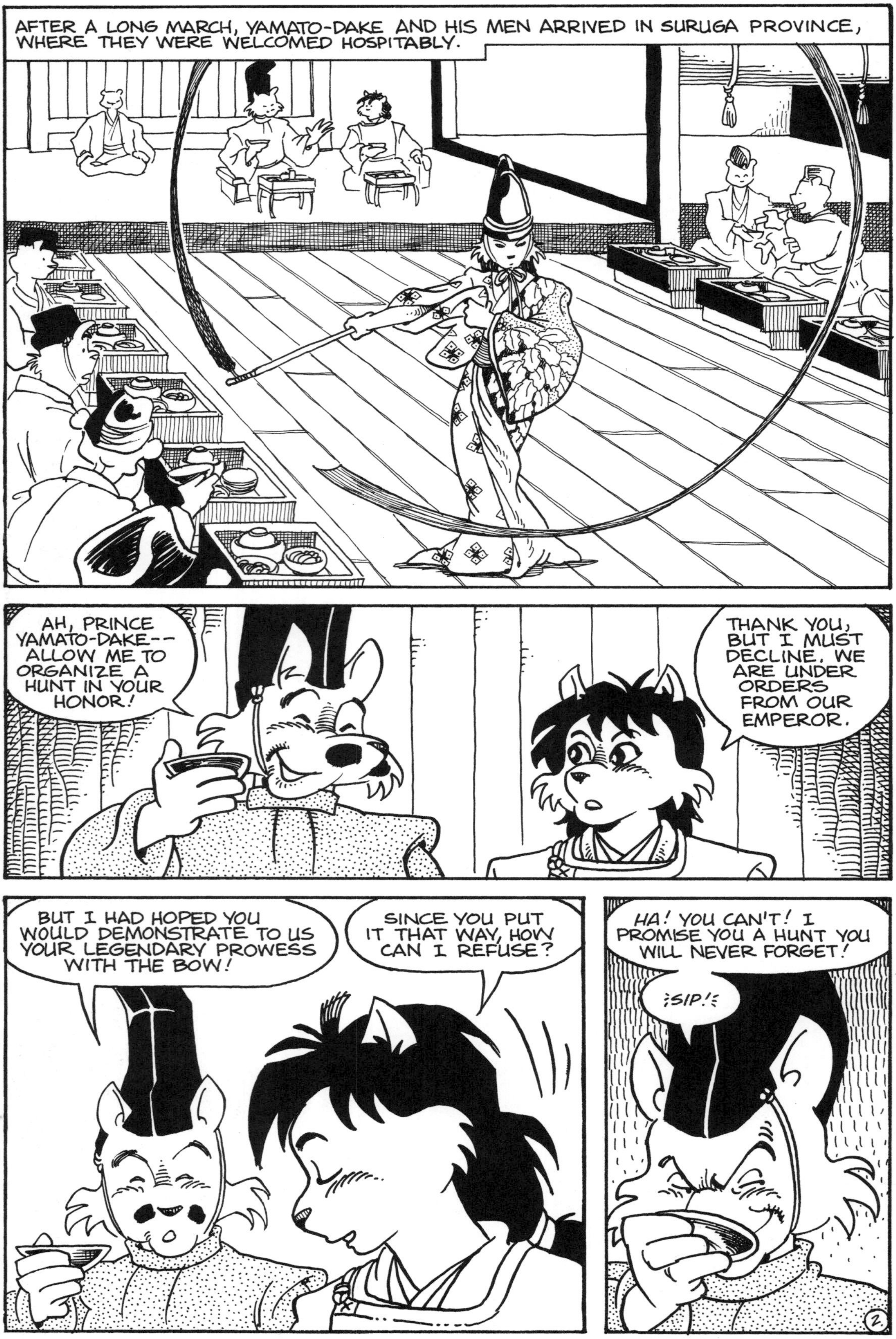
AFTER A LONG MARCH, YAMATO-DAKE AND HIS MEN ARRIVED IN SURUGA PROVINCE, WHERE THEY WERE WELCOMED HOSPITABLY.
AH, PRINCE YAMATO-DAKE-- ALLOW ME TO ORGANIZE A HUNT IN YOUR HONOR!
THANK YOU, BUT I MUST DECLINE. WE ARE UNDER ORDERS FROM OUR EMPEROR.
BUT I HAD HOPED YOU WOULD DEMONSTRATE TO US YOUR LEGENDARY PROWESS WITH THE BOW!
SINCE YOU PUT IT THAT WAY, HOW CAN I REFUSE?
HA! YOU CAN'T! I PROMISE YOU A HUNT YOU WILL NEVER FORGET!
SIP!
2

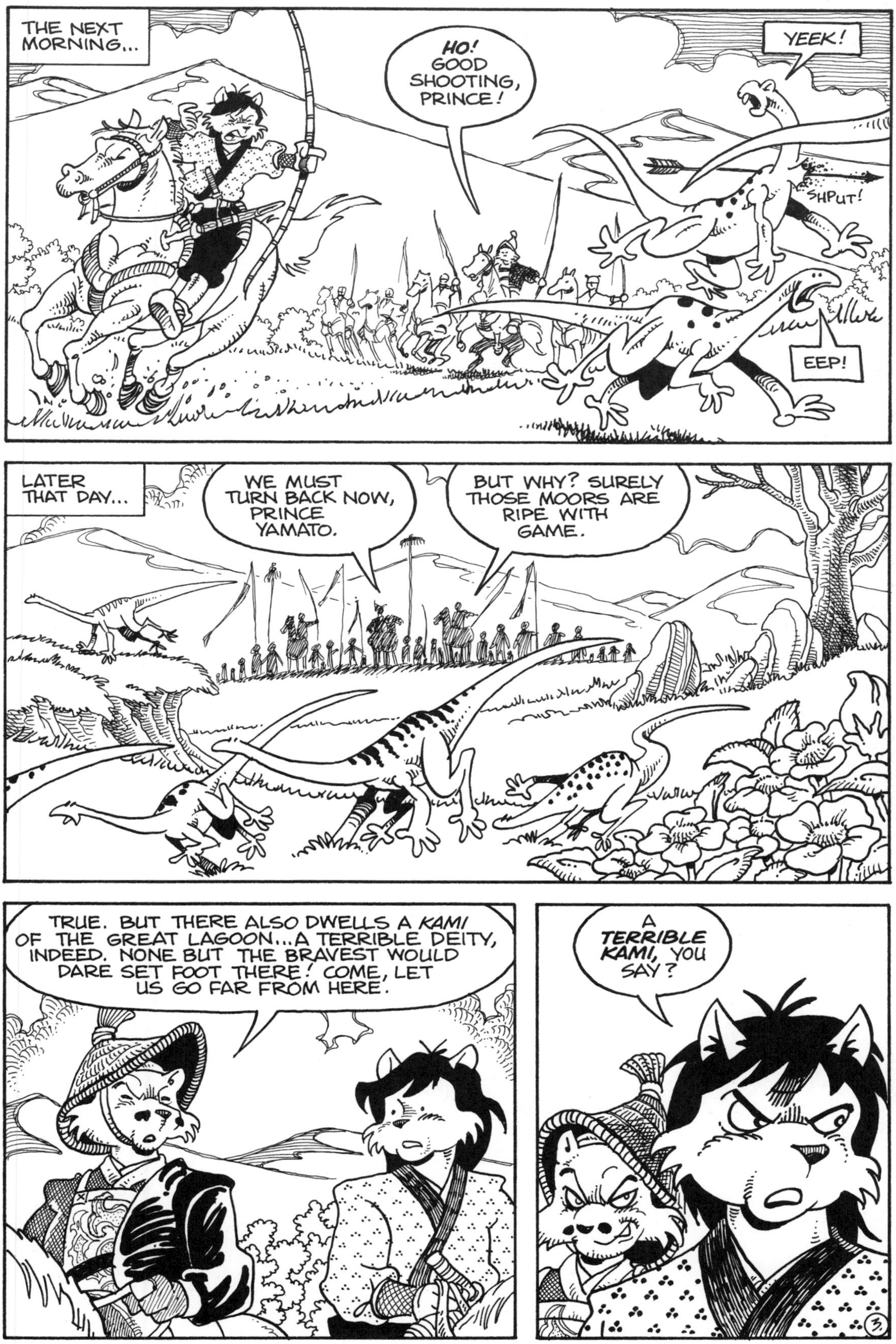
THE NEXT MORNING...
HO! GOOD SHOOTING, PRINCE!
YEEK!
SHPUT!
EEP!
LATER THAT DAY...
WE MUST TURN BACK NOW, PRINCE YAMATO.
BUT WHY? SURELY THOSE MOORS ARE RIPE WITH GAME.
TRUE. BUT THERE ALSO DWELLS A *KAMI* OF THE GREAT LAGOON...A TERRIBLE DEITY, INDEED. NONE BUT THE BRAVEST WOULD DARE SET FOOT THERE! COME, LET US GO FAR FROM HERE.
A *TERRIBLE KAMI,* YOU SAY?
3.

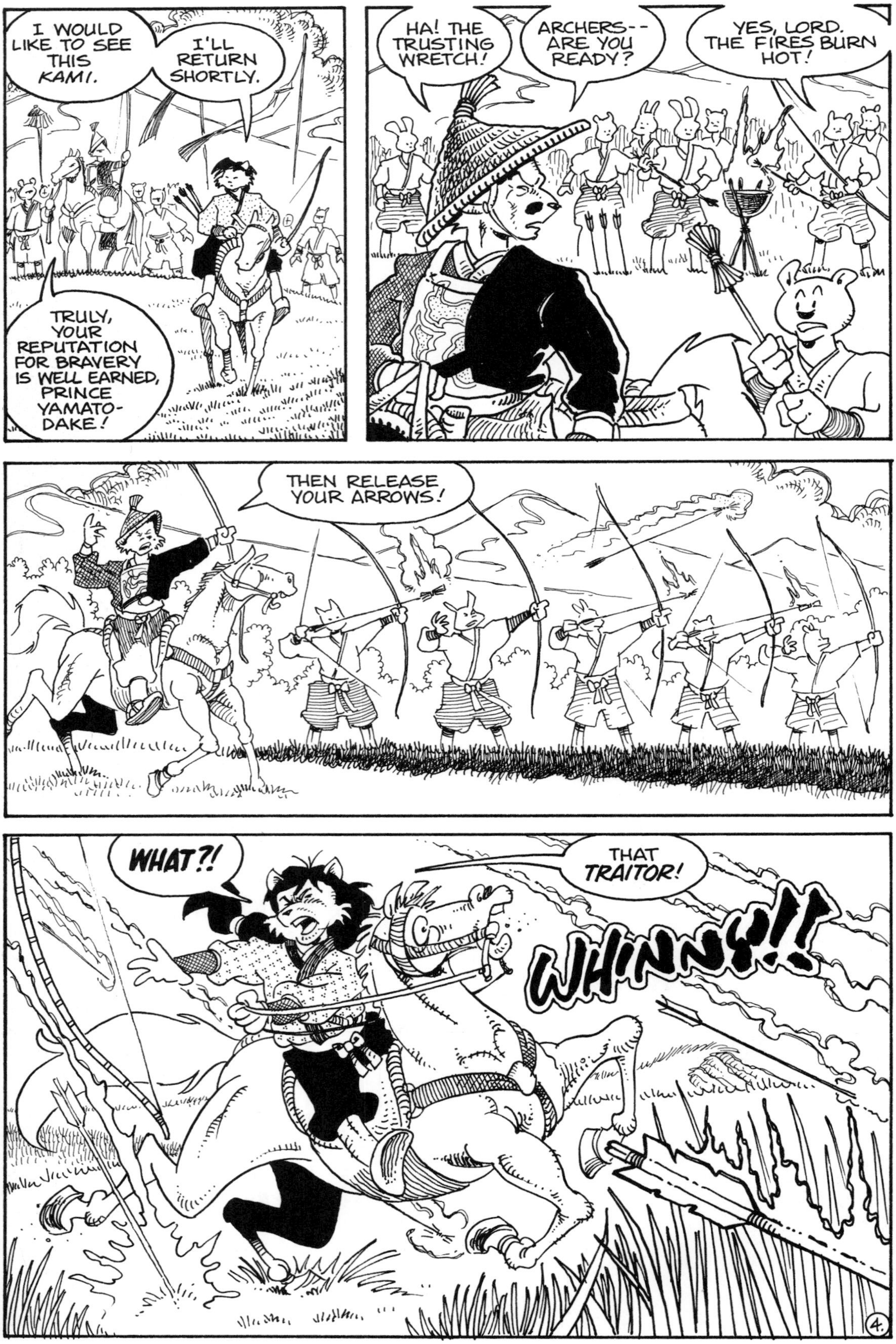
I WOULD LIKE TO SEE THIS KAMI.
I'LL RETURN SHORTLY.
TRULY, YOUR REPUTATION FOR BRAVERY IS WELL EARNED, PRINCE YAMATO-DAKE!
HA! THE TRUSTING WRETCH!
ARCHERS-- ARE YOU READY?
YES, LORD. THE FIRES BURN HOT!
THEN RELEASE YOUR ARROWS!
WHAT?!
THAT TRAITOR!
WHINNY!!
4.

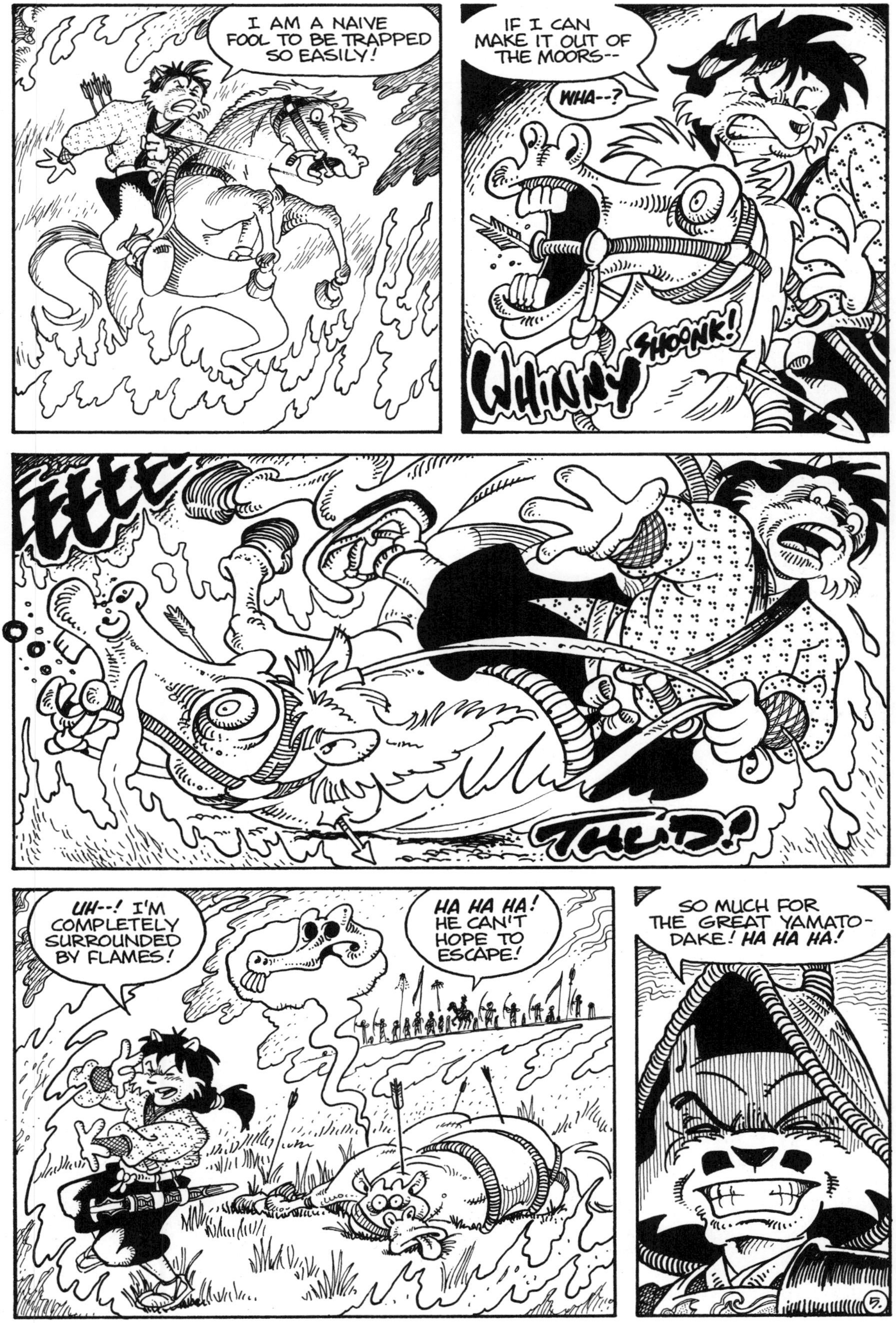
I AM A NAIVE FOOL TO BE TRAPPED SO EASILY!
IF I CAN MAKE IT OUT OF THE MOORS--
WHA--?
SHOONK!
WHINNY
EEEEE
THUD!
UH--! I'M COMPLETELY SURROUNDED BY FLAMES!
HA HA HA! HE CAN'T HOPE TO ESCAPE!
SO MUCH FOR THE GREAT YAMATO-DAKE! HA HA HA!

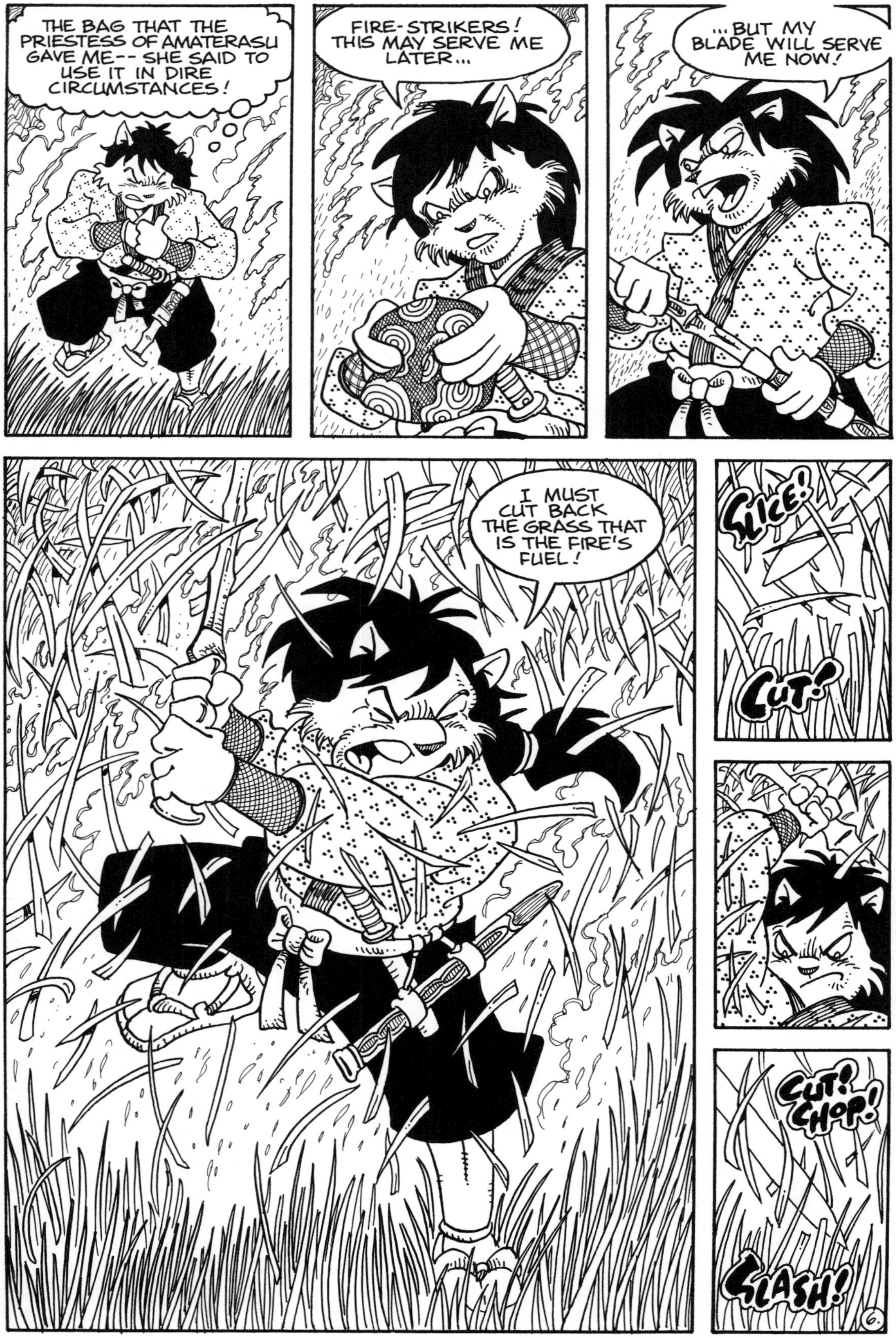
THE BAG THAT THE PRIESTESS OF AMATERASU GAVE ME-- SHE SAID TO USE IT IN DIRE CIRCUMSTANCES!
FIRE-STRIKERS! THIS MAY SERVE ME LATER...
...BUT MY BLADE WILL SERVE ME NOW!
I MUST CUT BACK THE GRASS THAT IS THE FIRE'S FUEL!
SLICE!
CUT!
CUT! CHOP!
SLASH!
6.

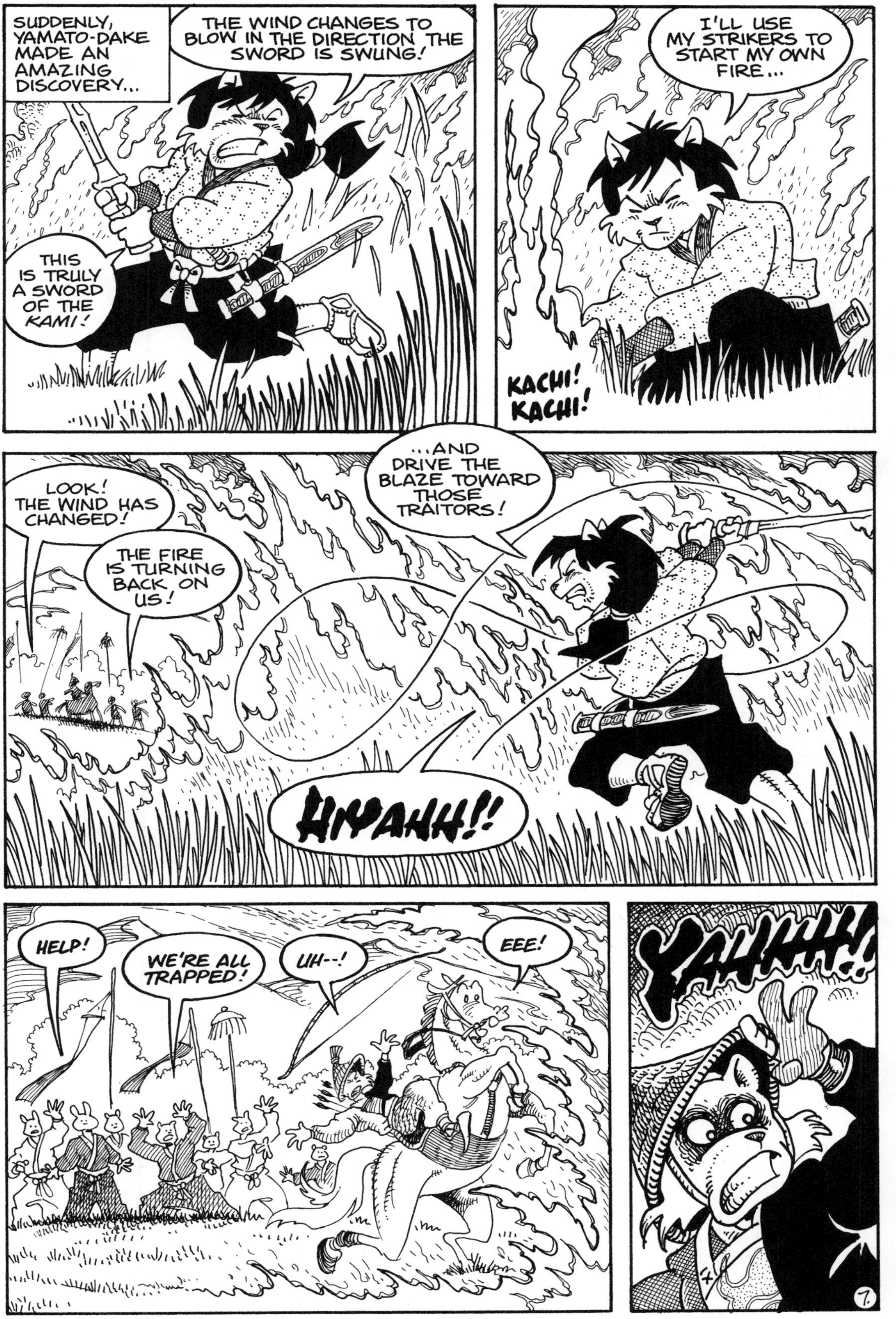
SUDDENLY, YAMATO-DAKE MADE AN AMAZING DISCOVERY...
THE WIND CHANGES TO BLOW IN THE DIRECTION THE SWORD IS SWUNG!
THIS IS TRULY A SWORD OF THE *KAMI*!
I'LL USE MY STRIKERS TO START MY OWN FIRE...
KACHI! KACHI!
LOOK! THE WIND HAS CHANGED!
THE FIRE IS TURNING BACK ON US!
...AND DRIVE THE BLAZE TOWARD THOSE TRAITORS!
HIYAHH!!
HELP!
WE'RE ALL TRAPPED!
UH--!
EEE!
YAHHH!
7.

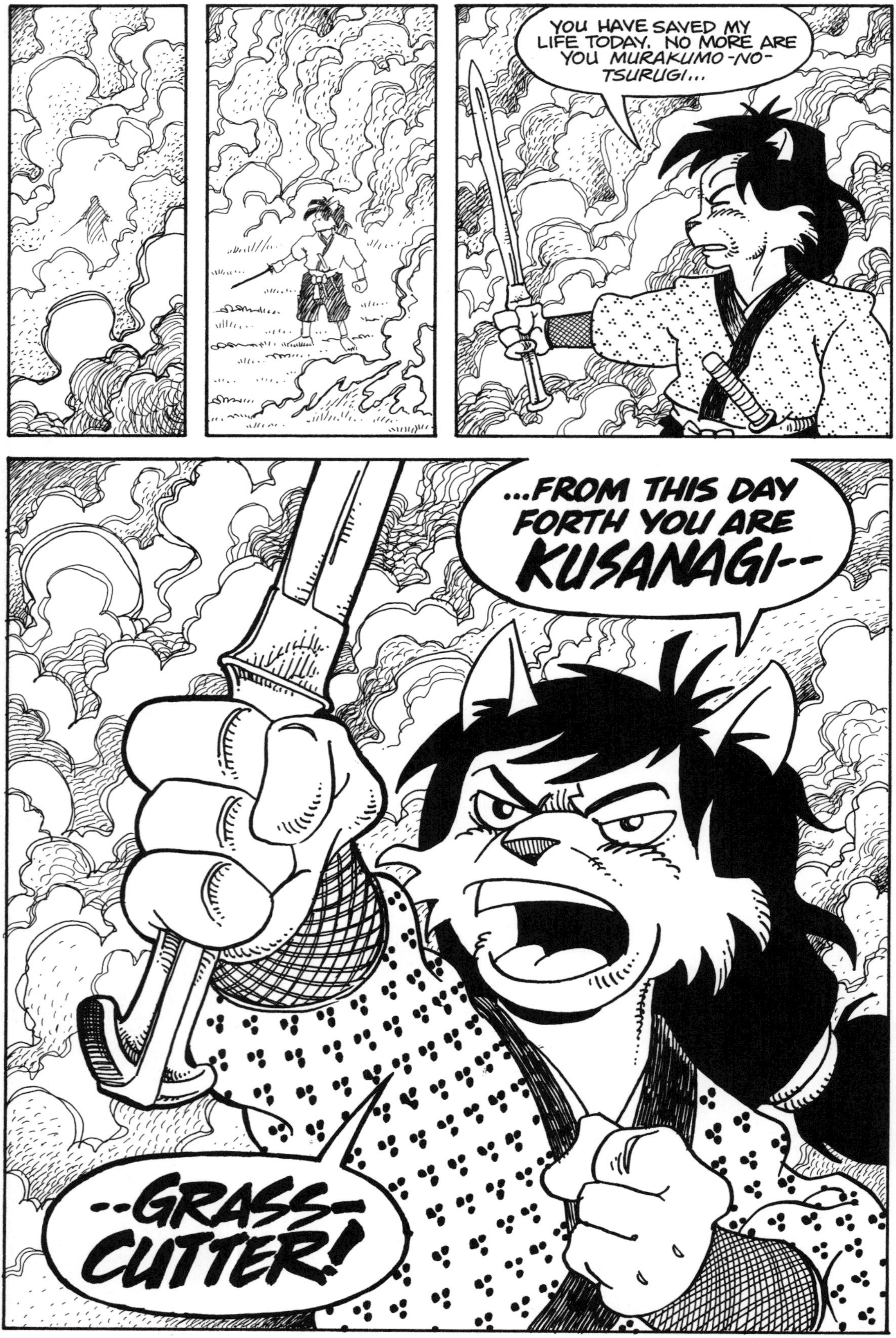
YOU HAVE SAVED MY LIFE TODAY. NO MORE ARE YOU MURAKUMO-NO-TSURUGI...
...FROM THIS DAY FORTH YOU ARE KUSANAGI--
--GRASS-CUTTER!

END OF PROLOGUE 3

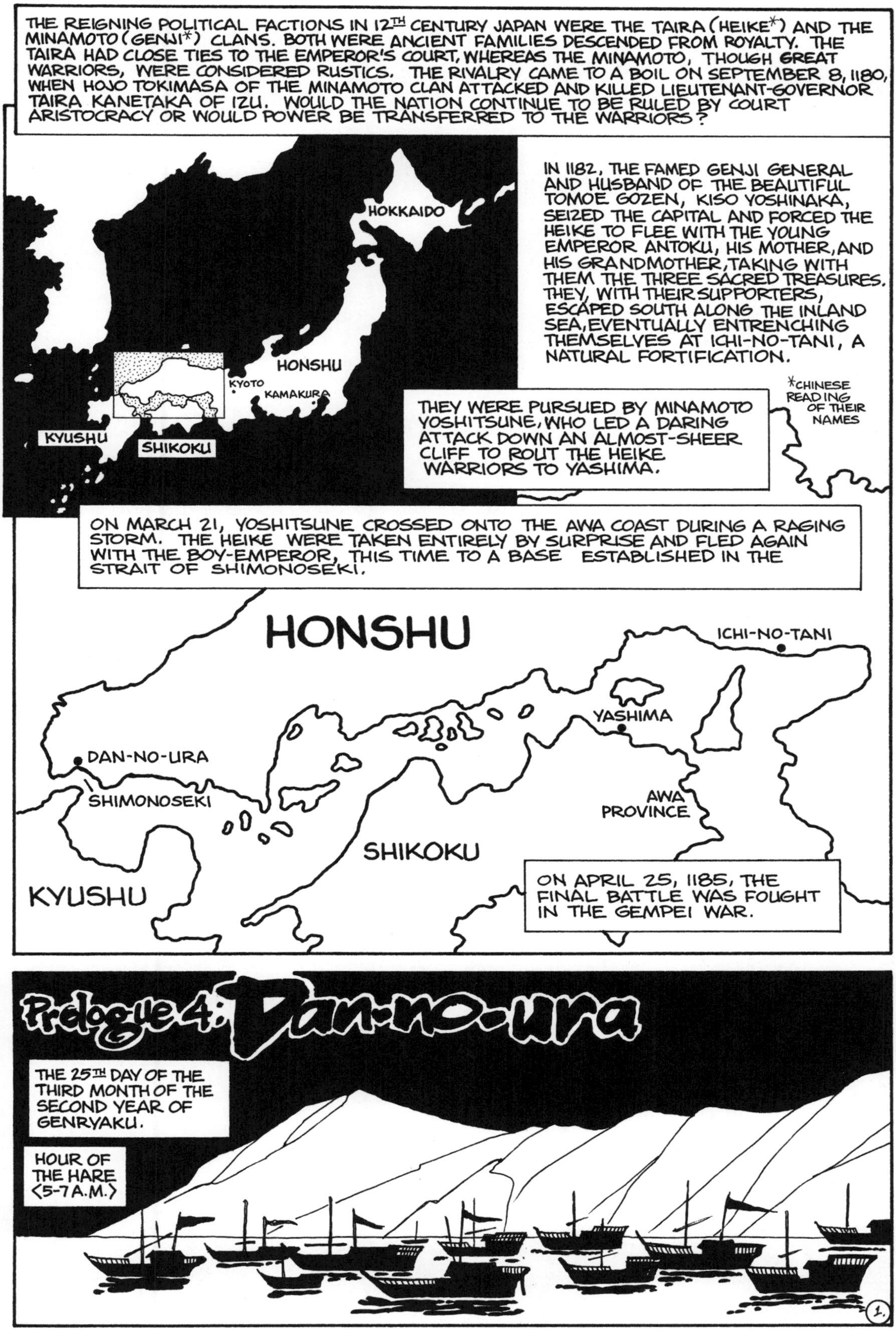

THE REIGNING POLITICAL FACTIONS IN 12TH CENTURY JAPAN WERE THE TAIRA (HEIKE*) AND THE MINAMOTO (GENJI*) CLANS. BOTH WERE ANCIENT FAMILIES DESCENDED FROM ROYALTY. THE TAIRA HAD CLOSE TIES TO THE EMPEROR'S COURT, WHEREAS THE MINAMOTO, THOUGH GREAT WARRIORS, WERE CONSIDERED RUSTICS. THE RIVALRY CAME TO A BOIL ON SEPTEMBER 8, 1180, WHEN HOJO TOKIMASA OF THE MINAMOTO CLAN ATTACKED AND KILLED LIEUTENANT-GOVERNOR TAIRA KANETAKA OF IZU. WOULD THE NATION CONTINUE TO BE RULED BY COURT ARISTOCRACY OR WOULD POWER BE TRANSFERRED TO THE WARRIORS?

HOKKAIDO

HONSHU

KYOTO
KAMAKURA

KYUSHU   SHIKOKU

IN 1182, THE FAMED GENJI GENERAL AND HUSBAND OF THE BEAUTIFUL TOMOE GOZEN, KISO YOSHINAKA, SEIZED THE CAPITAL AND FORCED THE HEIKE TO FLEE WITH THE YOUNG EMPEROR ANTOKU, HIS MOTHER, AND HIS GRANDMOTHER, TAKING WITH THEM THE THREE SACRED TREASURES. THEY, WITH THEIR SUPPORTERS, ESCAPED SOUTH ALONG THE INLAND SEA, EVENTUALLY ENTRENCHING THEMSELVES AT ICHI-NO-TANI, A NATURAL FORTIFICATION.

THEY WERE PURSUED BY MINAMOTO YOSHITSUNE, WHO LED A DARING ATTACK DOWN AN ALMOST-SHEER CLIFF TO ROUT THE HEIKE WARRIORS TO YASHIMA.

*CHINESE READING OF THEIR NAMES

ON MARCH 21, YOSHITSUNE CROSSED ONTO THE AWA COAST DURING A RAGING STORM. THE HEIKE WERE TAKEN ENTIRELY BY SURPRISE AND FLED AGAIN WITH THE BOY-EMPEROR, THIS TIME TO A BASE ESTABLISHED IN THE STRAIT OF SHIMONOSEKI.

HONSHU

ICHI-NO-TANI

YASHIMA

DAN-NO-URA

SHIMONOSEKI

AWA PROVINCE

SHIKOKU

KYUSHU

ON APRIL 25, 1185, THE FINAL BATTLE WAS FOUGHT IN THE GEMPEI WAR.

Prologue 4: Dan-no-ura

THE 25TH DAY OF THE THIRD MONTH OF THE SECOND YEAR OF GENRYAKU.

HOUR OF THE HARE 〈5-7 A.M.〉

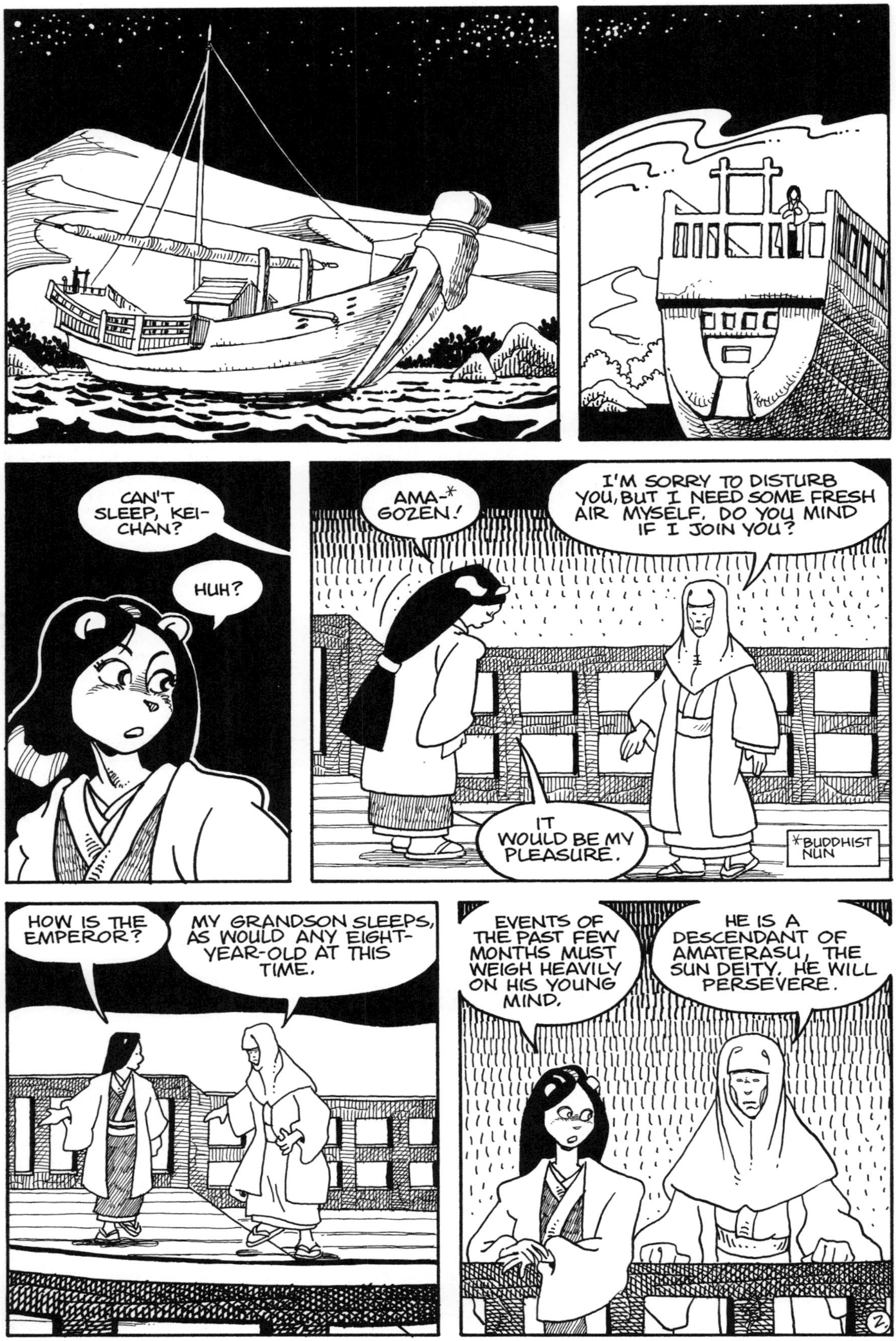
CAN'T SLEEP, KEI-CHAN?
HUH?
AMA-* GOZEN!
I'M SORRY TO DISTURB YOU, BUT I NEED SOME FRESH AIR MYSELF. DO YOU MIND IF I JOIN YOU?
IT WOULD BE MY PLEASURE.
*BUDDHIST NUN
HOW IS THE EMPEROR?
MY GRANDSON SLEEPS, AS WOULD ANY EIGHT-YEAR-OLD AT THIS TIME.
EVENTS OF THE PAST FEW MONTHS MUST WEIGH HEAVILY ON HIS YOUNG MIND.
HE IS A DESCENDANT OF AMATERASU, THE SUN DEITY. HE WILL PERSEVERE.
2.

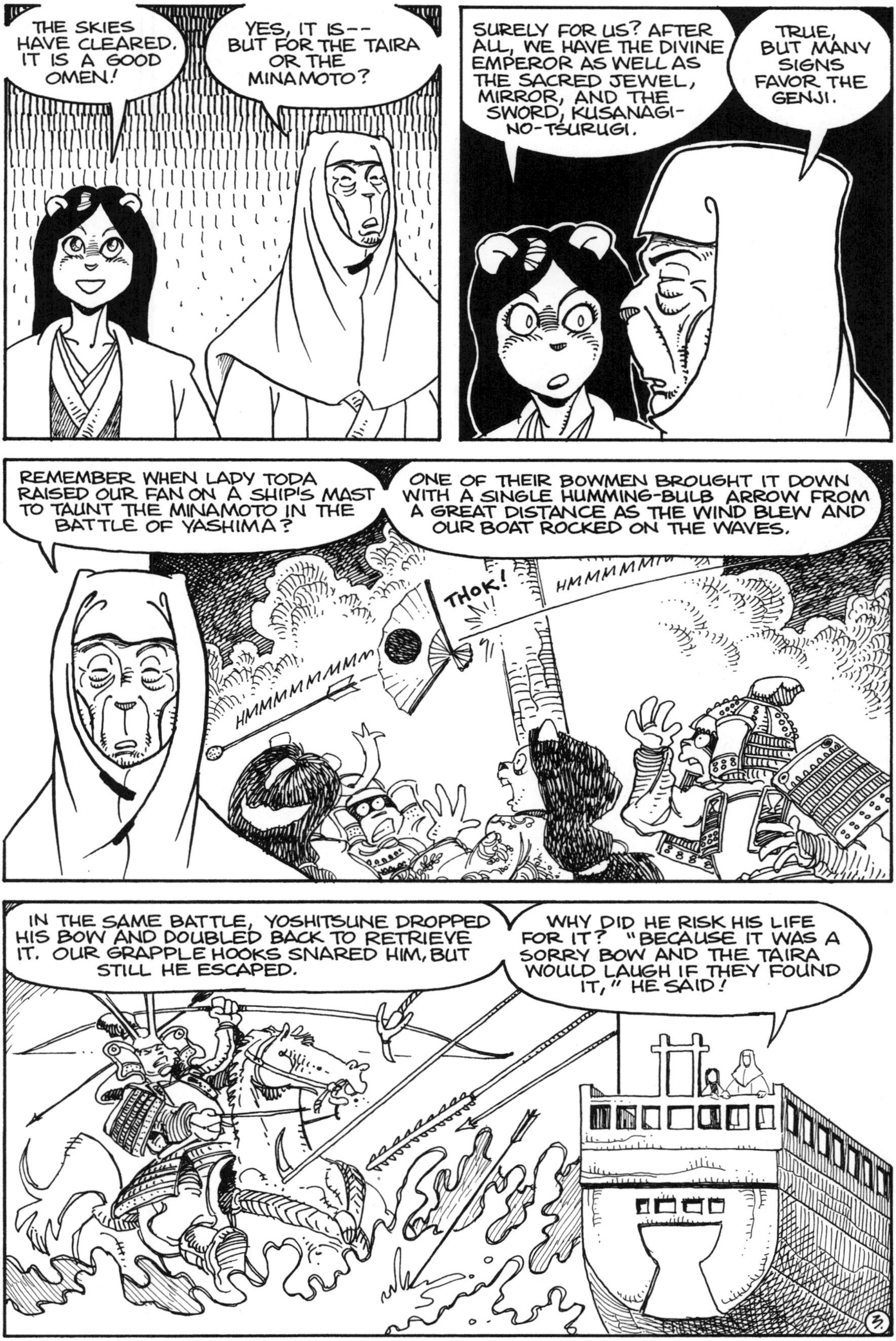
THE SKIES HAVE CLEARED. IT IS A GOOD OMEN!
YES, IT IS-- BUT FOR THE TAIRA OR THE MINAMOTO?
SURELY FOR US? AFTER ALL, WE HAVE THE DIVINE EMPEROR AS WELL AS THE SACRED JEWEL, MIRROR, AND THE SWORD, KUSANAGI-NO-TSURUGI.
TRUE, BUT MANY SIGNS FAVOR THE GENJI.
REMEMBER WHEN LADY TODA RAISED OUR FAN ON A SHIP'S MAST TO TAUNT THE MINAMOTO IN THE BATTLE OF YASHIMA?
ONE OF THEIR BOWMEN BROUGHT IT DOWN WITH A SINGLE HUMMING-BULB ARROW FROM A GREAT DISTANCE AS THE WIND BLEW AND OUR BOAT ROCKED ON THE WAVES.
THOK!
HMMMMMMM
HMMMMMMMMM
IN THE SAME BATTLE, YOSHITSUNE DROPPED HIS BOW AND DOUBLED BACK TO RETRIEVE IT. OUR GRAPPLE HOOKS SNARED HIM, BUT STILL HE ESCAPED.
WHY DID HE RISK HIS LIFE FOR IT? "BECAUSE IT WAS A SORRY BOW AND THE TAIRA WOULD LAUGH IF THEY FOUND IT," HE SAID!
3.

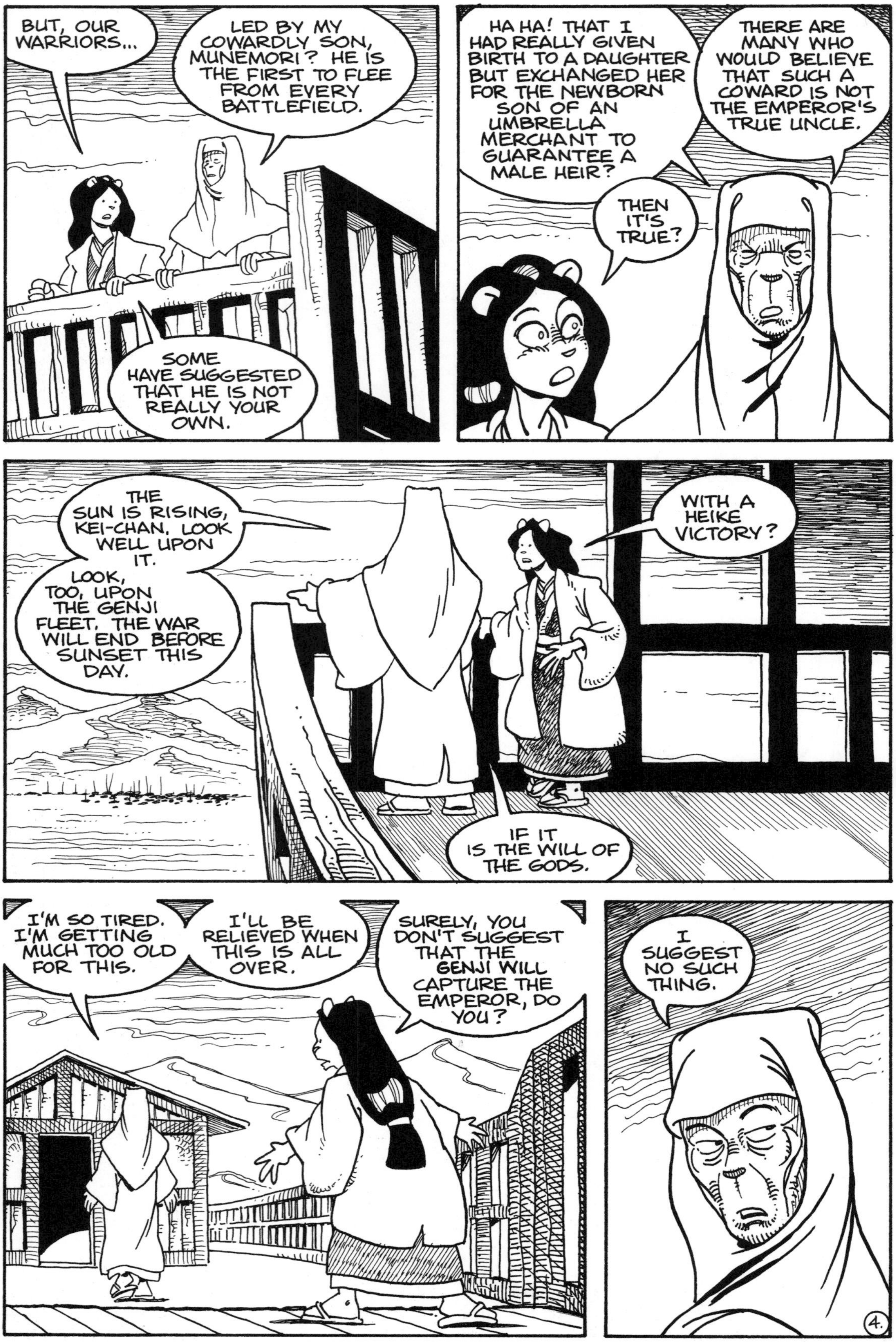
BUT, OUR WARRIORS...
LED BY MY COWARDLY SON, MUNEMORI? HE IS THE FIRST TO FLEE FROM EVERY BATTLEFIELD.
SOME HAVE SUGGESTED THAT HE IS NOT REALLY YOUR OWN.
HA HA! THAT I HAD REALLY GIVEN BIRTH TO A DAUGHTER BUT EXCHANGED HER FOR THE NEWBORN SON OF AN UMBRELLA MERCHANT TO GUARANTEE A MALE HEIR?
THERE ARE MANY WHO WOULD BELIEVE THAT SUCH A COWARD IS NOT THE EMPEROR'S TRUE UNCLE.
THEN IT'S TRUE?
THE SUN IS RISING, KEI-CHAN. LOOK WELL UPON IT.
LOOK, TOO, UPON THE GENJI FLEET. THE WAR WILL END BEFORE SUNSET THIS DAY.
WITH A HEIKE VICTORY?
IF IT IS THE WILL OF THE GODS.
I'M SO TIRED. I'M GETTING MUCH TOO OLD FOR THIS.
I'LL BE RELIEVED WHEN THIS IS ALL OVER.
SURELY, YOU DON'T SUGGEST THAT THE GENJI WILL CAPTURE THE EMPEROR, DO YOU?
I SUGGEST NO SUCH THING.
4.

HOUR OF THE DRAGON ⟨7–9 A.M.⟩

LORD YOSHITSUNE?

THE SKIES ARE CLEAR AFTER TWO DAYS OF RAIN. IT IS A GOOD DAY FOR BATTLE, BENKEI.

THE SEA WILL RUN RED WITH HEIKE BLOOD.

AND WITH GENJI BLOOD AS WELL.

THEY WILL BE REMEMBERED FOREVER! IT IS DISHONOR WE SHOULD FEAR-- NOT DEATH.

LOOK AT THEM, BENKEI. THEIR THOUSAND SHIPS AGAINST OUR FLEET THREE TIMES THEIR NUMBER!

IT WILL BE A FINE VICTORY. MY OLDER BROTHER WILL BE PLEASED.

YES, SIR!

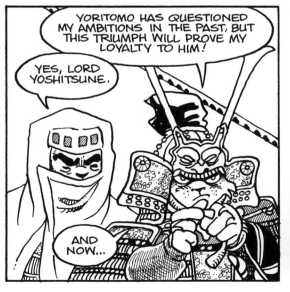

YORITOMO HAS QUESTIONED MY AMBITIONS IN THE PAST, BUT THIS TRIUMPH WILL PROVE MY LOYALTY TO HIM!

YES, LORD YOSHITSUNE.

AND NOW...

FORWARD!

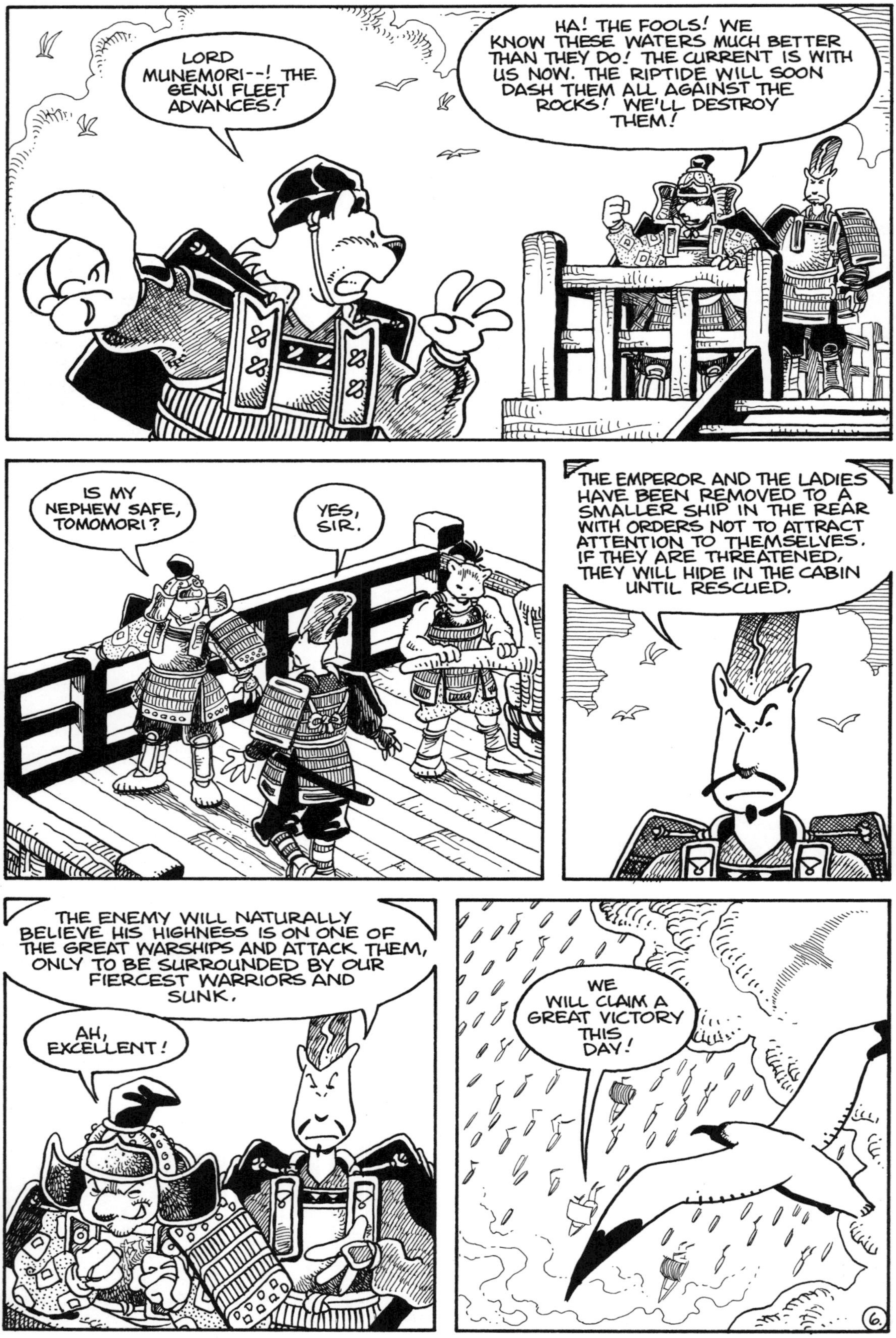
LORD MUNEMORI--! THE GENJI FLEET ADVANCES!
HA! THE FOOLS! WE KNOW THESE WATERS MUCH BETTER THAN THEY DO! THE CURRENT IS WITH US NOW. THE RIPTIDE WILL SOON DASH THEM ALL AGAINST THE ROCKS! WE'LL DESTROY THEM!
IS MY NEPHEW SAFE, TOMOMORI?
YES, SIR.
THE EMPEROR AND THE LADIES HAVE BEEN REMOVED TO A SMALLER SHIP IN THE REAR WITH ORDERS NOT TO ATTRACT ATTENTION TO THEMSELVES. IF THEY ARE THREATENED, THEY WILL HIDE IN THE CABIN UNTIL RESCUED.
THE ENEMY WILL NATURALLY BELIEVE HIS HIGHNESS IS ON ONE OF THE GREAT WARSHIPS AND ATTACK THEM, ONLY TO BE SURROUNDED BY OUR FIERCEST WARRIORS AND SUNK.
AH, EXCELLENT!
WE WILL CLAIM A GREAT VICTORY THIS DAY!
6.

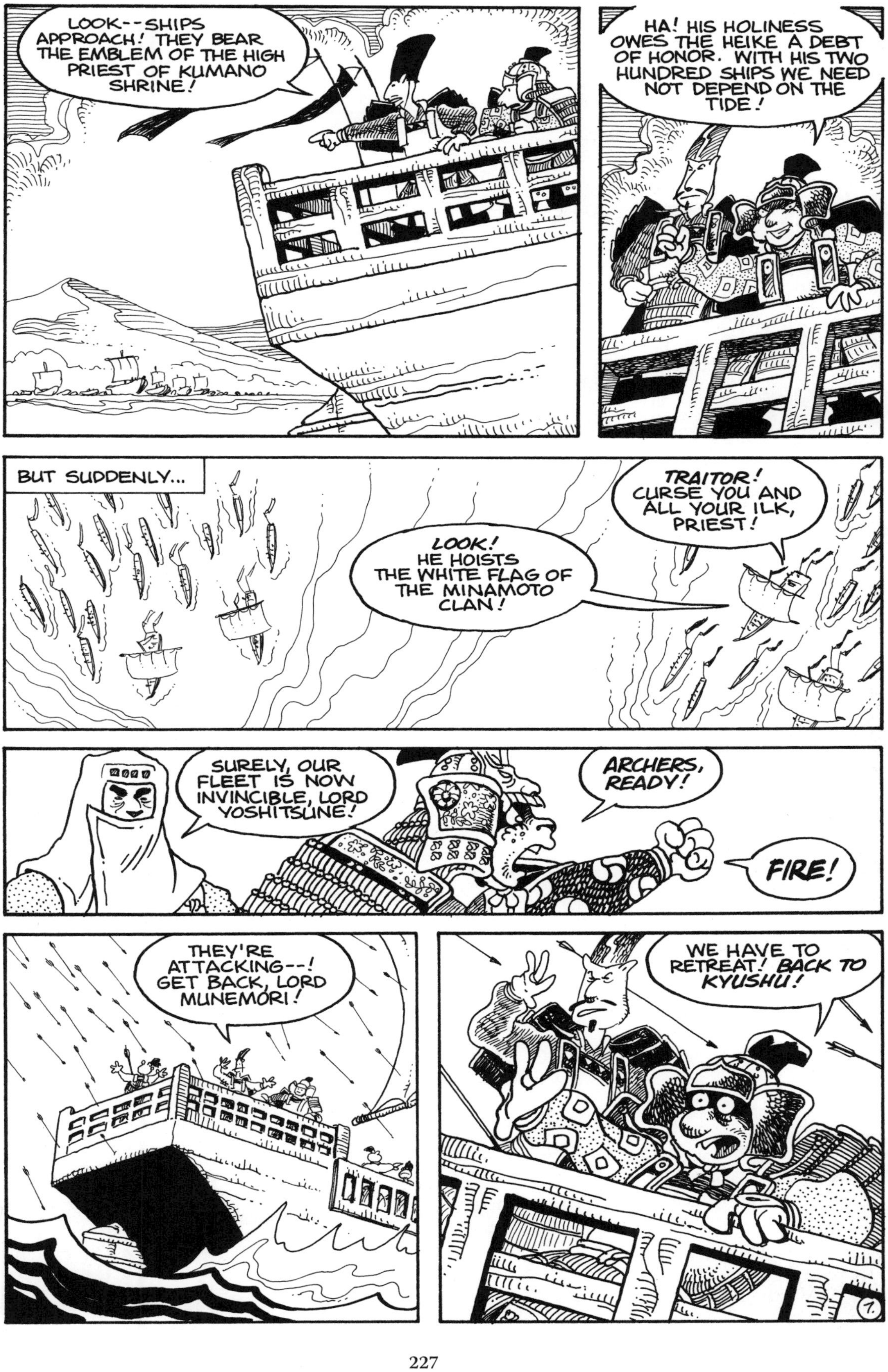

LOOK--SHIPS APPROACH! THEY BEAR THE EMBLEM OF THE HIGH PRIEST OF KUMANO SHRINE!
HA! HIS HOLINESS OWES THE HEIKE A DEBT OF HONOR. WITH HIS TWO HUNDRED SHIPS WE NEED NOT DEPEND ON THE TIDE!
BUT SUDDENLY...
LOOK! HE HOISTS THE WHITE FLAG OF THE MINAMOTO CLAN!
TRAITOR! CURSE YOU AND ALL YOUR ILK, PRIEST!
SURELY, OUR FLEET IS NOW INVINCIBLE, LORD YOSHITSUNE!
ARCHERS, READY!
FIRE!
THEY'RE ATTACKING--! GET BACK, LORD MUNEMORI!
WE HAVE TO RETREAT! BACK TO KYUSHU!
7.

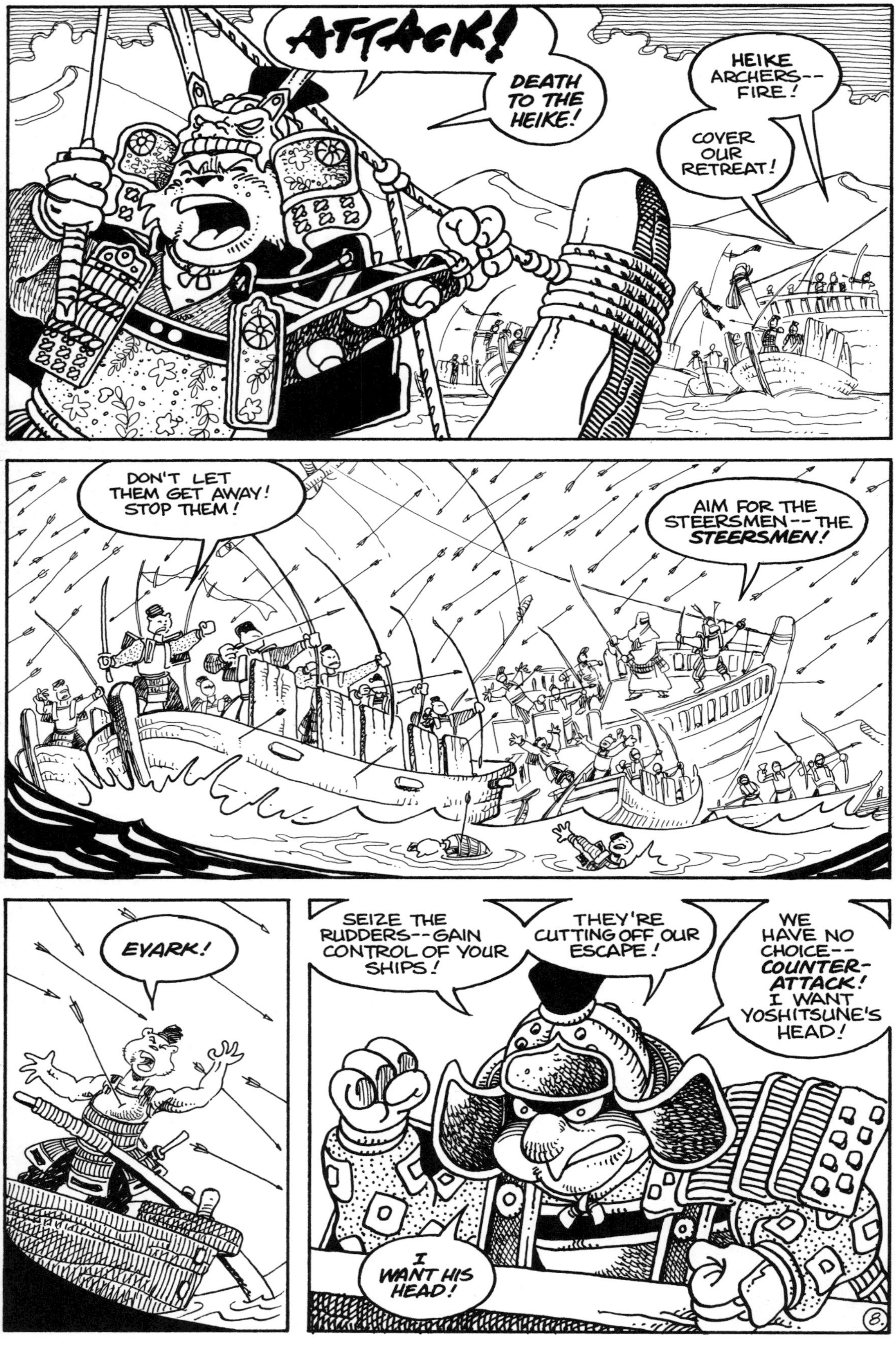
ATTACK!
DEATH TO THE HEIKE!
HEIKE ARCHERS--FIRE!
COVER OUR RETREAT!
DON'T LET THEM GET AWAY! STOP THEM!
AIM FOR THE STEERSMEN--THE STEERSMEN!
EYARK!
SEIZE THE RUDDERS--GAIN CONTROL OF YOUR SHIPS!
THEY'RE CUTTING OFF OUR ESCAPE!
WE HAVE NO CHOICE--COUNTER-ATTACK! I WANT YOSHITSUNE'S HEAD!
I WANT HIS HEAD!
8.

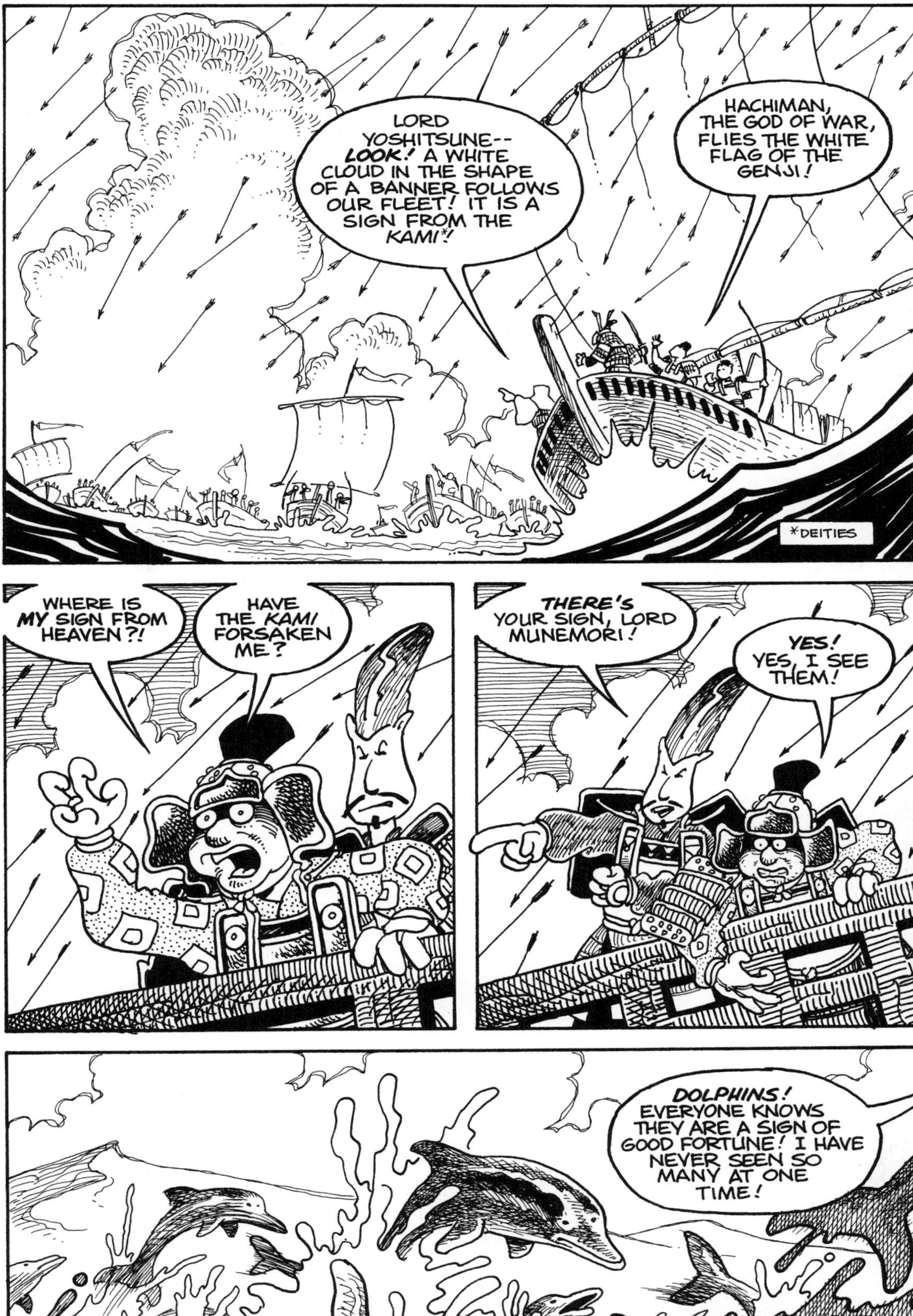
LORD YOSHITSUNE-- **LOOK!** A WHITE CLOUD IN THE SHAPE OF A BANNER FOLLOWS OUR FLEET! IT IS A SIGN FROM THE *KAMI**!
HACHIMAN, THE GOD OF WAR, FLIES THE WHITE FLAG OF THE GENJI!
*DEITIES
WHERE IS **MY** SIGN FROM HEAVEN?!
HAVE THE *KAMI* FORSAKEN ME?
THERE'S YOUR SIGN, LORD MUNEMORI!
YES! YES, I SEE THEM!
DOLPHINS! EVERYONE KNOWS THEY ARE A SIGN OF GOOD FORTUNE! I HAVE NEVER SEEN SO MANY AT ONE TIME!
9.

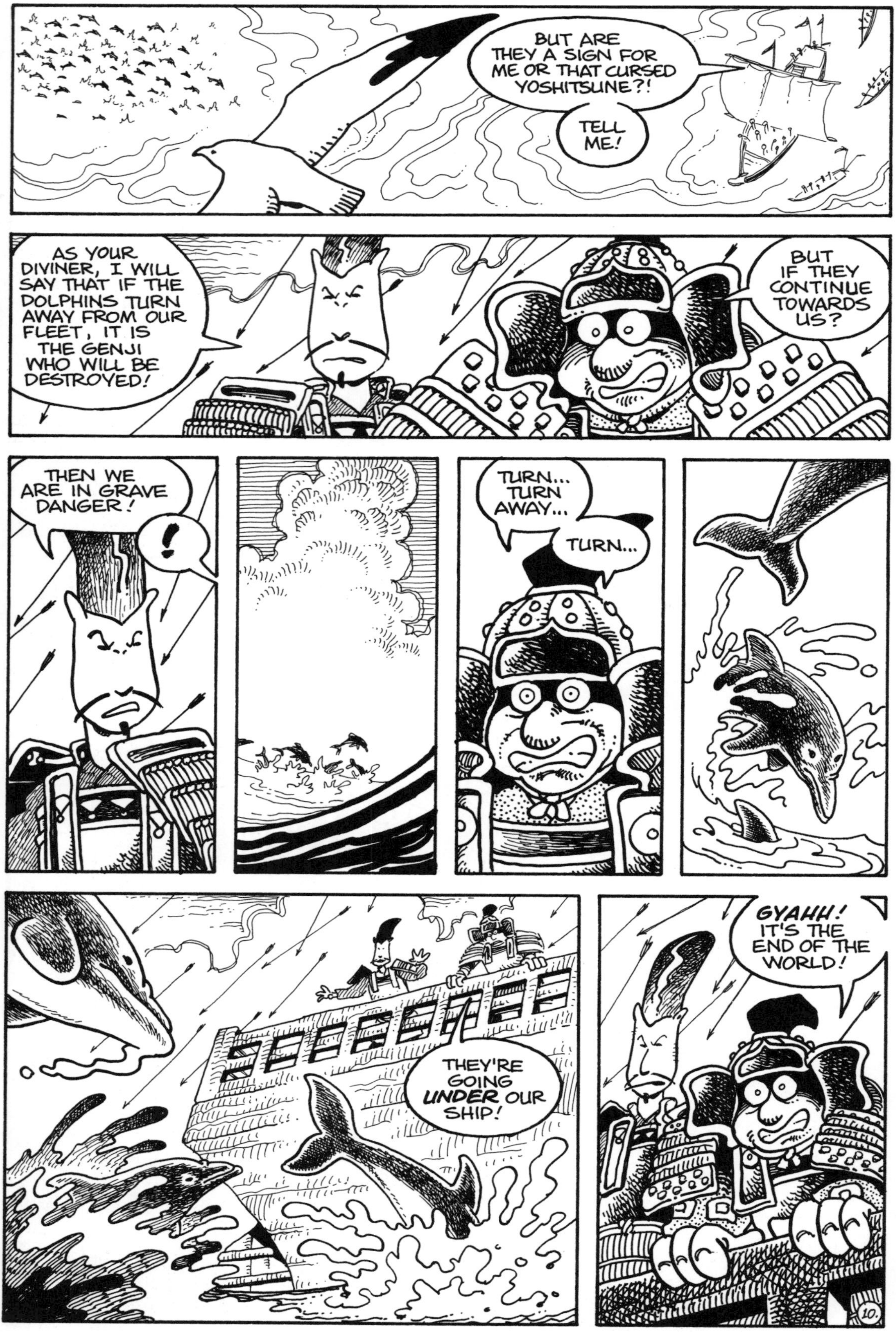
BUT ARE THEY A SIGN FOR ME OR THAT CURSED YOSHITSUNE?!
TELL ME!
AS YOUR DIVINER, I WILL SAY THAT IF THE DOLPHINS TURN AWAY FROM OUR FLEET, IT IS THE GENJI WHO WILL BE DESTROYED!
BUT IF THEY CONTINUE TOWARDS US?
THEN WE ARE IN GRAVE DANGER!
!
TURN... TURN AWAY...
TURN...
THEY'RE GOING **UNDER** OUR SHIP!
GYAHH! IT'S THE END OF THE WORLD!
10.

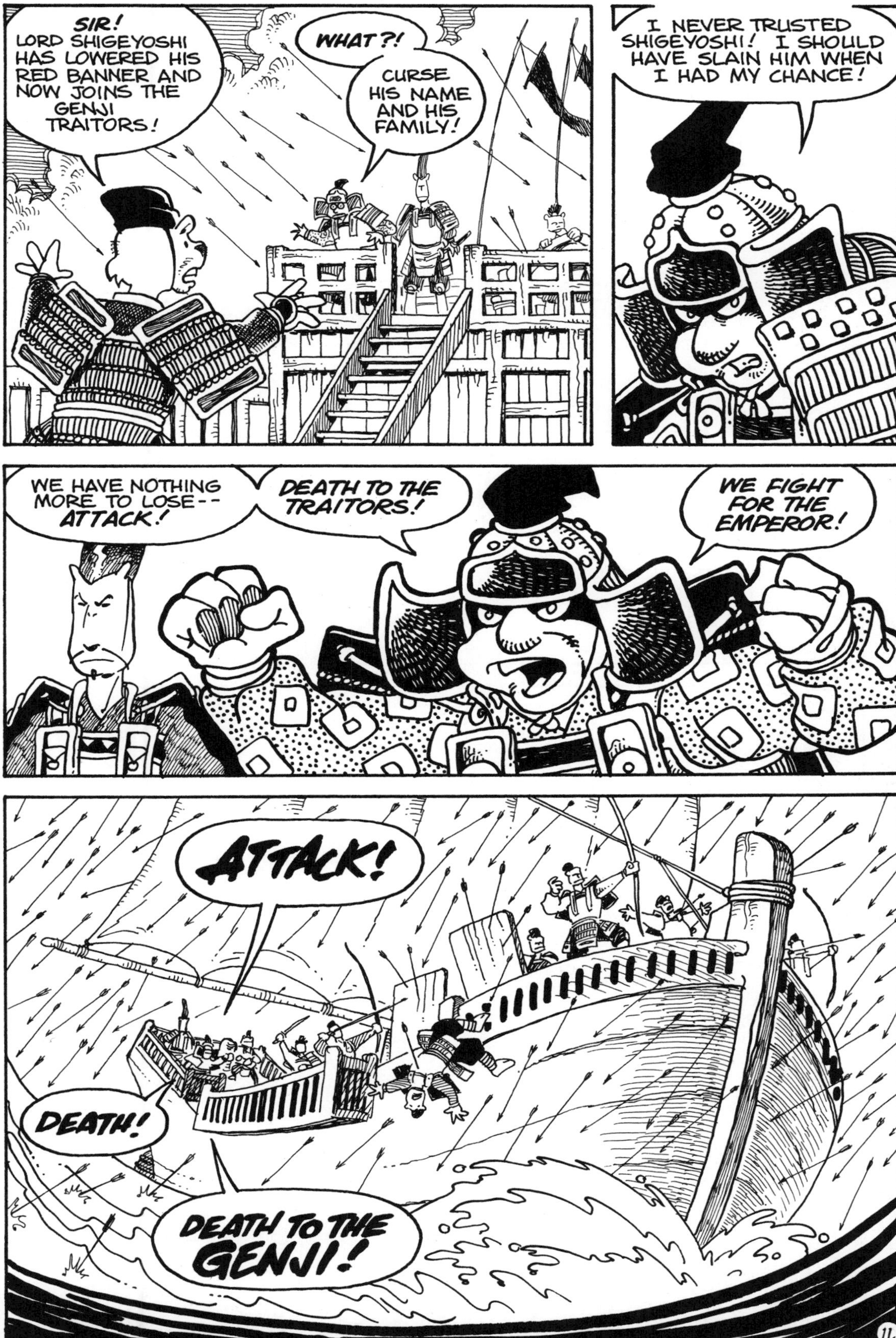
SIR! LORD SHIGEYOSHI HAS LOWERED HIS RED BANNER AND NOW JOINS THE GENJI TRAITORS!
WHAT?!
CURSE HIS NAME AND HIS FAMILY!
I NEVER TRUSTED SHIGEYOSHI! I SHOULD HAVE SLAIN HIM WHEN I HAD MY CHANCE!
WE HAVE NOTHING MORE TO LOSE-- ATTACK!
DEATH TO THE TRAITORS!
WE FIGHT FOR THE EMPEROR!
ATTACK!
DEATH!
DEATH TO THE GENJI!
11.

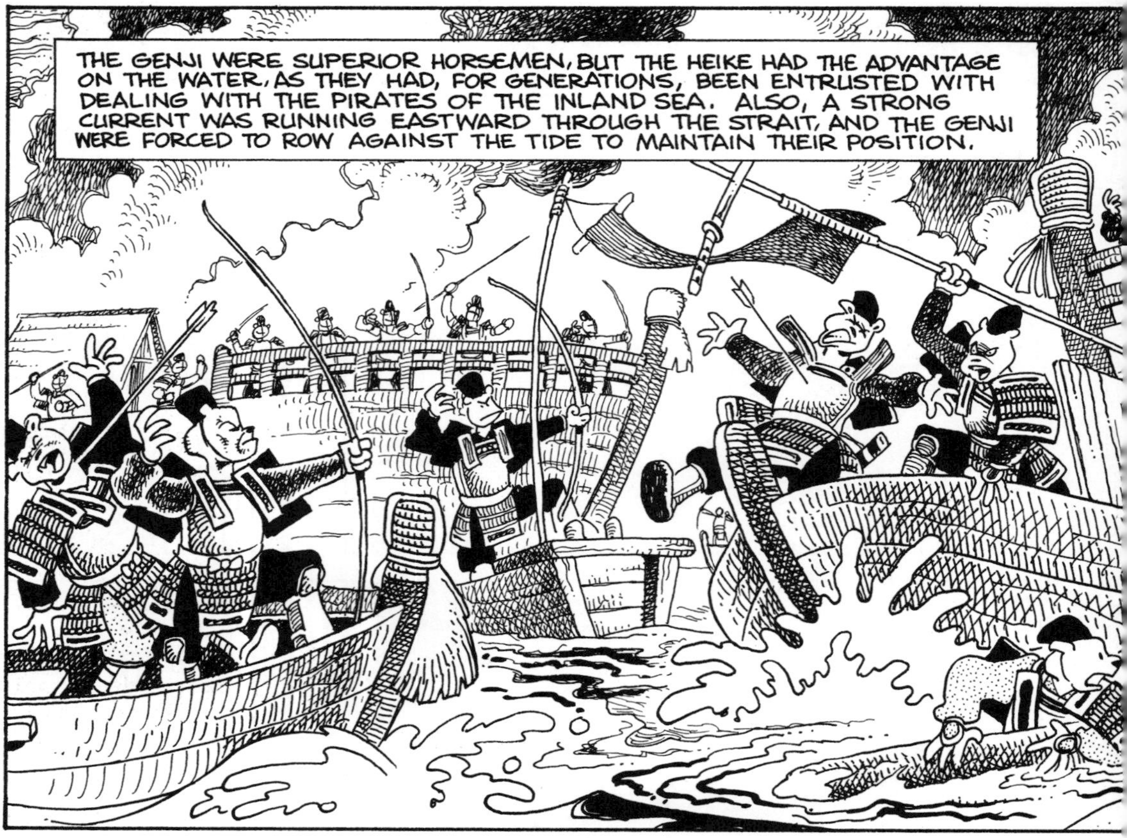
THE GENJI WERE SUPERIOR HORSEMEN, BUT THE HEIKE HAD THE ADVANTAGE ON THE WATER, AS THEY HAD, FOR GENERATIONS, BEEN ENTRUSTED WITH DEALING WITH THE PIRATES OF THE INLAND SEA. ALSO, A STRONG CURRENT WAS RUNNING EASTWARD THROUGH THE STRAIT, AND THE GENJI WERE FORCED TO ROW AGAINST THE TIDE TO MAINTAIN THEIR POSITION.

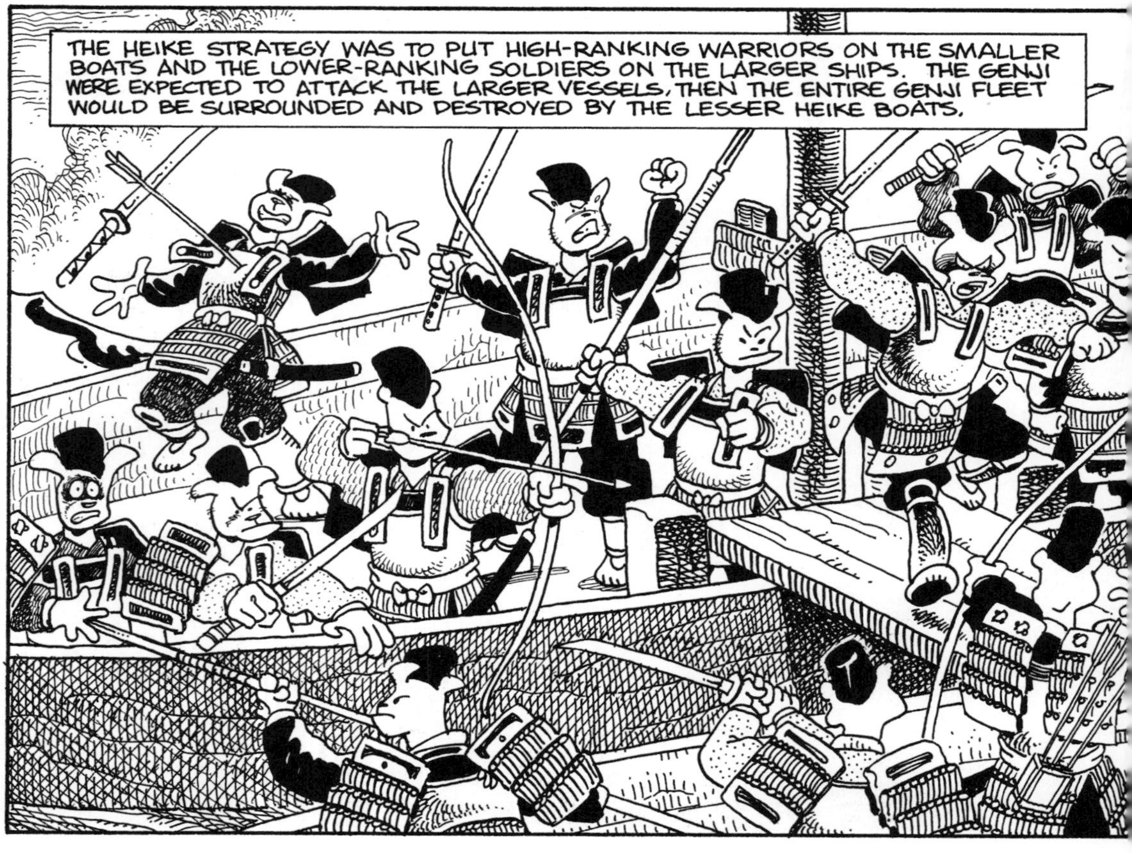
THE HEIKE STRATEGY WAS TO PUT HIGH-RANKING WARRIORS ON THE SMALLER BOATS AND THE LOWER-RANKING SOLDIERS ON THE LARGER SHIPS. THE GENJI WERE EXPECTED TO ATTACK THE LARGER VESSELS, THEN THE ENTIRE GENJI FLEET WOULD BE SURROUNDED AND DESTROYED BY THE LESSER HEIKE BOATS.

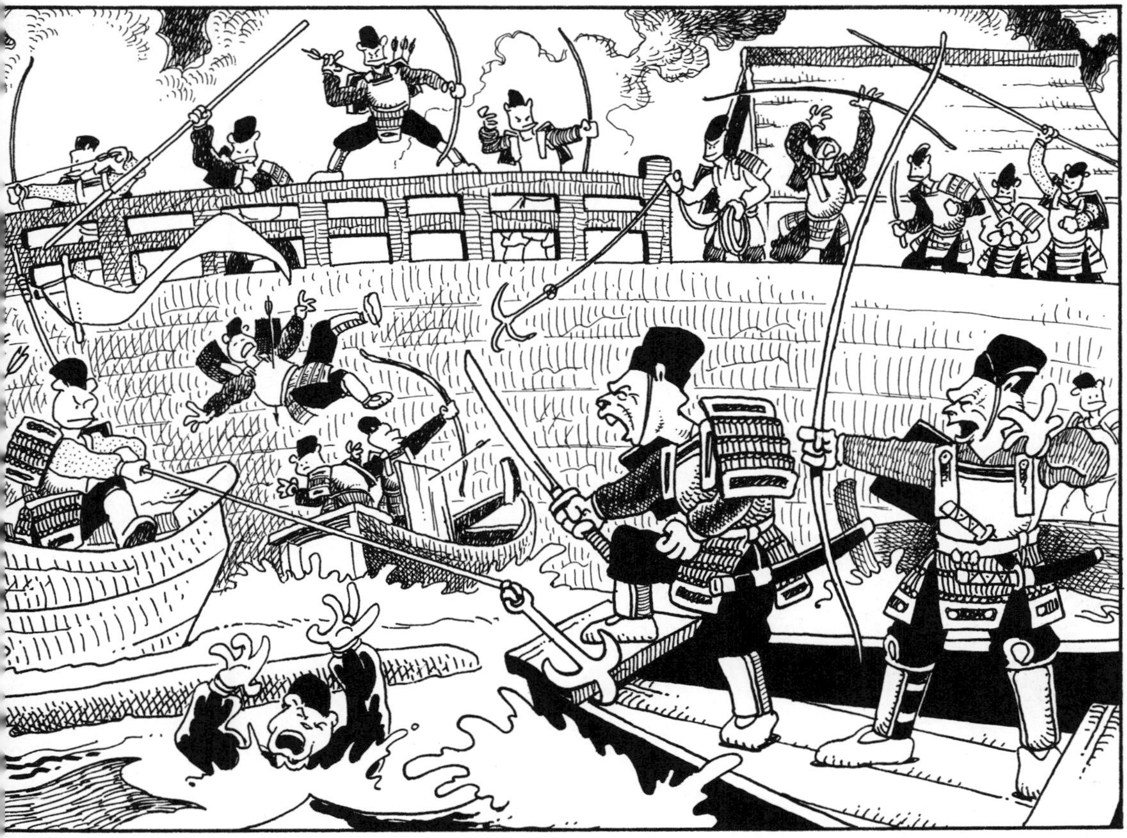

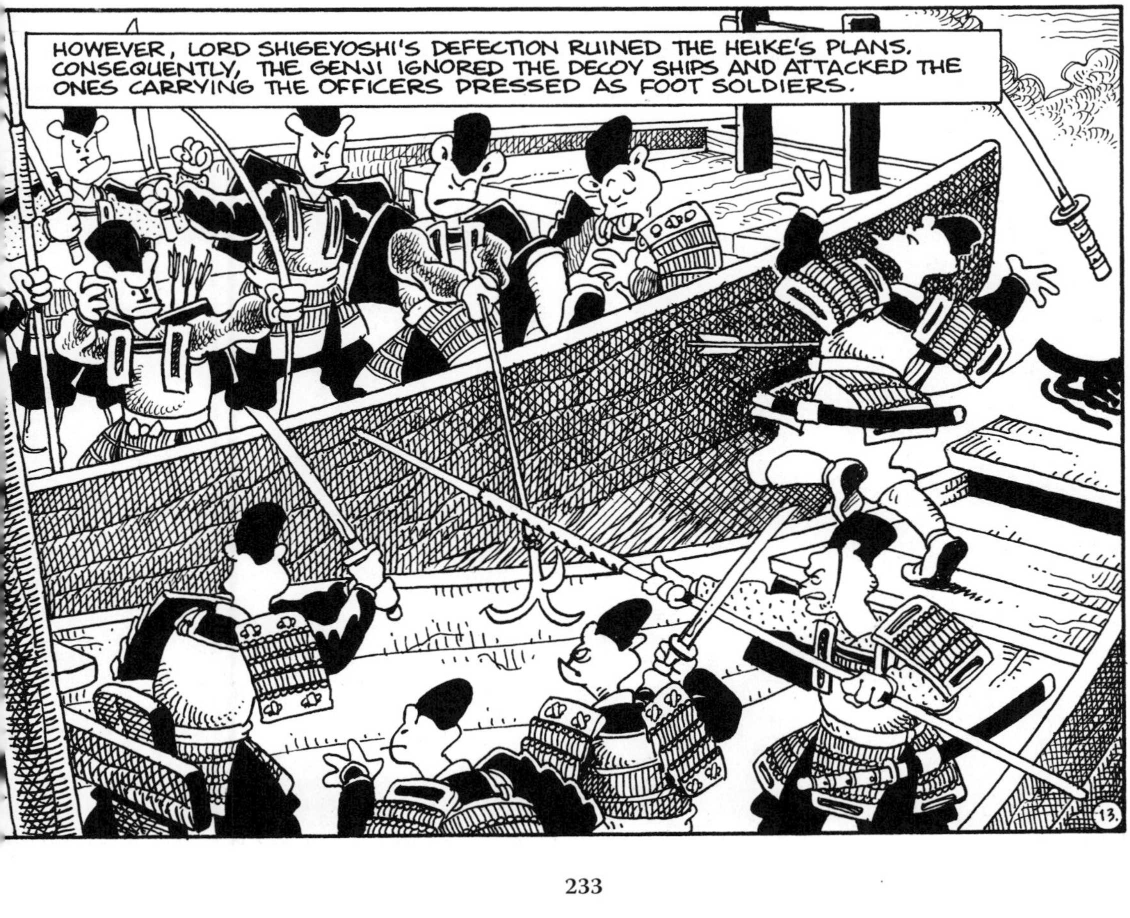
HOWEVER, LORD SHIGEYOSHI'S DEFECTION RUINED THE HEIKE'S PLANS. CONSEQUENTLY, THE GENJI IGNORED THE DECOY SHIPS AND ATTACKED THE ONES CARRYING THE OFFICERS DRESSED AS FOOT SOLDIERS.
13.

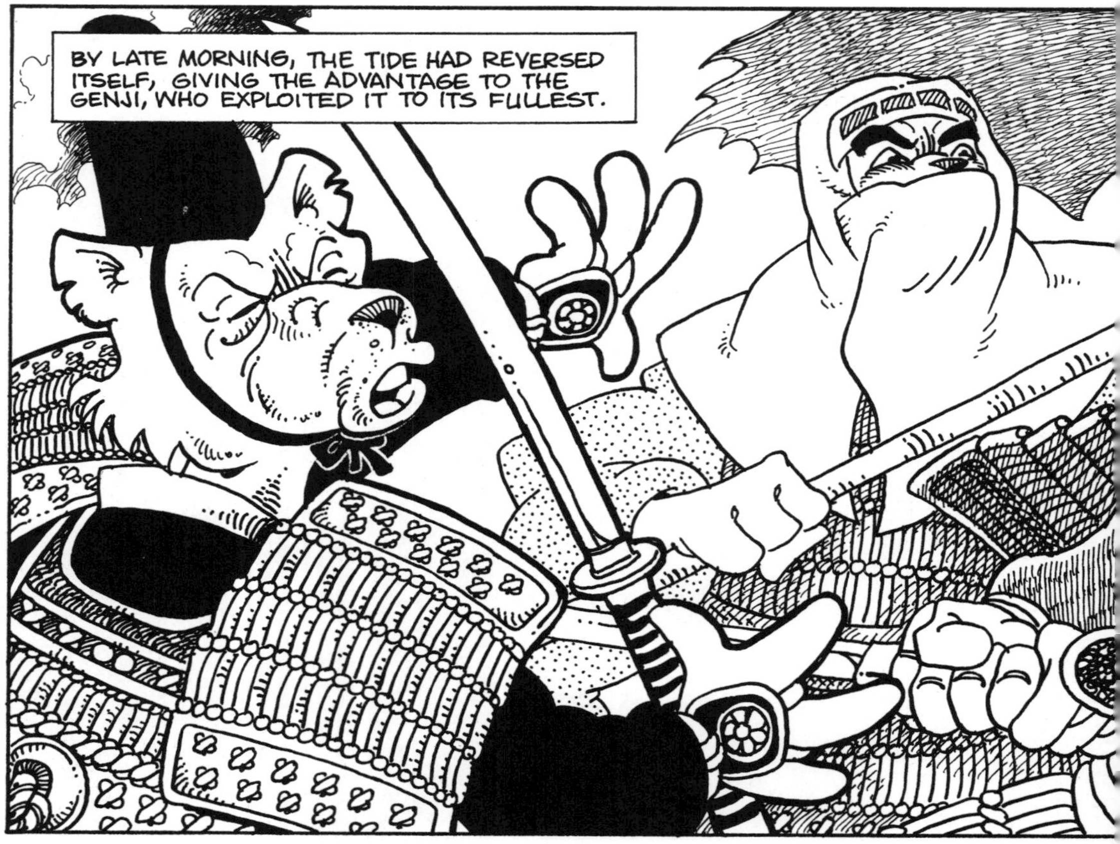
BY LATE MORNING, THE TIDE HAD REVERSED ITSELF, GIVING THE ADVANTAGE TO THE GENJI, WHO EXPLOITED IT TO ITS FULLEST.

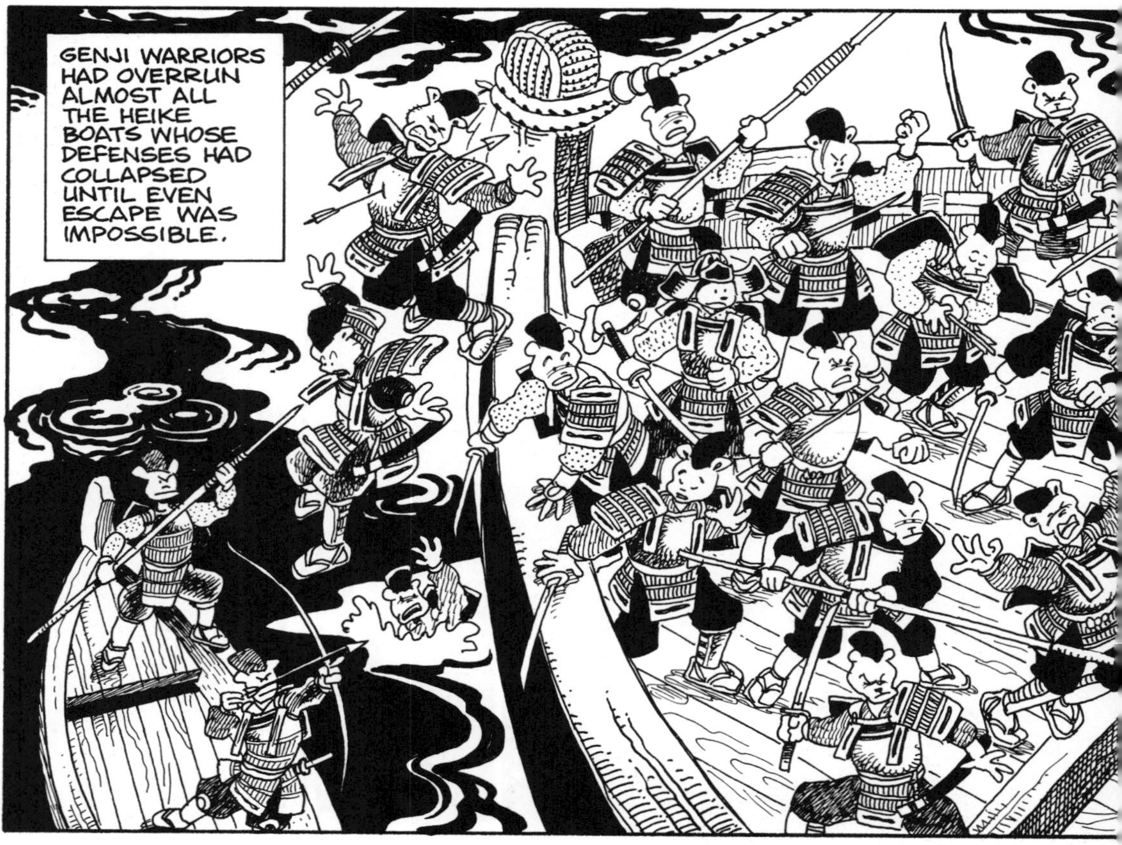
GENJI WARRIORS HAD OVERRUN ALMOST ALL THE HEIKE BOATS WHOSE DEFENSES HAD COLLAPSED UNTIL EVEN ESCAPE WAS IMPOSSIBLE.

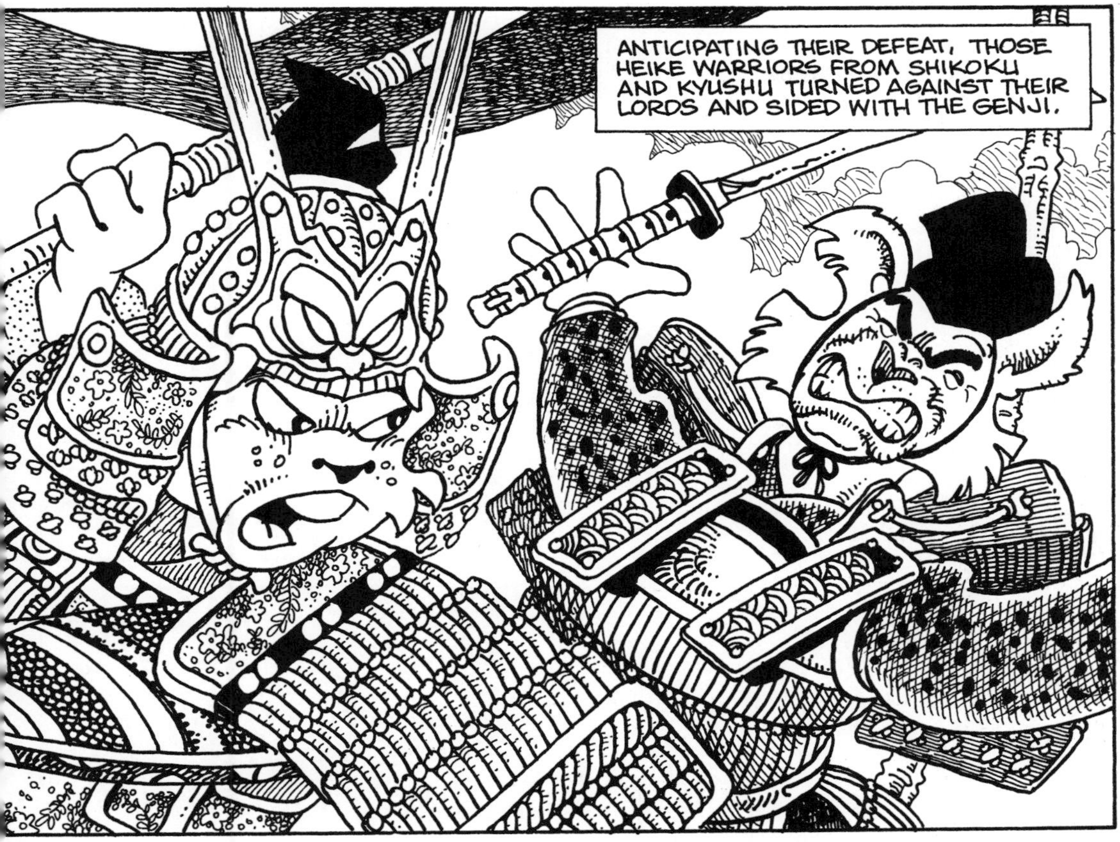
ANTICIPATING THEIR DEFEAT, THOSE HEIKE WARRIORS FROM SHIKOKU AND KYUSHU TURNED AGAINST THEIR LORDS AND SIDED WITH THE GENJI.

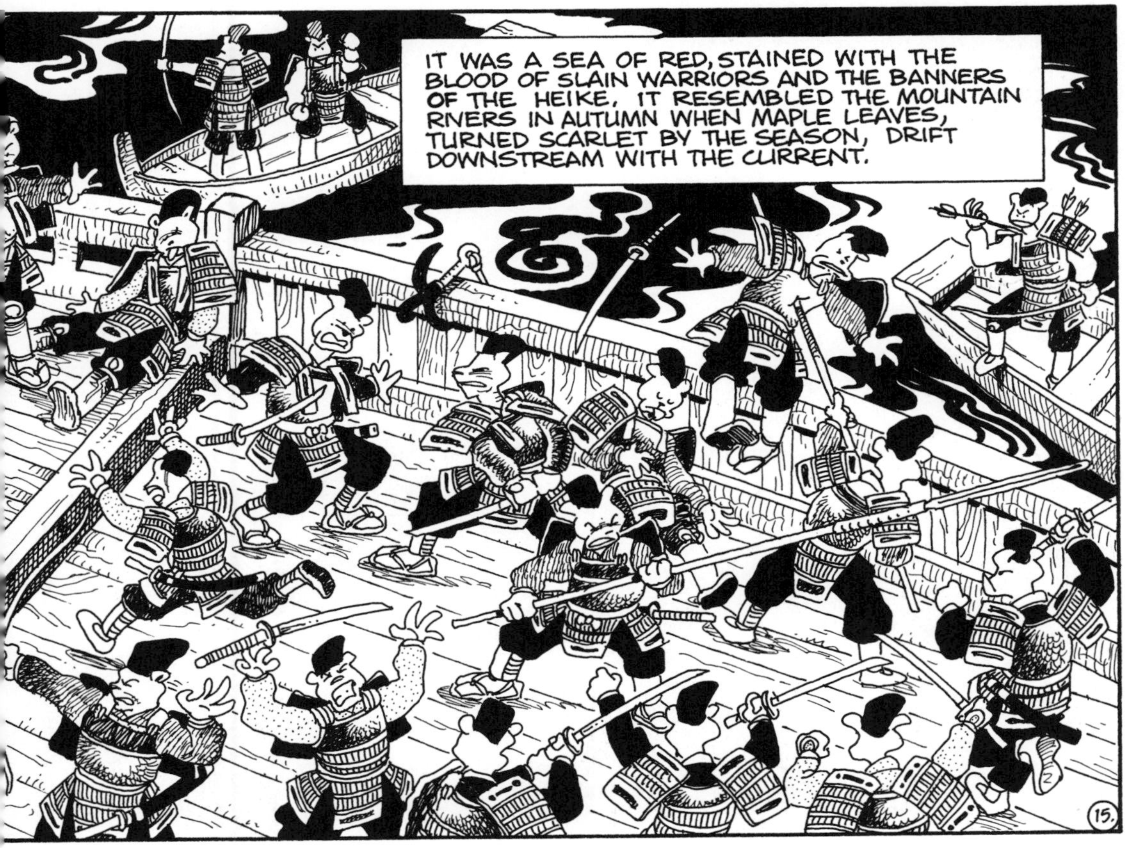
IT WAS A SEA OF RED, STAINED WITH THE BLOOD OF SLAIN WARRIORS AND THE BANNERS OF THE HEIKE. IT RESEMBLED THE MOUNTAIN RIVERS IN AUTUMN WHEN MAPLE LEAVES, TURNED SCARLET BY THE SEASON, DRIFT DOWNSTREAM WITH THE CURRENT.
15.

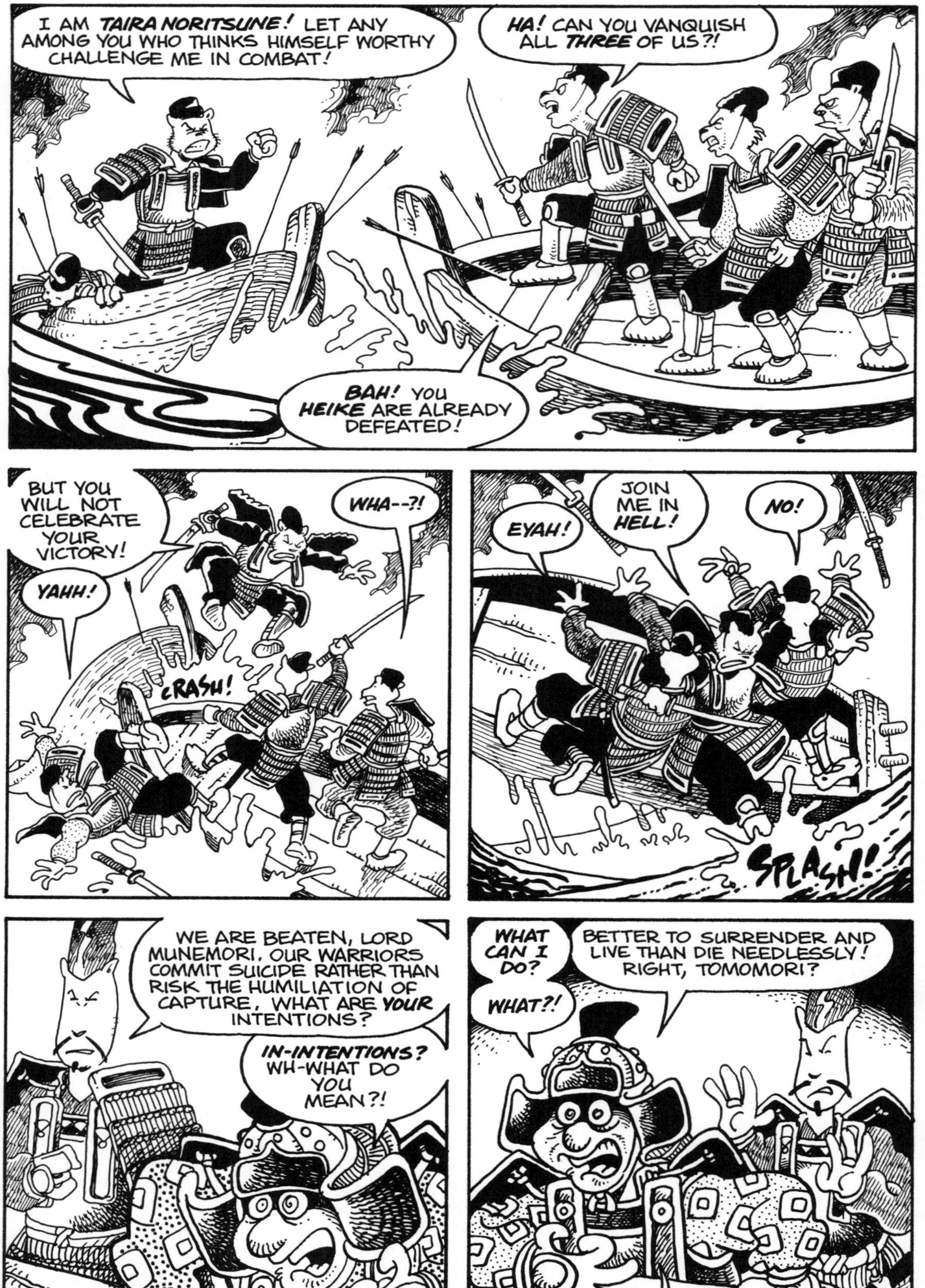
I AM TAIRA NORITSUNE! LET ANY AMONG YOU WHO THINKS HIMSELF WORTHY CHALLENGE ME IN COMBAT!
HA! CAN YOU VANQUISH ALL THREE OF US?!
BAH! YOU HEIKE ARE ALREADY DEFEATED!
BUT YOU WILL NOT CELEBRATE YOUR VICTORY!
YAHH!
WHA--?!
CRASH!
EYAH!
JOIN ME IN HELL!
NO!
SPLASH!
WE ARE BEATEN, LORD MUNEMORI. OUR WARRIORS COMMIT SUICIDE RATHER THAN RISK THE HUMILIATION OF CAPTURE. WHAT ARE YOUR INTENTIONS?
IN-INTENTIONS? WH-WHAT DO YOU MEAN?!
WHAT CAN I DO?
WHAT?!
BETTER TO SURRENDER AND LIVE THAN DIE NEEDLESSLY! RIGHT, TOMOMORI?
TOMOMORI...?
16.

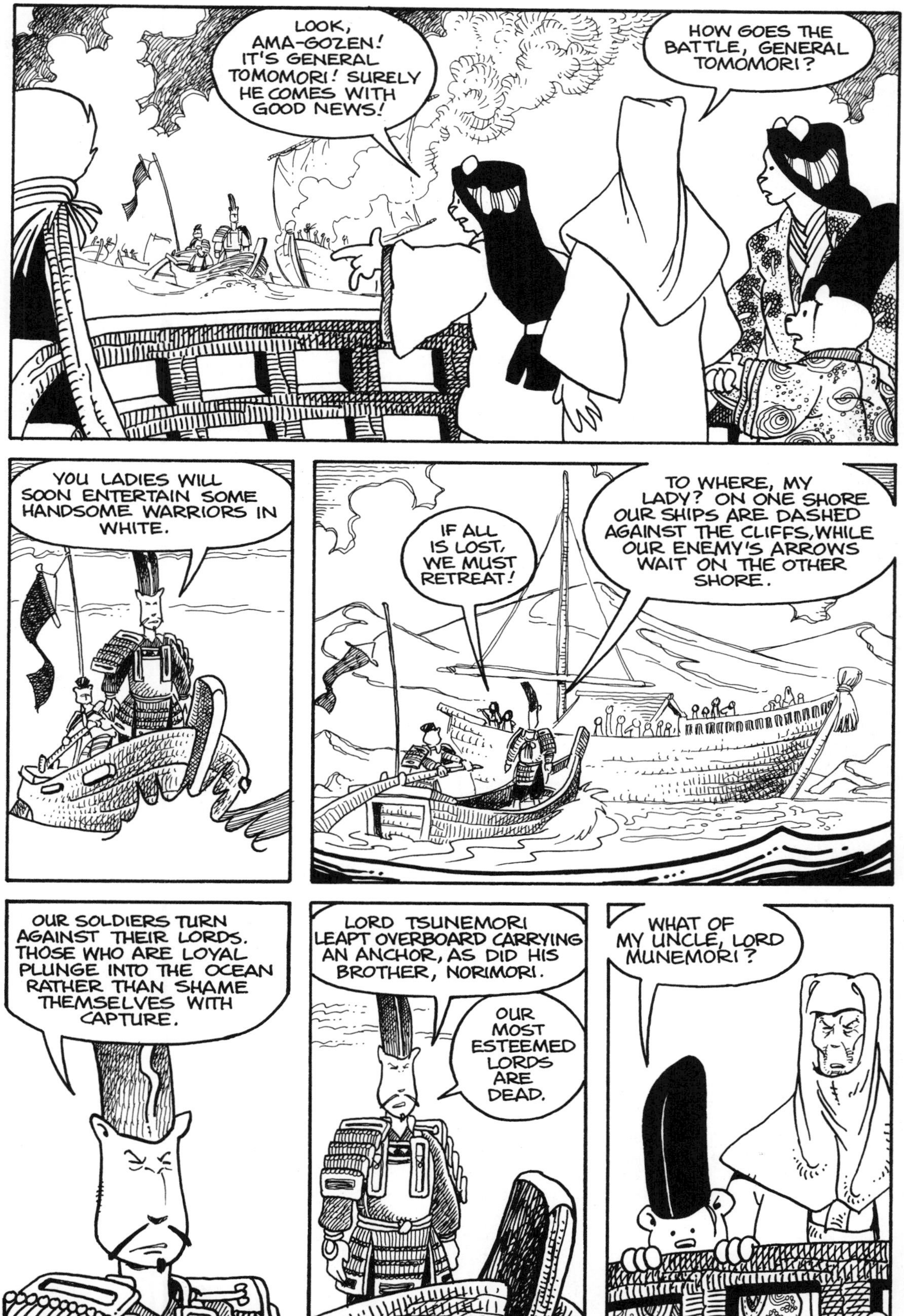
LOOK, AMA-GOZEN! IT'S GENERAL TOMOMORI! SURELY HE COMES WITH GOOD NEWS!
HOW GOES THE BATTLE, GENERAL TOMOMORI?
YOU LADIES WILL SOON ENTERTAIN SOME HANDSOME WARRIORS IN WHITE.
IF ALL IS LOST, WE MUST RETREAT!
TO WHERE, MY LADY? ON ONE SHORE OUR SHIPS ARE DASHED AGAINST THE CLIFFS, WHILE OUR ENEMY'S ARROWS WAIT ON THE OTHER SHORE.
OUR SOLDIERS TURN AGAINST THEIR LORDS. THOSE WHO ARE LOYAL PLUNGE INTO THE OCEAN RATHER THAN SHAME THEMSELVES WITH CAPTURE.
LORD TSUNEMORI LEAPT OVERBOARD CARRYING AN ANCHOR, AS DID HIS BROTHER, NORIMORI.
OUR MOST ESTEEMED LORDS ARE DEAD.
WHAT OF MY UNCLE, LORD MUNEMORI?
17.

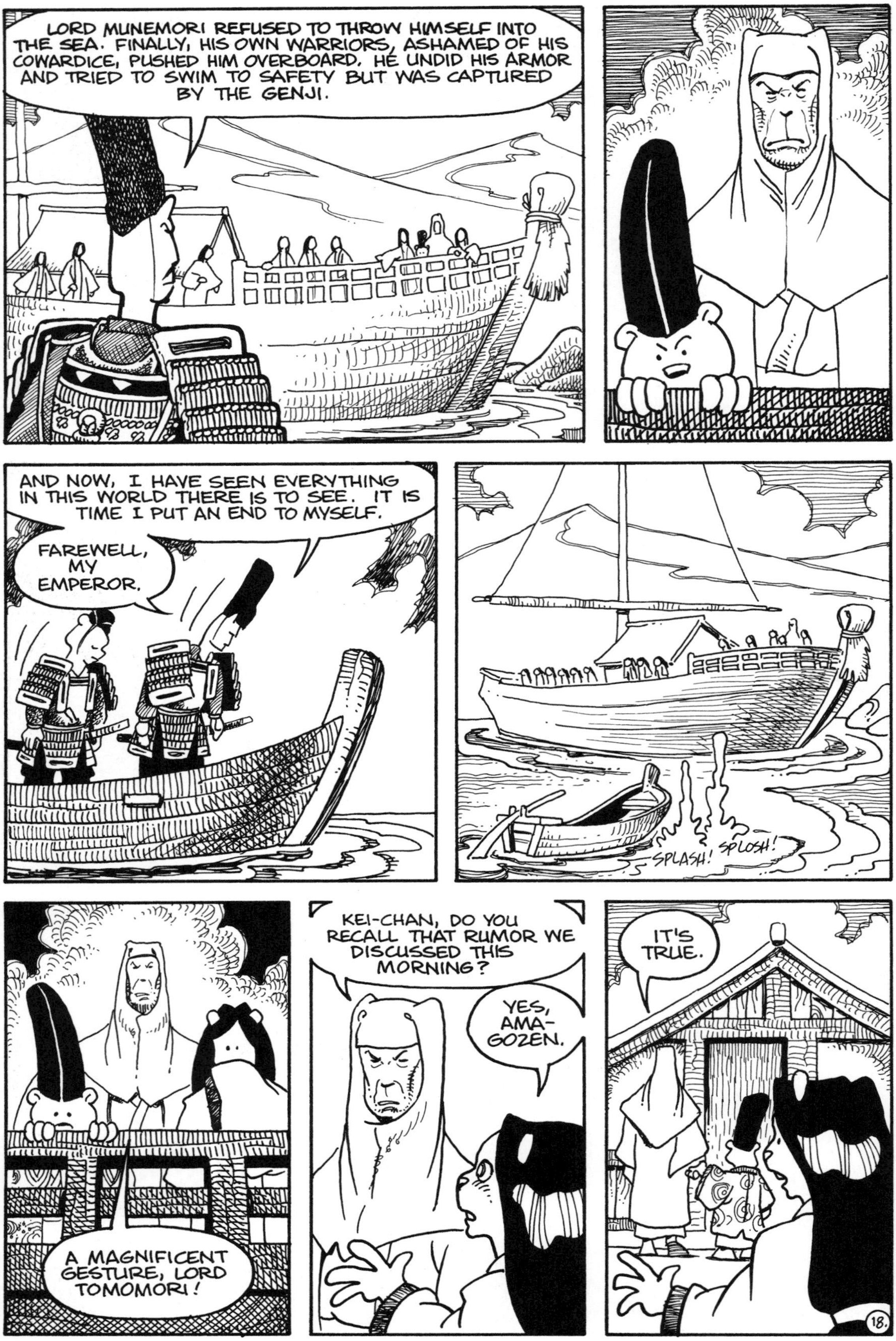
LORD MUNEMORI REFUSED TO THROW HIMSELF INTO THE SEA. FINALLY, HIS OWN WARRIORS, ASHAMED OF HIS COWARDICE, PUSHED HIM OVERBOARD. HE UNDID HIS ARMOR AND TRIED TO SWIM TO SAFETY BUT WAS CAPTURED BY THE GENJI.
AND NOW, I HAVE SEEN EVERYTHING IN THIS WORLD THERE IS TO SEE. IT IS TIME I PUT AN END TO MYSELF.
FAREWELL, MY EMPEROR.
SPLASH! SPLOSH!
A MAGNIFICENT GESTURE, LORD TOMOMORI!
KEI-CHAN, DO YOU RECALL THAT RUMOR WE DISCUSSED THIS MORNING?
YES, AMA-GOZEN.
IT'S TRUE.
18.

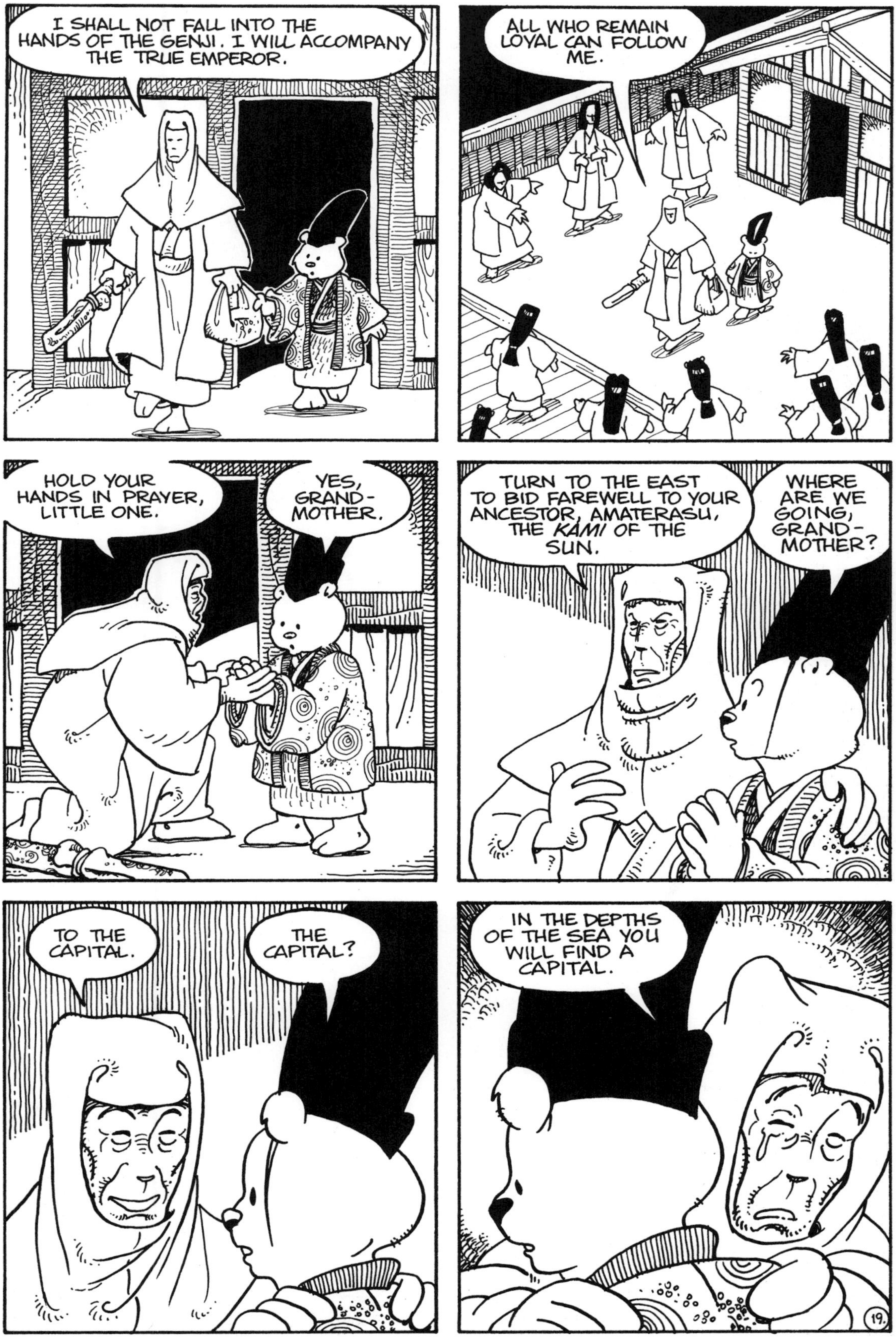

I SHALL NOT FALL INTO THE HANDS OF THE GENJI. I WILL ACCOMPANY THE TRUE EMPEROR.
ALL WHO REMAIN LOYAL CAN FOLLOW ME.
HOLD YOUR HANDS IN PRAYER, LITTLE ONE.
YES, GRAND-MOTHER.
TURN TO THE EAST TO BID FAREWELL TO YOUR ANCESTOR, AMATERASU, THE *KAMI* OF THE SUN.
WHERE ARE WE GOING, GRAND-MOTHER?
TO THE CAPITAL.
THE CAPITAL?
IN THE DEPTHS OF THE SEA YOU WILL FIND A CAPITAL.
19.

I WILL TAKE THE SWORD, *KUSANAGI-NO-TSURUGI,* AND THE SACRED JEWEL, *YASAKANI-NO-MAGATAMA.*

I TRUST *YATA-NO-KAGAMI,* THE STAR-HAND MIRROR, WILL NOT BE LEFT FOR THE MINAMOTO RABBLE.

HAIL, AMIDA BUDDHA!

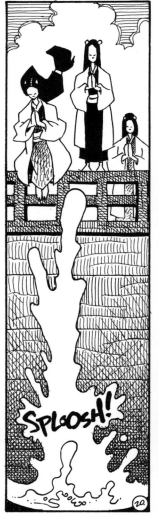

SPLOOSH!

20

THERE'S THE EMPEROR'S SHIP!

HURRY-- THEY'RE JUMPING OVER THE SIDE!

READY WITH YOUR GRAPPLES!

FISH THEM OUT!

NICE GOING!

YOU'VE RESCUED ONE!

THE GODS BE PRAISED! IT IS LADY KENREIMON-IN ... THE EMPEROR'S MOTHER!

BUT WHERE IS HIS HIGHNESS?!

I'VE GOT TO HURRY! I PRAY I'LL HAVE ENOUGH TIME TO DO WHAT I HAVE TO DO!

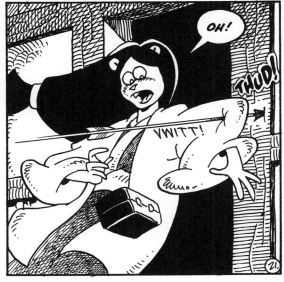

OH!

THUD!

VWITT!

21.

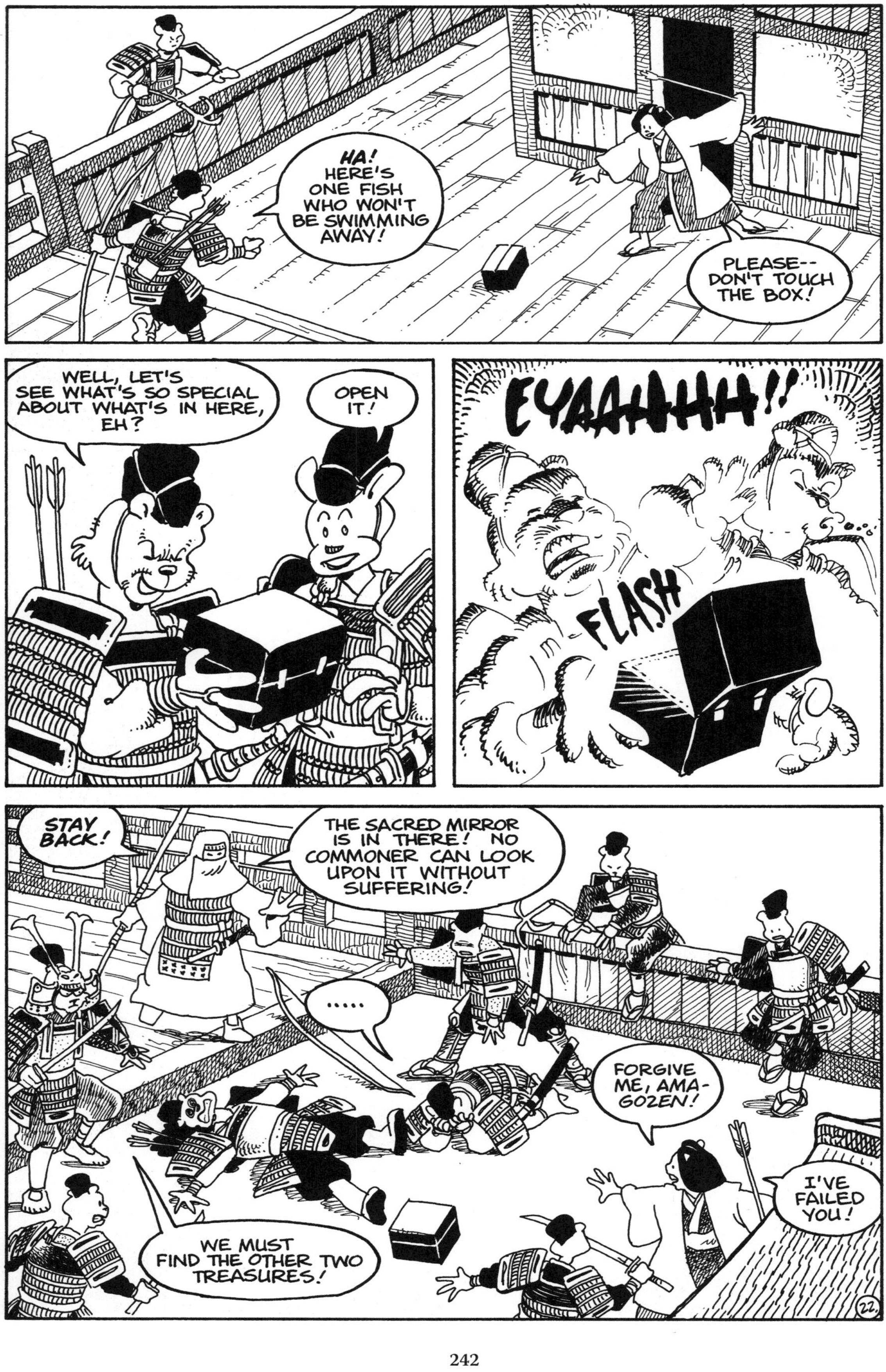
HA! HERE'S ONE FISH WHO WON'T BE SWIMMING AWAY!
PLEASE-- DON'T TOUCH THE BOX!
WELL, LET'S SEE WHAT'S SO SPECIAL ABOUT WHAT'S IN HERE, EH?
OPEN IT!
EYAAHHH!!
FLASH
STAY BACK!
THE SACRED MIRROR IS IN THERE! NO COMMONER CAN LOOK UPON IT WITHOUT SUFFERING!
.....
FORGIVE ME, AMA-GOZEN!
I'VE FAILED YOU!
WE MUST FIND THE OTHER TWO TREASURES!
22.

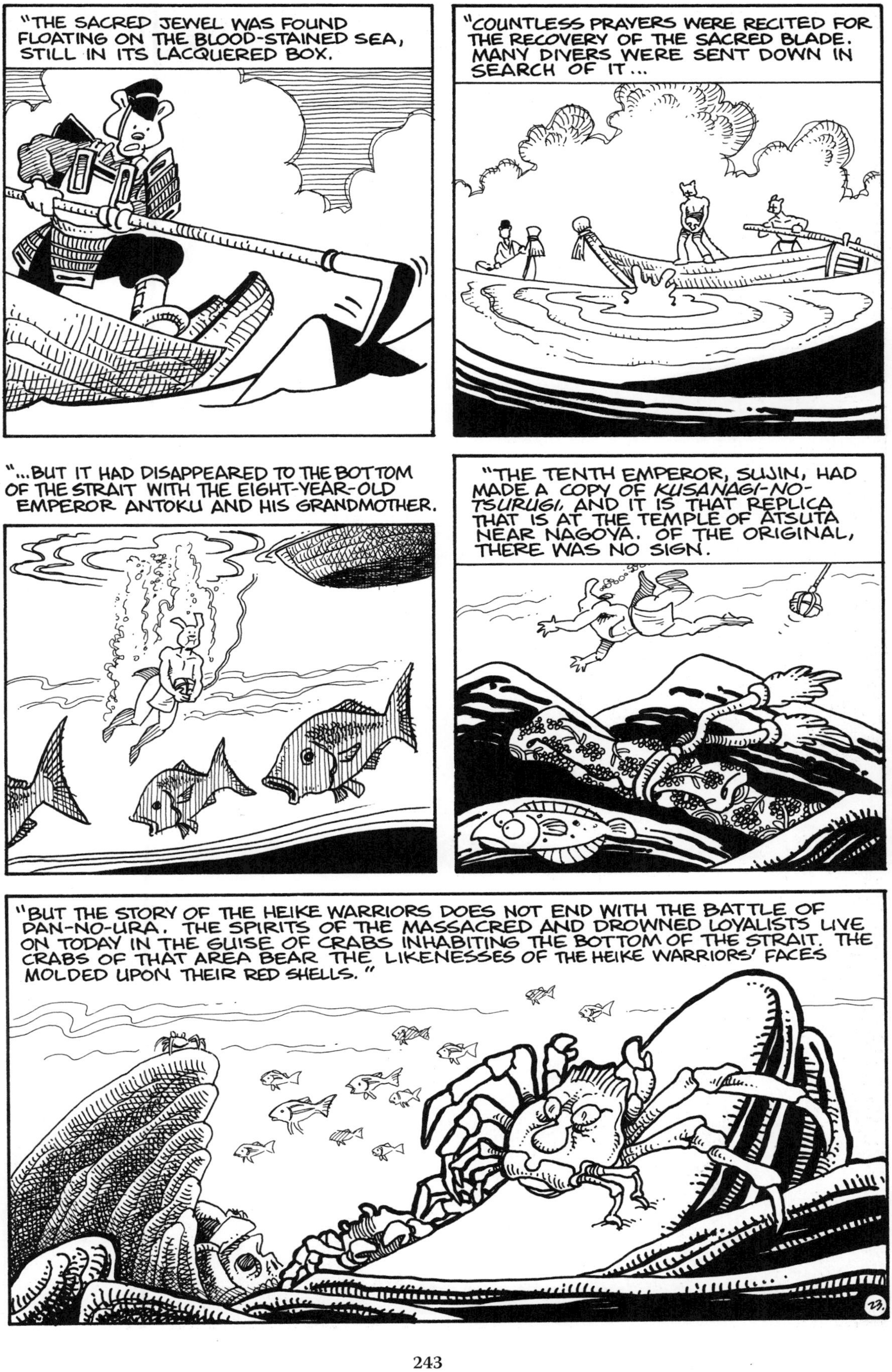
"THE SACRED JEWEL WAS FOUND FLOATING ON THE BLOOD-STAINED SEA, STILL IN ITS LACQUERED BOX.
"COUNTLESS PRAYERS WERE RECITED FOR THE RECOVERY OF THE SACRED BLADE. MANY DIVERS WERE SENT DOWN IN SEARCH OF IT...
"...BUT IT HAD DISAPPEARED TO THE BOTTOM OF THE STRAIT WITH THE EIGHT-YEAR-OLD EMPEROR ANTOKU AND HIS GRANDMOTHER.
"THE TENTH EMPEROR, SUJIN, HAD MADE A COPY OF *KUSANAGI-NO-TSURUGI,* AND IT IS THAT REPLICA THAT IS AT THE TEMPLE OF ATSUTA NEAR NAGOYA. OF THE ORIGINAL, THERE WAS NO SIGN.
"BUT THE STORY OF THE HEIKE WARRIORS DOES NOT END WITH THE BATTLE OF DAN-NO-URA. THE SPIRITS OF THE MASSACRED AND DROWNED LOYALISTS LIVE ON TODAY IN THE GUISE OF CRABS INHABITING THE BOTTOM OF THE STRAIT. THE CRABS OF THAT AREA BEAR THE LIKENESSES OF THE HEIKE WARRIORS' FACES MOLDED UPON THEIR RED SHELLS."
23.

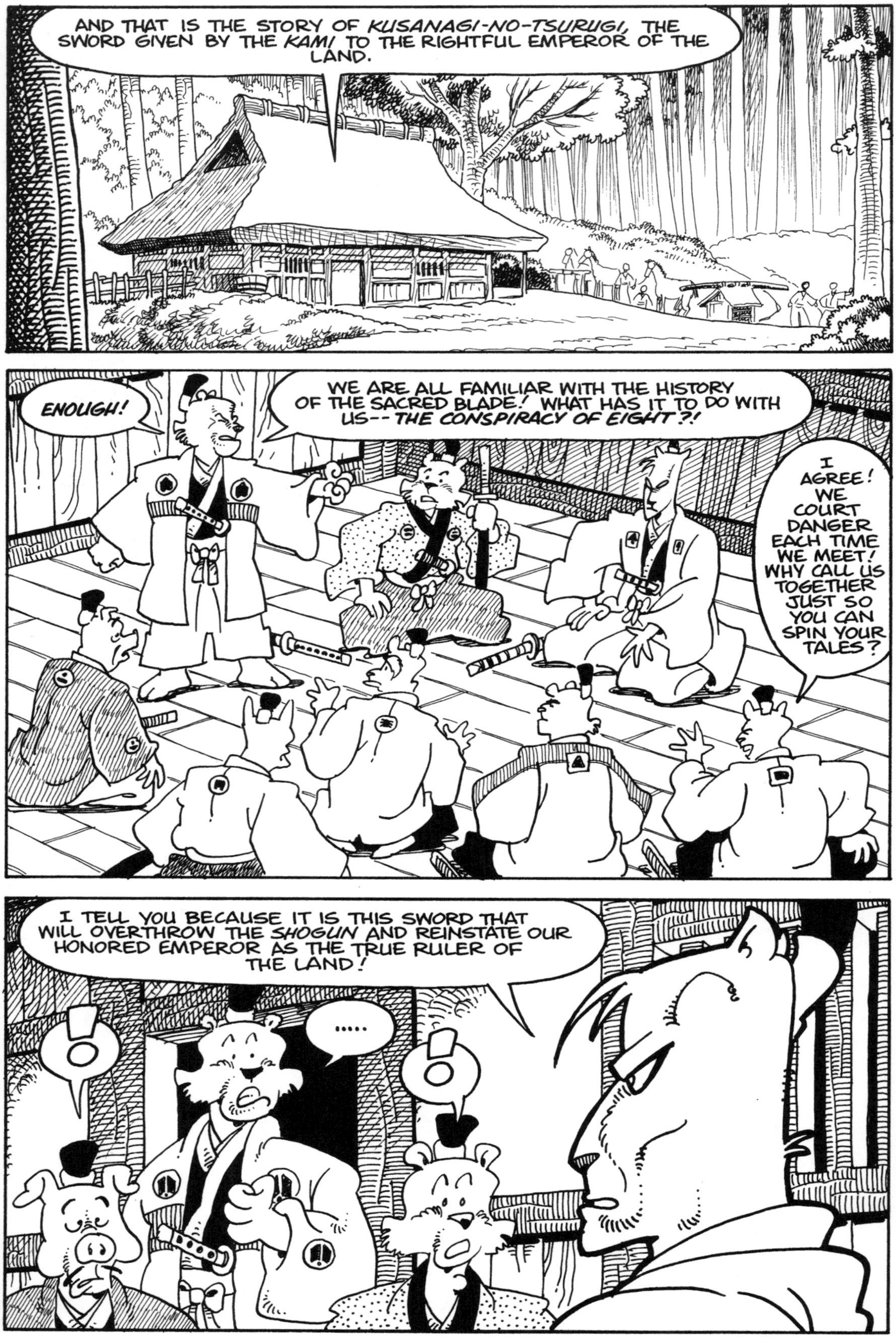
AND THAT IS THE STORY OF KUSANAGI-NO-TSURUGI, THE SWORD GIVEN BY THE KAMI TO THE RIGHTFUL EMPEROR OF THE LAND.
ENOUGH!
WE ARE ALL FAMILIAR WITH THE HISTORY OF THE SACRED BLADE! WHAT HAS IT TO DO WITH US-- THE CONSPIRACY OF EIGHT?!
I AGREE! WE COURT DANGER EACH TIME WE MEET! WHY CALL US TOGETHER JUST SO YOU CAN SPIN YOUR TALES?
I TELL YOU BECAUSE IT IS THIS SWORD THAT WILL OVERTHROW THE SHOGUN AND REINSTATE OUR HONORED EMPEROR AS THE TRUE RULER OF THE LAND!
!
.....
!

END of PROLOGUE 4

草薙の剣

THE *KANJI* READS
"*KUSANAGI-NO-TSURUGI*" —
"THE GRASSCUTTING SWORD."

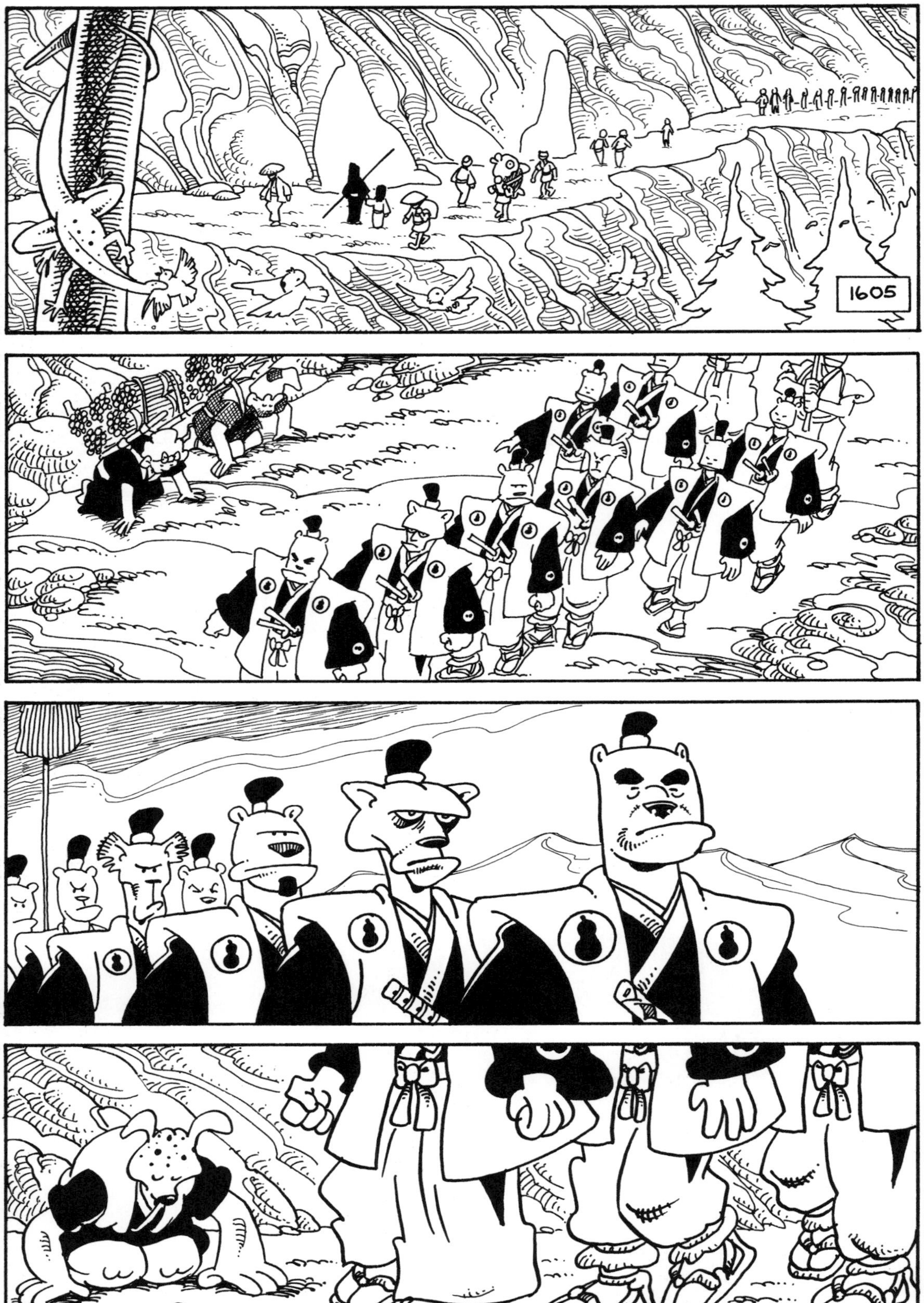
1605

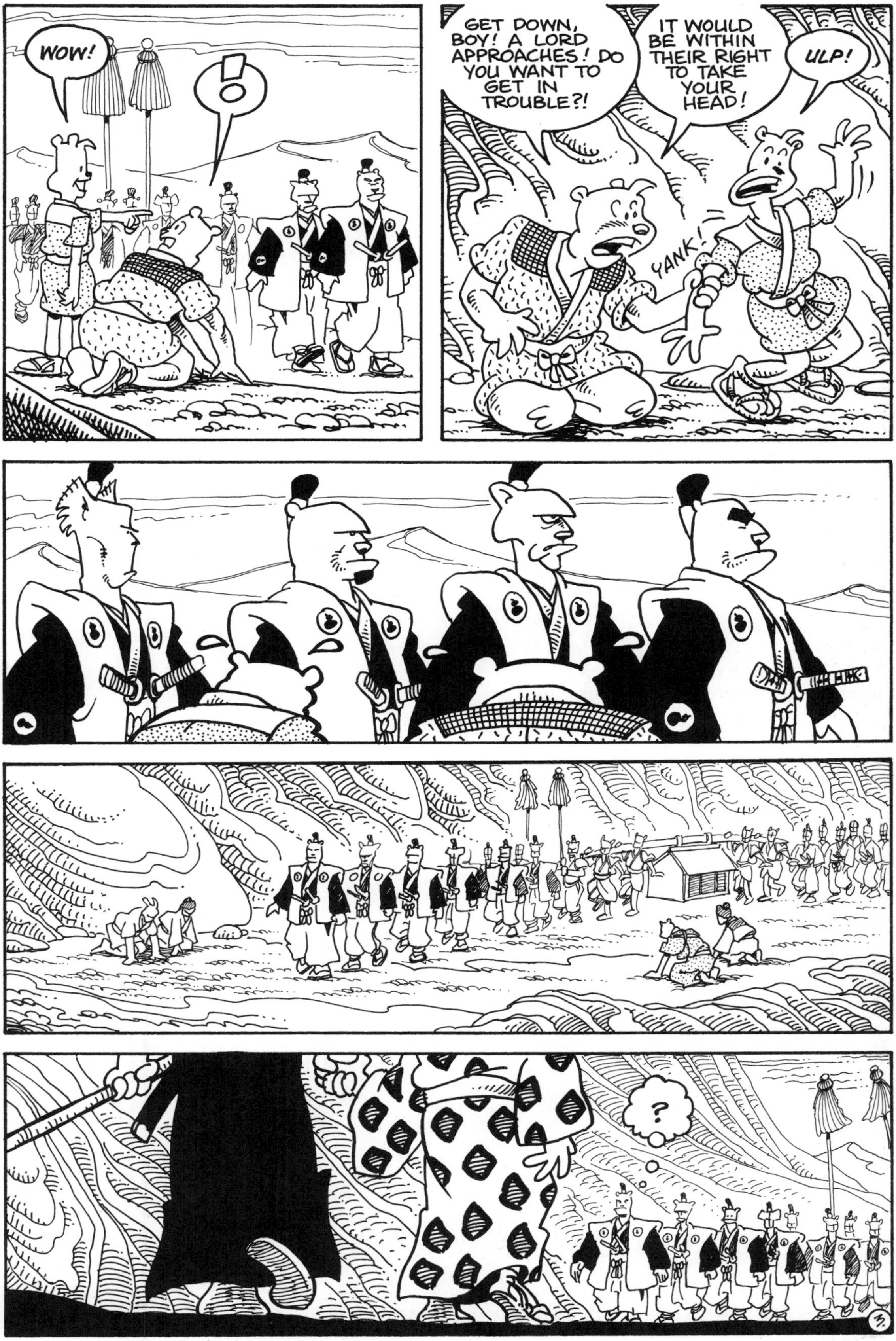
WOW!
!
GET DOWN, BOY! A LORD APPROACHES! DO YOU WANT TO GET IN TROUBLE?!
IT WOULD BE WITHIN THEIR RIGHT TO TAKE YOUR HEAD!
ULP!
YANK!
?
3.

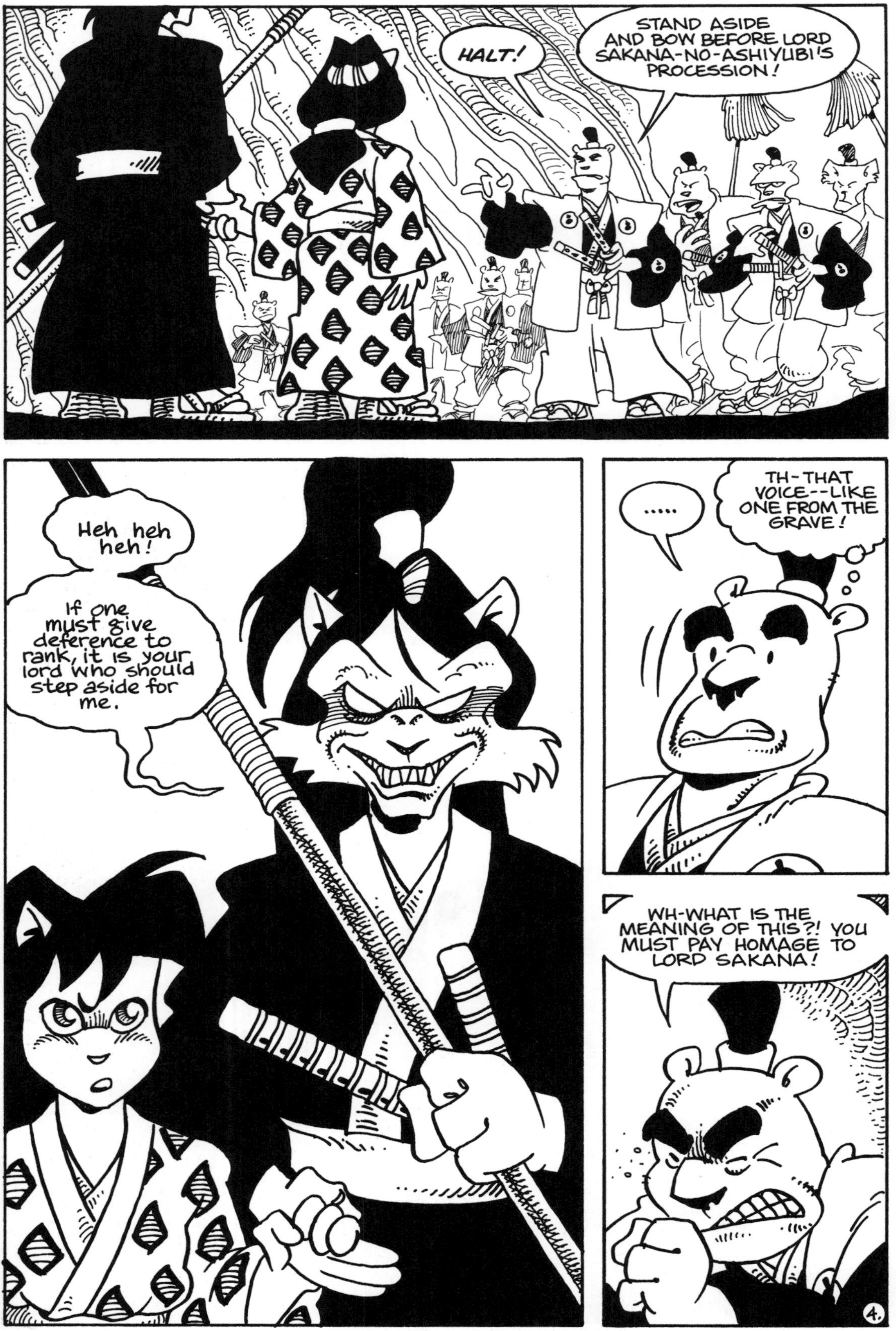
HALT!
STAND ASIDE AND BOW BEFORE LORD SAKANA-NO-ASHIYUBI'S PROCESSION!
Heh heh heh!
If one must give deference to rank, it is your lord who should step aside for me.
.....
TH-THAT VOICE--LIKE ONE FROM THE GRAVE!
WH-WHAT IS THE MEANING OF THIS?! YOU MUST PAY HOMAGE TO LORD SAKANA!
4.

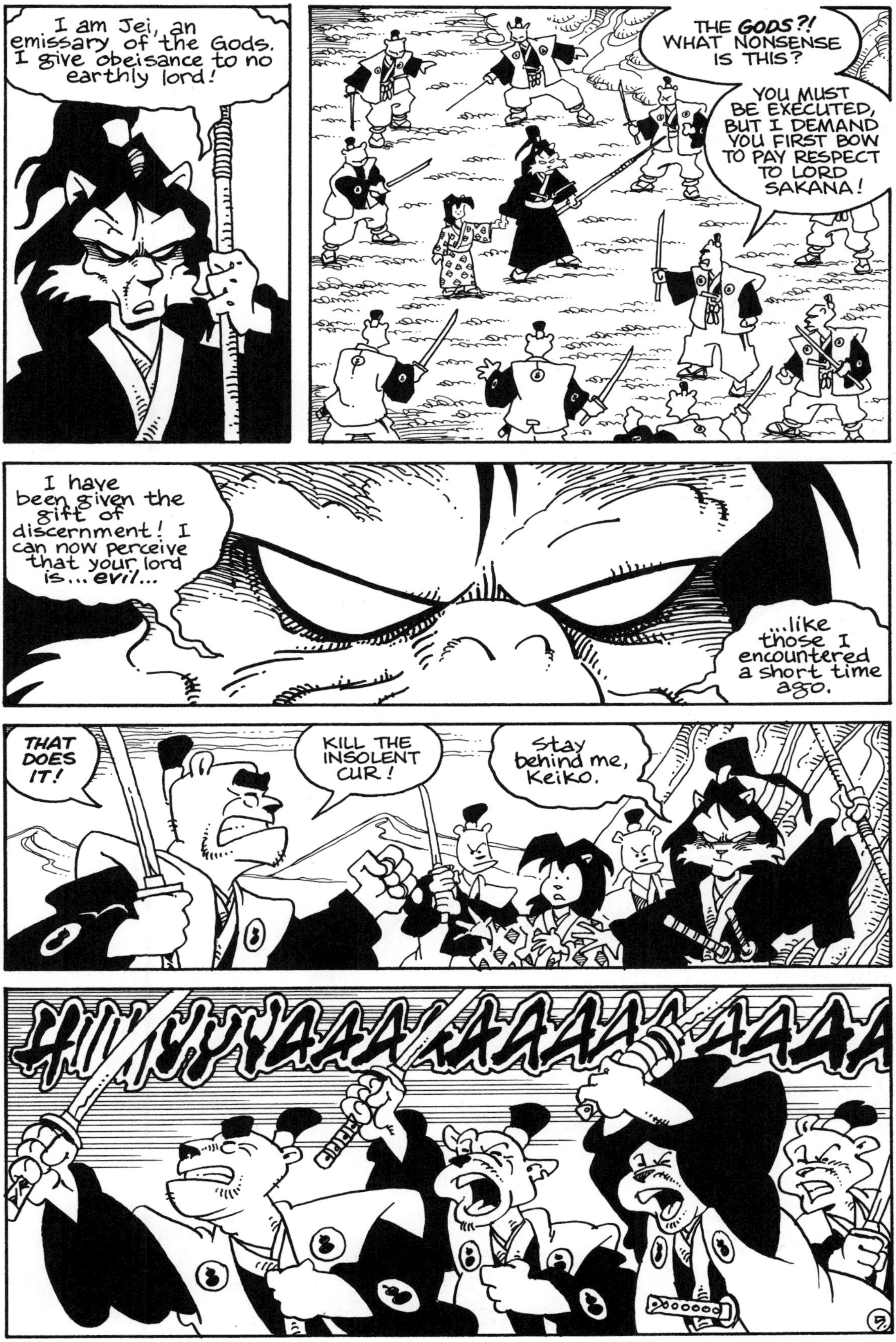
I am Jei, an emissary of the Gods. I give obeisance to no earthly lord!
THE *GODS*?! WHAT NONSENSE IS THIS?
YOU MUST BE EXECUTED, BUT I DEMAND YOU FIRST BOW TO PAY RESPECT TO LORD SAKANA!
I have been given the gift of discernment! I can now perceive that your lord is... *evil*...
...like those I encountered a short time ago.
THAT DOES IT!
KILL THE INSOLENT CUR!
Stay behind me, Keiko.
HIIYYYAAAAAAAAAAAA

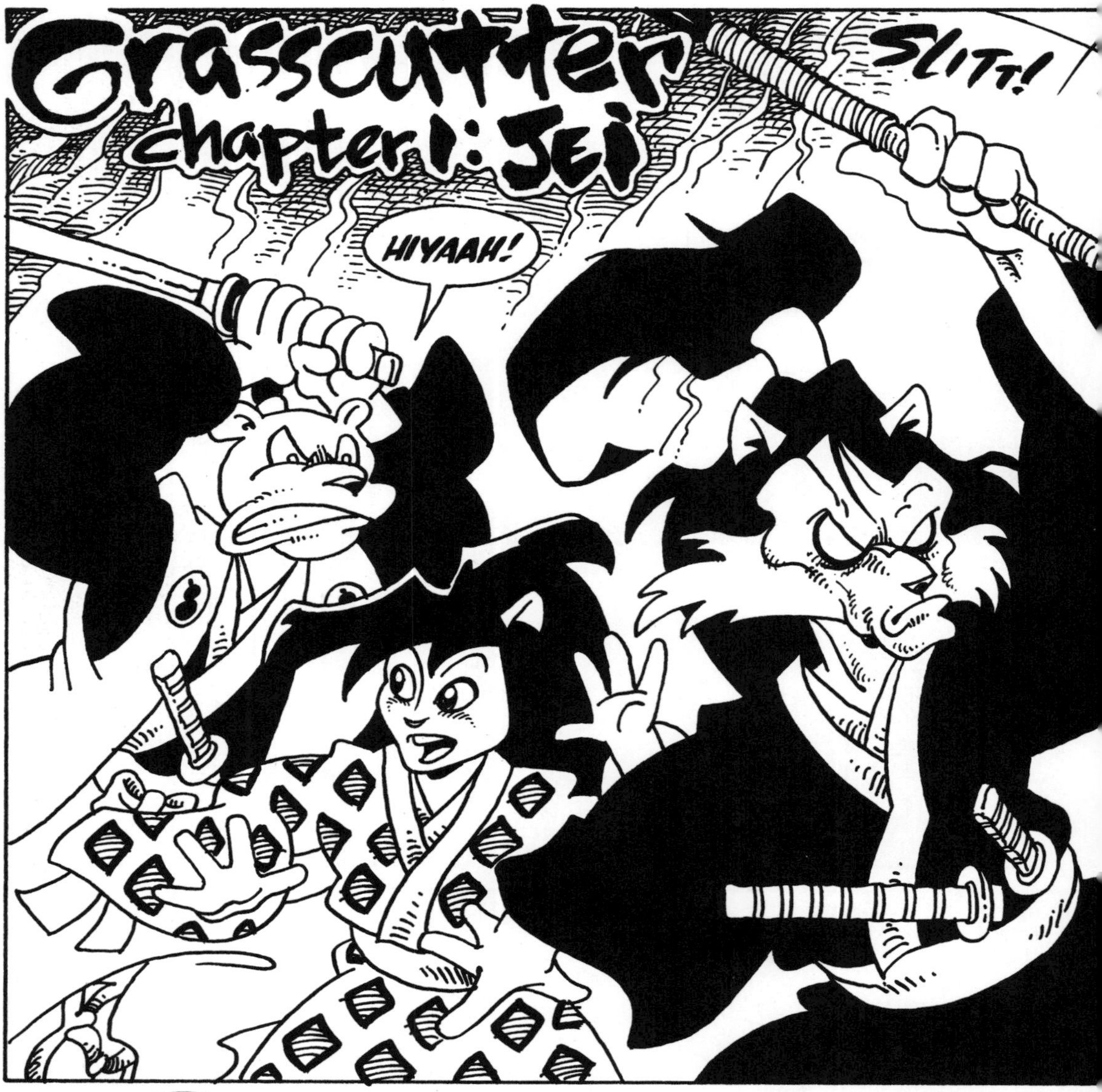
Grasscutter
chapter 1: Jei
SLITT!
HIYAAH!

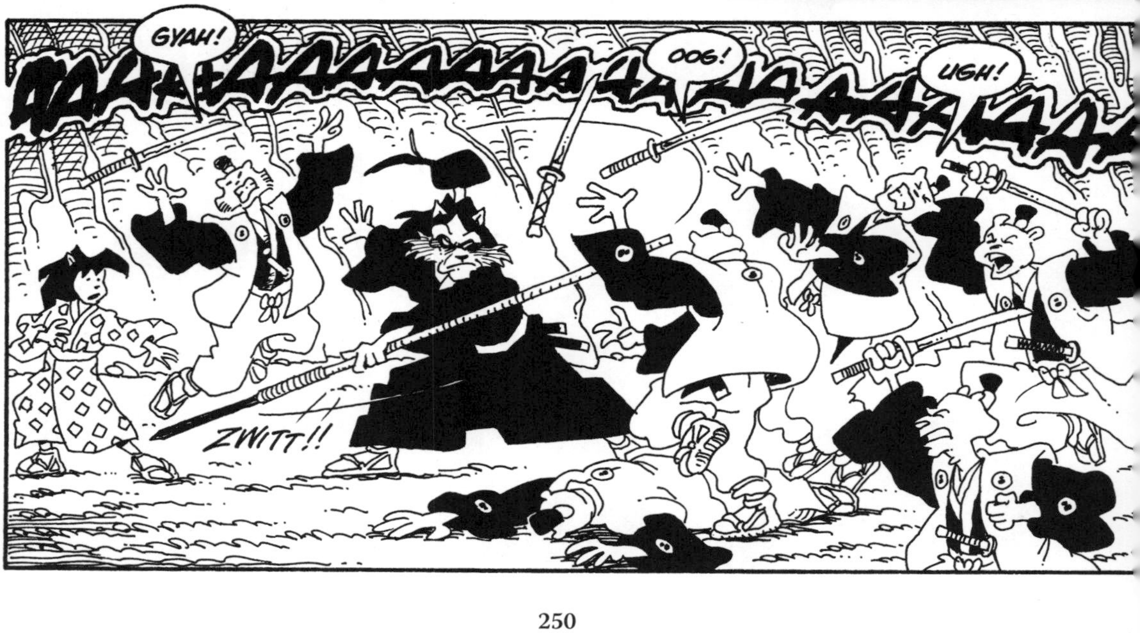
GYAH!
OOG!
UGH!
ZWITT!!

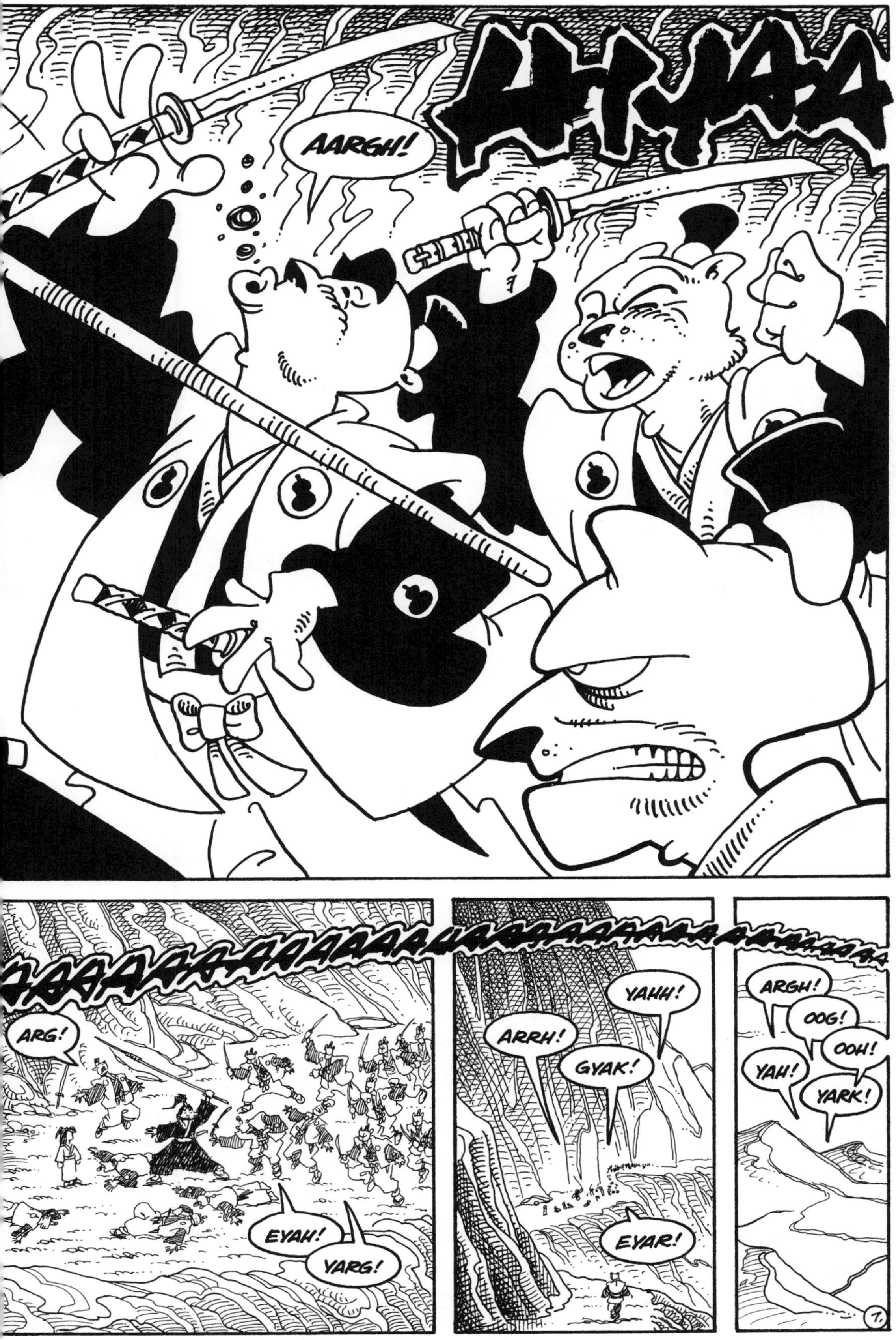
AARGH!
HI-YAA
AAAAAAAAAAAAAAAAAAAAAAAAAAAAAAAAAAAAAAAAAAAAAAAAAA
ARG!
EYAH!
YARG!
YAHH!
ARRH!
GYAK!
EYAR!
ARGH!
OOG!
OOH!
YAH!
YARK!
7.

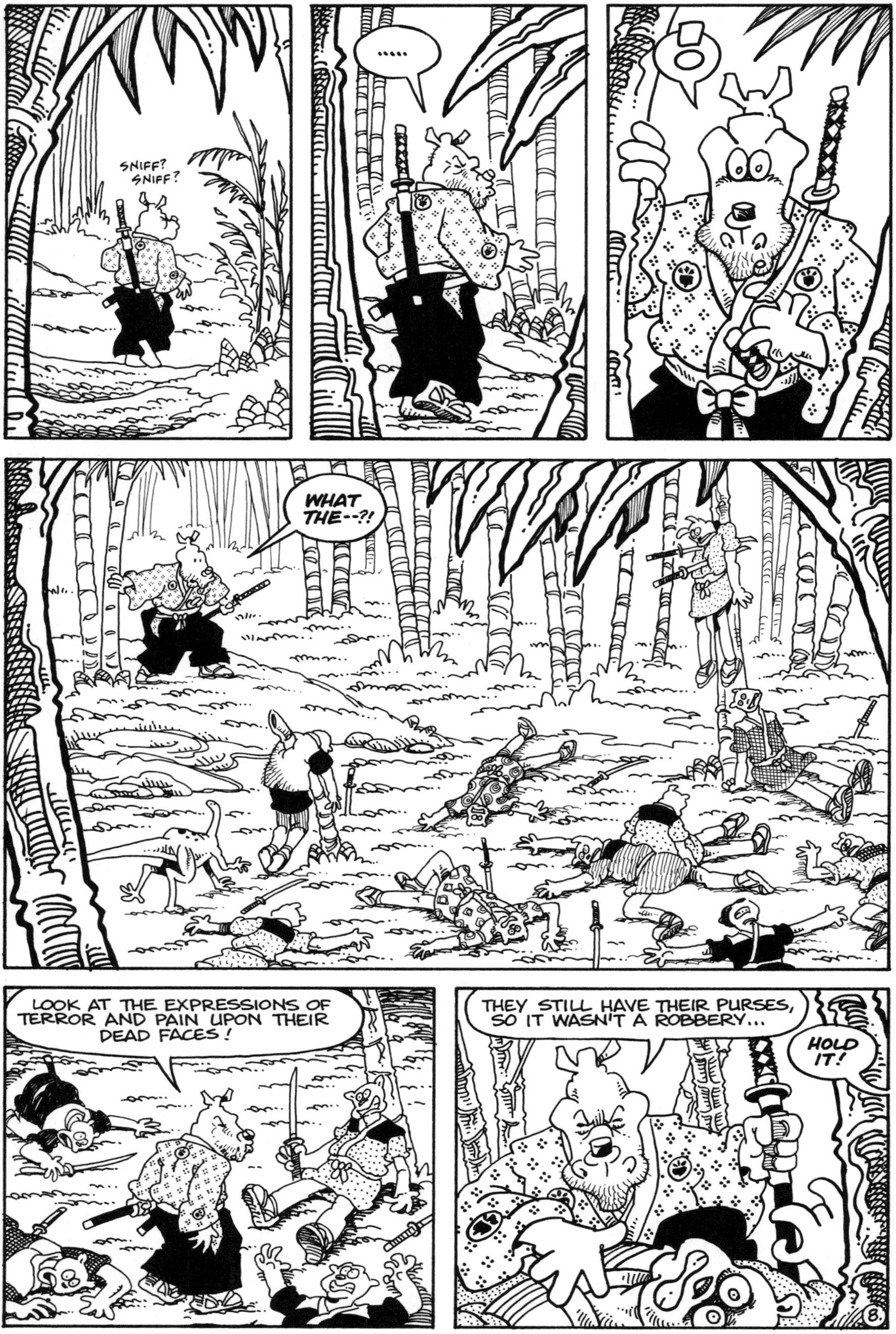
SNIFF? SNIFF?
......
!
WHAT THE--?!
LOOK AT THE EXPRESSIONS OF TERROR AND PAIN UPON THEIR DEAD FACES!
THEY STILL HAVE THEIR PURSES, SO IT WASN'T A ROBBERY...
HOLD IT!
8.

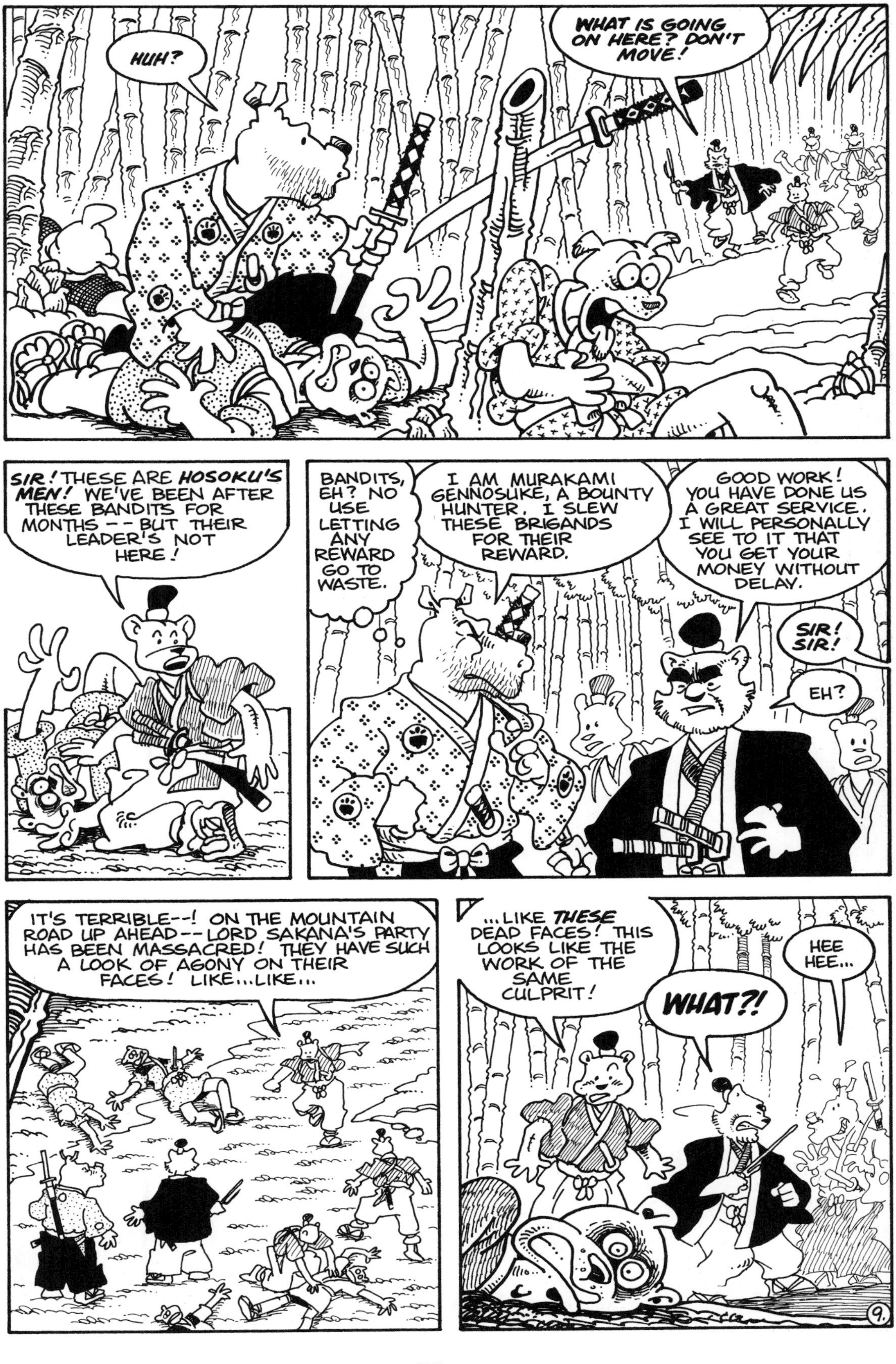
HUH?
WHAT IS GOING ON HERE? DON'T MOVE!
SIR! THESE ARE HOSOKU'S MEN! WE'VE BEEN AFTER THESE BANDITS FOR MONTHS -- BUT THEIR LEADER'S NOT HERE!
BANDITS, EH? NO USE LETTING ANY REWARD GO TO WASTE.
I AM MURAKAMI GENNOSUKE, A BOUNTY HUNTER. I SLEW THESE BRIGANDS FOR THEIR REWARD.
GOOD WORK! YOU HAVE DONE US A GREAT SERVICE. I WILL PERSONALLY SEE TO IT THAT YOU GET YOUR MONEY WITHOUT DELAY.
SIR! SIR!
EH?
IT'S TERRIBLE--! ON THE MOUNTAIN ROAD UP AHEAD--LORD SAKANA'S PARTY HAS BEEN MASSACRED! THEY HAVE SUCH A LOOK OF AGONY ON THEIR FACES! LIKE...LIKE...
...LIKE THESE DEAD FACES! THIS LOOKS LIKE THE WORK OF THE SAME CULPRIT!
WHAT?!
HEE HEE...
9.

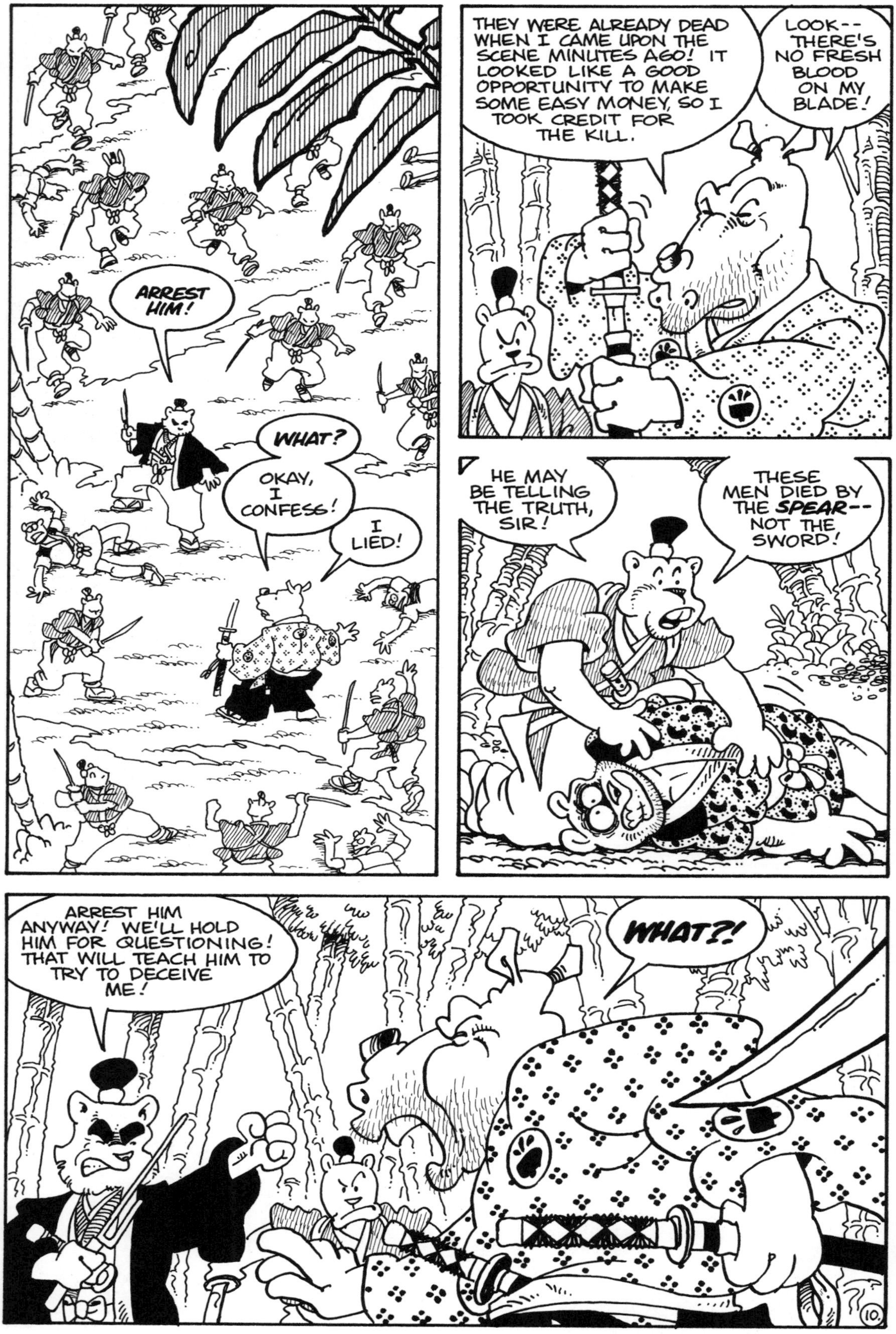
ARREST HIM!
WHAT?
OKAY, I CONFESS!
I LIED!
THEY WERE ALREADY DEAD WHEN I CAME UPON THE SCENE MINUTES AGO! IT LOOKED LIKE A GOOD OPPORTUNITY TO MAKE SOME EASY MONEY, SO I TOOK CREDIT FOR THE KILL.
LOOK-- THERE'S NO FRESH BLOOD ON MY BLADE!
HE MAY BE TELLING THE TRUTH, SIR!
THESE MEN DIED BY THE SPEAR-- NOT THE SWORD!
ARREST HIM ANYWAY! WE'LL HOLD HIM FOR QUESTIONING! THAT WILL TEACH HIM TO TRY TO DECEIVE ME!
WHAT?!
10.

HERE'S YOUR TEA, MA'AM. DRINK IT WHILE IT'S STILL HOT.

GO ON, DRINK IT.

GO ON!

IT'S GOOD!

YUMMY.

ZZZZ...

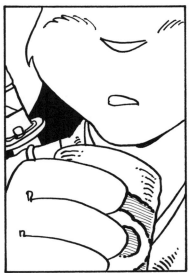

HERE, INNKEEPER. YOU DRINK IT.

WHAT? ME? UH... UH...

N-NO! I CAN'T! I-I MEAN, I'M ALLERGIC TO TEA. IT DOESN'T AGREE WITH ME....ER...I'LL SWELL UP...BREAK OUT IN A RASH... AND...UH....AND...

11.

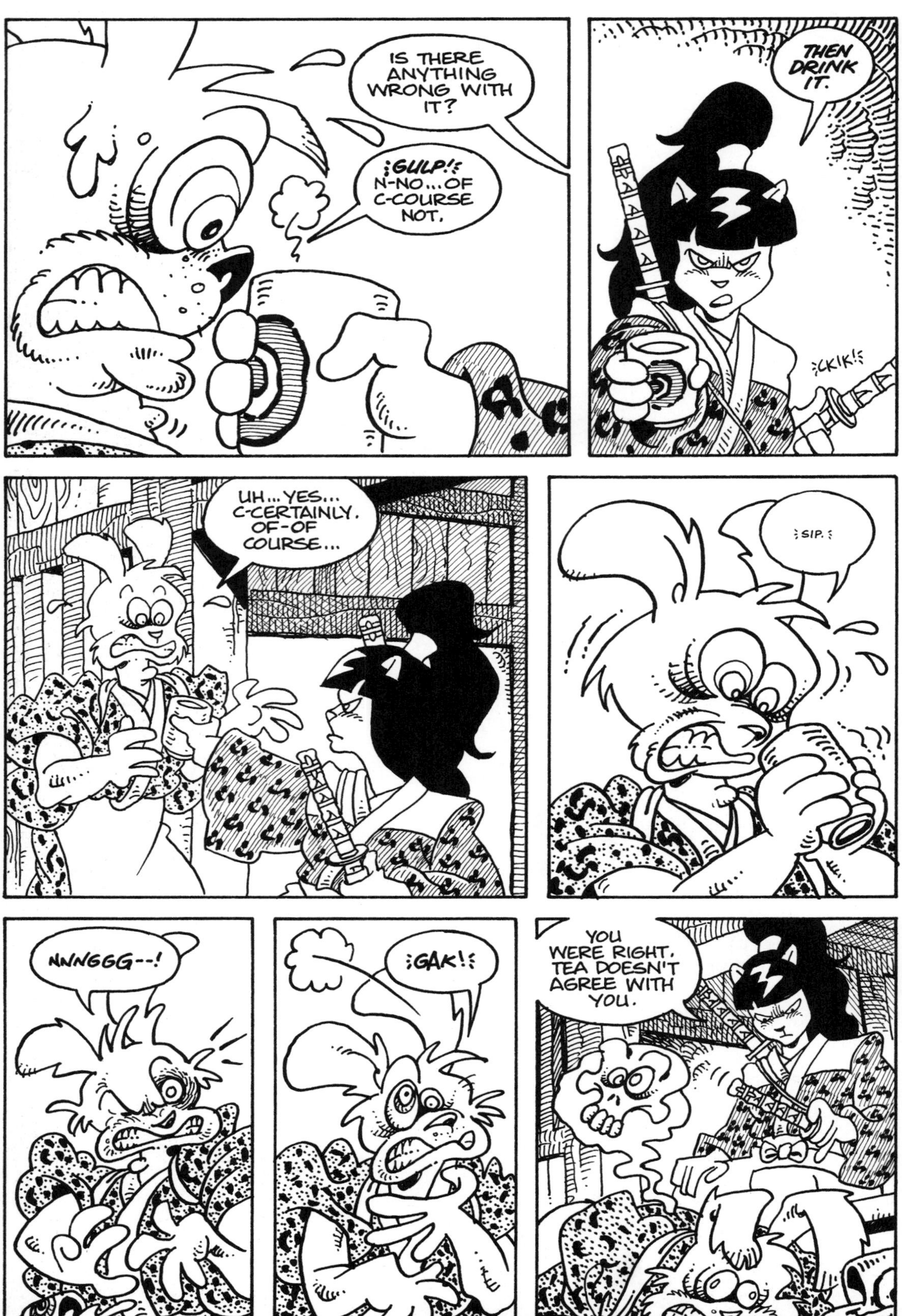
IS THERE ANYTHING WRONG WITH IT?
¡GULP!¡ N-NO...OF C-COURSE NOT.
THEN DRINK IT.
¡CKIK!¡
UH...YES... C-CERTAINLY. OF-OF COURSE...
¡SIP.¡
NNNGGG--!
¡GAK!¡
YOU WERE RIGHT. TEA DOESN'T AGREE WITH YOU.
12.

ASSASSINATION IS A DANGEROUS GAME--ESPECIALLY FOR AN AMATEUR!

YOU SHOULD HAVE STUCK TO RUNNING YOUR INN.

¡YAWN!¡ INNKEEPER! MORE SAKE!

I SAID, MORE SAKE!

HEY, YOU HEARD ME?!

YOU WANT ME TO COME BACK WITH MY GANG?

WHERE IS MY SAKE?!

¡ULP!¡

TH-THAT'S INAZUMA!

THEY SAY SHE'S UNMATCHED WITH THE SWORD!

BOSS BAKUCHI PUT A PRICE ON HER HEAD. THERE ARE MANY WHO WOULD LIKE TO CLAIM IT!

MAYBE I SHOULD GATHER THE GANG AND GO AFTER HER.

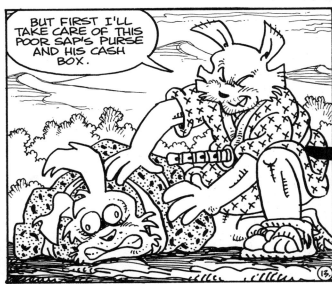

BUT FIRST I'LL TAKE CARE OF THIS POOR SAP'S PURSE AND HIS CASH BOX.

13.

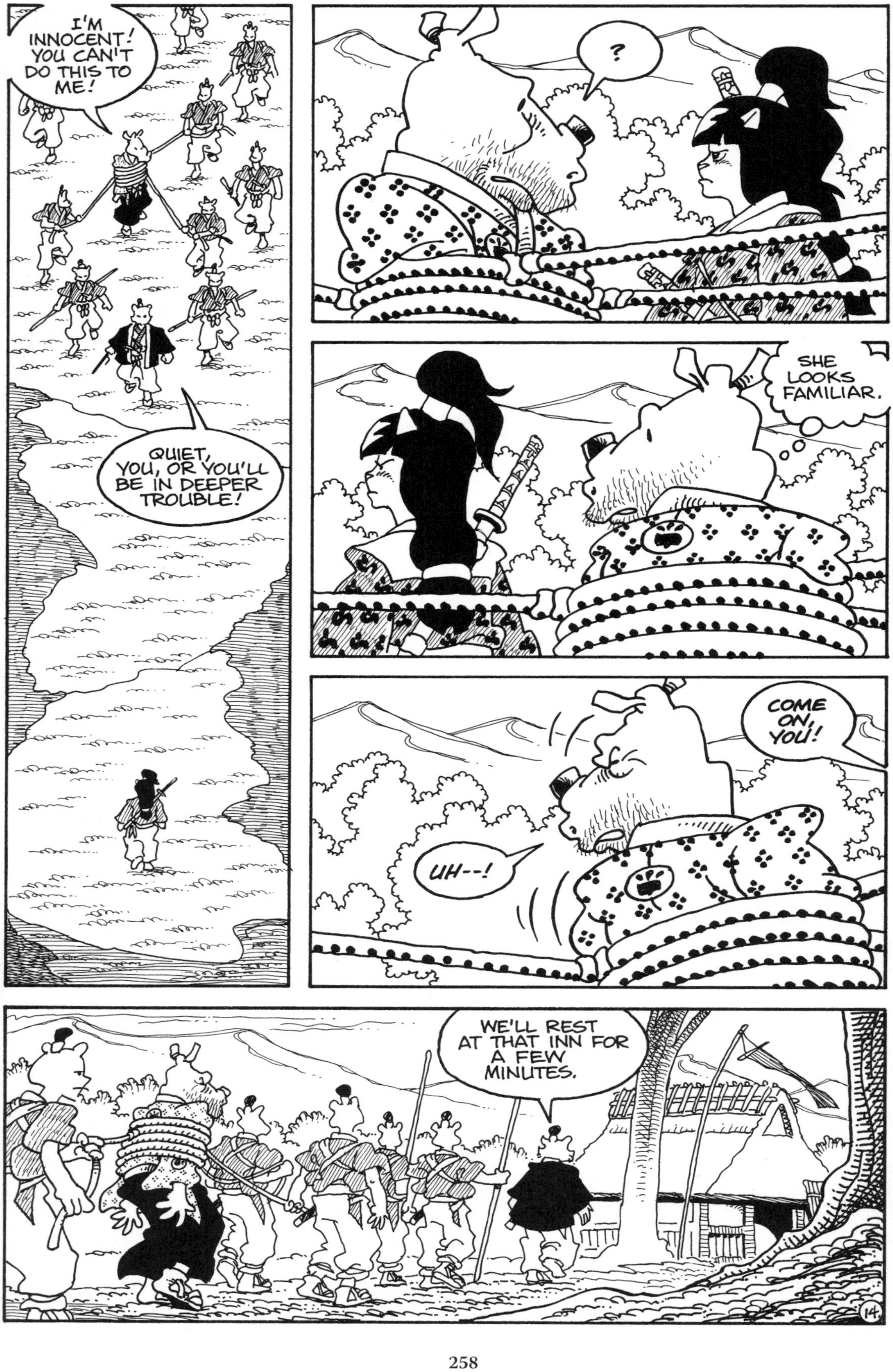
I'M INNOCENT! YOU CAN'T DO THIS TO ME!
QUIET, YOU, OR YOU'LL BE IN DEEPER TROUBLE!
?
SHE LOOKS FAMILIAR.
COME ON, YOU!
UH--!
WE'LL REST AT THAT INN FOR A FEW MINUTES.
14.

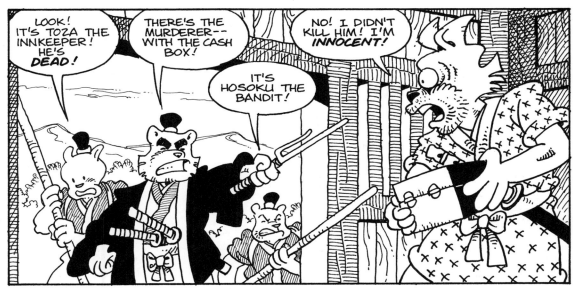

LOOK! IT'S TOZA THE INNKEEPER! HE'S *DEAD!*

THERE'S THE MURDERER-- WITH THE CASH BOX!

IT'S HOSOKU THE BANDIT!

NO! I DIDN'T KILL HIM! I'M *INNOCENT!*

AND SO...

I'M INNOCENT! *INNOCENT!*

SAVE YOUR BREATH!

BUT IT'S *TRUE!* I DIDN'T KILL THE INNKEEPER! IT WAS *INAZUMA!*

INAZUMA?!

THAT'S WHO THAT WAS! I WOULD LOVE TO GET BAKUCHI'S REWARD FOR HER!

INNOCENT!

COME ON, YOU TWO! STOP DAWDLING!

15

259

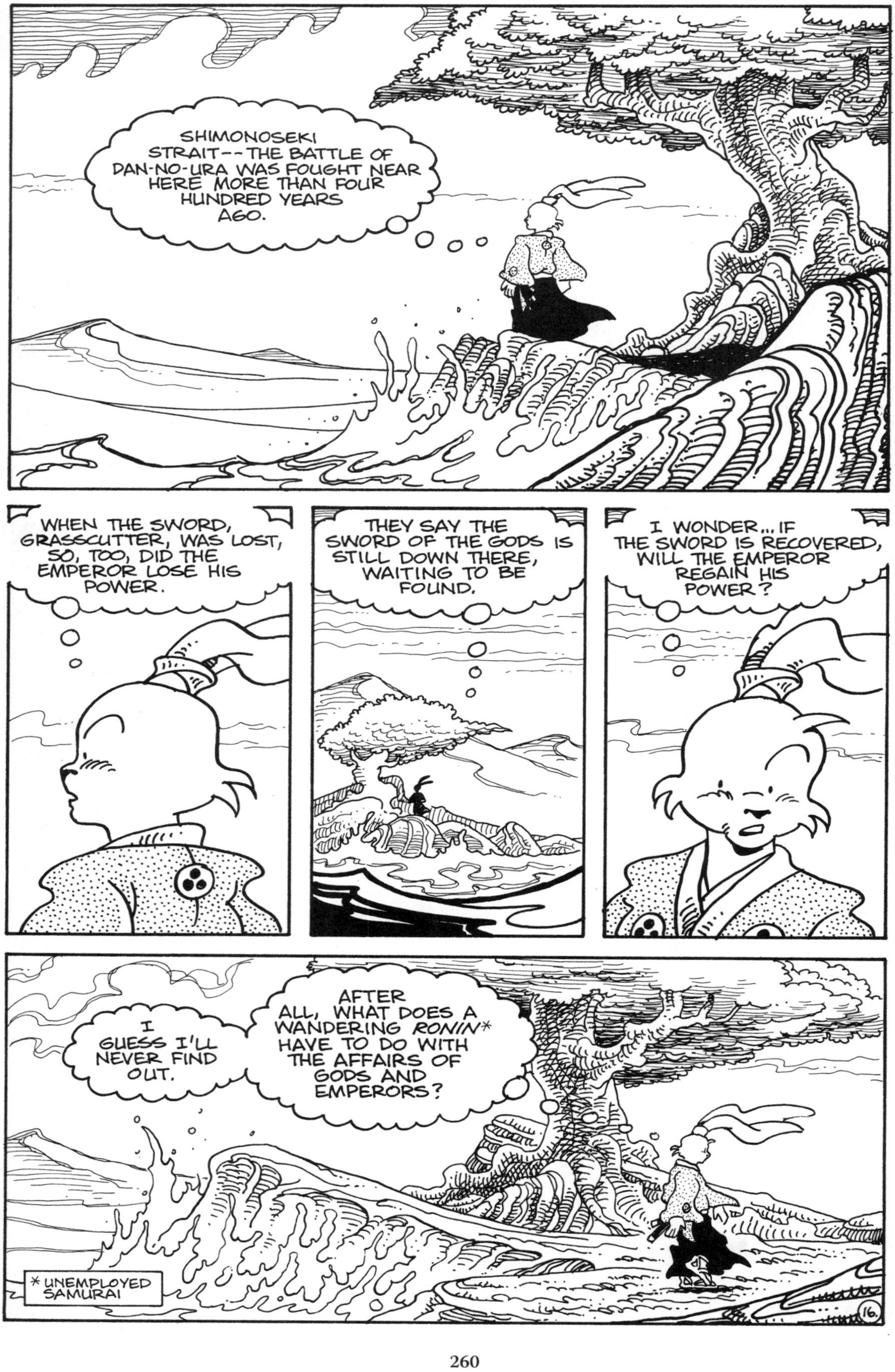
SHIMONOSEKI STRAIT--THE BATTLE OF DAN-NO-URA WAS FOUGHT NEAR HERE MORE THAN FOUR HUNDRED YEARS AGO.
WHEN THE SWORD, GRASSCUTTER, WAS LOST, SO, TOO, DID THE EMPEROR LOSE HIS POWER.
THEY SAY THE SWORD OF THE GODS IS STILL DOWN THERE, WAITING TO BE FOUND.
I WONDER... IF THE SWORD IS RECOVERED, WILL THE EMPEROR REGAIN HIS POWER?
I GUESS I'LL NEVER FIND OUT.
AFTER ALL, WHAT DOES A WANDERING *RONIN** HAVE TO DO WITH THE AFFAIRS OF GODS AND EMPERORS?
* UNEMPLOYED SAMURAI
16.

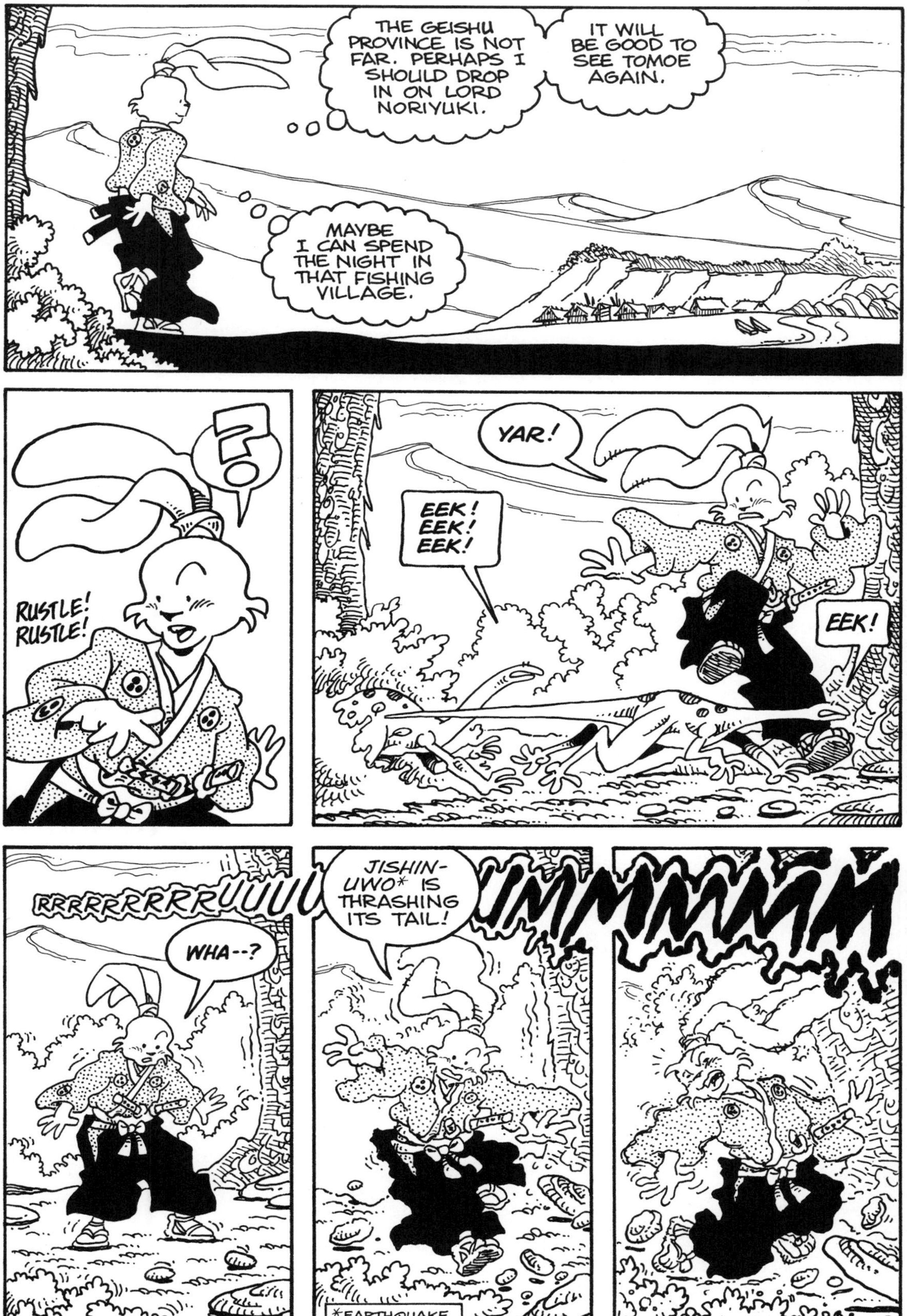
THE GEISHU PROVINCE IS NOT FAR. PERHAPS I SHOULD DROP IN ON LORD NORIYUKI.
IT WILL BE GOOD TO SEE TOMOE AGAIN.
MAYBE I CAN SPEND THE NIGHT IN THAT FISHING VILLAGE.
?
RUSTLE! RUSTLE!
YAR!
EEK! EEK! EEK!
EEK!
RRRRRRRRRRUUUU
WHA--?
JISHIN-UWO* IS THRASHING ITS TAIL!
*EARTHQUAKE FISH
UMMMMMM
17

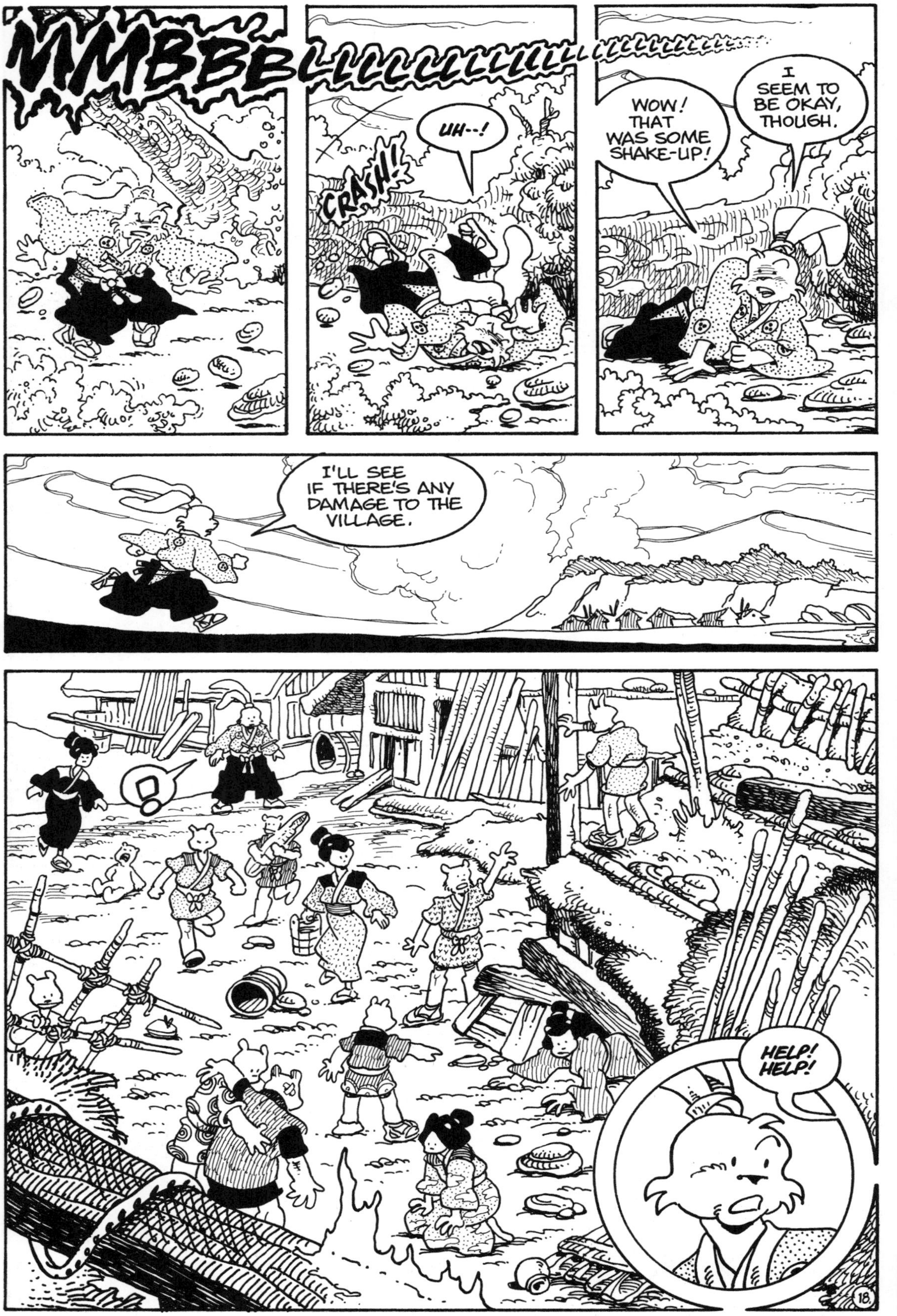
MMBBBLLLLLLLLLLLLLLLLLLLLLLLL
CRASH!
UH--!
WOW! THAT WAS SOME SHAKE-UP!
I SEEM TO BE OKAY, THOUGH.
I'LL SEE IF THERE'S ANY DAMAGE TO THE VILLAGE.
HELP! HELP!
18

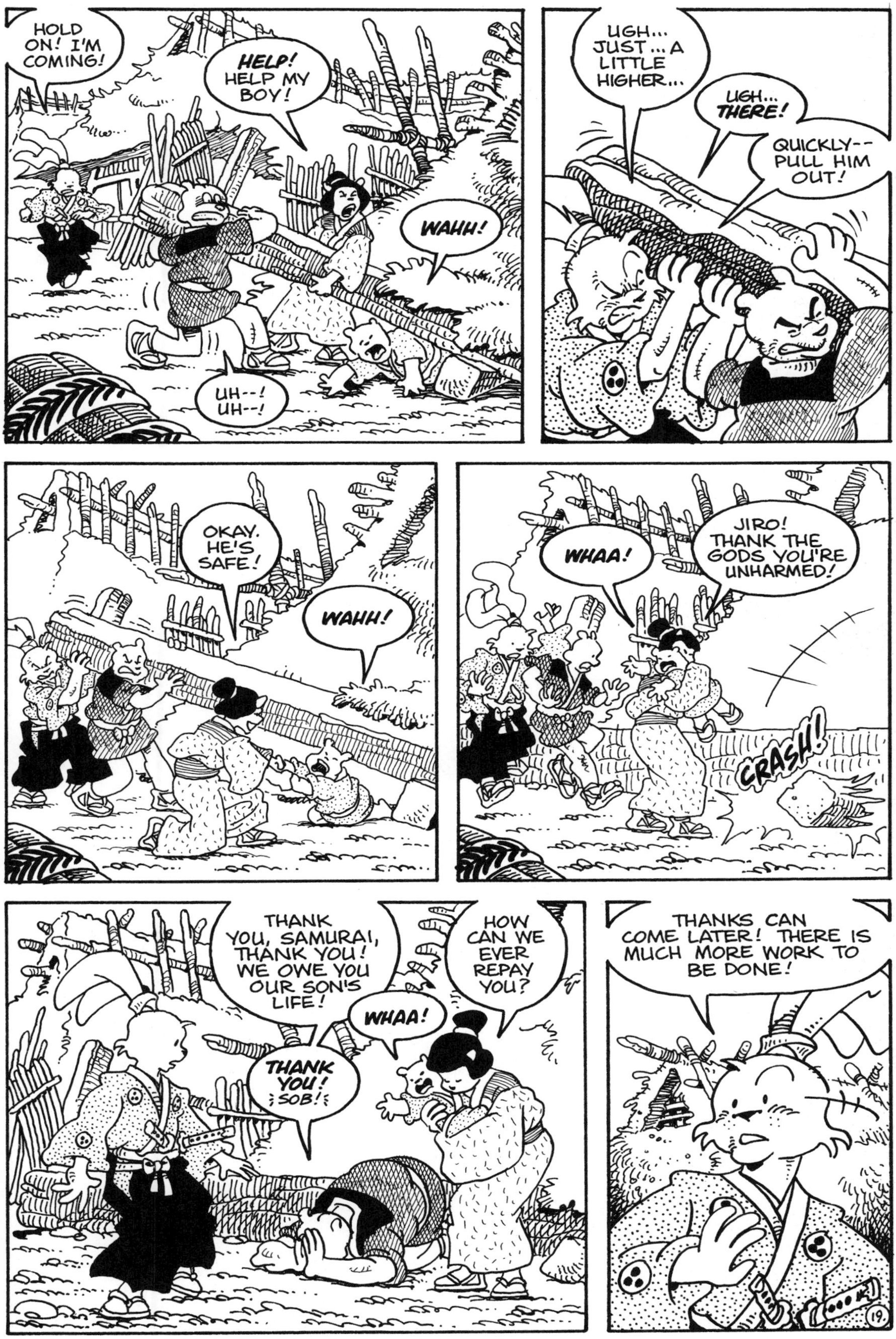
HOLD ON! I'M COMING!
HELP! HELP MY BOY!
WAHH!
UH--! UH--!
UGH... JUST... A LITTLE HIGHER...
UGH... THERE!
QUICKLY-- PULL HIM OUT!
OKAY. HE'S SAFE!
WAHH!
WHAA!
JIRO! THANK THE GODS YOU'RE UNHARMED!
CRASH!
THANK YOU, SAMURAI, THANK YOU! WE OWE YOU OUR SON'S LIFE!
THANK YOU! SOB!
WHAA!
HOW CAN WE EVER REPAY YOU?
THANKS CAN COME LATER! THERE IS MUCH MORE WORK TO BE DONE!
19.

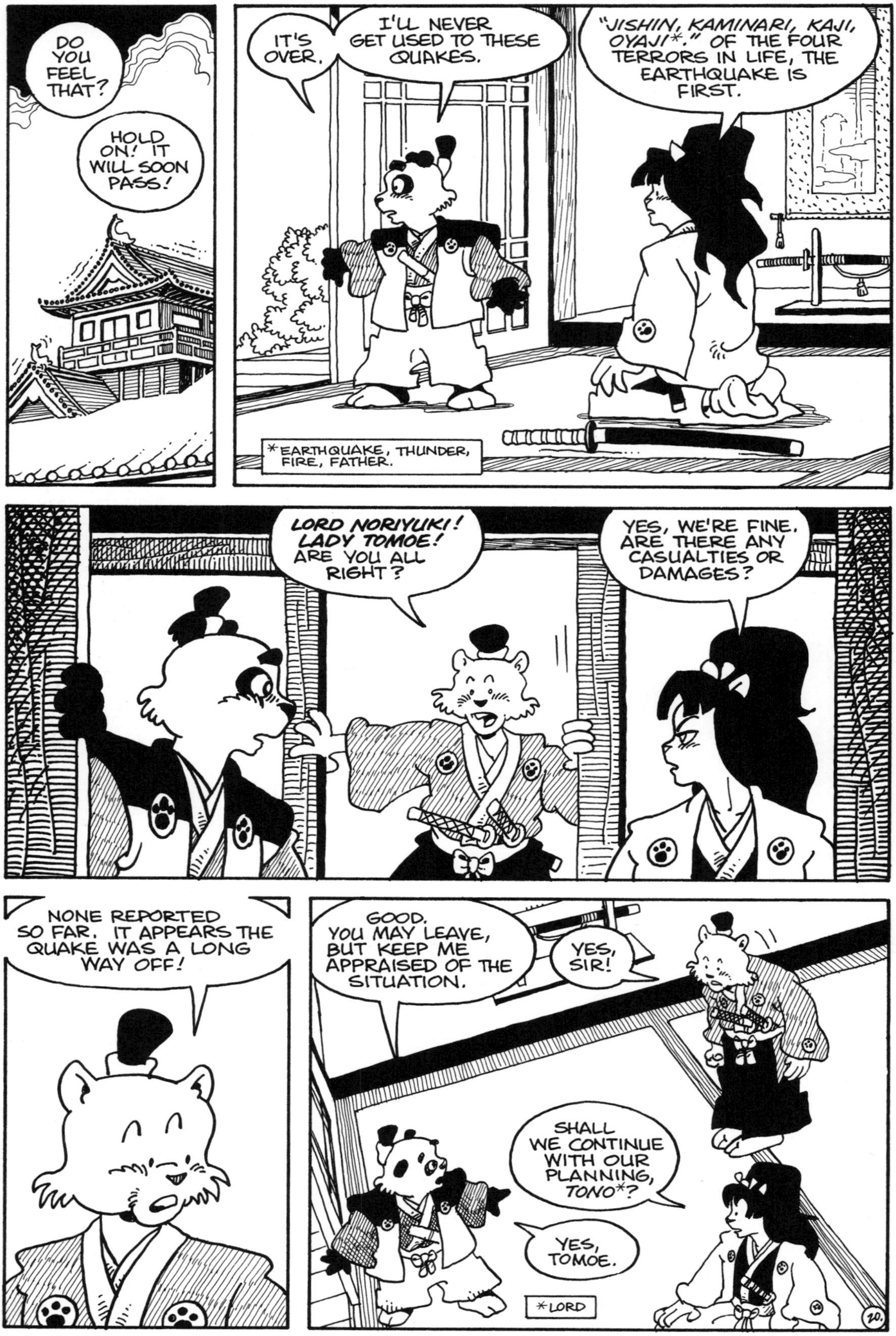
DO YOU FEEL THAT?
HOLD ON! IT WILL SOON PASS!
IT'S OVER.
I'LL NEVER GET USED TO THESE QUAKES.
"JISHIN, KAMINARI, KAJI, OYAJI*." OF THE FOUR TERRORS IN LIFE, THE EARTHQUAKE IS FIRST.
*EARTHQUAKE, THUNDER, FIRE, FATHER.
LORD NORIYUKI! LADY TOMOE! ARE YOU ALL RIGHT?
YES, WE'RE FINE. ARE THERE ANY CASUALTIES OR DAMAGES?
NONE REPORTED SO FAR. IT APPEARS THE QUAKE WAS A LONG WAY OFF!
GOOD. YOU MAY LEAVE, BUT KEEP ME APPRAISED OF THE SITUATION.
YES, SIR!
SHALL WE CONTINUE WITH OUR PLANNING, TONO*?
YES, TOMOE.
*LORD
20.

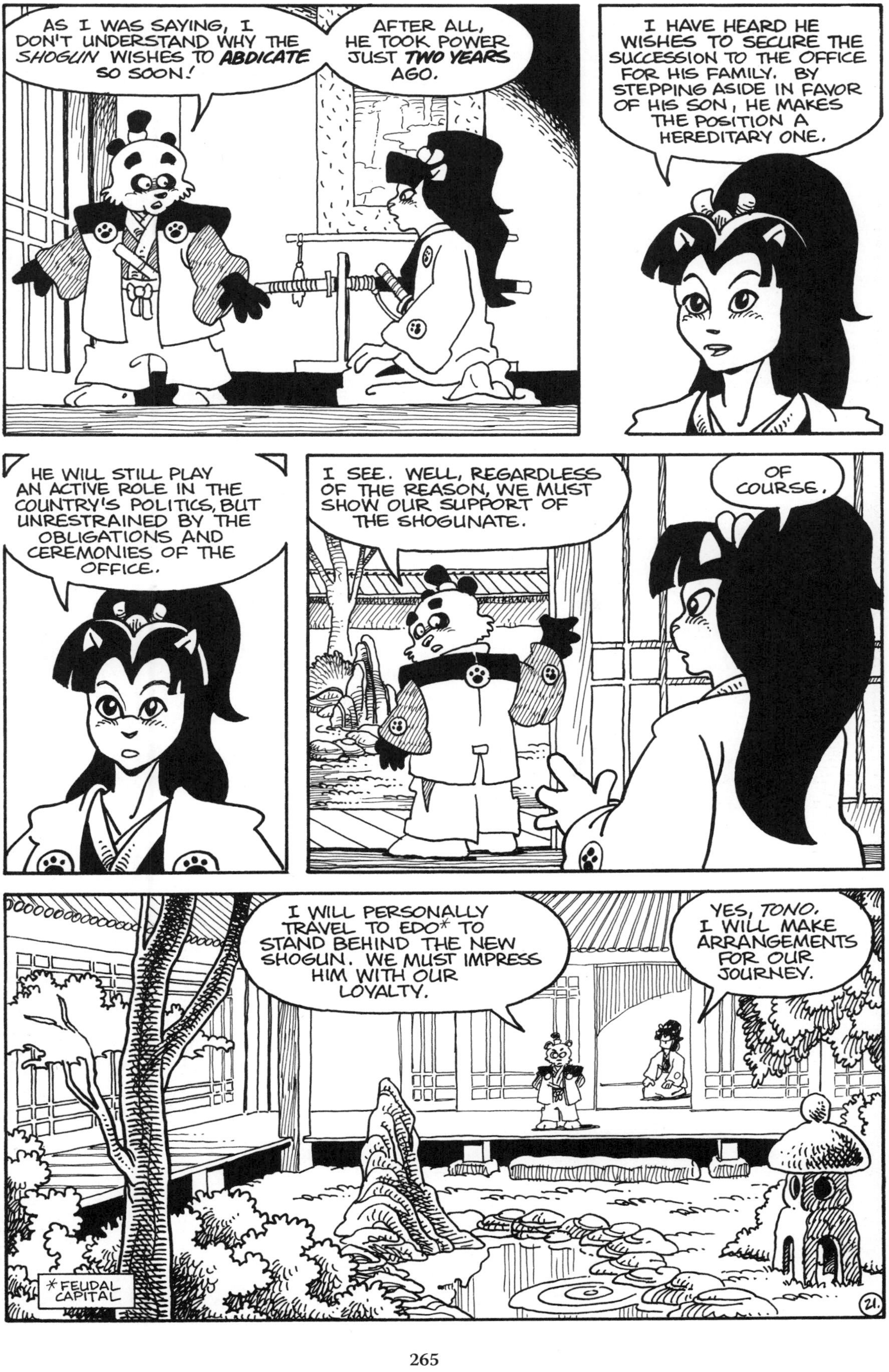

AS I WAS SAYING, I DON'T UNDERSTAND WHY THE *SHOGUN* WISHES TO ***ABDICATE*** SO SOON!
AFTER ALL, HE TOOK POWER JUST ***TWO YEARS*** AGO.
I HAVE HEARD HE WISHES TO SECURE THE SUCCESSION TO THE OFFICE FOR HIS FAMILY. BY STEPPING ASIDE IN FAVOR OF HIS SON, HE MAKES THE POSITION A HEREDITARY ONE.
HE WILL STILL PLAY AN ACTIVE ROLE IN THE COUNTRY'S POLITICS, BUT UNRESTRAINED BY THE OBLIGATIONS AND CEREMONIES OF THE OFFICE.
I SEE. WELL, REGARDLESS OF THE REASON, WE MUST SHOW OUR SUPPORT OF THE SHOGUNATE.
OF COURSE.
I WILL PERSONALLY TRAVEL TO EDO* TO STAND BEHIND THE NEW SHOGUN. WE MUST IMPRESS HIM WITH OUR LOYALTY.
YES, *TONO*. I WILL MAKE ARRANGEMENTS FOR OUR JOURNEY.
*FEUDAL CAPITAL
21.

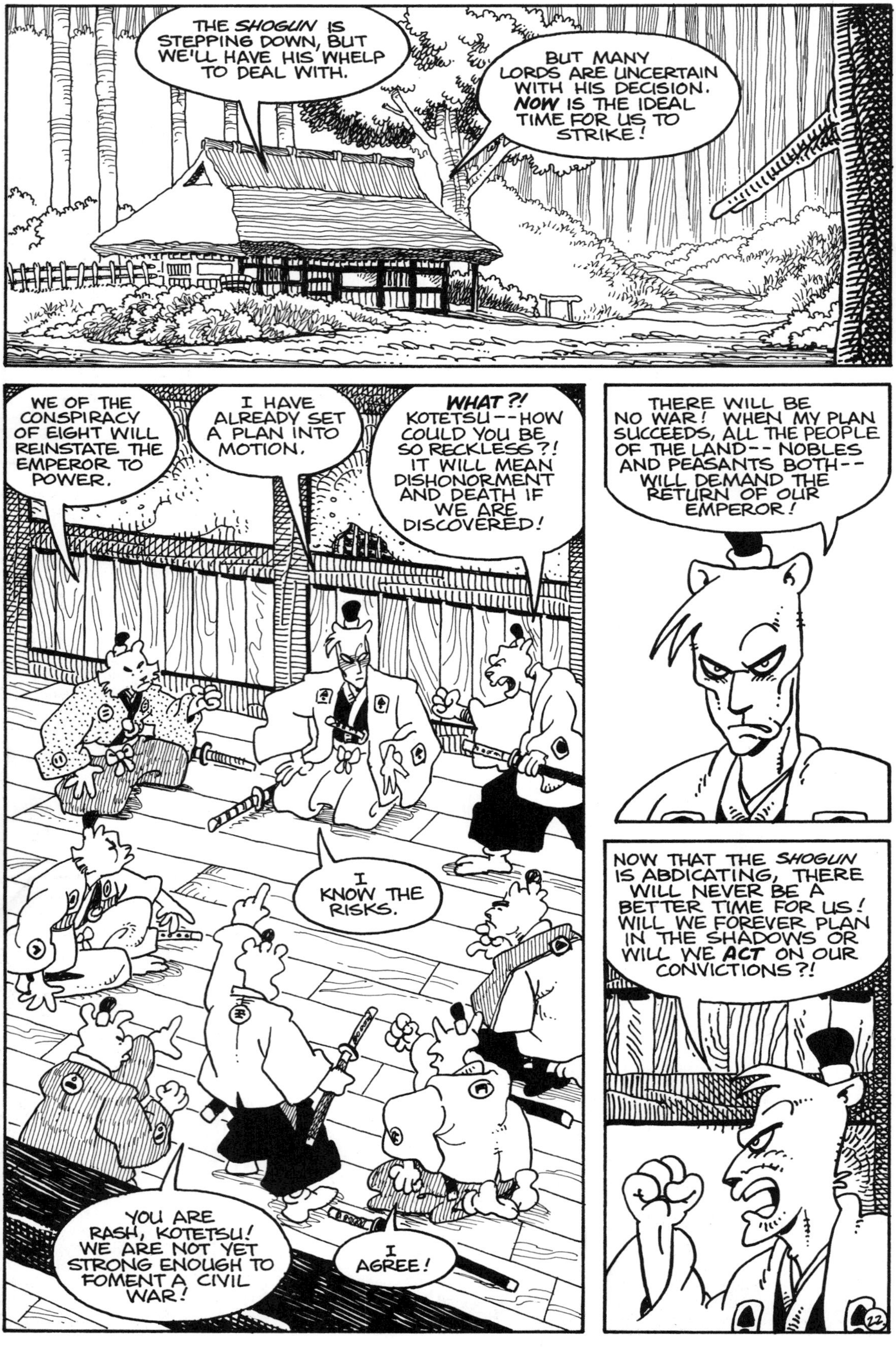
THE SHOGUN IS STEPPING DOWN, BUT WE'LL HAVE HIS WHELP TO DEAL WITH.
BUT MANY LORDS ARE UNCERTAIN WITH HIS DECISION. NOW IS THE IDEAL TIME FOR US TO STRIKE!
WE OF THE CONSPIRACY OF EIGHT WILL REINSTATE THE EMPEROR TO POWER.
I HAVE ALREADY SET A PLAN INTO MOTION.
WHAT?! KOTETSU--HOW COULD YOU BE SO RECKLESS?! IT WILL MEAN DISHONORMENT AND DEATH IF WE ARE DISCOVERED!
I KNOW THE RISKS.
YOU ARE RASH, KOTETSU! WE ARE NOT YET STRONG ENOUGH TO FOMENT A CIVIL WAR!
I AGREE!
THERE WILL BE NO WAR! WHEN MY PLAN SUCCEEDS, ALL THE PEOPLE OF THE LAND-- NOBLES AND PEASANTS BOTH-- WILL DEMAND THE RETURN OF OUR EMPEROR!
NOW THAT THE SHOGUN IS ABDICATING, THERE WILL NEVER BE A BETTER TIME FOR US! WILL WE FOREVER PLAN IN THE SHADOWS OR WILL WE ACT ON OUR CONVICTIONS?!
22

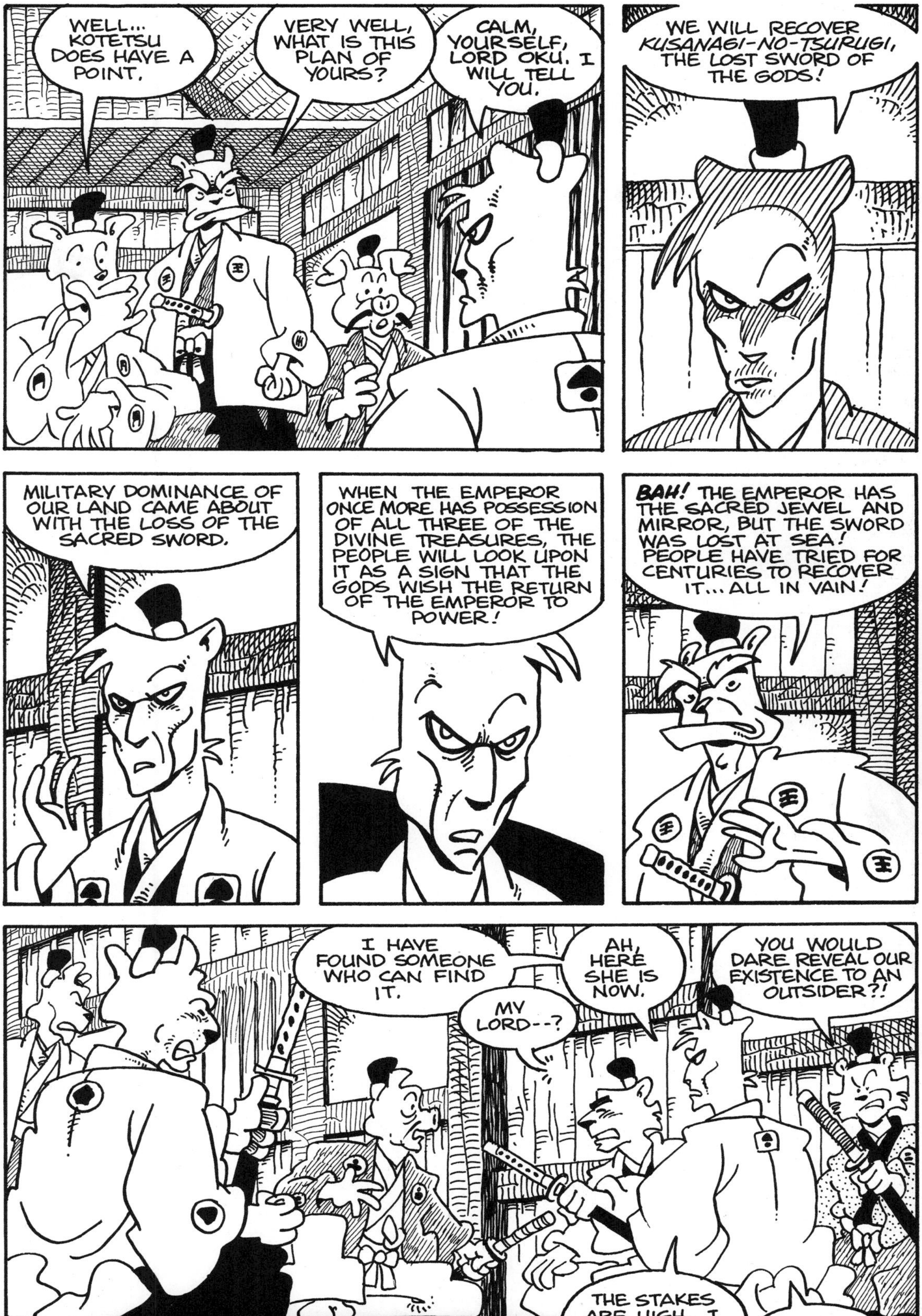
WELL... KOTETSU DOES HAVE A POINT.
VERY WELL, WHAT IS THIS PLAN OF YOURS?
CALM, YOURSELF, LORD OKU. I WILL TELL YOU.
WE WILL RECOVER *KUSANAGI-NO-TSURUGI*, THE LOST SWORD OF THE GODS!
MILITARY DOMINANCE OF OUR LAND CAME ABOUT WITH THE LOSS OF THE SACRED SWORD.
WHEN THE EMPEROR ONCE MORE HAS POSSESSION OF ALL THREE OF THE DIVINE TREASURES, THE PEOPLE WILL LOOK UPON IT AS A SIGN THAT THE GODS WISH THE RETURN OF THE EMPEROR TO POWER!
BAH! THE EMPEROR HAS THE SACRED JEWEL AND MIRROR, BUT THE SWORD WAS LOST AT SEA! PEOPLE HAVE TRIED FOR CENTURIES TO RECOVER IT... ALL IN VAIN!
I HAVE FOUND SOMEONE WHO CAN FIND IT.
MY LORD--?
AH, HERE SHE IS NOW.
YOU WOULD DARE REVEAL OUR EXISTENCE TO AN OUTSIDER?!
THE STAKES ARE HIGH. I WOULD DARE ANYTHING!
ENTER!
23.

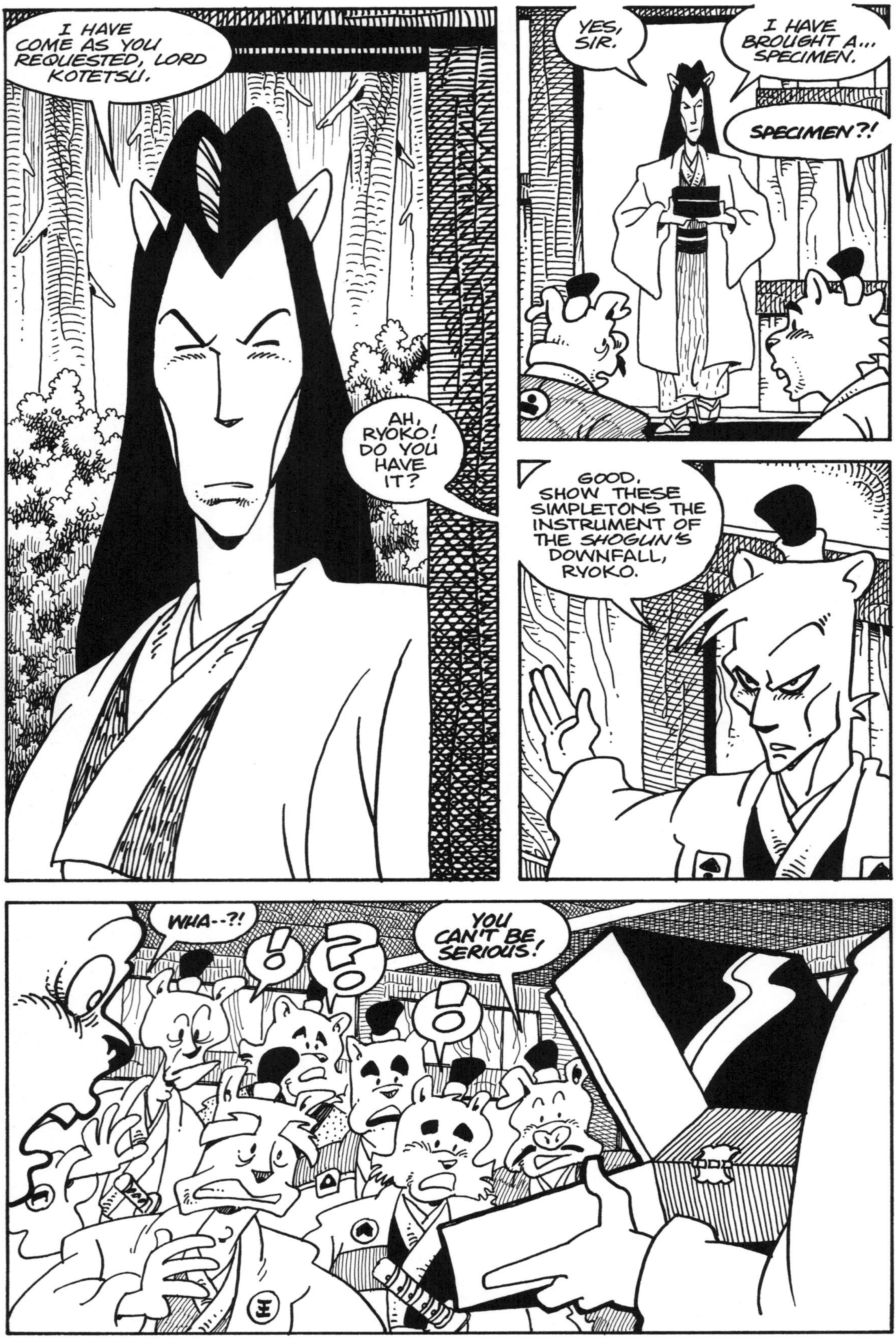
I HAVE COME AS YOU REQUESTED, LORD KOTETSU.
AH, RYOKO! DO YOU HAVE IT?
YES, SIR.
I HAVE BROUGHT A... SPECIMEN.
SPECIMEN?!
GOOD, SHOW THESE SIMPLETONS THE INSTRUMENT OF THE SHOGUN'S DOWNFALL, RYOKO.
WHA--?!
!
?
YOU CAN'T BE SERIOUS!
!

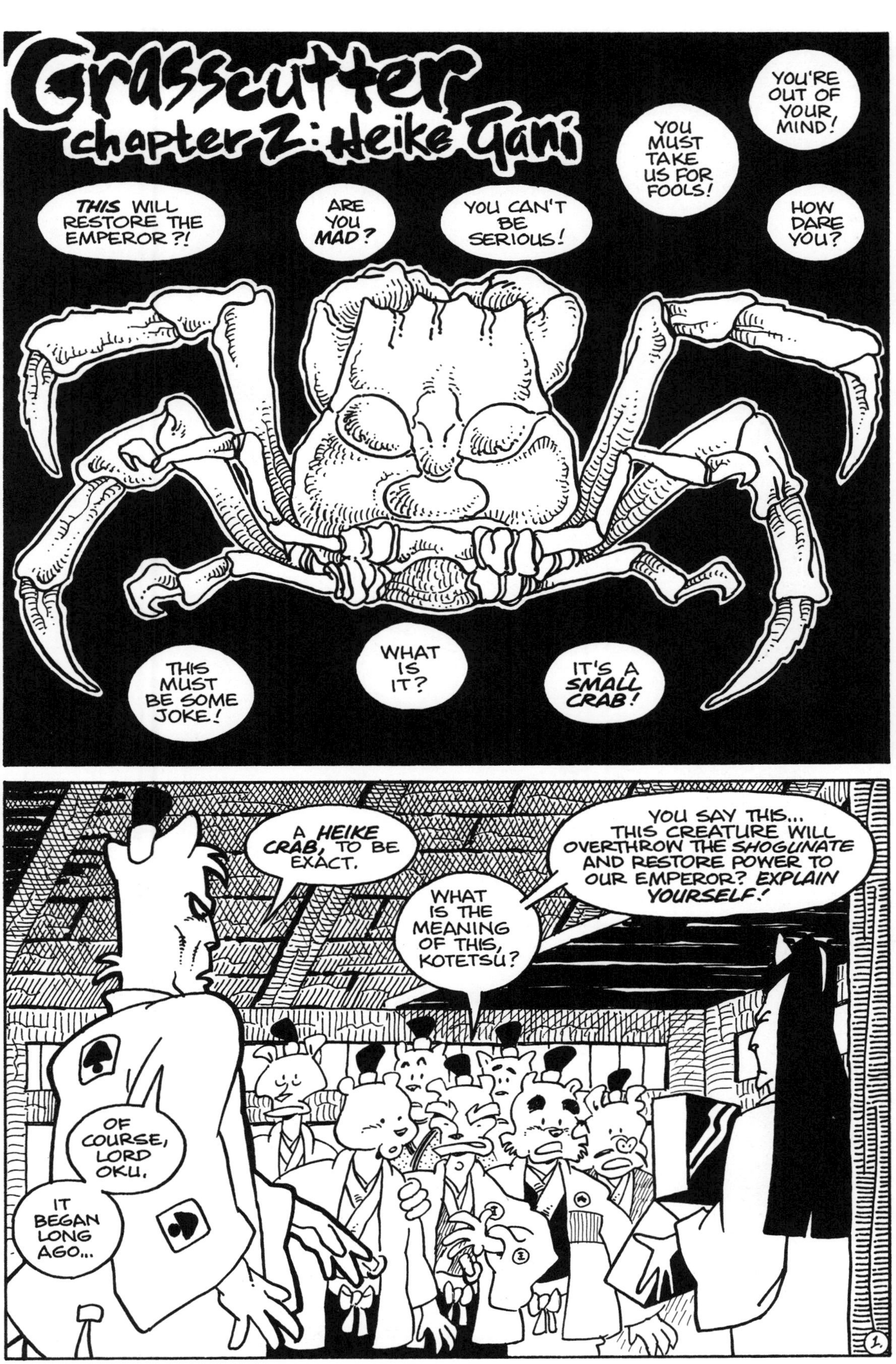
Grasscutter
chapter 2: Heike Gani
THIS WILL RESTORE THE EMPEROR?!
ARE YOU MAD?
YOU CAN'T BE SERIOUS!
YOU MUST TAKE US FOR FOOLS!
YOU'RE OUT OF YOUR MIND!
HOW DARE YOU?
THIS MUST BE SOME JOKE!
WHAT IS IT?
IT'S A SMALL CRAB!
A HEIKE CRAB, TO BE EXACT.
WHAT IS THE MEANING OF THIS, KOTETSU?
YOU SAY THIS... THIS CREATURE WILL OVERTHROW THE SHOGUNATE AND RESTORE POWER TO OUR EMPEROR? EXPLAIN YOURSELF!
OF COURSE, LORD OKU.
IT BEGAN LONG AGO...
1.

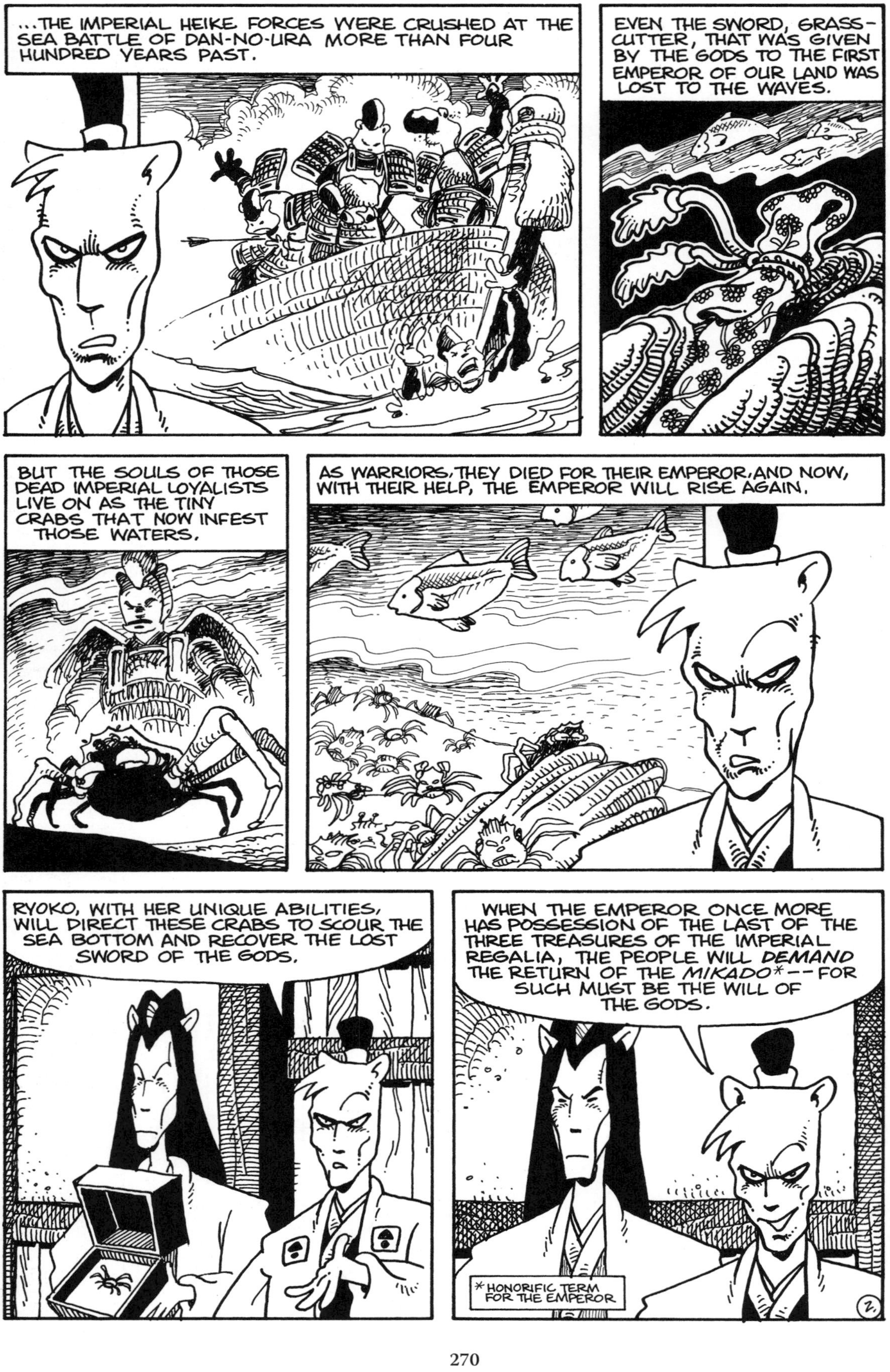
...THE IMPERIAL HEIKE FORCES WERE CRUSHED AT THE SEA BATTLE OF DAN-NO-URA MORE THAN FOUR HUNDRED YEARS PAST.
EVEN THE SWORD, GRASS-CUTTER, THAT WAS GIVEN BY THE GODS TO THE FIRST EMPEROR OF OUR LAND WAS LOST TO THE WAVES.
BUT THE SOULS OF THOSE DEAD IMPERIAL LOYALISTS LIVE ON AS THE TINY CRABS THAT NOW INFEST THOSE WATERS.
AS WARRIORS, THEY DIED FOR THEIR EMPEROR, AND NOW, WITH THEIR HELP, THE EMPEROR WILL RISE AGAIN.
RYOKO, WITH HER UNIQUE ABILITIES, WILL DIRECT THESE CRABS TO SCOUR THE SEA BOTTOM AND RECOVER THE LOST SWORD OF THE GODS.
WHEN THE EMPEROR ONCE MORE HAS POSSESSION OF THE LAST OF THE THREE TREASURES OF THE IMPERIAL REGALIA, THE PEOPLE WILL *DEMAND* THE RETURN OF THE *MIKADO**--FOR SUCH MUST BE THE WILL OF THE GODS.
*HONORIFIC TERM FOR THE EMPEROR
2

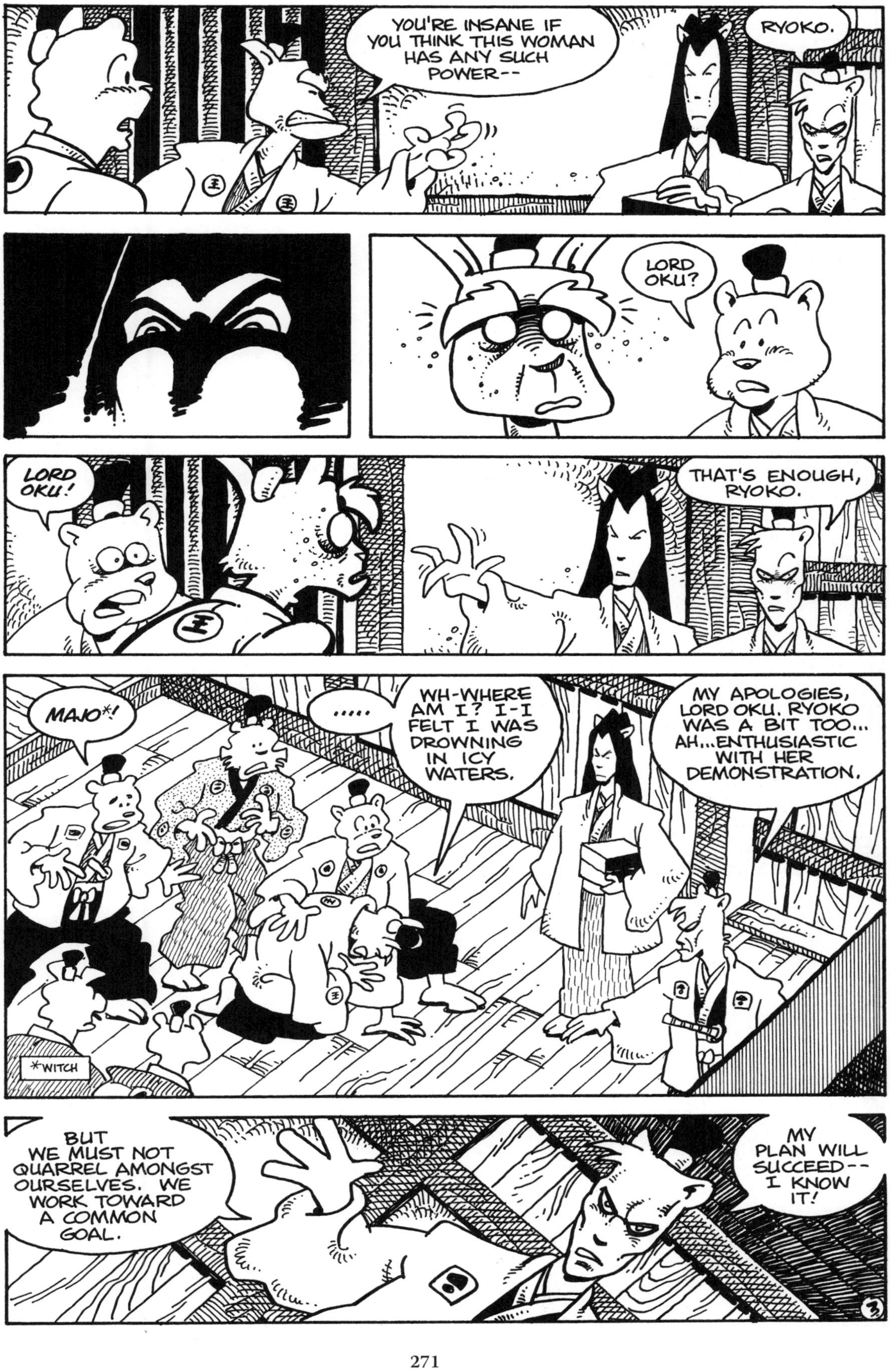

YOU'RE INSANE IF YOU THINK THIS WOMAN HAS ANY SUCH POWER--
RYOKO.
LORD OKU?
LORD OKU!
THAT'S ENOUGH, RYOKO.
MAJO*!
.....
WH-WHERE AM I? I-I FELT I WAS DROWNING IN ICY WATERS.
MY APOLOGIES, LORD OKU. RYOKO WAS A BIT TOO... AH...ENTHUSIASTIC WITH HER DEMONSTRATION.
*WITCH
BUT WE MUST NOT QUARREL AMONGST OURSELVES. WE WORK TOWARD A COMMON GOAL.
MY PLAN WILL SUCCEED-- I KNOW IT!
3

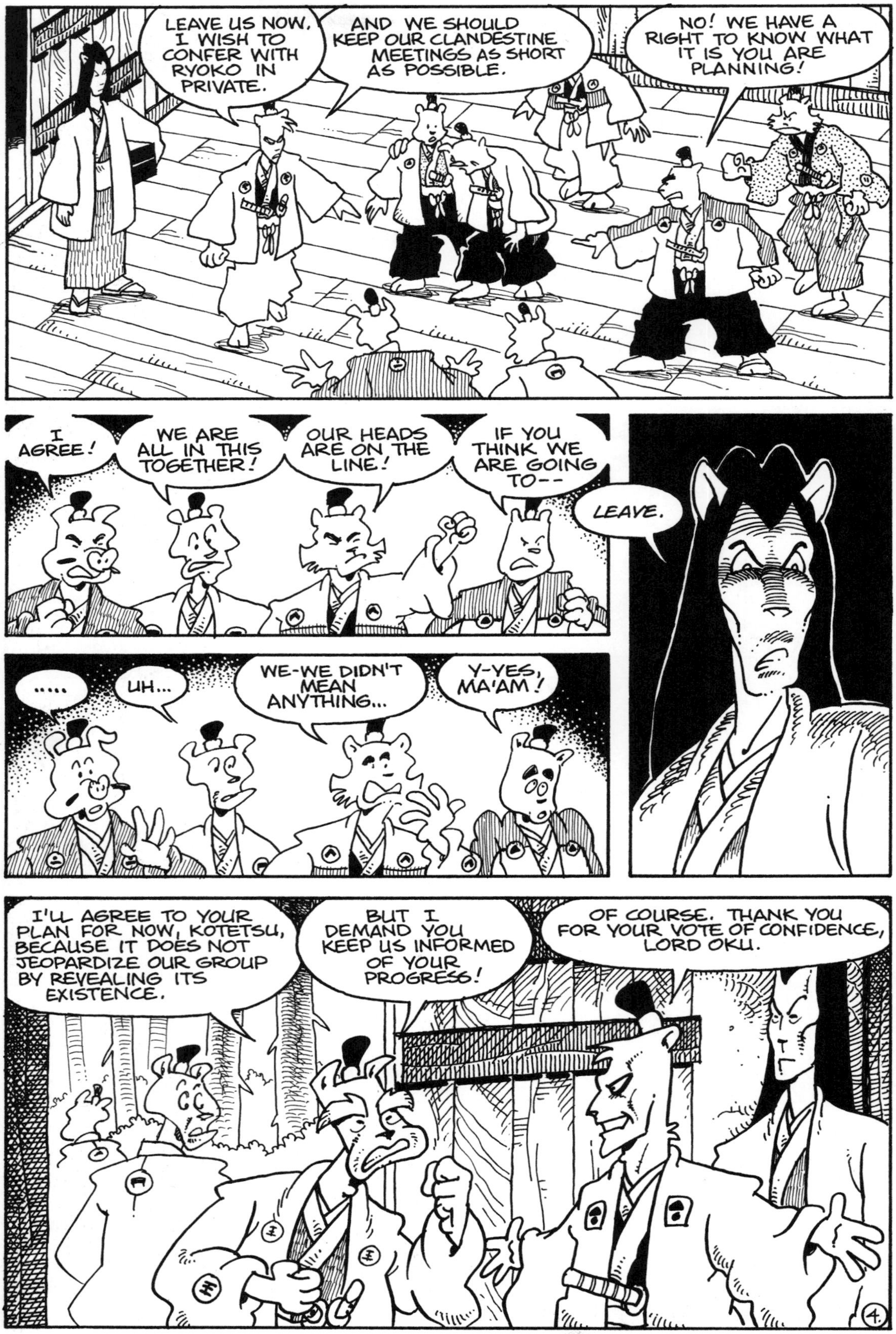
LEAVE US NOW. I WISH TO CONFER WITH RYOKO IN PRIVATE.
AND WE SHOULD KEEP OUR CLANDESTINE MEETINGS AS SHORT AS POSSIBLE.
NO! WE HAVE A RIGHT TO KNOW WHAT IT IS YOU ARE PLANNING!
I AGREE!
WE ARE ALL IN THIS TOGETHER!
OUR HEADS ARE ON THE LINE!
IF YOU THINK WE ARE GOING TO--
.....
UH...
WE-WE DIDN'T MEAN ANYTHING...
Y-YES, MA'AM!
LEAVE.
I'LL AGREE TO YOUR PLAN FOR NOW, KOTETSU, BECAUSE IT DOES NOT JEOPARDIZE OUR GROUP BY REVEALING ITS EXISTENCE.
BUT I DEMAND YOU KEEP US INFORMED OF YOUR PROGRESS!
OF COURSE. THANK YOU FOR YOUR VOTE OF CONFIDENCE, LORD OKU.
4.

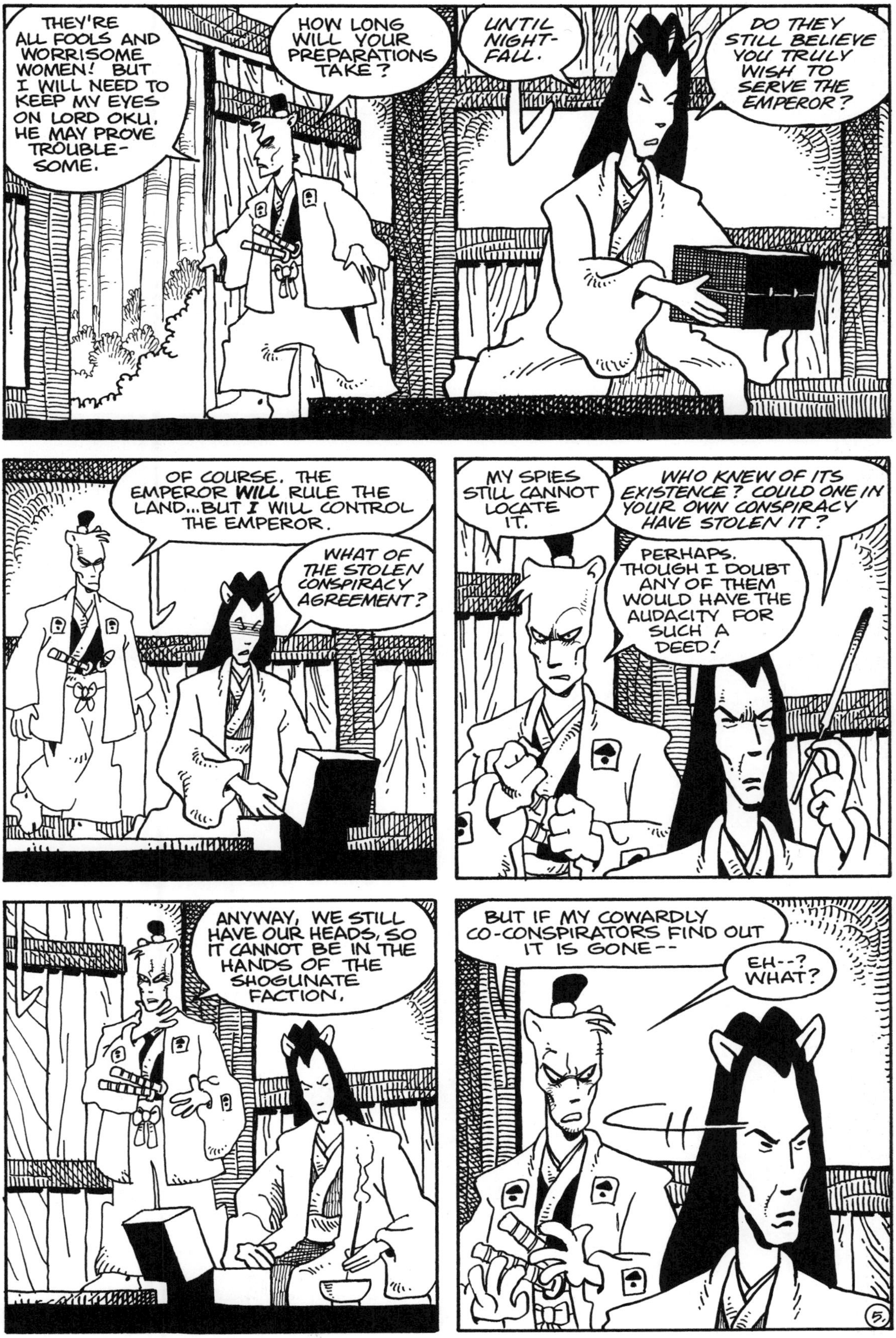
THEY'RE ALL FOOLS AND WORRISOME WOMEN! BUT I WILL NEED TO KEEP MY EYES ON LORD OKU. HE MAY PROVE TROUBLE-SOME.
HOW LONG WILL YOUR PREPARATIONS TAKE?
UNTIL NIGHT-FALL.
DO THEY STILL BELIEVE YOU TRULY WISH TO SERVE THE EMPEROR?
OF COURSE. THE EMPEROR **WILL** RULE THE LAND...BUT ***I*** WILL CONTROL THE EMPEROR.
WHAT OF THE STOLEN CONSPIRACY AGREEMENT?
MY SPIES STILL CANNOT LOCATE IT.
WHO KNEW OF ITS EXISTENCE? COULD ONE IN YOUR OWN CONSPIRACY HAVE STOLEN IT?
PERHAPS. THOUGH I DOUBT ANY OF THEM WOULD HAVE THE AUDACITY FOR SUCH A DEED!
ANYWAY, WE STILL HAVE OUR HEADS, SO IT CANNOT BE IN THE HANDS OF THE SHOGUNATE FACTION.
BUT IF MY COWARDLY CO-CONSPIRATORS FIND OUT IT IS GONE--
EH--? WHAT?
5.

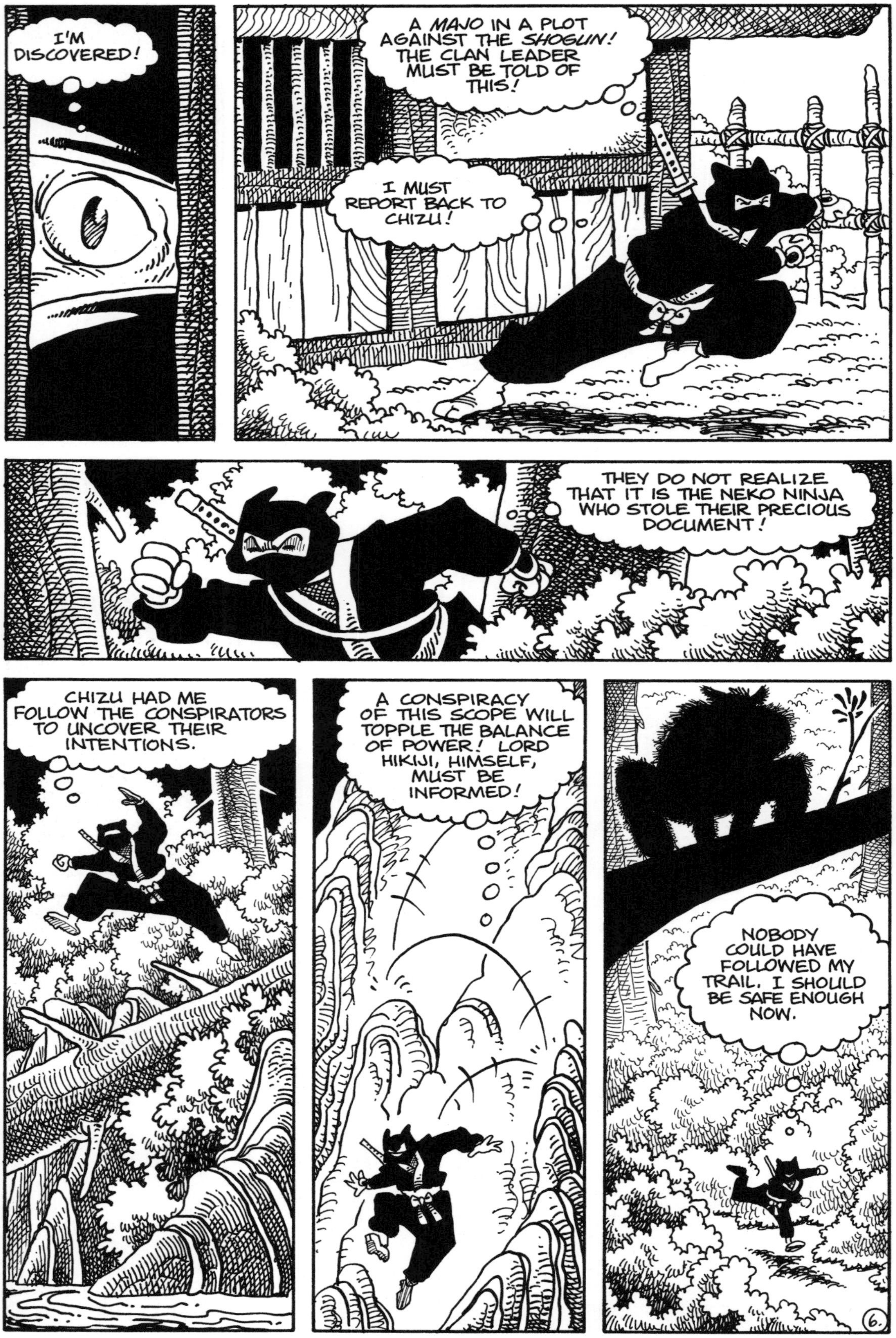
I'M DISCOVERED!
A *MAJO* IN A PLOT AGAINST THE *SHOGUN*! THE CLAN LEADER MUST BE TOLD OF THIS!
I MUST REPORT BACK TO CHIZU!
THEY DO NOT REALIZE THAT IT IS THE NEKO NINJA WHO STOLE THEIR PRECIOUS DOCUMENT!
CHIZU HAD ME FOLLOW THE CONSPIRATORS TO UNCOVER THEIR INTENTIONS.
A CONSPIRACY OF THIS SCOPE WILL TOPPLE THE BALANCE OF POWER! LORD HIKIJI, HIMSELF, MUST BE INFORMED!
NOBODY COULD HAVE FOLLOWED MY TRAIL. I SHOULD BE SAFE ENOUGH NOW.
6.

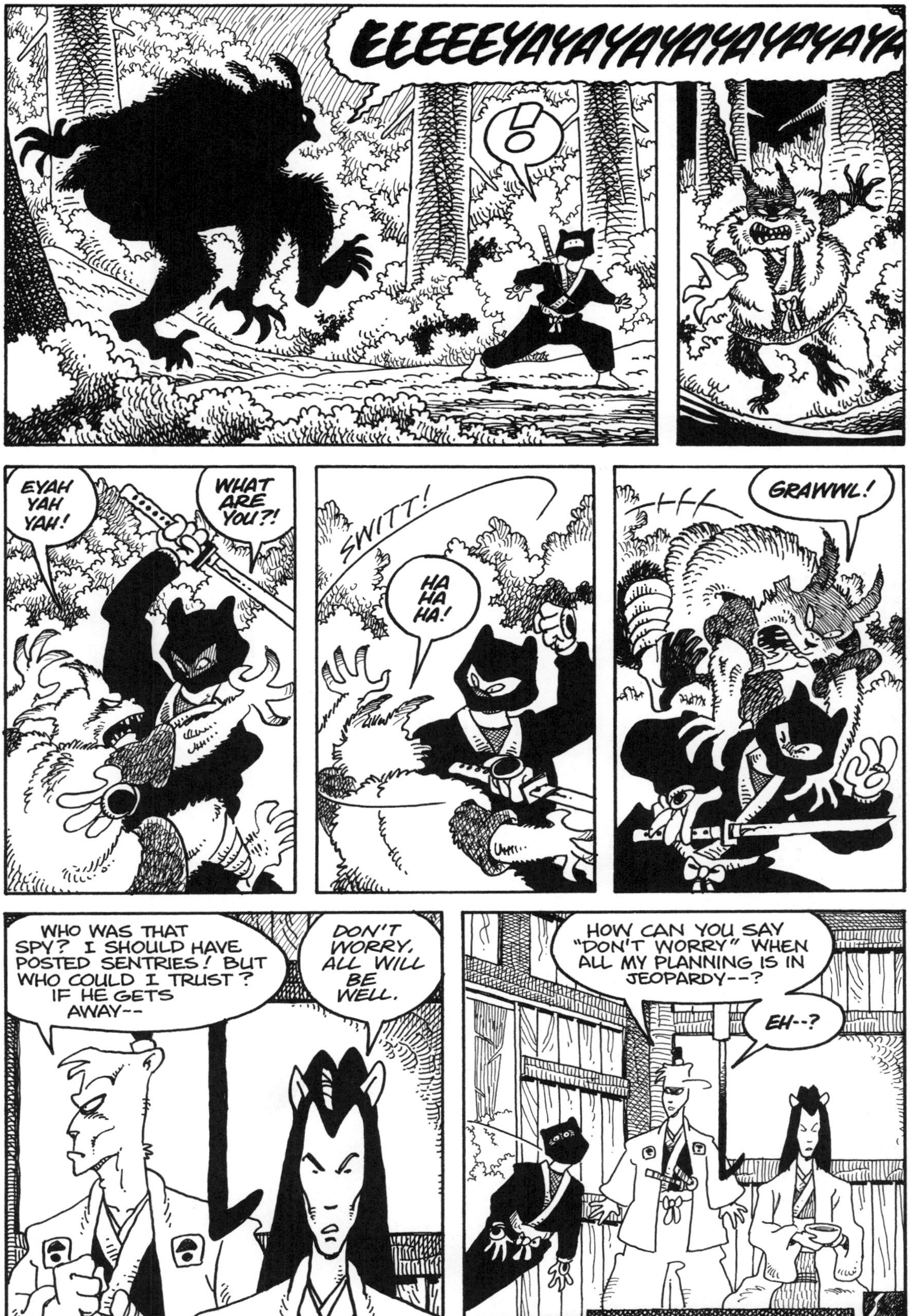
EEEEEYAYAYAYAYAYAYAYAYA
!
EYAH YAH YAH!
WHAT ARE YOU?!
SWITT!
HA HA HA!
GRAWWL!
WHO WAS THAT SPY? I SHOULD HAVE POSTED SENTRIES! BUT WHO COULD I TRUST? IF HE GETS AWAY--
DON'T WORRY. ALL WILL BE WELL.
HOW CAN YOU SAY "DON'T WORRY" WHEN ALL MY PLANNING IS IN JEOPARDY--?
EH--?
7.

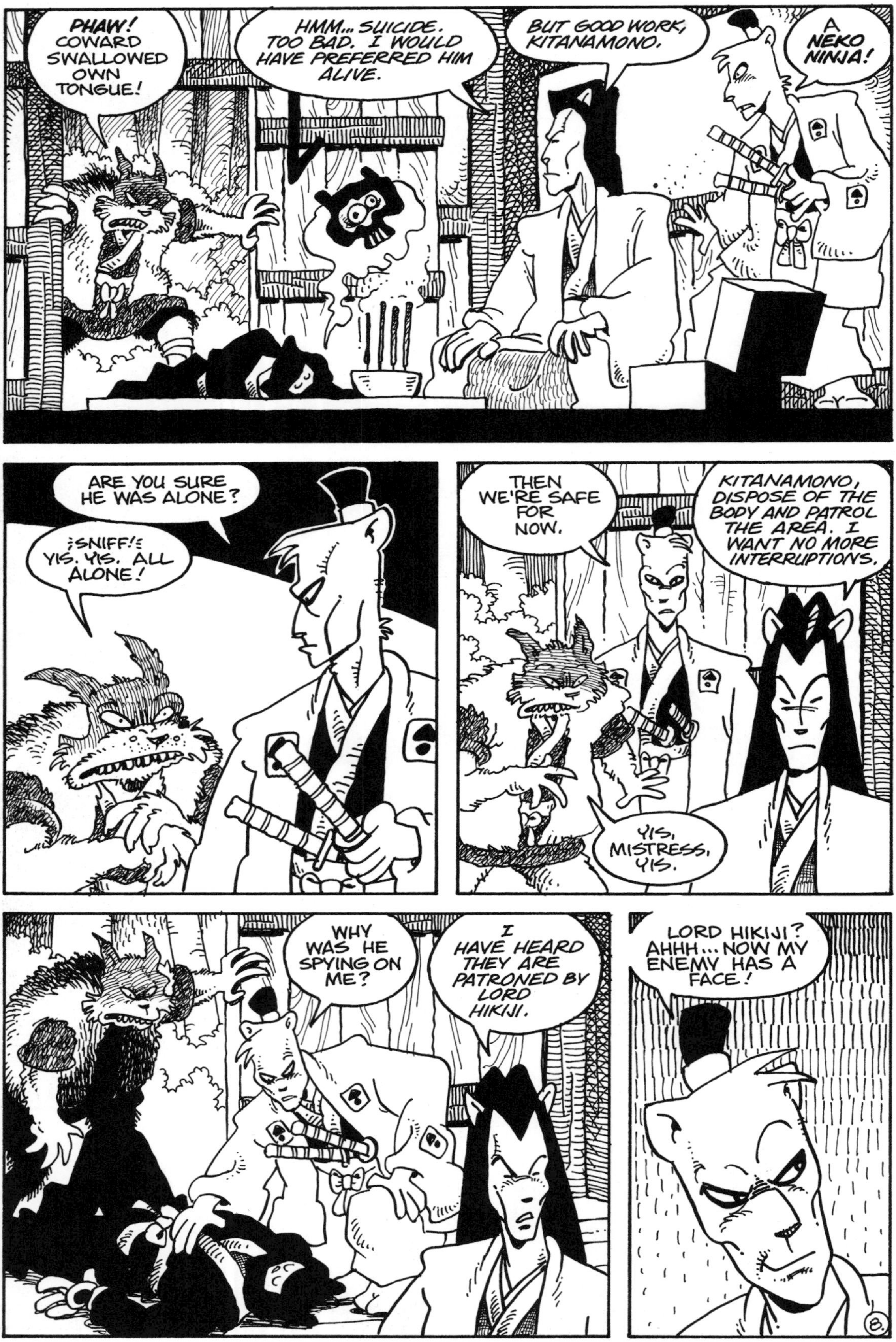
PHAW! COWARD SWALLOWED OWN TONGUE!
HMM... SUICIDE. TOO BAD. I WOULD HAVE PREFERRED HIM ALIVE.
BUT GOOD WORK, KITANAMONO.
A NEKO NINJA!
ARE YOU SURE HE WAS ALONE?
¡SNIFF!¡ YIS. YIS. ALL ALONE!
THEN WE'RE SAFE FOR NOW.
KITANAMONO, DISPOSE OF THE BODY AND PATROL THE AREA. I WANT NO MORE INTERRUPTIONS.
YIS, MISTRESS, YIS.
WHY WAS HE SPYING ON ME?
I HAVE HEARD THEY ARE PATRONED BY LORD HIKIJI.
LORD HIKIJI? AHHH... NOW MY ENEMY HAS A FACE!
8.

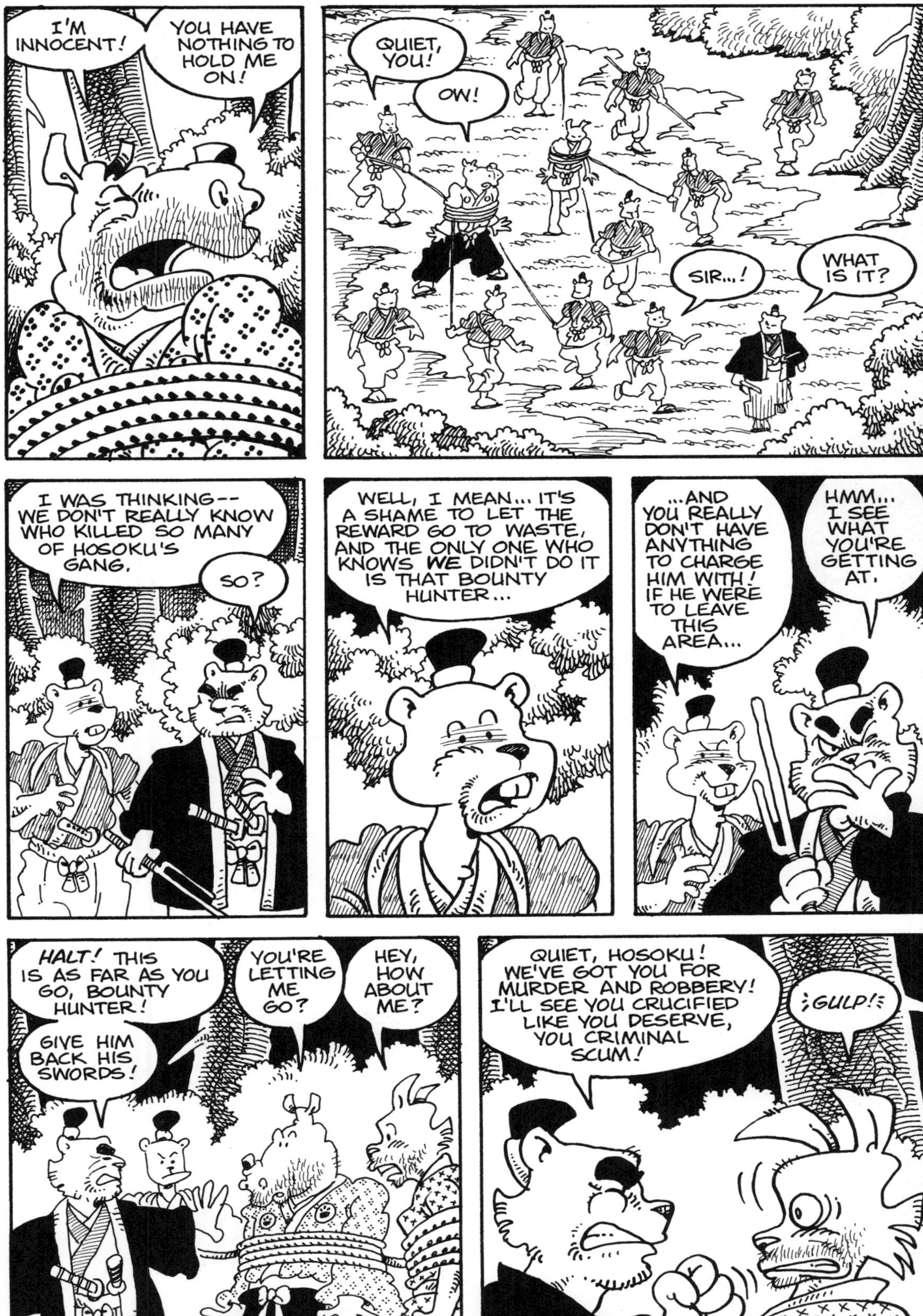

I'M INNOCENT!
YOU HAVE NOTHING TO HOLD ME ON!
QUIET, YOU!
OW!
SIR...!
WHAT IS IT?
I WAS THINKING-- WE DON'T REALLY KNOW WHO KILLED SO MANY OF HOSOKU'S GANG.
SO?
WELL, I MEAN... IT'S A SHAME TO LET THE REWARD GO TO WASTE, AND THE ONLY ONE WHO KNOWS WE DIDN'T DO IT IS THAT BOUNTY HUNTER...
...AND YOU REALLY DON'T HAVE ANYTHING TO CHARGE HIM WITH! IF HE WERE TO LEAVE THIS AREA...
HMM... I SEE WHAT YOU'RE GETTING AT.
HALT! THIS IS AS FAR AS YOU GO, BOUNTY HUNTER!
GIVE HIM BACK HIS SWORDS!
YOU'RE LETTING ME GO?
HEY, HOW ABOUT ME?
QUIET, HOSOKU! WE'VE GOT YOU FOR MURDER AND ROBBERY! I'LL SEE YOU CRUCIFIED LIKE YOU DESERVE, YOU CRIMINAL SCUM!
GULP!
9.

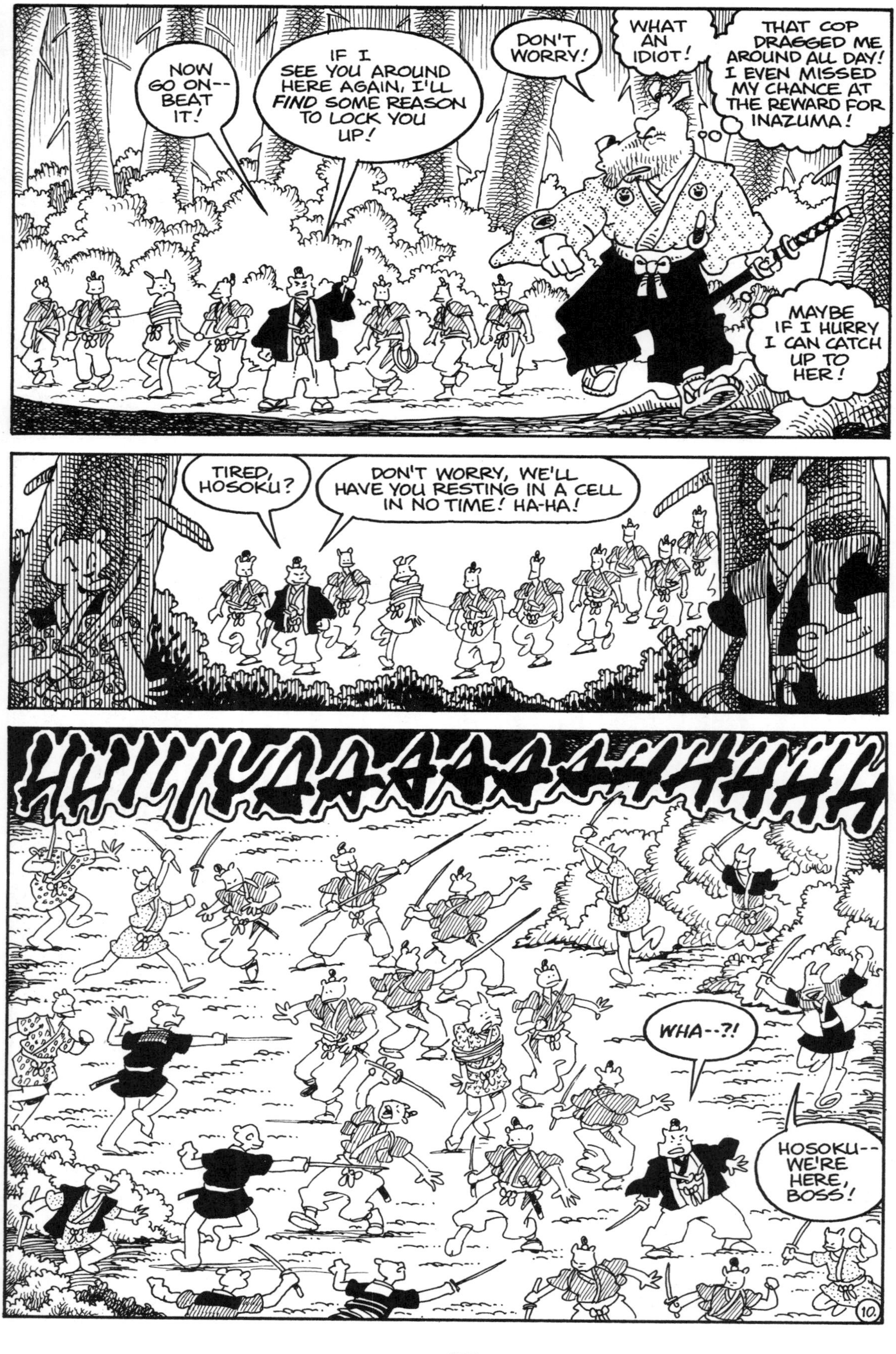

NOW GO ON-- BEAT IT!
IF I SEE YOU AROUND HERE AGAIN, I'LL *FIND* SOME REASON TO LOCK YOU UP!
DON'T WORRY!
WHAT AN IDIOT!
THAT COP DRAGGED ME AROUND ALL DAY! I EVEN MISSED MY CHANCE AT THE REWARD FOR INAZUMA!
MAYBE IF I HURRY I CAN CATCH UP TO HER!
TIRED, HOSOKU?
DON'T WORRY, WE'LL HAVE YOU RESTING IN A CELL IN NO TIME! HA-HA!
HHIIYAAAAAAAAHHHH
WHA--?!
HOSOKU-- WE'RE HERE, BOSS!
10.

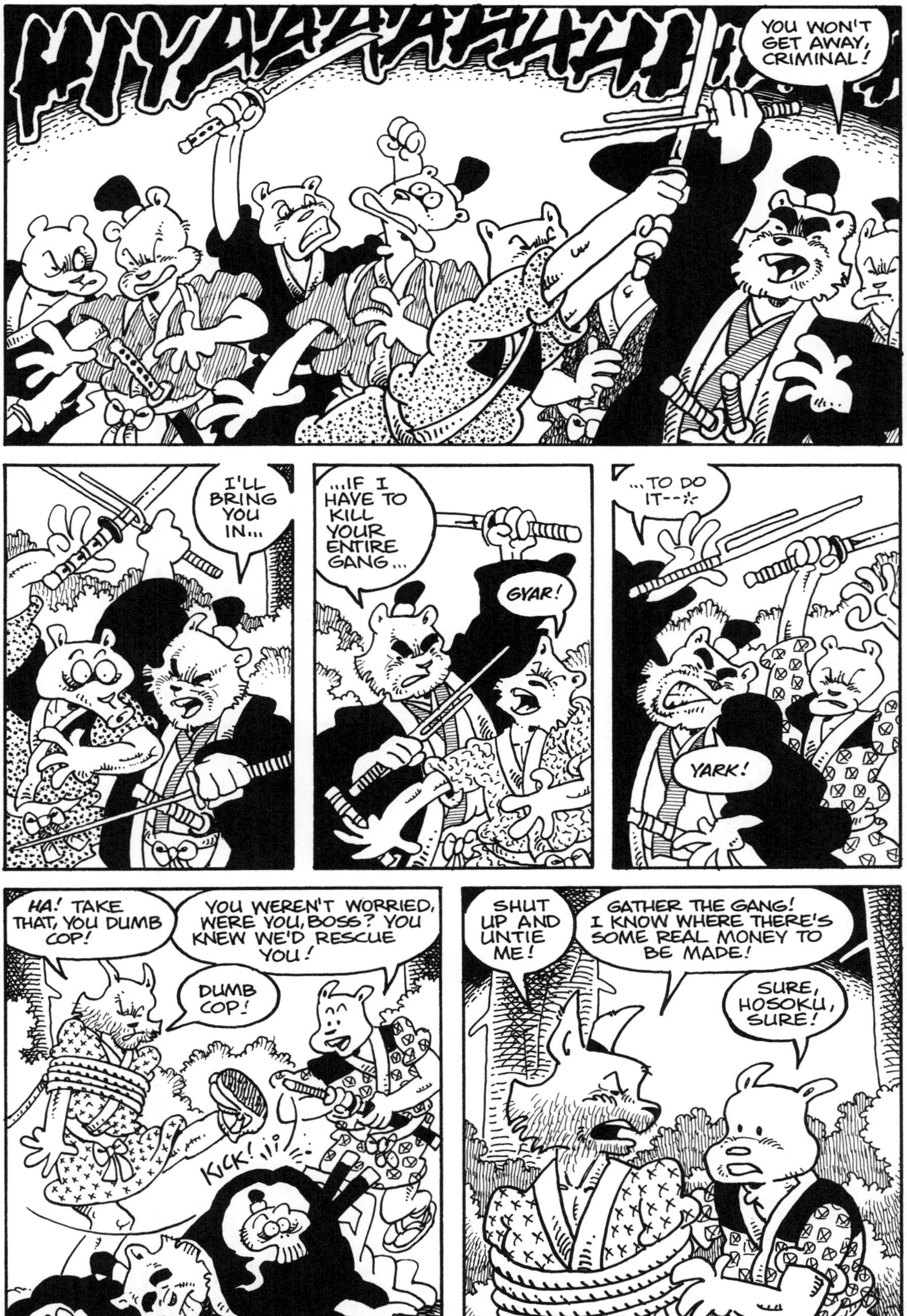
HIYAAAAAAAAAHH
YOU WON'T GET AWAY, CRIMINAL!
I'LL BRING YOU IN...
...IF I HAVE TO KILL YOUR ENTIRE GANG...
GYAR!
...TO DO IT--
YARK!
HA! TAKE THAT, YOU DUMB COP!
YOU WEREN'T WORRIED, WERE YOU, BOSS? YOU KNEW WE'D RESCUE YOU!
DUMB COP!
KICK!
SHUT UP AND UNTIE ME!
GATHER THE GANG! I KNOW WHERE THERE'S SOME REAL MONEY TO BE MADE!
SURE, HOSOKU, SURE!
11.

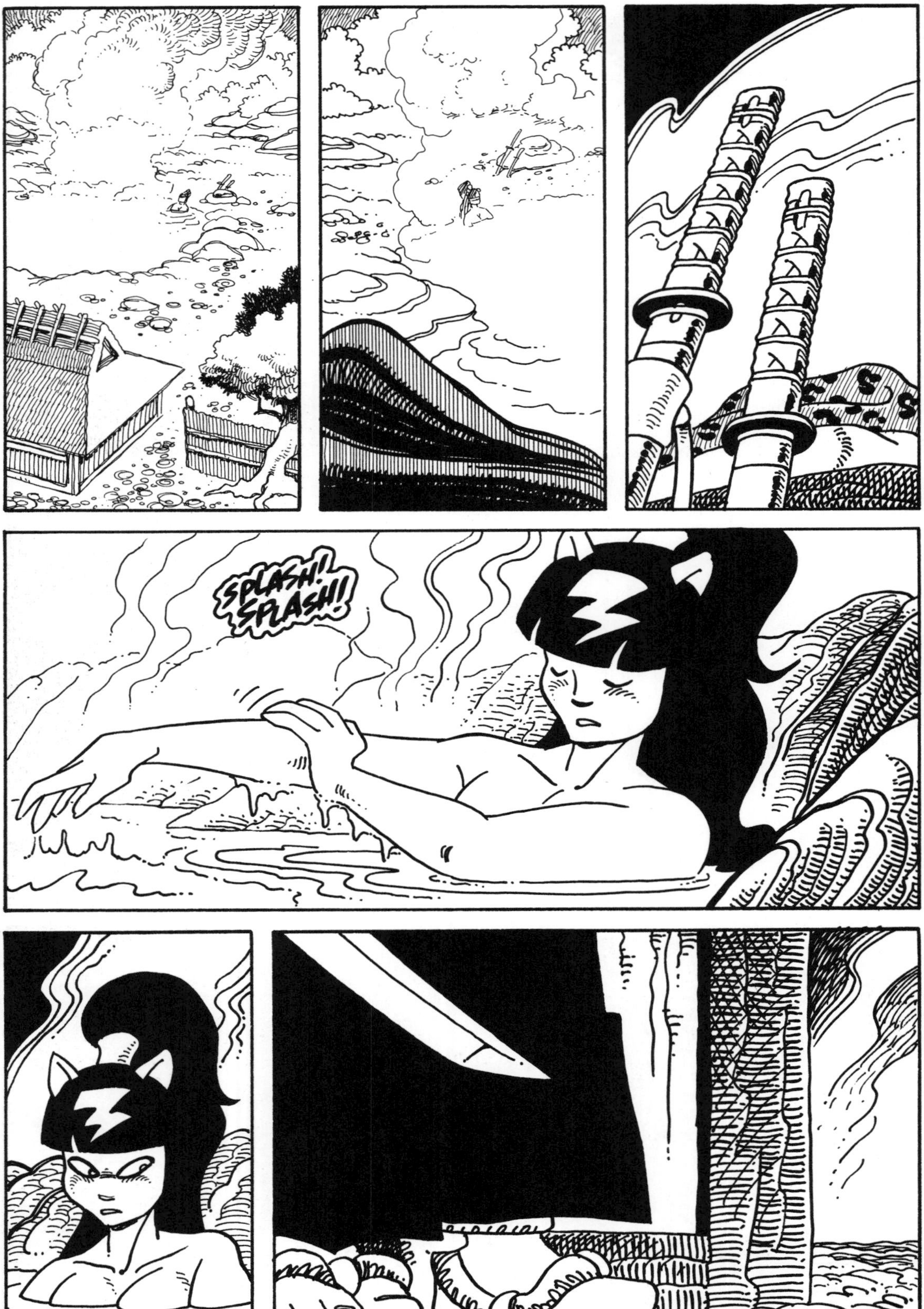
SPLASH! SPLASH!
12.

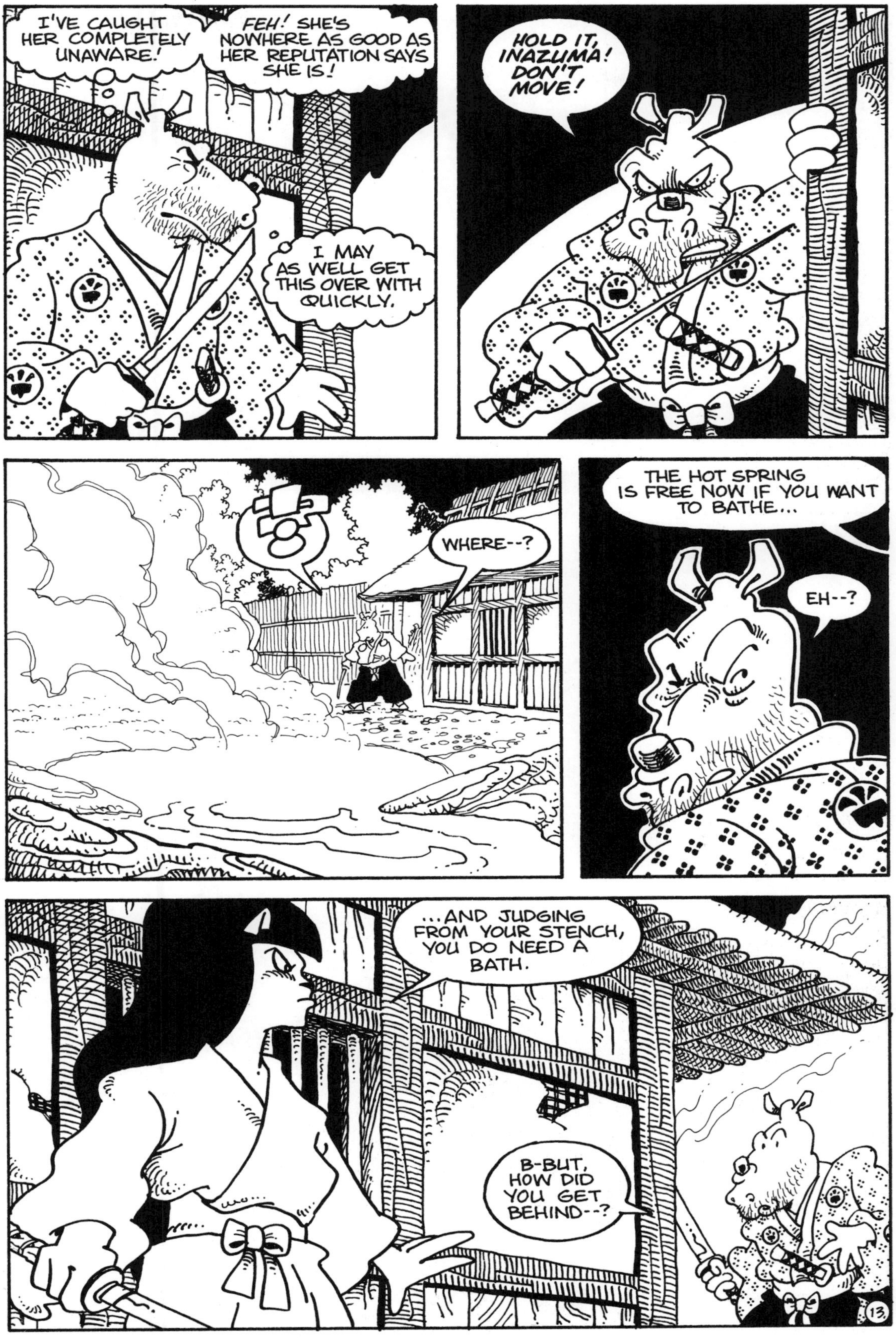
I'VE CAUGHT HER COMPLETELY UNAWARE!
FEH! SHE'S NOWHERE AS GOOD AS HER REPUTATION SAYS SHE IS!
I MAY AS WELL GET THIS OVER WITH QUICKLY.
HOLD IT, INAZUMA! DON'T MOVE!
WHERE--?
THE HOT SPRING IS FREE NOW IF YOU WANT TO BATHE...
EH--?
...AND JUDGING FROM YOUR STENCH, YOU DO NEED A BATH.
B-BUT, HOW DID YOU GET BEHIND--?
13

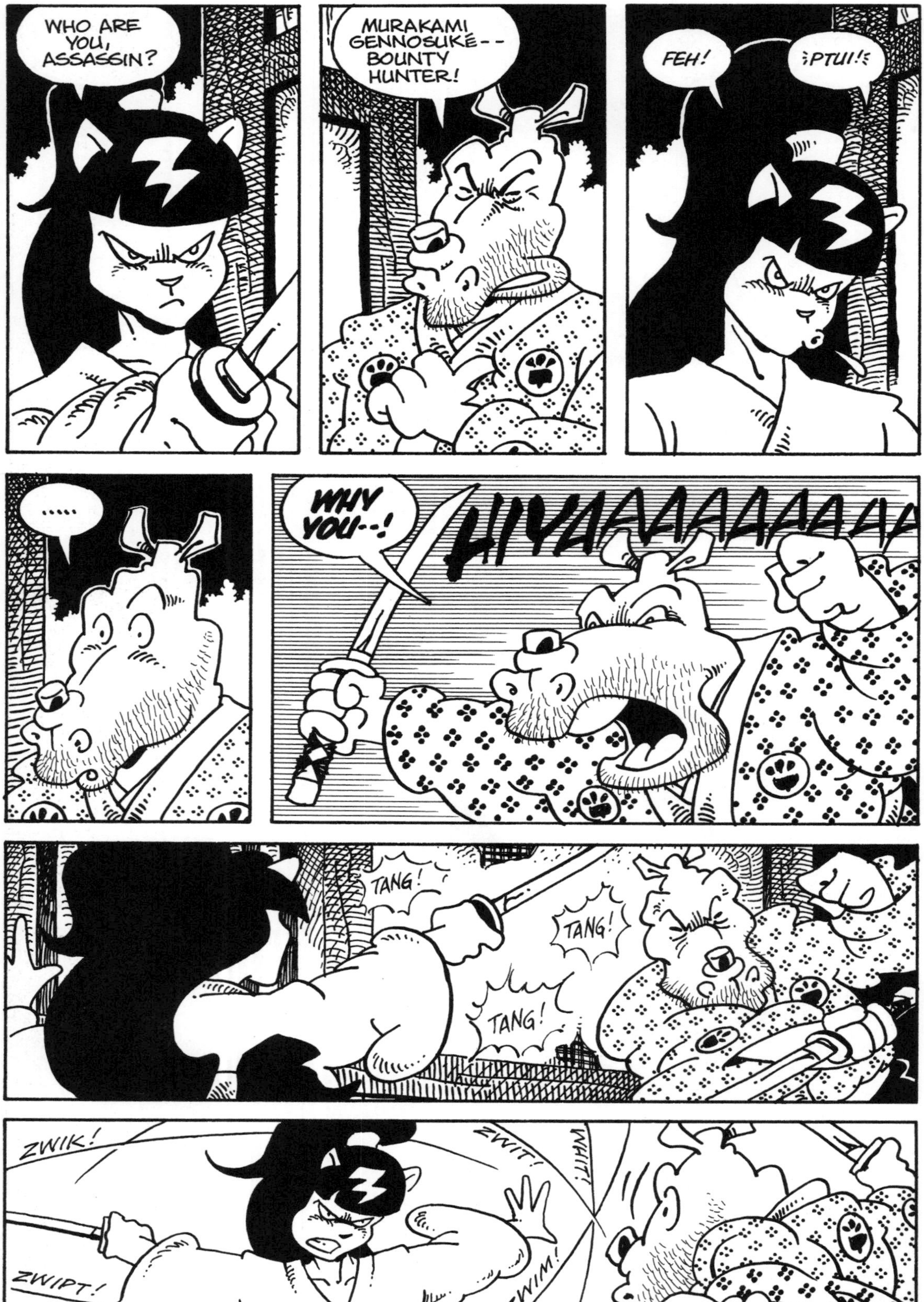
WHO ARE YOU, ASSASSIN?
MURAKAMI GENNOSUKE-- BOUNTY HUNTER!
FEH!
PTUI!
.....
WHY YOU--!
HIYAAAAAAAAA
TANG!
TANG!
TANG!
ZWIK!
ZWIT!
WHIT!
ZWIPT!
ZWIM!
14.

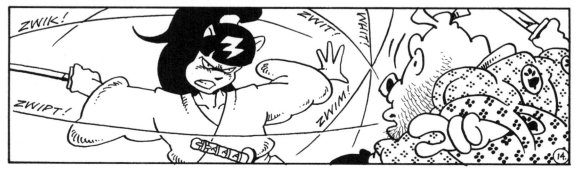

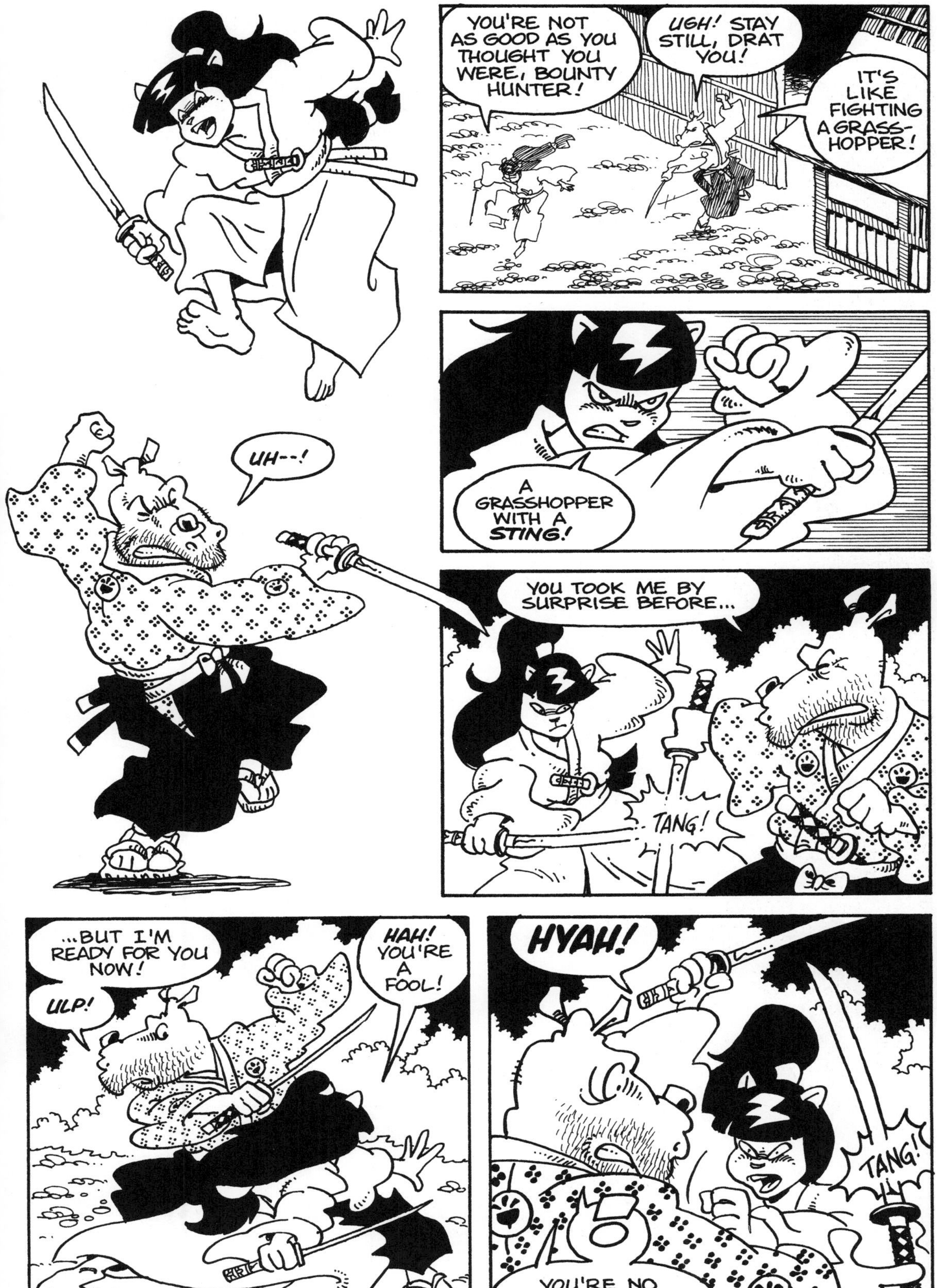
YOU'RE NOT AS GOOD AS YOU THOUGHT YOU WERE, BOUNTY HUNTER!
UGH! STAY STILL, DRAT YOU!
IT'S LIKE FIGHTING A GRASS-HOPPER!
UH--!
A GRASSHOPPER WITH A STING!
YOU TOOK ME BY SURPRISE BEFORE...
TANG!
...BUT I'M READY FOR YOU NOW!
ULP!
HAH! YOU'RE A FOOL!
HYAH!
TANG!
YOU'RE NO SWORDSWOMAN! YOU'RE THE DEVIL IN DISGUISE!
15.

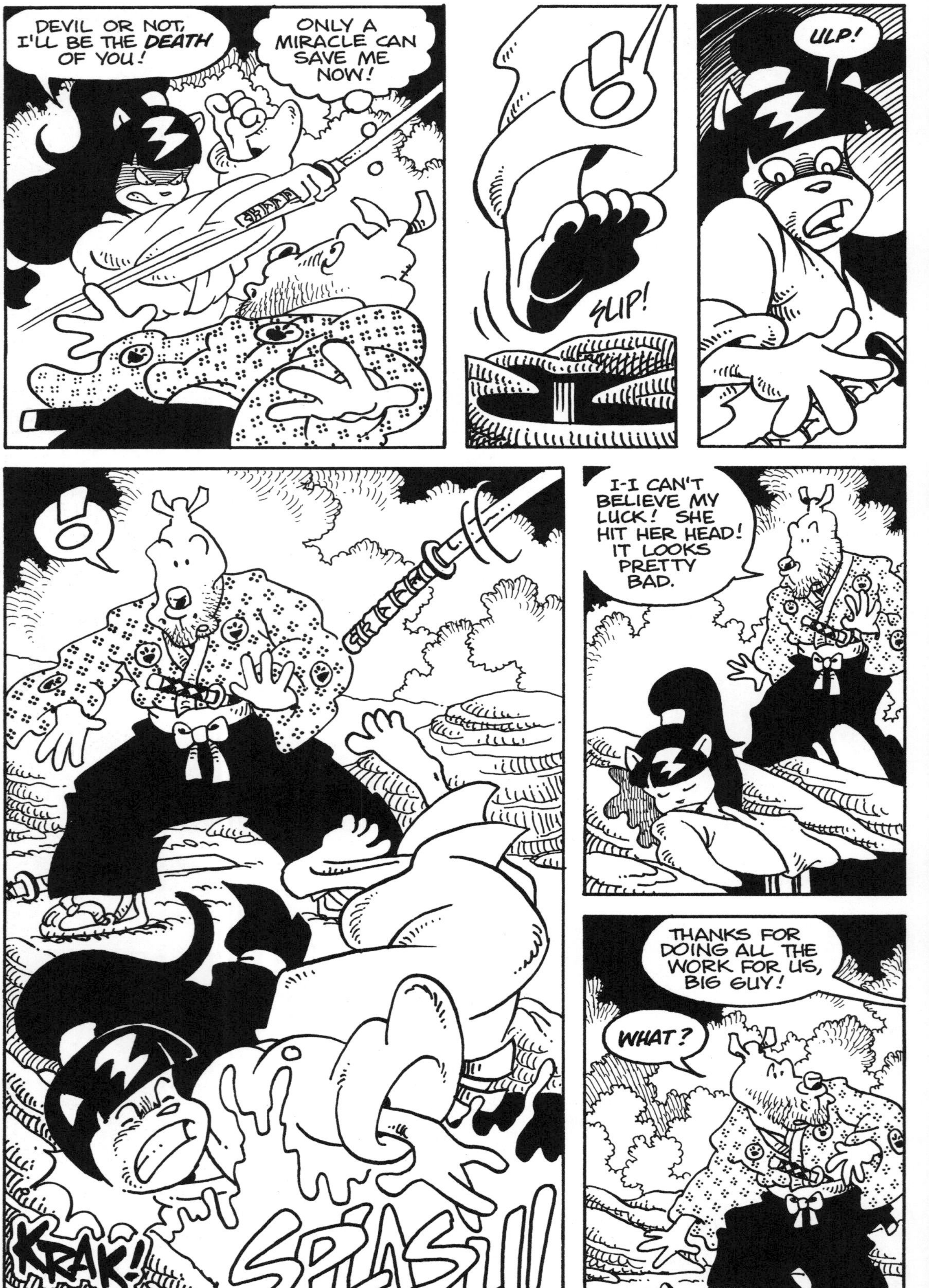
DEVIL OR NOT, I'LL BE THE *DEATH* OF YOU!
ONLY A MIRACLE CAN SAVE ME NOW!
!
SLIP!
ULP!
!
KRAK!
SPLASH!
I-I CAN'T BELIEVE MY LUCK! SHE HIT HER HEAD! IT LOOKS PRETTY BAD.
THANKS FOR DOING ALL THE WORK FOR US, BIG GUY!
WHAT?
16.

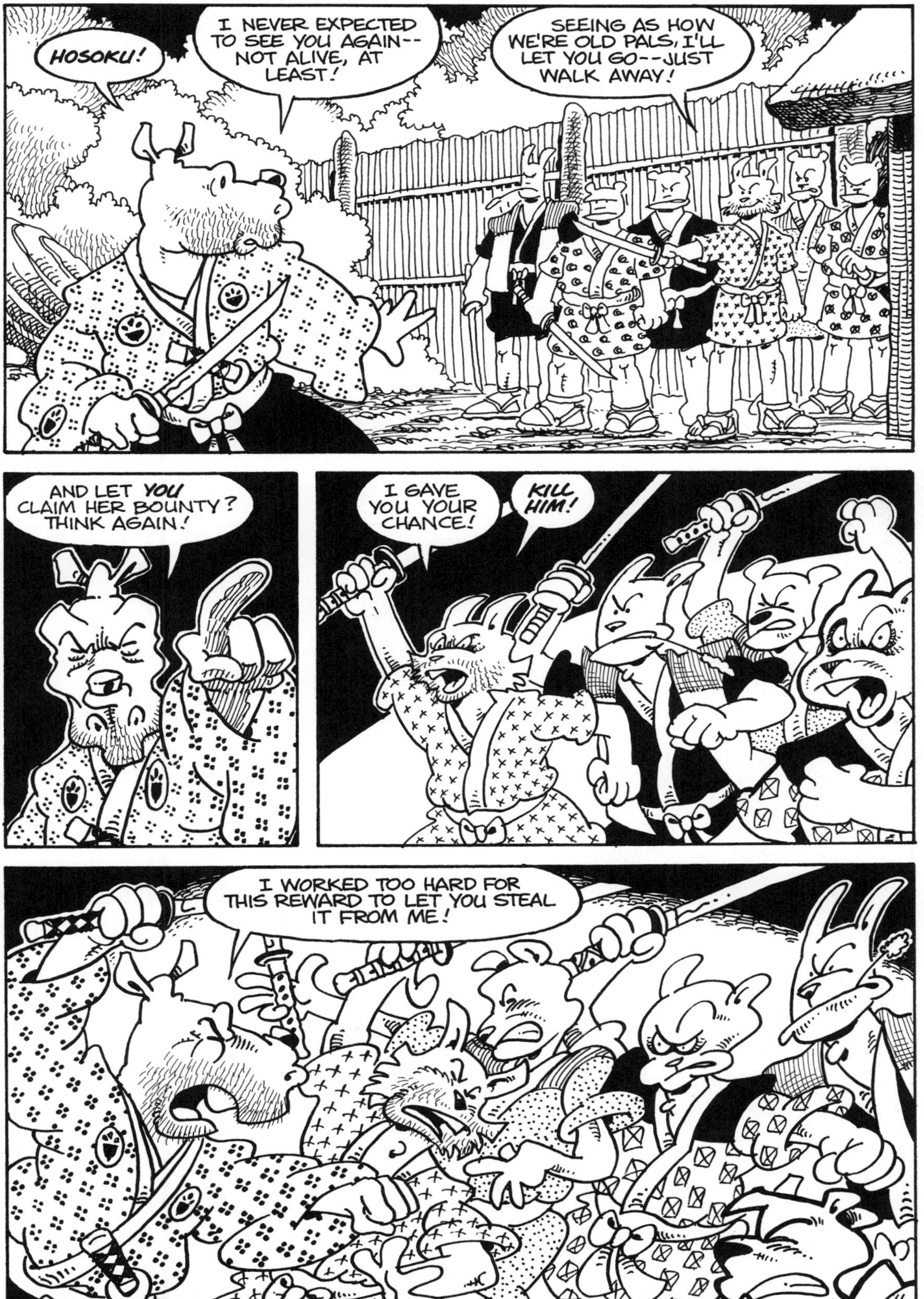
HOSOKU!
I NEVER EXPECTED TO SEE YOU AGAIN-- NOT ALIVE, AT LEAST!
SEEING AS HOW WE'RE OLD PALS, I'LL LET YOU GO--JUST WALK AWAY!
AND LET YOU CLAIM HER BOUNTY? THINK AGAIN!
I GAVE YOU YOUR CHANCE!
KILL HIM!
I WORKED TOO HARD FOR THIS REWARD TO LET YOU STEAL IT FROM ME!
17.

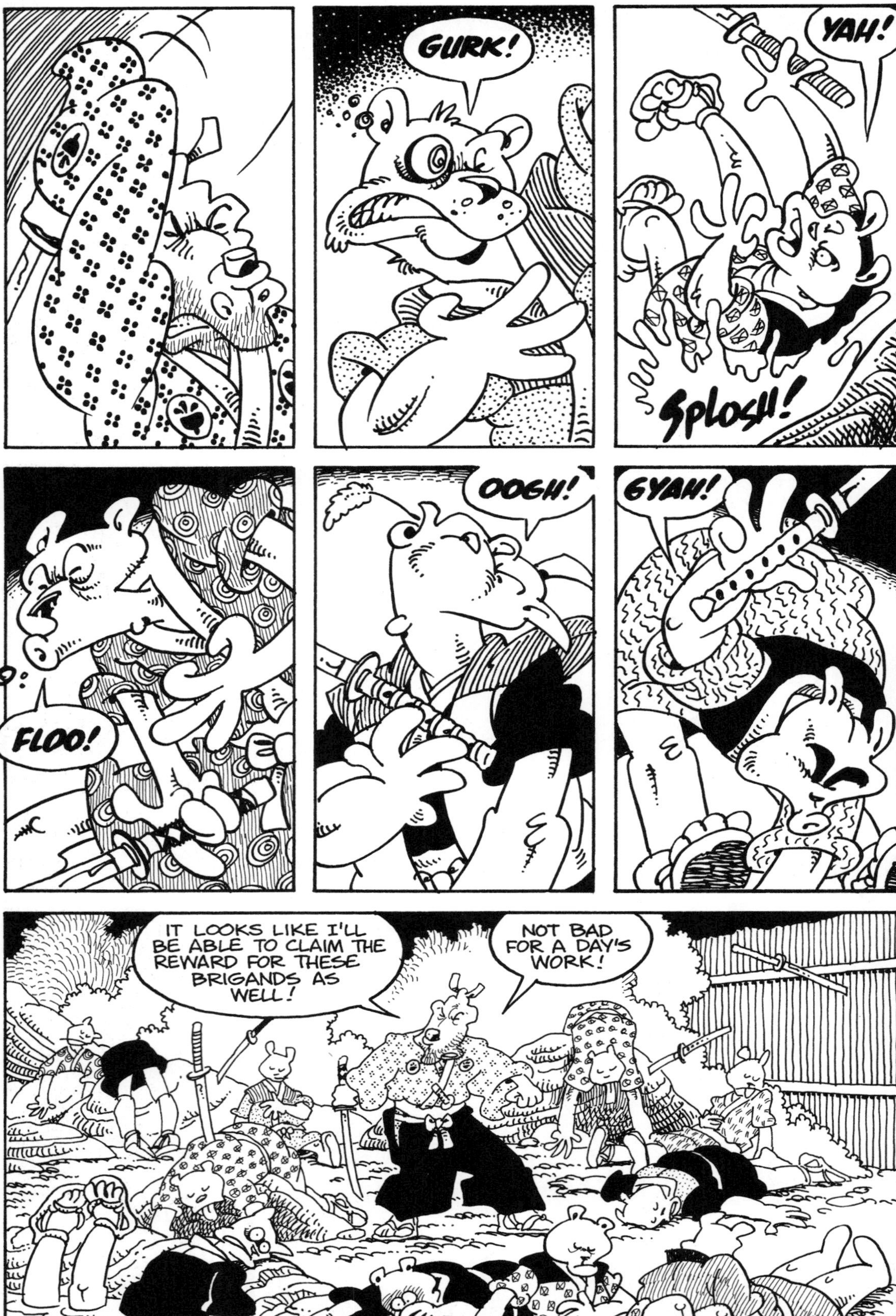

GURK!
YAH!
SPLOSH!
FLOO!
OOGH!
GYAH!
IT LOOKS LIKE I'LL BE ABLE TO CLAIM THE REWARD FOR THESE BRIGANDS AS WELL!
NOT BAD FOR A DAY'S WORK!
18.

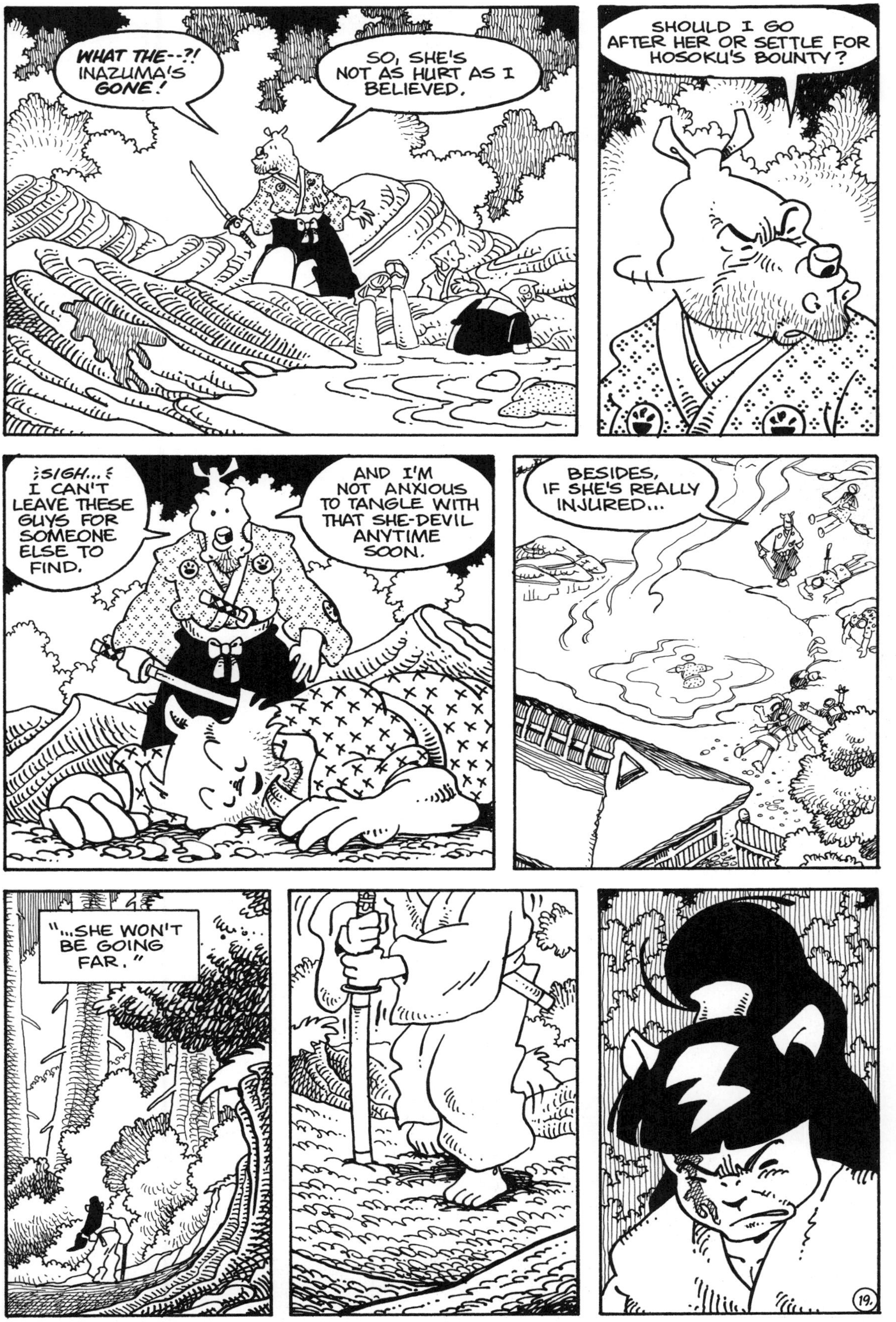
WHAT THE--?! INAZUMA'S GONE!
SO, SHE'S NOT AS HURT AS I BELIEVED.
SHOULD I GO AFTER HER OR SETTLE FOR HOSOKU'S BOUNTY?
SIGH... I CAN'T LEAVE THESE GUYS FOR SOMEONE ELSE TO FIND.
AND I'M NOT ANXIOUS TO TANGLE WITH THAT SHE-DEVIL ANYTIME SOON.
BESIDES, IF SHE'S REALLY INJURED...
"...SHE WON'T BE GOING FAR."
19.

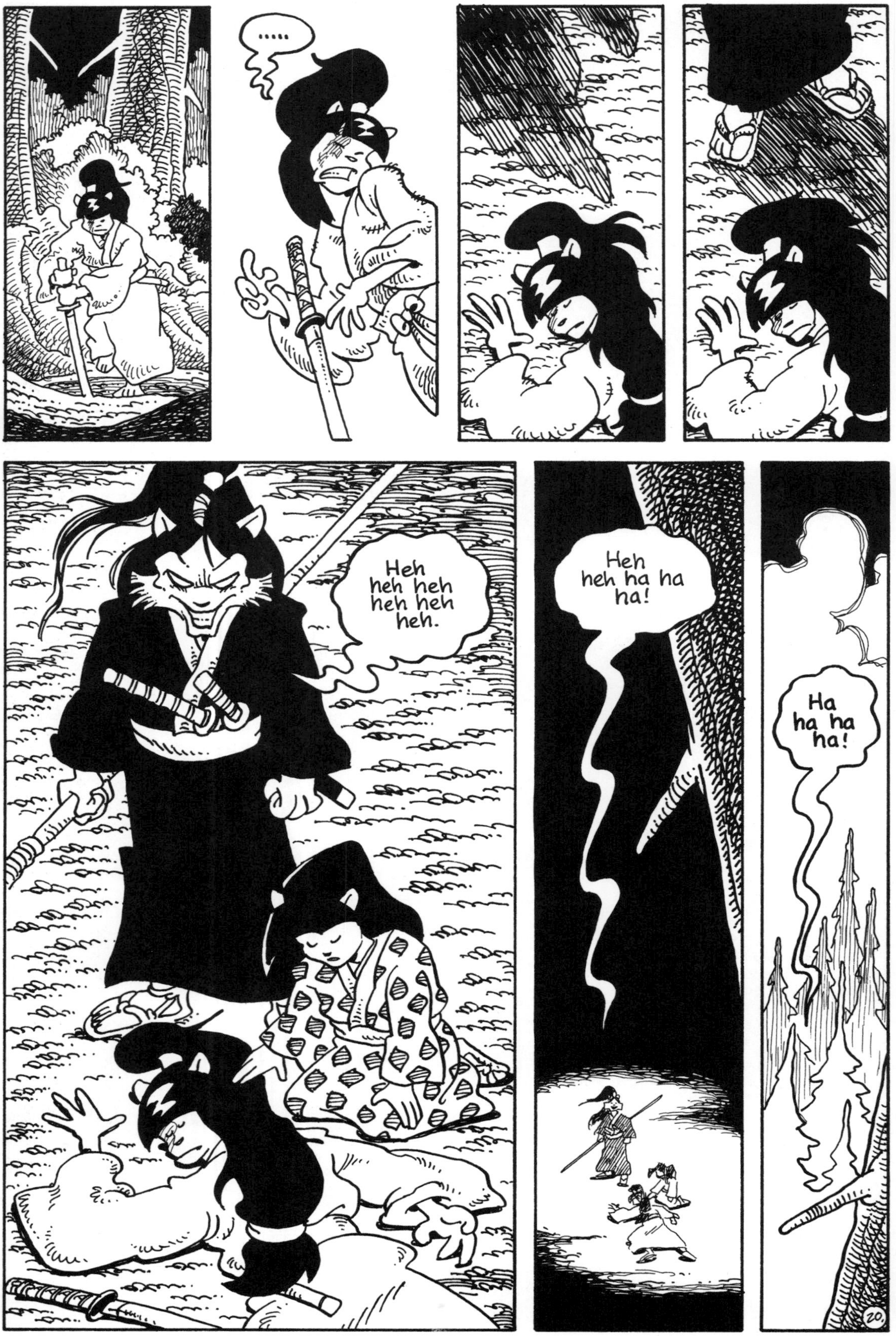
......
Heh heh heh heh heh heh.
Heh heh ha ha ha!
Ha ha ha ha!

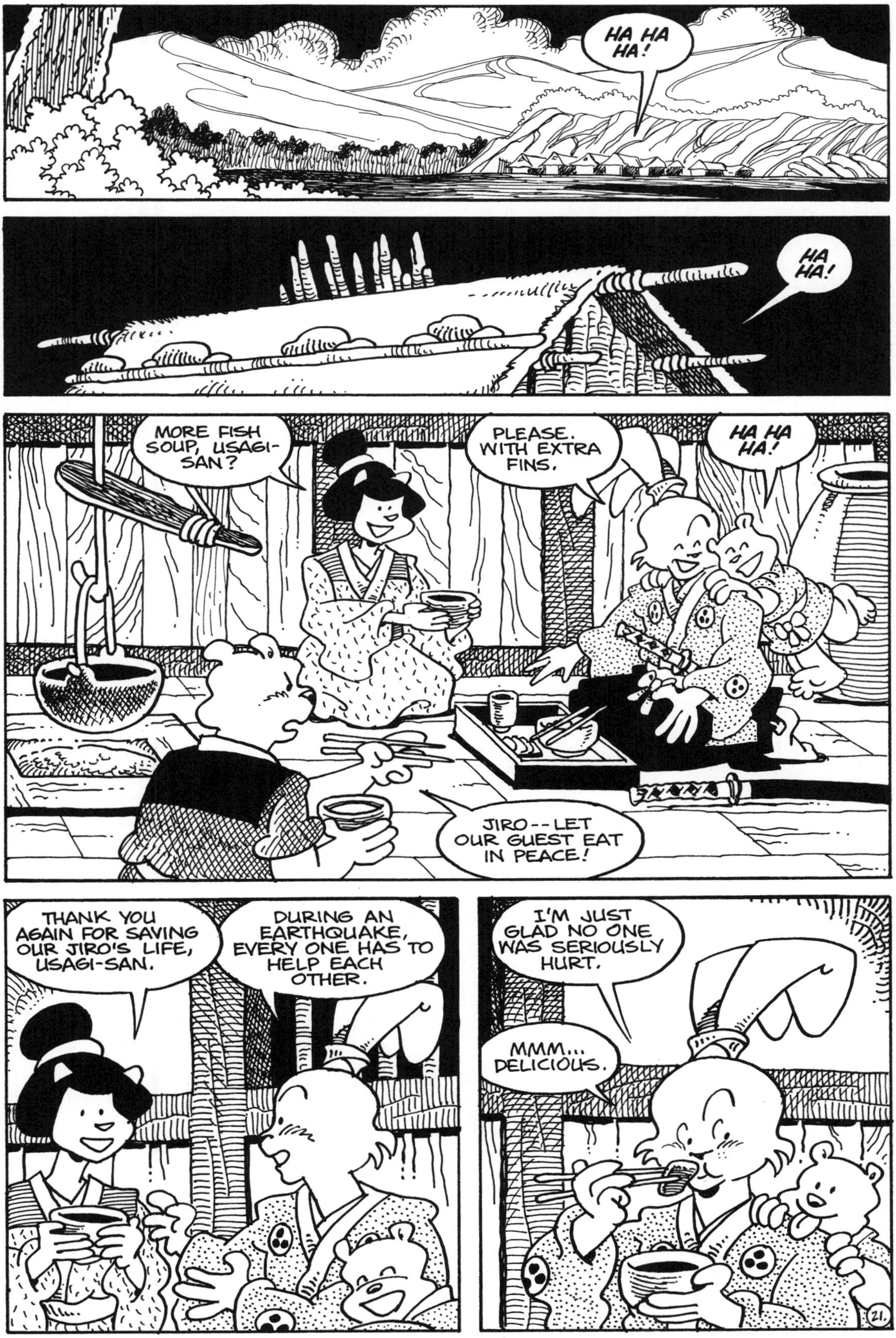

HA HA HA!
HA HA!
MORE FISH SOUP, USAGI-SAN?
PLEASE. WITH EXTRA FINS.
HA HA HA!
JIRO--LET OUR GUEST EAT IN PEACE!
THANK YOU AGAIN FOR SAVING OUR JIRO'S LIFE, USAGI-SAN.
DURING AN EARTHQUAKE, EVERY ONE HAS TO HELP EACH OTHER.
I'M JUST GLAD NO ONE WAS SERIOUSLY HURT.
MMM... DELICIOUS.
21.

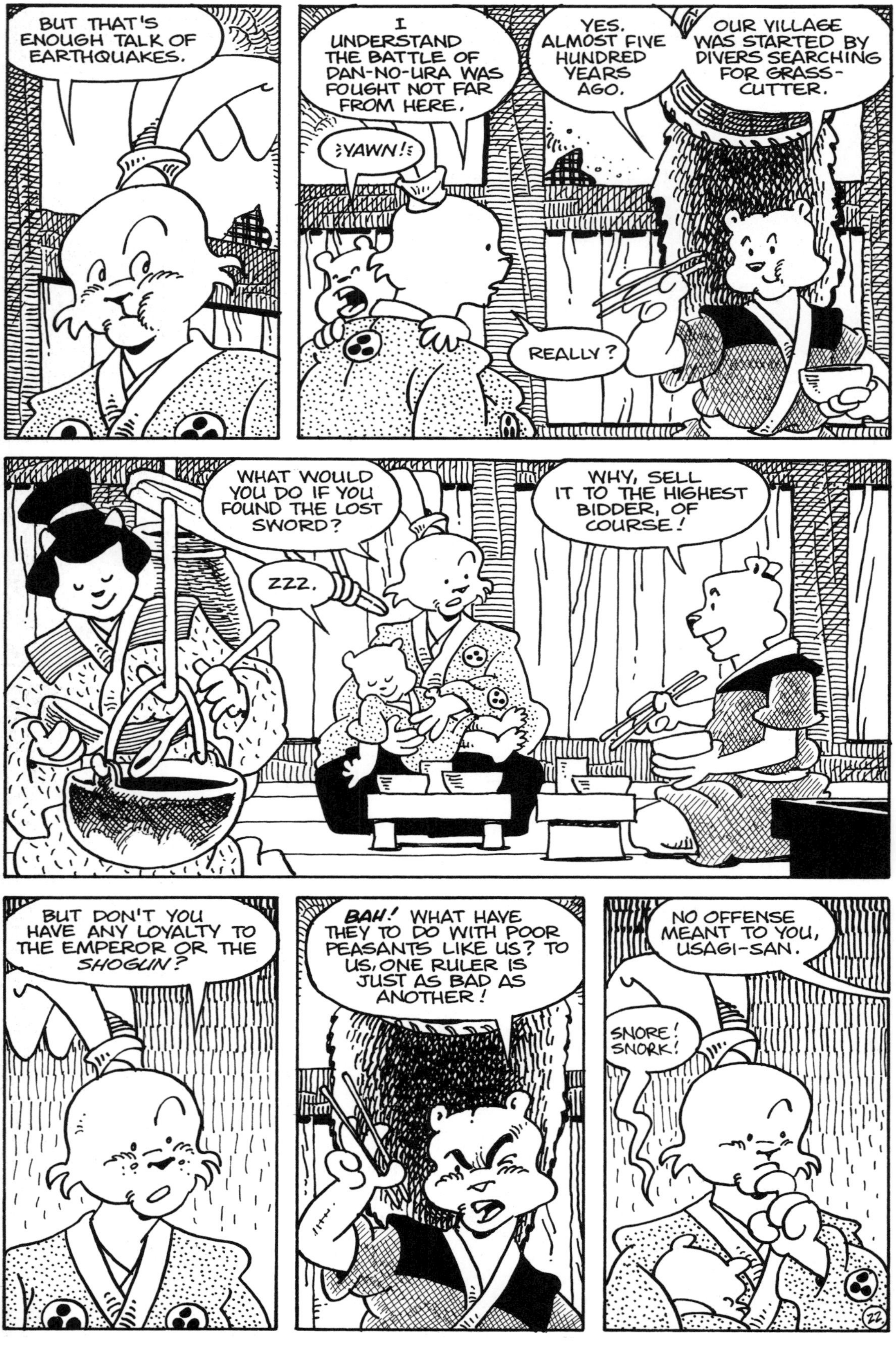
BUT THAT'S ENOUGH TALK OF EARTHQUAKES.
I UNDERSTAND THE BATTLE OF DAN-NO-URA WAS FOUGHT NOT FAR FROM HERE.
YAWN!
YES. ALMOST FIVE HUNDRED YEARS AGO.
OUR VILLAGE WAS STARTED BY DIVERS SEARCHING FOR GRASS-CUTTER.
REALLY?
WHAT WOULD YOU DO IF YOU FOUND THE LOST SWORD?
ZZZ.
WHY, SELL IT TO THE HIGHEST BIDDER, OF COURSE!
BUT DON'T YOU HAVE ANY LOYALTY TO THE EMPEROR OR THE *SHOGUN*?
BAH! WHAT HAVE THEY TO DO WITH POOR PEASANTS LIKE US? TO US, ONE RULER IS JUST AS BAD AS ANOTHER!
NO OFFENSE MEANT TO YOU, USAGI-SAN.
SNORE! SNORK!
22

LATER...

SPLASH!

SPLASH!

IT'S UNDER THERE SOMEWHERE.

AND NO DOUBT IT WILL STAY THERE FOR ANOTHER FIVE HUNDRED YEARS.

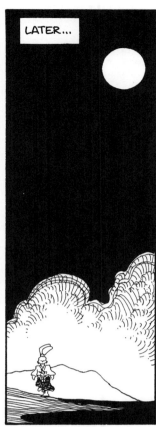

PREPARATIONS ARE COMPLETED.

FINALLY!

WHAT OF *YOUR* PREPARATIONS?

DON'T WORRY ABOUT ME. I'VE ALREADY DISPATCHED MY SAMURAI TO THE AREA.

WHAT TOKENS DO YOU HAVE?

HAIR AND FINGERNAIL CLIPPINGS FROM TWO OF THEM.

GOOD. I WILL NEED THEM LATER.

23.

291

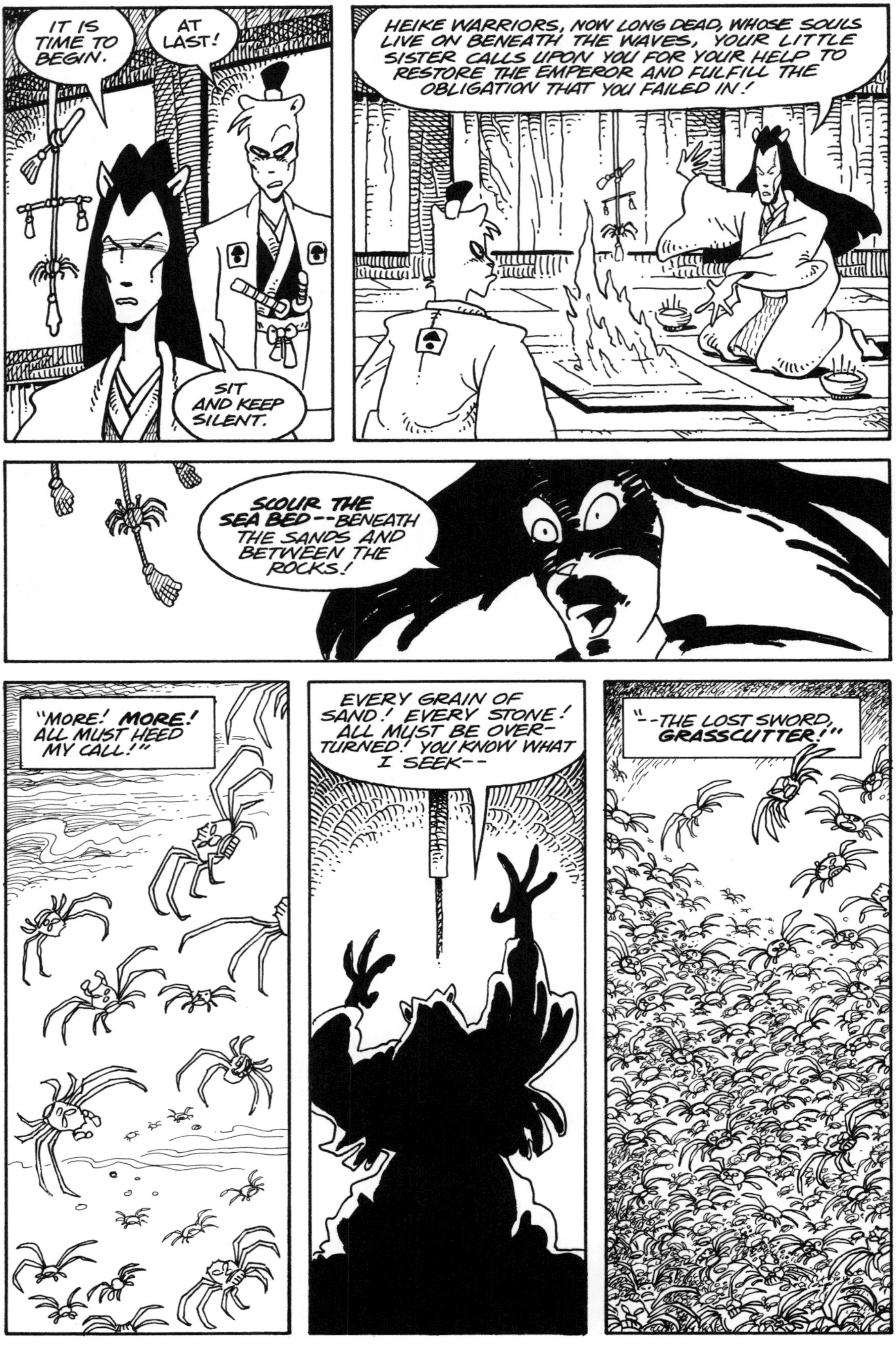
IT IS TIME TO BEGIN.
AT LAST!
SIT AND KEEP SILENT.
HEIKE WARRIORS, NOW LONG DEAD, WHOSE SOULS LIVE ON BENEATH THE WAVES, YOUR LITTLE SISTER CALLS UPON YOU FOR YOUR HELP TO RESTORE THE EMPEROR AND FULFILL THE OBLIGATION THAT YOU FAILED IN!
SCOUR THE SEA BED--BENEATH THE SANDS AND BETWEEN THE ROCKS!
"MORE! MORE! ALL MUST HEED MY CALL!"
EVERY GRAIN OF SAND! EVERY STONE! ALL MUST BE OVER-TURNED! YOU KNOW WHAT I SEEK--
"--THE LOST SWORD, GRASSCUTTER!"

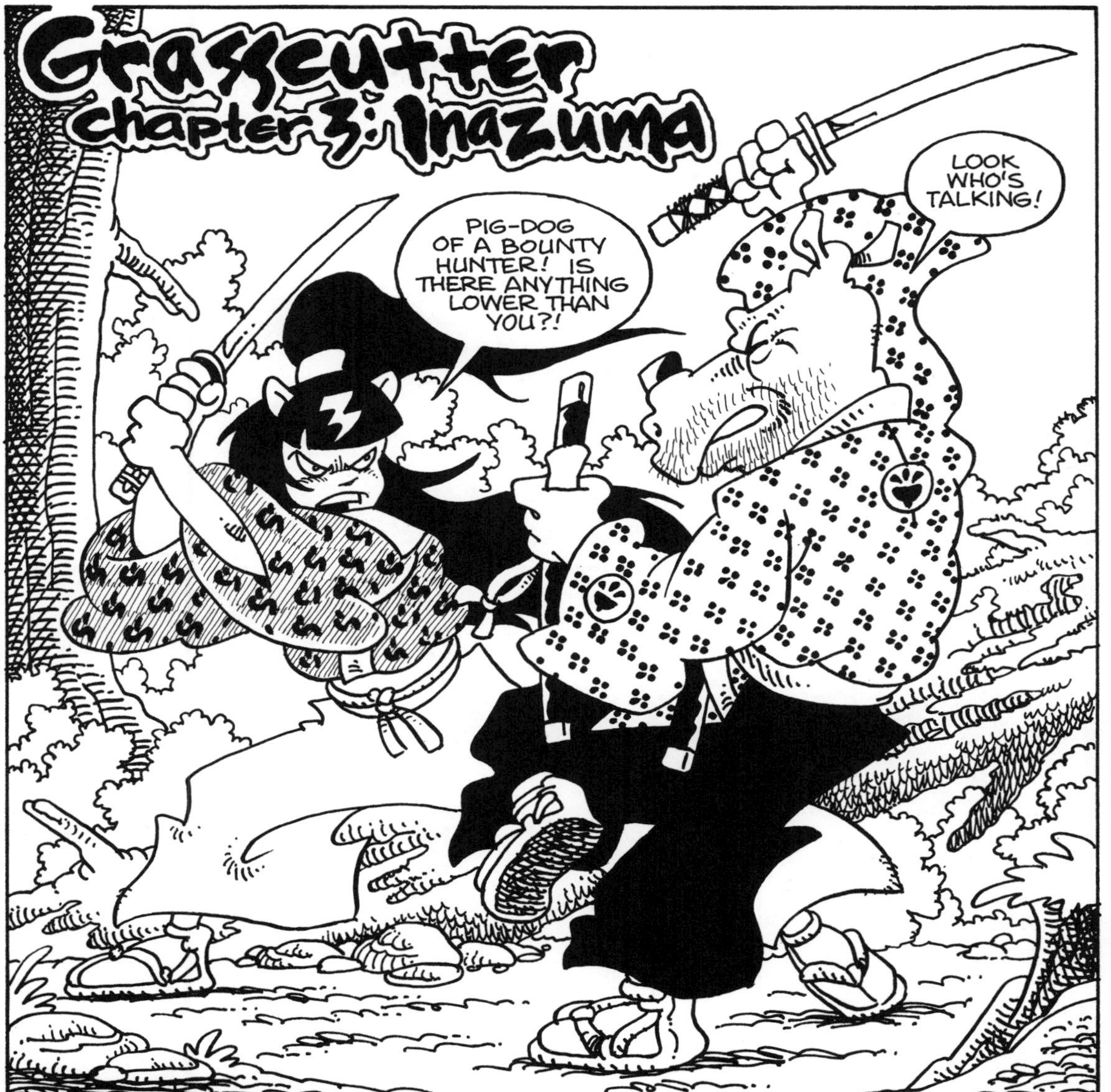
Grasscutter
Chapter 3: Inazuma
PIG-DOG OF A BOUNTY HUNTER! IS THERE ANYTHING LOWER THAN YOU?!
LOOK WHO'S TALKING!

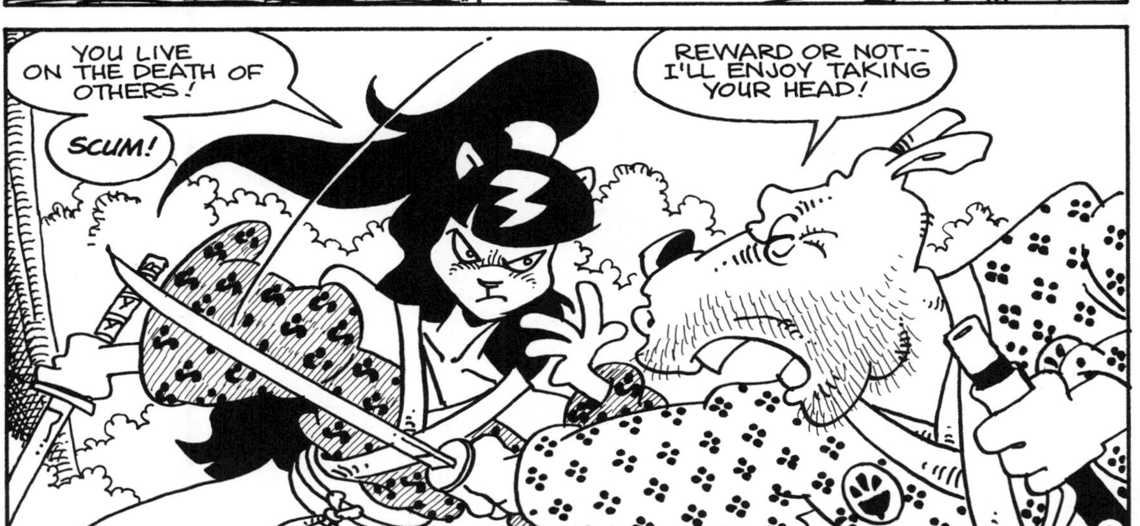
YOU LIVE ON THE DEATH OF OTHERS!
SCUM!
REWARD OR NOT-- I'LL ENJOY TAKING YOUR HEAD!
1.

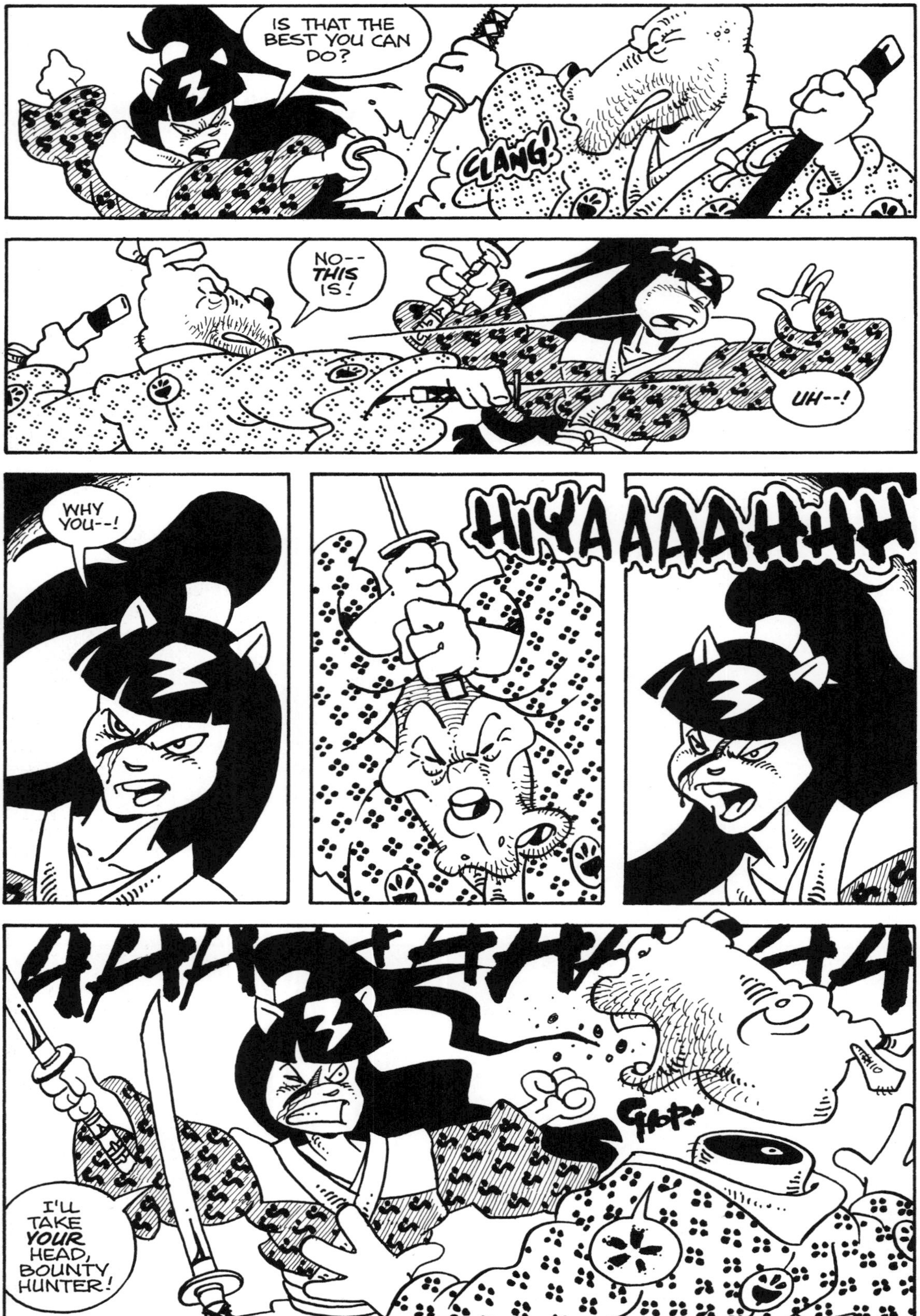
IS THAT THE BEST YOU CAN DO?
CLANG!
NO-- THIS IS!
UH--!
WHY YOU--!
HIYAAAAHHH
AAAAAAAAAAAAAA
GLOP!
I'LL TAKE YOUR HEAD, BOUNTY HUNTER!

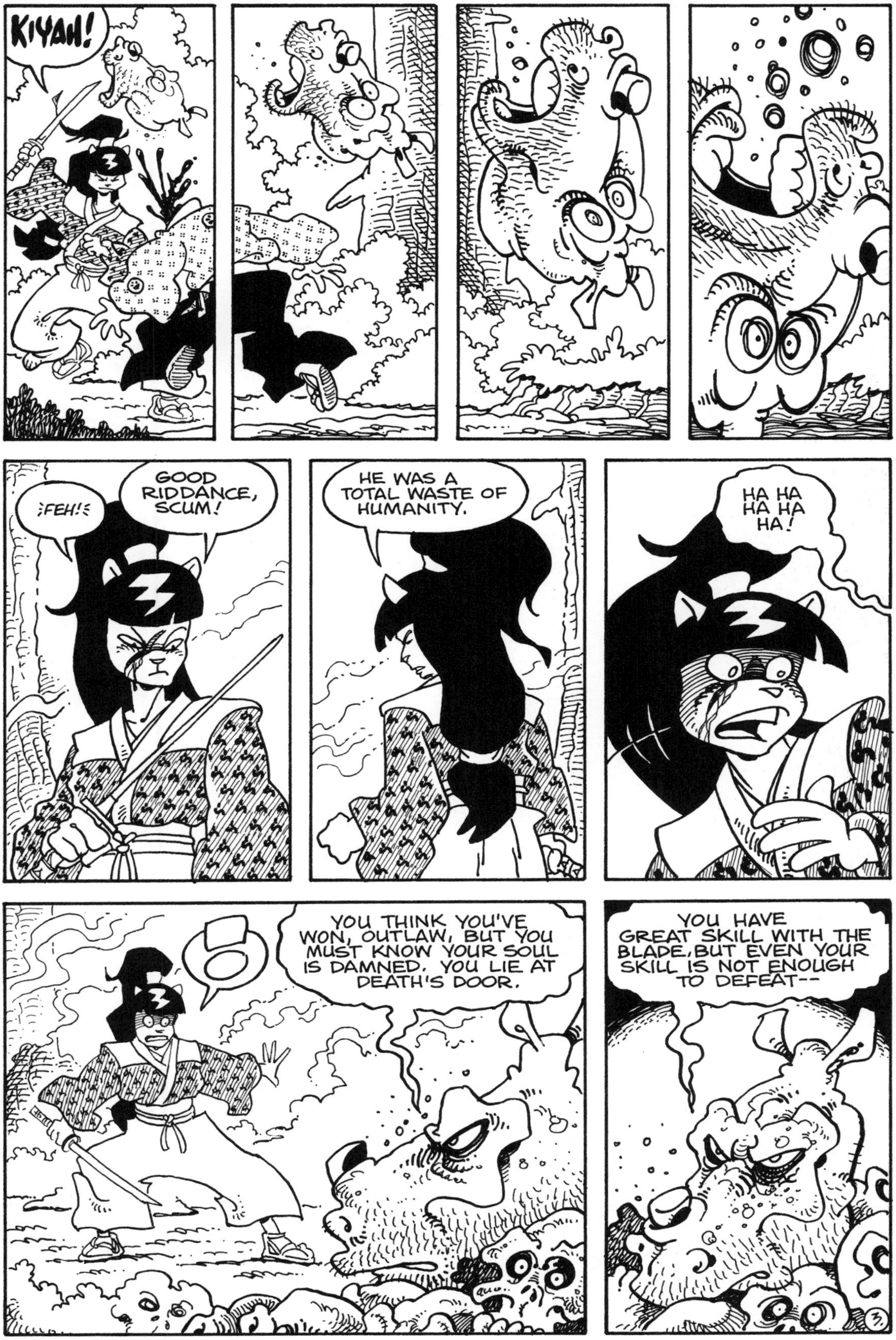
KIYAH!
¡FEH!¡
GOOD RIDDANCE, SCUM!
HE WAS A TOTAL WASTE OF HUMANITY.
HA HA HA HA HA!
YOU THINK YOU'VE WON, OUTLAW, BUT YOU MUST KNOW YOUR SOUL IS DAMNED. YOU LIE AT DEATH'S DOOR.
YOU HAVE GREAT SKILL WITH THE BLADE, BUT EVEN YOUR SKILL IS NOT ENOUGH TO DEFEAT--

--THE FORCES OF *YOMI**!

THAT BLACK FIGURE--!

HA HA HA HA!

LORD ENMA** HIMSELF?!

*HELL
**LORD OF HELL

NO. THAT IS YOUR SAVIOR!

THAT IS, IF YOU CAN GET TO HIM!

WHO IS HE?!

GO TO HIM IF YOU CAN-- AND DARE!

HAHAHAHAHAHAHA

EEYAHH!

HAHA, HAHAHA HA HA, HAHAHA HAHAHAHAHAHA HAHAHA

HAHAHA AHAHAHA HAHAHAHAHAHAHAHAHHIHHAHA HAHAHA

SHUT UP, BOUNTY HUNTER!

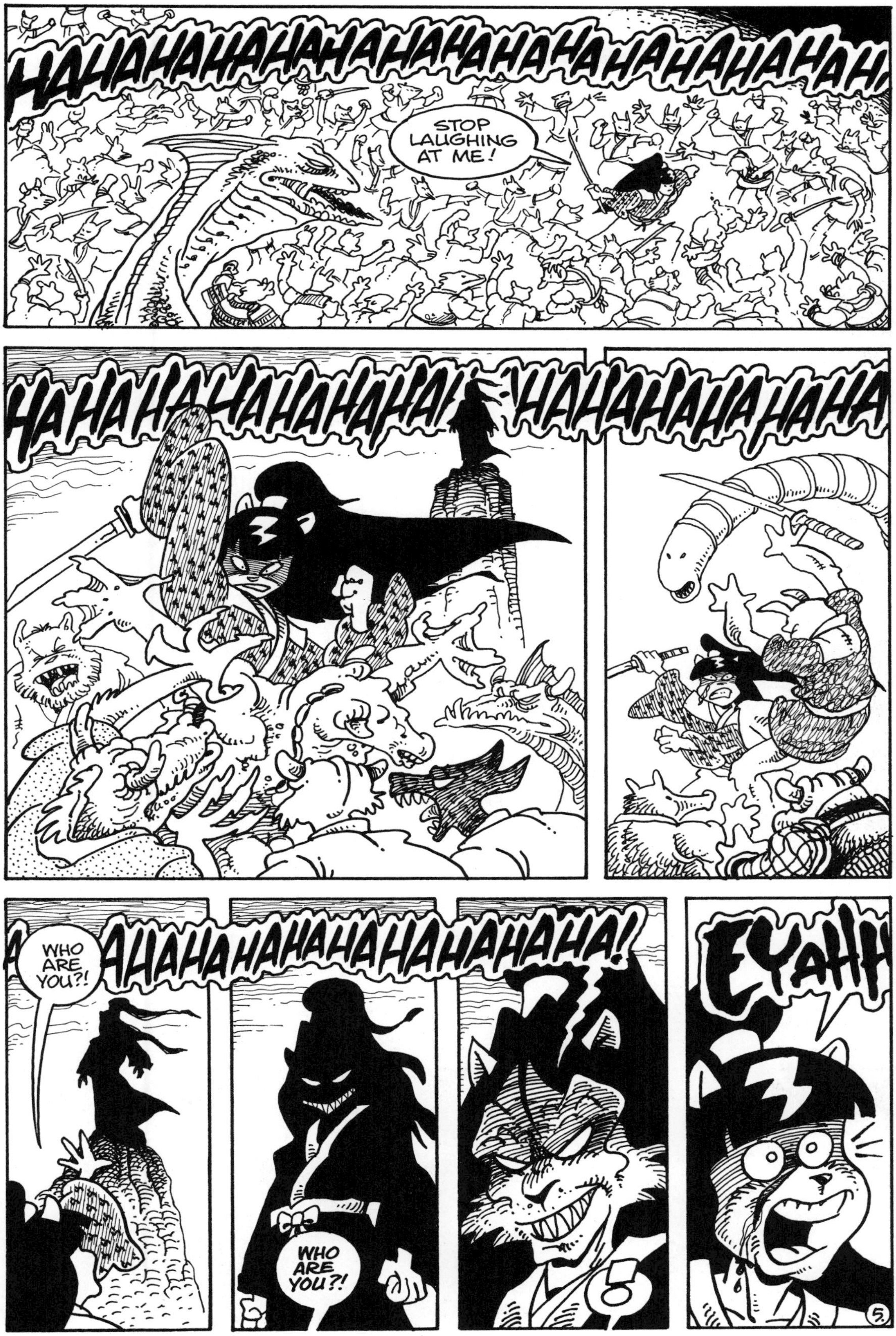
HAHAHAHAHAHAHAHAHAHAHAHAHAHAHAHAH
STOP LAUGHING AT ME!
HAHAHAHAHAHAHAHAHAHAHAHAHAHAHAHA
WHO ARE YOU?!
AHAHAHAHAHAHAHAHAHA!
WHO ARE YOU?!
EYAHH
5

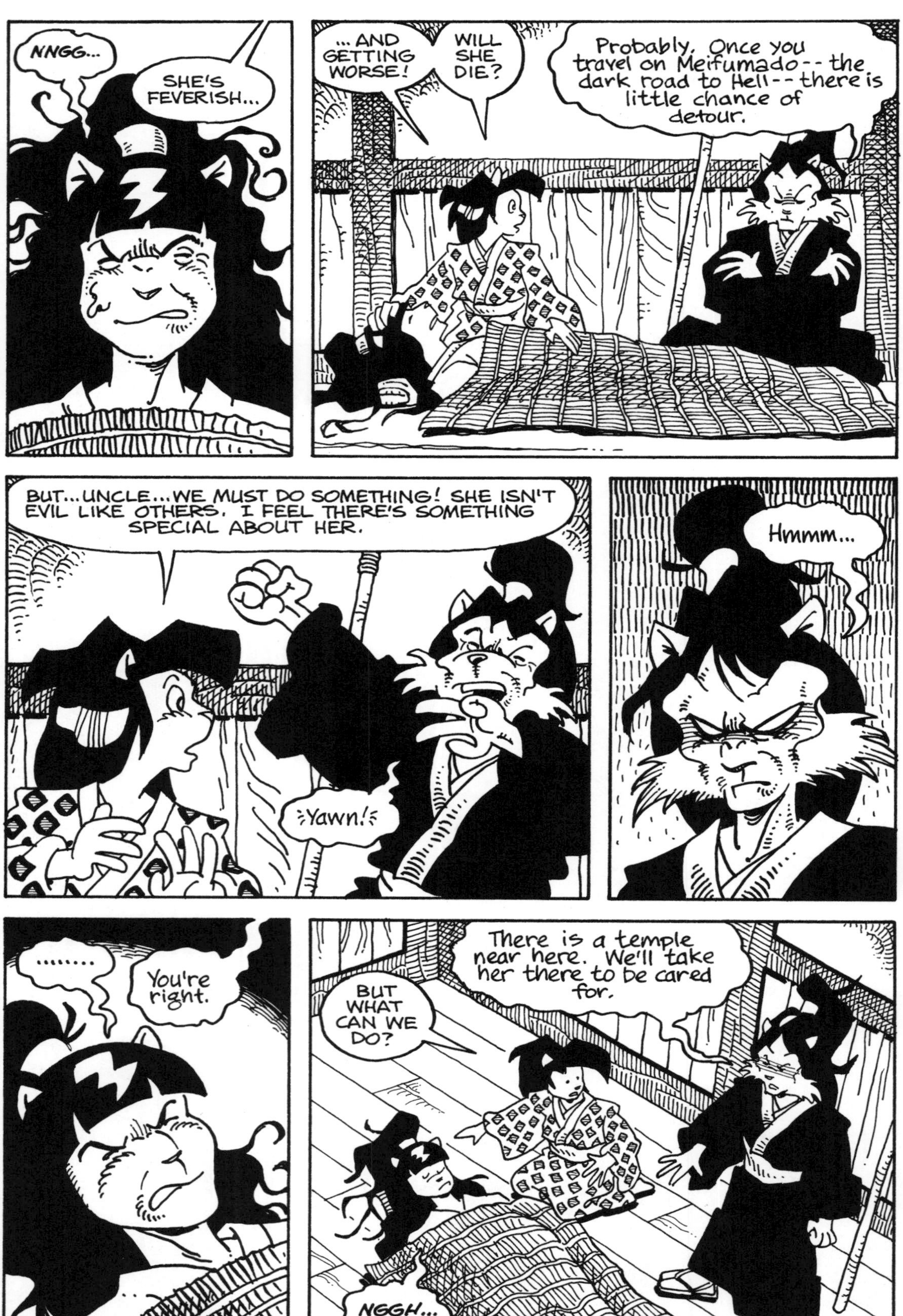
NNGG...
SHE'S FEVERISH...
...AND GETTING WORSE!
WILL SHE DIE?
Probably. Once you travel on Meifumado-- the dark road to Hell-- there is little chance of detour.
BUT...UNCLE...WE MUST DO SOMETHING! SHE ISN'T EVIL LIKE OTHERS. I FEEL THERE'S SOMETHING SPECIAL ABOUT HER.
Yawn!
Hmmm...
....
You're right.
There is a temple near here. We'll take her there to be cared for.
BUT WHAT CAN WE DO?
NGGH...
6.

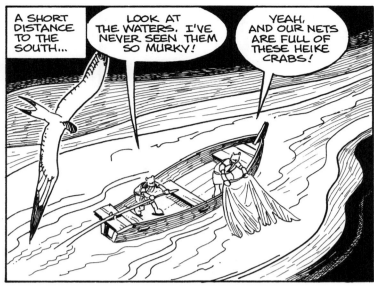

A SHORT DISTANCE TO THE SOUTH...

LOOK AT THE WATERS. I'VE NEVER SEEN THEM SO MURKY!

YEAH, AND OUR NETS ARE FULL OF THESE HEIKE CRABS!

IT'S AS IF SOMETHING IS CHURNING UP THE OCEAN BED.

PROBABLY BECAUSE OF YESTERDAY'S EARTHQUAKE.

IT SHOULD CLEAR UP IN A DAY OR TWO.

¡PHAW!¡ WE MIGHT AS WELL CALL IT A DAY AND WAIT FOR THE GODS TO GRANT US SOME CLEARER WATERS.

BUT IT WILL MEAN DAYS OF NO INCOME.

YEAH, BUT WHAT CAN WE DO? WE CATCH NOTHING BUT THOSE RED CRABS.

DEEP BENEATH THE WAVES, THOSE RED CRABS CONTINUE THEIR SEARCH FOR THE LOST SWORD.

WORKING IN UNISON, THEY OVERTURN ROCKS AND BURROW UNDER THE SAND...

...UNTIL...

SUCCESS!

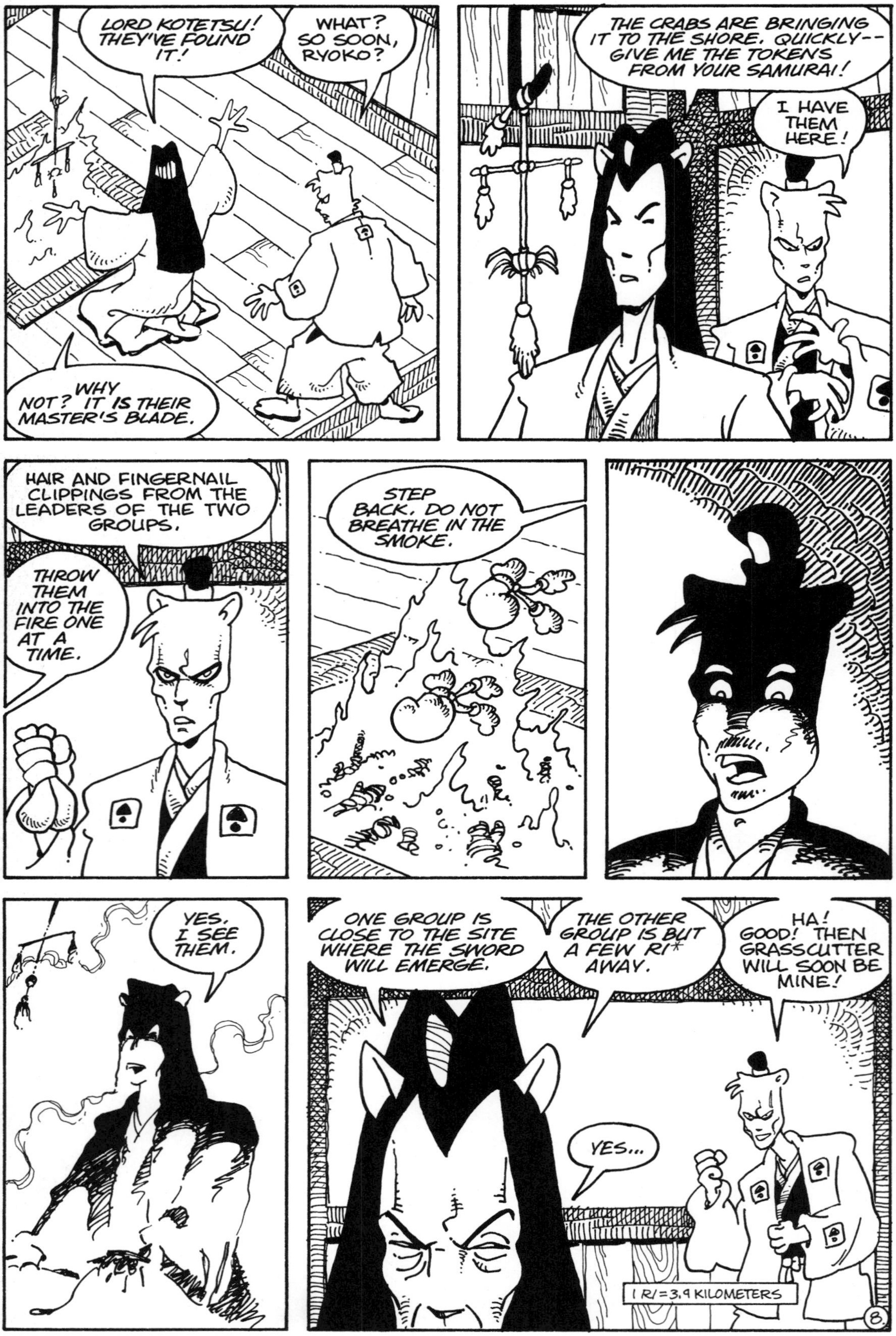
LORD KOTETSU! THEY'VE FOUND IT!
WHAT? SO SOON, RYOKO?
WHY NOT? IT IS THEIR MASTER'S BLADE.
THE CRABS ARE BRINGING IT TO THE SHORE. QUICKLY-- GIVE ME THE TOKENS FROM YOUR SAMURAI!
I HAVE THEM HERE!
HAIR AND FINGERNAIL CLIPPINGS FROM THE LEADERS OF THE TWO GROUPS.
THROW THEM INTO THE FIRE ONE AT A TIME.
STEP BACK. DO NOT BREATHE IN THE SMOKE.
YES. I SEE THEM.
ONE GROUP IS CLOSE TO THE SITE WHERE THE SWORD WILL EMERGE.
THE OTHER GROUP IS BUT A FEW RI* AWAY.
HA! GOOD! THEN GRASSCUTTER WILL SOON BE MINE!
YES...
1 RI = 3.9 KILOMETERS
8.

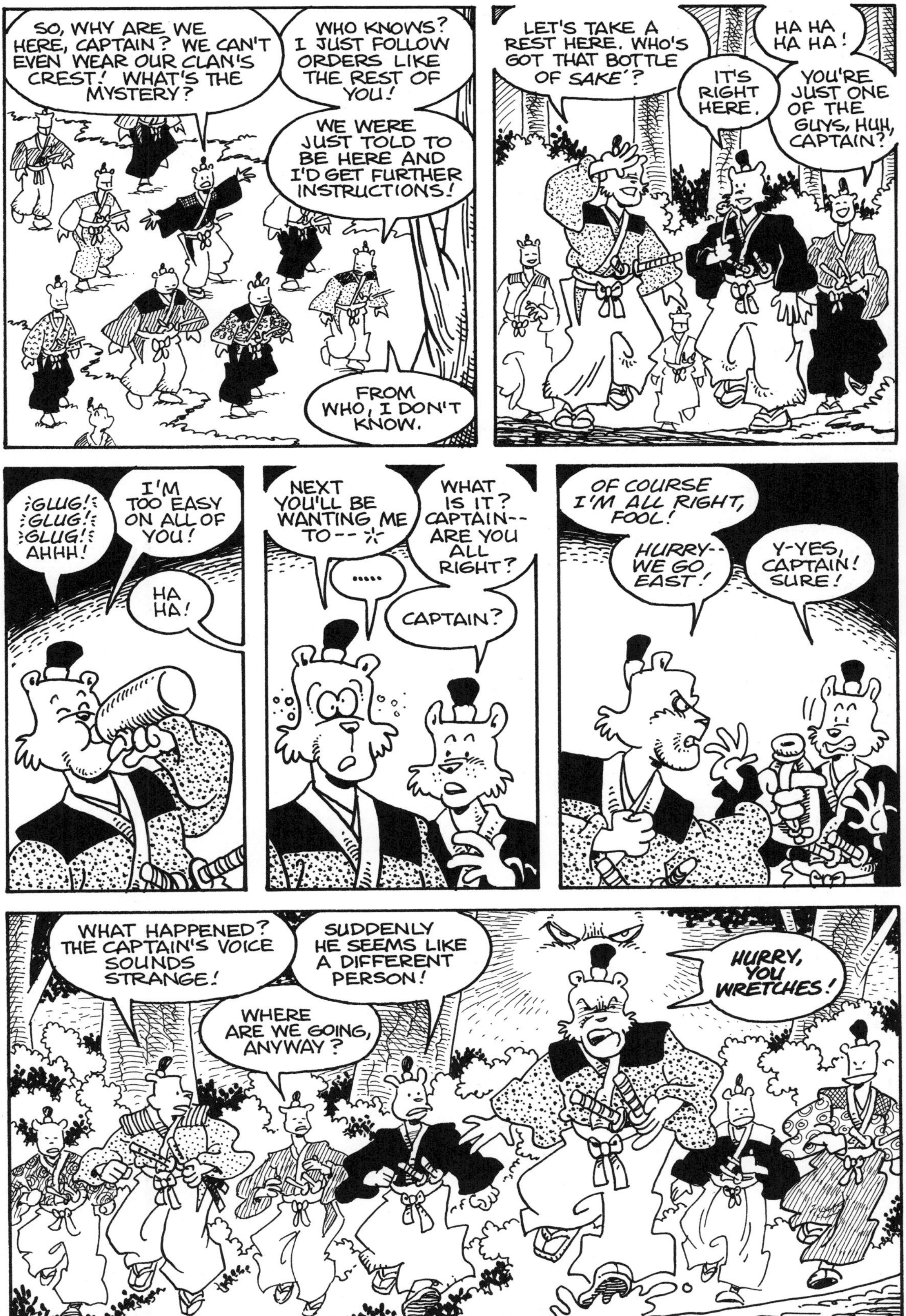
SO, WHY ARE WE HERE, CAPTAIN? WE CAN'T EVEN WEAR OUR CLAN'S CREST! WHAT'S THE MYSTERY?
WHO KNOWS? I JUST FOLLOW ORDERS LIKE THE REST OF YOU!
WE WERE JUST TOLD TO BE HERE AND I'D GET FURTHER INSTRUCTIONS!
FROM WHO, I DON'T KNOW.
LET'S TAKE A REST HERE. WHO'S GOT THAT BOTTLE OF SAKÉ?
IT'S RIGHT HERE.
HA HA HA HA!
YOU'RE JUST ONE OF THE GUYS, HUH, CAPTAIN?
¡GLUG! ¡GLUG! ¡GLUG! AHHH!
I'M TOO EASY ON ALL OF YOU!
HA HA!
NEXT YOU'LL BE WANTING ME TO--
.....
WHAT IS IT? CAPTAIN-- ARE YOU ALL RIGHT?
CAPTAIN?
OF COURSE I'M ALL RIGHT, FOOL!
HURRY-- WE GO EAST!
Y-YES, CAPTAIN! SURE!
WHAT HAPPENED? THE CAPTAIN'S VOICE SOUNDS STRANGE!
SUDDENLY HE SEEMS LIKE A DIFFERENT PERSON!
WHERE ARE WE GOING, ANYWAY?
HURRY, YOU WRETCHES!
9.

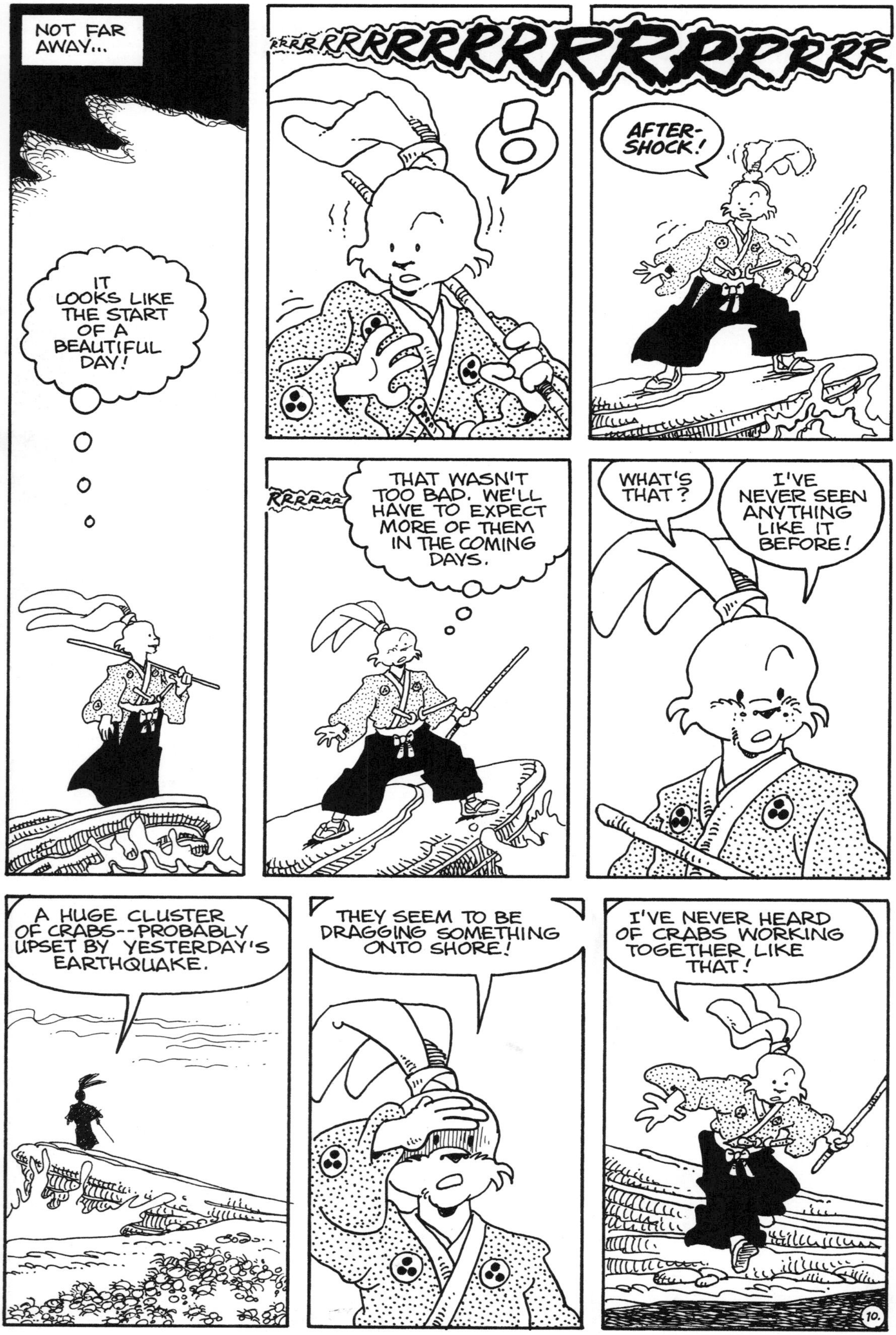
NOT FAR AWAY...
IT LOOKS LIKE THE START OF A BEAUTIFUL DAY!
RRRRRRRRRRRRRRRRRRRRRRR
!
AFTER-SHOCK!
RRRRRR
THAT WASN'T TOO BAD. WE'LL HAVE TO EXPECT MORE OF THEM IN THE COMING DAYS.
WHAT'S THAT?
I'VE NEVER SEEN ANYTHING LIKE IT BEFORE!
A HUGE CLUSTER OF CRABS--PROBABLY UPSET BY YESTERDAY'S EARTHQUAKE.
THEY SEEM TO BE DRAGGING SOMETHING ONTO SHORE!
I'VE NEVER HEARD OF CRABS WORKING TOGETHER LIKE THAT!
10.

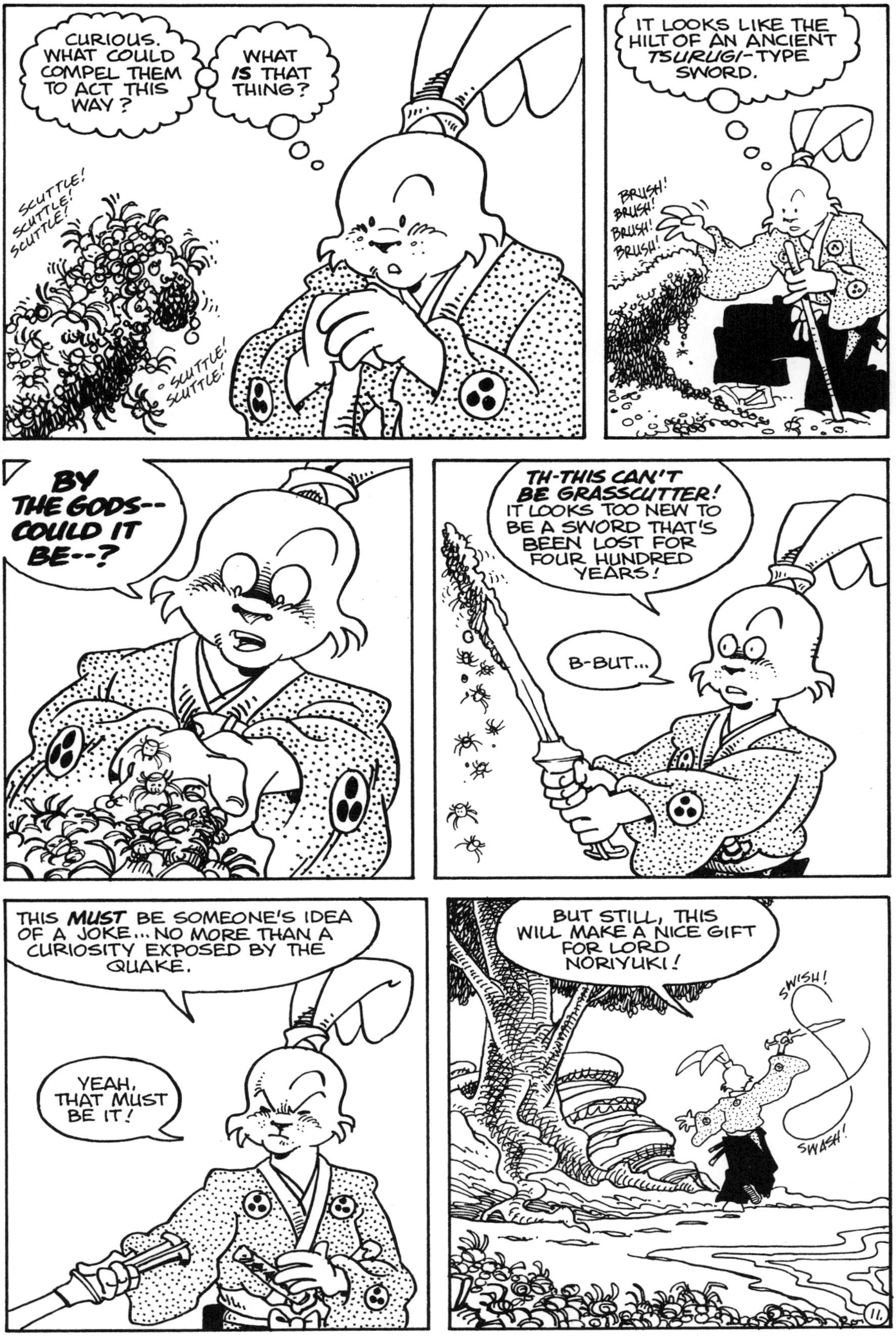
CURIOUS. WHAT COULD COMPEL THEM TO ACT THIS WAY?
WHAT *IS* THAT THING?
SCUTTLE! SCUTTLE! SCUTTLE!
SCUTTLE! SCUTTLE!
IT LOOKS LIKE THE HILT OF AN ANCIENT *TSURUGI*-TYPE SWORD.
BRUSH! BRUSH! BRUSH! BRUSH!
BY THE GODS-- COULD IT BE--?
TH-THIS CAN'T BE GRASSCUTTER! IT LOOKS TOO NEW TO BE A SWORD THAT'S BEEN LOST FOR FOUR HUNDRED YEARS!
B-BUT...
THIS **MUST** BE SOMEONE'S IDEA OF A JOKE... NO MORE THAN A CURIOSITY EXPOSED BY THE QUAKE.
YEAH, THAT MUST BE IT!
BUT STILL, THIS WILL MAKE A NICE GIFT FOR LORD NORIYUKI!
SWISH!
SWASH!
11.

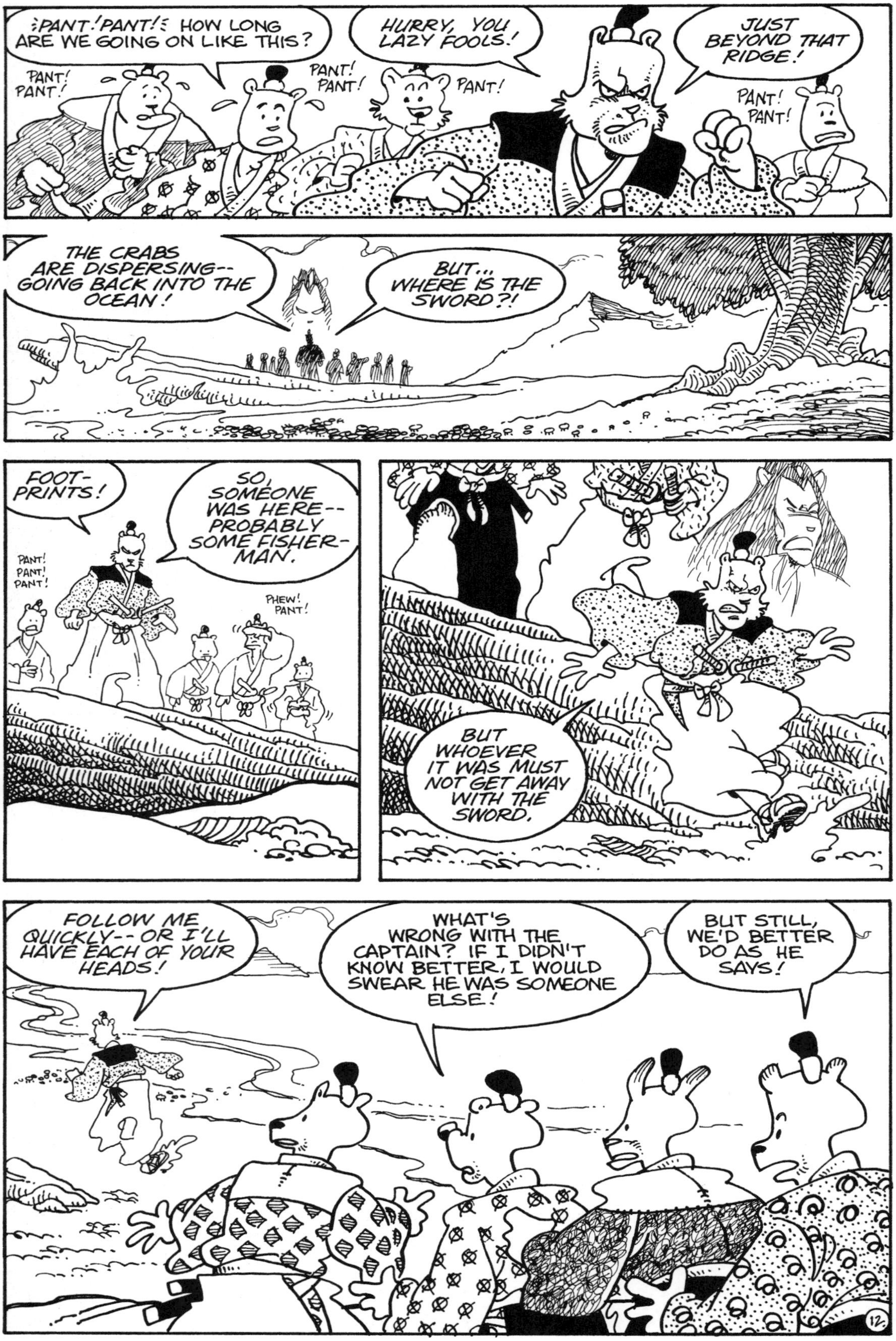

:PANT!PANT!: HOW LONG ARE WE GOING ON LIKE THIS?
PANT! PANT!
PANT! PANT!
HURRY, YOU LAZY FOOLS!
PANT!
JUST BEYOND THAT RIDGE!
PANT! PANT!
THE CRABS ARE DISPERSING-- GOING BACK INTO THE OCEAN!
BUT... WHERE IS THE SWORD?!
FOOT-PRINTS!
SO, SOMEONE WAS HERE-- PROBABLY SOME FISHER-MAN.
PANT! PANT! PANT!
PHEW! PANT!
BUT WHOEVER IT WAS MUST NOT GET AWAY WITH THE SWORD.
FOLLOW ME QUICKLY-- OR I'LL HAVE EACH OF YOUR HEADS!
WHAT'S WRONG WITH THE CAPTAIN? IF I DIDN'T KNOW BETTER, I WOULD SWEAR HE WAS SOMEONE ELSE!
BUT STILL, WE'D BETTER DO AS HE SAYS!
12.

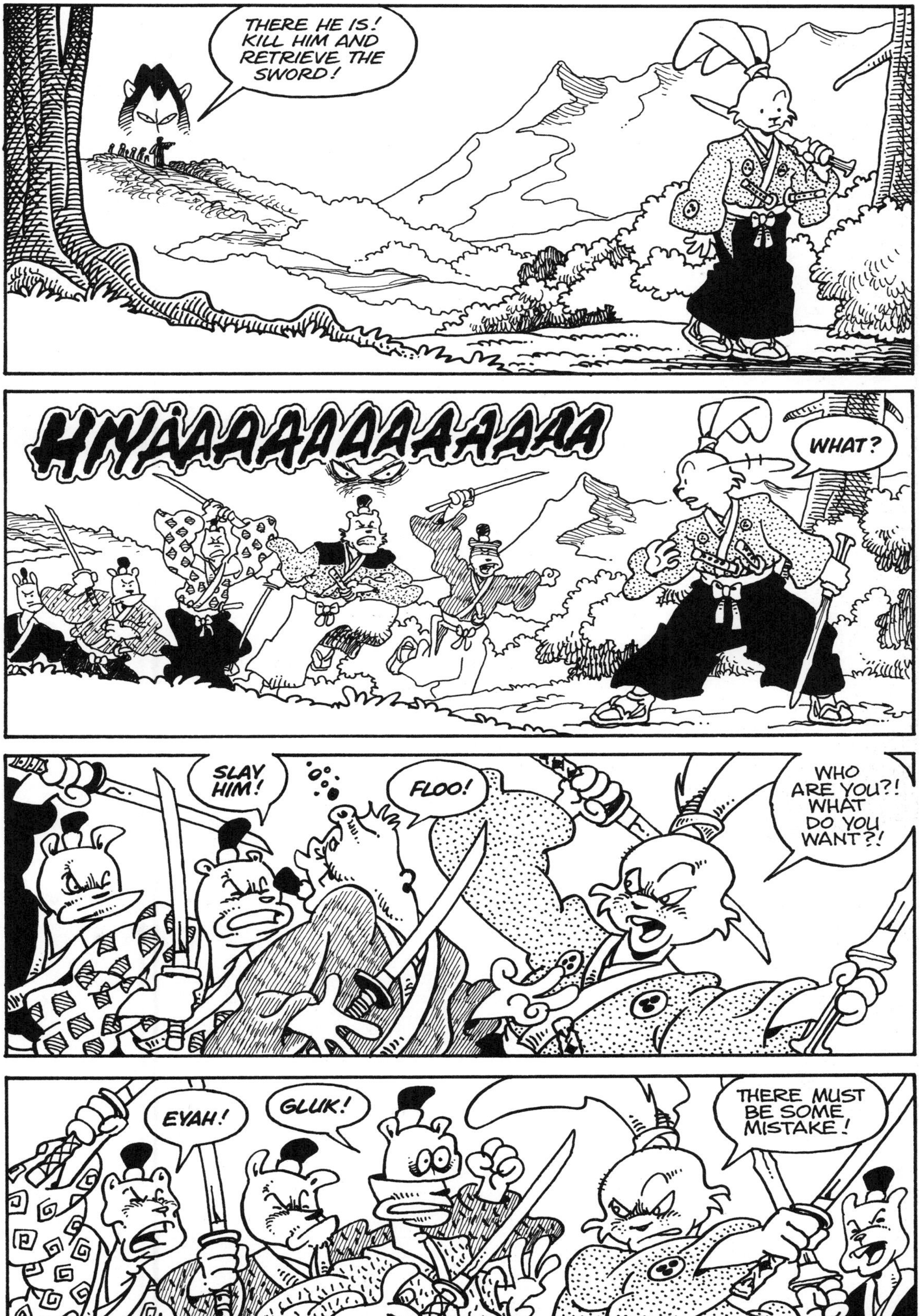
THERE HE IS! KILL HIM AND RETRIEVE THE SWORD!
HIYAAAAAAAAAAAA
WHAT?
SLAY HIM!
FLOO!
WHO ARE YOU?! WHAT DO YOU WANT?!
EYAH!
GLUK!
THERE MUST BE SOME MISTAKE!
13.

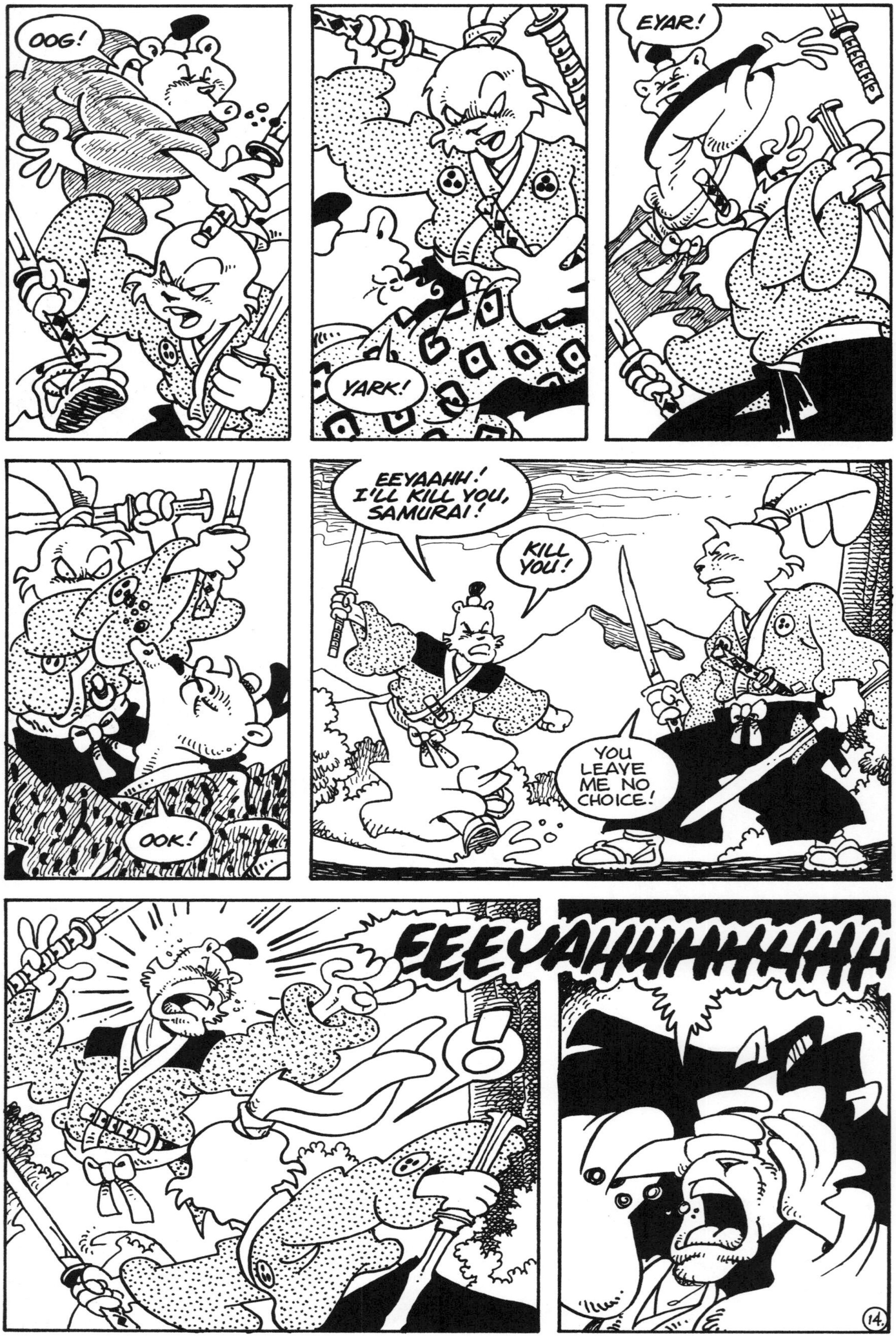

OOG!
YARK!
EYAR!
OOK!
EEYAAHH! I'LL KILL YOU, SAMURAI!
KILL YOU!
YOU LEAVE ME NO CHOICE!
EEEYAHHHHHHHH
14.

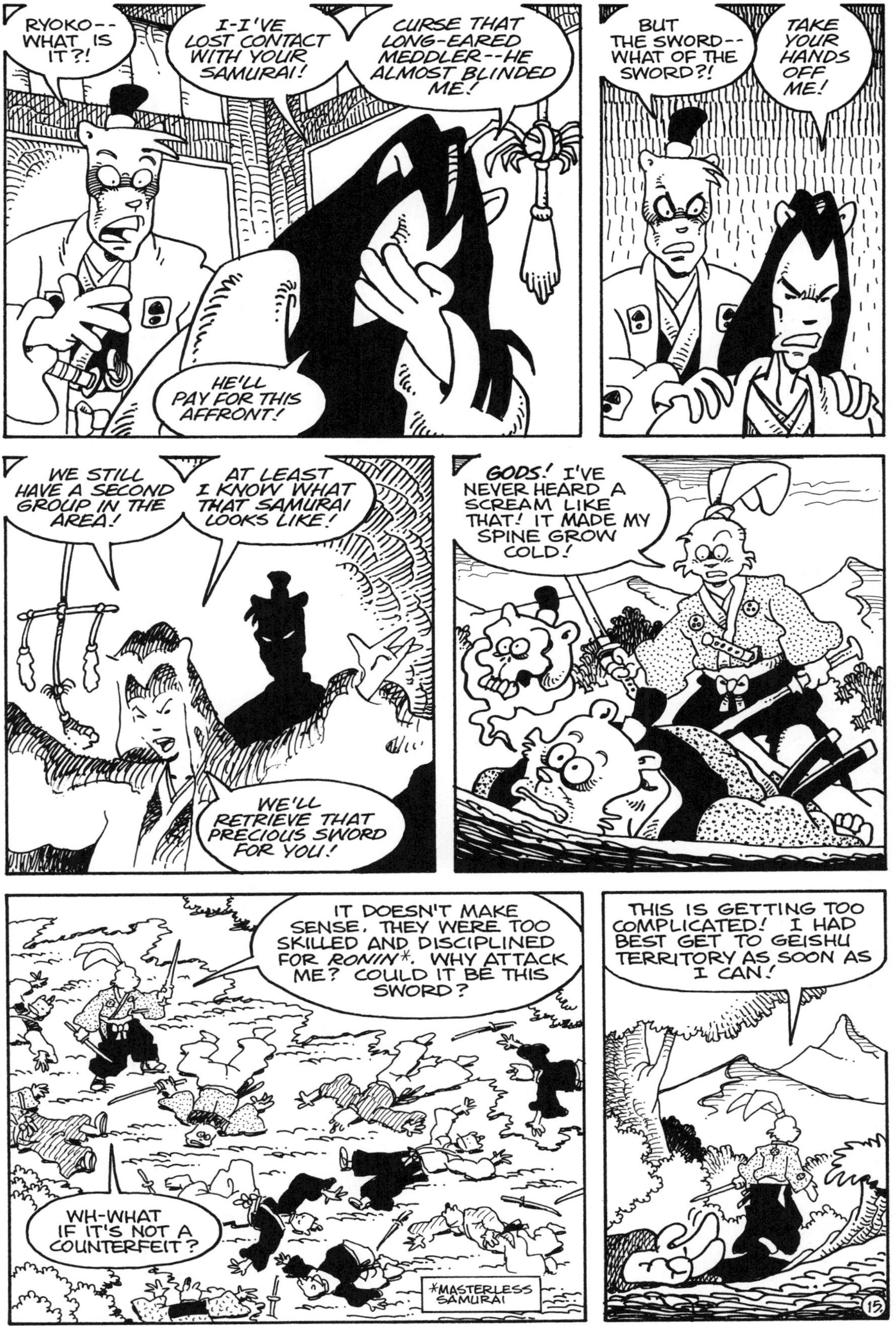
RYOKO-- WHAT IS IT?!
I-I'VE LOST CONTACT WITH YOUR SAMURAI!
CURSE THAT LONG-EARED MEDDLER--HE ALMOST BLINDED ME!
HE'LL PAY FOR THIS AFFRONT!
BUT THE SWORD-- WHAT OF THE SWORD?!
TAKE YOUR HANDS OFF ME!
WE STILL HAVE A SECOND GROUP IN THE AREA!
AT LEAST I KNOW WHAT THAT SAMURAI LOOKS LIKE!
WE'LL RETRIEVE THAT PRECIOUS SWORD FOR YOU!
GODS! I'VE NEVER HEARD A SCREAM LIKE THAT! IT MADE MY SPINE GROW COLD!
IT DOESN'T MAKE SENSE. THEY WERE TOO SKILLED AND DISCIPLINED FOR RONIN*. WHY ATTACK ME? COULD IT BE THIS SWORD?
WH-WHAT IF IT'S NOT A COUNTERFEIT?
*MASTERLESS SAMURAI
THIS IS GETTING TOO COMPLICATED! I HAD BEST GET TO GEISHU TERRITORY AS SOON AS I CAN!
15

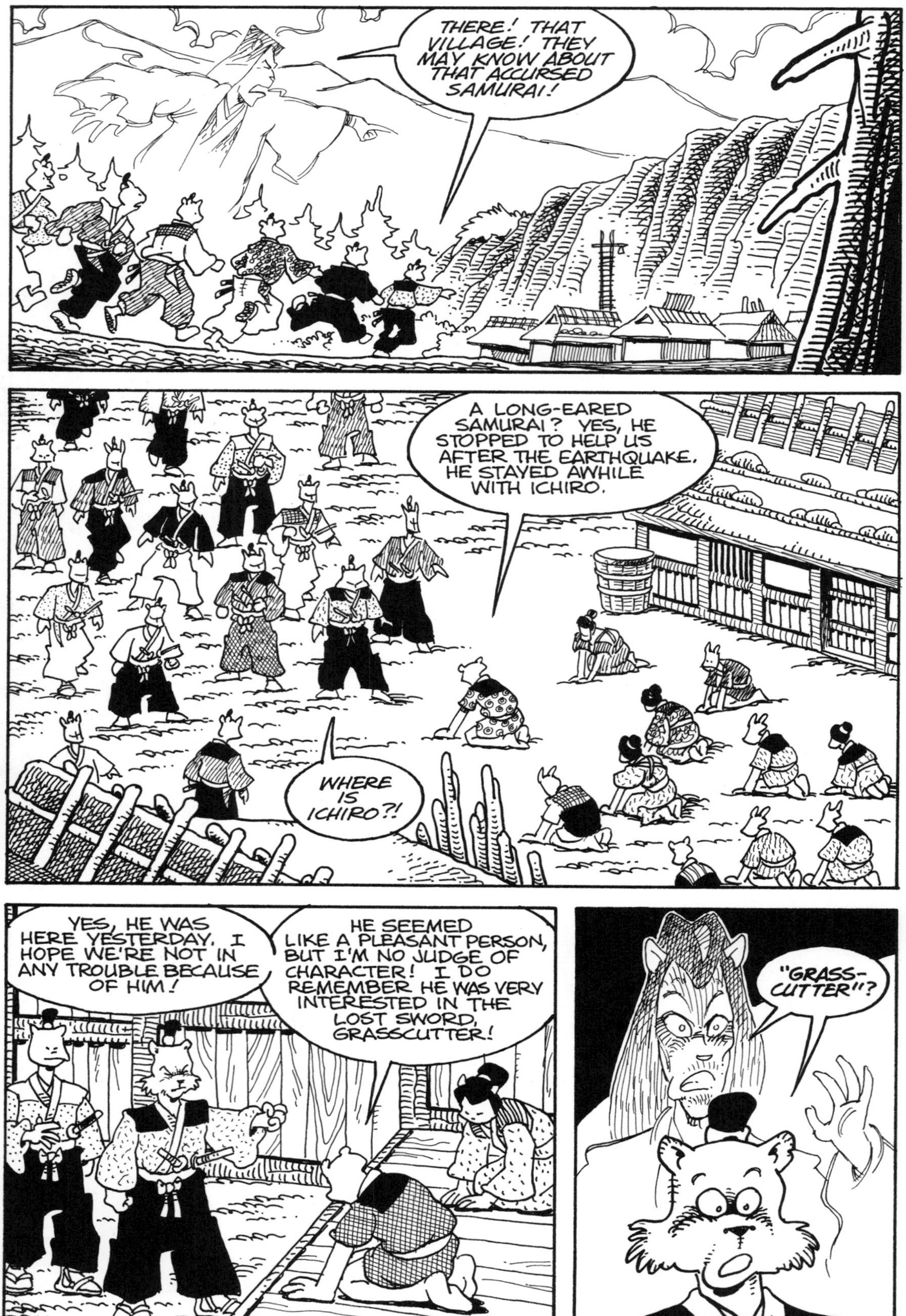
THERE! THAT VILLAGE! THEY MAY KNOW ABOUT THAT ACCURSED SAMURAI!
A LONG-EARED SAMURAI? YES, HE STOPPED TO HELP US AFTER THE EARTHQUAKE. HE STAYED AWHILE WITH ICHIRO.
WHERE IS ICHIRO?!
YES, HE WAS HERE YESTERDAY. I HOPE WE'RE NOT IN ANY TROUBLE BECAUSE OF HIM!
HE SEEMED LIKE A PLEASANT PERSON, BUT I'M NO JUDGE OF CHARACTER! I DO REMEMBER HE WAS VERY INTERESTED IN THE LOST SWORD, GRASSCUTTER!
"GRASS-CUTTER"?
16.

FORGIVE US ANY WRONGDOING. WE WOULDN'T HAVE HAD ANYTHING TO DO WITH HIM, BUT HE DID SAVE OUR SON...

WHAT ELSE DID HE SAY? WHICH WAY DID HE GO?

HE WENT TO THE NORTH-EAST.

TOWARD THE GEISHU PROVINCE. I UNDERSTAND HE IS TRAVELING TO SEE LORD NORIYUKI HIMSELF!

IS HE A FUGITIVE? IS THERE A REWARD?

LORD NORIYUKI?!

ARE YOU SURE?!

I JUST REPORT WHAT I HEAR.

NORIYUKI IS A SUPPORTER OF THE *SHOGUN*. IF HE GETS HIS HANDS ON GRASSCUTTER, MY PLAN IS *RUINED!*

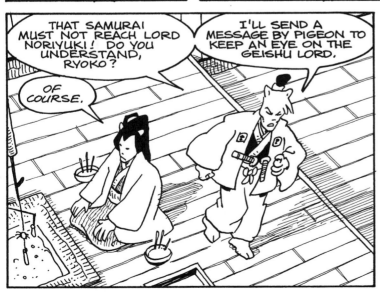

THAT SAMURAI MUST NOT REACH LORD NORIYUKI! DO YOU UNDERSTAND, RYOKO?

OF COURSE.

I'LL SEND A MESSAGE BY PIGEON TO KEEP AN EYE ON THE GEISHU LORD.

AND DESTROY THAT FISHING VILLAGE. I WANT NO ONE TO KNOW WE ARE AFTER THAT SAMURAI!

17.

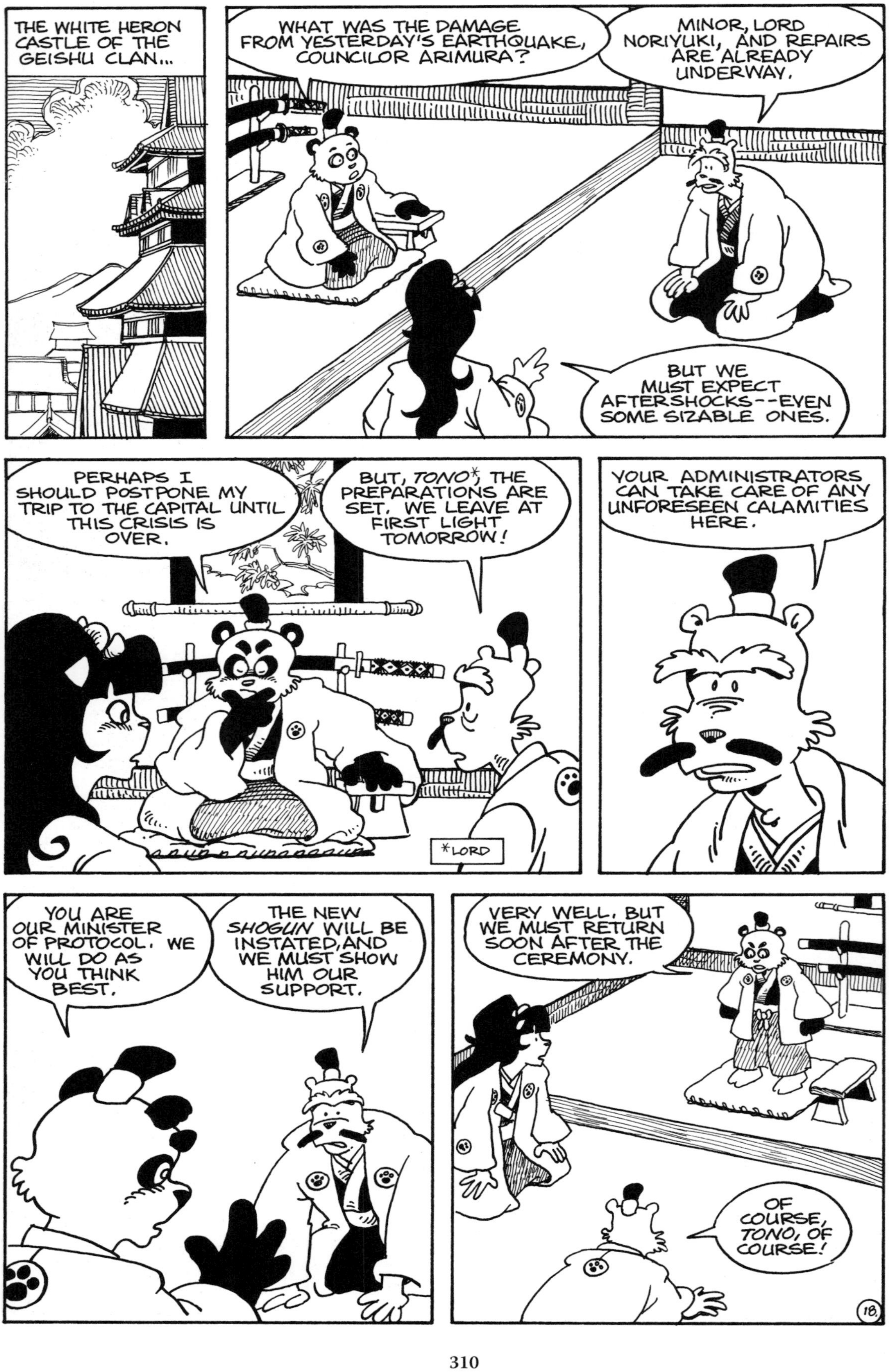
THE WHITE HERON CASTLE OF THE GEISHU CLAN...
WHAT WAS THE DAMAGE FROM YESTERDAY'S EARTHQUAKE, COUNCILOR ARIMURA?
MINOR, LORD NORIYUKI, AND REPAIRS ARE ALREADY UNDERWAY.
BUT WE MUST EXPECT AFTERSHOCKS--EVEN SOME SIZABLE ONES.
PERHAPS I SHOULD POSTPONE MY TRIP TO THE CAPITAL UNTIL THIS CRISIS IS OVER.
BUT, *TONO**, THE PREPARATIONS ARE SET. WE LEAVE AT FIRST LIGHT TOMORROW!
*LORD
YOUR ADMINISTRATORS CAN TAKE CARE OF ANY UNFORESEEN CALAMITIES HERE.
YOU ARE OUR MINISTER OF PROTOCOL. WE WILL DO AS YOU THINK BEST.
THE NEW *SHOGUN* WILL BE INSTATED, AND WE MUST SHOW HIM OUR SUPPORT.
VERY WELL, BUT WE MUST RETURN SOON AFTER THE CEREMONY.
OF COURSE, *TONO*, OF COURSE!
18.

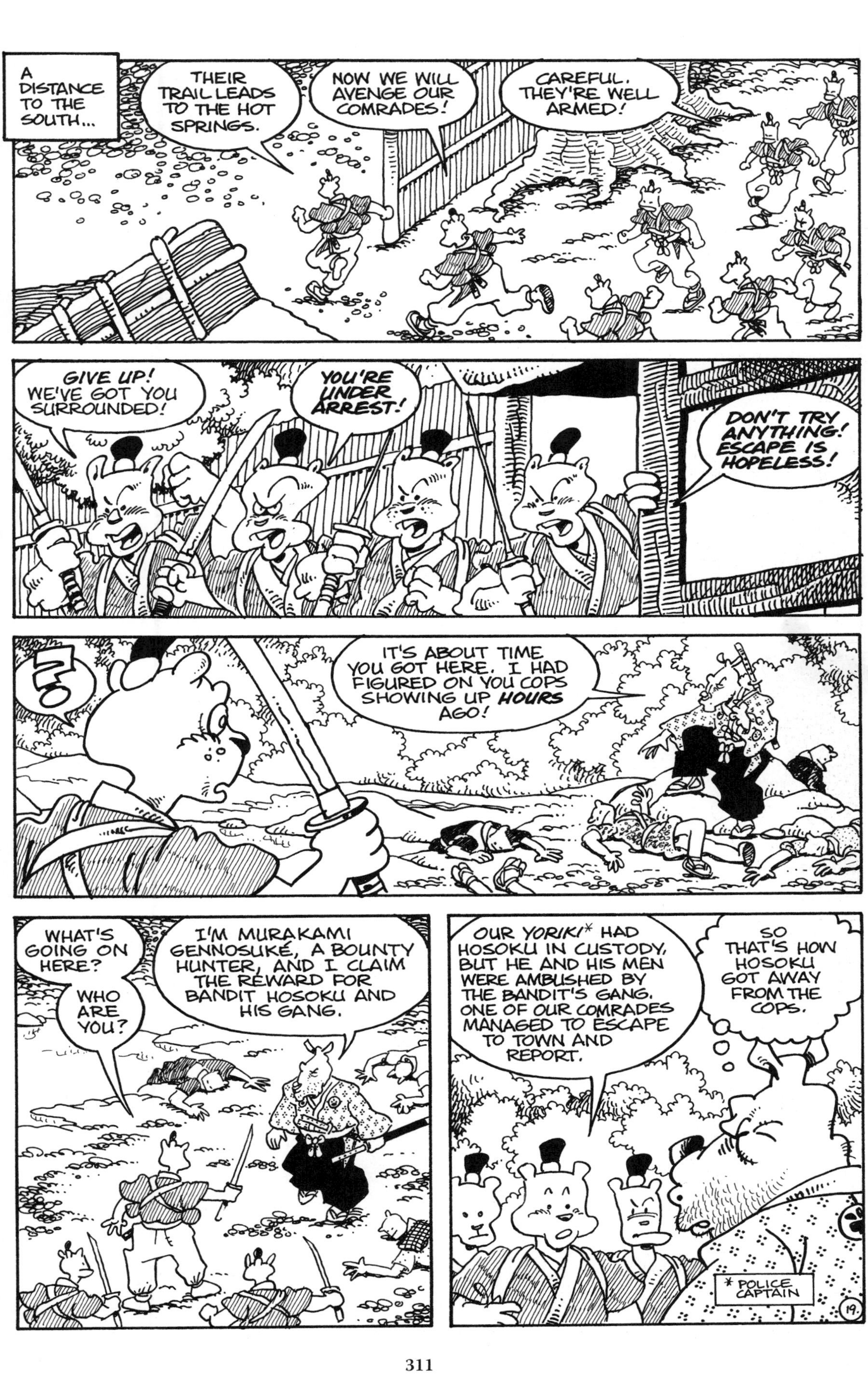
A DISTANCE TO THE SOUTH...
THEIR TRAIL LEADS TO THE HOT SPRINGS.
NOW WE WILL AVENGE OUR COMRADES!
CAREFUL. THEY'RE WELL ARMED!
GIVE UP! WE'VE GOT YOU SURROUNDED!
YOU'RE UNDER ARREST!
DON'T TRY ANYTHING! ESCAPE IS HOPELESS!
?!
IT'S ABOUT TIME YOU GOT HERE. I HAD FIGURED ON YOU COPS SHOWING UP HOURS AGO!
WHAT'S GOING ON HERE?
WHO ARE YOU?
I'M MURAKAMI GENNOSUKÉ, A BOUNTY HUNTER, AND I CLAIM THE REWARD FOR BANDIT HOSOKU AND HIS GANG.
OUR YORIKI* HAD HOSOKU IN CUSTODY, BUT HE AND HIS MEN WERE AMBUSHED BY THE BANDIT'S GANG. ONE OF OUR COMRADES MANAGED TO ESCAPE TO TOWN AND REPORT.
SO THAT'S HOW HOSOKU GOT AWAY FROM THE COPS.
*POLICE CAPTAIN
19.

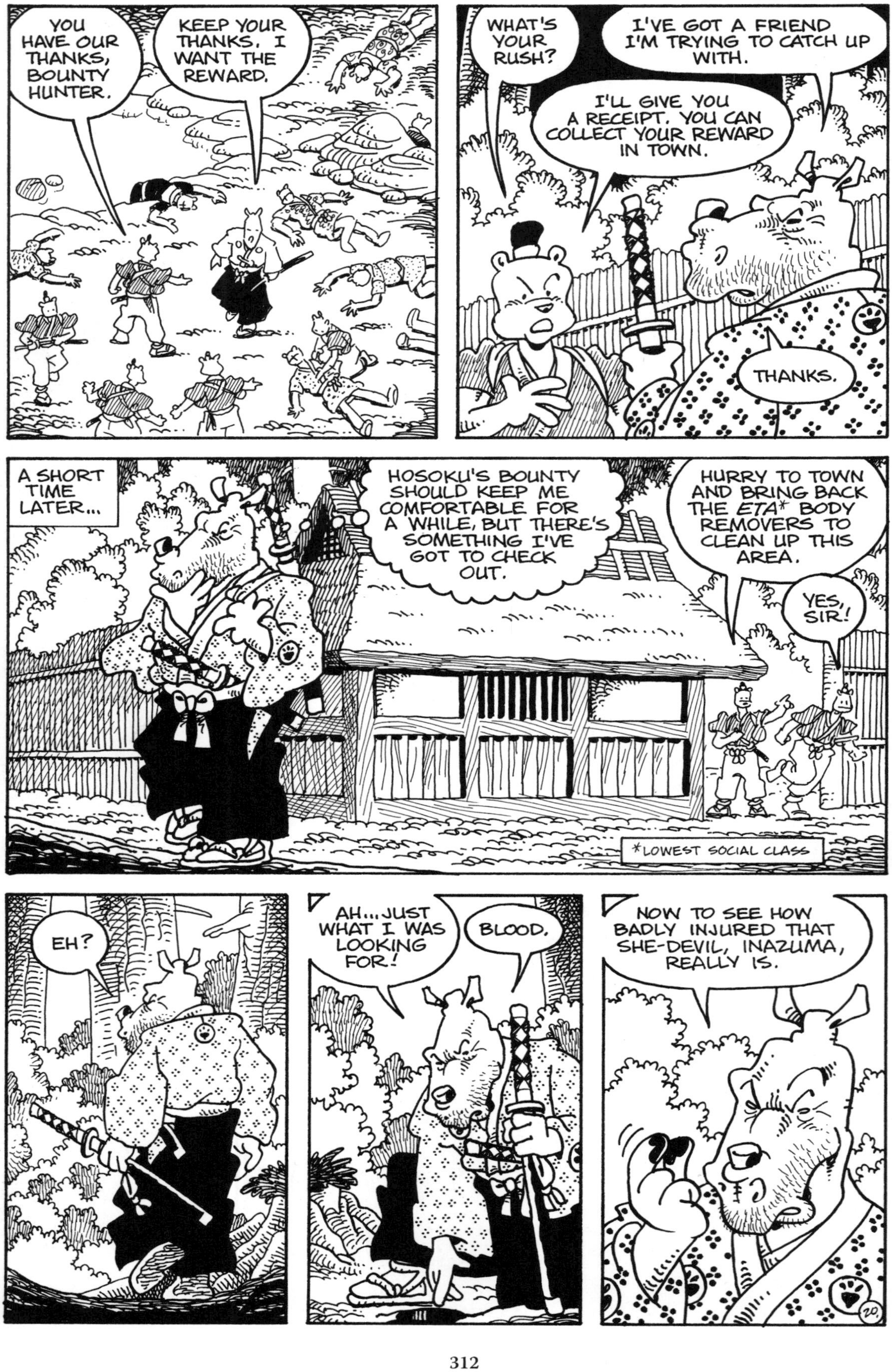
YOU HAVE OUR THANKS, BOUNTY HUNTER.
KEEP YOUR THANKS. I WANT THE REWARD.
WHAT'S YOUR RUSH?
I'VE GOT A FRIEND I'M TRYING TO CATCH UP WITH.
I'LL GIVE YOU A RECEIPT. YOU CAN COLLECT YOUR REWARD IN TOWN.
THANKS.
A SHORT TIME LATER...
HOSOKU'S BOUNTY SHOULD KEEP ME COMFORTABLE FOR A WHILE, BUT THERE'S SOMETHING I'VE GOT TO CHECK OUT.
HURRY TO TOWN AND BRING BACK THE ETA* BODY REMOVERS TO CLEAN UP THIS AREA.
YES, SIR!
*LOWEST SOCIAL CLASS
EH?
AH... JUST WHAT I WAS LOOKING FOR!
BLOOD.
NOW TO SEE HOW BADLY INJURED THAT SHE-DEVIL, INAZUMA, REALLY IS.
20.

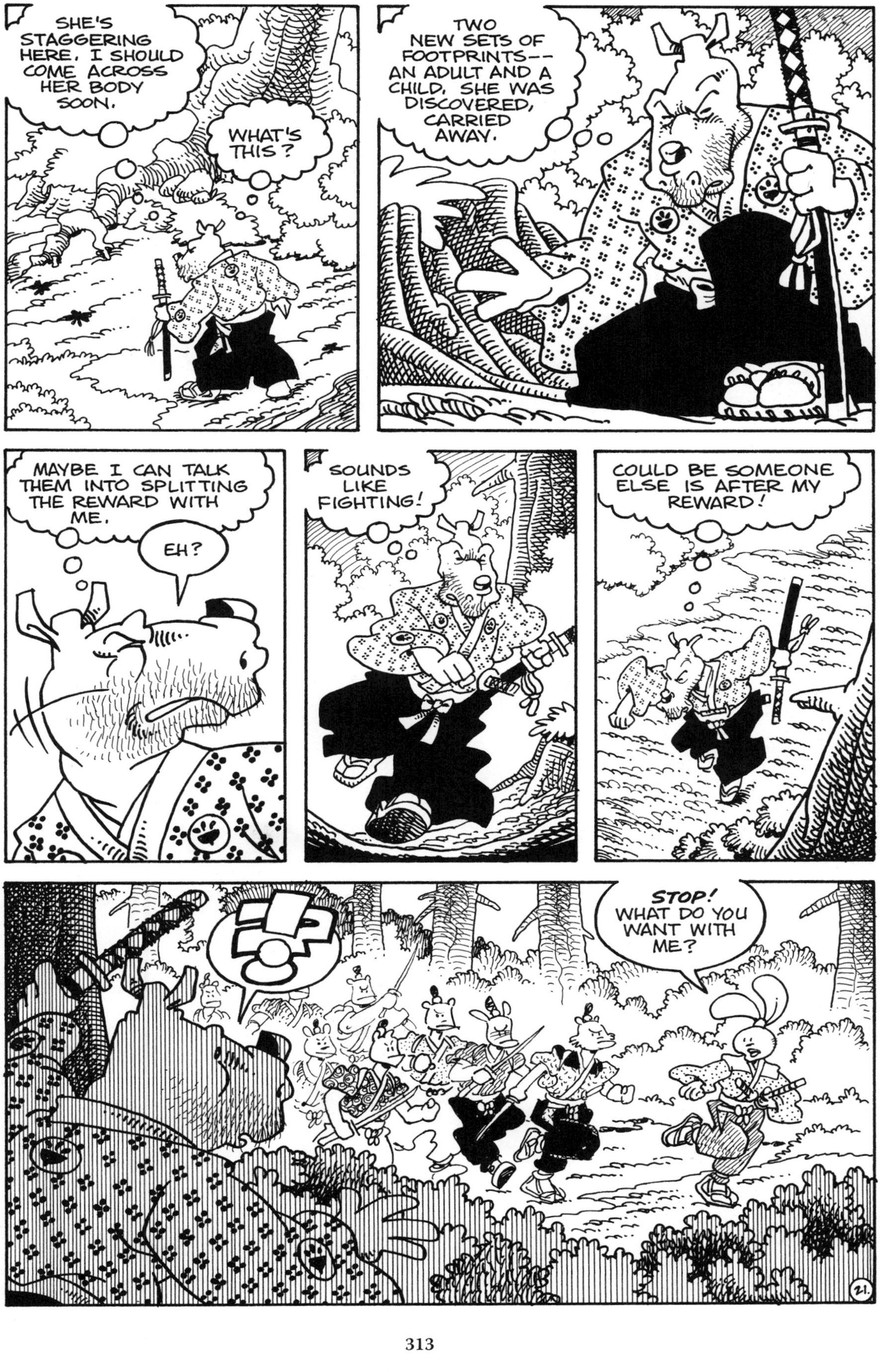
SHE'S STAGGERING HERE. I SHOULD COME ACROSS HER BODY SOON.
WHAT'S THIS?
TWO NEW SETS OF FOOTPRINTS-- AN ADULT AND A CHILD. SHE WAS DISCOVERED, CARRIED AWAY.
MAYBE I CAN TALK THEM INTO SPLITTING THE REWARD WITH ME.
EH?
SOUNDS LIKE FIGHTING!
COULD BE SOMEONE ELSE IS AFTER MY REWARD!
!
STOP! WHAT DO YOU WANT WITH ME?
21.

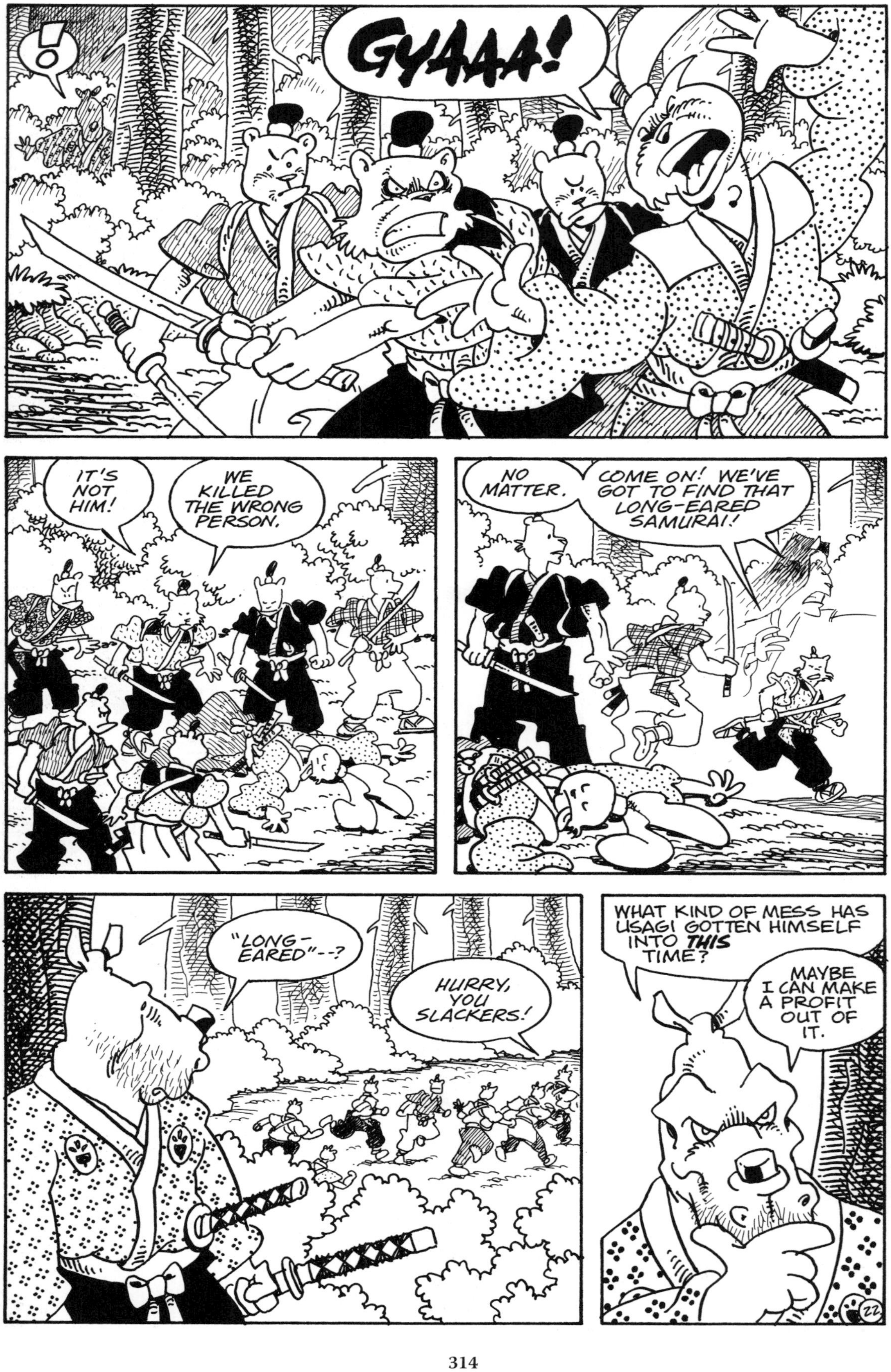
!
GYAAA!
IT'S NOT HIM!
WE KILLED THE WRONG PERSON.
NO MATTER.
COME ON! WE'VE GOT TO FIND THAT LONG-EARED SAMURAI!
"LONG-EARED"--?
HURRY, YOU SLACKERS!
WHAT KIND OF MESS HAS USAGI GOTTEN HIMSELF INTO THIS TIME?
MAYBE I CAN MAKE A PROFIT OUT OF IT.
22

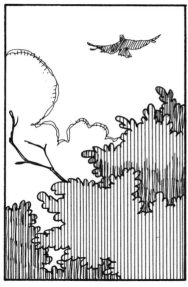

COO. COO.

AH, GOOD, A REPLY.

LORD NORIYUKI IS PREPARING TO TRAVEL TO EDO!

IT COULD BE A COINCIDENCE... THE RETIREMENT OF THE SHOGUN IN FAVOR OF HIS SON...

A GEISHU RETAINER INQUIRING ABOUT GRASSCUTTER AND THEN FINDING IT BEFORE MY OWN SAMURAI? NOW NORIYUKI'S TRIP TO THE CAPITAL? IT MUST BE MORE THAN COINCIDENCE!

YOU SUGGEST HE IS INVOLVED IN A COUNTER-CONSPIRACY?

WHAT BETTER WAY FOR NORIYUKI TO DEMONSTRATE HIS ALLEGIANCE TO THE NEW SHOGUN THAN TO PRESENT HIM WITH THE SWORD OF THE GODS?

BUT HOW DID HE KNOW OF MY PLAN TO RETRIEVE THE SACRED SWORD?

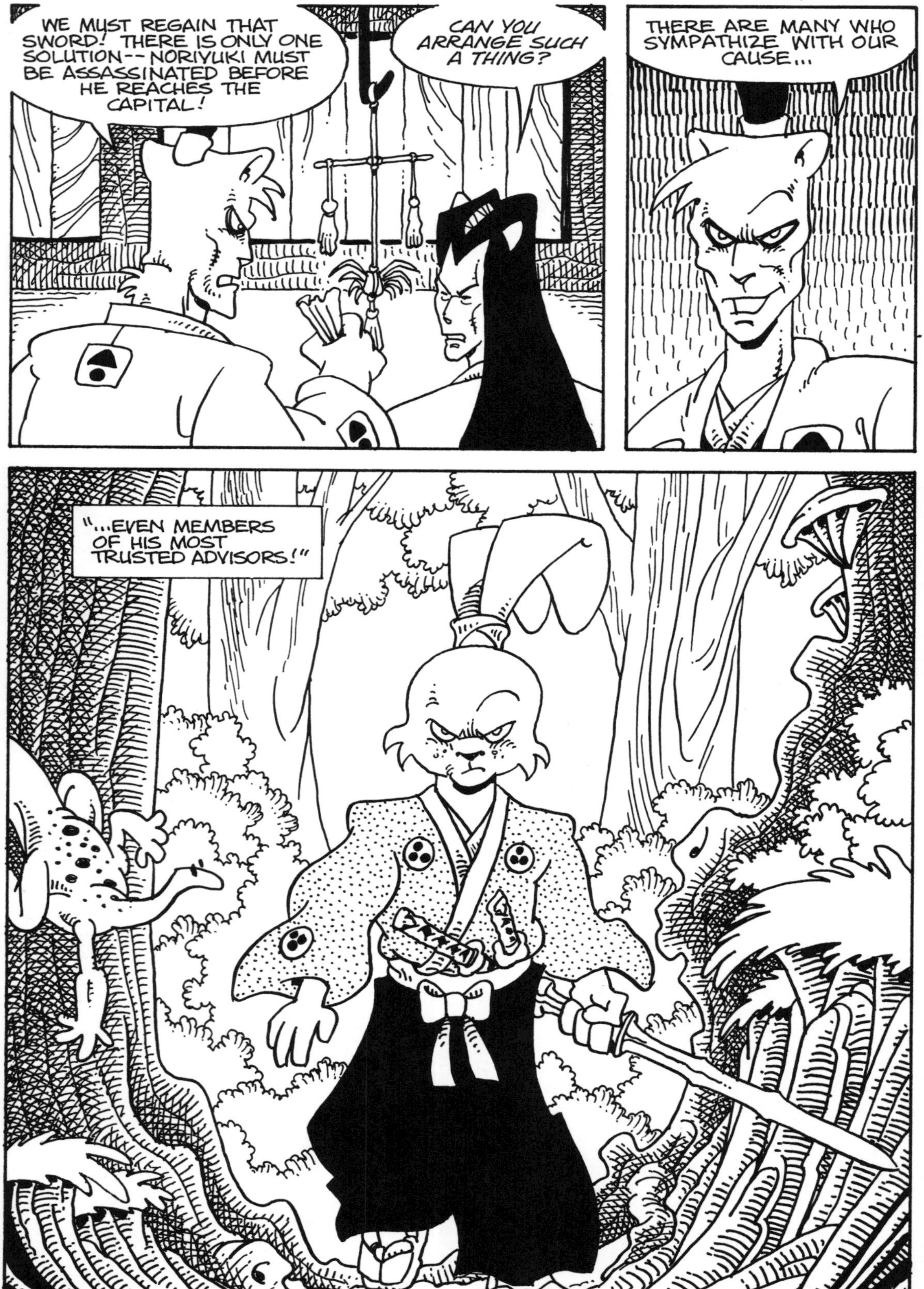
WE MUST REGAIN THAT SWORD! THERE IS ONLY ONE SOLUTION-- NORIYUKI MUST BE ASSASSINATED BEFORE HE REACHES THE CAPITAL!
CAN YOU ARRANGE SUCH A THING?
THERE ARE MANY WHO SYMPATHIZE WITH OUR CAUSE...
"...EVEN MEMBERS OF HIS MOST TRUSTED ADVISORS!"

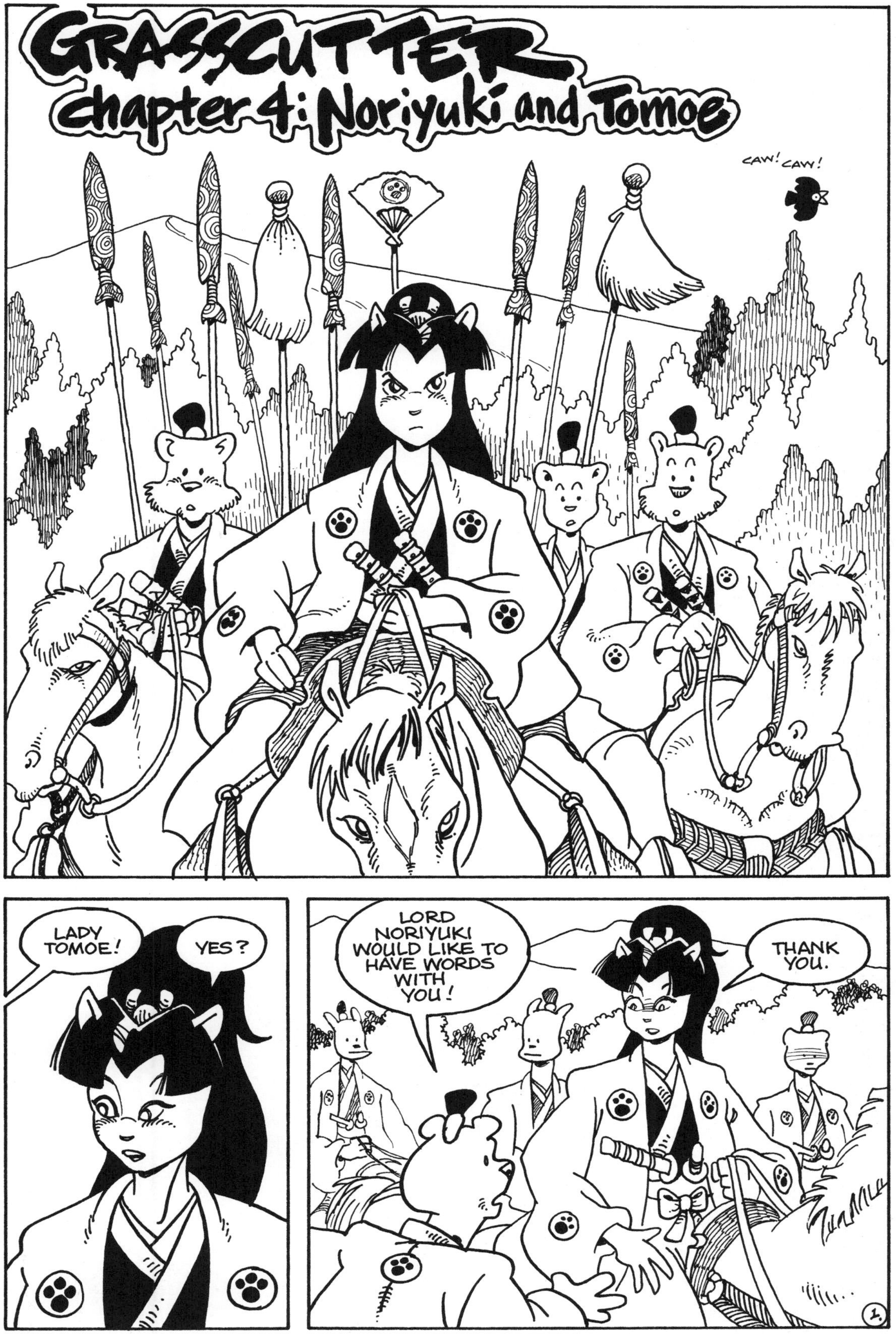
GRASSCUTTER
Chapter 4: Noriyuki and Tomoe
CAW! CAW!
LADY TOMOE!
YES?
LORD NORIYUKI WOULD LIKE TO HAVE WORDS WITH YOU!
THANK YOU.
1.

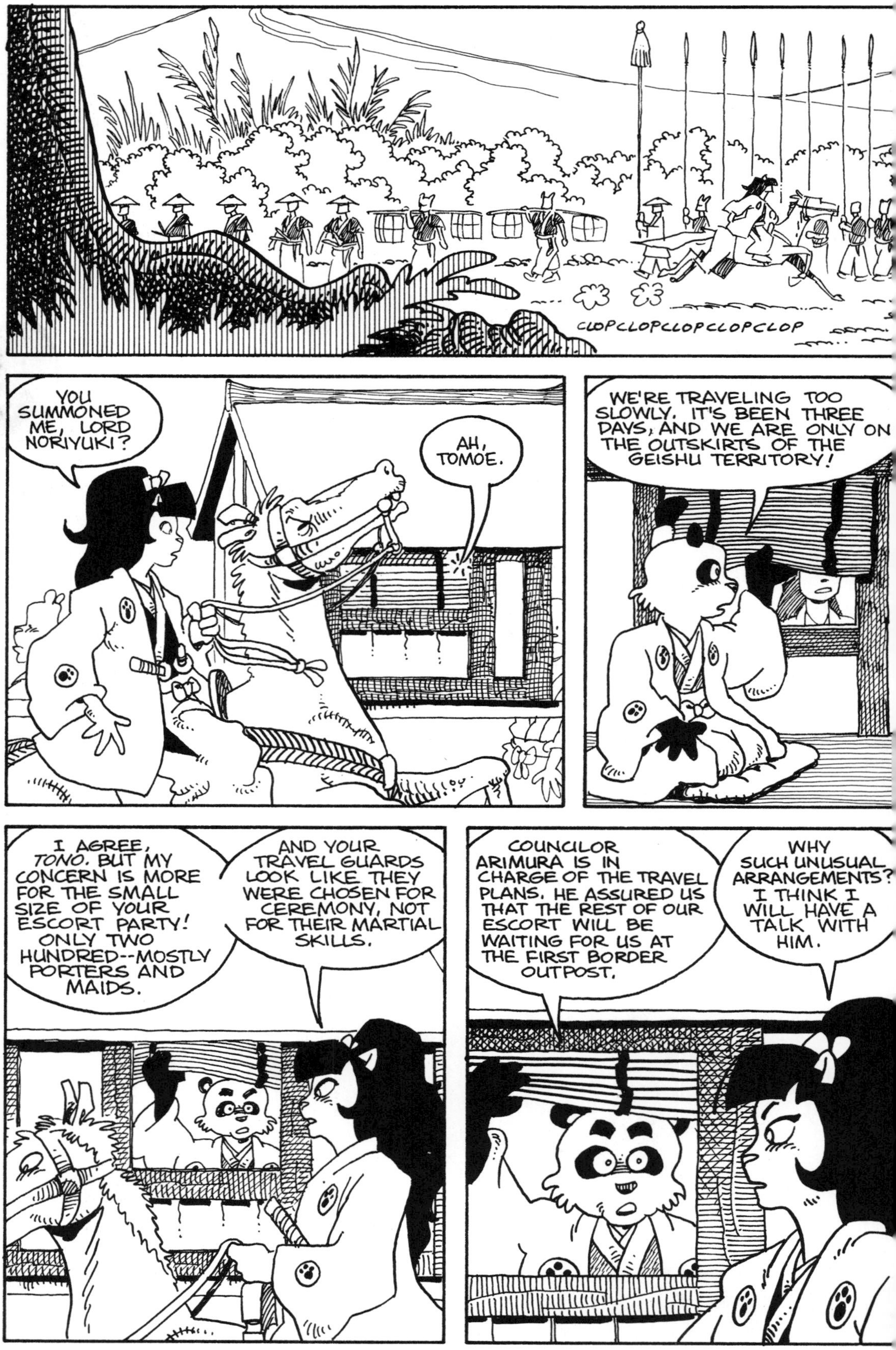
CLOPCLOPCLOPCLOPCLOP
YOU SUMMONED ME, LORD NORIYUKI?
AH, TOMOE.
WE'RE TRAVELING TOO SLOWLY. IT'S BEEN THREE DAYS, AND WE ARE ONLY ON THE OUTSKIRTS OF THE GEISHU TERRITORY!
I AGREE, *TONO*. BUT MY CONCERN IS MORE FOR THE SMALL SIZE OF YOUR ESCORT PARTY! ONLY TWO HUNDRED--MOSTLY PORTERS AND MAIDS.
AND YOUR TRAVEL GUARDS LOOK LIKE THEY WERE CHOSEN FOR CEREMONY, NOT FOR THEIR MARTIAL SKILLS.
COUNCILOR ARIMURA IS IN CHARGE OF THE TRAVEL PLANS. HE ASSURED US THAT THE REST OF OUR ESCORT WILL BE WAITING FOR US AT THE FIRST BORDER OUTPOST.
WHY SUCH UNUSUAL ARRANGEMENTS? I THINK I WILL HAVE A TALK WITH HIM.

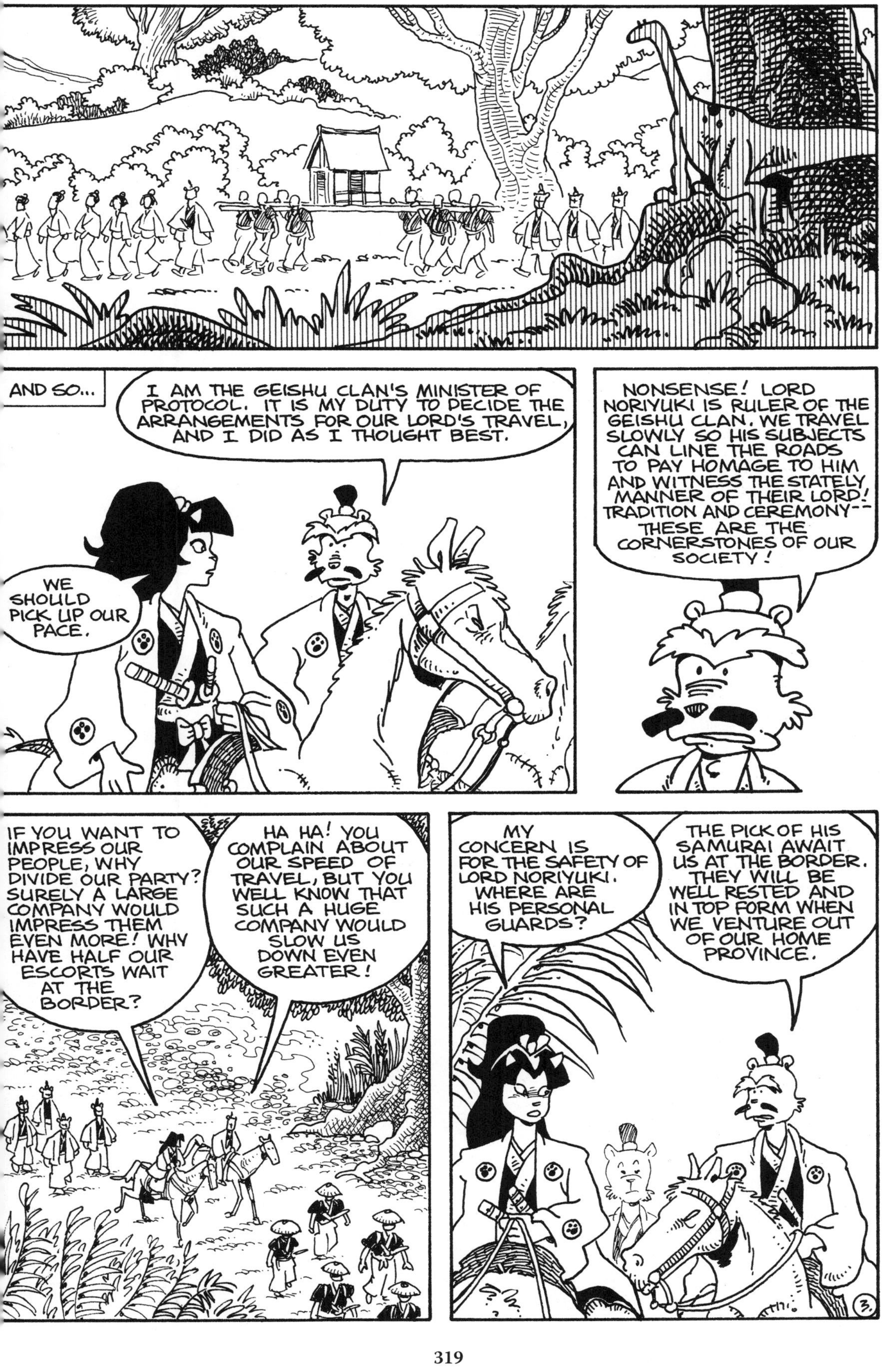
AND SO...
I AM THE GEISHU CLAN'S MINISTER OF PROTOCOL. IT IS MY DUTY TO DECIDE THE ARRANGEMENTS FOR OUR LORD'S TRAVEL, AND I DID AS I THOUGHT BEST.
WE SHOULD PICK UP OUR PACE.
NONSENSE! LORD NORIYUKI IS RULER OF THE GEISHU CLAN. WE TRAVEL SLOWLY SO HIS SUBJECTS CAN LINE THE ROADS TO PAY HOMAGE TO HIM AND WITNESS THE STATELY MANNER OF THEIR LORD! TRADITION AND CEREMONY-- THESE ARE THE CORNERSTONES OF OUR SOCIETY!
IF YOU WANT TO IMPRESS OUR PEOPLE, WHY DIVIDE OUR PARTY? SURELY A LARGE COMPANY WOULD IMPRESS THEM EVEN MORE! WHY HAVE HALF OUR ESCORTS WAIT AT THE BORDER?
HA HA! YOU COMPLAIN ABOUT OUR SPEED OF TRAVEL, BUT YOU WELL KNOW THAT SUCH A HUGE COMPANY WOULD SLOW US DOWN EVEN GREATER!
MY CONCERN IS FOR THE SAFETY OF LORD NORIYUKI. WHERE ARE HIS PERSONAL GUARDS?
THE PICK OF HIS SAMURAI AWAIT US AT THE BORDER. THEY WILL BE WELL RESTED AND IN TOP FORM WHEN WE VENTURE OUT OF OUR HOME PROVINCE.
3.

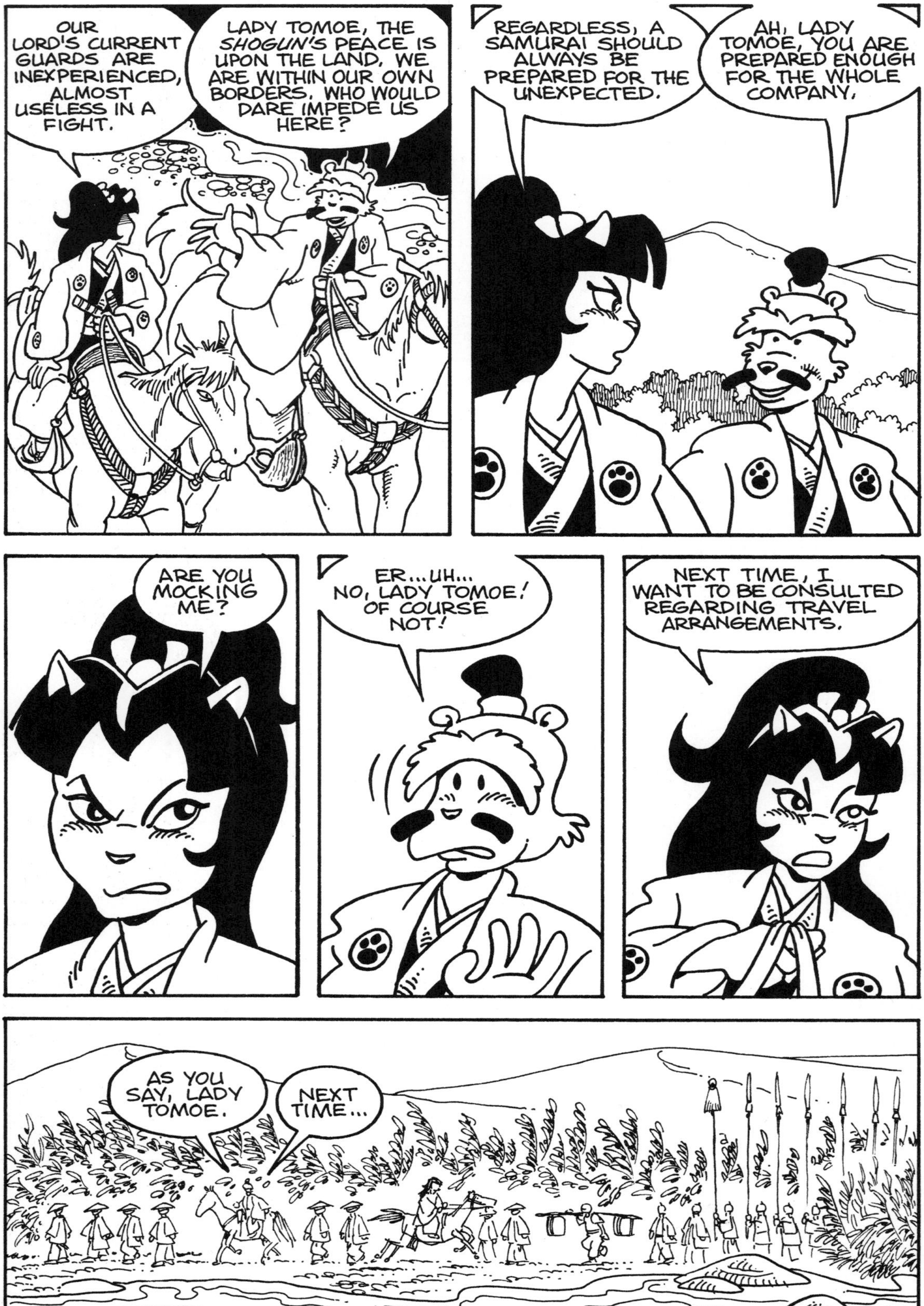
OUR LORD'S CURRENT GUARDS ARE INEXPERIENCED, ALMOST USELESS IN A FIGHT.
LADY TOMOE, THE *SHOGUN'S* PEACE IS UPON THE LAND. WE ARE WITHIN OUR OWN BORDERS. WHO WOULD DARE IMPEDE US HERE?
REGARDLESS, A SAMURAI SHOULD ALWAYS BE PREPARED FOR THE UNEXPECTED.
AH, LADY TOMOE, YOU ARE PREPARED ENOUGH FOR THE WHOLE COMPANY.
ARE YOU MOCKING ME?
ER...UH... NO, LADY TOMOE! OF COURSE NOT!
NEXT TIME, I WANT TO BE CONSULTED REGARDING TRAVEL ARRANGEMENTS.
AS YOU SAY, LADY TOMOE.
NEXT TIME...
4.

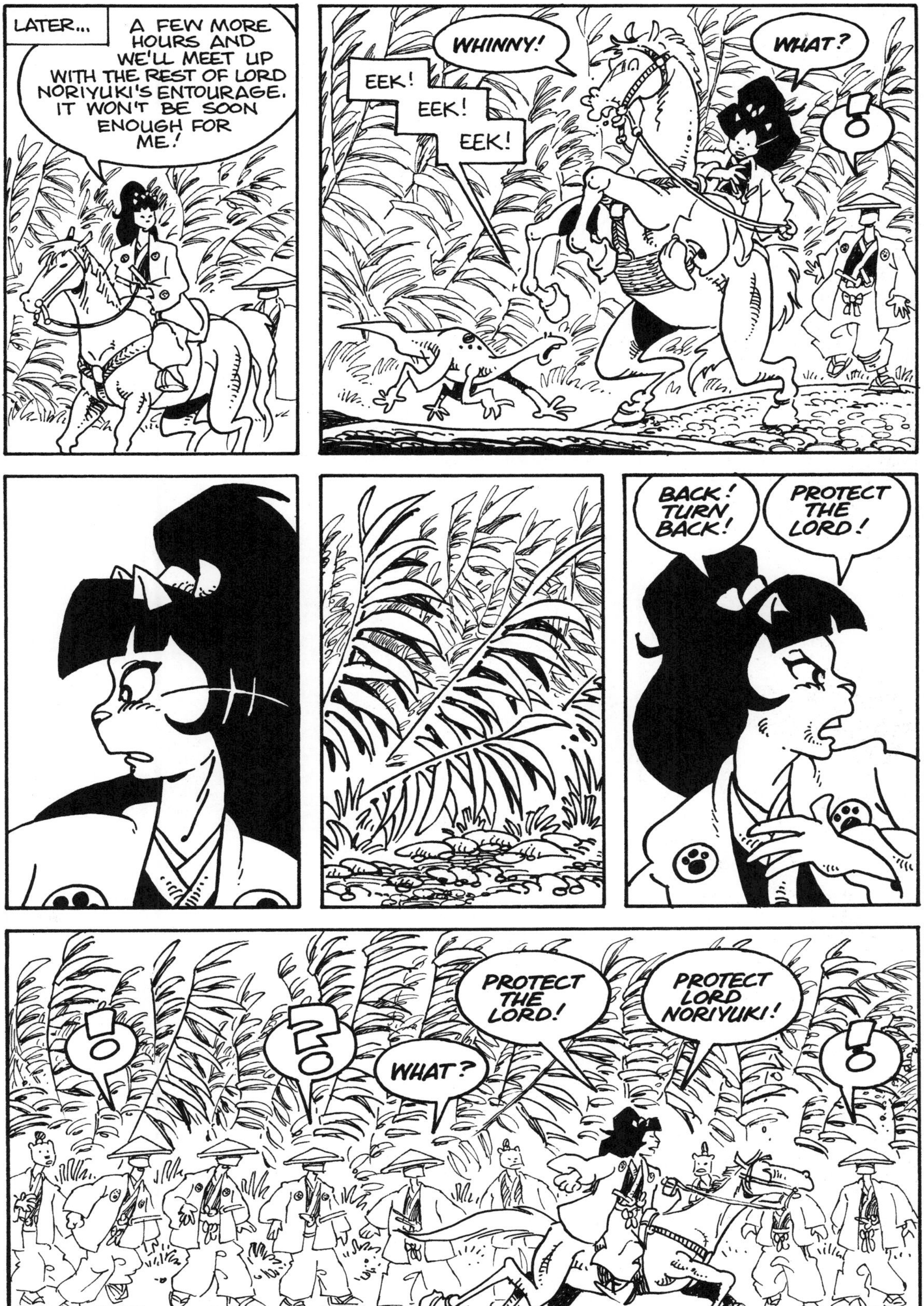
LATER...
A FEW MORE HOURS AND WE'LL MEET UP WITH THE REST OF LORD NORIYUKI'S ENTOURAGE. IT WON'T BE SOON ENOUGH FOR ME!
EEK! EEK! EEK!
WHINNY!
WHAT?
BACK! TURN BACK!
PROTECT THE LORD!
WHAT?
PROTECT THE LORD!
PROTECT LORD NORIYUKI!

WHAT IS LADY TOMOE TALKING ABOUT?

NO DOUBT THE SUN'S GOTTEN TO HER.

IT SERVES HER RIGHT! SHE SHOULD WEAR A HAT LIKE WE--*UH!*

SHONK!

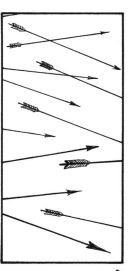

ASSASSINS IN THE RUSHES! ASSASSINS IN THE RUSHES!

HIIIYAAHHHHHHHHHH

6.

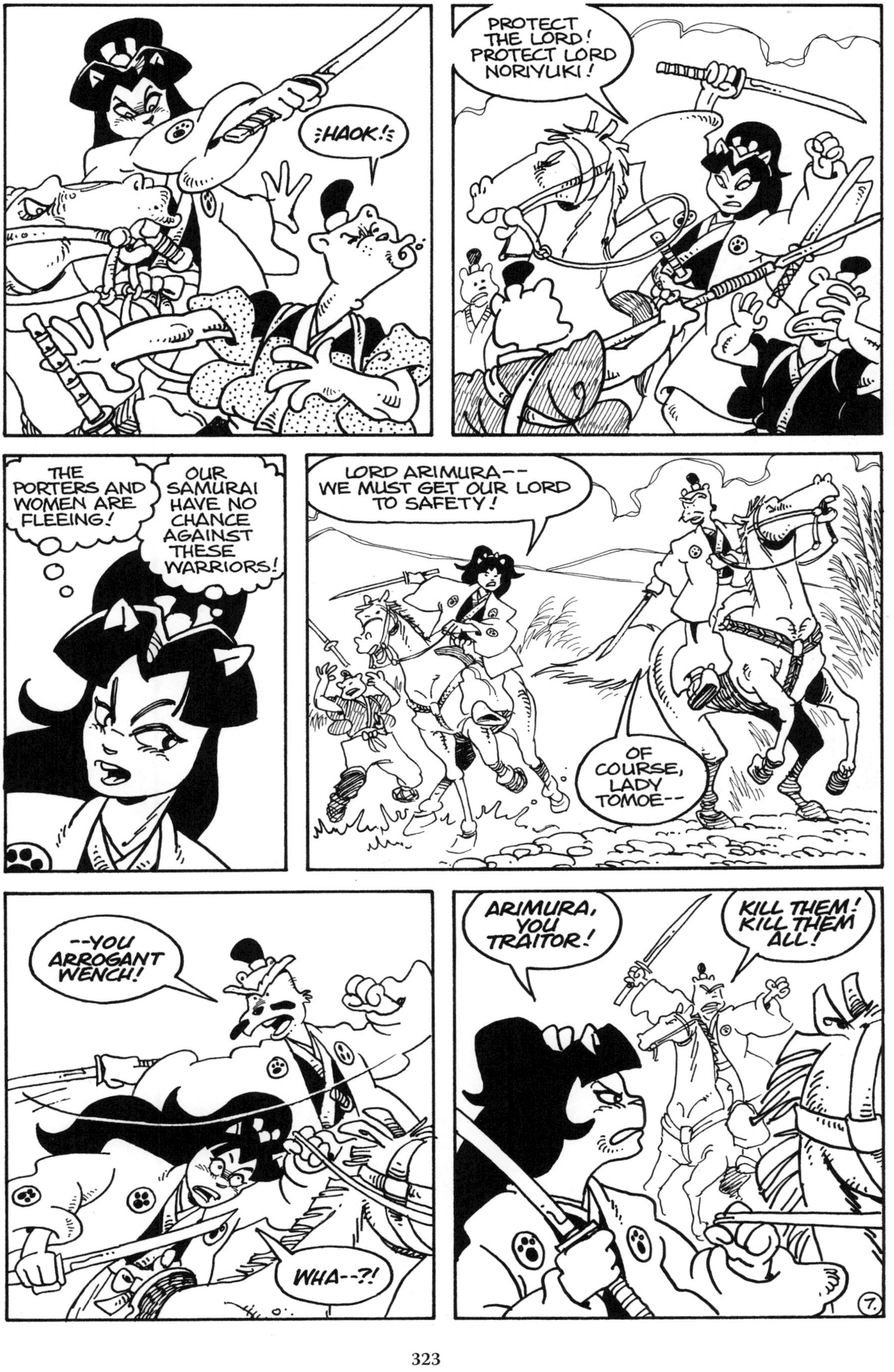
HAOK!
PROTECT THE LORD! PROTECT LORD NORIYUKI!
THE PORTERS AND WOMEN ARE FLEEING!
OUR SAMURAI HAVE NO CHANCE AGAINST THESE WARRIORS!
LORD ARIMURA-- WE MUST GET OUR LORD TO SAFETY!
OF COURSE, LADY TOMOE--
--YOU ARROGANT WENCH!
WHA--?!
ARIMURA, YOU TRAITOR!
KILL THEM! KILL THEM ALL!
7.

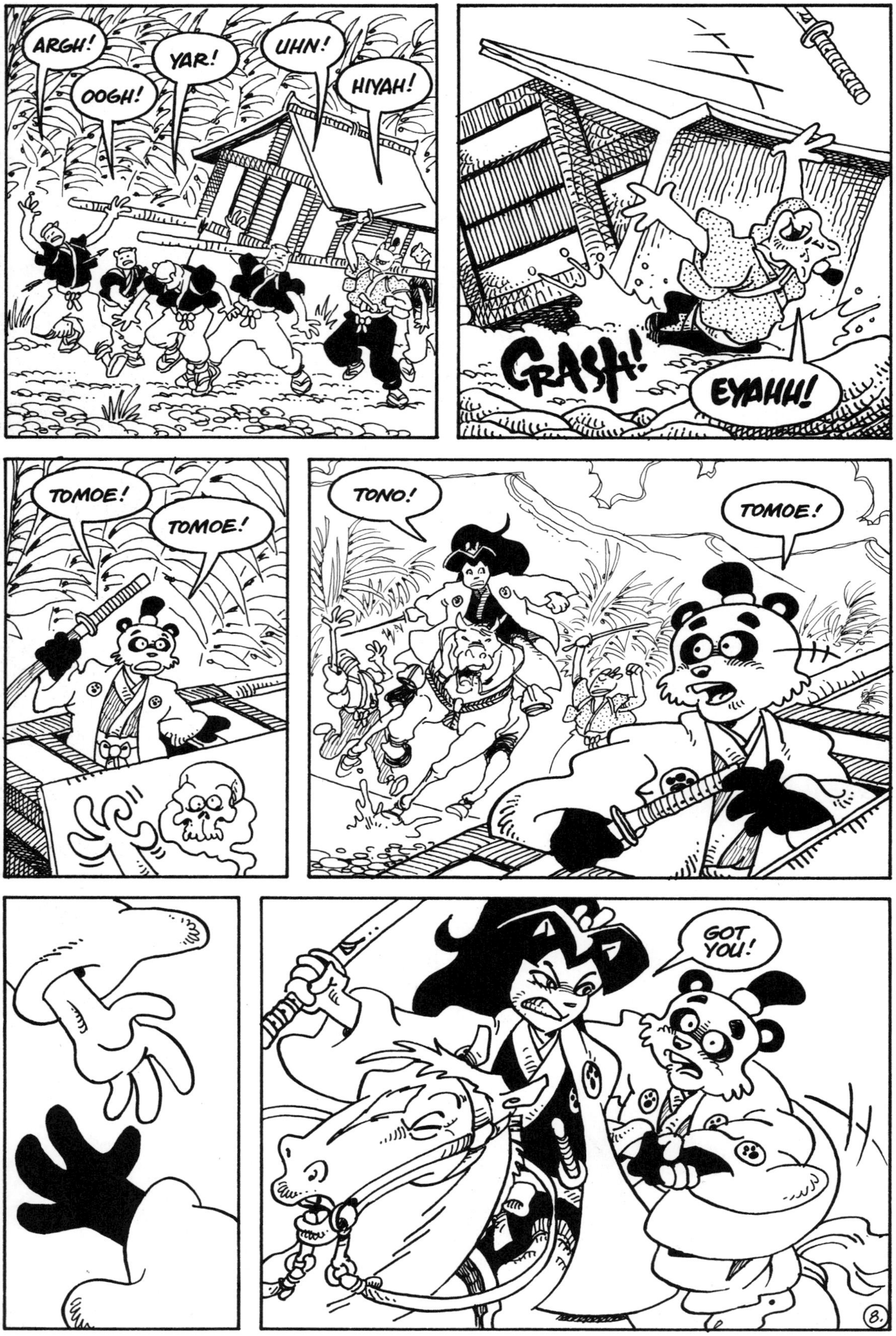
ARGH!
OOGH!
YAR!
UHN!
HIYAH!
CRASH!
EYAHH!
TOMOE!
TOMOE!
TONO!
TOMOE!
GOT YOU!
8.

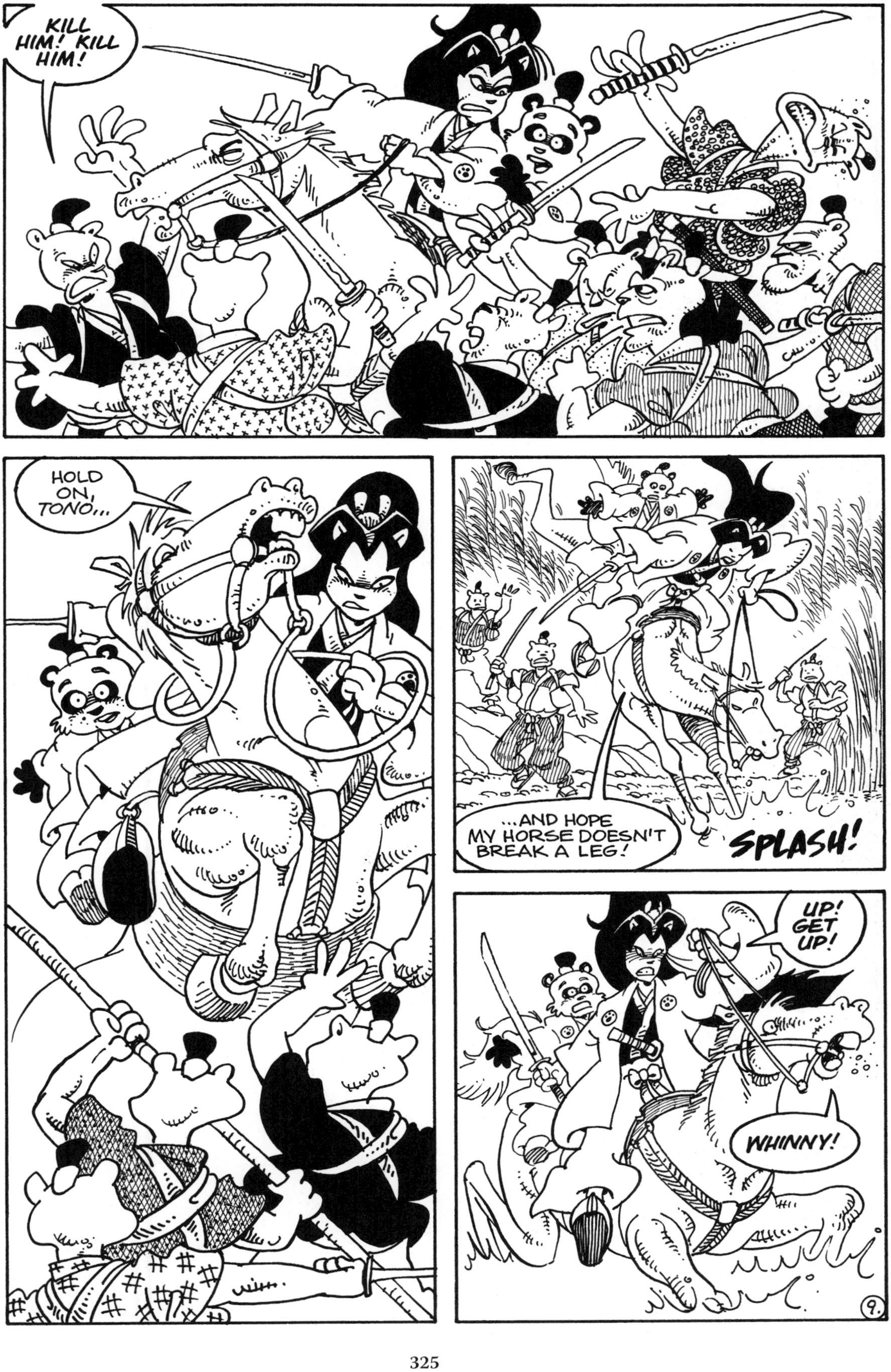
KILL HIM! KILL HIM!
HOLD ON, TONO...
...AND HOPE MY HORSE DOESN'T BREAK A LEG!
SPLASH!
UP! GET UP!
WHINNY!
9.

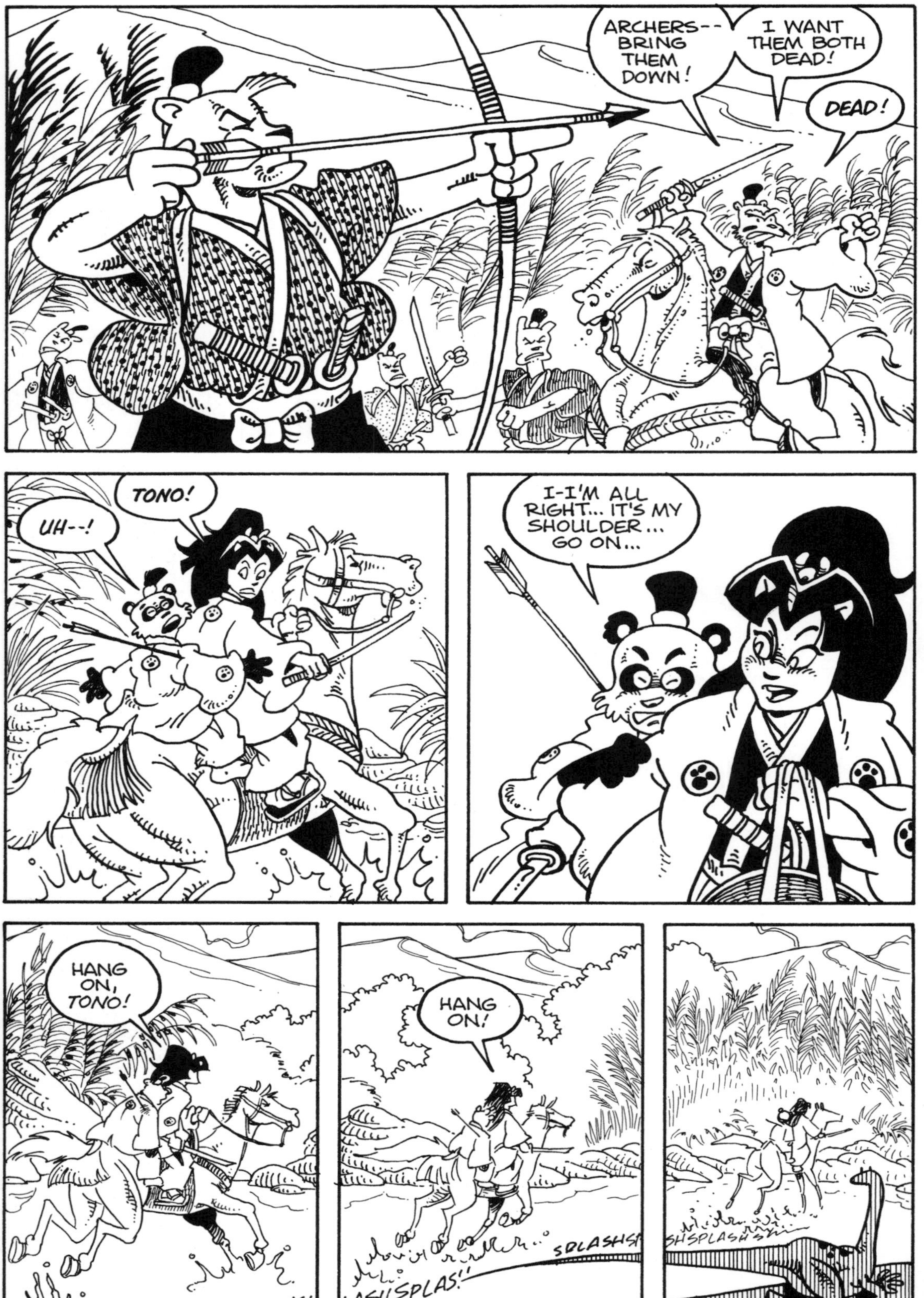
ARCHERS-- BRING THEM DOWN!
I WANT THEM BOTH DEAD!
DEAD!
UH--!
TONO!
I-I'M ALL RIGHT... IT'S MY SHOULDER... GO ON...
HANG ON, TONO!
SHSPLASHSPLASHSPLASHSPLASH
HANG ON!
SPLASHSPLASHSPLAS!
SHSPLASHSPLASHSH
10.

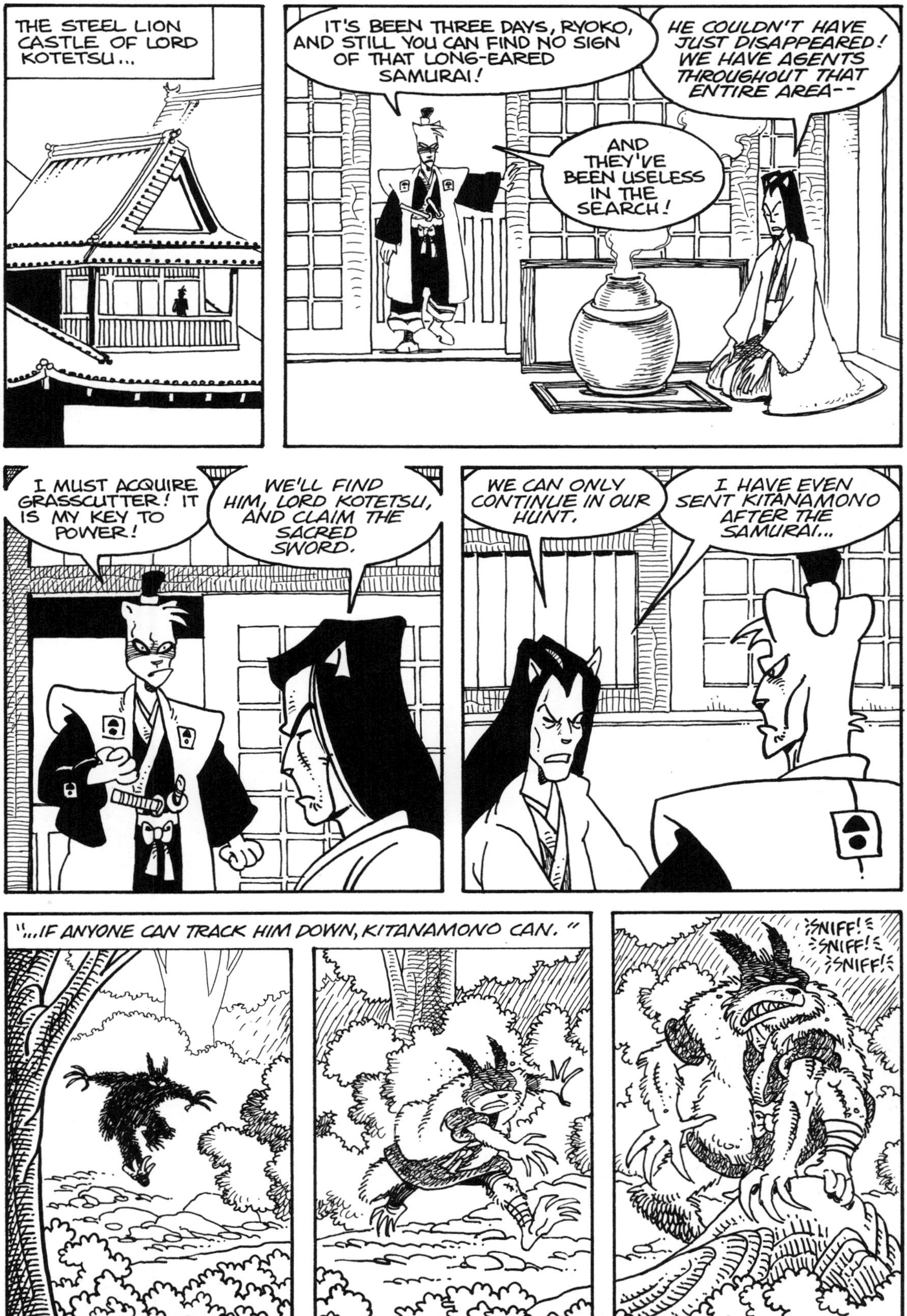
THE STEEL LION CASTLE OF LORD KOTETSU...
IT'S BEEN THREE DAYS, RYOKO, AND STILL YOU CAN FIND NO SIGN OF THAT LONG-EARED SAMURAI!
HE COULDN'T HAVE JUST DISAPPEARED! WE HAVE AGENTS THROUGHOUT THAT ENTIRE AREA--
AND THEY'VE BEEN USELESS IN THE SEARCH!
I MUST ACQUIRE GRASSCUTTER! IT IS MY KEY TO POWER!
WE'LL FIND HIM, LORD KOTETSU, AND CLAIM THE SACRED SWORD.
WE CAN ONLY CONTINUE IN OUR HUNT.
I HAVE EVEN SENT KITANAMONO AFTER THE SAMURAI...
"...IF ANYONE CAN TRACK HIM DOWN, KITANAMONO CAN."
SNIFF! SNIFF! SNIFF!
11.

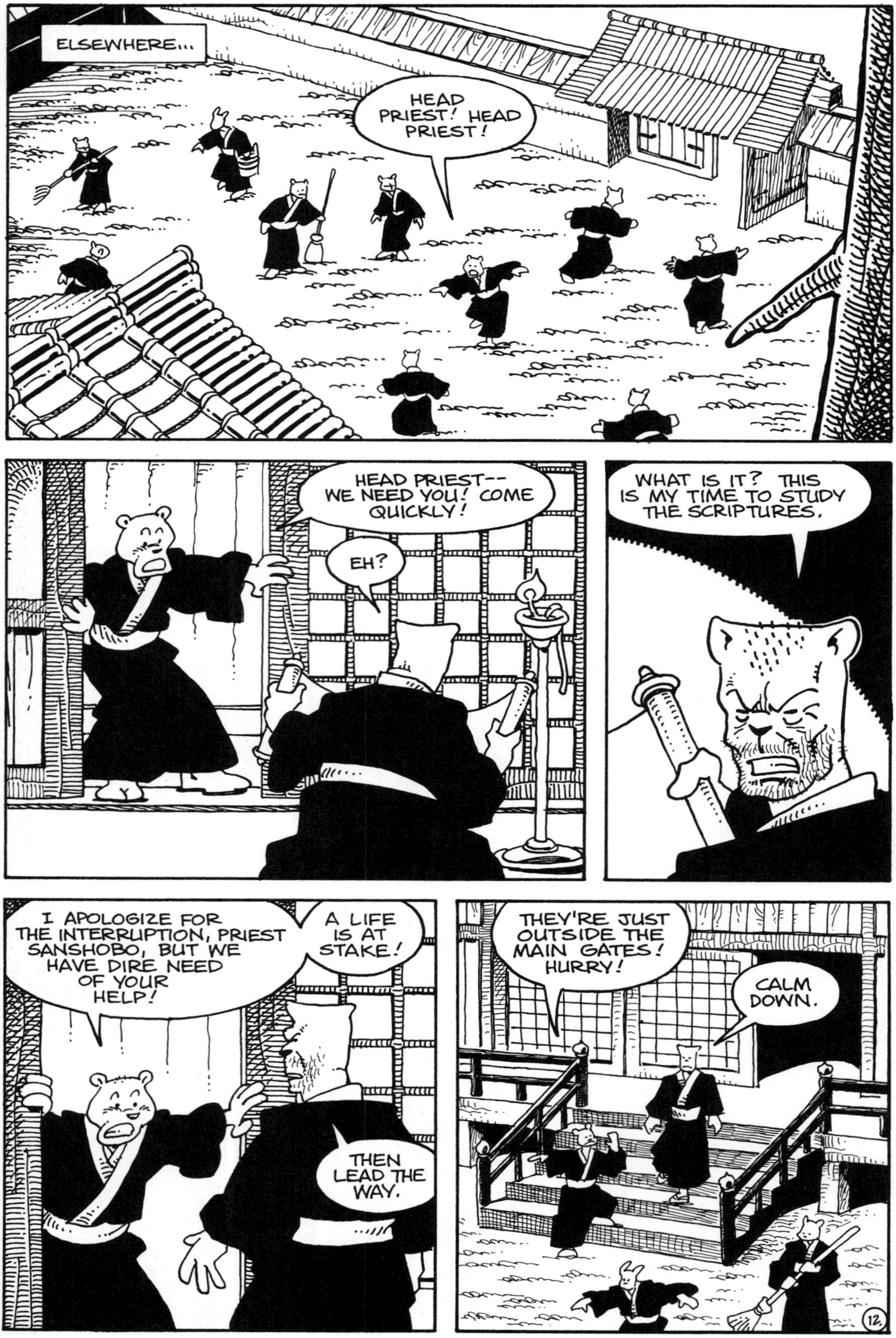
ELSEWHERE...
HEAD PRIEST! HEAD PRIEST!
HEAD PRIEST-- WE NEED YOU! COME QUICKLY!
EH?
WHAT IS IT? THIS IS MY TIME TO STUDY THE SCRIPTURES.
I APOLOGIZE FOR THE INTERRUPTION, PRIEST SANSHOBO, BUT WE HAVE DIRE NEED OF YOUR HELP!
A LIFE IS AT STAKE!
THEN LEAD THE WAY.
THEY'RE JUST OUTSIDE THE MAIN GATES! HURRY!
CALM DOWN.
12

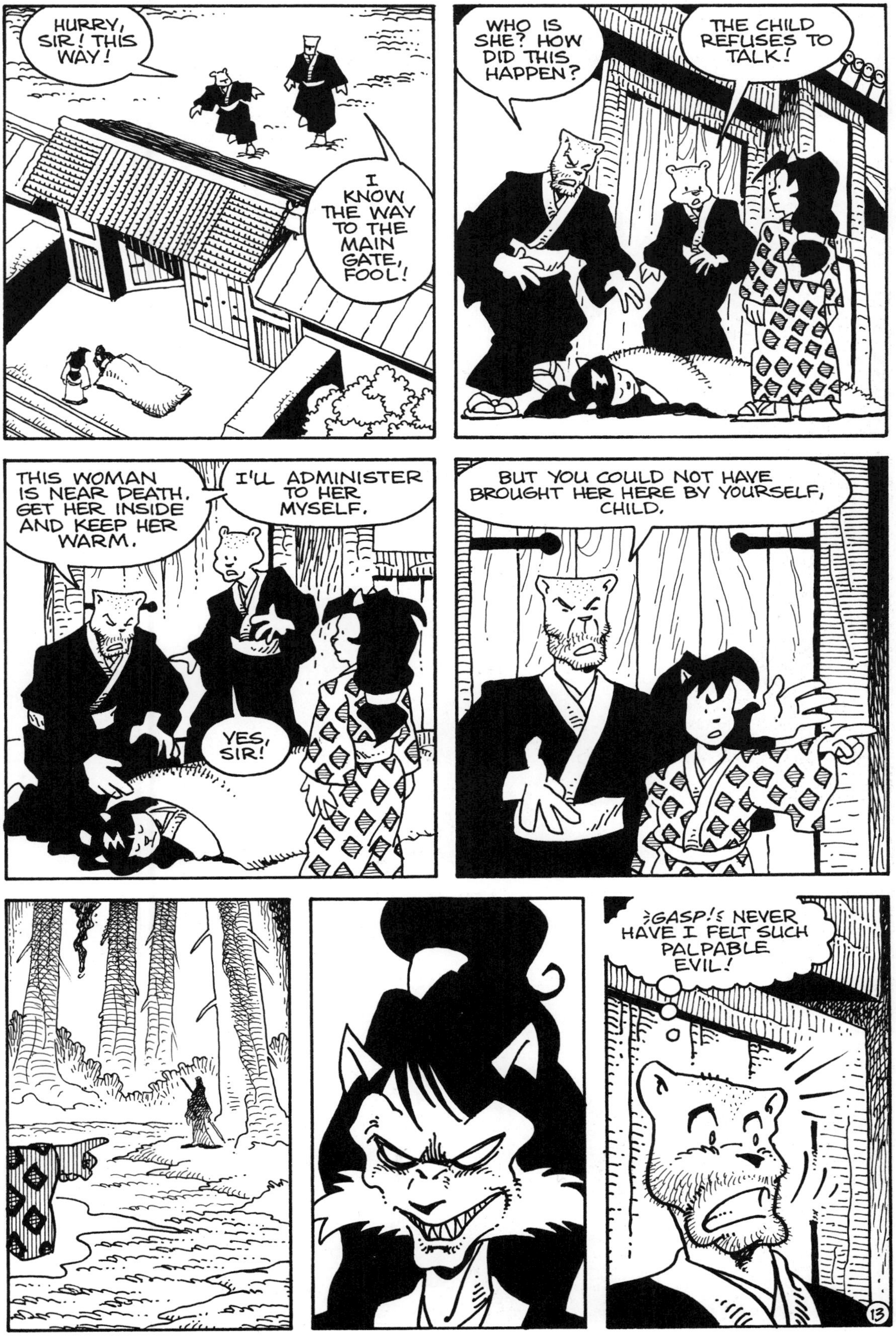
HURRY, SIR! THIS WAY!
I KNOW THE WAY TO THE MAIN GATE, FOOL!
WHO IS SHE? HOW DID THIS HAPPEN?
THE CHILD REFUSES TO TALK!
THIS WOMAN IS NEAR DEATH. GET HER INSIDE AND KEEP HER WARM.
I'LL ADMINISTER TO HER MYSELF.
YES, SIR!
BUT YOU COULD NOT HAVE BROUGHT HER HERE BY YOURSELF, CHILD.
GASP! NEVER HAVE I FELT SUCH PALPABLE EVIL!
13

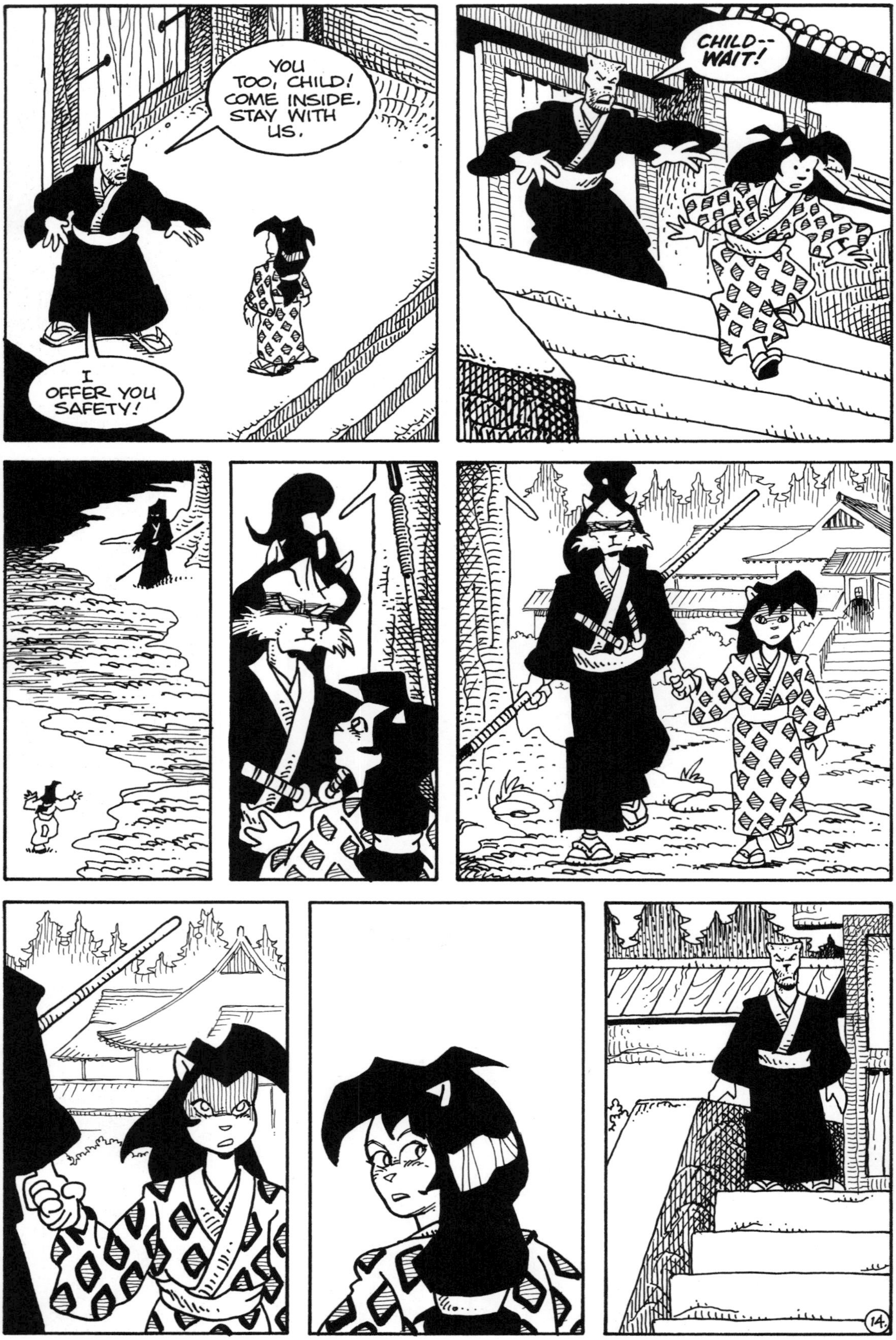
YOU TOO, CHILD! COME INSIDE, STAY WITH US.
I OFFER YOU SAFETY!
CHILD-- WAIT!
14.

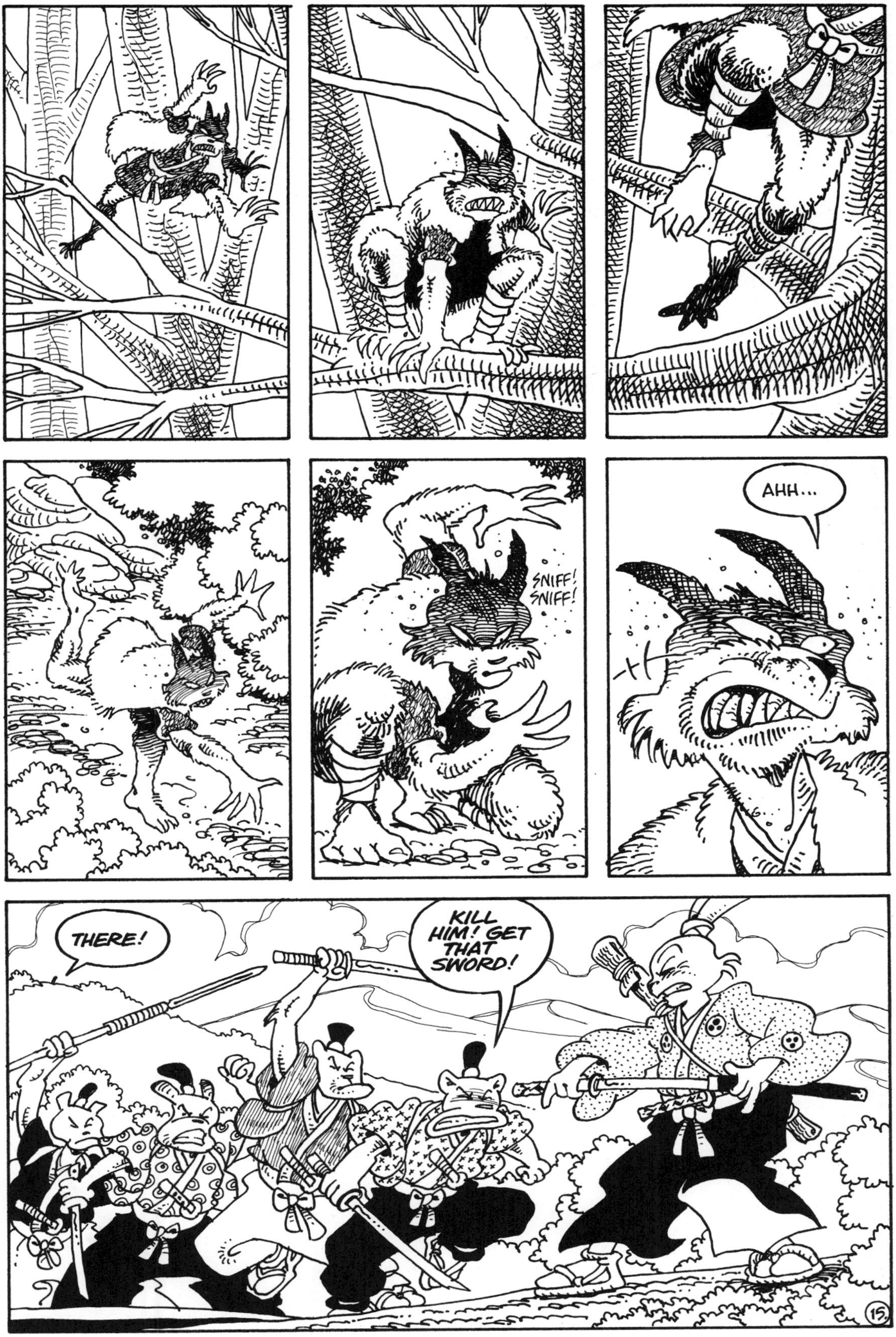
SNIFF! SNIFF!
AHH...
THERE!
KILL HIM! GET THAT SWORD!
15

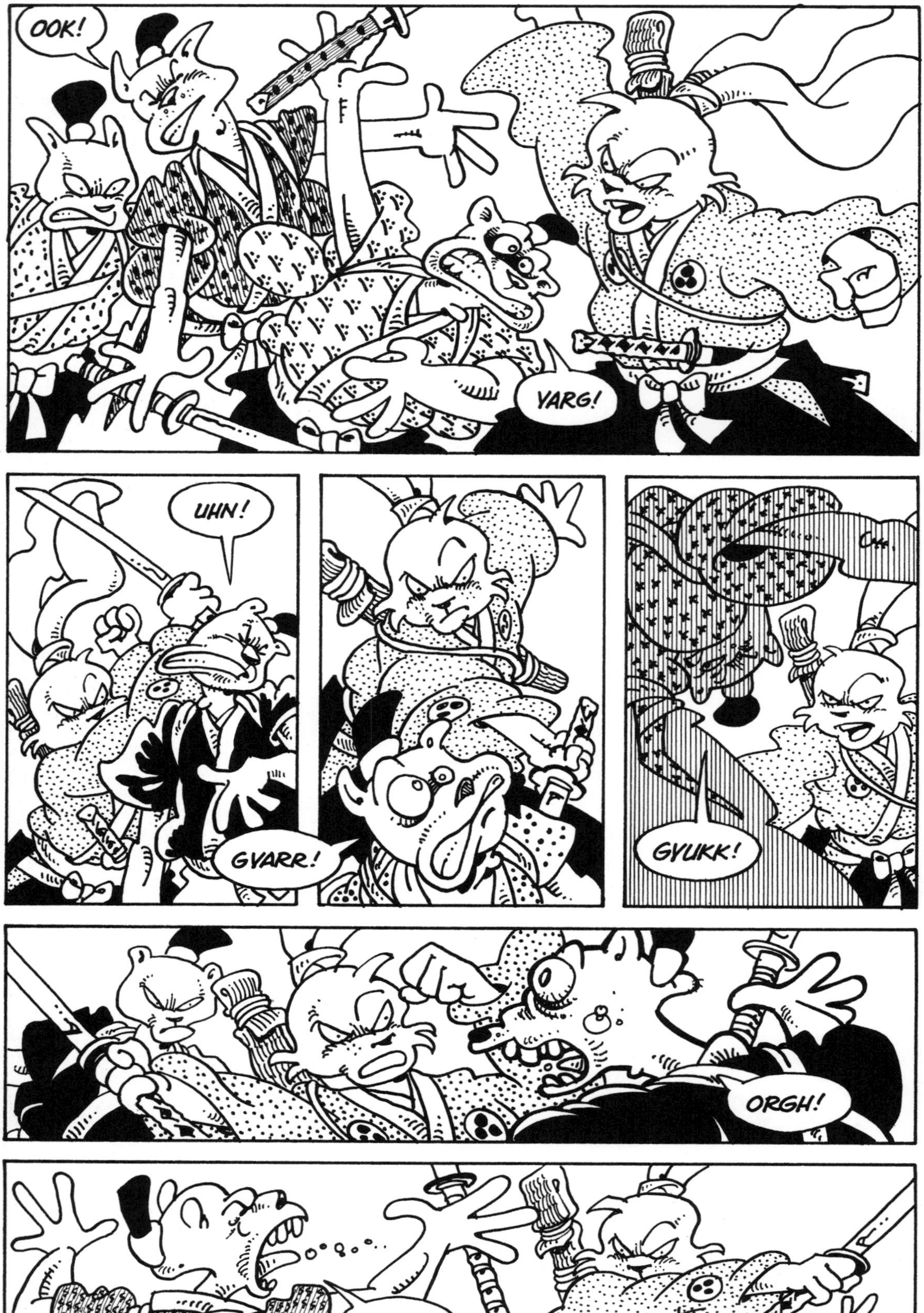
OOK!
YARG!
UHN!
GVARR!
GYUKK!
ORGH!
HYAK!
16.

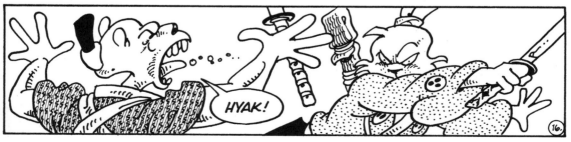

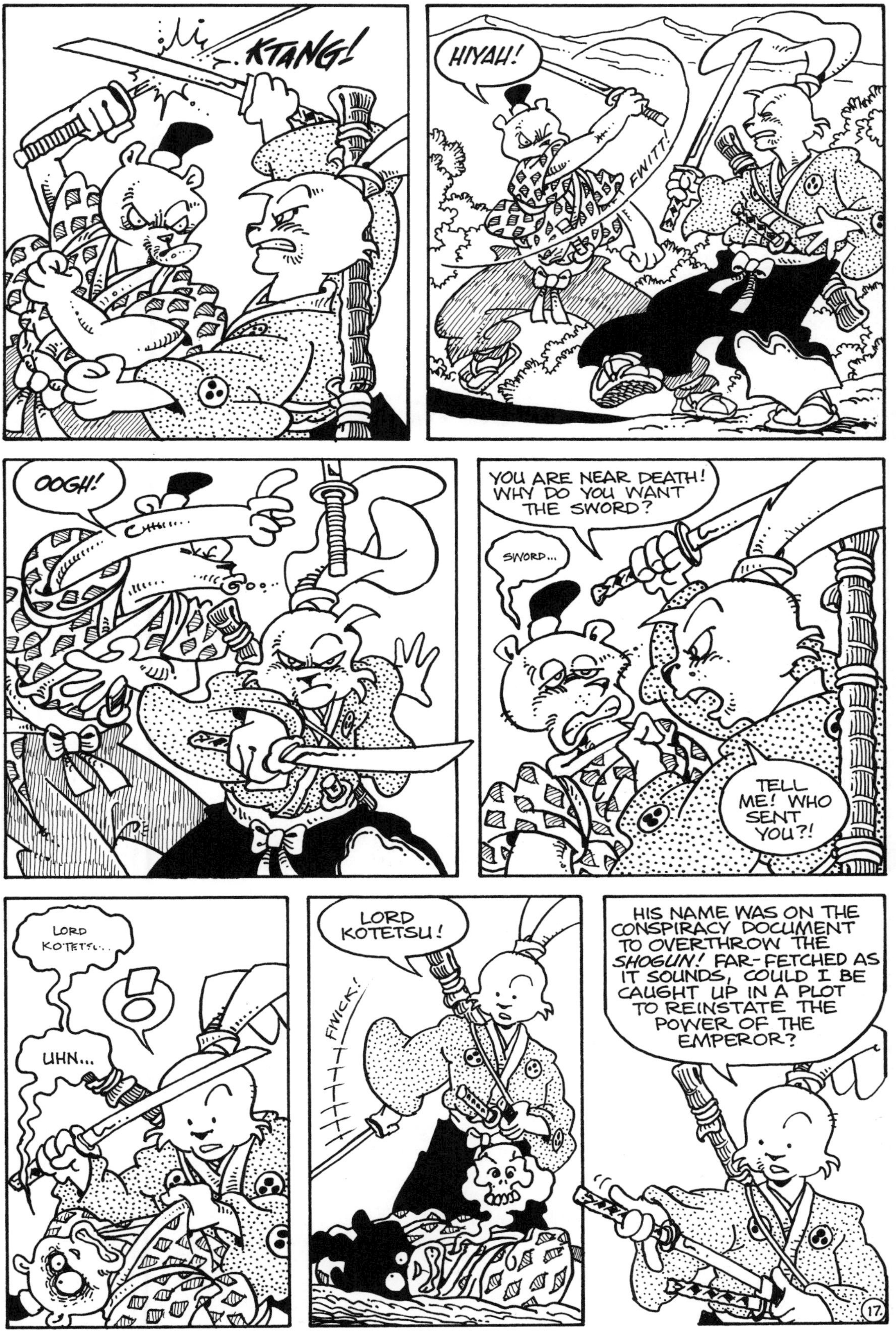
KTANG!
HIYAH!
FWITT!
OOGH!
YOU ARE NEAR DEATH! WHY DO YOU WANT THE SWORD?
SWORD...
TELL ME! WHO SENT YOU?!
LORD KOTETSU...
UHN...
LORD KOTETSU!
FWICK!
HIS NAME WAS ON THE CONSPIRACY DOCUMENT TO OVERTHROW THE SHOGUN! FAR-FETCHED AS IT SOUNDS, COULD I BE CAUGHT UP IN A PLOT TO REINSTATE THE POWER OF THE EMPEROR?
17

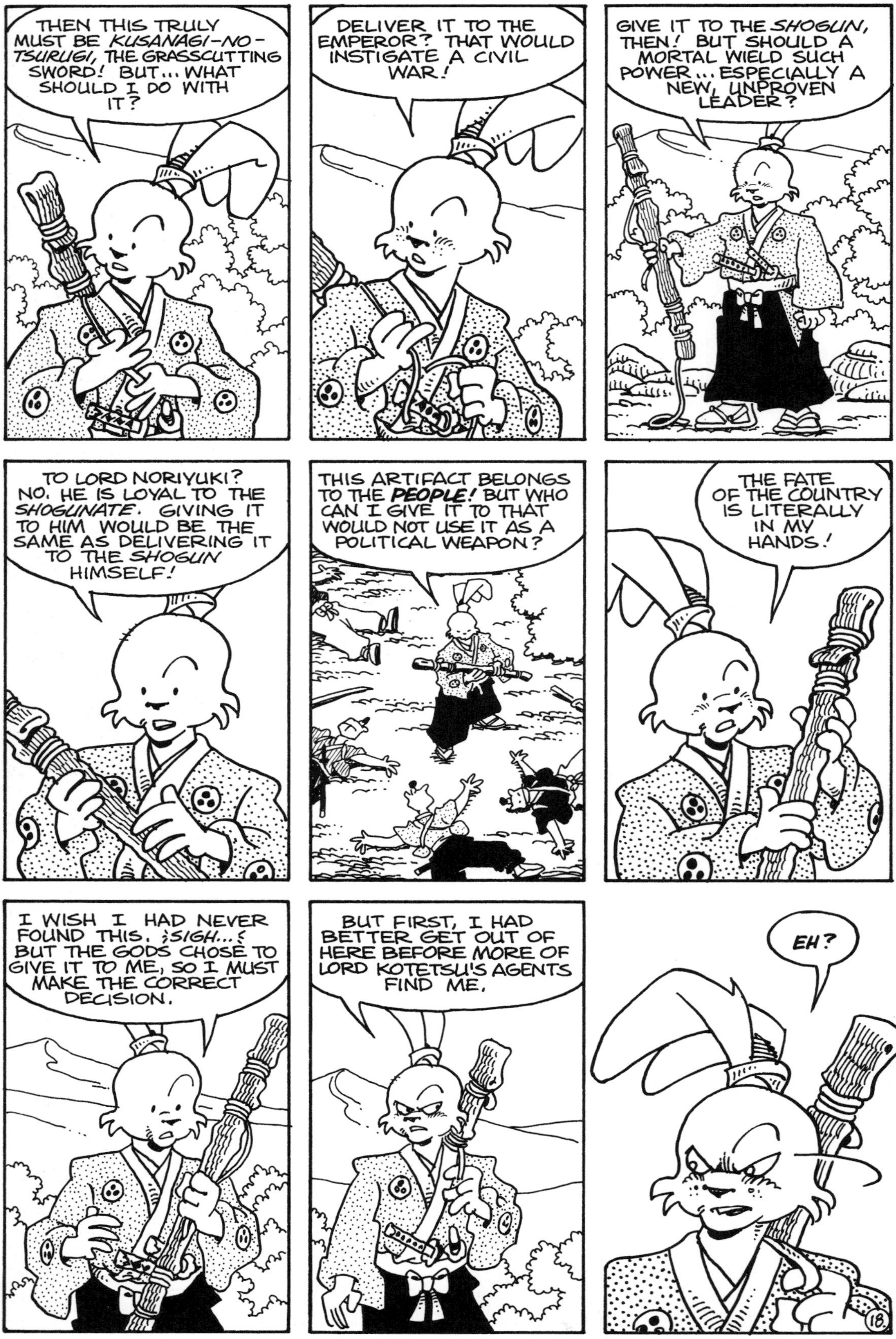
THEN THIS TRULY MUST BE KUSANAGI-NO-TSURUGI, THE GRASSCUTTING SWORD! BUT... WHAT SHOULD I DO WITH IT?
DELIVER IT TO THE EMPEROR? THAT WOULD INSTIGATE A CIVIL WAR!
GIVE IT TO THE SHOGUN, THEN! BUT SHOULD A MORTAL WIELD SUCH POWER... ESPECIALLY A NEW, UNPROVEN LEADER?
TO LORD NORIYUKI? NO. HE IS LOYAL TO THE SHOGUNATE. GIVING IT TO HIM WOULD BE THE SAME AS DELIVERING IT TO THE SHOGUN HIMSELF!
THIS ARTIFACT BELONGS TO THE PEOPLE! BUT WHO CAN I GIVE IT TO THAT WOULD NOT USE IT AS A POLITICAL WEAPON?
THE FATE OF THE COUNTRY IS LITERALLY IN MY HANDS!
I WISH I HAD NEVER FOUND THIS. ;SIGH...; BUT THE GODS CHOSE TO GIVE IT TO ME, SO I MUST MAKE THE CORRECT DECISION.
BUT FIRST, I HAD BETTER GET OUT OF HERE BEFORE MORE OF LORD KOTETSU'S AGENTS FIND ME.
EH?
18

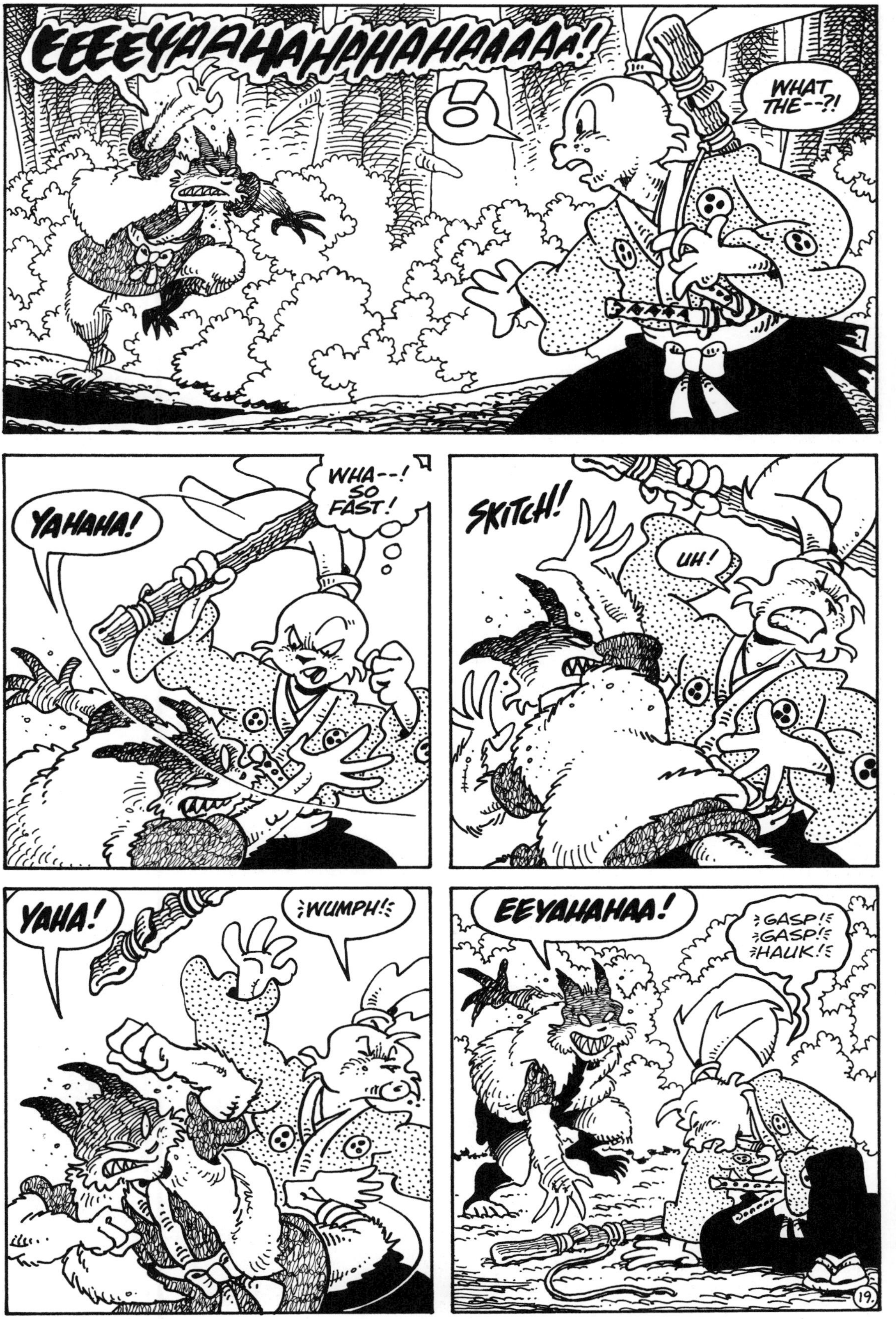
EEEEYAAHAHAHAHAAAAA!
!
WHAT THE--?!
YAHAHA!
WHA--! SO FAST!
SKITCH!
UH!
YAHA!
WUMPH!
EEYAHAHAA!
GASP! GASP! HAUK!
19.

WHOEVER--OR **WHAT**EVER--HE IS, HE'S GETTING AWAY WITH THE SWORD!

EEEYAHAAHAHA!

A MINUTE AGO I WISHED I HAD NEVER LAID EYES ON THAT SWORD...

...BUT NOW...

...I'VE GOT TO GET IT BACK!

SUCCESS! KITANAMONO HAS THE SWORD! HE WILL DELIVER IT HERE DIRECTLY.

ARE YOU SURE? HOW CAN YOU BE SO CONFIDENT?

KITANAMONO IS MY FAMILIAR. HE IS PART OF ME, JUST AS I AM A PART OF HIM. HE WOULD NOT FAIL ME... NO MORE THAN I WOULD FAIL YOU, LORD KOTETSU.

20.

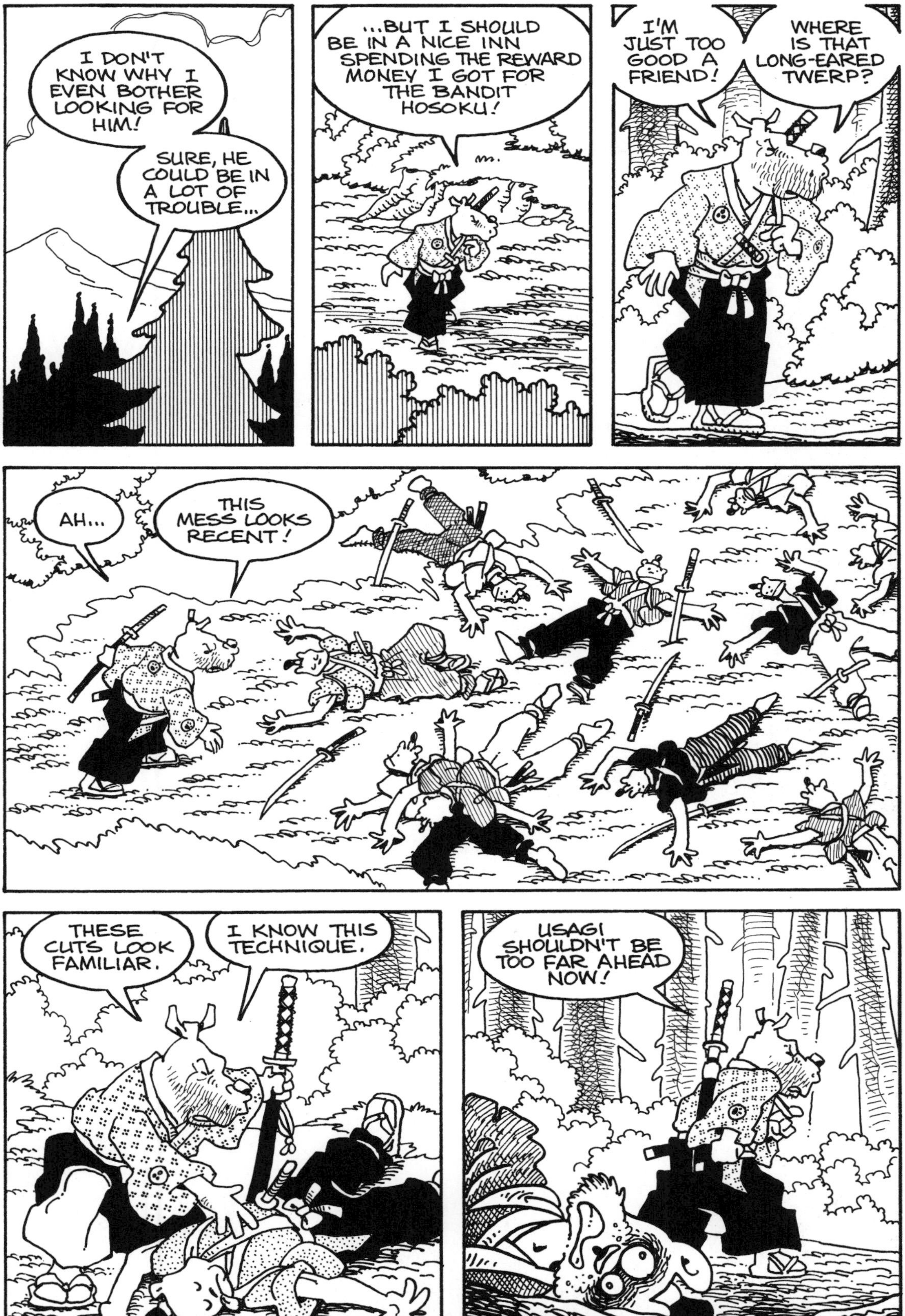
I DON'T KNOW WHY I EVEN BOTHER LOOKING FOR HIM!
SURE, HE COULD BE IN A LOT OF TROUBLE...
...BUT I SHOULD BE IN A NICE INN SPENDING THE REWARD MONEY I GOT FOR THE BANDIT HOSOKU!
I'M JUST TOO GOOD A FRIEND!
WHERE IS THAT LONG-EARED TWERP?
AH...
THIS MESS LOOKS RECENT!
THESE CUTS LOOK FAMILIAR.
I KNOW THIS TECHNIQUE.
USAGI SHOULDN'T BE TOO FAR AHEAD NOW!
21.

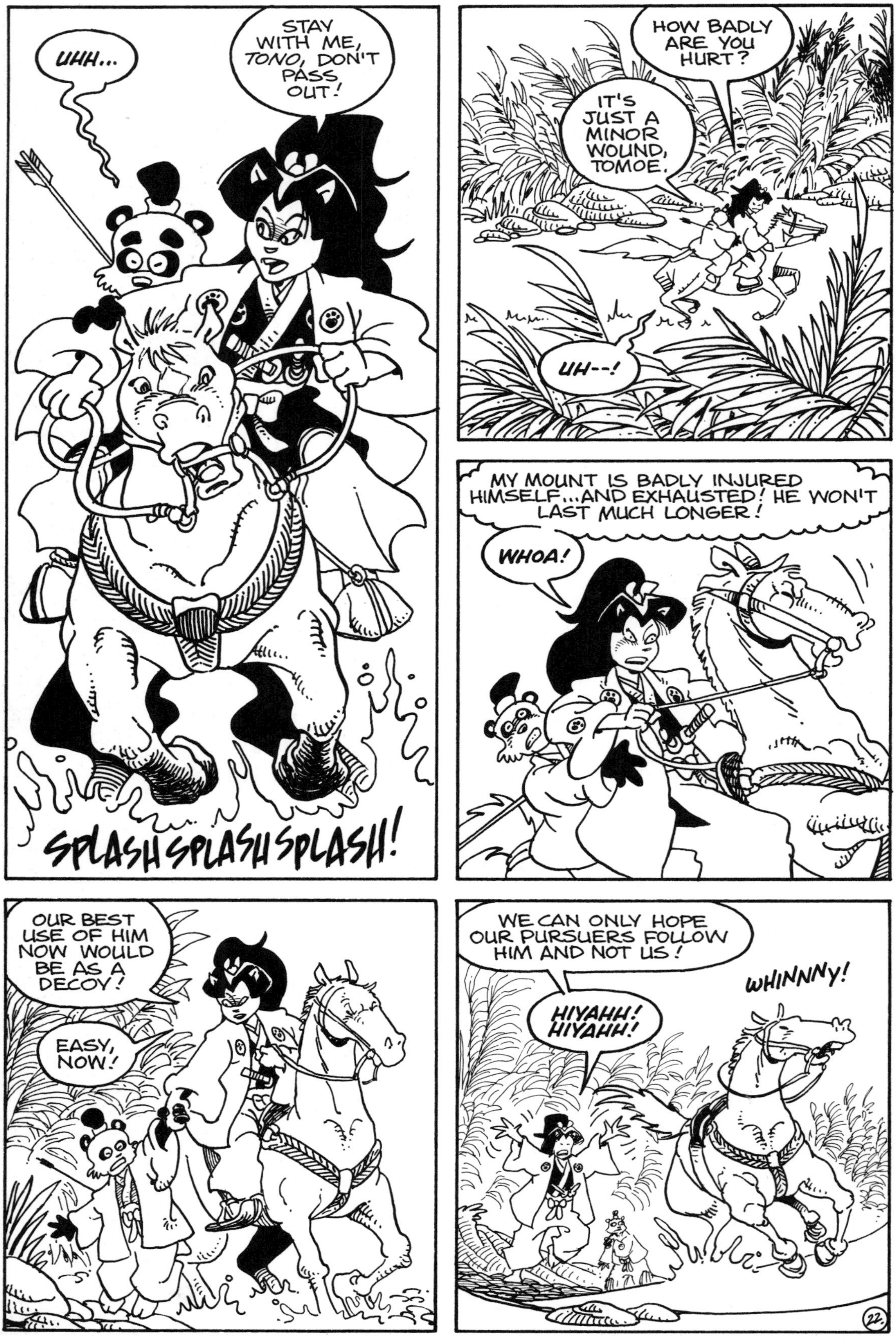
UHH...
STAY WITH ME, TONO, DON'T PASS OUT!
SPLASH SPLASH SPLASH!
HOW BADLY ARE YOU HURT?
IT'S JUST A MINOR WOUND, TOMOE.
UH--!
MY MOUNT IS BADLY INJURED HIMSELF...AND EXHAUSTED! HE WON'T LAST MUCH LONGER!
WHOA!
OUR BEST USE OF HIM NOW WOULD BE AS A DECOY!
EASY, NOW!
WE CAN ONLY HOPE OUR PURSUERS FOLLOW HIM AND NOT US!
HIYAHH! HIYAHH!
WHINNNY!
22.

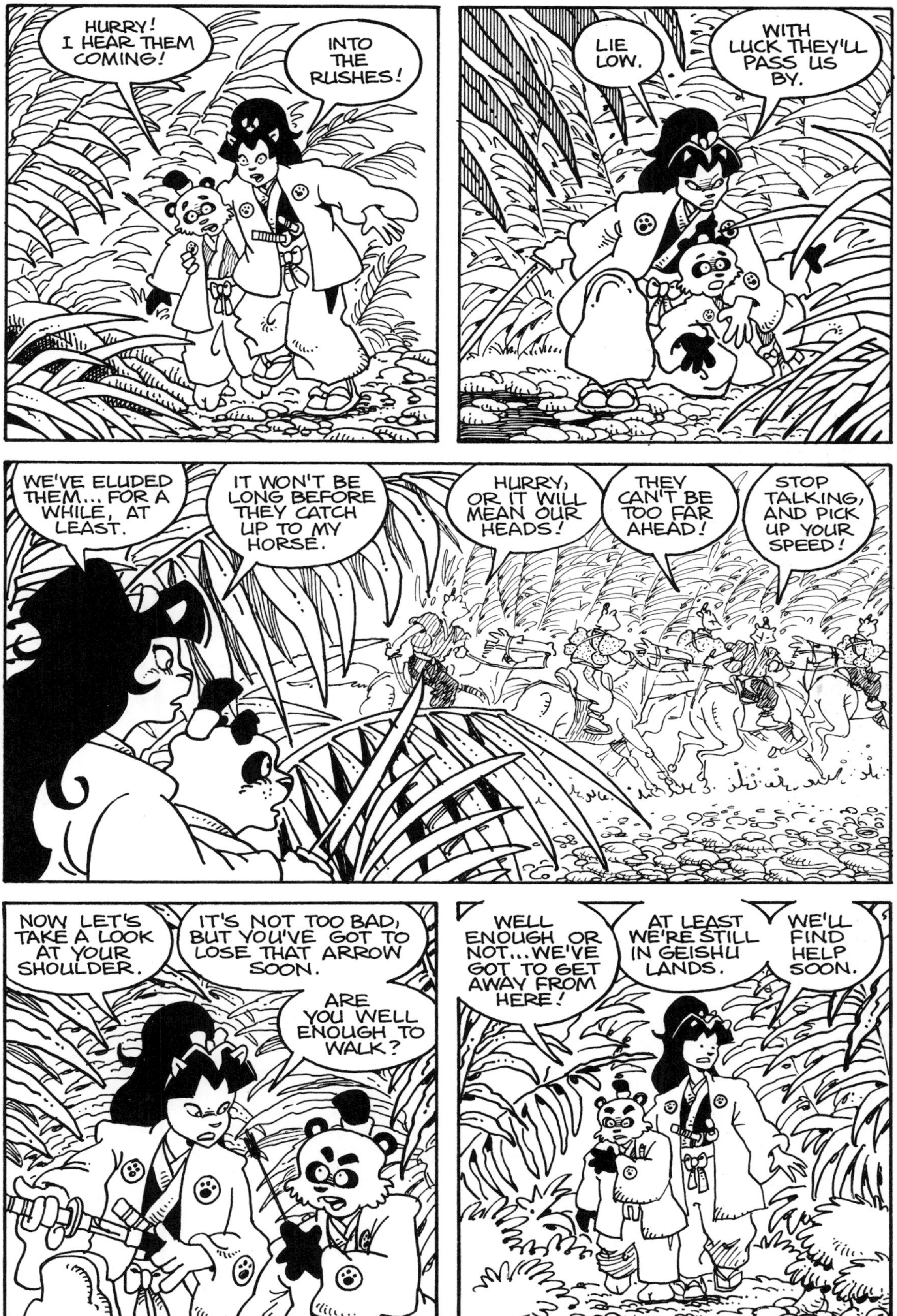
HURRY! I HEAR THEM COMING!
INTO THE RUSHES!
LIE LOW.
WITH LUCK THEY'LL PASS US BY.
WE'VE ELUDED THEM... FOR A WHILE, AT LEAST.
IT WON'T BE LONG BEFORE THEY CATCH UP TO MY HORSE.
HURRY, OR IT WILL MEAN OUR HEADS!
THEY CAN'T BE TOO FAR AHEAD!
STOP TALKING, AND PICK UP YOUR SPEED!
NOW LET'S TAKE A LOOK AT YOUR SHOULDER.
IT'S NOT TOO BAD, BUT YOU'VE GOT TO LOSE THAT ARROW SOON.
ARE YOU WELL ENOUGH TO WALK?
WELL ENOUGH OR NOT... WE'VE GOT TO GET AWAY FROM HERE!
AT LEAST WE'RE STILL IN GEISHU LANDS.
WE'LL FIND HELP SOON.
23

LATER...

TOMOE... I'VE GOT TO REST FOR A WHILE.

FORGIVE ME, *TONO,* I'VE BEEN INCONSIDERATE OF YOUR INJURY.

THERE'S A FARMHOUSE. WE CAN SEEK HELP THERE!

PEASANT-- YOUR LORD NEEDS YOUR HELP!

YOU WILL BE WELL REWARDED FOR YOUR AID.

DIDN'T YOU HEAR ME? I SAID LORD NORIYUKI NEEDS YOUR HELP!

I HEARD, I HEARD.

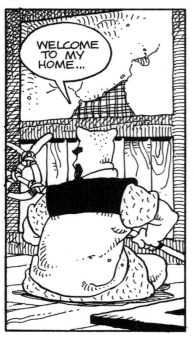

WELCOME TO MY HOME...

...LORD NORIYUKI.

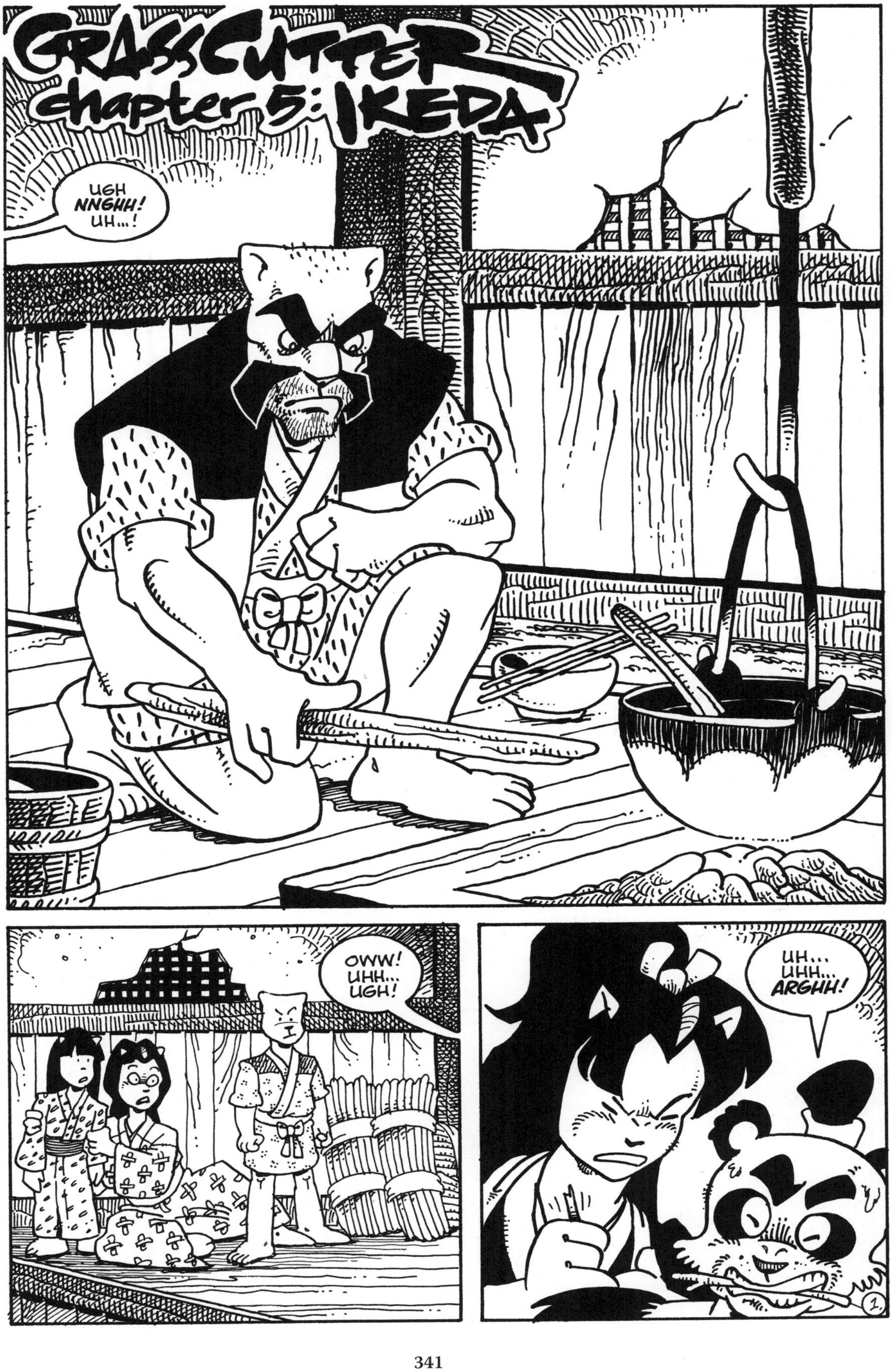
GRASSCUTTER
chapter 5: IKEDA
UGH NNGHH! UH...!
OWW! UHH... UGH!
UH... UHH... ARGHH!
1.

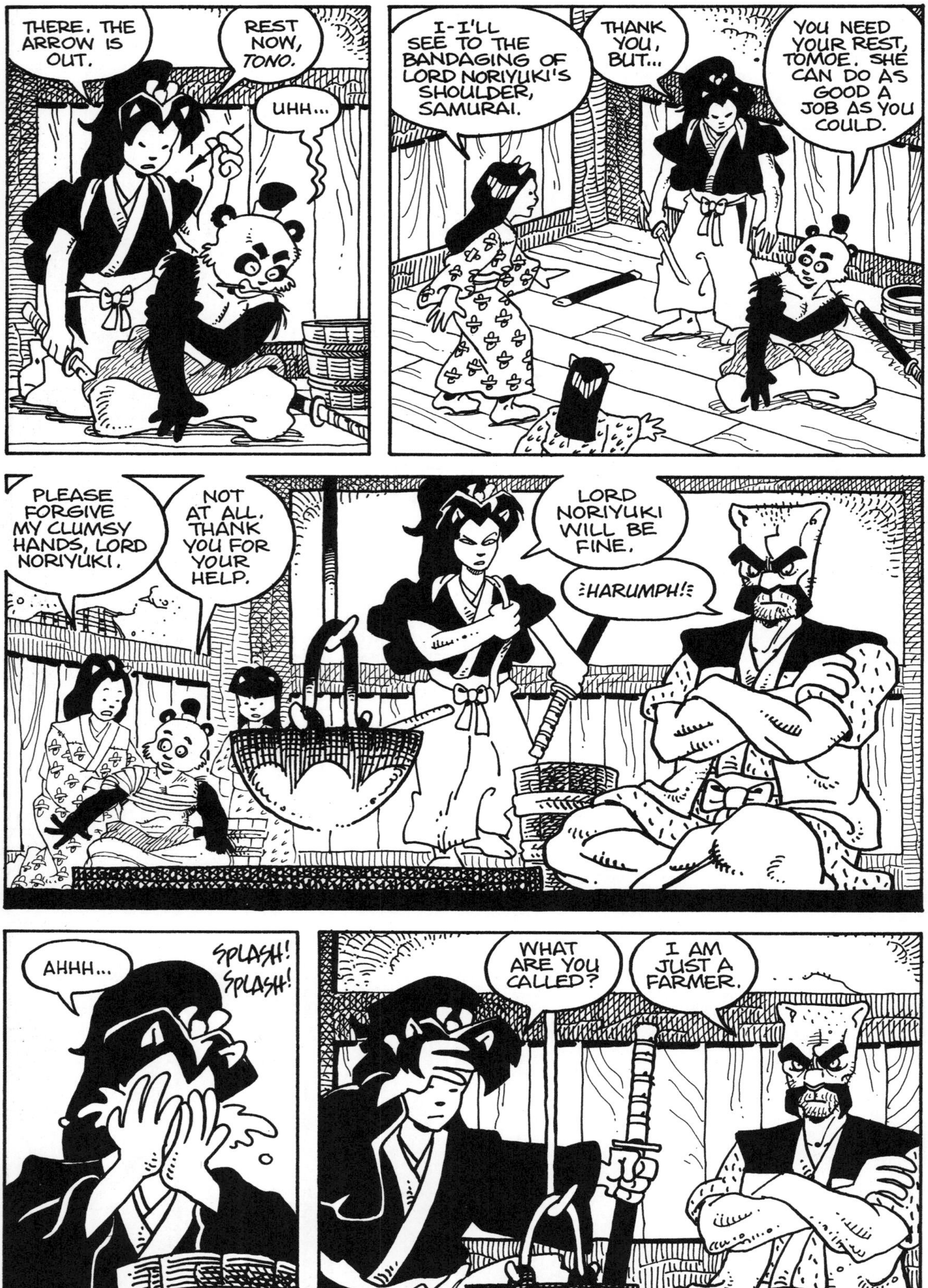
THERE. THE ARROW IS OUT.
REST NOW, *TONO.*
UHH...
I-I'LL SEE TO THE BANDAGING OF LORD NORIYUKI'S SHOULDER, SAMURAI.
THANK YOU, BUT...
YOU NEED YOUR REST, TOMOE. SHE CAN DO AS GOOD A JOB AS YOU COULD.
PLEASE FORGIVE MY CLUMSY HANDS, LORD NORIYUKI.
NOT AT ALL. THANK YOU FOR YOUR HELP.
LORD NORIYUKI WILL BE FINE.
HARUMPH!
AHHH...
SPLASH! SPLASH!
WHAT ARE YOU CALLED?
I AM JUST A FARMER.
2

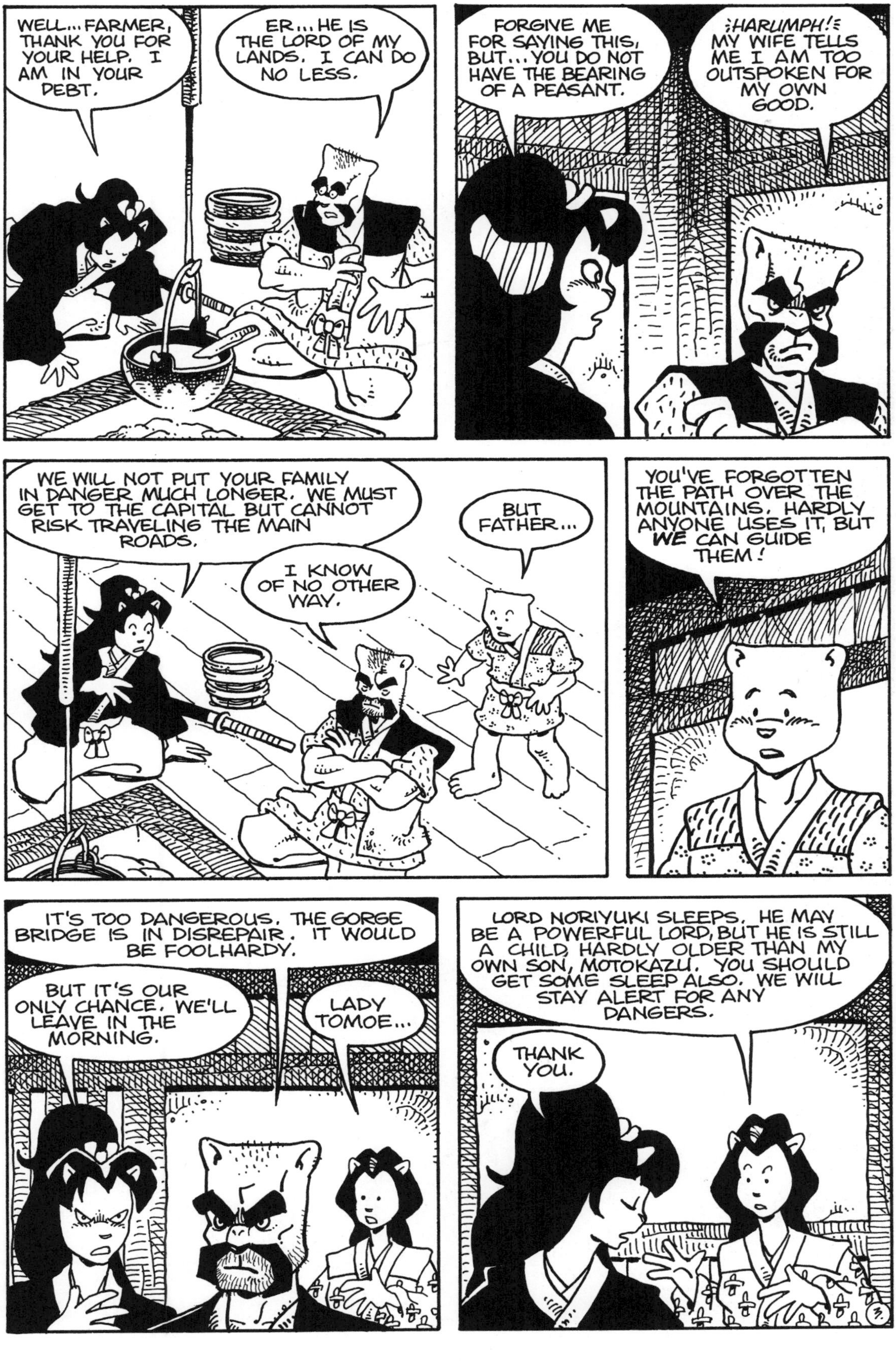
WELL... FARMER, THANK YOU FOR YOUR HELP. I AM IN YOUR DEBT.
ER... HE IS THE LORD OF MY LANDS. I CAN DO NO LESS.
FORGIVE ME FOR SAYING THIS, BUT... YOU DO NOT HAVE THE BEARING OF A PEASANT.
HARUMPH! MY WIFE TELLS ME I AM TOO OUTSPOKEN FOR MY OWN GOOD.
WE WILL NOT PUT YOUR FAMILY IN DANGER MUCH LONGER. WE MUST GET TO THE CAPITAL BUT CANNOT RISK TRAVELING THE MAIN ROADS.
I KNOW OF NO OTHER WAY.
BUT FATHER...
YOU'VE FORGOTTEN THE PATH OVER THE MOUNTAINS. HARDLY ANYONE USES IT, BUT WE CAN GUIDE THEM!
IT'S TOO DANGEROUS. THE GORGE BRIDGE IS IN DISREPAIR. IT WOULD BE FOOLHARDY.
BUT IT'S OUR ONLY CHANCE. WE'LL LEAVE IN THE MORNING.
LADY TOMOE...
LORD NORIYUKI SLEEPS. HE MAY BE A POWERFUL LORD, BUT HE IS STILL A CHILD, HARDLY OLDER THAN MY OWN SON, MOTOKAZU. YOU SHOULD GET SOME SLEEP ALSO. WE WILL STAY ALERT FOR ANY DANGERS.
THANK YOU.

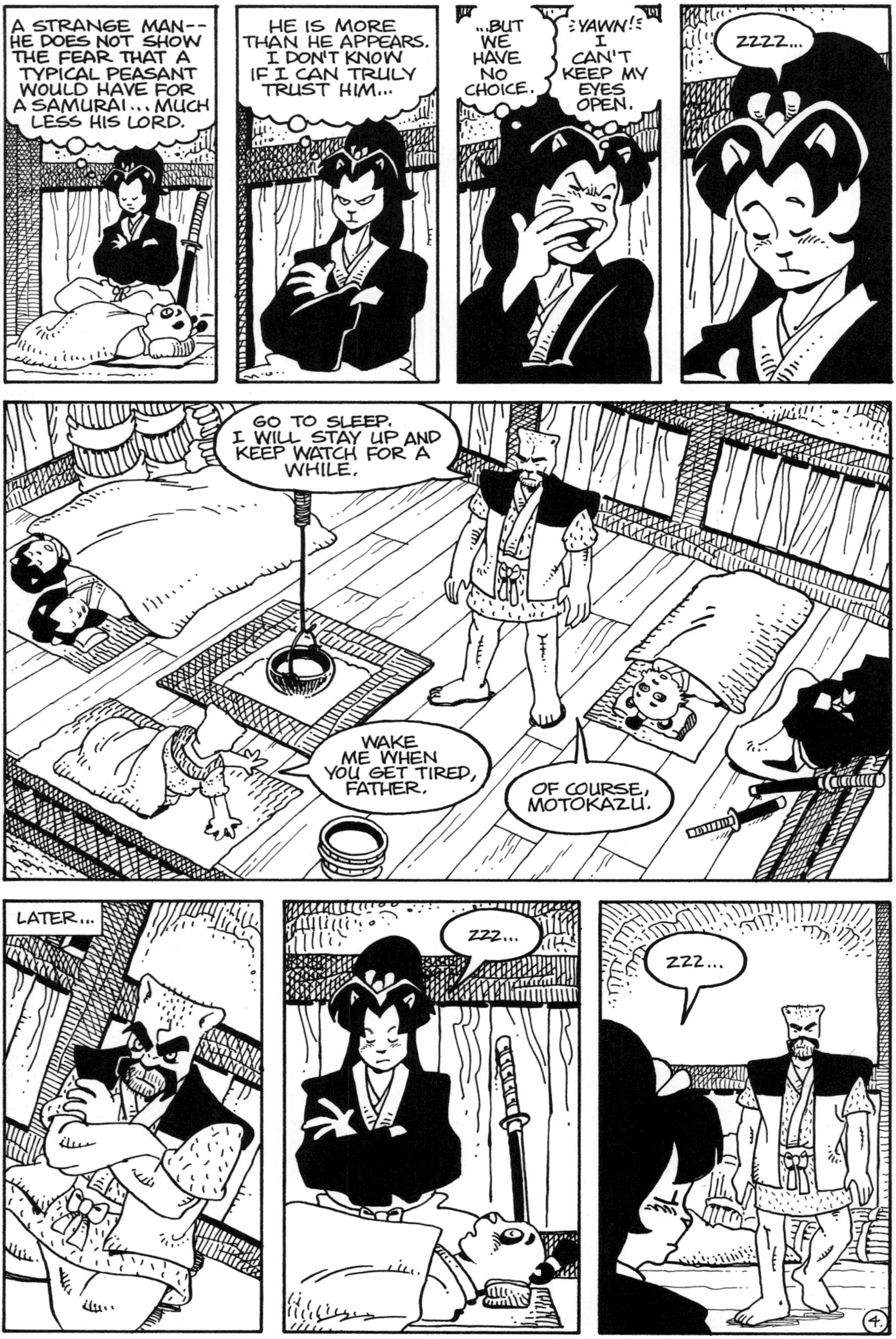
A STRANGE MAN--HE DOES NOT SHOW THE FEAR THAT A TYPICAL PEASANT WOULD HAVE FOR A SAMURAI... MUCH LESS HIS LORD.
HE IS MORE THAN HE APPEARS. I DON'T KNOW IF I CAN TRULY TRUST HIM...
...BUT WE HAVE NO CHOICE.
YAWN! I CAN'T KEEP MY EYES OPEN.
ZZZZ...
GO TO SLEEP. I WILL STAY UP AND KEEP WATCH FOR A WHILE.
WAKE ME WHEN YOU GET TIRED, FATHER.
OF COURSE, MOTOKAZU.
LATER...
ZZZ...
ZZZ...
4.

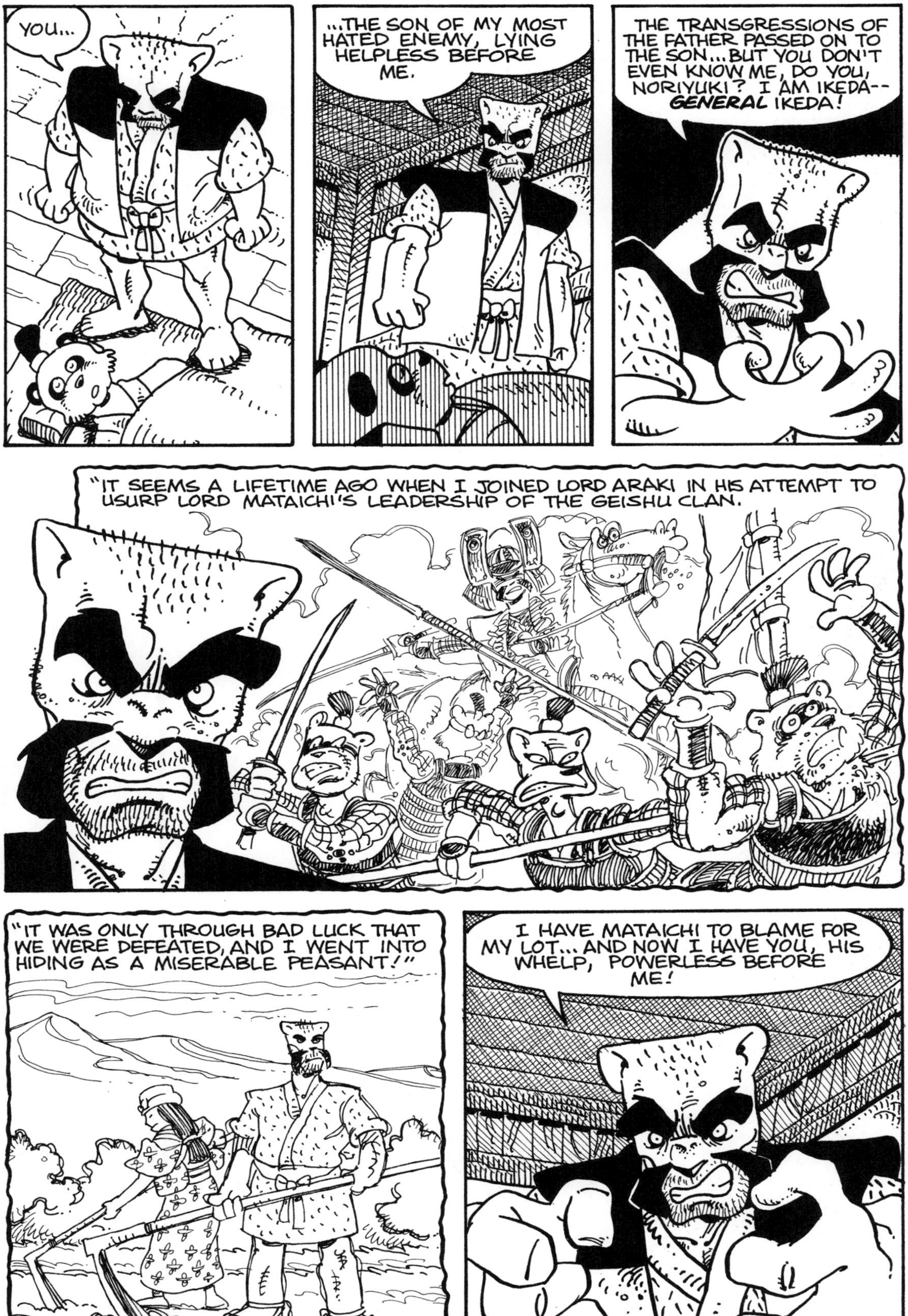
YOU...
...THE SON OF MY MOST HATED ENEMY, LYING HELPLESS BEFORE ME.
THE TRANSGRESSIONS OF THE FATHER PASSED ON TO THE SON... BUT YOU DON'T EVEN KNOW ME, DO YOU, NORIYUKI? I AM IKEDA-- GENERAL IKEDA!
"IT SEEMS A LIFETIME AGO WHEN I JOINED LORD ARAKI IN HIS ATTEMPT TO USURP LORD MATAICHI'S LEADERSHIP OF THE GEISHU CLAN.
"IT WAS ONLY THROUGH BAD LUCK THAT WE WERE DEFEATED, AND I WENT INTO HIDING AS A MISERABLE PEASANT!"
I HAVE MATAICHI TO BLAME FOR MY LOT... AND NOW I HAVE YOU, HIS WHELP, POWERLESS BEFORE ME!
5

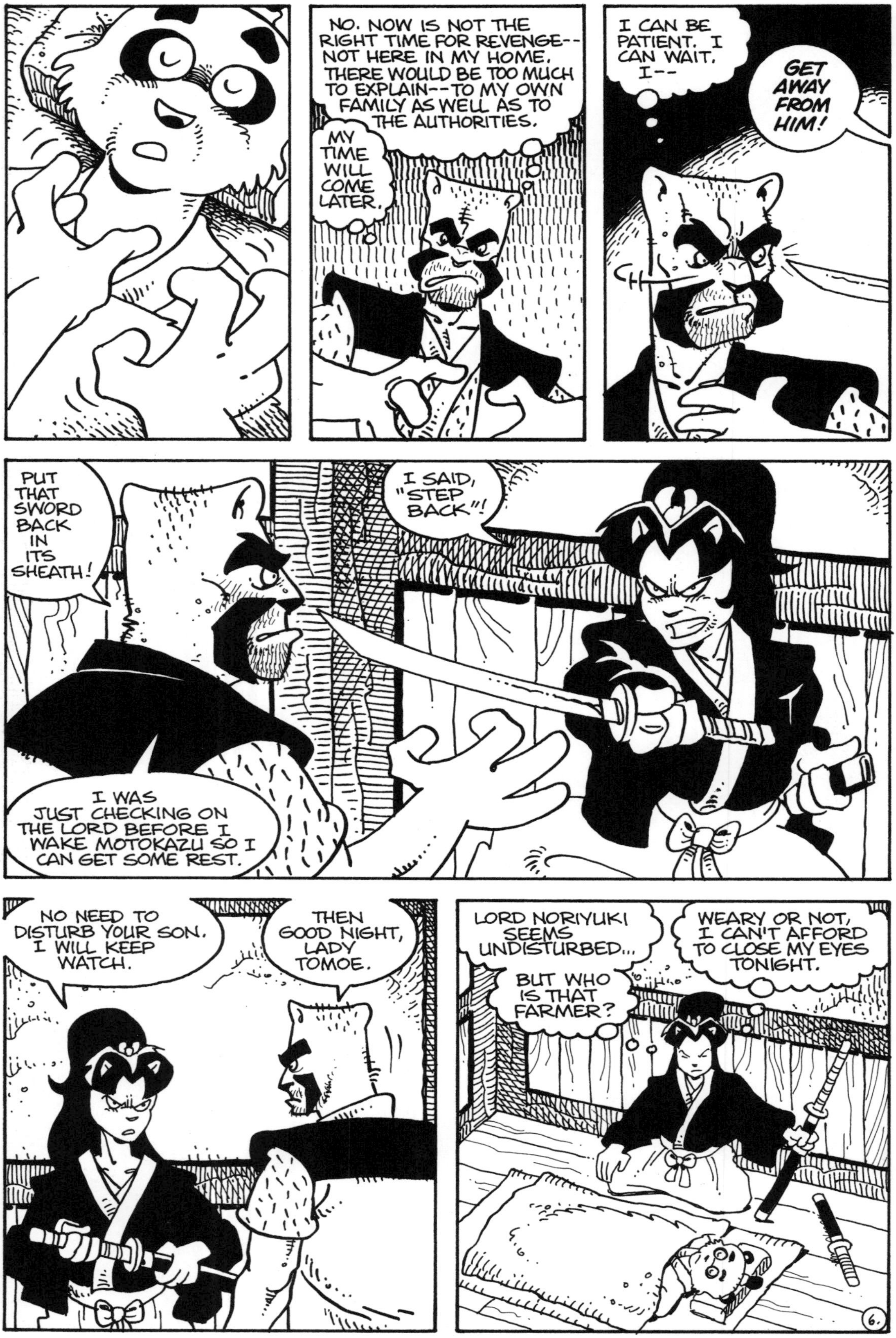
NO. NOW IS NOT THE RIGHT TIME FOR REVENGE-- NOT HERE IN MY HOME. THERE WOULD BE TOO MUCH TO EXPLAIN--TO MY OWN FAMILY AS WELL AS TO THE AUTHORITIES.
MY TIME WILL COME LATER.
I CAN BE PATIENT. I CAN WAIT. I--
GET AWAY FROM HIM!
PUT THAT SWORD BACK IN ITS SHEATH!
I SAID, "STEP BACK"!
I WAS JUST CHECKING ON THE LORD BEFORE I WAKE MOTOKAZU SO I CAN GET SOME REST.
NO NEED TO DISTURB YOUR SON. I WILL KEEP WATCH.
THEN GOOD NIGHT, LADY TOMOE.
LORD NORIYUKI SEEMS UNDISTURBED...
BUT WHO IS THAT FARMER?
WEARY OR NOT, I CAN'T AFFORD TO CLOSE MY EYES TONIGHT.
6.

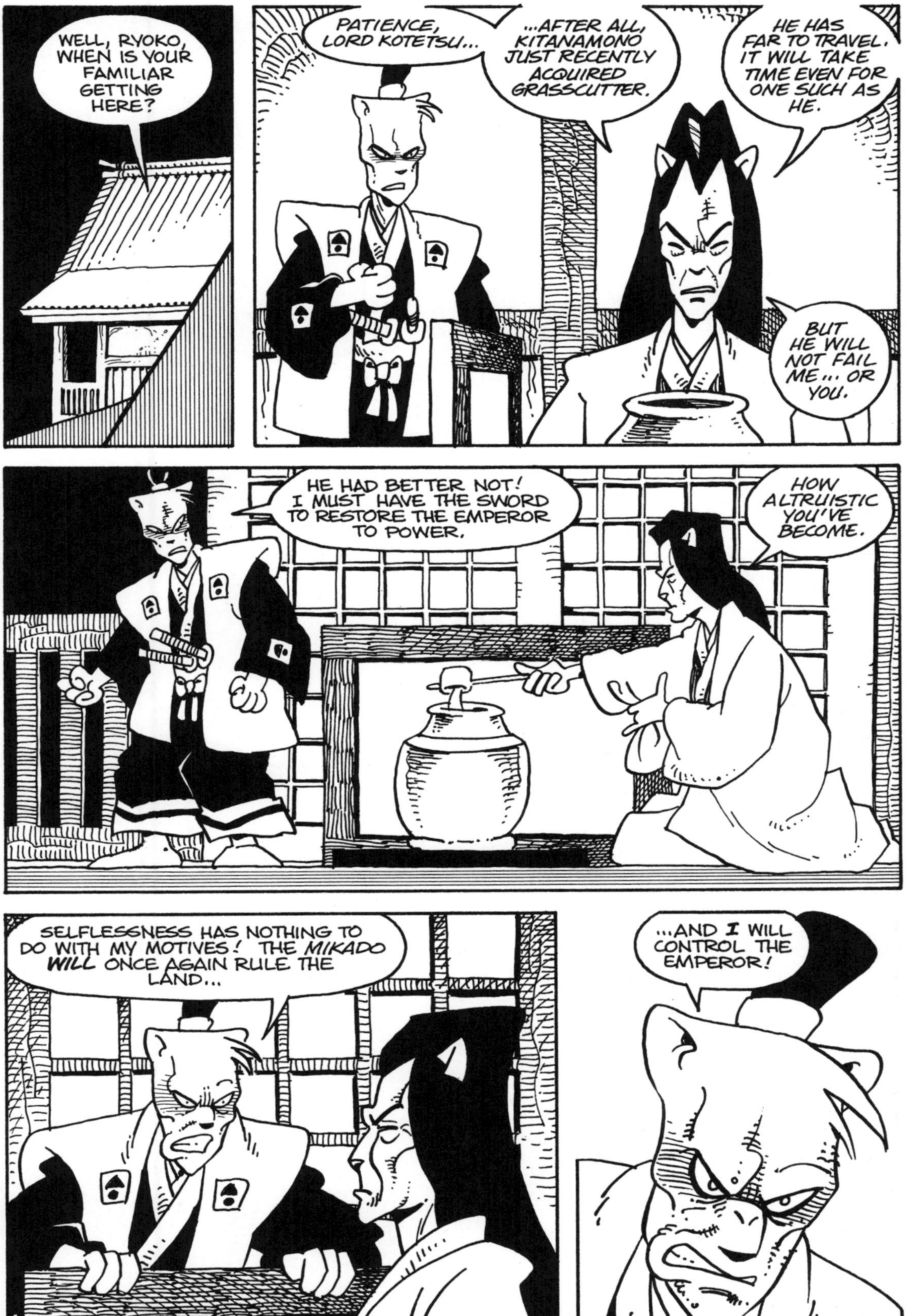
WELL, RYOKO, WHEN IS YOUR FAMILIAR GETTING HERE?
PATIENCE, LORD KOTETSU...
...AFTER ALL, KITANAMONO JUST RECENTLY ACQUIRED GRASSCUTTER.
HE HAS FAR TO TRAVEL. IT WILL TAKE TIME EVEN FOR ONE SUCH AS HE.
BUT HE WILL NOT FAIL ME... OR YOU.
HE HAD BETTER NOT! I MUST HAVE THE SWORD TO RESTORE THE EMPEROR TO POWER.
HOW ALTRUISTIC YOU'VE BECOME.
SELFLESSNESS HAS NOTHING TO DO WITH MY MOTIVES! THE MIKADO WILL ONCE AGAIN RULE THE LAND...
...AND I WILL CONTROL THE EMPEROR!
1.

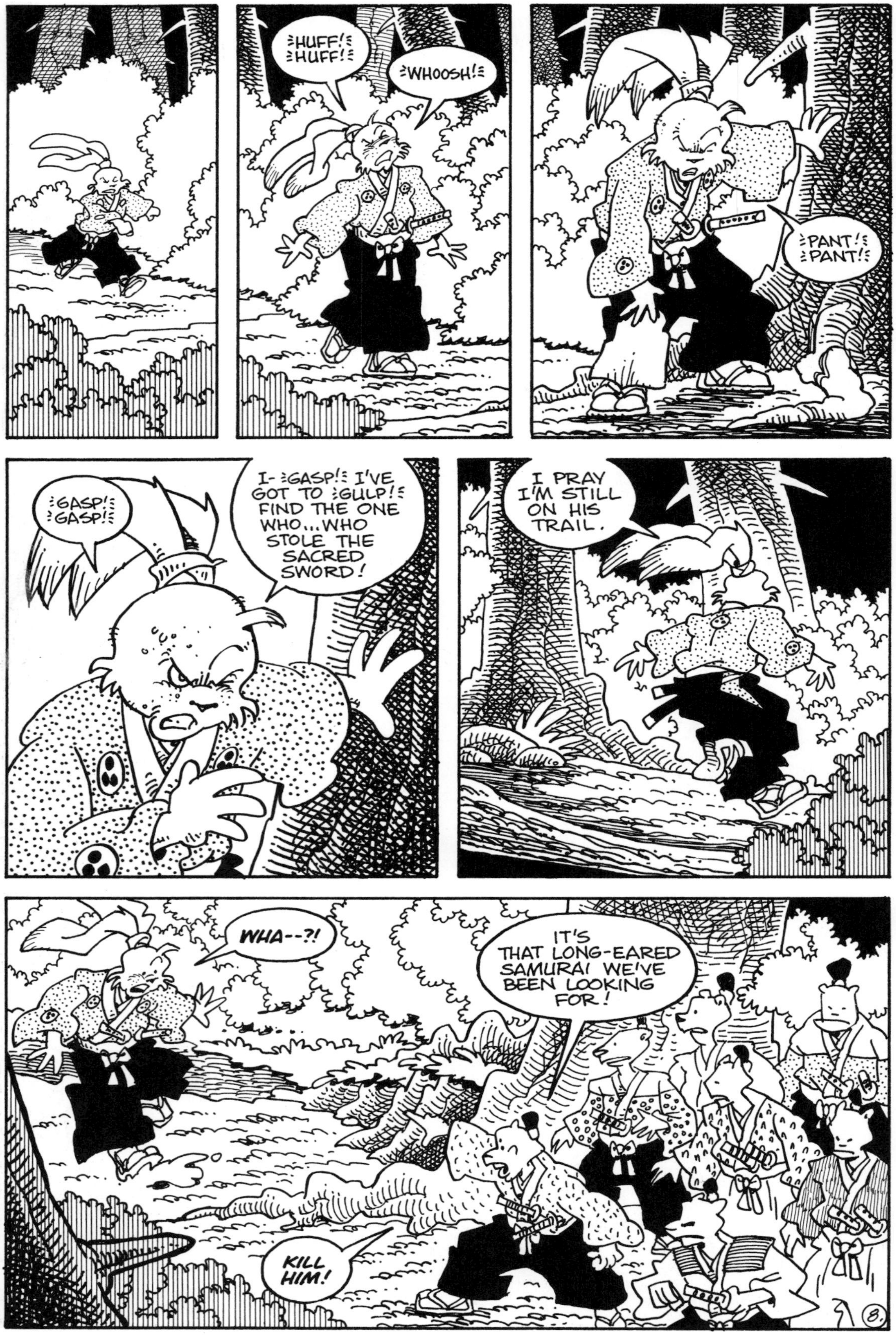
HUFF! HUFF!
WHOOSH!
PANT! PANT!
GASP! GASP!
I- GASP! I'VE GOT TO GULP! FIND THE ONE WHO... WHO STOLE THE SACRED SWORD!
I PRAY I'M STILL ON HIS TRAIL.
WHA--?!
IT'S THAT LONG-EARED SAMURAI WE'VE BEEN LOOKING FOR!
KILL HIM!
8.

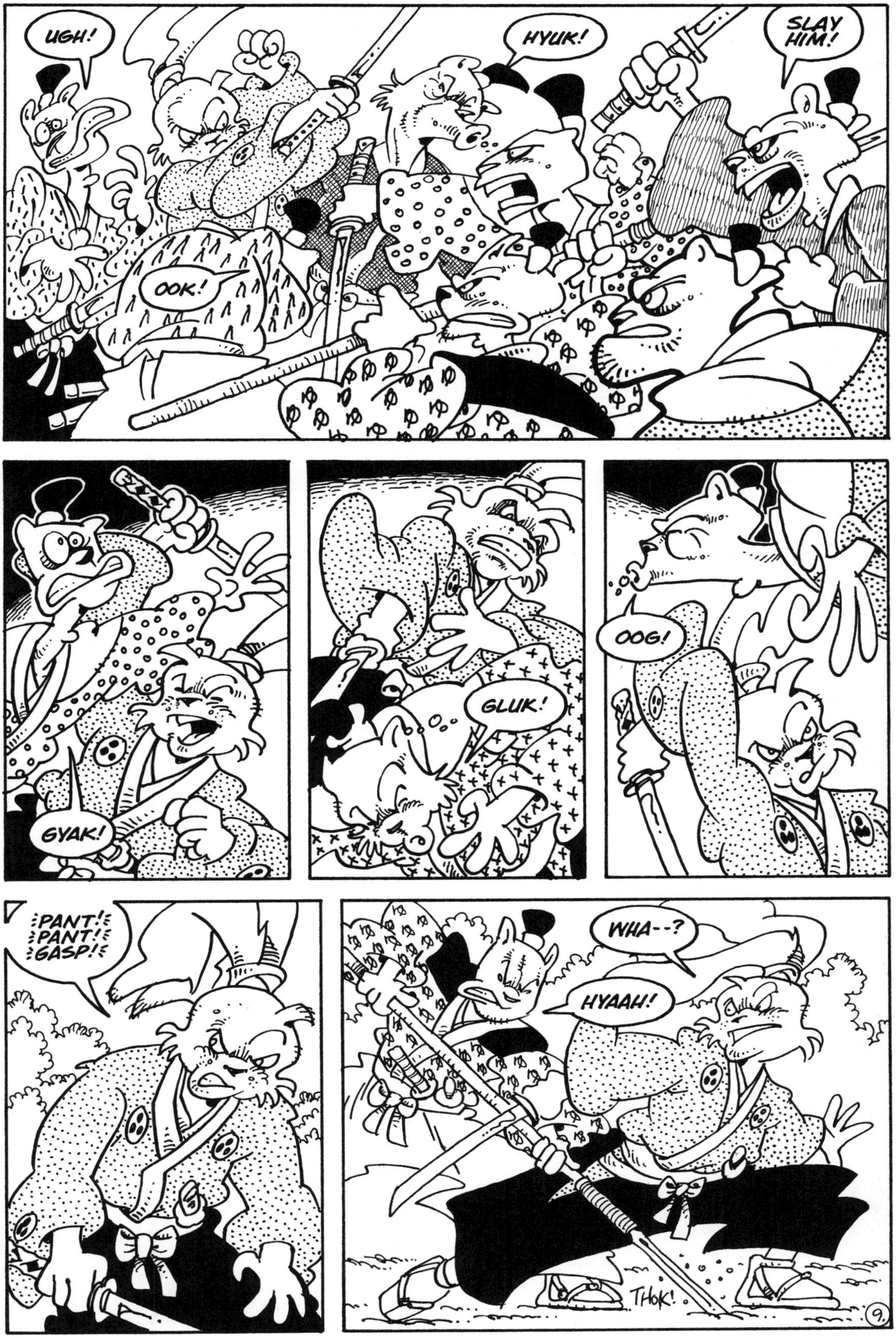
UGH!
OOK!
HYUK!
SLAY HIM!
GYAK!
GLUK!
OOG!
PANT! PANT! GASP!
WHA--?
HYAAH!
THOK!
9.

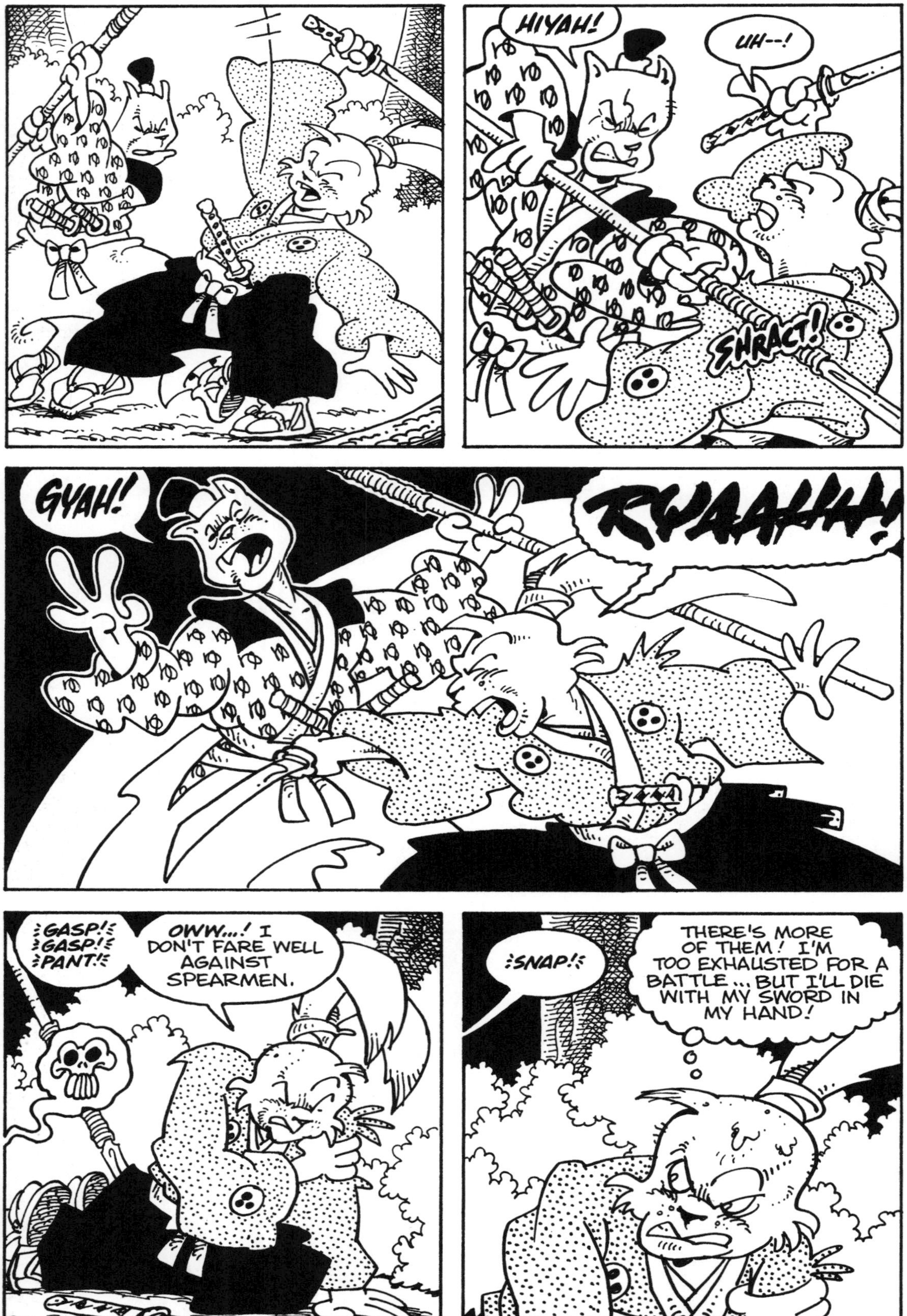
HIYAH!
UH--!
SHRACT!
GYAH!
RWAAHH!
GASP! GASP! PANT!
OWW...! I DON'T FARE WELL AGAINST SPEARMEN.
SNAP!
THERE'S MORE OF THEM! I'M TOO EXHAUSTED FOR A BATTLE... BUT I'LL DIE WITH MY SWORD IN MY HAND!
10.

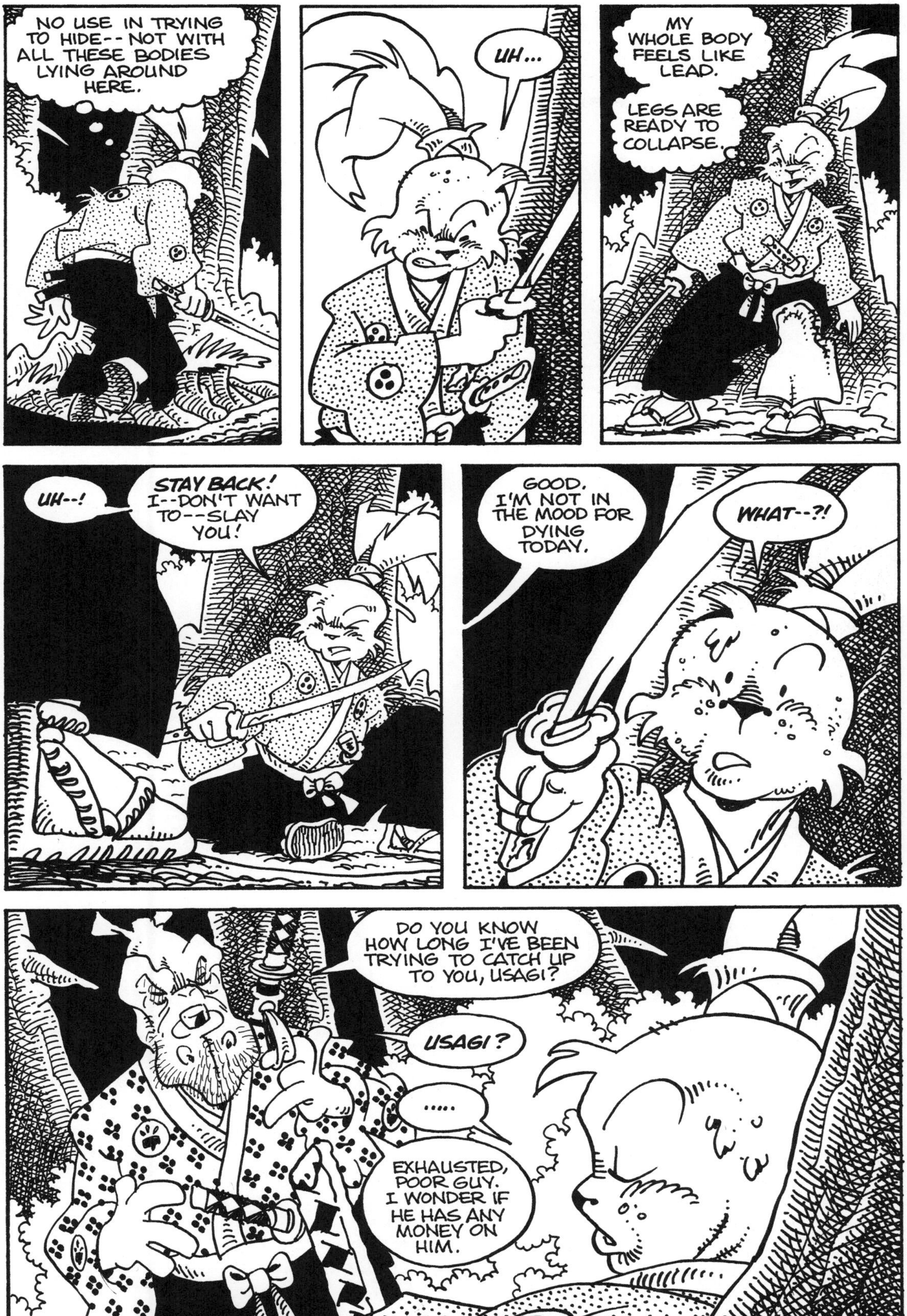
NO USE IN TRYING TO HIDE--NOT WITH ALL THESE BODIES LYING AROUND HERE.
UH...
MY WHOLE BODY FEELS LIKE LEAD.
LEGS ARE READY TO COLLAPSE.
UH--!
STAY BACK! I--DON'T WANT TO--SLAY YOU!
GOOD. I'M NOT IN THE MOOD FOR DYING TODAY.
WHAT--?!
DO YOU KNOW HOW LONG I'VE BEEN TRYING TO CATCH UP TO YOU, USAGI?
USAGI?
.....
EXHAUSTED, POOR GUY. I WONDER IF HE HAS ANY MONEY ON HIM.
17.

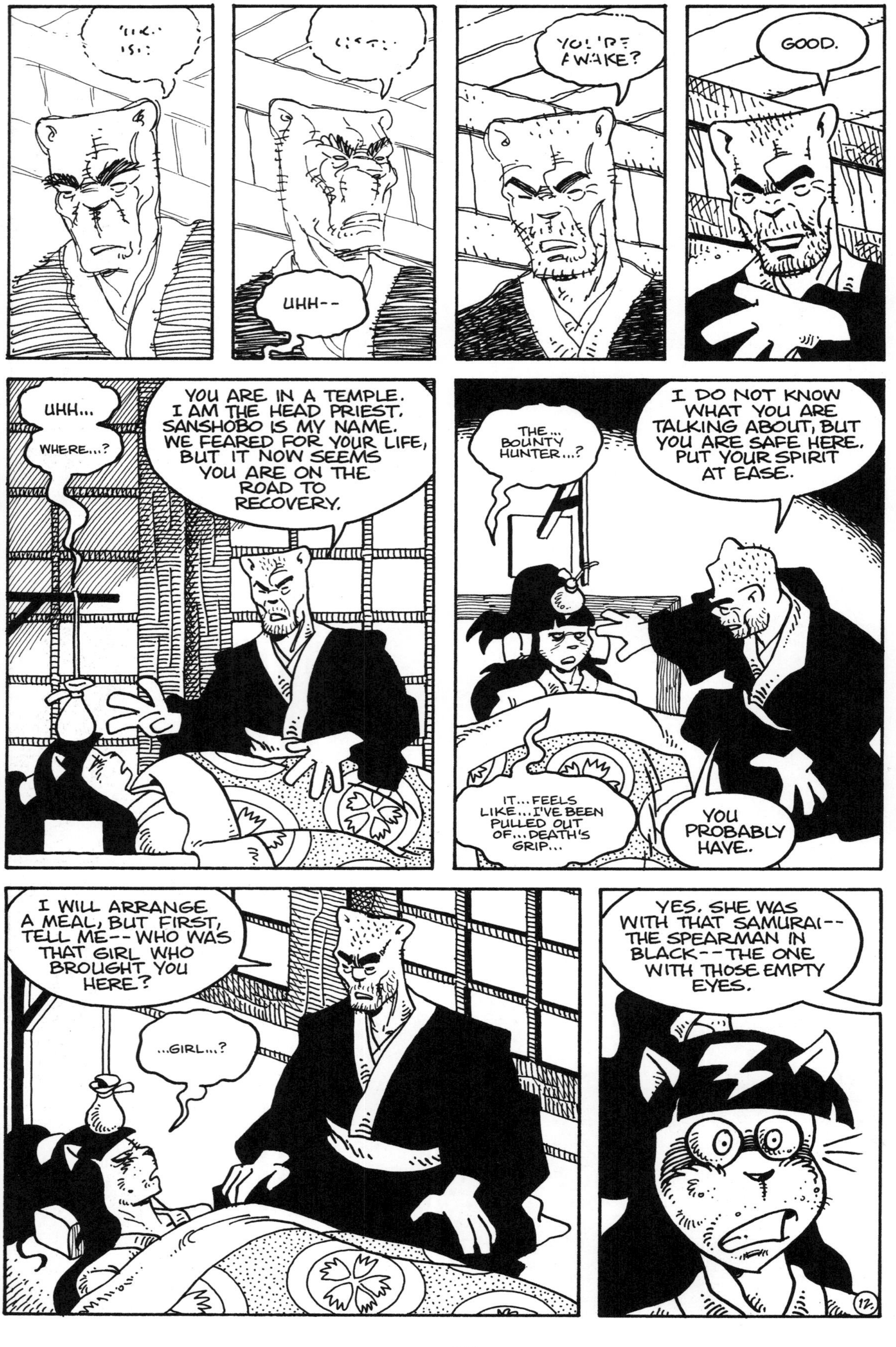
UHH--
YOU'RE AWAKE?
GOOD.
UHH... WHERE...?
YOU ARE IN A TEMPLE. I AM THE HEAD PRIEST. SANSHOBO IS MY NAME. WE FEARED FOR YOUR LIFE, BUT IT NOW SEEMS YOU ARE ON THE ROAD TO RECOVERY.
THE... BOUNTY HUNTER...?
I DO NOT KNOW WHAT YOU ARE TALKING ABOUT, BUT YOU ARE SAFE HERE. PUT YOUR SPIRIT AT EASE.
IT... FEELS LIKE... I'VE BEEN PULLED OUT OF... DEATH'S GRIP...
YOU PROBABLY HAVE.
I WILL ARRANGE A MEAL, BUT FIRST, TELL ME-- WHO WAS THAT GIRL WHO BROUGHT YOU HERE?
...GIRL...?
YES. SHE WAS WITH THAT SAMURAI-- THE SPEARMAN IN BLACK-- THE ONE WITH THOSE EMPTY EYES.
12.

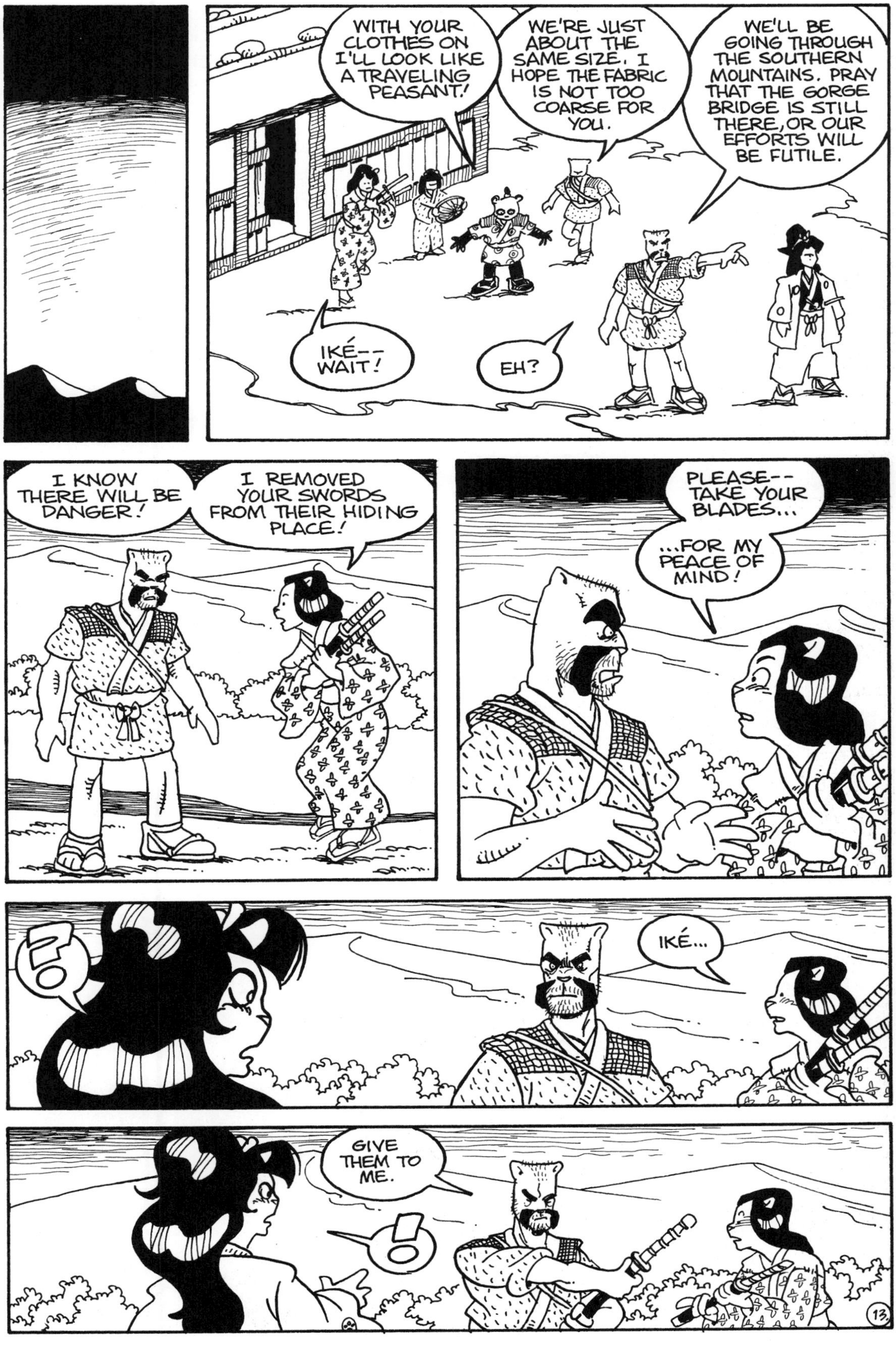
WITH YOUR CLOTHES ON I'LL LOOK LIKE A TRAVELING PEASANT!
WE'RE JUST ABOUT THE SAME SIZE. I HOPE THE FABRIC IS NOT TOO COARSE FOR YOU.
WE'LL BE GOING THROUGH THE SOUTHERN MOUNTAINS. PRAY THAT THE GORGE BRIDGE IS STILL THERE, OR OUR EFFORTS WILL BE FUTILE.
IKÉ-- WAIT!
EH?
I KNOW THERE WILL BE DANGER!
I REMOVED YOUR SWORDS FROM THEIR HIDING PLACE!
PLEASE-- TAKE YOUR BLADES...
...FOR MY PEACE OF MIND!
!?
IKÉ...
GIVE THEM TO ME.
!
13

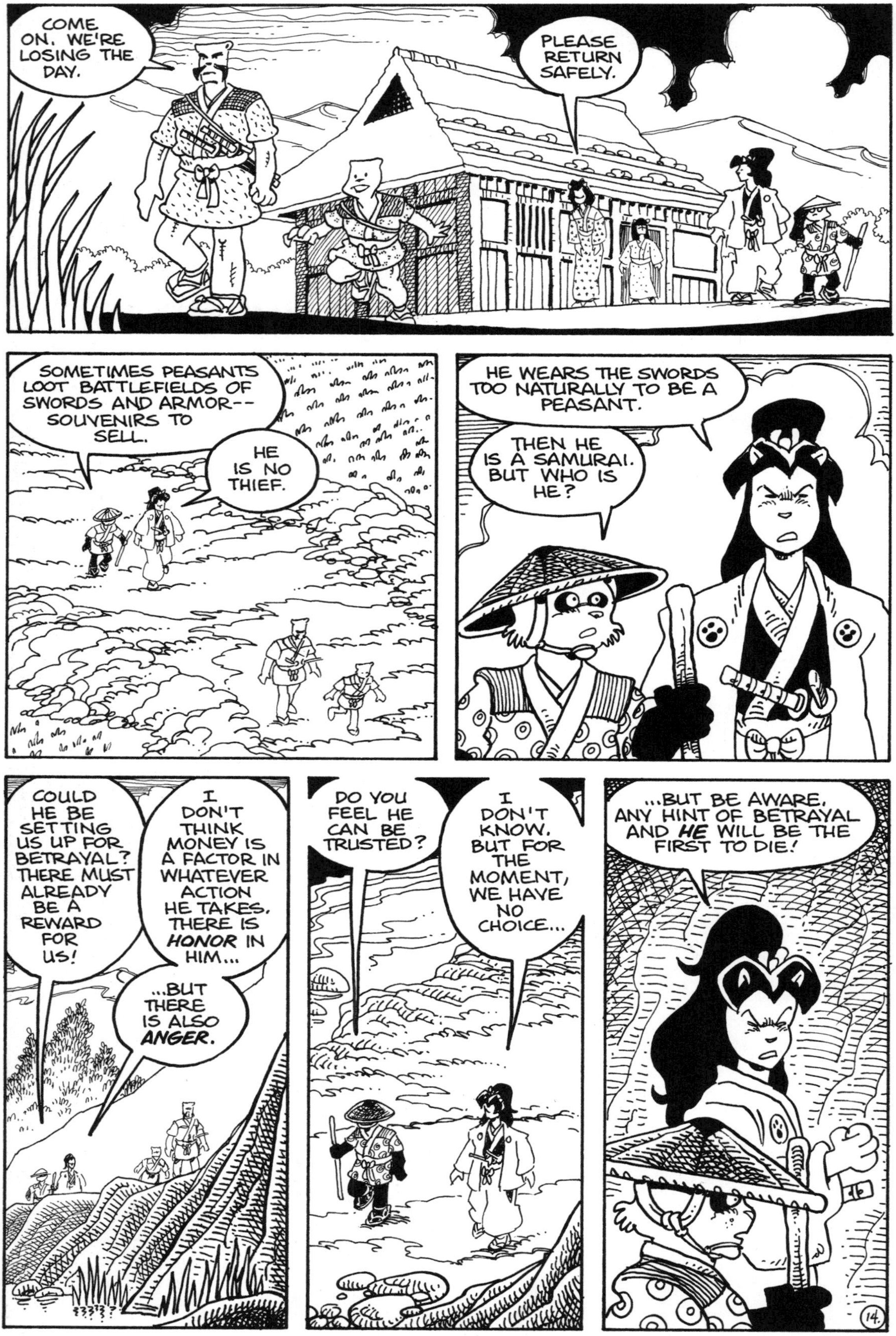
COME ON. WE'RE LOSING THE DAY.
PLEASE RETURN SAFELY.
SOMETIMES PEASANTS LOOT BATTLEFIELDS OF SWORDS AND ARMOR-- SOUVENIRS TO SELL.
HE IS NO THIEF.
HE WEARS THE SWORDS TOO NATURALLY TO BE A PEASANT.
THEN HE IS A SAMURAI. BUT WHO IS HE?
COULD HE BE SETTING US UP FOR BETRAYAL? THERE MUST ALREADY BE A REWARD FOR US!
I DON'T THINK MONEY IS A FACTOR IN WHATEVER ACTION HE TAKES. THERE IS *HONOR* IN HIM...
...BUT THERE IS ALSO *ANGER*.
DO YOU FEEL HE CAN BE TRUSTED?
I DON'T KNOW. BUT FOR THE MOMENT, WE HAVE NO CHOICE...
...BUT BE AWARE. ANY HINT OF BETRAYAL AND *HE* WILL BE THE FIRST TO DIE!
14.

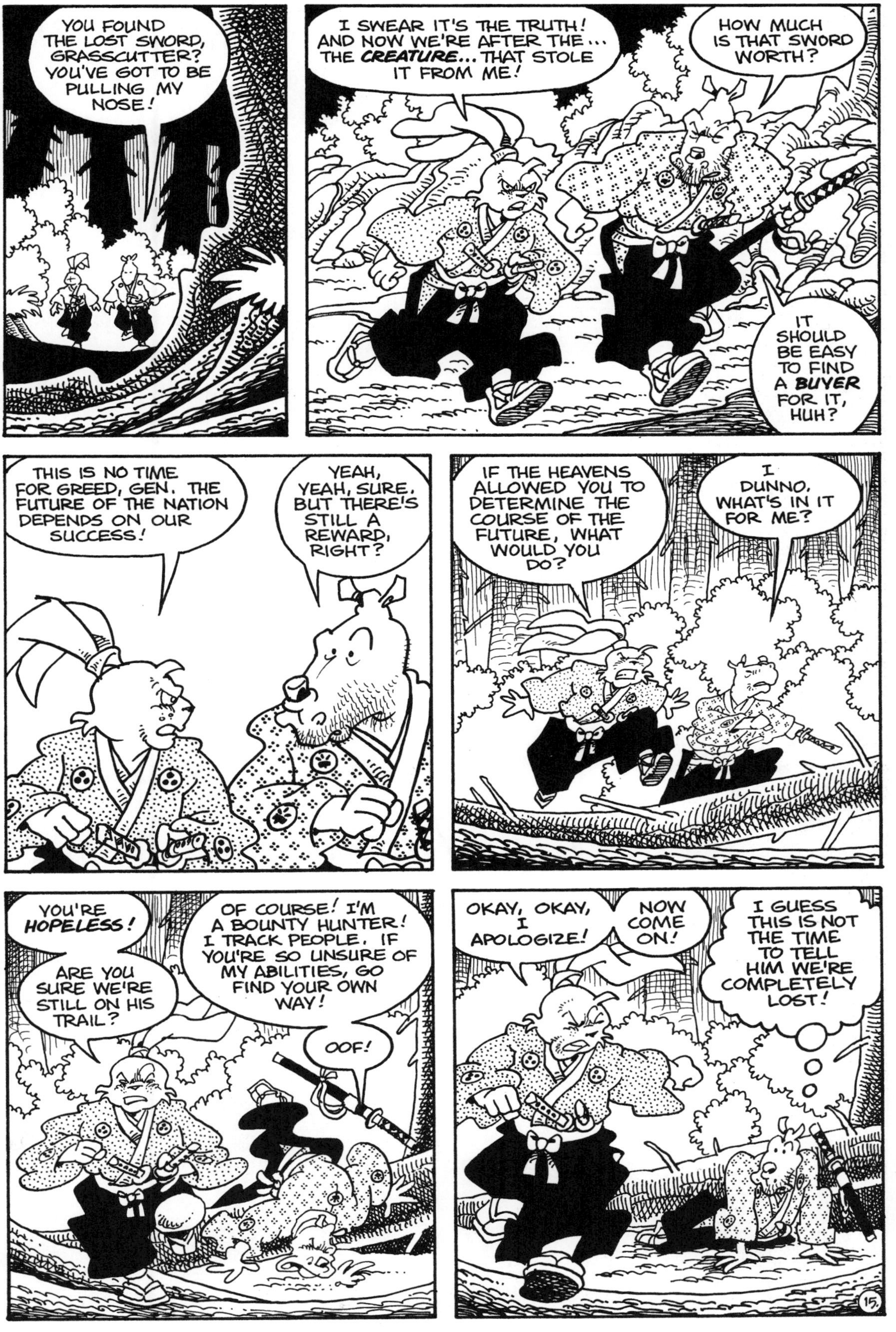
YOU FOUND THE LOST SWORD, GRASSCUTTER? YOU'VE GOT TO BE PULLING MY NOSE!
I SWEAR IT'S THE TRUTH! AND NOW WE'RE AFTER THE... THE CREATURE... THAT STOLE IT FROM ME!
HOW MUCH IS THAT SWORD WORTH?
IT SHOULD BE EASY TO FIND A BUYER FOR IT, HUH?
THIS IS NO TIME FOR GREED, GEN. THE FUTURE OF THE NATION DEPENDS ON OUR SUCCESS!
YEAH, YEAH, SURE. BUT THERE'S STILL A REWARD, RIGHT?
IF THE HEAVENS ALLOWED YOU TO DETERMINE THE COURSE OF THE FUTURE, WHAT WOULD YOU DO?
I DUNNO. WHAT'S IN IT FOR ME?
YOU'RE HOPELESS!
ARE YOU SURE WE'RE STILL ON HIS TRAIL?
OF COURSE! I'M A BOUNTY HUNTER! I TRACK PEOPLE. IF YOU'RE SO UNSURE OF MY ABILITIES, GO FIND YOUR OWN WAY!
OOF!
OKAY, OKAY, I APOLOGIZE!
NOW COME ON!
I GUESS THIS IS NOT THE TIME TO TELL HIM WE'RE COMPLETELY LOST!
15.

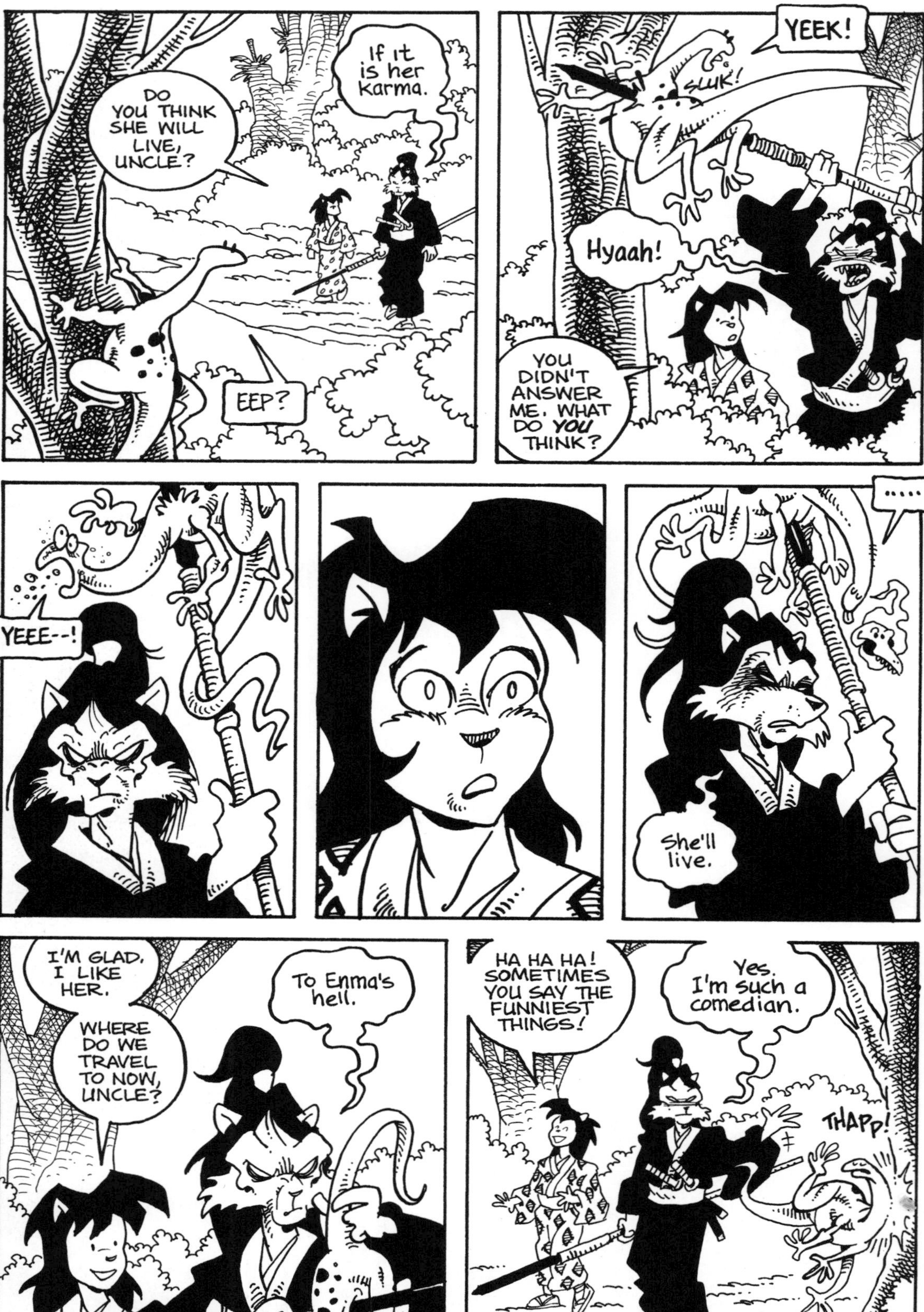
DO YOU THINK SHE WILL LIVE, UNCLE?
If it is her karma.
EEP?
YEEK!
SLUK!
Hyaah!
YOU DIDN'T ANSWER ME. WHAT DO *YOU* THINK?
YEEE--!
.....
She'll live.
I'M GLAD. I LIKE HER.
WHERE DO WE TRAVEL TO NOW, UNCLE?
To Enma's hell.
HA HA HA! SOMETIMES YOU SAY THE FUNNIEST THINGS!
Yes. I'm such a comedian.
THAPp!
16.

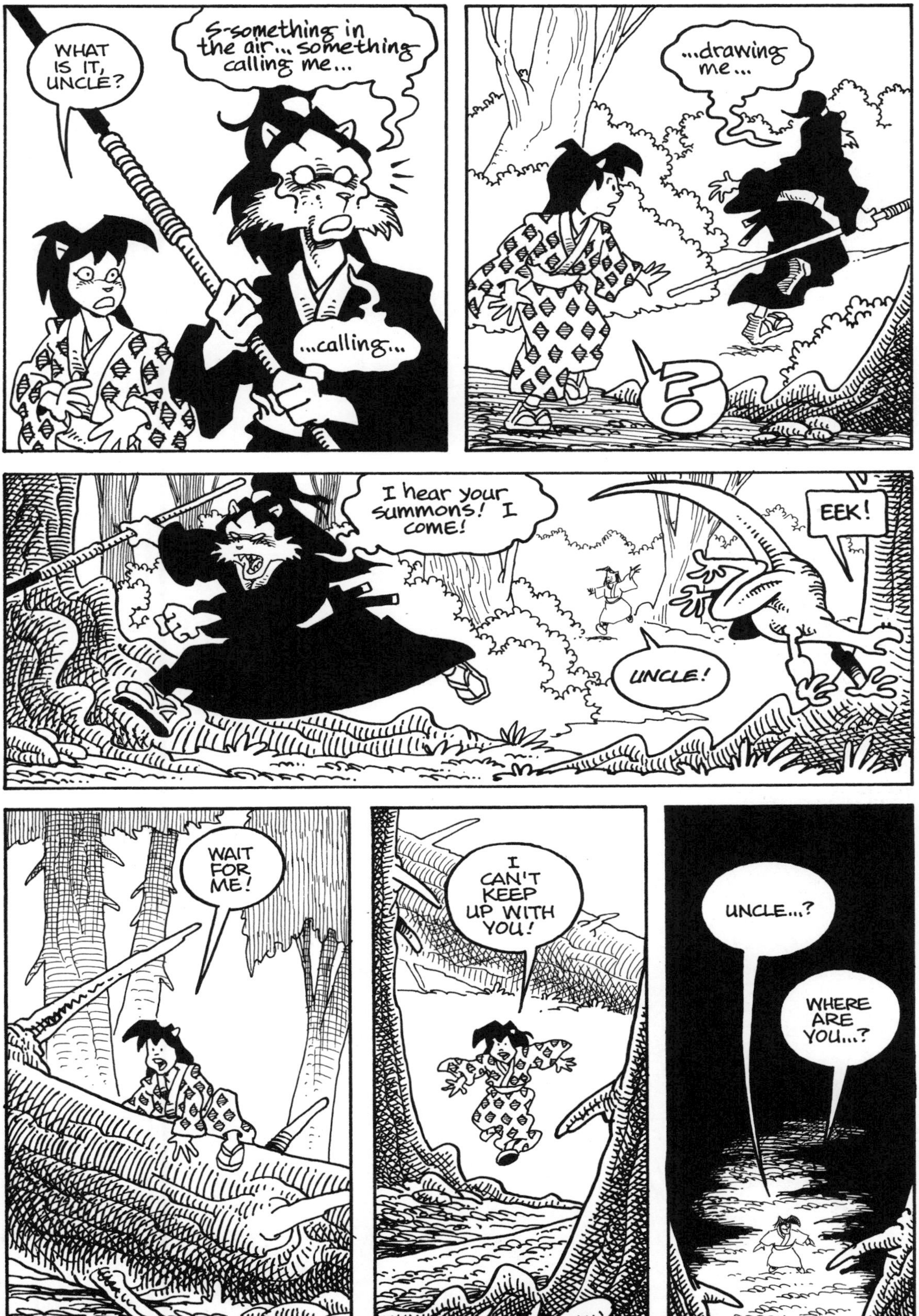
WHAT IS IT, UNCLE?
S-something in the air... something calling me...
...calling...
...drawing me...
?
I hear your summons! I come!
EEK!
UNCLE!
WAIT FOR ME!
I CAN'T KEEP UP WITH YOU!
UNCLE...?
WHERE ARE YOU...?
17.

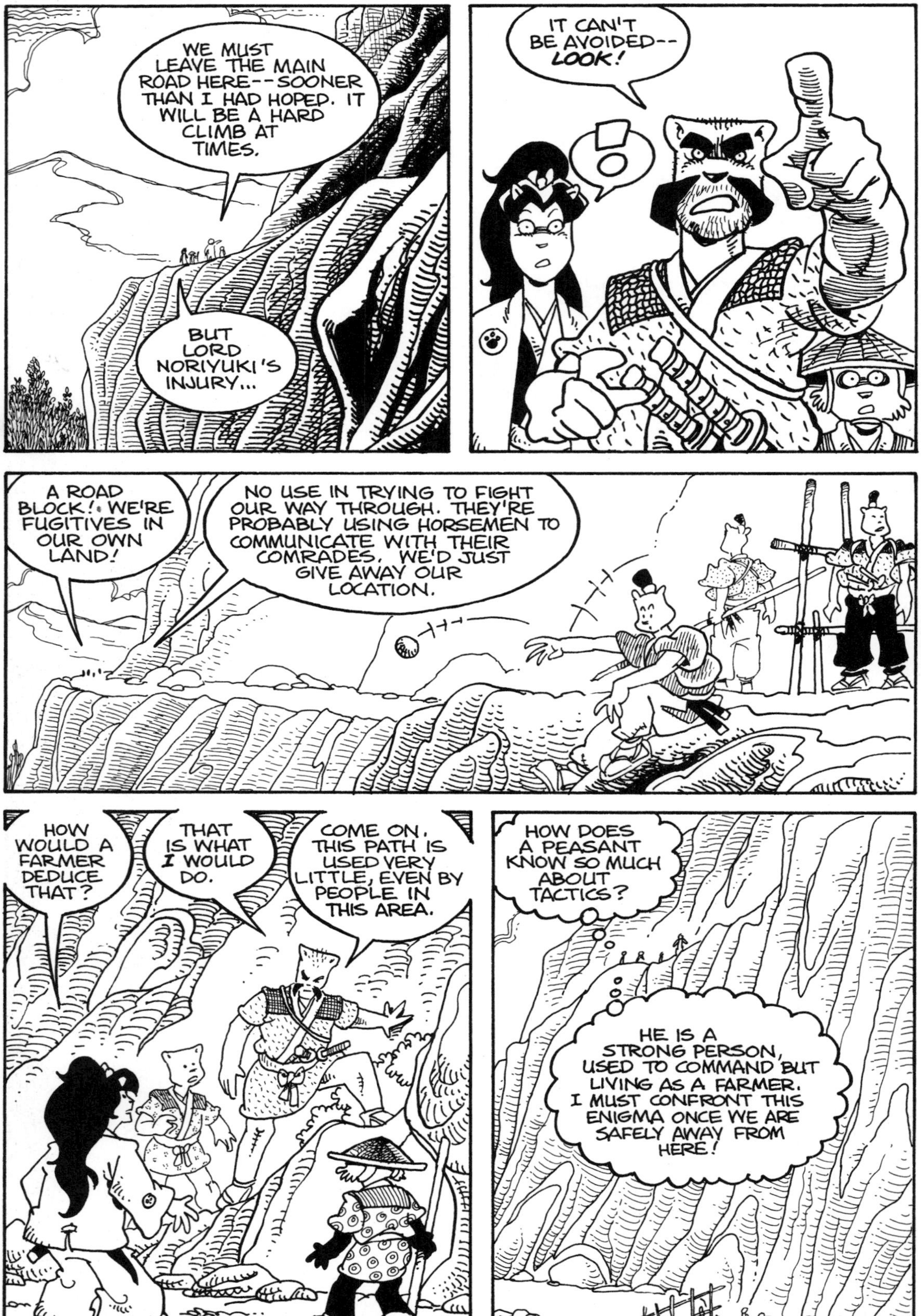
WE MUST LEAVE THE MAIN ROAD HERE--SOONER THAN I HAD HOPED. IT WILL BE A HARD CLIMB AT TIMES.
BUT LORD NORIYUKI'S INJURY...
IT CAN'T BE AVOIDED-- LOOK!
!
A ROAD BLOCK! WE'RE FUGITIVES IN OUR OWN LAND!
NO USE IN TRYING TO FIGHT OUR WAY THROUGH. THEY'RE PROBABLY USING HORSEMEN TO COMMUNICATE WITH THEIR COMRADES. WE'D JUST GIVE AWAY OUR LOCATION.
HOW WOULD A FARMER DEDUCE THAT?
THAT IS WHAT I WOULD DO.
COME ON. THIS PATH IS USED VERY LITTLE, EVEN BY PEOPLE IN THIS AREA.
HOW DOES A PEASANT KNOW SO MUCH ABOUT TACTICS?
HE IS A STRONG PERSON, USED TO COMMAND BUT LIVING AS A FARMER. I MUST CONFRONT THIS ENIGMA ONCE WE ARE SAFELY AWAY FROM HERE!
18.

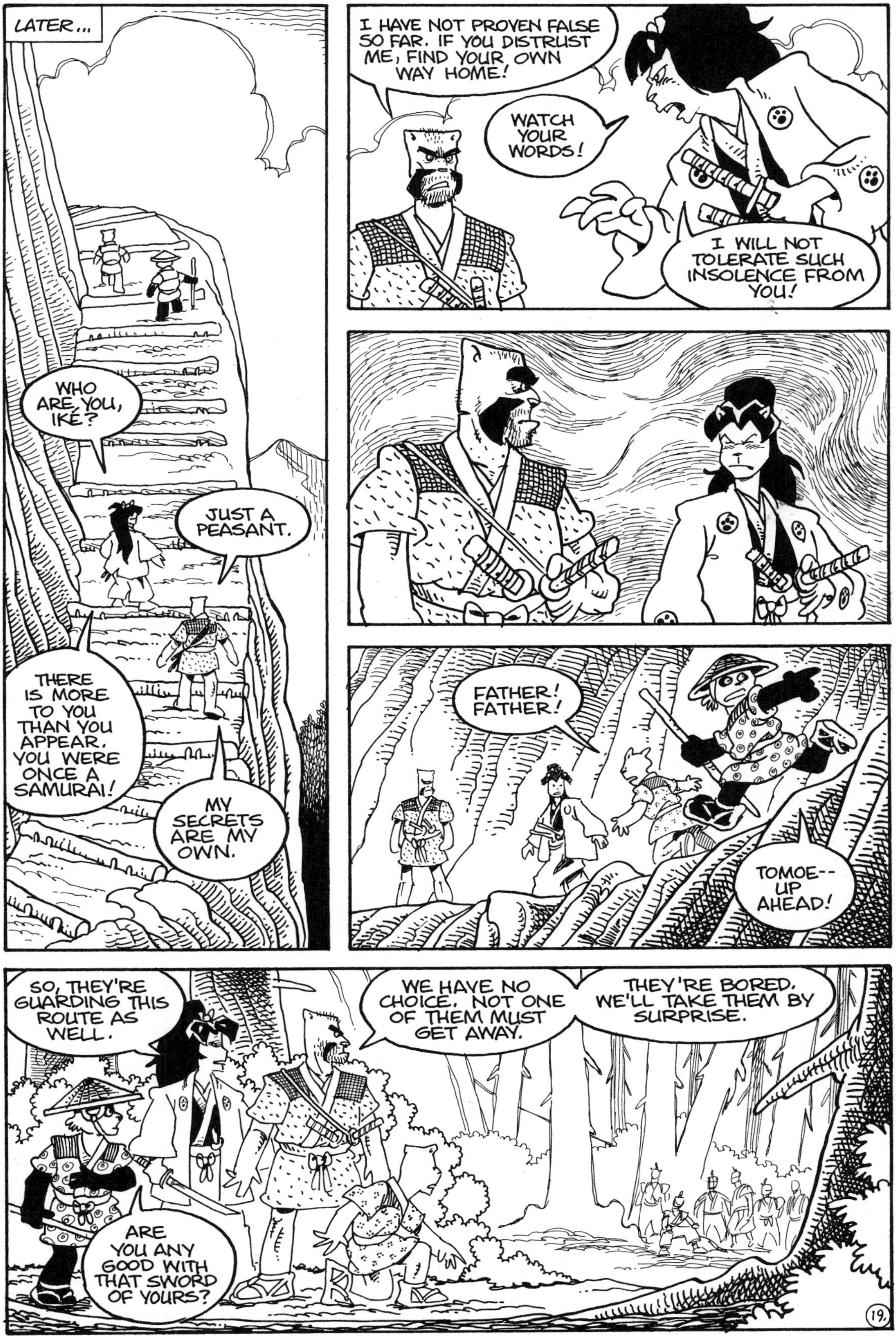
LATER...
WHO ARE YOU, IKÉ?
JUST A PEASANT.
THERE IS MORE TO YOU THAN YOU APPEAR. YOU WERE ONCE A SAMURAI!
MY SECRETS ARE MY OWN.
I HAVE NOT PROVEN FALSE SO FAR. IF YOU DISTRUST ME, FIND YOUR OWN WAY HOME!
WATCH YOUR WORDS!
I WILL NOT TOLERATE SUCH INSOLENCE FROM YOU!
FATHER! FATHER!
TOMOE-- UP AHEAD!
SO, THEY'RE GUARDING THIS ROUTE AS WELL.
ARE YOU ANY GOOD WITH THAT SWORD OF YOURS?
WE HAVE NO CHOICE. NOT ONE OF THEM MUST GET AWAY.
THEY'RE BORED. WE'LL TAKE THEM BY SURPRISE.
19.

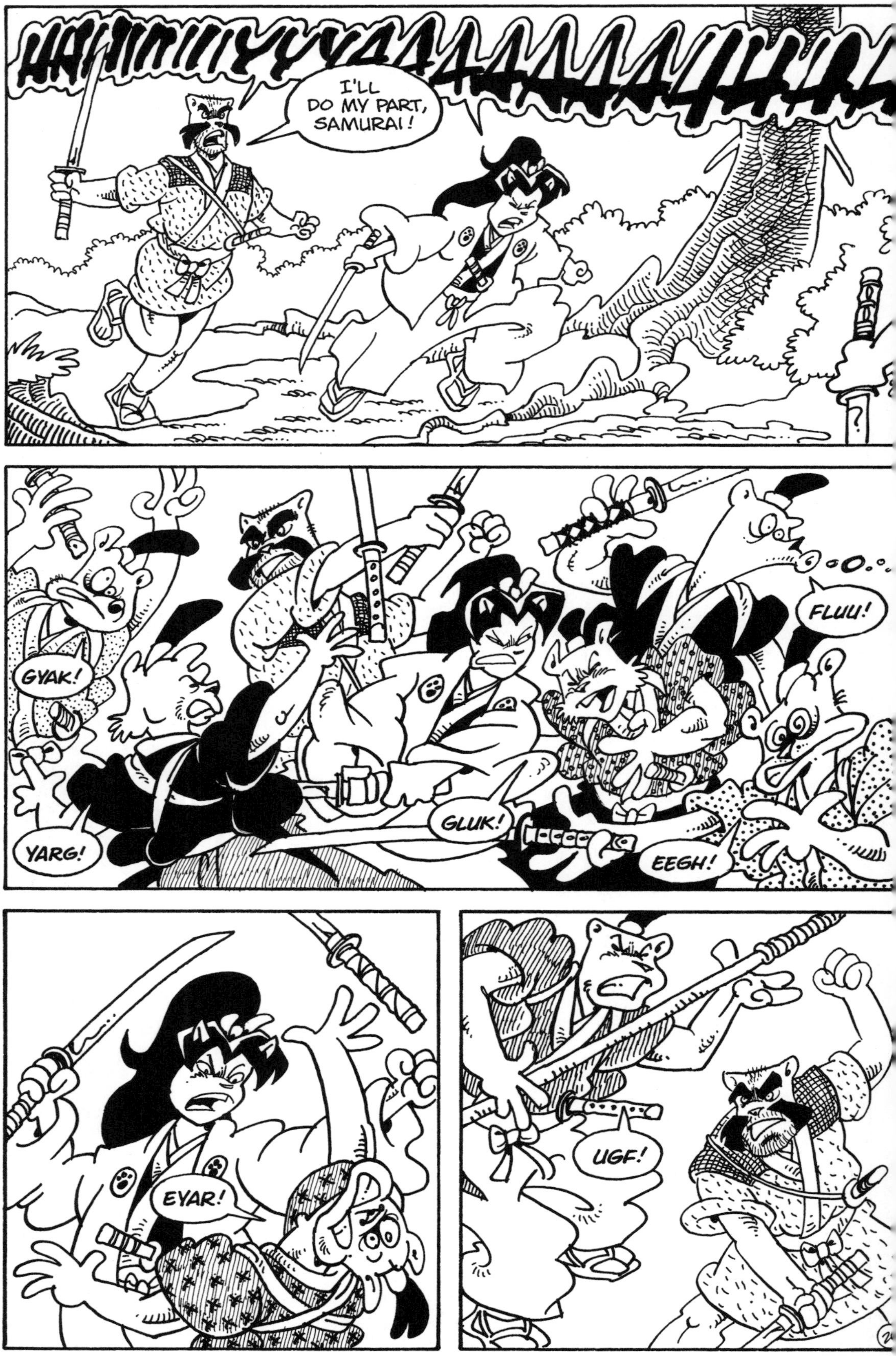
I'LL DO MY PART, SAMURAI!
GYAK!
FLUU!
YARG!
GLUK!
EEGH!
EYAR!
UGF!

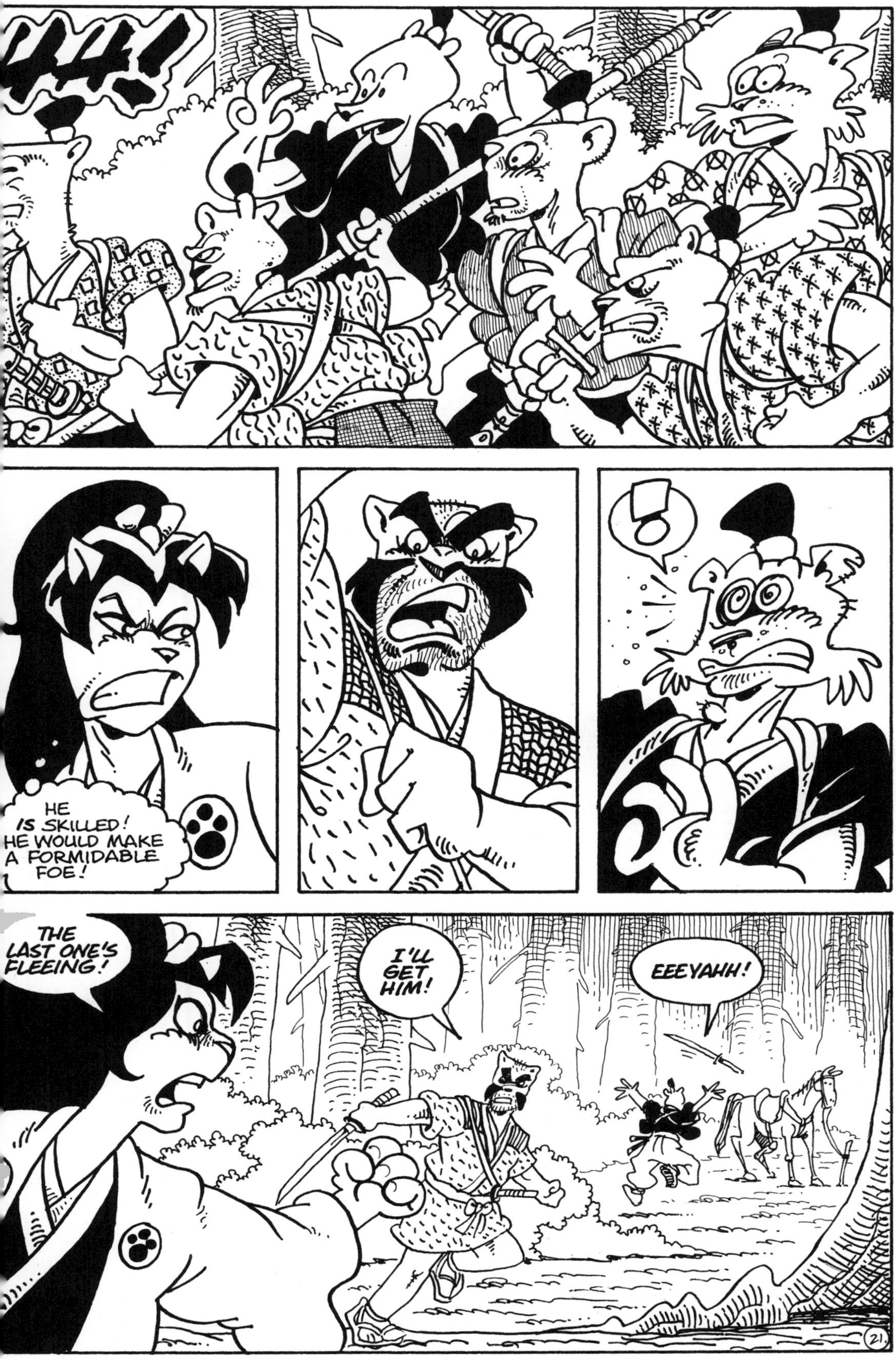
HE IS SKILLED! HE WOULD MAKE A FORMIDABLE FOE!
!
THE LAST ONE'S FLEEING!
I'LL GET HIM!
EEEYAHH!
21.

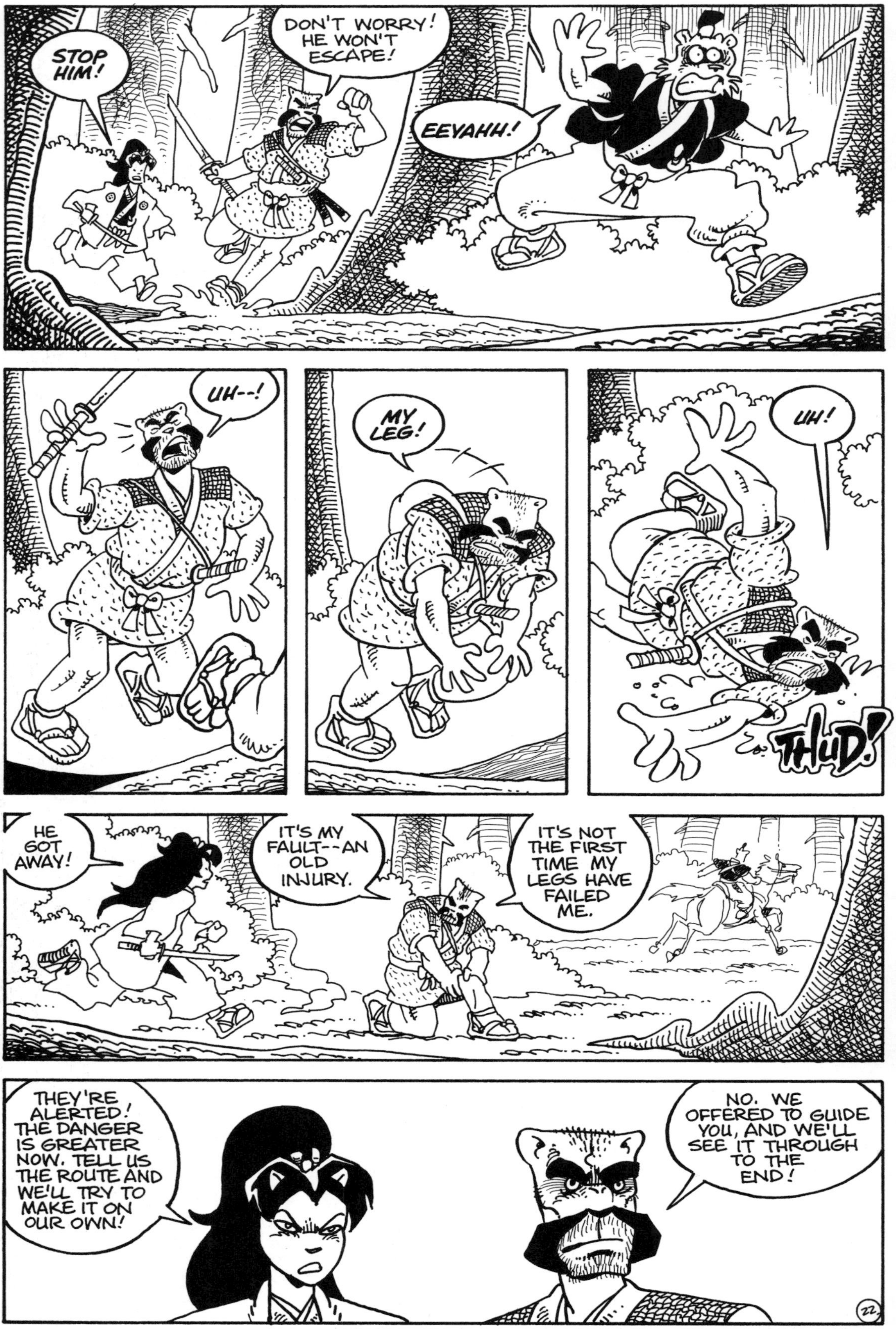
STOP HIM!
DON'T WORRY! HE WON'T ESCAPE!
EEYAHH!
UH--!
MY LEG!
UH!
THUD!
HE GOT AWAY!
IT'S MY FAULT--AN OLD INJURY.
IT'S NOT THE FIRST TIME MY LEGS HAVE FAILED ME.
THEY'RE ALERTED! THE DANGER IS GREATER NOW. TELL US THE ROUTE AND WE'LL TRY TO MAKE IT ON OUR OWN!
NO. WE OFFERED TO GUIDE YOU, AND WE'LL SEE IT THROUGH TO THE END!
22

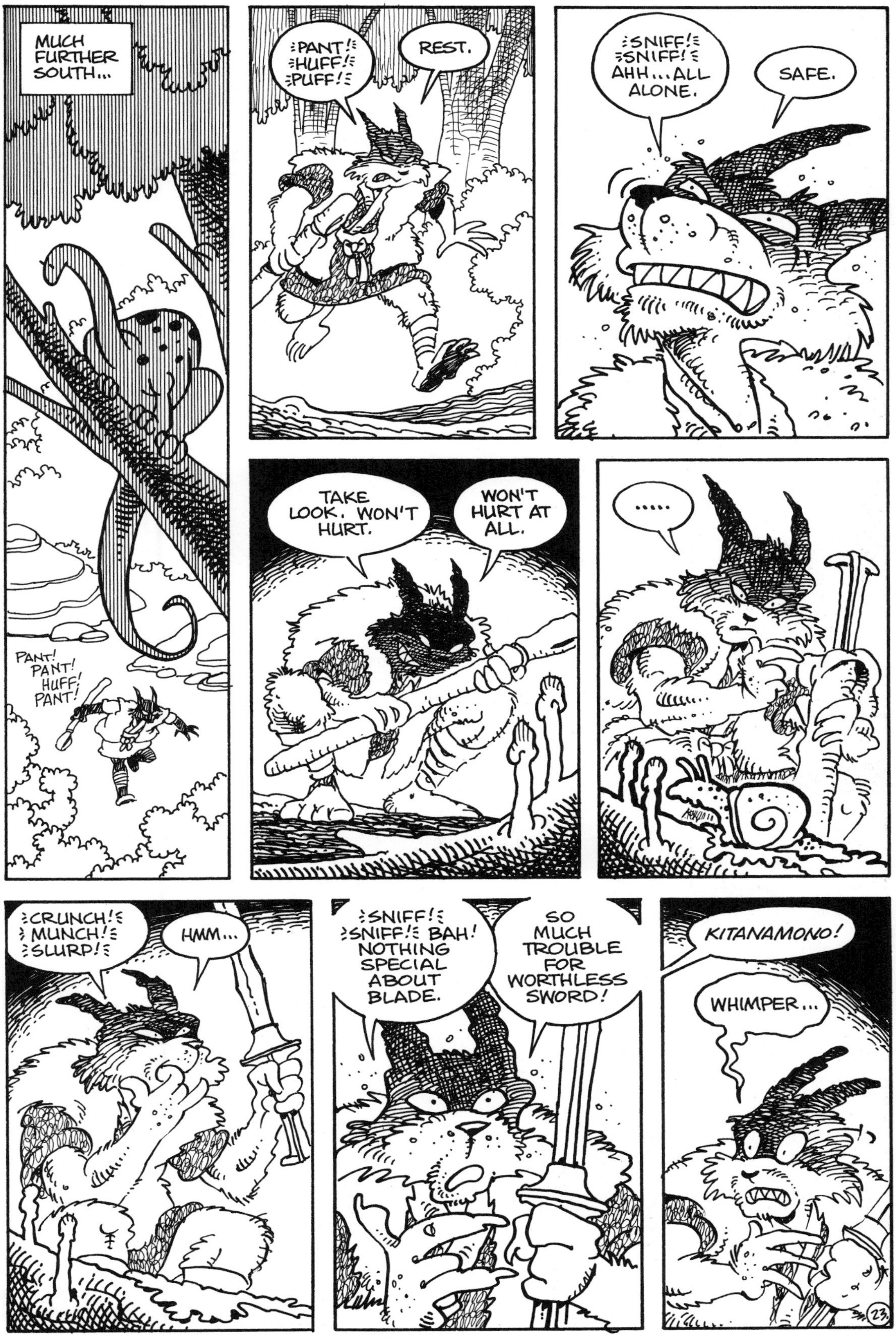
MUCH FURTHER SOUTH...
PANT! PANT! HUFF! PANT!
PANT! HUFF! PUFF!
REST.
SNIFF! SNIFF! AHH... ALL ALONE.
SAFE.
TAKE LOOK. WON'T HURT.
WON'T HURT AT ALL.
.....
CRUNCH! MUNCH! SLURP!
HMM...
SNIFF! SNIFF! BAH! NOTHING SPECIAL ABOUT BLADE.
SO MUCH TROUBLE FOR WORTHLESS SWORD!
KITANAMONO!
WHIMPER...
23

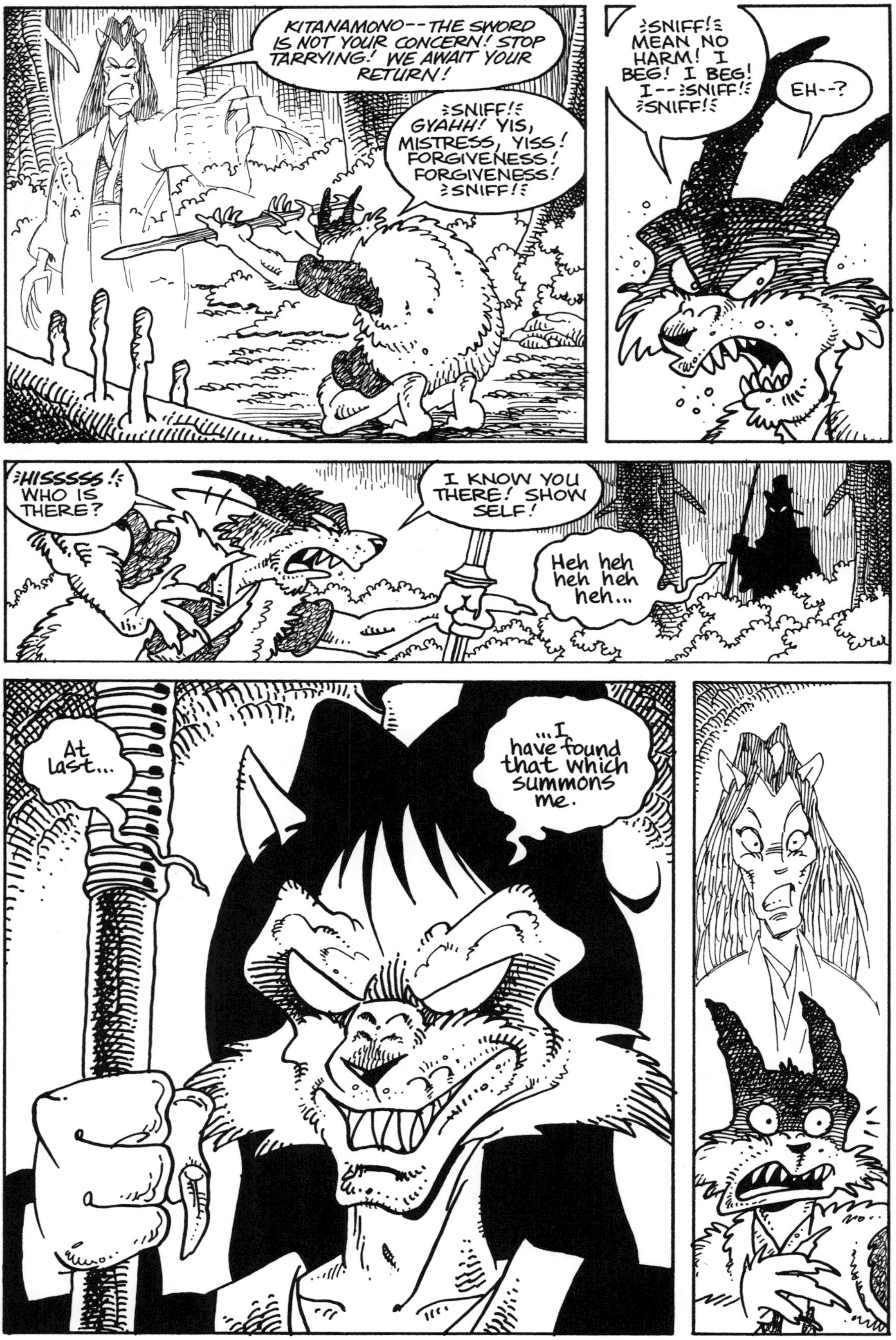
KITANAMONO--THE SWORD IS NOT YOUR CONCERN! STOP TARRYING! WE AWAIT YOUR RETURN!
SNIFF! GYAHH! YIS, MISTRESS, YISS! FORGIVENESS! FORGIVENESS! SNIFF!
SNIFF! MEAN NO HARM! I BEG! I BEG! I--SNIFF! SNIFF!
EH--?
HISSSSS! WHO IS THERE?
I KNOW YOU THERE! SHOW SELF!
Heh heh heh heh heh...
At last...
...I have found that which summons me.

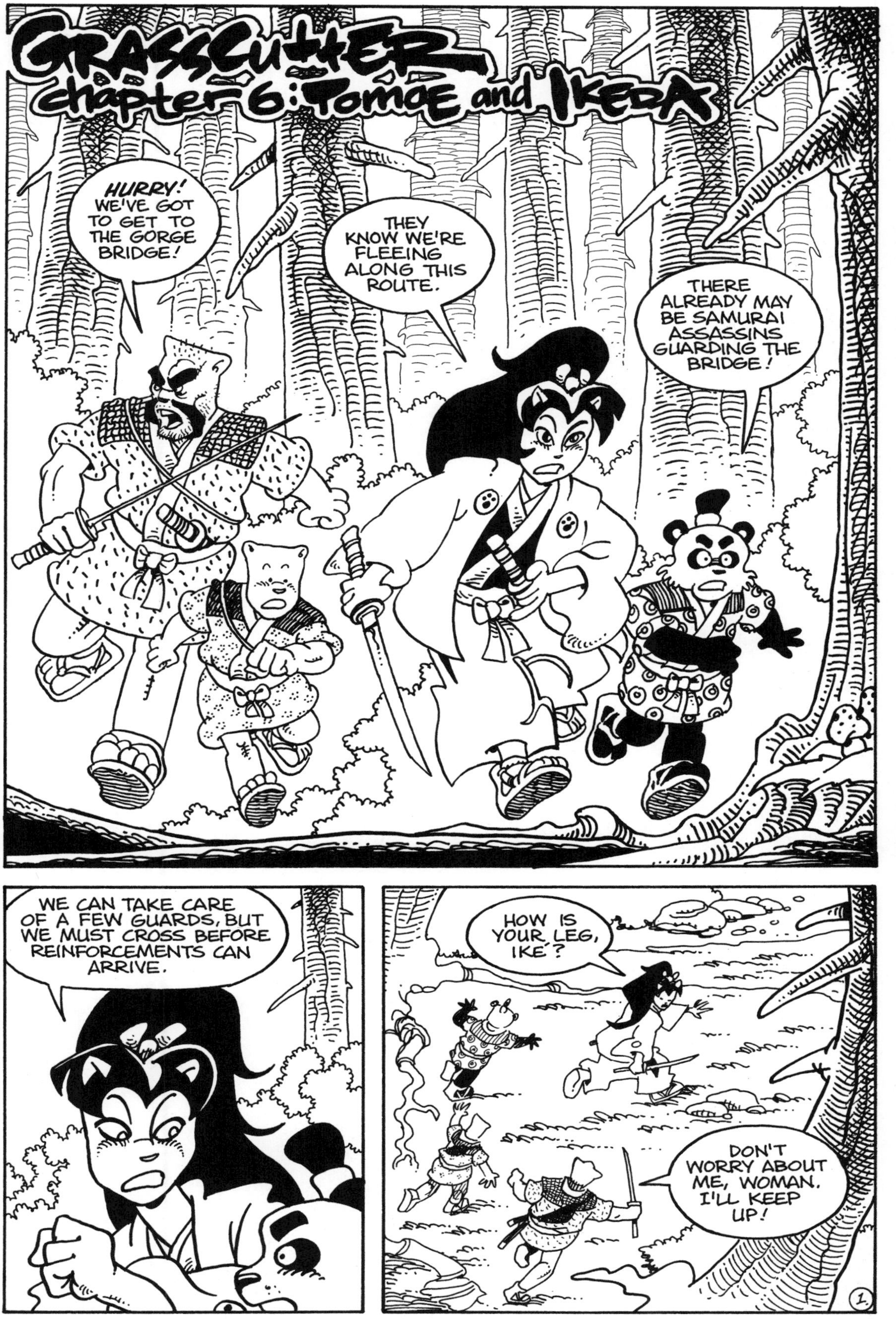
GRASSCUTTER
chapter 6: TOMOE and IKEDA
HURRY! WE'VE GOT TO GET TO THE GORGE BRIDGE!
THEY KNOW WE'RE FLEEING ALONG THIS ROUTE.
THERE ALREADY MAY BE SAMURAI ASSASSINS GUARDING THE BRIDGE!
WE CAN TAKE CARE OF A FEW GUARDS, BUT WE MUST CROSS BEFORE REINFORCEMENTS CAN ARRIVE.
HOW IS YOUR LEG, IKE?
DON'T WORRY ABOUT ME, WOMAN. I'LL KEEP UP!
1.

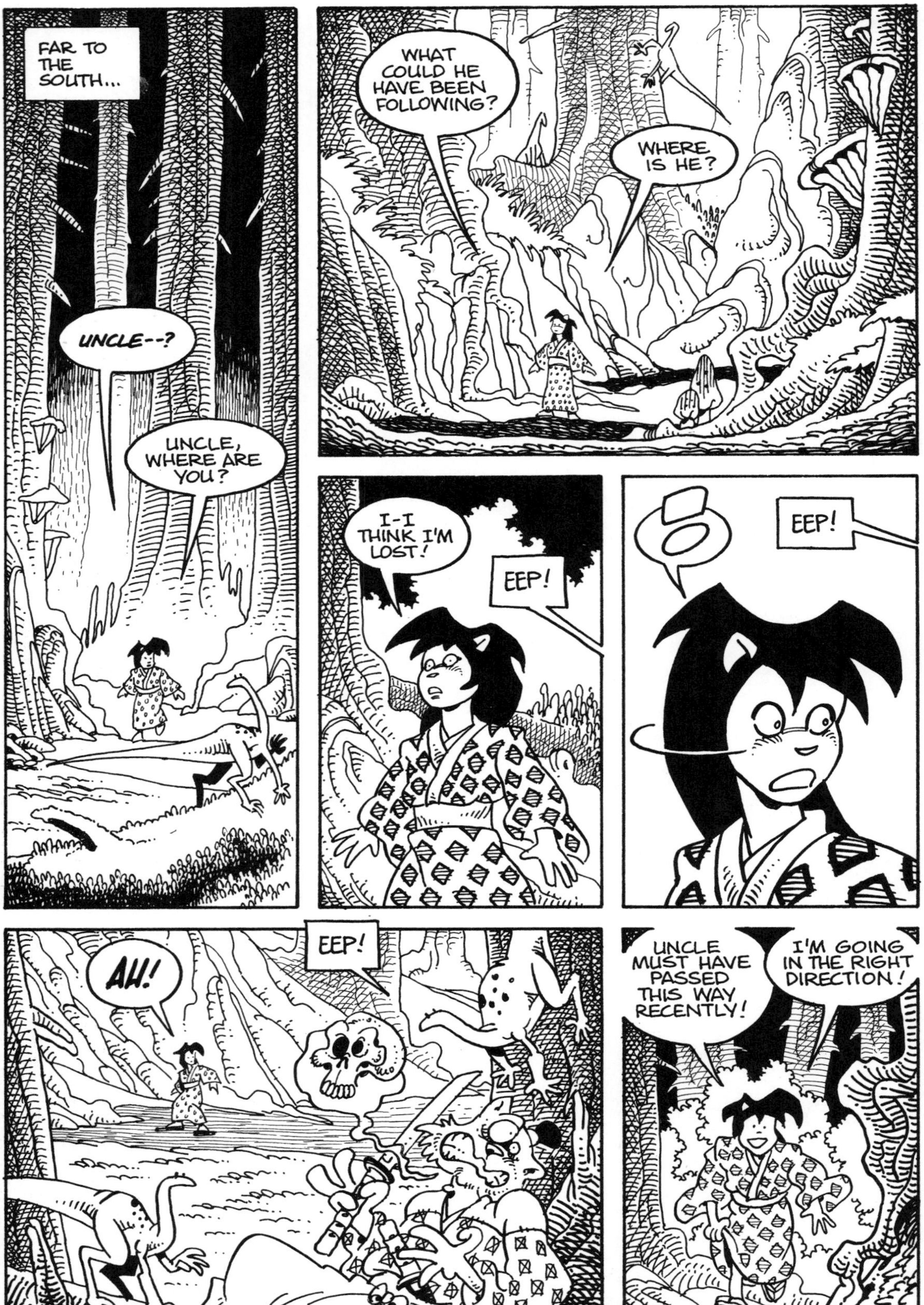
FAR TO THE SOUTH...
UNCLE--?
UNCLE, WHERE ARE YOU?
WHAT COULD HE HAVE BEEN FOLLOWING?
WHERE IS HE?
I-I THINK I'M LOST!
EEP!
EEP!
AH!
EEP!
UNCLE MUST HAVE PASSED THIS WAY RECENTLY!
I'M GOING IN THE RIGHT DIRECTION!
2.

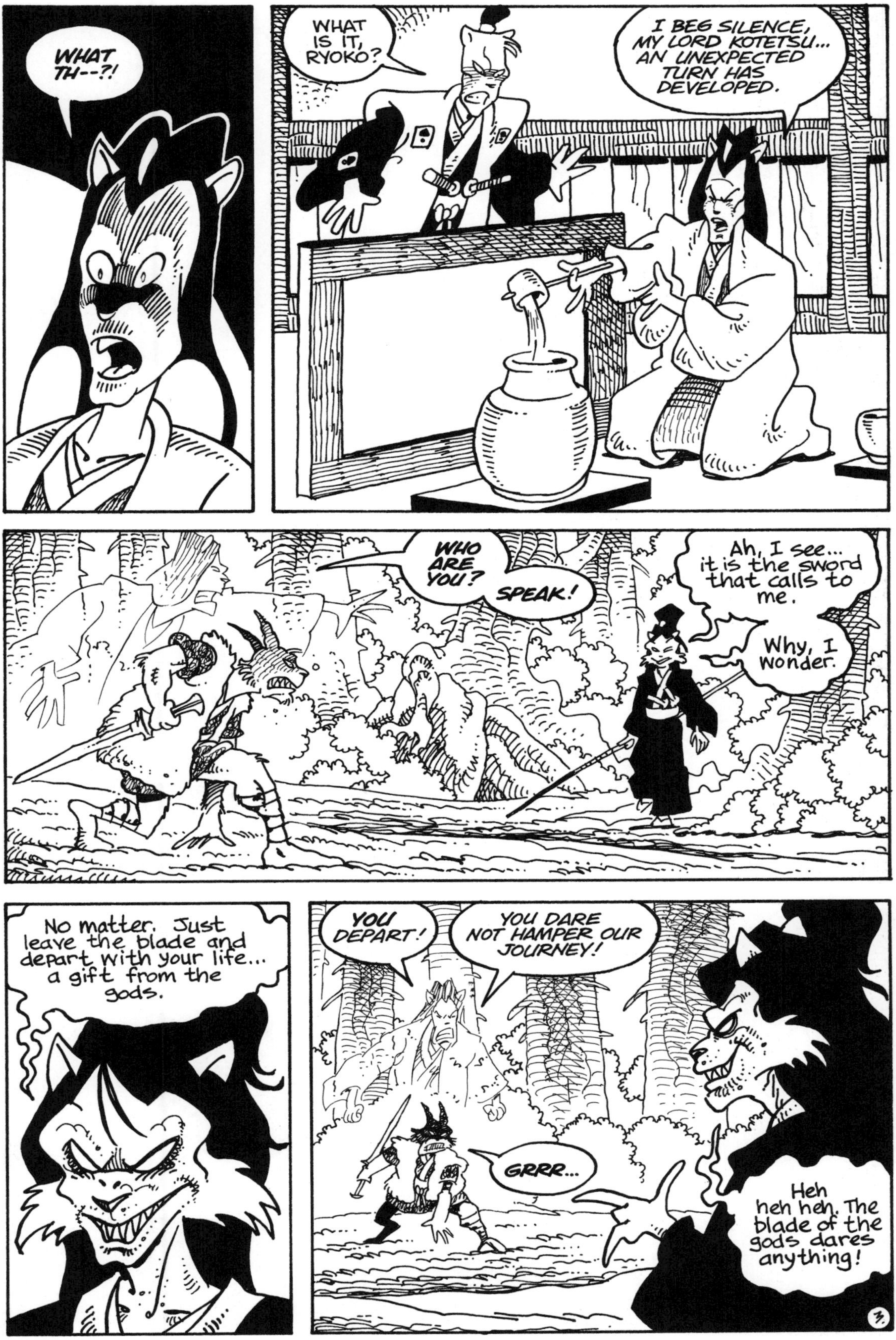
WHAT TH--?!
WHAT IS IT, RYOKO?
I BEG SILENCE, MY LORD KOTETSU... AN UNEXPECTED TURN HAS DEVELOPED.
WHO ARE YOU?
SPEAK!
Ah, I see... it is the sword that calls to me.
Why, I wonder.
No matter. Just leave the blade and depart with your life... a gift from the gods.
YOU DEPART!
YOU DARE NOT HAMPER OUR JOURNEY!
GRRR...
Heh heh heh. The blade of the gods dares anything!
3.

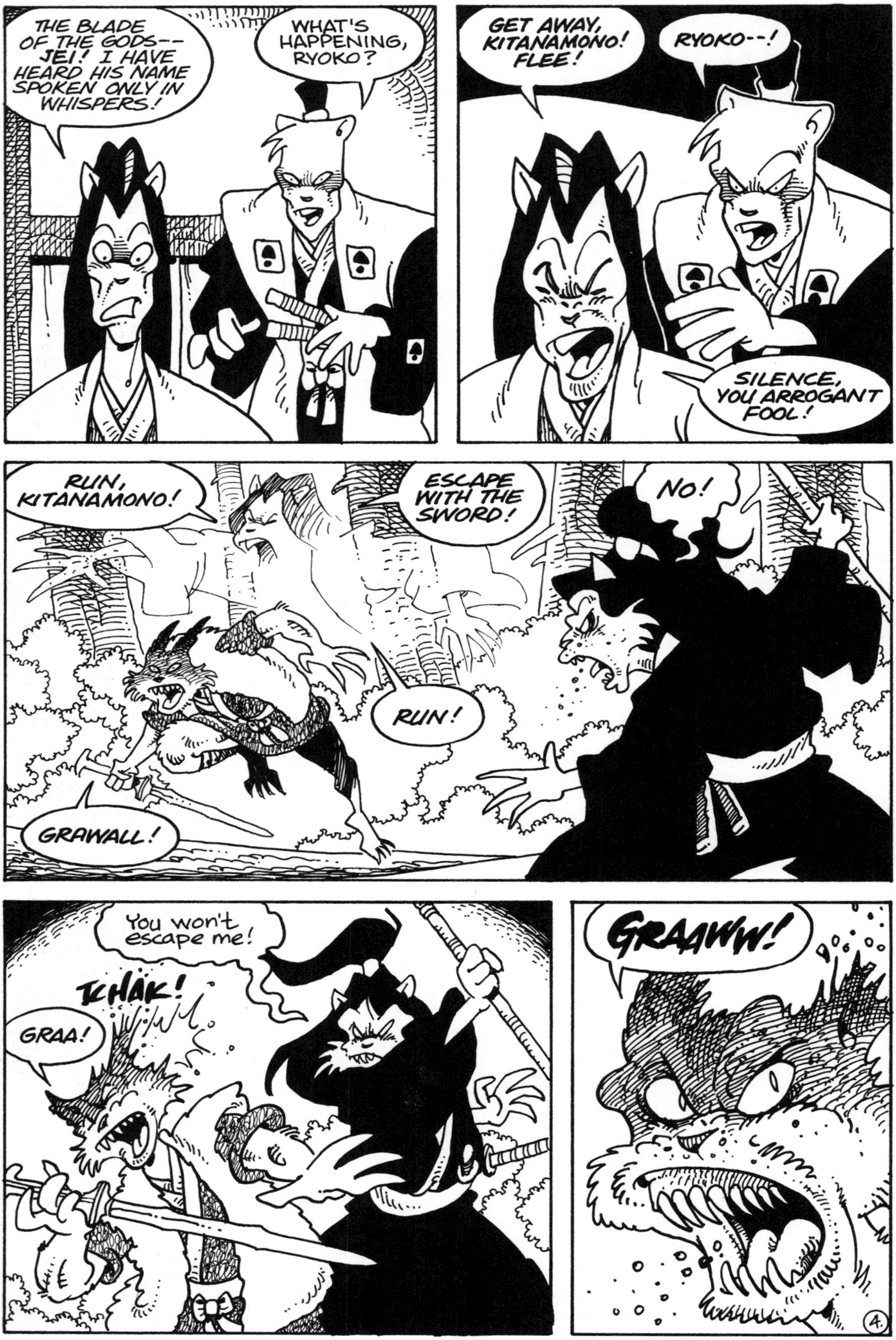
THE BLADE OF THE GODS-- JEI! I HAVE HEARD HIS NAME SPOKEN ONLY IN WHISPERS!
WHAT'S HAPPENING, RYOKO?
GET AWAY, KITANAMONO! FLEE!
RYOKO--!
SILENCE, YOU ARROGANT FOOL!
RUN, KITANAMONO!
ESCAPE WITH THE SWORD!
NO!
RUN!
GRAWALL!
You won't escape me!
KHAK!
GRAA!
GRAAWW!
4.

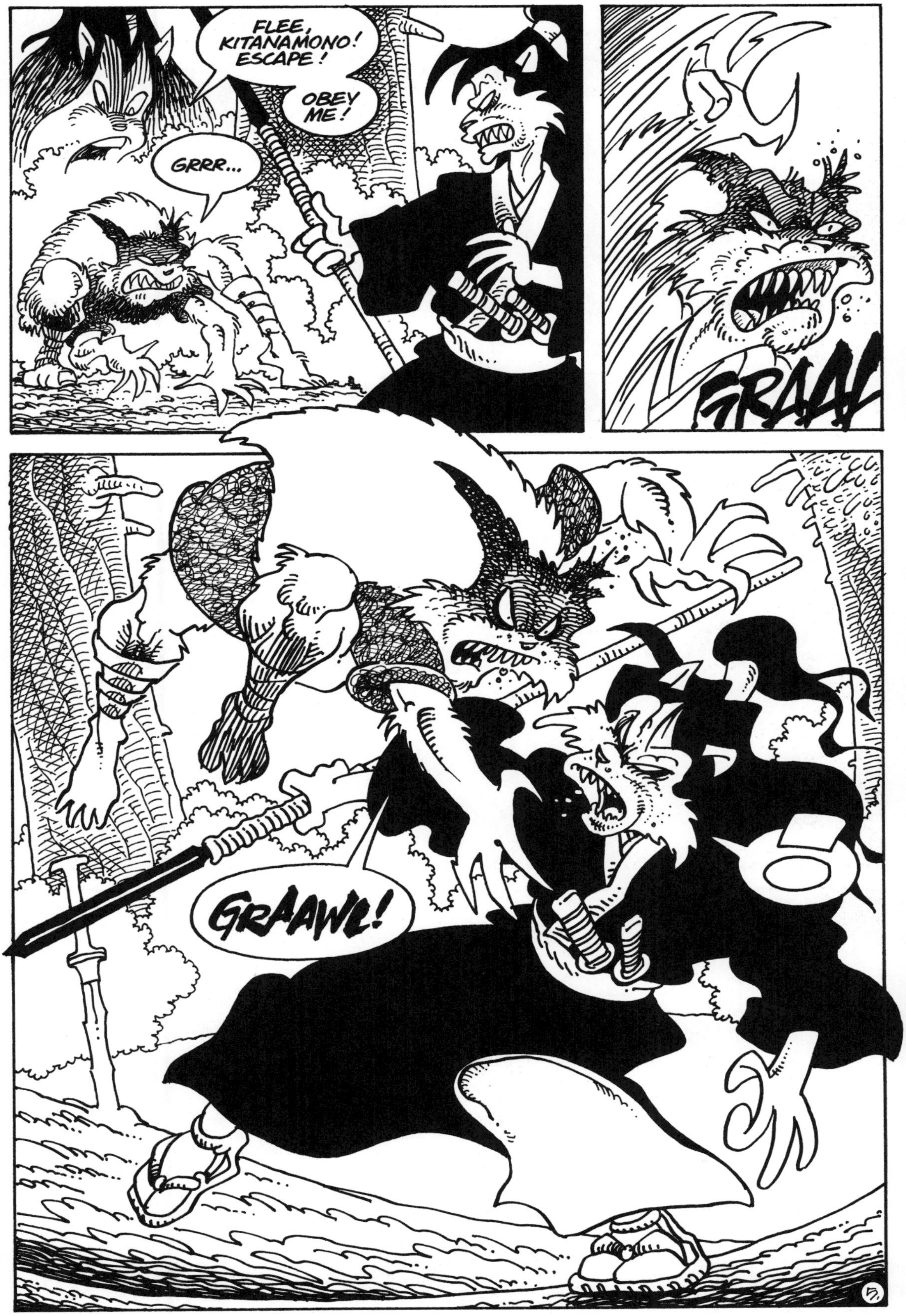
FLEE, KITANAMONO! ESCAPE!
OBEY ME!
GRRR...
GRAAA
GRAAWL!

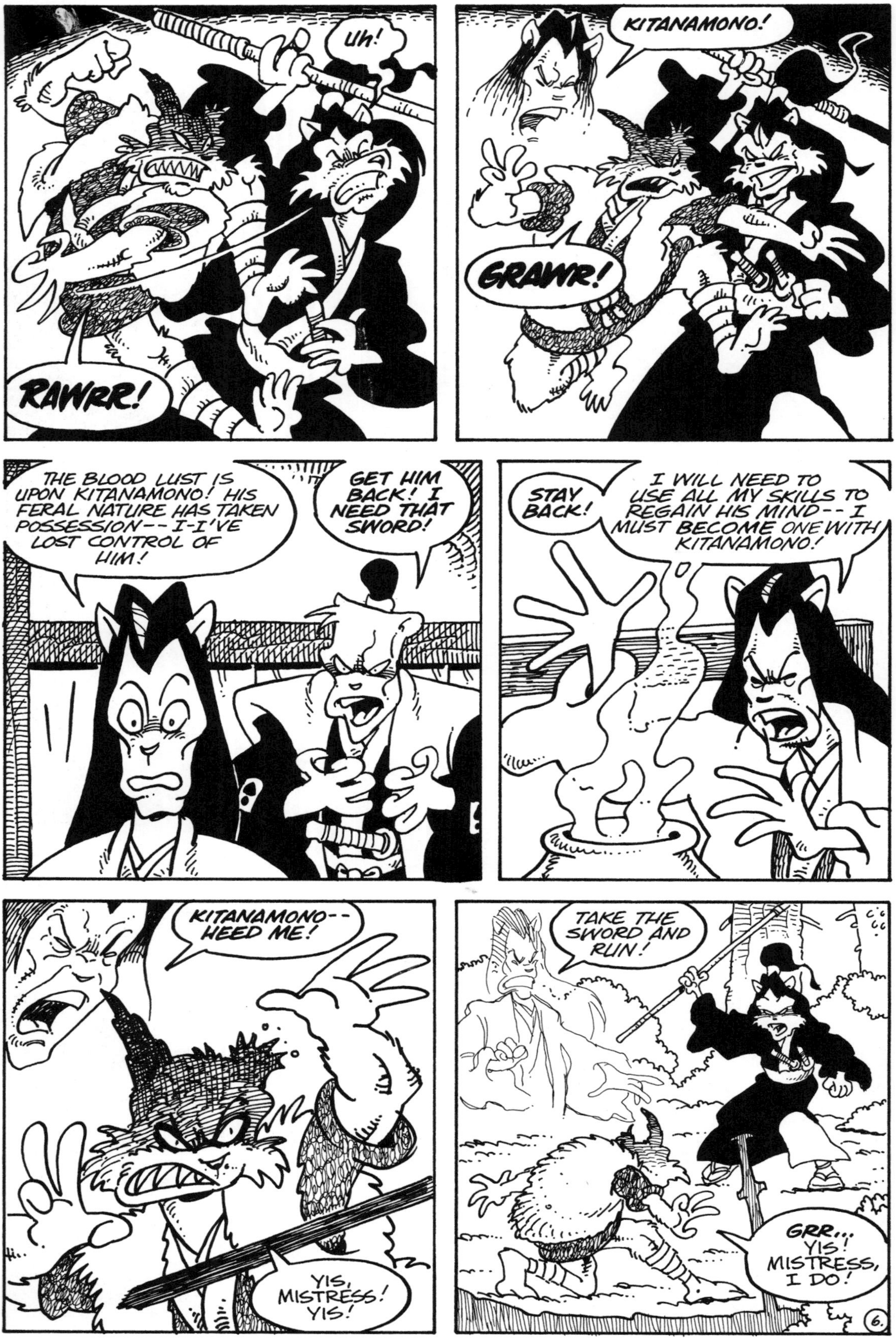
Uh!
RAWRR!
KITANAMONO!
GRAWR!
THE BLOOD LUST IS UPON KITANAMONO! HIS FERAL NATURE HAS TAKEN POSSESSION-- I-I'VE LOST CONTROL OF HIM!
GET HIM BACK! I NEED THAT SWORD!
STAY BACK!
I WILL NEED TO USE ALL MY SKILLS TO REGAIN HIS MIND-- I MUST BECOME ONE WITH KITANAMONO!
KITANAMONO-- HEED ME!
YIS, MISTRESS! YIS!
TAKE THE SWORD AND RUN!
GRR... YIS! MISTRESS, I DO!
6.

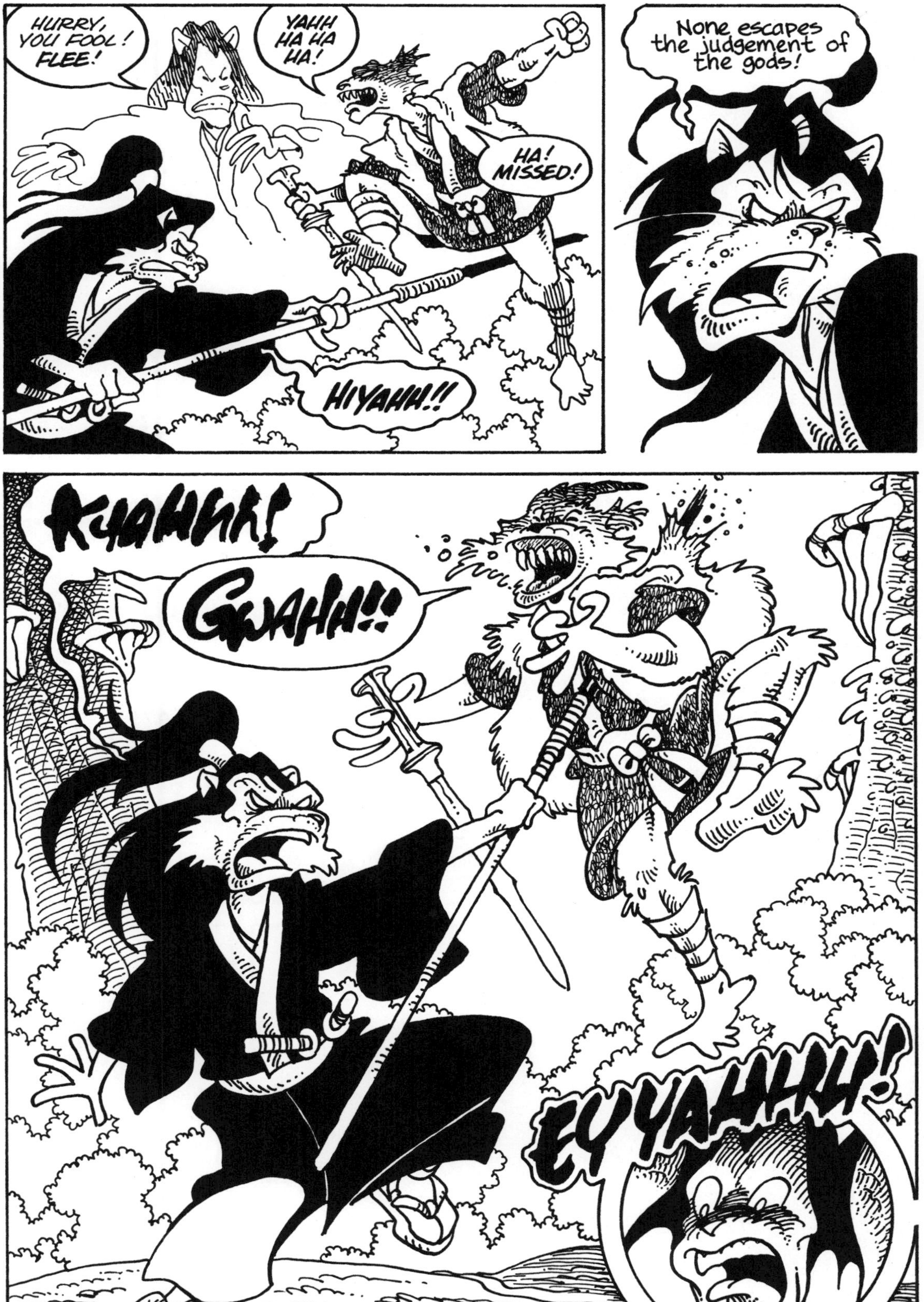
HURRY, YOU FOOL! FLEE!
YAHH HA HA HA!
HA! MISSED!
HIYAHH!!
None escapes the judgement of the gods!
KYAHHH!
GWAHH!!
EIYAHHH!
7.

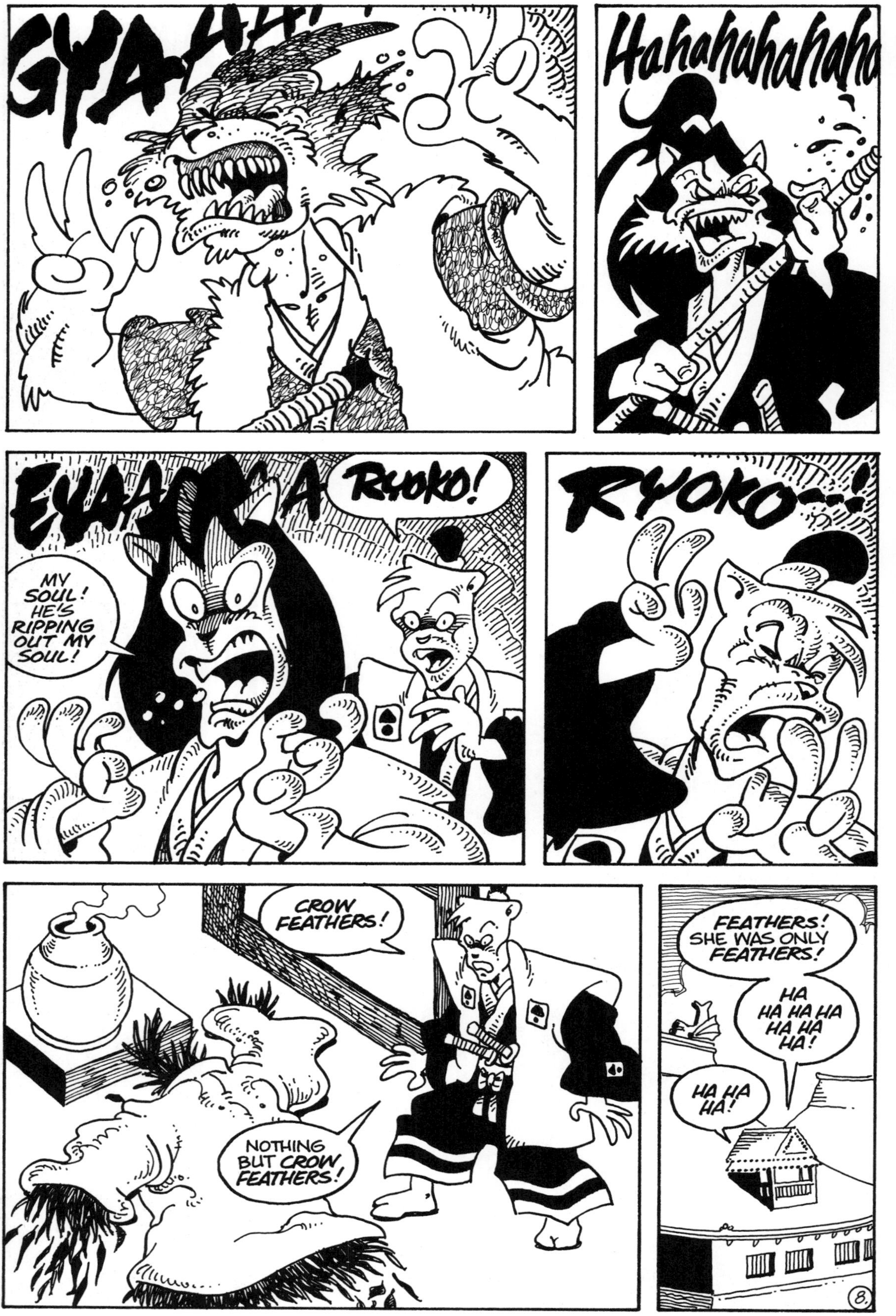
RYOKO!
MY SOUL! HE'S RIPPING OUT MY SOUL!
RYOKO--!
CROW FEATHERS!
NOTHING BUT CROW FEATHERS!
FEATHERS! SHE WAS ONLY FEATHERS!
HA HA HA HA HA HA HA!
HA HA HA!
8.

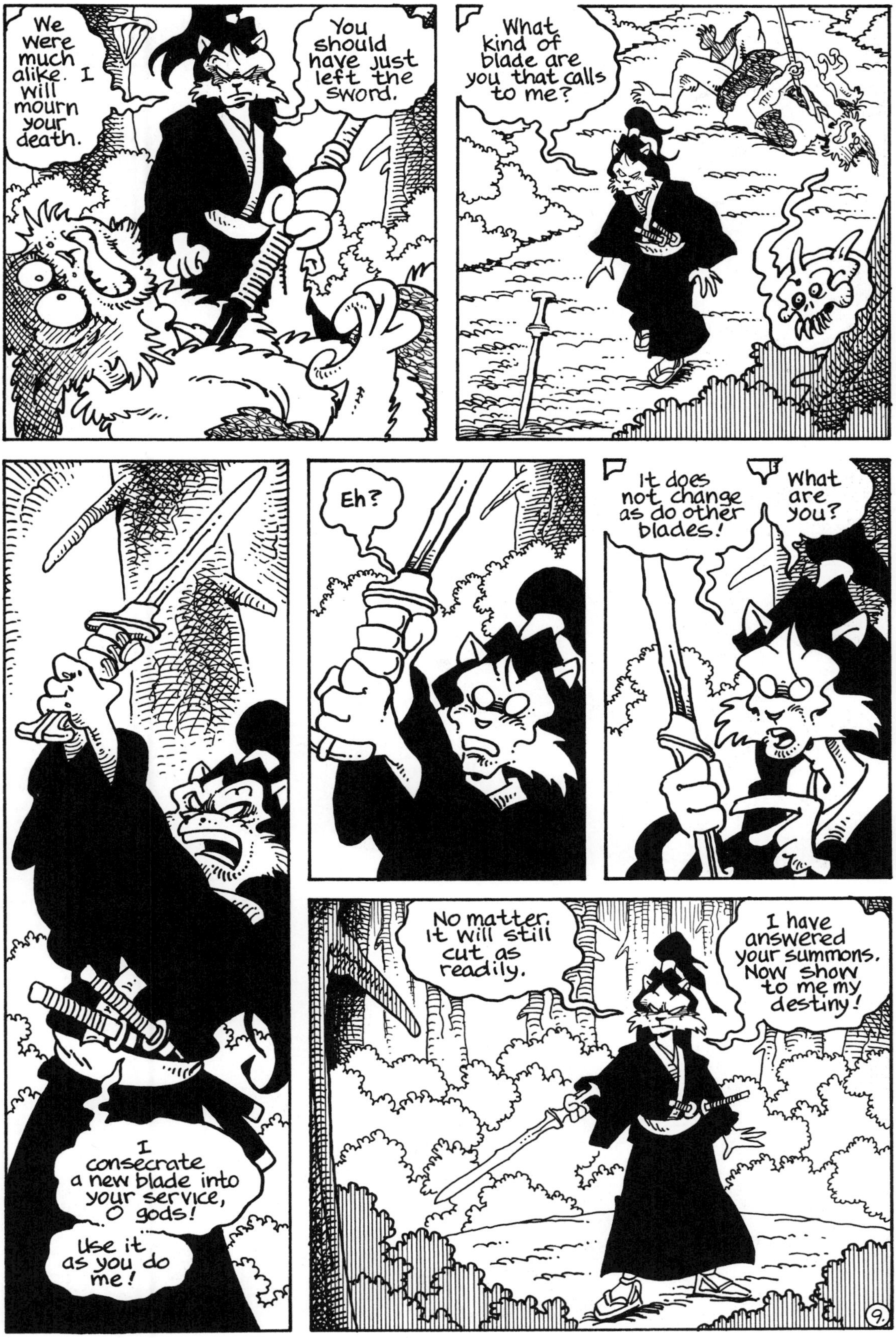
We were much alike. I will mourn your death.
You should have just left the sword.
What kind of blade are you that calls to me?
I consecrate a new blade into your service, O gods!
Use it as you do me!
Eh?
It does not change as do other blades!
What are you?
No matter. It will still cut as readily.
I have answered your summons. Now show to me my destiny!
9.

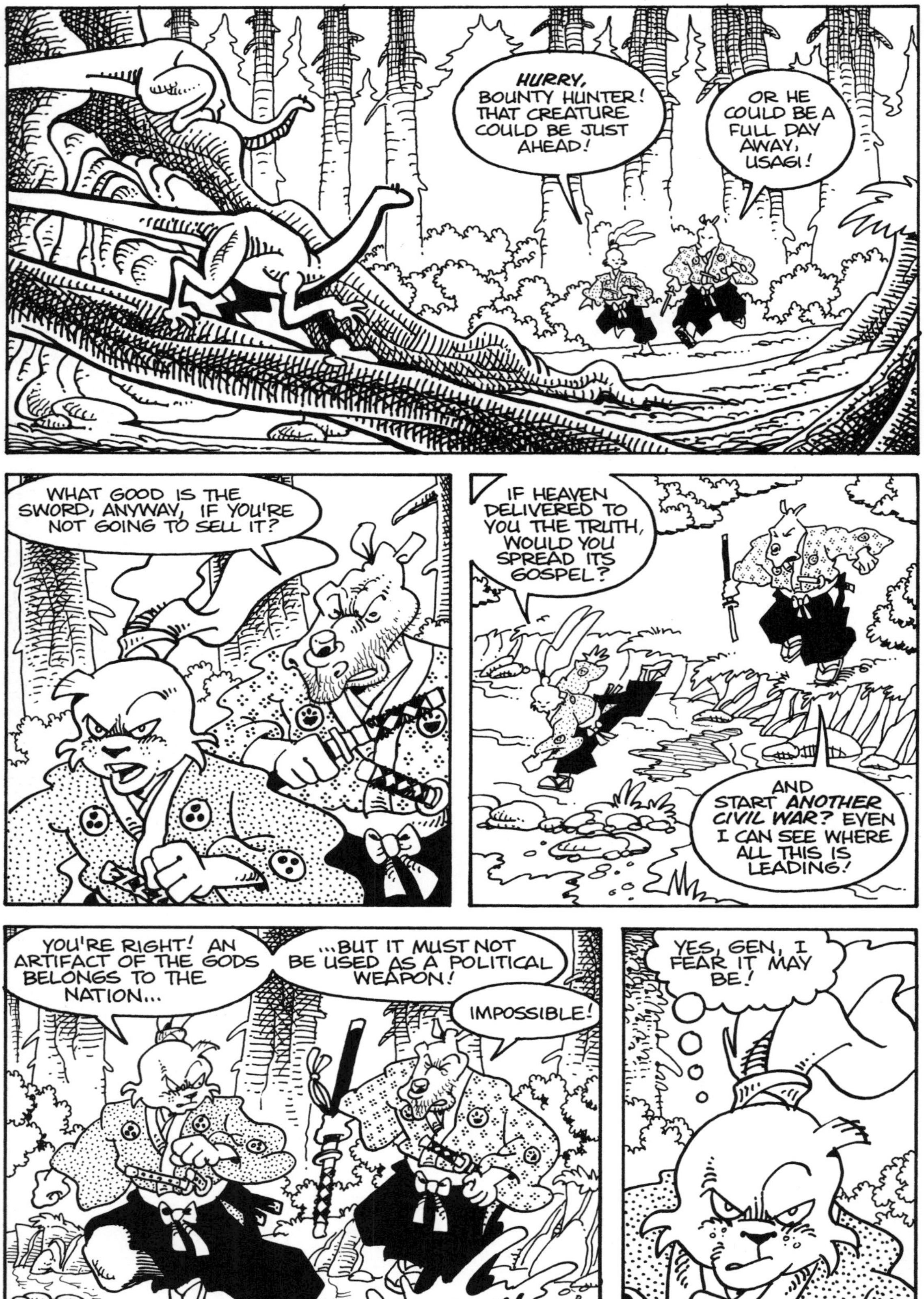
HURRY, BOUNTY HUNTER! THAT CREATURE COULD BE JUST AHEAD!
OR HE COULD BE A FULL DAY AWAY, USAGI!
WHAT GOOD IS THE SWORD, ANYWAY, IF YOU'RE NOT GOING TO SELL IT?
IF HEAVEN DELIVERED TO YOU THE TRUTH, WOULD YOU SPREAD ITS GOSPEL?
AND START ANOTHER CIVIL WAR? EVEN I CAN SEE WHERE ALL THIS IS LEADING!
YOU'RE RIGHT! AN ARTIFACT OF THE GODS BELONGS TO THE NATION...
...BUT IT MUST NOT BE USED AS A POLITICAL WEAPON!
IMPOSSIBLE!
SPLASH!
YES, GEN, I FEAR IT MAY BE!
10.

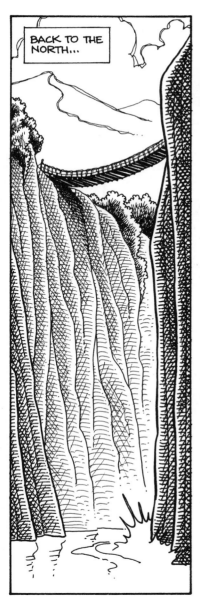

BACK TO THE NORTH...

SO, THE GORGE BRIDGE IS GUARDED.

YES, BUT WE EXPECTED THAT.

THEY DON'T LOOK LIKE THEY'RE PREPARED FOR US.

THE SAMURAI THAT ESCAPED US MUST HAVE GONE TO THEIR MAIN FORCES INSTEAD OF WARNING THESE GUARDS.

THEN WE'D BETTER CROSS QUICKLY BEFORE OTHERS ARRIVE!

STAY BACK, MOTOKAZU, LORD NORIYUKI!

11.

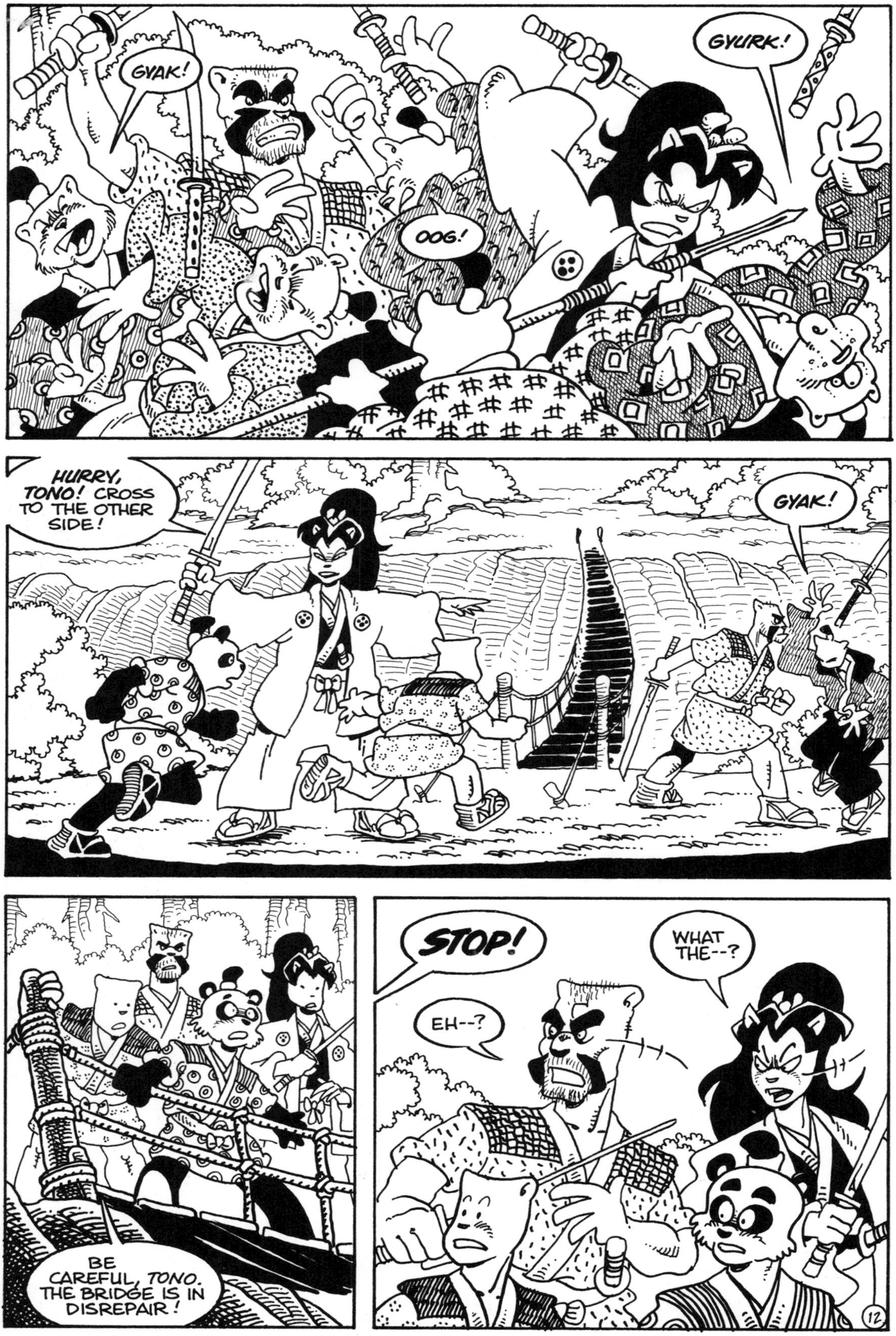
GYAK!
OOG!
GYURK!
HURRY, TONO! CROSS TO THE OTHER SIDE!
GYAK!
BE CAREFUL, TONO. THE BRIDGE IS IN DISREPAIR!
STOP!
EH--?
WHAT THE--?
12

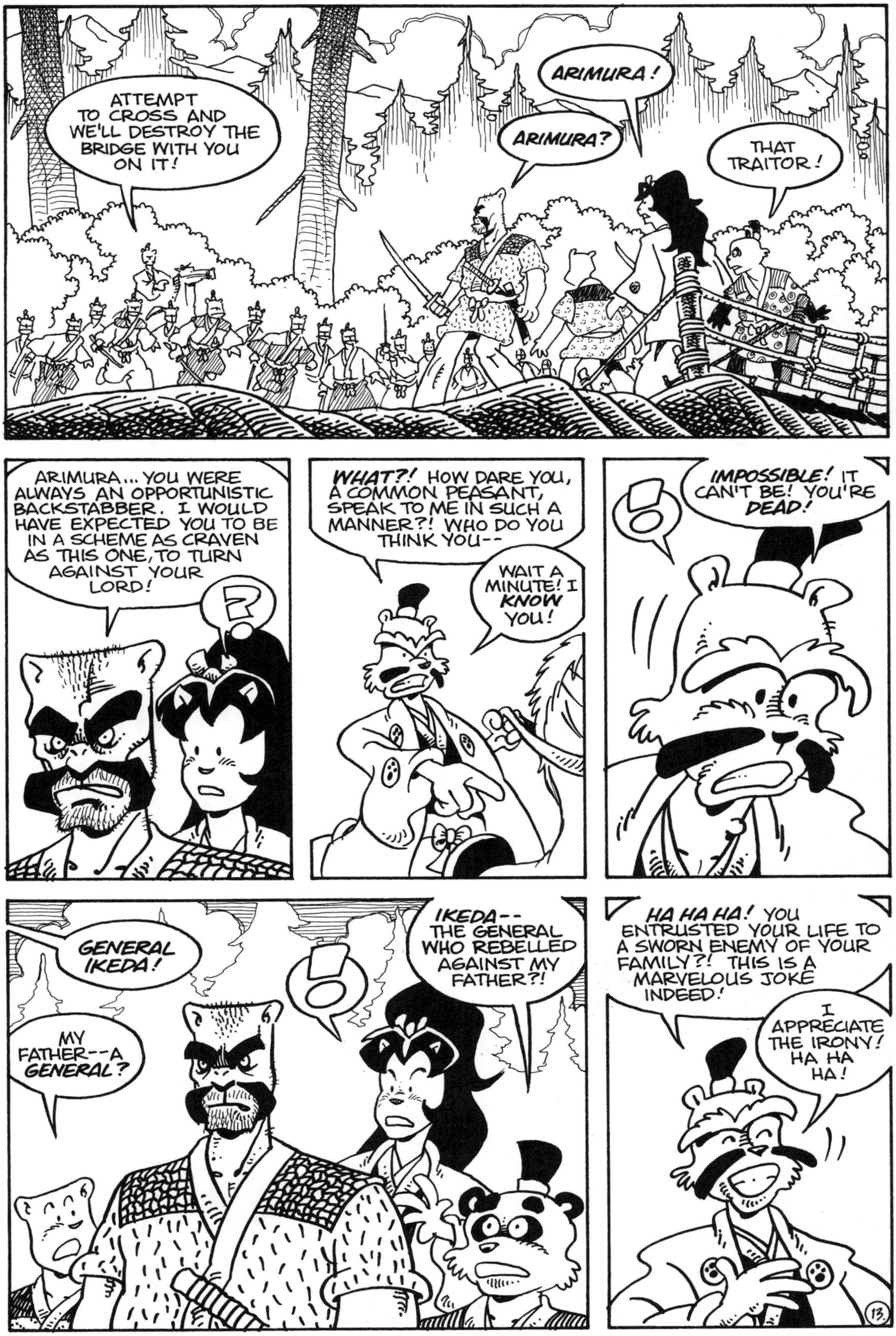

ATTEMPT TO CROSS AND WE'LL DESTROY THE BRIDGE WITH YOU ON IT!
ARIMURA!
ARIMURA?
THAT TRAITOR!
ARIMURA... YOU WERE ALWAYS AN OPPORTUNISTIC BACKSTABBER. I WOULD HAVE EXPECTED YOU TO BE IN A SCHEME AS CRAVEN AS THIS ONE, TO TURN AGAINST YOUR LORD!
?
WHAT?! HOW DARE YOU, A COMMON PEASANT, SPEAK TO ME IN SUCH A MANNER?! WHO DO YOU THINK YOU--
WAIT A MINUTE! I KNOW YOU!
!
IMPOSSIBLE! IT CAN'T BE! YOU'RE DEAD!
GENERAL IKEDA!
MY FATHER--A GENERAL?
!
IKEDA-- THE GENERAL WHO REBELLED AGAINST MY FATHER?!
HA HA HA! YOU ENTRUSTED YOUR LIFE TO A SWORN ENEMY OF YOUR FAMILY?! THIS IS A MARVELOUS JOKE INDEED!
I APPRECIATE THE IRONY! HA HA HA!
13.

YOU WENT UP AGAINST HIS FATHER, SO YOU MUST HAVE NO LOYALTY TO THE BRAT NORIYUKI. COME AND JOIN ME, IKEDA, AND REAP THE REWARDS ONCE I COME INTO POWER!

I KNEW YOU WHEN YOU WERE A POWER-HUNGRY JUNIOR COUNSELOR. YOU WERE AMBITIOUS BUT A COWARD! YOU WOULD NEVER ATTEMPT A COUP ON YOUR OWN! YOU ARE A PUPPET. WHO CONTROLS YOU, ARIMURA?

I DON'T KNOW IF IKEDA WILL DECIDE TO JOIN THEM.

GET READY TO RUN, *TONO!*

I NEED NOT ANSWER TO THE LIKES OF YOU, IKEDA! JUST KNOW THAT IT IS THE BOY WHO IS YOUR ENEMY. JOIN ME AND I WILL BECOME YOUR BENEFACTOR!

YOU'LL BE A *LORD* AGAIN... INSTEAD OF A GROVELLING PEASANT!

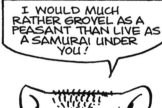

I WOULD MUCH RATHER GROVEL AS A PEASANT THAN LIVE AS A SAMURAI UNDER YOU!

YOU ARROGANT WRETCH -- A PEASANT'S LIFE HAS NOT TAUGHT YOU HUMILITY TOWARDS YOUR BETTERS! VERY WELL, THEN DIE AS YOU'VE LIVED!

KILL THEM! KILL THEM ALL!

14.

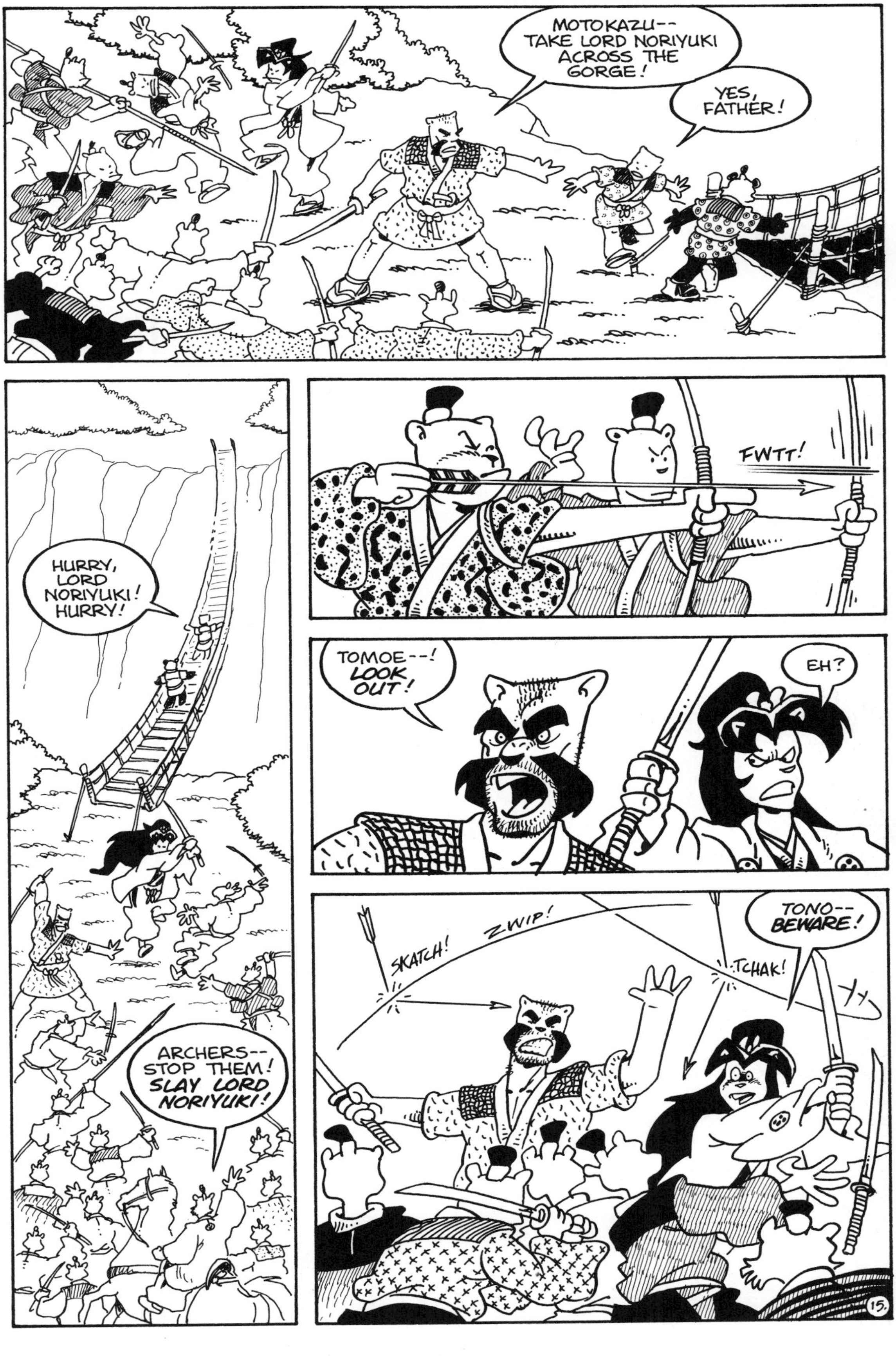
MOTOKAZU-- TAKE LORD NORIYUKI ACROSS THE GORGE!
YES, FATHER!
HURRY, LORD NORIYUKI! HURRY!
ARCHERS-- STOP THEM! SLAY LORD NORIYUKI!
FWTT!
TOMOE--! LOOK OUT!
EH?
SKATCH!
ZWIP!
TCHAK!
TONO-- BEWARE!
15.

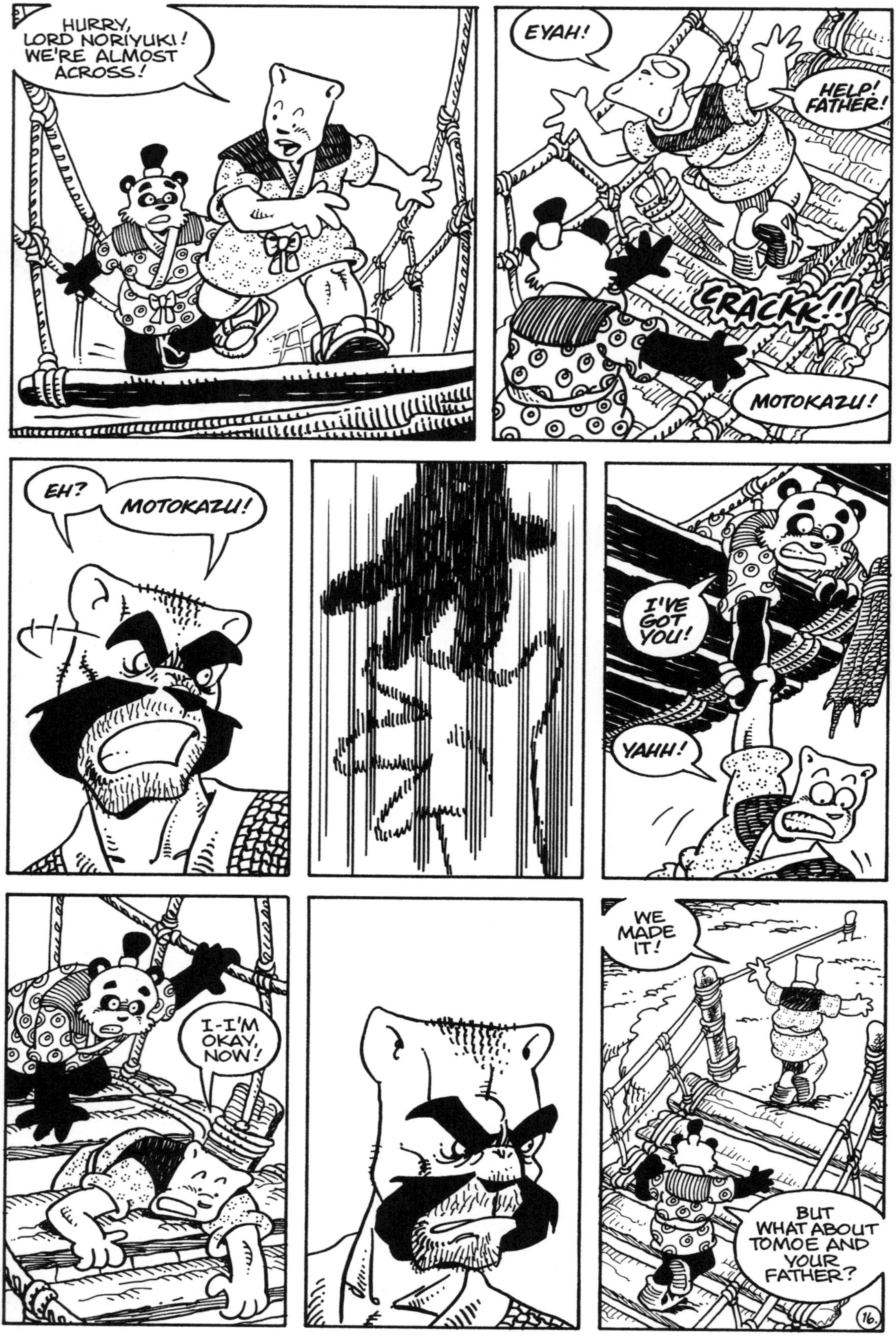
HURRY, LORD NORIYUKI! WE'RE ALMOST ACROSS!
EYAH!
HELP! FATHER!
CRACKK!!
MOTOKAZU!
EH?
MOTOKAZU!
I'VE GOT YOU!
YAHH!
I-I'M OKAY, NOW!
WE MADE IT!
BUT WHAT ABOUT TOMOE AND YOUR FATHER?
16.

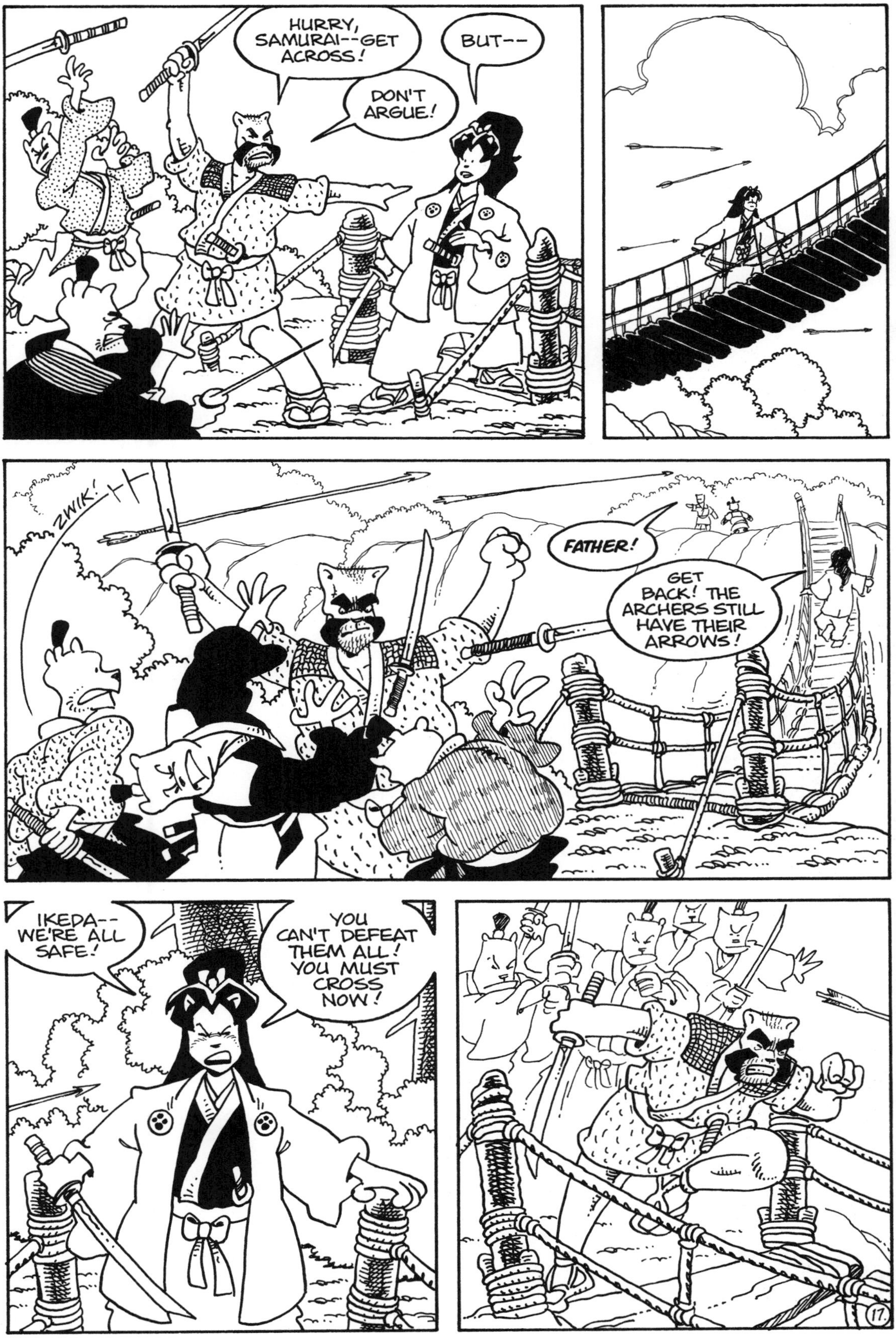
HURRY, SAMURAI--GET ACROSS!
BUT--
DON'T ARGUE!
ZWIK!
FATHER!
GET BACK! THE ARCHERS STILL HAVE THEIR ARROWS!
IKEDA-- WE'RE ALL SAFE!
YOU CAN'T DEFEAT THEM ALL! YOU MUST CROSS NOW!
17

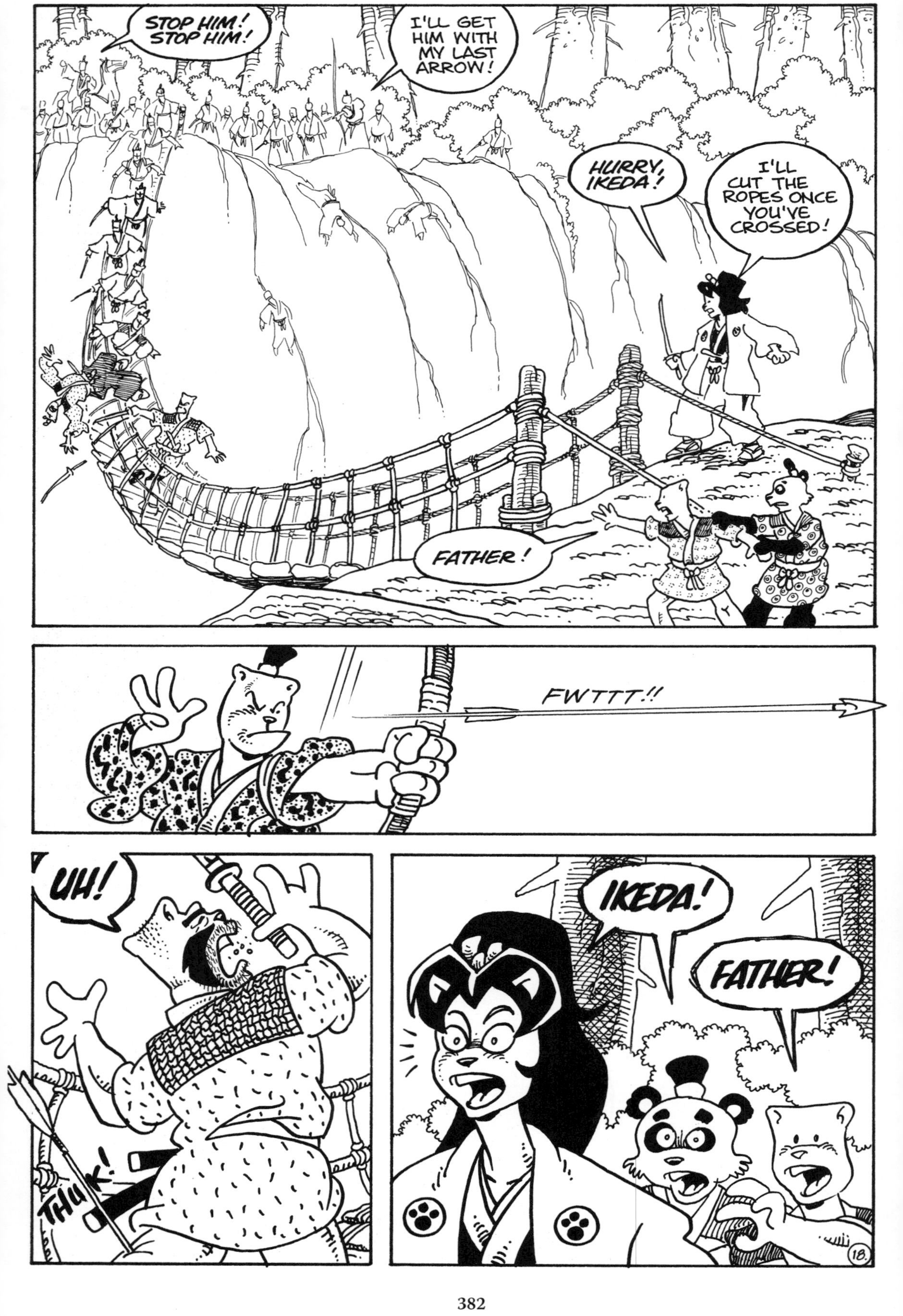
STOP HIM! STOP HIM!
I'LL GET HIM WITH MY LAST ARROW!
HURRY, IKEDA!
I'LL CUT THE ROPES ONCE YOU'VE CROSSED!
FATHER!
FWTTT!!
UH!
THUK!
IKEDA!
FATHER!
18.

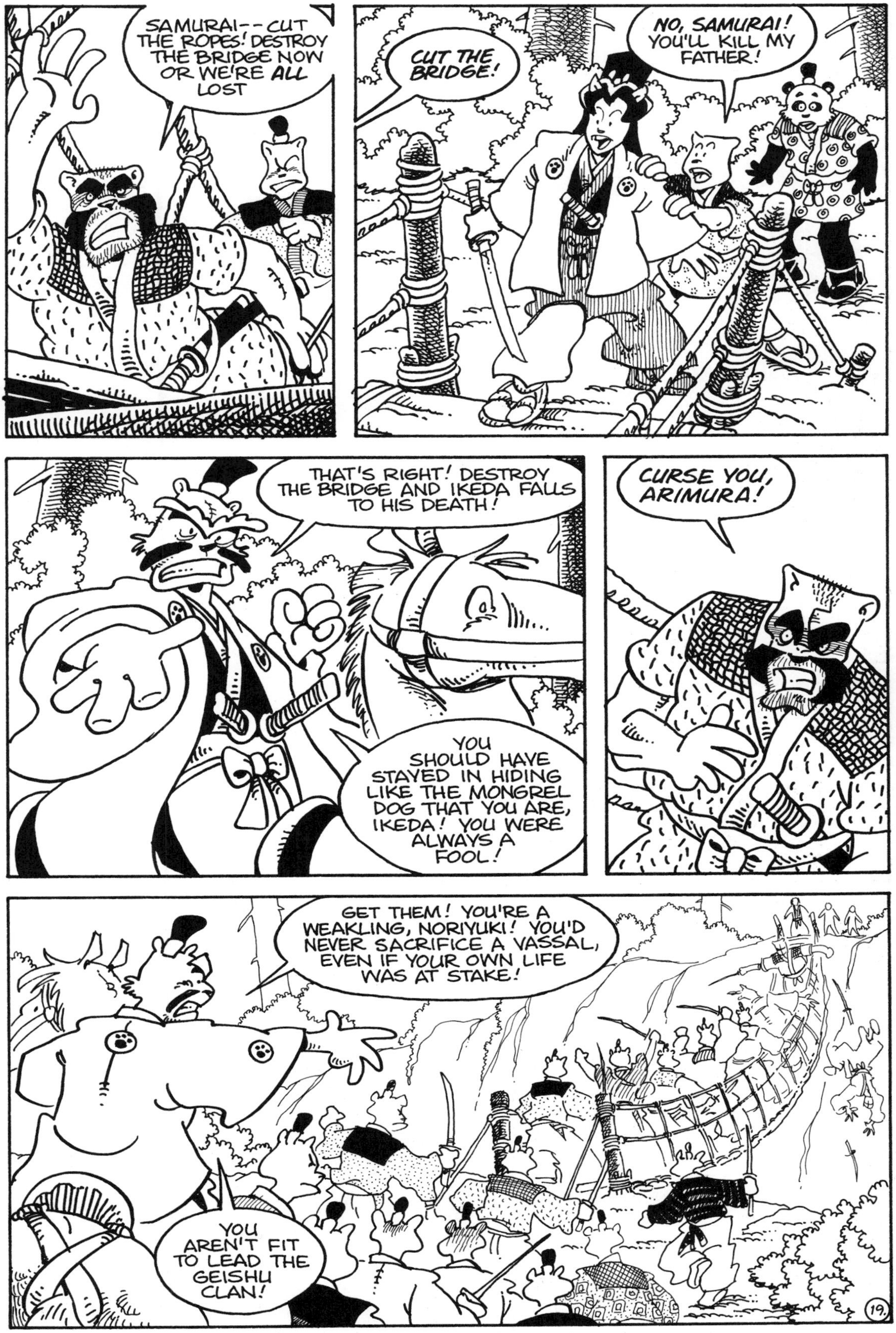
SAMURAI--CUT THE ROPES! DESTROY THE BRIDGE NOW OR WE'RE ALL LOST
CUT THE BRIDGE!
NO, SAMURAI! YOU'LL KILL MY FATHER!
THAT'S RIGHT! DESTROY THE BRIDGE AND IKEDA FALLS TO HIS DEATH!
YOU SHOULD HAVE STAYED IN HIDING LIKE THE MONGREL DOG THAT YOU ARE, IKEDA! YOU WERE ALWAYS A FOOL!
CURSE YOU, ARIMURA!
GET THEM! YOU'RE A WEAKLING, NORIYUKI! YOU'D NEVER SACRIFICE A VASSAL, EVEN IF YOUR OWN LIFE WAS AT STAKE!
YOU AREN'T FIT TO LEAD THE GEISHU CLAN!
19.

WE LEARN VALUABLE LESSONS AS WE FACE DEATH, LORD NORIYUKI.

I WAS WRONG.

YOU ARE A TRUE LORD!

THANK YOU FOR MY SON'S LIFE!

I GLADLY GIVE *MY* LIFE TO REGAIN LOST HONOR

NO!

FWWT!

TCK!

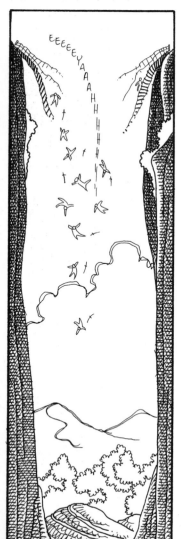

EEEEEYAAAHHHHH

NNNGG!

THEY'RE LEAVING!

FATHER! OH, FATHER!

20.

YOUR FATHER WAS A GOOD WARRIOR.

HE WILL BE GIVEN A HERO'S MEMORIAL.

F-FATHER! ≥SOB!≥

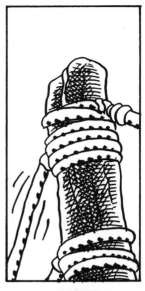

HMM...?

TONO! MOTOKAZU!

WELL?!

ARE YOU GOING TO HELP ME UP OR JUST LEAVE ME DANGLING HERE?!

ARIMURA WILL BE CIRCLING AROUND TO INTERCEPT US AGAIN, AND WE WON'T BE ABLE TO TRAVEL AS FAST WITH AN ARROW IN MY LEG!

21.

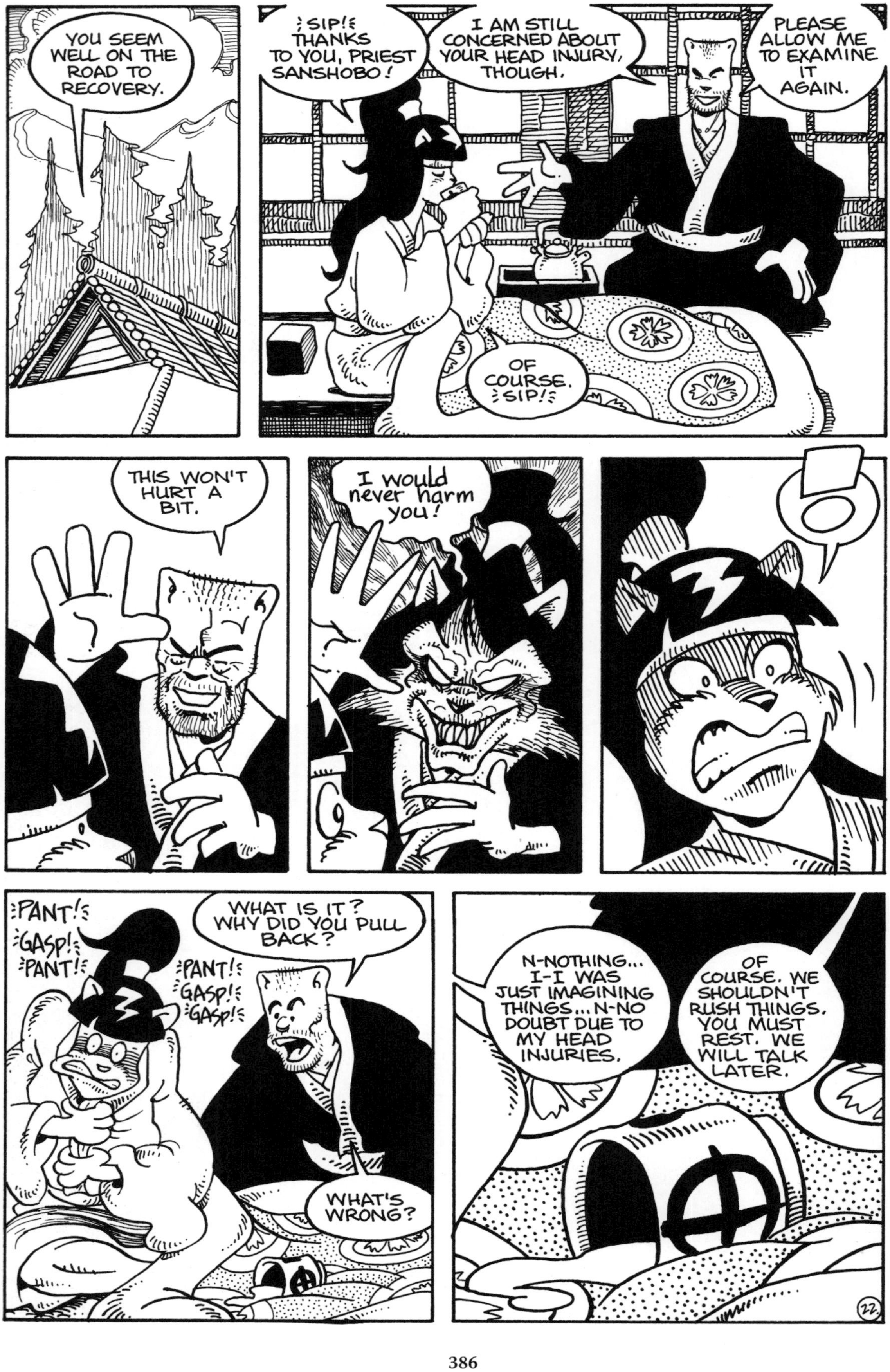
YOU SEEM WELL ON THE ROAD TO RECOVERY.
SIP! THANKS TO YOU, PRIEST SANSHOBO!
I AM STILL CONCERNED ABOUT YOUR HEAD INJURY, THOUGH.
PLEASE ALLOW ME TO EXAMINE IT AGAIN.
OF COURSE. SIP!
THIS WON'T HURT A BIT.
I would never harm you!
PANT! GASP! PANT!
WHAT IS IT? WHY DID YOU PULL BACK?
PANT! GASP! GASP!
WHAT'S WRONG?
N-NOTHING... I-I WAS JUST IMAGINING THINGS... N-NO DOUBT DUE TO MY HEAD INJURIES.
OF COURSE. WE SHOULDN'T RUSH THINGS. YOU MUST REST. WE WILL TALK LATER.
22.

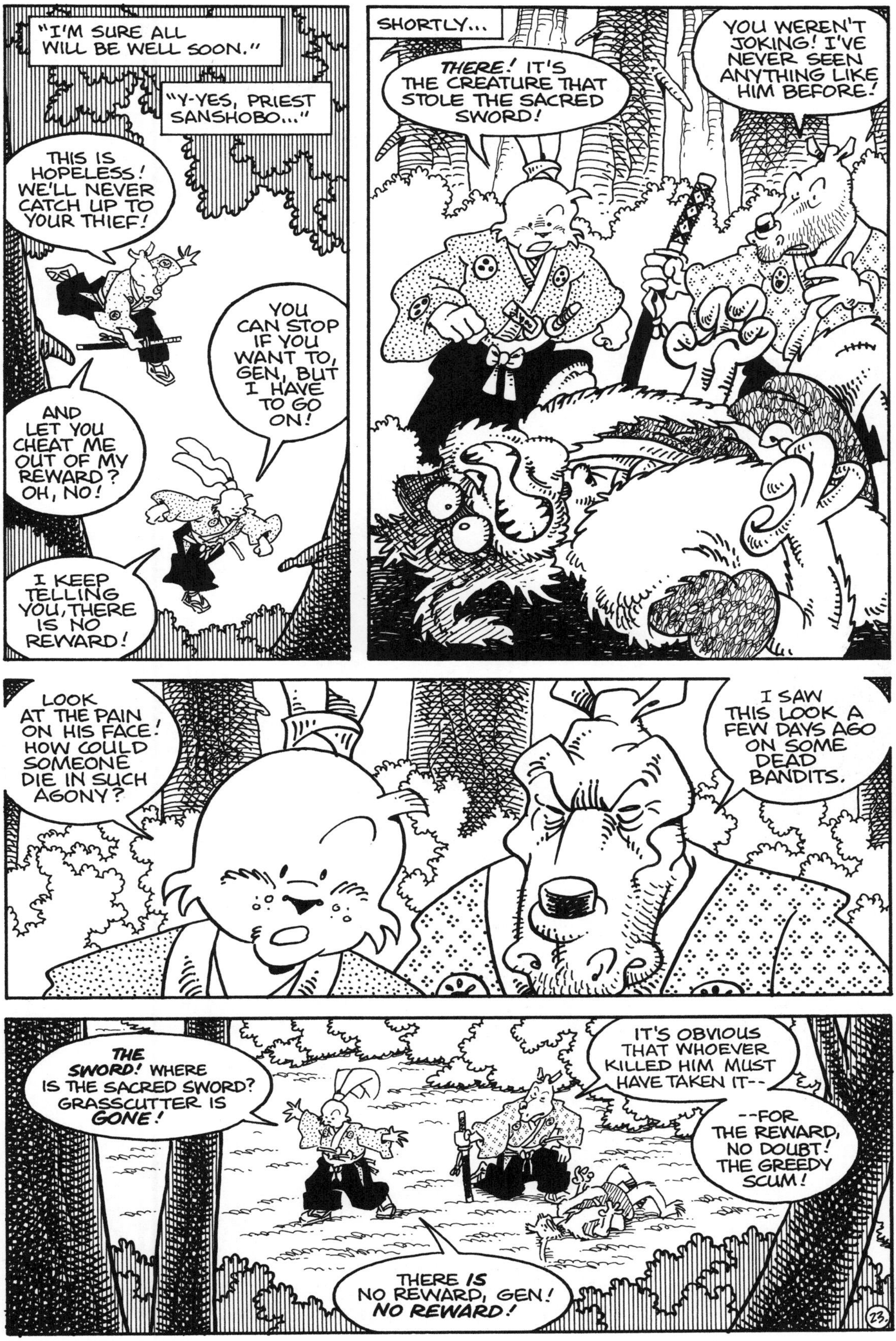
"I'M SURE ALL WILL BE WELL SOON."
"Y-YES, PRIEST SANSHOBO..."
THIS IS HOPELESS! WE'LL NEVER CATCH UP TO YOUR THIEF!
YOU CAN STOP IF YOU WANT TO, GEN, BUT I HAVE TO GO ON!
AND LET YOU CHEAT ME OUT OF MY REWARD? OH, NO!
I KEEP TELLING YOU, THERE IS NO REWARD!
SHORTLY...
THERE! IT'S THE CREATURE THAT STOLE THE SACRED SWORD!
YOU WEREN'T JOKING! I'VE NEVER SEEN ANYTHING LIKE HIM BEFORE!
LOOK AT THE PAIN ON HIS FACE! HOW COULD SOMEONE DIE IN SUCH AGONY?
I SAW THIS LOOK A FEW DAYS AGO ON SOME DEAD BANDITS.
THE SWORD! WHERE IS THE SACRED SWORD? GRASSCUTTER IS GONE!
IT'S OBVIOUS THAT WHOEVER KILLED HIM MUST HAVE TAKEN IT--
--FOR THE REWARD, NO DOUBT! THE GREEDY SCUM!
THERE IS NO REWARD, GEN! NO REWARD!
23.

COME ON! WE'VE GOT TO FIND WHOEVER TOOK THAT SWORD!

ARE YOU CRAZY? IT'S GETTING DARK!

YOU'LL NEVER FIND HIS TRAIL NOW!

Heh heh heh. No need to look for me, Usagi! I've been hunting *you* for some time now!

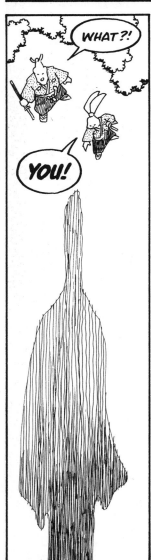

WHAT?!

YOU!

Heh heh heh heh heh.

So, this is the *true* blade of the gods? I have finally met my *destiny!*

HE'S EVEN STRANGER THAN THAT DEAD THING! YOU'VE GOT SOME *WEIRD* FRIENDS, USAGI!

"HURRY, MY LORDS, HURRY!"

GRASSCUTTER
CHAPTER 7: USAGI AND JEI

THIS WAY, MY LORDS, PLEASE HURRY!

I HAD ORDERS NOT TO DISTURB THEM, BUT THEN I HEARD THE LAUGHTER...

"LAUGHTER"? YOU SUMMONED US BECAUSE OF SOME LAUGHING?!

I UNDERSTAND YOUR ANGER, LORD OKU. BUT CONTRARY TO MY ORDERS, I DID LOOK IN ON THEM, AND WHAT I SAW MADE ME SEND FOR YOU IMMEDIATELY...YOU ALL BEING HIS CLOSE FRIENDS, THAT IS!

WHAT IS THE PROBLEM WITH YOUR MASTER?

WELL, SIRS, I OPENED THE DOORS AND--

THIS HAD BETTER BE WORTH OUR RUSHING HERE! IF NOT, WE'LL SEE THAT YOU'LL LOSE YOUR HEAD!

--THIS IS WHAT I SAW!

¡GASP!

WHAT HAPPENED HERE?

WHAT THE--?!

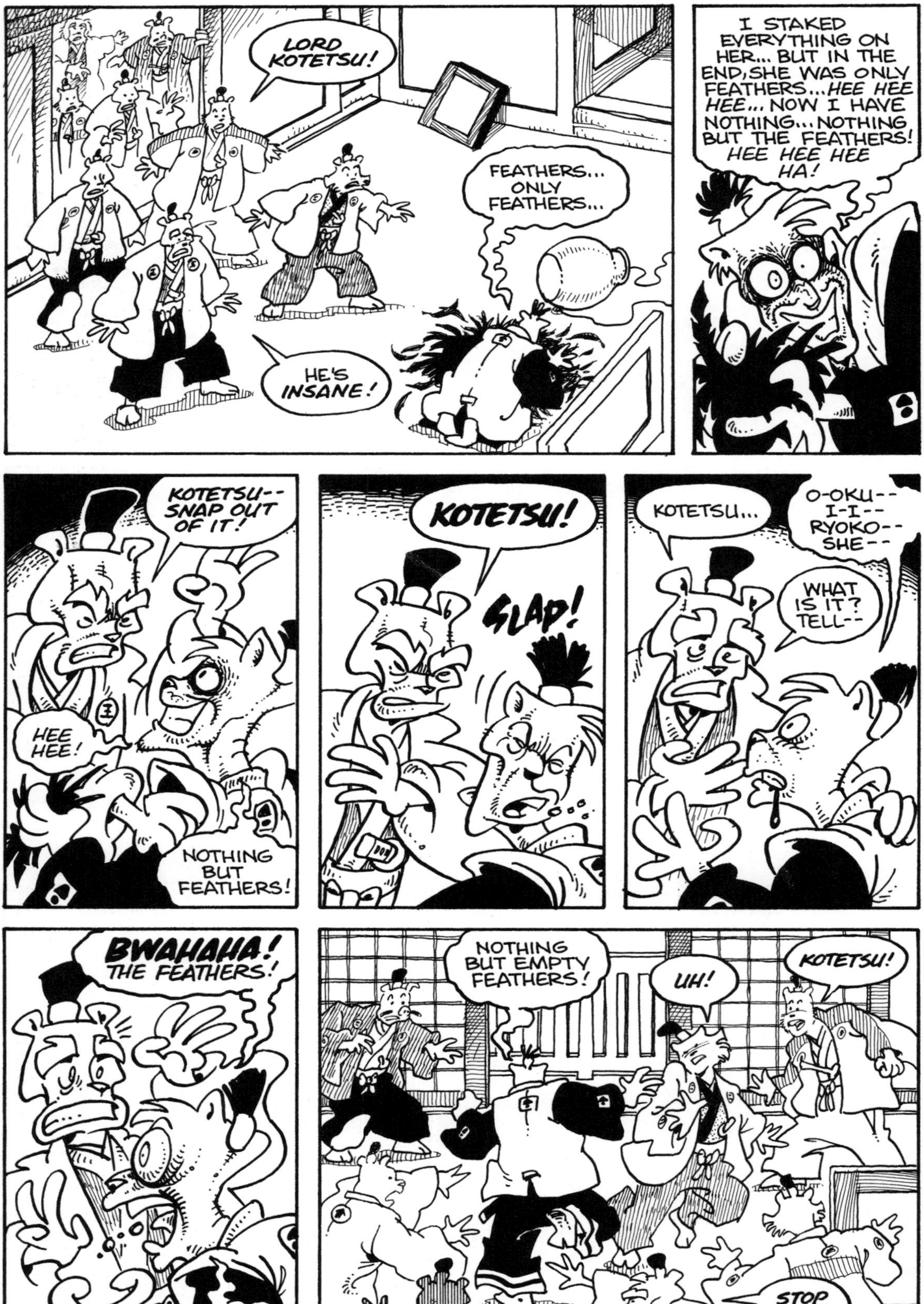
LORD KOTETSU!
FEATHERS... ONLY FEATHERS...
HE'S INSANE!
I STAKED EVERYTHING ON HER... BUT IN THE END, SHE WAS ONLY FEATHERS... HEE HEE HEE... NOW I HAVE NOTHING... NOTHING BUT THE FEATHERS! HEE HEE HEE HA!
KOTETSU-- SNAP OUT OF IT!
HEE HEE!
NOTHING BUT FEATHERS!
KOTETSU!
SLAP!
KOTETSU...
O-OKU-- I-I-- RYOKO-- SHE--
WHAT IS IT? TELL--
BWAHAHA! THE FEATHERS!
HA HA HEEE!
NOTHING BUT EMPTY FEATHERS!
UH!
KOTETSU!
STOP HIM!
2.

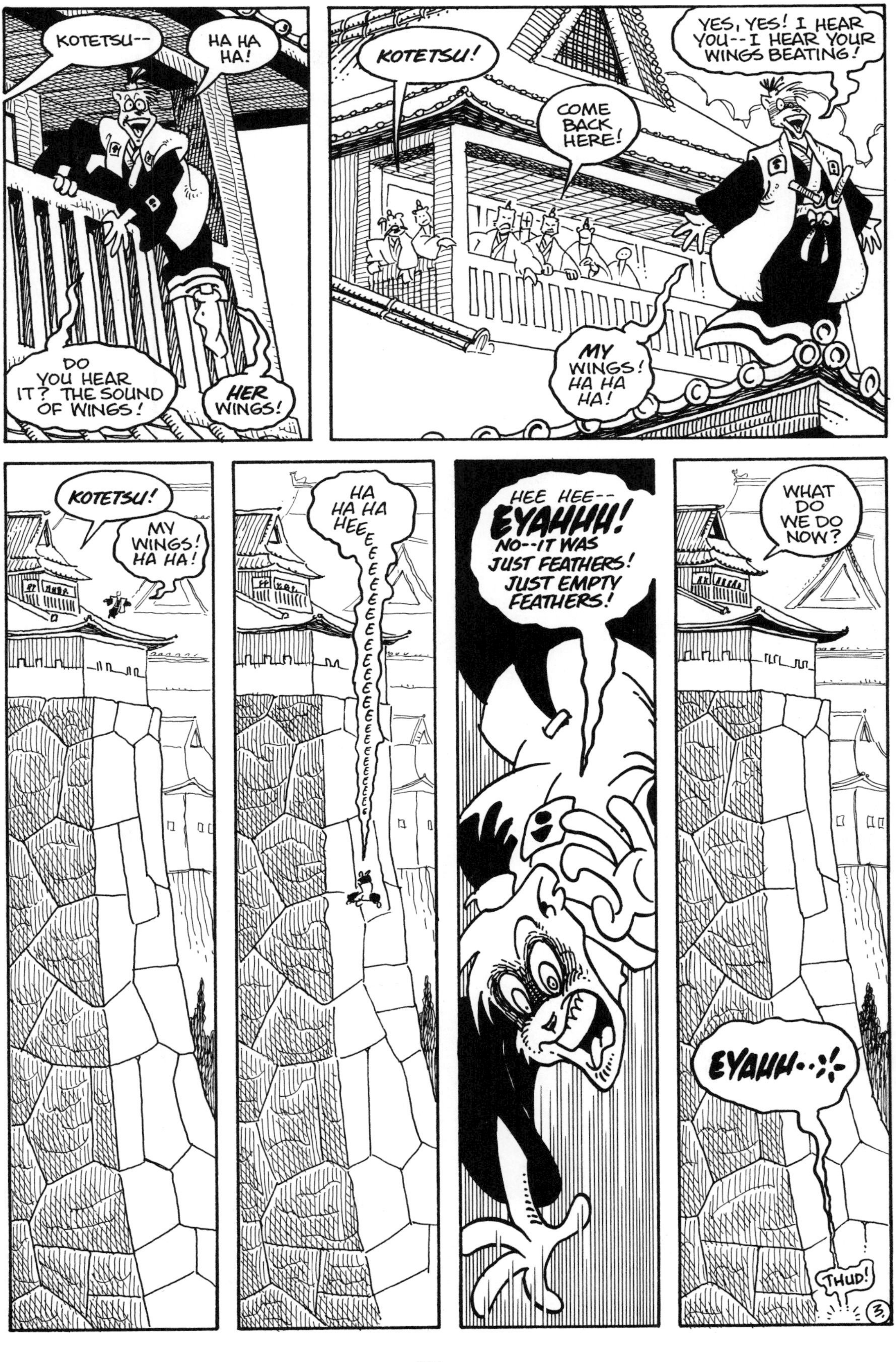
KOTETSU--
HA HA HA!
DO YOU HEAR IT? THE SOUND OF WINGS!
HER WINGS!
KOTETSU!
COME BACK HERE!
YES, YES! I HEAR YOU--I HEAR YOUR WINGS BEATING!
MY WINGS! HA HA HA!
KOTETSU!
MY WINGS! HA HA!
HA HA HA HEEEEEEEEEEEEEEEEEEEEEEEEEEEE
HEE HEE-- EYAHHH! NO--IT WAS JUST FEATHERS! JUST EMPTY FEATHERS!
WHAT DO WE DO NOW?
EYAHH..!
THUD!
3.

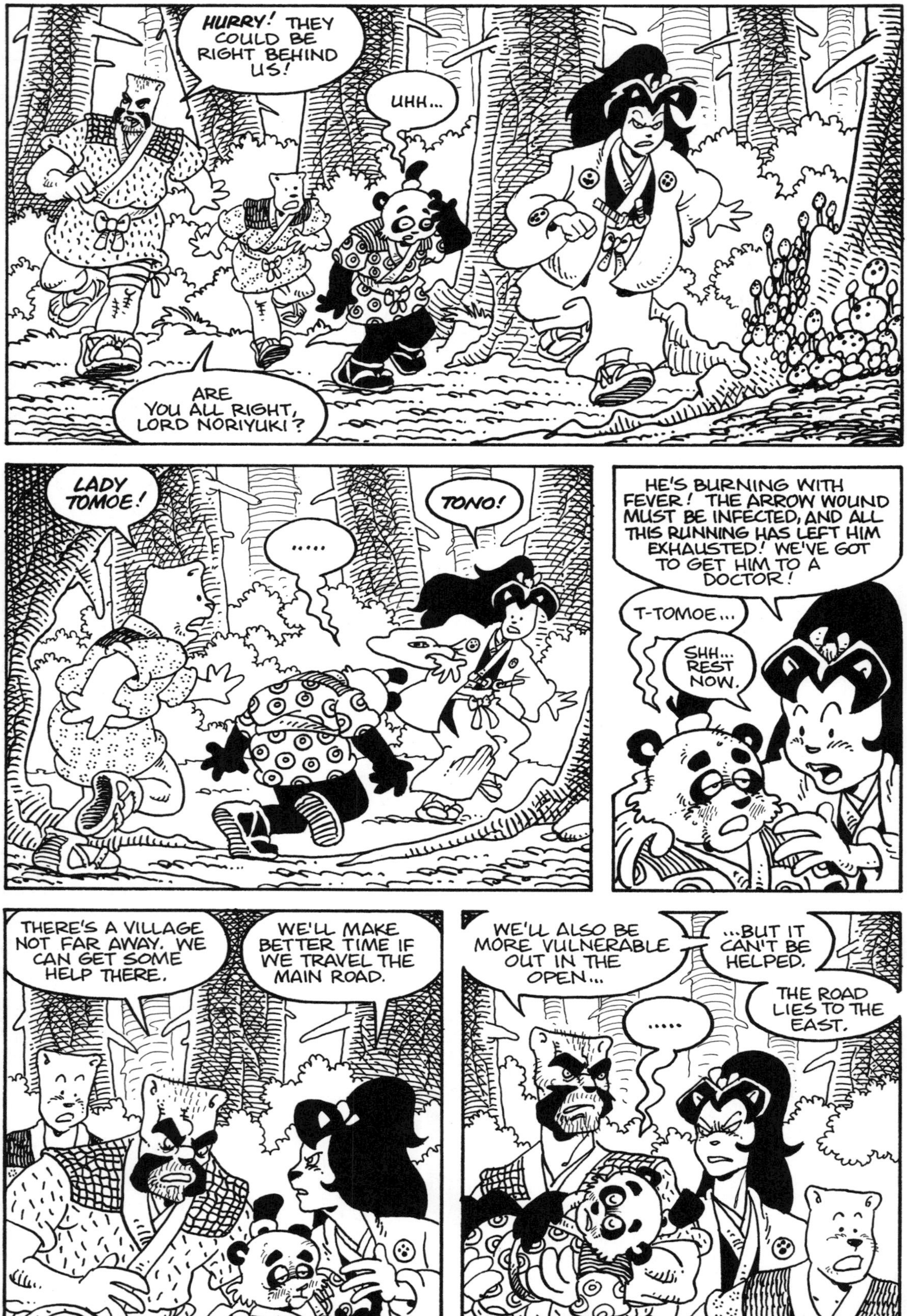
HURRY! THEY COULD BE RIGHT BEHIND US!
UHH...
ARE YOU ALL RIGHT, LORD NORIYUKI?
LADY TOMOE!
.....
TONO!
HE'S BURNING WITH FEVER! THE ARROW WOUND MUST BE INFECTED, AND ALL THIS RUNNING HAS LEFT HIM EXHAUSTED! WE'VE GOT TO GET HIM TO A DOCTOR!
T-TOMOE...
SHH... REST NOW.
THERE'S A VILLAGE NOT FAR AWAY. WE CAN GET SOME HELP THERE.
WE'LL MAKE BETTER TIME IF WE TRAVEL THE MAIN ROAD.
WE'LL ALSO BE MORE VULNERABLE OUT IN THE OPEN...
...BUT IT CAN'T BE HELPED.
.....
THE ROAD LIES TO THE EAST.
4

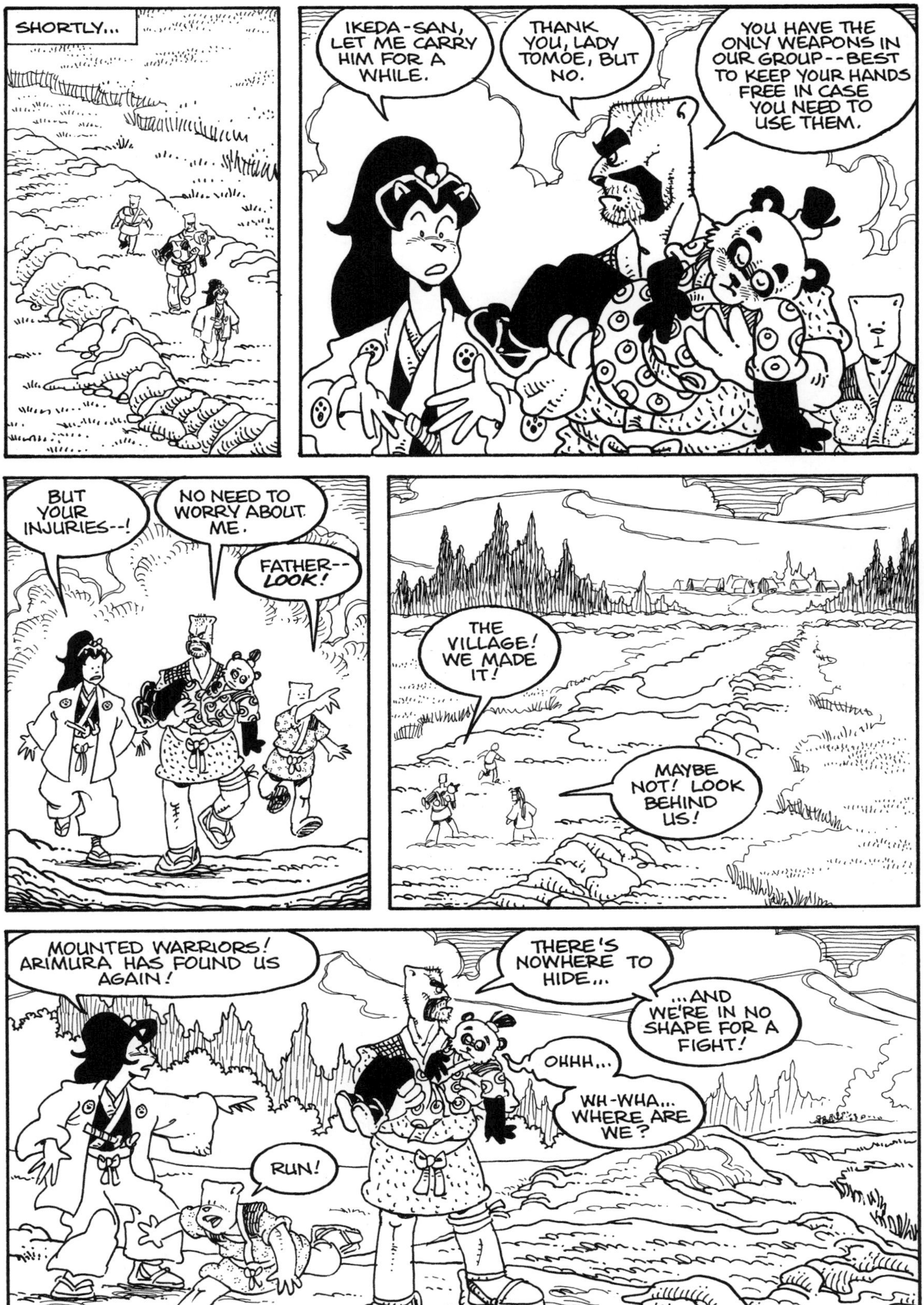
SHORTLY...
IKEDA-SAN, LET ME CARRY HIM FOR A WHILE.
THANK YOU, LADY TOMOE, BUT NO.
YOU HAVE THE ONLY WEAPONS IN OUR GROUP--BEST TO KEEP YOUR HANDS FREE IN CASE YOU NEED TO USE THEM.
BUT YOUR INJURIES--!
NO NEED TO WORRY ABOUT ME.
FATHER--LOOK!
THE VILLAGE! WE MADE IT!
MAYBE NOT! LOOK BEHIND US!
MOUNTED WARRIORS! ARIMURA HAS FOUND US AGAIN!
RUN!
THERE'S NOWHERE TO HIDE...
...AND WE'RE IN NO SHAPE FOR A FIGHT!
OHHH...
WH-WHA... WHERE ARE WE?
5

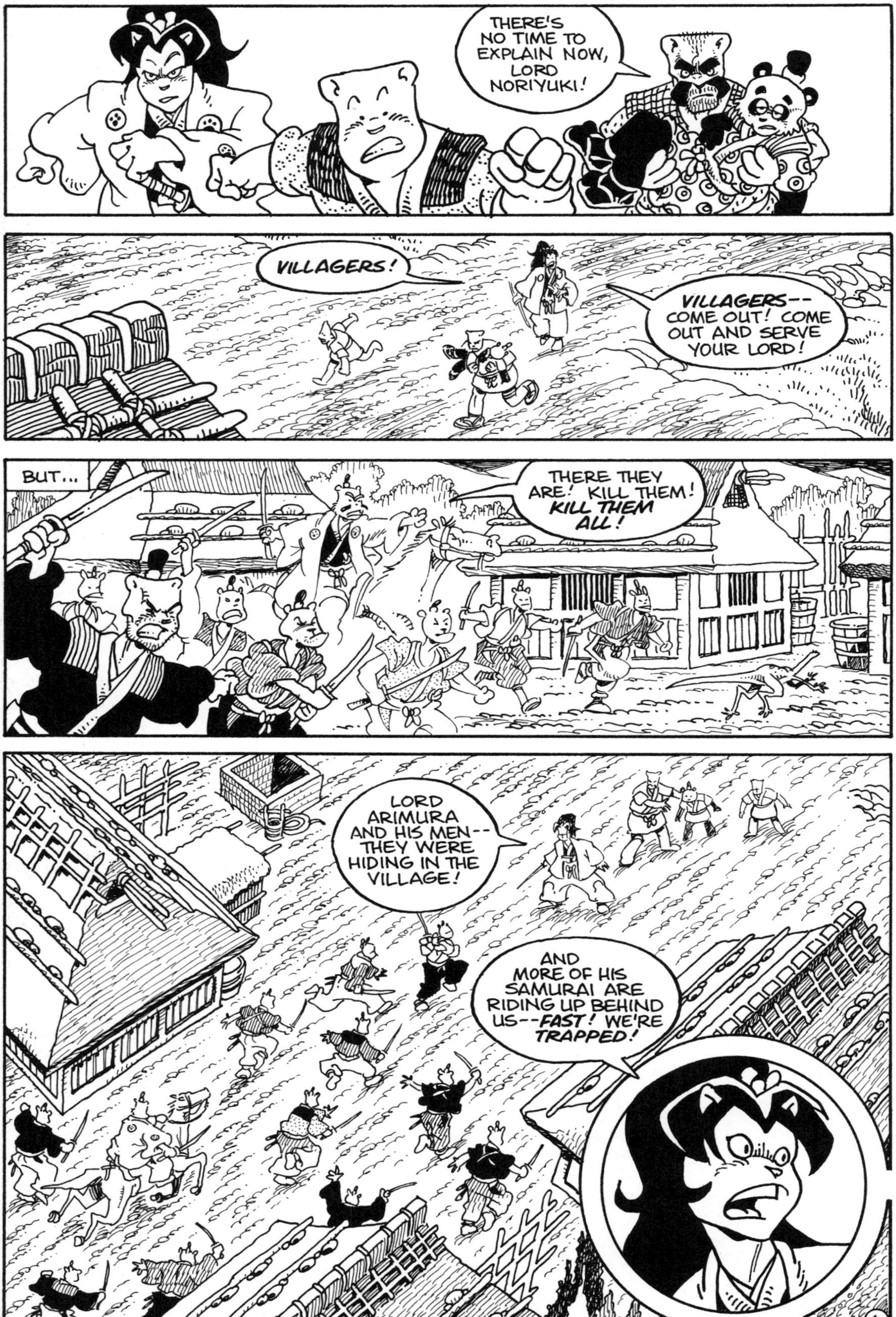
THERE'S NO TIME TO EXPLAIN NOW, LORD NORIYUKI!
VILLAGERS!
VILLAGERS-- COME OUT! COME OUT AND SERVE YOUR LORD!
BUT...
THERE THEY ARE! KILL THEM! KILL THEM ALL!
LORD ARIMURA AND HIS MEN-- THEY WERE HIDING IN THE VILLAGE!
AND MORE OF HIS SAMURAI ARE RIDING UP BEHIND US--FAST! WE'RE TRAPPED!
6.

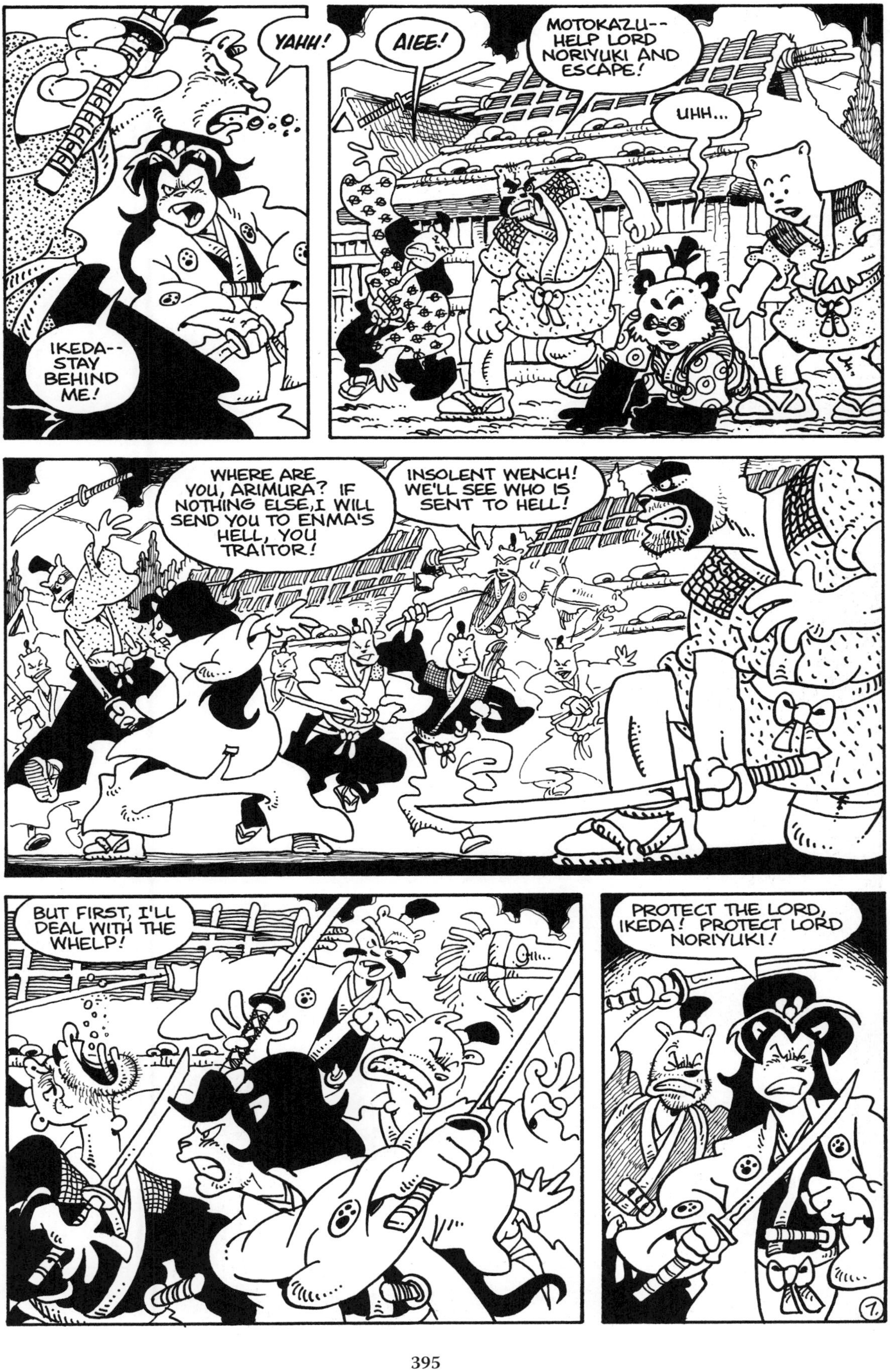
YAHH!
IKEDA--
STAY
BEHIND
ME!
AIEE!
MOTOKAZU--
HELP LORD
NORIYUKI AND
ESCAPE!
UHH...
WHERE ARE
YOU, ARIMURA? IF
NOTHING ELSE, I WILL
SEND YOU TO ENMA'S
HELL, YOU
TRAITOR!
INSOLENT WENCH!
WE'LL SEE WHO IS
SENT TO HELL!
BUT FIRST, I'LL
DEAL WITH THE
WHELP!
PROTECT THE LORD,
IKEDA! PROTECT LORD
NORIYUKI!
7.

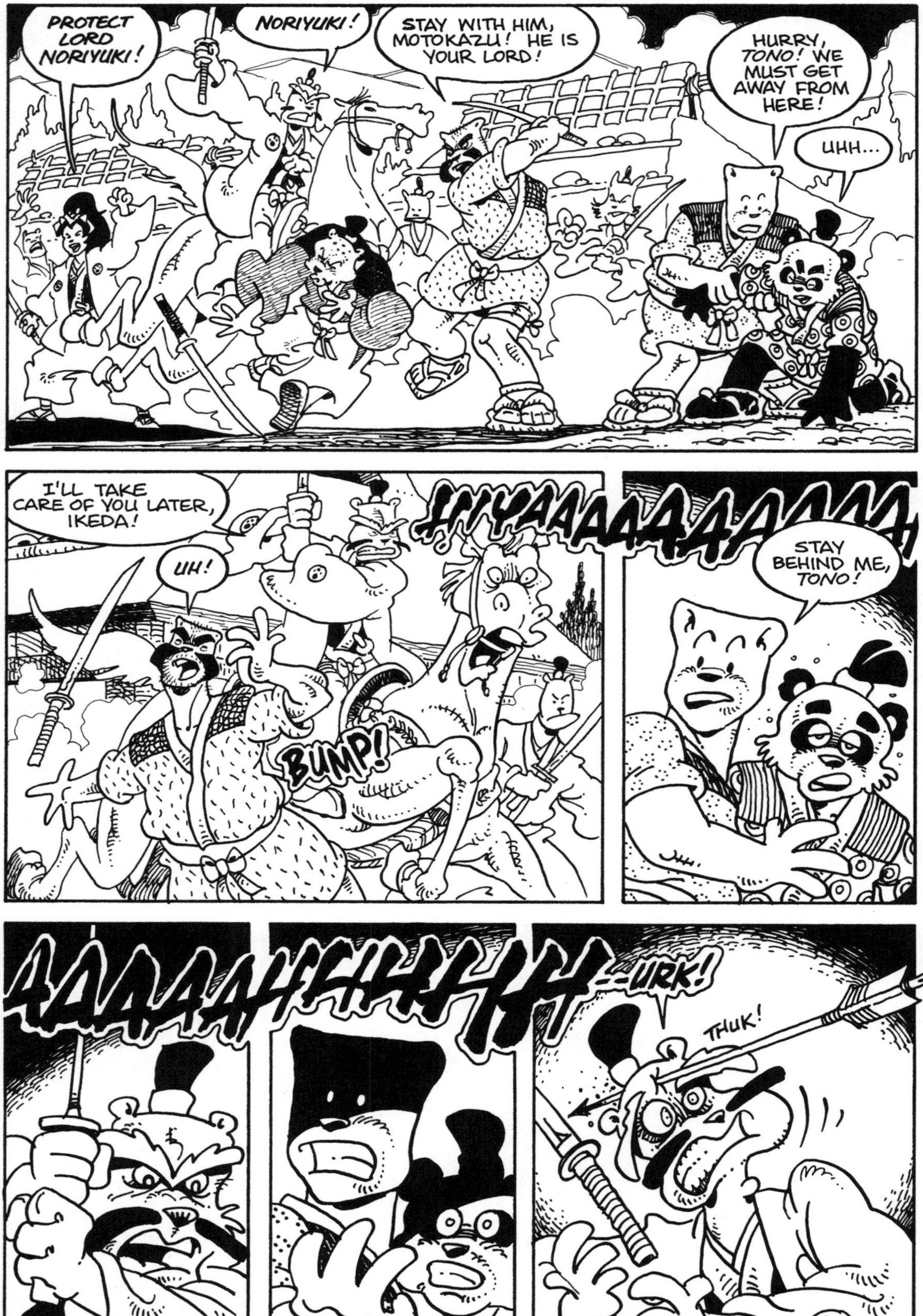
PROTECT LORD NORIYUKI!
NORIYUKI!
STAY WITH HIM, MOTOKAZU! HE IS YOUR LORD!
HURRY, TONO! WE MUST GET AWAY FROM HERE!
UHH...
I'LL TAKE CARE OF YOU LATER, IKEDA!
UH!
BUMP!
IIIYAAAAAAAAAAA
STAY BEHIND ME, TONO!
AAAAAHHHHHH
--URK!
THUK!
8.

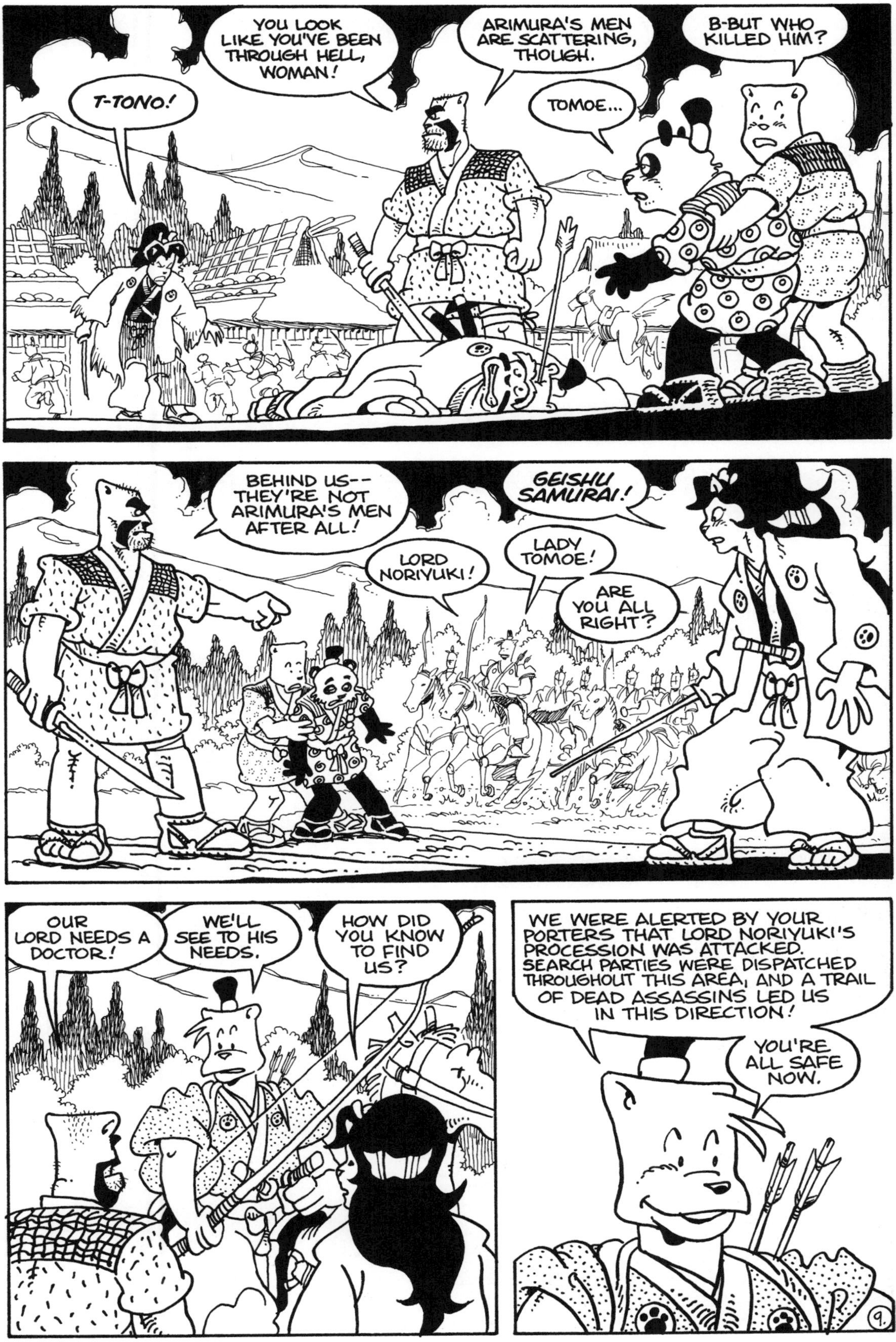
T-TONO!
YOU LOOK LIKE YOU'VE BEEN THROUGH HELL, WOMAN!
ARIMURA'S MEN ARE SCATTERING, THOUGH.
TOMOE...
B-BUT WHO KILLED HIM?
BEHIND US-- THEY'RE NOT ARIMURA'S MEN AFTER ALL!
LORD NORIYUKI!
GEISHU SAMURAI!
LADY TOMOE!
ARE YOU ALL RIGHT?
OUR LORD NEEDS A DOCTOR!
WE'LL SEE TO HIS NEEDS.
HOW DID YOU KNOW TO FIND US?
WE WERE ALERTED BY YOUR PORTERS THAT LORD NORIYUKI'S PROCESSION WAS ATTACKED. SEARCH PARTIES WERE DISPATCHED THROUGHOUT THIS AREA, AND A TRAIL OF DEAD ASSASSINS LED US IN THIS DIRECTION!
YOU'RE ALL SAFE NOW.
9.

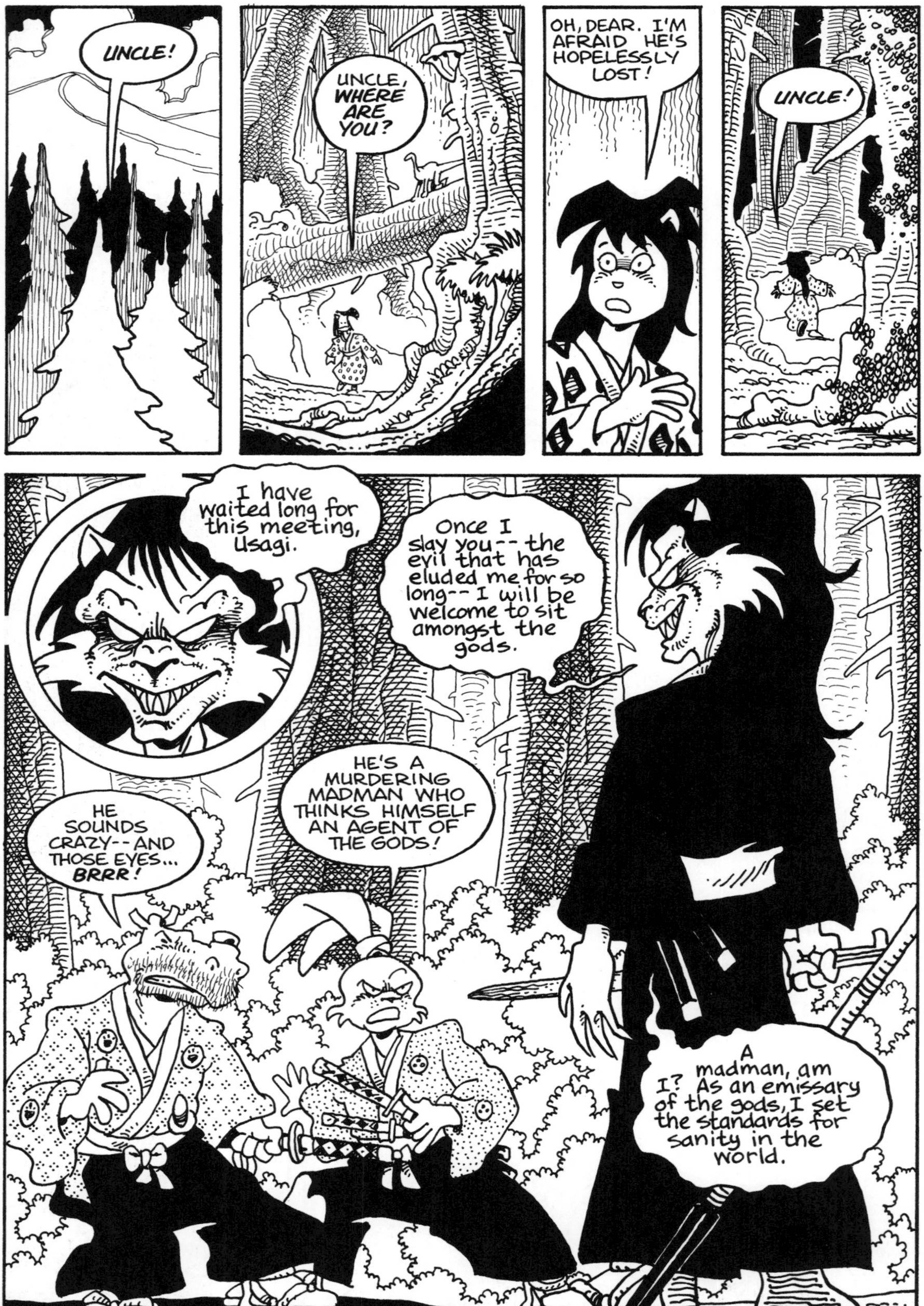
UNCLE!
UNCLE, WHERE ARE YOU?
OH, DEAR. I'M AFRAID HE'S HOPELESSLY LOST!
UNCLE!
I have waited long for this meeting, Usagi.
Once I slay you-- the evil that has eluded me for so long-- I will be welcome to sit amongst the gods.
HE SOUNDS CRAZY--AND THOSE EYES... BRRR!
HE'S A MURDERING MADMAN WHO THINKS HIMSELF AN AGENT OF THE GODS!
A madman, am I? As an emissary of the gods, I set the standards for sanity in the world.
10.

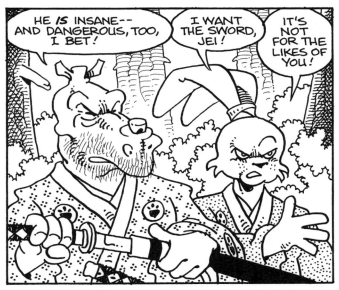

HE *IS* INSANE-- AND DANGEROUS, TOO, I BET!

I WANT THE SWORD, JEI!

IT'S NOT FOR THE LIKES OF YOU!

You want it?

Then it is yours for the taking.

I was unable to consecrate it...

...but it will make a fine trophy for the victor!

THUNK!

RRRRRRRR

RRRRRR

AN *EARTHQUAKE!* HE'S CREATED AN EARTHQUAKE WITH THAT THING!

UH--!

NO--IT'S A COINCIDENCE-- AN AFTERSHOCK!

RRRR

"Coincidence"? You're a fool, Usagi! It is the power of the Gods when wielded by the hand of their servant!

11.

399

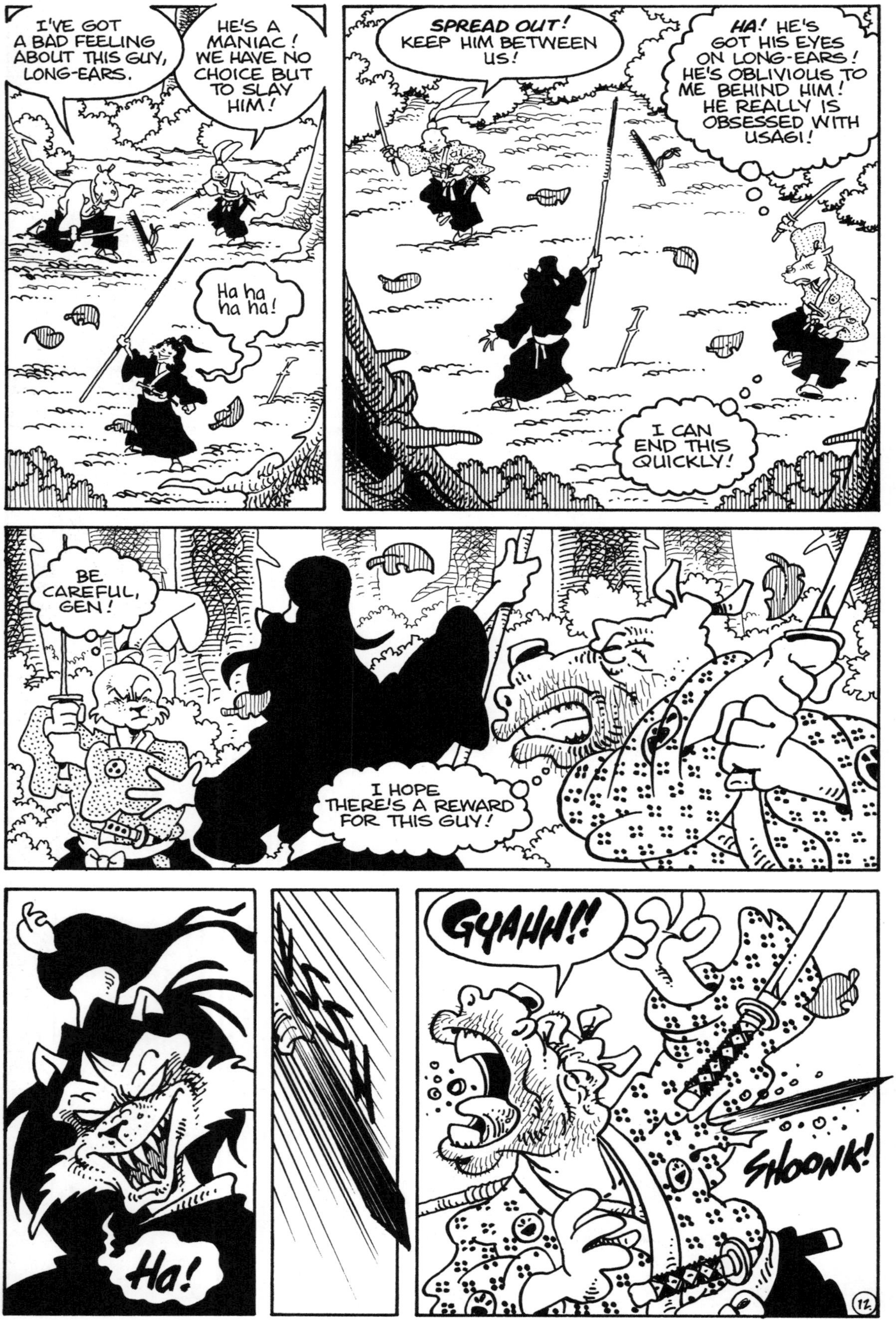
I'VE GOT A BAD FEELING ABOUT THIS GUY, LONG-EARS.
HE'S A MANIAC! WE HAVE NO CHOICE BUT TO SLAY HIM!
Ha ha ha ha!
SPREAD OUT! KEEP HIM BETWEEN US!
HA! HE'S GOT HIS EYES ON LONG-EARS! HE'S OBLIVIOUS TO ME BEHIND HIM! HE REALLY IS OBSESSED WITH USAGI!
I CAN END THIS QUICKLY!
BE CAREFUL, GEN!
I HOPE THERE'S A REWARD FOR THIS GUY!
Ha!
GYAHH!!
SHOONK!
12

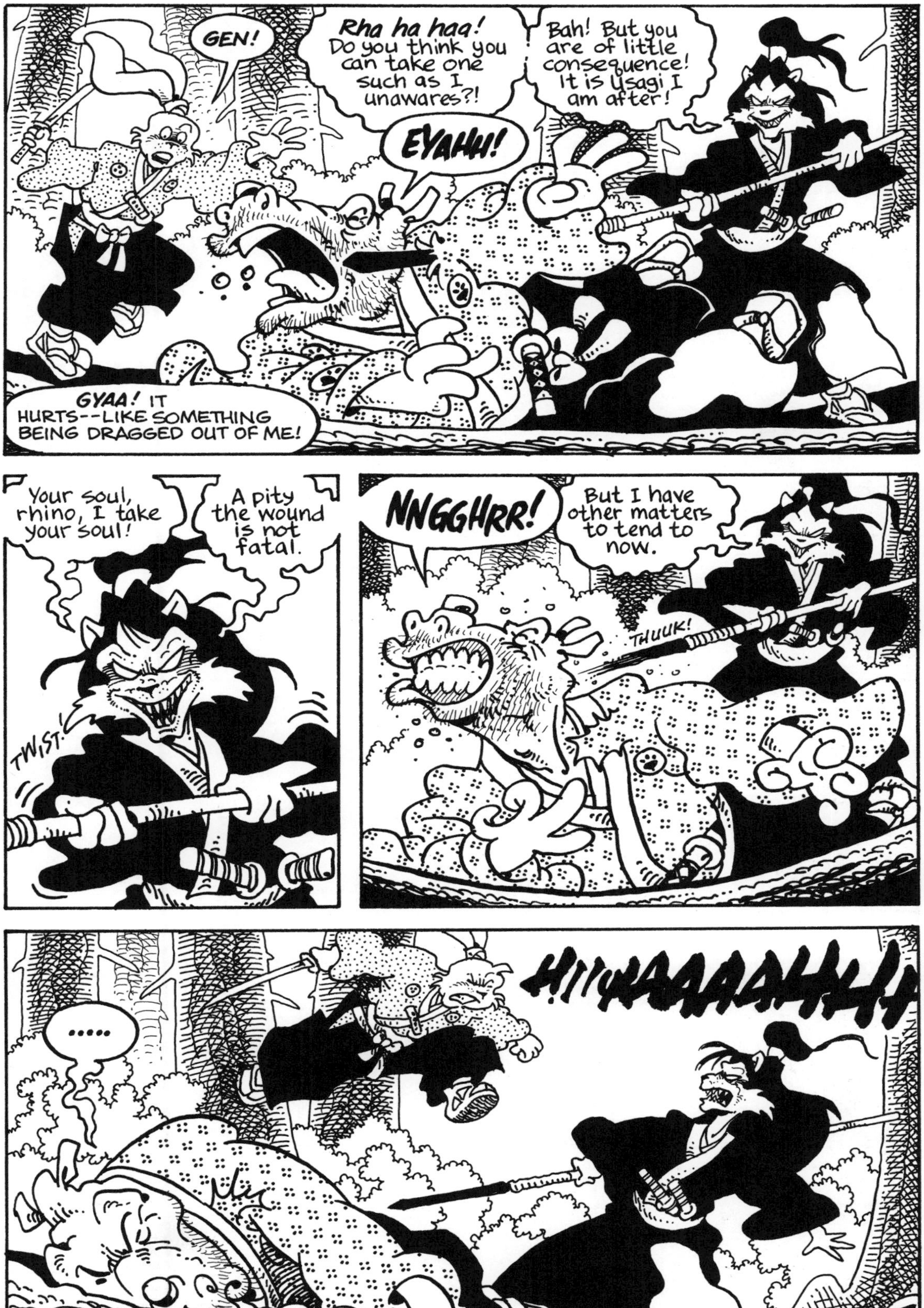
GEN!
Rha ha haa! Do you think you can take one such as I unawares?!
Bah! But you are of little consequence! It is Usagi I am after!
EYAHH!
GYAA! IT HURTS--LIKE SOMETHING BEING DRAGGED OUT OF ME!
Your soul, rhino, I take your soul!
A pity the wound is not fatal.
TWIST!
NNGGHRR!
But I have other matters to tend to now.
THUUK!
.....
HIIYAAAAAHHH
13

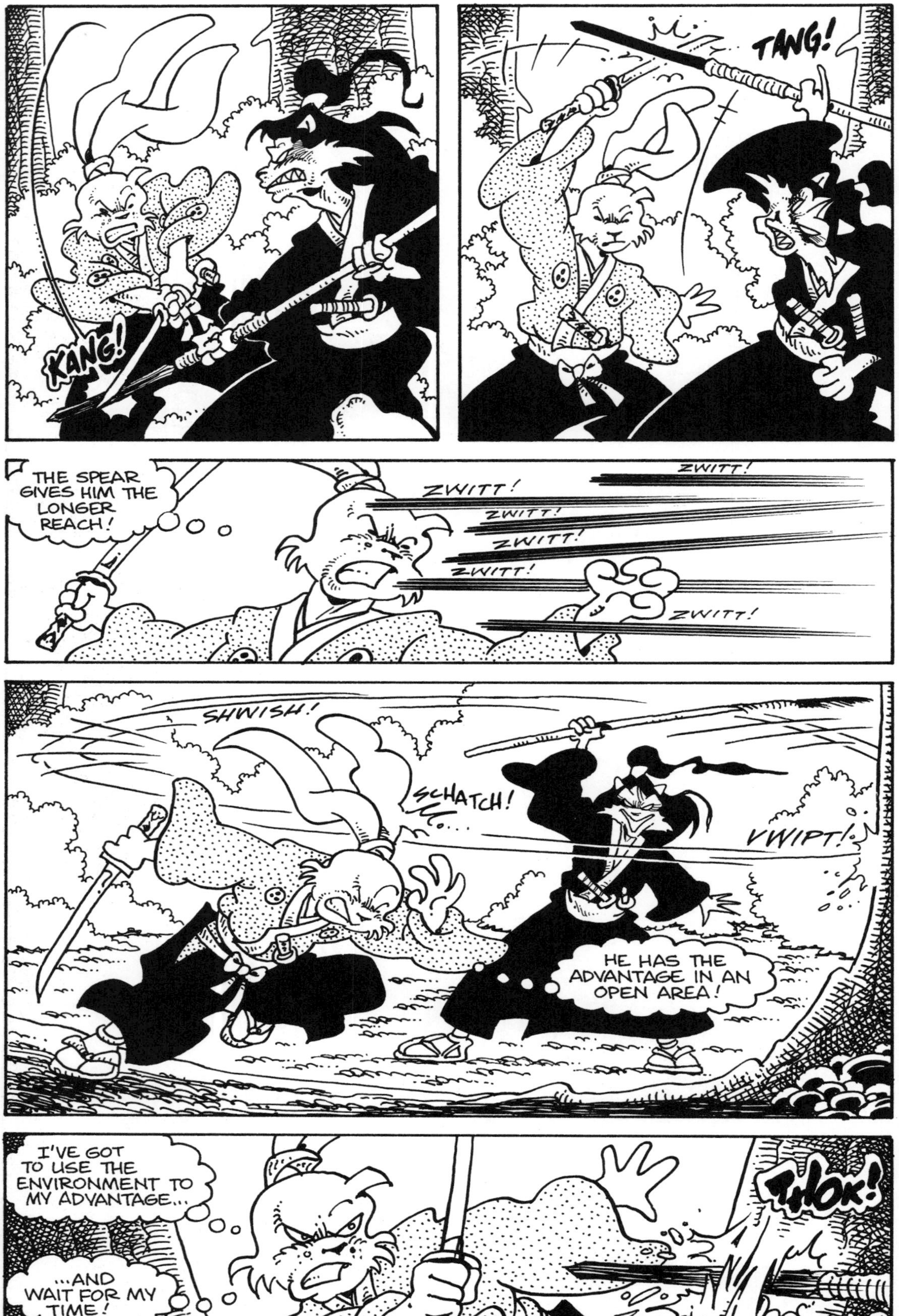
KANG!
TANG!
THE SPEAR GIVES HIM THE LONGER REACH!
ZWITT!
ZWITT!
ZWITT!
ZWITT!
ZWITT!
ZWITT!
SHWISH!
SCHATCH!
VWIPT!
HE HAS THE ADVANTAGE IN AN OPEN AREA!
I'VE GOT TO USE THE ENVIRONMENT TO MY ADVANTAGE...
...AND WAIT FOR MY TIME!
THOK!
14.

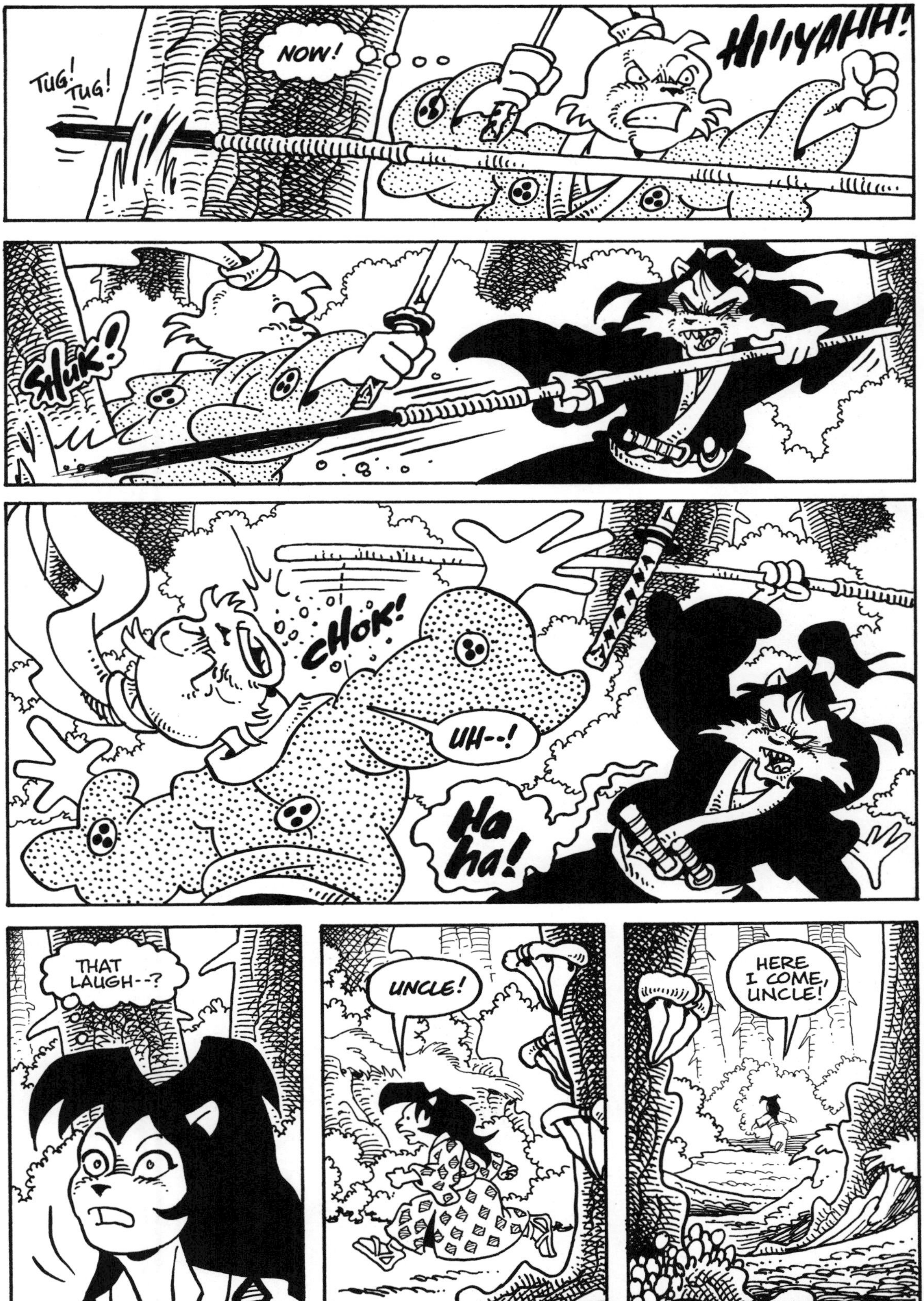
NOW!
TUG! TUG!
HI'YAHH!
SHUK!
CHOK!
UH--!
Ha ha!
THAT LAUGH--?
UNCLE!
HERE I COME, UNCLE!
15.

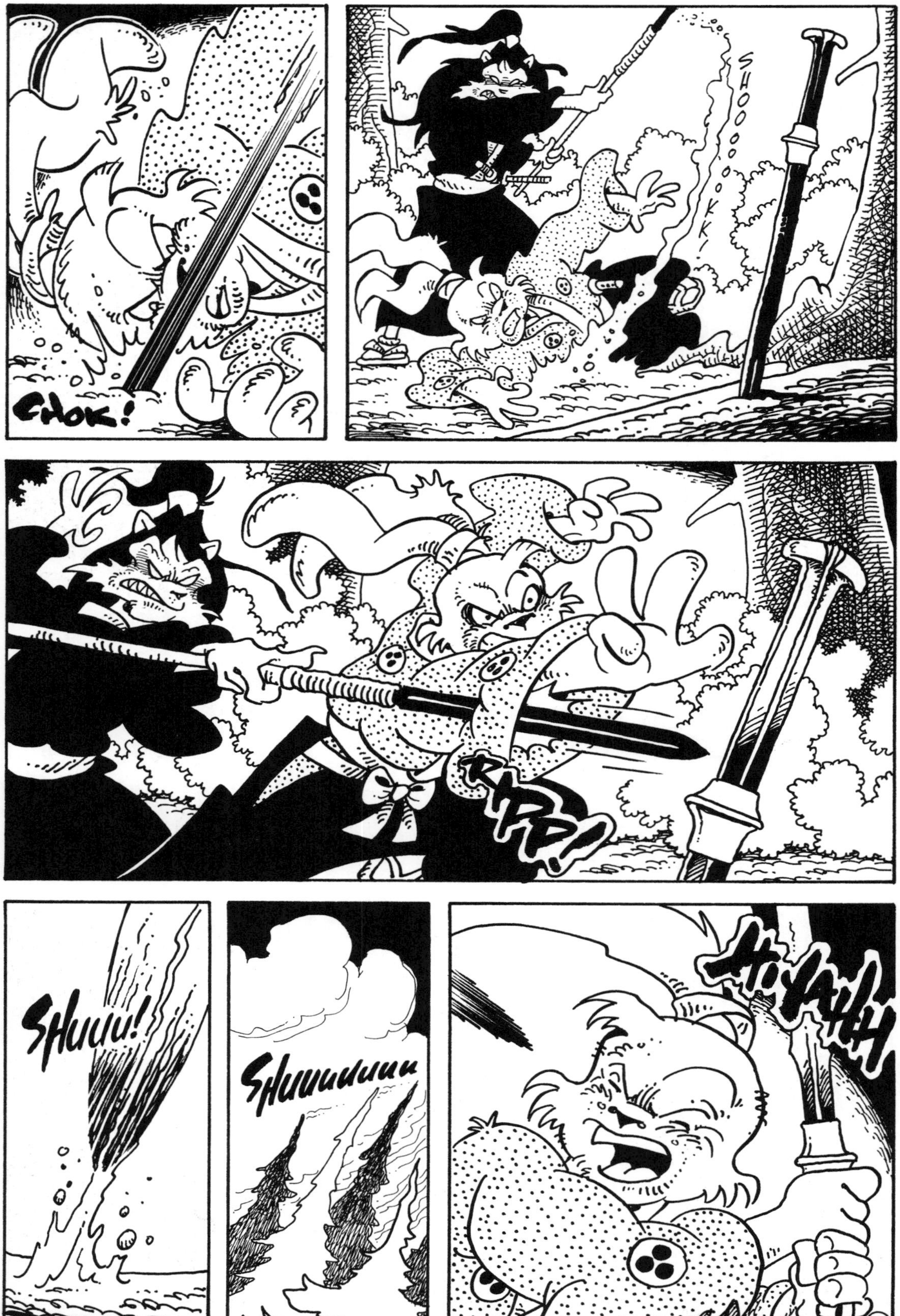
CHOK!
SHOOOOOOOOKK!
RIPPP!
SHUUU!
SHUUUUUUUU
AI-YAHH
16.

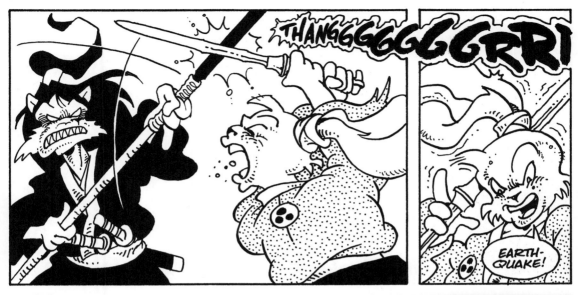

THANGGGGGGGRRI

EARTH-QUAKE!

RRRRK

Ha ha ha ha!

A perfect setting in which to die, Usagi!

KIIII!!!

R

BUT IT WON'T BE MY DEATH, DEMON!

RRRRRRRRR GYAHHHHHHHYAAHHHHHH,

17.

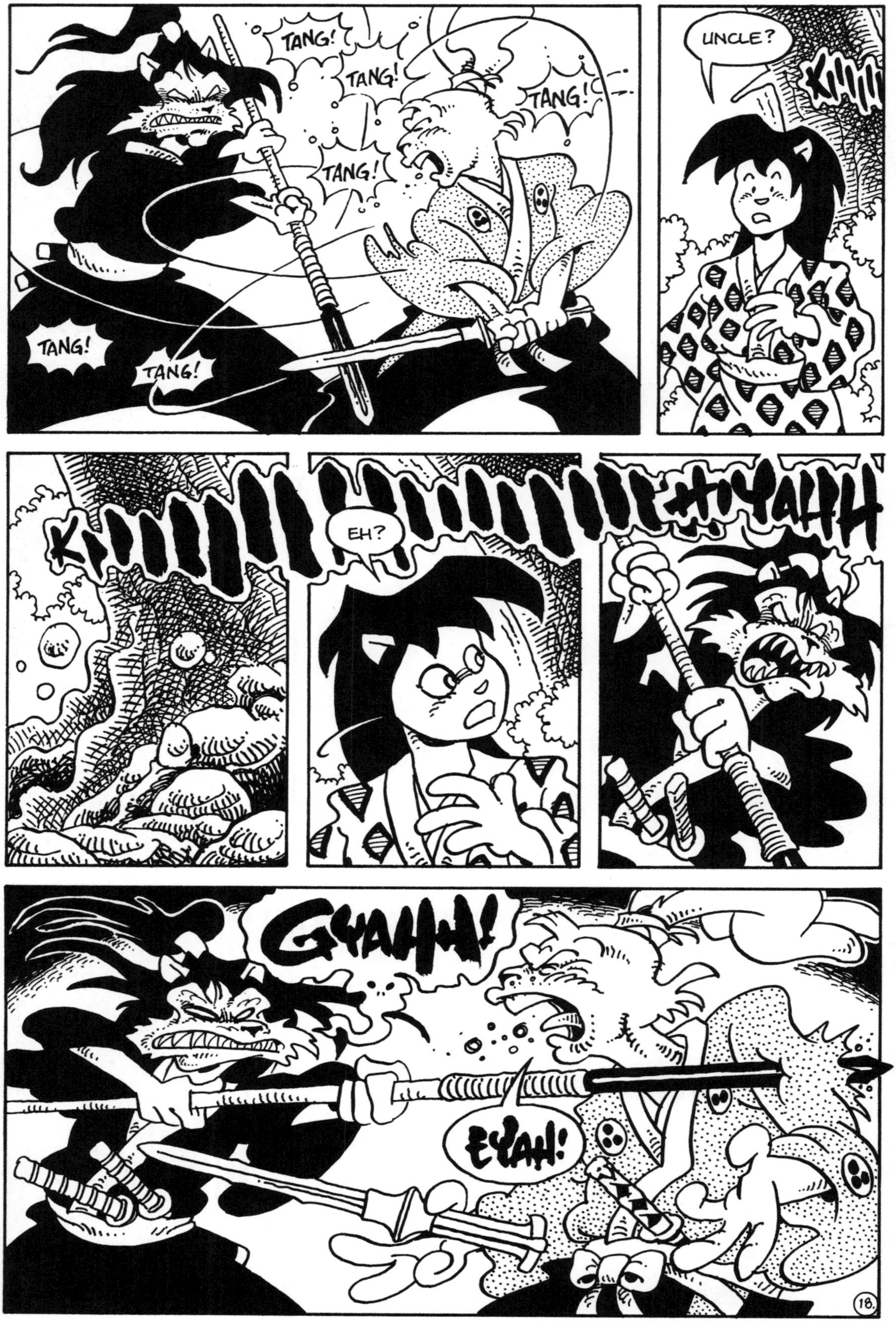
TANG!
TANG!
TANG!
TANG!
TANG!
TANG!
UNCLE?
KIIIII
KIIIIIIIIIIIIIIIIIIIIIIIII
EH?
HIYAHH
GYAHH!
EYAH!
18.

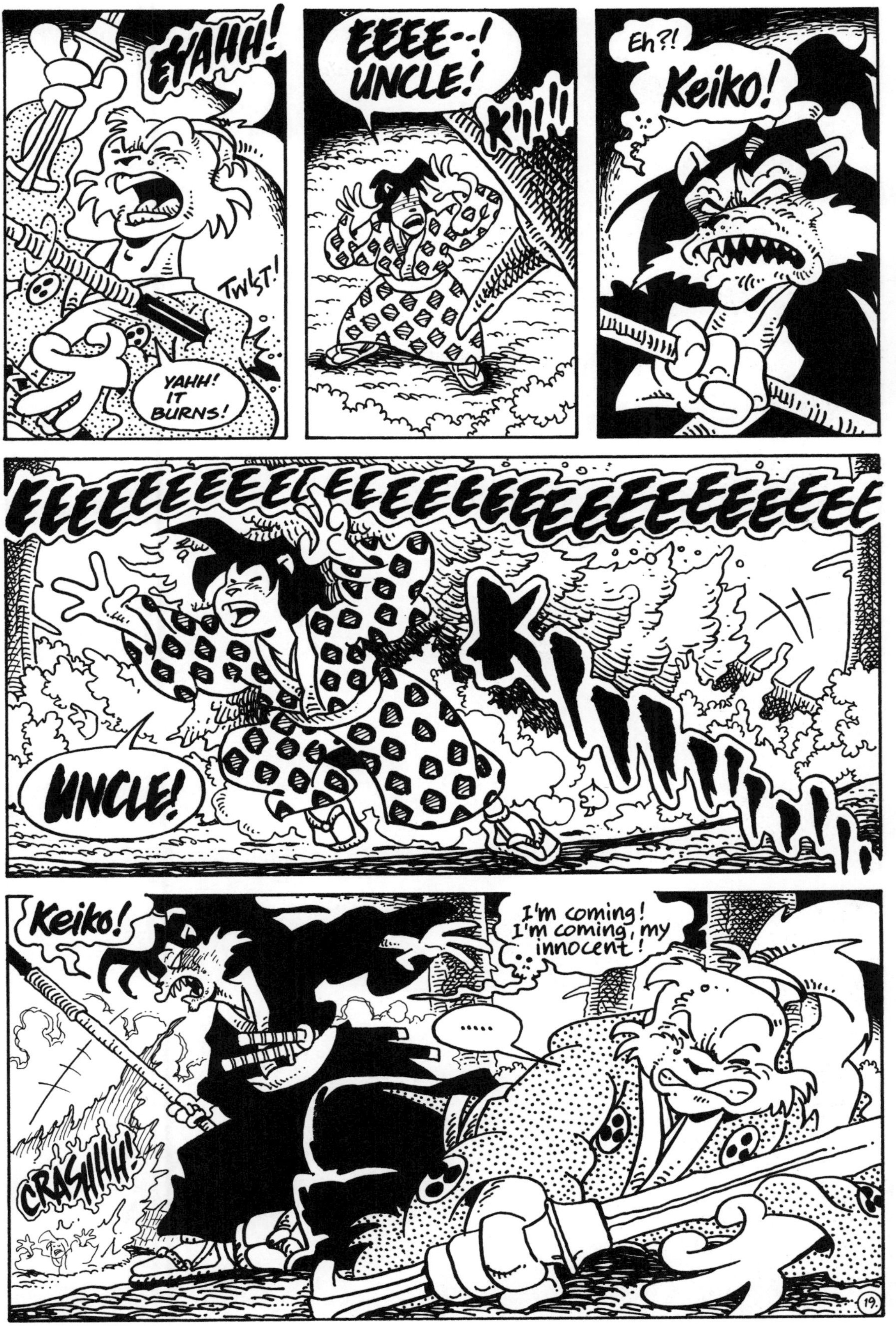
EYAHH!
TWIST!
YAHH! IT BURNS!
EEEE--! UNCLE!
K'I!!!
Eh?!
Keiko!
EEEEEEEEEEEEEEEEEEEEEEEEEEEEEEE
UNCLE!
Keiko!
I'm coming! I'm coming, my innocent!
.....
CRASHHH!
19.

MONSTER!
RRRYAA!
AAAAAAAHHHH!
SHOONK!
GYAHH!
20.

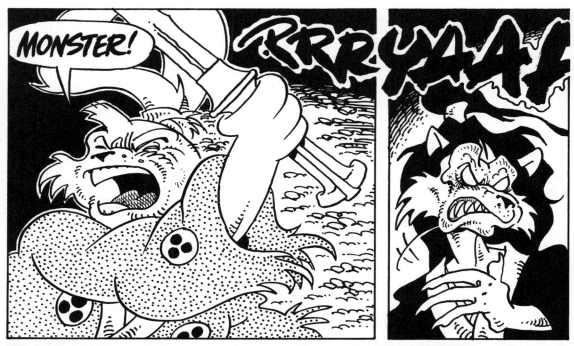

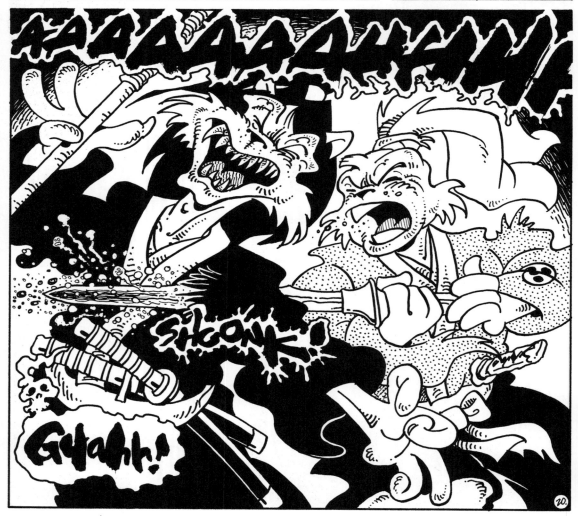

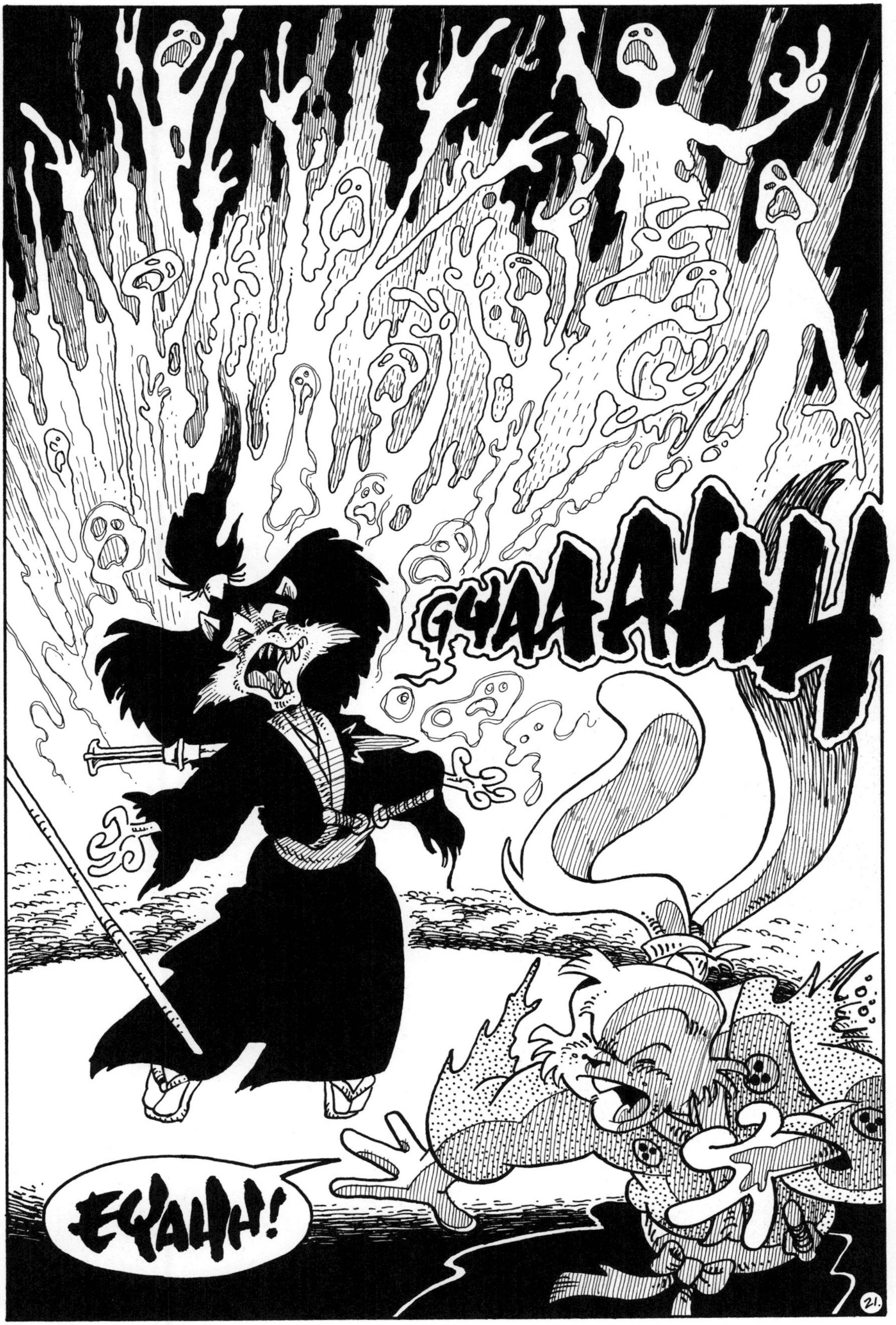
GYAAAAHH
EYAHH!
21.

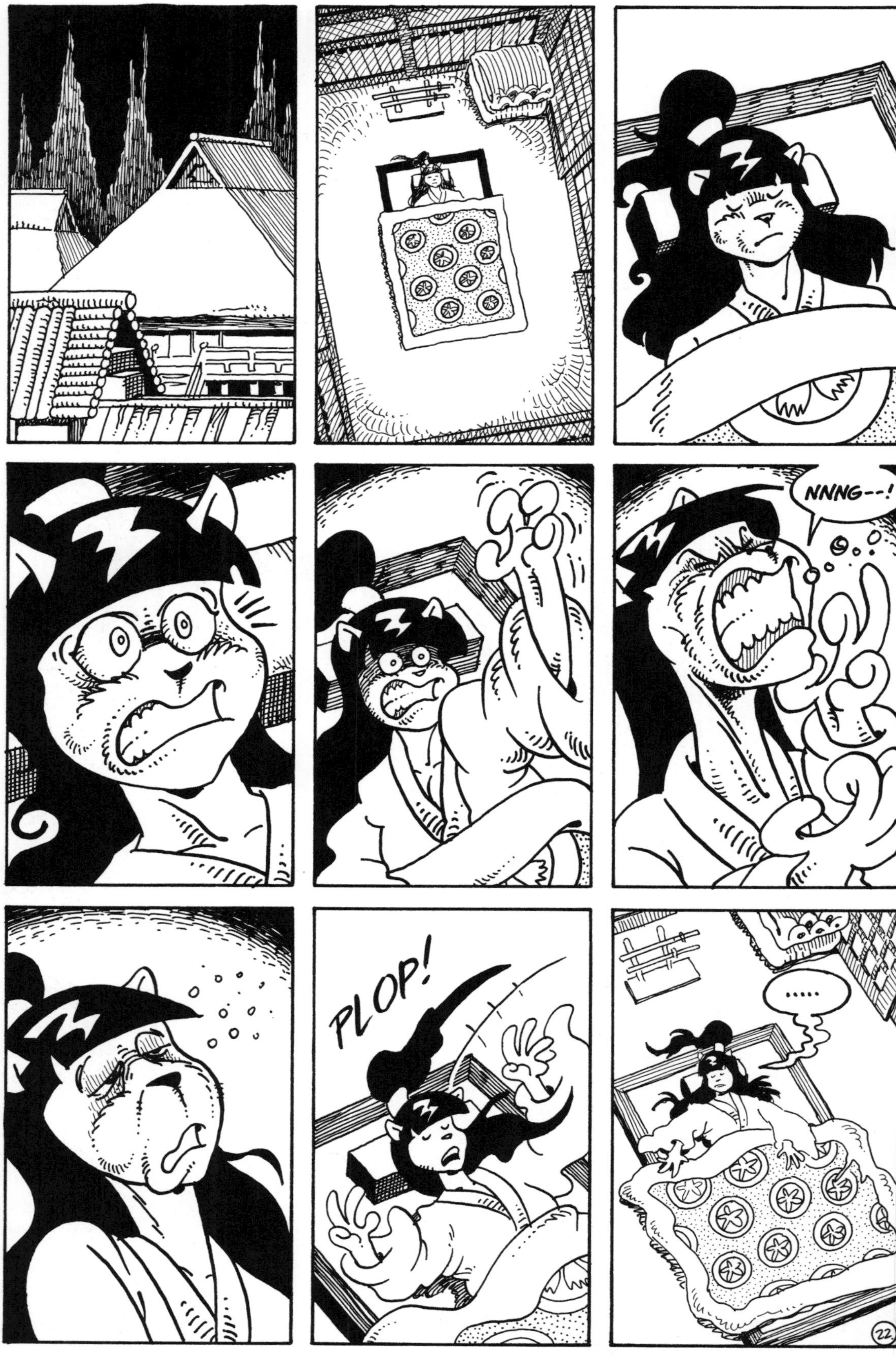
NNNG--!
PLOP!
.....
22.

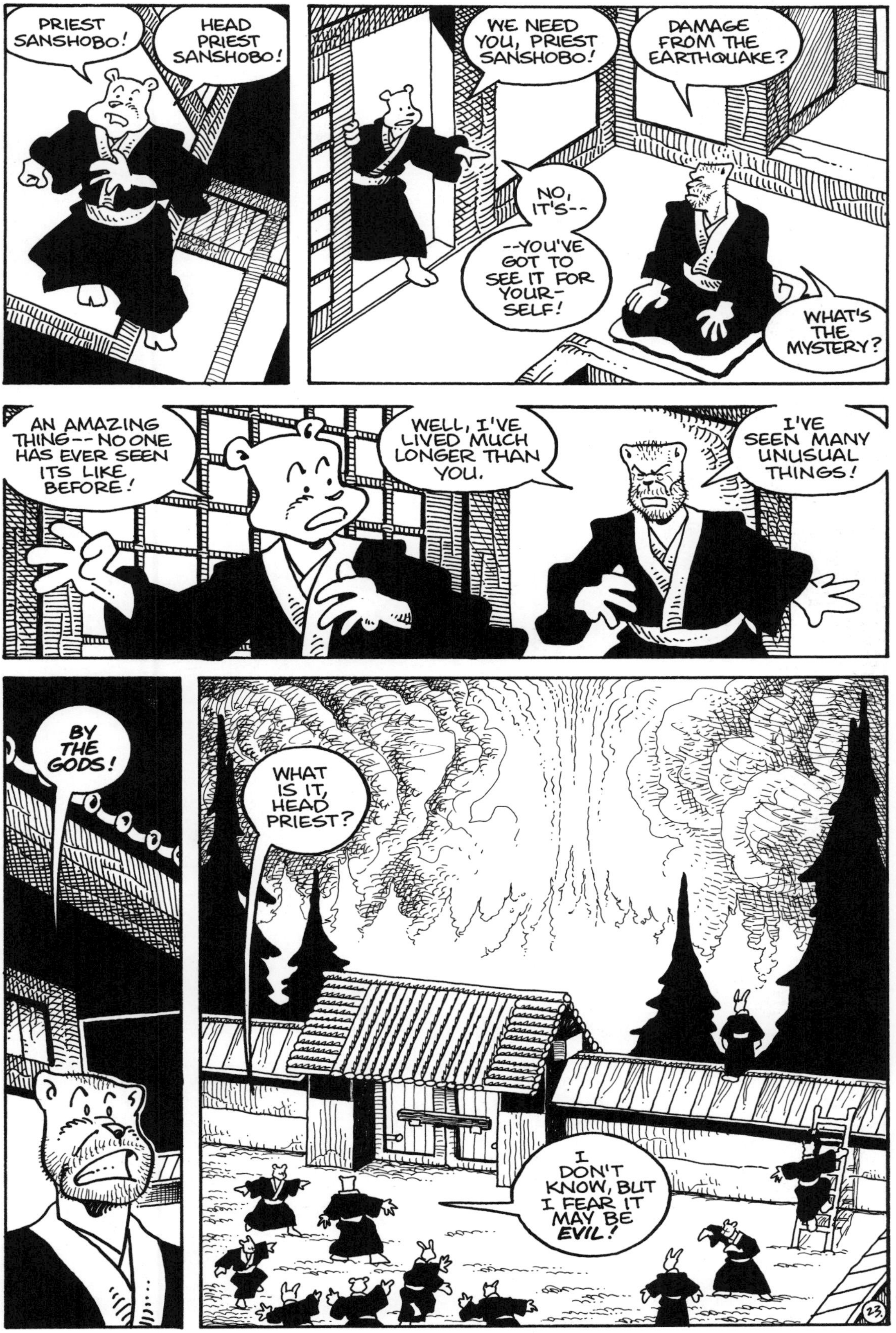
PRIEST SANSHOBO!
HEAD PRIEST SANSHOBO!
WE NEED YOU, PRIEST SANSHOBO!
DAMAGE FROM THE EARTHQUAKE?
NO, IT'S--
--YOU'VE GOT TO SEE IT FOR YOUR-SELF!
WHAT'S THE MYSTERY?
AN AMAZING THING--NO ONE HAS EVER SEEN ITS LIKE BEFORE!
WELL, I'VE LIVED MUCH LONGER THAN YOU.
I'VE SEEN MANY UNUSUAL THINGS!
BY THE GODS!
WHAT IS IT, HEAD PRIEST?
I DON'T KNOW, BUT I FEAR IT MAY BE EVIL!
23.

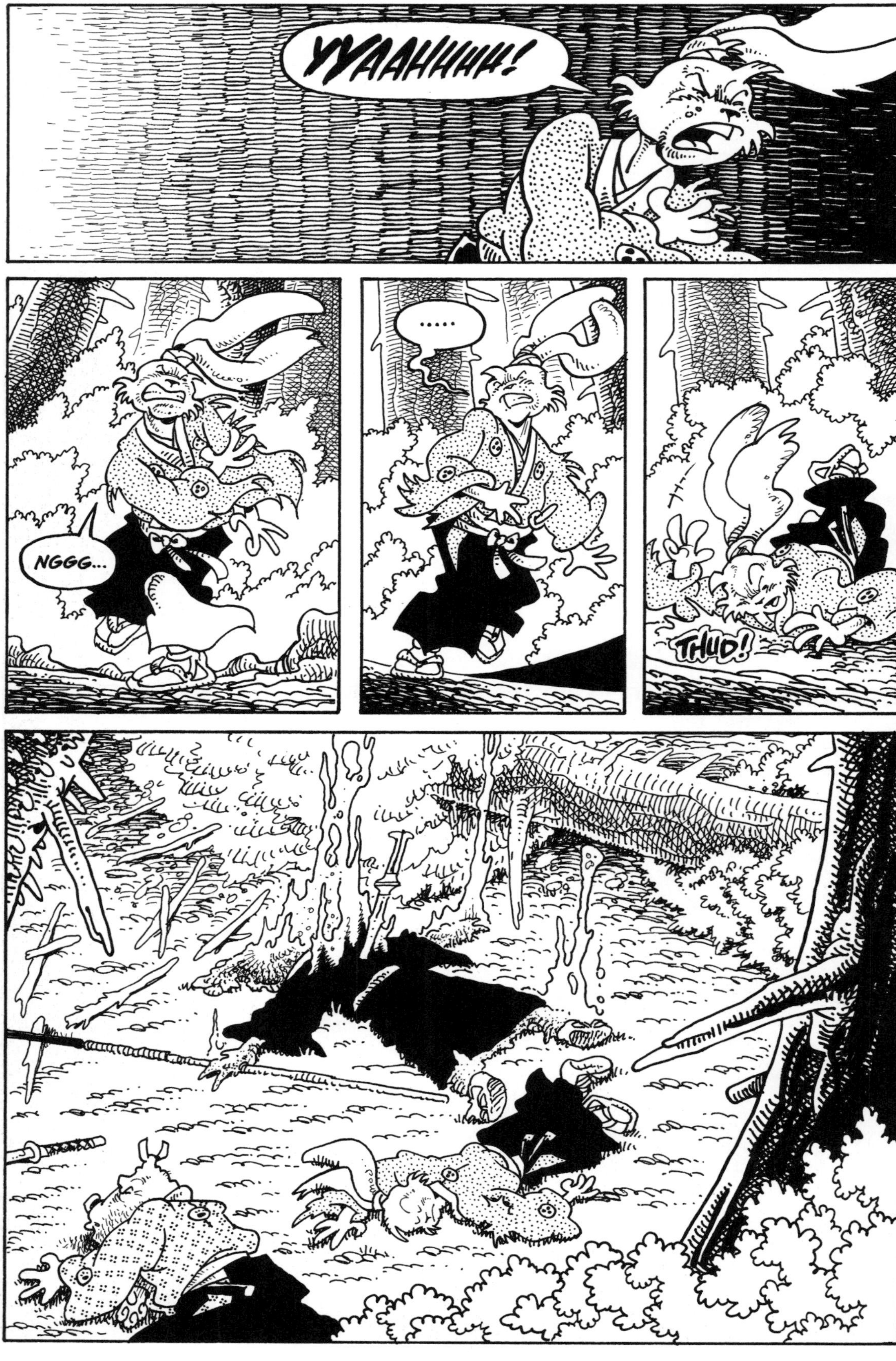
YYAAHHHH!
NGGG...
.....
THUD!

GRASSCUTTER
CHAPTER 8
SANSHOBO

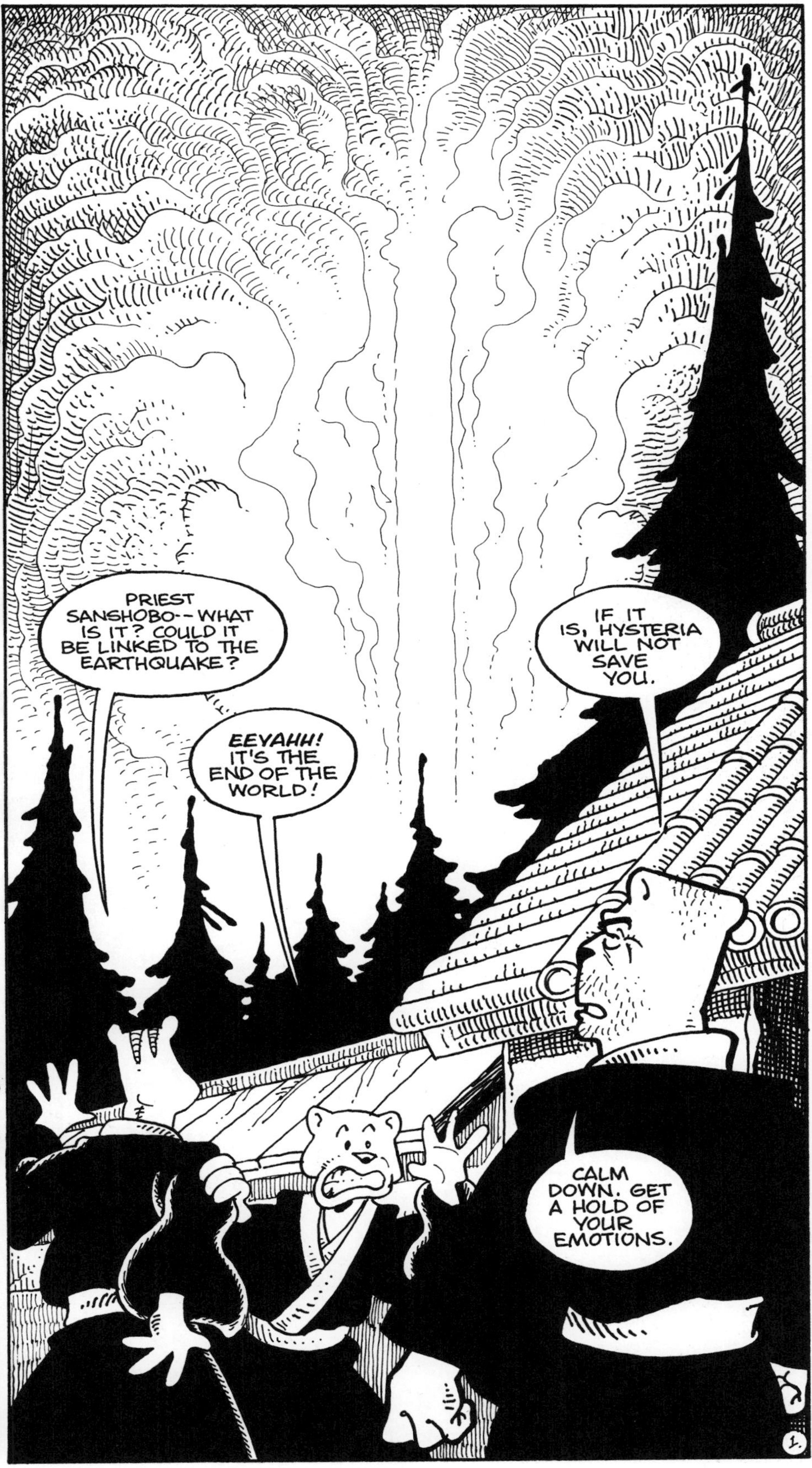

PRIEST SANSHOBO-- WHAT IS IT? COULD IT BE LINKED TO THE EARTHQUAKE?
EEYAHH! IT'S THE END OF THE WORLD!
CALM DOWN. GET A HOLD OF YOUR EMOTIONS.
IF IT IS, HYSTERIA WILL NOT SAVE YOU.

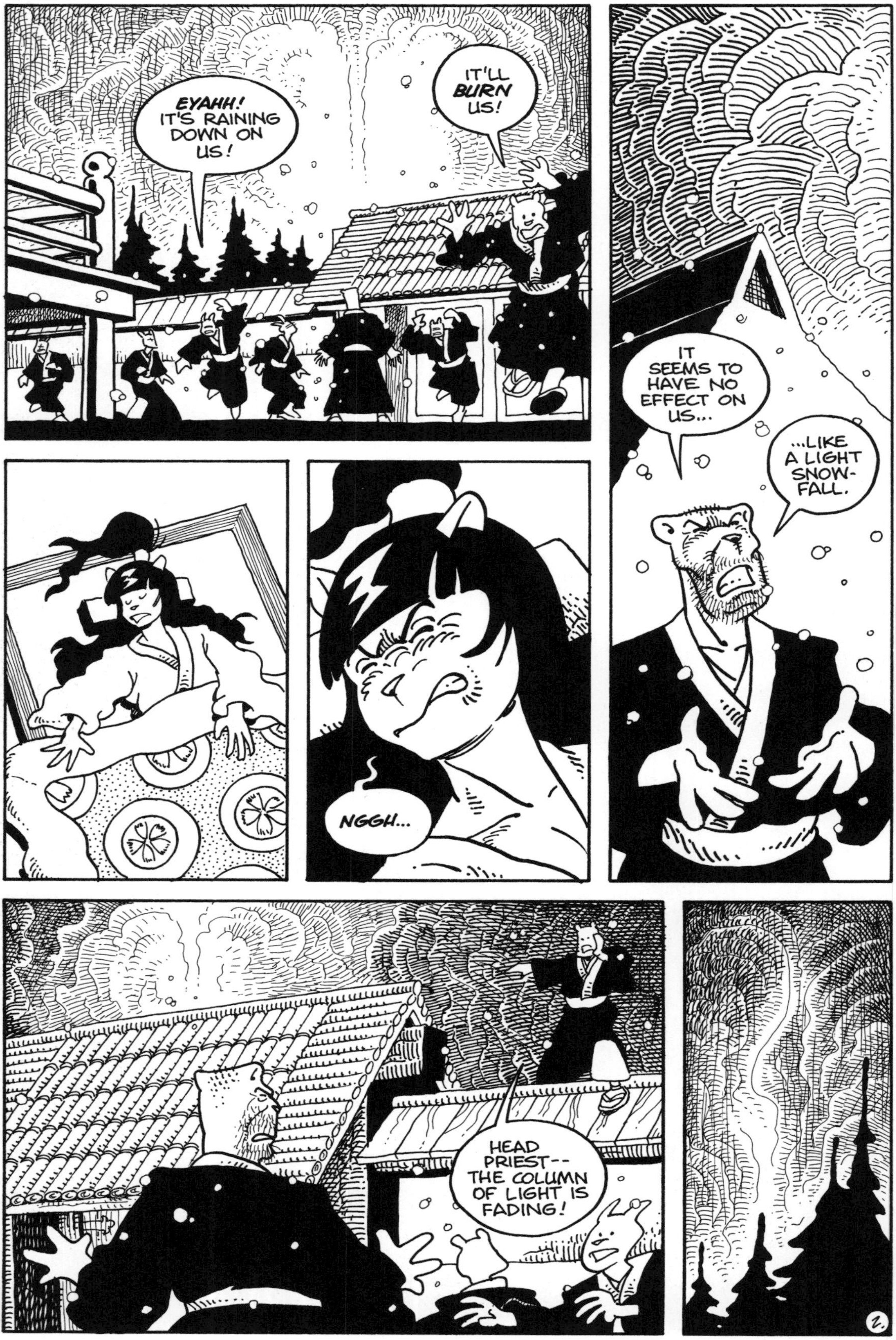
EYAHH! IT'S RAINING DOWN ON US!
IT'LL BURN US!
NGGH...
IT SEEMS TO HAVE NO EFFECT ON US...
...LIKE A LIGHT SNOW-FALL.
HEAD PRIEST-- THE COLUMN OF LIGHT IS FADING!

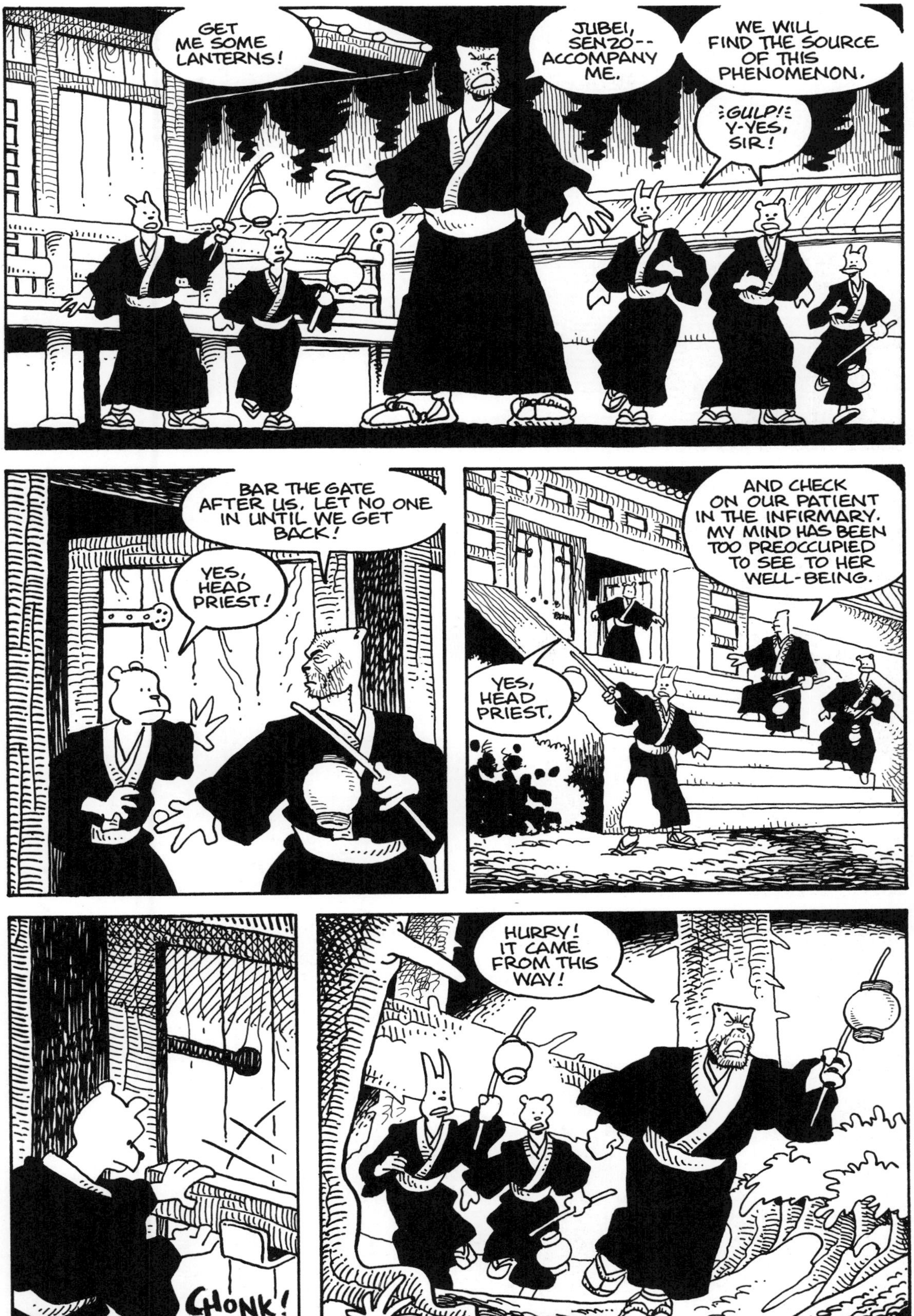
GET ME SOME LANTERNS!
JUBEI, SENZO-- ACCOMPANY ME.
WE WILL FIND THE SOURCE OF THIS PHENOMENON.
GULP! Y-YES, SIR!
BAR THE GATE AFTER US. LET NO ONE IN UNTIL WE GET BACK!
YES, HEAD PRIEST!
AND CHECK ON OUR PATIENT IN THE INFIRMARY. MY MIND HAS BEEN TOO PREOCCUPIED TO SEE TO HER WELL-BEING.
YES, HEAD PRIEST.
CHONK!
HURRY! IT CAME FROM THIS WAY!
3.

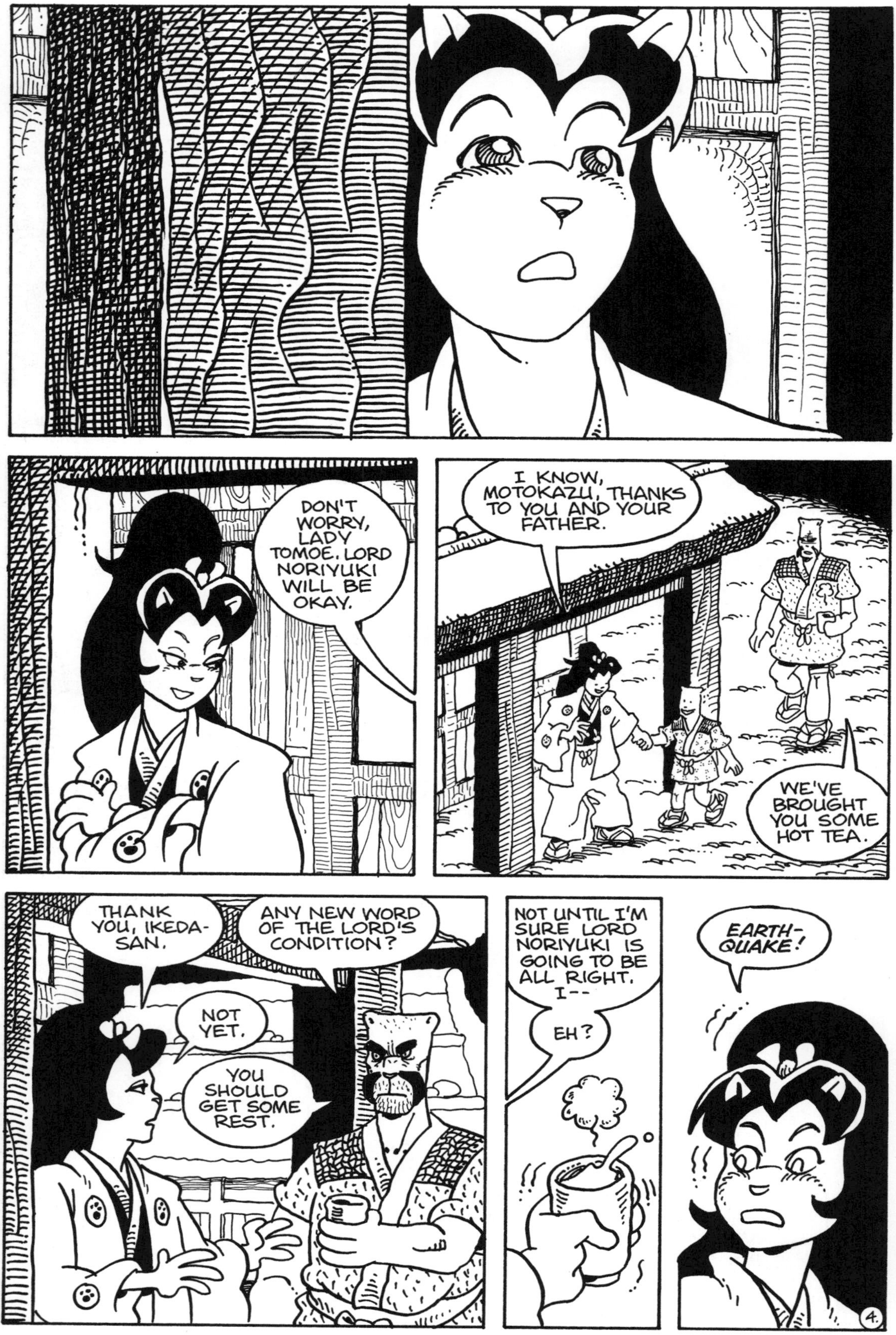
DON'T WORRY, LADY TOMOE. LORD NORIYUKI WILL BE OKAY.
I KNOW, MOTOKAZU, THANKS TO YOU AND YOUR FATHER.
WE'VE BROUGHT YOU SOME HOT TEA.
THANK YOU, IKEDA-SAN.
ANY NEW WORD OF THE LORD'S CONDITION?
NOT YET.
YOU SHOULD GET SOME REST.
NOT UNTIL I'M SURE LORD NORIYUKI IS GOING TO BE ALL RIGHT. I--
EH?
EARTH-QUAKE!
4.

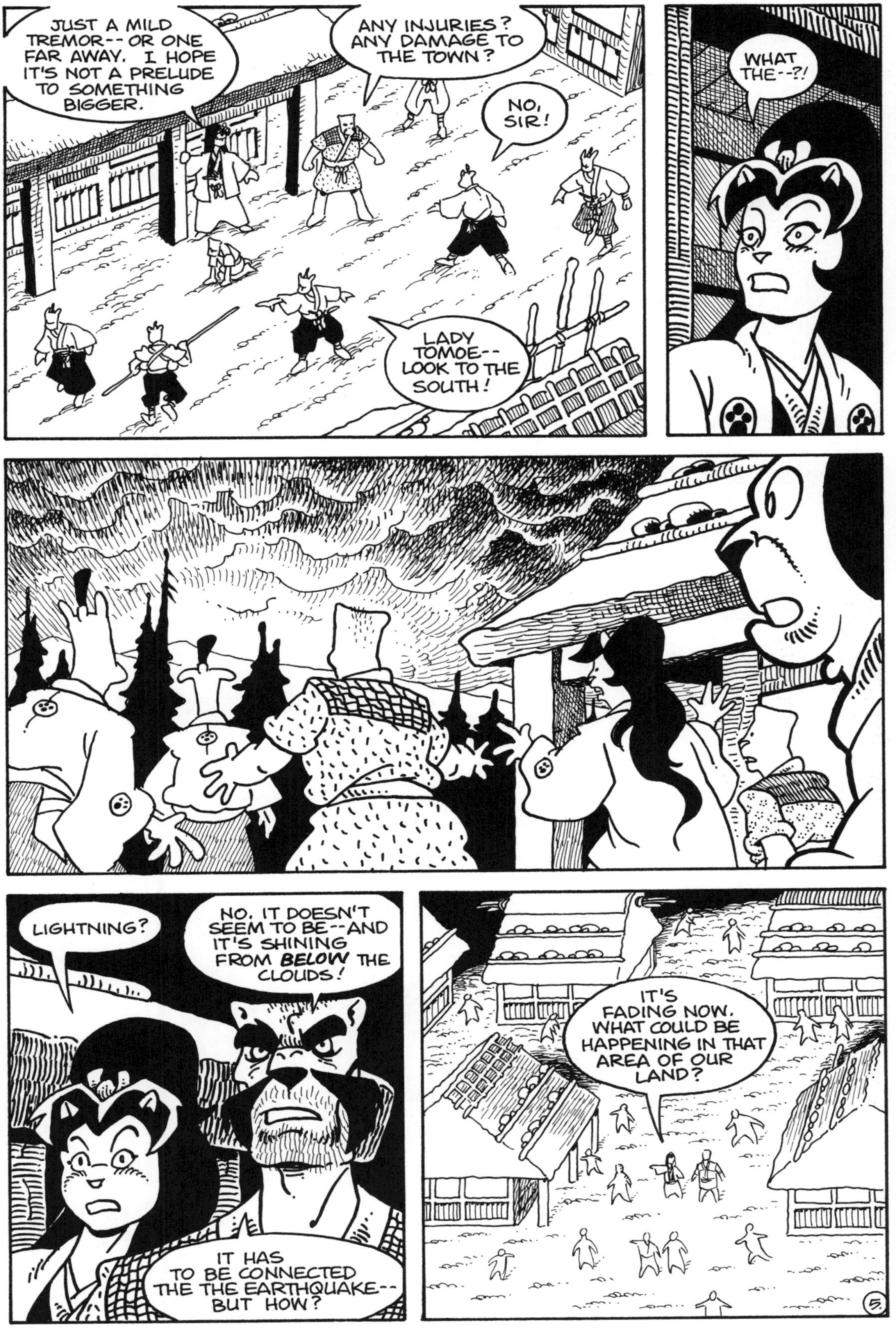
JUST A MILD TREMOR--OR ONE FAR AWAY. I HOPE IT'S NOT A PRELUDE TO SOMETHING BIGGER.
ANY INJURIES? ANY DAMAGE TO THE TOWN?
NO, SIR!
LADY TOMOE-- LOOK TO THE SOUTH!
WHAT THE--?!
LIGHTNING?
NO. IT DOESN'T SEEM TO BE--AND IT'S SHINING FROM BELOW THE CLOUDS!
IT HAS TO BE CONNECTED THE THE EARTHQUAKE-- BUT HOW?
IT'S FADING NOW. WHAT COULD BE HAPPENING IN THAT AREA OF OUR LAND?
5.

INAZUMA-SAN, FORGIVE THE INTRUSION...

...BUT PRIEST SANSHOBO ASKED US TO LOOK IN ON YOU.

Kllllll...

WHAT HAPPENED HERE?!

INAZUMA-SAN! INAZUMA-SAN! ARE YOU ALL RIGHT?!

DON'T FRET! I'LL BE BACK WITH SOME MEDICINE!

WHA--?! NO!

NOOOOOOOO!!

6.

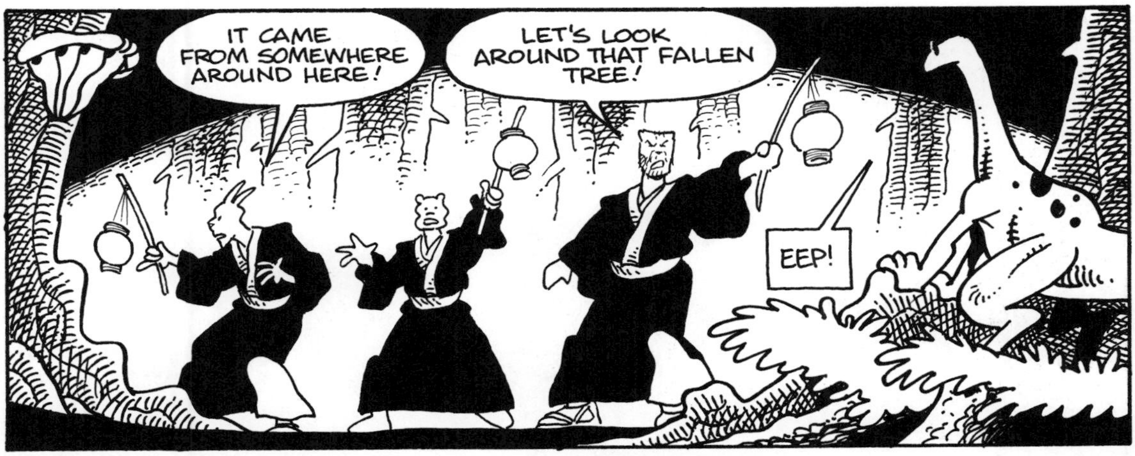
IT CAME FROM SOMEWHERE AROUND HERE!
LET'S LOOK AROUND THAT FALLEN TREE!
EEP!
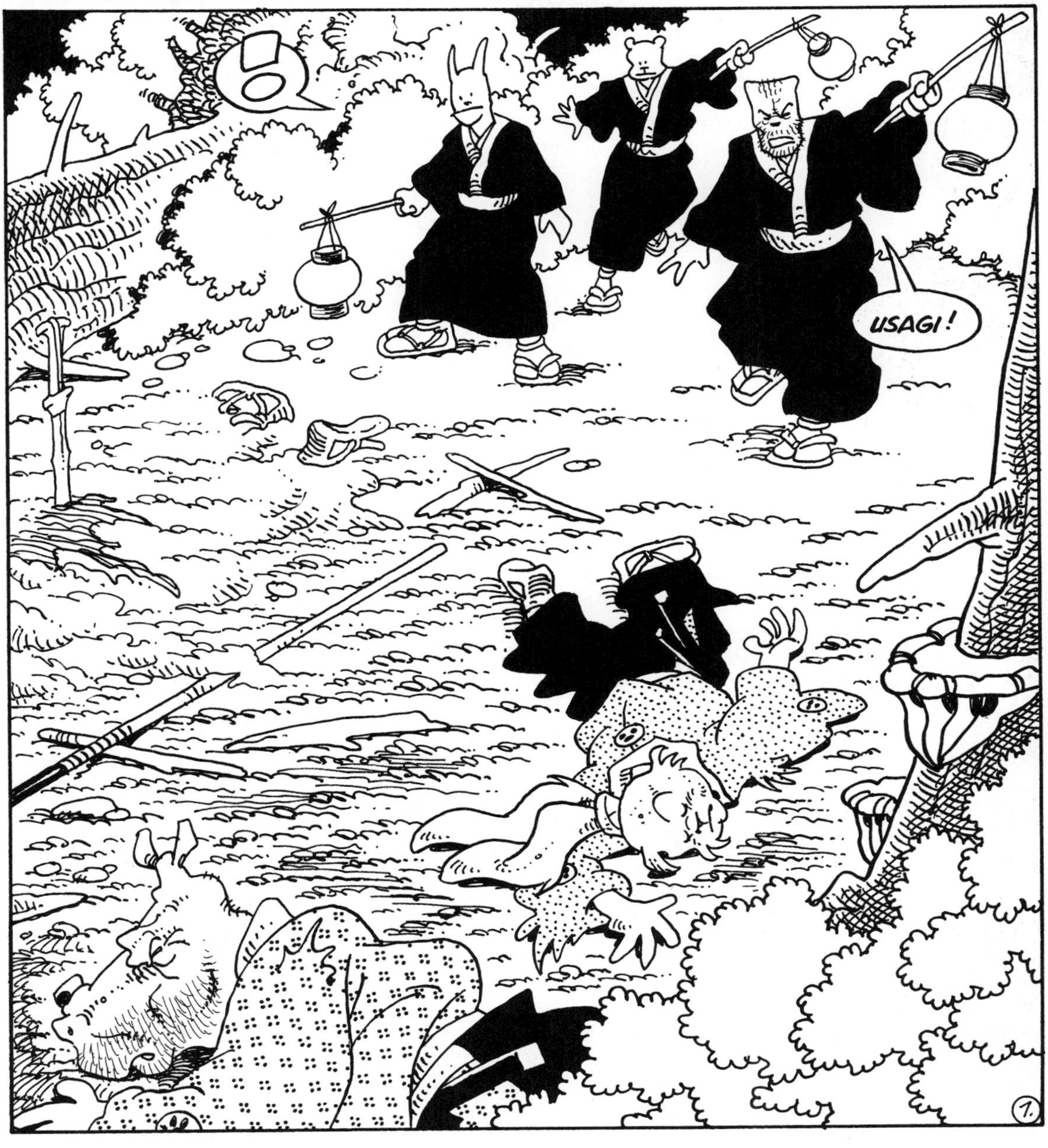
!
USAGI!
1.

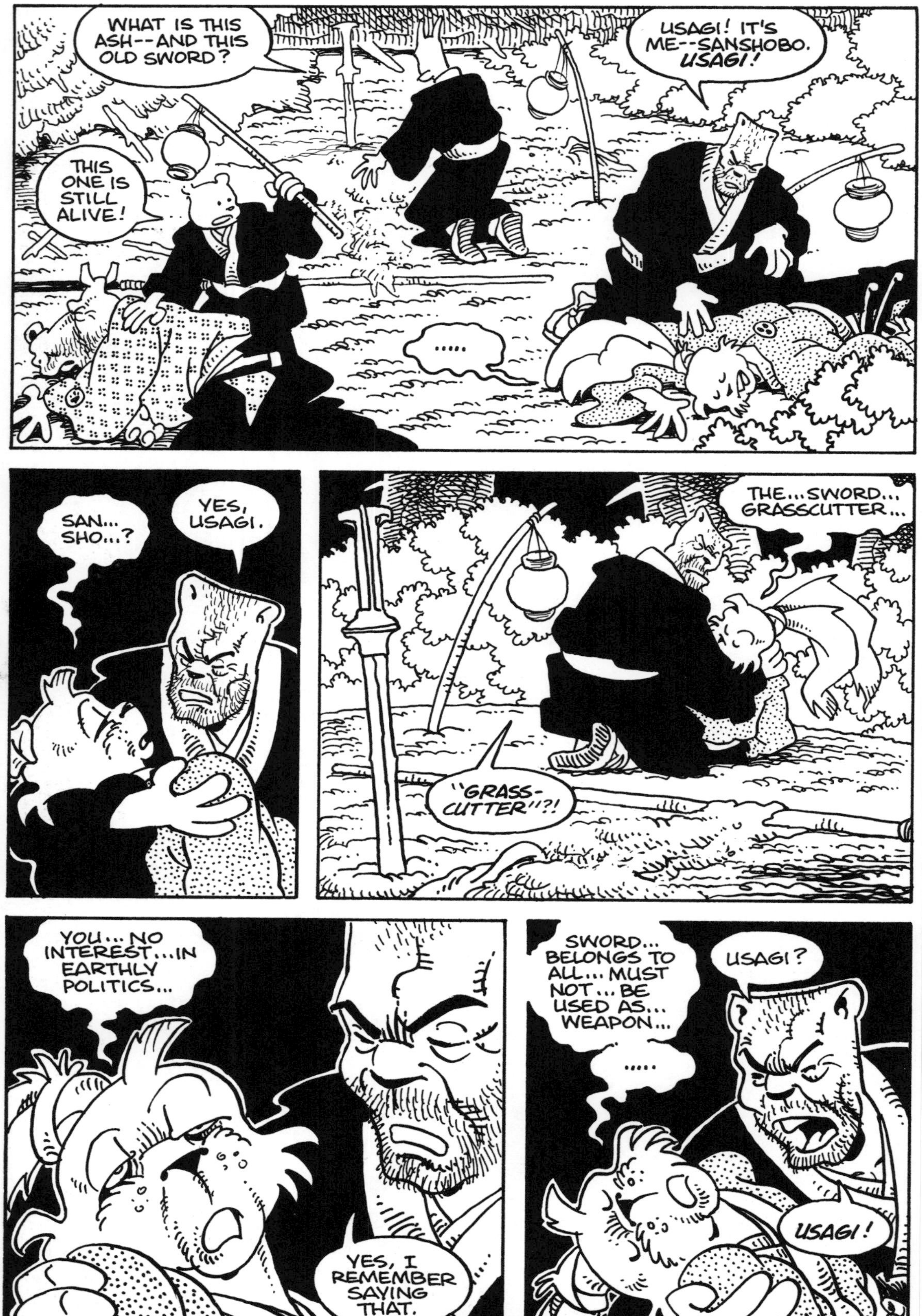
WHAT IS THIS ASH--AND THIS OLD SWORD?
THIS ONE IS STILL ALIVE!
USAGI! IT'S ME--SANSHOBO. *USAGI!*
.....
SAN... SHO...?
YES, USAGI.
THE... SWORD... GRASSCUTTER...
"*GRASS-CUTTER*"?!
YOU... NO INTEREST... IN EARTHLY POLITICS...
YES, I REMEMBER SAYING THAT.
SWORD... BELONGS TO ALL... MUST NOT... BE USED AS... WEAPON...
USAGI?
.....
USAGI!
8.

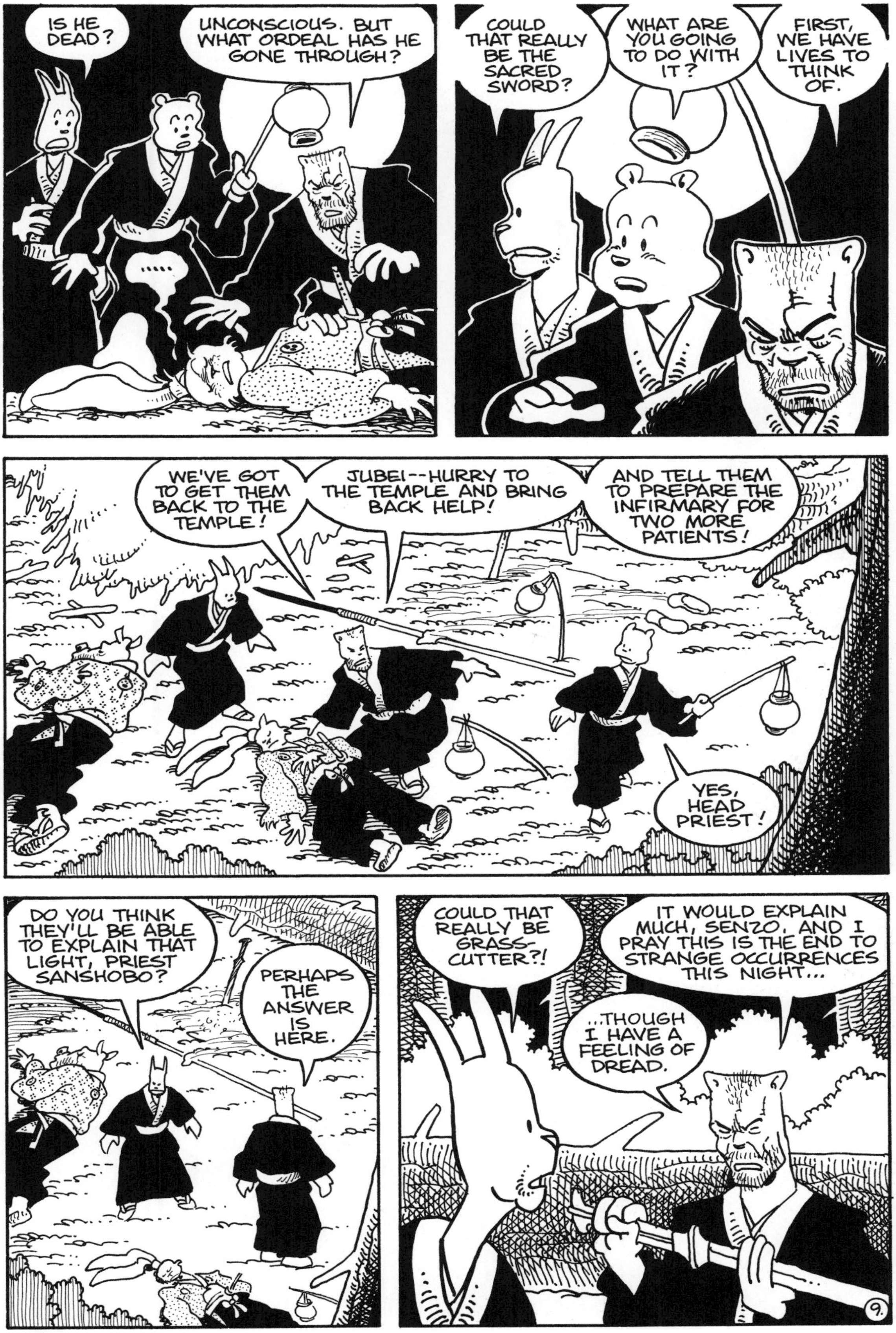
IS HE DEAD?
UNCONSCIOUS. BUT WHAT ORDEAL HAS HE GONE THROUGH?
......
COULD THAT REALLY BE THE SACRED SWORD?
WHAT ARE YOU GOING TO DO WITH IT?
FIRST, WE HAVE LIVES TO THINK OF.
WE'VE GOT TO GET THEM BACK TO THE TEMPLE!
JUBEI--HURRY TO THE TEMPLE AND BRING BACK HELP!
AND TELL THEM TO PREPARE THE INFIRMARY FOR TWO MORE PATIENTS!
YES, HEAD PRIEST!
DO YOU THINK THEY'LL BE ABLE TO EXPLAIN THAT LIGHT, PRIEST SANSHOBO?
PERHAPS THE ANSWER IS HERE.
COULD THAT REALLY BE GRASS-CUTTER?!
IT WOULD EXPLAIN MUCH, SENZO, AND I PRAY THIS IS THE END TO STRANGE OCCURRENCES THIS NIGHT...
...THOUGH I HAVE A FEELING OF DREAD.
9.

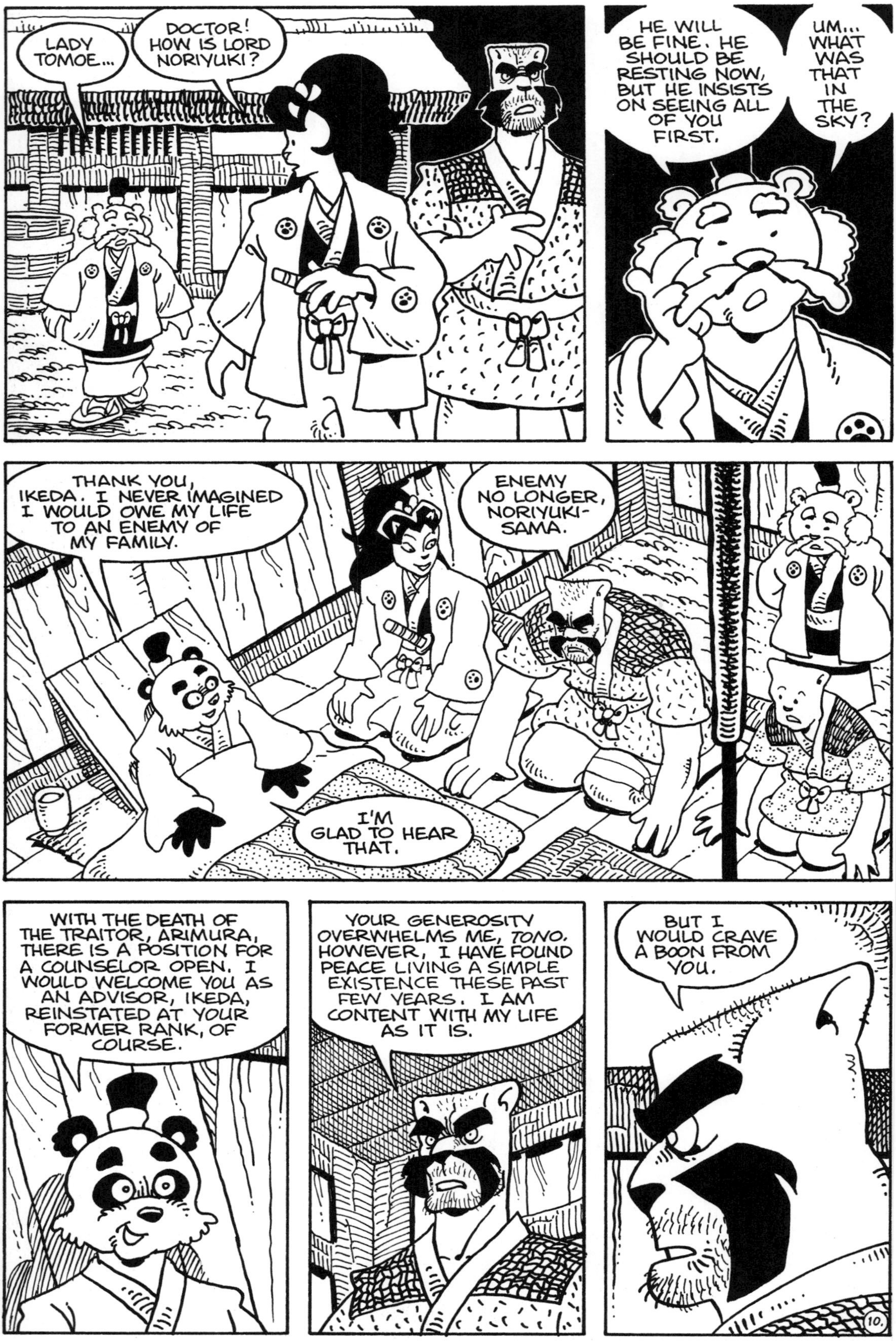
LADY TOMOE...
DOCTOR! HOW IS LORD NORIYUKI?
HE WILL BE FINE. HE SHOULD BE RESTING NOW, BUT HE INSISTS ON SEEING ALL OF YOU FIRST.
UM... WHAT WAS THAT IN THE SKY?
THANK YOU, IKEDA. I NEVER IMAGINED I WOULD OWE MY LIFE TO AN ENEMY OF MY FAMILY.
ENEMY NO LONGER, NORIYUKI-SAMA.
I'M GLAD TO HEAR THAT.
WITH THE DEATH OF THE TRAITOR, ARIMURA, THERE IS A POSITION FOR A COUNSELOR OPEN. I WOULD WELCOME YOU AS AN ADVISOR, IKEDA, REINSTATED AT YOUR FORMER RANK, OF COURSE.
YOUR GENEROSITY OVERWHELMS ME, *TONO*. HOWEVER, I HAVE FOUND PEACE LIVING A SIMPLE EXISTENCE THESE PAST FEW YEARS. I AM CONTENT WITH MY LIFE AS IT IS.
BUT I WOULD CRAVE A BOON FROM YOU.
10.

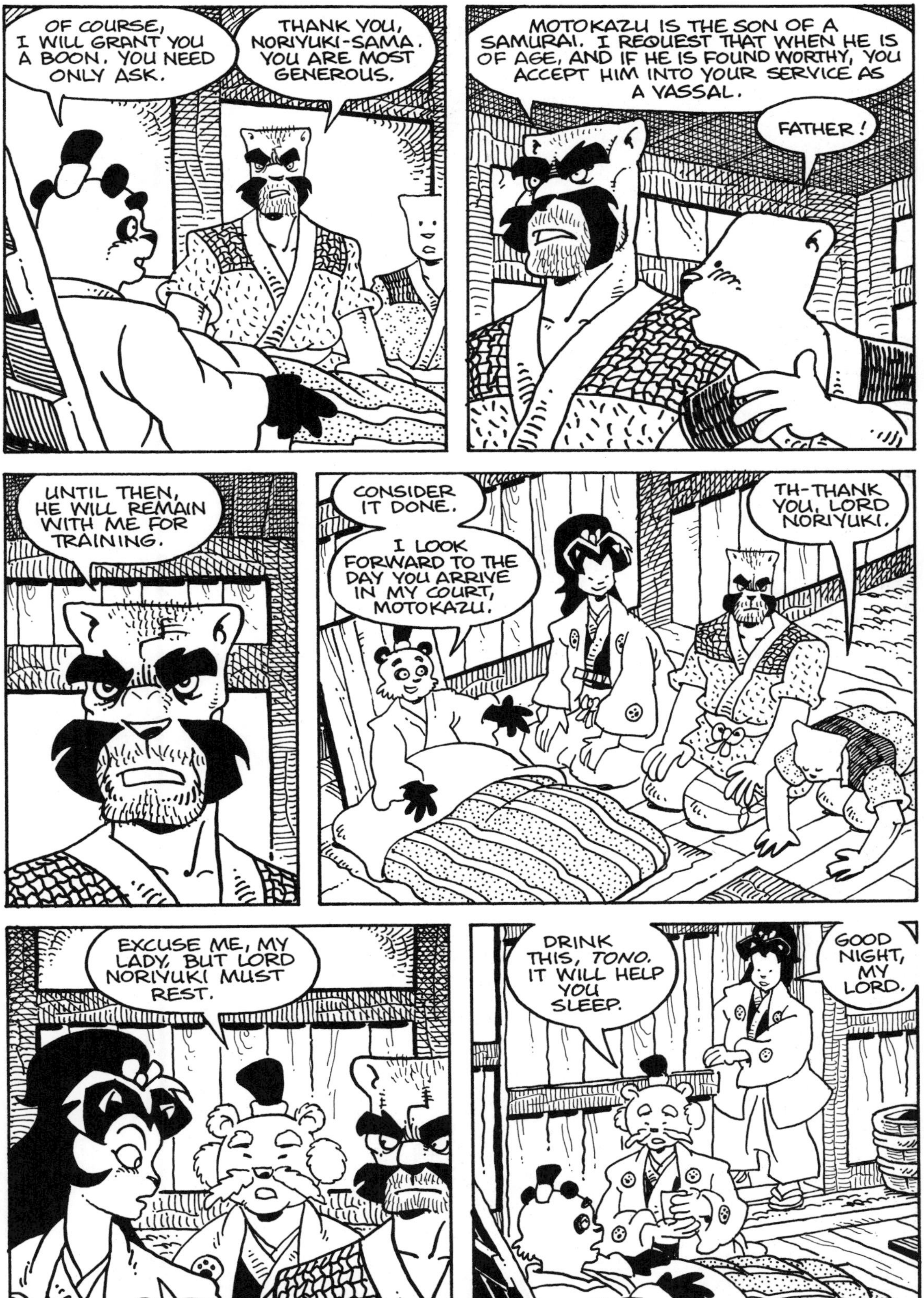
OF COURSE, I WILL GRANT YOU A BOON. YOU NEED ONLY ASK.
THANK YOU, NORIYUKI-SAMA. YOU ARE MOST GENEROUS.
MOTOKAZU IS THE SON OF A SAMURAI. I REQUEST THAT WHEN HE IS OF AGE, AND IF HE IS FOUND WORTHY, YOU ACCEPT HIM INTO YOUR SERVICE AS A VASSAL.
FATHER!
UNTIL THEN, HE WILL REMAIN WITH ME FOR TRAINING.
CONSIDER IT DONE.
I LOOK FORWARD TO THE DAY YOU ARRIVE IN MY COURT, MOTOKAZU.
TH-THANK YOU, LORD NORIYUKI.
EXCUSE ME, MY LADY, BUT LORD NORIYUKI MUST REST.
OF COURSE, DOCTOR.
DRINK THIS, *TONO*. IT WILL HELP YOU SLEEP.
GOOD NIGHT, MY LORD.
11.

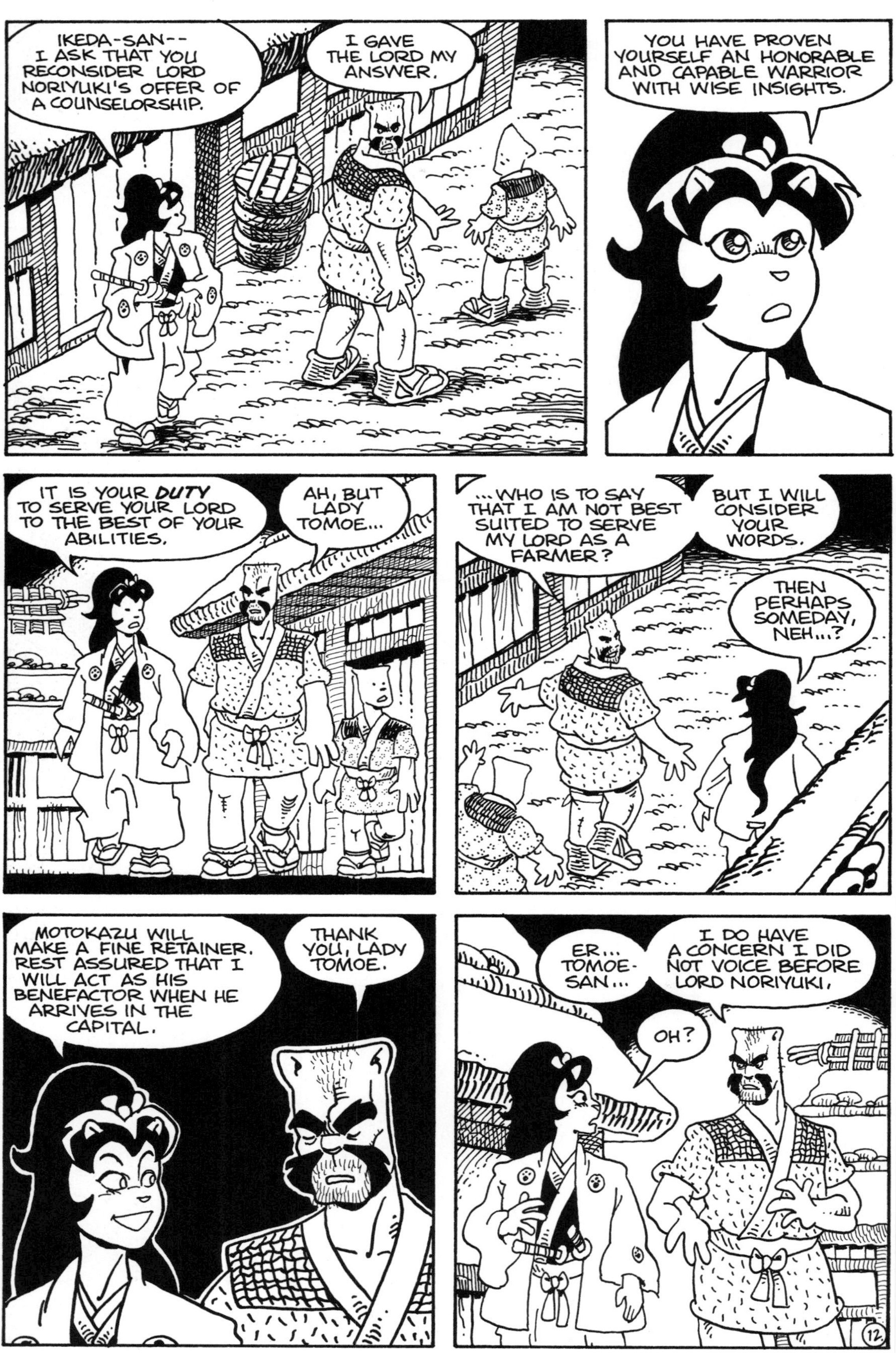
IKEDA-SAN-- I ASK THAT YOU RECONSIDER LORD NORIYUKI'S OFFER OF A COUNSELORSHIP.
I GAVE THE LORD MY ANSWER.
YOU HAVE PROVEN YOURSELF AN HONORABLE AND CAPABLE WARRIOR WITH WISE INSIGHTS.
IT IS YOUR DUTY TO SERVE YOUR LORD TO THE BEST OF YOUR ABILITIES.
AH, BUT LADY TOMOE...
...WHO IS TO SAY THAT I AM NOT BEST SUITED TO SERVE MY LORD AS A FARMER?
BUT I WILL CONSIDER YOUR WORDS.
THEN PERHAPS SOMEDAY, NEH...?
MOTOKAZU WILL MAKE A FINE RETAINER. REST ASSURED THAT I WILL ACT AS HIS BENEFACTOR WHEN HE ARRIVES IN THE CAPITAL.
THANK YOU, LADY TOMOE.
ER... TOMOE-SAN...
I DO HAVE A CONCERN I DID NOT VOICE BEFORE LORD NORIYUKI,
OH?
12

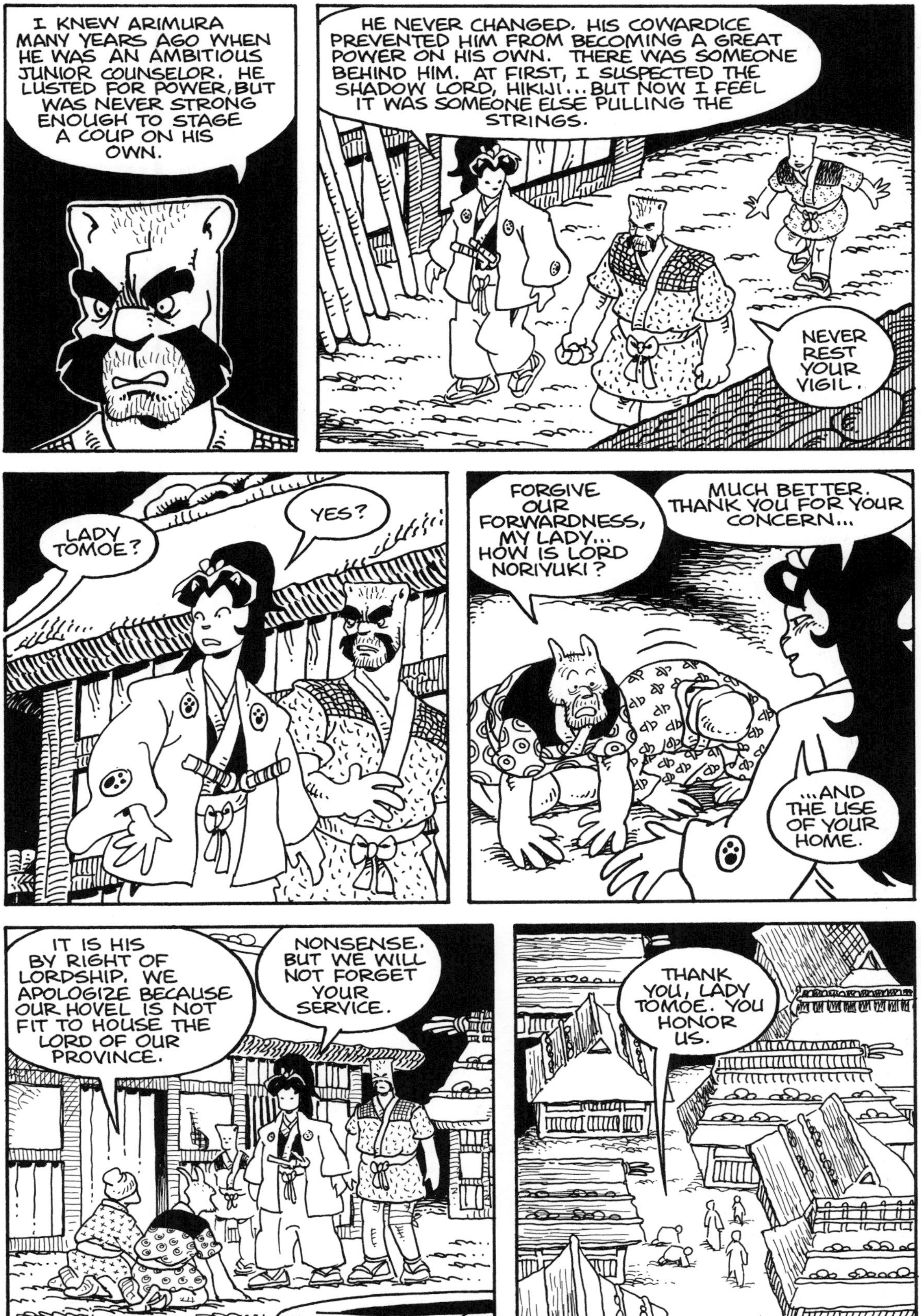
I KNEW ARIMURA MANY YEARS AGO WHEN HE WAS AN AMBITIOUS JUNIOR COUNSELOR. HE LUSTED FOR POWER, BUT WAS NEVER STRONG ENOUGH TO STAGE A COUP ON HIS OWN.
HE NEVER CHANGED. HIS COWARDICE PREVENTED HIM FROM BECOMING A GREAT POWER ON HIS OWN. THERE WAS SOMEONE BEHIND HIM. AT FIRST, I SUSPECTED THE SHADOW LORD, HIKIJI... BUT NOW I FEEL IT WAS SOMEONE ELSE PULLING THE STRINGS.
NEVER REST YOUR VIGIL.
LADY TOMOE?
YES?
FORGIVE OUR FORWARDNESS, MY LADY... HOW IS LORD NORIYUKI?
MUCH BETTER. THANK YOU FOR YOUR CONCERN...
...AND THE USE OF YOUR HOME.
IT IS HIS BY RIGHT OF LORDSHIP. WE APOLOGIZE BECAUSE OUR HOVEL IS NOT FIT TO HOUSE THE LORD OF OUR PROVINCE.
NONSENSE. BUT WE WILL NOT FORGET YOUR SERVICE.
THANK YOU, LADY TOMOE. YOU HONOR US.
13.

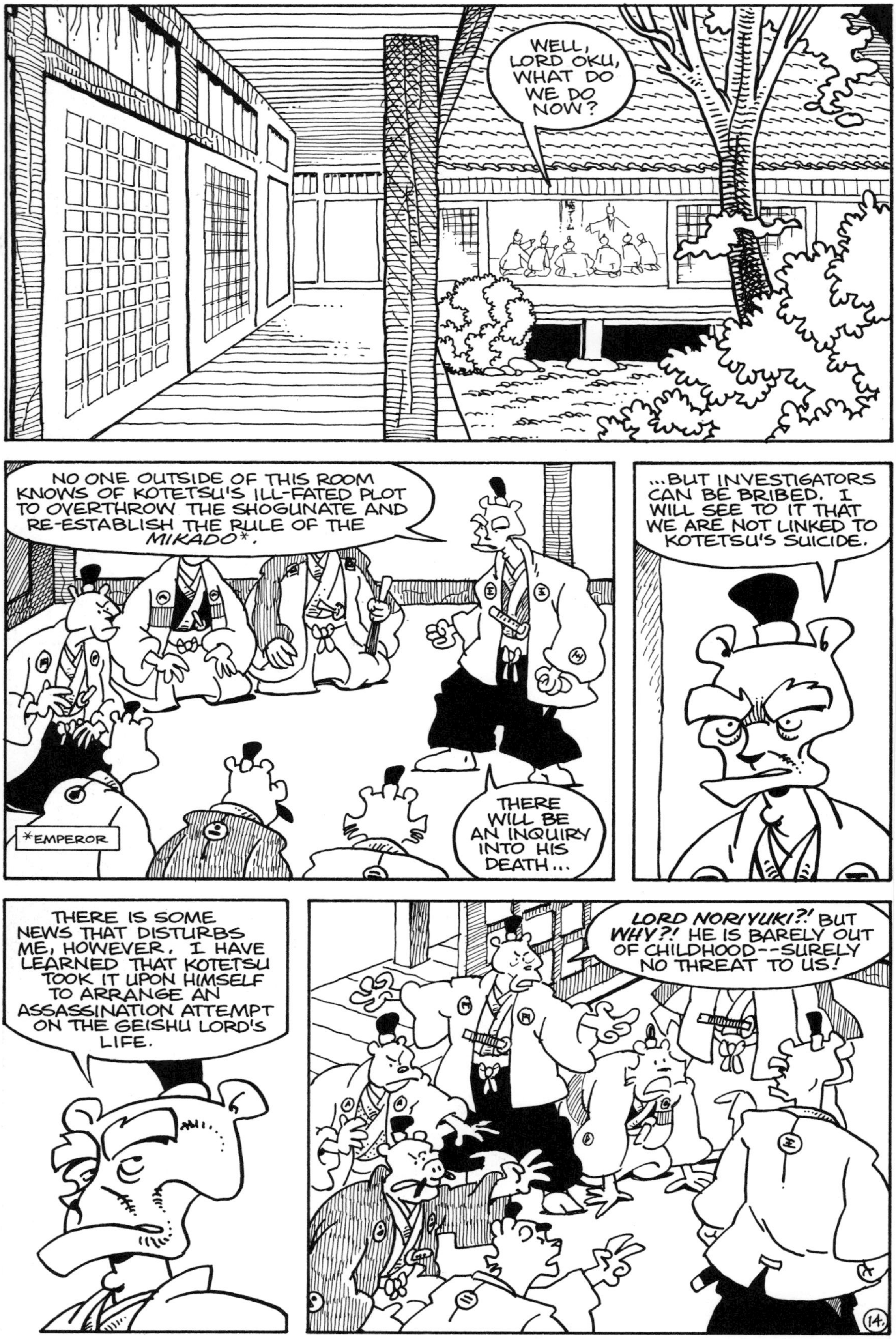
WELL, LORD OKU, WHAT DO WE DO NOW?
NO ONE OUTSIDE OF THIS ROOM KNOWS OF KOTETSU'S ILL-FATED PLOT TO OVERTHROW THE SHOGUNATE AND RE-ESTABLISH THE RULE OF THE *MIKADO**.
*EMPEROR
THERE WILL BE AN INQUIRY INTO HIS DEATH...
...BUT INVESTIGATORS CAN BE BRIBED. I WILL SEE TO IT THAT WE ARE NOT LINKED TO KOTETSU'S SUICIDE.
THERE IS SOME NEWS THAT DISTURBS ME, HOWEVER. I HAVE LEARNED THAT KOTETSU TOOK IT UPON HIMSELF TO ARRANGE AN ASSASSINATION ATTEMPT ON THE GEISHU LORD'S LIFE.
LORD NORIYUKI?! BUT *WHY?!* HE IS BARELY OUT OF CHILDHOOD--SURELY NO THREAT TO US!
14.

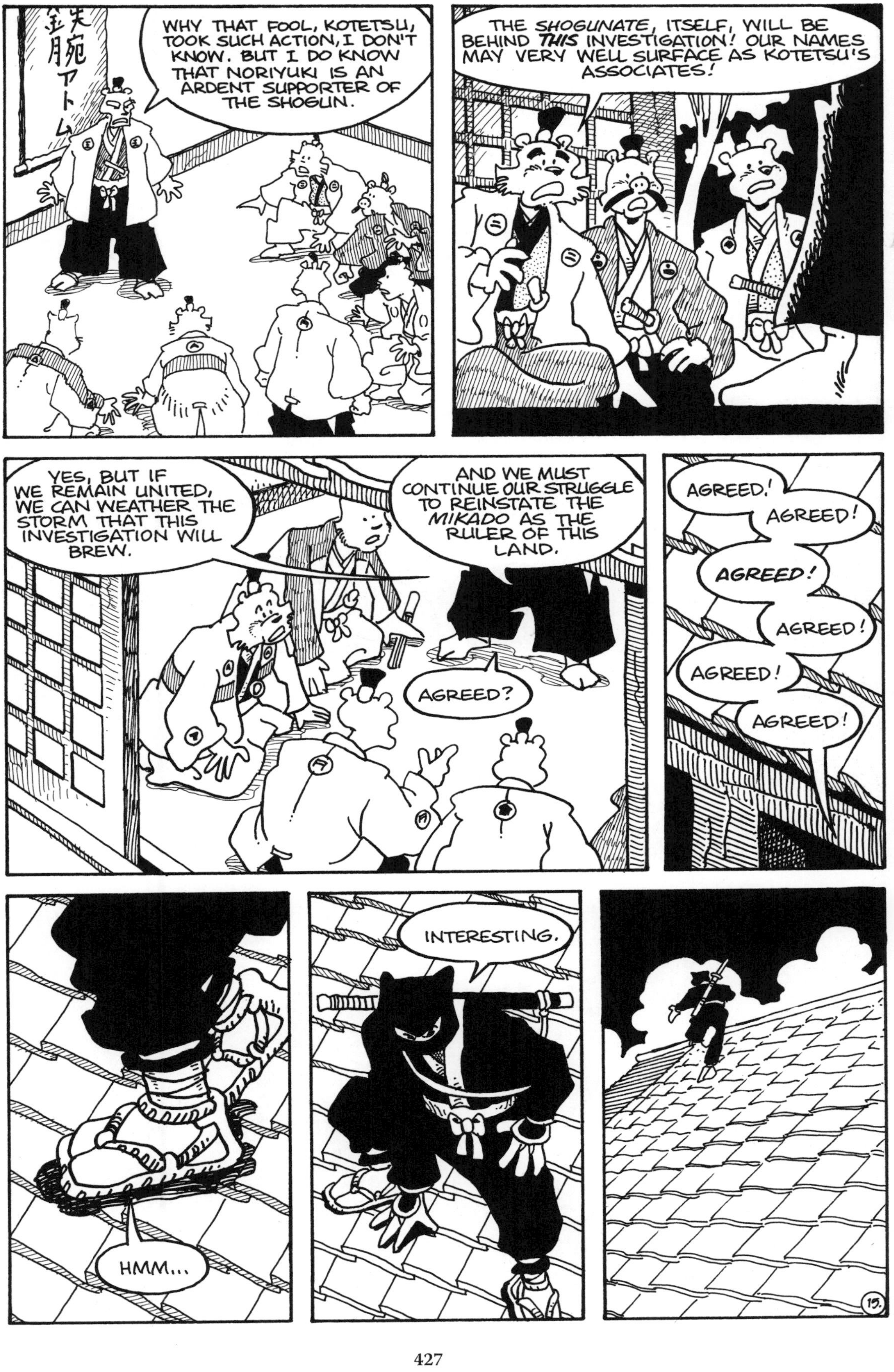
WHY THAT FOOL, KOTETSU, TOOK SUCH ACTION, I DON'T KNOW. BUT I DO KNOW THAT NORIYUKI IS AN ARDENT SUPPORTER OF THE SHOGUN.
THE *SHOGUNATE*, ITSELF, WILL BE BEHIND ***THIS*** INVESTIGATION! OUR NAMES MAY VERY WELL SURFACE AS KOTETSU'S ASSOCIATES!
YES, BUT IF WE REMAIN UNITED, WE CAN WEATHER THE STORM THAT THIS INVESTIGATION WILL BREW.
AND WE MUST CONTINUE OUR STRUGGLE TO REINSTATE THE *MIKADO* AS THE RULER OF THIS LAND.
AGREED?
AGREED!
AGREED!
AGREED!
AGREED!
AGREED!
AGREED!
HMM...
INTERESTING.
15.

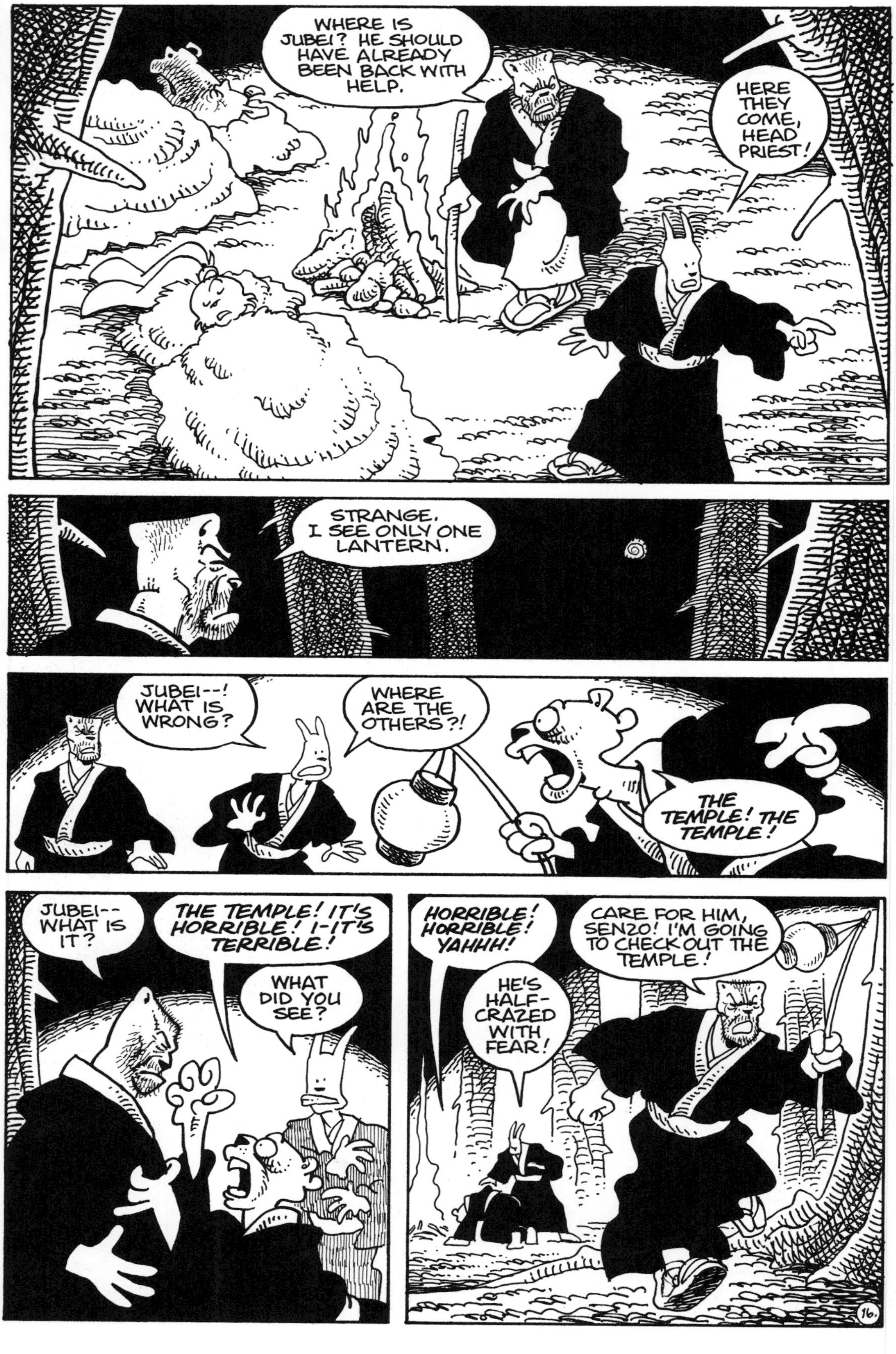
WHERE IS JUBEI? HE SHOULD HAVE ALREADY BEEN BACK WITH HELP.
HERE THEY COME, HEAD PRIEST!
STRANGE. I SEE ONLY ONE LANTERN.
JUBEI--! WHAT IS WRONG?
WHERE ARE THE OTHERS?!
THE TEMPLE! THE TEMPLE!
JUBEI-- WHAT IS IT?
THE TEMPLE! IT'S HORRIBLE! I-IT'S TERRIBLE!
WHAT DID YOU SEE?
HORRIBLE! HORRIBLE! YAHHH!
HE'S HALF-CRAZED WITH FEAR!
CARE FOR HIM, SENZO! I'M GOING TO CHECK OUT THE TEMPLE!
16.

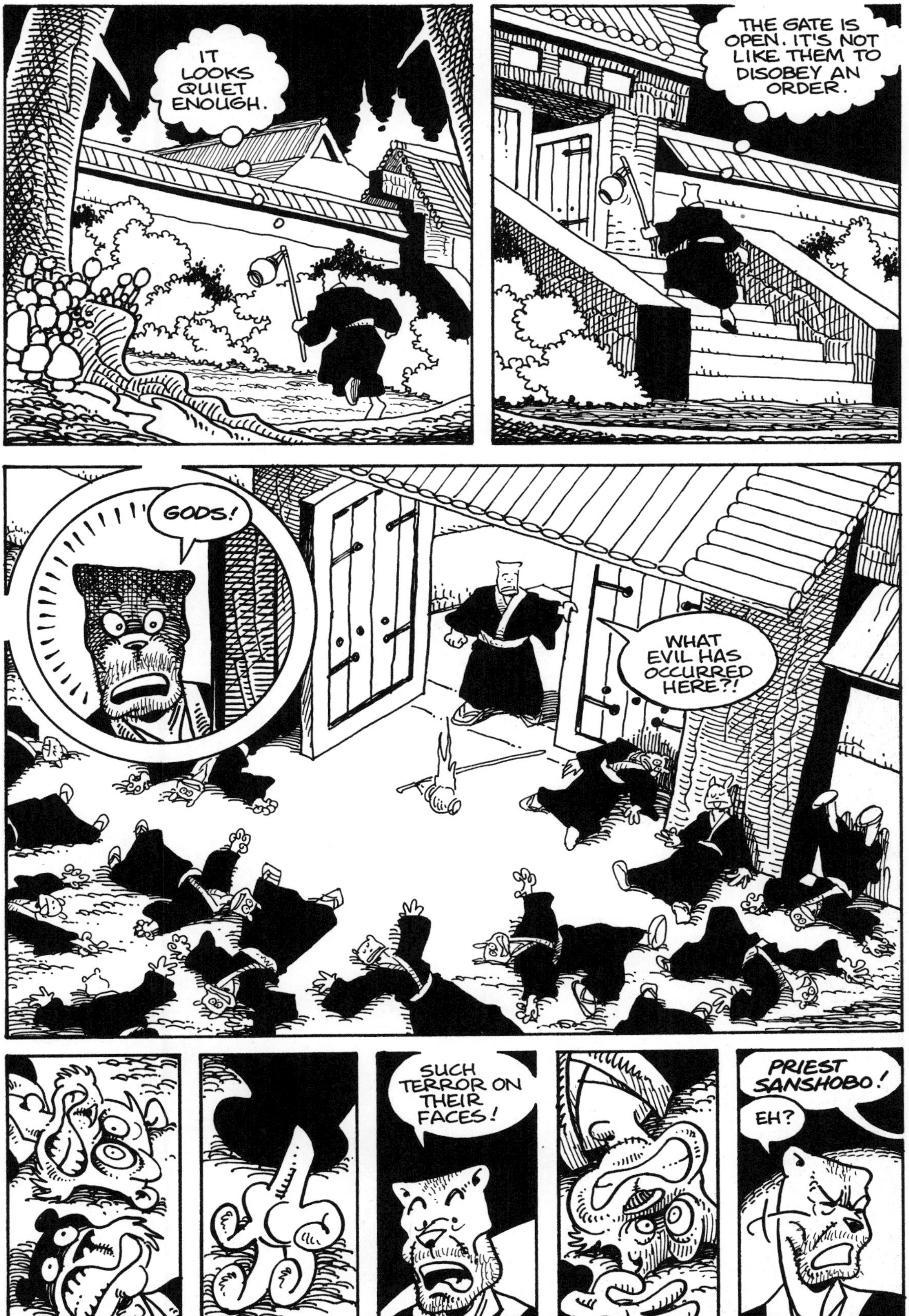
IT LOOKS QUIET ENOUGH.
THE GATE IS OPEN. IT'S NOT LIKE THEM TO DISOBEY AN ORDER.
GODS!
WHAT EVIL HAS OCCURRED HERE?!
SUCH TERROR ON THEIR FACES!
PRIEST SANSHOBO!
EH?
17.

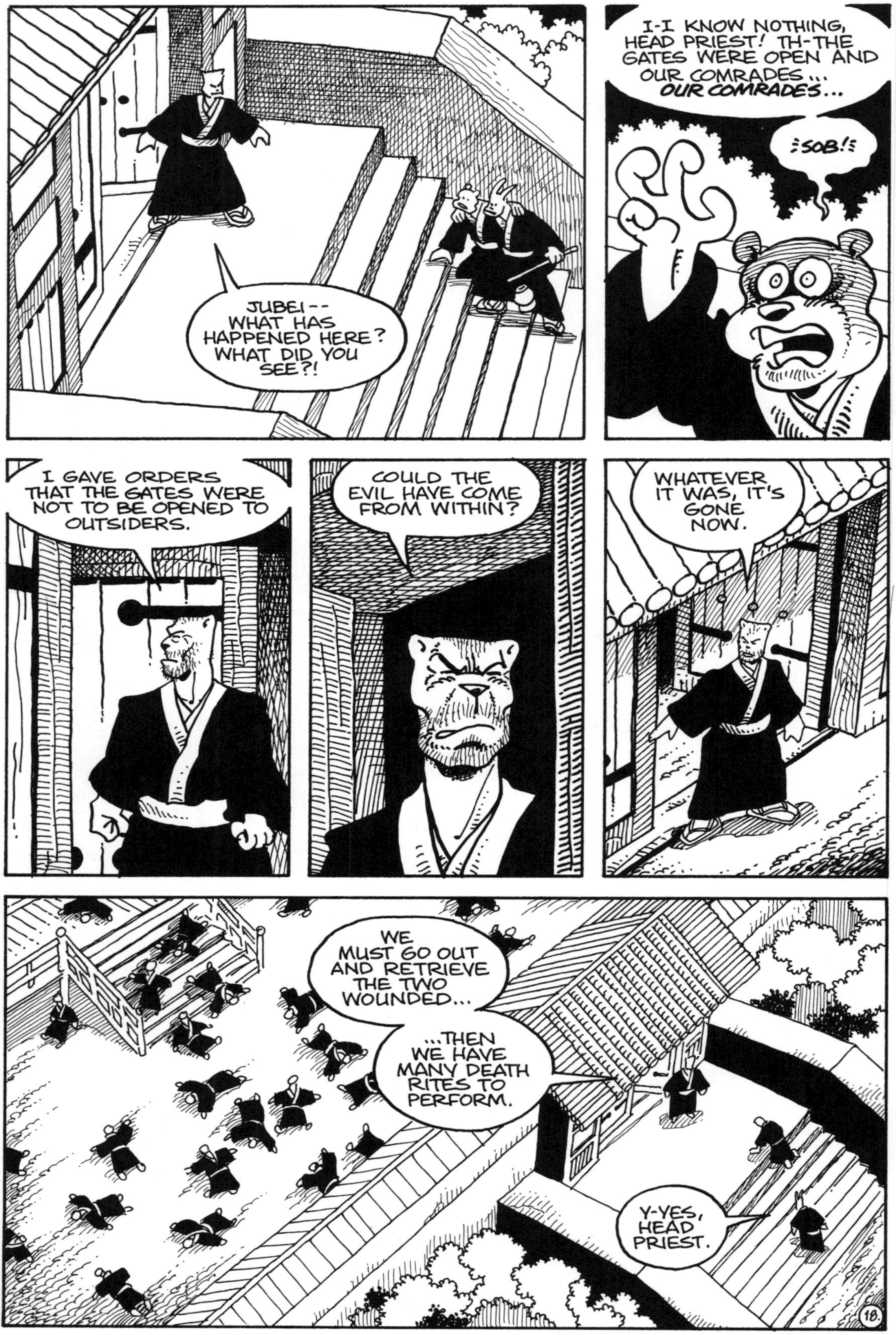
JUBEI-- WHAT HAS HAPPENED HERE? WHAT DID YOU SEE?!
I-I KNOW NOTHING, HEAD PRIEST! TH-THE GATES WERE OPEN AND OUR COMRADES... OUR COMRADES...
SOB!
I GAVE ORDERS THAT THE GATES WERE NOT TO BE OPENED TO OUTSIDERS.
COULD THE EVIL HAVE COME FROM WITHIN?
WHATEVER IT WAS, IT'S GONE NOW.
WE MUST GO OUT AND RETRIEVE THE TWO WOUNDED...
...THEN WE HAVE MANY DEATH RITES TO PERFORM.
Y-YES, HEAD PRIEST.
18.

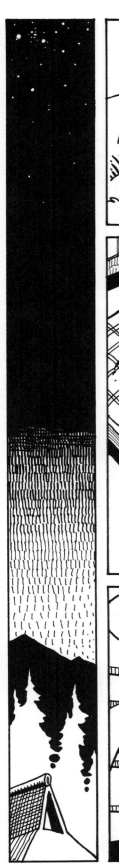

UHH...

YOU'RE AWAKE, ARE YOU, USAGI? I'LL BRING YOU SOME BROTH.

YOU'RE IN MY TEMPLE, BY THE WAY.

SAN... SHOBO..?

YES, IT'S ME.

YOU'LL BE FINE AFTER A FEW DAYS OF REST, BUT YOUR FRIEND THERE WILL TAKE MUCH LONGER TO MEND.

WHEN YOU'RE BETTER, I'D LIKE TO HEAR WHAT YOU WENT THROUGH. IT COULD BE CONNECTED TO THE DEATHS OF THIRTY PRIESTS...

...AND THE DISAPPEARANCE OF A WOMAN WE WERE CARING FOR, I WOULD SUSPECT HER OF THE MURDERS, EXCEPT SHE WAS TOO INJURED HERSELF TO CAUSE THE CARNAGE THAT I SAW.

BUT I VOW I'LL FIND THAT KILLER.

19.

431

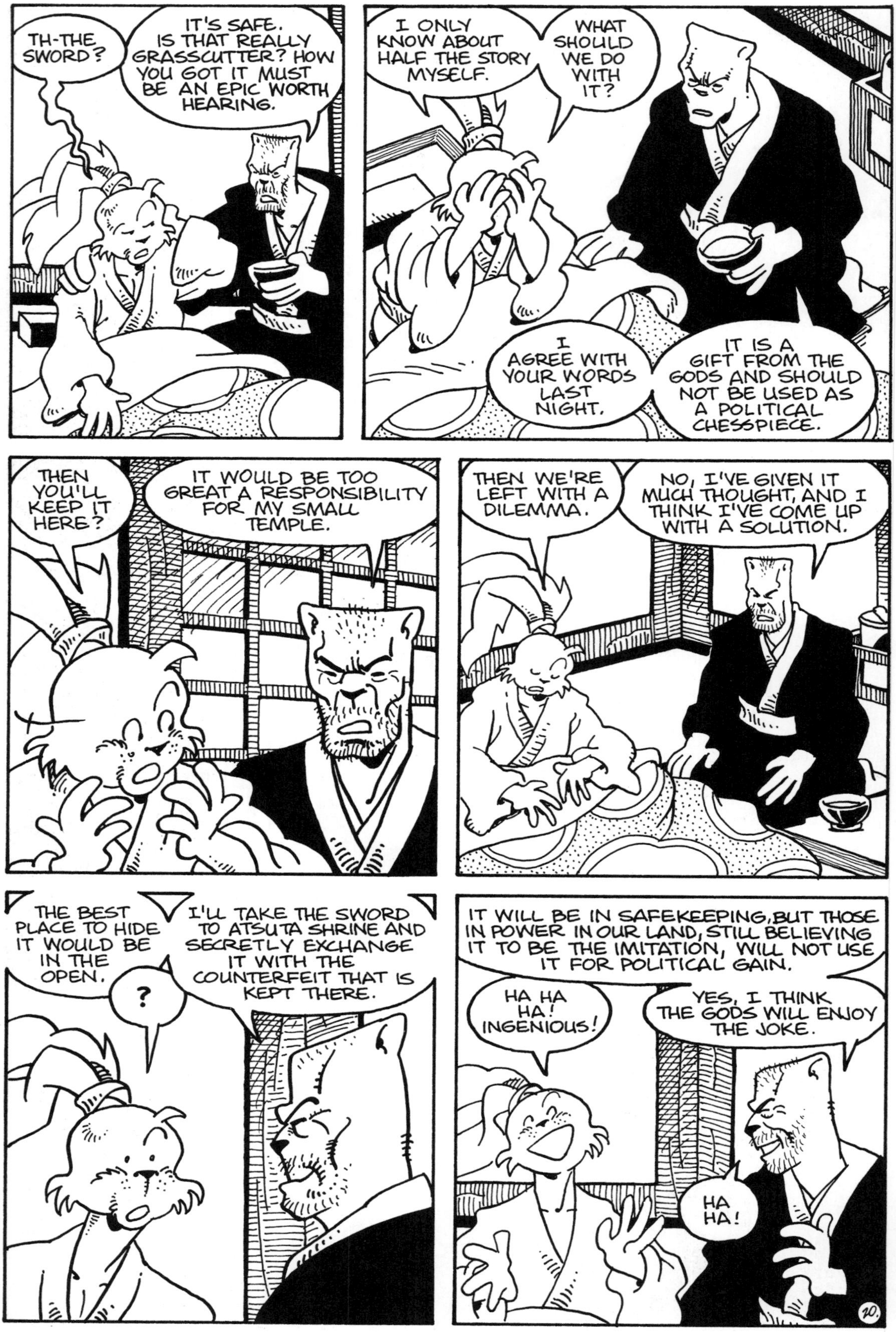
TH-THE SWORD?
IT'S SAFE. IS THAT REALLY GRASSCUTTER? HOW YOU GOT IT MUST BE AN EPIC WORTH HEARING.
I ONLY KNOW ABOUT HALF THE STORY MYSELF.
WHAT SHOULD WE DO WITH IT?
I AGREE WITH YOUR WORDS LAST NIGHT.
IT IS A GIFT FROM THE GODS AND SHOULD NOT BE USED AS A POLITICAL CHESSPIECE.
THEN YOU'LL KEEP IT HERE?
IT WOULD BE TOO GREAT A RESPONSIBILITY FOR MY SMALL TEMPLE.
THEN WE'RE LEFT WITH A DILEMMA.
NO, I'VE GIVEN IT MUCH THOUGHT, AND I THINK I'VE COME UP WITH A SOLUTION.
THE BEST PLACE TO HIDE IT WOULD BE IN THE OPEN.
?
I'LL TAKE THE SWORD TO ATSUTA SHRINE AND SECRETLY EXCHANGE IT WITH THE COUNTERFEIT THAT IS KEPT THERE.
IT WILL BE IN SAFEKEEPING, BUT THOSE IN POWER IN OUR LAND, STILL BELIEVING IT TO BE THE IMITATION, WILL NOT USE IT FOR POLITICAL GAIN.
HA HA HA! INGENIOUS!
YES, I THINK THE GODS WILL ENJOY THE JOKE.
HA HA!
20.

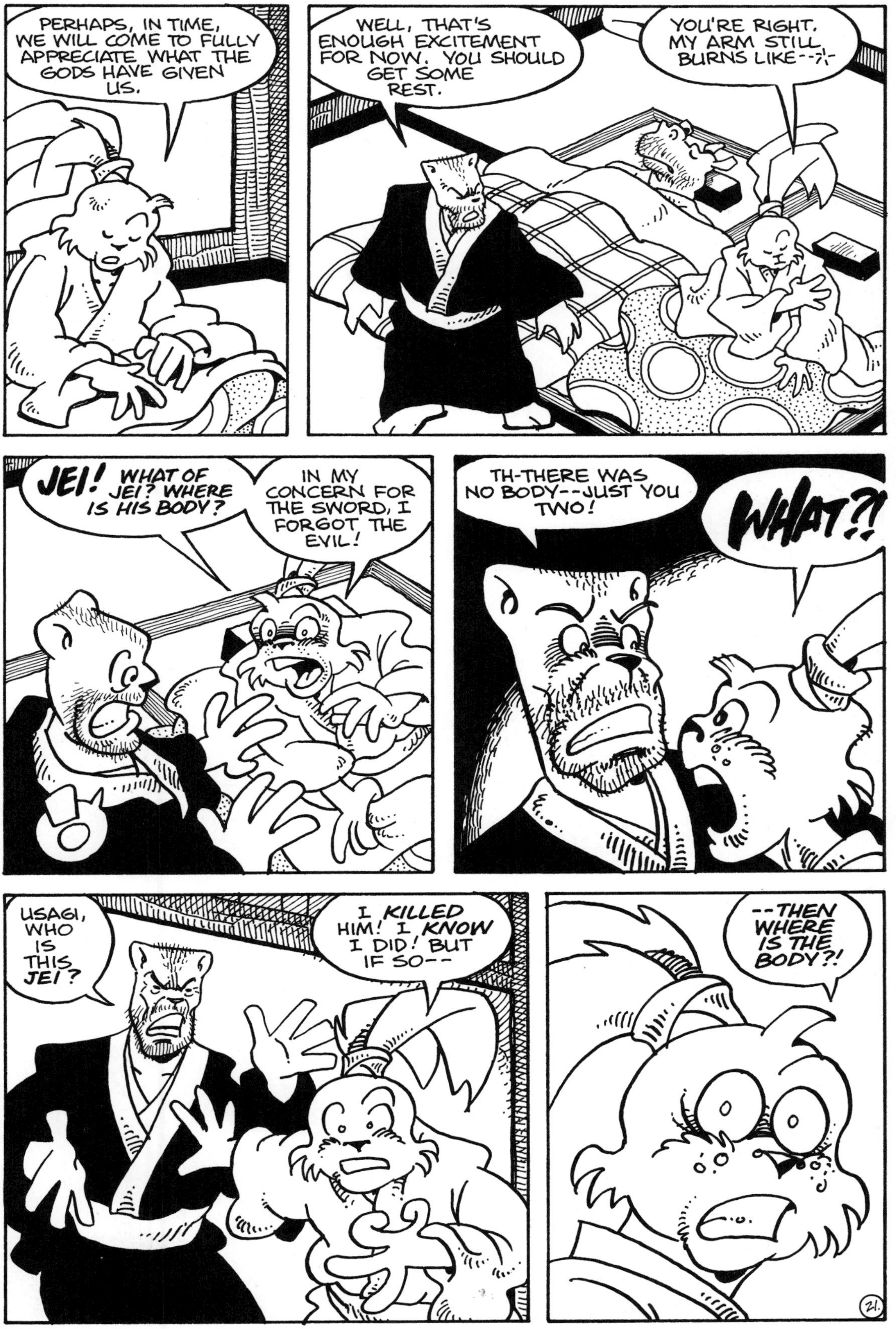
PERHAPS, IN TIME, WE WILL COME TO FULLY APPRECIATE WHAT THE GODS HAVE GIVEN US.
WELL, THAT'S ENOUGH EXCITEMENT FOR NOW. YOU SHOULD GET SOME REST.
YOU'RE RIGHT. MY ARM STILL BURNS LIKE--!
JEI! WHAT OF JEI? WHERE IS HIS BODY?
IN MY CONCERN FOR THE SWORD, I FORGOT THE EVIL!
TH-THERE WAS NO BODY--JUST YOU TWO!
WHAT?!
USAGI, WHO IS THIS JEI?
I KILLED HIM! I KNOW I DID! BUT IF SO--
--THEN WHERE IS THE BODY?!
21.

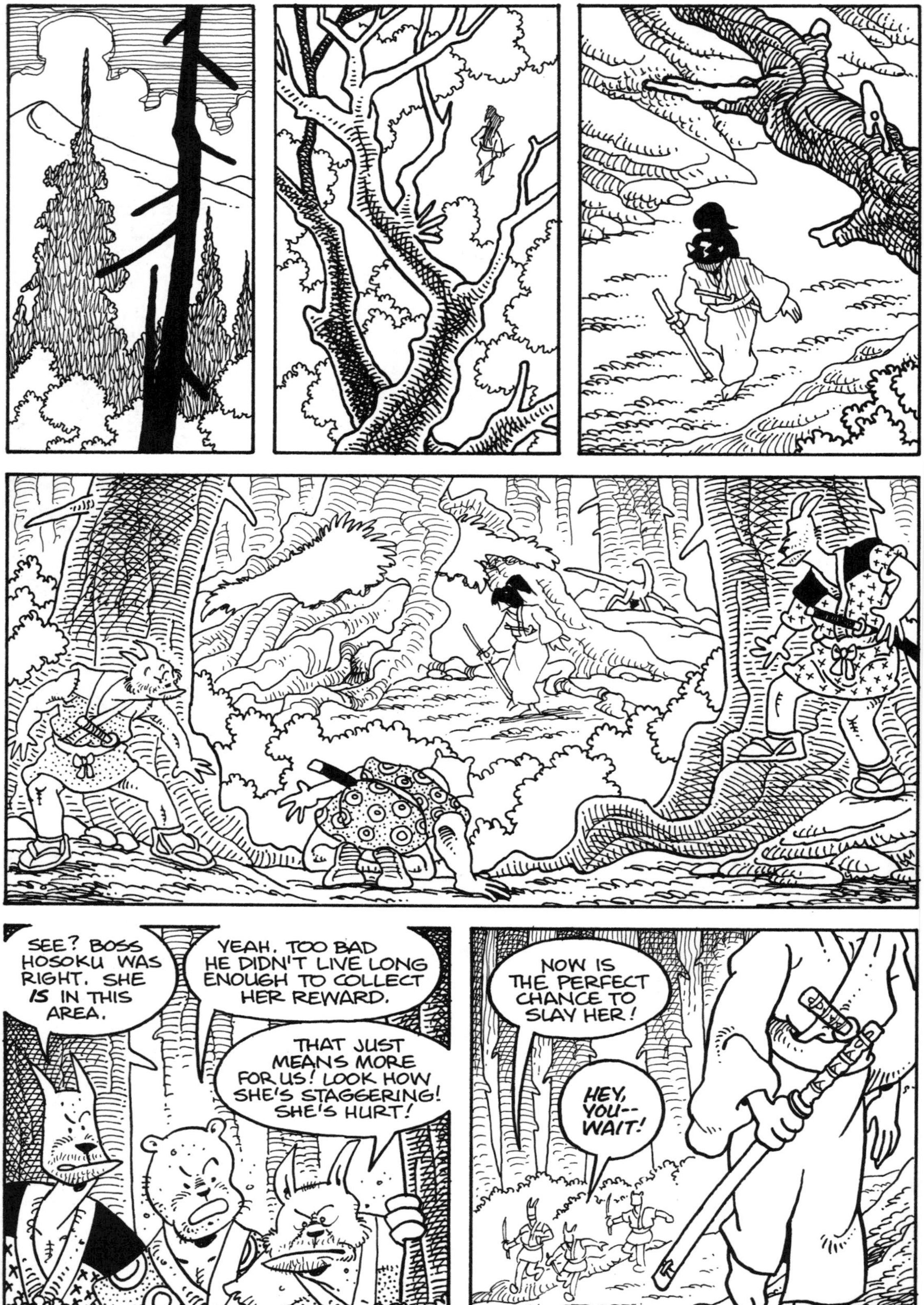
SEE? BOSS HOSOKU WAS RIGHT. SHE *IS* IN THIS AREA.
YEAH. TOO BAD HE DIDN'T LIVE LONG ENOUGH TO COLLECT HER REWARD.
THAT JUST MEANS MORE FOR US! LOOK HOW SHE'S STAGGERING! SHE'S HURT!
NOW IS THE PERFECT CHANCE TO SLAY HER!
HEY, YOU-- WAIT!
22.

INAZUMA!

YOU'RE GOING TO MAKE US RICH, GIRL!

TURN AND FACE US!

BLOOD WILL BE SPILLED THIS DAY!

I KNOW.

TH-THAT V-VOICE-- IT'S LIKE ONE FROM THE GRAVE!

AND THOSE EYES!

¡GASP!¡

EYES OR NO EYES-- THERE'S STILL A REWARD ON HER HEAD!

YOU'RE RIGHT!

KILL HER!

VWIT! FWIT! FWIT! VWITT! EYAUGH! YAHHH! GYAHHH.!!

435

THERE YOU ARE. I'VE BEEN LOOKING ALL OVER FOR YOU...

...AUNTY.

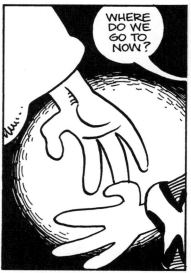

WHERE DO WE GO TO NOW?

To hell, my innocent, to hell.

436

GREY SHADOWS

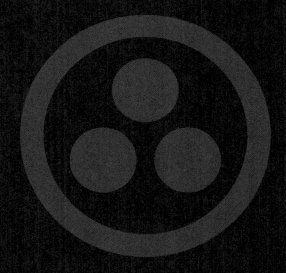

I AM GRATEFUL TO STAN SAKAI for a number of reasons.

First, and foremost, he has created one of the best and longest-running independent comic-book series in the history of the medium.

Second, he has been nice enough to acknowledge me, in the story notes for "The Hairpin Murders," as one of his two favorite mystery writers. (His other favorite is Ed McBain, whose 87th Precinct novels I have followed since I was about the age that my son Nathan discovered *Usagi Yojimbo*.)

And, finally, Stan Sakai did the impossible: he (however briefly) managed to make my teenage son impressed with his old man.

Stan Sakai is Nate's favorite cartoonist, and *Usagi Yojimbo* is his favorite comic book. None of this is surprising, because Stan's work is about as good as current comics get, and Nate was raised on a steady diet of *Lone Wolf and Cub* manga, John Woo movies, and Japanese video games.

For my entire life (short as it may be), I have been a great fan of comics. Living with a writer of comics made it inevitable: I grew up on everything from Teenage Mutant Ninja Turtles *to* Calvin and Hobbes. *But at the tender age of eleven, I was subjected by my father to a different type of comic book—the manga. After I had read graphic novels like* Barefoot Gen *and the* Lone Wolf and Cub *series, my father steered me to* Usagi Yojimbo.

These brief moments of respect I receive from Nate—however fleeting—have occurred at comics conventions when we have approached Stan, to get copies of Nate's *Usagi* comics signed. And, invariably, inevitably, Stan lights up, seeing me, and informs Nate and me that he —the creator of *Usagi Yojimbo!*—has brought books of mine to have me sign.

This admiration of course bewilders my son, but somewhere in the confusion is a stirring notion that his father may have some value . . . After all, Stan Sakai approves.

Which is fine with me, because I sure approve of Stan Sakai. Having worked, off and on, in this field since the late seventies, I've become pretty jaded and little impresses me, particularly new stuff. But Stan Sakai is an exception: he stirs in me memories of the classic comic strips, where the likes of Dick Tracy and Little Orphan Annie and Wash Tubbs could—despite their cartoony depictions—enjoy thrilling adventures. His "funny animal" approach evokes the great Carl Barks guiding Uncle Scrooge through journeys of mystery and excitement, in exotic settings, thrilling tales that dared not to be terribly funny . . . just terrific. His boyish yet courageous Usagi summons the ghost of Hergé's Tintin, that kid reporter whose exploits managed to have a childlike innocence while being extremely adult.

I quickly became addicted to the cute rabbit and his adventures. I was drawn in by many aspects of the comic: the beautiful artwork, so detailed and simple at the same time; the Japanese culture and mythology, with demons, ninja, and sword fights; and the rich story lines that held it all together, stories that brought alive Japanese folklore to an audience that would never have seen it otherwise . . . and fueled my interest in Japanese culture.

Stan Sakai has written and drawn a series that both Nate and I can read—and that Nate has been able to keep reading as he grows to adulthood.

In the stories in this book, Stan introduces one of his best characters, Inspector Ishida, who shares the same real-life role model as Charlie Chan: Honolulu detective Chang Apana. Ishida—who spouts wisdom in a vaguely Chan-like manner—is more like the hard-boiled Apana than the mild-mannered Chan of Earl Derr Biggers's novels (and the many films they spawned). Ishida is an action hero, and Usagi makes a great, sword-slinging Watson for him in mystery yarns that are involving, exciting, and deftly plotted.

Besides being an expert storyteller and artist, Stan Sakai is a genuinely kind man. He has always been very nice and personable to me and the rest of his fans I have met at various conventions. Stan Sakai deserves every bit of praise and respect that he has received, and I have no doubt that after reading this collection, you would agree with me.

MAX ALLAN COLLINS (*WITH NATHAN COLLINS*)

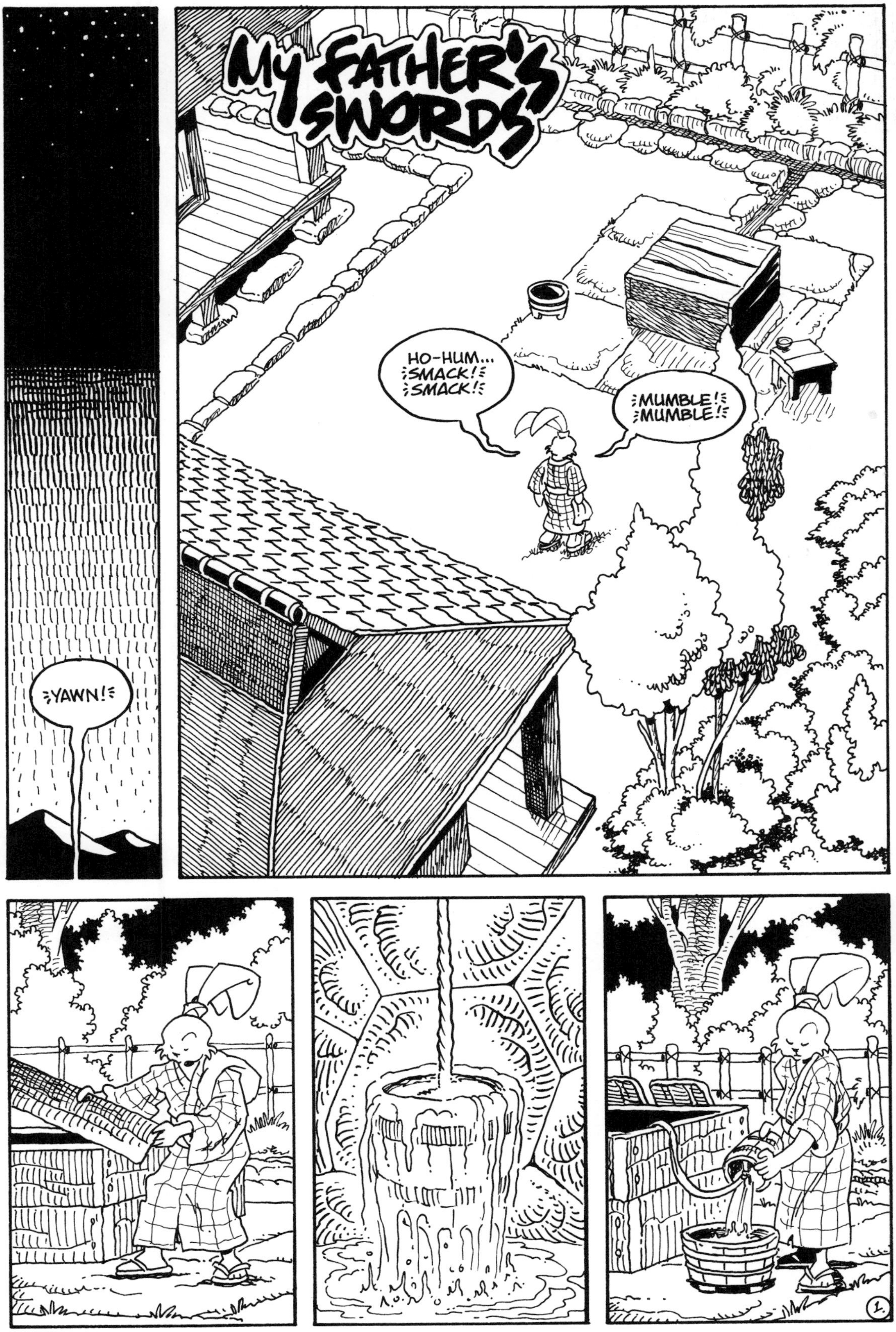
YAWN!
MY FATHER'S SWORDS
HO-HUM... SMACK! SMACK!
MUMBLE! MUMBLE!
1.

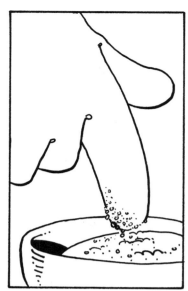

SCRUB! SCRUB!

SIP! SIP! SWISH! SWISH!

SPIT!

≥BLURGG!≤ ≥GLURKK!≤

SPLASH! SPLASH!

WIPE! WIPE!

AH...

CRAK!

GOOD MORNING, USAGI!

AH, PRIEST SANSHOBO! WELCOME BACK!

THANK YOU, MY FRIEND!

HOW ARE YOU TODAY?

MUCH BETTER. MY ARM IS HEALING NICELY-- SEE?

BUT I AM CONCERNED ABOUT GEN.

IT'S BEEN A WEEK, AND HIS RECOVERY IS STEADY...BUT SLOW.

HMM...

IT SEEMED A CLEAN SPEAR WOUND, NOT VERY SERIOUS.

THERE WAS NOTHING CLEAN ABOUT THE WEAPON ...OR ITS WIELDER!

IS THE WOUND FESTERING?

IT'S MORE THAN THE WOUND. IT'S AS IF HE HAD BEEN... DRAINED.

LET US CHECK IN ON HIM.

WELCOME BACK, HEAD PRIEST.

HOW IS YOUR PATIENT TODAY, SENZO?

HIS RECOVERY WOULD BE QUICKER IF HE WEREN'T SO MELANCHOLY. IT'S ALMOST AS IF HE NEEDS A REASON TO LIVE.

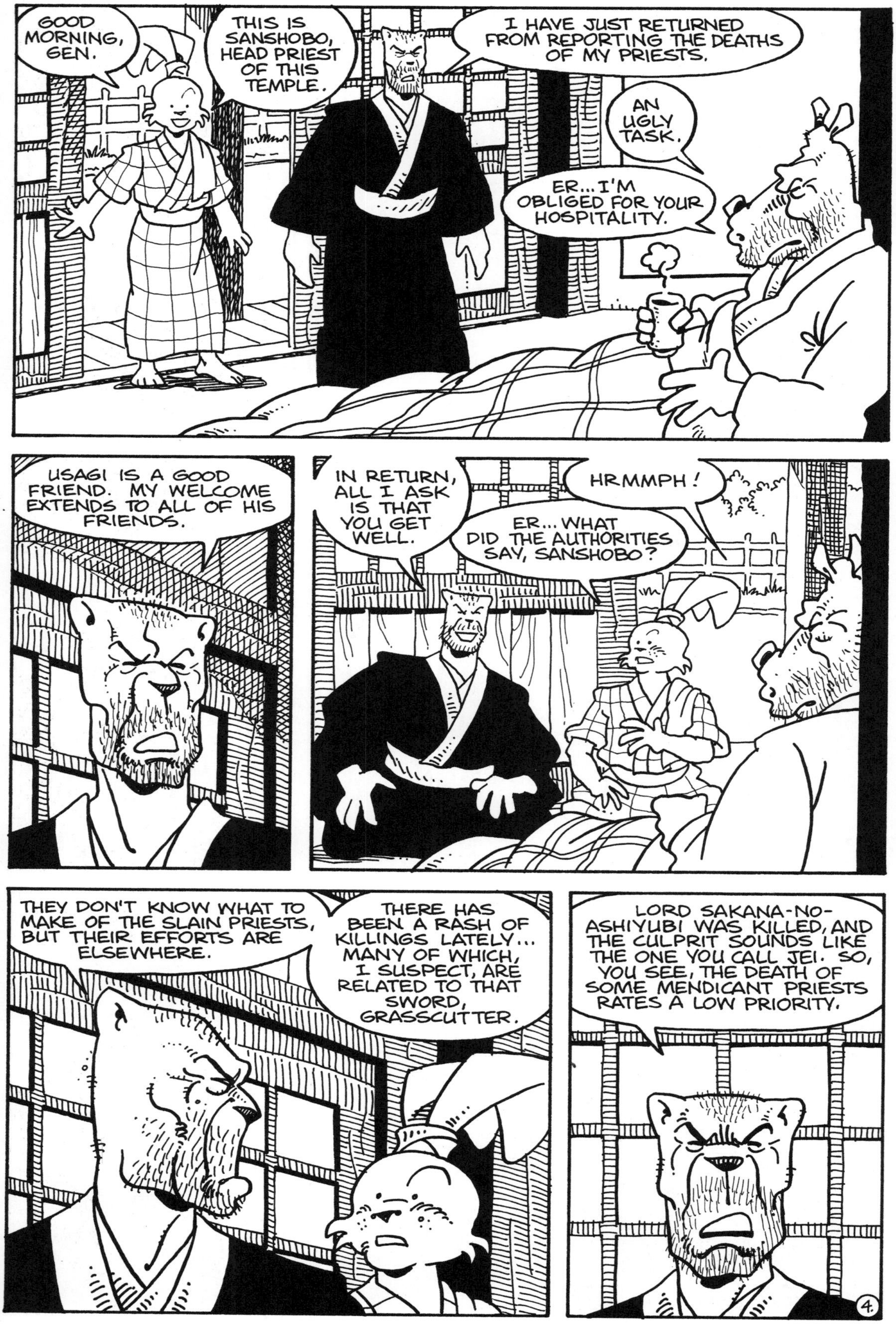
GOOD MORNING, GEN.
THIS IS SANSHOBO, HEAD PRIEST OF THIS TEMPLE.
I HAVE JUST RETURNED FROM REPORTING THE DEATHS OF MY PRIESTS.
AN UGLY TASK.
ER... I'M OBLIGED FOR YOUR HOSPITALITY.
USAGI IS A GOOD FRIEND. MY WELCOME EXTENDS TO ALL OF HIS FRIENDS.
IN RETURN, ALL I ASK IS THAT YOU GET WELL.
HRMMPH!
ER... WHAT DID THE AUTHORITIES SAY, SANSHOBO?
THEY DON'T KNOW WHAT TO MAKE OF THE SLAIN PRIESTS, BUT THEIR EFFORTS ARE ELSEWHERE.
THERE HAS BEEN A RASH OF KILLINGS LATELY... MANY OF WHICH, I SUSPECT, ARE RELATED TO THAT SWORD, GRASSCUTTER.
LORD SAKANA-NO-ASHIYUBI WAS KILLED, AND THE CULPRIT SOUNDS LIKE THE ONE YOU CALL JEI. SO, YOU SEE, THE DEATH OF SOME MENDICANT PRIESTS RATES A LOW PRIORITY.
4.

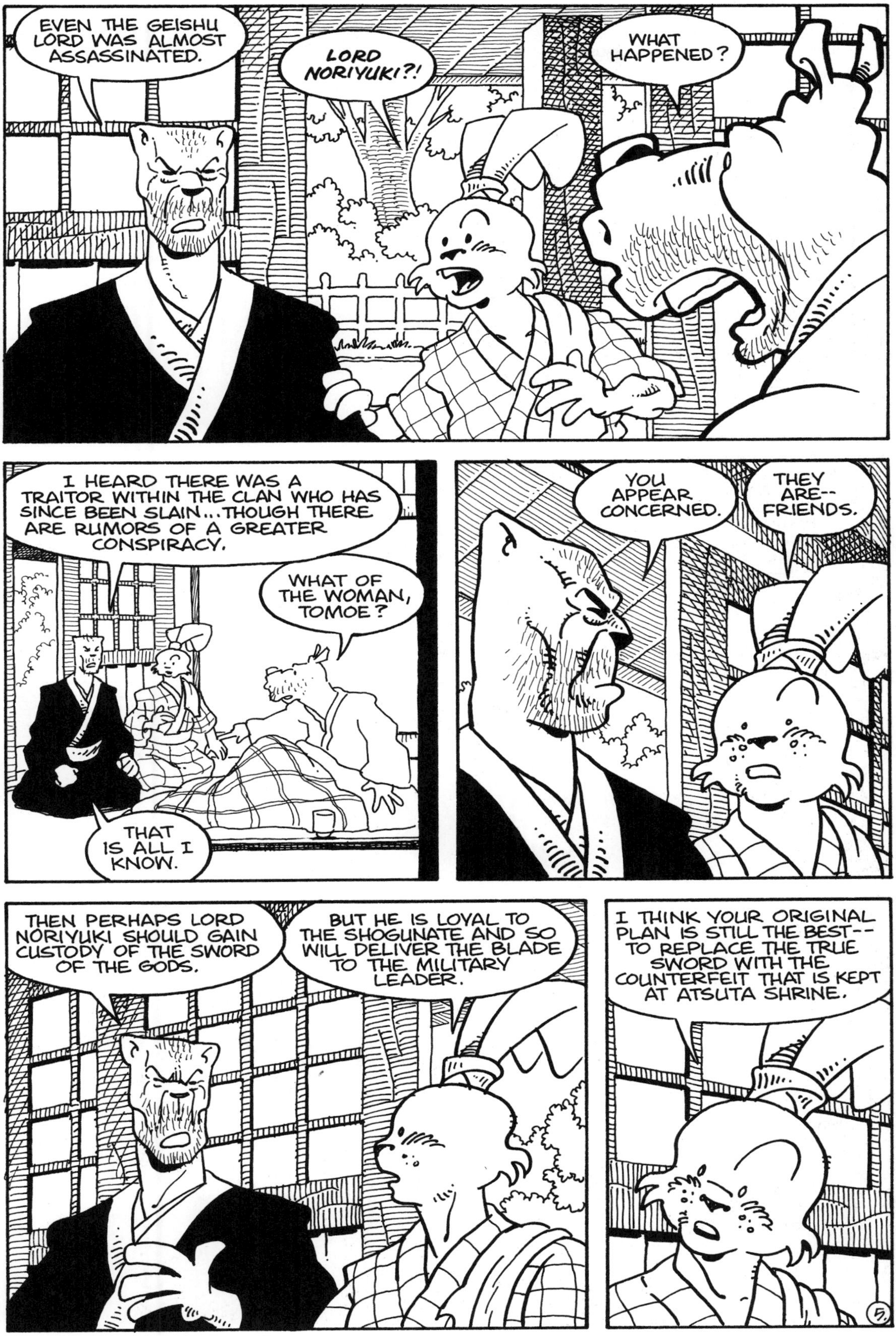
EVEN THE GEISHU LORD WAS ALMOST ASSASSINATED.
LORD NORIYUKI?!
WHAT HAPPENED?
I HEARD THERE WAS A TRAITOR WITHIN THE CLAN WHO HAS SINCE BEEN SLAIN... THOUGH THERE ARE RUMORS OF A GREATER CONSPIRACY.
WHAT OF THE WOMAN, TOMOE?
THAT IS ALL I KNOW.
YOU APPEAR CONCERNED.
THEY ARE-- FRIENDS.
THEN PERHAPS LORD NORIYUKI SHOULD GAIN CUSTODY OF THE SWORD OF THE GODS.
BUT HE IS LOYAL TO THE SHOGUNATE AND SO WILL DELIVER THE BLADE TO THE MILITARY LEADER.
I THINK YOUR ORIGINAL PLAN IS STILL THE BEST-- TO REPLACE THE TRUE SWORD WITH THE COUNTERFEIT THAT IS KEPT AT ATSUTA SHRINE.
5

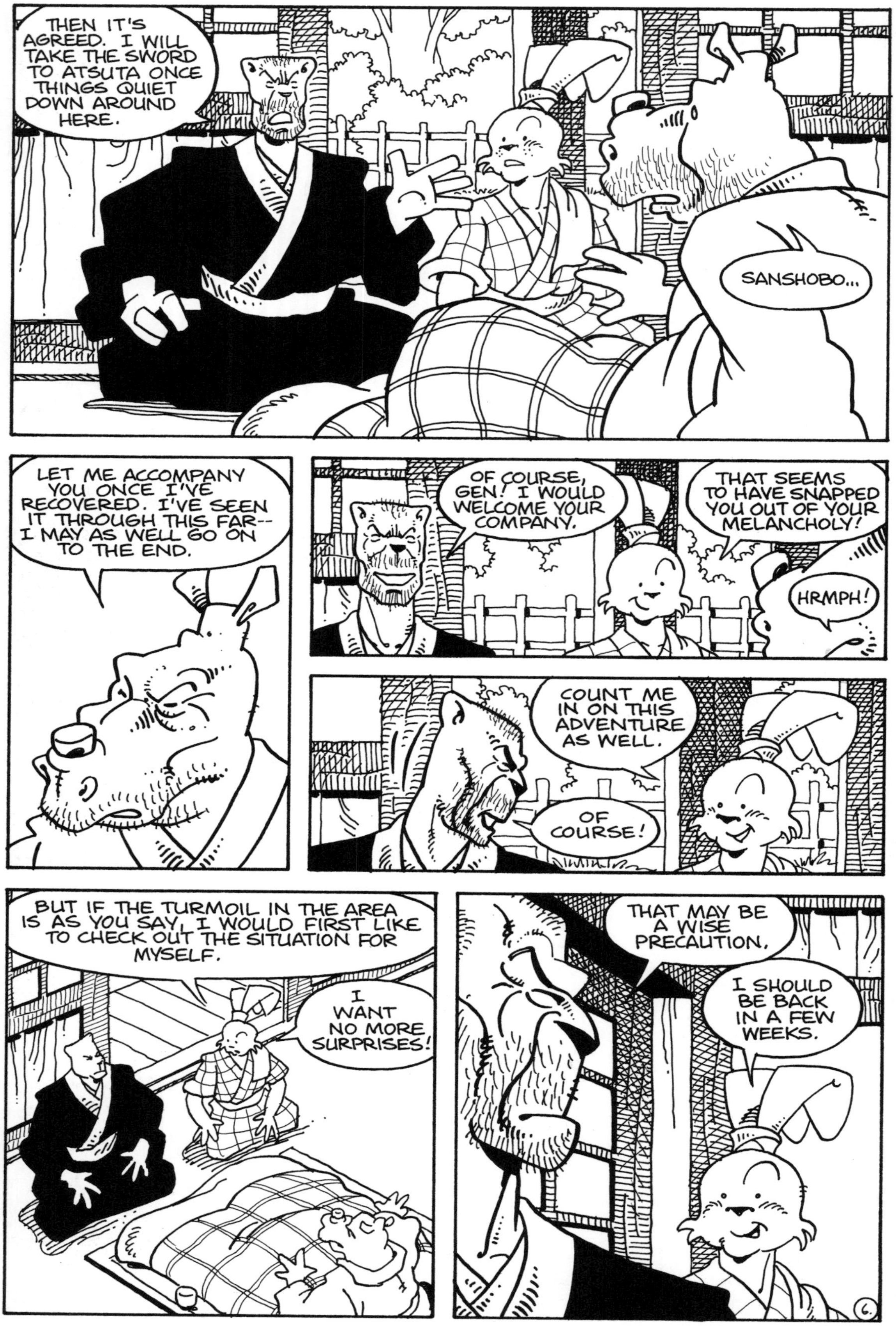
THEN IT'S AGREED. I WILL TAKE THE SWORD TO ATSUTA ONCE THINGS QUIET DOWN AROUND HERE.
SANSHOBO...
LET ME ACCOMPANY YOU ONCE I'VE RECOVERED. I'VE SEEN IT THROUGH THIS FAR-- I MAY AS WELL GO ON TO THE END.
OF COURSE, GEN! I WOULD WELCOME YOUR COMPANY.
THAT SEEMS TO HAVE SNAPPED YOU OUT OF YOUR MELANCHOLY!
HRMPH!
COUNT ME IN ON THIS ADVENTURE AS WELL.
OF COURSE!
BUT IF THE TURMOIL IN THE AREA IS AS YOU SAY, I WOULD FIRST LIKE TO CHECK OUT THE SITUATION FOR MYSELF.
I WANT NO MORE SURPRISES!
THAT MAY BE A WISE PRECAUTION.
I SHOULD BE BACK IN A FEW WEEKS.
6.

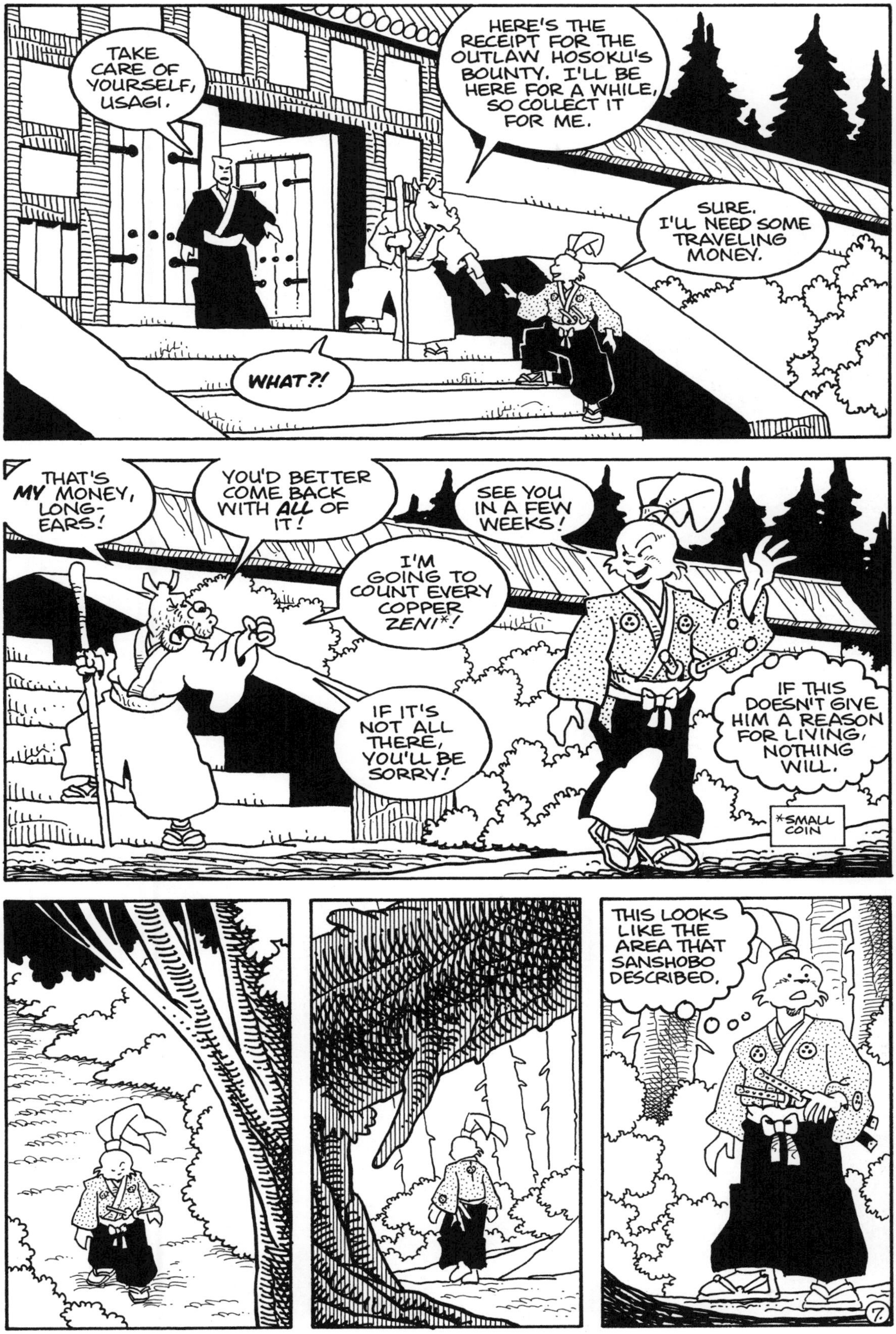
TAKE CARE OF YOURSELF, USAGI.
HERE'S THE RECEIPT FOR THE OUTLAW HOSOKU'S BOUNTY. I'LL BE HERE FOR A WHILE, SO COLLECT IT FOR ME.
SURE. I'LL NEED SOME TRAVELING MONEY.
WHAT?!
THAT'S MY MONEY, LONG-EARS!
YOU'D BETTER COME BACK WITH ALL OF IT!
SEE YOU IN A FEW WEEKS!
I'M GOING TO COUNT EVERY COPPER ZENI*!
IF IT'S NOT ALL THERE, YOU'LL BE SORRY!
IF THIS DOESN'T GIVE HIM A REASON FOR LIVING, NOTHING WILL.
*SMALL COIN
THIS LOOKS LIKE THE AREA THAT SANSHOBO DESCRIBED.
7.

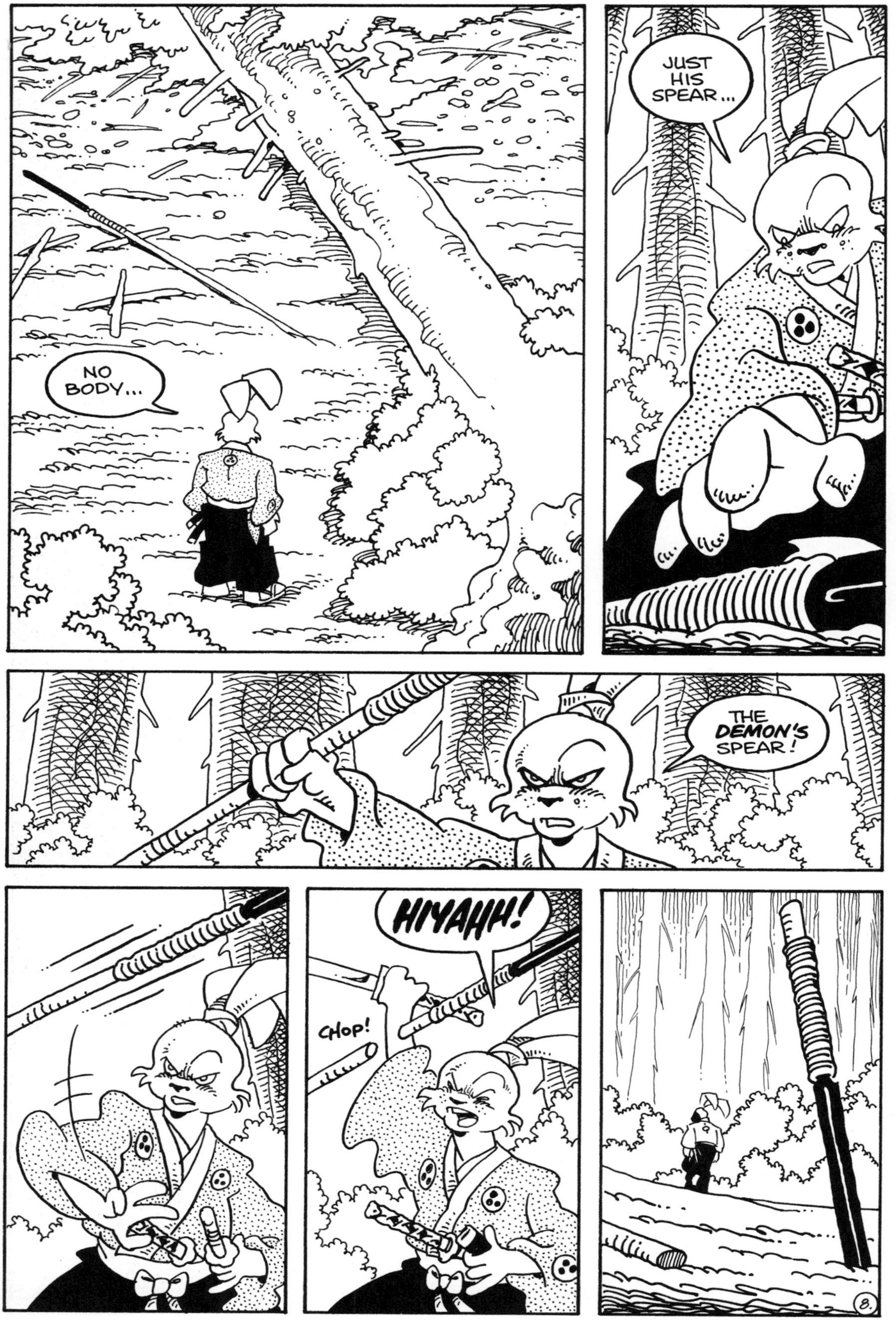
NO BODY...
JUST HIS SPEAR...
THE DEMON'S SPEAR!
HIYAHH!
CHOP!
8.

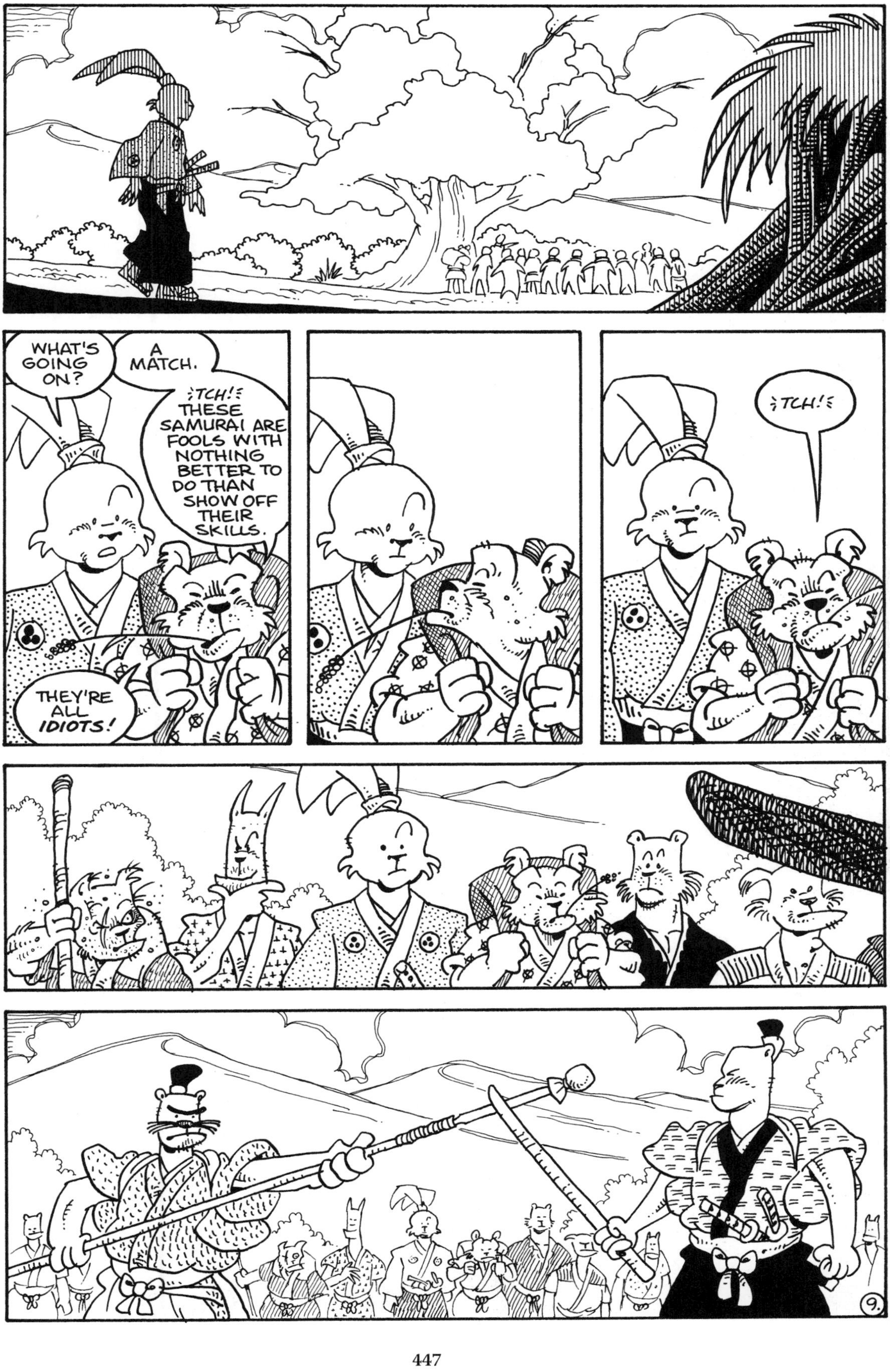
WHAT'S GOING ON?
A MATCH.
TCH! THESE SAMURAI ARE FOOLS WITH NOTHING BETTER TO DO THAN SHOW OFF THEIR SKILLS.
THEY'RE ALL IDIOTS!
TCH!
9.

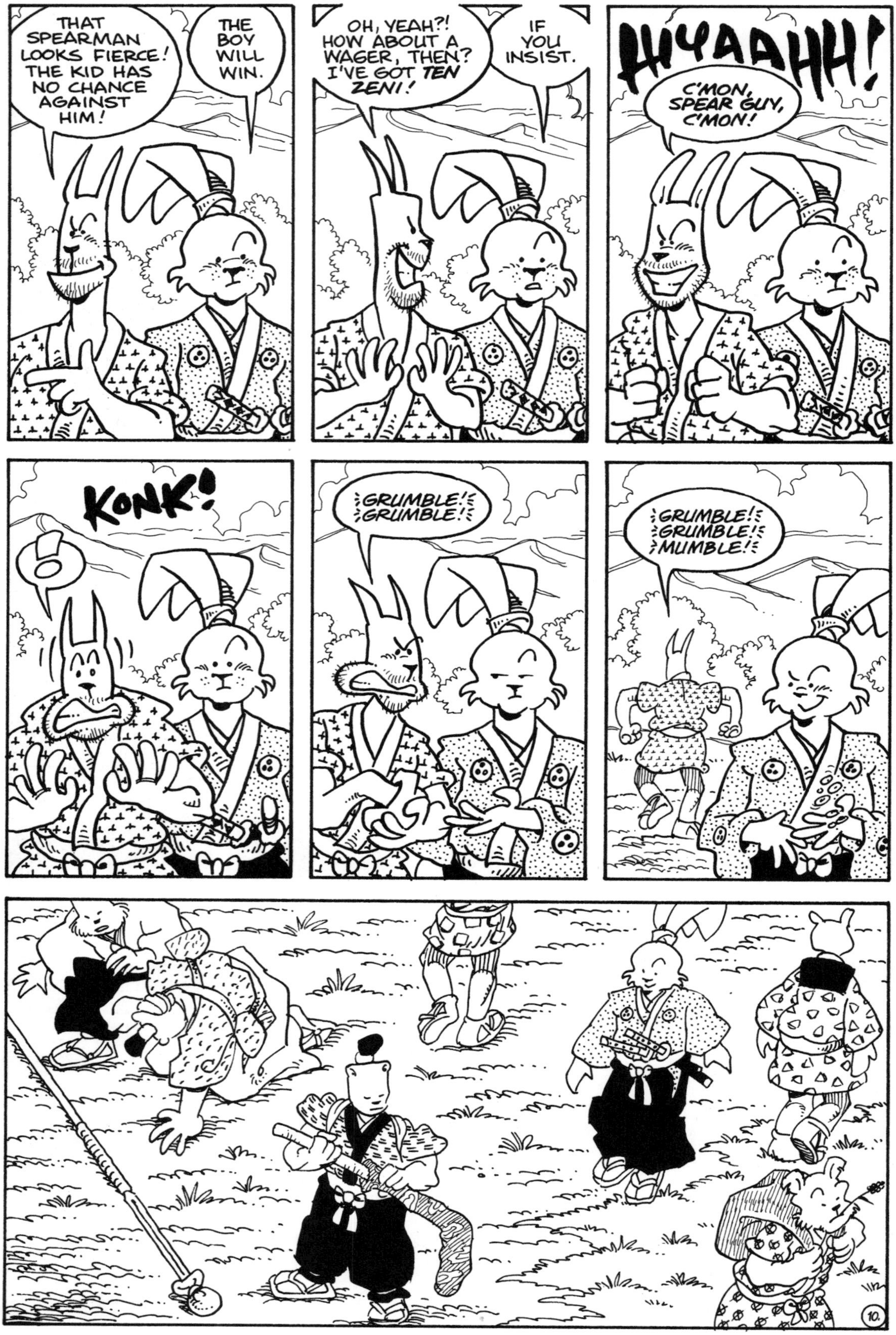
THAT SPEARMAN LOOKS FIERCE! THE KID HAS NO CHANCE AGAINST HIM!
THE BOY WILL WIN.
OH, YEAH?! HOW ABOUT A WAGER, THEN? I'VE GOT TEN ZENI!
IF YOU INSIST.
HIYAAHH!
C'MON, SPEAR GUY, C'MON!
KONK!
!
GRUMBLE! GRUMBLE!
GRUMBLE! GRUMBLE! MUMBLE!
10.

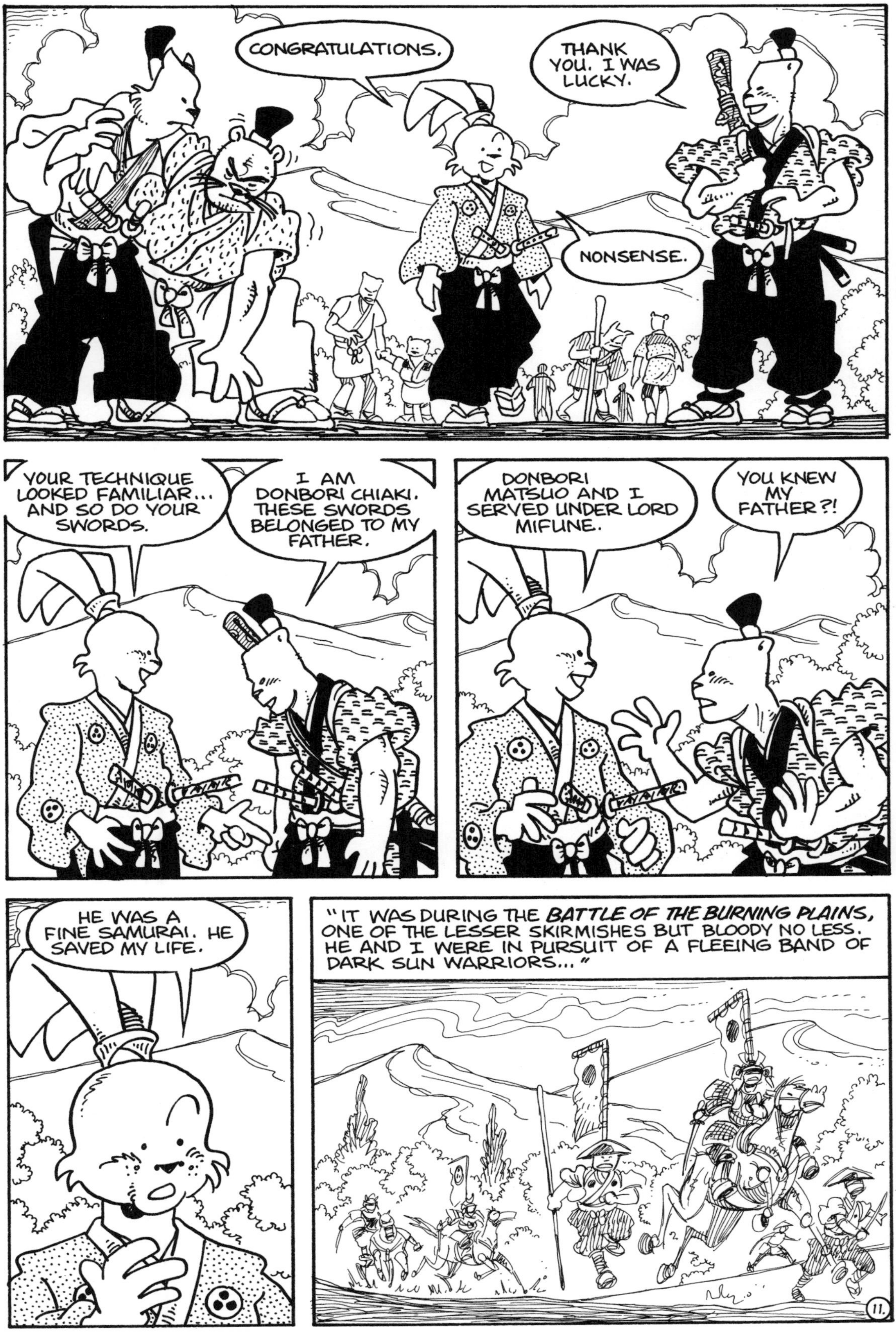
CONGRATULATIONS.
THANK YOU. I WAS LUCKY.
NONSENSE.
YOUR TECHNIQUE LOOKED FAMILIAR... AND SO DO YOUR SWORDS.
I AM DONBORI CHIAKI. THESE SWORDS BELONGED TO MY FATHER.
DONBORI MATSUO AND I SERVED UNDER LORD MIFUNE.
YOU KNEW MY FATHER?!
HE WAS A FINE SAMURAI. HE SAVED MY LIFE.
"IT WAS DURING THE *BATTLE OF THE BURNING PLAINS,* ONE OF THE LESSER SKIRMISHES BUT BLOODY NO LESS. HE AND I WERE IN PURSUIT OF A FLEEING BAND OF DARK SUN WARRIORS..."
11.

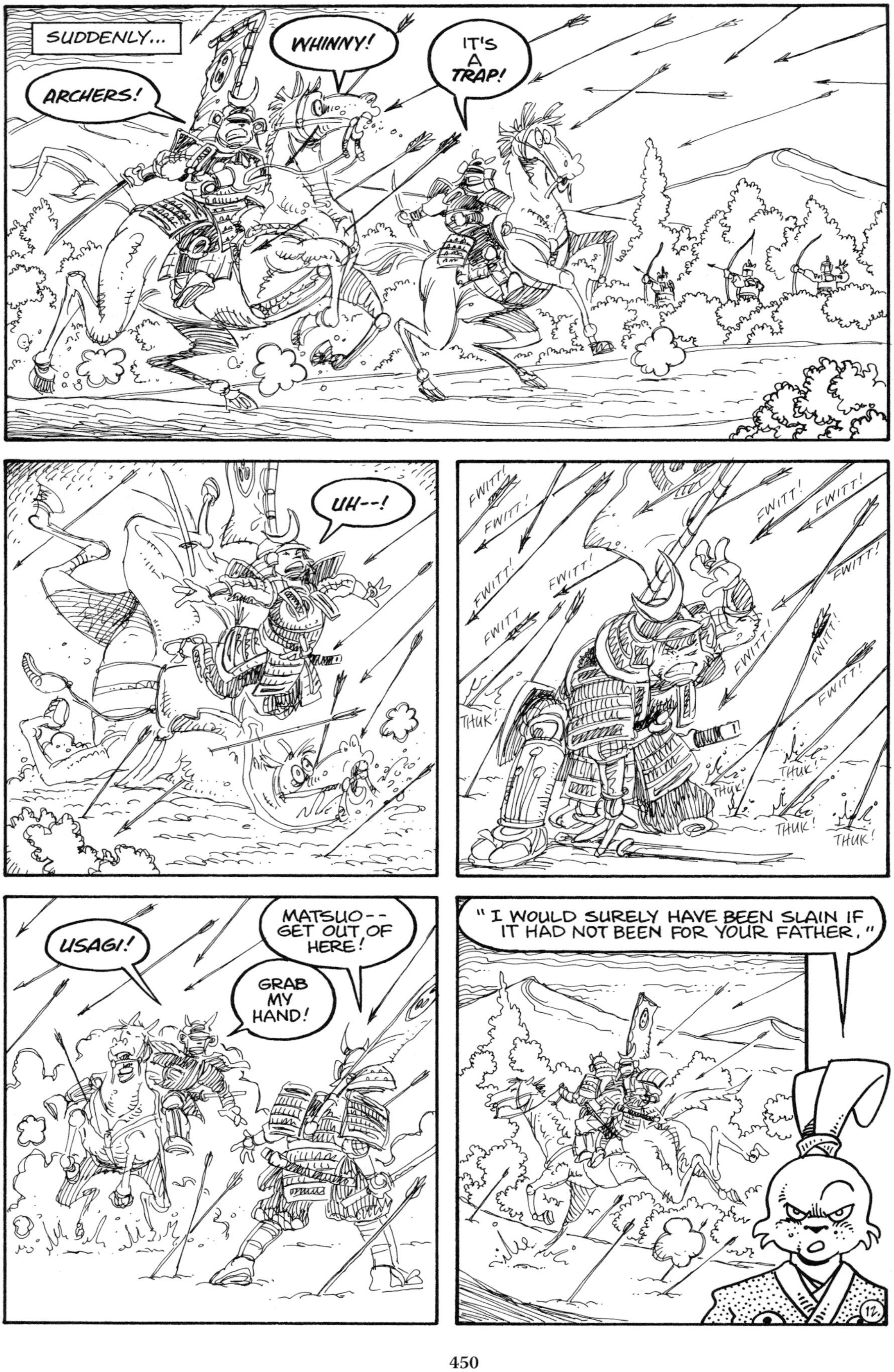
SUDDENLY...
ARCHERS!
WHINNY!
IT'S A TRAP!
UH--!
FWITT!
FWITT!
FWITT!
FWITT!
FWITT
FWITT!
FWITT!
FWITT!
FWITT!
FWITT!
FWITT!
FWITT!
THUK!
THUK!
THUK!
THUK!
THUK!
USAGI!
MATSUO-- GET OUT OF HERE!
GRAB MY HAND!
"I WOULD SURELY HAVE BEEN SLAIN IF IT HAD NOT BEEN FOR YOUR FATHER."
12

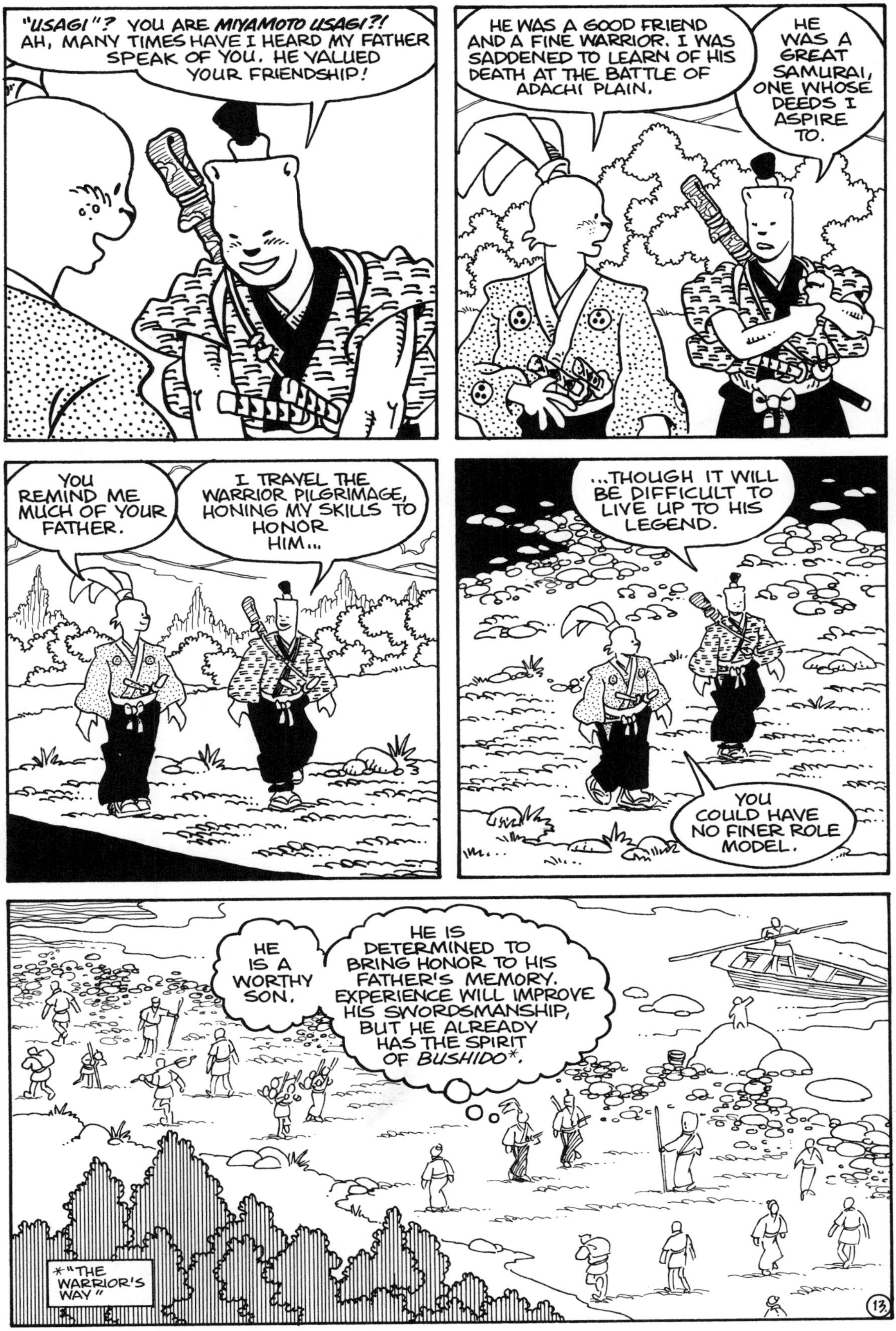
"USAGI"? YOU ARE MIYAMOTO USAGI?! AH, MANY TIMES HAVE I HEARD MY FATHER SPEAK OF YOU. HE VALUED YOUR FRIENDSHIP!
HE WAS A GOOD FRIEND AND A FINE WARRIOR. I WAS SADDENED TO LEARN OF HIS DEATH AT THE BATTLE OF ADACHI PLAIN.
HE WAS A GREAT SAMURAI, ONE WHOSE DEEDS I ASPIRE TO.
YOU REMIND ME MUCH OF YOUR FATHER.
I TRAVEL THE WARRIOR PILGRIMAGE, HONING MY SKILLS TO HONOR HIM...
...THOUGH IT WILL BE DIFFICULT TO LIVE UP TO HIS LEGEND.
YOU COULD HAVE NO FINER ROLE MODEL.
HE IS A WORTHY SON.
HE IS DETERMINED TO BRING HONOR TO HIS FATHER'S MEMORY. EXPERIENCE WILL IMPROVE HIS SWORDSMANSHIP, BUT HE ALREADY HAS THE SPIRIT OF BUSHIDO*.
*"THE WARRIOR'S WAY"
13

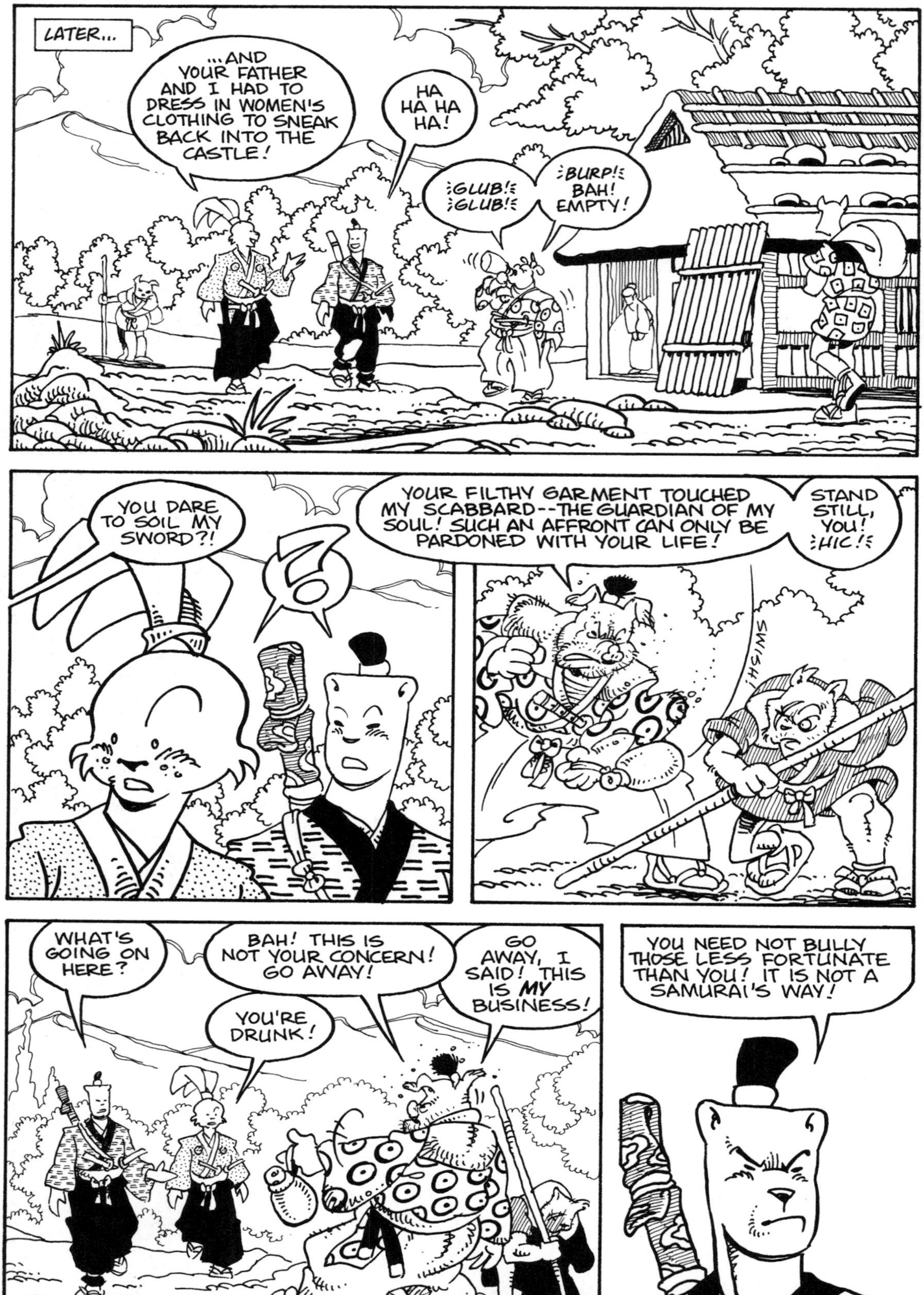
LATER...
...AND YOUR FATHER AND I HAD TO DRESS IN WOMEN'S CLOTHING TO SNEAK BACK INTO THE CASTLE!
HA HA HA HA!
GLUB! GLUB!
BURP! BAH! EMPTY!
YOU DARE TO SOIL MY SWORD?!
YOUR FILTHY GARMENT TOUCHED MY SCABBARD--THE GUARDIAN OF MY SOUL! SUCH AN AFFRONT CAN ONLY BE PARDONED WITH YOUR LIFE!
STAND STILL, YOU! HIC!
SWISH!
WHAT'S GOING ON HERE?
BAH! THIS IS NOT YOUR CONCERN! GO AWAY!
YOU'RE DRUNK!
GO AWAY, I SAID! THIS IS MY BUSINESS!
YOU NEED NOT BULLY THOSE LESS FORTUNATE THAN YOU! IT IS NOT A SAMURAI'S WAY!
14.

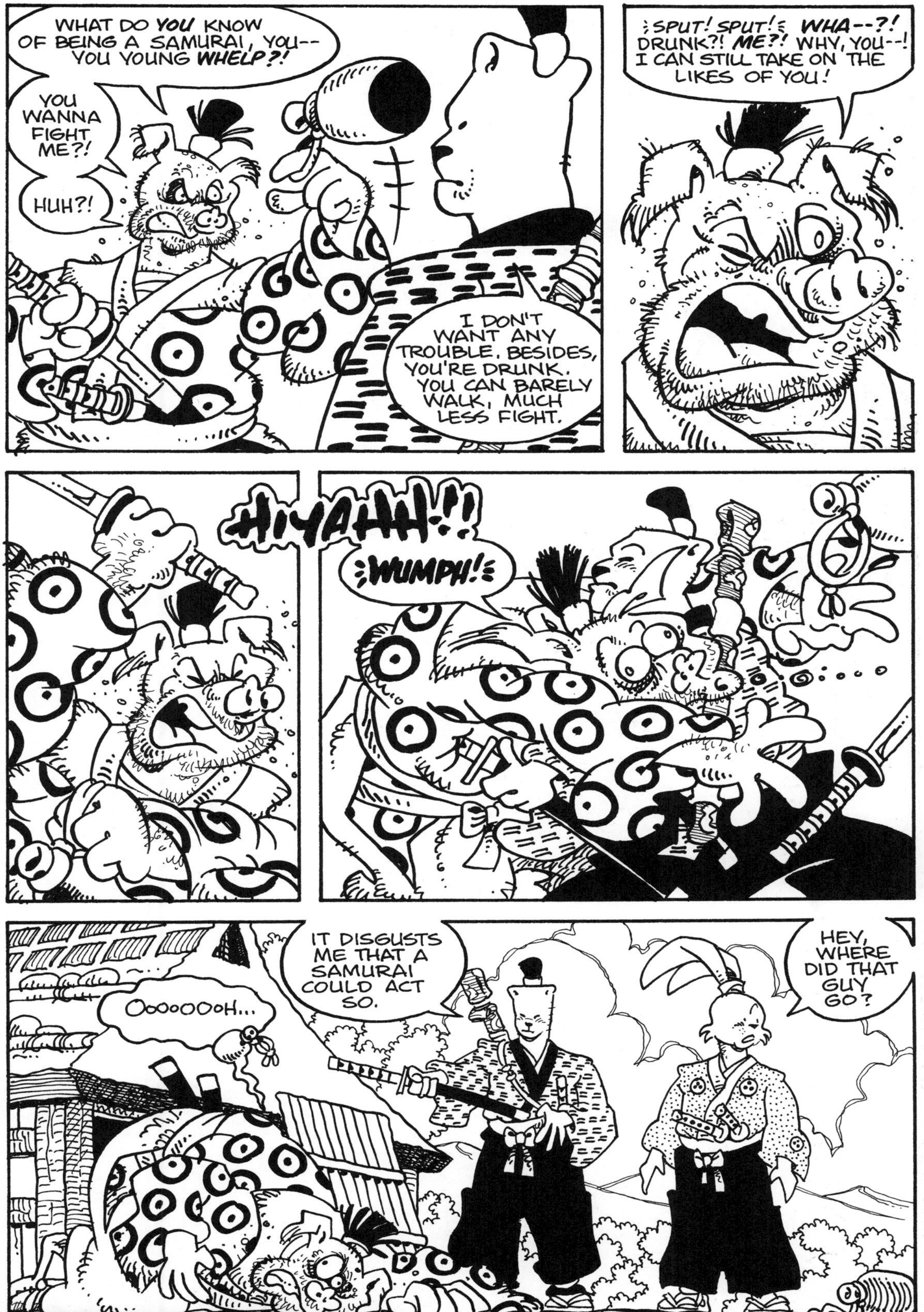
WHAT DO YOU KNOW OF BEING A SAMURAI, YOU-- YOU YOUNG WHELP?!
YOU WANNA FIGHT ME?!
HUH?!
I DON'T WANT ANY TROUBLE. BESIDES, YOU'RE DRUNK. YOU CAN BARELY WALK, MUCH LESS FIGHT.
SPUT! SPUT! WHA--?! DRUNK?! ME?! WHY, YOU--! I CAN STILL TAKE ON THE LIKES OF YOU!
HIYAHH!!
WUMPH!
OOOOOOOH...
IT DISGUSTS ME THAT A SAMURAI COULD ACT SO.
HEY, WHERE DID THAT GUY GO?
15

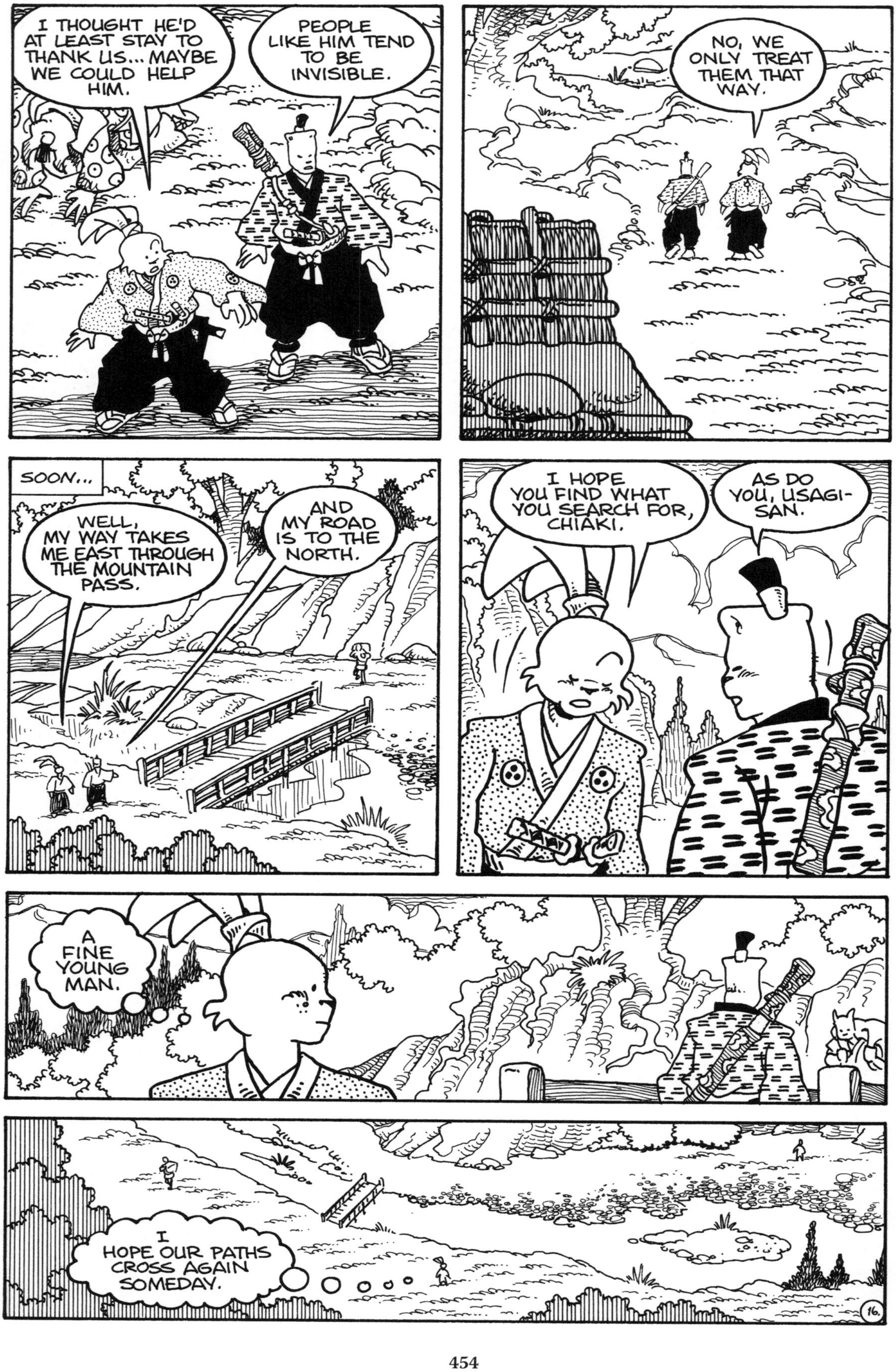
I THOUGHT HE'D AT LEAST STAY TO THANK US... MAYBE WE COULD HELP HIM.
PEOPLE LIKE HIM TEND TO BE INVISIBLE.
NO, WE ONLY TREAT THEM THAT WAY.
SOON...
WELL, MY WAY TAKES ME EAST THROUGH THE MOUNTAIN PASS.
AND MY ROAD IS TO THE NORTH.
I HOPE YOU FIND WHAT YOU SEARCH FOR, CHIAKI.
AS DO YOU, USAGI-SAN.
A FINE YOUNG MAN.
I HOPE OUR PATHS CROSS AGAIN SOMEDAY.
16.

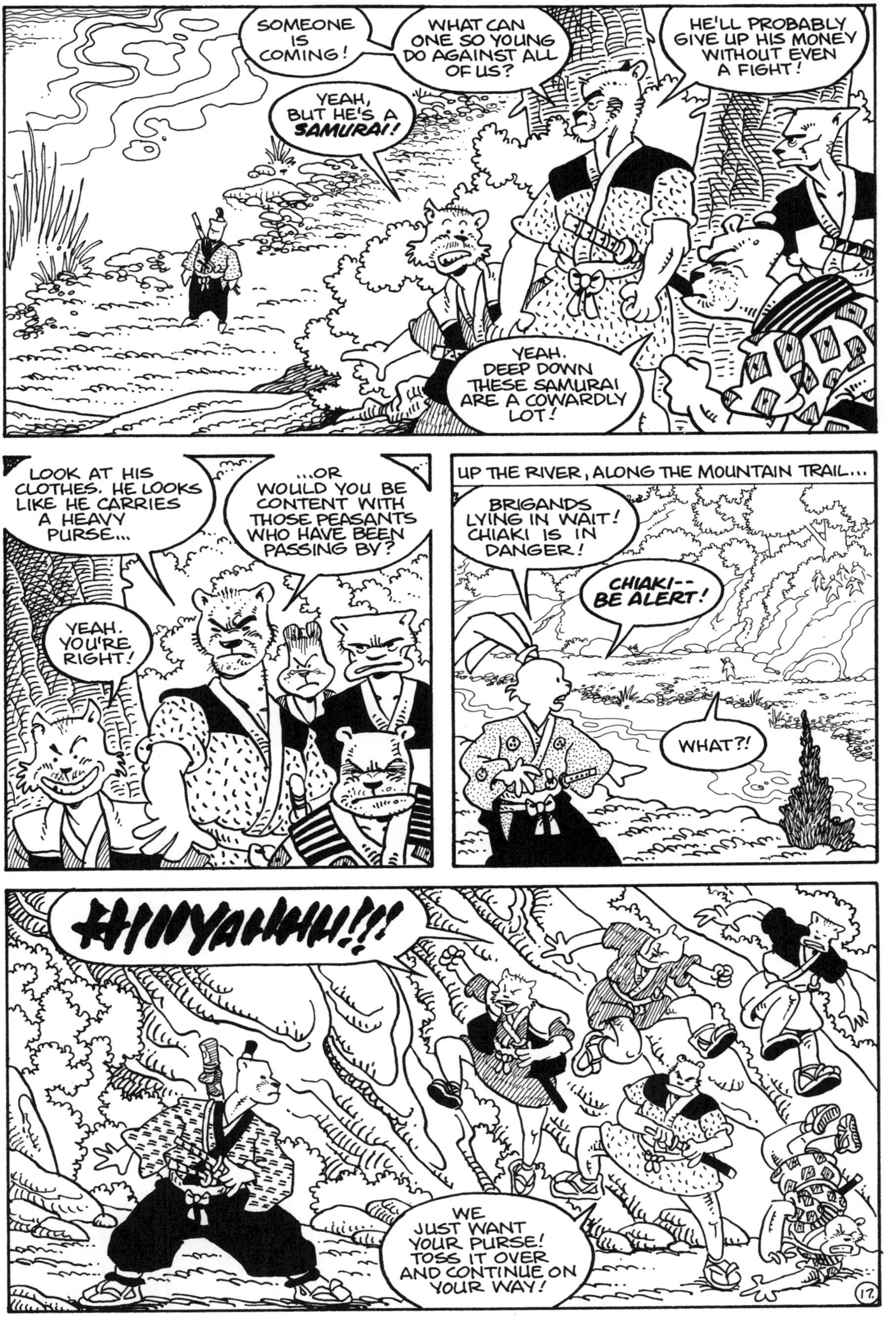
SOMEONE IS COMING!
WHAT CAN ONE SO YOUNG DO AGAINST ALL OF US?
YEAH, BUT HE'S A SAMURAI!
HE'LL PROBABLY GIVE UP HIS MONEY WITHOUT EVEN A FIGHT!
YEAH. DEEP DOWN THESE SAMURAI ARE A COWARDLY LOT!
LOOK AT HIS CLOTHES. HE LOOKS LIKE HE CARRIES A HEAVY PURSE...
...OR WOULD YOU BE CONTENT WITH THOSE PEASANTS WHO HAVE BEEN PASSING BY?
YEAH. YOU'RE RIGHT!
UP THE RIVER, ALONG THE MOUNTAIN TRAIL...
BRIGANDS LYING IN WAIT! CHIAKI IS IN DANGER!
CHIAKI-- BE ALERT!
WHAT?!
HIIIYAAAHH!!!
WE JUST WANT YOUR PURSE! TOSS IT OVER AND CONTINUE ON YOUR WAY!
17.

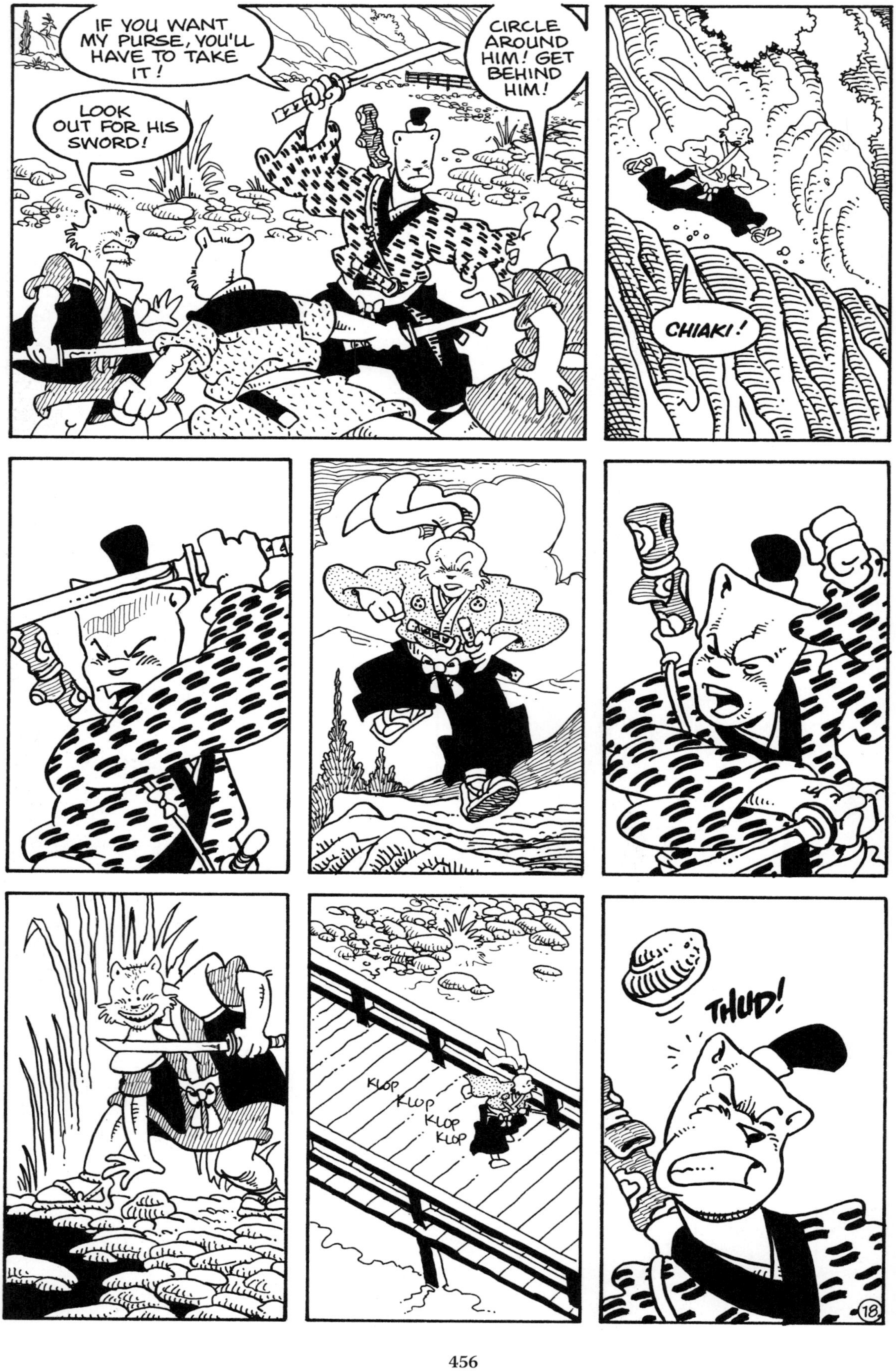
IF YOU WANT MY PURSE, YOU'LL HAVE TO TAKE IT!
LOOK OUT FOR HIS SWORD!
CIRCLE AROUND HIM! GET BEHIND HIM!
CHIAKI!
KLOP KLOP KLOP KLOP
THUD!
18

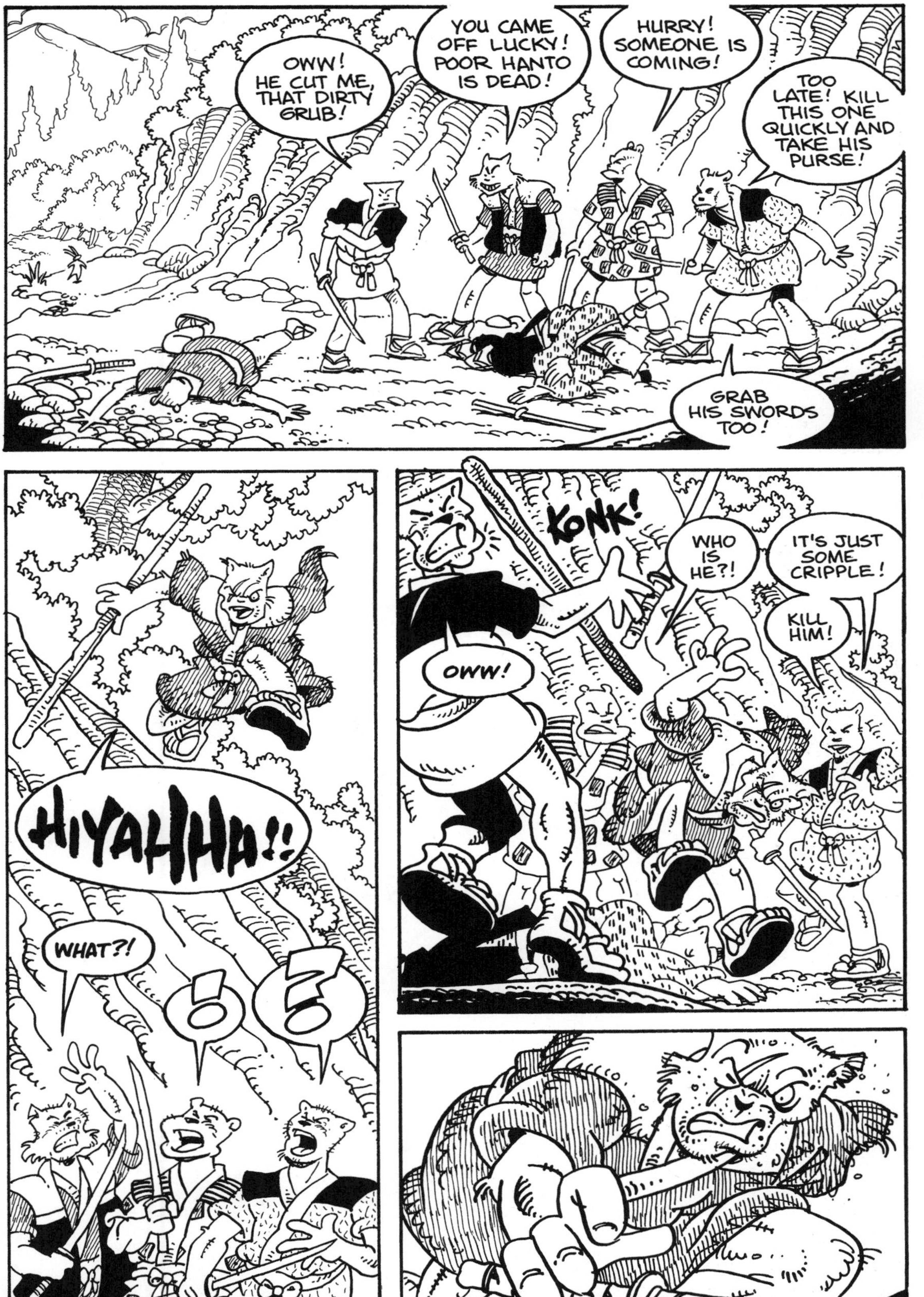
OWW! HE CUT ME, THAT DIRTY GRUB!
YOU CAME OFF LUCKY! POOR HANTO IS DEAD!
HURRY! SOMEONE IS COMING!
TOO LATE! KILL THIS ONE QUICKLY AND TAKE HIS PURSE!
GRAB HIS SWORDS TOO!
HIYAHHA!!
WHAT?!
!
?
KONK!
WHO IS HE?!
IT'S JUST SOME CRIPPLE!
KILL HIM!
OWW!
19.

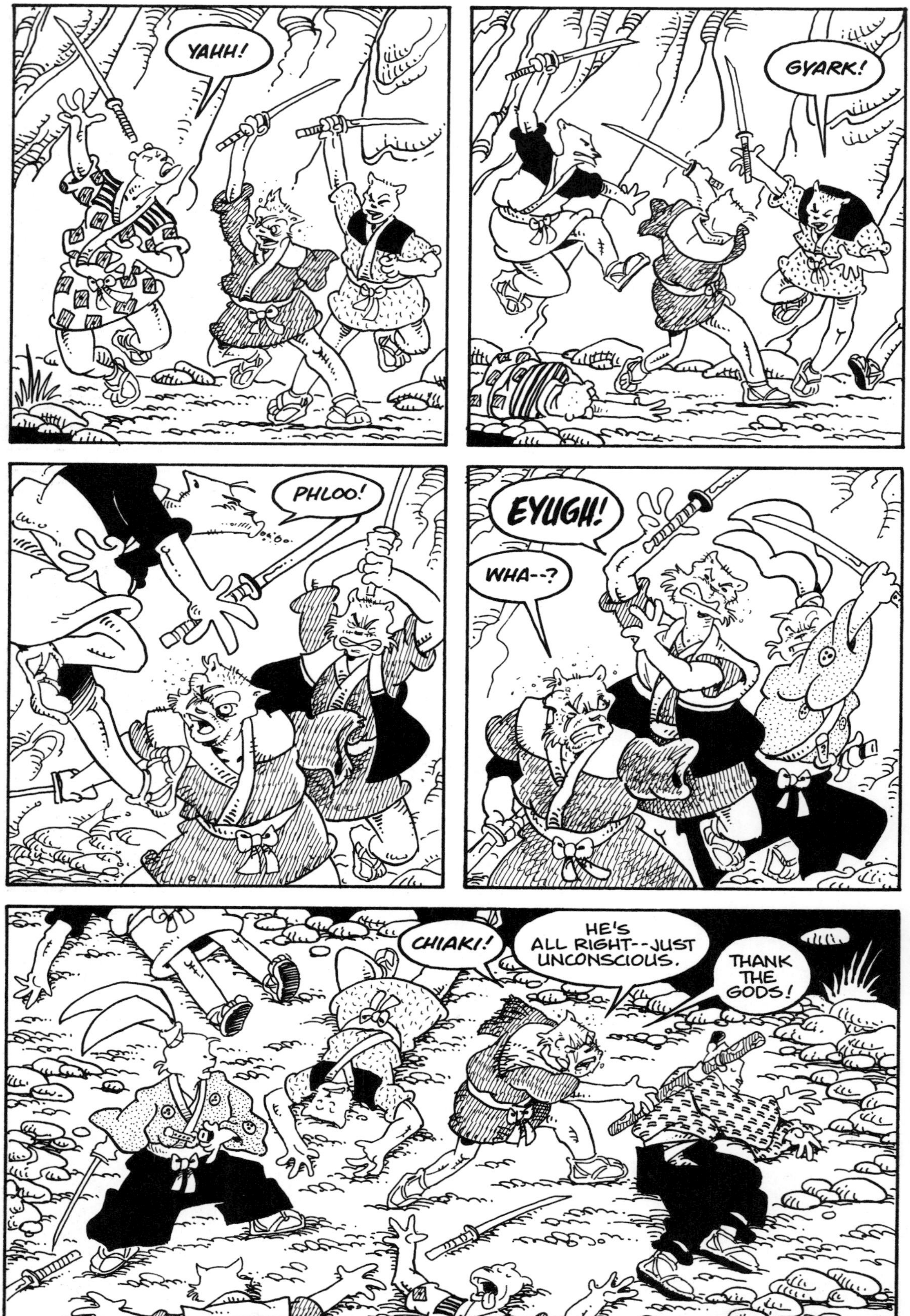
YAHH!
GYARK!
PHLOO!
EYUGH!
WHA--?
CHIAKI!
HE'S ALL RIGHT--JUST UNCONSCIOUS.
THANK THE GODS!
20.

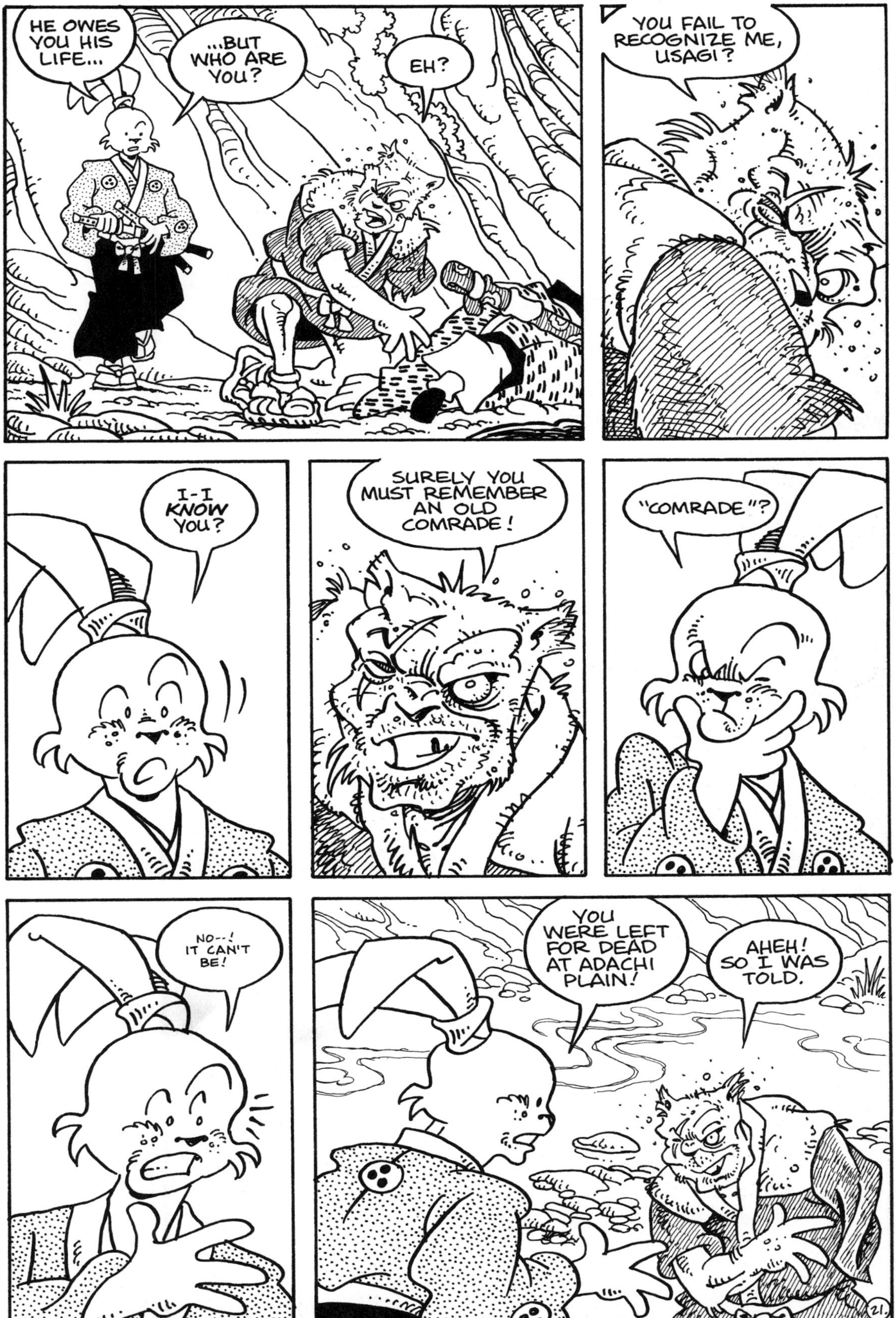
HE OWES YOU HIS LIFE...
...BUT WHO ARE YOU?
EH?
YOU FAIL TO RECOGNIZE ME, USAGI?
I-I *KNOW* YOU?
SURELY YOU MUST REMEMBER AN OLD COMRADE!
"COMRADE"?
NO--! IT CAN'T BE!
YOU WERE LEFT FOR DEAD AT ADACHI PLAIN!
AHEH! SO I WAS TOLD.
21.

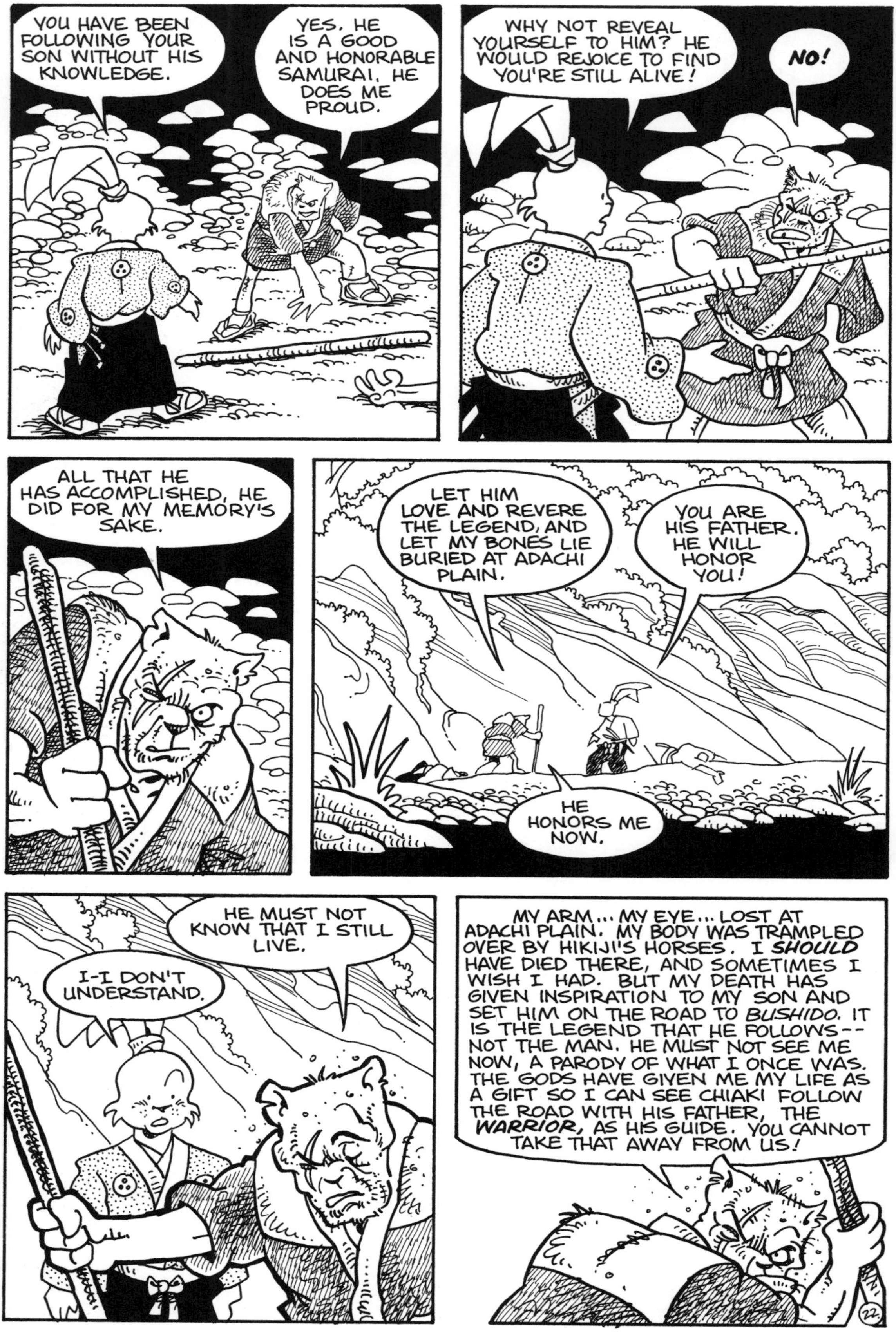
YOU HAVE BEEN FOLLOWING YOUR SON WITHOUT HIS KNOWLEDGE.
YES. HE IS A GOOD AND HONORABLE SAMURAI. HE DOES ME PROUD.
WHY NOT REVEAL YOURSELF TO HIM? HE WOULD REJOICE TO FIND YOU'RE STILL ALIVE!
NO!
ALL THAT HE HAS ACCOMPLISHED, HE DID FOR MY MEMORY'S SAKE.
LET HIM LOVE AND REVERE THE LEGEND, AND LET MY BONES LIE BURIED AT ADACHI PLAIN.
YOU ARE HIS FATHER. HE WILL HONOR YOU!
HE HONORS ME NOW.
HE MUST NOT KNOW THAT I STILL LIVE.
I-I DON'T UNDERSTAND.
MY ARM... MY EYE... LOST AT ADACHI PLAIN. MY BODY WAS TRAMPLED OVER BY HIKIJI'S HORSES. I ***SHOULD*** HAVE DIED THERE, AND SOMETIMES I WISH I HAD. BUT MY DEATH HAS GIVEN INSPIRATION TO MY SON AND SET HIM ON THE ROAD TO *BUSHIDO.* IT IS THE LEGEND THAT HE FOLLOWS--NOT THE MAN. HE MUST NOT SEE ME NOW, A PARODY OF WHAT I ONCE WAS. THE GODS HAVE GIVEN ME MY LIFE AS A GIFT SO I CAN SEE CHIAKI FOLLOW THE ROAD WITH HIS FATHER, THE ***WARRIOR,*** AS HIS GUIDE. YOU CANNOT TAKE THAT AWAY FROM US!
22.

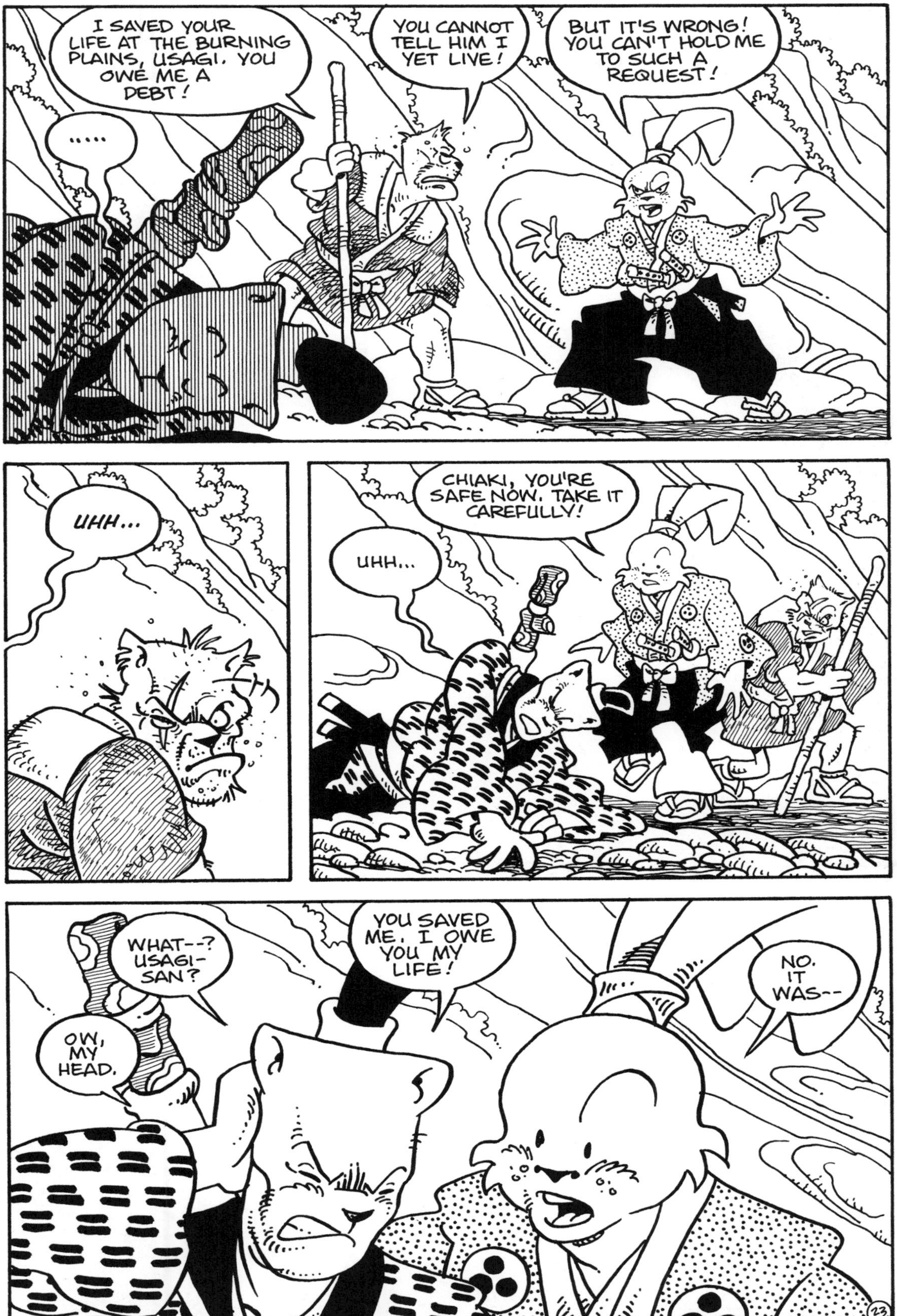
I SAVED YOUR LIFE AT THE BURNING PLAINS, USAGI. YOU OWE ME A DEBT!
.....
YOU CANNOT TELL HIM I YET LIVE!
BUT IT'S WRONG! YOU CAN'T HOLD ME TO SUCH A REQUEST!
UHH...
CHIAKI, YOU'RE SAFE NOW. TAKE IT CAREFULLY!
UHH...
WHAT--? USAGI-SAN?
OW, MY HEAD.
YOU SAVED ME. I OWE YOU MY LIFE!
NO. IT WAS--
23

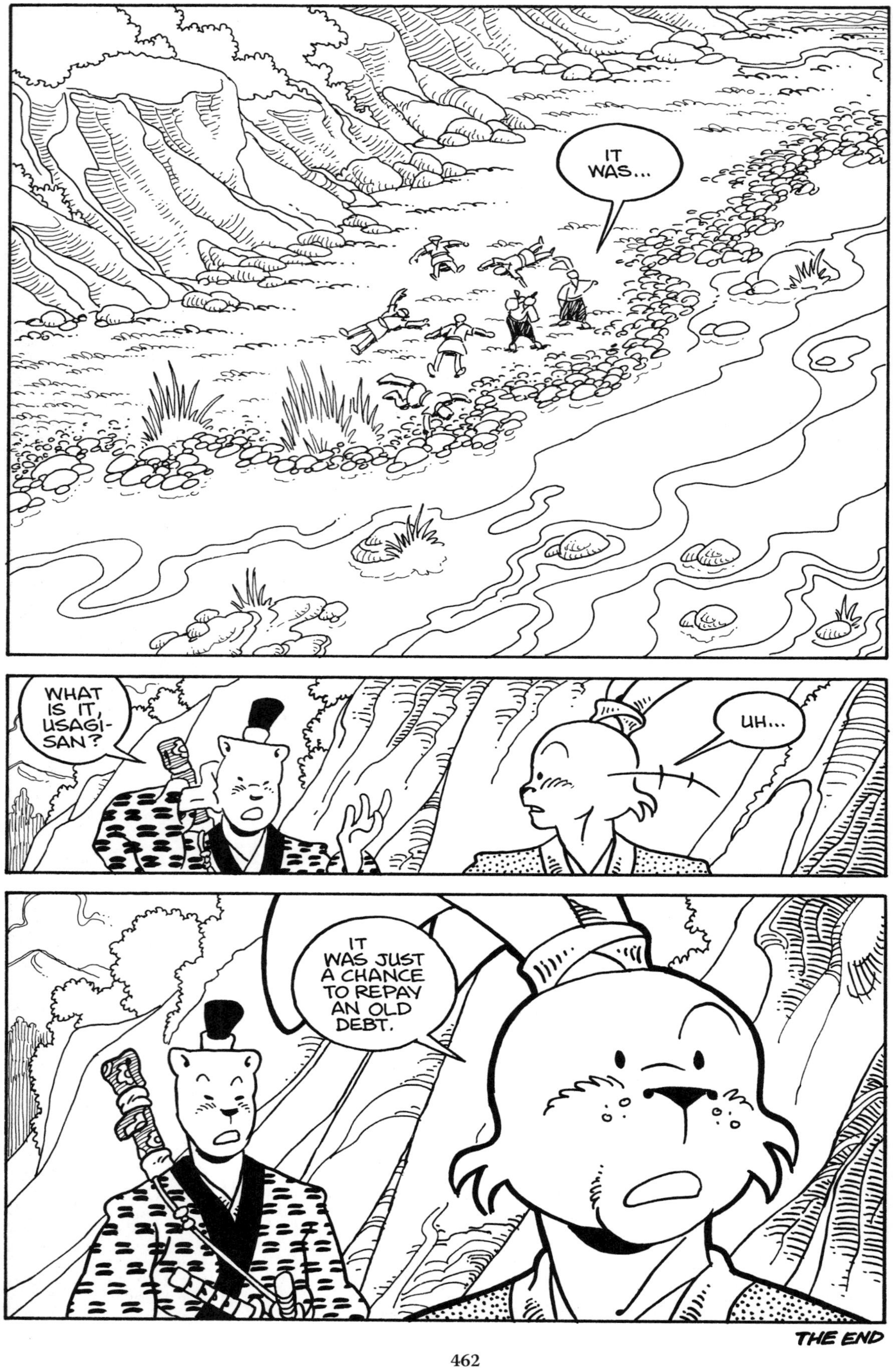
IT WAS...
WHAT IS IT, USAGI-SAN?
UH...
IT WAS JUST A CHANCE TO REPAY AN OLD DEBT.

THE END

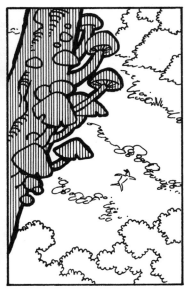

UHH--!

THUD!

I'M FAR FROM THE VILLAGE...I PRAY I'M SAFE NOW!

¡GASP!¿

I-I HEAR MUSIC--FAR AWAY BUT GETTING CLOSER!

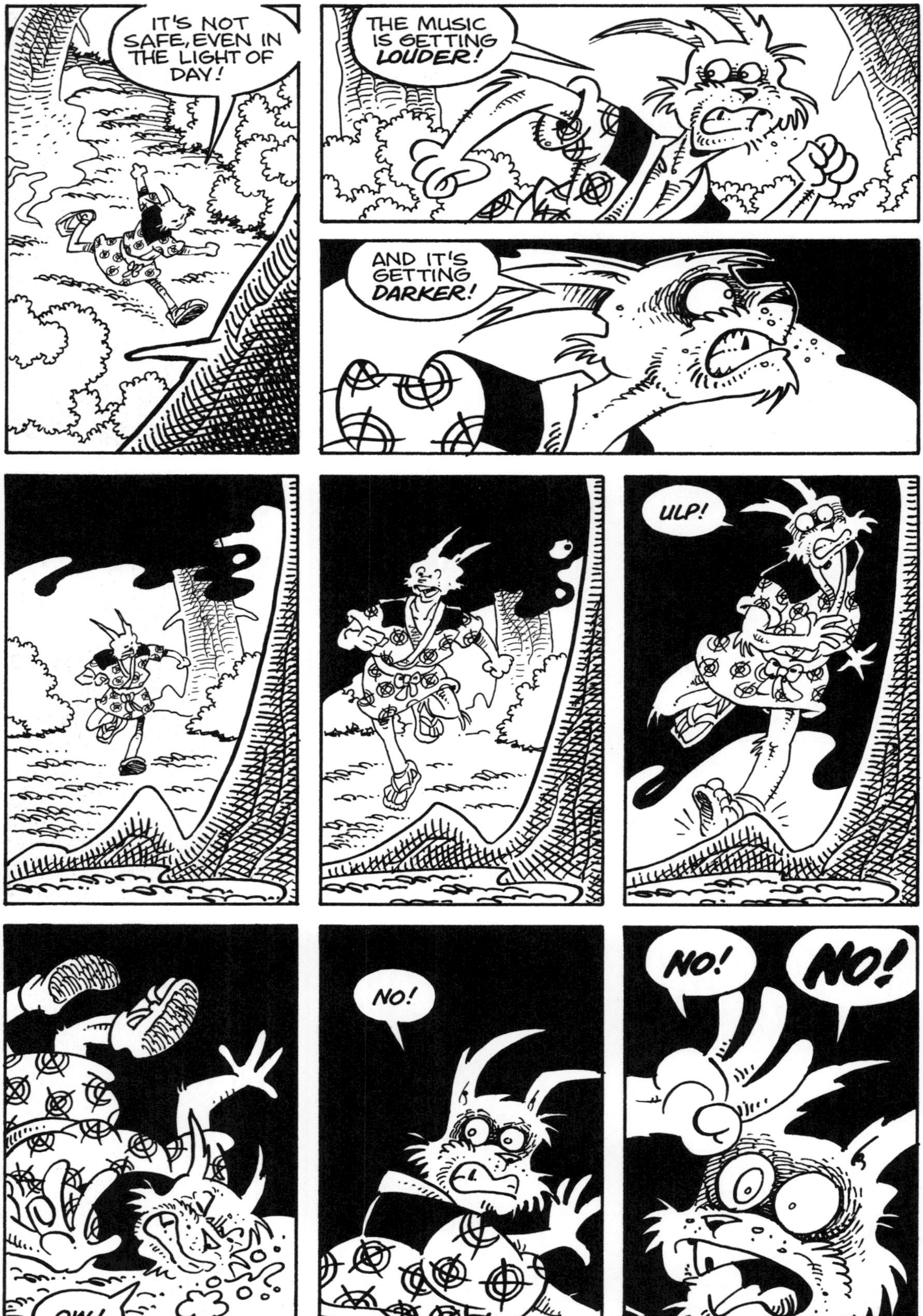
IT'S NOT SAFE, EVEN IN THE LIGHT OF DAY!
THE MUSIC IS GETTING LOUDER!
AND IT'S GETTING DARKER!
ULP!
OW!
NO!
NO!
NO!
2.

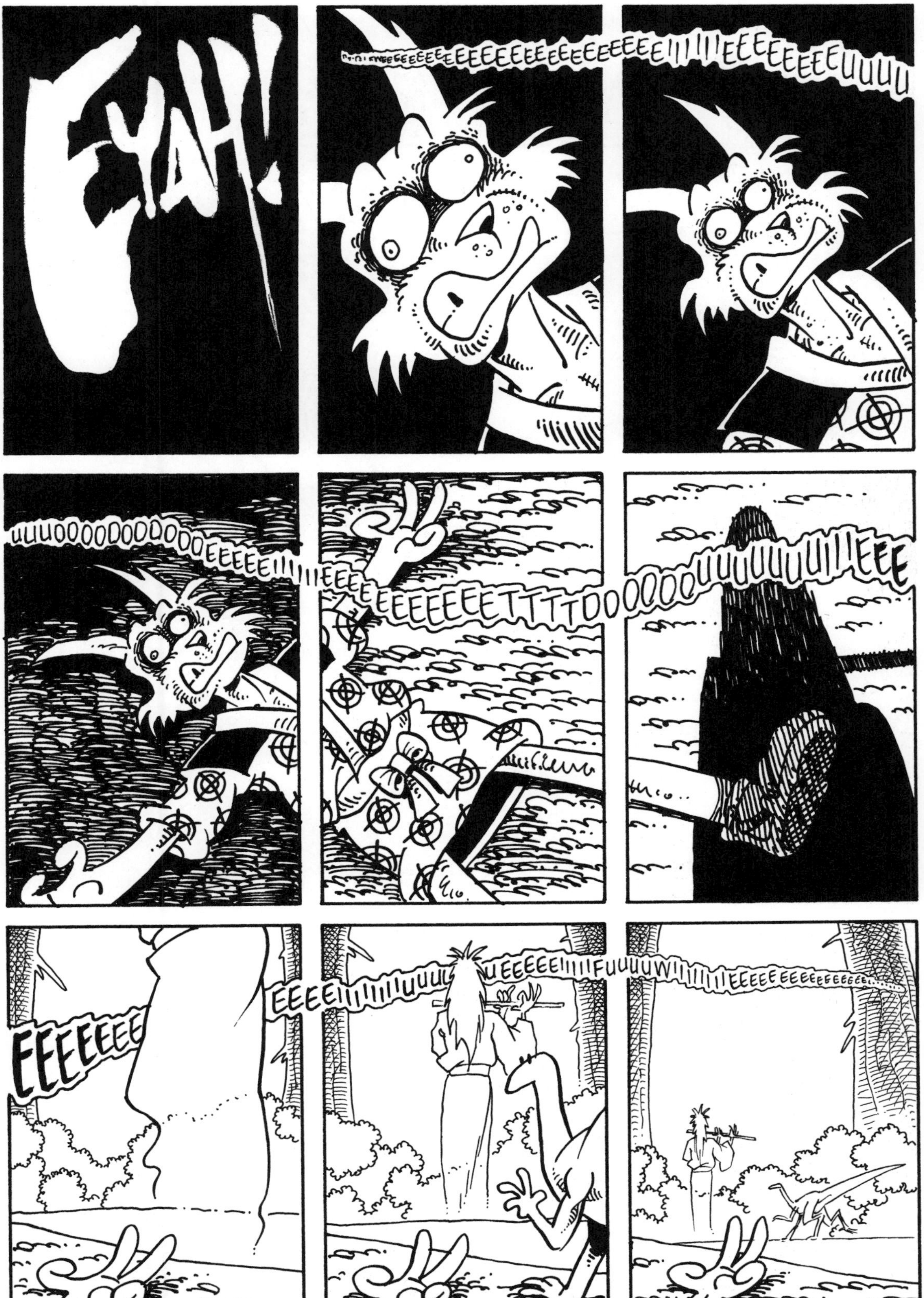

EYAH!
EEEEEEEEEEEEEEEEEEEE!!!!!EEEEEEEEUUUU
UUUOOOOODOOOOOOOEEEEE!!!!!!EEEEEEEEEEETTTTOOOOOOOUUUUUUU!!EEE
EEEEEEE
EEEE!!!!!UUUUUUEEEEE!!!!FUUUUW!!!!!!!EEEEEEEEEEEEEEEE
3

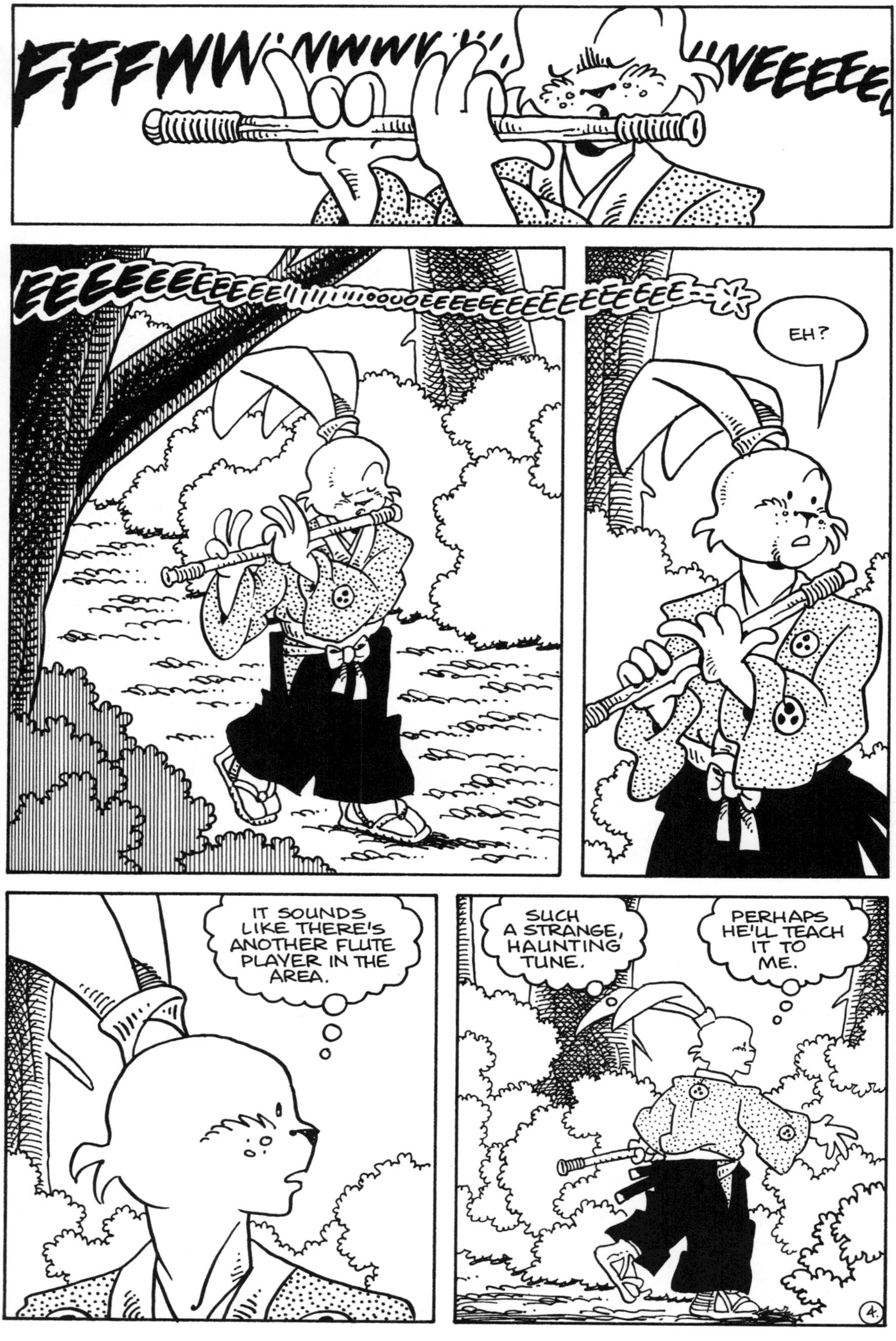
EH?
IT SOUNDS LIKE THERE'S ANOTHER FLUTE PLAYER IN THE AREA.
SUCH A STRANGE, HAUNTING TUNE.
PERHAPS HE'LL TEACH IT TO ME.
4.

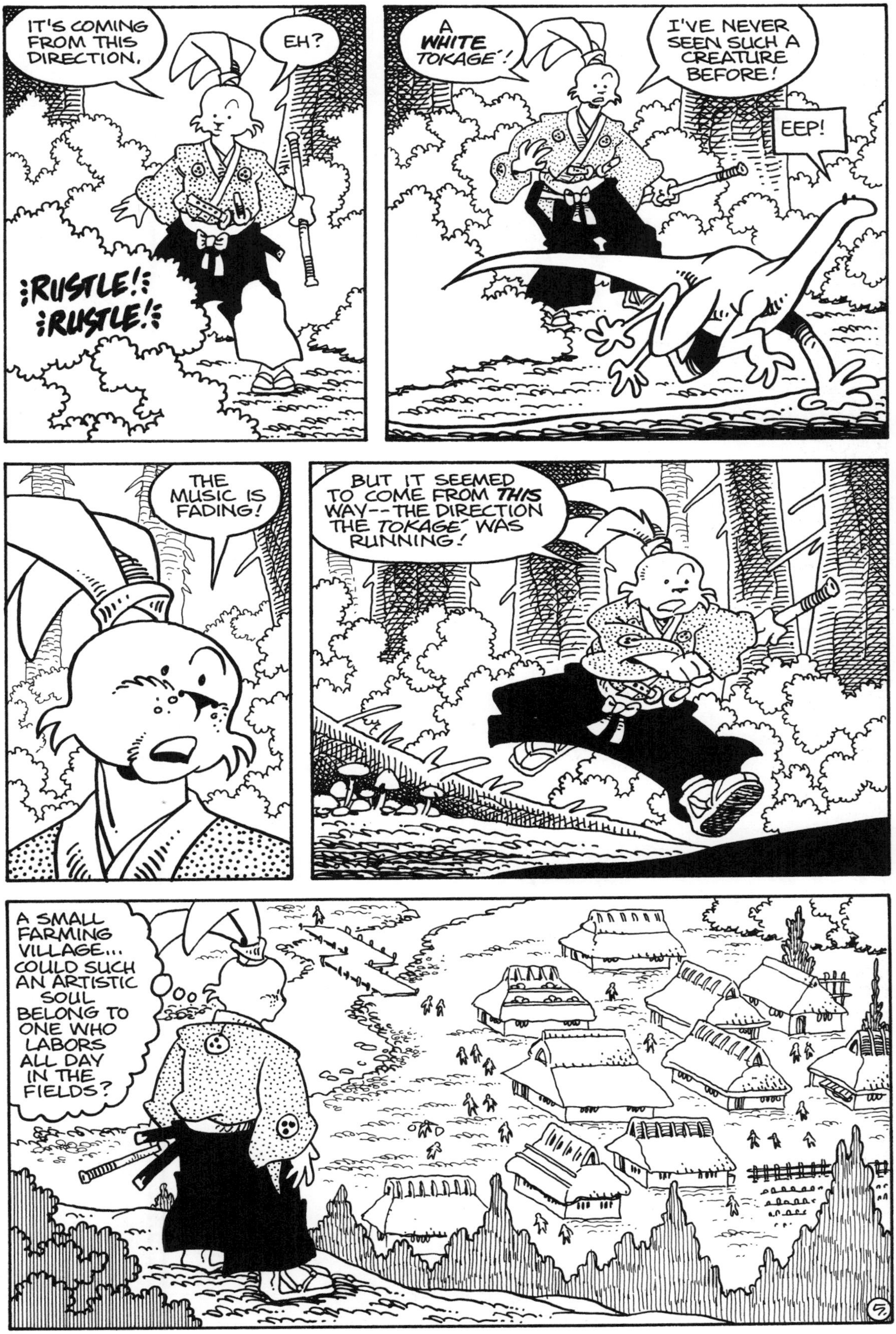

IT'S COMING FROM THIS DIRECTION.
EH?
RUSTLE! RUSTLE!
A WHITE TOKAGE'!
I'VE NEVER SEEN SUCH A CREATURE BEFORE!
EEP!
THE MUSIC IS FADING!
BUT IT SEEMED TO COME FROM THIS WAY--THE DIRECTION THE TOKAGE' WAS RUNNING!
A SMALL FARMING VILLAGE... COULD SUCH AN ARTISTIC SOUL BELONG TO ONE WHO LABORS ALL DAY IN THE FIELDS?
5

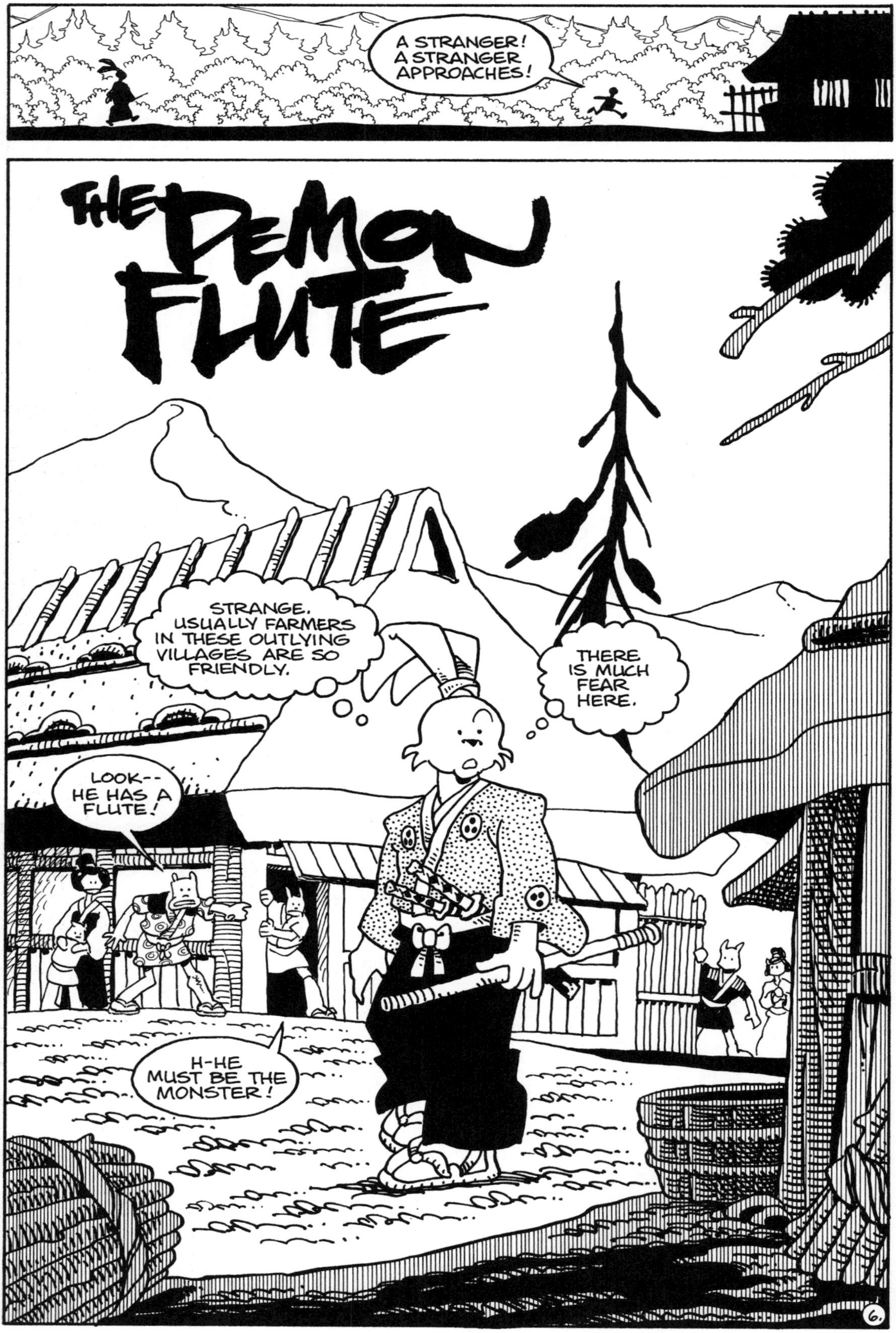
A STRANGER! A STRANGER APPROACHES!
THE DEMON FLUTE
STRANGE. USUALLY FARMERS IN THESE OUTLYING VILLAGES ARE SO FRIENDLY.
THERE IS MUCH FEAR HERE.
LOOK-- HE HAS A FLUTE!
H-HE MUST BE THE MONSTER!
6.

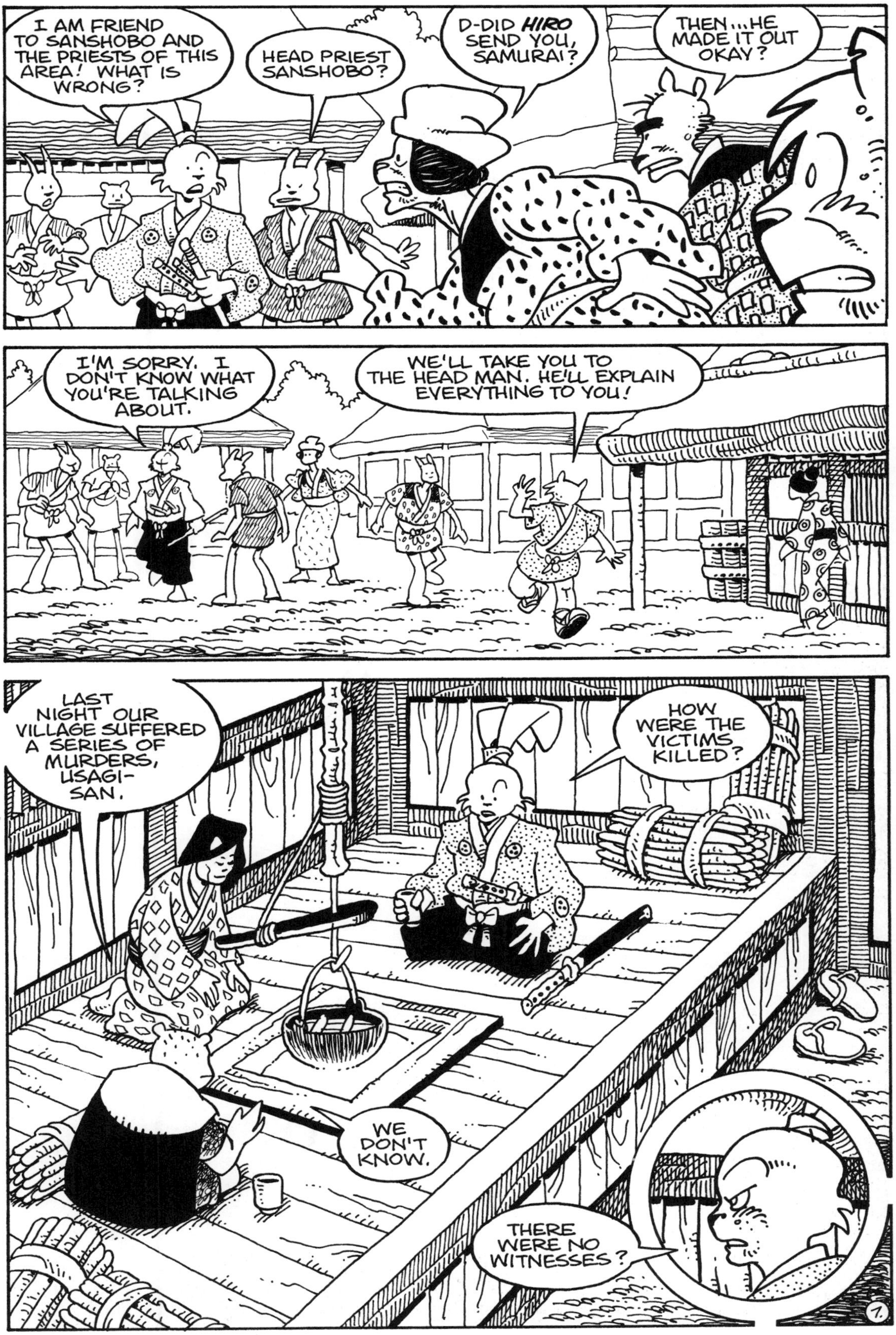
I AM FRIEND TO SANSHOBO AND THE PRIESTS OF THIS AREA! WHAT IS WRONG?
HEAD PRIEST SANSHOBO?
D-DID HIRO SEND YOU, SAMURAI?
THEN...HE MADE IT OUT OKAY?
I'M SORRY. I DON'T KNOW WHAT YOU'RE TALKING ABOUT.
WE'LL TAKE YOU TO THE HEAD MAN. HE'LL EXPLAIN EVERYTHING TO YOU!
LAST NIGHT OUR VILLAGE SUFFERED A SERIES OF MURDERS, USAGI-SAN.
HOW WERE THE VICTIMS KILLED?
WE DON'T KNOW.
THERE WERE NO WITNESSES?
7.

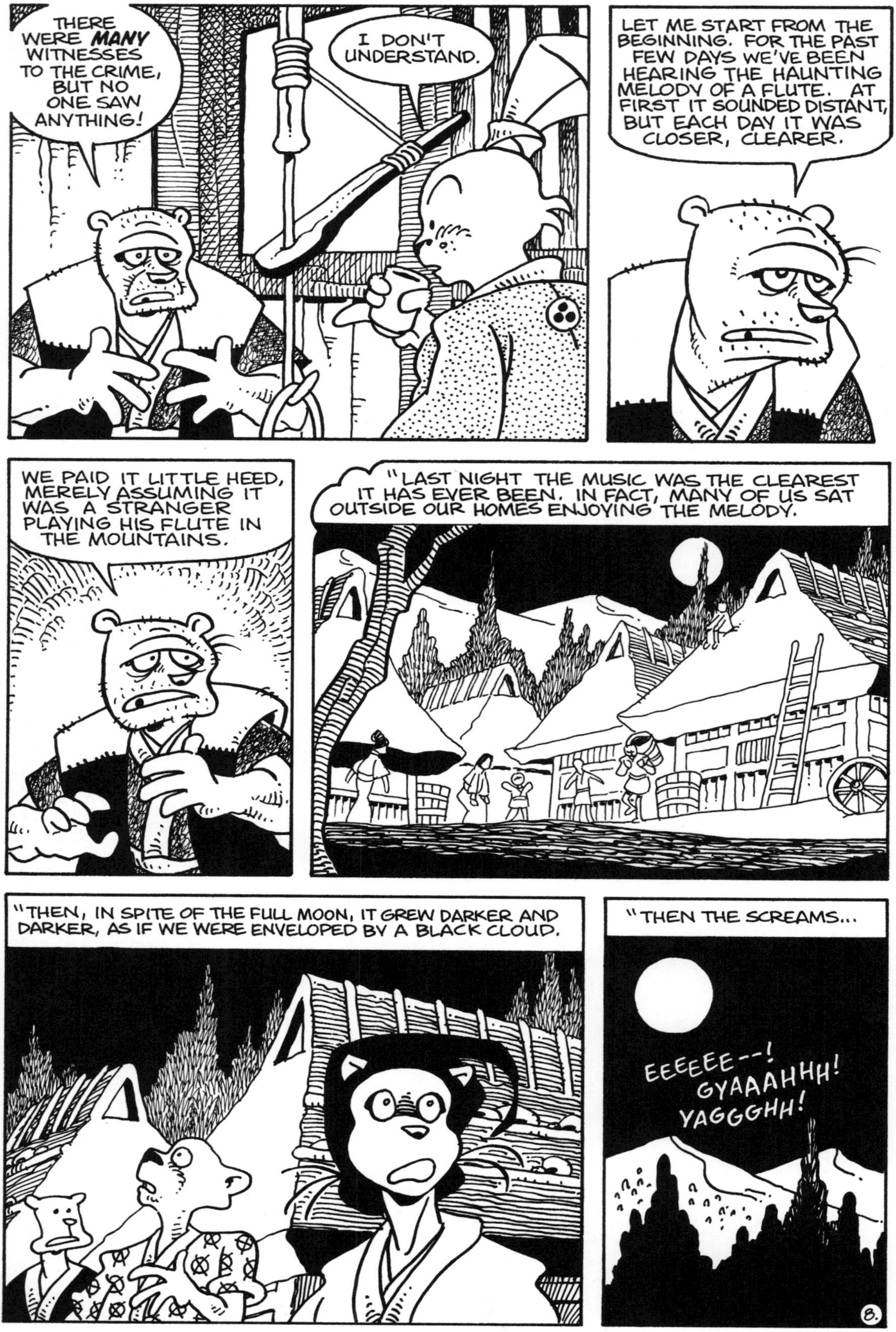
THERE WERE MANY WITNESSES TO THE CRIME, BUT NO ONE SAW ANYTHING!
I DON'T UNDERSTAND.
LET ME START FROM THE BEGINNING. FOR THE PAST FEW DAYS WE'VE BEEN HEARING THE HAUNTING MELODY OF A FLUTE. AT FIRST IT SOUNDED DISTANT, BUT EACH DAY IT WAS CLOSER, CLEARER.
WE PAID IT LITTLE HEED, MERELY ASSUMING IT WAS A STRANGER PLAYING HIS FLUTE IN THE MOUNTAINS.
"LAST NIGHT THE MUSIC WAS THE CLEAREST IT HAS EVER BEEN. IN FACT, MANY OF US SAT OUTSIDE OUR HOMES ENJOYING THE MELODY.
"THEN, IN SPITE OF THE FULL MOON, IT GREW DARKER AND DARKER, AS IF WE WERE ENVELOPED BY A BLACK CLOUD.
"THEN THE SCREAMS...
EEEEEE--!
GYAAAHHH!
YAGGGHH!
8.

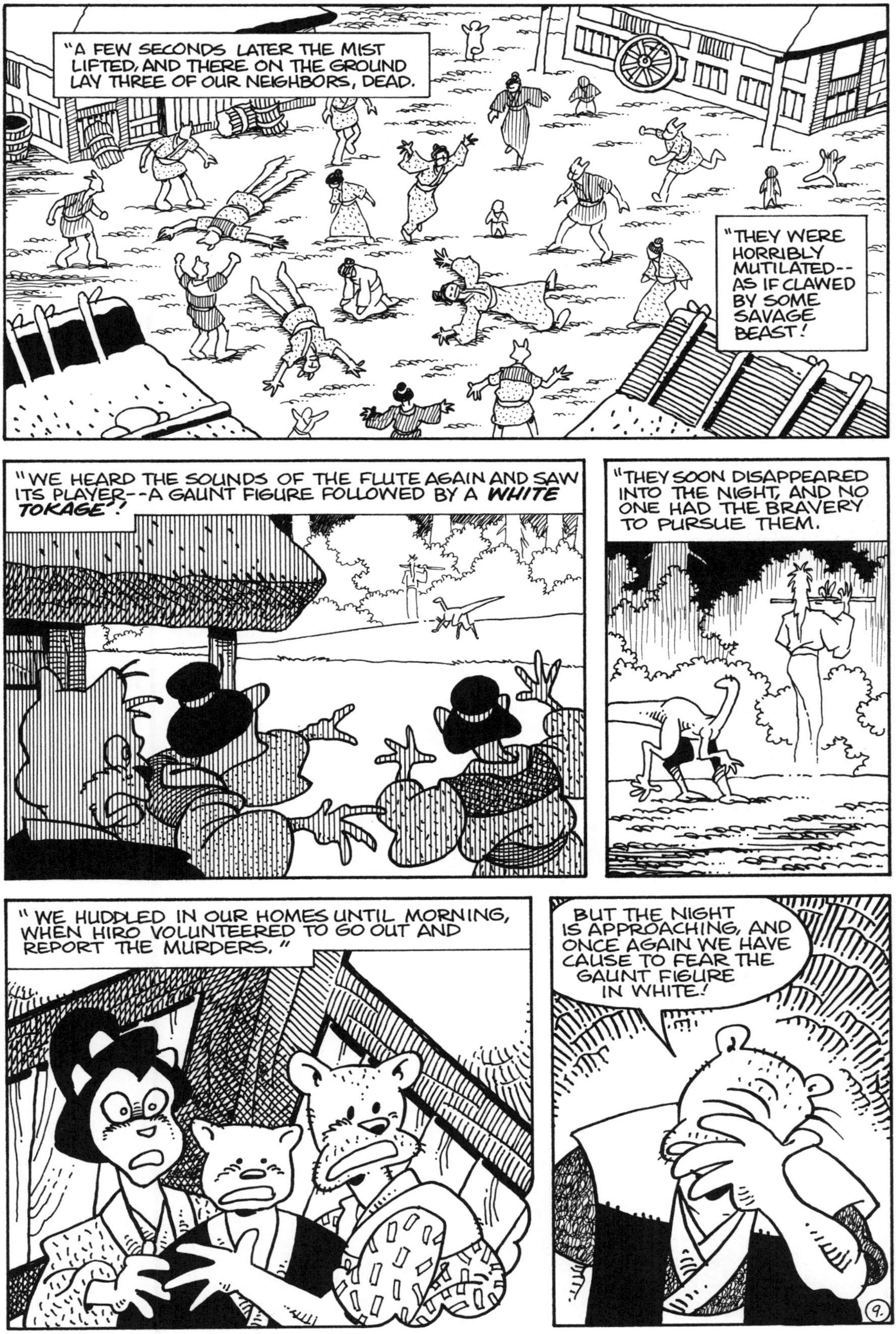
"A FEW SECONDS LATER THE MIST LIFTED, AND THERE ON THE GROUND LAY THREE OF OUR NEIGHBORS, DEAD.
"THEY WERE HORRIBLY MUTILATED--AS IF CLAWED BY SOME SAVAGE BEAST!
"WE HEARD THE SOUNDS OF THE FLUTE AGAIN AND SAW ITS PLAYER--A GAUNT FIGURE FOLLOWED BY A *WHITE TOKAGE*!
"THEY SOON DISAPPEARED INTO THE NIGHT, AND NO ONE HAD THE BRAVERY TO PURSUE THEM.
"WE HUDDLED IN OUR HOMES UNTIL MORNING, WHEN HIRO VOLUNTEERED TO GO OUT AND REPORT THE MURDERS."
BUT THE NIGHT IS APPROACHING, AND ONCE AGAIN WE HAVE CAUSE TO FEAR THE GAUNT FIGURE IN WHITE!
9.

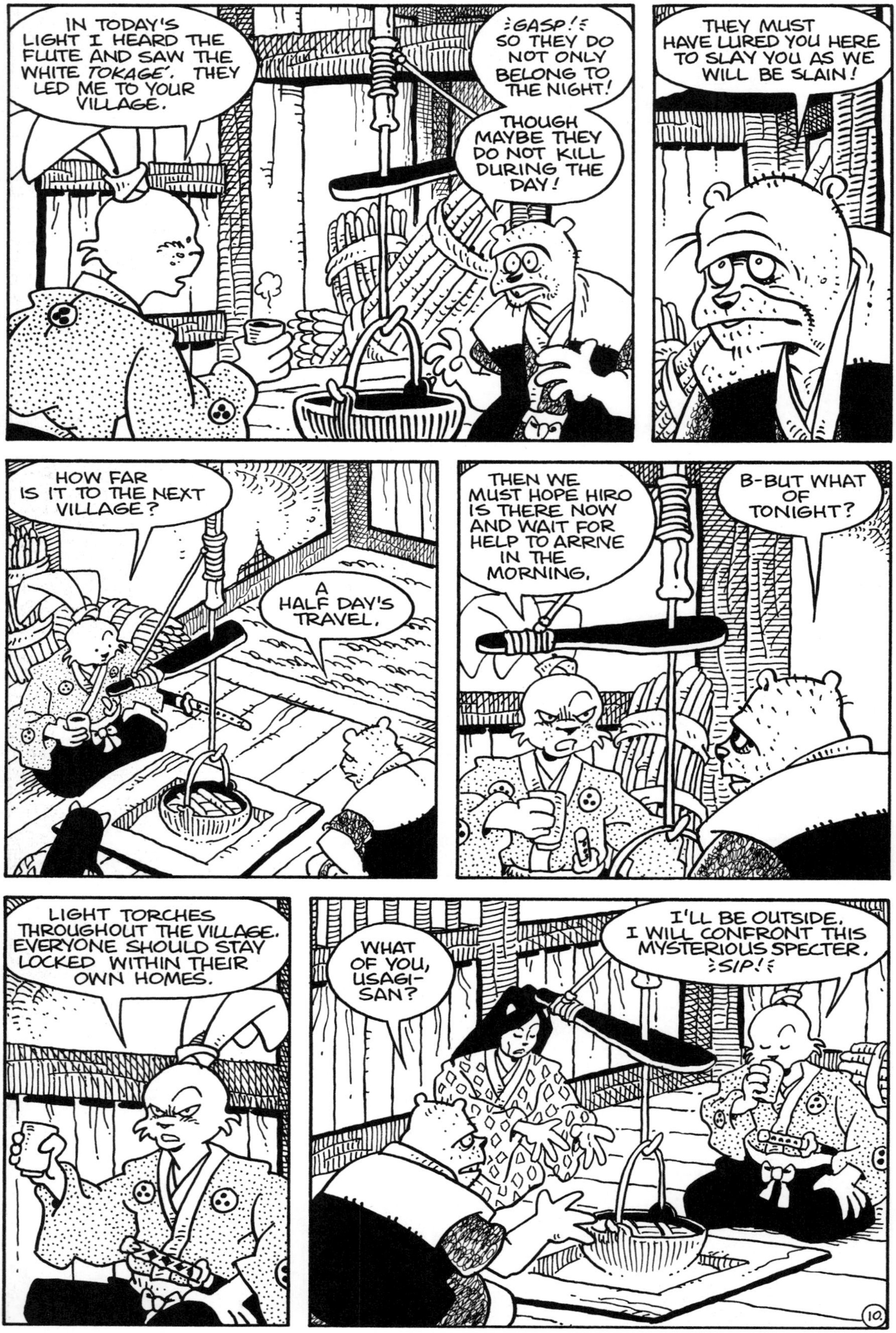
IN TODAY'S LIGHT I HEARD THE FLUTE AND SAW THE WHITE *TOKAGE*. THEY LED ME TO YOUR VILLAGE.
GASP! SO THEY DO NOT ONLY BELONG TO THE NIGHT!
THOUGH MAYBE THEY DO NOT KILL DURING THE DAY!
THEY MUST HAVE LURED YOU HERE TO SLAY YOU AS WE WILL BE SLAIN!
HOW FAR IS IT TO THE NEXT VILLAGE?
A HALF DAY'S TRAVEL.
THEN WE MUST HOPE HIRO IS THERE NOW AND WAIT FOR HELP TO ARRIVE IN THE MORNING.
B-BUT WHAT OF TONIGHT?
LIGHT TORCHES THROUGHOUT THE VILLAGE. EVERYONE SHOULD STAY LOCKED WITHIN THEIR OWN HOMES.
WHAT OF YOU, USAGI-SAN?
I'LL BE OUTSIDE. I WILL CONFRONT THIS MYSTERIOUS SPECTER.
SIP!
10

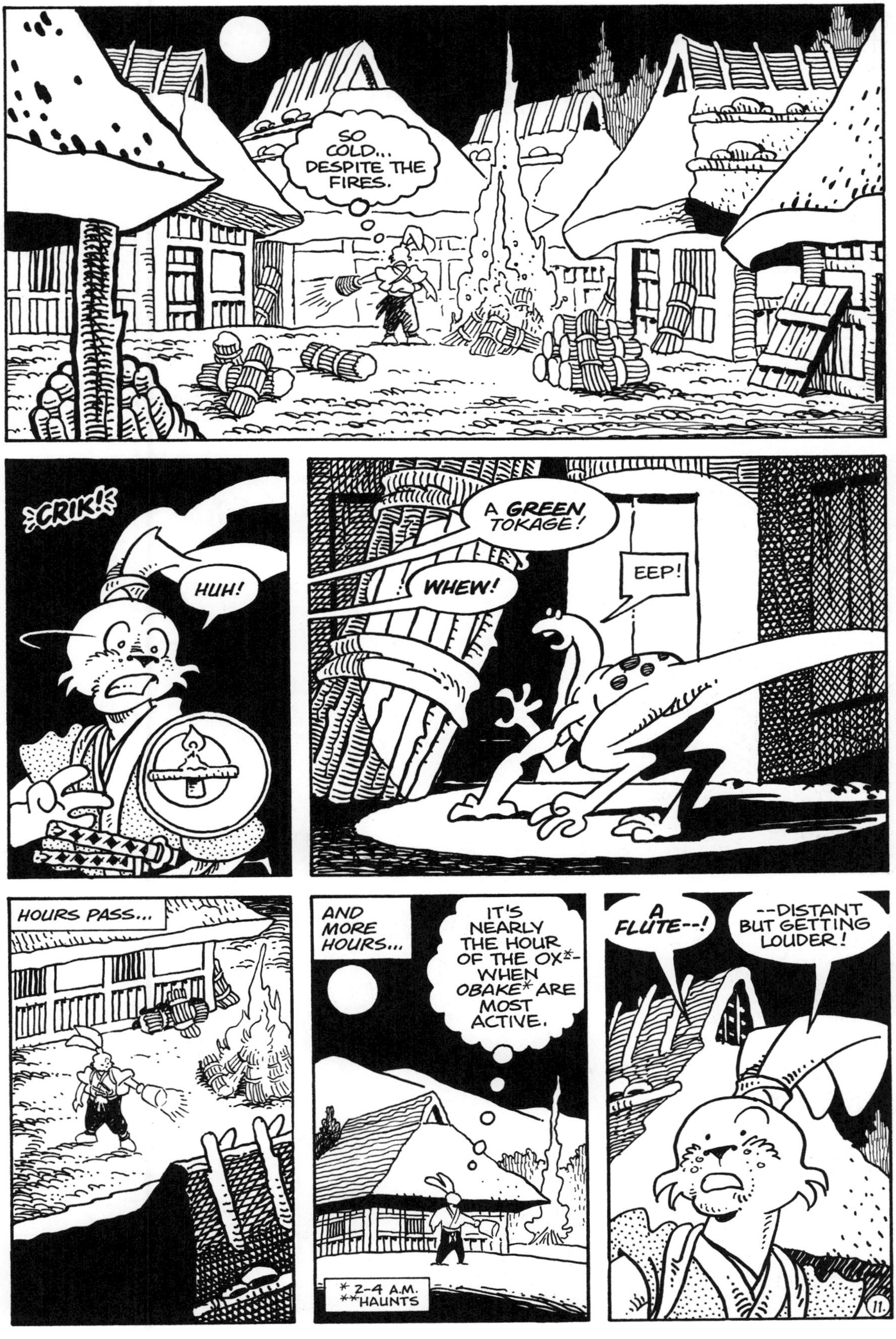

SO COLD... DESPITE THE FIRES.
CRIK!
HUH!
A GREEN TOKAGE!
WHEW!
EEP!
HOURS PASS...
AND MORE HOURS...
IT'S NEARLY THE HOUR OF THE OX*- WHEN OBAKE* ARE MOST ACTIVE.
* 2-4 A.M.
** HAUNTS
A FLUTE--!
--DISTANT BUT GETTING LOUDER!
11.

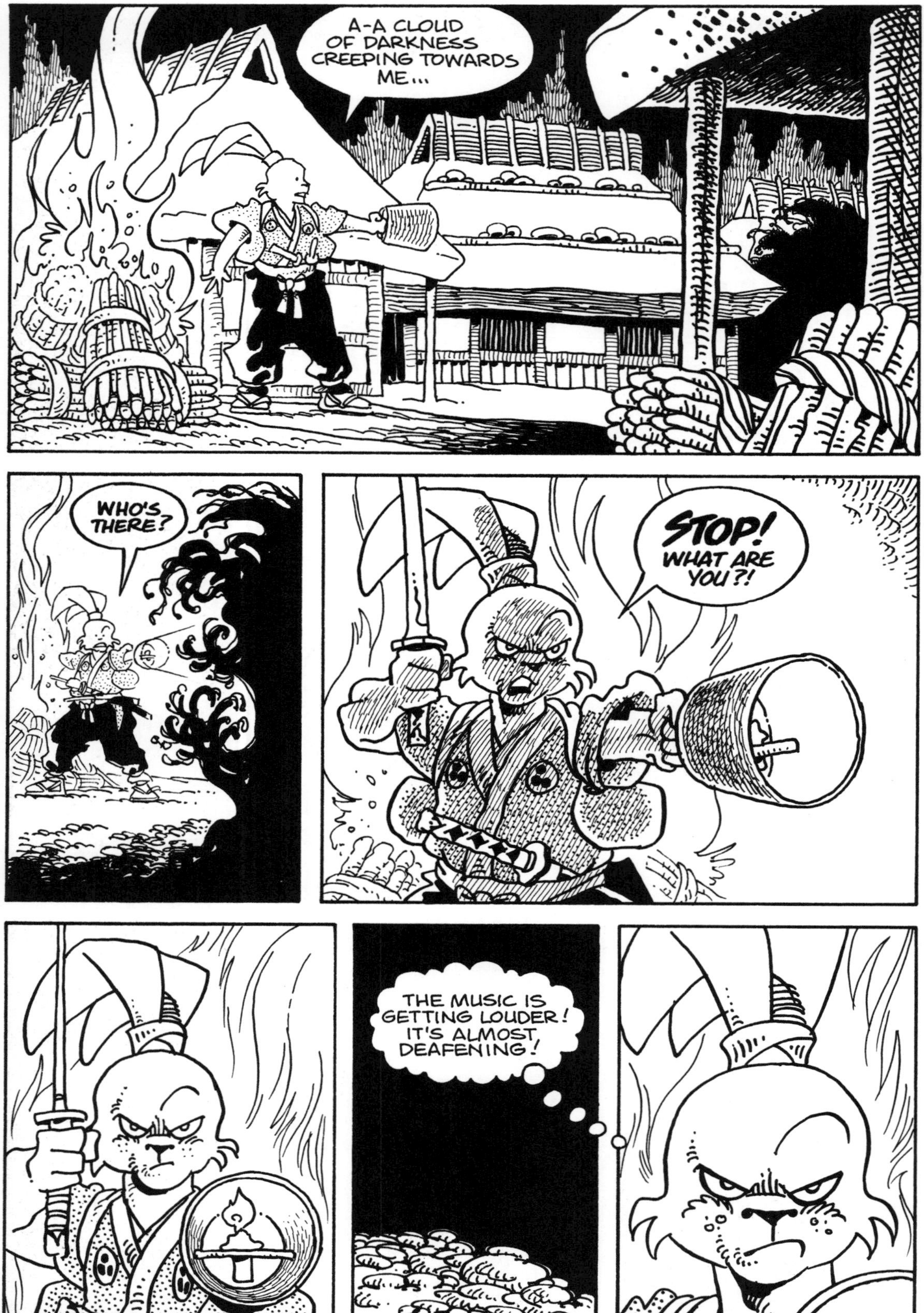
A-A CLOUD OF DARKNESS CREEPING TOWARDS ME...
WHO'S THERE?
STOP! WHAT ARE YOU?!
THE MUSIC IS GETTING LOUDER! IT'S ALMOST DEAFENING!
12

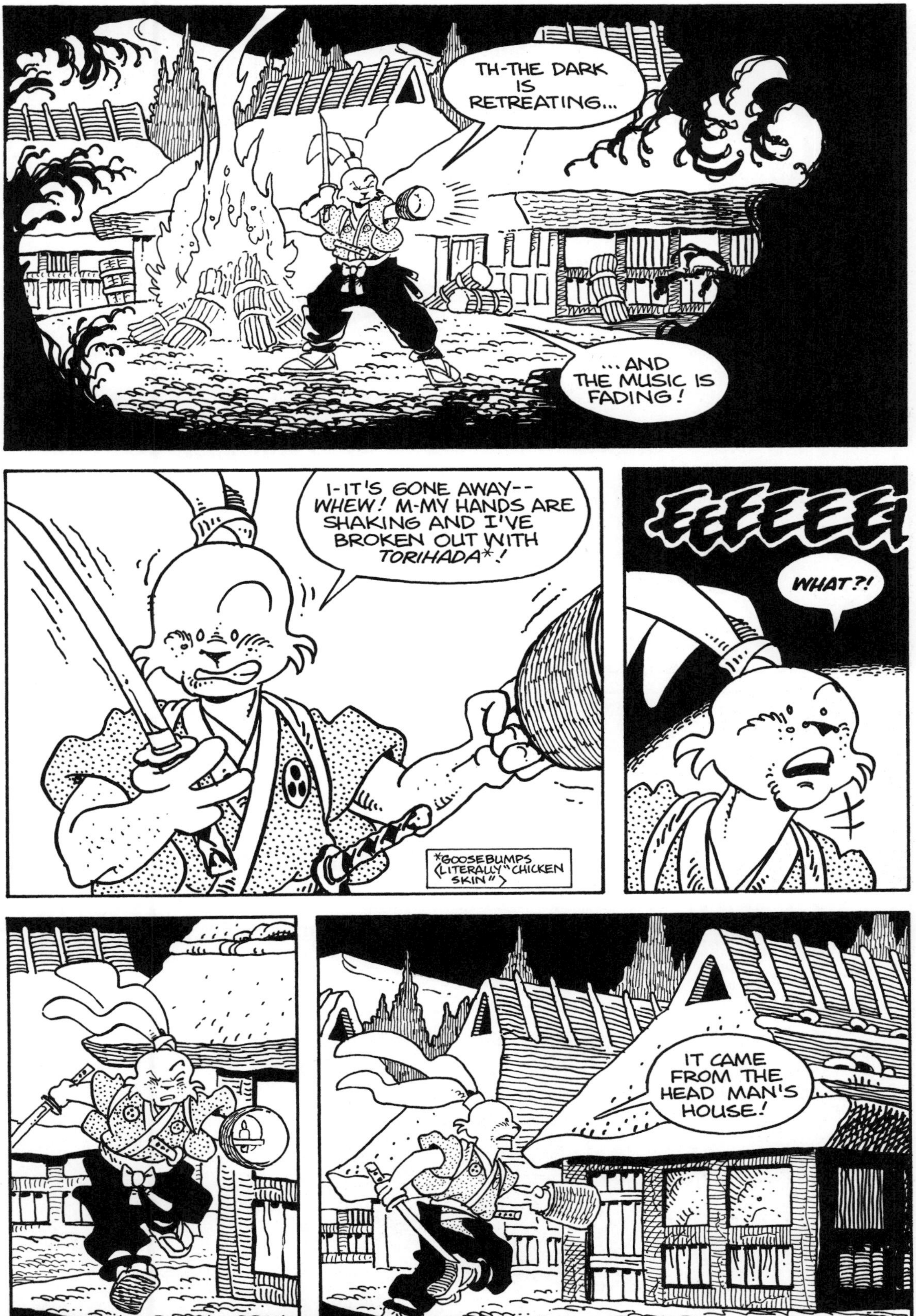
TH-THE DARK IS RETREATING...
...AND THE MUSIC IS FADING!
I-IT'S GONE AWAY-- WHEW! M-MY HANDS ARE SHAKING AND I'VE BROKEN OUT WITH TORIHADA*!
*GOOSEBUMPS (LITERALLY "CHICKEN SKIN")
EEEEEE
WHAT?!
IT CAME FROM THE HEAD MAN'S HOUSE!
13.

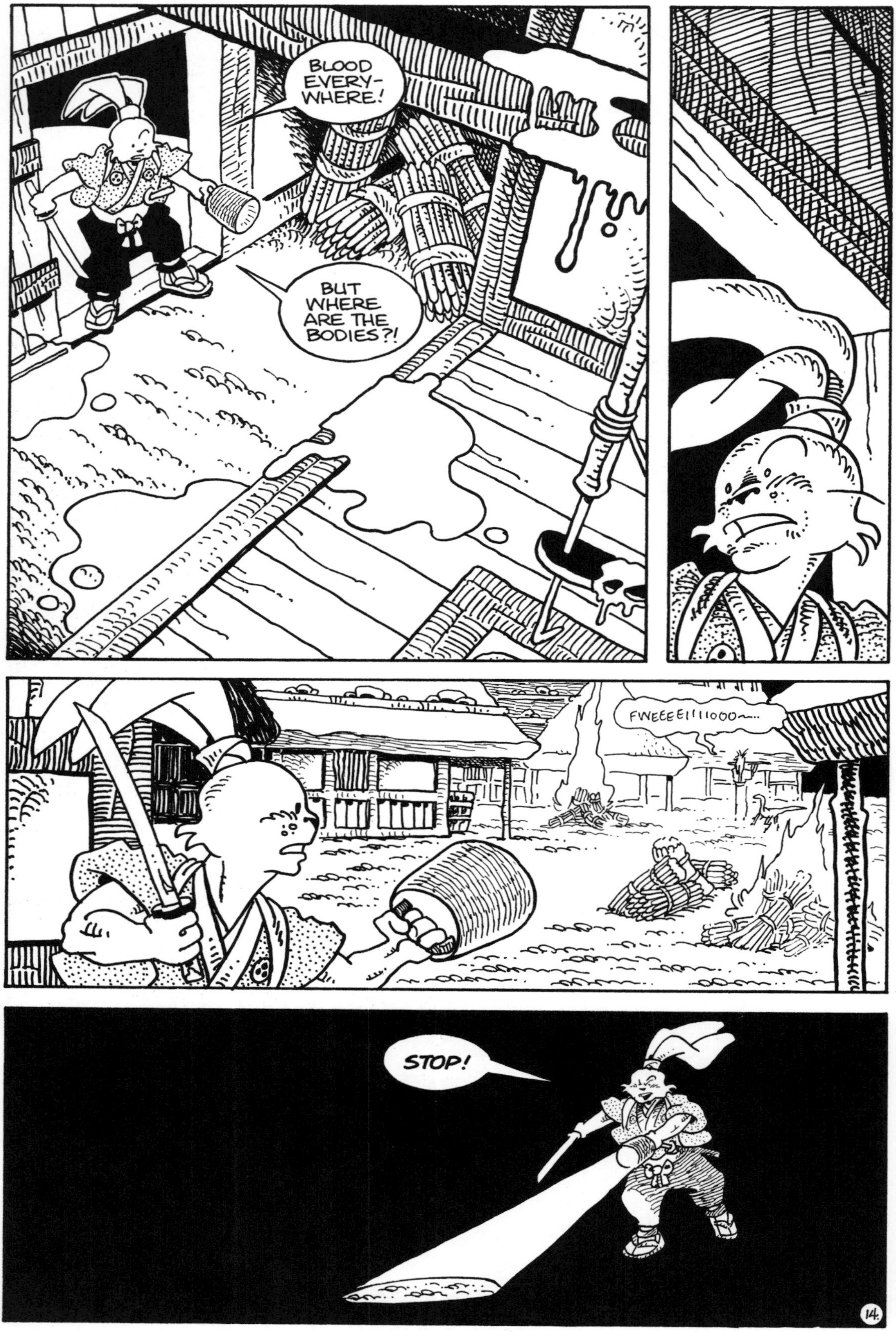
BLOOD EVERY-WHERE!
BUT WHERE ARE THE BODIES?!
FWEEEEIIIIOOO~...
STOP!
14.

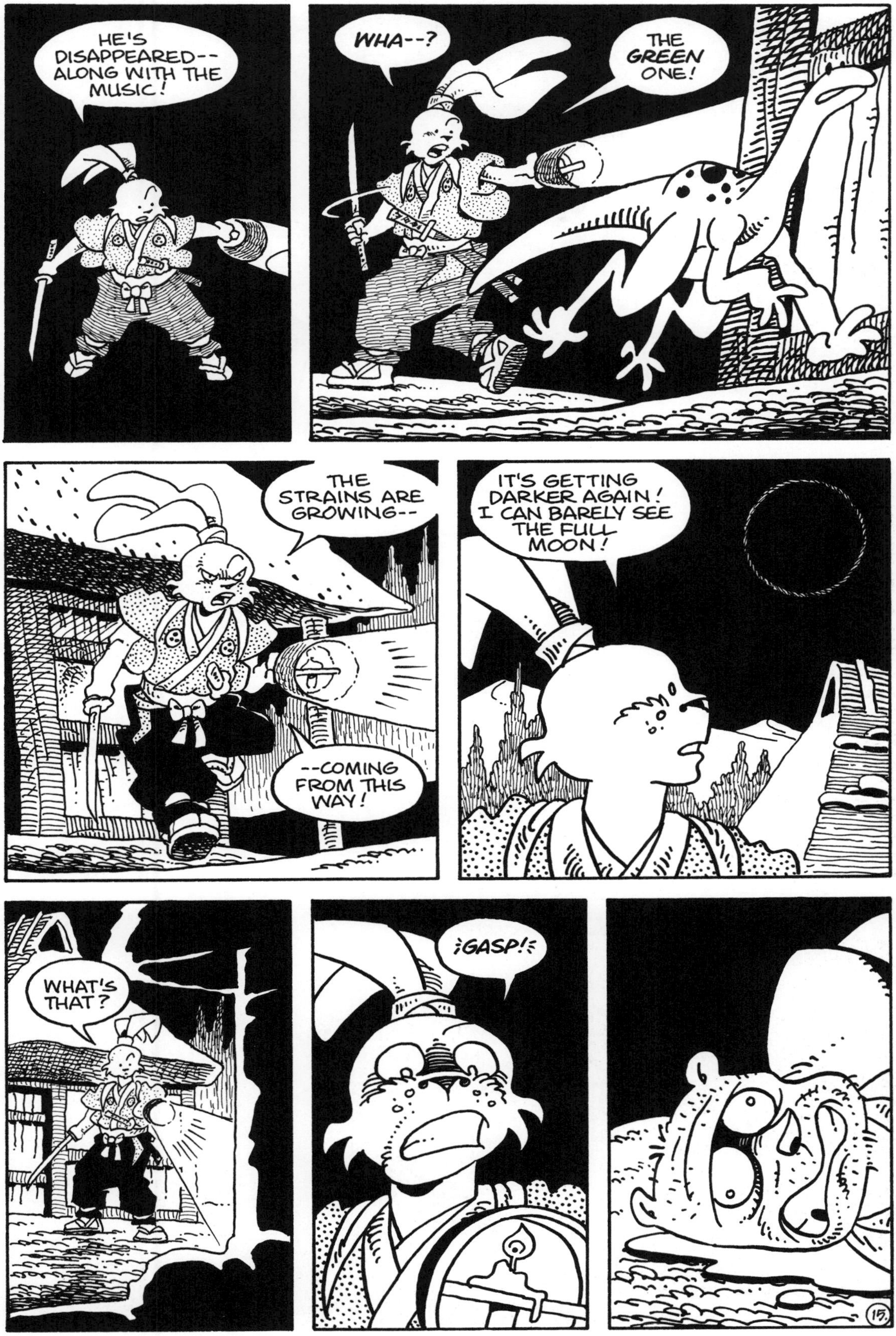

HE'S DISAPPEARED-- ALONG WITH THE MUSIC!
WHA--?
THE GREEN ONE!
THE STRAINS ARE GROWING--
--COMING FROM THIS WAY!
IT'S GETTING DARKER AGAIN! I CAN BARELY SEE THE FULL MOON!
WHAT'S THAT?
¡GASP!¡
15.

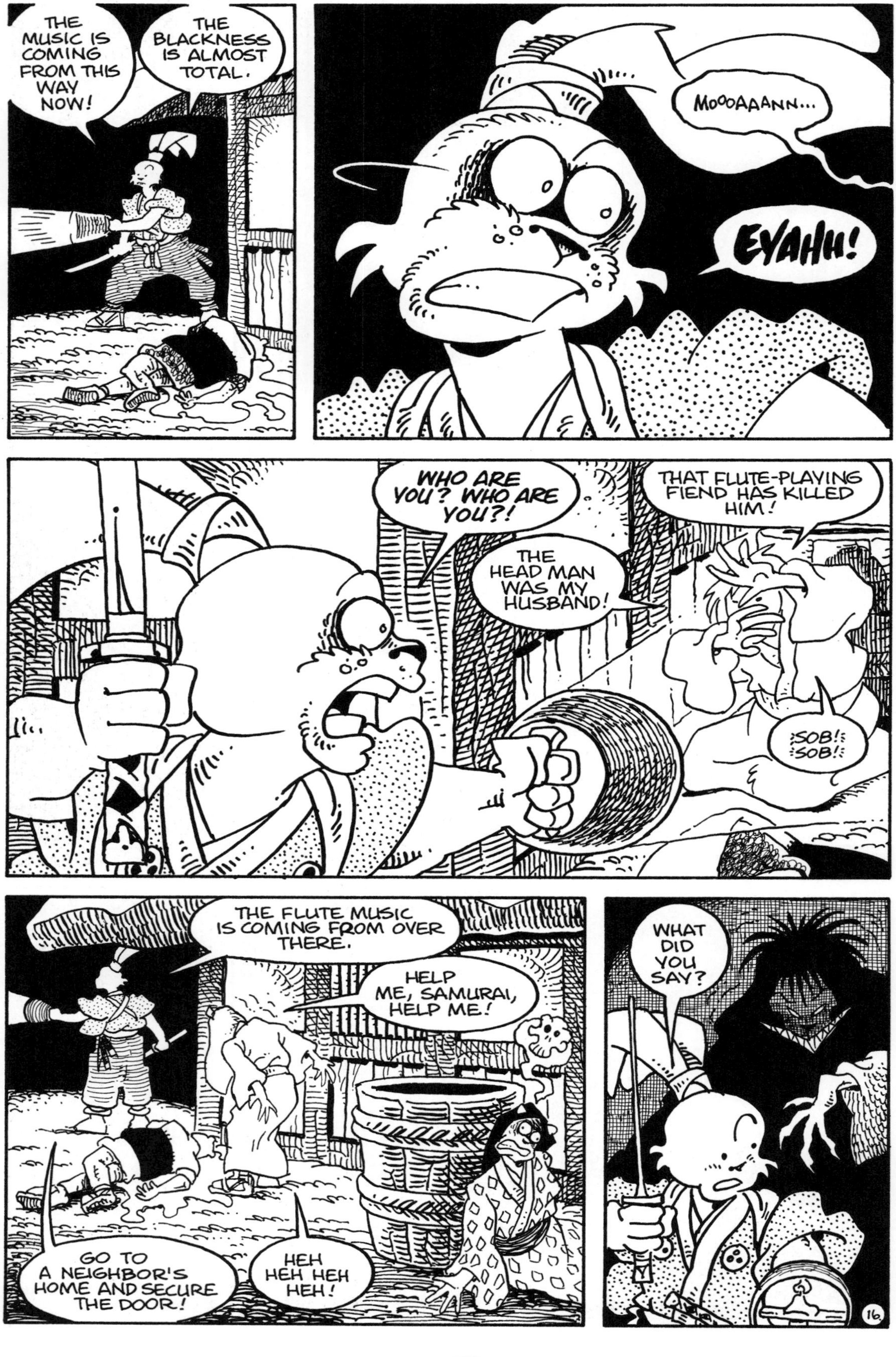
THE MUSIC IS COMING FROM THIS WAY NOW!
THE BLACKNESS IS ALMOST TOTAL.
MOOOAAANN...
EYAHH!
WHO ARE YOU? WHO ARE YOU?!
THAT FLUTE-PLAYING FIEND HAS KILLED HIM!
THE HEAD MAN WAS MY HUSBAND!
SOB! SOB!
THE FLUTE MUSIC IS COMING FROM OVER THERE.
HELP ME, SAMURAI, HELP ME!
GO TO A NEIGHBOR'S HOME AND SECURE THE DOOR!
HEH HEH HEH HEH!
WHAT DID YOU SAY?
16

EEYAAHHHH

HANYA!

*FEMALE DEMON

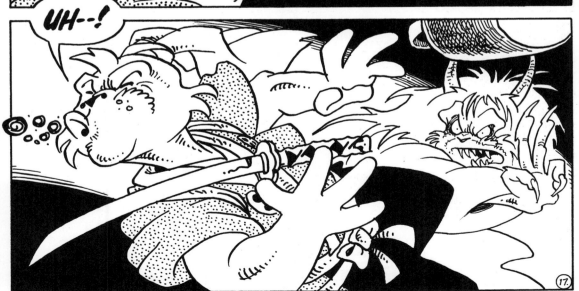

UH--!

17.

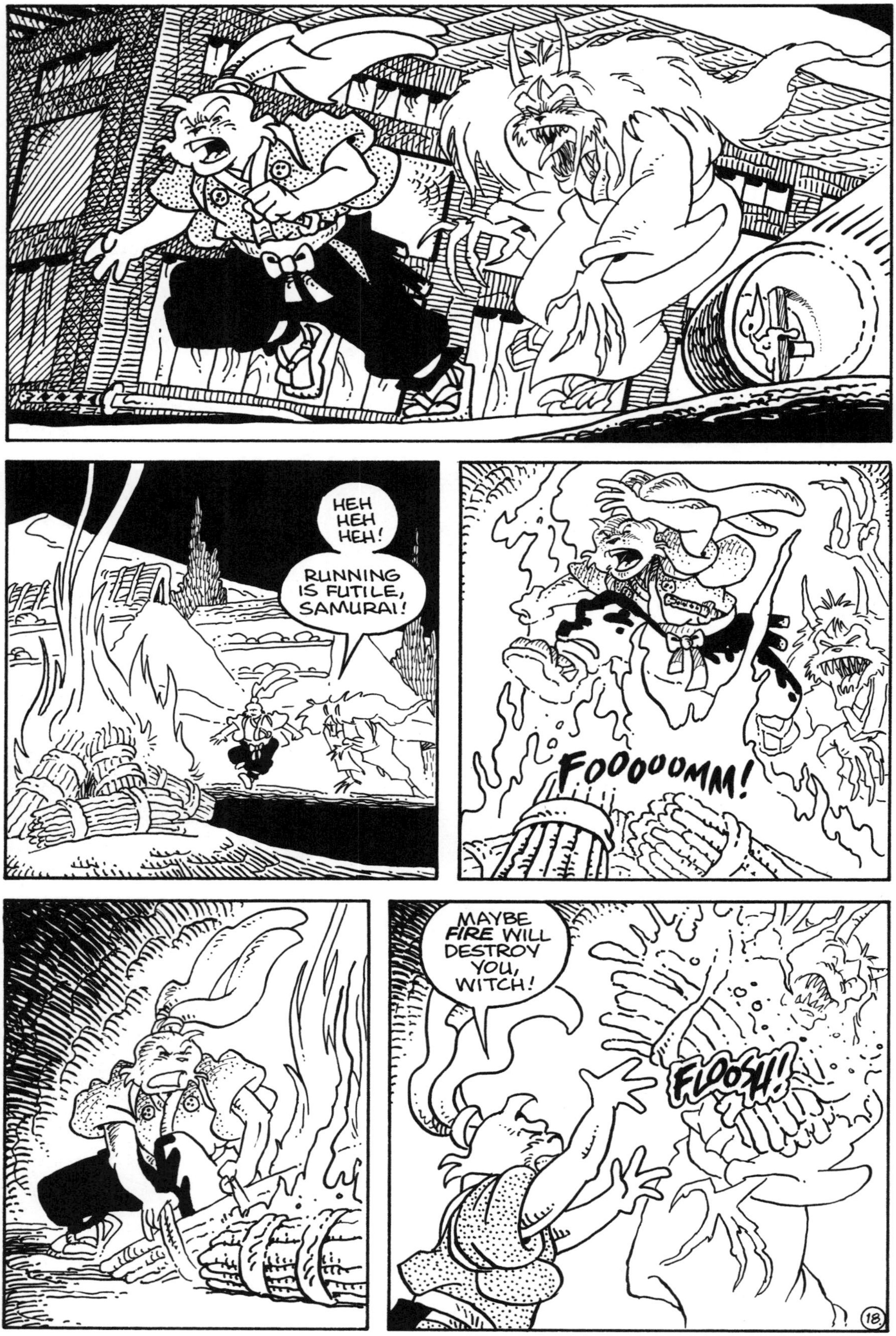
HEH HEH HEH!
RUNNING IS FUTILE, SAMURAI!
FOOOOOMM!
MAYBE FIRE WILL DESTROY YOU, WITCH!
FLOOSH!
18

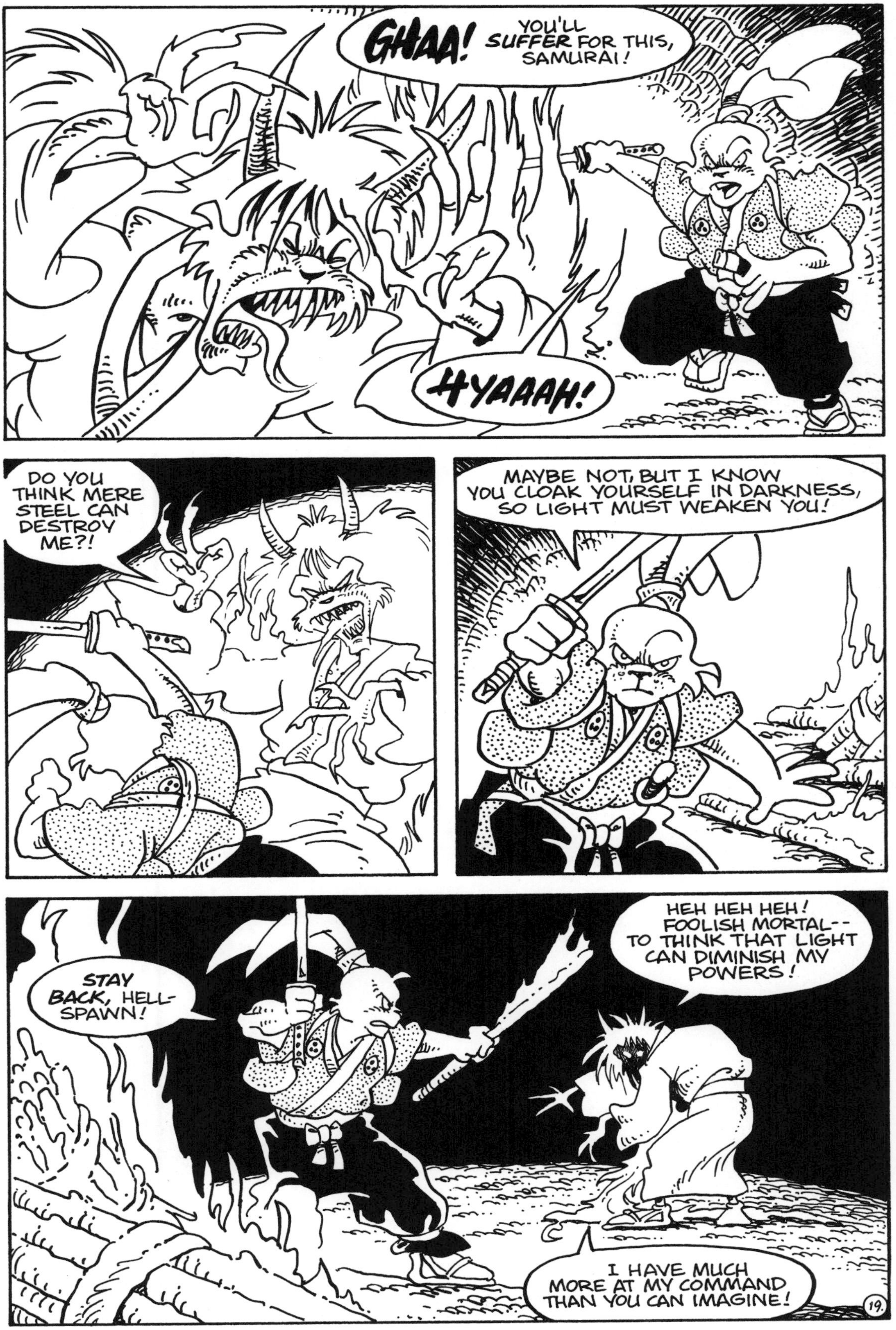
GHAA! YOU'LL SUFFER FOR THIS, SAMURAI!
HYAAAH!
DO YOU THINK MERE STEEL CAN DESTROY ME?!
MAYBE NOT, BUT I KNOW YOU CLOAK YOURSELF IN DARKNESS, SO LIGHT MUST WEAKEN YOU!
STAY BACK, HELL-SPAWN!
HEH HEH HEH! FOOLISH MORTAL-- TO THINK THAT LIGHT CAN DIMINISH MY POWERS!
I HAVE MUCH MORE AT MY COMMAND THAN YOU CAN IMAGINE!
19.

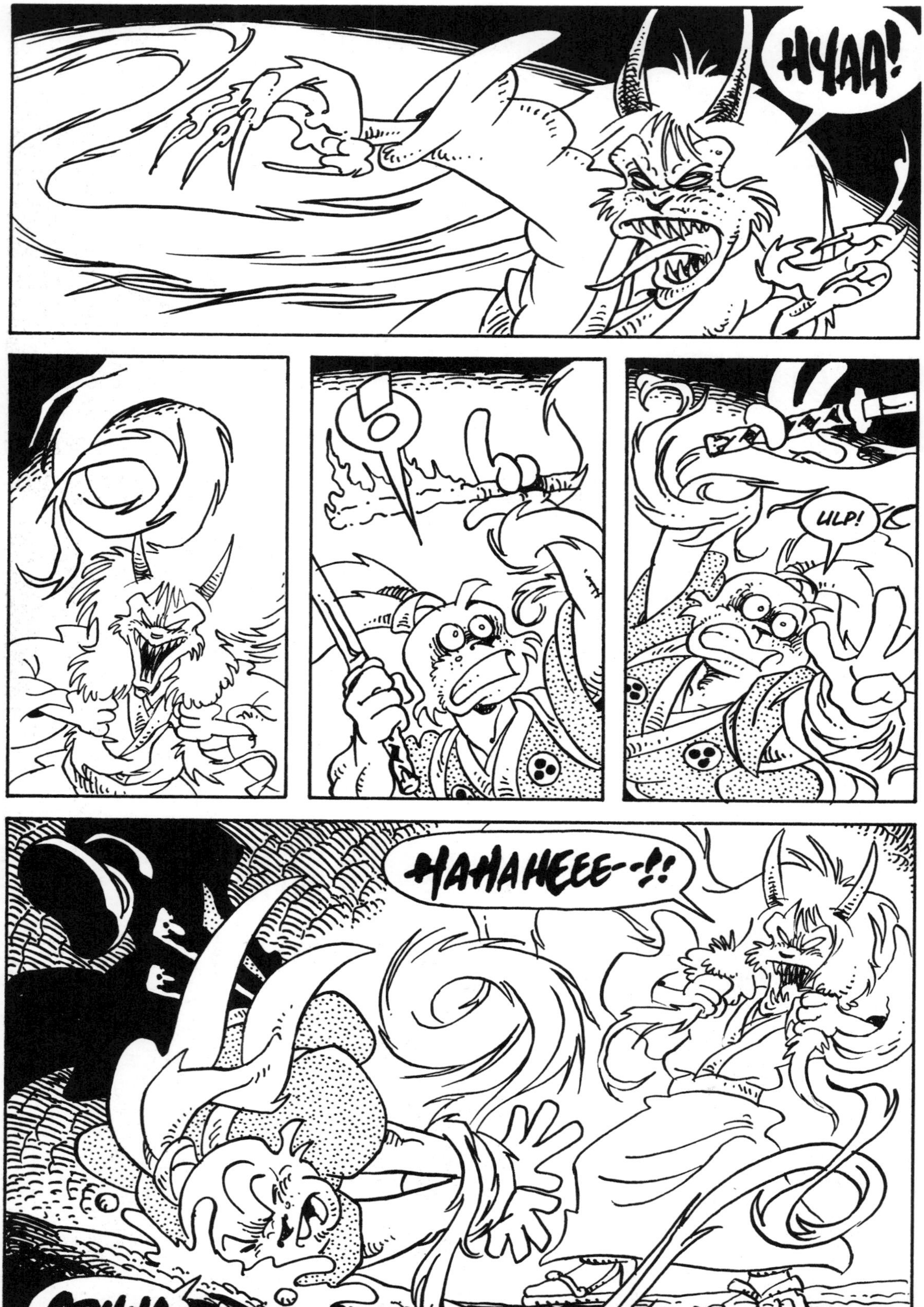
HYAA!
ULP!
HAHAHEEE--!!
ARHH!
20.

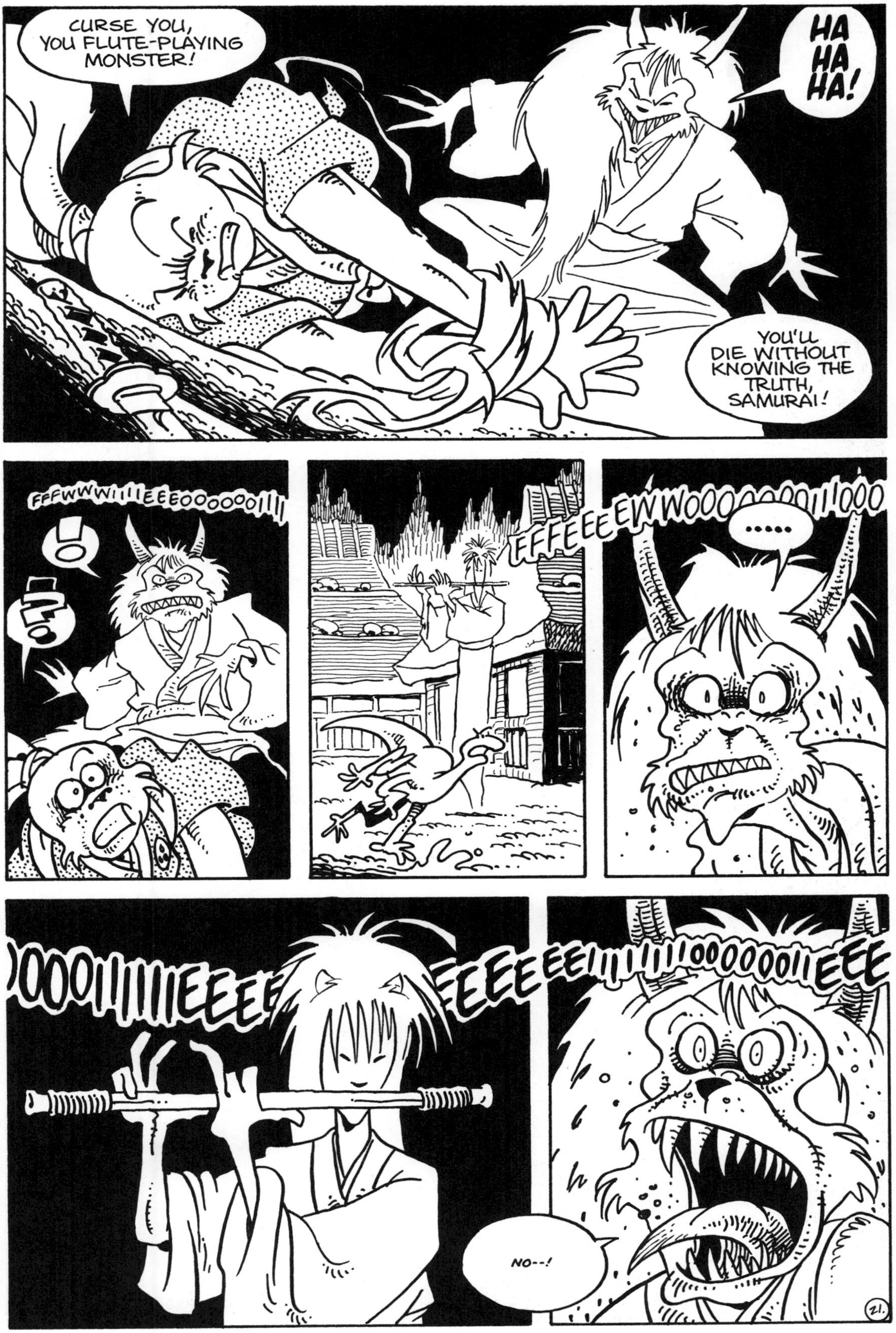
CURSE YOU, YOU FLUTE-PLAYING MONSTER!
HA HA HA!
YOU'LL DIE WITHOUT KNOWING THE TRUTH, SAMURAI!
FFFWWWIIIEEEOOOOOOIIII
!
?!
FFFEEEEWWOOOOOOOIIIOOO
.....
OOOOIIIIIIEEEE
EEEEEEIIIIIIIOOOOOOIIEEE
NO--!
21.

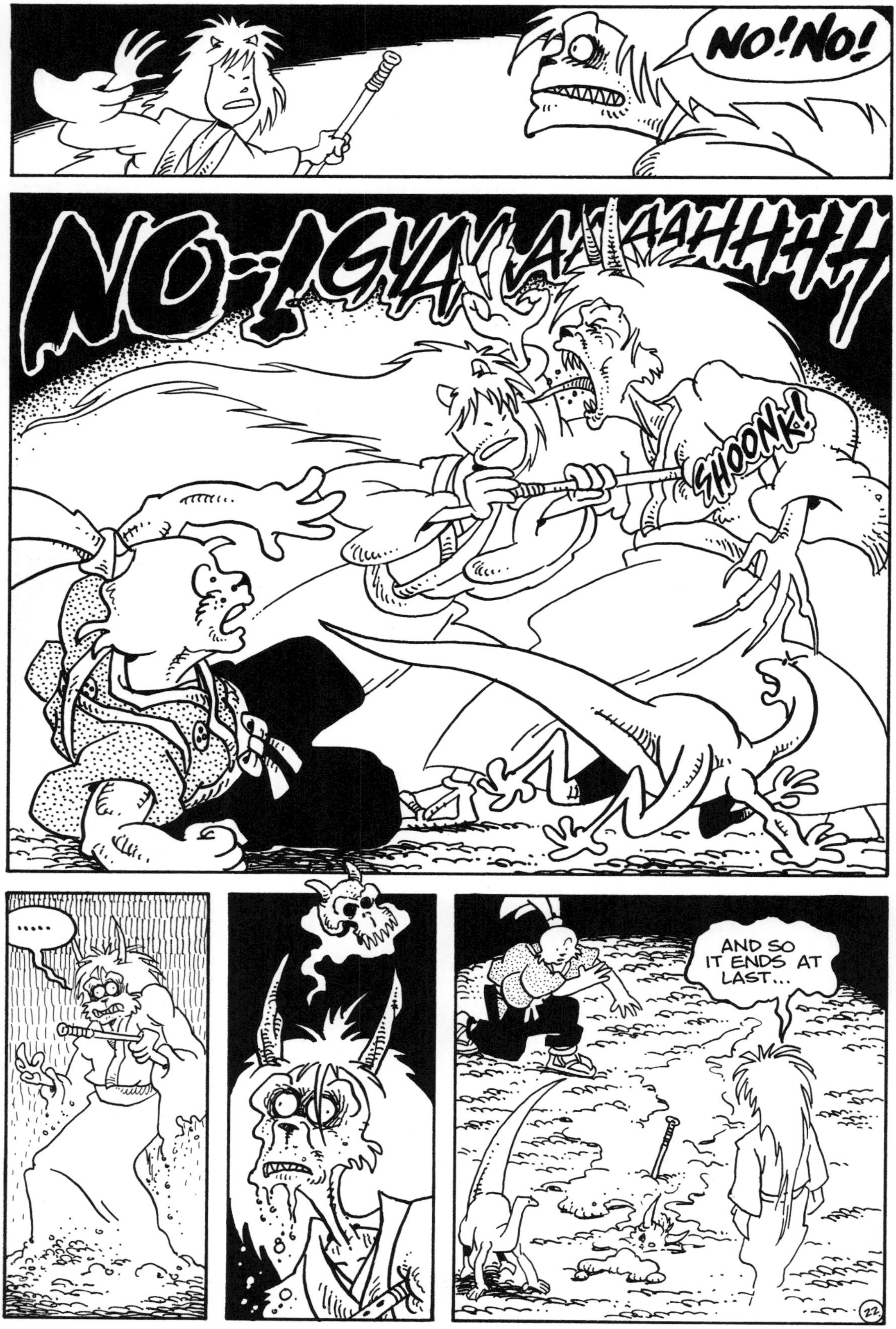

NO! NO!
NO-AGYAAAAAAHHHHH
SHOONK!
.....
AND SO IT ENDS AT LAST...
22.

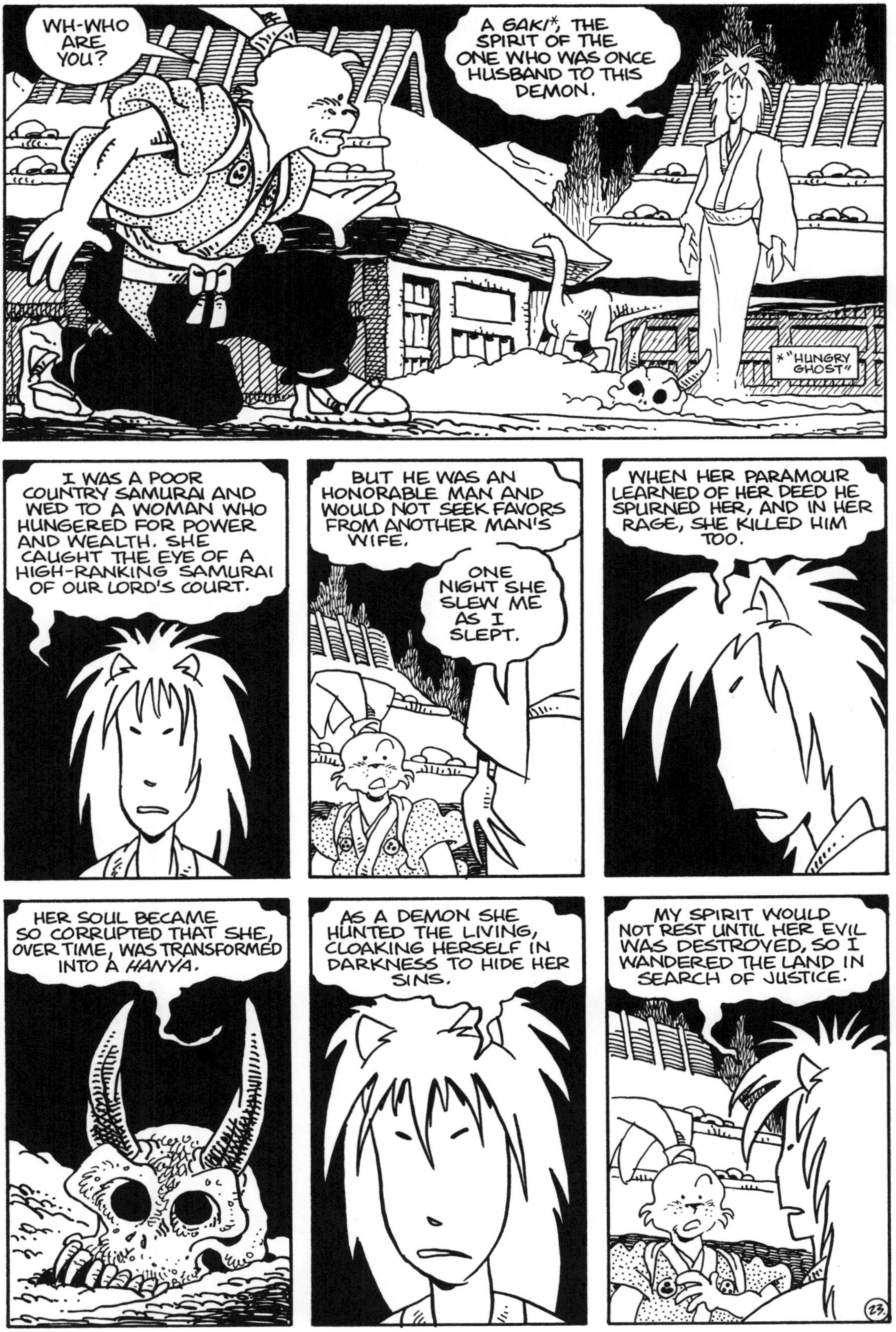
WH-WHO ARE YOU?
A GAKI*, THE SPIRIT OF THE ONE WHO WAS ONCE HUSBAND TO THIS DEMON.
*"HUNGRY GHOST"
I WAS A POOR COUNTRY SAMURAI AND WED TO A WOMAN WHO HUNGERED FOR POWER AND WEALTH. SHE CAUGHT THE EYE OF A HIGH-RANKING SAMURAI OF OUR LORD'S COURT.
BUT HE WAS AN HONORABLE MAN AND WOULD NOT SEEK FAVORS FROM ANOTHER MAN'S WIFE.
ONE NIGHT SHE SLEW ME AS I SLEPT.
WHEN HER PARAMOUR LEARNED OF HER DEED HE SPURNED HER, AND IN HER RAGE, SHE KILLED HIM TOO.
HER SOUL BECAME SO CORRUPTED THAT SHE, OVER TIME, WAS TRANSFORMED INTO A *HANYA*.
AS A DEMON SHE HUNTED THE LIVING, CLOAKING HERSELF IN DARKNESS TO HIDE HER SINS.
MY SPIRIT WOULD NOT REST UNTIL HER EVIL WAS DESTROYED, SO I WANDERED THE LAND IN SEARCH OF JUSTICE.
23.

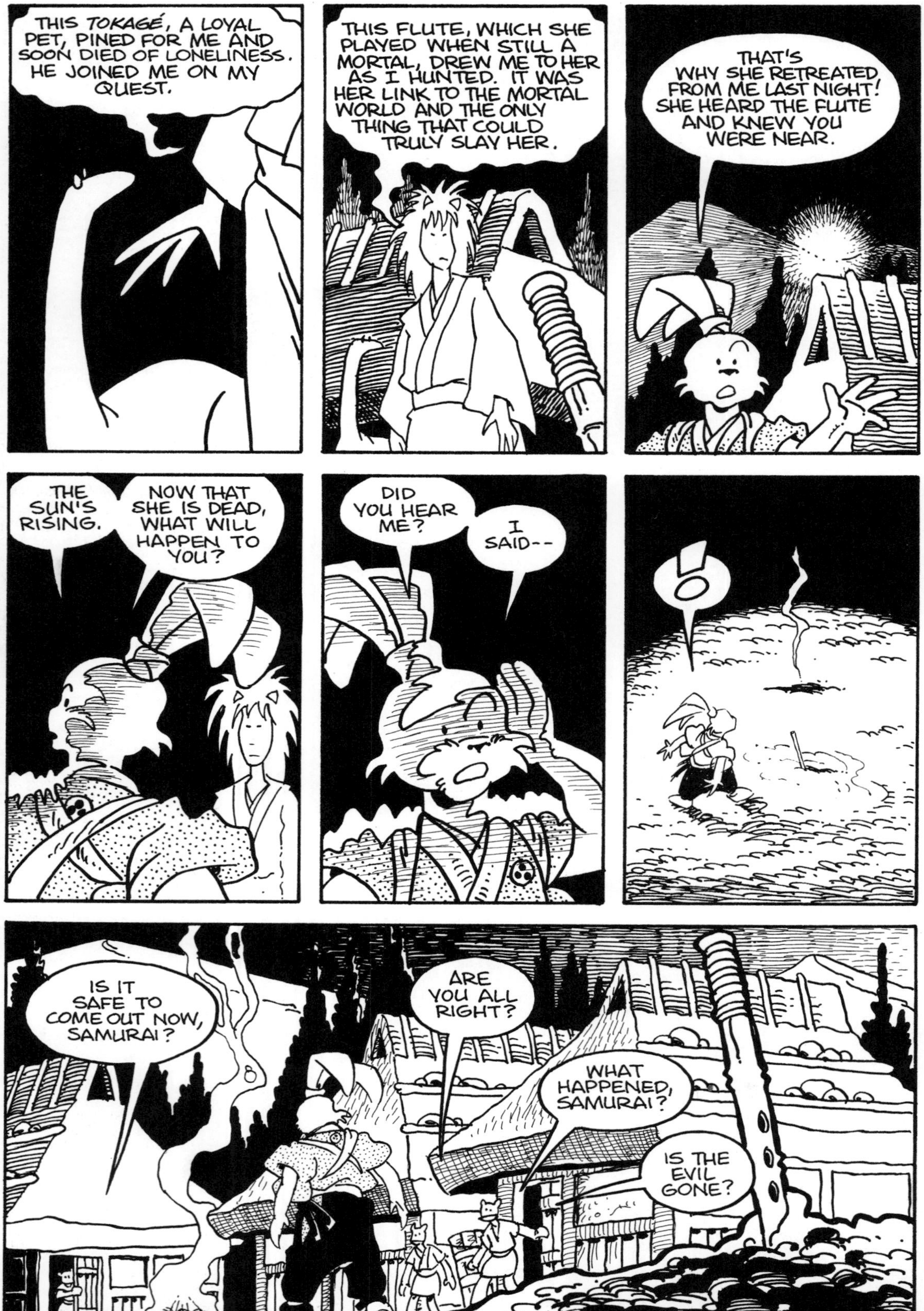
THIS *TOKAGÉ*, A LOYAL PET, PINED FOR ME AND SOON DIED OF LONELINESS. HE JOINED ME ON MY QUEST.
THIS FLUTE, WHICH SHE PLAYED WHEN STILL A MORTAL, DREW ME TO HER AS I HUNTED. IT WAS HER LINK TO THE MORTAL WORLD AND THE ONLY THING THAT COULD TRULY SLAY HER.
THAT'S WHY SHE RETREATED FROM ME LAST NIGHT! SHE HEARD THE FLUTE AND KNEW YOU WERE NEAR.
THE SUN'S RISING.
NOW THAT SHE IS DEAD, WHAT WILL HAPPEN TO YOU?
DID YOU HEAR ME?
I SAID--
!
IS IT SAFE TO COME OUT NOW, SAMURAI?
ARE YOU ALL RIGHT?
WHAT HAPPENED, SAMURAI?
IS THE EVIL GONE?

THE END

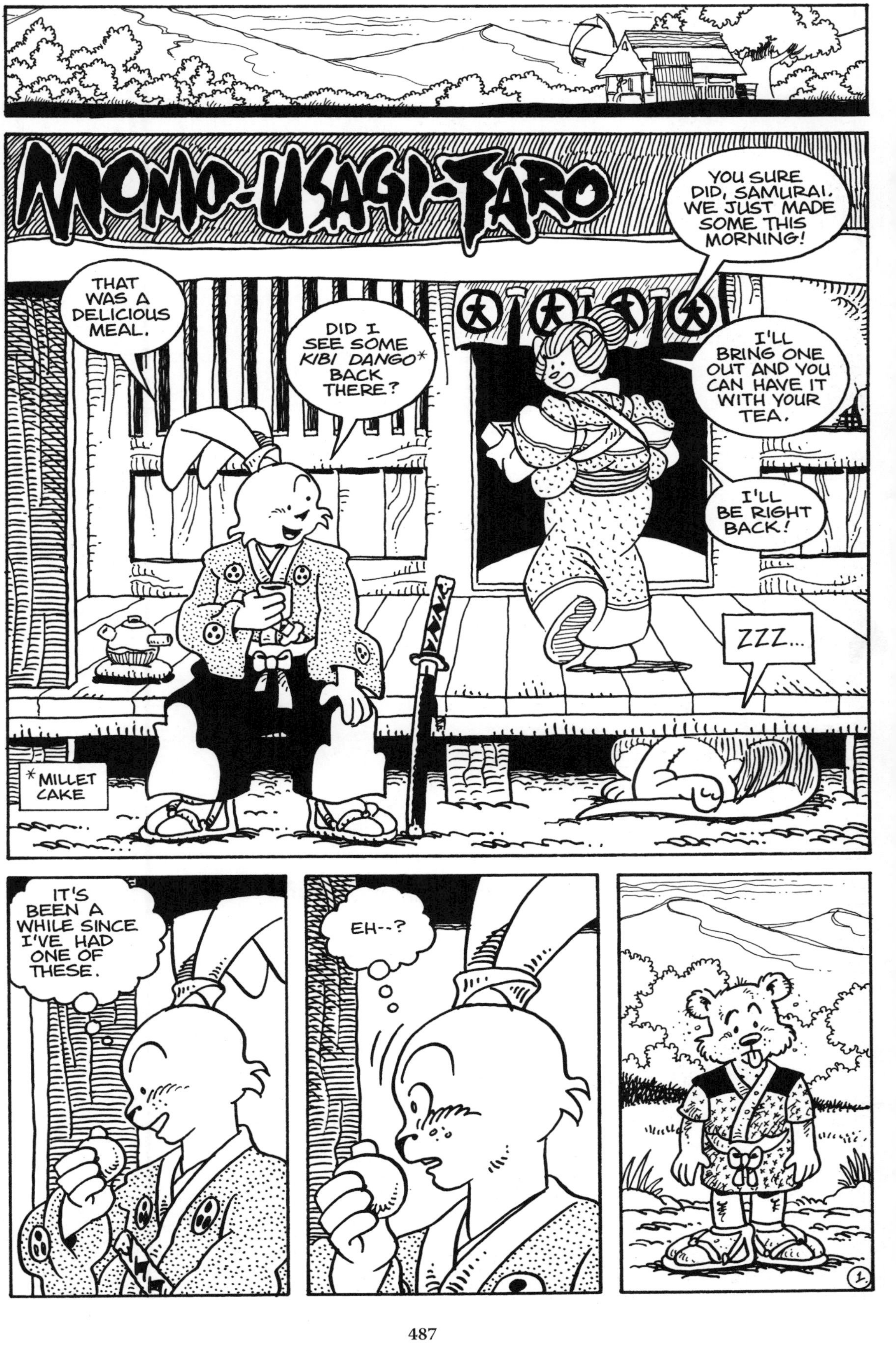
MOMO-USAGI-TARO
THAT WAS A DELICIOUS MEAL.
DID I SEE SOME KIBI DANGO* BACK THERE?
YOU SURE DID, SAMURAI. WE JUST MADE SOME THIS MORNING!
I'LL BRING ONE OUT AND YOU CAN HAVE IT WITH YOUR TEA.
I'LL BE RIGHT BACK!
ZZZ...
*MILLET CAKE
IT'S BEEN A WHILE SINCE I'VE HAD ONE OF THESE.
EH--?

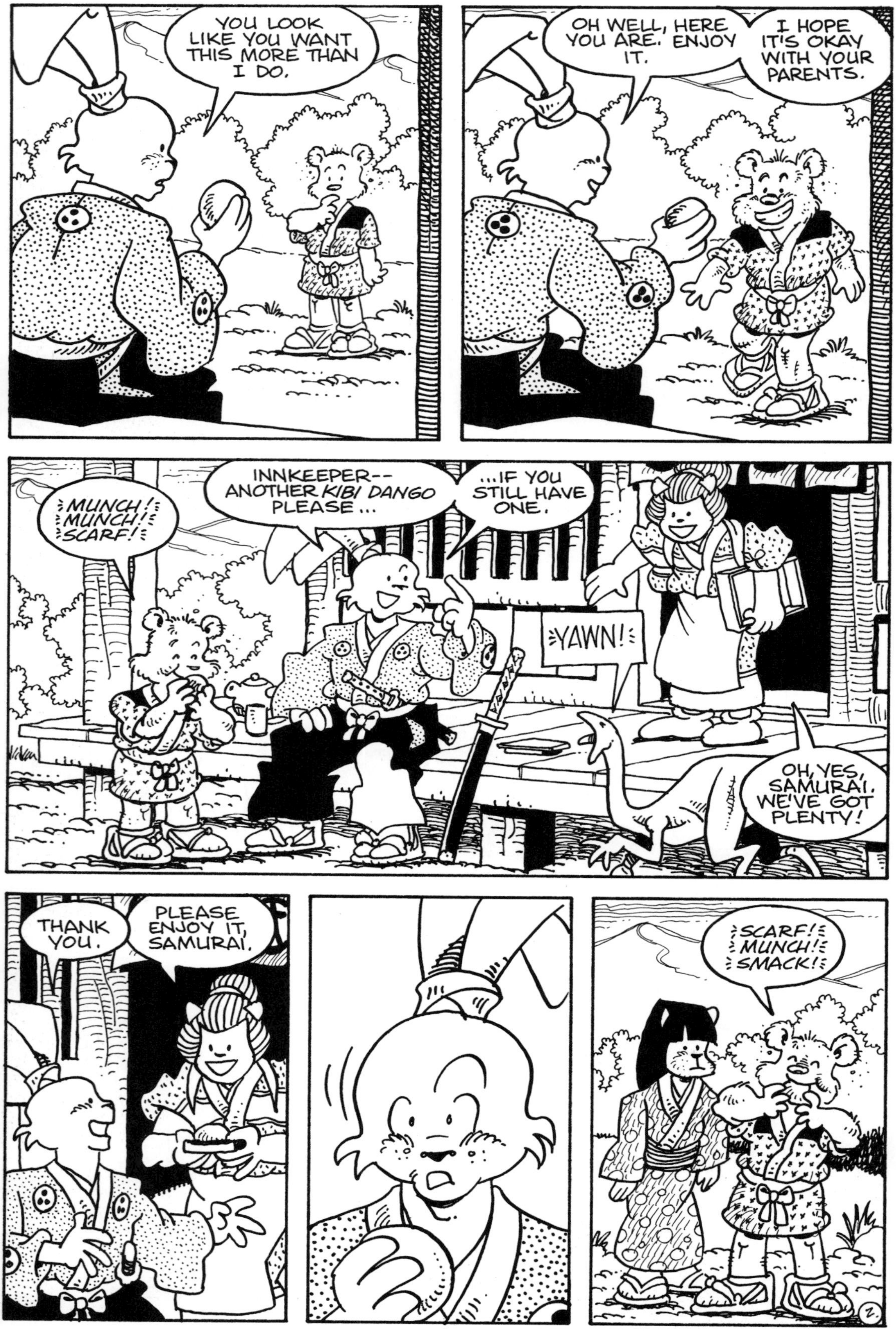
YOU LOOK LIKE YOU WANT THIS MORE THAN I DO.
OH WELL, HERE YOU ARE. ENJOY IT.
I HOPE IT'S OKAY WITH YOUR PARENTS.
MUNCH! MUNCH! SCARF!
INNKEEPER-- ANOTHER KIBI DANGO PLEASE...
...IF YOU STILL HAVE ONE.
YAWN!
OH, YES, SAMURAI. WE'VE GOT PLENTY!
THANK YOU.
PLEASE ENJOY IT, SAMURAI.
SCARF! MUNCH! SMACK!
2.

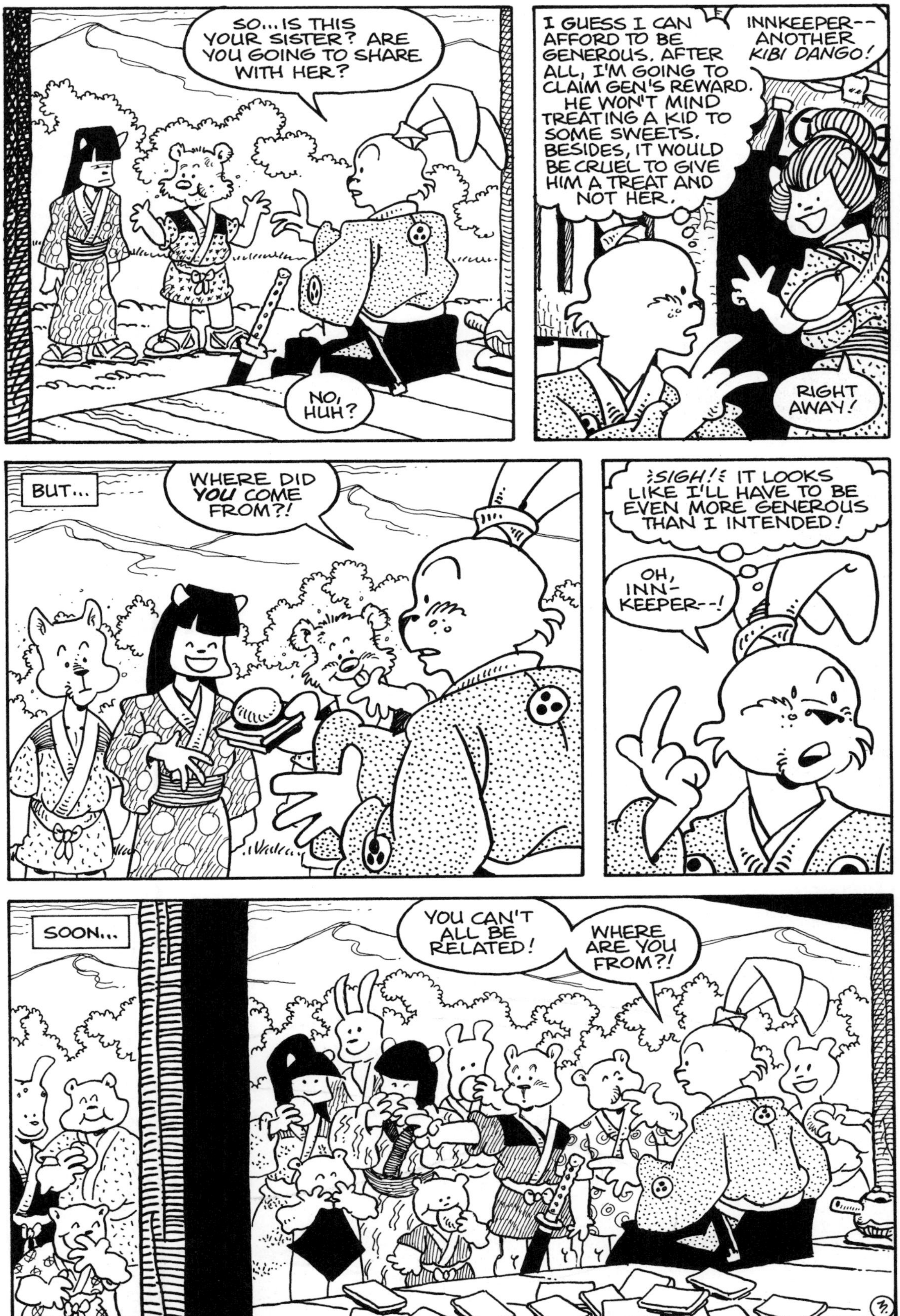
SO... IS THIS YOUR SISTER? ARE YOU GOING TO SHARE WITH HER?
NO, HUH?
I GUESS I CAN AFFORD TO BE GENEROUS. AFTER ALL, I'M GOING TO CLAIM GEN'S REWARD. HE WON'T MIND TREATING A KID TO SOME SWEETS. BESIDES, IT WOULD BE CRUEL TO GIVE HIM A TREAT AND NOT HER.
INNKEEPER-- ANOTHER *KIBI DANGO*!
RIGHT AWAY!
BUT...
WHERE DID ***YOU*** COME FROM?!
SIGH! IT LOOKS LIKE I'LL HAVE TO BE EVEN MORE GENEROUS THAN I INTENDED!
OH, INN-KEEPER--!
SOON...
YOU CAN'T ALL BE RELATED!
WHERE ARE YOU FROM?!

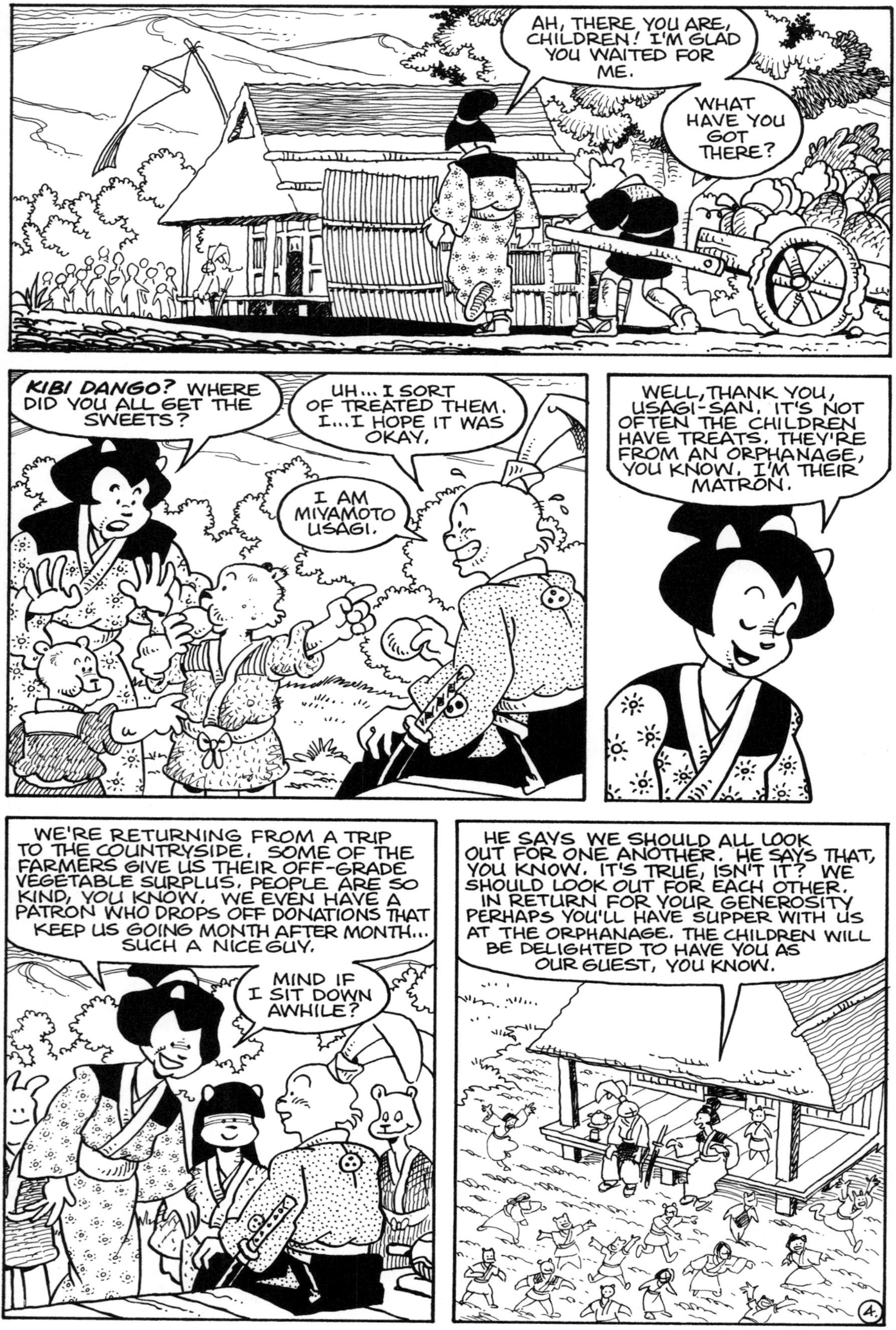
AH, THERE YOU ARE, CHILDREN! I'M GLAD YOU WAITED FOR ME.
WHAT HAVE YOU GOT THERE?
KIBI DANGO? WHERE DID YOU ALL GET THE SWEETS?
UH... I SORT OF TREATED THEM. I...I HOPE IT WAS OKAY.
I AM MIYAMOTO USAGI.
WELL, THANK YOU, USAGI-SAN. IT'S NOT OFTEN THE CHILDREN HAVE TREATS. THEY'RE FROM AN ORPHANAGE, YOU KNOW. I'M THEIR MATRON.
WE'RE RETURNING FROM A TRIP TO THE COUNTRYSIDE. SOME OF THE FARMERS GIVE US THEIR OFF-GRADE VEGETABLE SURPLUS. PEOPLE ARE SO KIND, YOU KNOW. WE EVEN HAVE A PATRON WHO DROPS OFF DONATIONS THAT KEEP US GOING MONTH AFTER MONTH... SUCH A NICE GUY.
MIND IF I SIT DOWN AWHILE?
HE SAYS WE SHOULD ALL LOOK OUT FOR ONE ANOTHER. HE SAYS THAT, YOU KNOW. IT'S TRUE, ISN'T IT? WE SHOULD LOOK OUT FOR EACH OTHER. IN RETURN FOR YOUR GENEROSITY PERHAPS YOU'LL HAVE SUPPER WITH US AT THE ORPHANAGE. THE CHILDREN WILL BE DELIGHTED TO HAVE YOU AS OUR GUEST, YOU KNOW.
4.

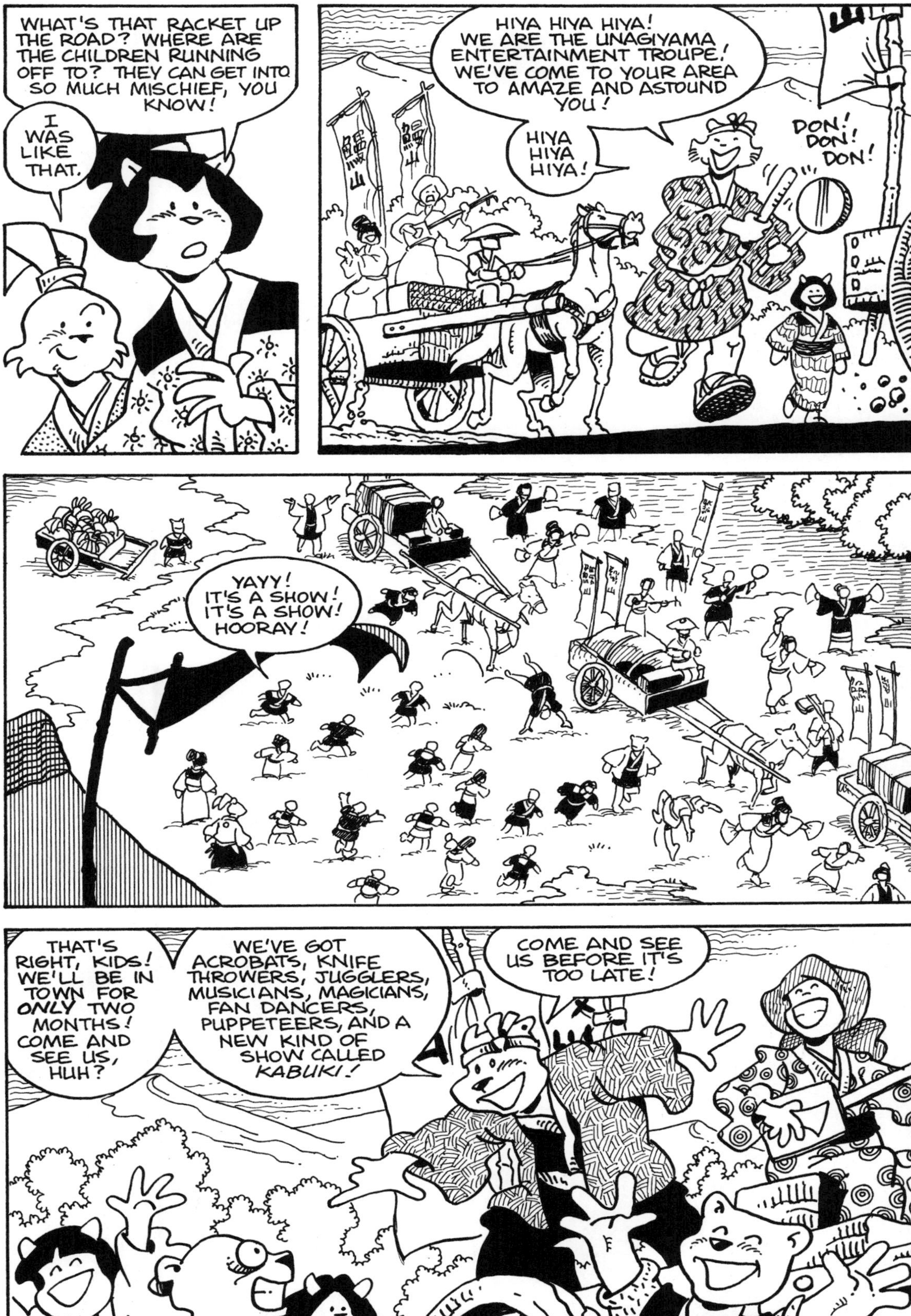
WHAT'S THAT RACKET UP THE ROAD? WHERE ARE THE CHILDREN RUNNING OFF TO? THEY CAN GET INTO SO MUCH MISCHIEF, YOU KNOW!
I WAS LIKE THAT.
HIYA HIYA HIYA! WE ARE THE UNAGIYAMA ENTERTAINMENT TROUPE! WE'VE COME TO YOUR AREA TO AMAZE AND ASTOUND YOU!
HIYA HIYA HIYA!
DON! DON! DON!
YAYY! IT'S A SHOW! IT'S A SHOW! HOORAY!
THAT'S RIGHT, KIDS! WE'LL BE IN TOWN FOR ONLY TWO MONTHS! COME AND SEE US, HUH?
WE'VE GOT ACROBATS, KNIFE THROWERS, JUGGLERS, MUSICIANS, MAGICIANS, FAN DANCERS, PUPPETEERS, AND A NEW KIND OF SHOW CALLED KABUKI!
COME AND SEE US BEFORE IT'S TOO LATE!
5.

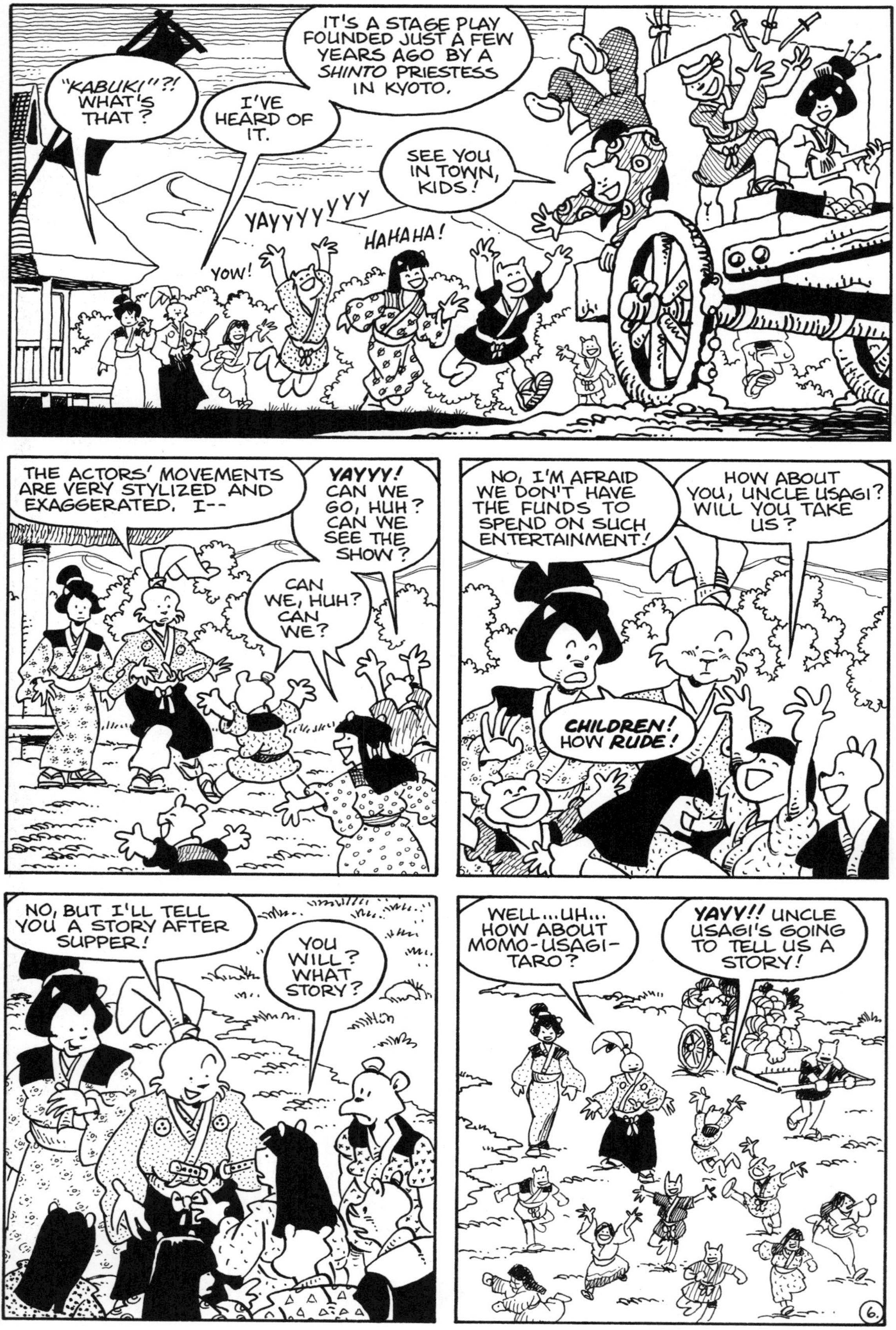
"KABUKI"?! WHAT'S THAT?
I'VE HEARD OF IT.
IT'S A STAGE PLAY FOUNDED JUST A FEW YEARS AGO BY A *SHINTO* PRIESTESS IN KYOTO.
SEE YOU IN TOWN, KIDS!
YAYYYYYYY
HAHAHA!
YOW!
THE ACTORS' MOVEMENTS ARE VERY STYLIZED AND EXAGGERATED. I--
YAYYY! CAN WE GO, HUH? CAN WE SEE THE SHOW?
CAN WE, HUH? CAN WE?
NO, I'M AFRAID WE DON'T HAVE THE FUNDS TO SPEND ON SUCH ENTERTAINMENT!
HOW ABOUT YOU, UNCLE USAGI? WILL YOU TAKE US?
CHILDREN! HOW **RUDE!**
NO, BUT I'LL TELL YOU A STORY AFTER SUPPER!
YOU WILL? WHAT STORY?
WELL...UH... HOW ABOUT MOMO-USAGI-TARO?
YAYY!! UNCLE USAGI'S GOING TO TELL US A STORY!
6.

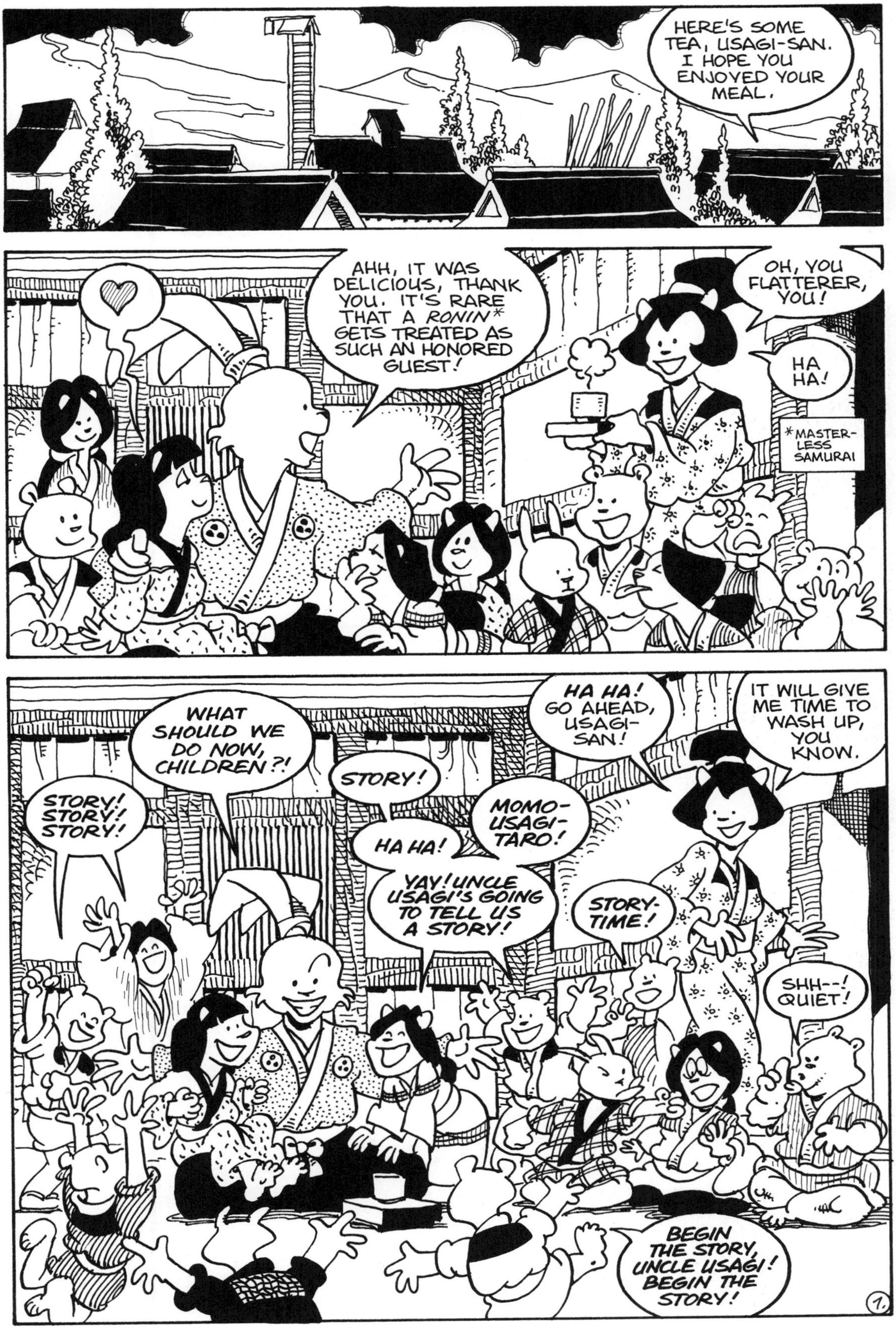
HERE'S SOME TEA, USAGI-SAN. I HOPE YOU ENJOYED YOUR MEAL.
AHH, IT WAS DELICIOUS, THANK YOU. IT'S RARE THAT A *RONIN** GETS TREATED AS SUCH AN HONORED GUEST!
OH, YOU FLATTERER, YOU!
HA HA!
*MASTER-LESS SAMURAI
WHAT SHOULD WE DO NOW, CHILDREN?!
STORY! STORY! STORY!
STORY!
HA HA!
MOMO-USAGI-TARO!
YAY! UNCLE USAGI'S GOING TO TELL US A STORY!
HA HA! GO AHEAD, USAGI-SAN!
IT WILL GIVE ME TIME TO WASH UP, YOU KNOW.
STORY-TIME!
SHH--! QUIET!
BEGIN THE STORY, UNCLE USAGI! BEGIN THE STORY!
1.

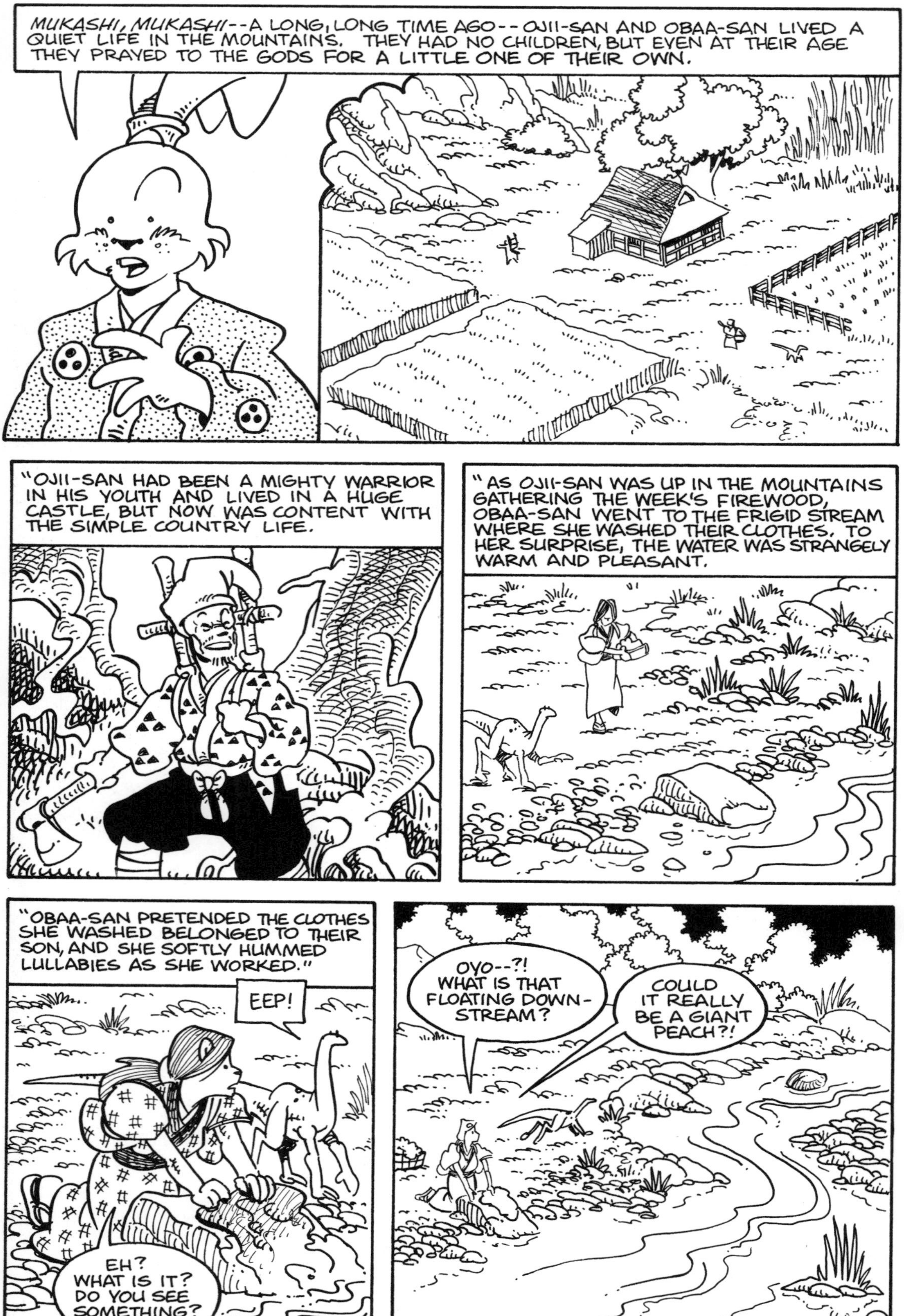
MUKASHI, MUKASHI--A LONG, LONG TIME AGO--OJII-SAN AND OBAA-SAN LIVED A QUIET LIFE IN THE MOUNTAINS. THEY HAD NO CHILDREN, BUT EVEN AT THEIR AGE THEY PRAYED TO THE GODS FOR A LITTLE ONE OF THEIR OWN.
"OJII-SAN HAD BEEN A MIGHTY WARRIOR IN HIS YOUTH AND LIVED IN A HUGE CASTLE, BUT NOW WAS CONTENT WITH THE SIMPLE COUNTRY LIFE.
"AS OJII-SAN WAS UP IN THE MOUNTAINS GATHERING THE WEEK'S FIREWOOD, OBAA-SAN WENT TO THE FRIGID STREAM WHERE SHE WASHED THEIR CLOTHES. TO HER SURPRISE, THE WATER WAS STRANGELY WARM AND PLEASANT.
"OBAA-SAN PRETENDED THE CLOTHES SHE WASHED BELONGED TO THEIR SON, AND SHE SOFTLY HUMMED LULLABIES AS SHE WORKED."
EEP!
EH? WHAT IS IT? DO YOU SEE SOMETHING?
OYO--?! WHAT IS THAT FLOATING DOWN-STREAM?
COULD IT REALLY BE A GIANT PEACH?!
8

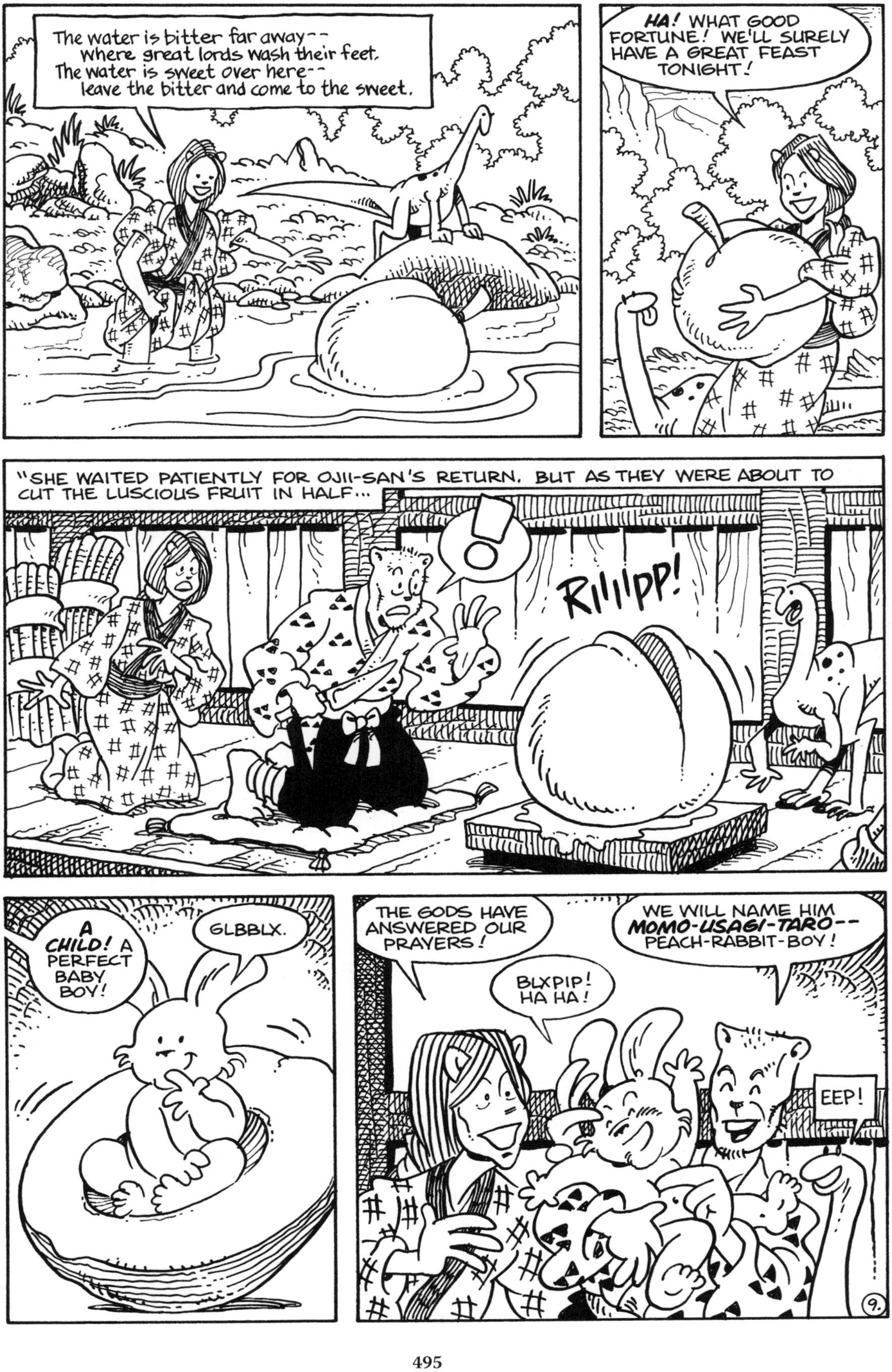

The water is bitter far away-- where great lords wash their feet. The water is sweet over here-- leave the bitter and come to the sweet.
HA! WHAT GOOD FORTUNE! WE'LL SURELY HAVE A GREAT FEAST TONIGHT!
"SHE WAITED PATIENTLY FOR OJII-SAN'S RETURN. BUT AS THEY WERE ABOUT TO CUT THE LUSCIOUS FRUIT IN HALF...
!
RIIIPP!
A CHILD! A PERFECT BABY BOY!
GLBBLX.
THE GODS HAVE ANSWERED OUR PRAYERS!
BLXPIP! HA HA!
WE WILL NAME HIM MOMO-USAGI-TARO-- PEACH-RABBIT-BOY!
EEP!
9.

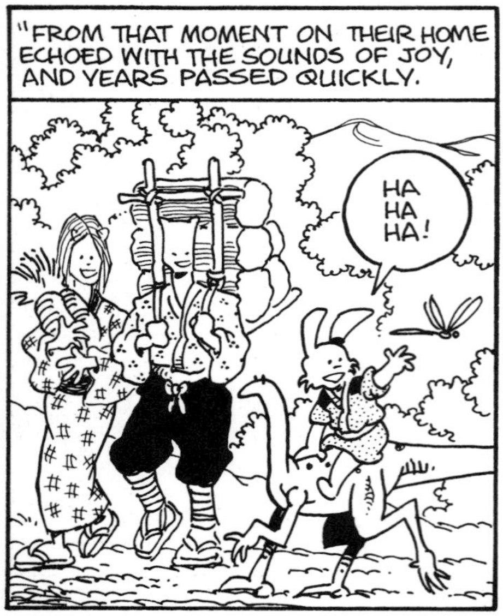
"FROM THAT MOMENT ON THEIR HOME ECHOED WITH THE SOUNDS OF JOY, AND YEARS PASSED QUICKLY.
HA HA HA!

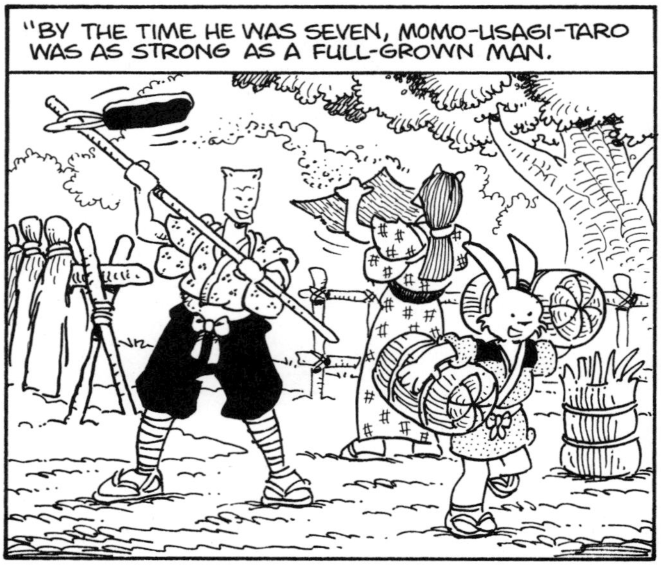
"BY THE TIME HE WAS SEVEN, MOMO-USAGI-TARO WAS AS STRONG AS A FULL-GROWN MAN.

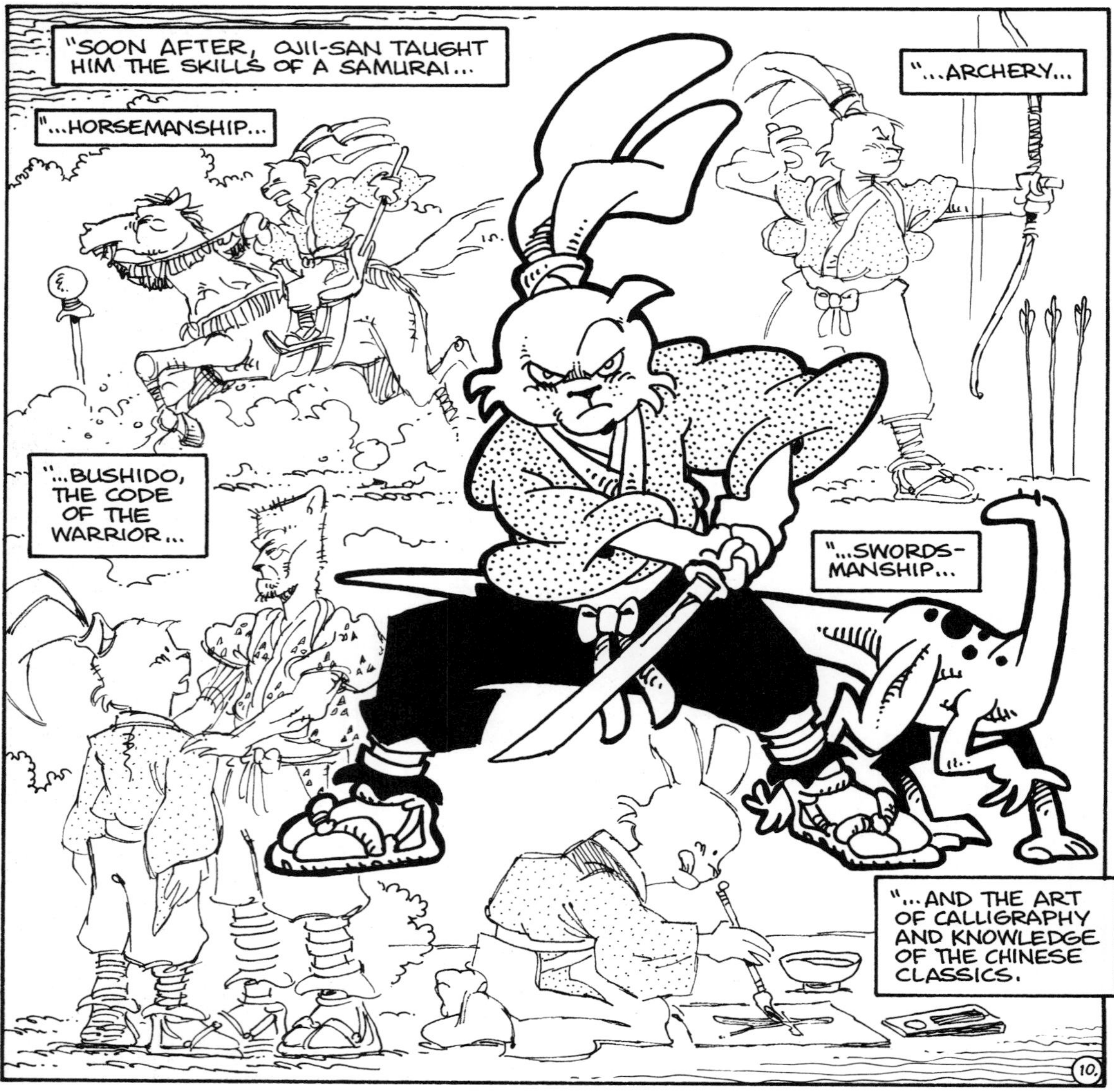
"SOON AFTER, OJII-SAN TAUGHT HIM THE SKILLS OF A SAMURAI...
"...HORSEMANSHIP...
"...ARCHERY...
"...BUSHIDO, THE CODE OF THE WARRIOR...
"...SWORDS-MANSHIP...
"...AND THE ART OF CALLIGRAPHY AND KNOWLEDGE OF THE CHINESE CLASSICS.
10.

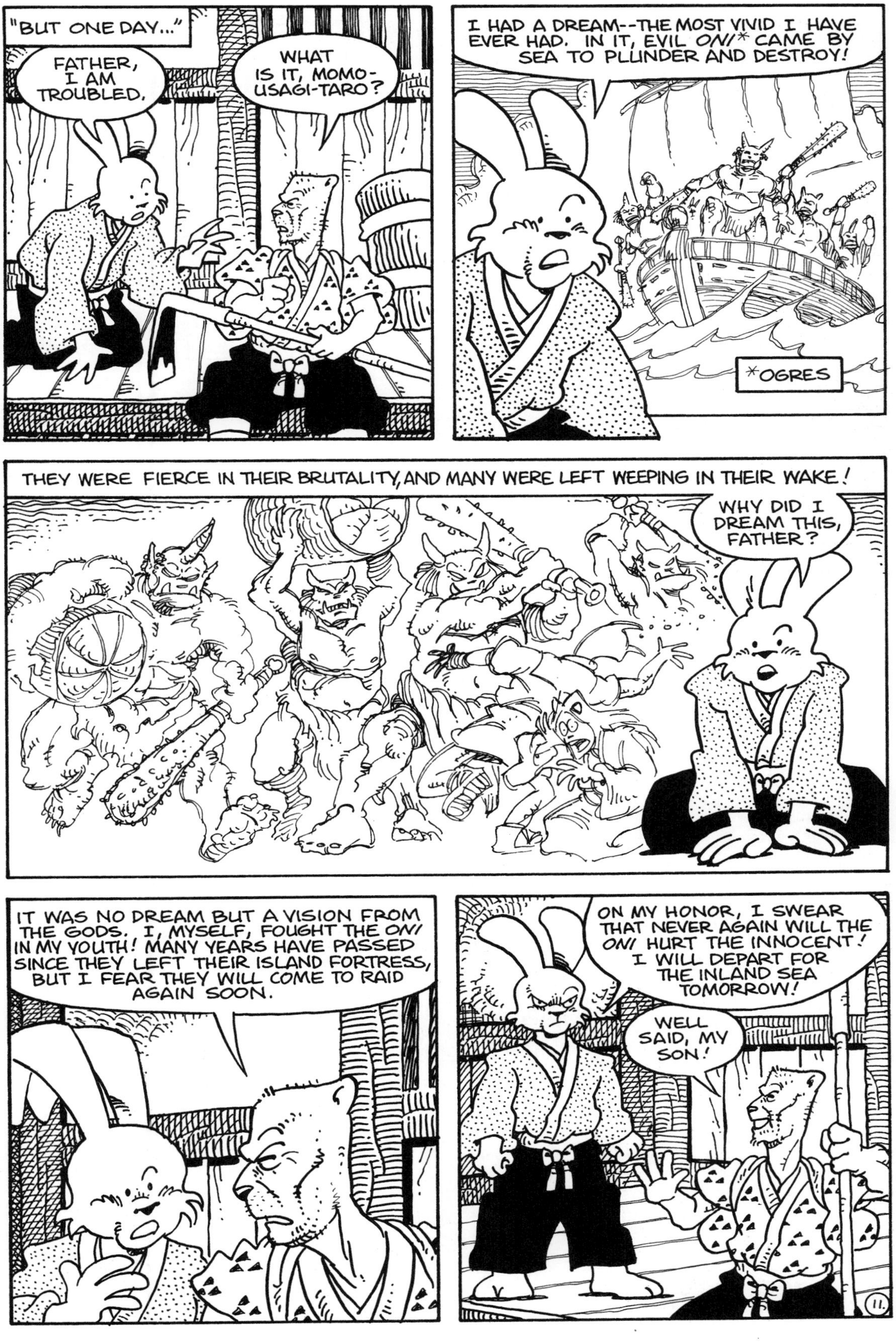
"BUT ONE DAY..."
FATHER, I AM TROUBLED.
WHAT IS IT, MOMO-USAGI-TARO?
I HAD A DREAM--THE MOST VIVID I HAVE EVER HAD. IN IT, EVIL ONI* CAME BY SEA TO PLUNDER AND DESTROY!
*OGRES
THEY WERE FIERCE IN THEIR BRUTALITY, AND MANY WERE LEFT WEEPING IN THEIR WAKE!
WHY DID I DREAM THIS, FATHER?
IT WAS NO DREAM BUT A VISION FROM THE GODS. I, MYSELF, FOUGHT THE ONI IN MY YOUTH! MANY YEARS HAVE PASSED SINCE THEY LEFT THEIR ISLAND FORTRESS, BUT I FEAR THEY WILL COME TO RAID AGAIN SOON.
ON MY HONOR, I SWEAR THAT NEVER AGAIN WILL THE ONI HURT THE INNOCENT! I WILL DEPART FOR THE INLAND SEA TOMORROW!
WELL SAID, MY SON!
11.

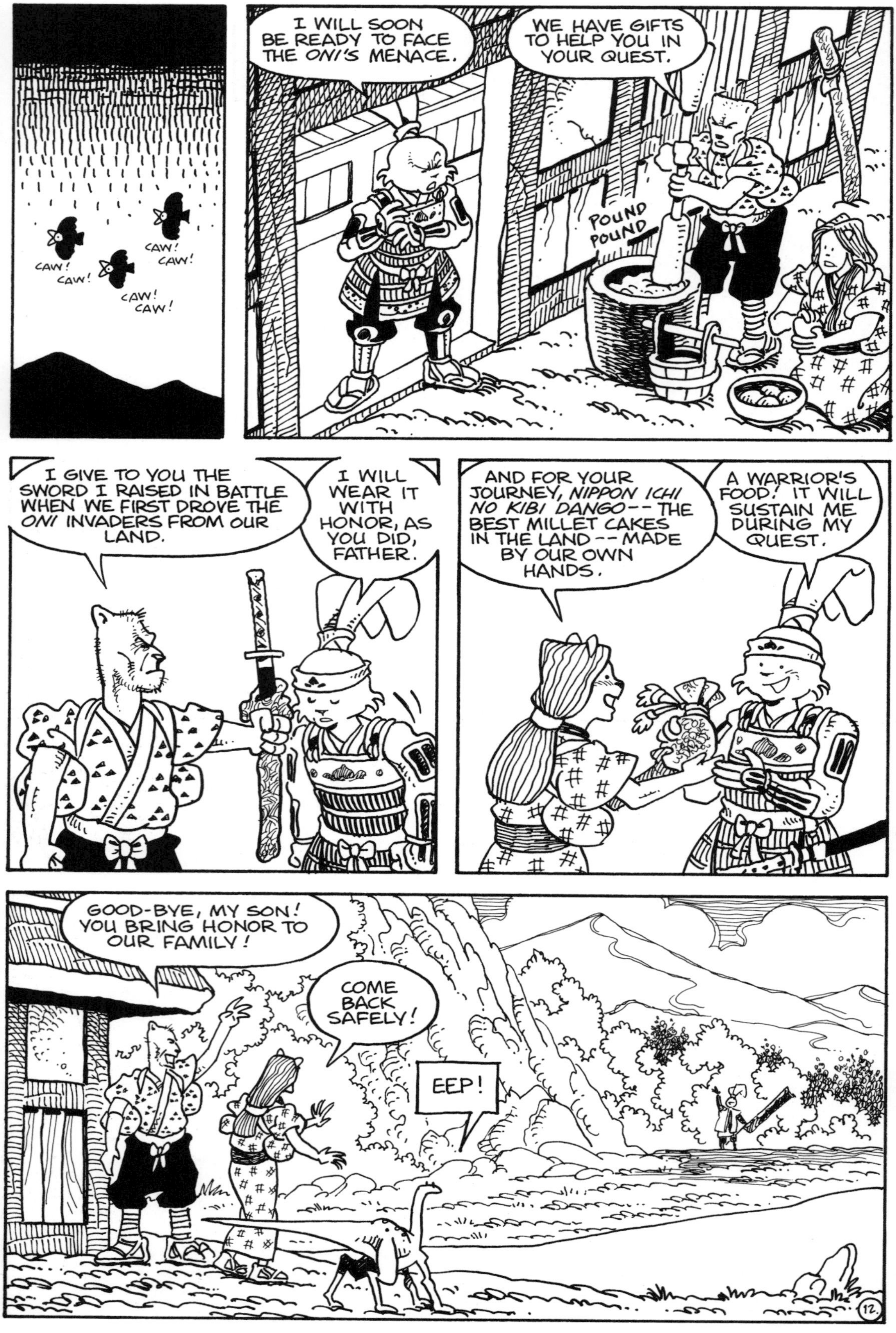
CAW! CAW!
CAW! CAW!
CAW! CAW!
I WILL SOON BE READY TO FACE THE *ONI'S* MENACE.
WE HAVE GIFTS TO HELP YOU IN YOUR QUEST.
POUND POUND
I GIVE TO YOU THE SWORD I RAISED IN BATTLE WHEN WE FIRST DROVE THE *ONI* INVADERS FROM OUR LAND.
I WILL WEAR IT WITH HONOR, AS YOU DID, FATHER.
AND FOR YOUR JOURNEY, *NIPPON ICHI NO KIBI DANGO*-- THE BEST MILLET CAKES IN THE LAND -- MADE BY OUR OWN HANDS.
A WARRIOR'S FOOD! IT WILL SUSTAIN ME DURING MY QUEST.
GOOD-BYE, MY SON! YOU BRING HONOR TO OUR FAMILY!
COME BACK SAFELY!
EEP!
12.

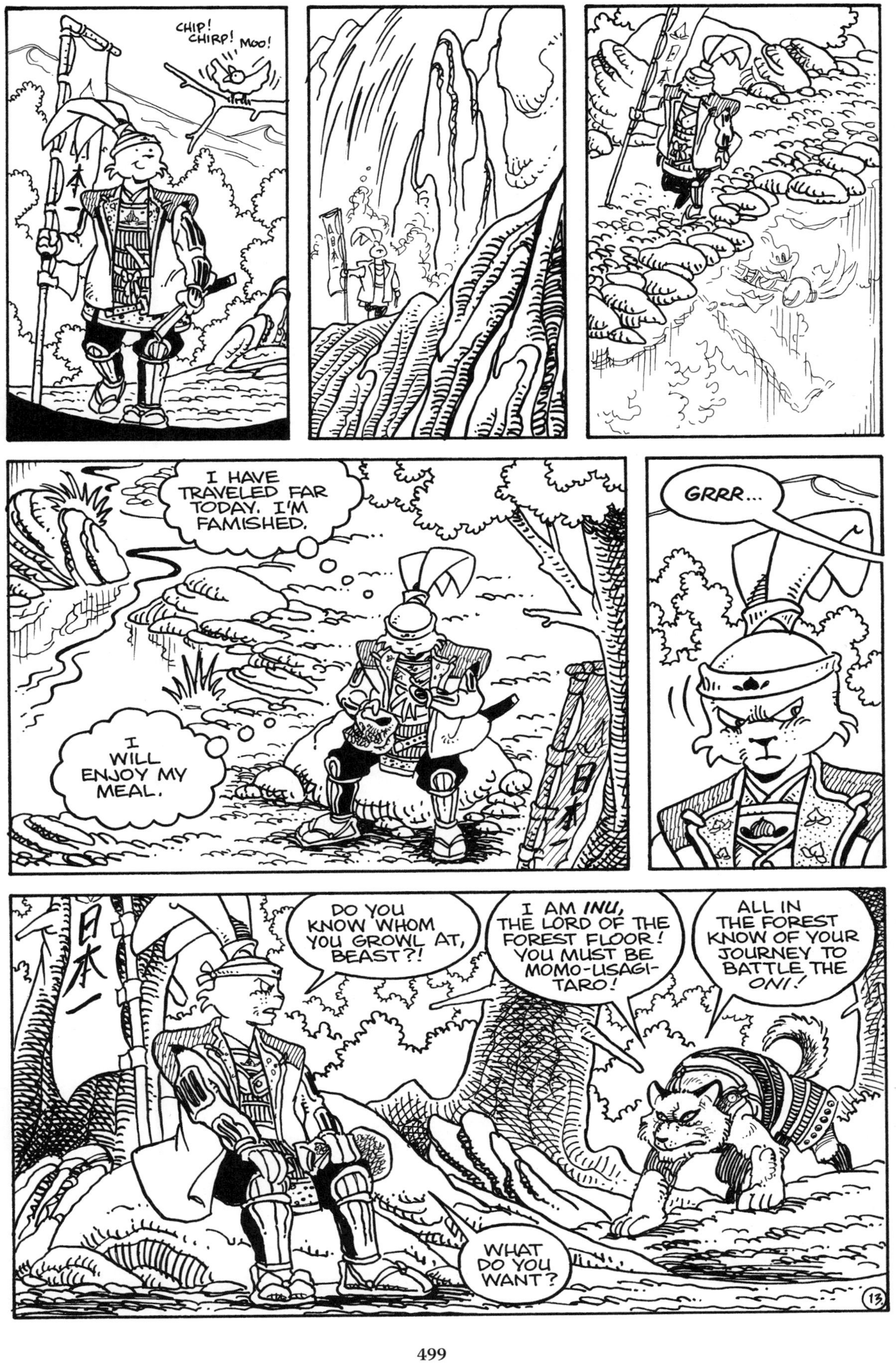
CHIP! CHIRP! MOO!
I HAVE TRAVELED FAR TODAY. I'M FAMISHED.
I WILL ENJOY MY MEAL.
GRRR...
DO YOU KNOW WHOM YOU GROWL AT, BEAST?!
I AM INU, THE LORD OF THE FOREST FLOOR! YOU MUST BE MOMO-USAGI-TARO!
ALL IN THE FOREST KNOW OF YOUR JOURNEY TO BATTLE THE ONI!
WHAT DO YOU WANT?
13

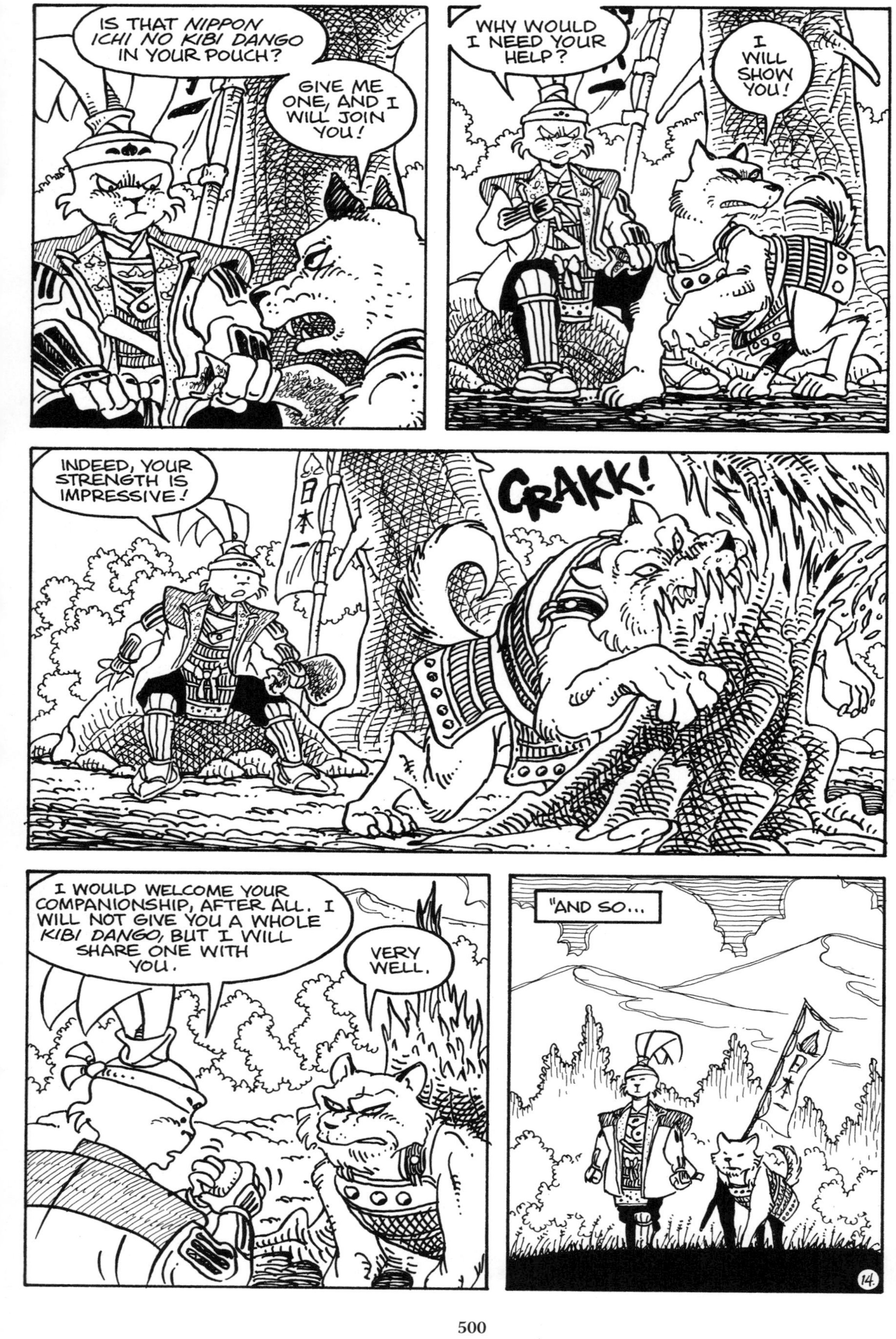
IS THAT *NIPPON ICHI NO KIBI DANGO* IN YOUR POUCH?
GIVE ME ONE, AND I WILL JOIN YOU!
WHY WOULD I NEED YOUR HELP?
I WILL SHOW YOU!
INDEED, YOUR STRENGTH IS IMPRESSIVE!
CRAKK!
I WOULD WELCOME YOUR COMPANIONSHIP, AFTER ALL. I WILL NOT GIVE YOU A WHOLE *KIBI DANGO*, BUT I WILL SHARE ONE WITH YOU.
VERY WELL.
"AND SO...
14.

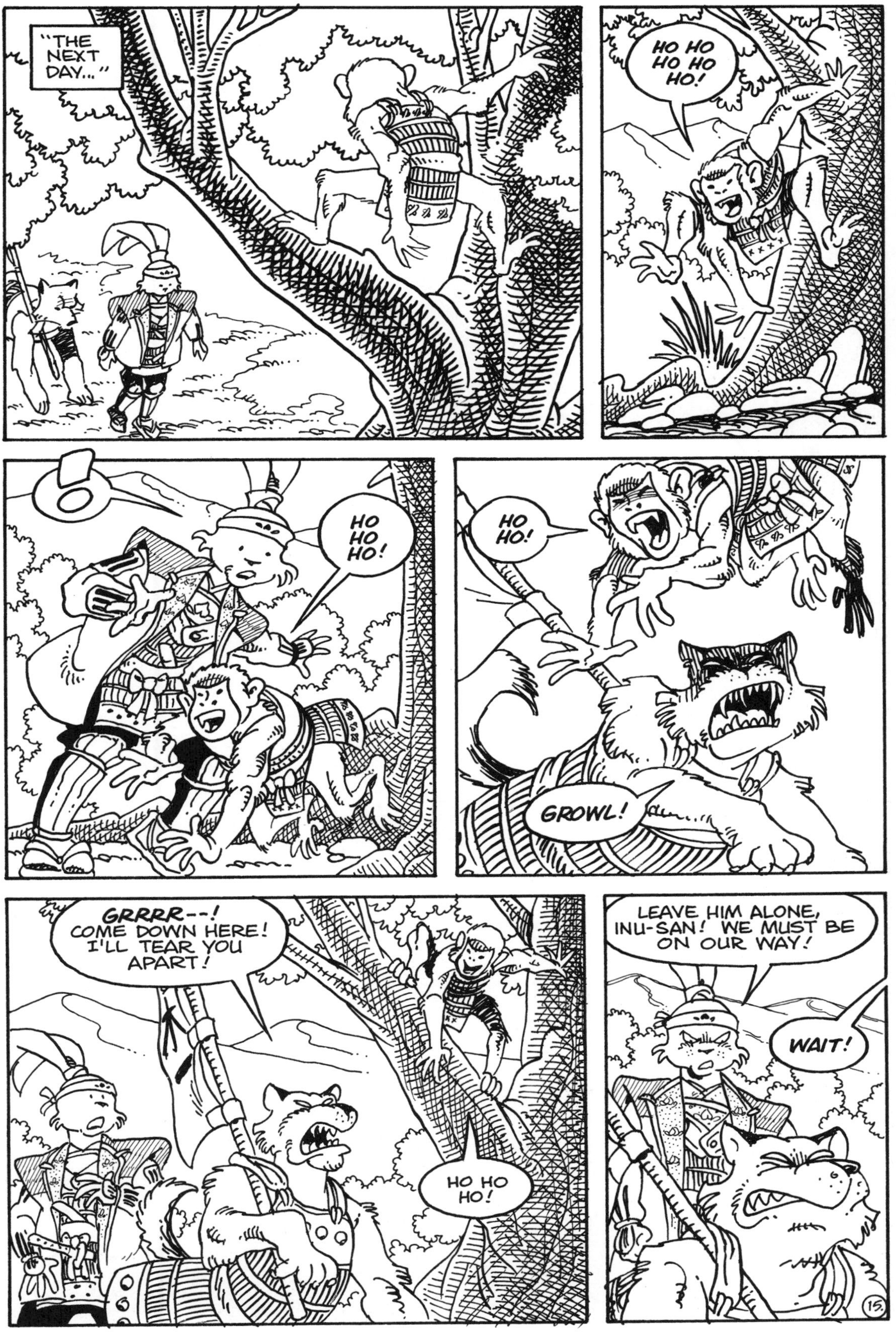
"THE NEXT DAY..."
HO HO HO HO HO!
!
HO HO HO!
HO HO!
GROWL!
GRRRR--! COME DOWN HERE! I'LL TEAR YOU APART!
HO HO HO!
LEAVE HIM ALONE, INU-SAN! WE MUST BE ON OUR WAY!
WAIT!
15.

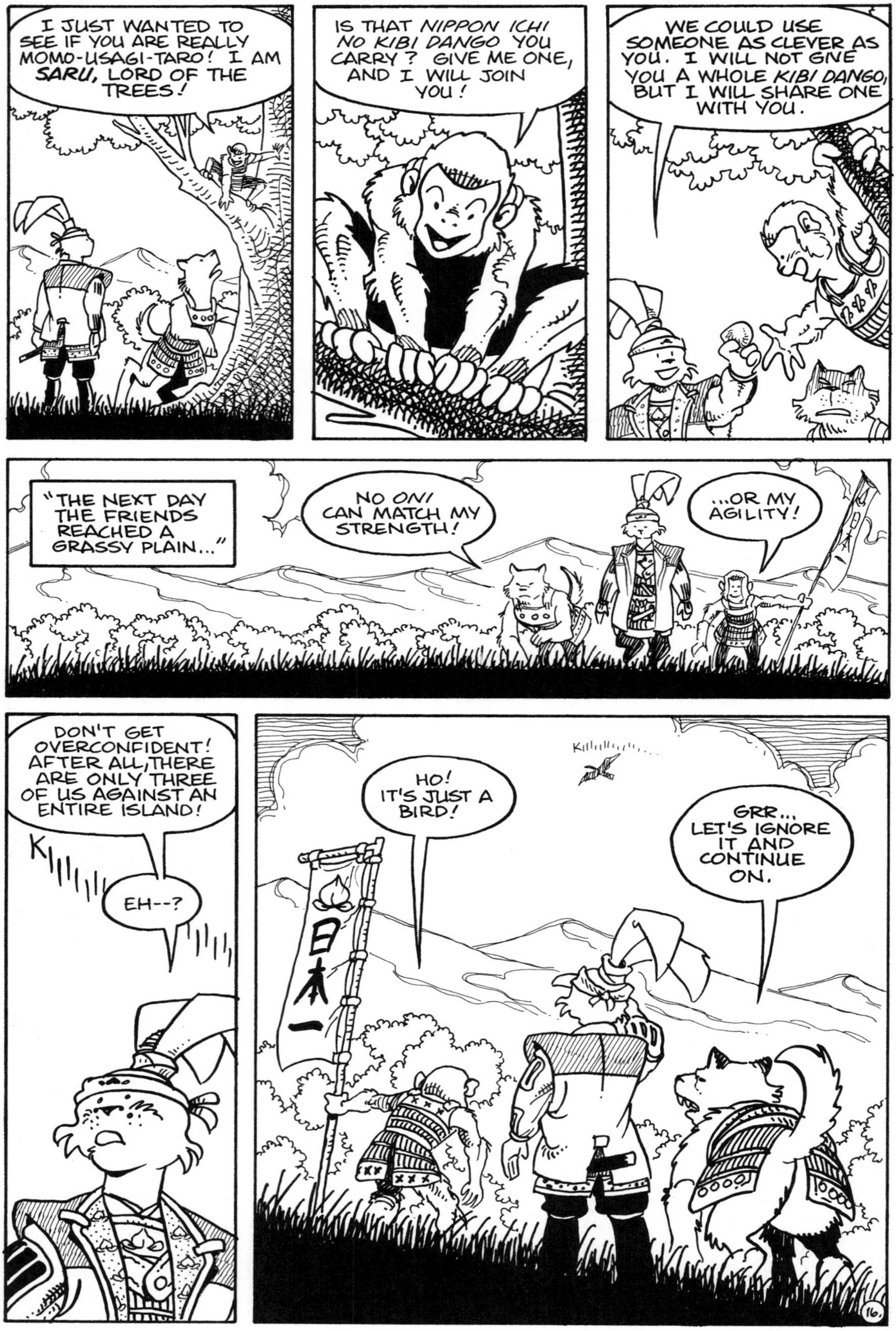
I JUST WANTED TO SEE IF YOU ARE REALLY MOMO-USAGI-TARO! I AM **SARU**, LORD OF THE TREES!
IS THAT *NIPPON ICHI NO KIBI DANGO* YOU CARRY? GIVE ME ONE, AND I WILL JOIN YOU!
WE COULD USE SOMEONE AS CLEVER AS YOU. I WILL NOT GIVE YOU A WHOLE *KIBI DANGO*, BUT I WILL SHARE ONE WITH YOU.
"THE NEXT DAY THE FRIENDS REACHED A GRASSY PLAIN..."
NO *ONI* CAN MATCH MY STRENGTH!
...OR MY AGILITY!
DON'T GET OVERCONFIDENT! AFTER ALL, THERE ARE ONLY THREE OF US AGAINST AN ENTIRE ISLAND!
KIIIIIII
EH--?
KIIIIIII......
HO! IT'S JUST A BIRD!
GRR... LET'S IGNORE IT AND CONTINUE ON.
日本一
16.

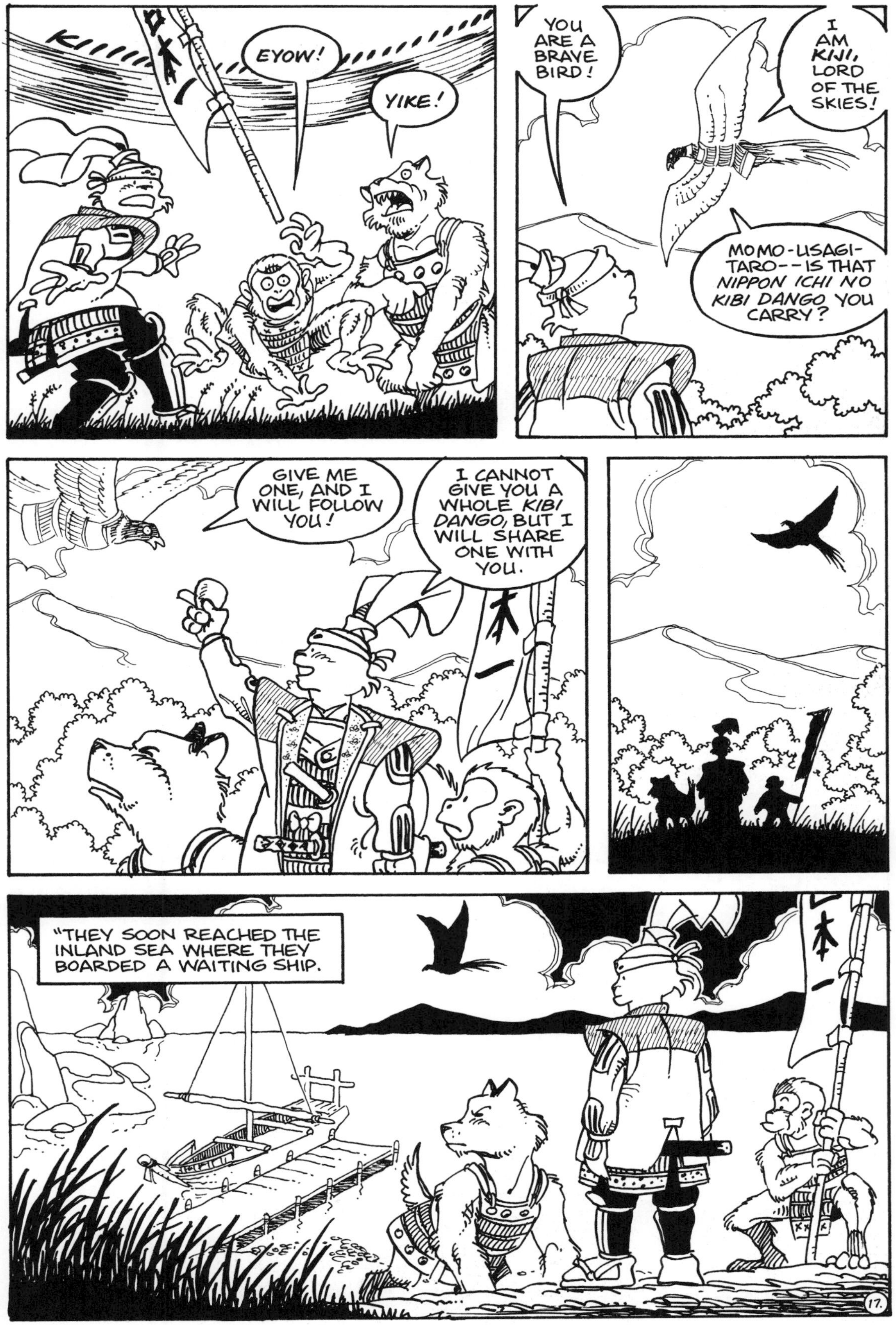
KI!!!!!!!!
EYOW!
YIKE!
YOU ARE A BRAVE BIRD!
I AM KIJI, LORD OF THE SKIES!
MOMO-USAGI-TARO--IS THAT NIPPON ICHI NO KIBI DANGO YOU CARRY?
GIVE ME ONE, AND I WILL FOLLOW YOU!
I CANNOT GIVE YOU A WHOLE KIBI DANGO, BUT I WILL SHARE ONE WITH YOU.
"THEY SOON REACHED THE INLAND SEA WHERE THEY BOARDED A WAITING SHIP.
17.

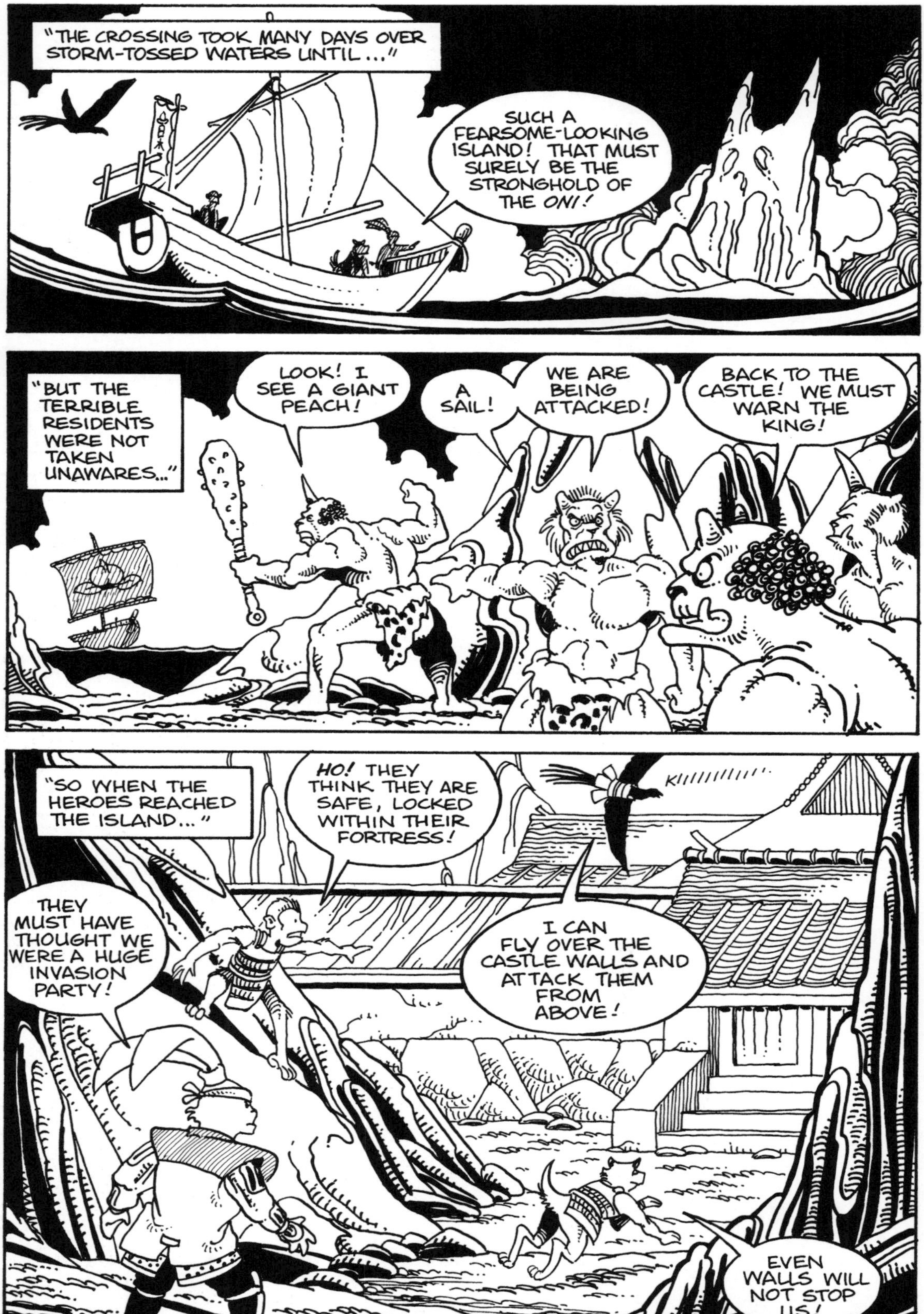
"THE CROSSING TOOK MANY DAYS OVER STORM-TOSSED WATERS UNTIL..."
SUCH A FEARSOME-LOOKING ISLAND! THAT MUST SURELY BE THE STRONGHOLD OF THE *ONI*!
"BUT THE TERRIBLE RESIDENTS WERE NOT TAKEN UNAWARES..."
LOOK! I SEE A GIANT PEACH!
A SAIL!
WE ARE BEING ATTACKED!
BACK TO THE CASTLE! WE MUST WARN THE KING!
"SO WHEN THE HEROES REACHED THE ISLAND..."
HO! THEY THINK THEY ARE SAFE, LOCKED WITHIN THEIR FORTRESS!
KIIIIIII
THEY MUST HAVE THOUGHT WE WERE A HUGE INVASION PARTY!
I CAN FLY OVER THE CASTLE WALLS AND ATTACK THEM FROM ABOVE!
EVEN WALLS WILL NOT STOP US!
18.

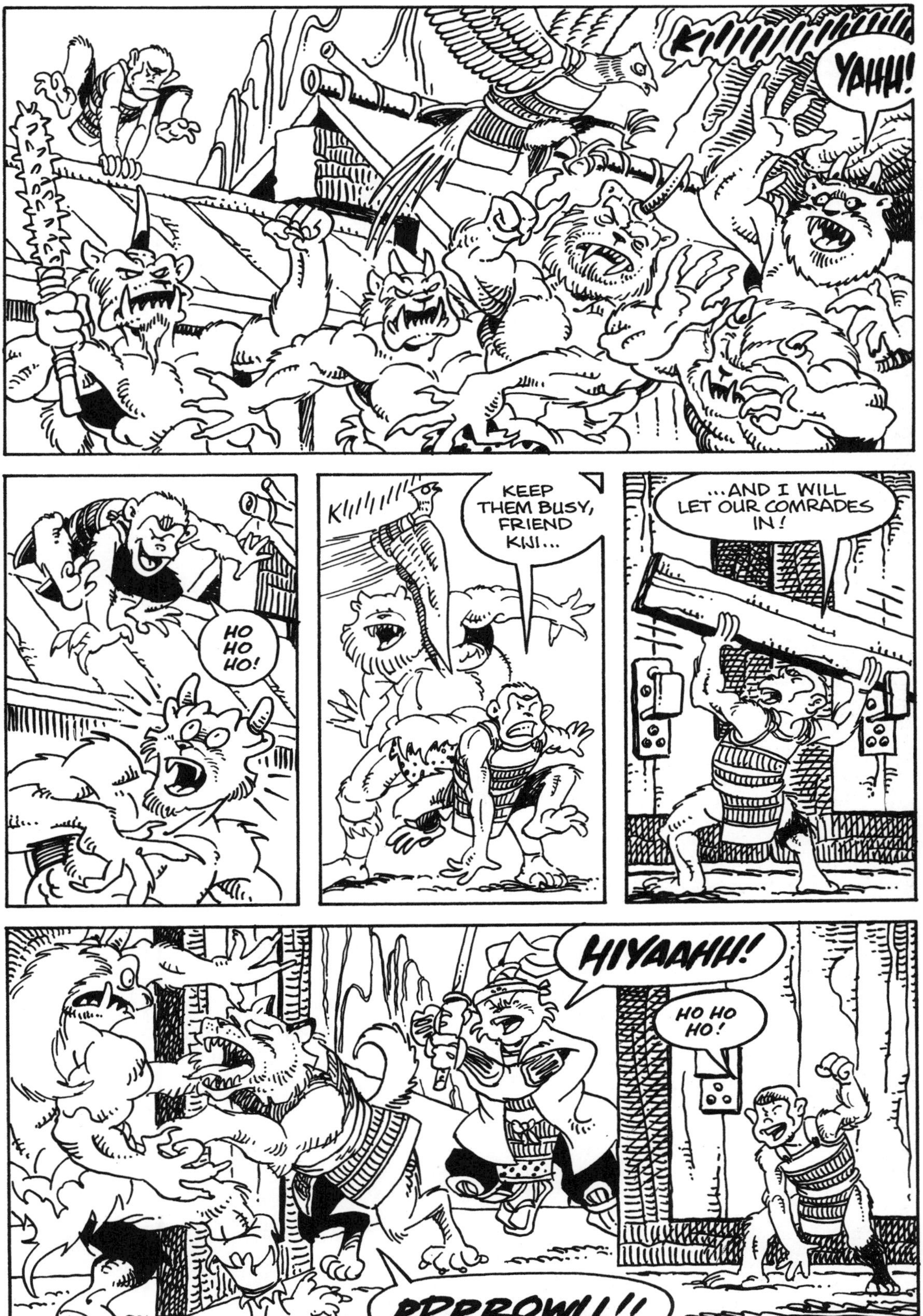
KIIIIIIIIIIIIII
YAHH!
HO HO HO!
KIIIIIIIII
KEEP THEM BUSY, FRIEND KIJI...
...AND I WILL LET OUR COMRADES IN!
HIYAAHH!
HO HO HO!
RRRROWLL!!
19.

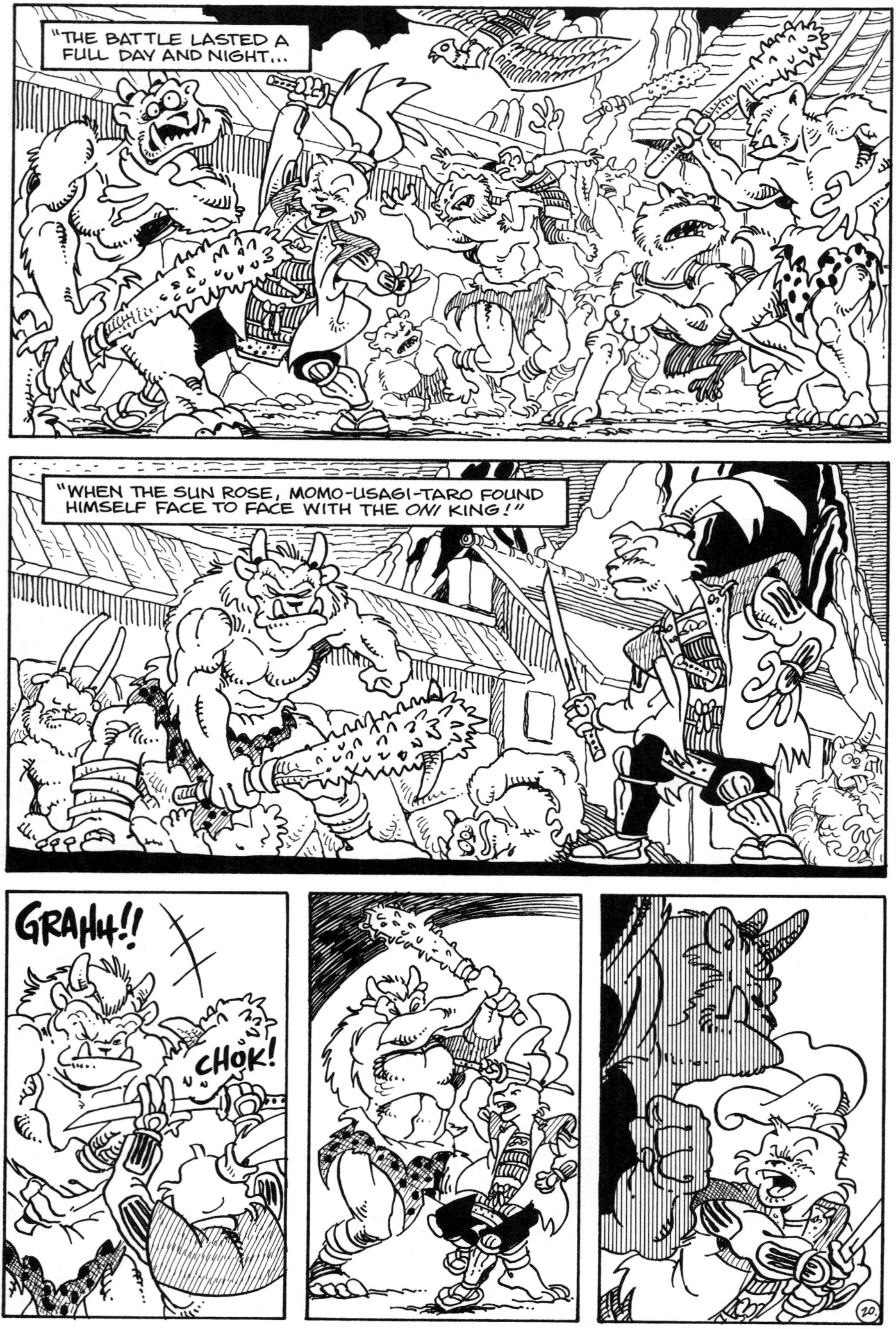
"THE BATTLE LASTED A FULL DAY AND NIGHT...
"WHEN THE SUN ROSE, MOMO-USAGI-TARO FOUND HIMSELF FACE TO FACE WITH THE *ONI* KING!"
GRAHH!!
CHOK!
20.

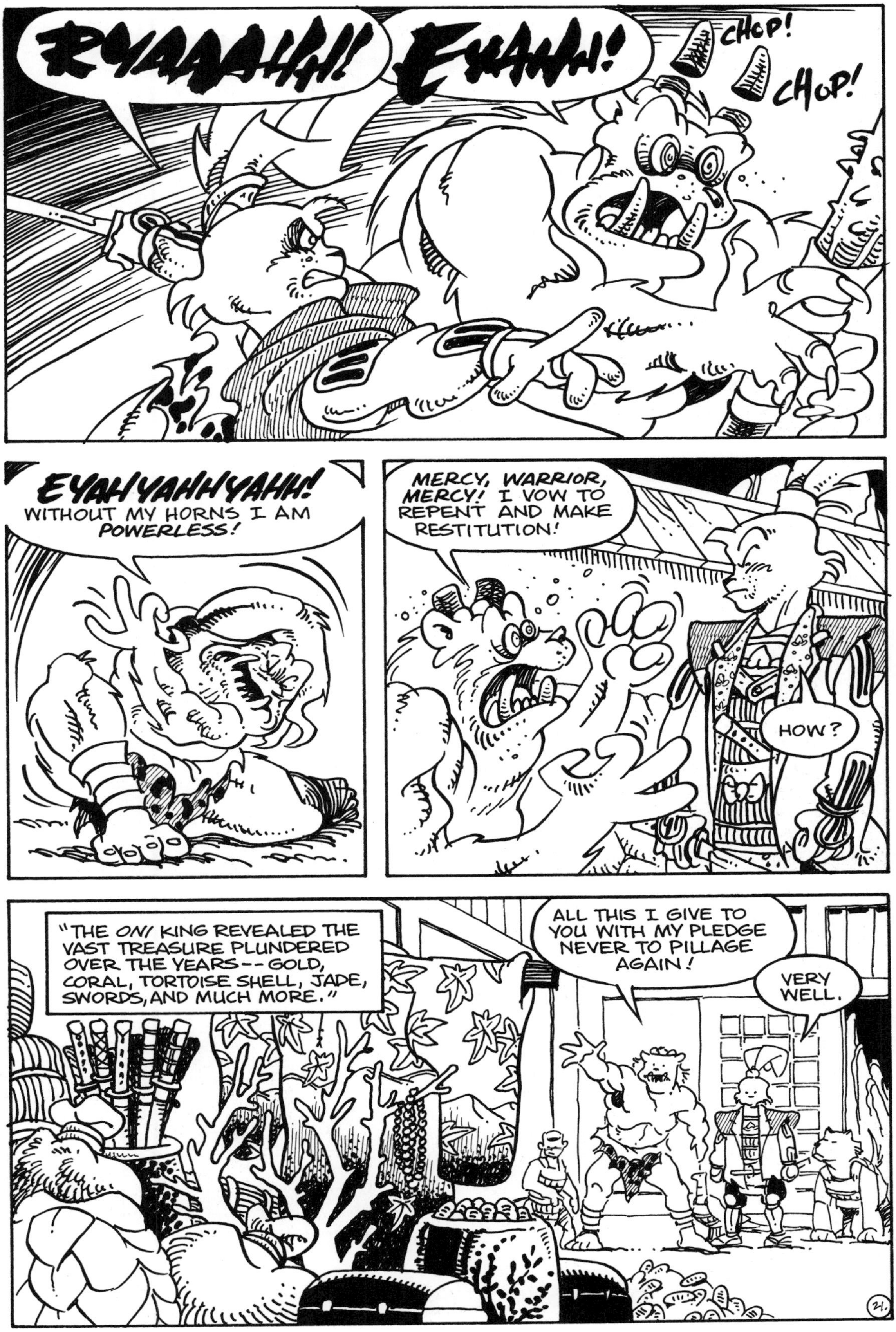
RYAAAAHH!
EYAHH!
CHOP!
CHOP!
EYAHYAHHYAHH! WITHOUT MY HORNS I AM POWERLESS!
MERCY, WARRIOR, MERCY! I VOW TO REPENT AND MAKE RESTITUTION!
HOW?
"THE ONI KING REVEALED THE VAST TREASURE PLUNDERED OVER THE YEARS--GOLD, CORAL, TORTOISE SHELL, JADE, SWORDS, AND MUCH MORE."
ALL THIS I GIVE TO YOU WITH MY PLEDGE NEVER TO PILLAGE AGAIN!
VERY WELL.
21.

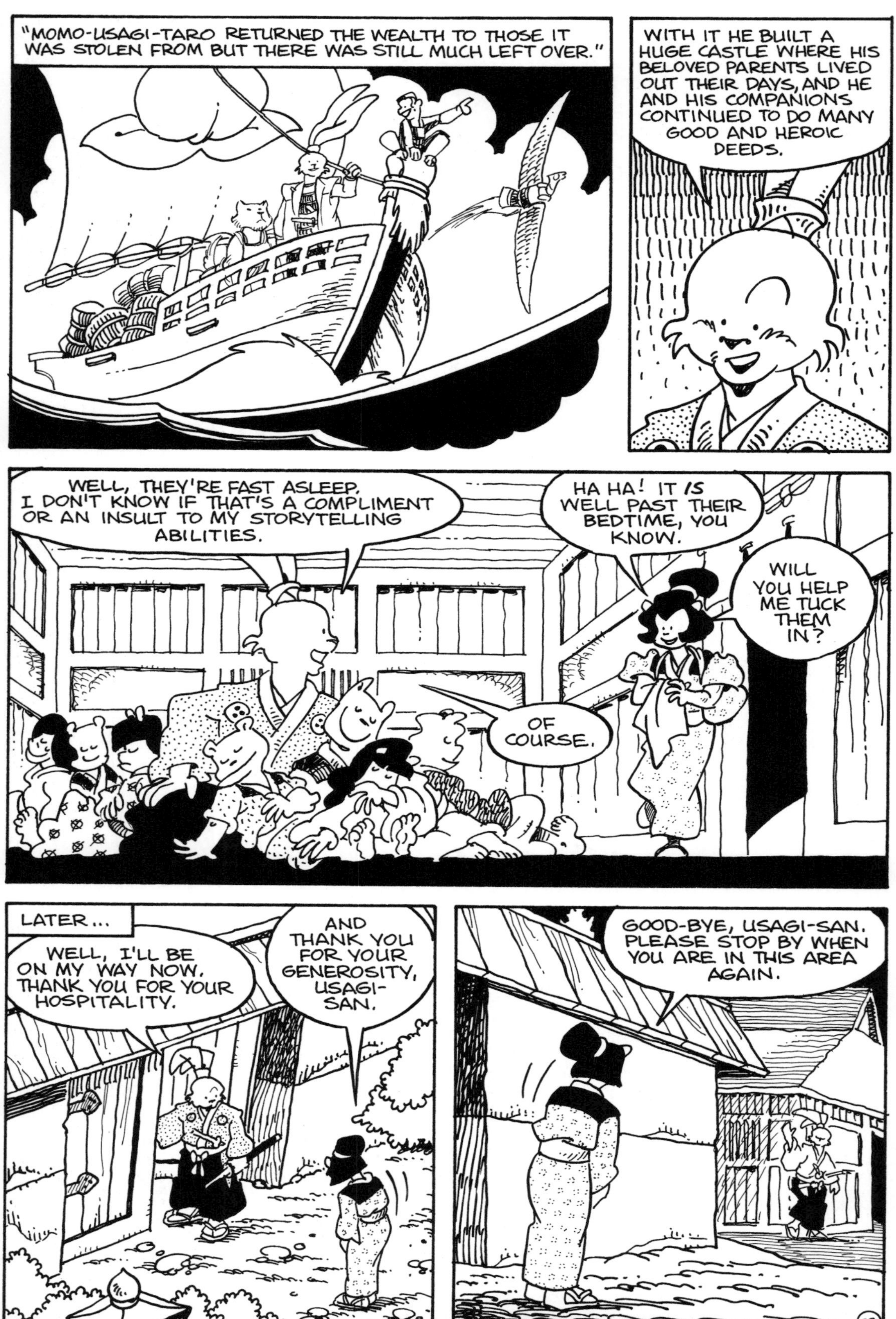
"MOMO-USAGI-TARO RETURNED THE WEALTH TO THOSE IT WAS STOLEN FROM BUT THERE WAS STILL MUCH LEFT OVER."
WITH IT HE BUILT A HUGE CASTLE WHERE HIS BELOVED PARENTS LIVED OUT THEIR DAYS, AND HE AND HIS COMPANIONS CONTINUED TO DO MANY GOOD AND HEROIC DEEDS.
WELL, THEY'RE FAST ASLEEP. I DON'T KNOW IF THAT'S A COMPLIMENT OR AN INSULT TO MY STORYTELLING ABILITIES.
HA HA! IT *IS* WELL PAST THEIR BEDTIME, YOU KNOW.
WILL YOU HELP ME TUCK THEM IN?
OF COURSE.
LATER...
WELL, I'LL BE ON MY WAY NOW. THANK YOU FOR YOUR HOSPITALITY.
AND THANK YOU FOR YOUR GENEROSITY, USAGI-SAN.
GOOD-BYE, USAGI-SAN. PLEASE STOP BY WHEN YOU ARE IN THIS AREA AGAIN.
22

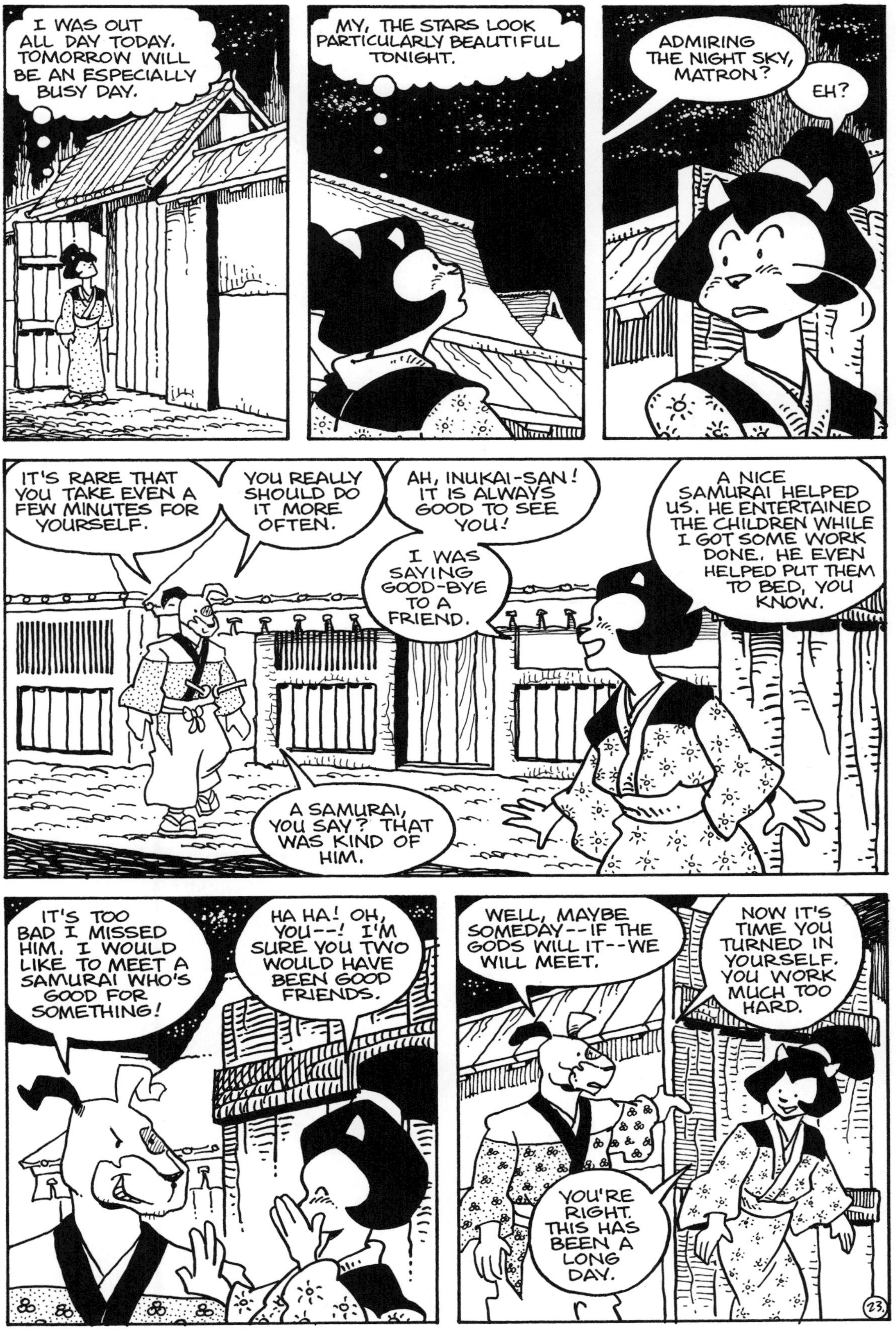
I WAS OUT ALL DAY TODAY. TOMORROW WILL BE AN ESPECIALLY BUSY DAY.
MY, THE STARS LOOK PARTICULARLY BEAUTIFUL TONIGHT.
ADMIRING THE NIGHT SKY, MATRON?
EH?
IT'S RARE THAT YOU TAKE EVEN A FEW MINUTES FOR YOURSELF.
YOU REALLY SHOULD DO IT MORE OFTEN.
AH, INUKAI-SAN! IT IS ALWAYS GOOD TO SEE YOU!
I WAS SAYING GOOD-BYE TO A FRIEND.
A NICE SAMURAI HELPED US. HE ENTERTAINED THE CHILDREN WHILE I GOT SOME WORK DONE. HE EVEN HELPED PUT THEM TO BED, YOU KNOW.
A SAMURAI, YOU SAY? THAT WAS KIND OF HIM.
IT'S TOO BAD I MISSED HIM. I WOULD LIKE TO MEET A SAMURAI WHO'S GOOD FOR SOMETHING!
HA HA! OH, YOU--! I'M SURE YOU TWO WOULD HAVE BEEN GOOD FRIENDS.
WELL, MAYBE SOMEDAY--IF THE GODS WILL IT--WE WILL MEET.
NOW IT'S TIME YOU TURNED IN YOURSELF. YOU WORK MUCH TOO HARD.
YOU'RE RIGHT. THIS HAS BEEN A LONG DAY.
23.

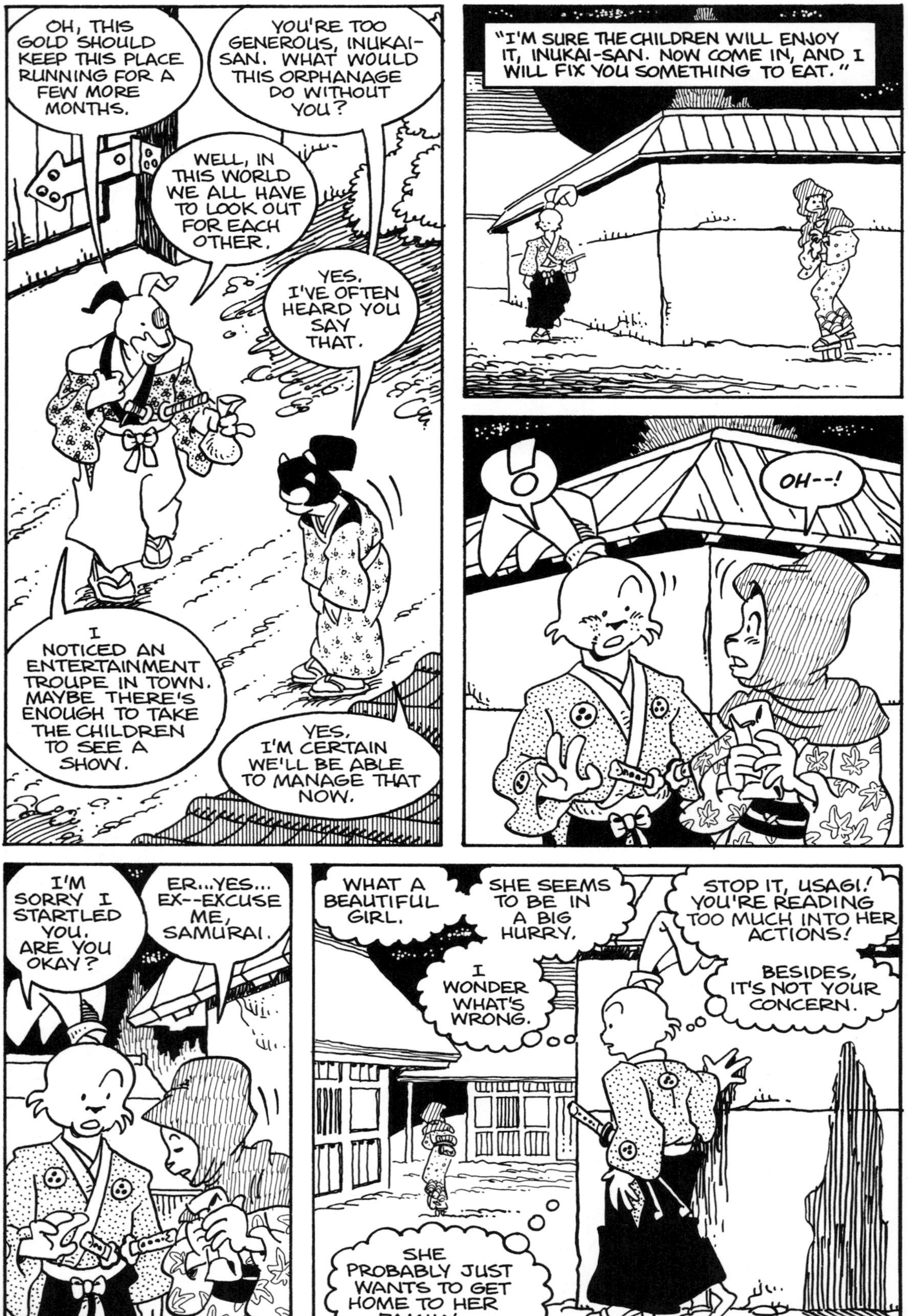

OH, THIS GOLD SHOULD KEEP THIS PLACE RUNNING FOR A FEW MORE MONTHS.
YOU'RE TOO GENEROUS, INUKAI-SAN. WHAT WOULD THIS ORPHANAGE DO WITHOUT YOU?
WELL, IN THIS WORLD WE ALL HAVE TO LOOK OUT FOR EACH OTHER.
YES. I'VE OFTEN HEARD YOU SAY THAT.
I NOTICED AN ENTERTAINMENT TROUPE IN TOWN. MAYBE THERE'S ENOUGH TO TAKE THE CHILDREN TO SEE A SHOW.
YES, I'M CERTAIN WE'LL BE ABLE TO MANAGE THAT NOW.
"I'M SURE THE CHILDREN WILL ENJOY IT, INUKAI-SAN. NOW COME IN, AND I WILL FIX YOU SOMETHING TO EAT."
!
OH--!
I'M SORRY I STARTLED YOU. ARE YOU OKAY?
ER...YES... EX--EXCUSE ME, SAMURAI.
WHAT A BEAUTIFUL GIRL.
SHE SEEMS TO BE IN A BIG HURRY.
I WONDER WHAT'S WRONG.
STOP IT, USAGI! YOU'RE READING TOO MUCH INTO HER ACTIONS!
BESIDES, IT'S NOT YOUR CONCERN.
SHE PROBABLY JUST WANTS TO GET HOME TO HER FAMILY.
THE END

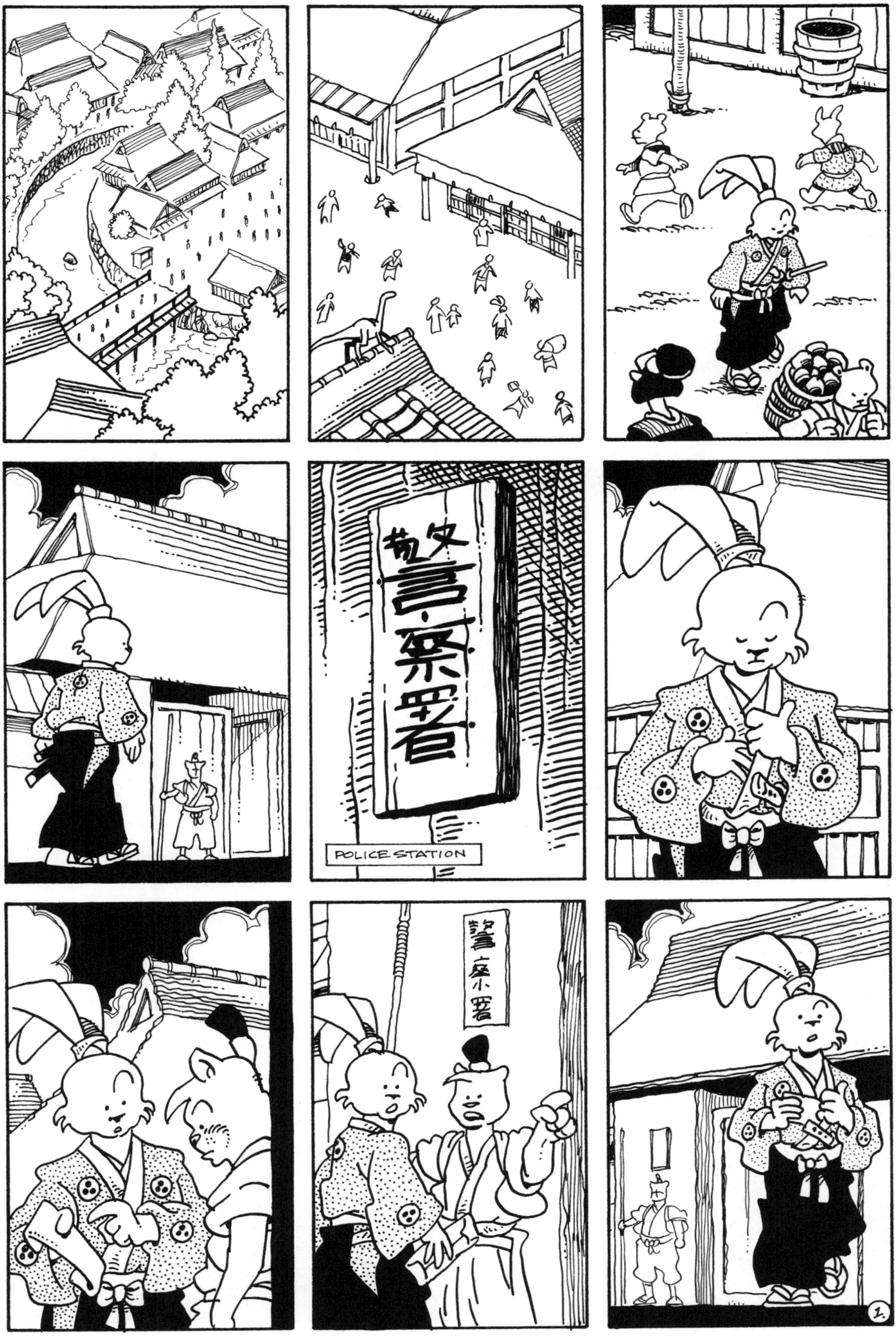
警察署
POLICE STATION

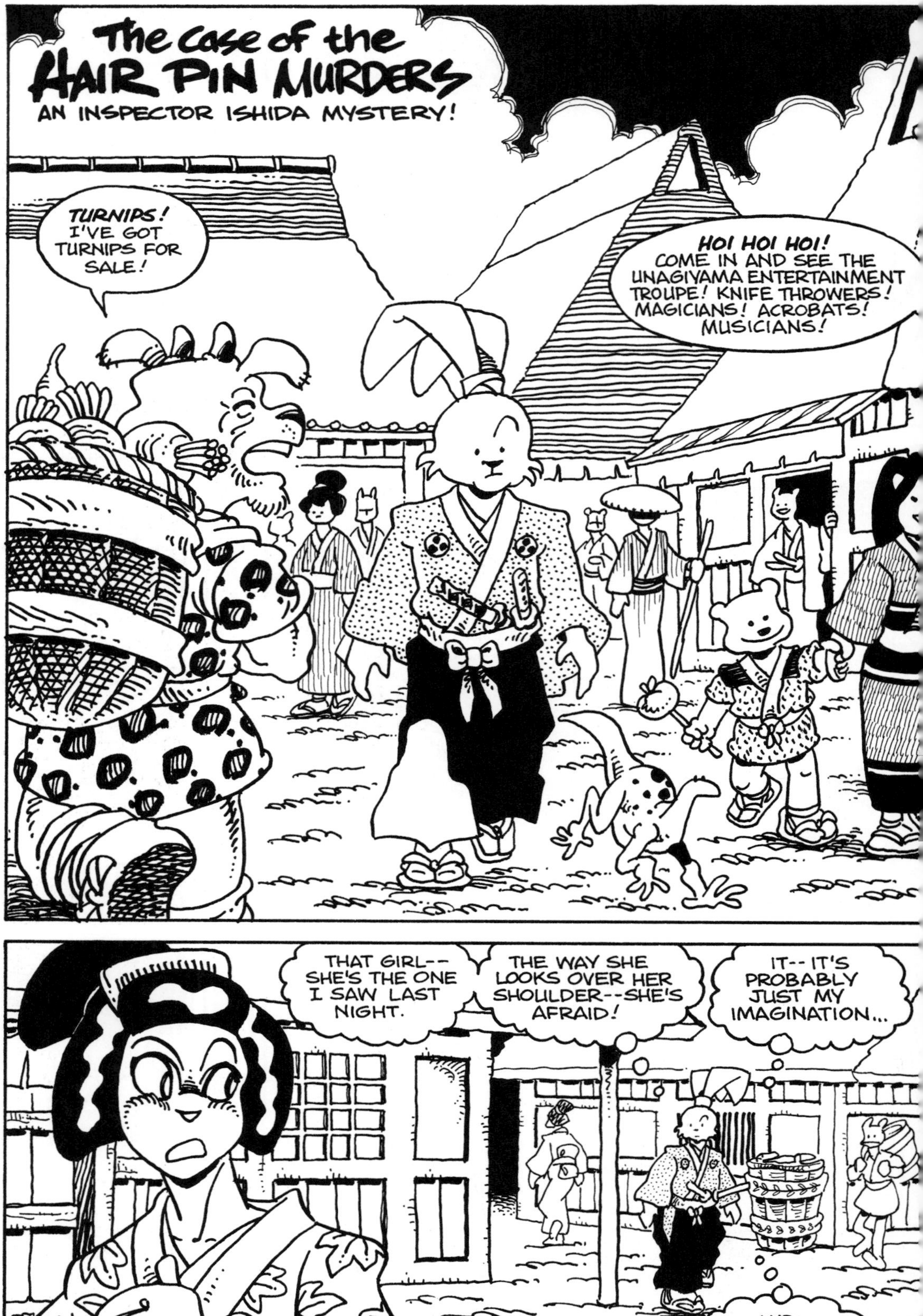

The Case of the
HAIR PIN MURDERS
AN INSPECTOR ISHIDA MYSTERY!
TURNIPS! I'VE GOT TURNIPS FOR SALE!
HOI HOI HOI! COME IN AND SEE THE UNAGIYAMA ENTERTAINMENT TROUPE! KNIFE THROWERS! MAGICIANS! ACROBATS! MUSICIANS!
THAT GIRL-- SHE'S THE ONE I SAW LAST NIGHT.
THE WAY SHE LOOKS OVER HER SHOULDER--SHE'S AFRAID!
IT-- IT'S PROBABLY JUST MY IMAGINATION...
...AND CERTAINLY NO CONCERN OF MINE.

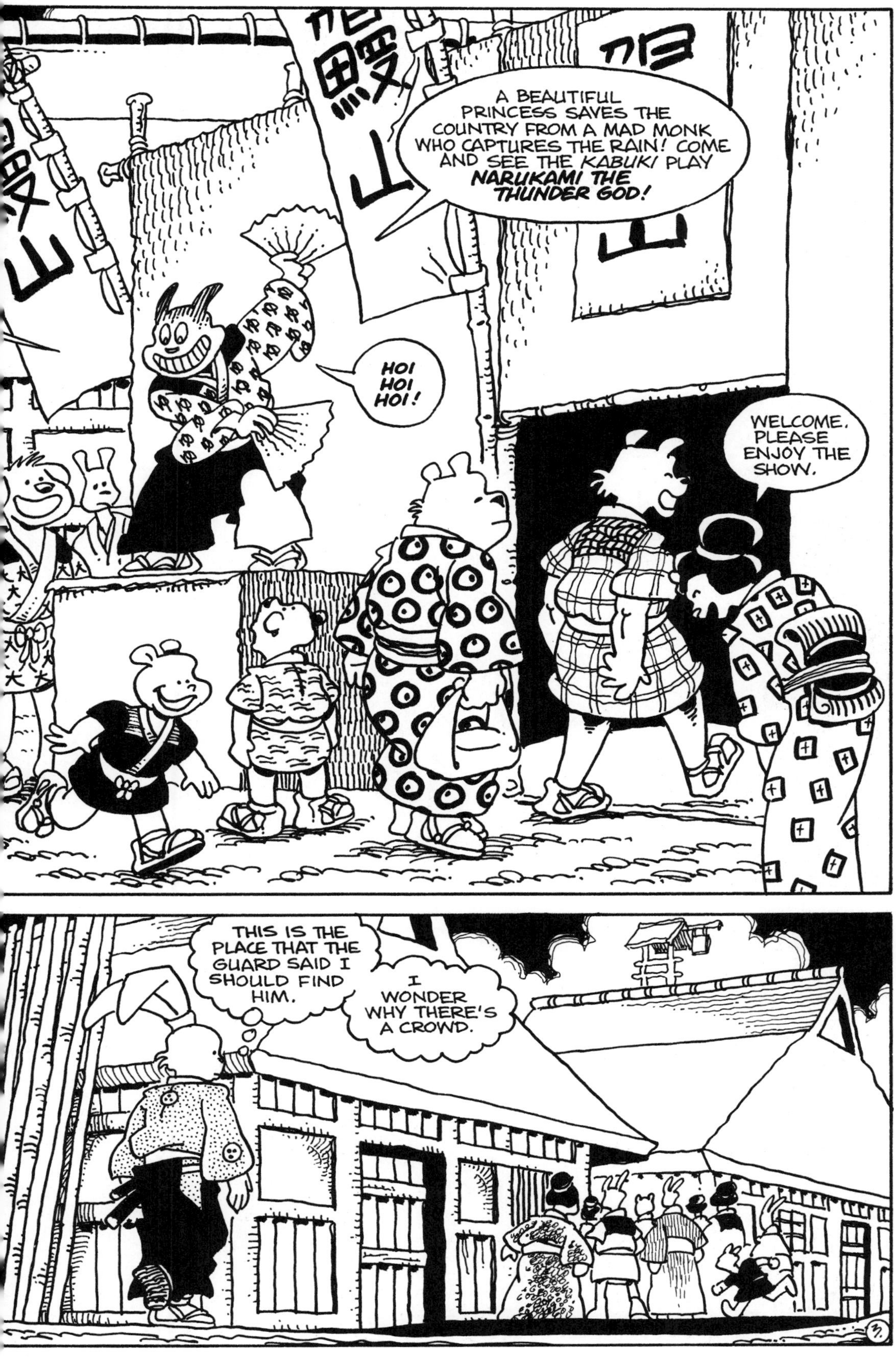
A BEAUTIFUL PRINCESS SAVES THE COUNTRY FROM A MAD MONK WHO CAPTURES THE RAIN! COME AND SEE THE *KABUKI* PLAY **NARUKAMI THE THUNDER GOD!**
HOI HOI HOI!
WELCOME. PLEASE ENJOY THE SHOW.
THIS IS THE PLACE THAT THE GUARD SAID I SHOULD FIND HIM.
I WONDER WHY THERE'S A CROWD.
3.

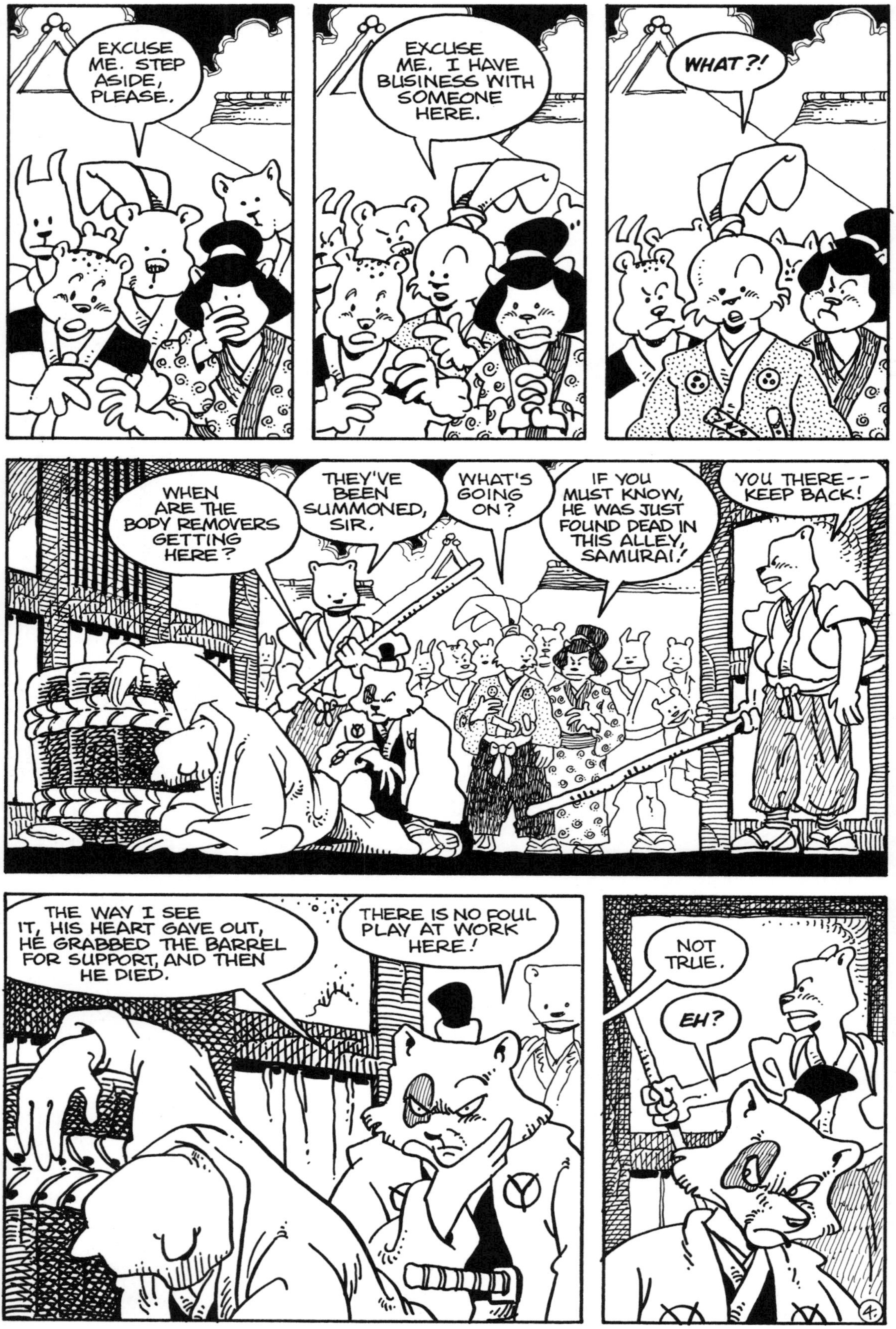
EXCUSE ME. STEP ASIDE, PLEASE.
EXCUSE ME. I HAVE BUSINESS WITH SOMEONE HERE.
WHAT?!
WHEN ARE THE BODY REMOVERS GETTING HERE?
THEY'VE BEEN SUMMONED, SIR.
WHAT'S GOING ON?
IF YOU MUST KNOW, HE WAS JUST FOUND DEAD IN THIS ALLEY, SAMURAI!
YOU THERE-- KEEP BACK!
THE WAY I SEE IT, HIS HEART GAVE OUT, HE GRABBED THE BARREL FOR SUPPORT, AND THEN HE DIED.
THERE IS NO FOUL PLAY AT WORK HERE!
NOT TRUE.
EH?
4.

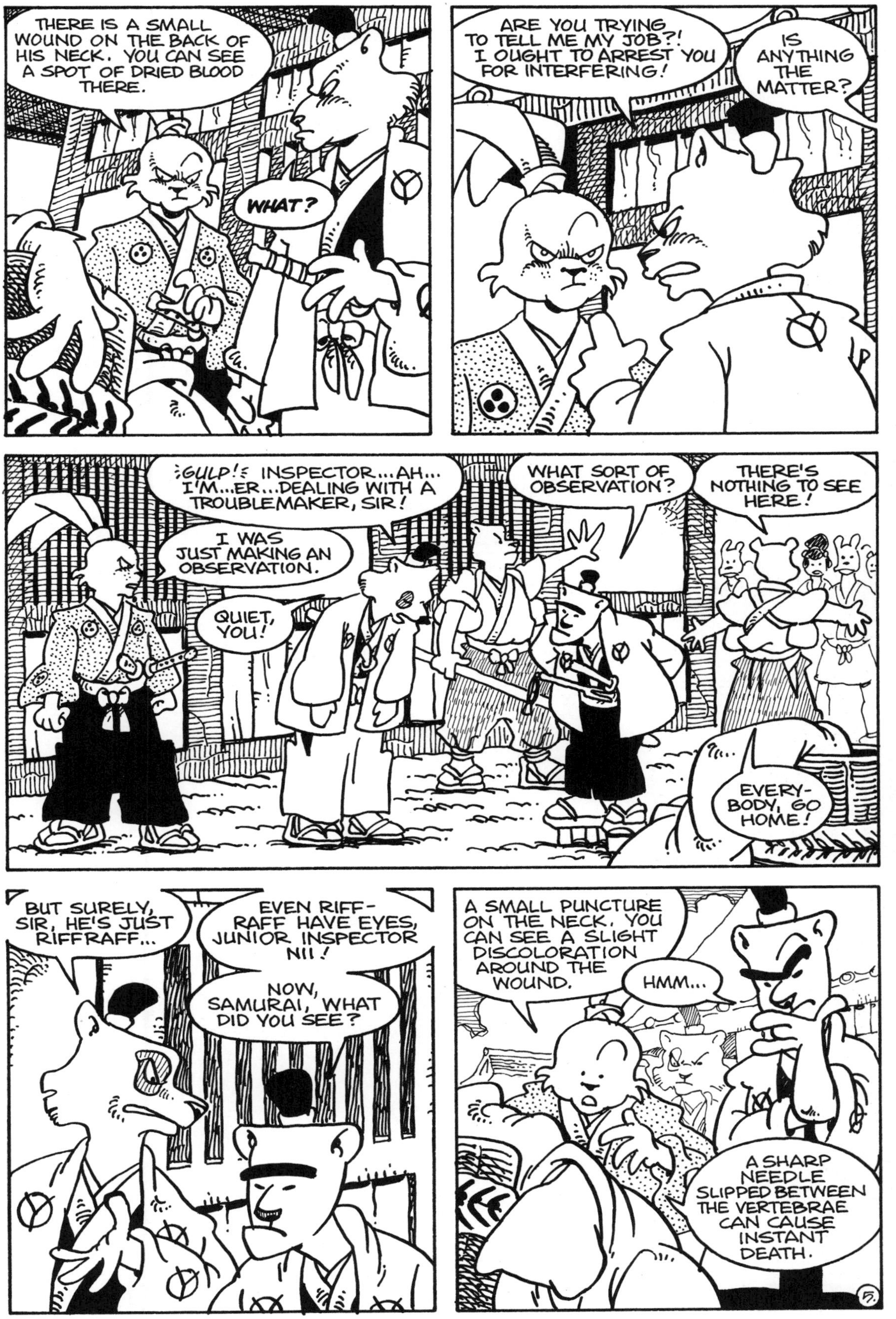
THERE IS A SMALL WOUND ON THE BACK OF HIS NECK. YOU CAN SEE A SPOT OF DRIED BLOOD THERE.
WHAT?
ARE YOU TRYING TO TELL ME MY JOB?! I OUGHT TO ARREST YOU FOR INTERFERING!
IS ANYTHING THE MATTER?
:GULP!: INSPECTOR...AH... I'M...ER...DEALING WITH A TROUBLEMAKER, SIR!
I WAS JUST MAKING AN OBSERVATION.
QUIET, YOU!
WHAT SORT OF OBSERVATION?
THERE'S NOTHING TO SEE HERE!
EVERY-BODY, GO HOME!
BUT SURELY, SIR, HE'S JUST RIFFRAFF...
EVEN RIFF-RAFF HAVE EYES, JUNIOR INSPECTOR NII!
NOW, SAMURAI, WHAT DID YOU SEE?
A SMALL PUNCTURE ON THE NECK. YOU CAN SEE A SLIGHT DISCOLORATION AROUND THE WOUND.
HMM...
A SHARP NEEDLE SLIPPED BETWEEN THE VERTEBRAE CAN CAUSE INSTANT DEATH.
5.

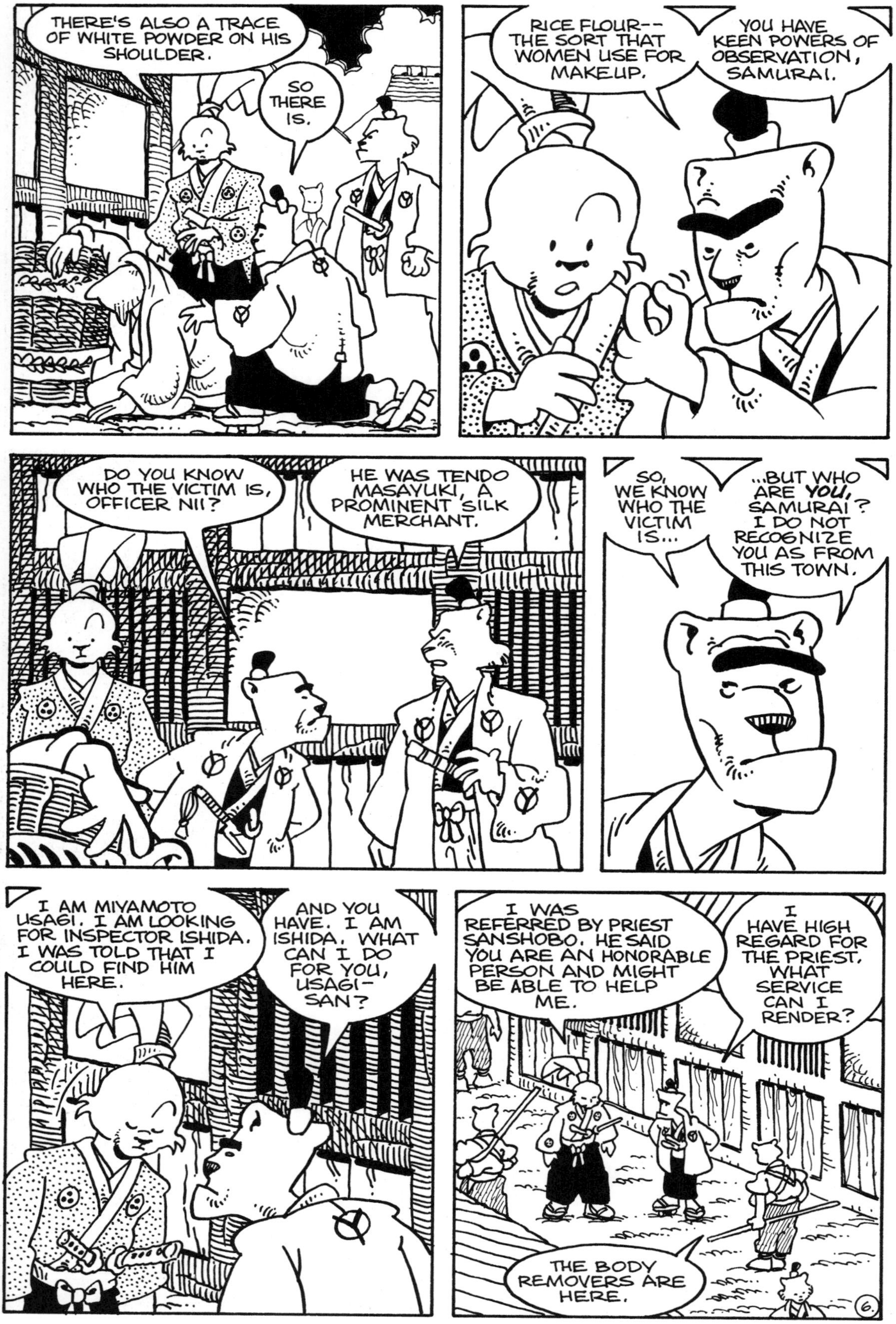
THERE'S ALSO A TRACE OF WHITE POWDER ON HIS SHOULDER.
SO THERE IS.
RICE FLOUR-- THE SORT THAT WOMEN USE FOR MAKEUP.
YOU HAVE KEEN POWERS OF OBSERVATION, SAMURAI.
DO YOU KNOW WHO THE VICTIM IS, OFFICER NII?
HE WAS TENDO MASAYUKI, A PROMINENT SILK MERCHANT.
SO, WE KNOW WHO THE VICTIM IS...
...BUT WHO ARE *YOU*, SAMURAI? I DO NOT RECOGNIZE YOU AS FROM THIS TOWN.
I AM MIYAMOTO USAGI. I AM LOOKING FOR INSPECTOR ISHIDA. I WAS TOLD THAT I COULD FIND HIM HERE.
AND YOU HAVE. I AM ISHIDA. WHAT CAN I DO FOR YOU, USAGI-SAN?
I WAS REFERRED BY PRIEST SANSHOBO. HE SAID YOU ARE AN HONORABLE PERSON AND MIGHT BE ABLE TO HELP ME.
I HAVE HIGH REGARD FOR THE PRIEST. WHAT SERVICE CAN I RENDER?
THE BODY REMOVERS ARE HERE.
6.

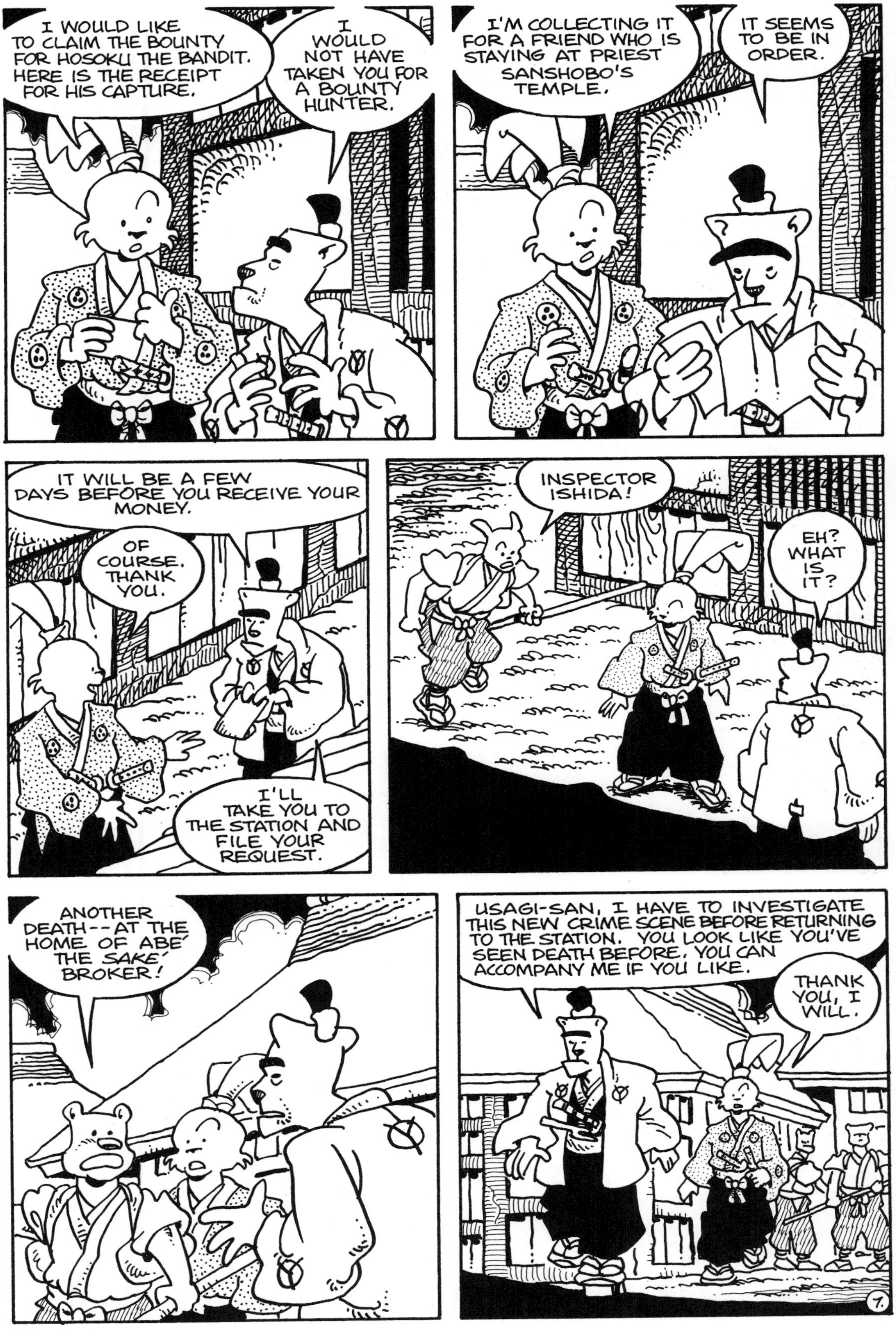

I WOULD LIKE TO CLAIM THE BOUNTY FOR HOSOKU THE BANDIT. HERE IS THE RECEIPT FOR HIS CAPTURE.
I WOULD NOT HAVE TAKEN YOU FOR A BOUNTY HUNTER.
I'M COLLECTING IT FOR A FRIEND WHO IS STAYING AT PRIEST SANSHOBO'S TEMPLE.
IT SEEMS TO BE IN ORDER.
IT WILL BE A FEW DAYS BEFORE YOU RECEIVE YOUR MONEY.
OF COURSE. THANK YOU.
I'LL TAKE YOU TO THE STATION AND FILE YOUR REQUEST.
INSPECTOR ISHIDA!
EH? WHAT IS IT?
ANOTHER DEATH--AT THE HOME OF ABE THE *SAKE* BROKER!
USAGI-SAN, I HAVE TO INVESTIGATE THIS NEW CRIME SCENE BEFORE RETURNING TO THE STATION. YOU LOOK LIKE YOU'VE SEEN DEATH BEFORE. YOU CAN ACCOMPANY ME IF YOU LIKE.
THANK YOU, I WILL.
7.

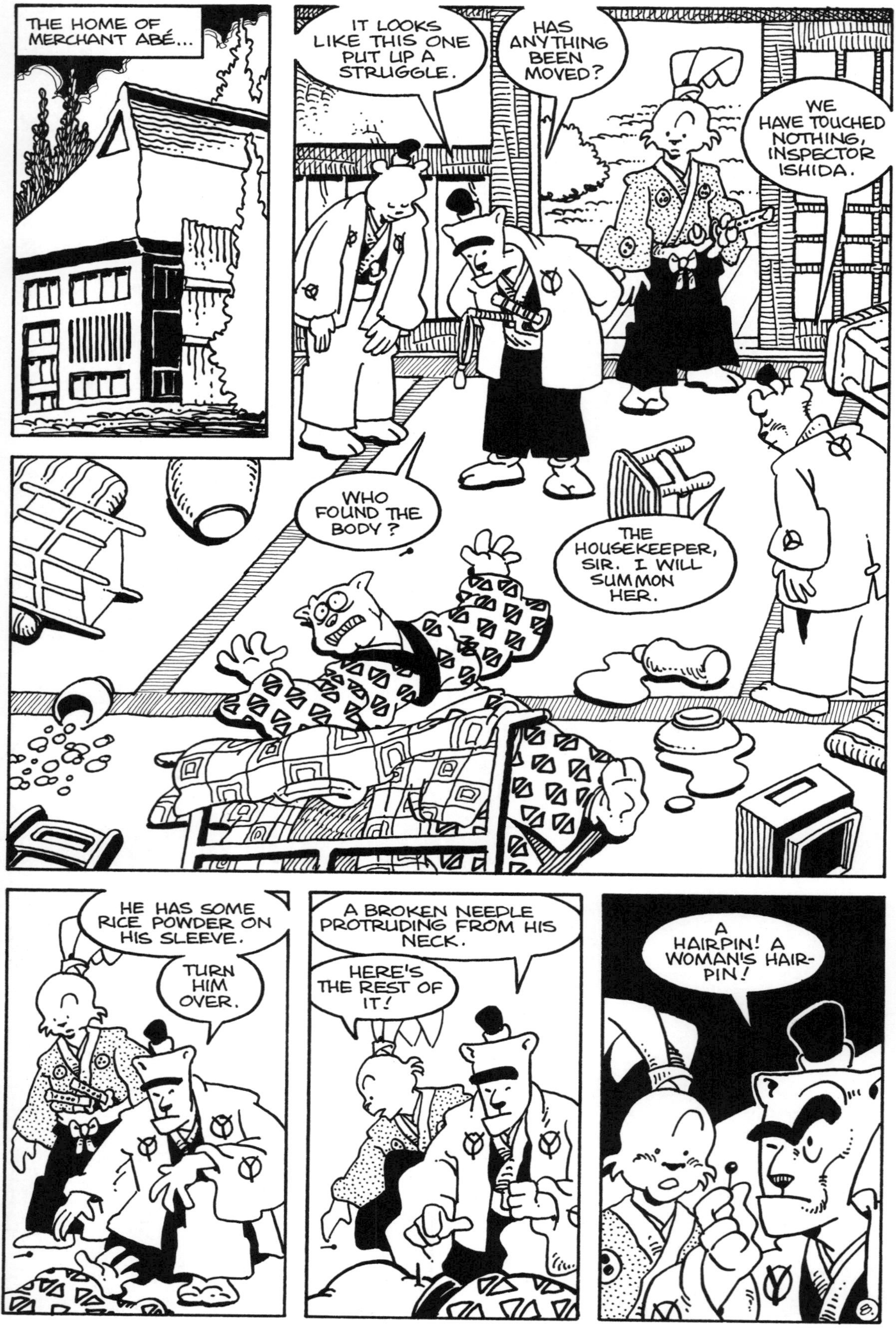
THE HOME OF MERCHANT ABÉ...
IT LOOKS LIKE THIS ONE PUT UP A STRUGGLE.
HAS ANYTHING BEEN MOVED?
WE HAVE TOUCHED NOTHING, INSPECTOR ISHIDA.
WHO FOUND THE BODY?
THE HOUSEKEEPER, SIR. I WILL SUMMON HER.
HE HAS SOME RICE POWDER ON HIS SLEEVE.
TURN HIM OVER.
A BROKEN NEEDLE PROTRUDING FROM HIS NECK.
HERE'S THE REST OF IT!
A HAIRPIN! A WOMAN'S HAIR-PIN!
8.

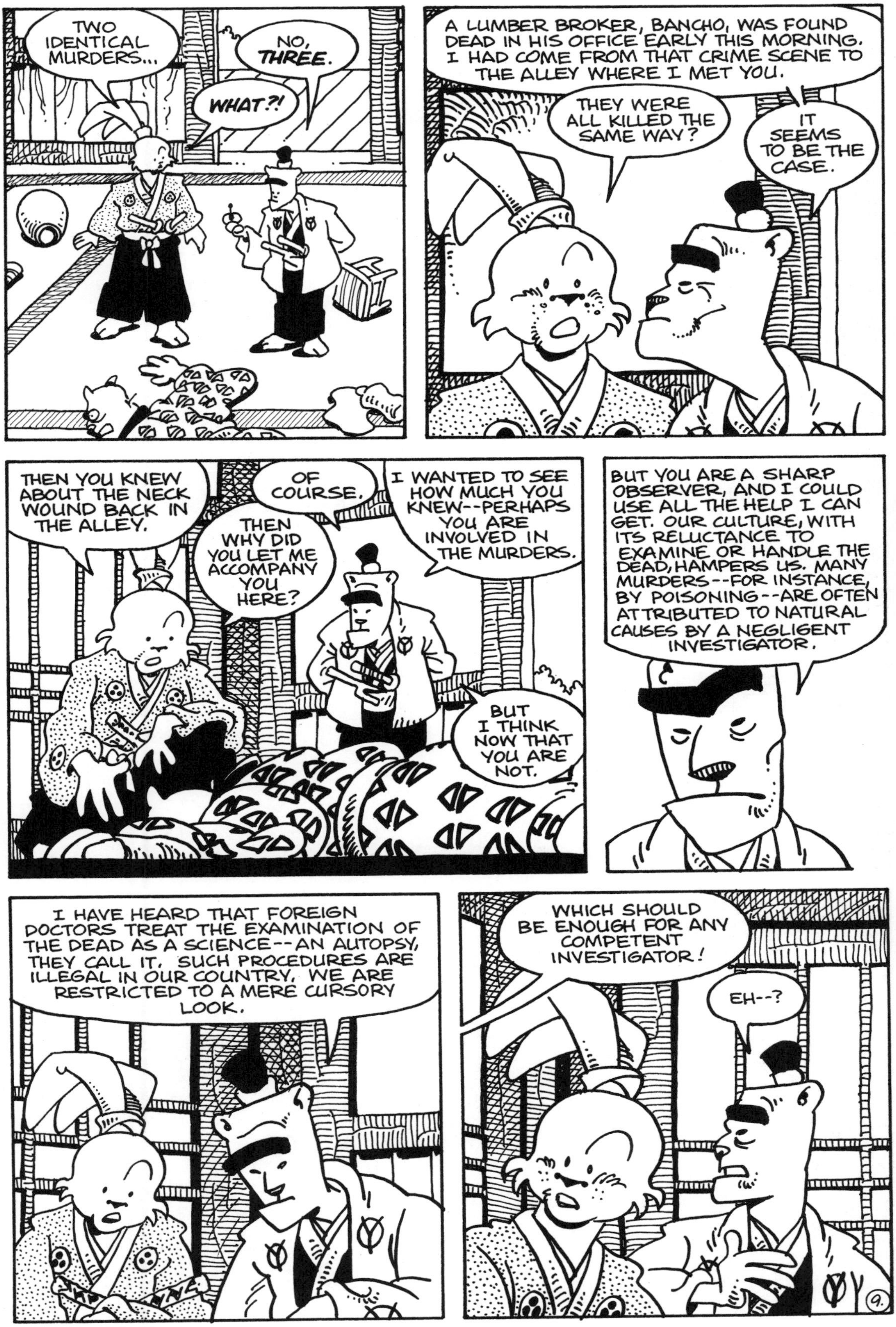

TWO IDENTICAL MURDERS...
NO, THREE.
WHAT?!
A LUMBER BROKER, BANCHO, WAS FOUND DEAD IN HIS OFFICE EARLY THIS MORNING. I HAD COME FROM THAT CRIME SCENE TO THE ALLEY WHERE I MET YOU.
THEY WERE ALL KILLED THE SAME WAY?
IT SEEMS TO BE THE CASE.
THEN YOU KNEW ABOUT THE NECK WOUND BACK IN THE ALLEY.
OF COURSE.
THEN WHY DID YOU LET ME ACCOMPANY YOU HERE?
I WANTED TO SEE HOW MUCH YOU KNEW--PERHAPS YOU ARE INVOLVED IN THE MURDERS.
BUT I THINK NOW THAT YOU ARE NOT.
BUT YOU ARE A SHARP OBSERVER, AND I COULD USE ALL THE HELP I CAN GET. OUR CULTURE, WITH ITS RELUCTANCE TO EXAMINE OR HANDLE THE DEAD, HAMPERS US. MANY MURDERS--FOR INSTANCE, BY POISONING--ARE OFTEN ATTRIBUTED TO NATURAL CAUSES BY A NEGLIGENT INVESTIGATOR.
I HAVE HEARD THAT FOREIGN DOCTORS TREAT THE EXAMINATION OF THE DEAD AS A SCIENCE--AN AUTOPSY, THEY CALL IT. SUCH PROCEDURES ARE ILLEGAL IN OUR COUNTRY. WE ARE RESTRICTED TO A MERE CURSORY LOOK.
WHICH SHOULD BE ENOUGH FOR ANY COMPETENT INVESTIGATOR!
EH--?
9.

THREE PROMINENT MERCHANTS WERE MURDERED LAST NIGHT!

SENIOR INSPECTOR OGAWA! WHAT A PLEASANT SURPRISE! I USUALLY DON'T SEE YOU SO EARLY IN THE MORNING!

DON'T BE A FOOL, ISHIDA! WHAT HAVE YOU LEARNED?

WE KNOW VERY LITTLE SO FAR, BUT THERE MUST BE SOME CONNECTION BETWEEN THE VICTIMS.

THINGS ARE NOT PROGRESSING! I THINK I SHOULD TAKE OVER THIS CASE.

NONSENSE. I WAS ON CALL WHEN THE REPORTS CAME IN. I REFUSE TO GIVE UP THIS CASE!

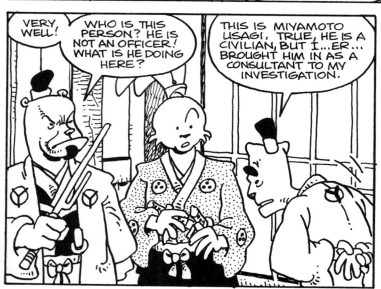

VERY WELL!

WHO IS THIS PERSON? HE IS NOT AN OFFICER! WHAT IS HE DOING HERE?

THIS IS MIYAMOTO USAGI, TRUE, HE IS A CIVILIAN, BUT I...ER... BROUGHT HIM IN AS A CONSULTANT TO MY INVESTIGATION.

HMM... MOST UNUSUAL. I WILL HAVE TO LOOK INTO THIS. IF THERE IS ANY IRREGULARITY, I WILL SEE TO YOUR DISMISSAL!

OF COURSE.

10.

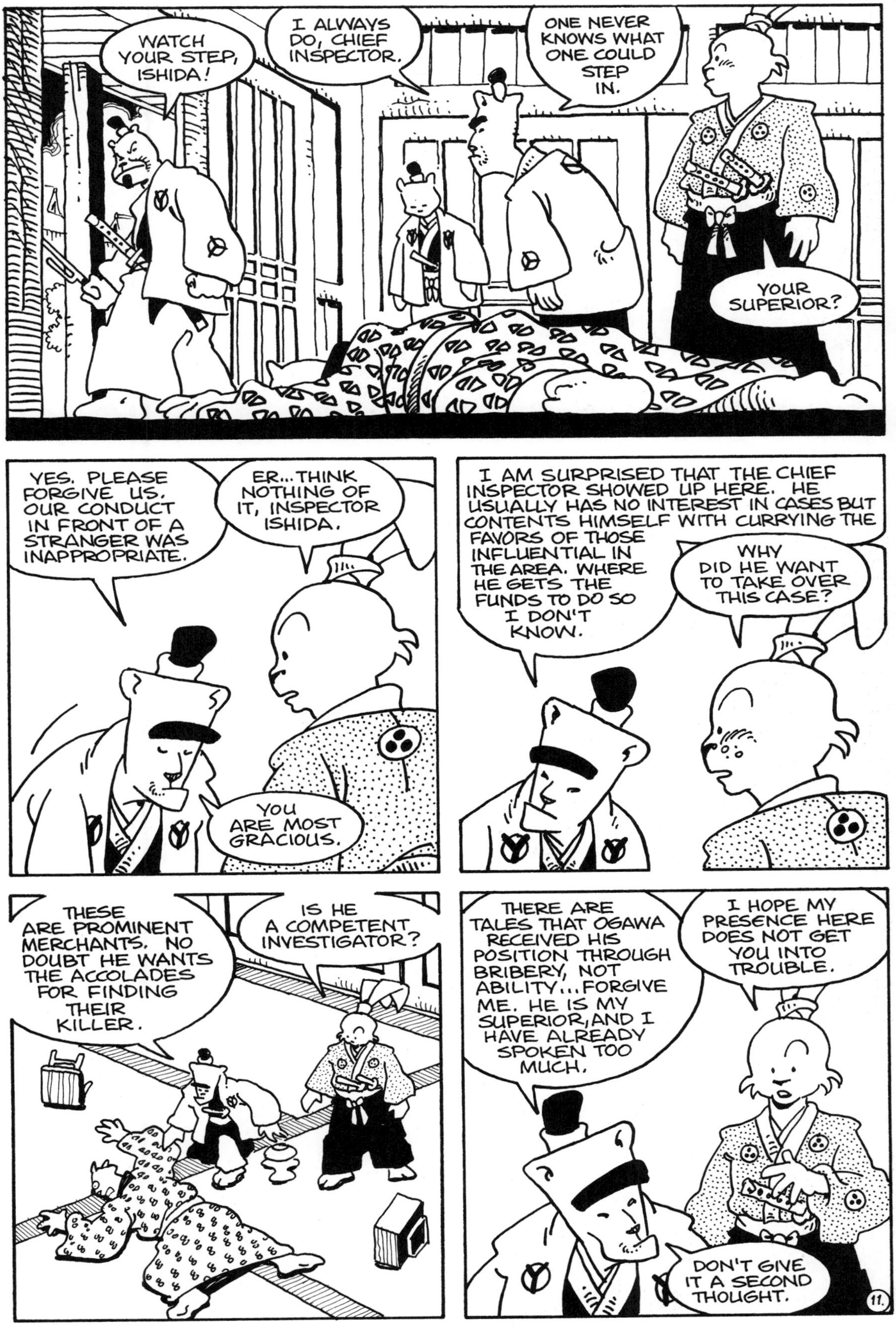
WATCH YOUR STEP, ISHIDA!
I ALWAYS DO, CHIEF INSPECTOR.
ONE NEVER KNOWS WHAT ONE COULD STEP IN.
YOUR SUPERIOR?
YES. PLEASE FORGIVE US. OUR CONDUCT IN FRONT OF A STRANGER WAS INAPPROPRIATE.
ER... THINK NOTHING OF IT, INSPECTOR ISHIDA.
YOU ARE MOST GRACIOUS.
I AM SURPRISED THAT THE CHIEF INSPECTOR SHOWED UP HERE. HE USUALLY HAS NO INTEREST IN CASES BUT CONTENTS HIMSELF WITH CURRYING THE FAVORS OF THOSE INFLUENTIAL IN THE AREA. WHERE HE GETS THE FUNDS TO DO SO I DON'T KNOW.
WHY DID HE WANT TO TAKE OVER THIS CASE?
THESE ARE PROMINENT MERCHANTS. NO DOUBT HE WANTS THE ACCOLADES FOR FINDING THEIR KILLER.
IS HE A COMPETENT INVESTIGATOR?
THERE ARE TALES THAT OGAWA RECEIVED HIS POSITION THROUGH BRIBERY, NOT ABILITY... FORGIVE ME. HE IS MY SUPERIOR, AND I HAVE ALREADY SPOKEN TOO MUCH.
I HOPE MY PRESENCE HERE DOES NOT GET YOU INTO TROUBLE.
DON'T GIVE IT A SECOND THOUGHT.
11.

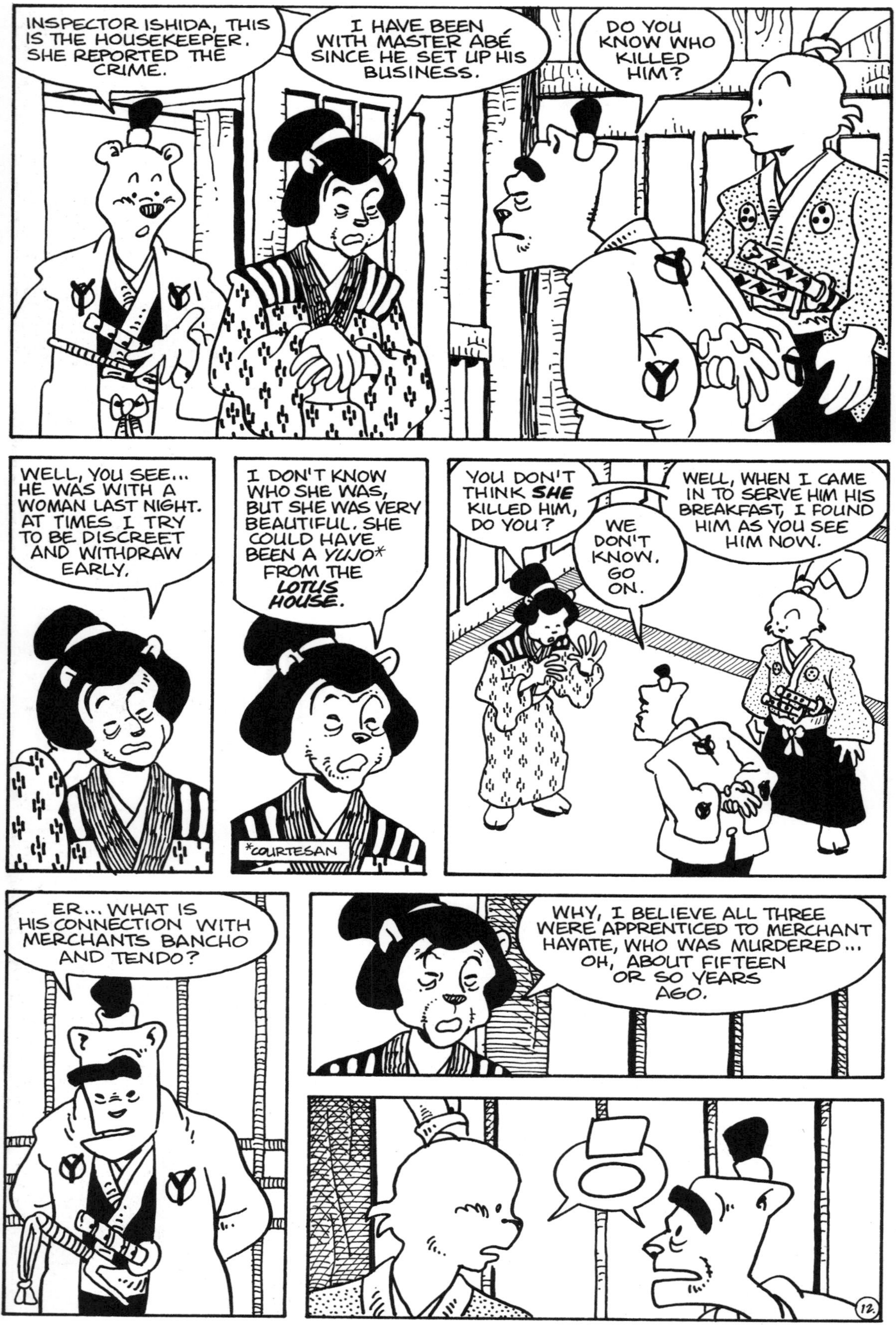
INSPECTOR ISHIDA, THIS IS THE HOUSEKEEPER. SHE REPORTED THE CRIME.
I HAVE BEEN WITH MASTER ABÉ SINCE HE SET UP HIS BUSINESS.
DO YOU KNOW WHO KILLED HIM?
WELL, YOU SEE... HE WAS WITH A WOMAN LAST NIGHT. AT TIMES I TRY TO BE DISCREET AND WITHDRAW EARLY.
I DON'T KNOW WHO SHE WAS, BUT SHE WAS VERY BEAUTIFUL. SHE COULD HAVE BEEN A YUJO* FROM THE LOTUS HOUSE.
*COURTESAN
YOU DON'T THINK SHE KILLED HIM, DO YOU?
WE DON'T KNOW. GO ON.
WELL, WHEN I CAME IN TO SERVE HIM HIS BREAKFAST, I FOUND HIM AS YOU SEE HIM NOW.
ER... WHAT IS HIS CONNECTION WITH MERCHANTS BANCHO AND TENDO?
WHY, I BELIEVE ALL THREE WERE APPRENTICED TO MERCHANT HAYATE, WHO WAS MURDERED... OH, ABOUT FIFTEEN OR SO YEARS AGO.
12.

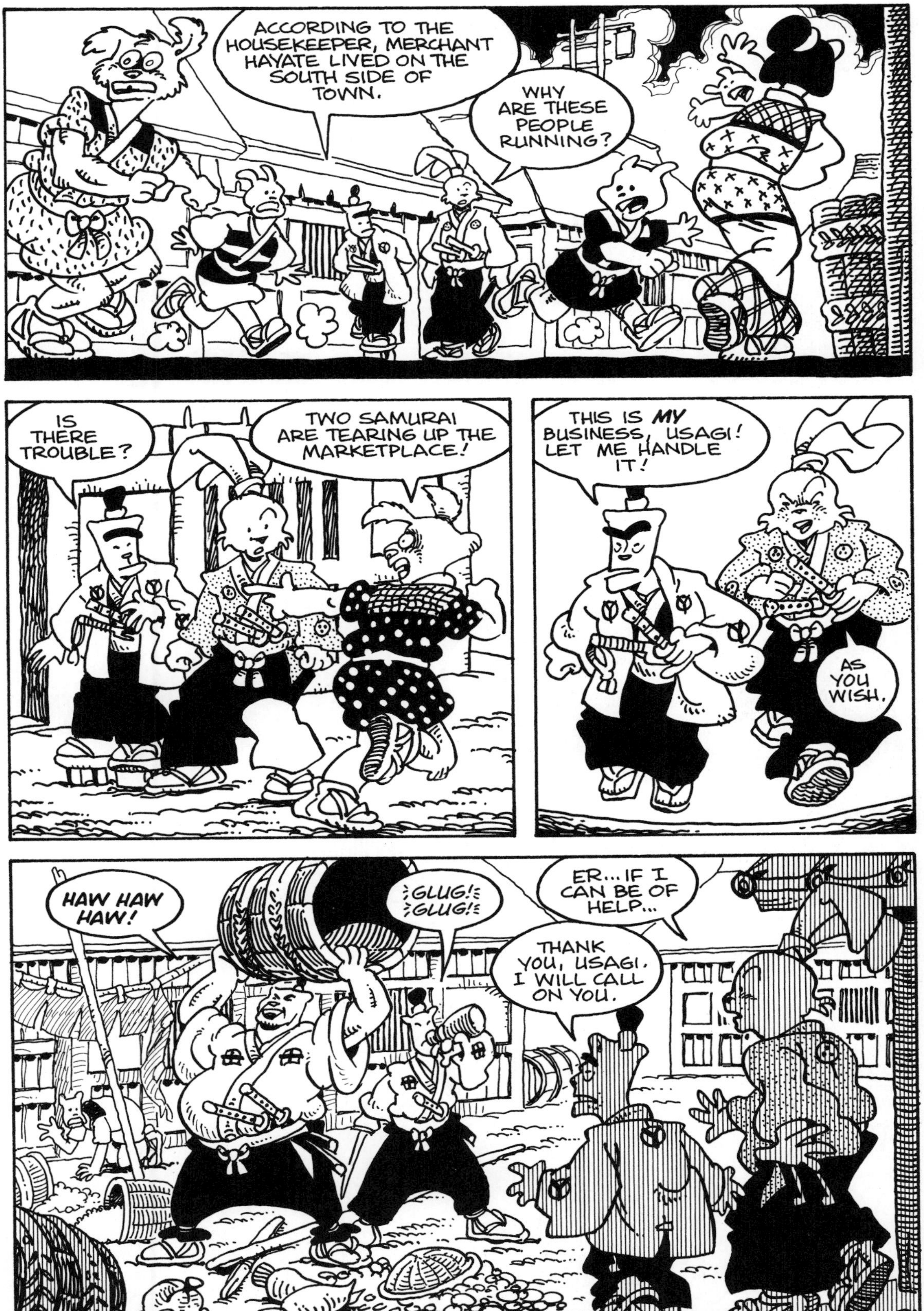

ACCORDING TO THE HOUSEKEEPER, MERCHANT HAYATE LIVED ON THE SOUTH SIDE OF TOWN.
WHY ARE THESE PEOPLE RUNNING?
IS THERE TROUBLE?
TWO SAMURAI ARE TEARING UP THE MARKETPLACE!
THIS IS *MY* BUSINESS, USAGI! LET ME HANDLE IT!
AS YOU WISH.
HAW HAW HAW!
GLUG! GLUG!
ER...IF I CAN BE OF HELP...
THANK YOU, USAGI. I WILL CALL ON YOU.
13

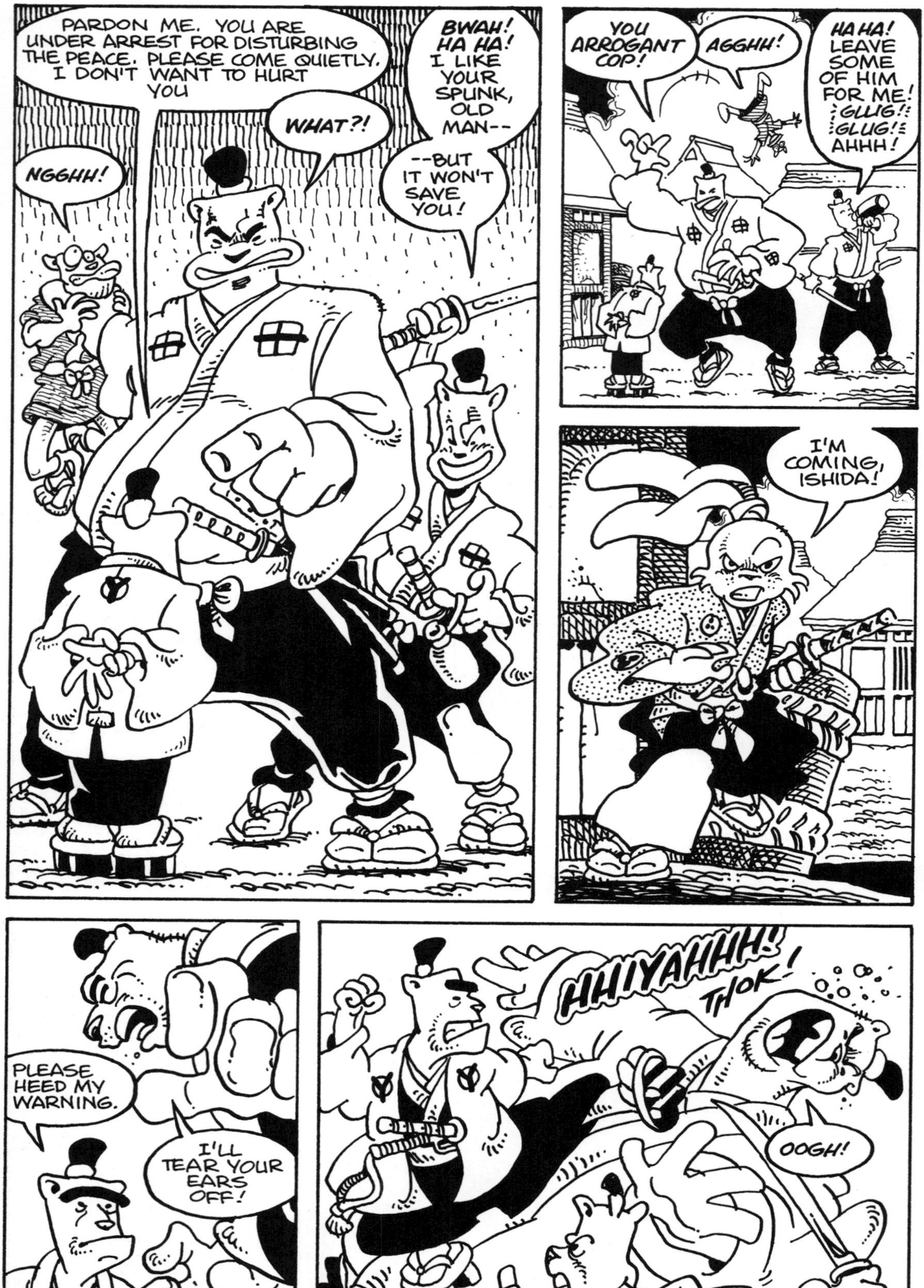
PARDON ME. YOU ARE UNDER ARREST FOR DISTURBING THE PEACE. PLEASE COME QUIETLY. I DON'T WANT TO HURT YOU
NGGHH!
WHAT?!
BWAH! HA HA! I LIKE YOUR SPUNK, OLD MAN--
--BUT IT WON'T SAVE YOU!
YOU ARROGANT COP!
AGGHH!
HA HA! LEAVE SOME OF HIM FOR ME! GLUG! GLUG! AHHH!
I'M COMING, ISHIDA!
PLEASE HEED MY WARNING.
I'LL TEAR YOUR EARS OFF!
HHIYAHHH!
THOK!
OOGH!
14.

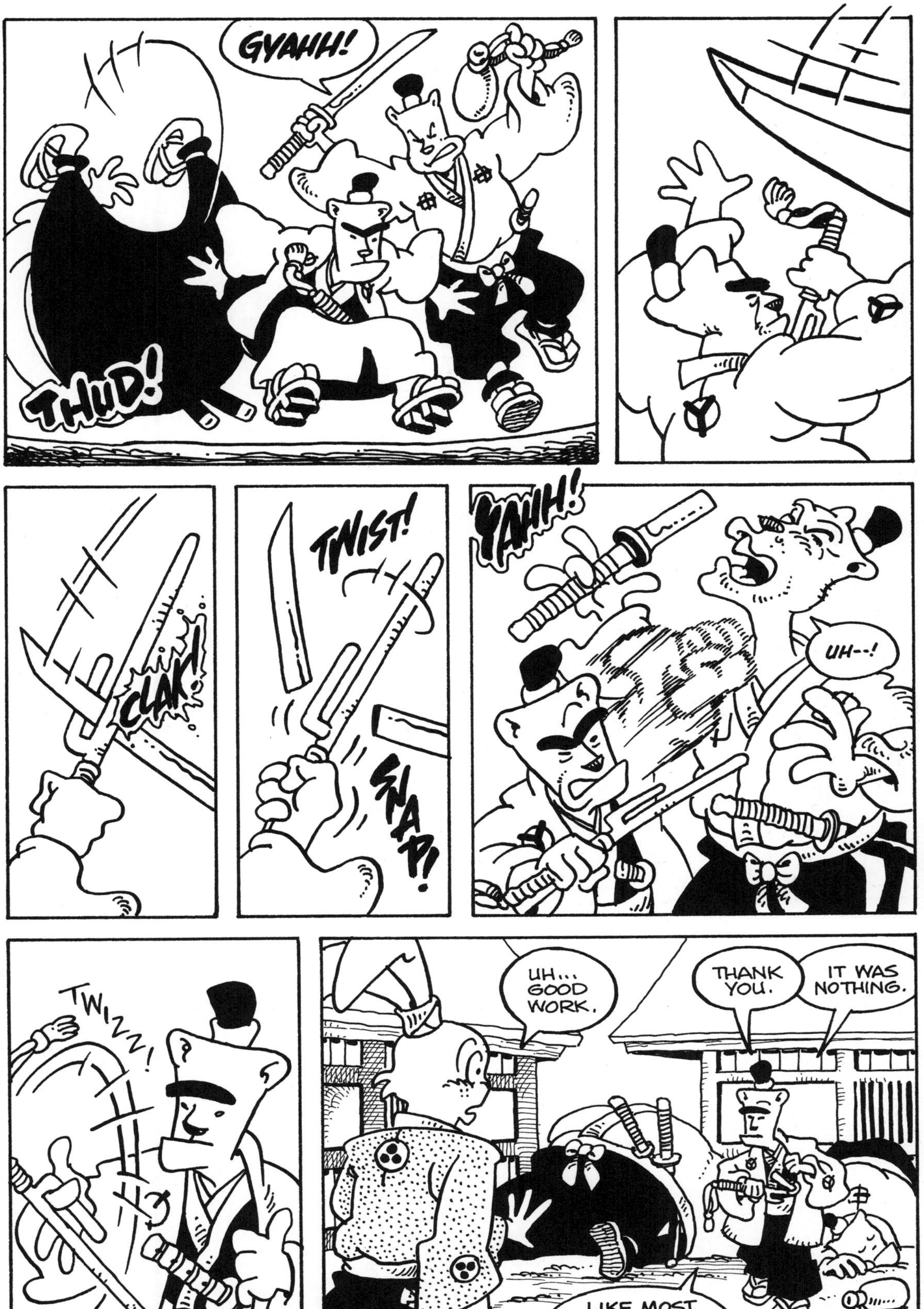
GYAHH!
THUD!
CLAK!
TWIST!
SNAP!
YAHH!
UH--!
TWIZZ!
UH... GOOD WORK.
THANK YOU.
IT WAS NOTHING.
LIKE MOST BIG BULLIES, THEY ARE UNSKILLED AS FIGHTERS.
15.

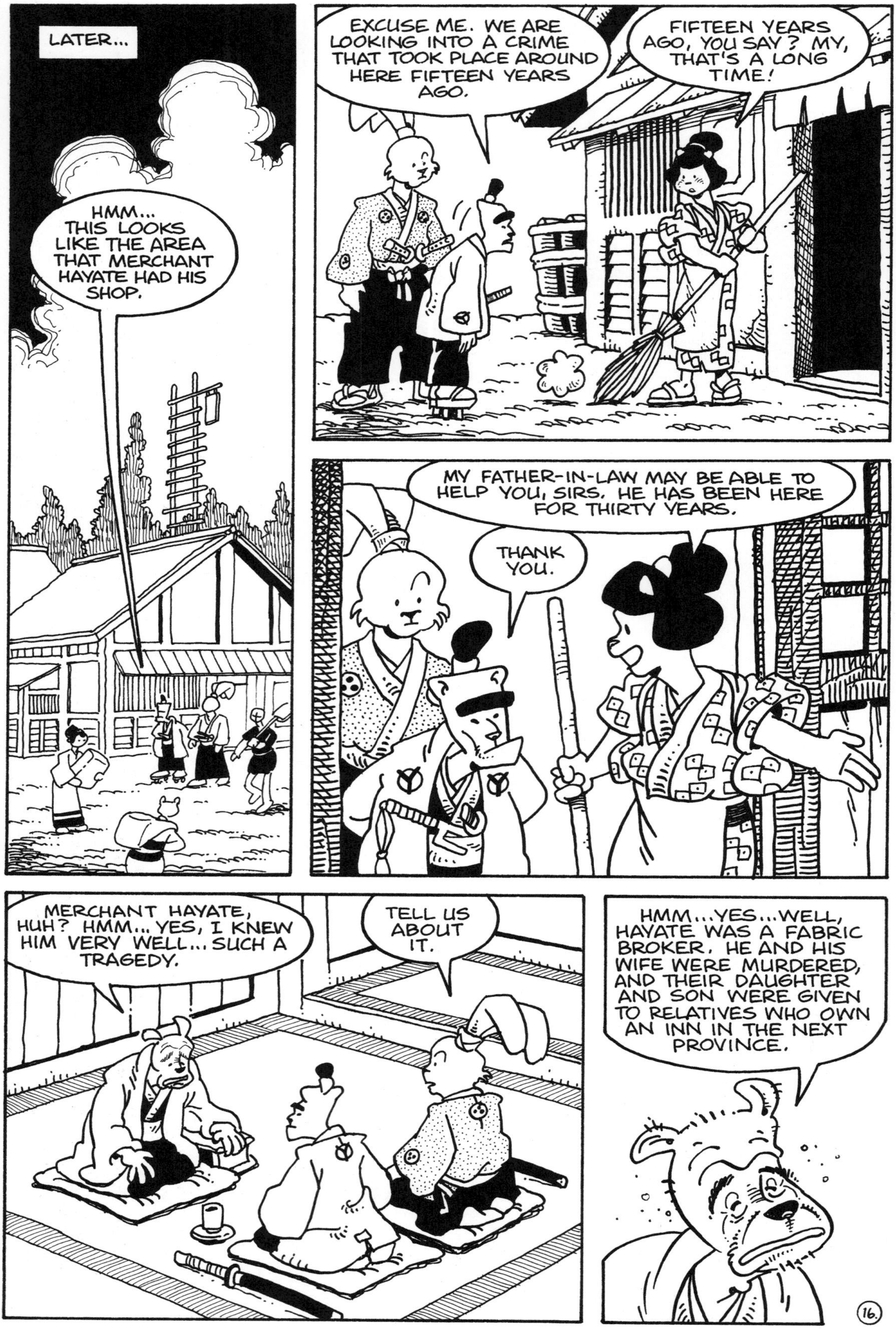
LATER...
HMM... THIS LOOKS LIKE THE AREA THAT MERCHANT HAYATE HAD HIS SHOP.
EXCUSE ME. WE ARE LOOKING INTO A CRIME THAT TOOK PLACE AROUND HERE FIFTEEN YEARS AGO.
FIFTEEN YEARS AGO, YOU SAY? MY, THAT'S A LONG TIME!
MY FATHER-IN-LAW MAY BE ABLE TO HELP YOU, SIRS. HE HAS BEEN HERE FOR THIRTY YEARS.
THANK YOU.
MERCHANT HAYATE, HUH? HMM... YES, I KNEW HIM VERY WELL... SUCH A TRAGEDY.
TELL US ABOUT IT.
HMM... YES... WELL, HAYATE WAS A FABRIC BROKER. HE AND HIS WIFE WERE MURDERED, AND THEIR DAUGHTER AND SON WERE GIVEN TO RELATIVES WHO OWN AN INN IN THE NEXT PROVINCE.
16.

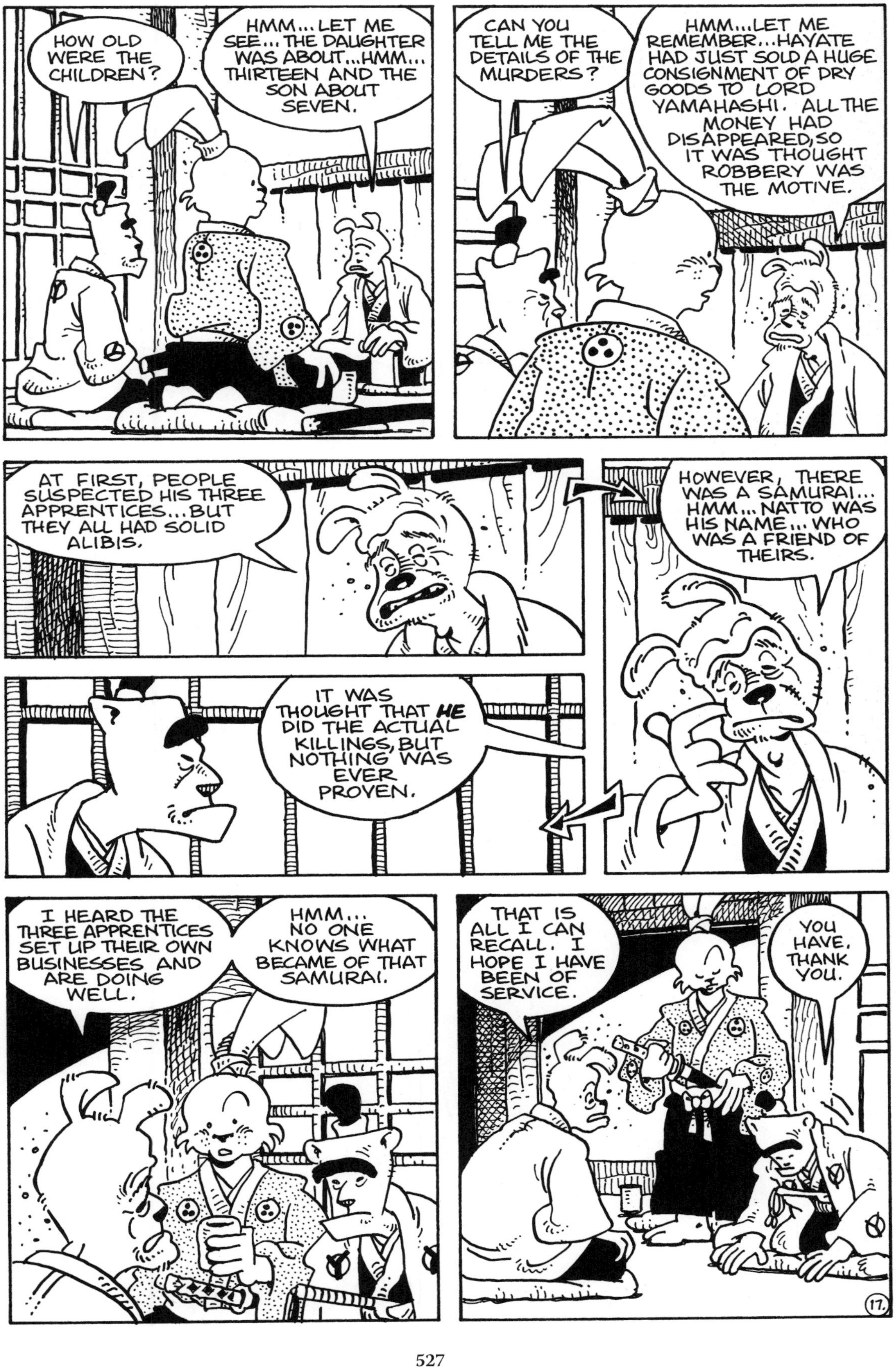
HOW OLD WERE THE CHILDREN?
HMM... LET ME SEE... THE DAUGHTER WAS ABOUT... HMM... THIRTEEN AND THE SON ABOUT SEVEN.
CAN YOU TELL ME THE DETAILS OF THE MURDERS?
HMM... LET ME REMEMBER... HAYATE HAD JUST SOLD A HUGE CONSIGNMENT OF DRY GOODS TO LORD YAMAHASHI. ALL THE MONEY HAD DISAPPEARED, SO IT WAS THOUGHT ROBBERY WAS THE MOTIVE.
AT FIRST, PEOPLE SUSPECTED HIS THREE APPRENTICES... BUT THEY ALL HAD SOLID ALIBIS.
HOWEVER, THERE WAS A SAMURAI... HMM... NATTO WAS HIS NAME... WHO WAS A FRIEND OF THEIRS.
IT WAS THOUGHT THAT ***HE*** DID THE ACTUAL KILLINGS, BUT NOTHING WAS EVER PROVEN.
I HEARD THE THREE APPRENTICES SET UP THEIR OWN BUSINESSES AND ARE DOING WELL.
HMM... NO ONE KNOWS WHAT BECAME OF THAT SAMURAI.
THAT IS ALL I CAN RECALL. I HOPE I HAVE BEEN OF SERVICE.
YOU HAVE. THANK YOU.
17.

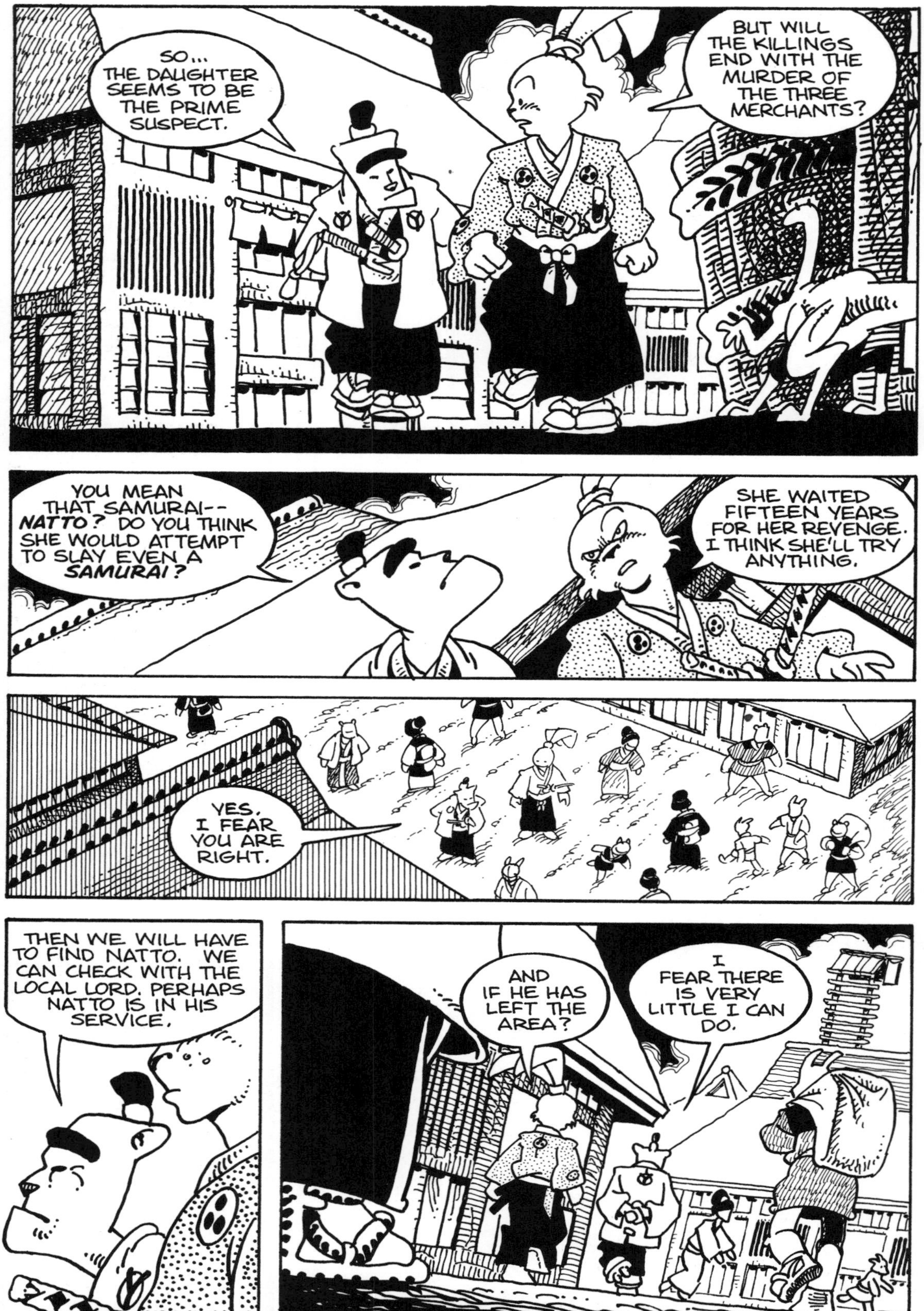
SO... THE DAUGHTER SEEMS TO BE THE PRIME SUSPECT.
BUT WILL THE KILLINGS END WITH THE MURDER OF THE THREE MERCHANTS?
YOU MEAN THAT SAMURAI-- NATTO? DO YOU THINK SHE WOULD ATTEMPT TO SLAY EVEN A SAMURAI?
SHE WAITED FIFTEEN YEARS FOR HER REVENGE. I THINK SHE'LL TRY ANYTHING.
YES, I FEAR YOU ARE RIGHT.
THEN WE WILL HAVE TO FIND NATTO. WE CAN CHECK WITH THE LOCAL LORD. PERHAPS NATTO IS IN HIS SERVICE.
AND IF HE HAS LEFT THE AREA?
I FEAR THERE IS VERY LITTLE I CAN DO.
18.

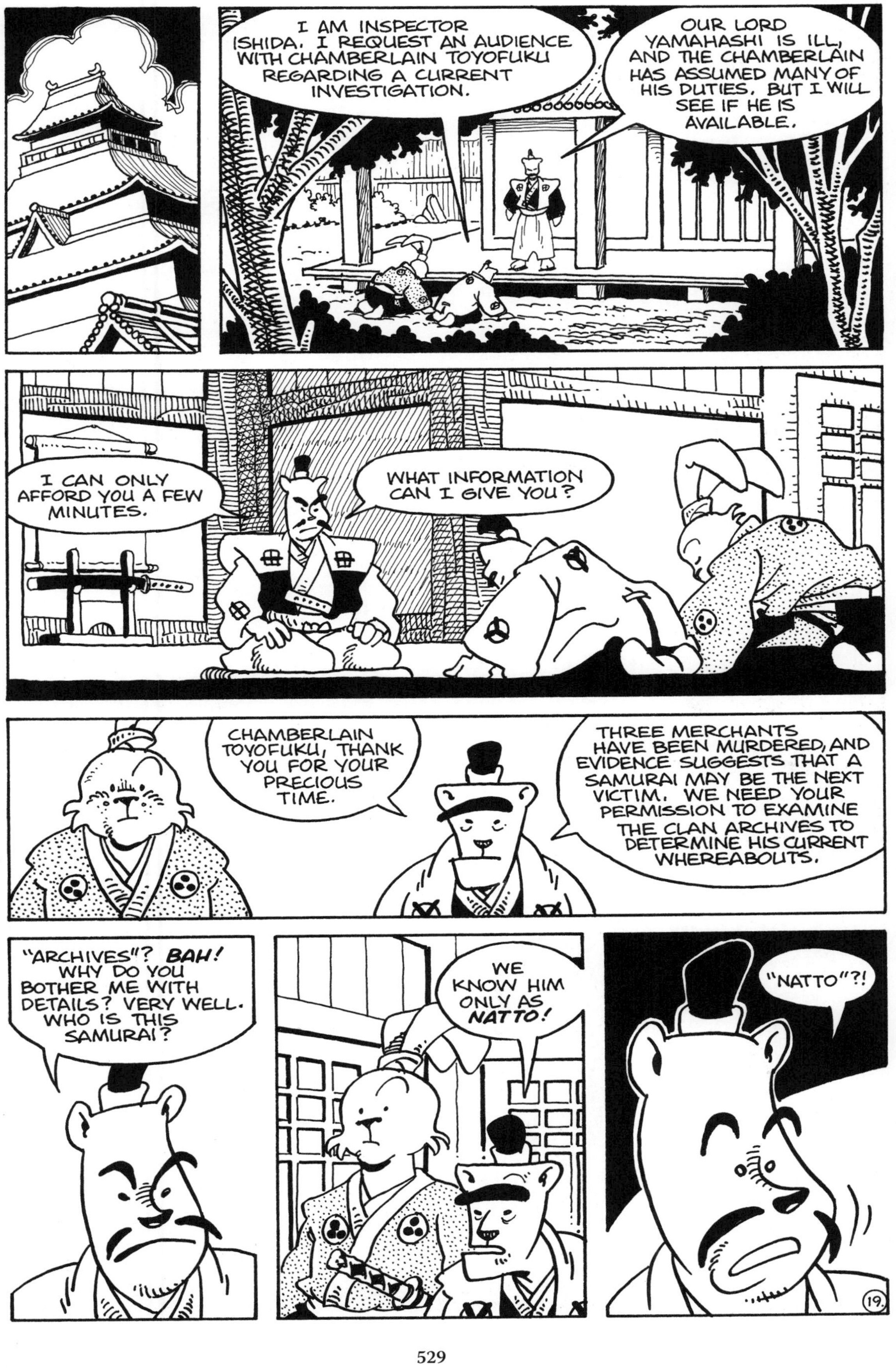
I AM INSPECTOR ISHIDA. I REQUEST AN AUDIENCE WITH CHAMBERLAIN TOYOFUKU REGARDING A CURRENT INVESTIGATION.
OUR LORD YAMAHASHI IS ILL, AND THE CHAMBERLAIN HAS ASSUMED MANY OF HIS DUTIES. BUT I WILL SEE IF HE IS AVAILABLE.
I CAN ONLY AFFORD YOU A FEW MINUTES.
WHAT INFORMATION CAN I GIVE YOU?
CHAMBERLAIN TOYOFUKU, THANK YOU FOR YOUR PRECIOUS TIME.
THREE MERCHANTS HAVE BEEN MURDERED, AND EVIDENCE SUGGESTS THAT A SAMURAI MAY BE THE NEXT VICTIM. WE NEED YOUR PERMISSION TO EXAMINE THE CLAN ARCHIVES TO DETERMINE HIS CURRENT WHEREABOUTS.
"ARCHIVES"? **BAH!** WHY DO YOU BOTHER ME WITH DETAILS? VERY WELL. WHO IS THIS SAMURAI?
WE KNOW HIM ONLY AS ***NATTO!***
"NATTO"?!
19.

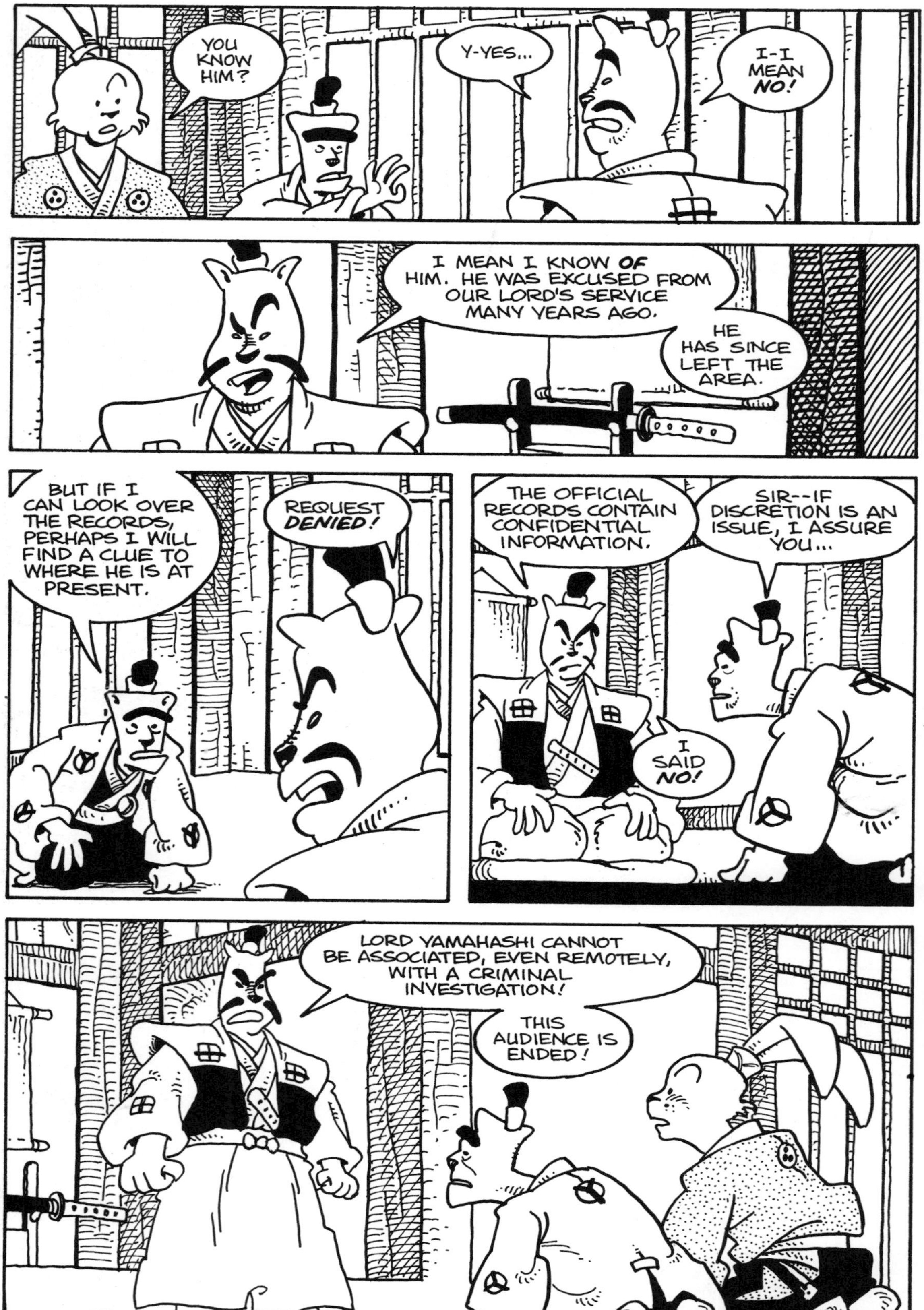
YOU KNOW HIM?
Y-YES...
I-I MEAN NO!
I MEAN I KNOW OF HIM. HE WAS EXCUSED FROM OUR LORD'S SERVICE MANY YEARS AGO.
HE HAS SINCE LEFT THE AREA.
BUT IF I CAN LOOK OVER THE RECORDS, PERHAPS I WILL FIND A CLUE TO WHERE HE IS AT PRESENT.
REQUEST DENIED!
THE OFFICIAL RECORDS CONTAIN CONFIDENTIAL INFORMATION.
SIR--IF DISCRETION IS AN ISSUE, I ASSURE YOU...
I SAID NO!
LORD YAMAHASHI CANNOT BE ASSOCIATED, EVEN REMOTELY, WITH A CRIMINAL INVESTIGATION!
THIS AUDIENCE IS ENDED!
20.

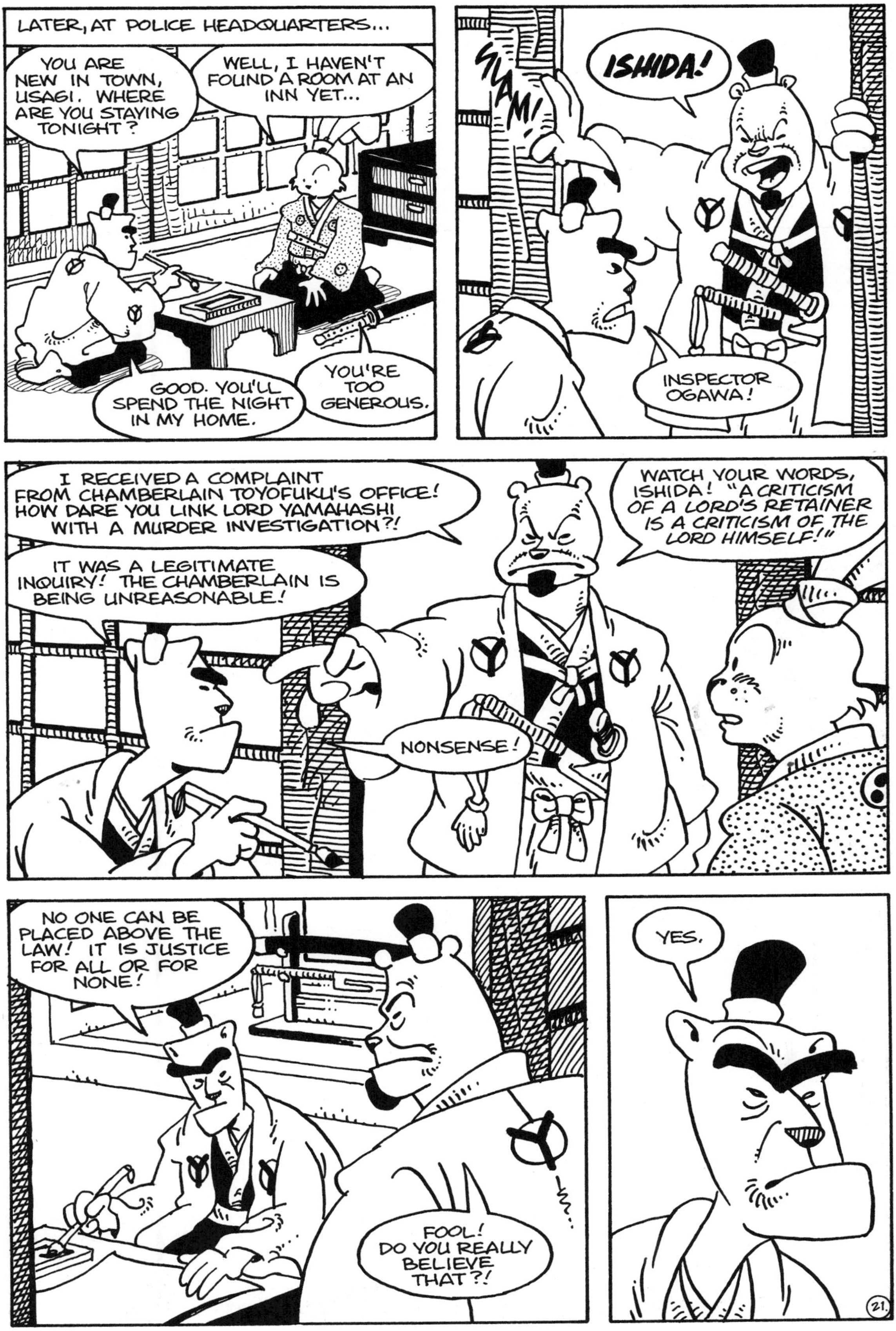
LATER, AT POLICE HEADQUARTERS...
YOU ARE NEW IN TOWN, USAGI. WHERE ARE YOU STAYING TONIGHT?
WELL, I HAVEN'T FOUND A ROOM AT AN INN YET...
GOOD. YOU'LL SPEND THE NIGHT IN MY HOME.
YOU'RE TOO GENEROUS.
SLAM!
ISHIDA!
INSPECTOR OGAWA!
I RECEIVED A COMPLAINT FROM CHAMBERLAIN TOYOFUKU'S OFFICE! HOW DARE YOU LINK LORD YAMAHASHI WITH A MURDER INVESTIGATION?!
IT WAS A LEGITIMATE INQUIRY! THE CHAMBERLAIN IS BEING UNREASONABLE!
WATCH YOUR WORDS, ISHIDA! "A CRITICISM OF A LORD'S RETAINER IS A CRITICISM OF THE LORD HIMSELF!"
NONSENSE!
NO ONE CAN BE PLACED ABOVE THE LAW! IT IS JUSTICE FOR ALL OR FOR NONE!
FOOL! DO YOU REALLY BELIEVE THAT?!
YES.
21.

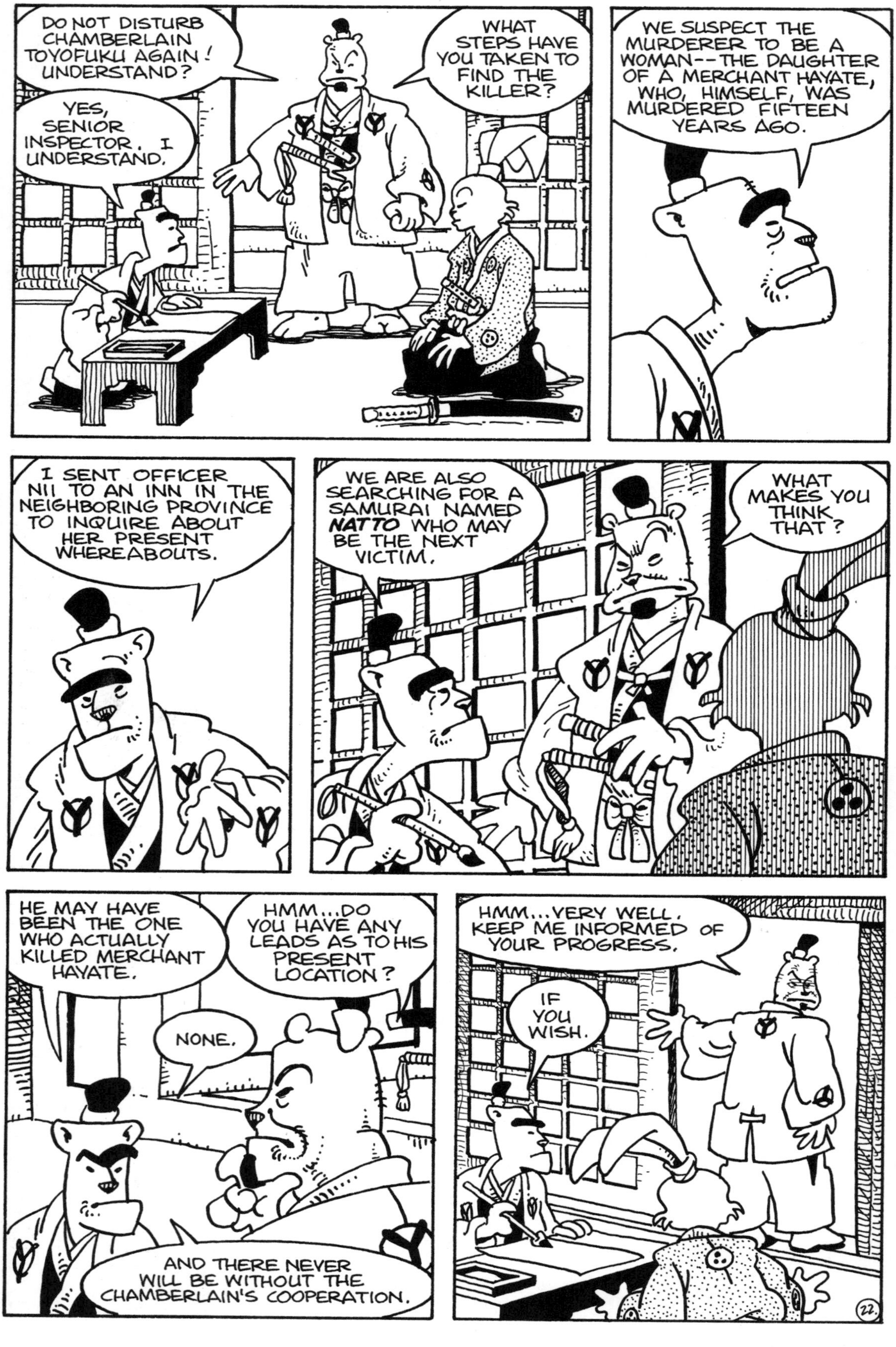
DO NOT DISTURB CHAMBERLAIN TOYOFUKU AGAIN! UNDERSTAND?
YES, SENIOR INSPECTOR. I UNDERSTAND.
WHAT STEPS HAVE YOU TAKEN TO FIND THE KILLER?
WE SUSPECT THE MURDERER TO BE A WOMAN--THE DAUGHTER OF A MERCHANT HAYATE, WHO, HIMSELF, WAS MURDERED FIFTEEN YEARS AGO.
I SENT OFFICER NII TO AN INN IN THE NEIGHBORING PROVINCE TO INQUIRE ABOUT HER PRESENT WHEREABOUTS.
WE ARE ALSO SEARCHING FOR A SAMURAI NAMED NATTO WHO MAY BE THE NEXT VICTIM.
WHAT MAKES YOU THINK THAT?
HE MAY HAVE BEEN THE ONE WHO ACTUALLY KILLED MERCHANT HAYATE.
HMM...DO YOU HAVE ANY LEADS AS TO HIS PRESENT LOCATION?
NONE.
AND THERE NEVER WILL BE WITHOUT THE CHAMBERLAIN'S COOPERATION.
HMM...VERY WELL. KEEP ME INFORMED OF YOUR PROGRESS.
IF YOU WISH.
22.

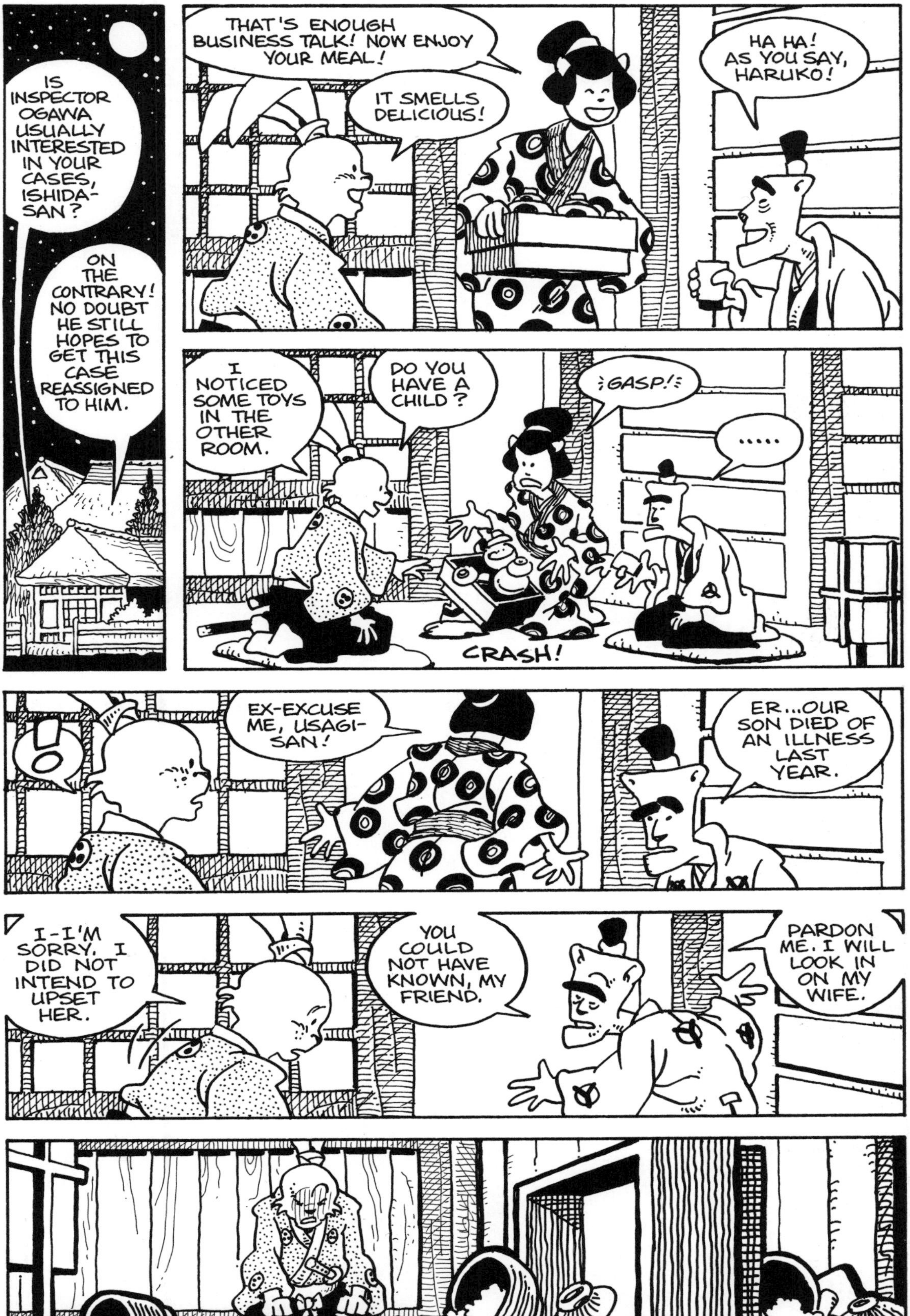

IS INSPECTOR OGAWA USUALLY INTERESTED IN YOUR CASES, ISHIDA-SAN?
ON THE CONTRARY! NO DOUBT HE STILL HOPES TO GET THIS CASE REASSIGNED TO HIM.
THAT'S ENOUGH BUSINESS TALK! NOW ENJOY YOUR MEAL!
IT SMELLS DELICIOUS!
HA HA! AS YOU SAY, HARUKO!
I NOTICED SOME TOYS IN THE OTHER ROOM.
DO YOU HAVE A CHILD?
GASP!
.....
CRASH!
!
EX-EXCUSE ME, USAGI-SAN!
ER...OUR SON DIED OF AN ILLNESS LAST YEAR.
I-I'M SORRY. I DID NOT INTEND TO UPSET HER.
YOU COULD NOT HAVE KNOWN, MY FRIEND.
PARDON ME. I WILL LOOK IN ON MY WIFE.
23

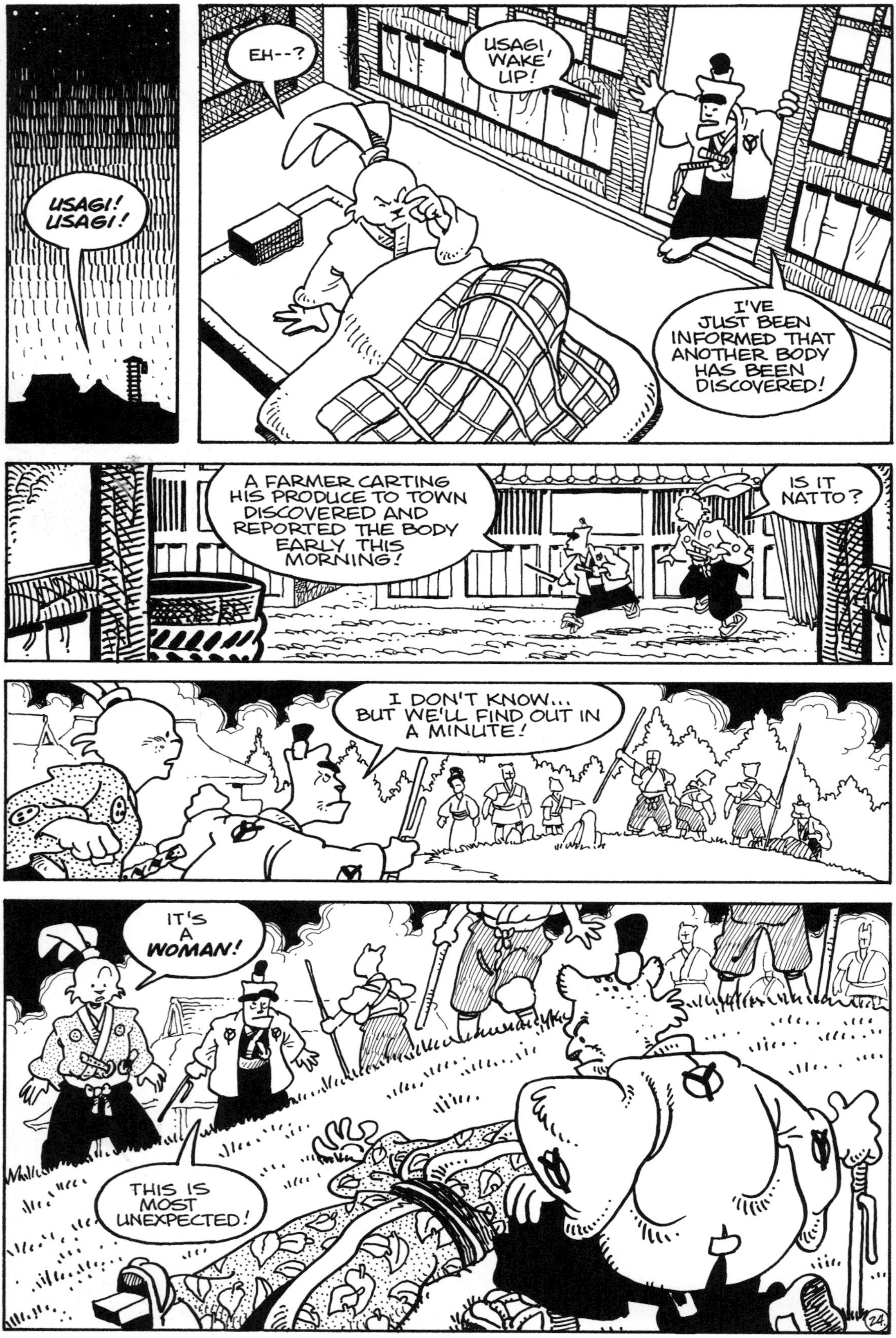
USAGI! USAGI!
EH--?
USAGI, WAKE UP!
I'VE JUST BEEN INFORMED THAT ANOTHER BODY HAS BEEN DISCOVERED!
A FARMER CARTING HIS PRODUCE TO TOWN DISCOVERED AND REPORTED THE BODY EARLY THIS MORNING!
IS IT NATTO?
I DON'T KNOW... BUT WE'LL FIND OUT IN A MINUTE!
IT'S A WOMAN!
THIS IS MOST UNEXPECTED!
24.

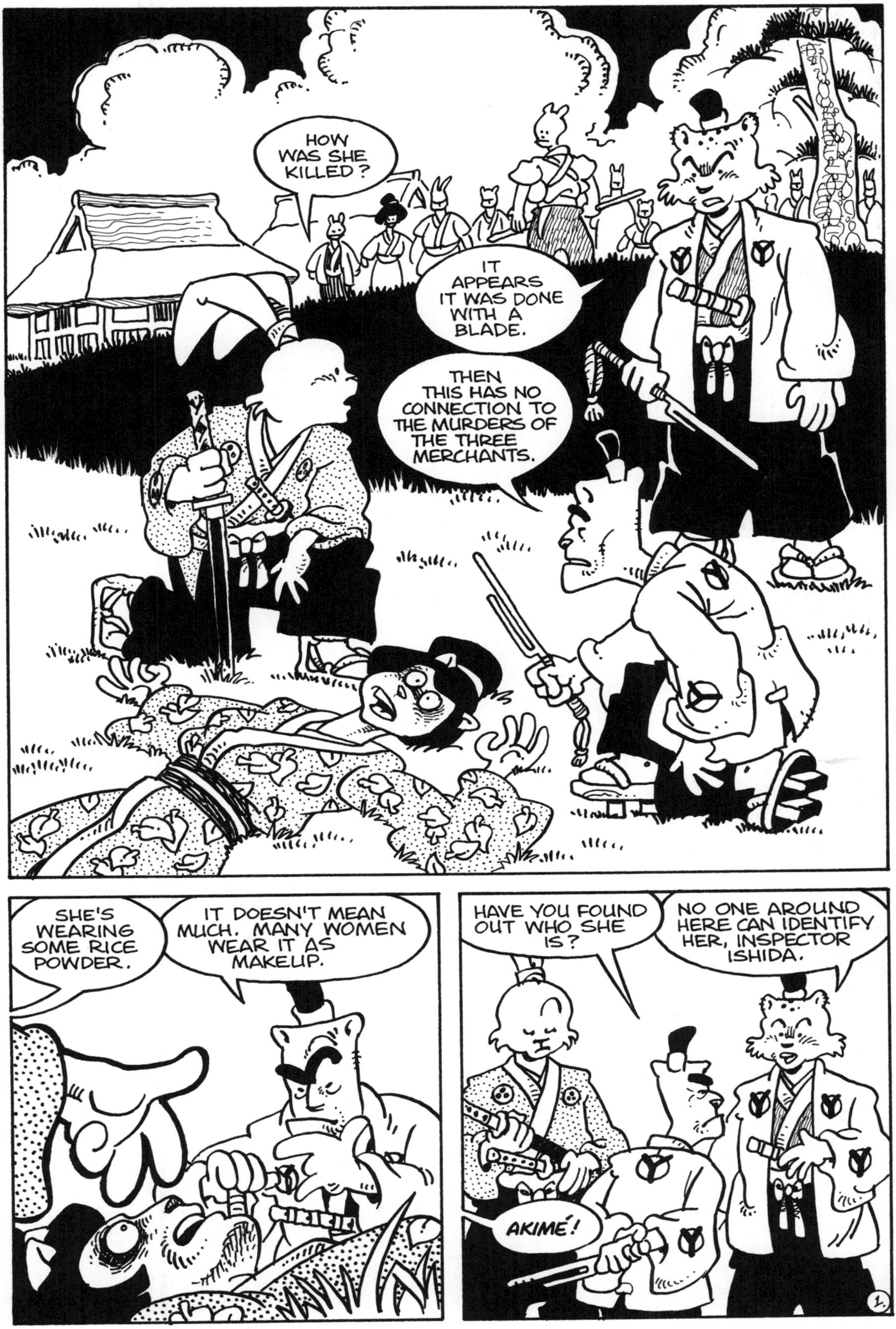

HOW WAS SHE KILLED?
IT APPEARS IT WAS DONE WITH A BLADE.
THEN THIS HAS NO CONNECTION TO THE MURDERS OF THE THREE MERCHANTS.
SHE'S WEARING SOME RICE POWDER.
IT DOESN'T MEAN MUCH. MANY WOMEN WEAR IT AS MAKEUP.
HAVE YOU FOUND OUT WHO SHE IS?
NO ONE AROUND HERE CAN IDENTIFY HER, INSPECTOR ISHIDA.
AKIMÉ!
1.

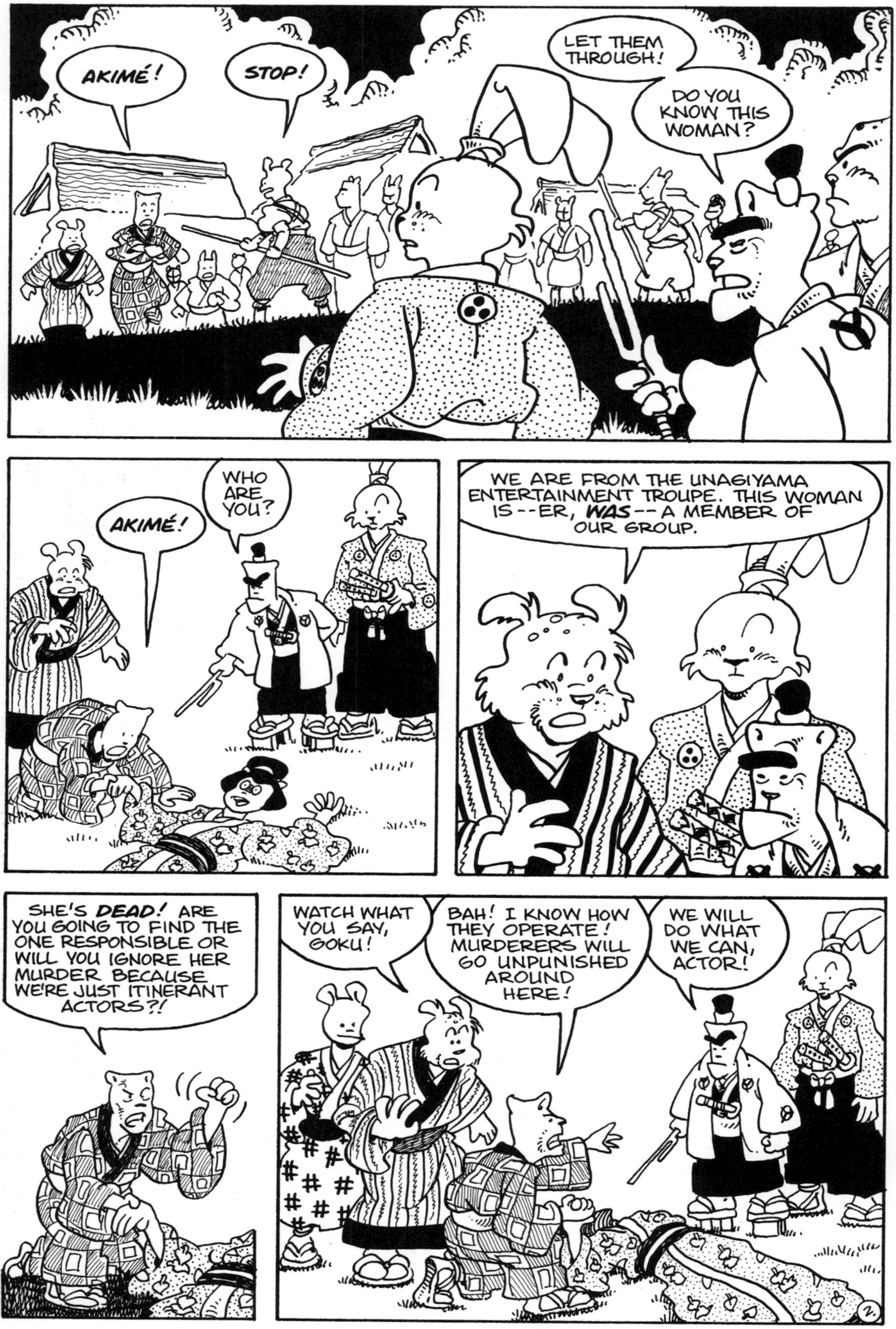
AKIMÉ!
STOP!
LET THEM THROUGH!
DO YOU KNOW THIS WOMAN?
AKIMÉ!
WHO ARE YOU?
WE ARE FROM THE UNAGIYAMA ENTERTAINMENT TROUPE. THIS WOMAN IS--ER, WAS--A MEMBER OF OUR GROUP.
SHE'S DEAD! ARE YOU GOING TO FIND THE ONE RESPONSIBLE OR WILL YOU IGNORE HER MURDER BECAUSE WE'RE JUST ITINERANT ACTORS?!
WATCH WHAT YOU SAY, GOKU!
BAH! I KNOW HOW THEY OPERATE! MURDERERS WILL GO UNPUNISHED AROUND HERE!
WE WILL DO WHAT WE CAN, ACTOR!
2

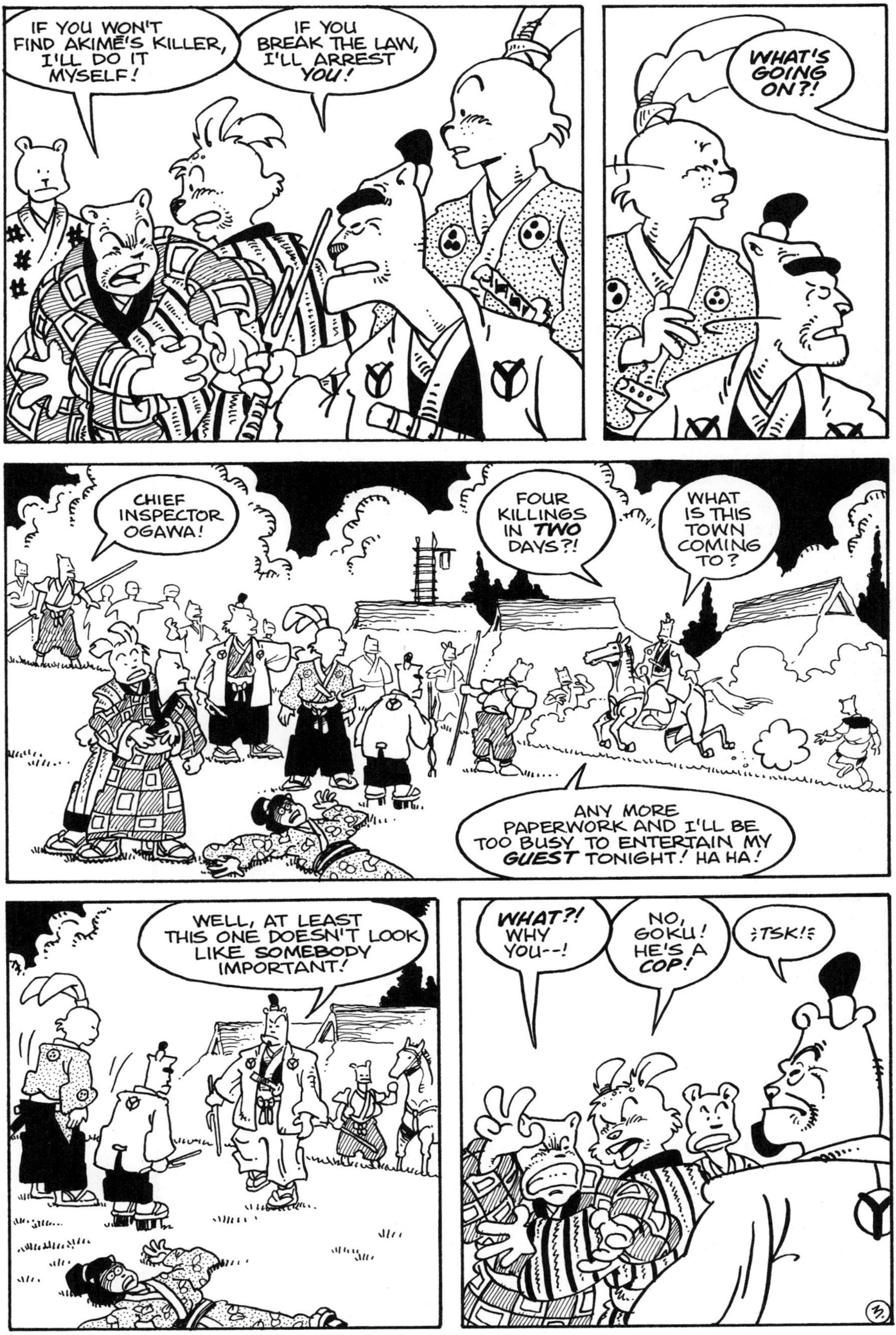

IF YOU WON'T FIND AKIME'S KILLER, I'LL DO IT MYSELF!
IF YOU BREAK THE LAW, I'LL ARREST YOU!
WHAT'S GOING ON?!
CHIEF INSPECTOR OGAWA!
FOUR KILLINGS IN TWO DAYS?!
WHAT IS THIS TOWN COMING TO?
ANY MORE PAPERWORK AND I'LL BE TOO BUSY TO ENTERTAIN MY GUEST TONIGHT! HA HA!
WELL, AT LEAST THIS ONE DOESN'T LOOK LIKE SOMEBODY IMPORTANT!
WHAT?! WHY YOU--!
NO, GOKU! HE'S A COP!
TSK!
3.

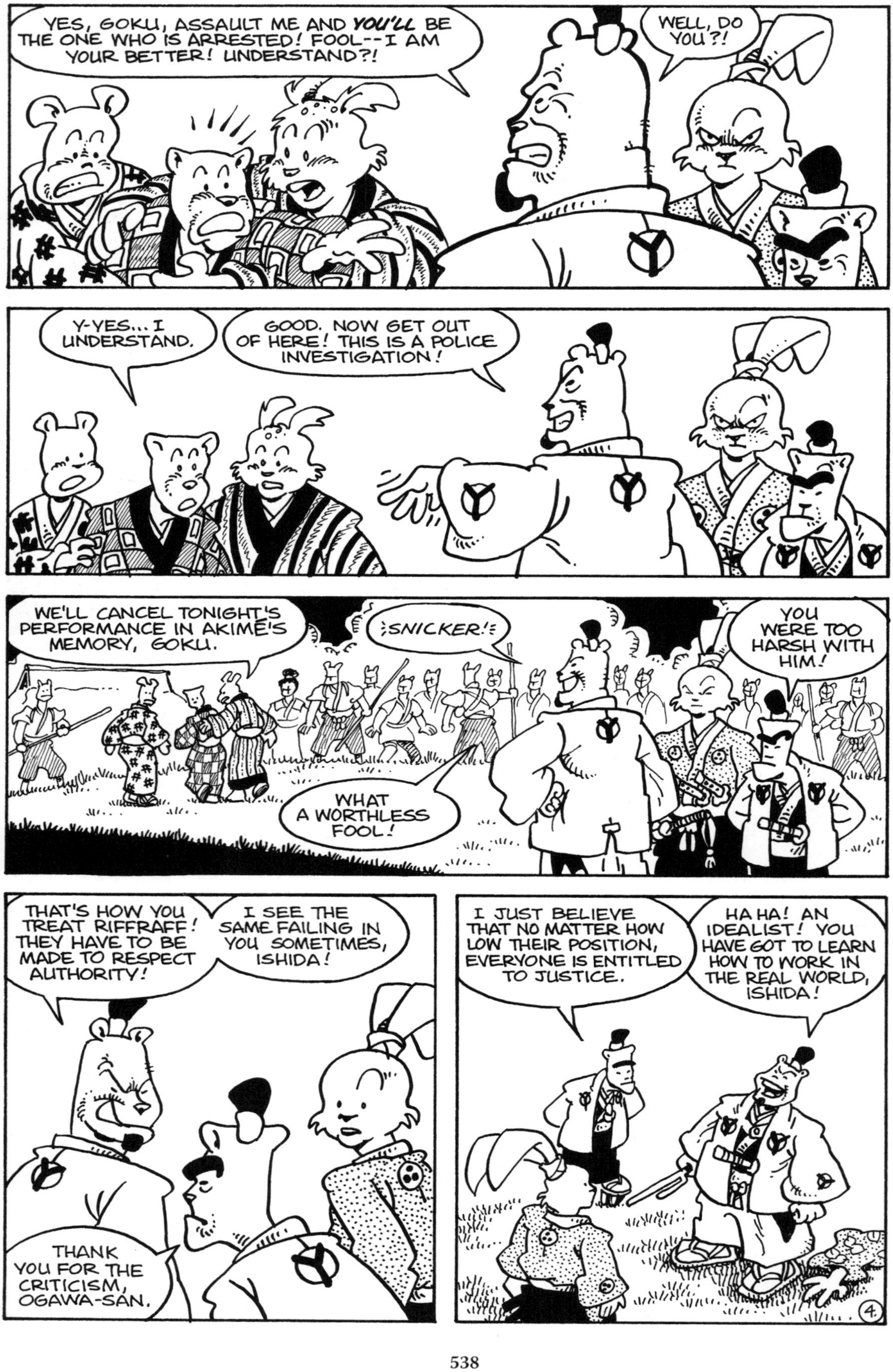
YES, GOKU, ASSAULT ME AND YOU'LL BE THE ONE WHO IS ARRESTED! FOOL--I AM YOUR BETTER! UNDERSTAND?!
WELL, DO YOU?!
Y-YES... I UNDERSTAND.
GOOD. NOW GET OUT OF HERE! THIS IS A POLICE INVESTIGATION!
WE'LL CANCEL TONIGHT'S PERFORMANCE IN AKIME'S MEMORY, GOKU.
SNICKER!
WHAT A WORTHLESS FOOL!
YOU WERE TOO HARSH WITH HIM!
THAT'S HOW YOU TREAT RIFFRAFF! THEY HAVE TO BE MADE TO RESPECT AUTHORITY!
I SEE THE SAME FAILING IN YOU SOMETIMES, ISHIDA!
THANK YOU FOR THE CRITICISM, OGAWA-SAN.
I JUST BELIEVE THAT NO MATTER HOW LOW THEIR POSITION, EVERYONE IS ENTITLED TO JUSTICE.
HA HA! AN IDEALIST! YOU HAVE GOT TO LEARN HOW TO WORK IN THE REAL WORLD, ISHIDA!
4

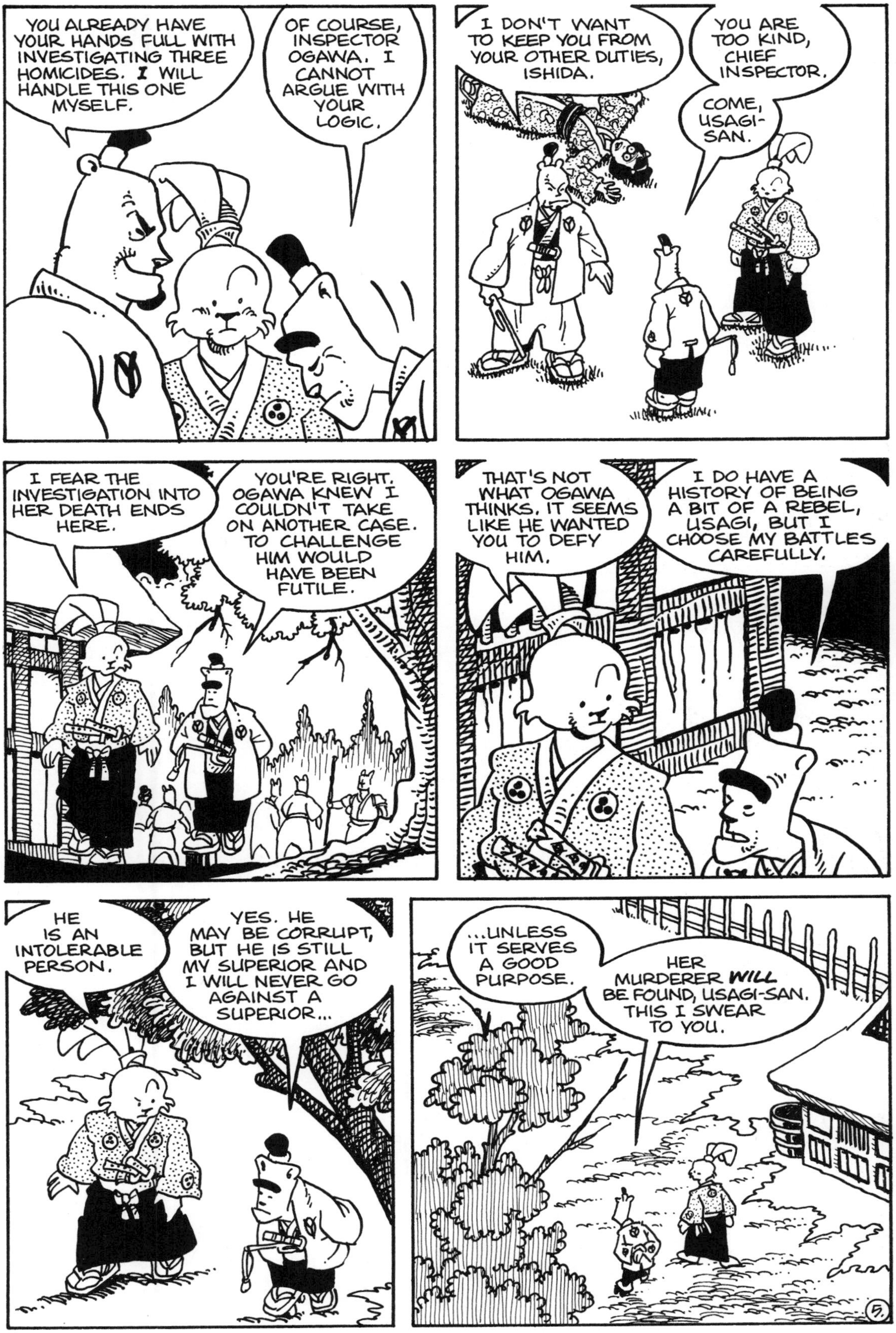
YOU ALREADY HAVE YOUR HANDS FULL WITH INVESTIGATING THREE HOMICIDES. I WILL HANDLE THIS ONE MYSELF.
OF COURSE, INSPECTOR OGAWA. I CANNOT ARGUE WITH YOUR LOGIC.
I DON'T WANT TO KEEP YOU FROM YOUR OTHER DUTIES, ISHIDA.
YOU ARE TOO KIND, CHIEF INSPECTOR.
COME, USAGI-SAN.
I FEAR THE INVESTIGATION INTO HER DEATH ENDS HERE.
YOU'RE RIGHT. OGAWA KNEW I COULDN'T TAKE ON ANOTHER CASE. TO CHALLENGE HIM WOULD HAVE BEEN FUTILE.
THAT'S NOT WHAT OGAWA THINKS. IT SEEMS LIKE HE WANTED YOU TO DEFY HIM.
I DO HAVE A HISTORY OF BEING A BIT OF A REBEL, USAGI, BUT I CHOOSE MY BATTLES CAREFULLY.
HE IS AN INTOLERABLE PERSON.
YES. HE MAY BE CORRUPT, BUT HE IS STILL MY SUPERIOR AND I WILL NEVER GO AGAINST A SUPERIOR...
...UNLESS IT SERVES A GOOD PURPOSE.
HER MURDERER WILL BE FOUND, USAGI-SAN. THIS I SWEAR TO YOU.
5.

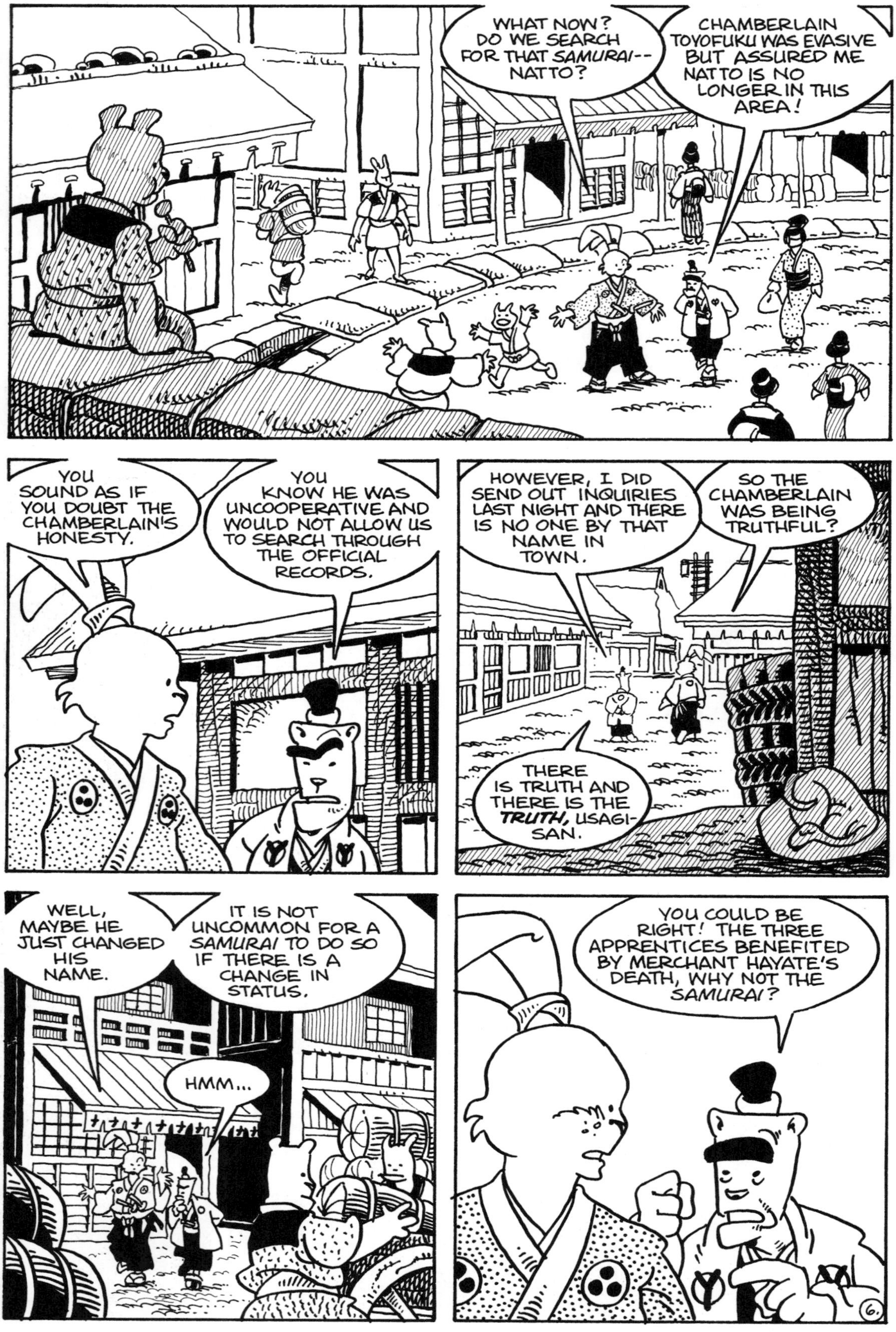

WHAT NOW? DO WE SEARCH FOR THAT *SAMURAI*-- NATTO?
CHAMBERLAIN TOYOFUKU WAS EVASIVE BUT ASSURED ME NATTO IS NO LONGER IN THIS AREA!
YOU SOUND AS IF YOU DOUBT THE CHAMBERLAIN'S HONESTY.
YOU KNOW HE WAS UNCOOPERATIVE AND WOULD NOT ALLOW US TO SEARCH THROUGH THE OFFICIAL RECORDS.
HOWEVER, I DID SEND OUT INQUIRIES LAST NIGHT AND THERE IS NO ONE BY THAT NAME IN TOWN.
SO THE CHAMBERLAIN WAS BEING TRUTHFUL?
THERE IS TRUTH AND THERE IS THE ***TRUTH***, USAGI-SAN.
WELL, MAYBE HE JUST CHANGED HIS NAME.
IT IS NOT UNCOMMON FOR A *SAMURAI* TO DO SO IF THERE IS A CHANGE IN STATUS.
HMM...
YOU COULD BE RIGHT! THE THREE APPRENTICES BENEFITED BY MERCHANT HAYATE'S DEATH, WHY NOT THE *SAMURAI*?
6.

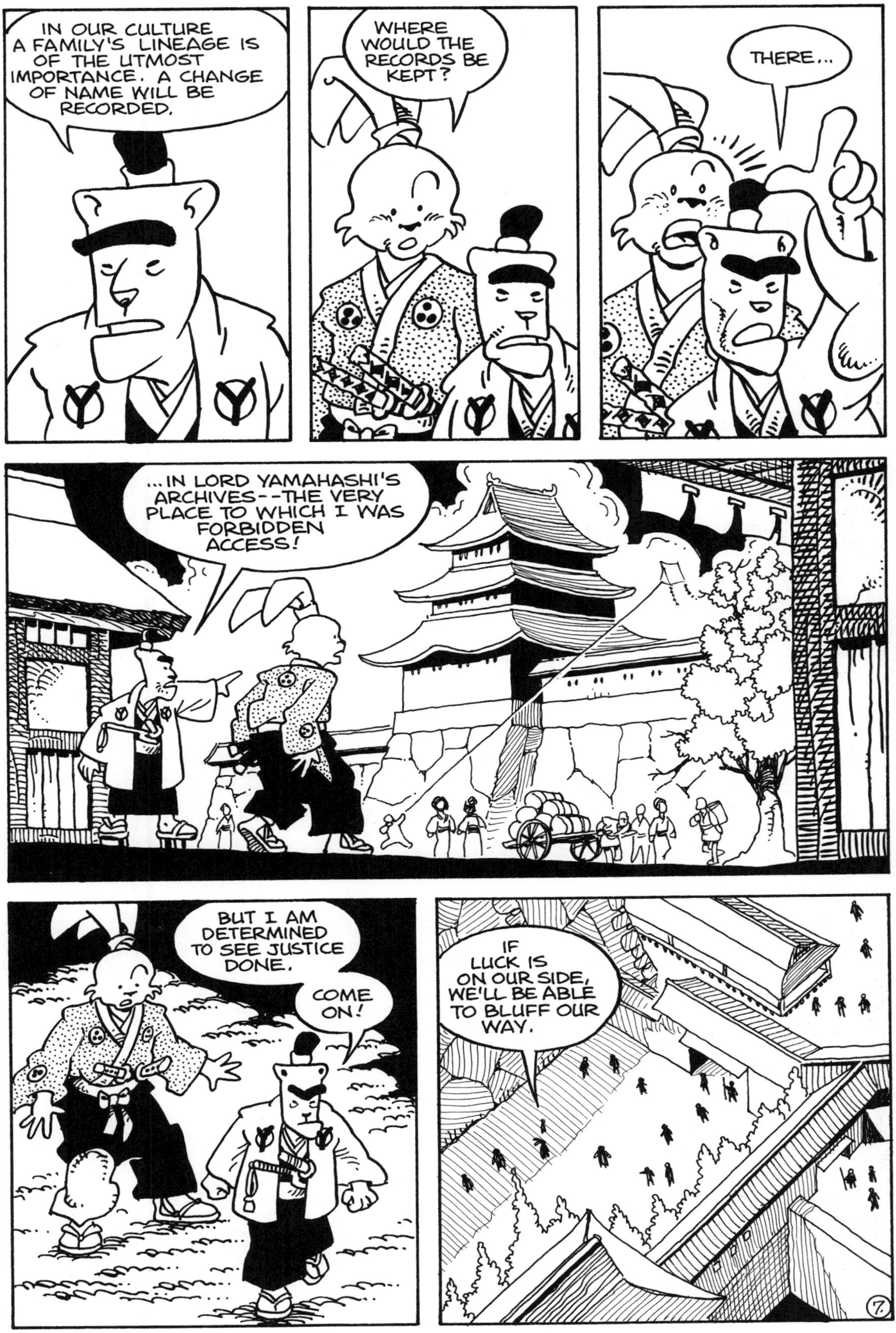
IN OUR CULTURE A FAMILY'S LINEAGE IS OF THE UTMOST IMPORTANCE. A CHANGE OF NAME WILL BE RECORDED.
WHERE WOULD THE RECORDS BE KEPT?
THERE...
...IN LORD YAMAHASHI'S ARCHIVES--THE VERY PLACE TO WHICH I WAS FORBIDDEN ACCESS!
BUT I AM DETERMINED TO SEE JUSTICE DONE.
COME ON!
IF LUCK IS ON OUR SIDE, WE'LL BE ABLE TO BLUFF OUR WAY.
7.

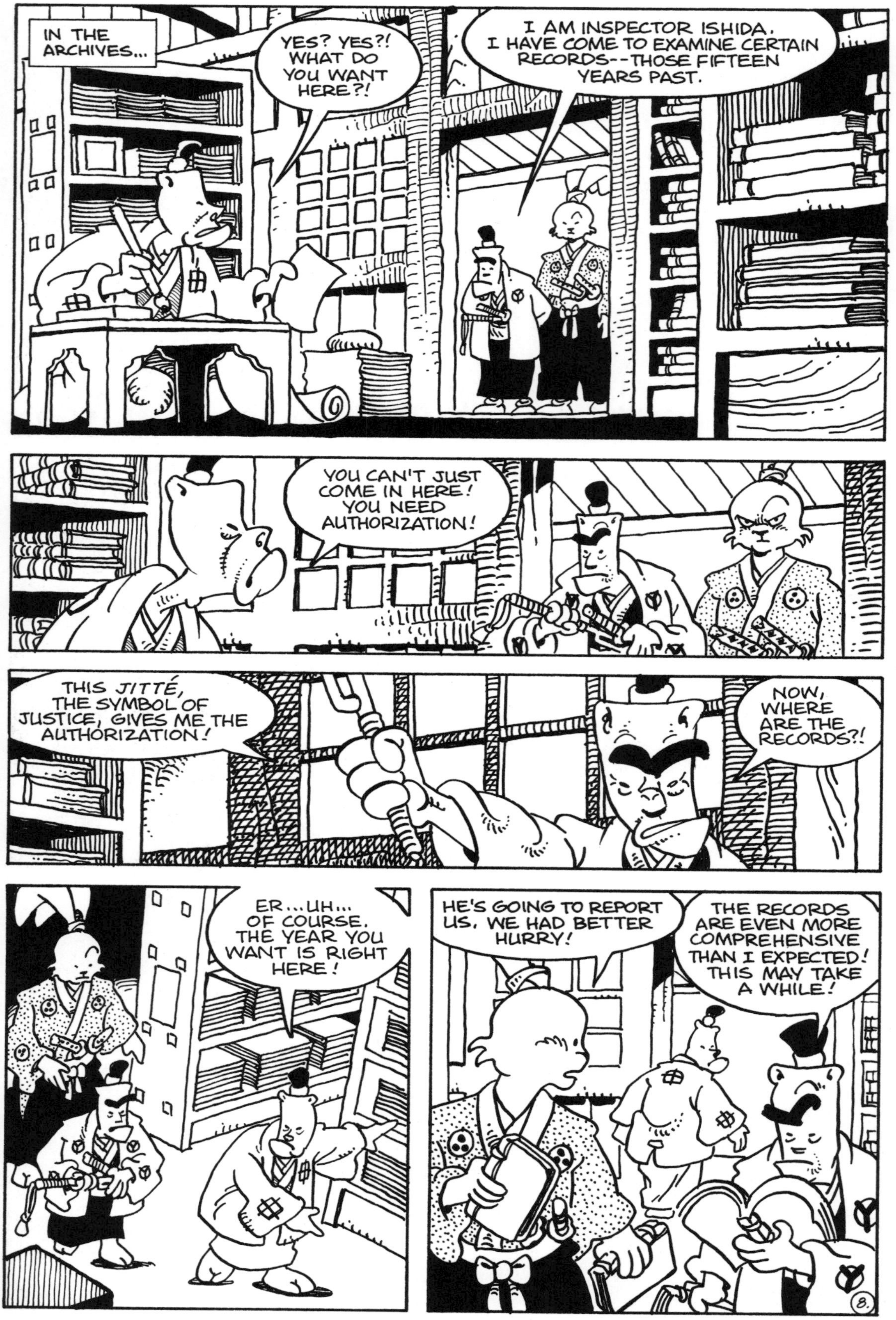
IN THE ARCHIVES...
YES? YES?! WHAT DO YOU WANT HERE?!
I AM INSPECTOR ISHIDA. I HAVE COME TO EXAMINE CERTAIN RECORDS--THOSE FIFTEEN YEARS PAST.
YOU CAN'T JUST COME IN HERE! YOU NEED AUTHORIZATION!
THIS JITTÉ, THE SYMBOL OF JUSTICE, GIVES ME THE AUTHORIZATION!
NOW, WHERE ARE THE RECORDS?!
ER...UH... OF COURSE. THE YEAR YOU WANT IS RIGHT HERE!
HE'S GOING TO REPORT US. WE HAD BETTER HURRY!
THE RECORDS ARE EVEN MORE COMPREHENSIVE THAN I EXPECTED! THIS MAY TAKE A WHILE!
8.

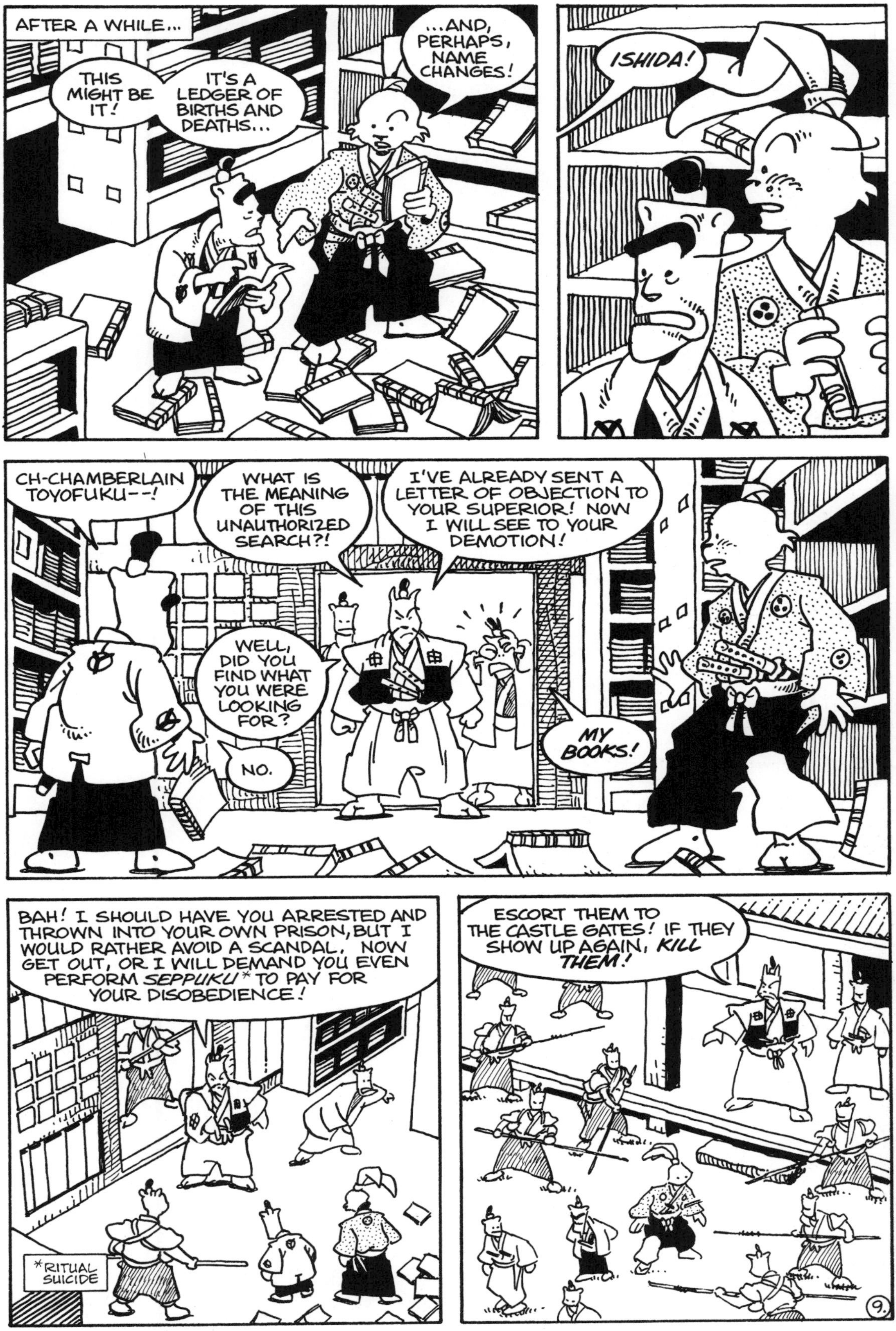
AFTER A WHILE...
THIS MIGHT BE IT!
IT'S A LEDGER OF BIRTHS AND DEATHS...
...AND, PERHAPS, NAME CHANGES!
ISHIDA!
CH-CHAMBERLAIN TOYOFUKU--!
WHAT IS THE MEANING OF THIS UNAUTHORIZED SEARCH?!
I'VE ALREADY SENT A LETTER OF OBJECTION TO YOUR SUPERIOR! NOW I WILL SEE TO YOUR DEMOTION!
WELL, DID YOU FIND WHAT YOU WERE LOOKING FOR?
NO.
MY BOOKS!
BAH! I SHOULD HAVE YOU ARRESTED AND THROWN INTO YOUR OWN PRISON, BUT I WOULD RATHER AVOID A SCANDAL. NOW GET OUT, OR I WILL DEMAND YOU EVEN PERFORM SEPPUKU* TO PAY FOR YOUR DISOBEDIENCE!
*RITUAL SUICIDE
ESCORT THEM TO THE CASTLE GATES! IF THEY SHOW UP AGAIN, KILL THEM!
9.

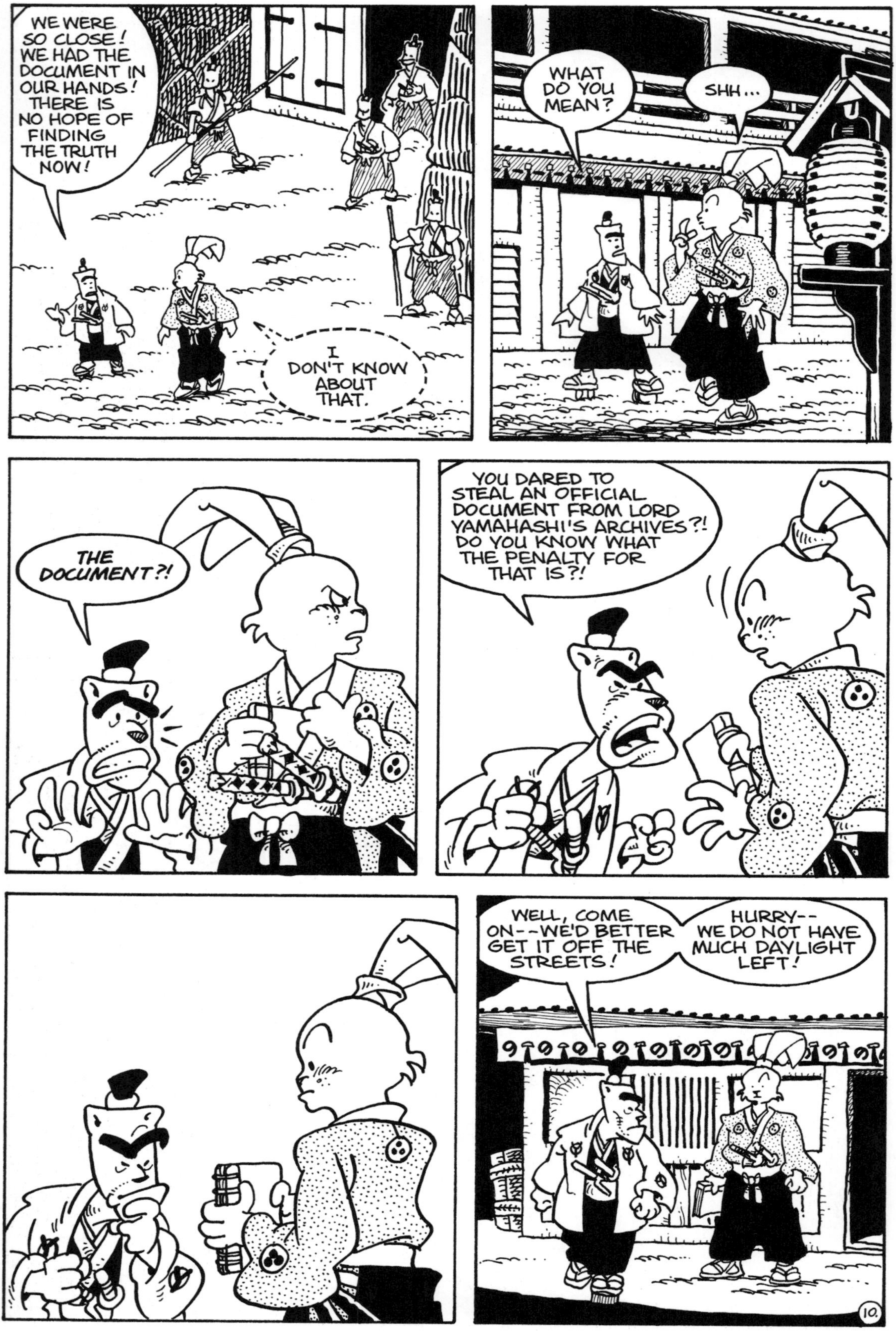
WE WERE SO CLOSE! WE HAD THE DOCUMENT IN OUR HANDS! THERE IS NO HOPE OF FINDING THE TRUTH NOW!
I DON'T KNOW ABOUT THAT.
WHAT DO YOU MEAN?
SHH...
THE DOCUMENT?!
YOU DARED TO STEAL AN OFFICIAL DOCUMENT FROM LORD YAMAHASHI'S ARCHIVES?! DO YOU KNOW WHAT THE PENALTY FOR THAT IS?!
WELL, COME ON--WE'D BETTER GET IT OFF THE STREETS!
HURRY--WE DO NOT HAVE MUCH DAYLIGHT LEFT!
10.

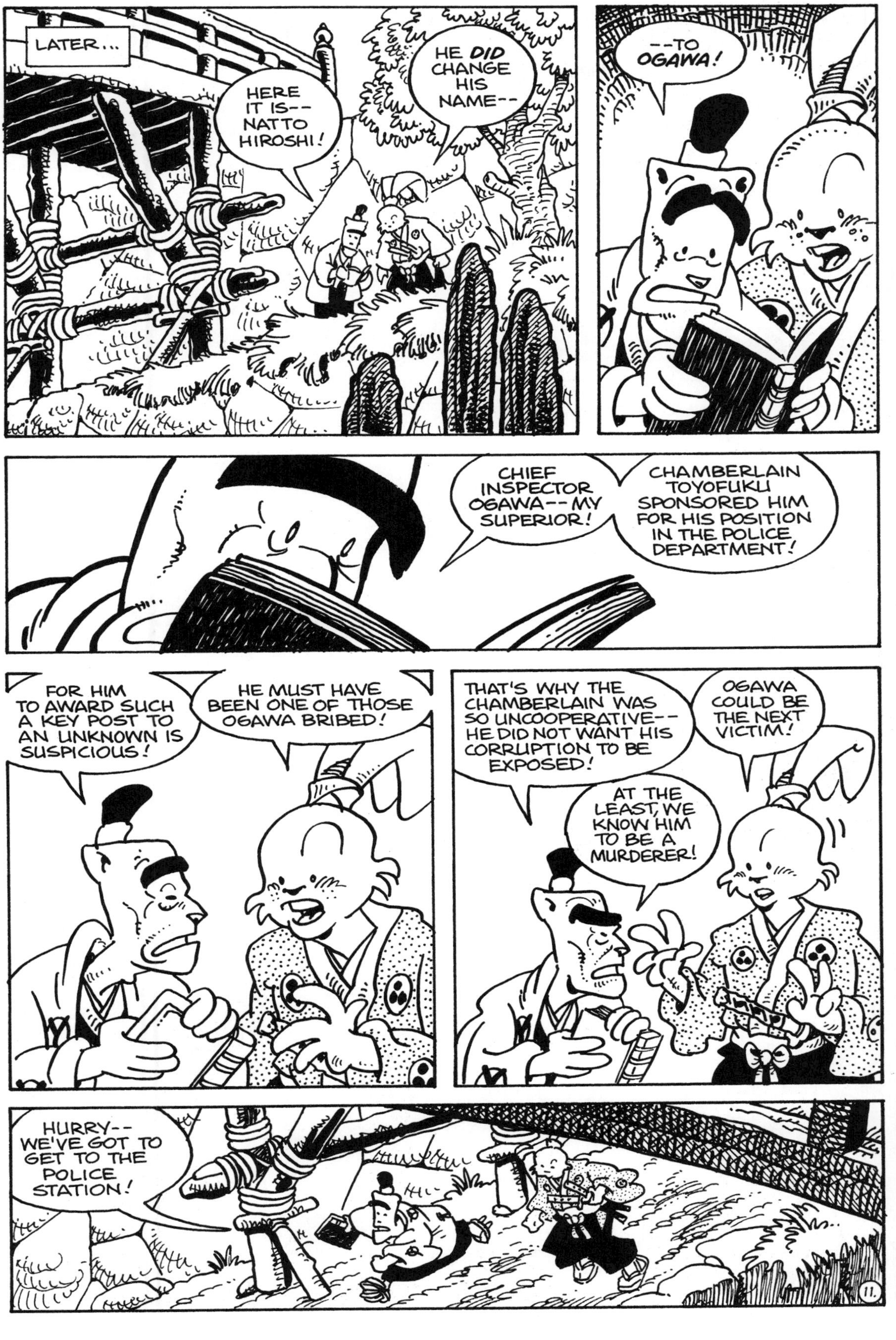
LATER...
HERE IT IS-- NATTO HIROSHI!
HE DID CHANGE HIS NAME--
--TO OGAWA!
CHIEF INSPECTOR OGAWA--MY SUPERIOR!
CHAMBERLAIN TOYOFUKU SPONSORED HIM FOR HIS POSITION IN THE POLICE DEPARTMENT!
FOR HIM TO AWARD SUCH A KEY POST TO AN UNKNOWN IS SUSPICIOUS!
HE MUST HAVE BEEN ONE OF THOSE OGAWA BRIBED!
THAT'S WHY THE CHAMBERLAIN WAS SO UNCOOPERATIVE-- HE DID NOT WANT HIS CORRUPTION TO BE EXPOSED!
OGAWA COULD BE THE NEXT VICTIM!
AT THE LEAST, WE KNOW HIM TO BE A MURDERER!
HURRY-- WE'VE GOT TO GET TO THE POLICE STATION!
11.

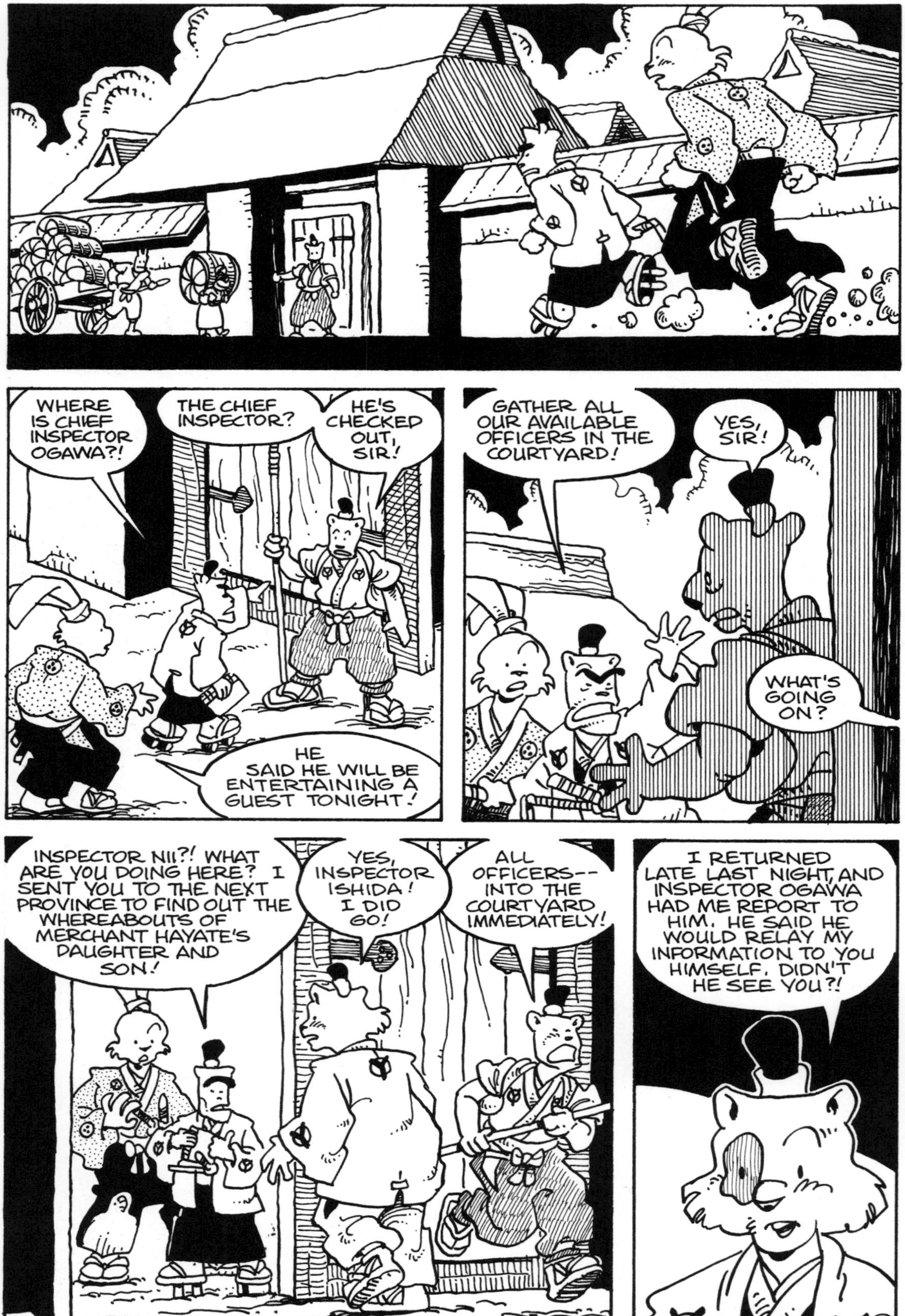
WHERE IS CHIEF INSPECTOR OGAWA?!
THE CHIEF INSPECTOR?
HE'S CHECKED OUT, SIR!
HE SAID HE WILL BE ENTERTAINING A GUEST TONIGHT!
GATHER ALL OUR AVAILABLE OFFICERS IN THE COURTYARD!
YES, SIR!
WHAT'S GOING ON?
INSPECTOR NII?! WHAT ARE YOU DOING HERE? I SENT YOU TO THE NEXT PROVINCE TO FIND OUT THE WHEREABOUTS OF MERCHANT HAYATE'S DAUGHTER AND SON!
YES, INSPECTOR ISHIDA! I DID GO!
ALL OFFICERS-- INTO THE COURTYARD IMMEDIATELY!
I RETURNED LATE LAST NIGHT, AND INSPECTOR OGAWA HAD ME REPORT TO HIM. HE SAID HE WOULD RELAY MY INFORMATION TO YOU HIMSELF. DIDN'T HE SEE YOU?!
12.

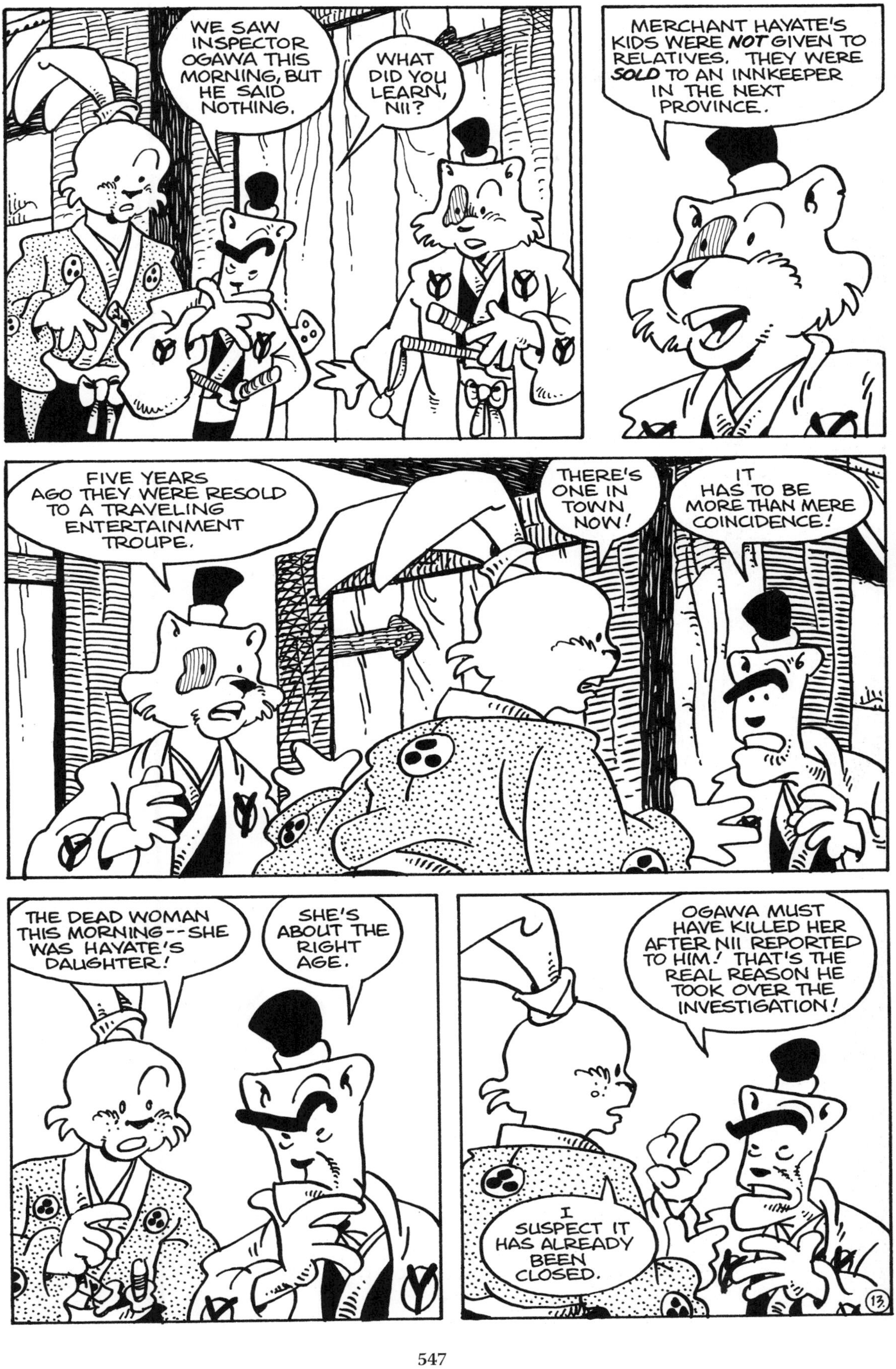
WE SAW INSPECTOR OGAWA THIS MORNING, BUT HE SAID NOTHING.
WHAT DID YOU LEARN, NII?
MERCHANT HAYATE'S KIDS WERE **NOT** GIVEN TO RELATIVES. THEY WERE **SOLD** TO AN INNKEEPER IN THE NEXT PROVINCE.
FIVE YEARS AGO THEY WERE RESOLD TO A TRAVELING ENTERTAINMENT TROUPE.
THERE'S ONE IN TOWN NOW!
IT HAS TO BE MORE THAN MERE COINCIDENCE!
THE DEAD WOMAN THIS MORNING--SHE WAS HAYATE'S DAUGHTER!
SHE'S ABOUT THE RIGHT AGE.
OGAWA MUST HAVE KILLED HER AFTER NII REPORTED TO HIM! THAT'S THE REAL REASON HE TOOK OVER THE INVESTIGATION!
I SUSPECT IT HAS ALREADY BEEN CLOSED.
13

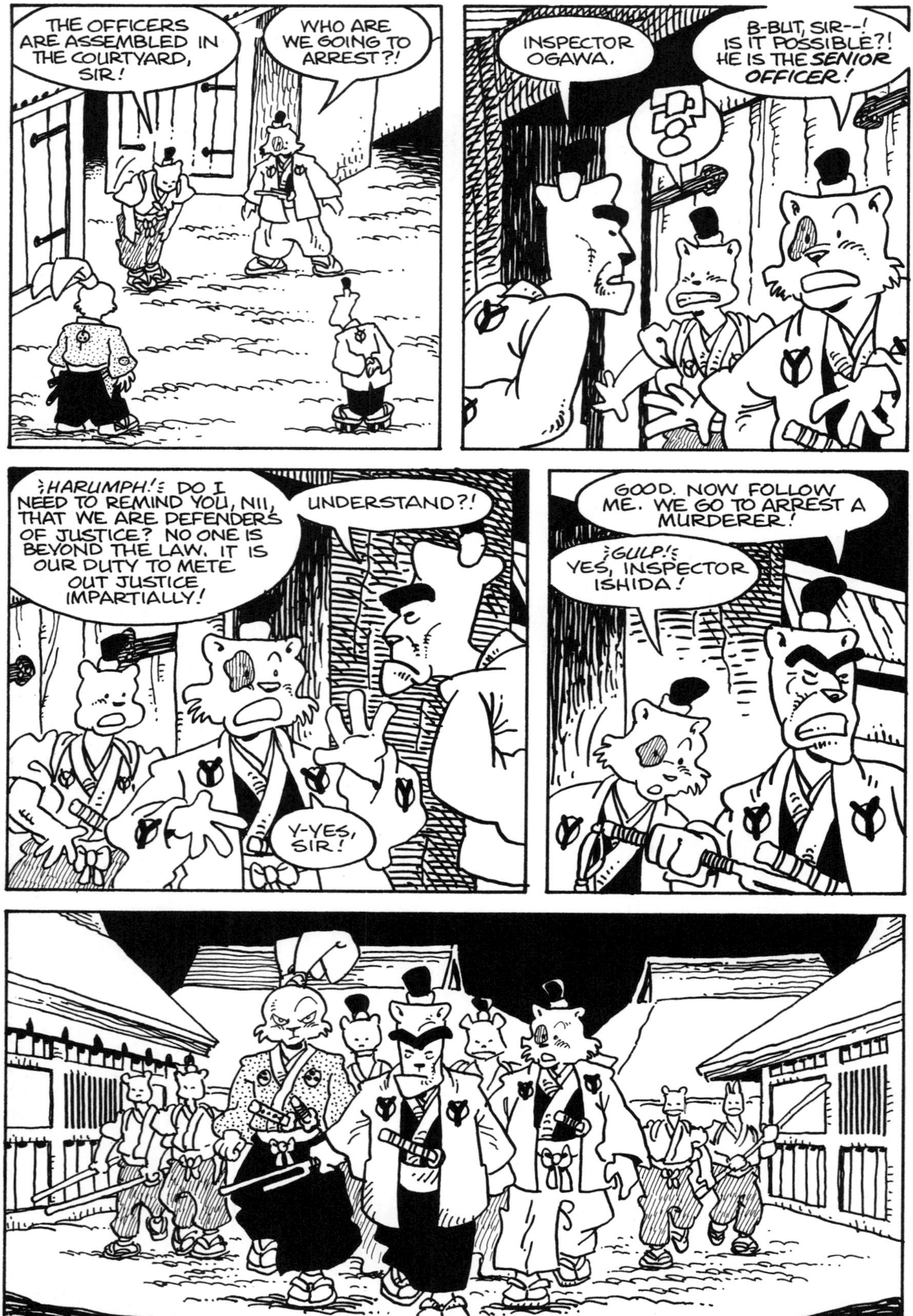
THE OFFICERS ARE ASSEMBLED IN THE COURTYARD, SIR!
WHO ARE WE GOING TO ARREST?!
INSPECTOR OGAWA.
B-BUT, SIR--! IS IT POSSIBLE?! HE IS THE *SENIOR OFFICER!*
HARUMPH! DO I NEED TO REMIND YOU, NII, THAT WE ARE DEFENDERS OF JUSTICE? NO ONE IS BEYOND THE LAW. IT IS OUR DUTY TO METE OUT JUSTICE IMPARTIALLY!
UNDERSTAND?!
Y-YES, SIR!
GOOD. NOW FOLLOW ME. WE GO TO ARREST A MURDERER!
GULP! YES, INSPECTOR ISHIDA!
14.

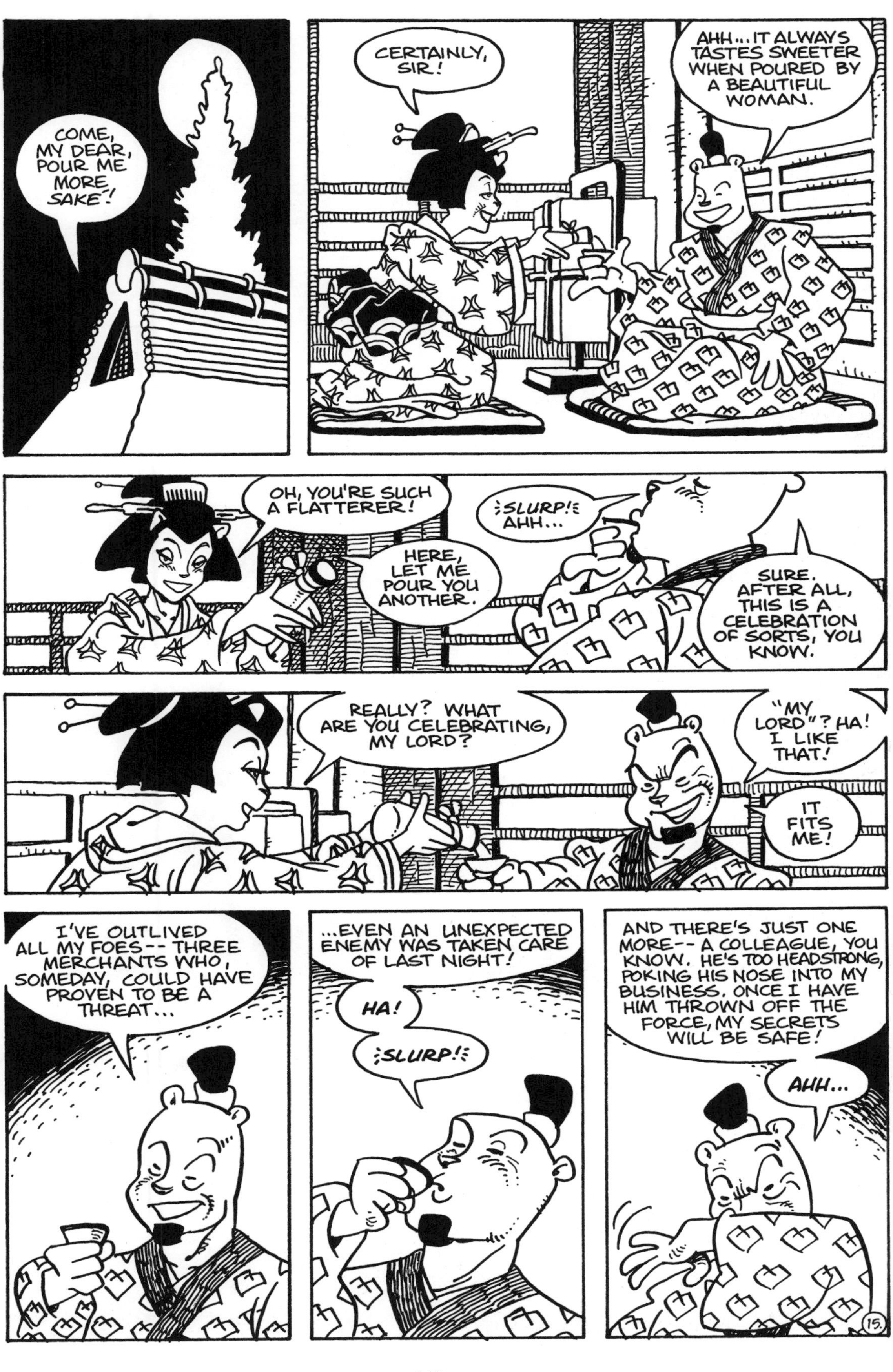
COME, MY DEAR, POUR ME MORE SAKE!
CERTAINLY, SIR!
AHH... IT ALWAYS TASTES SWEETER WHEN POURED BY A BEAUTIFUL WOMAN.
OH, YOU'RE SUCH A FLATTERER!
HERE, LET ME POUR YOU ANOTHER.
SLURP! AHH...
SURE. AFTER ALL, THIS IS A CELEBRATION OF SORTS, YOU KNOW.
REALLY? WHAT ARE YOU CELEBRATING, MY LORD?
"MY LORD"? HA! I LIKE THAT!
IT FITS ME!
I'VE OUTLIVED ALL MY FOES-- THREE MERCHANTS WHO, SOMEDAY, COULD HAVE PROVEN TO BE A THREAT...
...EVEN AN UNEXPECTED ENEMY WAS TAKEN CARE OF LAST NIGHT!
HA!
SLURP!
AND THERE'S JUST ONE MORE-- A COLLEAGUE, YOU KNOW. HE'S TOO HEADSTRONG, POKING HIS NOSE INTO MY BUSINESS. ONCE I HAVE HIM THROWN OFF THE FORCE, MY SECRETS WILL BE SAFE!
AHH...
15.

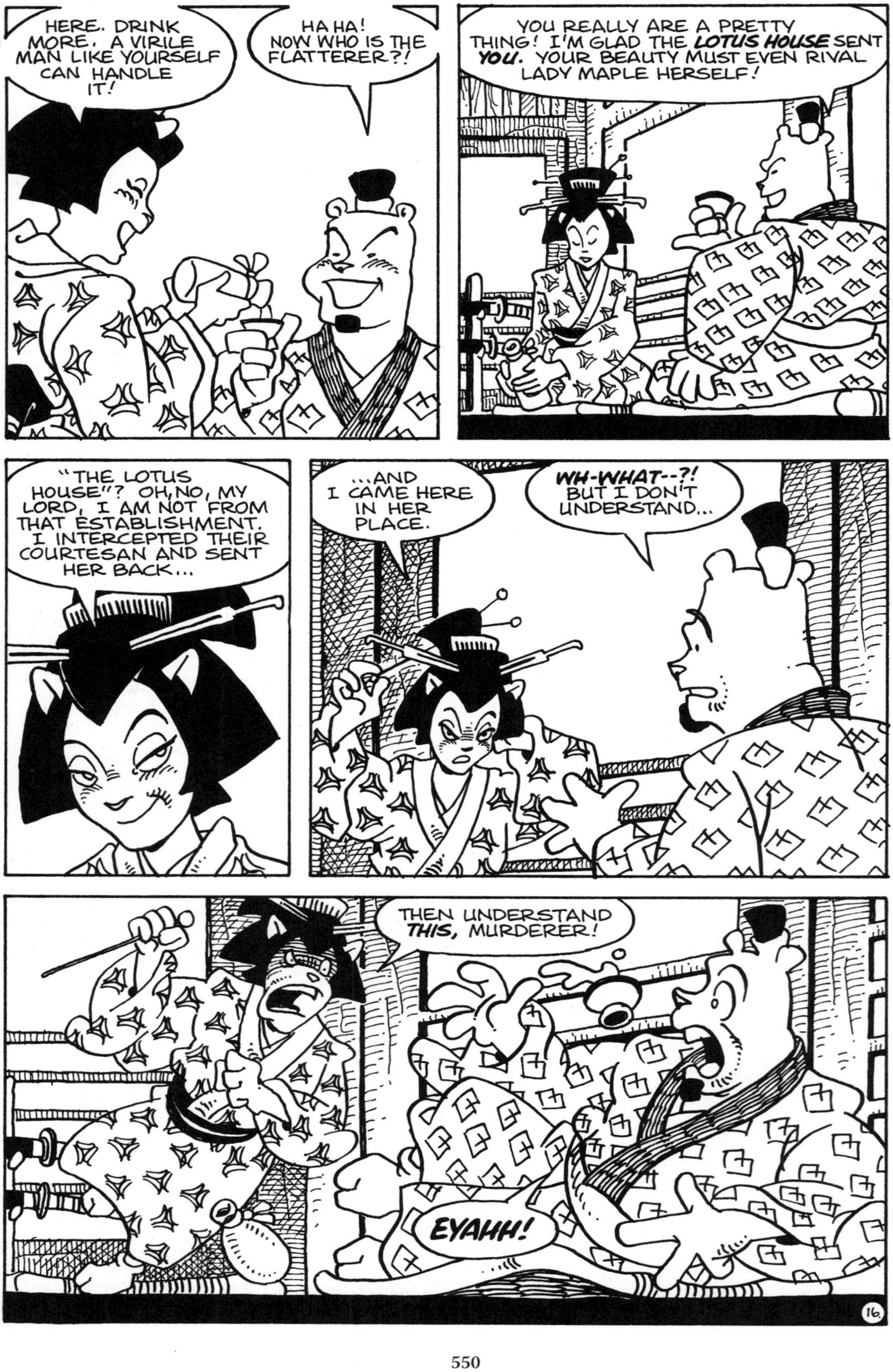
HERE. DRINK MORE. A VIRILE MAN LIKE YOURSELF CAN HANDLE IT!
HA HA! NOW WHO IS THE FLATTERER?!
YOU REALLY ARE A PRETTY THING! I'M GLAD THE LOTUS HOUSE SENT YOU. YOUR BEAUTY MUST EVEN RIVAL LADY MAPLE HERSELF!
"THE LOTUS HOUSE"? OH, NO, MY LORD, I AM NOT FROM THAT ESTABLISHMENT. I INTERCEPTED THEIR COURTESAN AND SENT HER BACK...
...AND I CAME HERE IN HER PLACE.
WH-WHAT--?! BUT I DON'T UNDERSTAND...
THEN UNDERSTAND THIS, MURDERER!
EYAHH!
16.

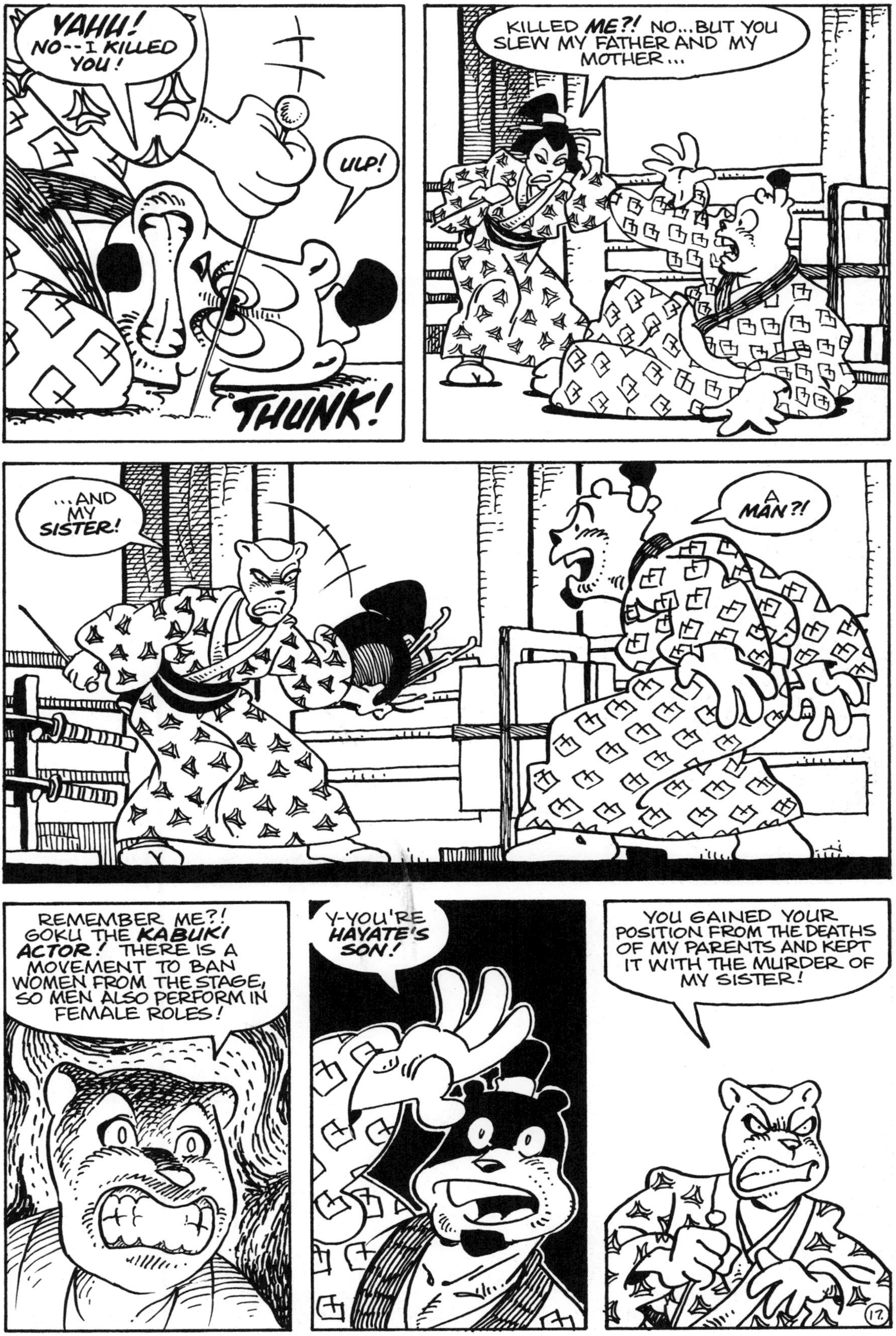
YAHH! NO--I KILLED YOU!
ULP!
THUNK!
KILLED ME?! NO...BUT YOU SLEW MY FATHER AND MY MOTHER...
...AND MY SISTER!
A MAN?!
REMEMBER ME?! GOKU THE KABUKI ACTOR! THERE IS A MOVEMENT TO BAN WOMEN FROM THE STAGE, SO MEN ALSO PERFORM IN FEMALE ROLES!
Y-YOU'RE HAYATE'S SON!
YOU GAINED YOUR POSITION FROM THE DEATHS OF MY PARENTS AND KEPT IT WITH THE MURDER OF MY SISTER!
17.

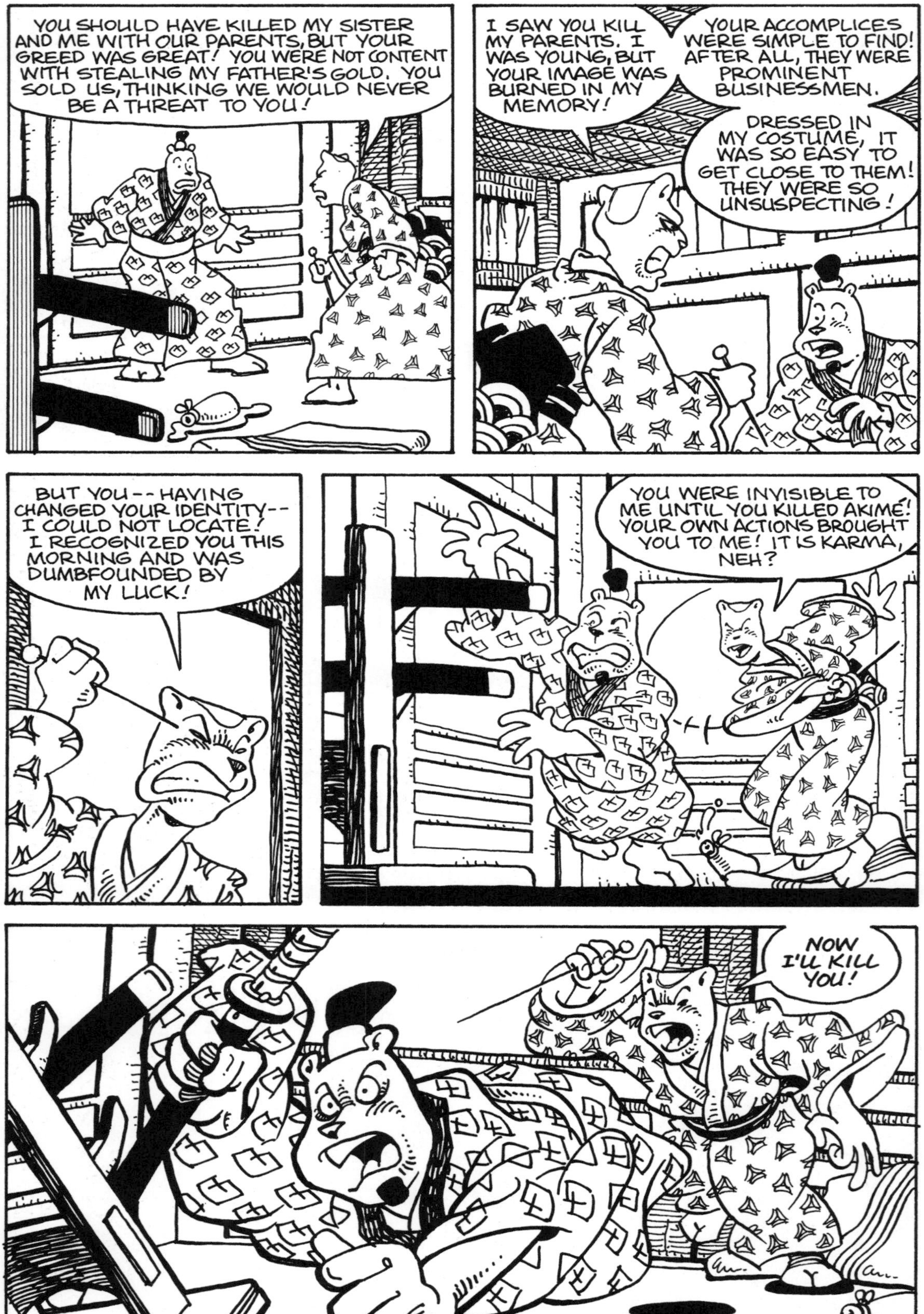
YOU SHOULD HAVE KILLED MY SISTER AND ME WITH OUR PARENTS, BUT YOUR GREED WAS GREAT! YOU WERE NOT CONTENT WITH STEALING MY FATHER'S GOLD. YOU SOLD US, THINKING WE WOULD NEVER BE A THREAT TO YOU!
I SAW YOU KILL MY PARENTS. I WAS YOUNG, BUT YOUR IMAGE WAS BURNED IN MY MEMORY!
YOUR ACCOMPLICES WERE SIMPLE TO FIND! AFTER ALL, THEY WERE PROMINENT BUSINESSMEN.
DRESSED IN MY COSTUME, IT WAS SO EASY TO GET CLOSE TO THEM! THEY WERE SO UNSUSPECTING!
BUT YOU -- HAVING CHANGED YOUR IDENTITY -- I COULD NOT LOCATE! I RECOGNIZED YOU THIS MORNING AND WAS DUMBFOUNDED BY MY LUCK!
YOU WERE INVISIBLE TO ME UNTIL YOU KILLED AKIMÉ! YOUR OWN ACTIONS BROUGHT YOU TO ME! IT IS KARMA, NEH?
NOW I'LL KILL YOU!
18.

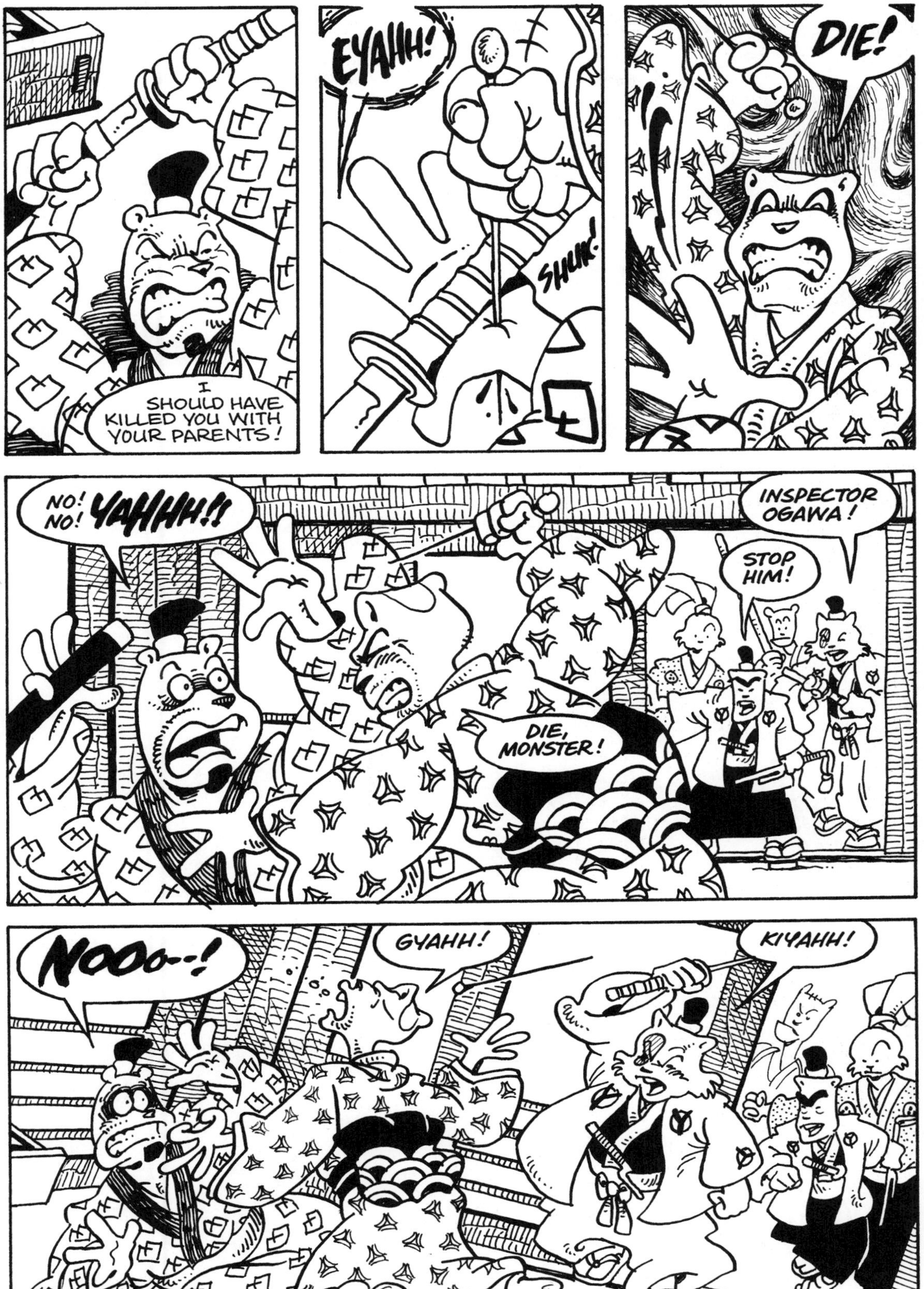
I SHOULD HAVE KILLED YOU WITH YOUR PARENTS!
EYAHH!
SHUK!
DIE!
NO! NO! YAHHH!!
DIE, MONSTER!
INSPECTOR OGAWA!
STOP HIM!
NOOo--!
GYAHH!
KIYAHH!
19.

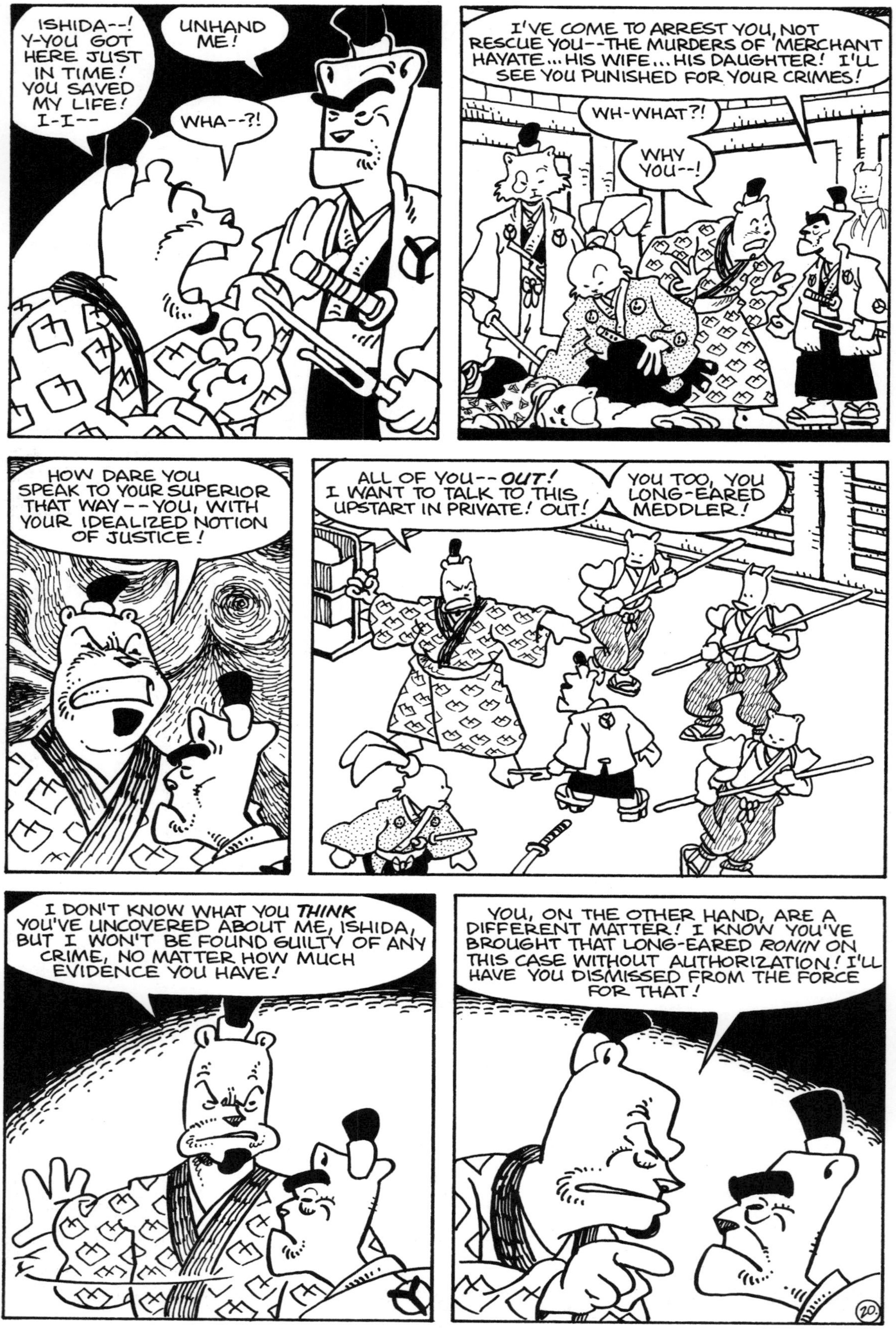
ISHIDA--! Y-YOU GOT HERE JUST IN TIME! YOU SAVED MY LIFE! I-I--
UNHAND ME!
WHA--?!
I'VE COME TO ARREST YOU, NOT RESCUE YOU--THE MURDERS OF MERCHANT HAYATE...HIS WIFE...HIS DAUGHTER! I'LL SEE YOU PUNISHED FOR YOUR CRIMES!
WH-WHAT?!
WHY YOU--!
HOW DARE YOU SPEAK TO YOUR SUPERIOR THAT WAY--YOU, WITH YOUR IDEALIZED NOTION OF JUSTICE!
ALL OF YOU--*OUT!* I WANT TO TALK TO THIS UPSTART IN PRIVATE! OUT!
YOU TOO, YOU LONG-EARED MEDDLER!
I DON'T KNOW WHAT YOU *THINK* YOU'VE UNCOVERED ABOUT ME, ISHIDA, BUT I WON'T BE FOUND GUILTY OF ANY CRIME, NO MATTER HOW MUCH EVIDENCE YOU HAVE!
YOU, ON THE OTHER HAND, ARE A DIFFERENT MATTER! I KNOW YOU'VE BROUGHT THAT LONG-EARED *RONIN* ON THIS CASE WITHOUT AUTHORIZATION! I'LL HAVE YOU DISMISSED FROM THE FORCE FOR THAT!
20.

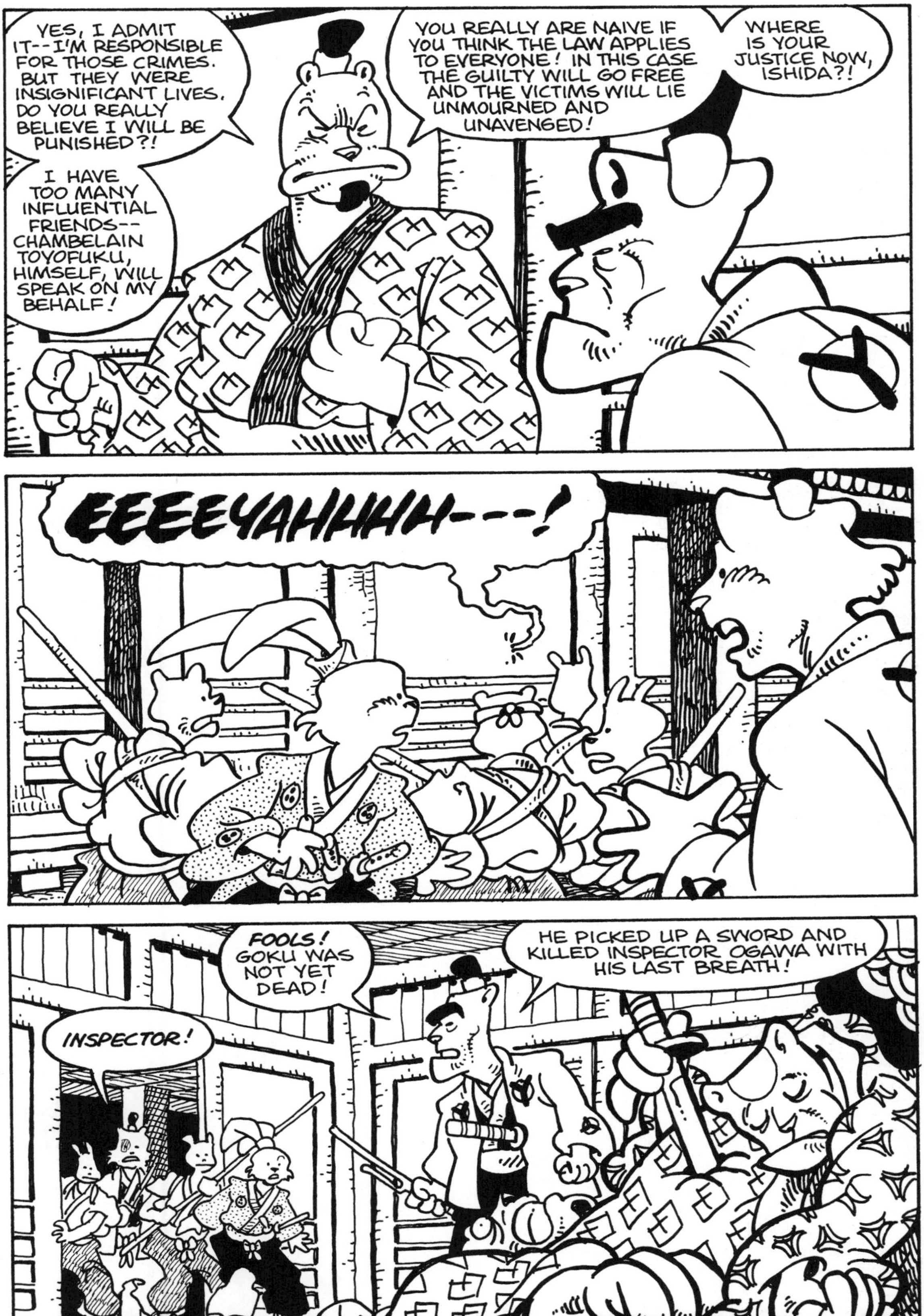
YES, I ADMIT IT-- I'M RESPONSIBLE FOR THOSE CRIMES. BUT THEY WERE INSIGNIFICANT LIVES. DO YOU REALLY BELIEVE I WILL BE PUNISHED?!
I HAVE TOO MANY INFLUENTIAL FRIENDS-- CHAMBELAIN TOYOFUKU, HIMSELF, WILL SPEAK ON MY BEHALF!
YOU REALLY ARE NAIVE IF YOU THINK THE LAW APPLIES TO EVERYONE! IN THIS CASE THE GUILTY WILL GO FREE AND THE VICTIMS WILL LIE UNMOURNED AND UNAVENGED!
WHERE IS YOUR JUSTICE NOW, ISHIDA?!
EEEEYAHHHHH---!
INSPECTOR!
FOOLS! GOKU WAS NOT YET DEAD!
HE PICKED UP A SWORD AND KILLED INSPECTOR OGAWA WITH HIS LAST BREATH!
21.

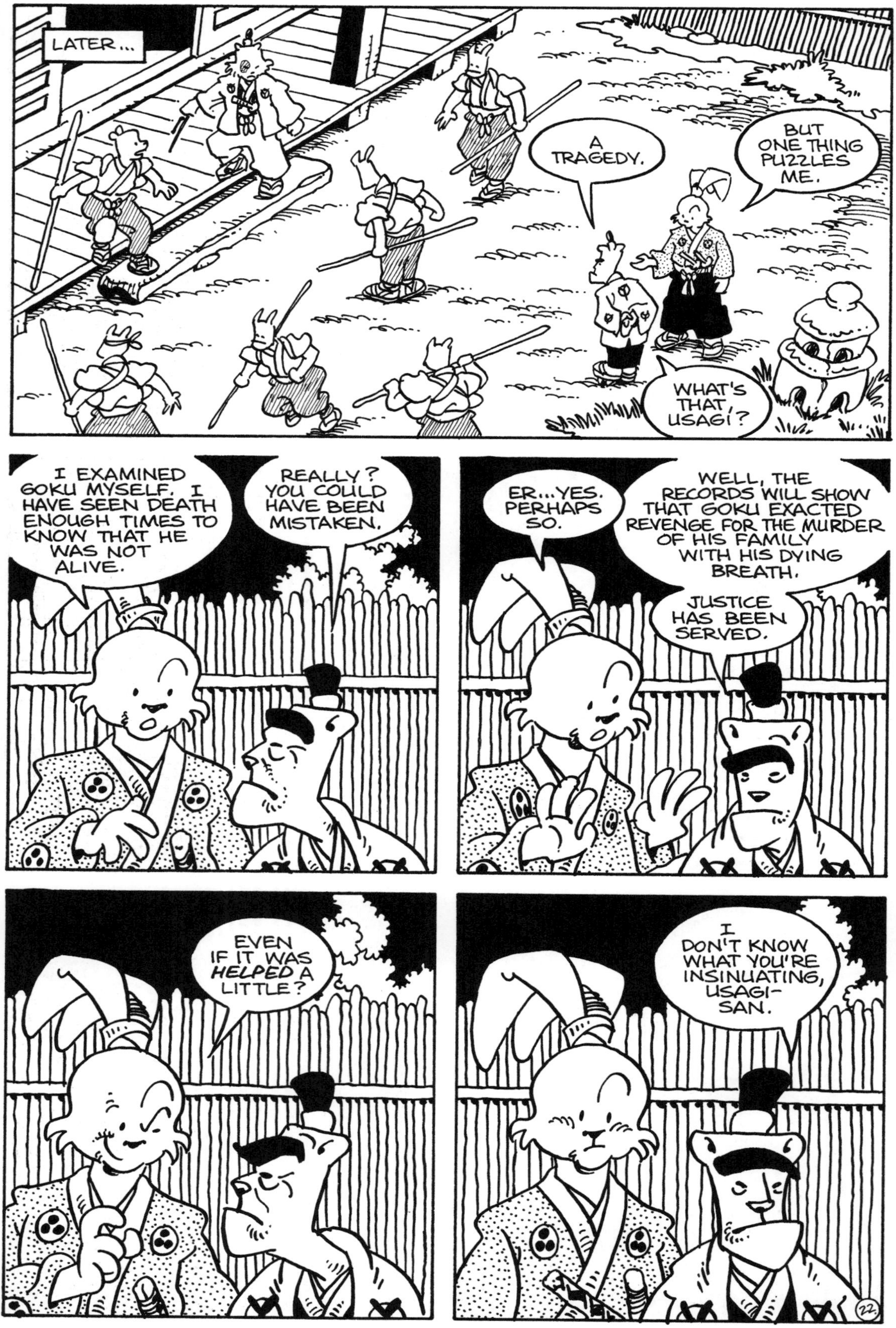
LATER...
A TRAGEDY.
BUT ONE THING PUZZLES ME.
WHAT'S THAT, USAGI?
I EXAMINED GOKU MYSELF. I HAVE SEEN DEATH ENOUGH TIMES TO KNOW THAT HE WAS NOT ALIVE.
REALLY? YOU COULD HAVE BEEN MISTAKEN.
ER...YES. PERHAPS SO.
WELL, THE RECORDS WILL SHOW THAT GOKU EXACTED REVENGE FOR THE MURDER OF HIS FAMILY WITH HIS DYING BREATH.
JUSTICE HAS BEEN SERVED.
EVEN IF IT WAS *HELPED* A LITTLE?
I DON'T KNOW WHAT YOU'RE INSINUATING, USAGI-SAN.
22

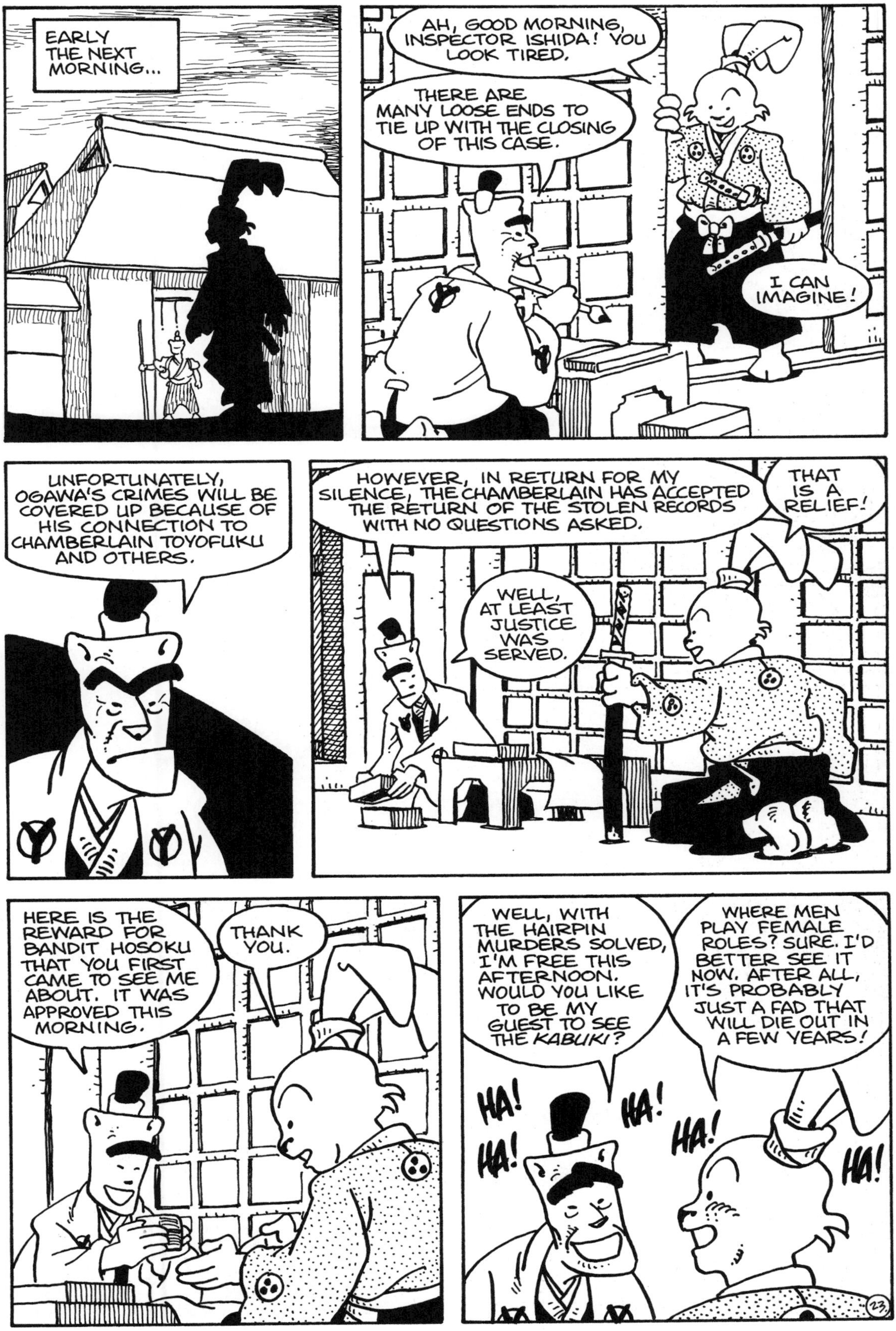
EARLY THE NEXT MORNING...
AH, GOOD MORNING, INSPECTOR ISHIDA! YOU LOOK TIRED.
THERE ARE MANY LOOSE ENDS TO TIE UP WITH THE CLOSING OF THIS CASE.
I CAN IMAGINE!
UNFORTUNATELY, OGAWA'S CRIMES WILL BE COVERED UP BECAUSE OF HIS CONNECTION TO CHAMBERLAIN TOYOFUKU AND OTHERS.
HOWEVER, IN RETURN FOR MY SILENCE, THE CHAMBERLAIN HAS ACCEPTED THE RETURN OF THE STOLEN RECORDS WITH NO QUESTIONS ASKED.
THAT IS A RELIEF!
WELL, AT LEAST JUSTICE WAS SERVED.
HERE IS THE REWARD FOR BANDIT HOSOKU THAT YOU FIRST CAME TO SEE ME ABOUT. IT WAS APPROVED THIS MORNING.
THANK YOU.
WELL, WITH THE HAIRPIN MURDERS SOLVED, I'M FREE THIS AFTERNOON. WOULD YOU LIKE TO BE MY GUEST TO SEE THE *KABUKI*?
WHERE MEN PLAY FEMALE ROLES? SURE. I'D BETTER SEE IT NOW. AFTER ALL, IT'S PROBABLY JUST A FAD THAT WILL DIE OUT IN A FEW YEARS!
HA! HA! HA! HA! HA!
23

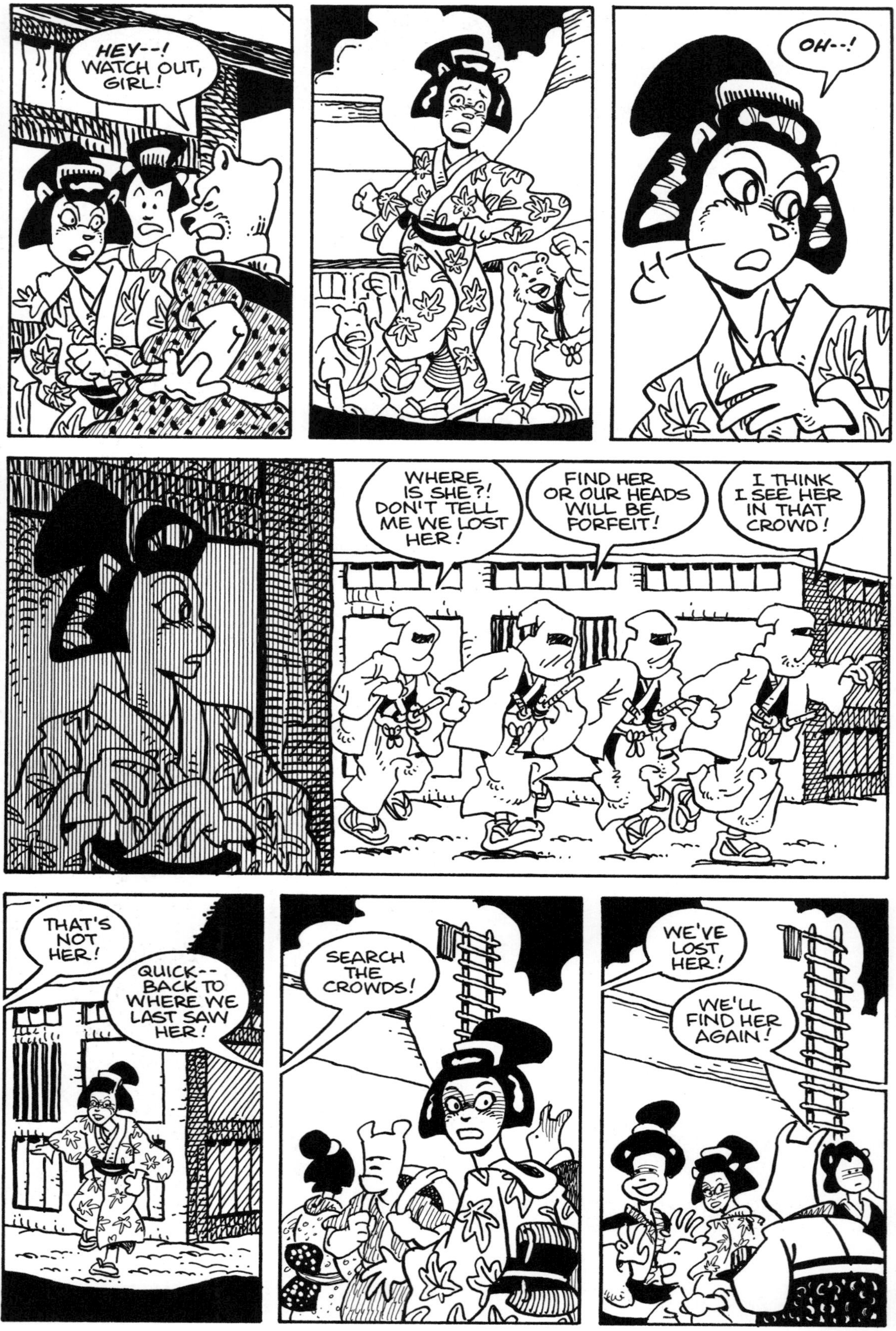
HEY--! WATCH OUT, GIRL!
OH--!
WHERE IS SHE?! DON'T TELL ME WE LOST HER!
FIND HER OR OUR HEADS WILL BE FORFEIT!
I THINK I SEE HER IN THAT CROWD!
THAT'S NOT HER!
QUICK-- BACK TO WHERE WE LAST SAW HER!
SEARCH THE CROWDS!
WE'VE LOST HER!
WE'LL FIND HER AGAIN!
THE END

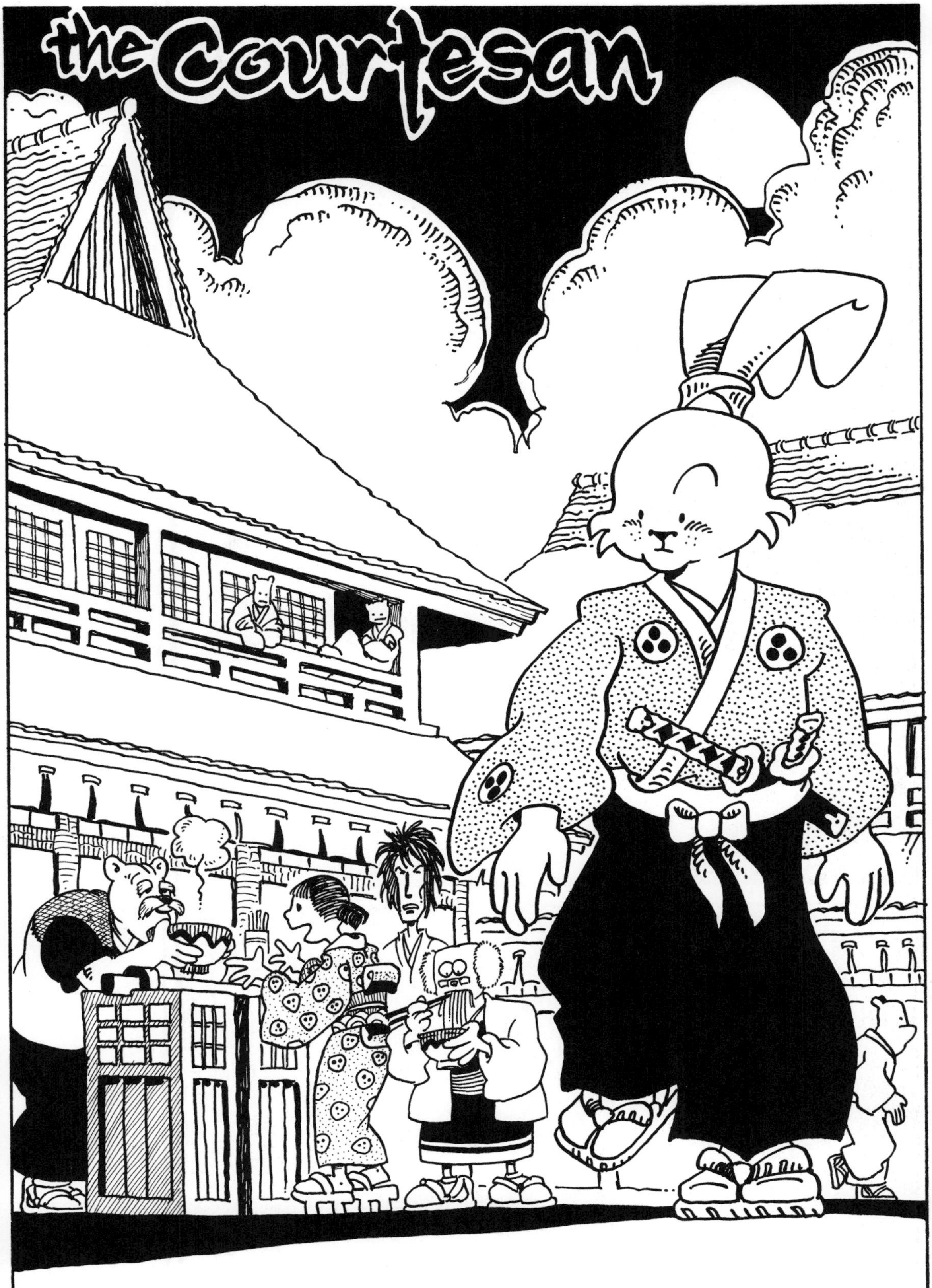
the Courtesan
1.

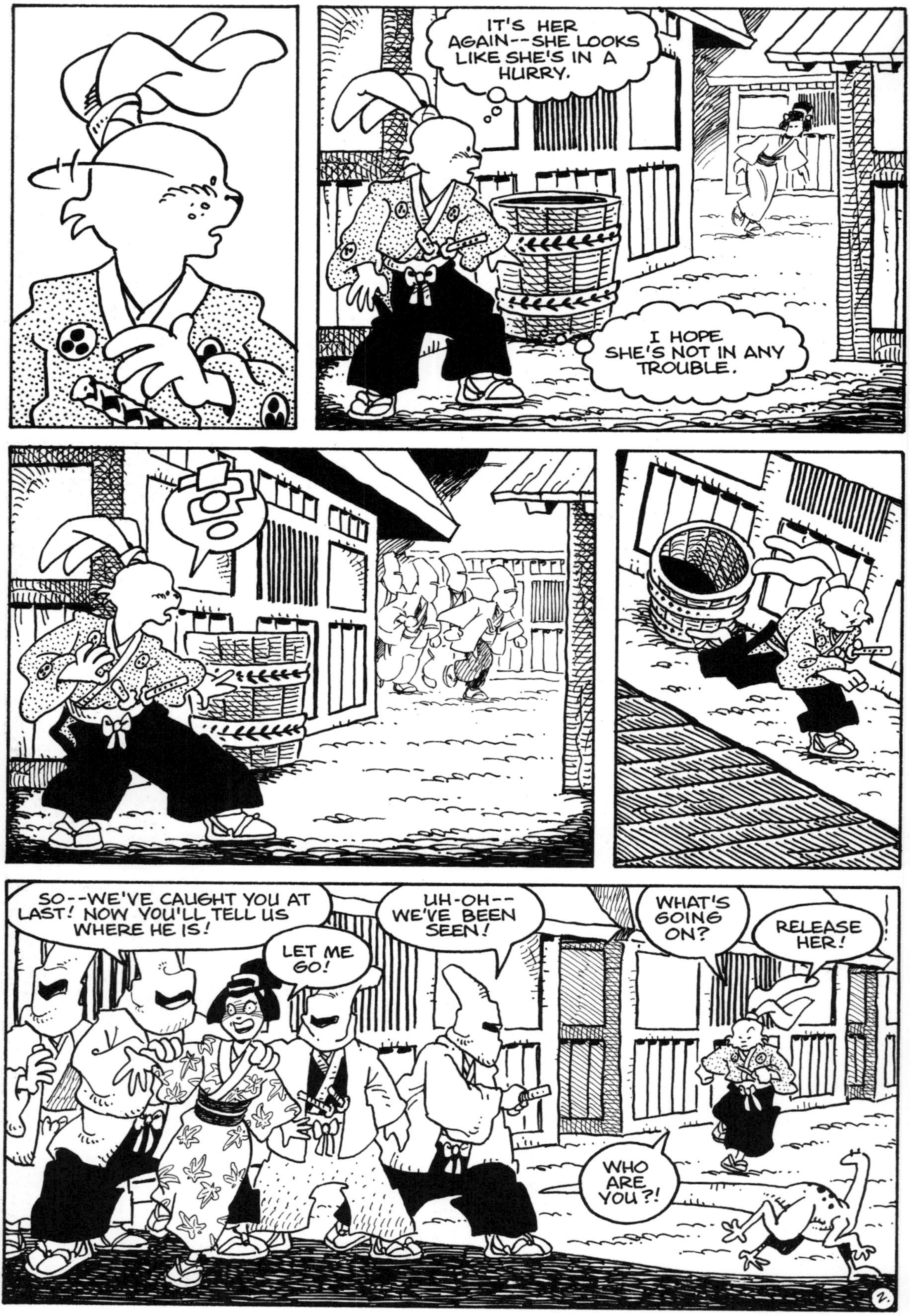
IT'S HER AGAIN--SHE LOOKS LIKE SHE'S IN A HURRY.
I HOPE SHE'S NOT IN ANY TROUBLE.
SO--WE'VE CAUGHT YOU AT LAST! NOW YOU'LL TELL US WHERE HE IS!
LET ME GO!
UH-OH--WE'VE BEEN SEEN!
WHAT'S GOING ON?
RELEASE HER!
WHO ARE YOU?!
2.

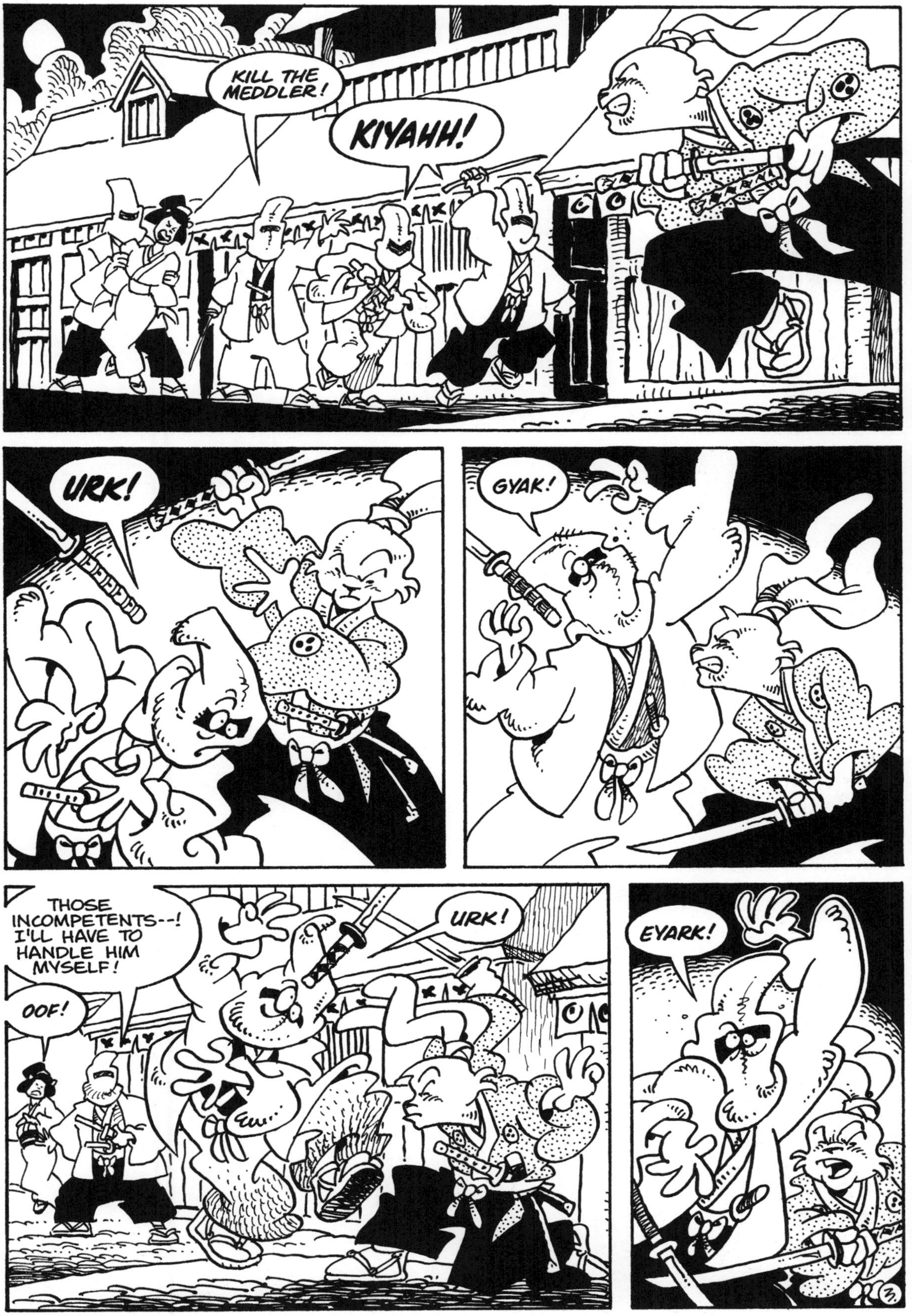
KILL THE MEDDLER!
KIYAHH!
URK!
GYAK!
THOSE INCOMPETENTS--! I'LL HAVE TO HANDLE HIM MYSELF!
OOF!
URK!
EYARK!
3

I AM MIYAMOTO USAGI. ARE YOU ALL RIGHT?

Y-YES. THANK YOU, USAGI-SAN.

I BUMPED INTO YOU THE OTHER NIGHT. YOU SEEMED AFRAID. WAS IT THESE MEN YOU WERE IN FEAR OF? IS THERE ANYTHING I CAN DO?

I HAVE ALREADY BEEN A GREAT IMPOSITION TO YOU. I MUST BE GOING. FORGIVE ME THAT I CANNOT THANK YOU PROPERLY.

AT LEAST LET ME SEE YOU TO YOUR DESTINATION SAFELY.

NO! AND YOU MUST GIVE ME YOUR WORD OF HONOR THAT YOU WILL NOT FOLLOW ME!

VERY WELL. I SHOULD REPORT THESE DEATHS, ANYWAY!

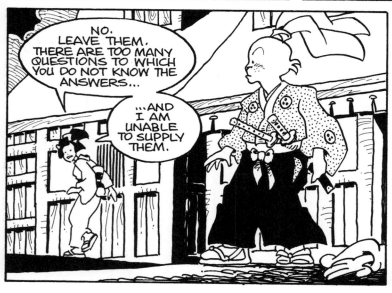

NO. LEAVE THEM. THERE ARE TOO MANY QUESTIONS TO WHICH YOU DO NOT KNOW THE ANSWERS...

...AND I AM UNABLE TO SUPPLY THEM.

SHE MAY BE RIGHT. THESE ARE NOT ORDINARY THIEVES.

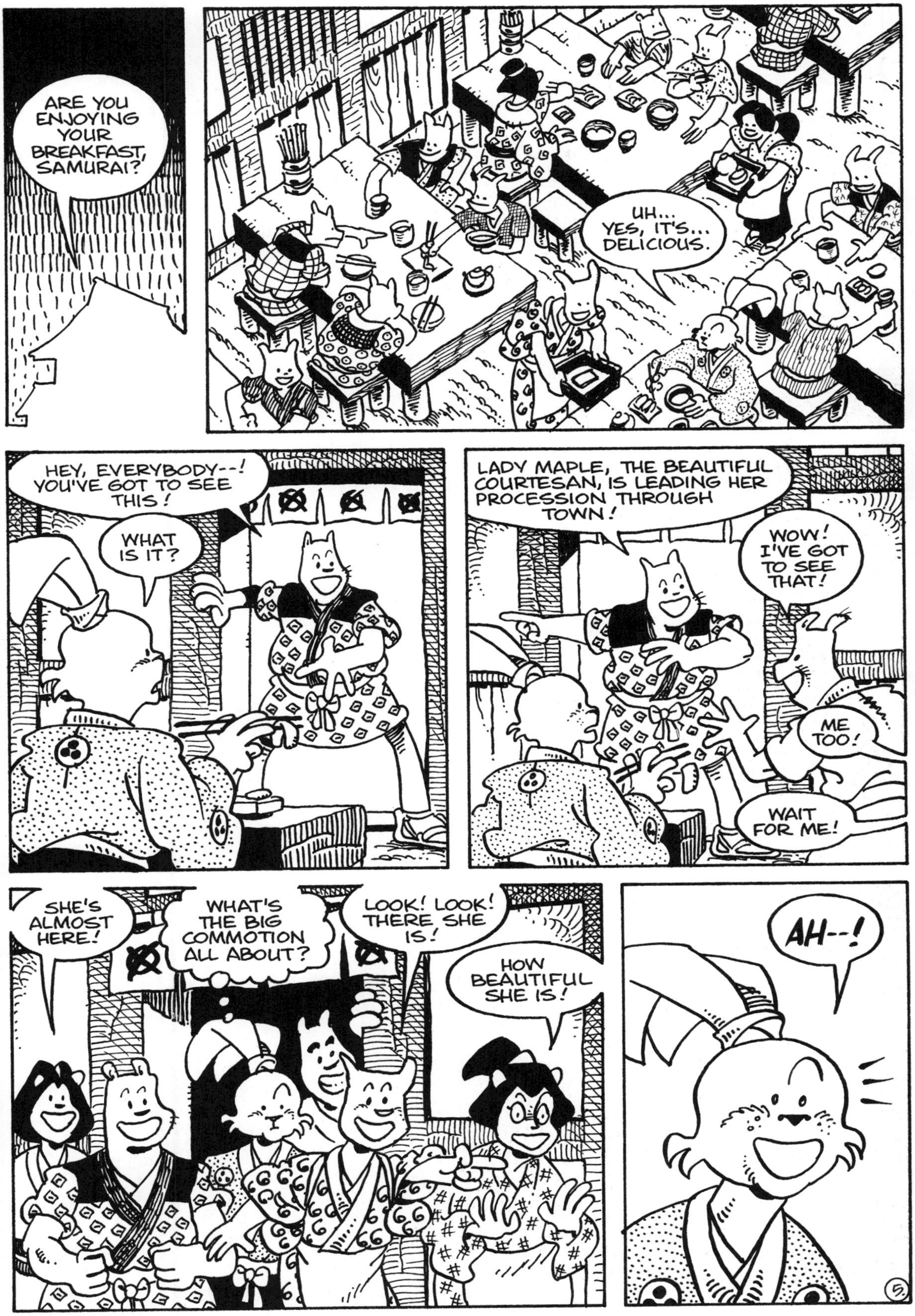

ARE YOU ENJOYING YOUR BREAKFAST, SAMURAI?
UH... YES, IT'S... DELICIOUS.
HEY, EVERYBODY--! YOU'VE GOT TO SEE THIS!
WHAT IS IT?
LADY MAPLE, THE BEAUTIFUL COURTESAN, IS LEADING HER PROCESSION THROUGH TOWN!
WOW! I'VE GOT TO SEE THAT!
ME TOO!
WAIT FOR ME!
SHE'S ALMOST HERE!
WHAT'S THE BIG COMMOTION ALL ABOUT?
LOOK! LOOK! THERE SHE IS!
HOW BEAUTIFUL SHE IS!
AH--!
5

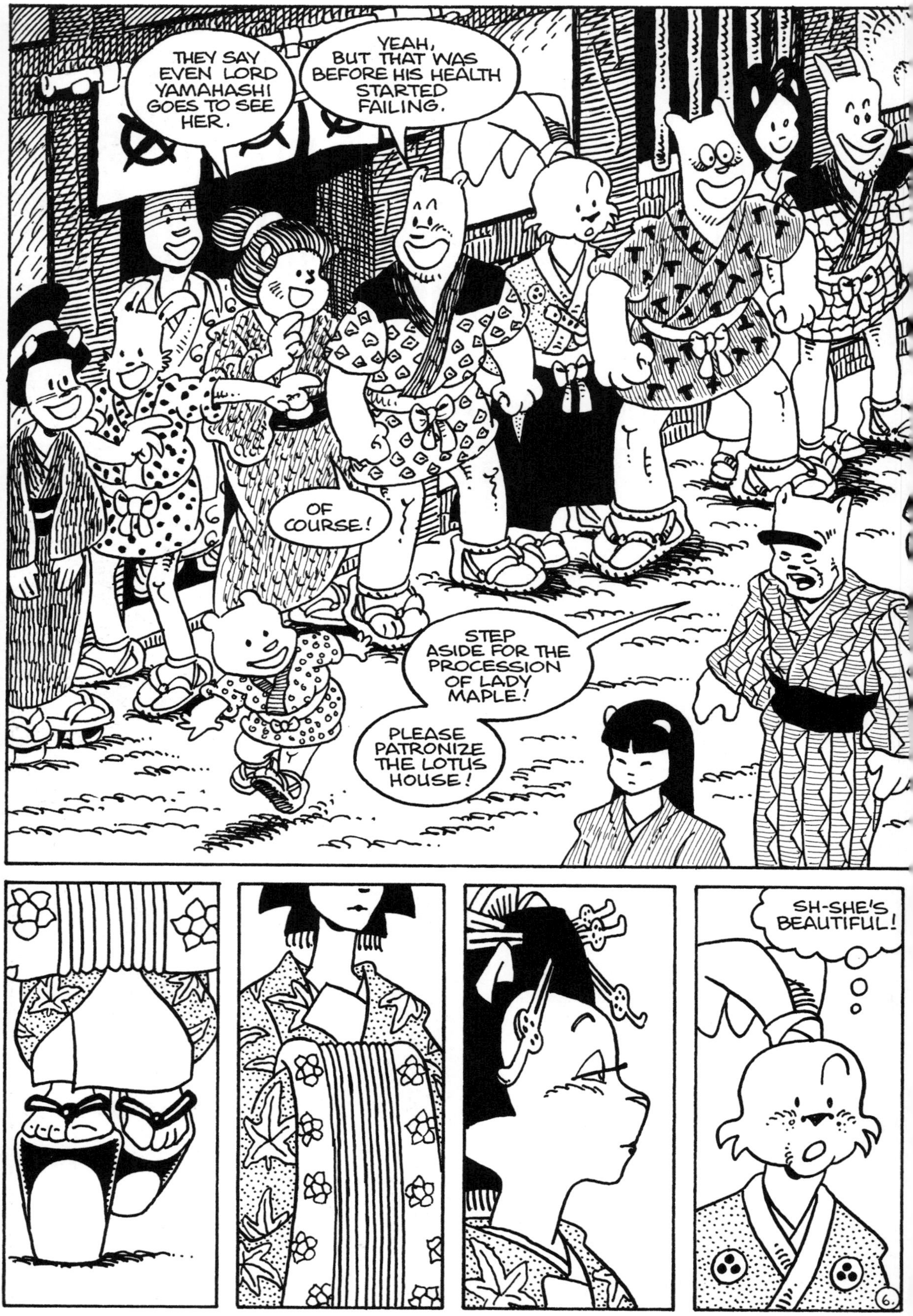
THEY SAY EVEN LORD YAMAHASHI GOES TO SEE HER.
YEAH, BUT THAT WAS BEFORE HIS HEALTH STARTED FAILING.
OF COURSE!
STEP ASIDE FOR THE PROCESSION OF LADY MAPLE!
PLEASE PATRONIZE THE LOTUS HOUSE!
SH-SHE'S BEAUTIFUL!
6.

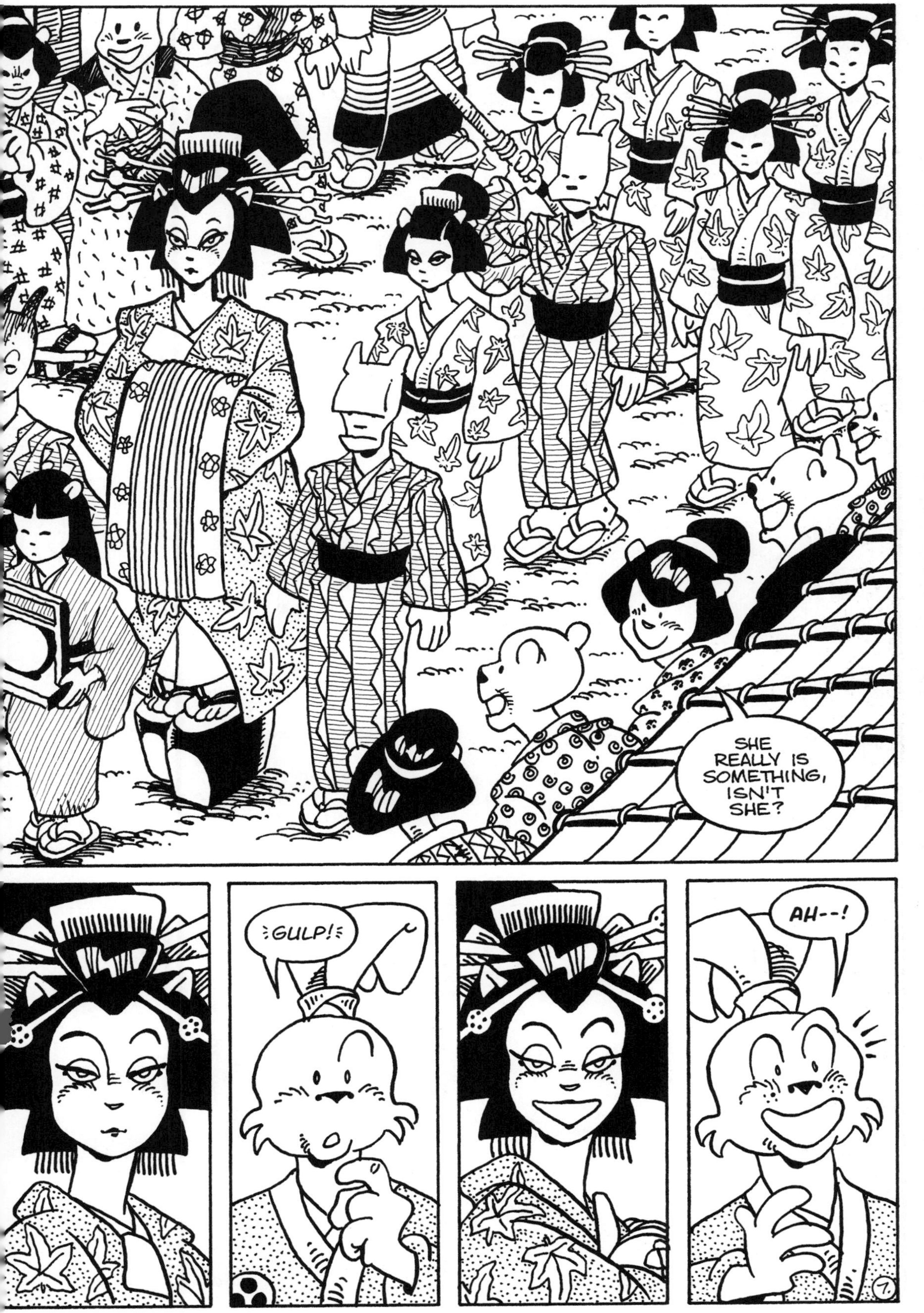
SHE REALLY IS SOMETHING, ISN'T SHE?
GULP!
AH--!
7.

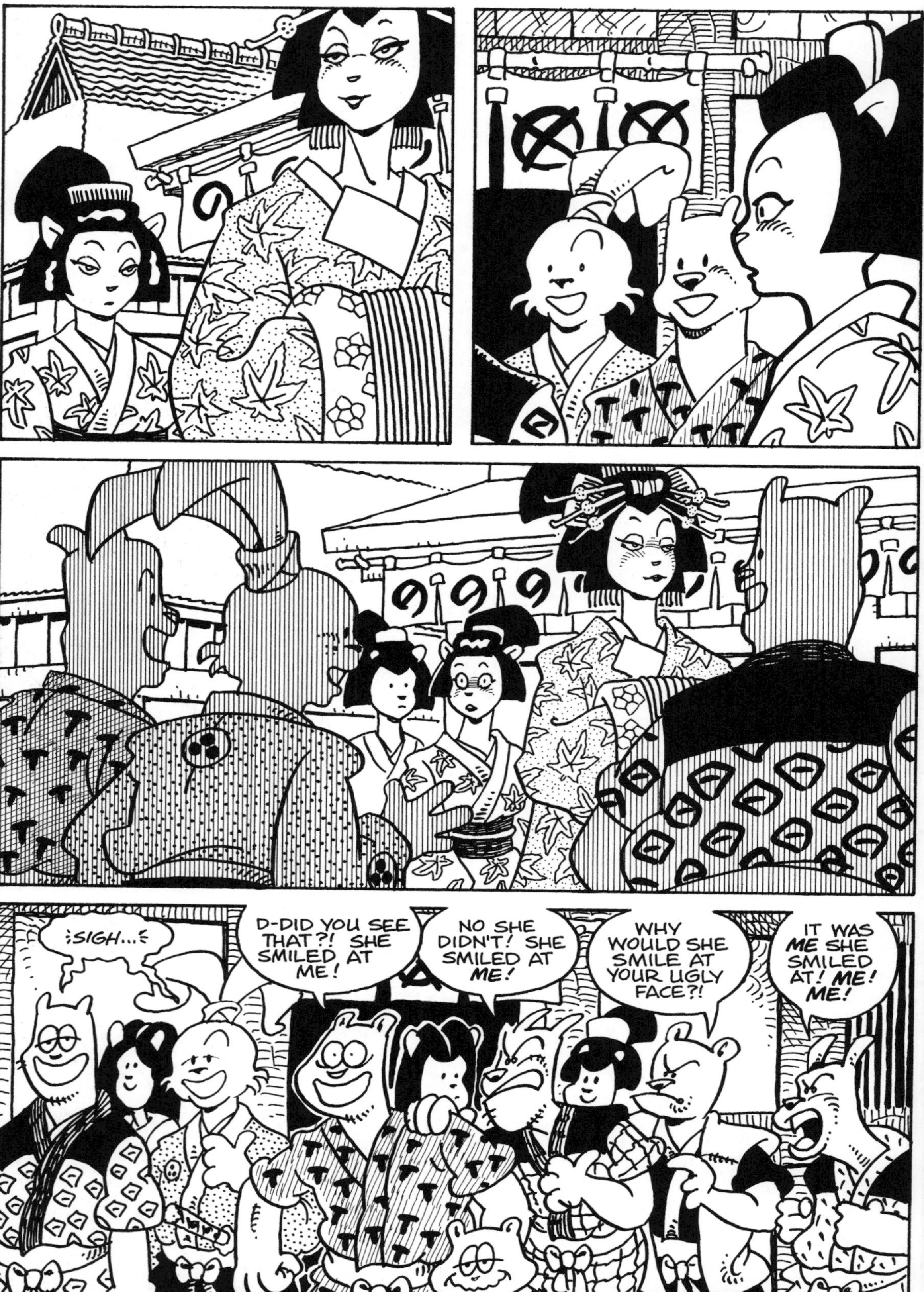
SIGH...
D-DID YOU SEE THAT?! SHE SMILED AT ME!
NO SHE DIDN'T! SHE SMILED AT **ME!**
WHY WOULD SHE SMILE AT YOUR UGLY FACE?!
IT WAS **ME** SHE SMILED AT! **ME! ME!**

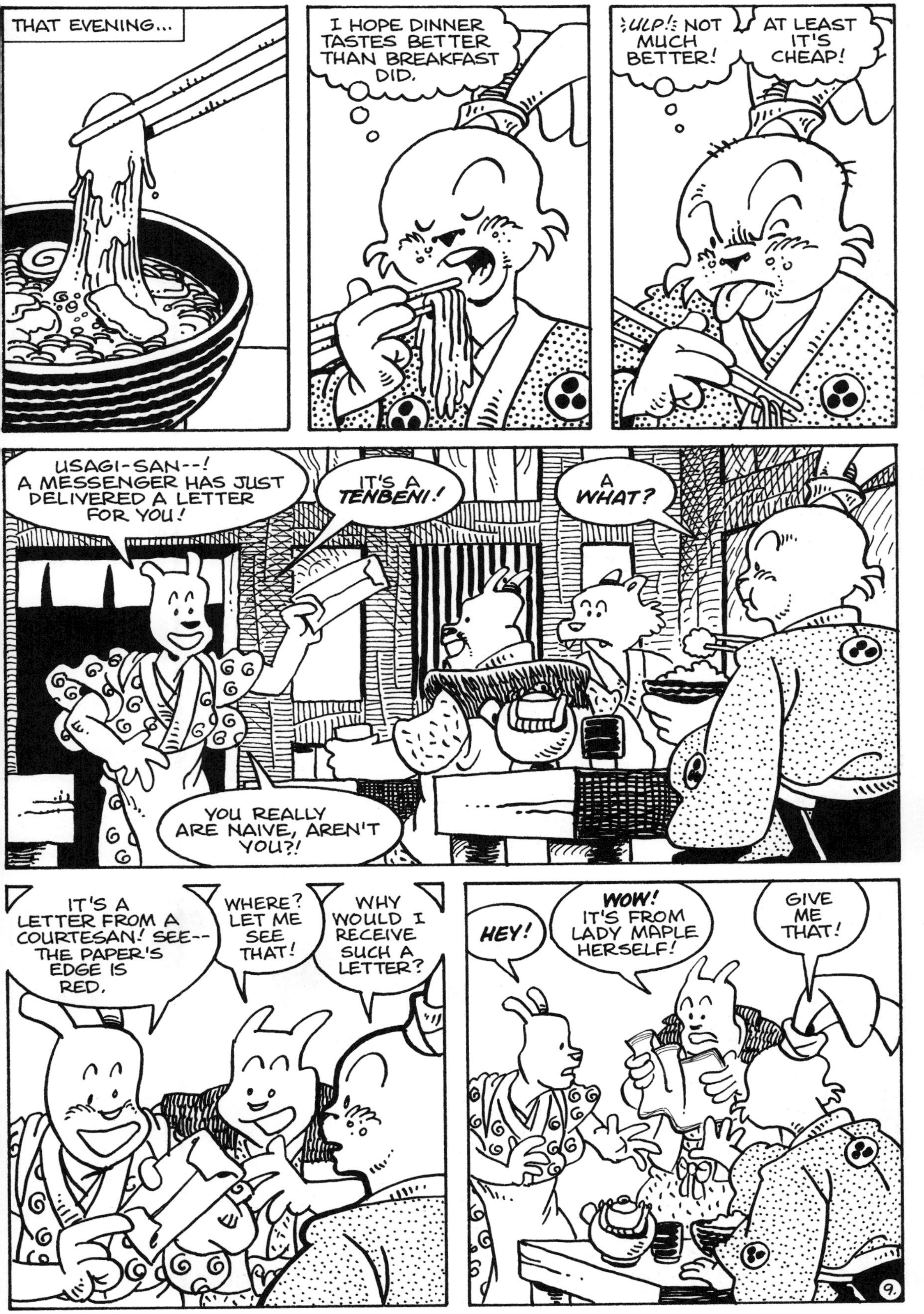
THAT EVENING...
I HOPE DINNER TASTES BETTER THAN BREAKFAST DID.
ULP! NOT MUCH BETTER!
AT LEAST IT'S CHEAP!
USAGI-SAN--! A MESSENGER HAS JUST DELIVERED A LETTER FOR YOU!
IT'S A TENBEN!!
A WHAT?
YOU REALLY ARE NAIVE, AREN'T YOU?!
IT'S A LETTER FROM A COURTESAN! SEE-- THE PAPER'S EDGE IS RED.
WHERE? LET ME SEE THAT!
WHY WOULD I RECEIVE SUCH A LETTER?
HEY!
WOW! IT'S FROM LADY MAPLE HERSELF!
GIVE ME THAT!
9.

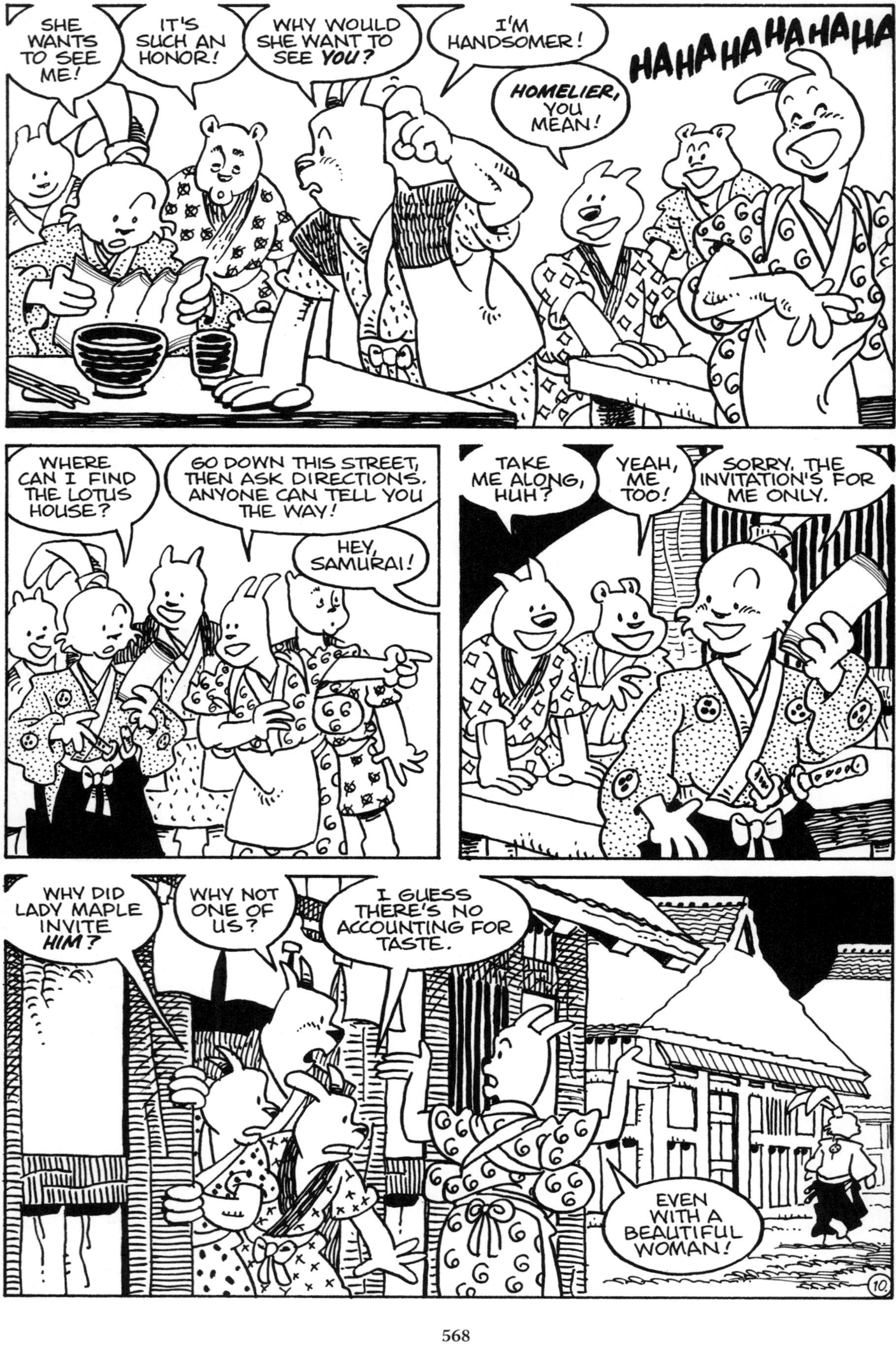
SHE WANTS TO SEE ME!
IT'S SUCH AN HONOR!
WHY WOULD SHE WANT TO SEE *YOU?*
I'M HANDSOMER!
HOMELIER, YOU MEAN!
HAHAHAHAHAHAHA
WHERE CAN I FIND THE LOTUS HOUSE?
GO DOWN THIS STREET, THEN ASK DIRECTIONS. ANYONE CAN TELL YOU THE WAY!
HEY, SAMURAI!
TAKE ME ALONG, HUH?
YEAH, ME TOO!
SORRY. THE INVITATION'S FOR ME ONLY.
WHY DID LADY MAPLE INVITE *HIM?*
WHY NOT ONE OF US?
I GUESS THERE'S NO ACCOUNTING FOR TASTE.
EVEN WITH A BEAUTIFUL WOMAN!
10.

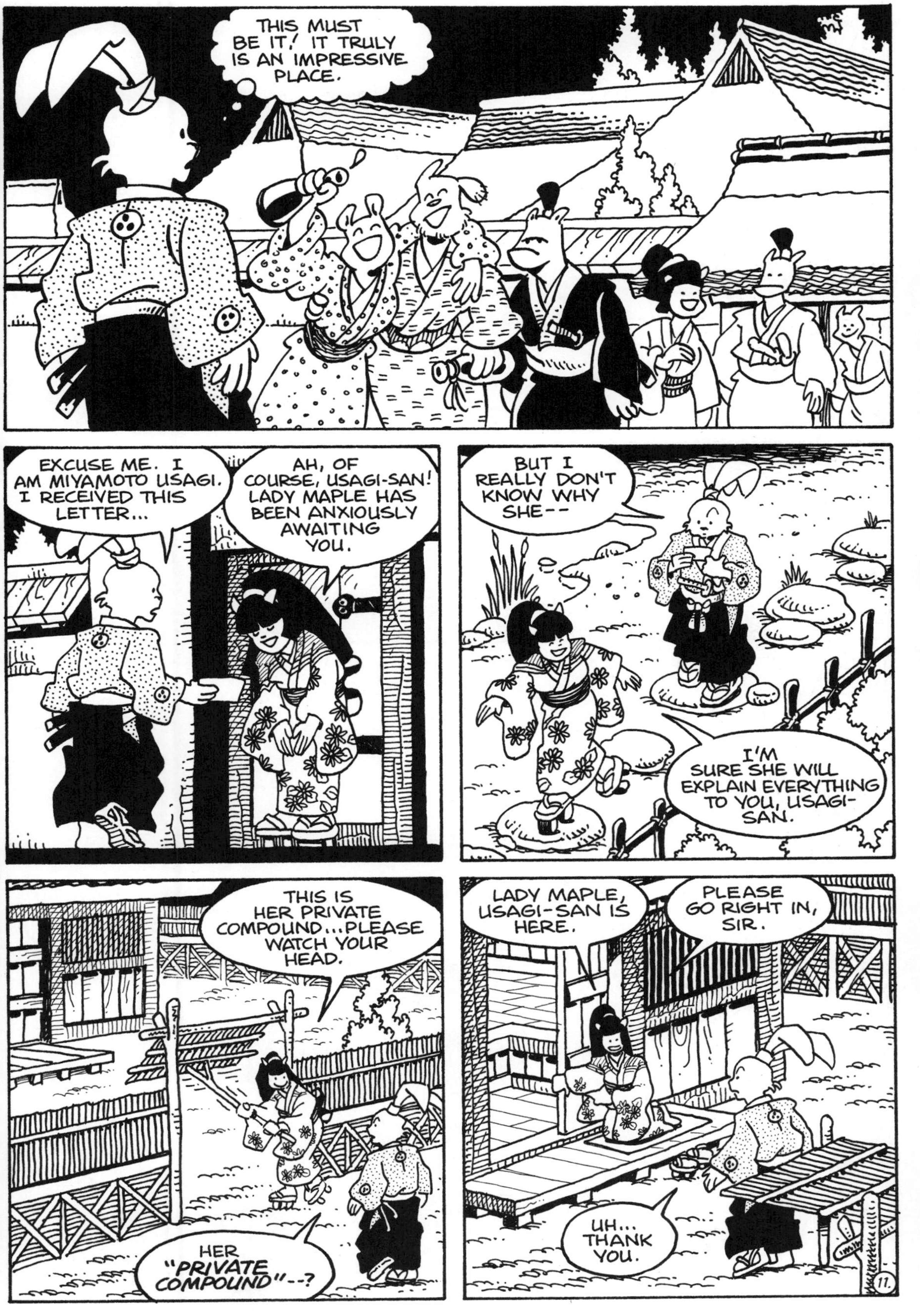
THIS MUST BE IT! IT TRULY IS AN IMPRESSIVE PLACE.
EXCUSE ME. I AM MIYAMOTO USAGI. I RECEIVED THIS LETTER...
AH, OF COURSE, USAGI-SAN! LADY MAPLE HAS BEEN ANXIOUSLY AWAITING YOU.
BUT I REALLY DON'T KNOW WHY SHE--
I'M SURE SHE WILL EXPLAIN EVERYTHING TO YOU, USAGI-SAN.
THIS IS HER PRIVATE COMPOUND...PLEASE WATCH YOUR HEAD.
HER "PRIVATE COMPOUND"--?
LADY MAPLE, USAGI-SAN IS HERE.
PLEASE GO RIGHT IN, SIR.
UH... THANK YOU.
11.

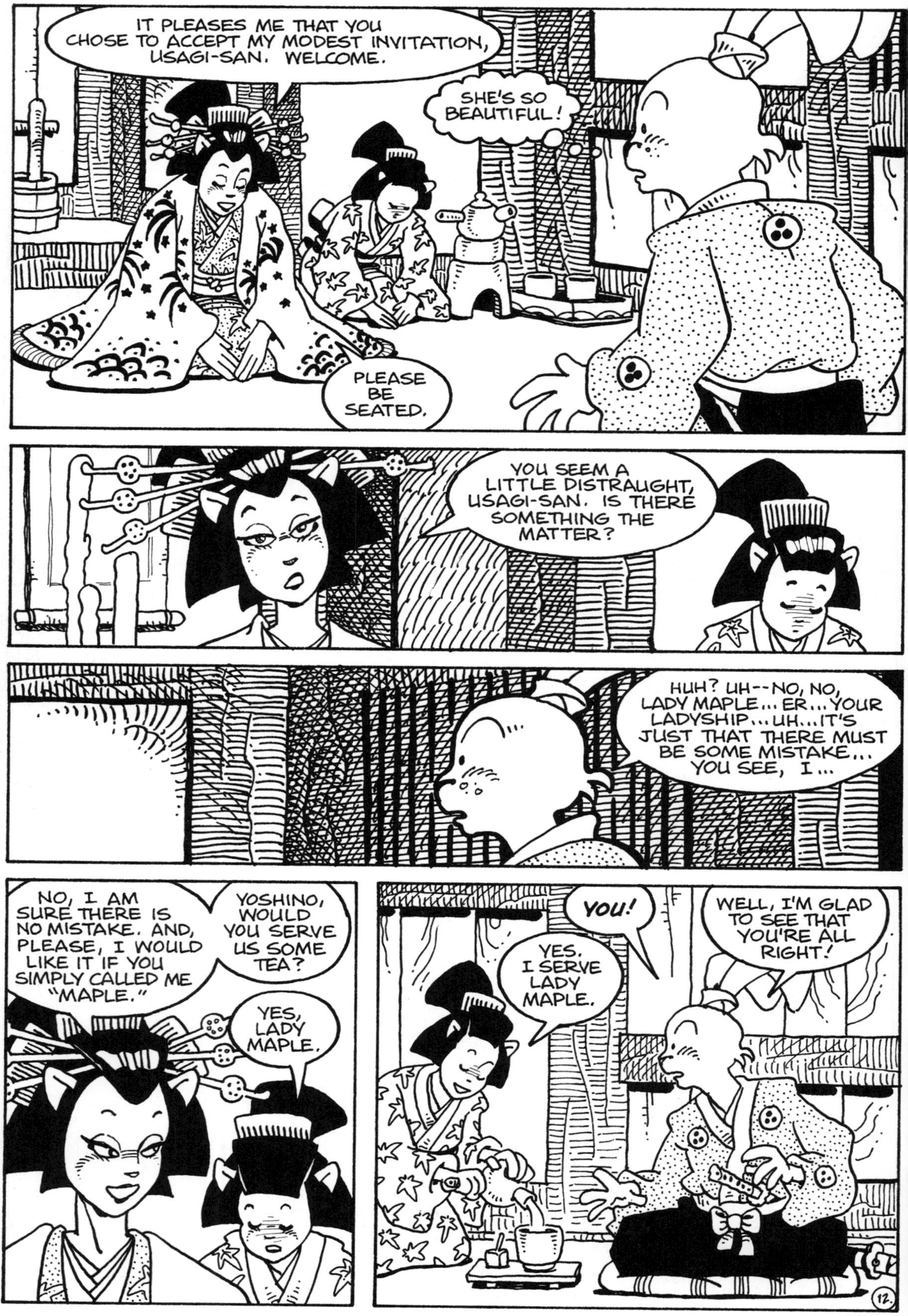
IT PLEASES ME THAT YOU CHOSE TO ACCEPT MY MODEST INVITATION, USAGI-SAN. WELCOME.
SHE'S SO BEAUTIFUL!
PLEASE BE SEATED.
YOU SEEM A LITTLE DISTRAUGHT, USAGI-SAN. IS THERE SOMETHING THE MATTER?
HUH? UH--NO, NO, LADY MAPLE... ER... YOUR LADYSHIP... UH... IT'S JUST THAT THERE MUST BE SOME MISTAKE... YOU SEE, I...
NO, I AM SURE THERE IS NO MISTAKE. AND, PLEASE, I WOULD LIKE IT IF YOU SIMPLY CALLED ME "MAPLE."
YOSHINO, WOULD YOU SERVE US SOME TEA?
YES, LADY MAPLE.
YOU!
YES. I SERVE LADY MAPLE.
WELL, I'M GLAD TO SEE THAT YOU'RE ALL RIGHT!
12.

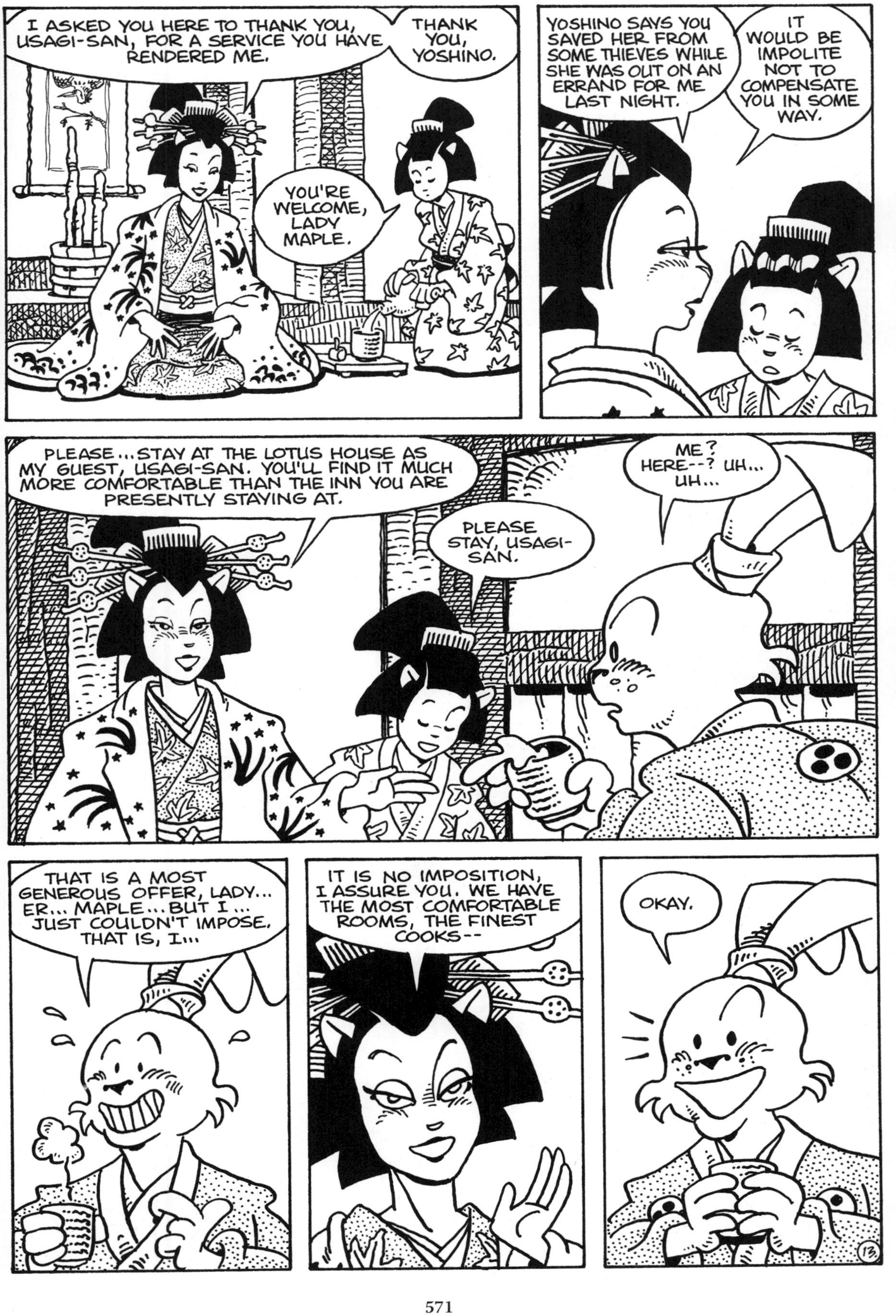
I ASKED YOU HERE TO THANK YOU, USAGI-SAN, FOR A SERVICE YOU HAVE RENDERED ME.
THANK YOU, YOSHINO.
YOU'RE WELCOME, LADY MAPLE.
YOSHINO SAYS YOU SAVED HER FROM SOME THIEVES WHILE SHE WAS OUT ON AN ERRAND FOR ME LAST NIGHT.
IT WOULD BE IMPOLITE NOT TO COMPENSATE YOU IN SOME WAY.
PLEASE... STAY AT THE LOTUS HOUSE AS MY GUEST, USAGI-SAN. YOU'LL FIND IT MUCH MORE COMFORTABLE THAN THE INN YOU ARE PRESENTLY STAYING AT.
PLEASE STAY, USAGI-SAN.
ME? HERE--? UH... UH...
THAT IS A MOST GENEROUS OFFER, LADY... ER... MAPLE... BUT I... JUST COULDN'T IMPOSE. THAT IS, I...
IT IS NO IMPOSITION, I ASSURE YOU. WE HAVE THE MOST COMFORTABLE ROOMS, THE FINEST COOKS--
OKAY.
13

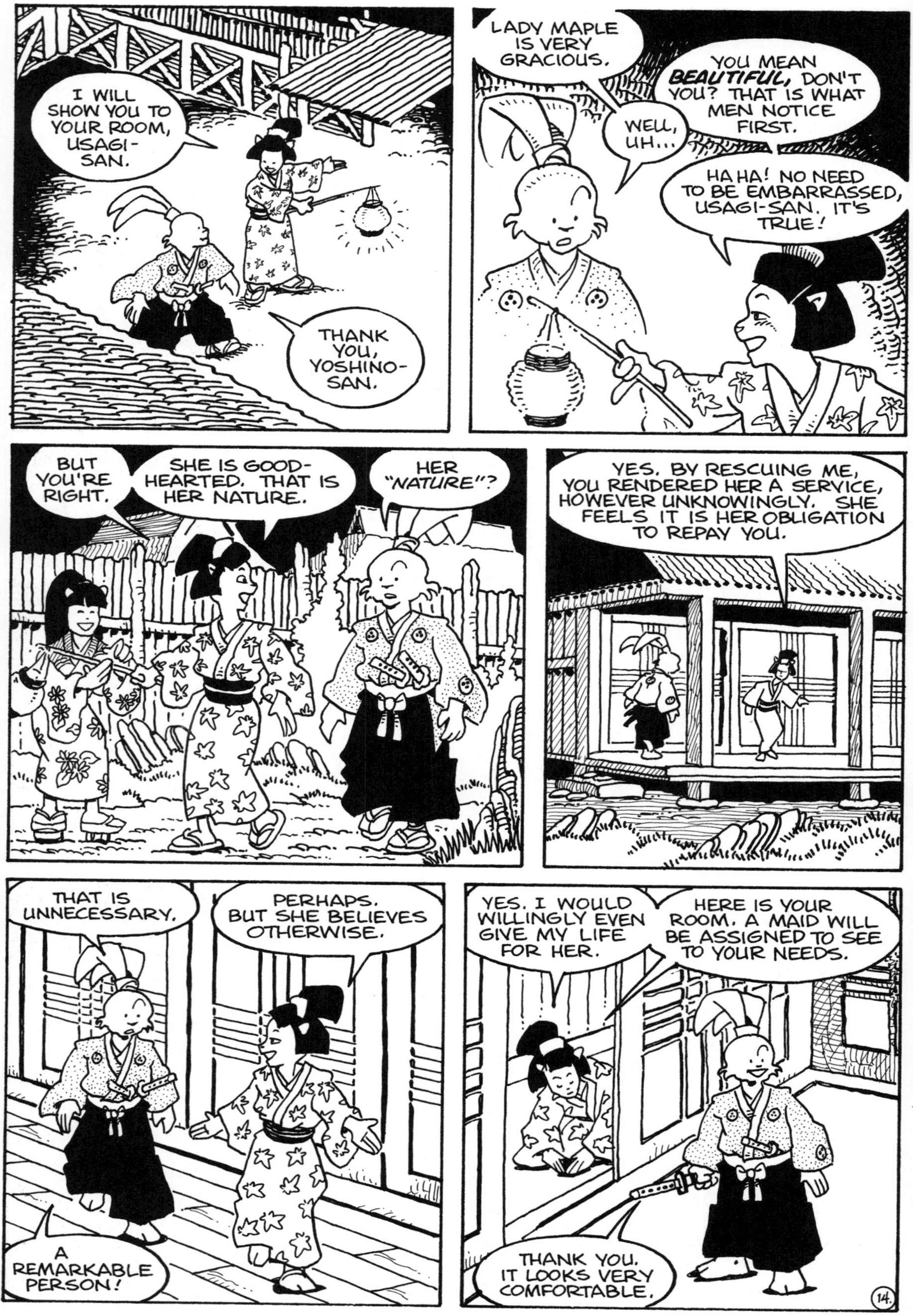
I WILL SHOW YOU TO YOUR ROOM, USAGI-SAN.
THANK YOU, YOSHINO-SAN.
LADY MAPLE IS VERY GRACIOUS.
WELL, UH...
YOU MEAN **BEAUTIFUL,** DON'T YOU? THAT IS WHAT MEN NOTICE FIRST.
HA HA! NO NEED TO BE EMBARRASSED, USAGI-SAN. IT'S TRUE!
BUT YOU'RE RIGHT.
SHE IS GOOD-HEARTED. THAT IS HER NATURE.
HER *"NATURE"*?
YES. BY RESCUING ME, YOU RENDERED HER A SERVICE, HOWEVER UNKNOWINGLY. SHE FEELS IT IS HER OBLIGATION TO REPAY YOU.
THAT IS UNNECESSARY.
PERHAPS. BUT SHE BELIEVES OTHERWISE.
A REMARKABLE PERSON!
YES. I WOULD WILLINGLY EVEN GIVE MY LIFE FOR HER.
HERE IS YOUR ROOM. A MAID WILL BE ASSIGNED TO SEE TO YOUR NEEDS.
THANK YOU. IT LOOKS VERY COMFORTABLE.
14.

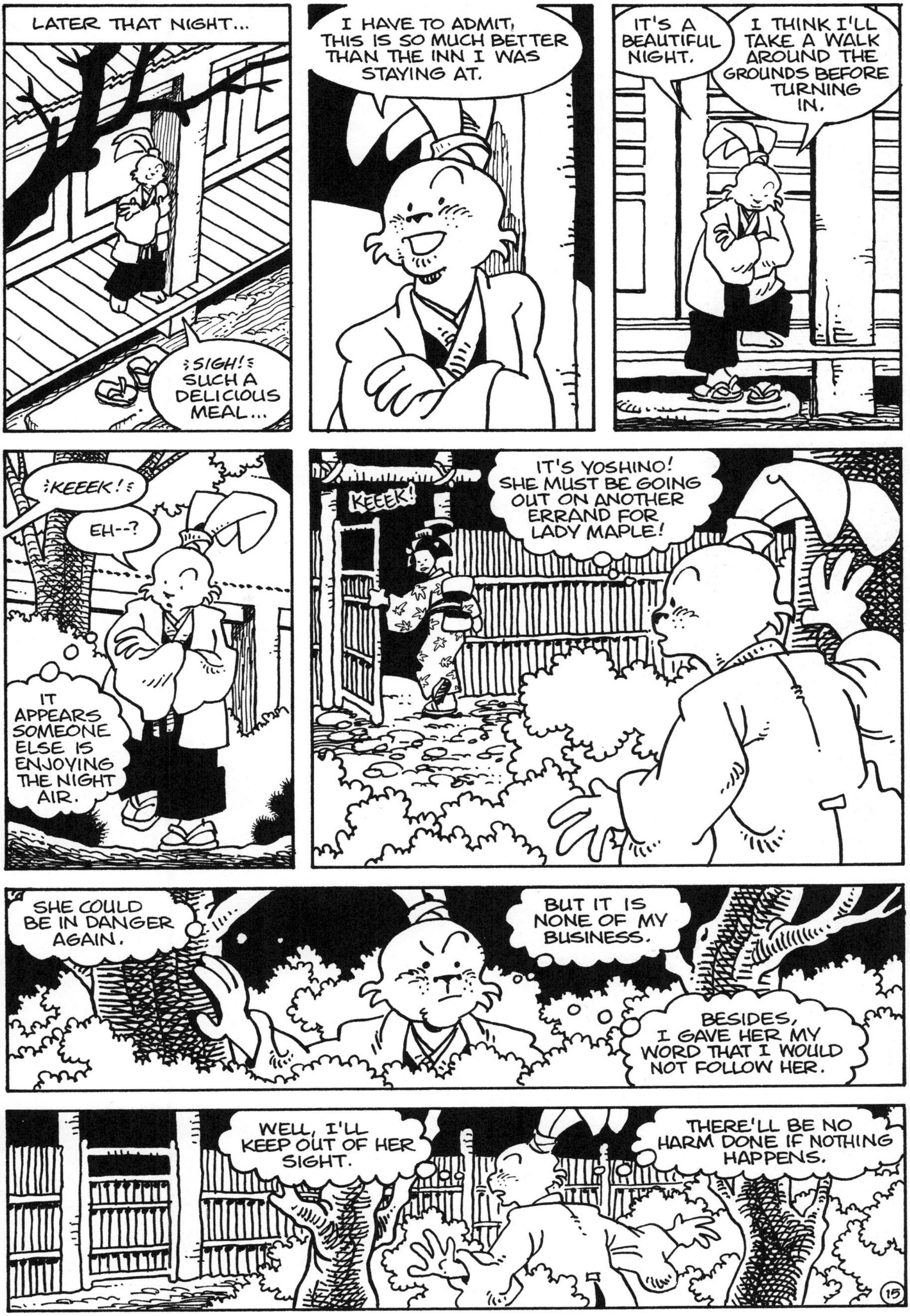

LATER THAT NIGHT...
:SIGH!: SUCH A DELICIOUS MEAL...
I HAVE TO ADMIT, THIS IS SO MUCH BETTER THAN THE INN I WAS STAYING AT.
IT'S A BEAUTIFUL NIGHT.
I THINK I'LL TAKE A WALK AROUND THE GROUNDS BEFORE TURNING IN.
:KEEEK!:
EH--?
IT APPEARS SOMEONE ELSE IS ENJOYING THE NIGHT AIR.
KEEEK!
IT'S YOSHINO! SHE MUST BE GOING OUT ON ANOTHER ERRAND FOR LADY MAPLE!
SHE COULD BE IN DANGER AGAIN.
BUT IT IS NONE OF MY BUSINESS.
BESIDES, I GAVE HER MY WORD THAT I WOULD NOT FOLLOW HER.
WELL, I'LL KEEP OUT OF HER SIGHT.
THERE'LL BE NO HARM DONE IF NOTHING HAPPENS.
15

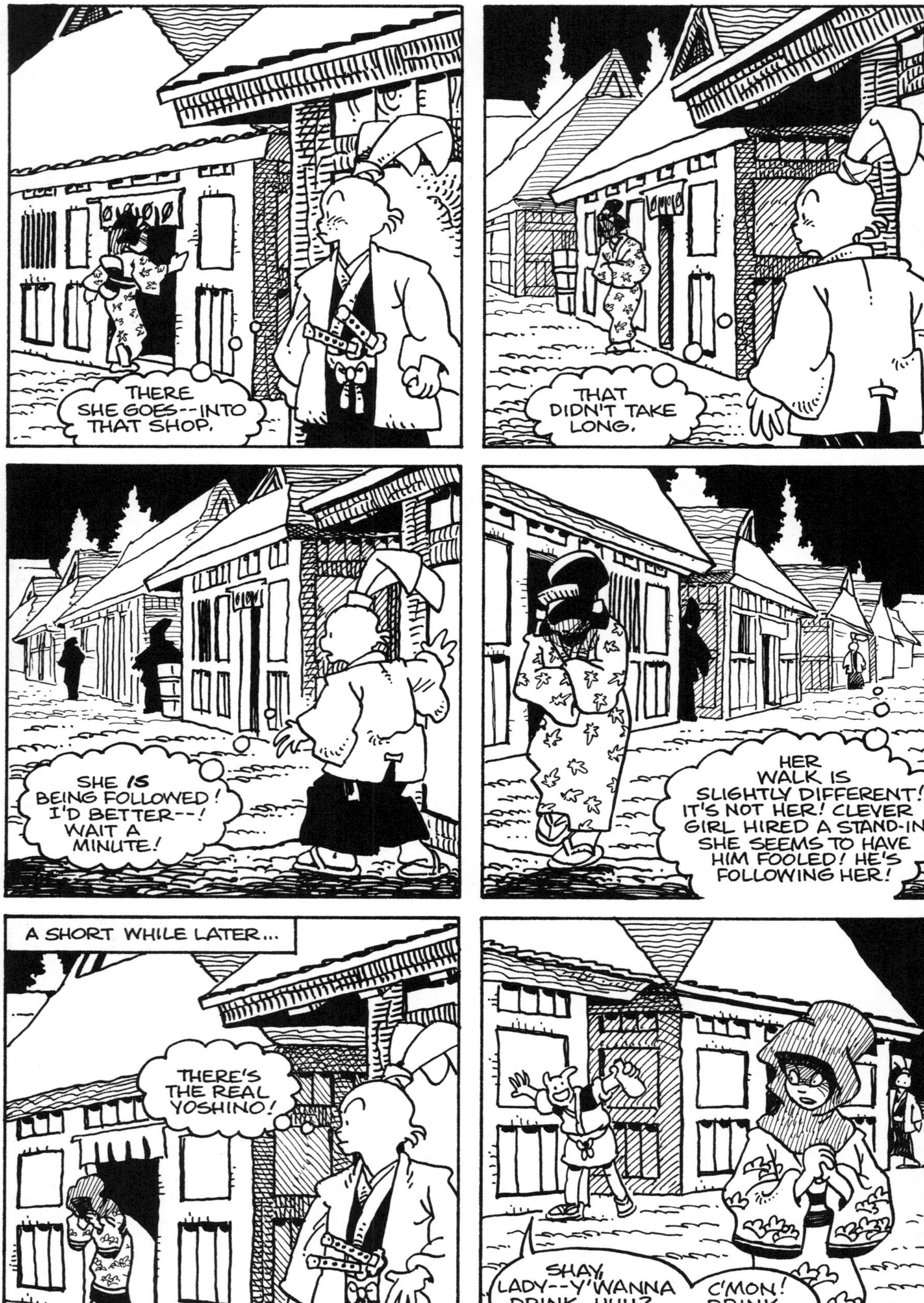
THERE SHE GOES--INTO THAT SHOP.
THAT DIDN'T TAKE LONG.
SHE IS BEING FOLLOWED! I'D BETTER--! WAIT A MINUTE!
HER WALK IS SLIGHTLY DIFFERENT! IT'S NOT HER! CLEVER GIRL HIRED A STAND-IN! SHE SEEMS TO HAVE HIM FOOLED! HE'S FOLLOWING HER!
A SHORT WHILE LATER...
THERE'S THE REAL YOSHINO!
SHAY, LADY--Y'WANNA DRINK, HUH? HUH? HIC!
C'MON! DRINK WI' ME! HICCUP!
16.

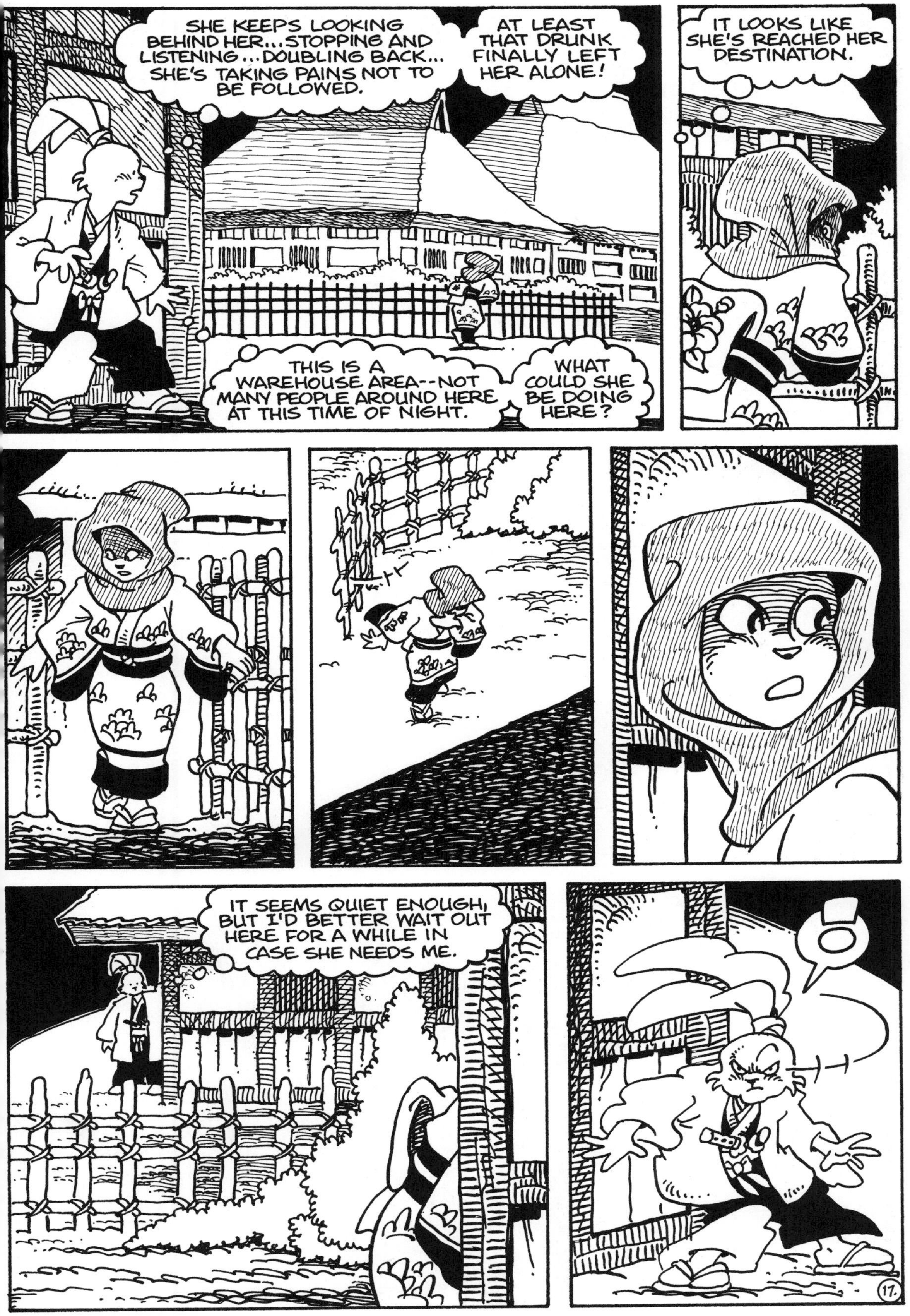
SHE KEEPS LOOKING BEHIND HER...STOPPING AND LISTENING...DOUBLING BACK... SHE'S TAKING PAINS NOT TO BE FOLLOWED.
AT LEAST THAT DRUNK FINALLY LEFT HER ALONE!
THIS IS A WAREHOUSE AREA--NOT MANY PEOPLE AROUND HERE AT THIS TIME OF NIGHT.
WHAT COULD SHE BE DOING HERE?
IT LOOKS LIKE SHE'S REACHED HER DESTINATION.
IT SEEMS QUIET ENOUGH, BUT I'D BETTER WAIT OUT HERE FOR A WHILE IN CASE SHE NEEDS ME.
!
17.

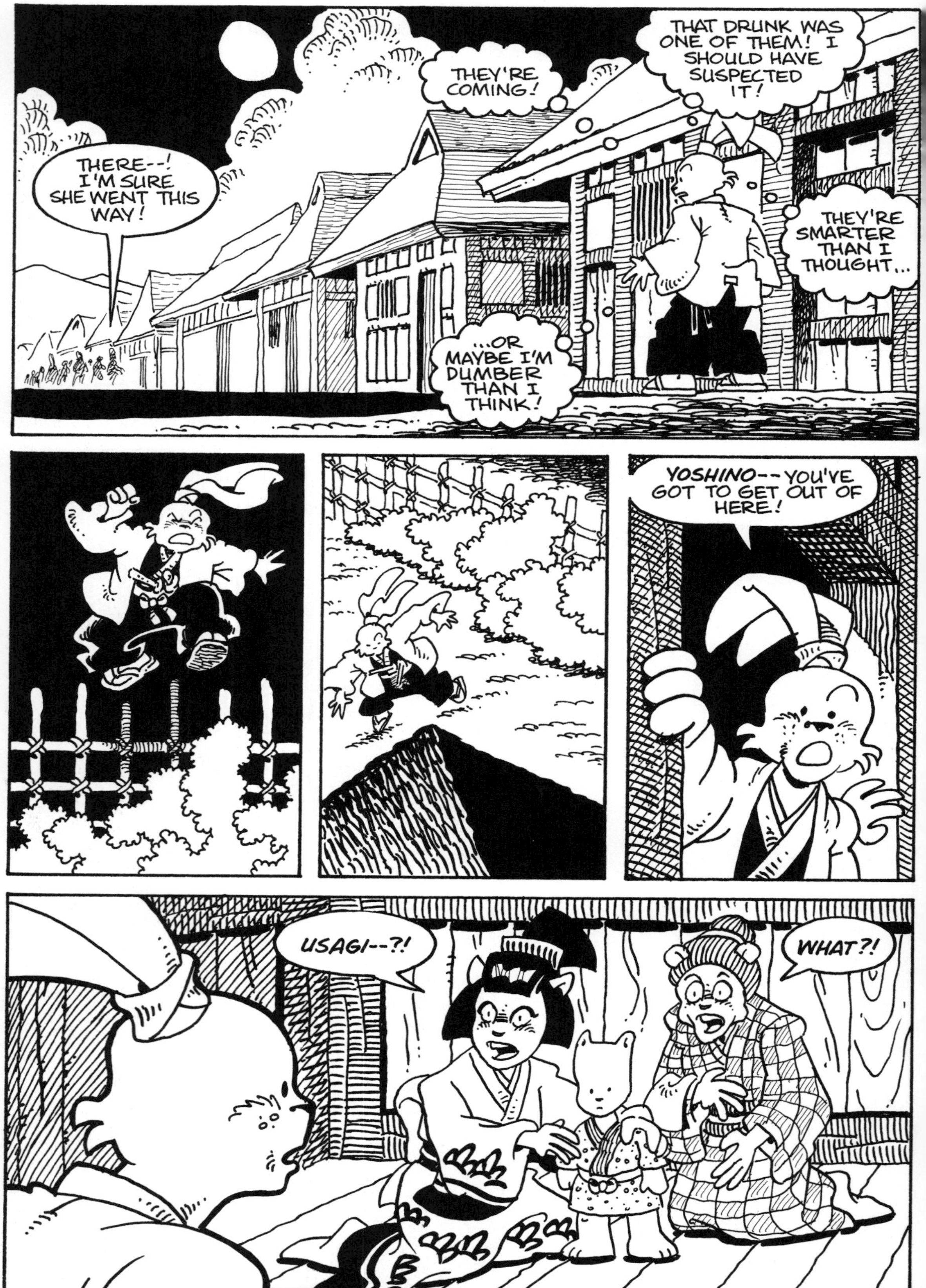
THERE--! I'M SURE SHE WENT THIS WAY!
THEY'RE COMING!
THAT DRUNK WAS ONE OF THEM! I SHOULD HAVE SUSPECTED IT!
THEY'RE SMARTER THAN I THOUGHT...
...OR MAYBE I'M DUMBER THAN I THINK!
YOSHINO--YOU'VE GOT TO GET OUT OF HERE!
USAGI--?!
WHAT?!
18.

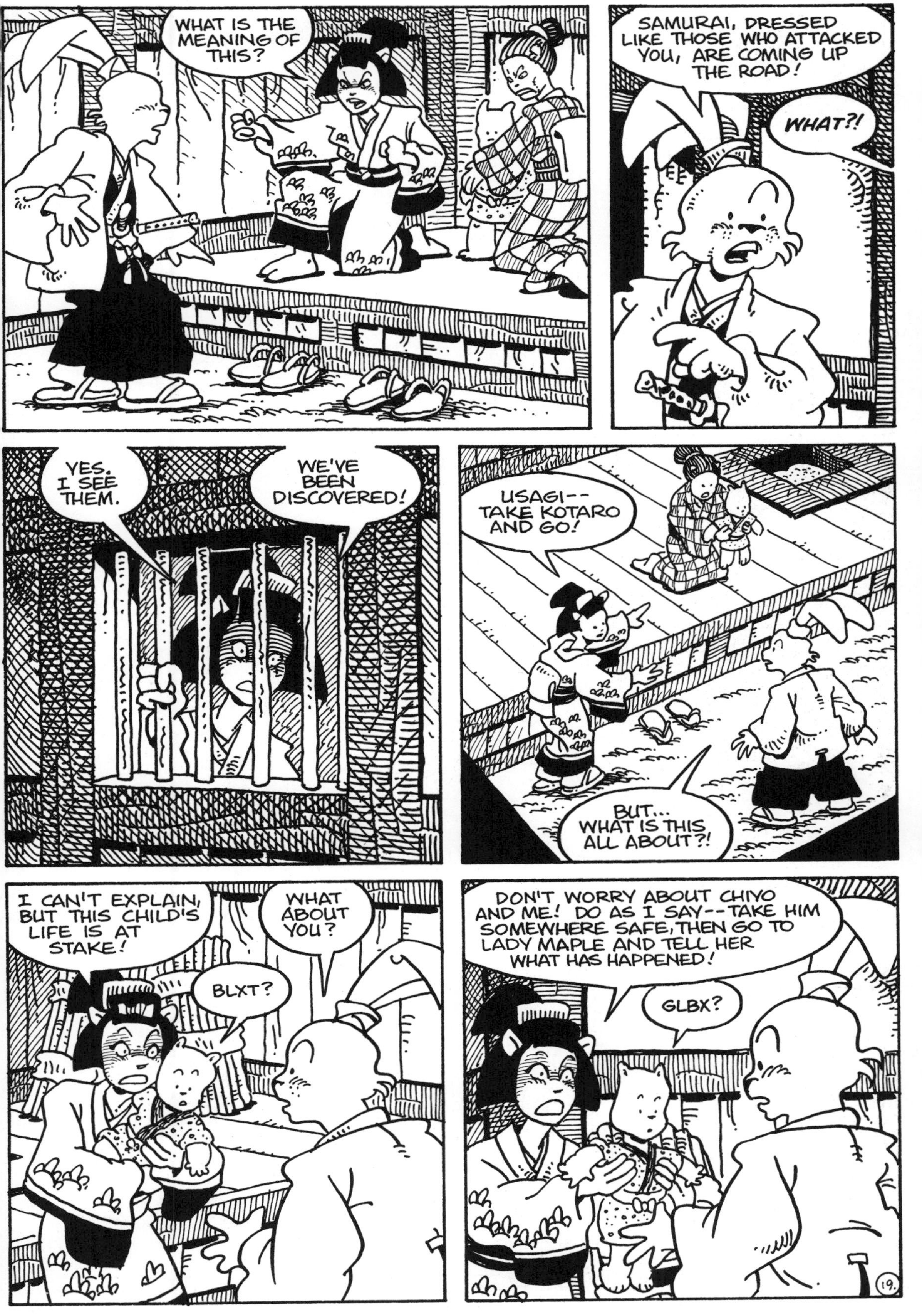

WHAT IS THE MEANING OF THIS?
SAMURAI, DRESSED LIKE THOSE WHO ATTACKED YOU, ARE COMING UP THE ROAD!
WHAT?!
YES. I SEE THEM.
WE'VE BEEN DISCOVERED!
USAGI-- TAKE KOTARO AND GO!
BUT... WHAT IS THIS ALL ABOUT?!
I CAN'T EXPLAIN, BUT THIS CHILD'S LIFE IS AT STAKE!
WHAT ABOUT YOU?
BLXT?
DON'T WORRY ABOUT CHIYO AND ME! DO AS I SAY--TAKE HIM SOMEWHERE SAFE, THEN GO TO LADY MAPLE AND TELL HER WHAT HAS HAPPENED!
GLBX?
19.

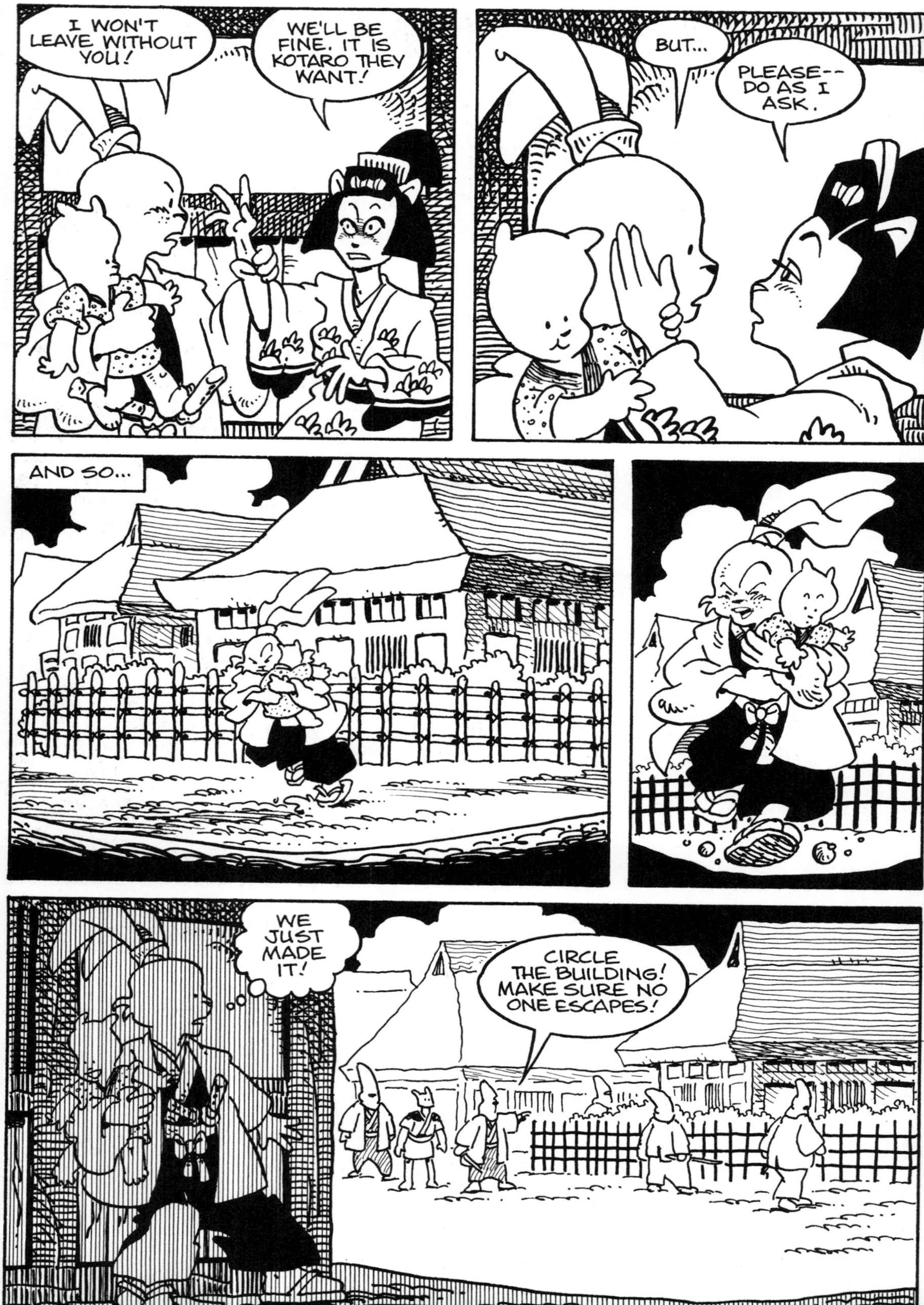

I WON'T LEAVE WITHOUT YOU!
WE'LL BE FINE. IT IS KOTARO THEY WANT!
BUT...
PLEASE--DO AS I ASK.
AND SO...
WE JUST MADE IT!
CIRCLE THE BUILDING! MAKE SURE NO ONE ESCAPES!
20.

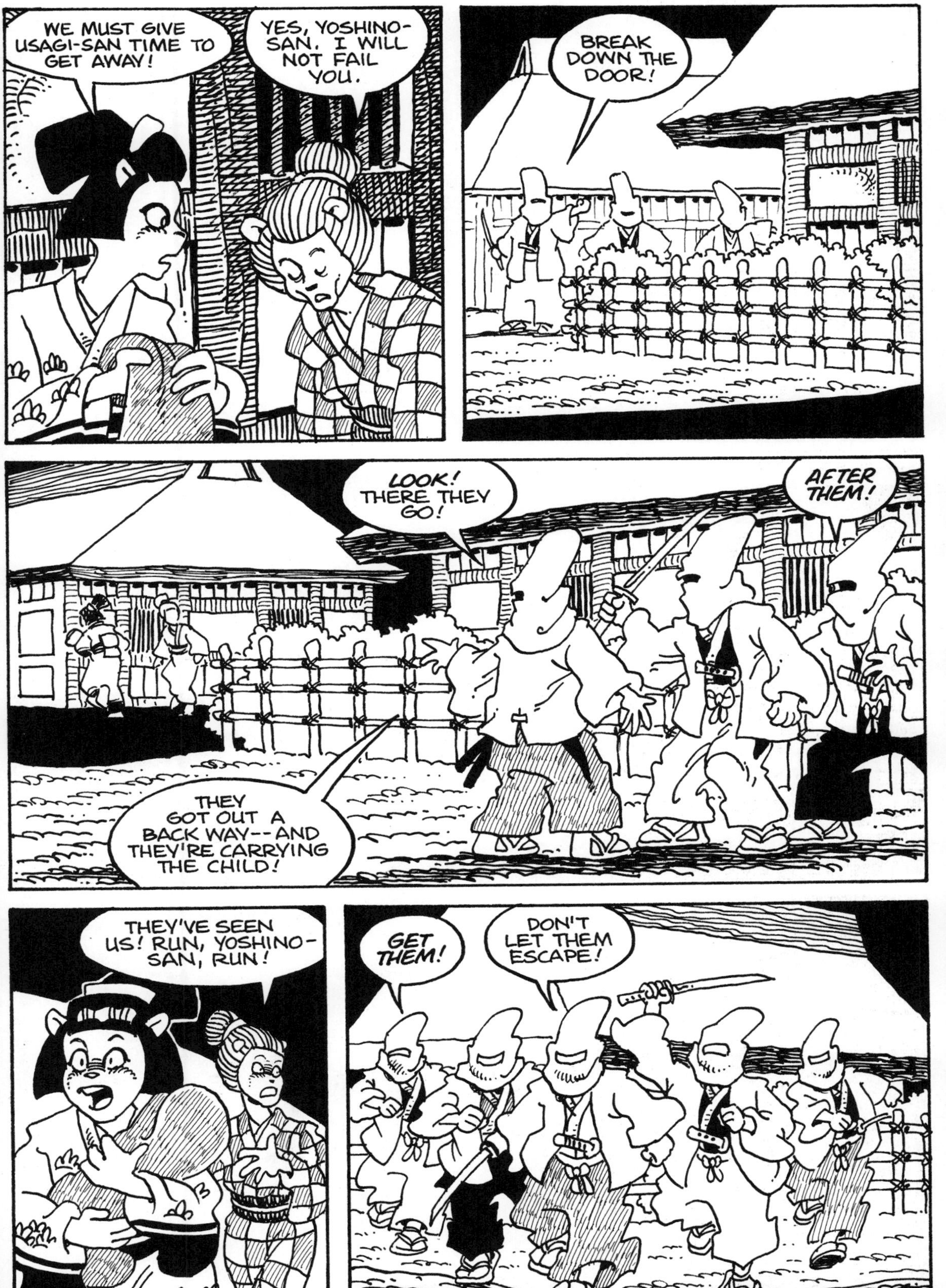
WE MUST GIVE USAGI-SAN TIME TO GET AWAY!
YES, YOSHINO-SAN. I WILL NOT FAIL YOU.
BREAK DOWN THE DOOR!
LOOK! THERE THEY GO!
AFTER THEM!
THEY GOT OUT A BACK WAY--AND THEY'RE CARRYING THE CHILD!
THEY'VE SEEN US! RUN, YOSHINO-SAN, RUN!
GET THEM!
DON'T LET THEM ESCAPE!
21.

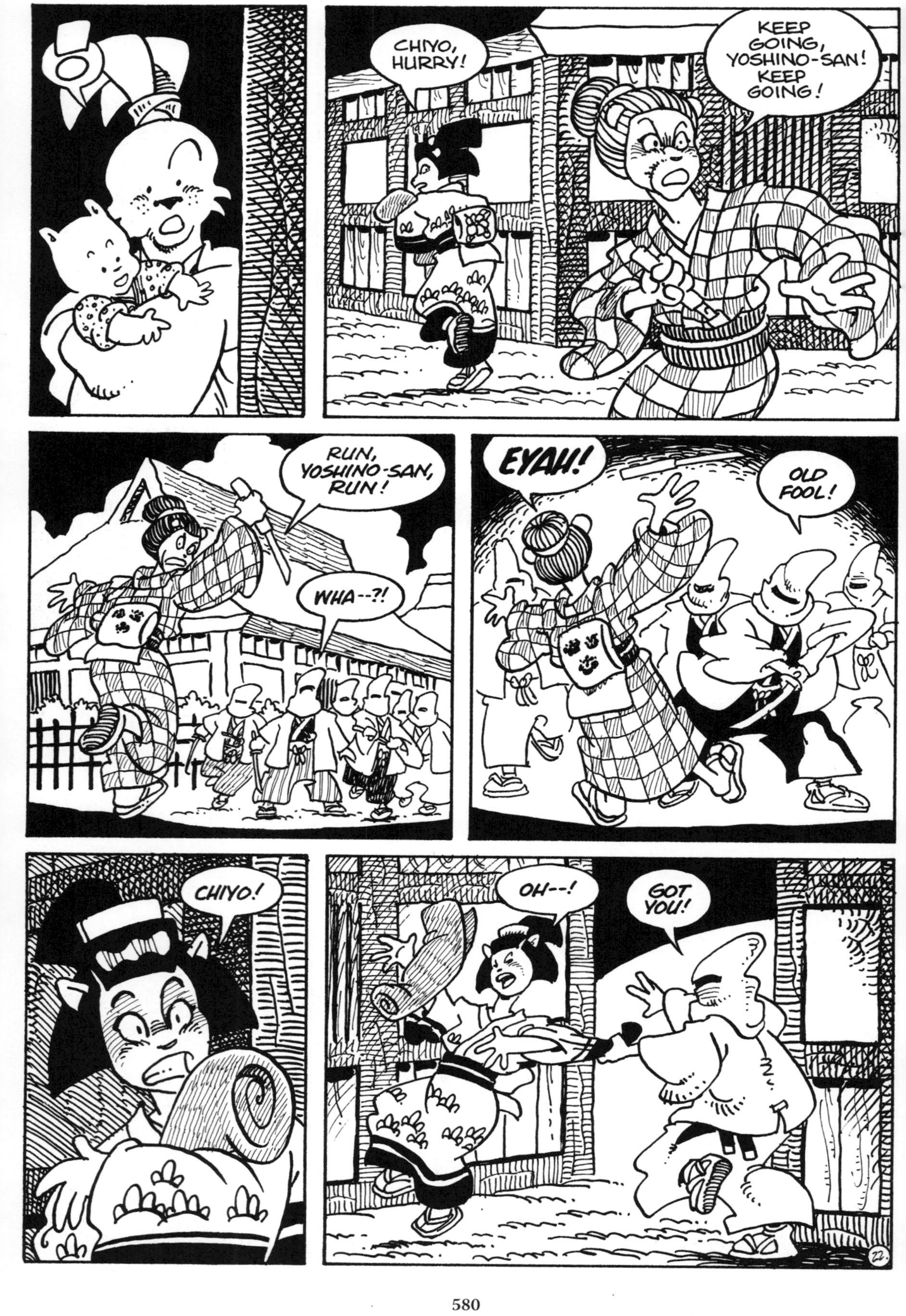
CHIYO, HURRY!
KEEP GOING, YOSHINO-SAN! KEEP GOING!
RUN, YOSHINO-SAN, RUN!
WHA--?!
EYAH!
OLD FOOL!
CHIYO!
OH--!
GOT YOU!
22.

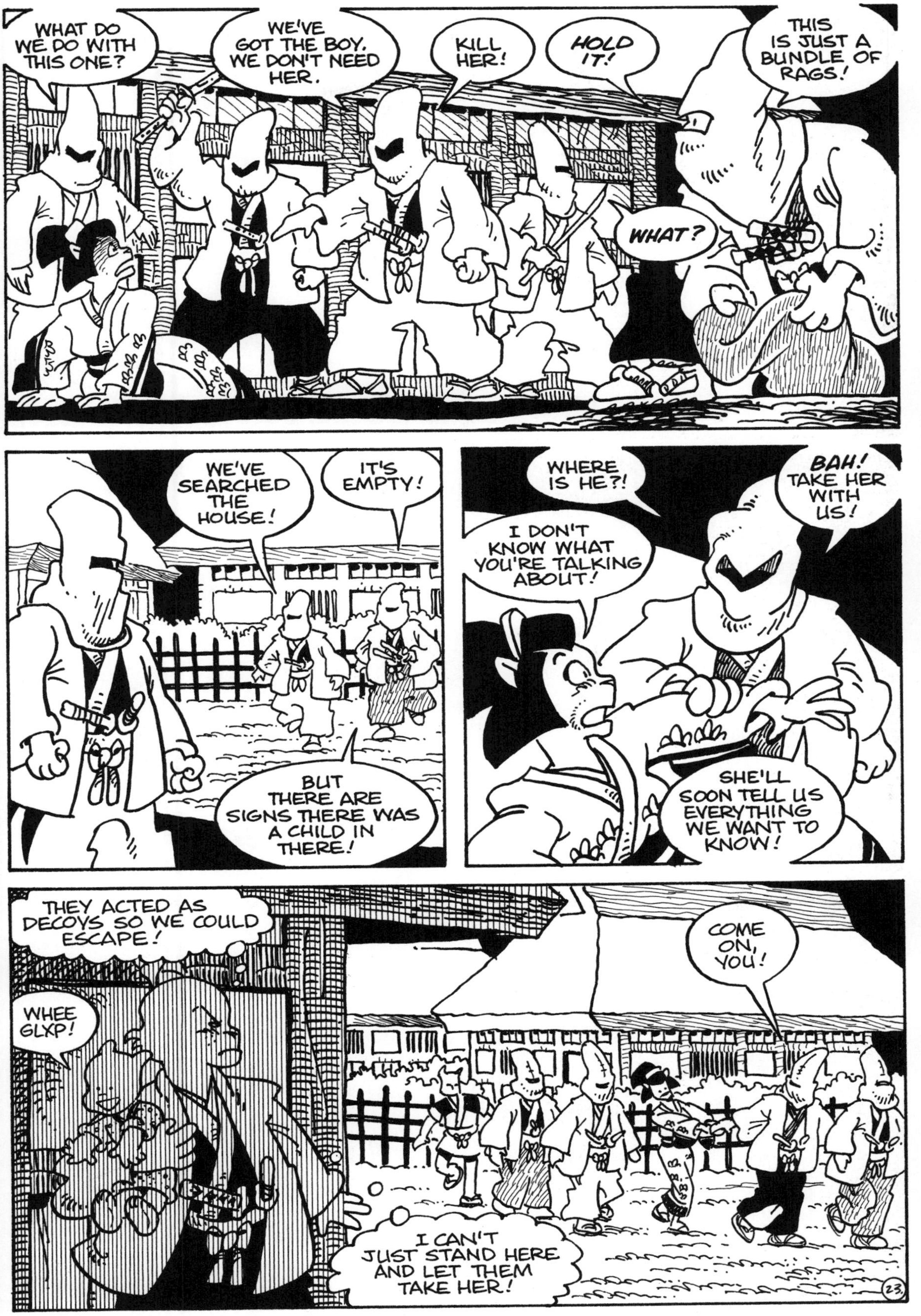
WHAT DO WE DO WITH THIS ONE?
WE'VE GOT THE BOY. WE DON'T NEED HER.
KILL HER!
HOLD IT!
THIS IS JUST A BUNDLE OF RAGS!
WHAT?
WE'VE SEARCHED THE HOUSE!
IT'S EMPTY!
BUT THERE ARE SIGNS THERE WAS A CHILD IN THERE!
WHERE IS HE?!
I DON'T KNOW WHAT YOU'RE TALKING ABOUT!
BAH! TAKE HER WITH US!
SHE'LL SOON TELL US EVERYTHING WE WANT TO KNOW!
THEY ACTED AS DECOYS SO WE COULD ESCAPE!
WHEE GLXP!
COME ON, YOU!
I CAN'T JUST STAND HERE AND LET THEM TAKE HER!
23

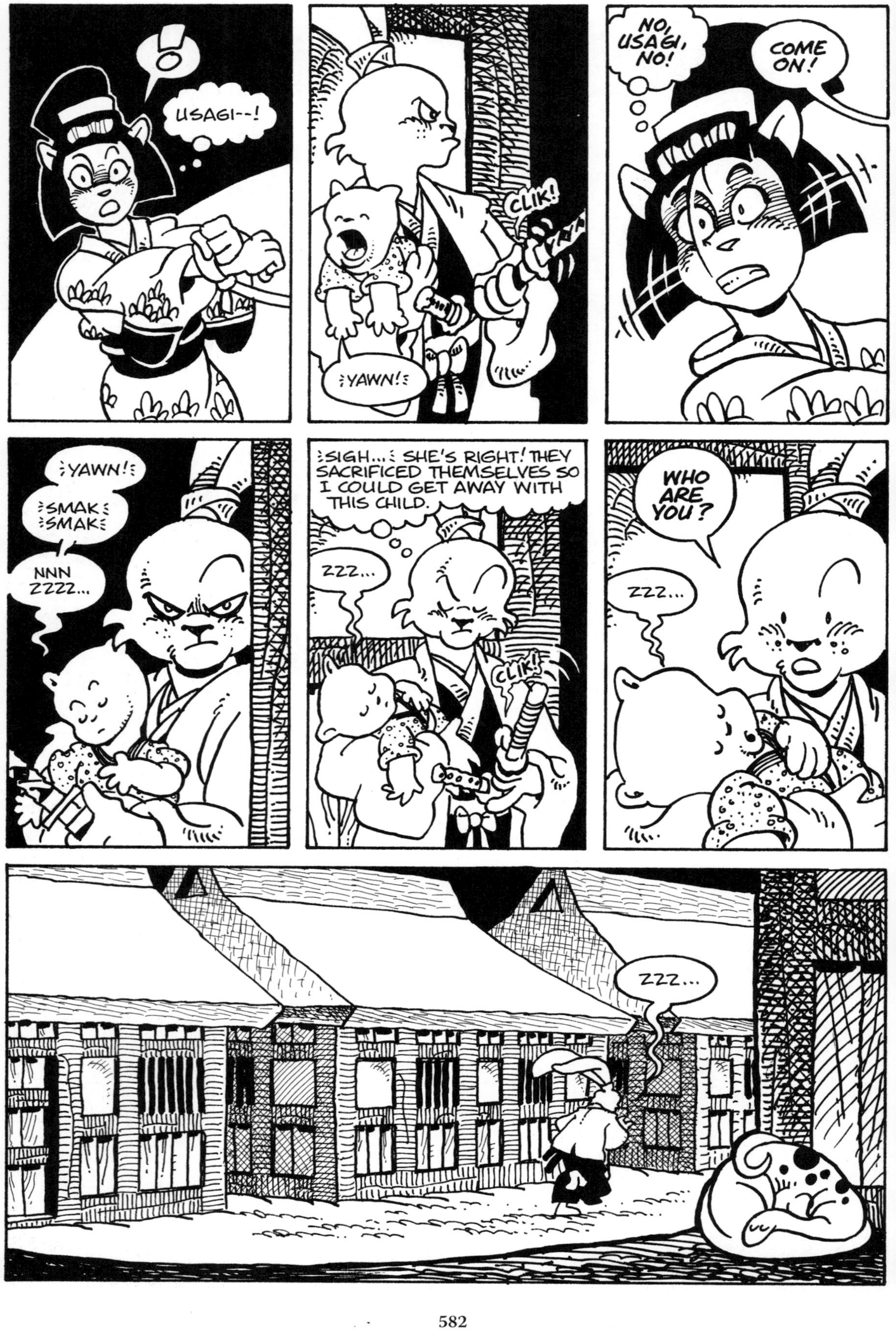
!
USAGI--!
:YAWN!:
CLIK!
NO, USAGI, NO!
COME ON!
:YAWN!:
:SMAK: :SMAK:
NNN ZZZZ...
:SIGH...: SHE'S RIGHT! THEY SACRIFICED THEMSELVES SO I COULD GET AWAY WITH THIS CHILD.
ZZZ...
CLIK!
WHO ARE YOU?
ZZZ...
ZZZ...

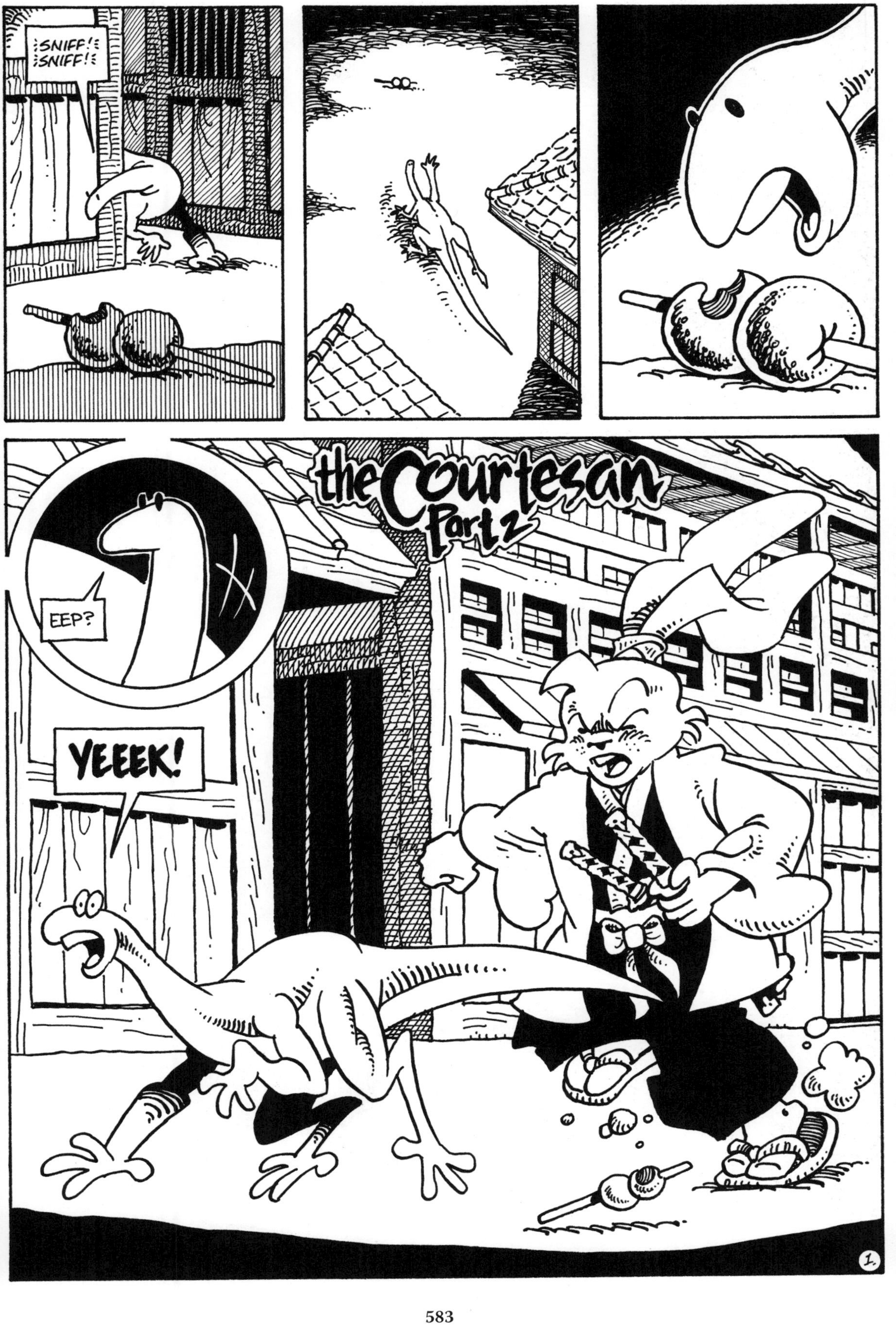
SNIFF! SNIFF!
EEP?
YEEEK!
the Courtesan Part 2
1.

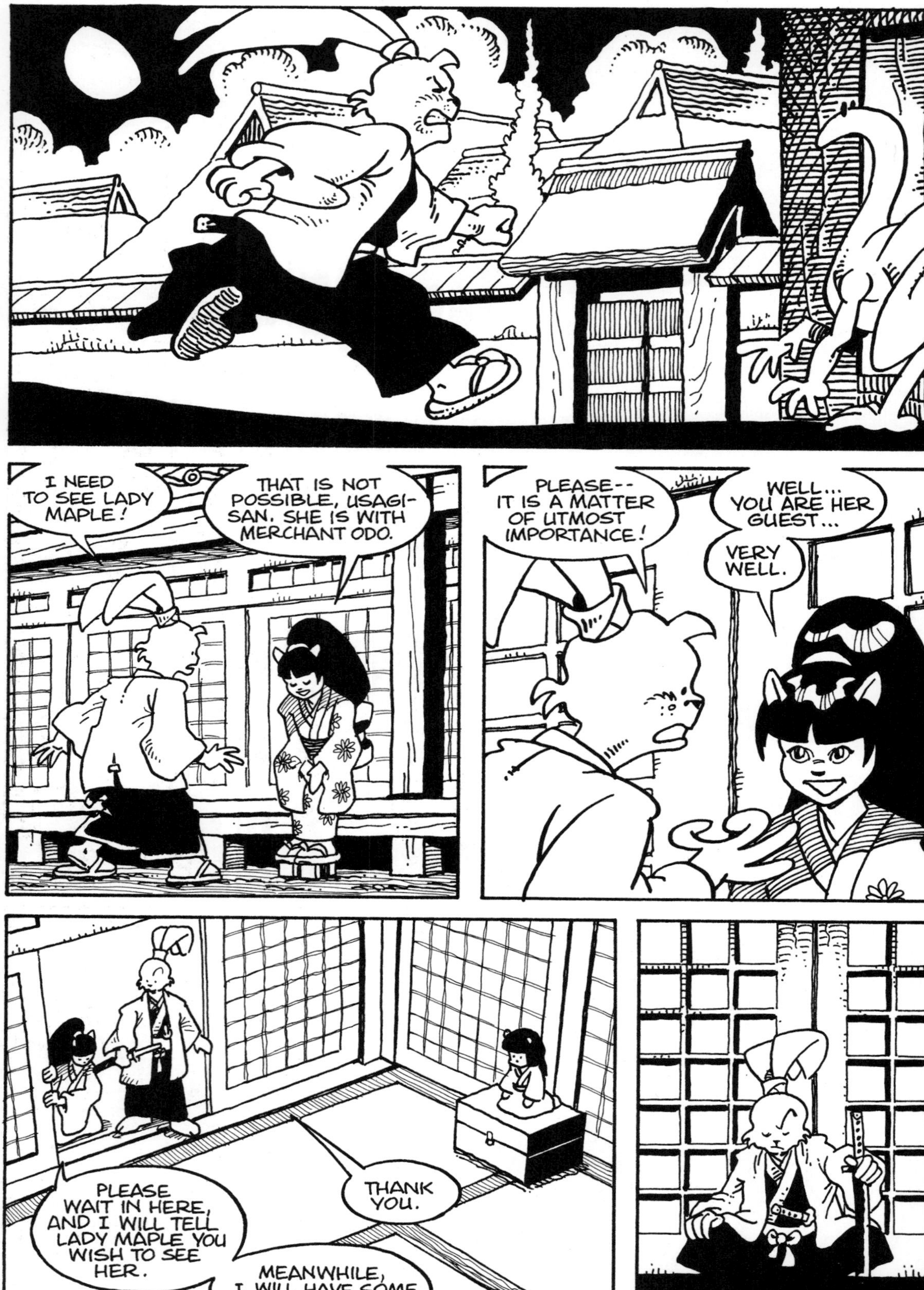

I NEED TO SEE LADY MAPLE!
THAT IS NOT POSSIBLE, USAGI-SAN. SHE IS WITH MERCHANT ODO.
PLEASE-- IT IS A MATTER OF UTMOST IMPORTANCE!
WELL... YOU ARE HER GUEST...
VERY WELL.
PLEASE WAIT IN HERE, AND I WILL TELL LADY MAPLE YOU WISH TO SEE HER.
MEANWHILE, I WILL HAVE SOME TEA BROUGHT IN TO YOU.
THANK YOU.
2.

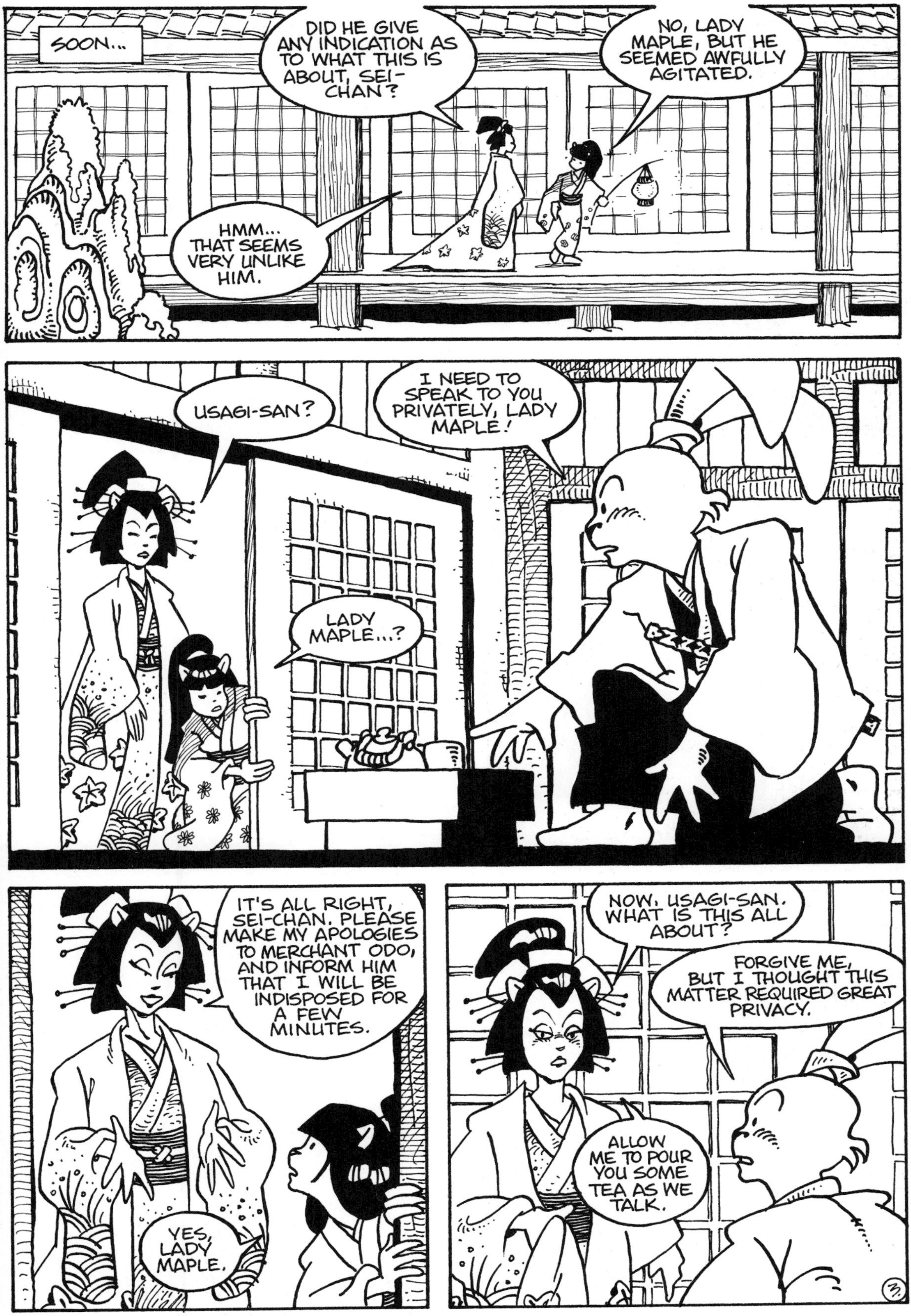
SOON...
DID HE GIVE ANY INDICATION AS TO WHAT THIS IS ABOUT, SEI-CHAN?
NO, LADY MAPLE, BUT HE SEEMED AWFULLY AGITATED.
HMM... THAT SEEMS VERY UNLIKE HIM.
USAGI-SAN?
I NEED TO SPEAK TO YOU PRIVATELY, LADY MAPLE!
LADY MAPLE...?
IT'S ALL RIGHT, SEI-CHAN. PLEASE MAKE MY APOLOGIES TO MERCHANT ODO, AND INFORM HIM THAT I WILL BE INDISPOSED FOR A FEW MINUTES.
YES, LADY MAPLE.
NOW, USAGI-SAN. WHAT IS THIS ALL ABOUT?
FORGIVE ME, BUT I THOUGHT THIS MATTER REQUIRED GREAT PRIVACY.
ALLOW ME TO POUR YOU SOME TEA AS WE TALK.
3.

I SAW YOSHINO LEAVE TONIGHT. I FEARED FOR HER SAFETY SO I FOLLOWED HER.

I AM DISAPPOINTED, USAGI-SAN.

THAT GOES BEYOND THE BOUNDARIES OF A GOOD GUEST.

I-I KNOW, BUT...

THEY TOOK HER!

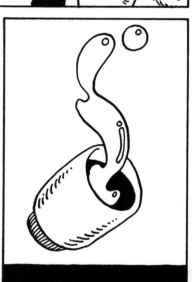

WHAT OF KOTARO?! DO THEY HAVE HIM AS WELL?

THE CHILD? NO. HE IS SAFE!

PRAISE THE GODS!

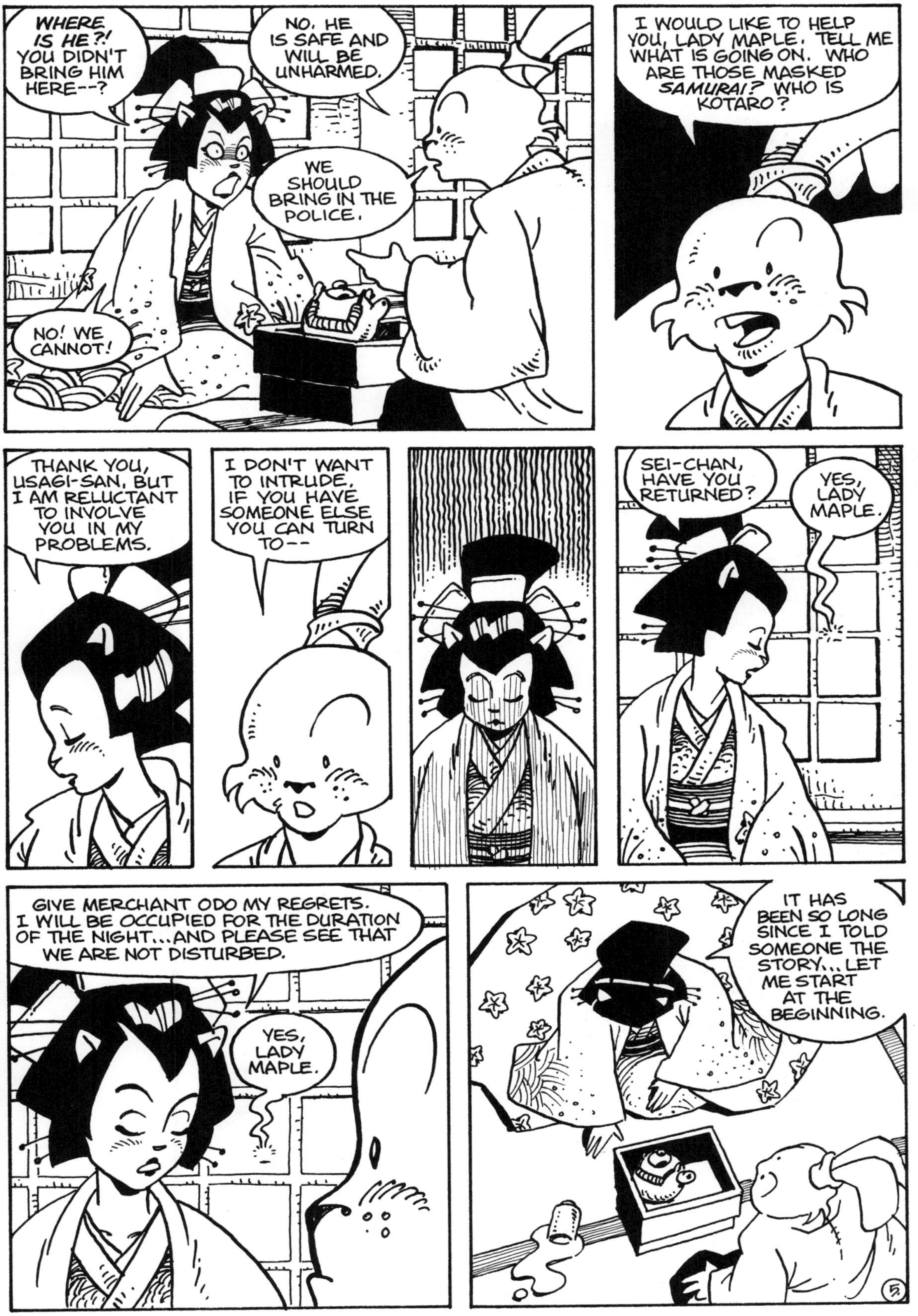
WHERE IS HE?! YOU DIDN'T BRING HIM HERE--?
NO. HE IS SAFE AND WILL BE UNHARMED.
WE SHOULD BRING IN THE POLICE.
NO! WE CANNOT!
I WOULD LIKE TO HELP YOU, LADY MAPLE. TELL ME WHAT IS GOING ON. WHO ARE THOSE MASKED SAMURAI? WHO IS KOTARO?
THANK YOU, USAGI-SAN, BUT I AM RELUCTANT TO INVOLVE YOU IN MY PROBLEMS.
I DON'T WANT TO INTRUDE, IF YOU HAVE SOMEONE ELSE YOU CAN TURN TO--
SEI-CHAN, HAVE YOU RETURNED?
YES, LADY MAPLE.
GIVE MERCHANT ODO MY REGRETS. I WILL BE OCCUPIED FOR THE DURATION OF THE NIGHT...AND PLEASE SEE THAT WE ARE NOT DISTURBED.
YES, LADY MAPLE.
IT HAS BEEN SO LONG SINCE I TOLD SOMEONE THE STORY... LET ME START AT THE BEGINNING.
5

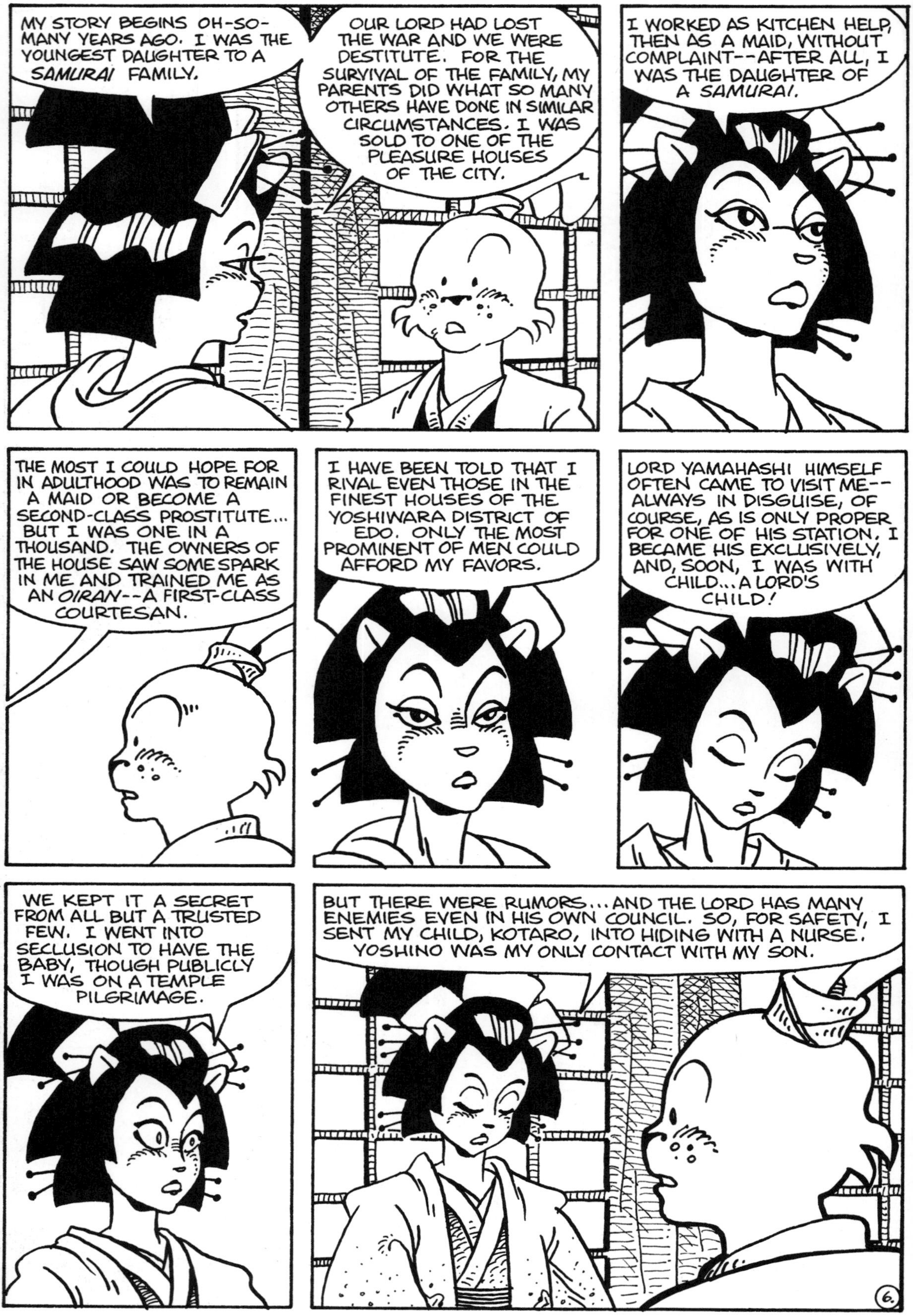
MY STORY BEGINS OH-SO-MANY YEARS AGO. I WAS THE YOUNGEST DAUGHTER TO A *SAMURAI* FAMILY.
OUR LORD HAD LOST THE WAR AND WE WERE DESTITUTE. FOR THE SURVIVAL OF THE FAMILY, MY PARENTS DID WHAT SO MANY OTHERS HAVE DONE IN SIMILAR CIRCUMSTANCES. I WAS SOLD TO ONE OF THE PLEASURE HOUSES OF THE CITY.
I WORKED AS KITCHEN HELP, THEN AS A MAID, WITHOUT COMPLAINT--AFTER ALL, I WAS THE DAUGHTER OF A *SAMURAI*.
THE MOST I COULD HOPE FOR IN ADULTHOOD WAS TO REMAIN A MAID OR BECOME A SECOND-CLASS PROSTITUTE... BUT I WAS ONE IN A THOUSAND. THE OWNERS OF THE HOUSE SAW SOME SPARK IN ME AND TRAINED ME AS AN *OIRAN*--A FIRST-CLASS COURTESAN.
I HAVE BEEN TOLD THAT I RIVAL EVEN THOSE IN THE FINEST HOUSES OF THE YOSHIWARA DISTRICT OF EDO. ONLY THE MOST PROMINENT OF MEN COULD AFFORD MY FAVORS.
LORD YAMAHASHI HIMSELF OFTEN CAME TO VISIT ME--ALWAYS IN DISGUISE, OF COURSE, AS IS ONLY PROPER FOR ONE OF HIS STATION. I BECAME HIS EXCLUSIVELY, AND, SOON, I WAS WITH CHILD...A LORD'S CHILD!
WE KEPT IT A SECRET FROM ALL BUT A TRUSTED FEW. I WENT INTO SECLUSION TO HAVE THE BABY, THOUGH PUBLICLY I WAS ON A TEMPLE PILGRIMAGE.
BUT THERE WERE RUMORS...AND THE LORD HAS MANY ENEMIES EVEN IN HIS OWN COUNCIL. SO, FOR SAFETY, I SENT MY CHILD, KOTARO, INTO HIDING WITH A NURSE. YOSHINO WAS MY ONLY CONTACT WITH MY SON.
6.

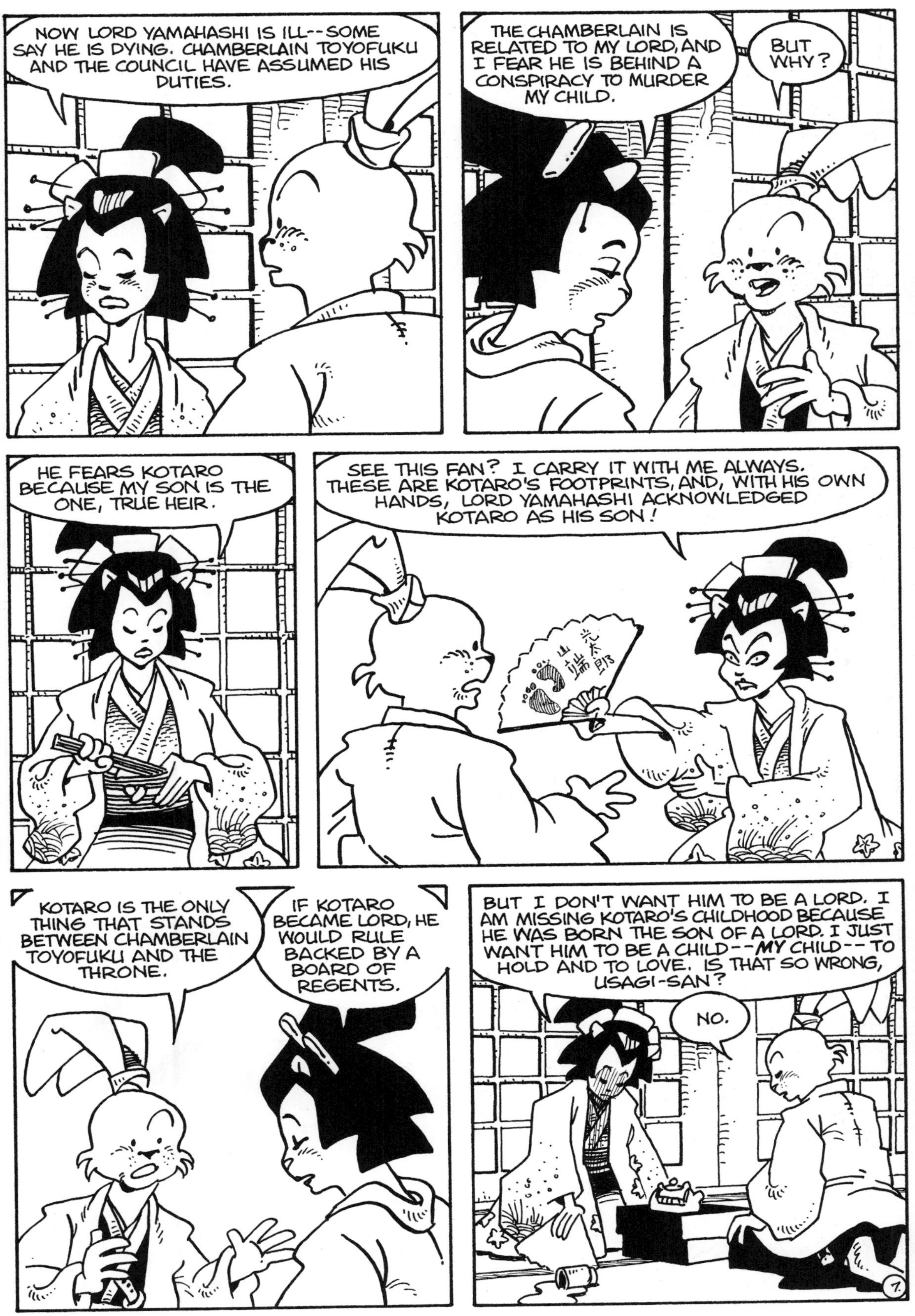
NOW LORD YAMAHASHI IS ILL--SOME SAY HE IS DYING. CHAMBERLAIN TOYOFUKU AND THE COUNCIL HAVE ASSUMED HIS DUTIES.
THE CHAMBERLAIN IS RELATED TO MY LORD, AND I FEAR HE IS BEHIND A CONSPIRACY TO MURDER MY CHILD.
BUT WHY?
HE FEARS KOTARO BECAUSE MY SON IS THE ONE, TRUE HEIR.
SEE THIS FAN? I CARRY IT WITH ME ALWAYS. THESE ARE KOTARO'S FOOTPRINTS, AND, WITH HIS OWN HANDS, LORD YAMAHASHI ACKNOWLEDGED KOTARO AS HIS SON!
KOTARO IS THE ONLY THING THAT STANDS BETWEEN CHAMBERLAIN TOYOFUKU AND THE THRONE.
IF KOTARO BECAME LORD, HE WOULD RULE BACKED BY A BOARD OF REGENTS.
BUT I DON'T WANT HIM TO BE A LORD. I AM MISSING KOTARO'S CHILDHOOD BECAUSE HE WAS BORN THE SON OF A LORD. I JUST WANT HIM TO BE A CHILD--*MY* CHILD--TO HOLD AND TO LOVE. IS THAT SO WRONG, USAGI-SAN?
NO.

"DO YOU KNOW WHERE THE HOODED ONES HAVE TAKEN YOSHINO, LADY MAPLE?"

"NO... BUT I FEAR WHAT THEY MAY BE DOING TO HER!"

WHACK! :UH!

SWISHHH!

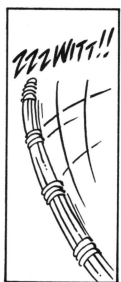

ZZZWITT!!

WHAK!

UH--!

WHERE IS HE?!

WHERE IS THE CHILD?!

I-I DON'T KNOW...

UH--!

WHACK!

SPEAK OR I'LL HAVE THE SKIN FLAYED OFF YOUR BODY!

I-I KNOW NOTHING...

LIAR!

ANSWER CHAMBERLAIN TOYOFUKU!

8.

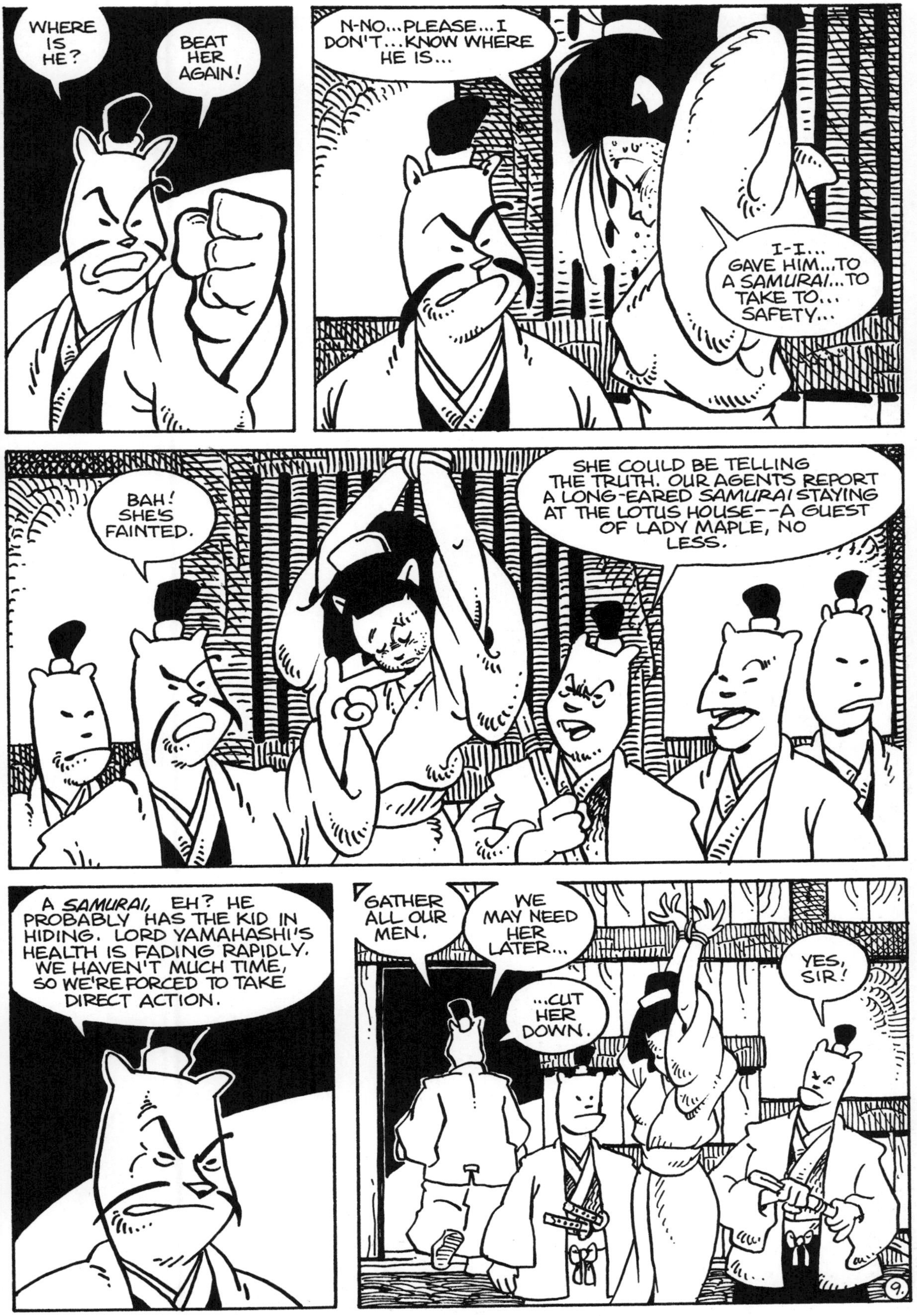
WHERE IS HE?
BEAT HER AGAIN!
N-NO...PLEASE...I DON'T...KNOW WHERE HE IS...
I-I... GAVE HIM...TO A SAMURAI...TO TAKE TO... SAFETY...
BAH! SHE'S FAINTED.
SHE COULD BE TELLING THE TRUTH. OUR AGENTS REPORT A LONG-EARED SAMURAI STAYING AT THE LOTUS HOUSE--A GUEST OF LADY MAPLE, NO LESS.
A SAMURAI, EH? HE PROBABLY HAS THE KID IN HIDING. LORD YAMAHASHI'S HEALTH IS FADING RAPIDLY. WE HAVEN'T MUCH TIME, SO WE'RE FORCED TO TAKE DIRECT ACTION.
GATHER ALL OUR MEN.
WE MAY NEED HER LATER...
...CUT HER DOWN.
YES, SIR!
9.

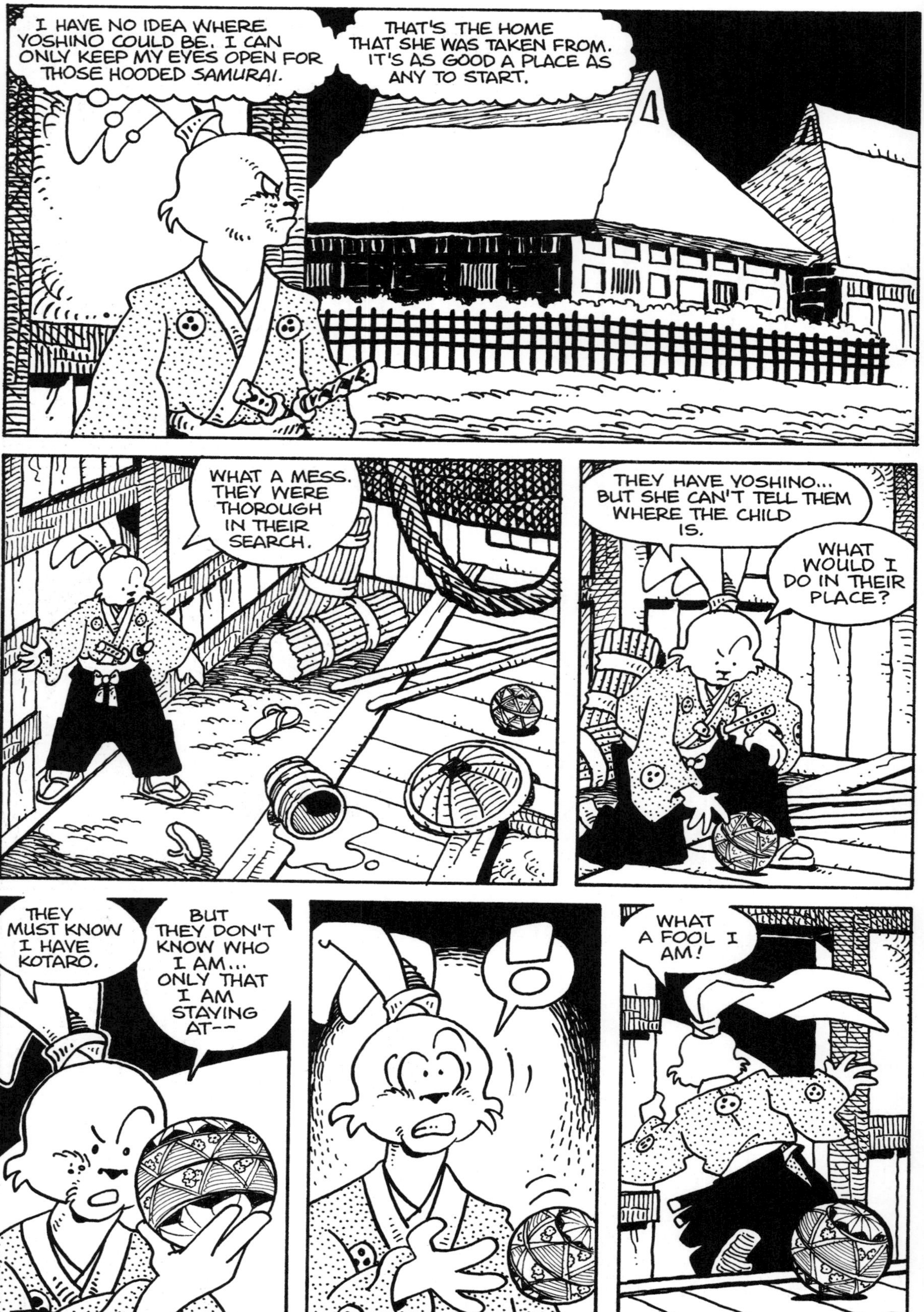
I HAVE NO IDEA WHERE YOSHINO COULD BE. I CAN ONLY KEEP MY EYES OPEN FOR THOSE HOODED *SAMURAI*.
THAT'S THE HOME THAT SHE WAS TAKEN FROM. IT'S AS GOOD A PLACE AS ANY TO START.
WHAT A MESS. THEY WERE THOROUGH IN THEIR SEARCH.
THEY HAVE YOSHINO... BUT SHE CAN'T TELL THEM WHERE THE CHILD IS.
WHAT WOULD I DO IN THEIR PLACE?
THEY MUST KNOW I HAVE KOTARO.
BUT THEY DON'T KNOW WHO I AM... ONLY THAT I AM STAYING AT--
!
WHAT A FOOL I AM!
10

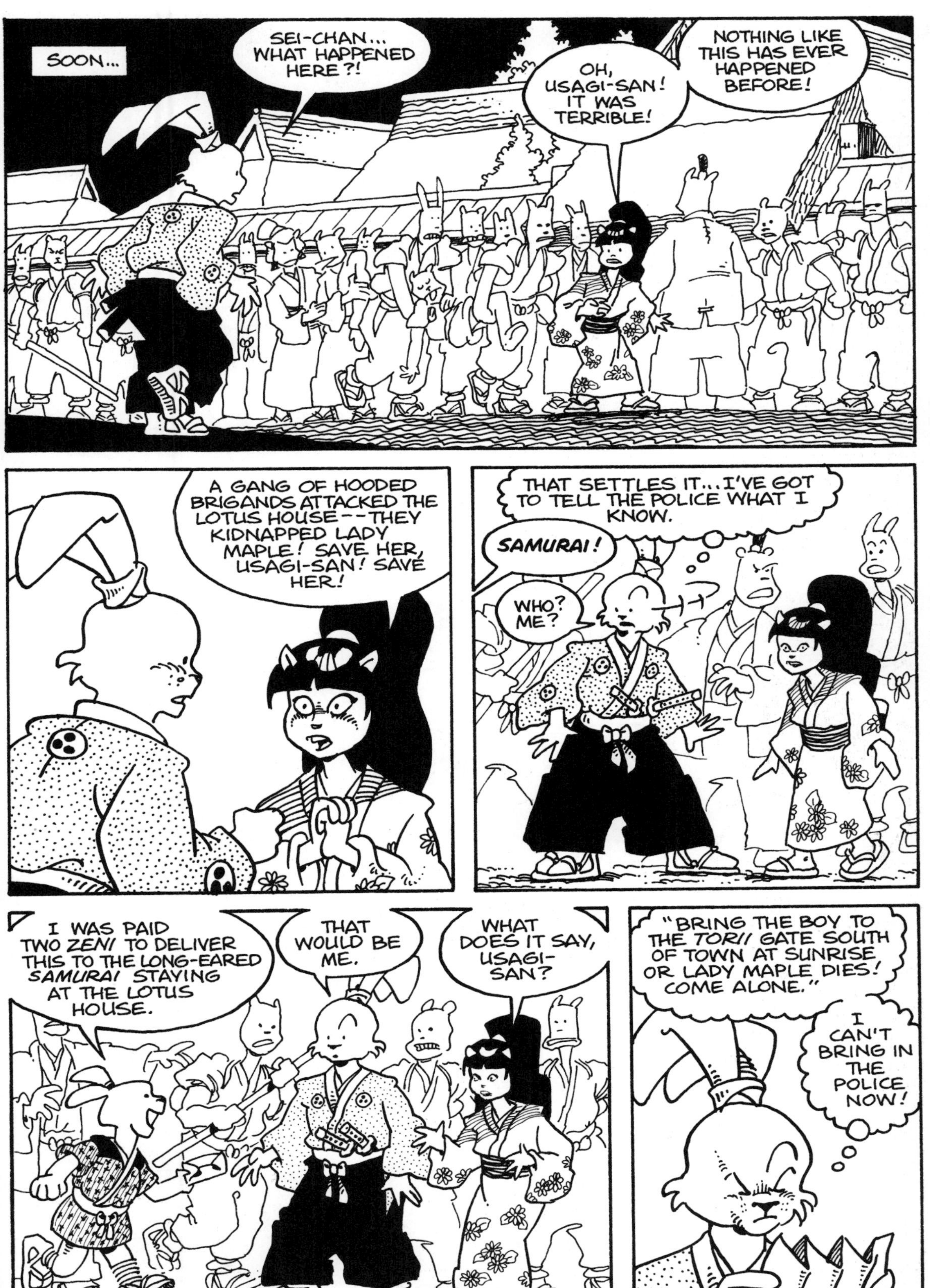
SOON...
SEI-CHAN... WHAT HAPPENED HERE?!
OH, USAGI-SAN! IT WAS TERRIBLE!
NOTHING LIKE THIS HAS EVER HAPPENED BEFORE!
A GANG OF HOODED BRIGANDS ATTACKED THE LOTUS HOUSE--THEY KIDNAPPED LADY MAPLE! SAVE HER, USAGI-SAN! SAVE HER!
THAT SETTLES IT... I'VE GOT TO TELL THE POLICE WHAT I KNOW.
SAMURAI!
WHO? ME?
I WAS PAID TWO ZENI TO DELIVER THIS TO THE LONG-EARED SAMURAI STAYING AT THE LOTUS HOUSE.
THAT WOULD BE ME.
WHAT DOES IT SAY, USAGI-SAN?
"BRING THE BOY TO THE TORII GATE SOUTH OF TOWN AT SUNRISE OR LADY MAPLE DIES! COME ALONE."
I CAN'T BRING IN THE POLICE NOW!
11.

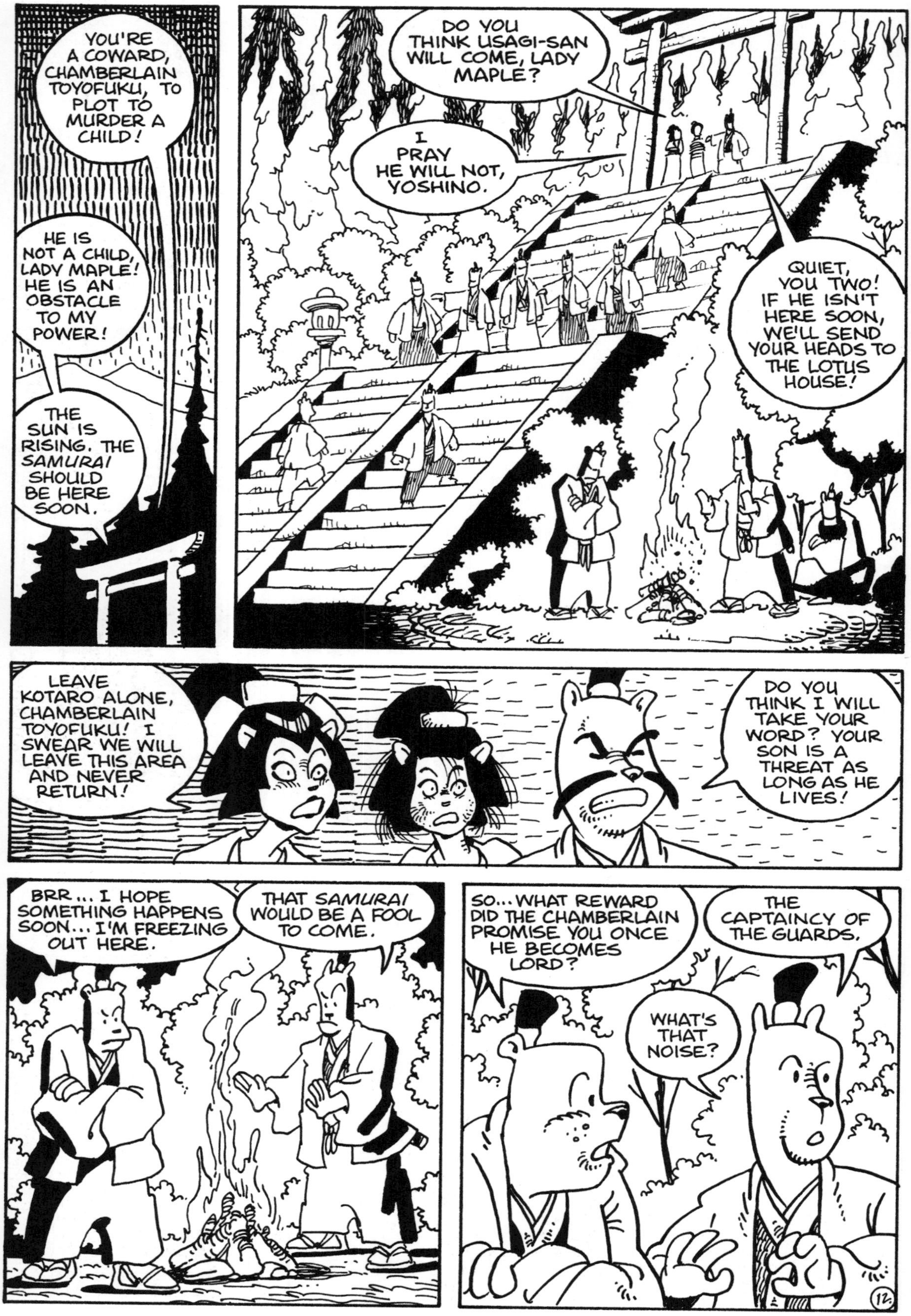
YOU'RE A COWARD, CHAMBERLAIN TOYOFUKU, TO PLOT TO MURDER A CHILD!
HE IS NOT A CHILD, LADY MAPLE! HE IS AN OBSTACLE TO MY POWER!
THE SUN IS RISING. THE *SAMURAI* SHOULD BE HERE SOON.
DO YOU THINK USAGI-SAN WILL COME, LADY MAPLE?
I PRAY HE WILL NOT, YOSHINO.
QUIET, YOU TWO! IF HE ISN'T HERE SOON, WE'LL SEND YOUR HEADS TO THE LOTUS HOUSE!
LEAVE KOTARO ALONE, CHAMBERLAIN TOYOFUKU! I SWEAR WE WILL LEAVE THIS AREA AND NEVER RETURN!
DO YOU THINK I WILL TAKE YOUR WORD? YOUR SON IS A THREAT AS LONG AS HE LIVES!
BRR... I HOPE SOMETHING HAPPENS SOON... I'M FREEZING OUT HERE.
THAT *SAMURAI* WOULD BE A FOOL TO COME.
SO... WHAT REWARD DID THE CHAMBERLAIN PROMISE YOU ONCE HE BECOMES LORD?
THE CAPTAINCY OF THE GUARDS.
WHAT'S THAT NOISE?
12.

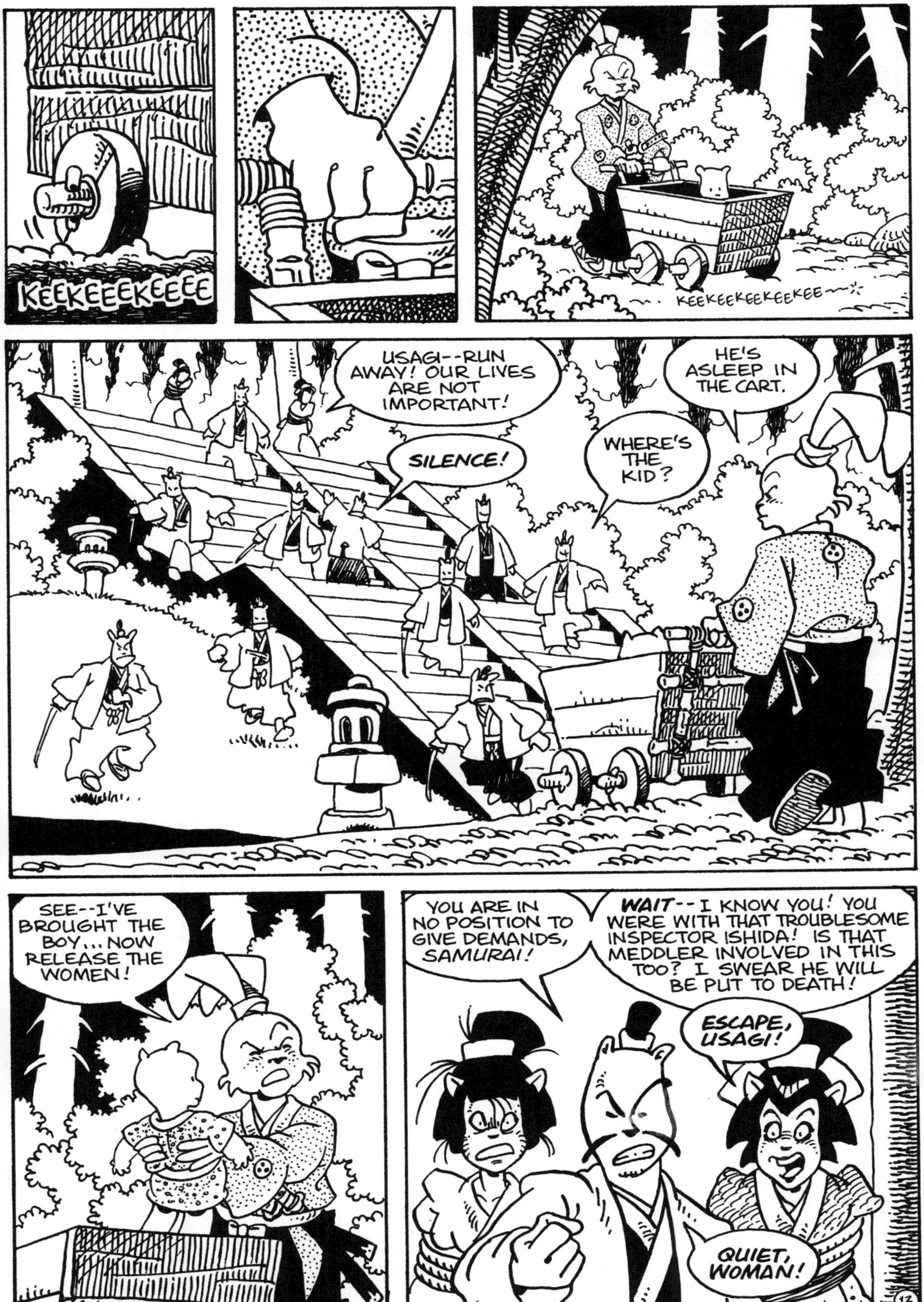
KEEKEEEKEEEE
KEEKEEKEEKEEKEE
USAGI--RUN AWAY! OUR LIVES ARE NOT IMPORTANT!
SILENCE!
WHERE'S THE KID?
HE'S ASLEEP IN THE CART.
SEE--I'VE BROUGHT THE BOY... NOW RELEASE THE WOMEN!
YOU ARE IN NO POSITION TO GIVE DEMANDS, SAMURAI!
WAIT--I KNOW YOU! YOU WERE WITH THAT TROUBLESOME INSPECTOR ISHIDA! IS THAT MEDDLER INVOLVED IN THIS TOO? I SWEAR HE WILL BE PUT TO DEATH!
ESCAPE, USAGI!
QUIET, WOMAN!
13

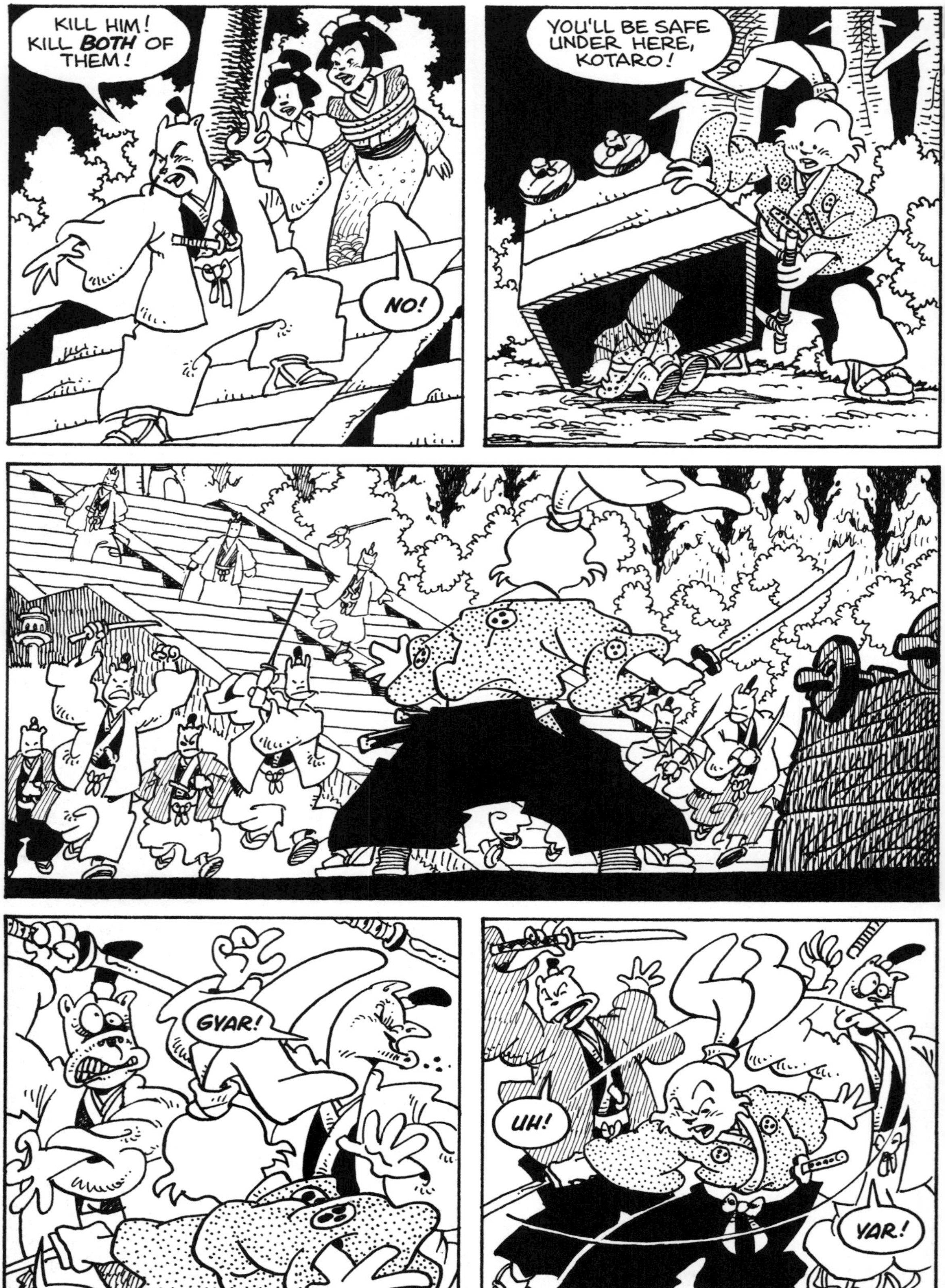
KILL HIM! KILL BOTH OF THEM!
NO!
YOU'LL BE SAFE UNDER HERE, KOTARO!
GYAR!
URK!
UH!
YAR!
14.

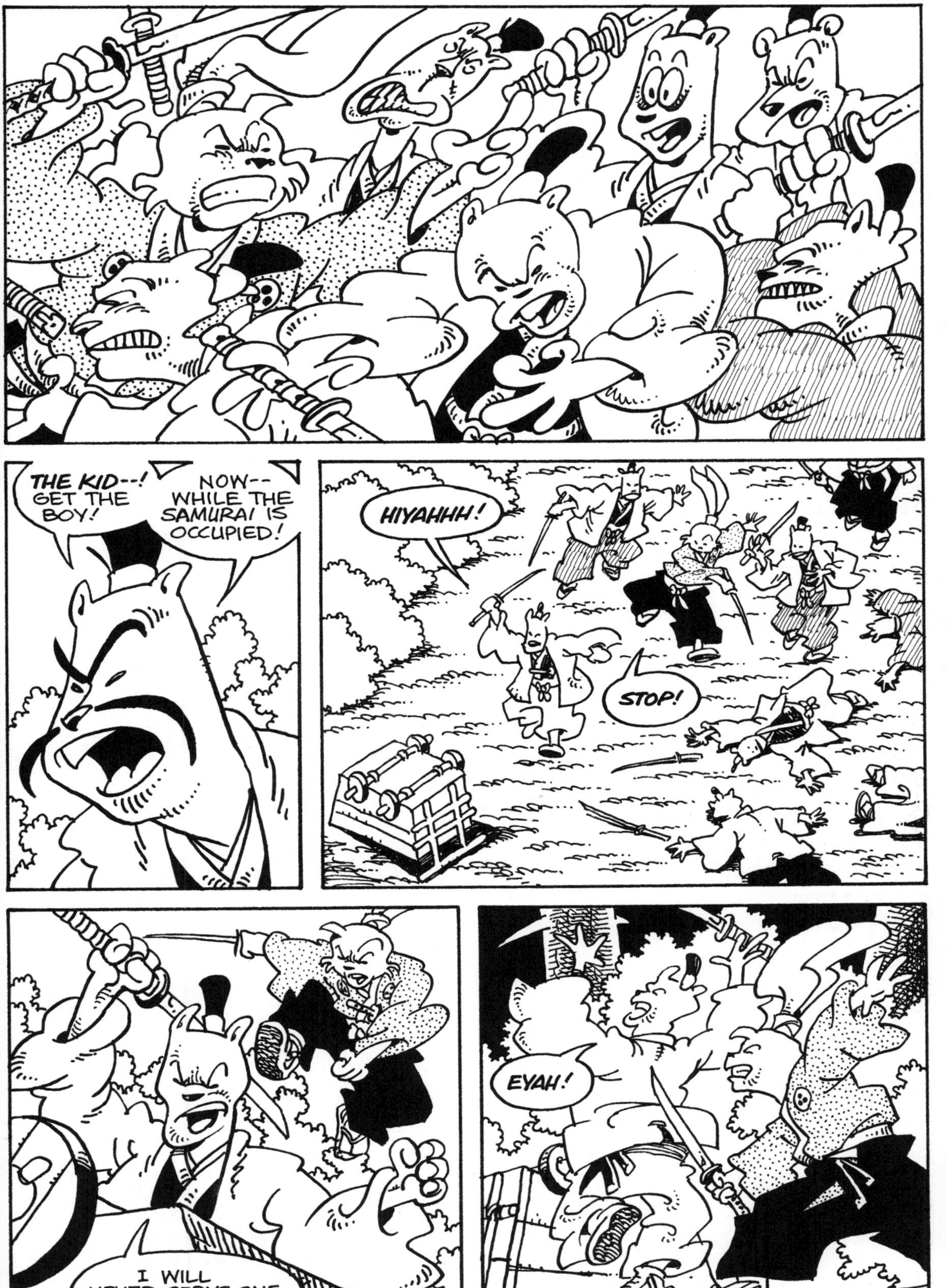
THE KID--! GET THE BOY!
NOW-- WHILE THE SAMURAI IS OCCUPIED!
HIYAHHH!
STOP!
I WILL NEVER SERVE ONE OTHER THAN LORD TOYOFUKU!
EYAH!
15

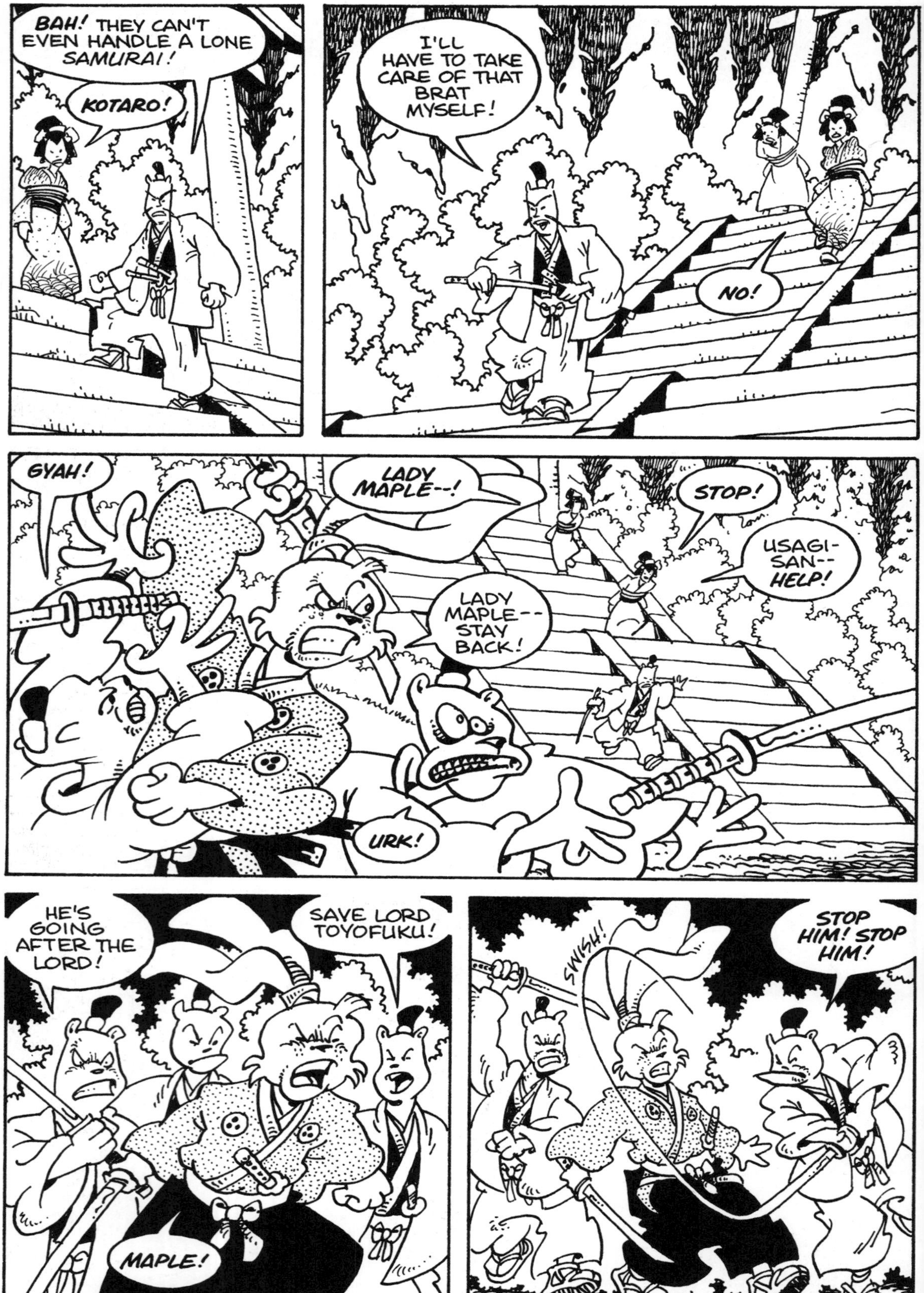
BAH! THEY CAN'T EVEN HANDLE A LONE SAMURAI!
KOTARO!
I'LL HAVE TO TAKE CARE OF THAT BRAT MYSELF!
NO!
GYAH!
LADY MAPLE--!
STOP!
USAGI-SAN-- HELP!
LADY MAPLE-- STAY BACK!
URK!
HE'S GOING AFTER THE LORD!
SAVE LORD TOYOFUKU!
MAPLE!
SWISH!
STOP HIM! STOP HIM!
16.

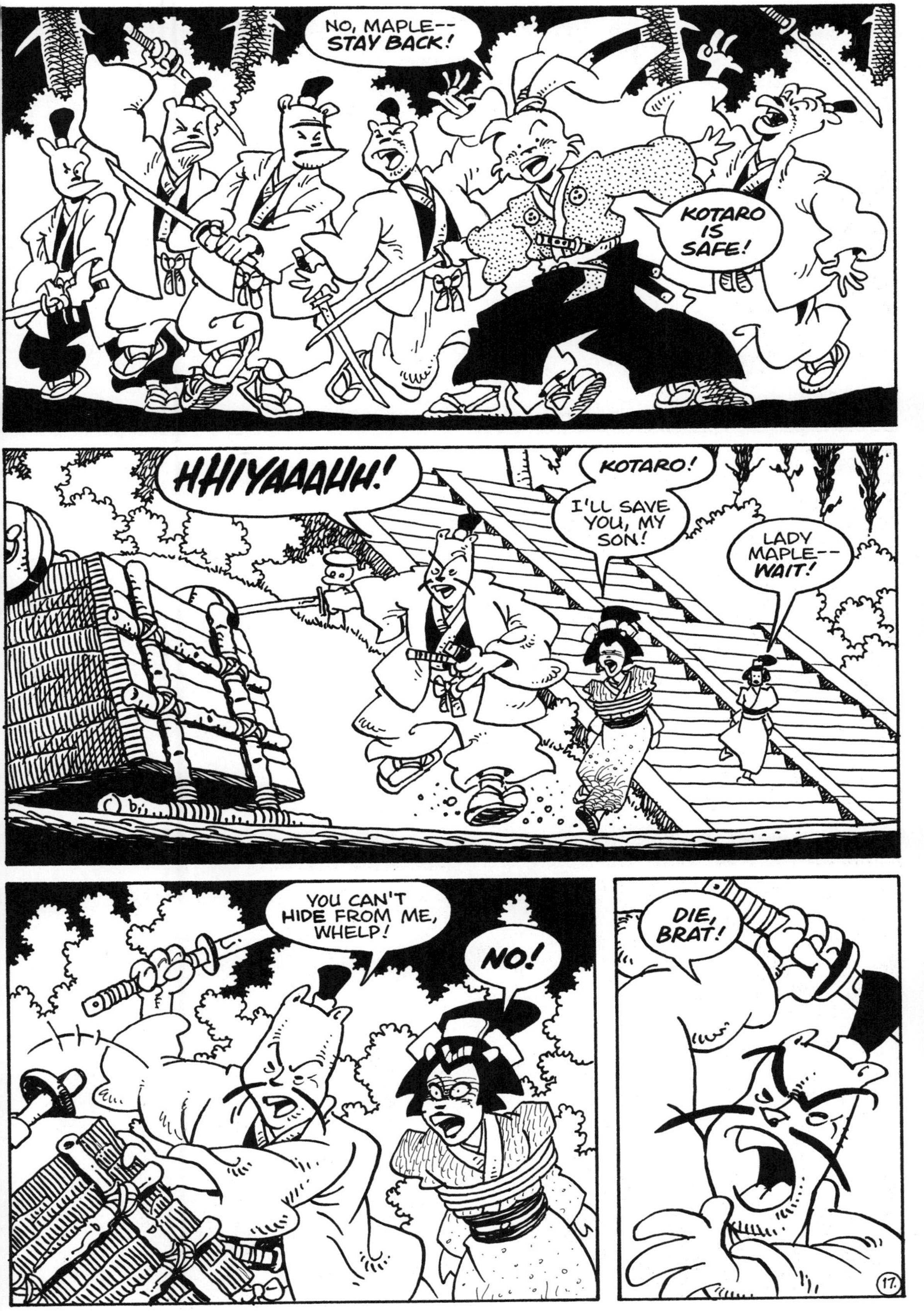
NO, MAPLE-- STAY BACK!
KOTARO IS SAFE!
HHIYAAAAHH!
KOTARO!
I'LL SAVE YOU, MY SON!
LADY MAPLE-- WAIT!
YOU CAN'T HIDE FROM ME, WHELP!
NO!
DIE, BRAT!
17.

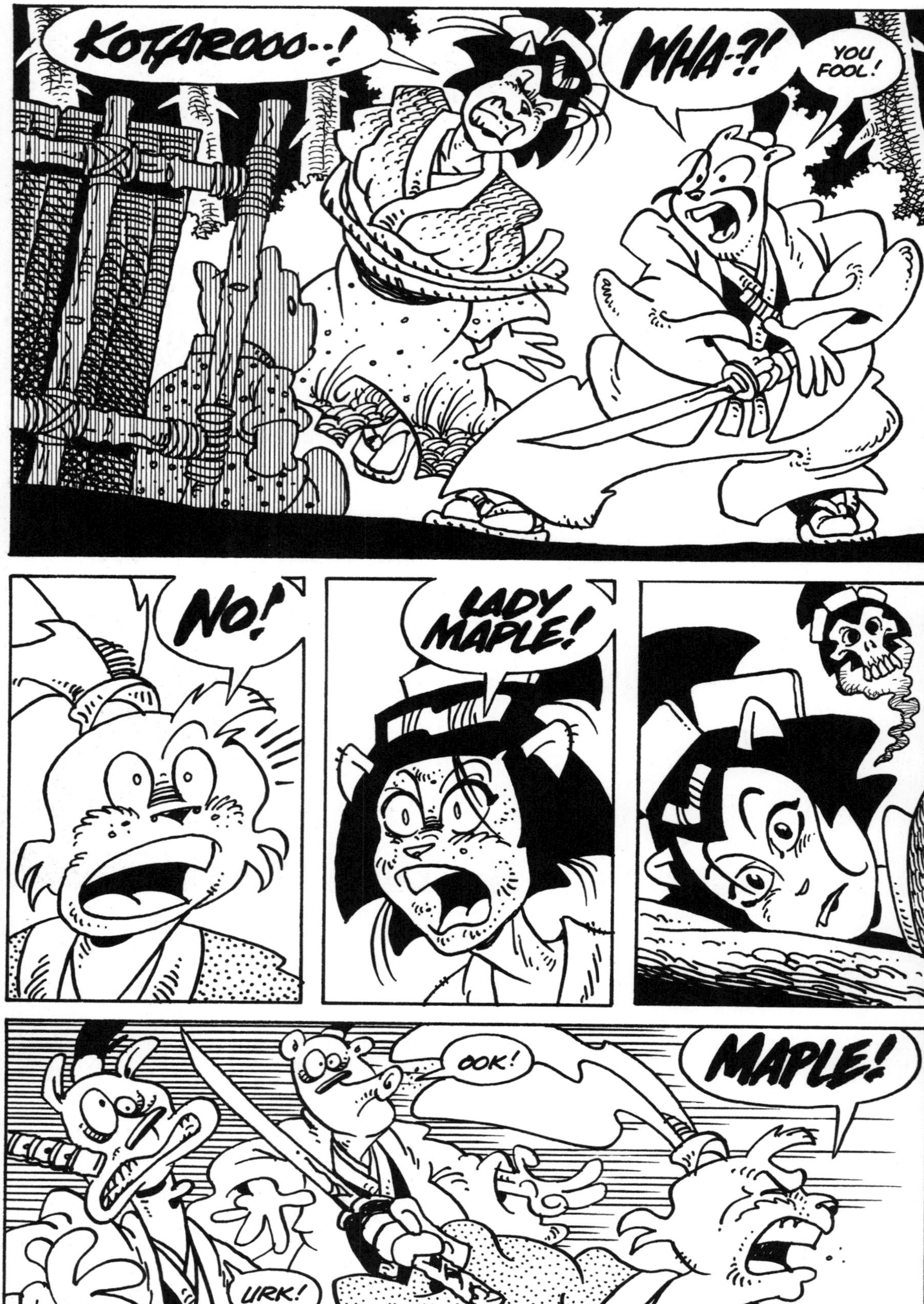
KOTAROOO..!
WHA-?!
YOU FOOL!
NO!
LADY MAPLE!
OOK!
MAPLE!
URK!
18

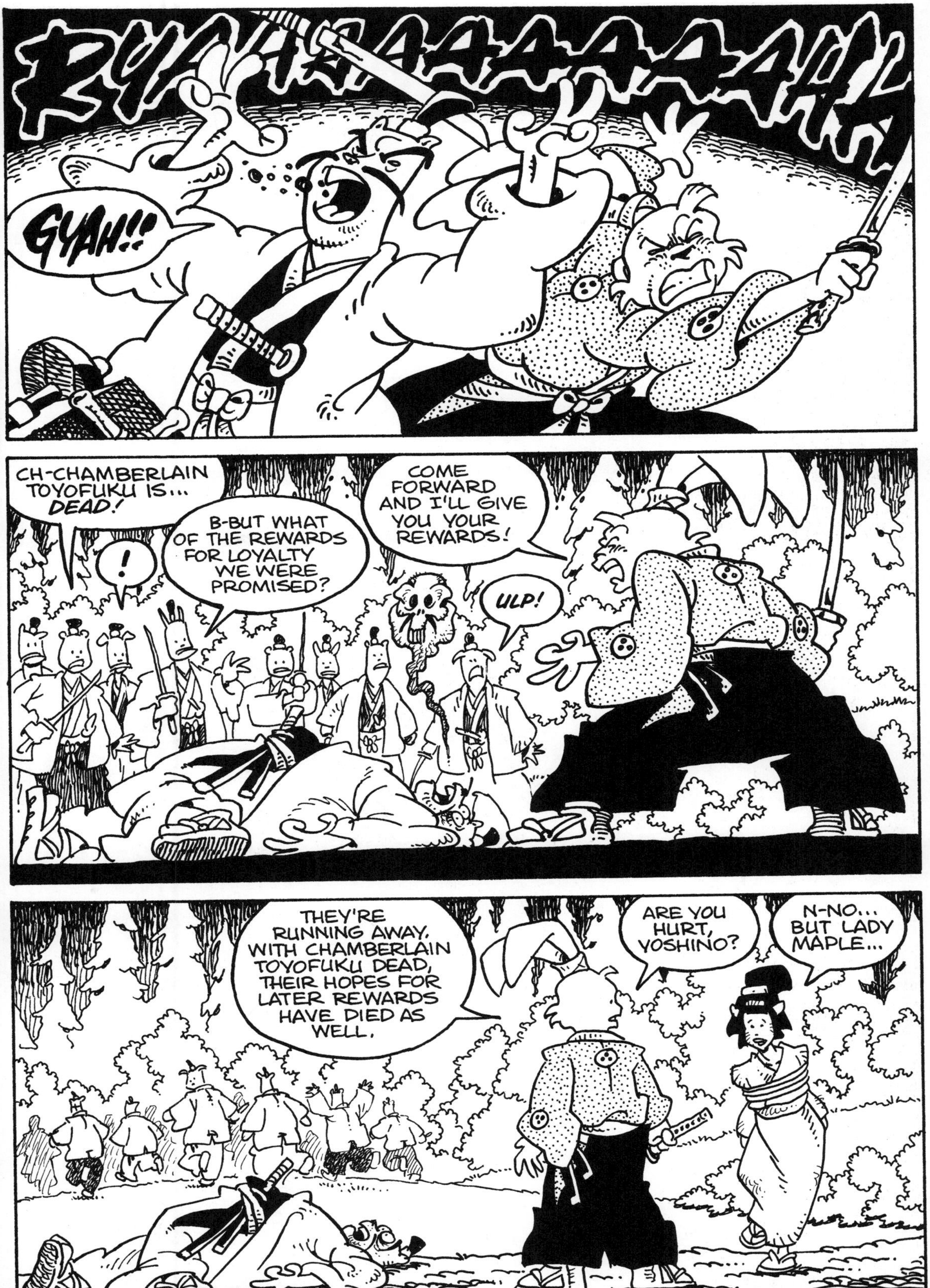
RYAAAAAAAAAH
GYAH!!
CH-CHAMBERLAIN TOYOFUKU IS... *DEAD!*
!
B-BUT WHAT OF THE REWARDS FOR LOYALTY WE WERE PROMISED?
COME FORWARD AND I'LL GIVE YOU YOUR REWARDS!
ULP!
THEY'RE RUNNING AWAY. WITH CHAMBERLAIN TOYOFUKU DEAD, THEIR HOPES FOR LATER REWARDS HAVE DIED AS WELL.
ARE YOU HURT, YOSHINO?
N-NO... BUT LADY MAPLE...
19.

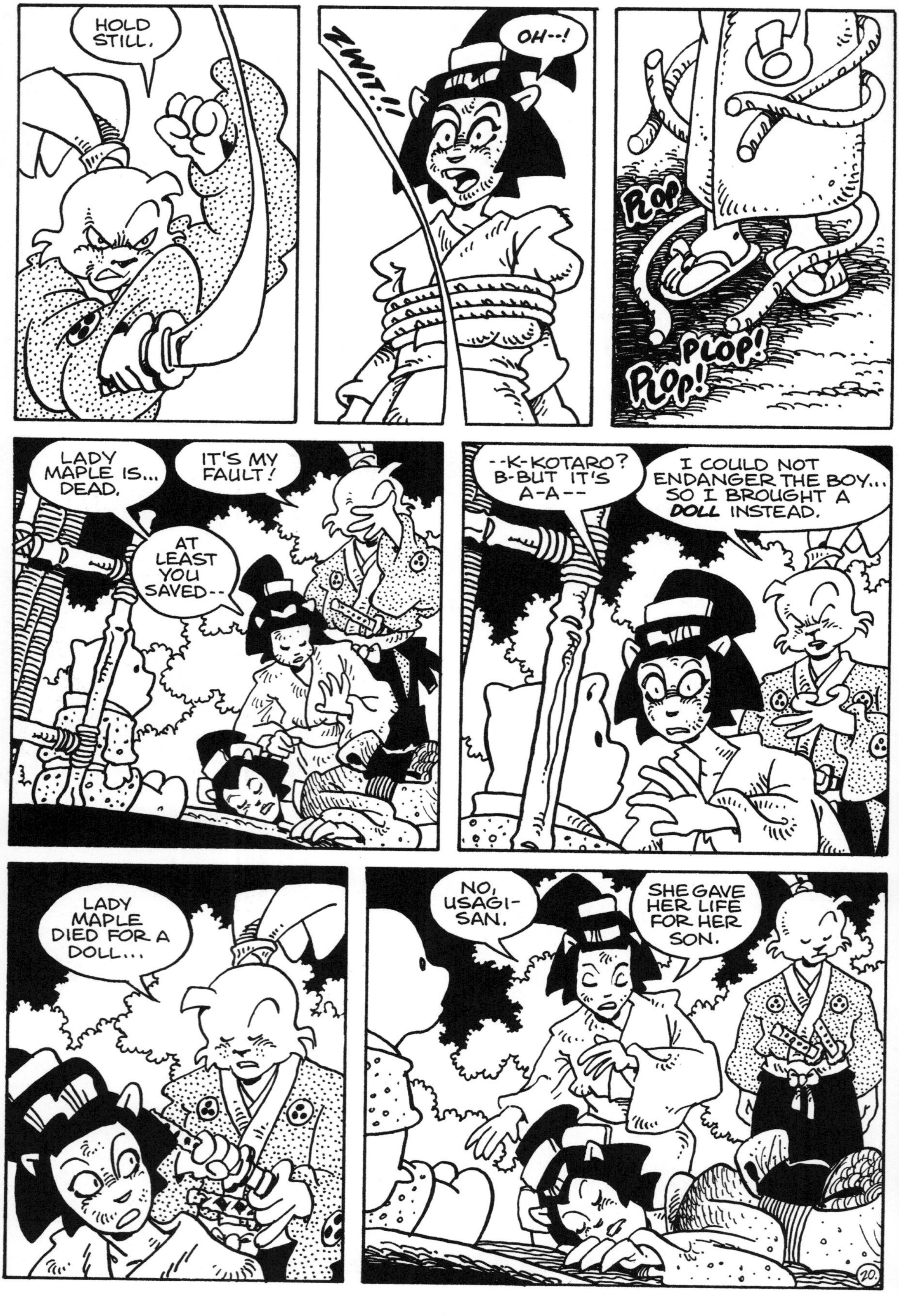
HOLD STILL.
ZWIT!!
OH--!
PLOP
PLOP!
PLOP!
LADY MAPLE IS... DEAD.
IT'S MY FAULT!
AT LEAST YOU SAVED--
--K-KOTARO? B-BUT IT'S A-A--
I COULD NOT ENDANGER THE BOY... SO I BROUGHT A DOLL INSTEAD.
LADY MAPLE DIED FOR A DOLL...
NO, USAGI-SAN.
SHE GAVE HER LIFE FOR HER SON.
20.

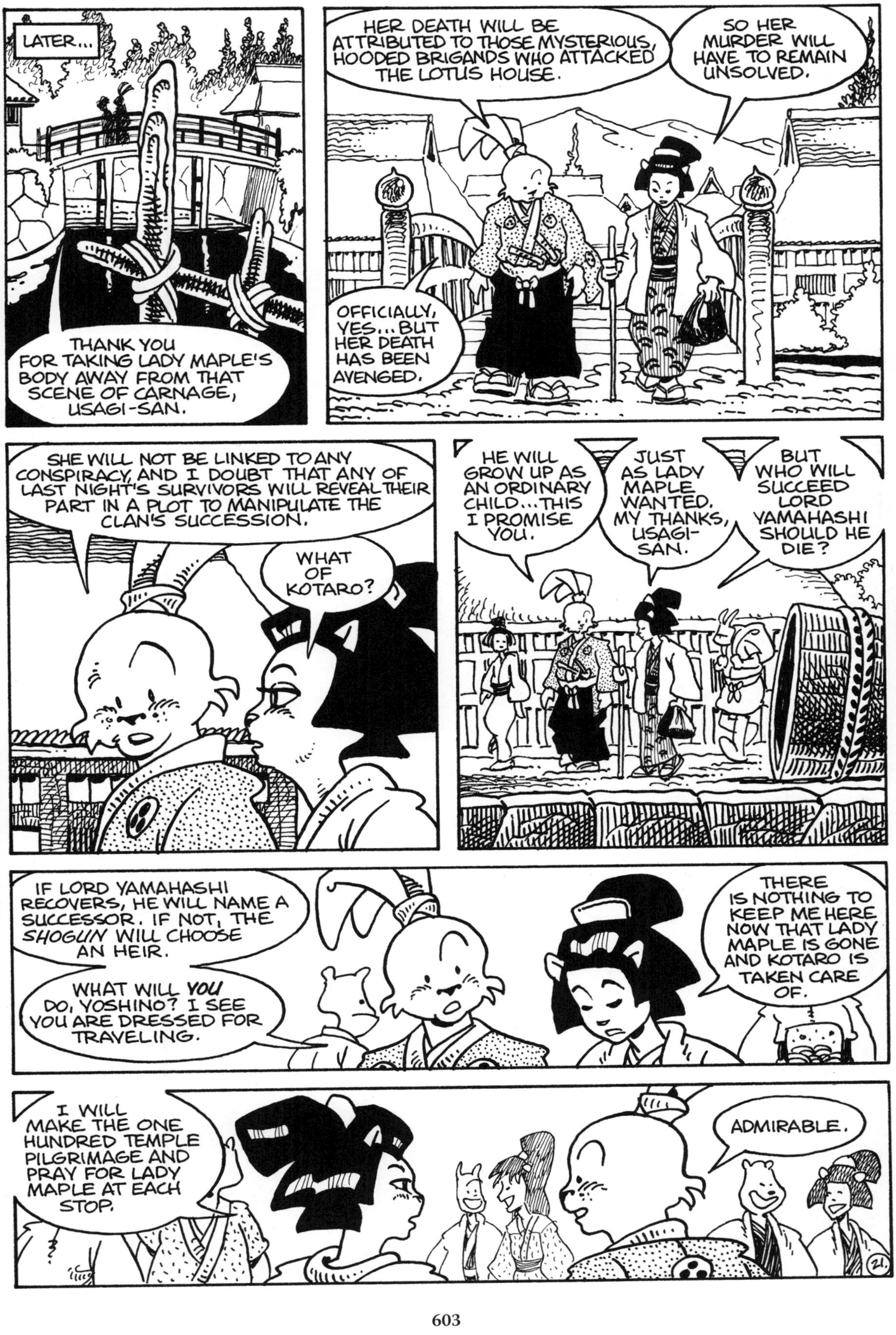
LATER...
THANK YOU FOR TAKING LADY MAPLE'S BODY AWAY FROM THAT SCENE OF CARNAGE, USAGI-SAN.
HER DEATH WILL BE ATTRIBUTED TO THOSE MYSTERIOUS, HOODED BRIGANDS WHO ATTACKED THE LOTUS HOUSE.
SO HER MURDER WILL HAVE TO REMAIN UNSOLVED.
OFFICIALLY, YES... BUT HER DEATH HAS BEEN AVENGED.
SHE WILL NOT BE LINKED TO ANY CONSPIRACY, AND I DOUBT THAT ANY OF LAST NIGHT'S SURVIVORS WILL REVEAL THEIR PART IN A PLOT TO MANIPULATE THE CLAN'S SUCCESSION.
WHAT OF KOTARO?
HE WILL GROW UP AS AN ORDINARY CHILD... THIS I PROMISE YOU.
JUST AS LADY MAPLE WANTED. MY THANKS, USAGI-SAN.
BUT WHO WILL SUCCEED LORD YAMAHASHI SHOULD HE DIE?
IF LORD YAMAHASHI RECOVERS, HE WILL NAME A SUCCESSOR. IF NOT, THE *SHOGUN* WILL CHOOSE AN HEIR.
WHAT WILL **YOU** DO, YOSHINO? I SEE YOU ARE DRESSED FOR TRAVELING.
THERE IS NOTHING TO KEEP ME HERE NOW THAT LADY MAPLE IS GONE AND KOTARO IS TAKEN CARE OF.
I WILL MAKE THE ONE HUNDRED TEMPLE PILGRIMAGE AND PRAY FOR LADY MAPLE AT EACH STOP.
ADMIRABLE.
21.

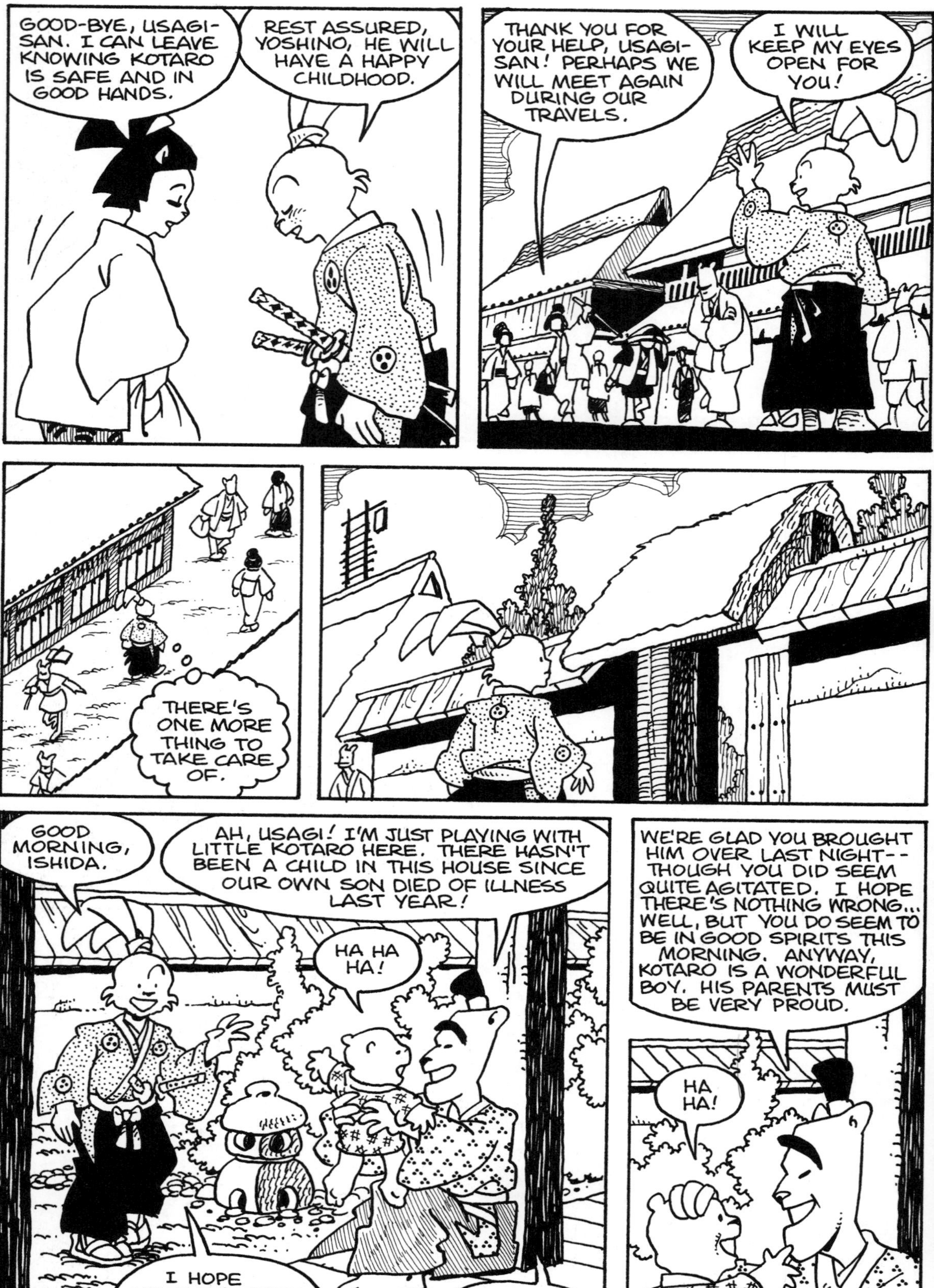
GOOD-BYE, USAGI-SAN. I CAN LEAVE KNOWING KOTARO IS SAFE AND IN GOOD HANDS.
REST ASSURED, YOSHINO, HE WILL HAVE A HAPPY CHILDHOOD.
THANK YOU FOR YOUR HELP, USAGI-SAN! PERHAPS WE WILL MEET AGAIN DURING OUR TRAVELS.
I WILL KEEP MY EYES OPEN FOR YOU!
THERE'S ONE MORE THING TO TAKE CARE OF.
GOOD MORNING, ISHIDA.
AH, USAGI! I'M JUST PLAYING WITH LITTLE KOTARO HERE. THERE HASN'T BEEN A CHILD IN THIS HOUSE SINCE OUR OWN SON DIED OF ILLNESS LAST YEAR!
HA HA HA!
I HOPE HE HASN'T BEEN TOO MUCH TROUBLE.
NONSENSE.
WE'RE GLAD YOU BROUGHT HIM OVER LAST NIGHT-- THOUGH YOU DID SEEM QUITE AGITATED. I HOPE THERE'S NOTHING WRONG... WELL, BUT YOU DO SEEM TO BE IN GOOD SPIRITS THIS MORNING. ANYWAY, KOTARO IS A WONDERFUL BOY. HIS PARENTS MUST BE VERY PROUD.
HA HA!
22

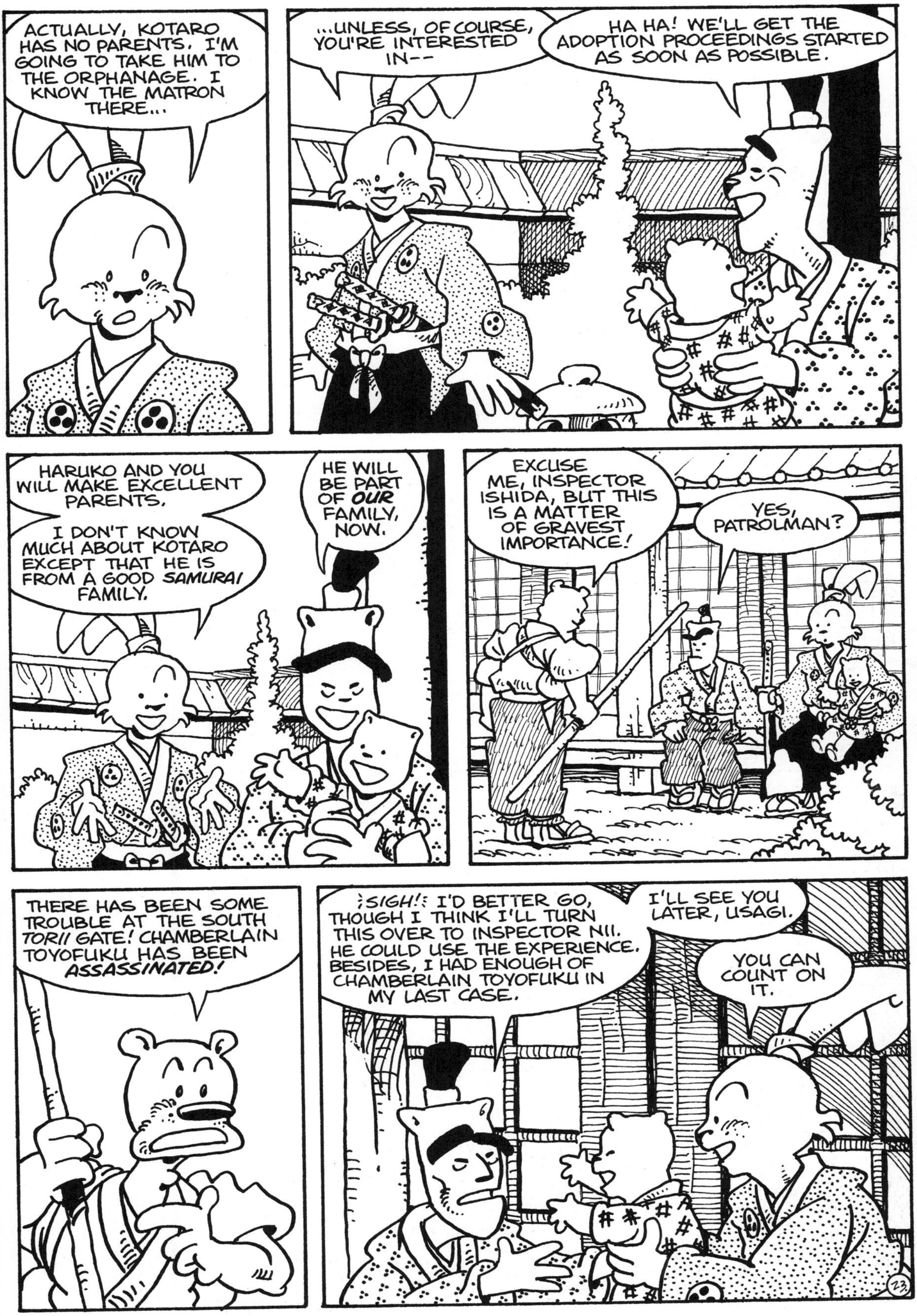
ACTUALLY, KOTARO HAS NO PARENTS. I'M GOING TO TAKE HIM TO THE ORPHANAGE. I KNOW THE MATRON THERE...
...UNLESS, OF COURSE, YOU'RE INTERESTED IN--
HA HA! WE'LL GET THE ADOPTION PROCEEDINGS STARTED AS SOON AS POSSIBLE.
HARUKO AND YOU WILL MAKE EXCELLENT PARENTS.
I DON'T KNOW MUCH ABOUT KOTARO EXCEPT THAT HE IS FROM A GOOD *SAMURAI* FAMILY.
HE WILL BE PART OF ***OUR*** FAMILY, NOW.
EXCUSE ME, INSPECTOR ISHIDA, BUT THIS IS A MATTER OF GRAVEST IMPORTANCE!
YES, PATROLMAN?
THERE HAS BEEN SOME TROUBLE AT THE SOUTH *TORII* GATE! CHAMBERLAIN TOYOFUKU HAS BEEN ***ASSASSINATED!***
SIGH! I'D BETTER GO, THOUGH I THINK I'LL TURN THIS OVER TO INSPECTOR NII. HE COULD USE THE EXPERIENCE. BESIDES, I HAD ENOUGH OF CHAMBERLAIN TOYOFUKU IN MY LAST CASE.
I'LL SEE YOU LATER, USAGI.
YOU CAN COUNT ON IT.
23

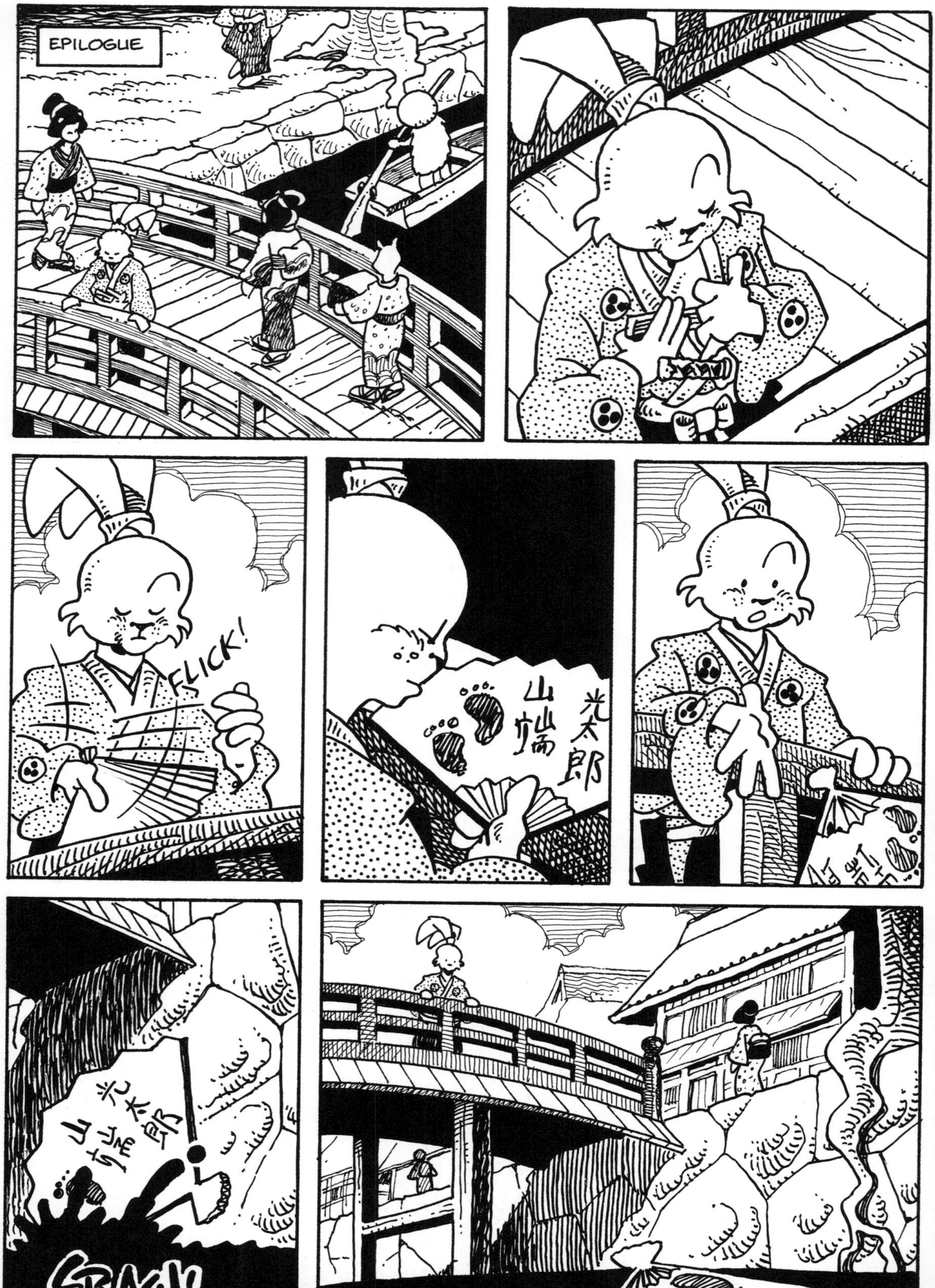
EPILOGUE
FLICK!
光太郎
山端
光太郎
山端
SPLASH!
THE END

ZWIT!

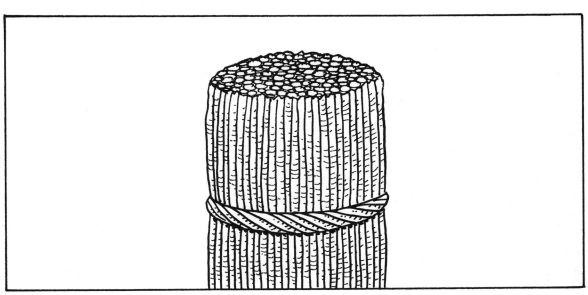

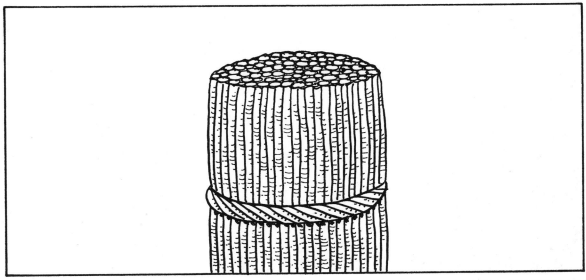

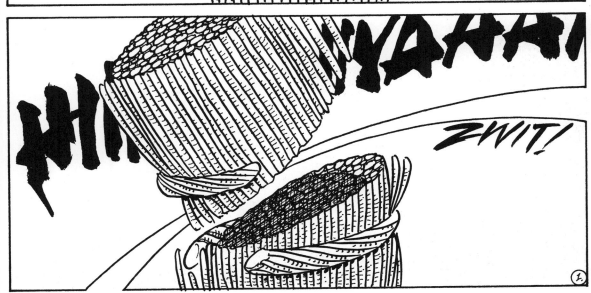

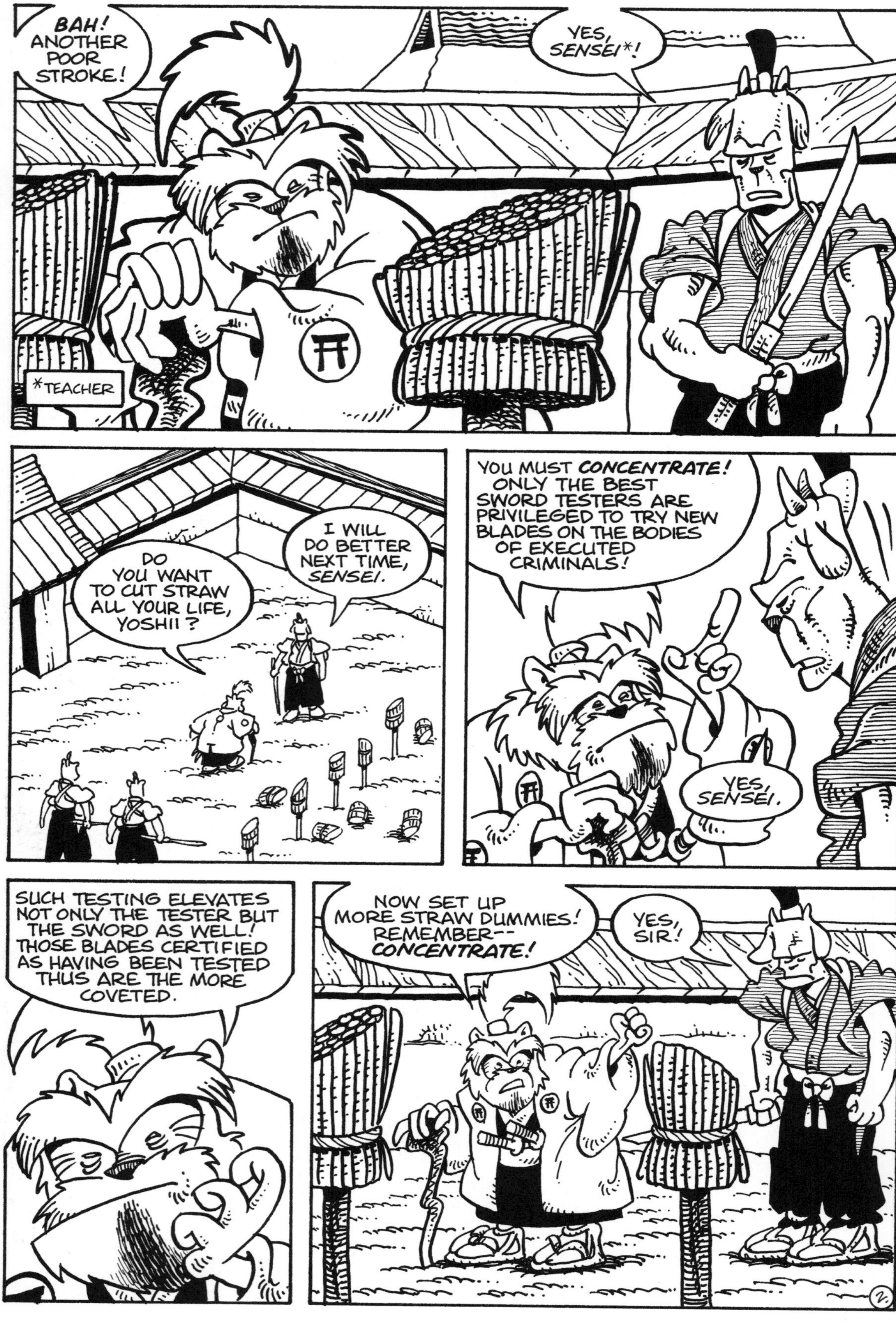
BAH! ANOTHER POOR STROKE!
YES, SENSEI*!
*TEACHER
DO YOU WANT TO CUT STRAW ALL YOUR LIFE, YOSHII?
I WILL DO BETTER NEXT TIME, SENSEI.
YOU MUST CONCENTRATE! ONLY THE BEST SWORD TESTERS ARE PRIVILEGED TO TRY NEW BLADES ON THE BODIES OF EXECUTED CRIMINALS!
YES, SENSEI.
SUCH TESTING ELEVATES NOT ONLY THE TESTER BUT THE SWORD AS WELL! THOSE BLADES CERTIFIED AS HAVING BEEN TESTED THUS ARE THE MORE COVETED.
NOW SET UP MORE STRAW DUMMIES! REMEMBER-- CONCENTRATE!
YES, SIR!
2.

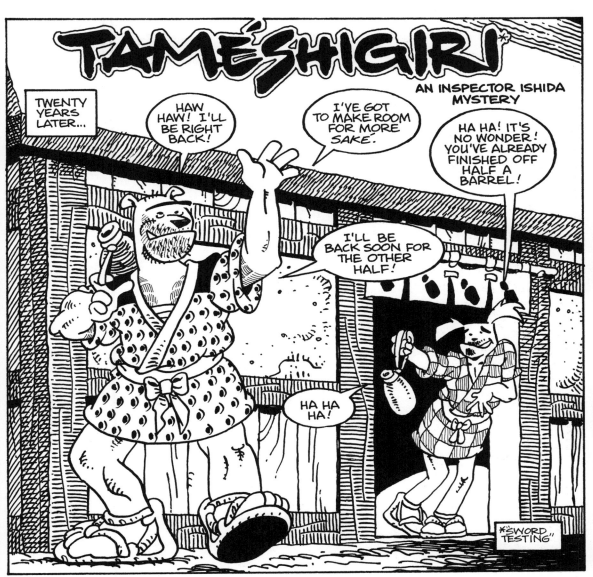

TAMÉSHIGIRI*

AN INSPECTOR ISHIDA MYSTERY

TWENTY YEARS LATER...

HAW HAW! I'LL BE RIGHT BACK!

I'VE GOT TO MAKE ROOM FOR MORE SAKÉ.

HA HA! IT'S NO WONDER! YOU'VE ALREADY FINISHED OFF HALF A BARREL!

I'LL BE BACK SOON FOR THE OTHER HALF!

HA HA HA!

*"SWORD TESTING"

HEY, SAMURAI-- NICE NIGHT, HUH? HAW! HAW!

¡BURP!

HEY, YA WANNA DRINK, HUH? C'MON, IT'S ON ME! HAW! HAW!

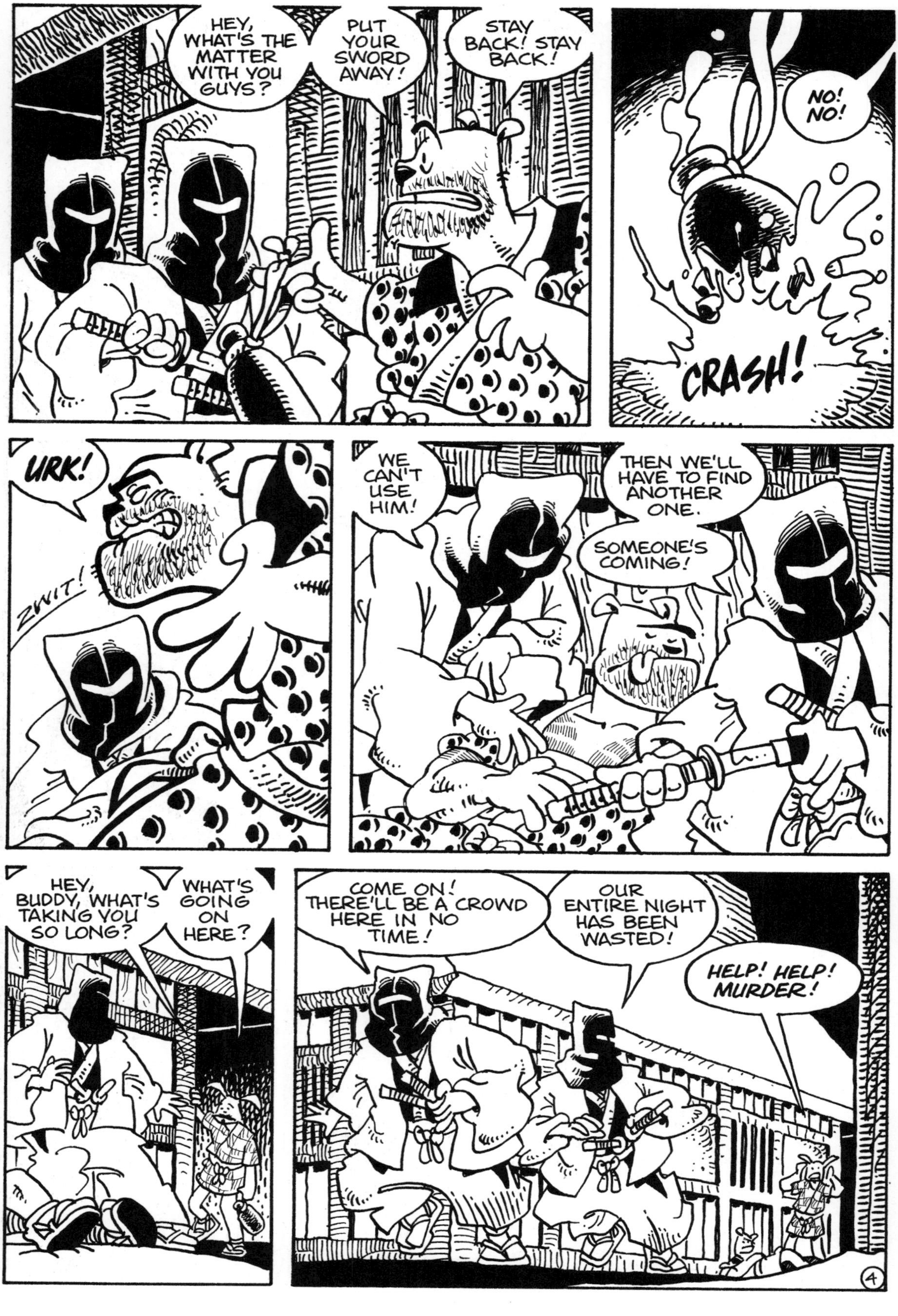
HEY, WHAT'S THE MATTER WITH YOU GUYS?
PUT YOUR SWORD AWAY!
STAY BACK! STAY BACK!
NO! NO!
CRASH!
URK!
ZWIT!
WE CAN'T USE HIM!
THEN WE'LL HAVE TO FIND ANOTHER ONE.
SOMEONE'S COMING!
HEY, BUDDY, WHAT'S TAKING YOU SO LONG?
WHAT'S GOING ON HERE?
COME ON! THERE'LL BE A CROWD HERE IN NO TIME!
OUR ENTIRE NIGHT HAS BEEN WASTED!
HELP! HELP! MURDER!
4

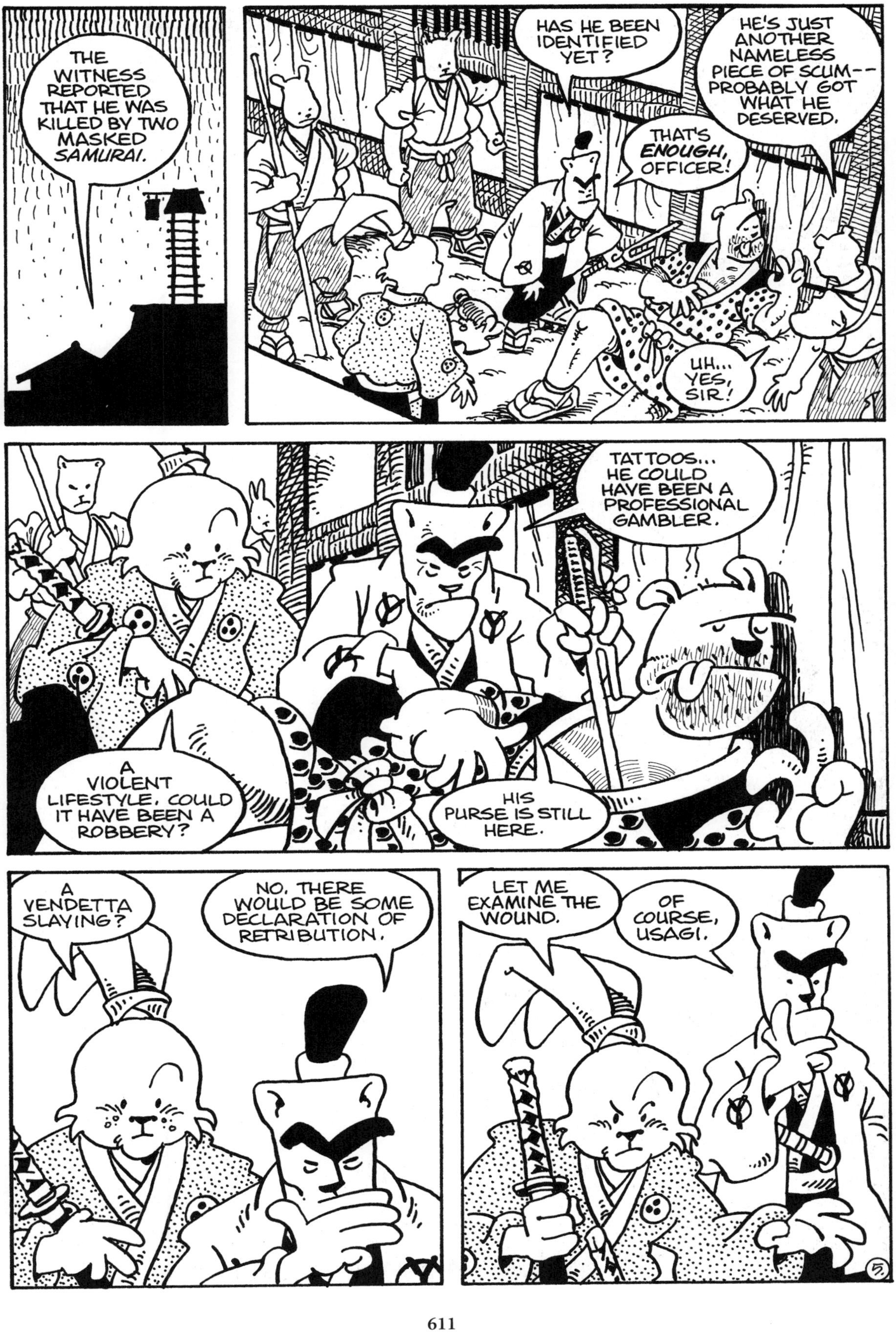
THE WITNESS REPORTED THAT HE WAS KILLED BY TWO MASKED *SAMURAI.*
HAS HE BEEN IDENTIFIED YET?
HE'S JUST ANOTHER NAMELESS PIECE OF SCUM-- PROBABLY GOT WHAT HE DESERVED.
THAT'S **ENOUGH,** OFFICER!
UH... YES, SIR!
TATTOOS... HE COULD HAVE BEEN A PROFESSIONAL GAMBLER.
A VIOLENT LIFESTYLE. COULD IT HAVE BEEN A ROBBERY?
HIS PURSE IS STILL HERE.
A VENDETTA SLAYING?
NO. THERE WOULD BE SOME DECLARATION OF RETRIBUTION.
LET ME EXAMINE THE WOUND.
OF COURSE, USAGI.
5

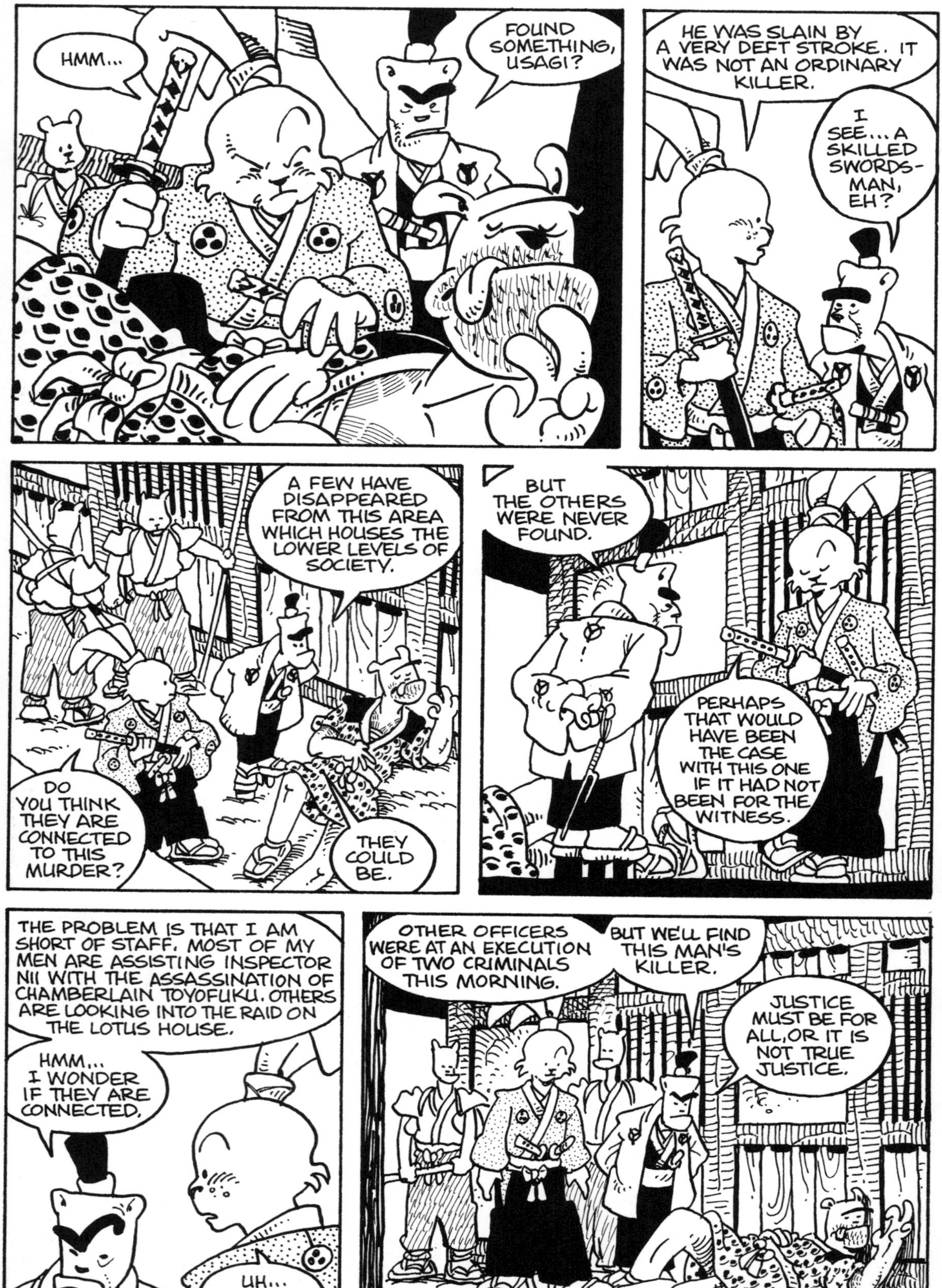
HMM...
FOUND SOMETHING, USAGI?
HE WAS SLAIN BY A VERY DEFT STROKE. IT WAS NOT AN ORDINARY KILLER.
I SEE... A SKILLED SWORDSMAN, EH?
A FEW HAVE DISAPPEARED FROM THIS AREA WHICH HOUSES THE LOWER LEVELS OF SOCIETY.
DO YOU THINK THEY ARE CONNECTED TO THIS MURDER?
THEY COULD BE.
BUT THE OTHERS WERE NEVER FOUND.
PERHAPS THAT WOULD HAVE BEEN THE CASE WITH THIS ONE IF IT HAD NOT BEEN FOR THE WITNESS.
THE PROBLEM IS THAT I AM SHORT OF STAFF. MOST OF MY MEN ARE ASSISTING INSPECTOR NII WITH THE ASSASSINATION OF CHAMBERLAIN TOYOFUKU. OTHERS ARE LOOKING INTO THE RAID ON THE LOTUS HOUSE.
HMM... I WONDER IF THEY ARE CONNECTED.
UH... I DOUBT IT.
OTHER OFFICERS WERE AT AN EXECUTION OF TWO CRIMINALS THIS MORNING.
BUT WE'LL FIND THIS MAN'S KILLER.
JUSTICE MUST BE FOR ALL, OR IT IS NOT TRUE JUSTICE.
6.

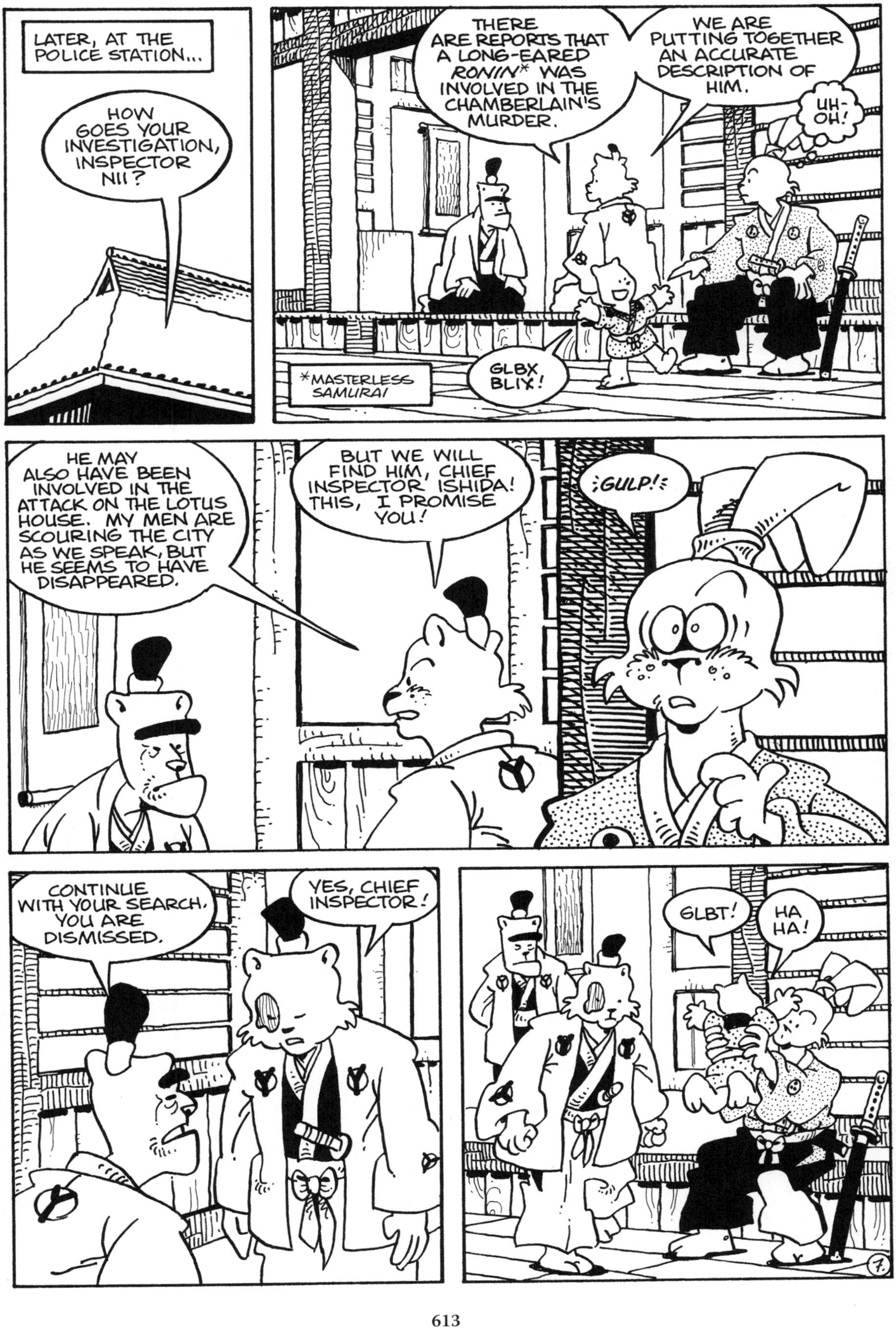
LATER, AT THE POLICE STATION...
HOW GOES YOUR INVESTIGATION, INSPECTOR NII?
THERE ARE REPORTS THAT A LONG-EARED *RONIN** WAS INVOLVED IN THE CHAMBERLAIN'S MURDER.
WE ARE PUTTING TOGETHER AN ACCURATE DESCRIPTION OF HIM.
UH-OH!
GLBX BLIX!
*MASTERLESS SAMURAI
HE MAY ALSO HAVE BEEN INVOLVED IN THE ATTACK ON THE LOTUS HOUSE. MY MEN ARE SCOURING THE CITY AS WE SPEAK, BUT HE SEEMS TO HAVE DISAPPEARED.
BUT WE WILL FIND HIM, CHIEF INSPECTOR ISHIDA! THIS, I PROMISE YOU!
GULP!
CONTINUE WITH YOUR SEARCH. YOU ARE DISMISSED.
YES, CHIEF INSPECTOR!
GLBT!
HA HA!
7.

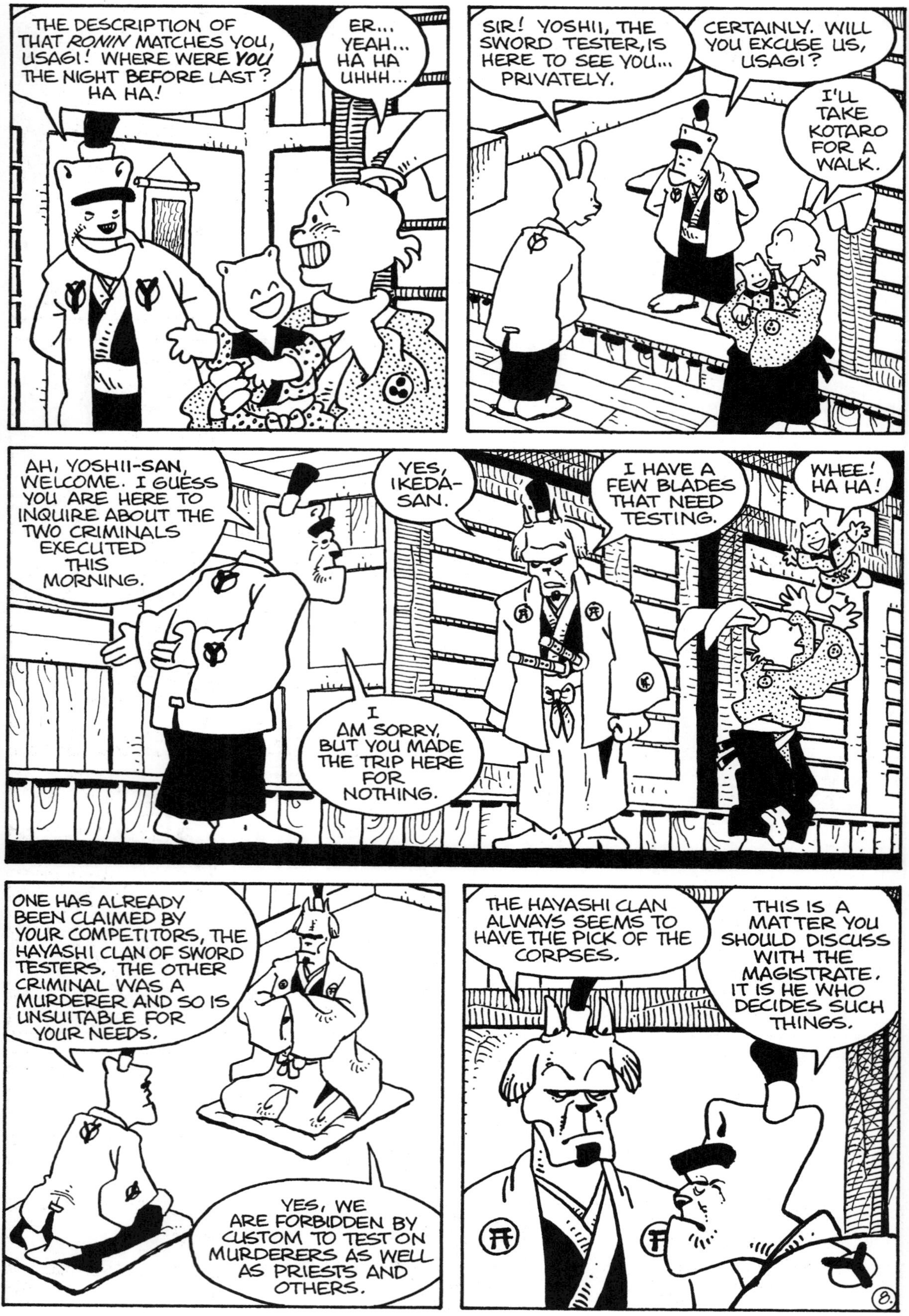
THE DESCRIPTION OF THAT *RONIN* MATCHES YOU, USAGI! WHERE WERE ***YOU*** THE NIGHT BEFORE LAST? HA HA!
ER... YEAH... HA HA UHHH...
SIR! YOSHII, THE SWORD TESTER, IS HERE TO SEE YOU... PRIVATELY.
CERTAINLY. WILL YOU EXCUSE US, USAGI?
I'LL TAKE KOTARO FOR A WALK.
AH, YOSHII-SAN, WELCOME. I GUESS YOU ARE HERE TO INQUIRE ABOUT THE TWO CRIMINALS EXECUTED THIS MORNING.
YES, IKEDA-SAN.
I HAVE A FEW BLADES THAT NEED TESTING.
WHEE! HA HA!
I AM SORRY, BUT YOU MADE THE TRIP HERE FOR NOTHING.
ONE HAS ALREADY BEEN CLAIMED BY YOUR COMPETITORS, THE HAYASHI CLAN OF SWORD TESTERS. THE OTHER CRIMINAL WAS A MURDERER AND SO IS UNSUITABLE FOR YOUR NEEDS.
YES, WE ARE FORBIDDEN BY CUSTOM TO TEST ON MURDERERS AS WELL AS PRIESTS AND OTHERS.
THE HAYASHI CLAN ALWAYS SEEMS TO HAVE THE PICK OF THE CORPSES.
THIS IS A MATTER YOU SHOULD DISCUSS WITH THE MAGISTRATE. IT IS HE WHO DECIDES SUCH THINGS.
8.

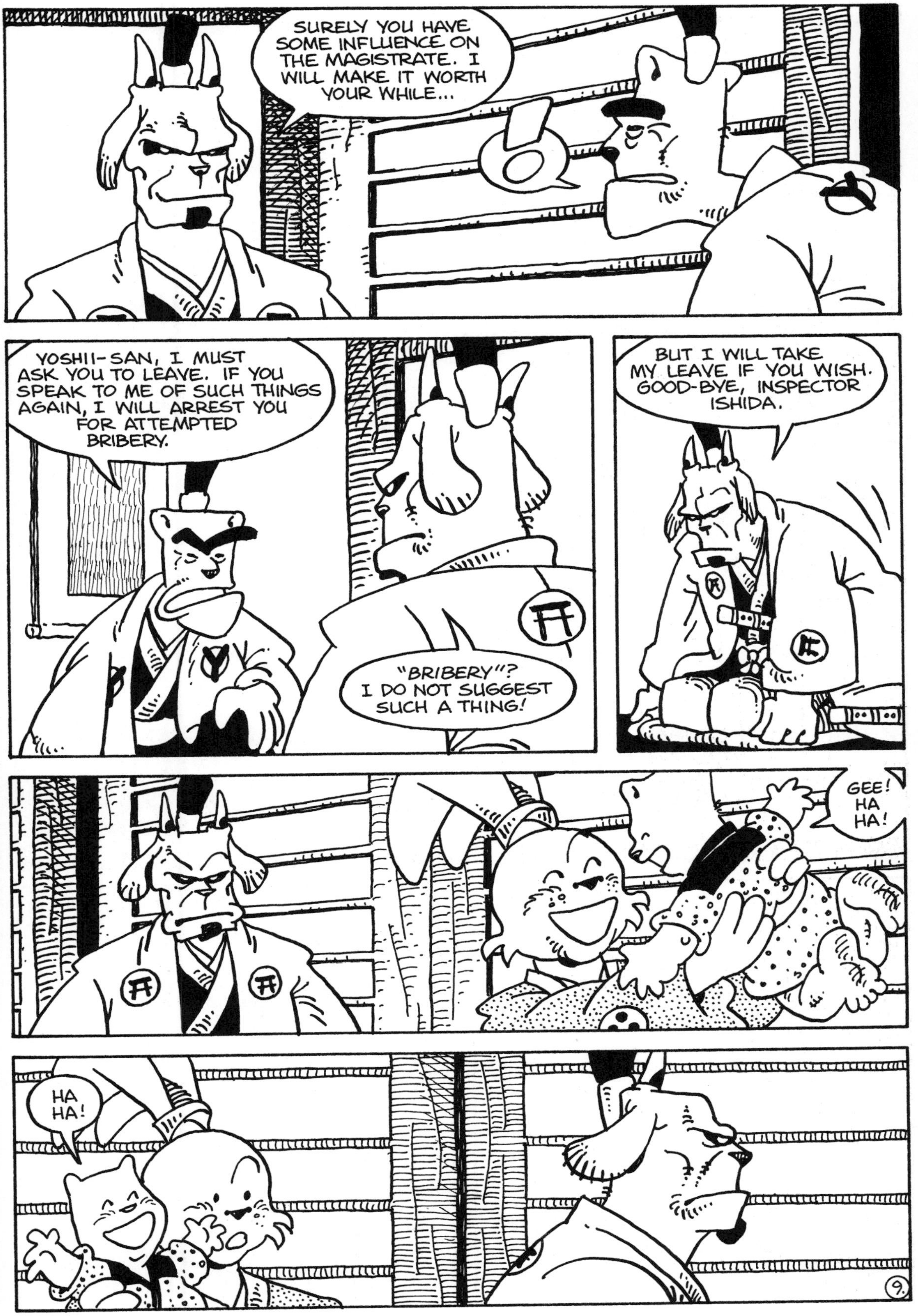
SURELY YOU HAVE SOME INFLUENCE ON THE MAGISTRATE. I WILL MAKE IT WORTH YOUR WHILE...
YOSHII-SAN, I MUST ASK YOU TO LEAVE. IF YOU SPEAK TO ME OF SUCH THINGS AGAIN, I WILL ARREST YOU FOR ATTEMPTED BRIBERY.
"BRIBERY"? I DO NOT SUGGEST SUCH A THING!
BUT I WILL TAKE MY LEAVE IF YOU WISH. GOOD-BYE, INSPECTOR ISHIDA.
GEE! HA HA!
HA HA!
9.

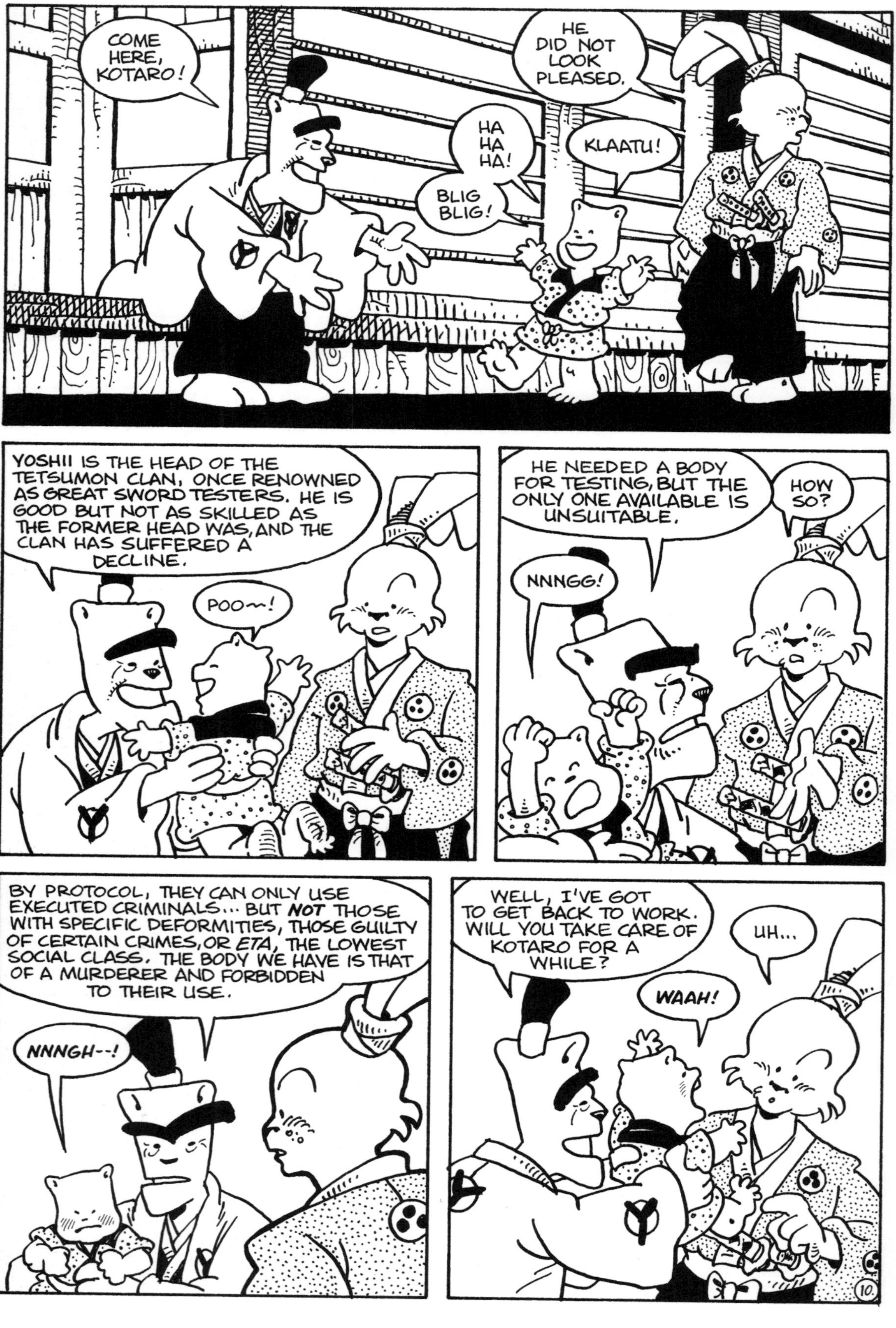
COME HERE, KOTARO!
HE DID NOT LOOK PLEASED.
HA HA HA!
BLIG BLIG!
KLAATU!
YOSHII IS THE HEAD OF THE TETSUMON CLAN, ONCE RENOWNED AS GREAT SWORD TESTERS. HE IS GOOD BUT NOT AS SKILLED AS THE FORMER HEAD WAS, AND THE CLAN HAS SUFFERED A DECLINE.
POO~!
HE NEEDED A BODY FOR TESTING, BUT THE ONLY ONE AVAILABLE IS UNSUITABLE.
HOW SO?
NNNGG!
BY PROTOCOL, THEY CAN ONLY USE EXECUTED CRIMINALS... BUT **NOT** THOSE WITH SPECIFIC DEFORMITIES, THOSE GUILTY OF CERTAIN CRIMES, OR *ETA*, THE LOWEST SOCIAL CLASS. THE BODY WE HAVE IS THAT OF A MURDERER AND FORBIDDEN TO THEIR USE.
NNNGH--!
WELL, I'VE GOT TO GET BACK TO WORK. WILL YOU TAKE CARE OF KOTARO FOR A WHILE?
UH...
WAAH!
10.

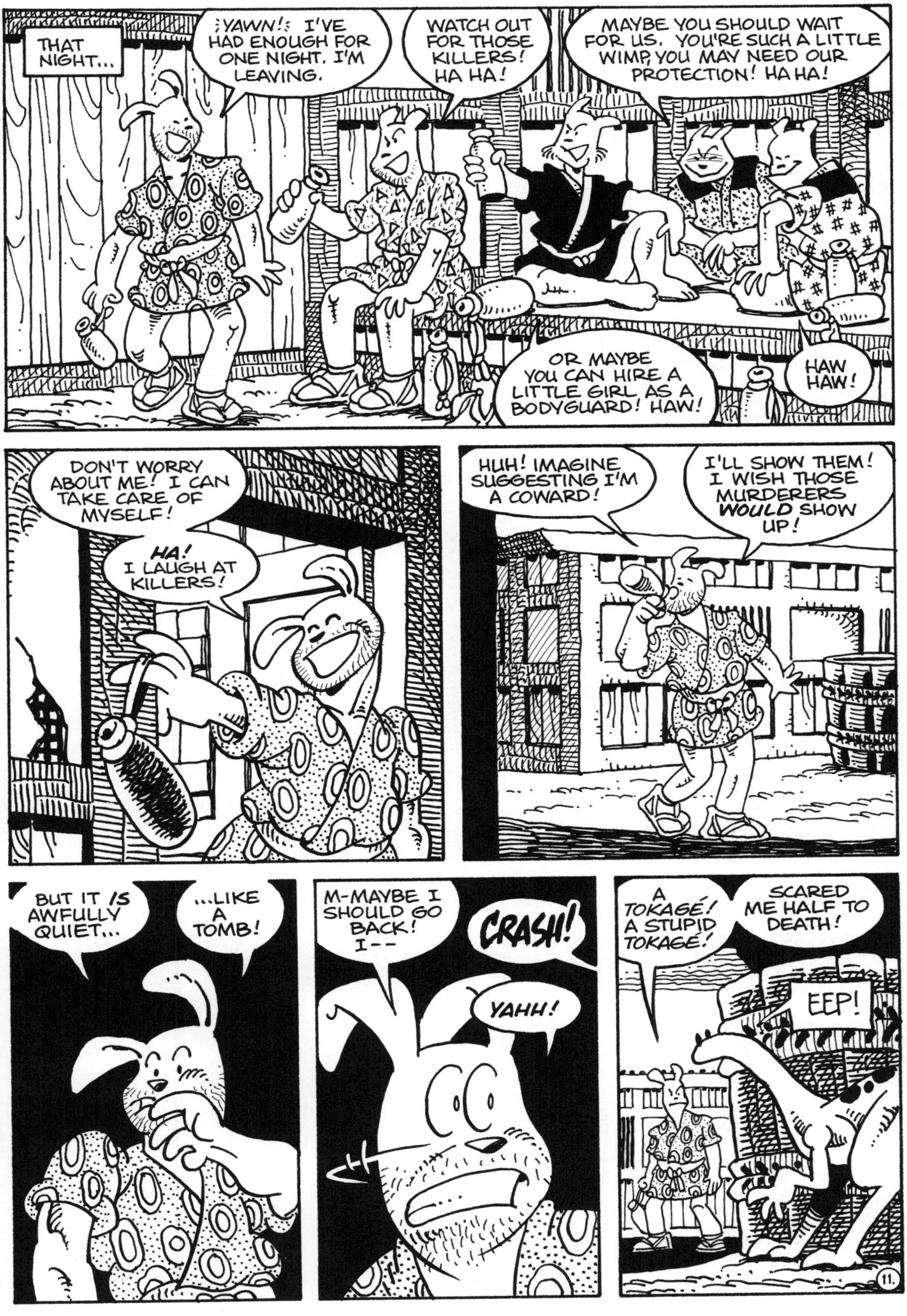

THAT NIGHT...
¡YAWN!¡ I'VE HAD ENOUGH FOR ONE NIGHT. I'M LEAVING.
WATCH OUT FOR THOSE KILLERS! HA HA!
MAYBE YOU SHOULD WAIT FOR US. YOU'RE SUCH A LITTLE WIMP, YOU MAY NEED OUR PROTECTION! HA HA!
OR MAYBE YOU CAN HIRE A LITTLE GIRL AS A BODYGUARD! HAW!
HAW HAW!
DON'T WORRY ABOUT ME! I CAN TAKE CARE OF MYSELF!
HA! I LAUGH AT KILLERS!
HUH! IMAGINE SUGGESTING I'M A COWARD!
I'LL SHOW THEM! I WISH THOSE MURDERERS WOULD SHOW UP!
BUT IT IS AWFULLY QUIET...
...LIKE A TOMB!
M-MAYBE I SHOULD GO BACK! I--
CRASH!
YAHH!
A TOKAGÉ! A STUPID TOKAGÉ!
SCARED ME HALF TO DEATH!
EEP!
11.

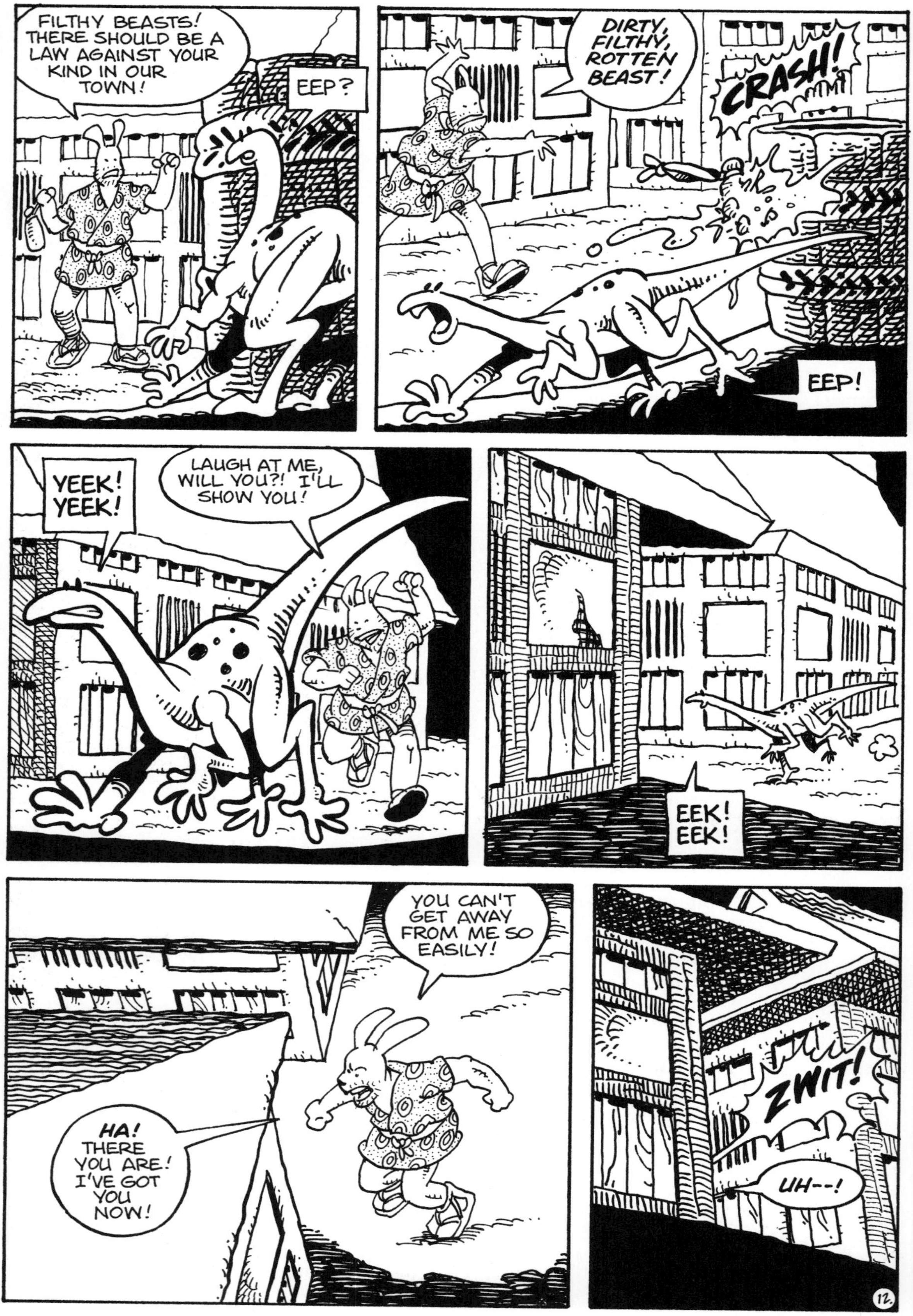
FILTHY BEASTS! THERE SHOULD BE A LAW AGAINST YOUR KIND IN OUR TOWN!
EEP?
DIRTY, FILTHY, ROTTEN BEAST!
CRASH!
EEP!
YEEK! YEEK!
LAUGH AT ME, WILL YOU?! I'LL SHOW YOU!
EEK! EEK!
YOU CAN'T GET AWAY FROM ME SO EASILY!
HA! THERE YOU ARE! I'VE GOT YOU NOW!
ZWIT!
UH--!
12.

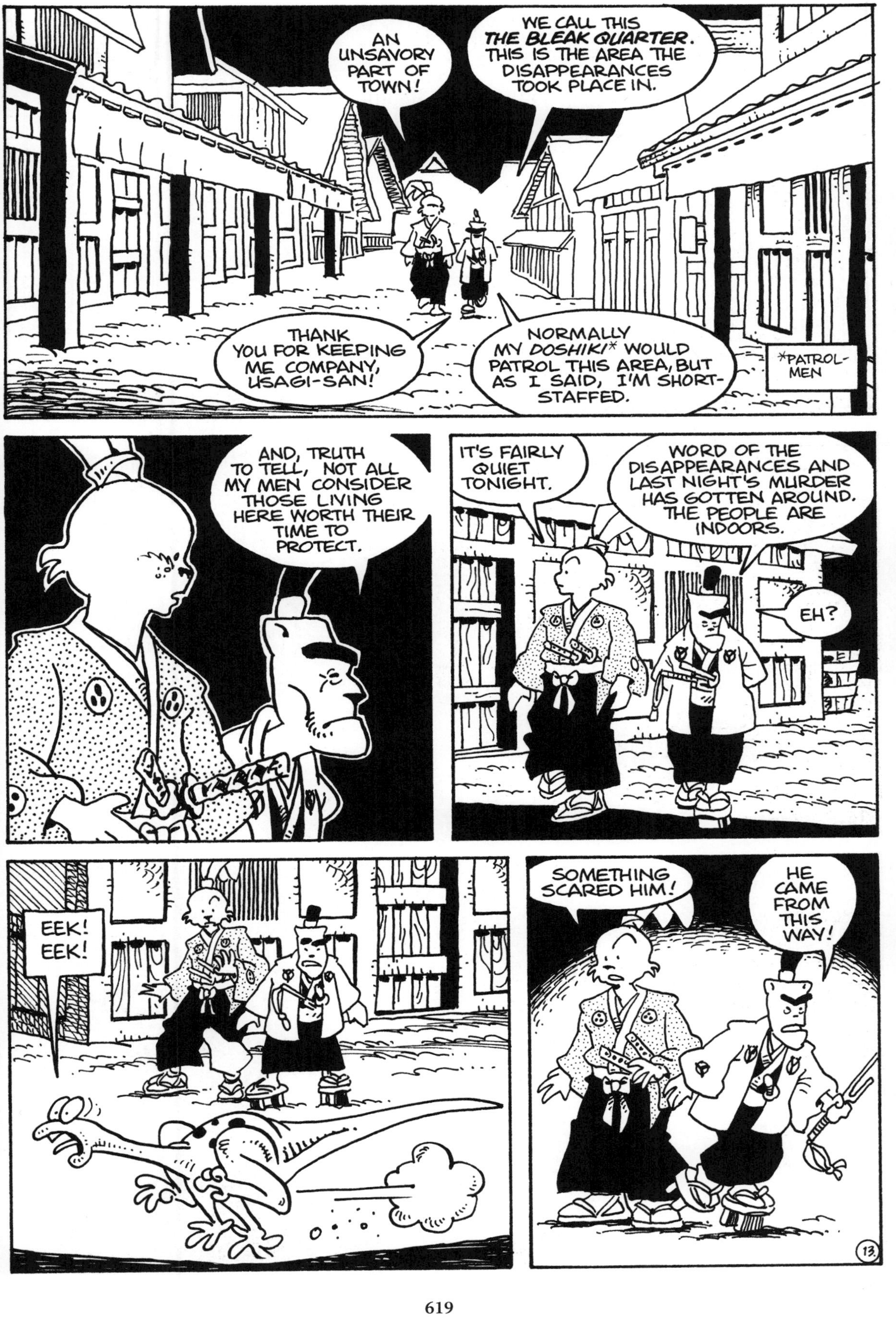
AN UNSAVORY PART OF TOWN!
WE CALL THIS **THE BLEAK QUARTER**. THIS IS THE AREA THE DISAPPEARANCES TOOK PLACE IN.
THANK YOU FOR KEEPING ME COMPANY, USAGI-SAN!
NORMALLY MY *DOSHIKI** WOULD PATROL THIS AREA, BUT AS I SAID, I'M SHORT-STAFFED.
*PATROL-MEN
AND, TRUTH TO TELL, NOT ALL MY MEN CONSIDER THOSE LIVING HERE WORTH THEIR TIME TO PROTECT.
IT'S FAIRLY QUIET TONIGHT.
WORD OF THE DISAPPEARANCES AND LAST NIGHT'S MURDER HAS GOTTEN AROUND. THE PEOPLE ARE INDOORS.
EH?
EEK! EEK!
SOMETHING SCARED HIM!
HE CAME FROM THIS WAY!
13

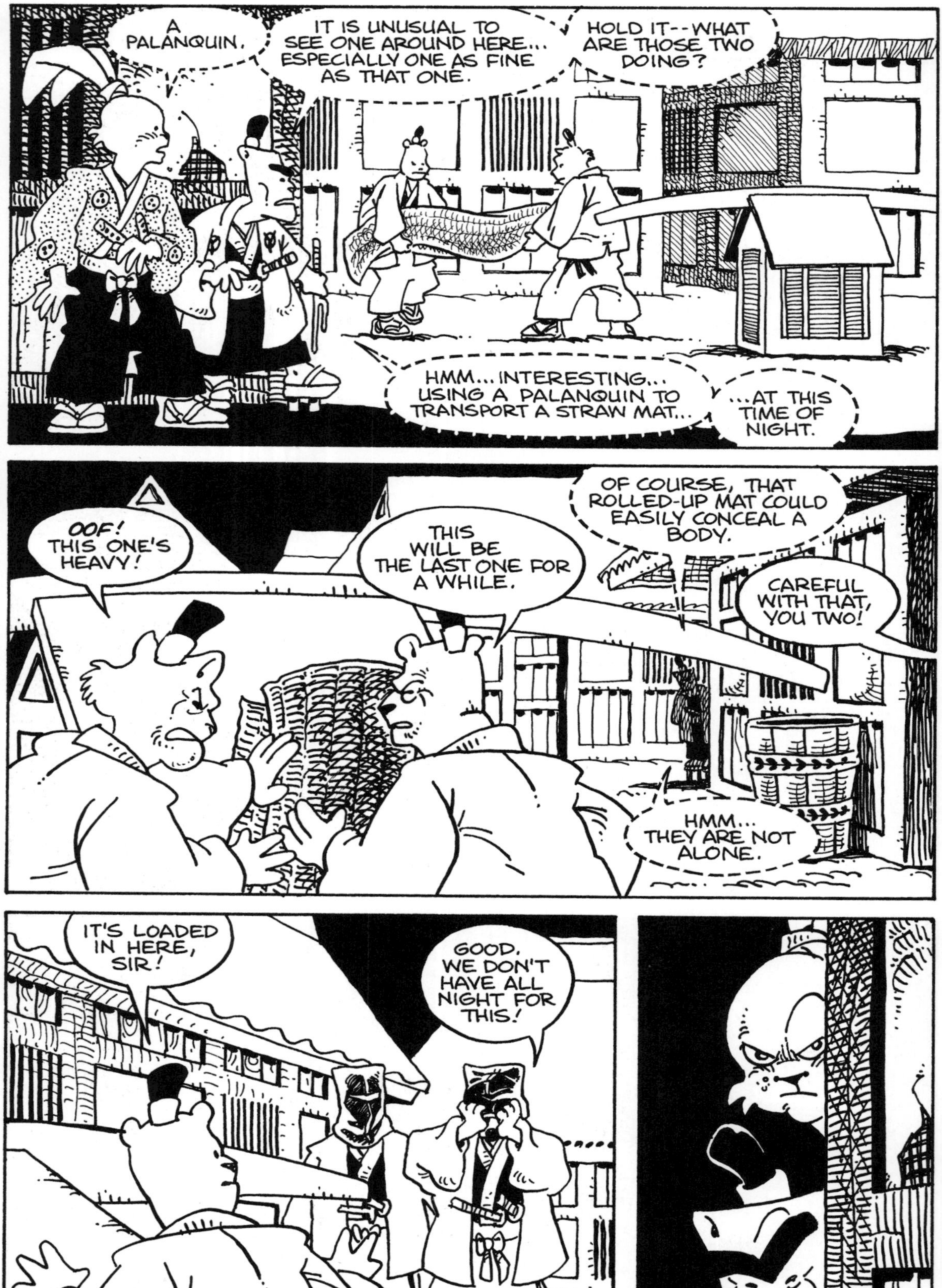
A PALANQUIN.
IT IS UNUSUAL TO SEE ONE AROUND HERE... ESPECIALLY ONE AS FINE AS THAT ONE.
HOLD IT-- WHAT ARE THOSE TWO DOING?
HMM... INTERESTING... USING A PALANQUIN TO TRANSPORT A STRAW MAT...
...AT THIS TIME OF NIGHT.
OOF! THIS ONE'S HEAVY!
THIS WILL BE THE LAST ONE FOR A WHILE.
OF COURSE, THAT ROLLED-UP MAT COULD EASILY CONCEAL A BODY.
CAREFUL WITH THAT, YOU TWO!
HMM... THEY ARE NOT ALONE.
IT'S LOADED IN HERE, SIR!
GOOD. WE DON'T HAVE ALL NIGHT FOR THIS!
14.

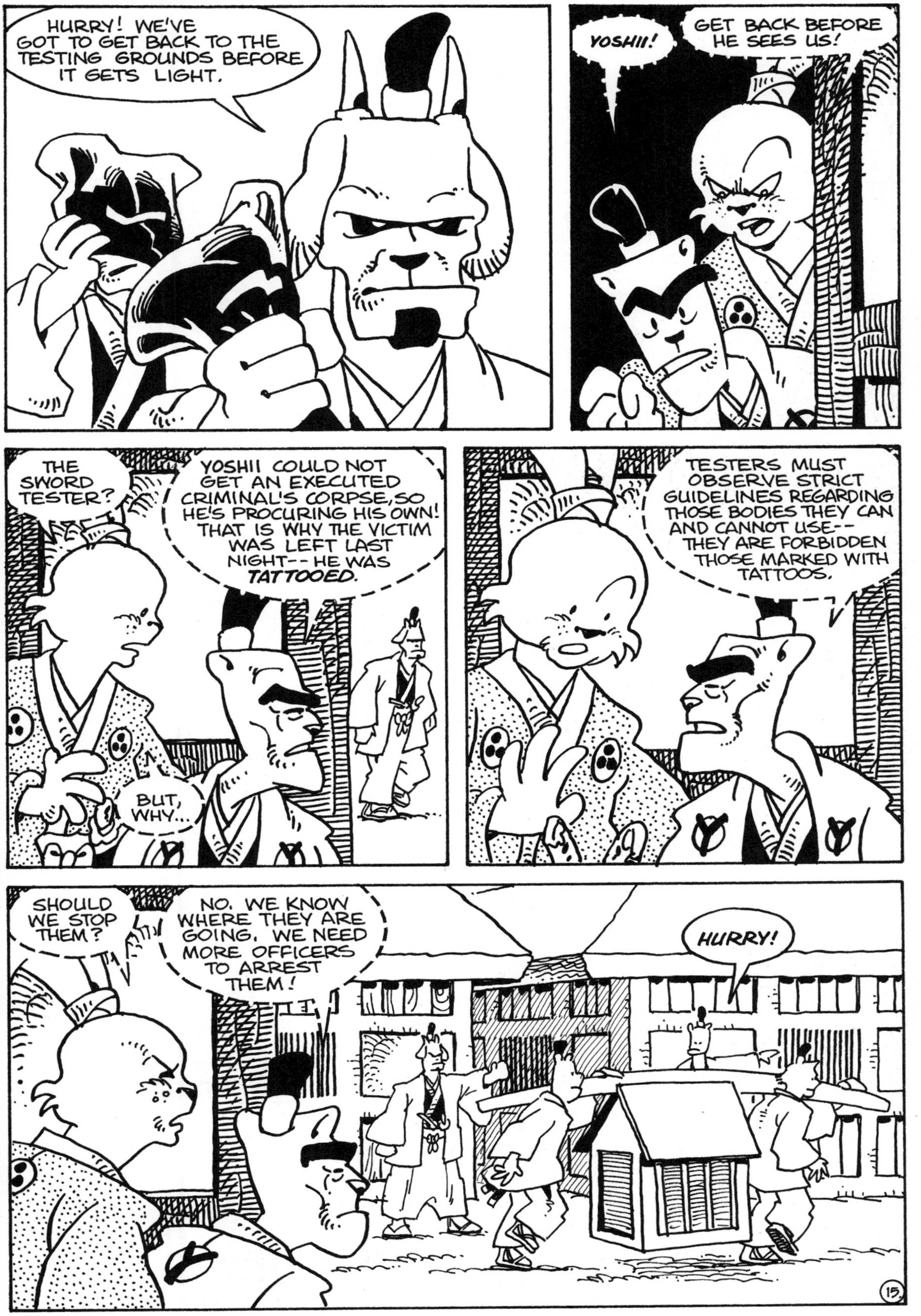
HURRY! WE'VE GOT TO GET BACK TO THE TESTING GROUNDS BEFORE IT GETS LIGHT.
YOSHII!
GET BACK BEFORE HE SEES US!
THE SWORD TESTER?
YOSHII COULD NOT GET AN EXECUTED CRIMINAL'S CORPSE, SO HE'S PROCURING HIS OWN! THAT IS WHY THE VICTIM WAS LEFT LAST NIGHT-- HE WAS TATTOOED.
BUT, WHY...
TESTERS MUST OBSERVE STRICT GUIDELINES REGARDING THOSE BODIES THEY CAN AND CANNOT USE-- THEY ARE FORBIDDEN THOSE MARKED WITH TATTOOS.
SHOULD WE STOP THEM?
NO. WE KNOW WHERE THEY ARE GOING. WE NEED MORE OFFICERS TO ARREST THEM!
HURRY!
15

LATER AT THE TETSUMON CLAN COMPOUND...

EVERYTHING IS IN READINESS, YOSHII-SAMA!

EXCELLENT.

WE HAVE FIVE BLADES TO TEST TONIGHT.

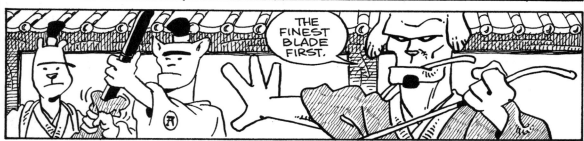

THE FINEST BLADE FIRST.

THIS IS FROM THE SWORDSMITH YAMAHIRA.

¡FEH!¿ A SECONDARY SMITH.

LET US SEE HOW WORTHY THIS BLADE IS.

SROOKH!

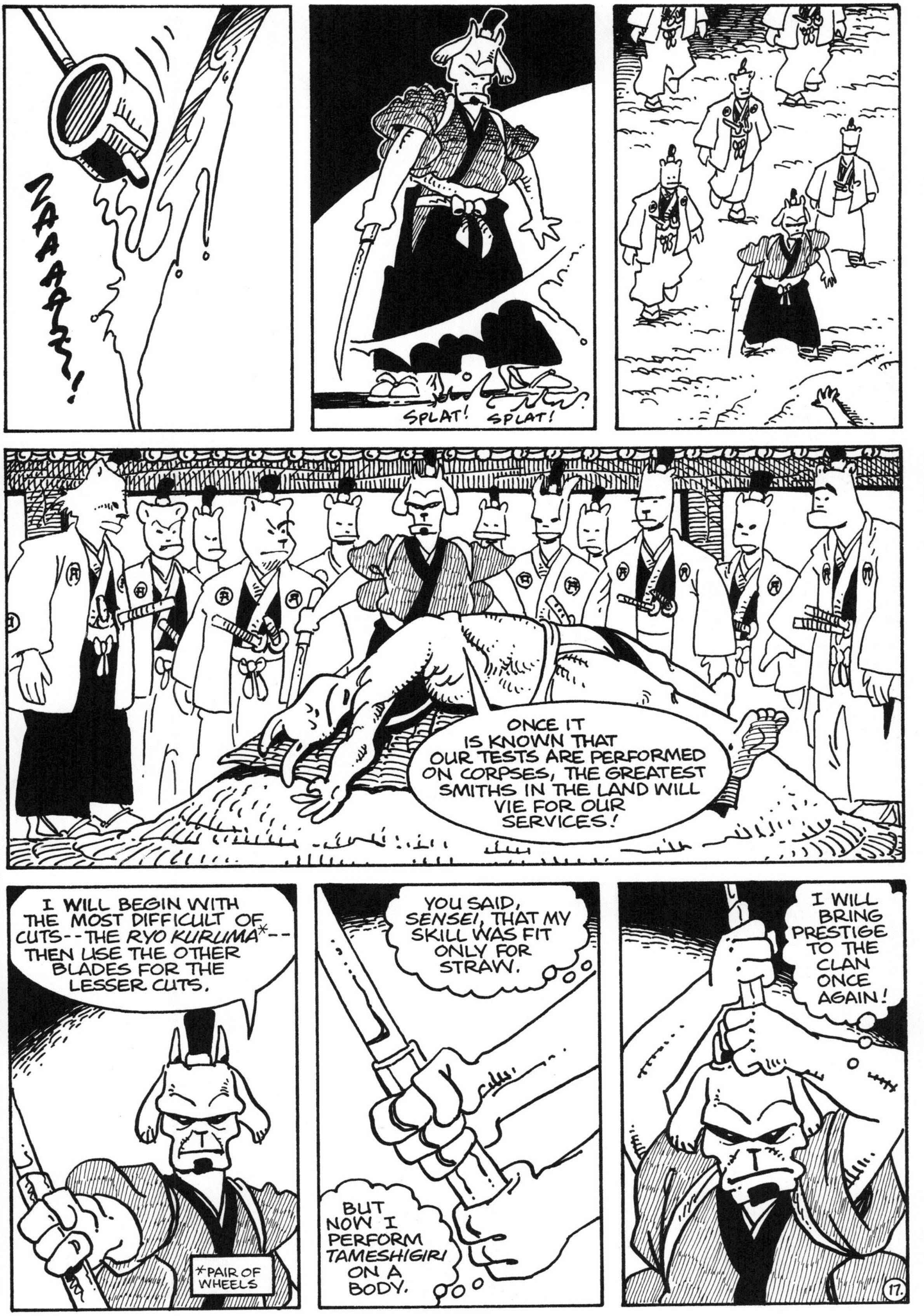
ZAAAAAZZ!
SPLAT! SPLAT!
ONCE IT IS KNOWN THAT OUR TESTS ARE PERFORMED ON CORPSES, THE GREATEST SMITHS IN THE LAND WILL VIE FOR OUR SERVICES!
I WILL BEGIN WITH THE MOST DIFFICULT OF CUTS--THE *RYO KURUMA**--THEN USE THE OTHER BLADES FOR THE LESSER CUTS.
*PAIR OF WHEELS
YOU SAID, *SENSEI*, THAT MY SKILL WAS FIT ONLY FOR STRAW.
BUT NOW I PERFORM *TAMESHIGIRI* ON A BODY.
I WILL BRING PRESTIGE TO THE CLAN ONCE AGAIN!
17.

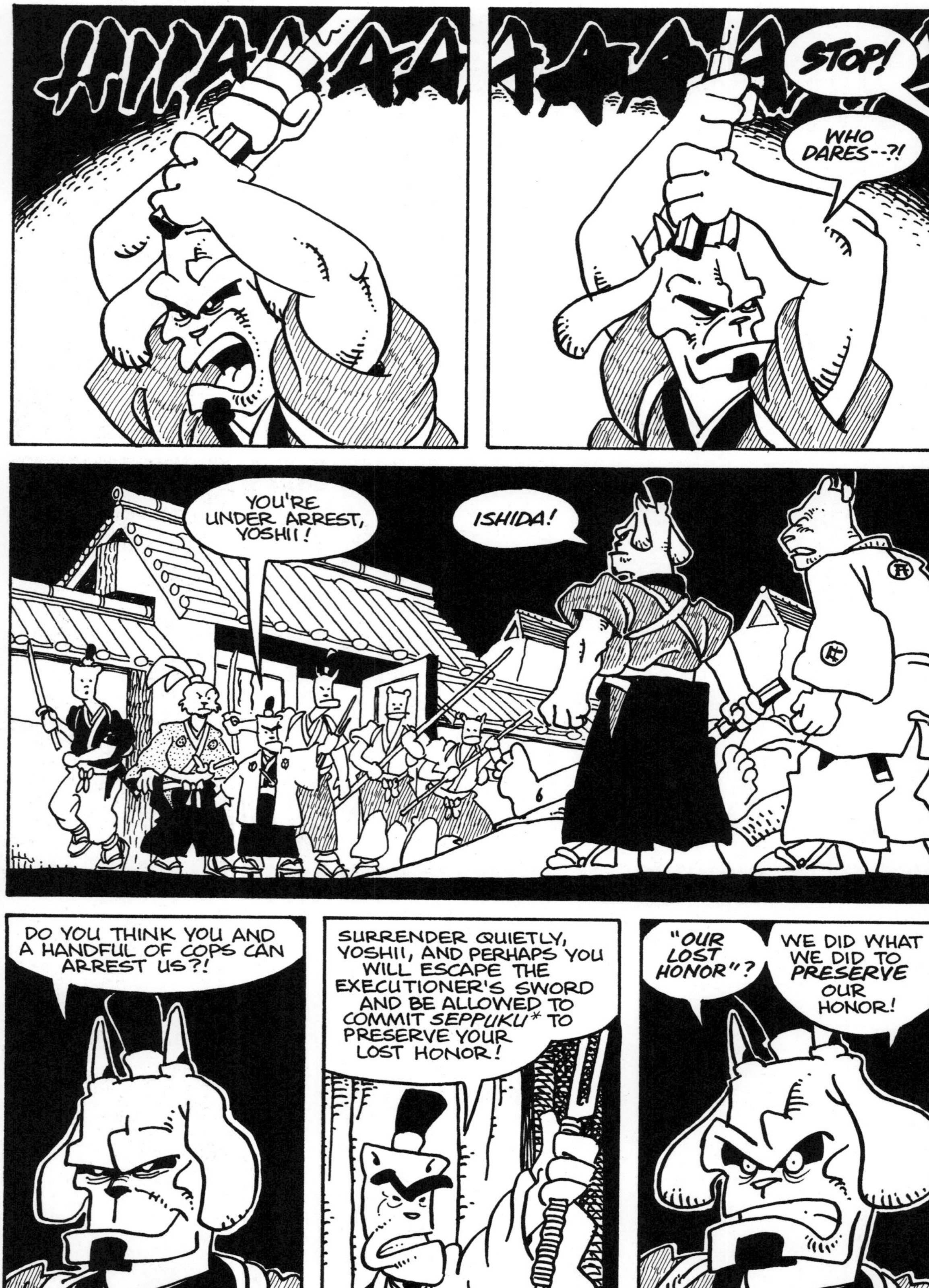
HIYAAAAAAAAAA
STOP!
WHO DARES--?!
YOU'RE UNDER ARREST, YOSHII!
ISHIDA!
DO YOU THINK YOU AND A HANDFUL OF COPS CAN ARREST US?!
SURRENDER QUIETLY, YOSHII, AND PERHAPS YOU WILL ESCAPE THE EXECUTIONER'S SWORD AND BE ALLOWED TO COMMIT SEPPUKU* TO PRESERVE YOUR LOST HONOR!
*RITUAL SUICIDE
"OUR LOST HONOR"?
WE DID WHAT WE DID TO PRESERVE OUR HONOR!
18.

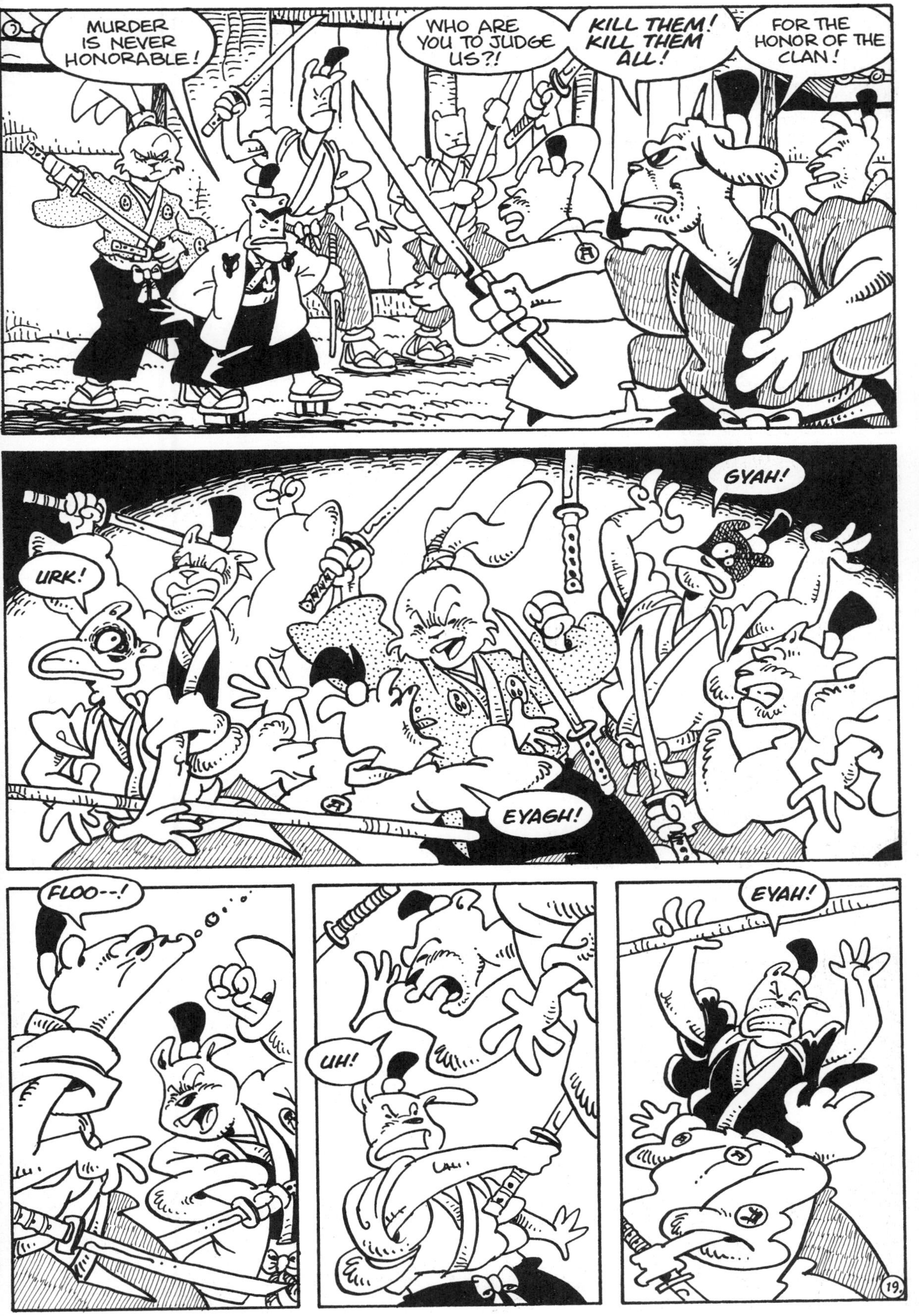

MURDER IS NEVER HONORABLE!
WHO ARE YOU TO JUDGE US?!
KILL THEM! KILL THEM ALL!
FOR THE HONOR OF THE CLAN!
URK!
GYAH!
EYAGH!
FLOO--!
UH!
EYAH!
19

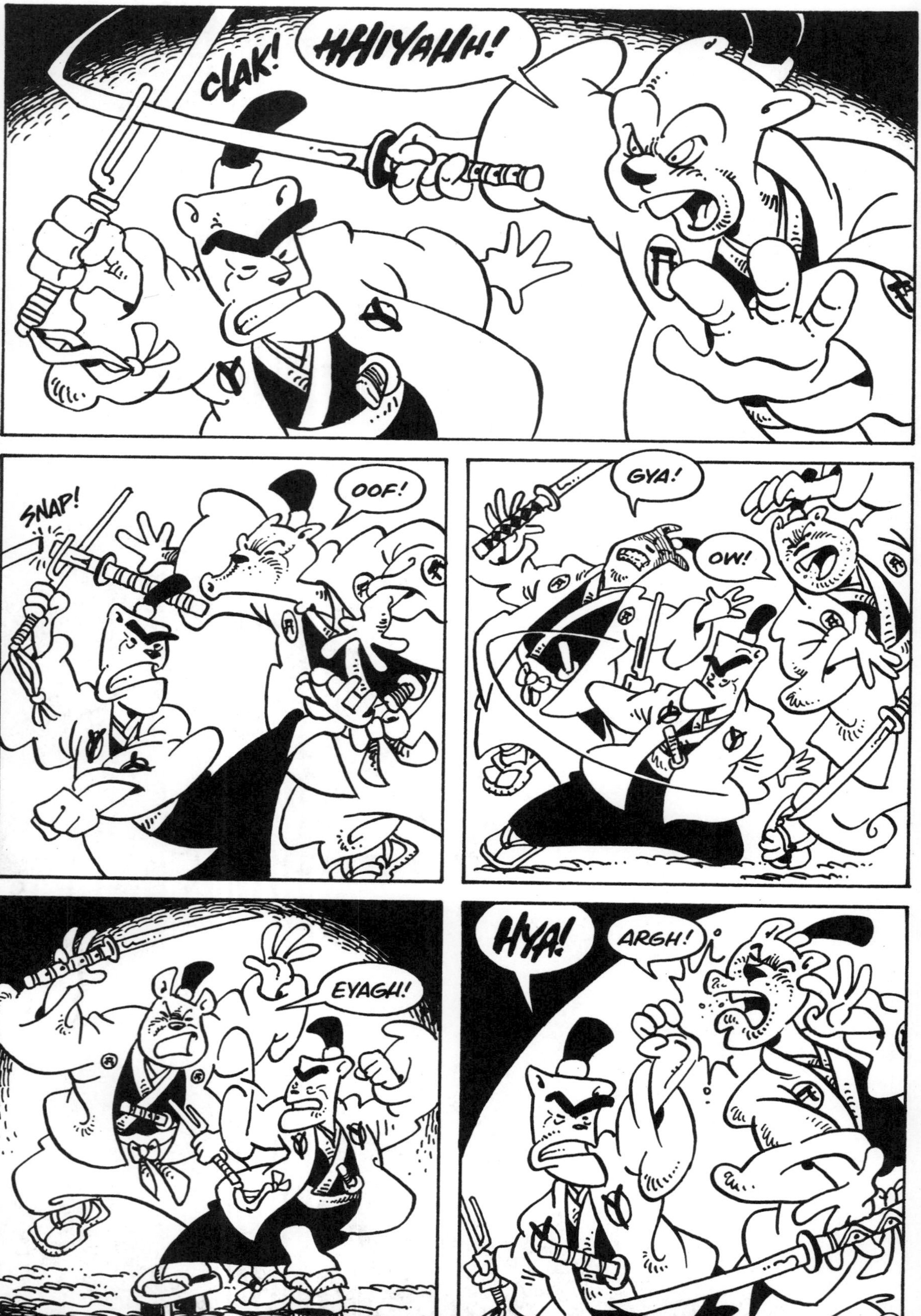
CLAK!
HHIYAHH!
SNAP!
OOF!
GYA!
OW!
EYAGH!
HYA!
ARGH!
20.

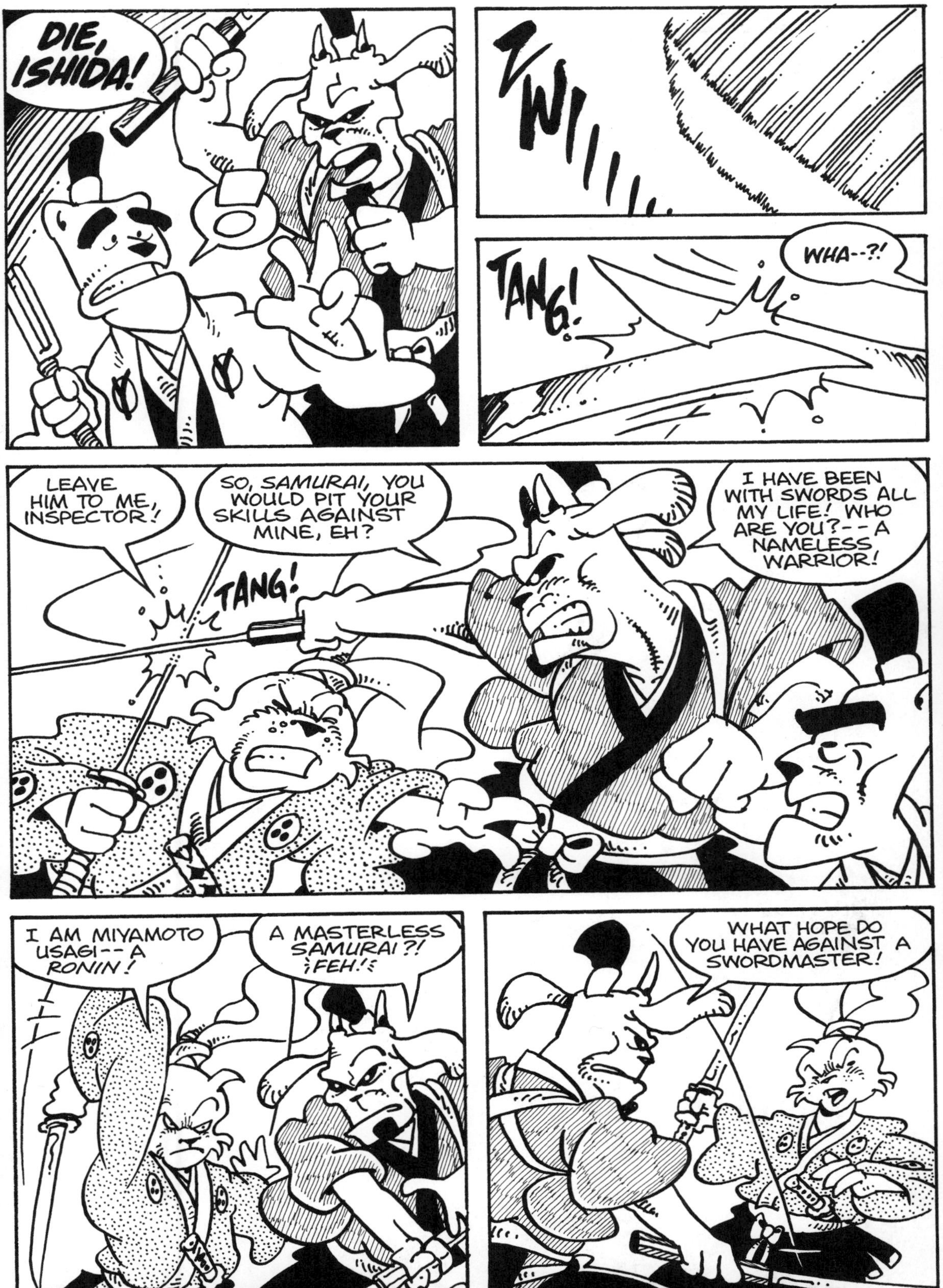
DIE, ISHIDA!
ZWIIIII...
TANG!
WHA--?!
LEAVE HIM TO ME, INSPECTOR!
SO, SAMURAI, YOU WOULD PIT YOUR SKILLS AGAINST MINE, EH?
TANG!
I HAVE BEEN WITH SWORDS ALL MY LIFE! WHO ARE YOU?--A NAMELESS WARRIOR!
I AM MIYAMOTO USAGI--A RONIN!
A MASTERLESS SAMURAI?! FEH!
WHAT HOPE DO YOU HAVE AGAINST A SWORDMASTER!
21.

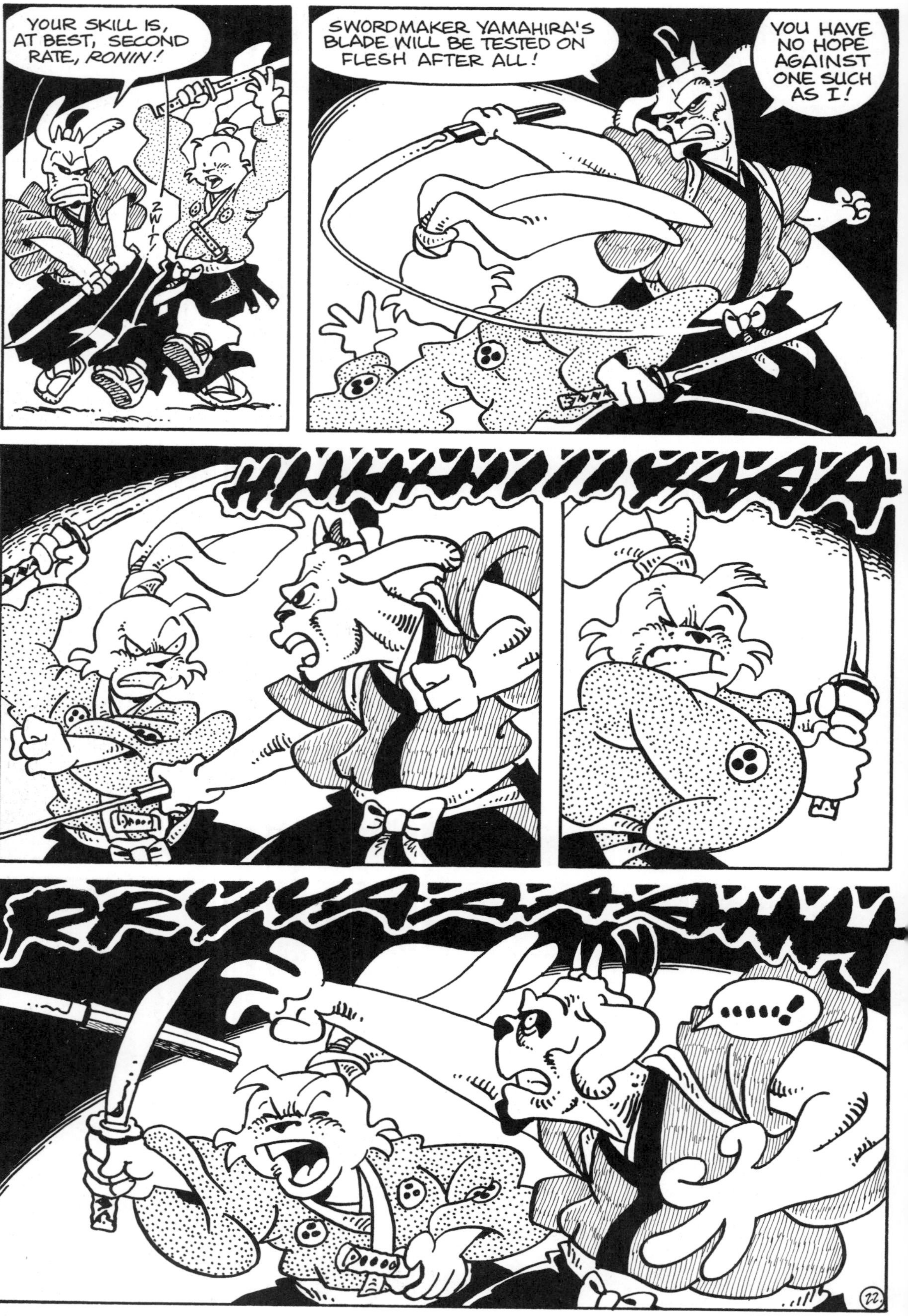
YOUR SKILL IS, AT BEST, SECOND RATE, *RONIN*!
ZWIT!
SWORDMAKER YAMAHIRA'S BLADE WILL BE TESTED ON FLESH AFTER ALL!
YOU HAVE NO HOPE AGAINST ONE SUCH AS I!
HHHHHIIIIYAAAA
RRYYAAAAAHHH
.....!
22

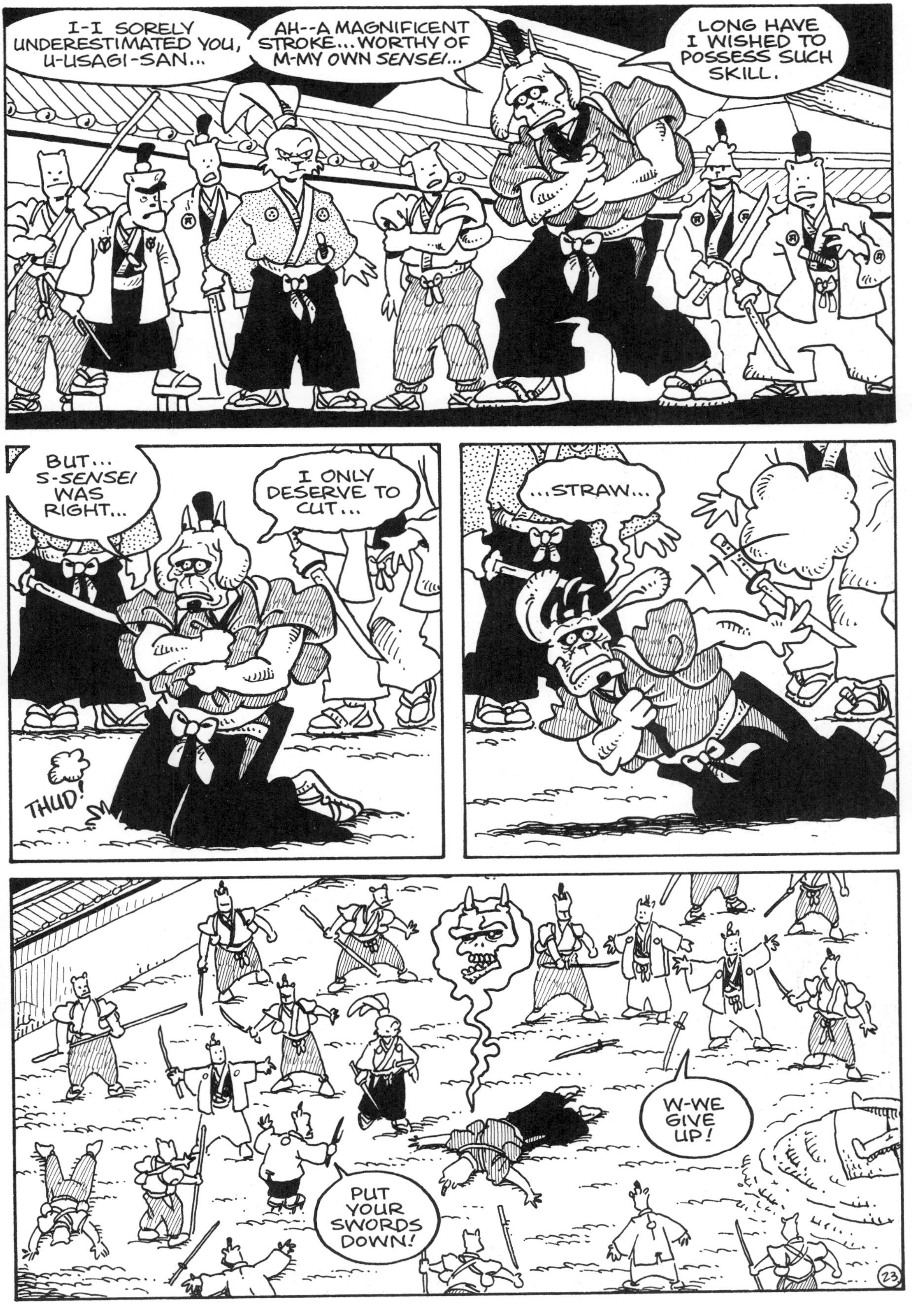
I-I SORELY UNDERESTIMATED YOU, U-USAGI-SAN...
AH--A MAGNIFICENT STROKE...WORTHY OF M-MY OWN SENSEI...
LONG HAVE I WISHED TO POSSESS SUCH SKILL.
BUT... S-SENSEI WAS RIGHT...
I ONLY DESERVE TO CUT...
THUD!
...STRAW...
PUT YOUR SWORDS DOWN!
W-WE GIVE UP!
23

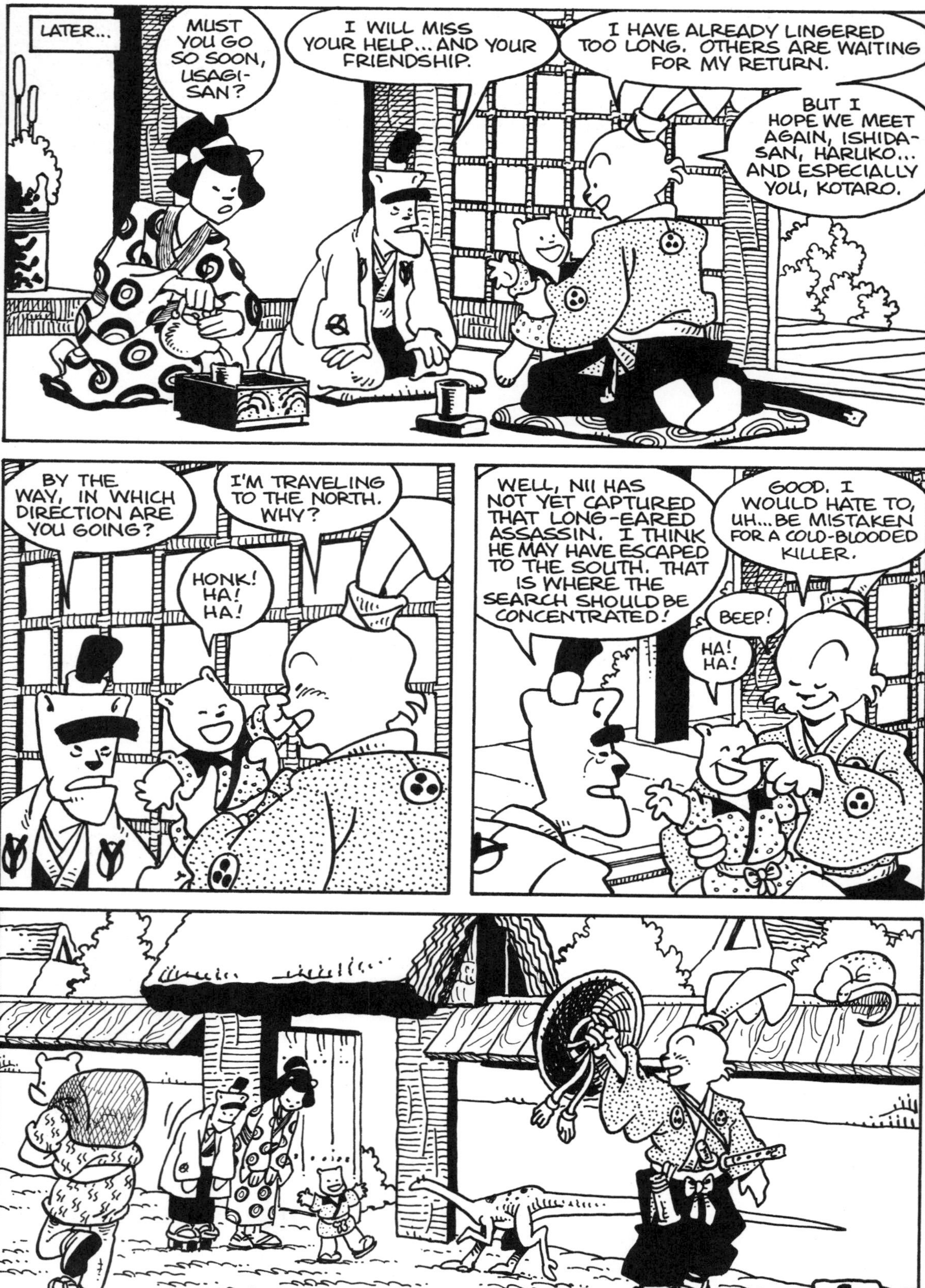
LATER...
MUST YOU GO SO SOON, USAGI-SAN?
I WILL MISS YOUR HELP... AND YOUR FRIENDSHIP.
I HAVE ALREADY LINGERED TOO LONG. OTHERS ARE WAITING FOR MY RETURN.
BUT I HOPE WE MEET AGAIN, ISHIDA-SAN, HARUKO... AND ESPECIALLY YOU, KOTARO.
BY THE WAY, IN WHICH DIRECTION ARE YOU GOING?
I'M TRAVELING TO THE NORTH. WHY?
HONK! HA! HA!
WELL, NII HAS NOT YET CAPTURED THAT LONG-EARED ASSASSIN. I THINK HE MAY HAVE ESCAPED TO THE SOUTH. THAT IS WHERE THE SEARCH SHOULD BE CONCENTRATED!
GOOD. I WOULD HATE TO, UH... BE MISTAKEN FOR A COLD-BLOODED KILLER.
BEEP!
HA! HA!
完

STORY NOTES by stan sakai

THE WITHERED FIELD

Challenging an established fencing school was a common practice for the *shugyosha*, or "student warriors," the samurai who went on the road seeking to hone their skills rather than serve a lord. Miyamoto Musashi did it a number of times, the most famous of which, his duel with the Yoshioka school, inspired a scene in "The Withered Field."

I heavily condensed the prefight etiquette ritual because of space, but for a more detailed depiction I refer you to *The Deity and the Sword*, by Risuke Otake. Another fine book is *Flashing Steel*, by Shimabukuro and Pellman (thank you, Chuck Arnold, for giving it to me). Both books contain lots of photographs and are excellent references. I also recommend the movies *Tange Sazen* and Inagaki's *Duel at Ichijoji Temple* (the second part of the *Samurai* trilogy), which has some nice sequences of duels in a school.

THE LORD OF OWLS

The owl was regarded as a symbol of bad luck in Japanese folklore, and its cry an omen of death. It was thought that an owl would devour its mother, and in a country where respect for parents and ancestors was stressed, ungrateful children were sometimes called "owls." The owl possessed the "evil eye," and so it was often depicted in traditional art with its back turned or its eyes closed.

The Ainu people of Hokkaido believed the eagle owl was a messenger of the gods and brought good luck during a hunt. The horned owl could discern a person's soul. If the owl narrowed its eyes when looking at someone, that person had a dark soul. If it stared with wide eyes, that person could be trusted.

In more recent times, however, the owl has been associated with good luck. The good luck stems from its name, *fukurou*. *Kurou* means "trouble" or "hardship," and *fu* can mean "no"—therefore, "no hardship." Ceramic owls might be given to newlyweds, or owl charms may be worn to ward off evil.

THE *OBAKÉNEKO* OF THE GEISHU CLAN

There is a Japanese saying: Feed a dog for three days, and he will remember your kindness for three years. Feed a cat for three years, and she will forget your kindness in three days.

The first cats were introduced to Japan by Fujiwara no Sanesuke, a nobleman at the court of Emperor Ichijo (986–1011). They were imported from China and were called "hand-fed tigers." They were very popular pets but were soon looked upon with suspicion and even fear. Besides being ungrateful, cats are destructive by nature. They tear straw *tatami* mats, make holes in paper *shoji* doors, and sharpen their claws on wooden pillars. They are also very fond of the oil in lamps and will often lap them dry.

The Japanese looked upon cats as being under a curse. Only the cat and the serpent did not weep at the death of Buddha. In fact, the cat killed the rat that was sent to get the medicine.

Like foxes and badgers, cats are able to bewitch human beings. Cats are also able to control the dead, even making them dance. Cats have a natural tendency to become *nekomata*, or "goblin cats." This can only be controlled by cutting off their tails, which was a common practice performed on kittens. When a *nekomata* ages, it becomes an *obakéneko*. *Obakéneko* (sometimes called *kaibyo*) literally translates as "supernatural cat," though it is also called "ghost cat" or "vampire cat." There is no single Western equivalent to this creature. Not only old cats but also those killed or wronged by a person can become *obakéneko* to take revenge.

There is a well-known story of the *obakéneko* of Saga Castle. During the Edo period, Lord Nabeshima, an avid player of the board game *go*, challenged a blind champion, Matahichiryo Ryuzoji, to a game. When it appeared that he was going to lose, Lord Nabeshima lost his temper and killed Matahichiryo. The blind man left an aged mother who, learning of her son's death, killed herself in grief. He also left a pet cat, Tama, who lapped up the mother's blood and became an *obakéneko* and, to this day, is responsible for strange occurrences in the castle.

However, not all cats are regarded with malice. Sailors prized cats, especially the three-colored *mikeneko*. People who drown at sea never find rest but lurk in the waves and extend their arms in the whitecaps in an effort to grab a victim. Cats, with their control over the dead, can keep those spirits away.

The *manekineko*, or "beckoning cat," is found in a spot of honor in many shops, because a cat with its paw raised invites customers in. The Sleeping Cat carving of Nikko Shrine, the burial place of Shogun Tokugawa Ieyasu, is said to keep the area free of mice and winks when rain is approaching.

Much of the research for this story came from *Yokai Yurei Dahyaku* (Many unnatural and ghost stories). Thanks to Bill Mimbu for sending me this book and to my parents, Akio and Teruko Sakai, for translating the sections on *obakéneko* and *kaibyo*. Also used were: *Myths and Legends of Japan*, by F. Hadland Davis; *Japanese Animal Art: Antique and Contemporary*, by Lea Baten; *The Mystery of Things: Evocations of the Japanese Supernatural*, by Akeji Sumiyoshi and Patrik Le Nestour; *Glimpses of Unfamiliar Japan*, by Lafcadio Hearn; and *Obake: Ghost Stories in Hawai'i*, by Glen Grant.

GRASSCUTTER

My apologies. I am not doing my reference materials justice. I can blame this on the restrictions placed by the comic-book medium, conflicting sources, and my own inadequacies as a storyteller. I have skirted over a lot of important events, choosing to tell only those that directly pertain to the plot. I have even made up scenes to enhance the story. But, hopefully, these more detailed story notes will resolve at least some of the problems.

Dates in Japanese history (especially prehistory) are very confusing at times because they are established in reference to the ruler of that period. For example: *The Kojiki: Records of Ancient Matters* states that the eighth emperor, Kogen, died at age fifty-seven; however, according to *The Nihongi: Chronicles of Japan*

from the Earliest Times to A.D. 697, he ascended the throne at age fifty-nine and ruled for fifty-six years. One source places the story of Yamato-Dake as occurring in 110 BC, while another has his father's reign as AD 71–130, having ascended the throne at the age of eighty-three.

There is no exact English equivalent to the word *kami*. Sometimes it's been translated as "god." However, ancestors can also be *kami*, and the government was once known as *okami*. I chose to translate it as "deity" or "divinity," though this is still inaccurate. According to *The Kojiki*, Japan has eight million good *kami* and ten million evil spirits.

A note of interest is that the number eight is sacred to the Japanese and is a recurring theme, much like how seven or forty bears significance to Christians.

PROLOGUE 1: IZANAGI & IZANAMI
There are seven generations of deities leading up to the creation of the Japanese islands. I skipped over the earlier ones as they had nothing to do with the story. Indeed, they seemed to do little except come into being and pass on (die). However, if you're interested in a complete genealogy, I suggest *The Kojiki* or *The Nihongi*.

The Bridge of Heaven is located at Miyazu Bay on the west coast of Honshu, Japan's main island. A pine-covered bar, about two miles long and sixty-six feet wide, is the remnant of the heavenly bridge.

Izanagi and Izanami learned the art of lovemaking from watching a pair of wagtails. These waterbirds are still associated with this couple. Even the *kami* of scarecrows cannot frighten wagtails, a result of a blessing given to them.

Izanagi and Izanami's first child was a leech-like creature, who at the age of three, could not stand upright and was set adrift in a reed boat. Again, for a detailed account of their children, I recommend the aforementioned books.

As Izanagi was being pursued by the hags of Yomi, he stalled them by tearing off a vine wreath from his head and dropping it behind him. It turned into a bunch of grapes, which the hags stopped to devour. He next cast his comb away and it turned into a grove of bamboo shoots which the hags ate. He fought the "eight thunders and fifteen hundred warriors" with his sword until he reached the entrance to Yomi. He plucked three peaches from a tree and hurled them at his enemies, driving them back. The peach was rewarded with the title of "Great Divine Fruit." Izanagi emerged at Himuka on the island of Kyushu. He blocked the path to Yomi with a rock that would take a thousand men to move.

When Izanagi washed himself after his escape, he inaugurated the Shinto rite of purification practiced to this day.

PROLOGUE 2: SUSANO-O

Some sources refer to Susano-o as "The God of Storms"; others as "The God of the Ocean" or "The God of Force." He is associated with the province of Izumo on the coast of the Sea of Japan on Honshu Island. It is from there that he forested the coasts of Korea, taking hairs from his beard and turning them into trees.

He is often mischievous and, at times, downright evil.

On one rampage, he destroyed fields, filled irrigation ditches, tore out dikes, and spread excrement about the temples where the Festival of the First Fruits was being held. He then flayed a horse and threw it through the roof into the room where Amaterasu and her attendants were weaving. This so frightened the maids that they committed suicide by stabbing themselves with their shuttles. The terrified Sun Deity hid herself in a cave, blocking the entrance with a great boulder. Everything was plunged into darkness and the deities of pestilence overran the world. The Eight Hundred Deities made an eight-span mirror, strings of jewels, and cloth streamers and hung them from a *sakaki* tree. They had a riotous celebration outside the cave, and when the curious Amaterasu emerged to investigate the noise, she was dazzled by her reflection in the mirror. One of the *kami* seized her arm and drew her out of the cave, while others stretched a straw rope across the cave entrance, preventing her retreat. She was then escorted to a new palace, and light was restored to the world.

As punishment, the deities cut off Susano-o's mustache and beard and pulled out his fingernails and toenails. He was then expelled from heaven.

Before he had gone too far, he met up with the Deity of Food and begged for something to eat. She offered a grand feast, but taken from her mouth, her nose, and other parts of her body. Susano-o was outraged because he thought she was offering him filth and slew her. From her body was borne rice, barley, millet, and bean seeds, as well as farm animals and grasses.

The scene in which Susano-o went off to look at the serpent himself was created from my own imagination, as I felt it was important that he see it with his own eyes, and it made for a stronger story. In legend, Susano-o merely asks the couple for the serpent's description:

> HIS EYES ARE FIERY AND RED LIKE THE WINTER CHERRY. HE HAS BUT ONE BODY, WITH EIGHT HEADS AND EIGHT SCALY TAILS. MOREOVER, ON HIS BODY GROWS MOSS, TOGETHER WITH THE FIR AND CRYPTOMERIA OF THE FOREST. IN HIS GOING, HE COVERS EIGHT VALLEYS AND EIGHT HILLS, AND UPON HIS UNDERSIDE HE IS RED AND GORY. —*Green Willow and Other Japanese Fairy Tales*

Susano-o presented the sword to Amaterasu. When she saw it, she exclaimed, "This is the sword that I lost at Takama-ga-hara ["Plain of the High Sky," a home of the heavenly deities] long ago!" (*The Tale of the Heike*). The blade became lodged in the serpent's tail and huge clouds billowed above the village, hence the name "Sword of the Village of the Clustering Clouds."

PROLOGUE 3: YAMATO-DAKE

Amaterasu's grandson, Ninigi, was sent to earth with three treasures: a mirror, a jewel, and the sword. He fell in love with Ko-No-Hana, the princess who makes trees blossom. Her father had an elder daughter, Iha-Naga (Princess Long-as-the-Rocks). Ninigi was given the choice of either daughter in marriage, but he remained true to the flower princess. Iha-Naga said, had he chosen her, their offspring would have lived as long as the rocks, but now his children would bloom and fade

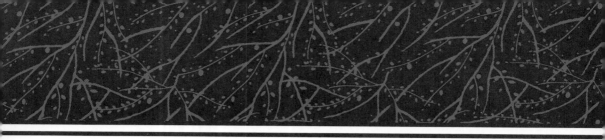

as do blossoms. Ninigi's great-grandson was Jimmu, the first emperor of Japan.

The temple of Amaterasu in Ise, located on the southern coast of the island of Honshu, is one of the oldest religious sites in Japan, but the current structure is not more than twenty years old. It has been rebuilt every two decades, with a few exceptions, since about 4 BC, using traditional methods. It is built of *hinoki* cypress (*Chamaecyparis obtusa*). Early carpenters' tools did not include the crosscut saw or plane, and these fragrant trees with their grain that runs straight along the length of the timber were ideal for that time of limited technology. There was also a great abundance of these trees.

Yamato-Dake was the youngest son of Emperor Keiko and the hero of numerous campaigns. Many of his victories, though, were the result of cunning, as well as strength—such as disguising himself as a beautiful woman to get close to the brigands of Kumaso or replacing the sword of the outlaw Takeru with a wooden imitation, then challenging him to a duel.

"Wo-Usu" was the birth name of this hero. He was given the name Yamato-Dake (Bravest of the Yamato) by one of the Kumaso bandits soon before the prince "ripped him up like a ripe melon and slew him."

Yamato-Dake was married to Princess Ototachibana, a faithful wife who followed him on all his campaigns. As a result, her skin became deeply tanned and her garments soiled and tattered. He met Princess Miyazu, a beauty with skin as delicate as cherry blossoms, and professed his love for her. He promised to one day return and make her his bride. Then he noticed Ototachibana had seen and heard everything. When Yamato-Dake and his entourage were crossing the straits of Kazusu, a great storm arose which threatened to capsize the boats. Ototachibana pleaded to the sea king to accept her life and deliver her husband safely to shore, whereupon she threw herself into the water. No sooner had she gone under than the storm abated and the clouds dispersed. Too late, Yamato-Dake realized what a treasure he had lost. Years later he stood on the mountains from which he could gaze upon the distant sea where Ototachibana had given her life for

him. He stretched out his arms, sighed three times, and said, "My wife!" To this day that area is called Azuma, "My Wife."

The Yemishi that Yamato-Dake was to subjugate are the ancestors of the modern Ainu of Hokkaido Island. In earlier times, the Yemishi extended from the north down the eastern section of Japan, as far south as present-day Tokyo. The Yemishi appear to have been a peaceful people and offered no resistance. In *The Nihongi*, they were called "*kami* of the country" and so were held in some respect by the Japanese. It should be noted that the people of Suruga were not Yemishi.

There are two versions of the story of how the hero was tricked onto the moors. In the first, the Suruga lord suggests a deer hunt. In the other, he invites Yamato-Dake to see an unusually violent lake *kami*. I chose to incorporate both versions in my story. The area this incident took place in is now called Yakizu, or "The Port of Burning."

Yamato-Dake died in the seventh month of his thirtieth year at Atsuta in Owari Province. It is unclear whether he died from fatigue and exposure or from poison. His spirit ascended to heaven in the form of a white bird.

Kusanagi is a *ken* or *tsurugi*-type sword. These swords are about two and a half to three feet long, straight, double edged, and very heavy. The scabbards were generally made of wood bound with metal bands.

Kusanagi was given to Atsuta Shrine. In the seventh year of the reign of Emperor Tenchi (AD 668), a Korean named Dogyo stole the sword, hoping to make it a treasure of his own country. During the voyage to his homeland, a terrible storm appeared. Dogyo begged forgiveness and returned the sword to the shrine. In 686, Emperor Temmu placed the sacred sword in his court.

PROLOGUE 4: DAN-NO-URA
The Genpei War, the great civil war of Japan (1180–1185), gets its name from the Chinese readings of the names of the two rival clans, the Genji (Minamoto) and the Heike (Taira).

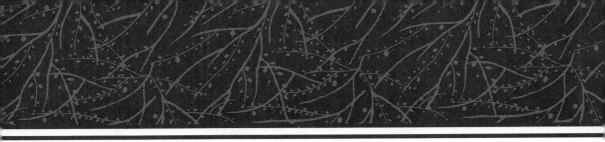

The Taira controlled the West and the imperial court, while the Minamoto were dominant in the East. In 1156, the Minamoto declared a revolt against the Taira which was soon crushed. As a result, the Minamoto family was almost exterminated. A few boys escaped, however, and when they grew to manhood, set out to avenge their clan. In 1180, minor outbreaks developed into a full-scale civil war. The leader of the Minamoto clan was Yoritomo. The Taira leader, Imperial Grandfather Kiyomori, died of a fever in 1181 and was succeeded by his son, Munemori, an incompetent whose own mother revealed that he was not a true Taira but the son of an umbrella merchant.

In 1182, Yoritomo's cousin, Minamoto Kiso no Yoshinaka, conquered Kyoto and set himself as shogun, or military ruler. This enraged Yoritomo, who sent his younger half brother, Yoshitsune, to retake the capital. After his defeat, Yoshinaka escaped with his wife, Tomoe Gozen, and a few retainers. They were ambushed and legend has it that Yoshinaka took his own life but refused to let Tomoe die with him. She killed some of the attackers and fled to a temple to become a nun.

While their enemies were fighting amongst themselves, the Taira fled south, taking the eight-year-old emperor Antoku. Yoshitsune hounded them until they made their final stand at Dan-no-Ura.

Again, I've taken a lot of liberties for the sake of the story. I have depicted a few events out of sequence and, for the sake of space, combined the actions of several people into one character. There are also many conflicting accounts of the battle, such as its date and time and the age of the emperor. In the case of conflicting resources, I've either chosen that which was best for the narrative or that which is agreed upon by most scholars.

Seagoing warfare was very similar to fighting on land, in that there was no maneuvering or much naval strategy involved. Ships were, for the most part, commandeered ferry or fishing boats whose main purpose was to get the armies into bow range and then sword reach. The number of boats actually involved in this battle varies greatly with researchers: anywhere from less than fourteen hundred to more than four thousand.

Keiko or Kei-*chan* is fictitious, as is her early-morning conversation with the emperor's grandmother. This sequence was invented to reveal a bit of the backstory.

Taira Munemori was the younger "son" of Kiyomori, but upon the death of his older, more capable brother, Shigemori, became the Taira heir. He and his son, Kiyomune, were captured at Dan-no-Ura and were later put to death at Shinowara.

My depiction of Taira Tomomori is a conglomeration of personages. True, he was a great general who defeated the Minamoto in three separate battles, but it was the imperial diviner Harenobu who accompanied Munemori and forecast the omen of the dolphins. I suggested that Tomomori, disgusted with his lord's cowardice, forced Munemori overboard; however, it was the fault of some unnamed soldiers who "accidentally" pushed him as he stood in shock and fear, at a loss as to what to do. Tomomori fought bravely, but after hearing of his lord's capture, donned a double set of armor and, with his uncle, jumped into the sea.

The defection of Lord Taguchi Shigeyoshi was not unexpected. His loyalty fell under suspicion after his son, who was captured by the Minamoto, came to side with them and urged his father to do so also. Shigeyoshi not only took his son's advice but chose the time most disastrous to the Taira to do so.

Emperor Antoku's age at the time of his death was somewhere between six and ten. I showed him as eight years old because that seems to be the most consistent age among researchers and eight is a significant number to the Japanese. As stated in *The Tale of the Heike*:

> THE GREAT SERPENT THAT WAS KILLED BY SUSANO-O-NO-MIKOTO LONG AGO AT THE UPPER PART OF THE HIGAWA RIVER MUST HAVE BORNE A GRUDGE BECAUSE OF THE LOSS OF THE SWORD. THEREFORE WITH HIS EIGHT HEADS AND EIGHT TAILS, HE HAS ENTERED INTO THE EIGHT-YEAR-OLD EMPEROR AFTER EIGHTY GENERATIONS, AND HAS TAKEN THE SWORD BACK TO THE DEPTHS OF THE SEA.

Antoku was succeeded by Emperor Go-Toba, his younger brother.

Yoshitsune is the most popular and most tragic of all the Japanese heroes. Always at his side was the warrior-monk Benkei, whom he had defeated in a duel and who had pledged eternal loyalty. Yoshitsune was twenty-one when he joined Yoritomo's rebellion, but his half brother became increasingly jealous and wary of Yoshitsune, especially in light of the traitorous actions of their cousin, Yoshinaka. Soon after the triumph over the Taira, Yoshitsune became a hunted man and was forced to flee Yoritomo's assassins. He was finally cornered in the northern province, and, as Benkei gave his life to defend the stronghold, Yoshitsune killed his wife and children before committing suicide. He was thirty-one years old. However, according to legend, Yoshitsune did not die then. He escaped further north and is now honored by the aboriginal Ainu under the name "Gikyo-daimyo-jin." Others say that he made his way to Mongolia, where Minamoto Yoshitsune (or "Genji-Kyo" in the Chinese reading) became Genghis Khan (1157–1226).

In 1192, Yoritomo was proclaimed shogun and set about to form his own government. The Heian period had ended and the Kamakura era had begun. Military dominance of Japan would continue until the Meiji Restoration in 1868.

CHAPTER 1: JEI
Usagi's adventures take place at the turn of seventeenth-century Japan.

I've deliberately kept exact dates vague to give myself more latitude in storytelling; however, I'm making an exception in this story with the retirement of the shogun Tokugawa Ieyasu.

In 1603, Ieyasu (1542–1616), the first of the Tokugawa shoguns, received the title *sei-i-tai shogun*, or "supreme military dictator," from Emperor Go-Yozei. Two years later, he abdicated in favor of his son, Hidetada, then twenty-six years old. He did this to guarantee the succession of the position within his family. Ieyasu retired to Shizuoka but still maintained an active role in politics.

And, after almost a lifetime on the battlefield, he now devoted his leisure time to literature and poetry.

Hidetada ruled until 1622, when he abdicated in favor of his son, Iemitsu.

The Tokugawa shogunate endured for fifteen successions and came to an end in 1868 with the Meiji Restoration, which gave power back to the emperor.

Jishin-Uwo (page 261) is a giant catfish that lives under Shimofusa and Hitachi Provinces. Its movements are responsible for Japan's many earthquakes. A stone in the temple of Kashima is the exposed part of a sword that the gods used to pin the fish in place.

The *kanji* characters on page 245 read "Kusanagi-no-Tsurugi," literally "The Grasscutting Sword."

CHAPTER 2: HEIKE GANI
The *Heike gani* or Heike crab (*Heikea japonica*) has, on its carapace (shell), the image of a scowling human face. According to legend, these crabs are the ghosts of the Heike warriors who died during the sea battle at Dan-no-Ura.

These small crabs reach a maximum size of 1.2 inches (31 mm) across their backs. The rear two legs on each side are much smaller and claw-like for carrying objects. Their red coloration further reinforced their connection to the Heike clan, whose banners were also red. There are actually two varieties of "face crabs" along Dan-no-Ura. I've drawn the smaller *Heike gani*, which are the spirits of the common warriors. The slightly larger, more ornate *taisho gani* (chieftain crab), or *tatsugashira* (dragon helmet), were animated by the ghosts of the clan leaders.

The shell images are not merely decorative but serve a specific purpose. They are the external grooves of support ridges, called apodemes, inside the carapace that are the sites where muscles are attached. These grooves occur in almost all species of crabs. There are other varieties of "face crabs"—the *kuei lien hsieh* (ghost crabs) of China and the *Paradorippe granulata*, a northwestern Pacific species, to name two.

BIBLIOGRAPHY

My ultimate references for Japanese prehistory are *The Kojiki: Records of Ancient Matters*, trans. Basil Hall Chamberlain (Boston: C. E. Tuttle & Co., 1981), and *The Nihongi: Chronicles of Japan from the Earliest Times to A.D. 697*, trans. William George Aston (Boston: C. E. Tuttle & Co., 1971).

Also used for the prologues: *The Japanese: People of the Three Treasures*, by Robert Newman (?: Atheneum, 1964); *A History of the Japanese People from the Earliest Times to the End of the Meiji Era*, by Capt. F. Brinkley, R. A. (New York: The Encyclopedia Britannica Co., 1915), contained both records of prehistory and the Genpei Wars, as well as a photo of the shrine at Ise and a statue of Emperor Jimmu, upon which I based the visuals of Susano-o); *Japanese Mythology*, by Juliet Piggott (New York: Hamlyn Publishing Group, 1969); *Ancient Tales and Folklore of Japan*, by Richard Gordon Smith (New York: Studio Editions, 1995); *Gods of Myth and Stone*, by Michael Czaja (New York: John Weatherhill, Inc., 1974), went into detail on the creation myth and Susano-o with an analysis of each act and artifact; *Green Willow and Other Japanese Fairy Tales*, by Grace James (New York: Avenel Books, 1987), contains stories on Susano-o and the land of Yomi; *The Book of the Samurai: The Warrior Class of Japan*, by Stephen R. Turnbull (New York: Arco, 1982), has woodcut prints of Yamato-Dake using Kusanagi, as well as Emperor Antoku and his grandmother; *Myths and Legends of Japan*, by F. Hadland Davis (New York: Dover Books, 1992); *Myths and Legends Series: China and Japan*, by Donald A. Mackenzie (London: Bracken Books, 1985); and *Vanishing Peoples of the Earth* (Washington: National Geographic Society, 1969) contains a section entitled "Mysterious Sky People: Japan's Dwindling Ainu," by Sister Mary Inez Hilger.

Photos of the temple of Ise can be found in *The Lesson of Japanese Architecture*, by Jiro Harada (New York: Dover Books, 1985), and *Japanese Folkhouses*, by Norman F. Carver Jr. (Kalamazoo: Documan Press, 1984). *The Creators: A History of Heroes of the Imagination* chronicles the Japanese use of wood in building, particularly in the temple of Ise.

The visuals for Yamato-Hime were based upon Shinto temple maidens found in *Festivals of Japan* and *A Look into Japan*, both published in 1985 by Japan Travel Bureau, Inc.

Resources on the history of the Genpei War: *The Tale of the Heike*, trans. Hiroshi Kitagawa and Bruce T. Tsuchida (Japan: University of Tokyo Press, 1975); *The Ten Foot Square Hut and Tales of the Heike*, trans. A. L. Sadler (Boston: C. E. Tuttle & Co.,1985); *Genpei*, by Hideo Takeda, is an art book chronicling the history of the war; *Of Nightingales That Weep*, by Katherine Paterson (New York: Harper Trophy, 1989), is a very enjoyable, well-researched young-adult novel; *Yoshitsune* is a Japanese television docudrama chronicling the life of this hero and helped with the visuals of my story.

Books that contain chapters on the war: *The Samurai: A Military History*, by Stephen R. Turnbull (New York: Macmillan Publishing, 1977), devotes chapters to the rivalry between the Minamoto and the Taira clans in detail; *Samurai Warriors*, by Turnbull (New York: Blandford Press, 1987); *The Samurai: Warriors of Medieval Japan, 940–1600*, by Anthony J. Bryant (London: Osprey Press, 1989), also has many photographs and paintings, including Yoshitsune's and Benkei's armor; and *Arms and Armor of the Samurai: The History of Weaponry in Ancient Japan*, by I. Bottomley and A. P. Hopson (New York: Crescent Books, 1988).

Additional war-related sources: *Historical and Geographical Dictionary of Japan*, by E. Papinot (Boston: C. E. Tuttle & Co., 1984); *Dictionary of Japanese Culture*, by Setsuko Kojima and Gene A. Crane (Torrance: Heian International, 1991); *Bushido, the Way of the Warrior: A New Perspective on the Japanese Military Tradition*, by John Newman (Leicester: Magna Books, 1989); *Battles of the Samurai*, by Turnbull (New York: Arms and Armor Press, 1987), has a chapter on the Battle of Kurikara during the early days of the war; and *Samurai Warfare*, by Turnbull (New York: Arms and Armor Press, 1996), has a section on naval warfare.

Research on the *Heike gani* crabs came from the periodical *Terra*, vol. 31, no. 4 (Los Angeles: Natural History Museum of Los Angeles County, September

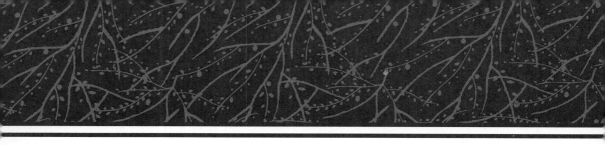

1993); *Kotto,* by Lafcadio Hearn (Rutland, VT/Tokyo: Charles E. Tuttle Co., Inc., 1971), contains a chapter and drawings of these unusual crustaceans; and *Japan Day by Day, 1877–1883,* by Edward Morse (Boston: Houghton Mifflin Co., 1945), has drawings and a brief history of the crabs.

The Hairpin Murders

Kabuki was founded in 1600 in Kyoto by Okuni, a priestess of the Oyashiro Shrine in Izumo Province. Her performances were an outgrowth of the *nembutsu odori* (dance of prayer to Buddha) and the belief that the principles of Buddhism could be more easily understood through song and dance.

Like many entertainers in Kyoto, Okuni performed on the dry riverbed of the Kamo River. She soon teamed up with Sanza, a samurai musician, and together they created dramas and ribald comedies borrowed freely from the No and Kyogen theaters. Okuni would often dress in a man's costume and Sanza in a woman's, to the approval of the audience. They soon put together a troupe and went into business for themselves. The needs of the shrine were forgotten, but that's showbiz.

In 1603 this type of entertainment was called Kabuki (Free Life).

There were different schools of Kabuki. The most notorious was the Yujo (pleasure woman) Kabuki, in which prostitutes found another means to charm and attract customers. In 1629, all women, in any capacity, were banned from the stage by the shogun's order, in an effort to protect public morals and limit interaction between the social classes. As a result, samurai were less likely to attend these shows, which were primarily frequented by commoners. The *onnagata* (female impersonator) was created to offset the boredom of watching an all-male cast.

I was very lax in historical accuracy in this story. *Narukami* was written well after Usagi's time, but I made reference to it because it is one of my favorites.

Also, though Sanza appeared in women's attire, the first true *onnagata* is credited as being Murayama Sakon in 1649.

Sharon and I were in Japan in January of 1998 as guests of Osamu Tezuka Productions. We made a trip to the Grand Kabuki Theatre in Tokyo, though we didn't have the time to actually see a performance. However, we were taken to Takarazuka outside Kyoto to visit the Tezuka museum—an incredible place—and see the Takarazuka Theatre, which is the antithesis of Kabuki in that all the actors are women. We first saw a historical drama and then a Las Vegas–type show. It was amazing to see the women take on male roles—subtle nuances in posture and the swagger as they walked made them absolutely convincing.

For information on Kabuki I referred to *Kabuki Costume,* by Ruth M. Shaver (Rutland, VT/Tokyo: Charles E. Tuttle Co., Inc., 1966). This is a lavishly illustrated book and is indispensable not only for Kabuki costumes but for all types of traditional clothing.

The Courtesan

The yearly courtesan procession was a sight to behold. The *oiran,* with her retinue, made an appearance in her finest gowns, walking on foot-high, black-lacquered clogs called *mitsuba-no-kuro-nuri-geta.* Her costume was so voluminous and heavy (fifty pounds or more) that she had to be assisted by one or two *wakaimono*—male servants of a brothel—on whose shoulders she could lean. Her skirts were tied up for easier walking, allowing spectators a view of her bare, white feet. Folded paper peeked out of her collar to be used as a handkerchief. J. E. de Becker, in *The Nightless City,* writes: "The sight of a lovely and bewitching *yujo* clad in rich silk brocades glittering with gold and polychromatic tints: of her wonderful pyramidal coiffure ornamented with numerous tortoiseshell and coral hairpins so closely thrust together as to suggest a halo of light encircling her head; and her stately graceful movements as she swept slowly and majestically through the Naka-no-cho, must indeed have appeared magnificent and awe-inspiring to the uninitiated."

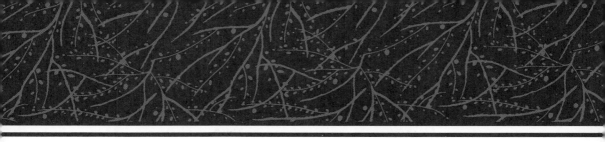

The *oiran* was a courtesan of high status. The term was supposedly derived from *oira no ane*, or "my elder sister," a term of respect used by apprentice courtesans in the Yoshiwara pleasure district of Edo.

The *oiran* should not be confused with the geisha (art person), who were women skilled in dancing, singing, playing musical instruments, and conversation. The geisha still exist, but the *oiran*, as portrayed in period movies and art, have all but disappeared.

There are still processions, however. The Bunsui Oiran Dochu in Nishikanbara, Niigata Prefecture, is celebrated usually on the third Sunday in April. The Senteisai Matsuri at Shimonoseki, Yamaguchi Prefecture, dates back to the times when court ladies who were widows of husbands lost in wars would become courtesans. In sympathy, women don the ceremonial attire to honor them.

The visual for Lady Maple was inspired by the character Agemaki from the Kabuki play *Sukeroku Yukari no Edo Zakura*.

The *torii* is the symbol and gate to a Shinto shrine. The sun is a symbol of Japan, and many early shrines were erected to Amaterasu, the sun goddess. The rooster is associated with the sun. *Torii* literally means "bird perch." A live rooster was placed on a perch as an offering. Over time, the perch itself came to symbolize the shrine and represents the division between the everyday world and the spiritual one. Some shrines, such as the Inari Shrine at Fushimi, have so many *torii* that they form long tunnels. The *torii* of the Itsukushima Shrine in Hiroshima Prefecture is regarded as one of the "three great sights" of Japan.

The Yoshiwara District was the licensed "pleasure quarters" of Edo. This was the only area where brothels were permitted in the city, so they could be controlled and regulated. The name originally meant "reed plain," but later the characters used in writing the name were changed, though the pronunciation remained intact, so that the name meant "lucky plain." The area was burnt down at least four times between 1617, the year it was founded, and 1643. As the city spread, Yoshiwara became embarrassingly close to the center, so it was moved to the eastern boundary, where it stayed until its dissolution after World War II.

References to this story also came from Ruth M. Shaver's *Kabuki Costume* (which contains a detailed description of a procession and the *oiran*'s costume); *Kabuki: Eighteen Traditional Dramas*, by Toshio Kawatake and Akira Iwata (San Francisco: Chronicle, 1985), which includes beautiful photographs with summaries of plays; *Japanese Festivals*, by Helen Bauer and Sherwin Carlquist (New York: Doubleday, 1965); and *Japan*, by Nebojsa Bato Tomasevic, Michael Random, and Louis Frederic (New York: Flint River Publishers, 1986). I also used *Samurai II: Duel at Ichijoji Temple*, directed by Inagaki (available on video), which has Miyamoto Musashi staying at the home of an *oiran*, on which I based the visuals of Maple's private residence, including that vertically swinging gate. An episode of the *Kage no Gundan II* TV series entitled "The Two-Faces Art of Kunoichi" featured a procession, albeit on a limited production budget.

TAMESHIGIRI

New swords were often tested for strength and sharpness on the bodies of beheaded criminals. The corpses were either suspended from a rope or laid on a mound of sand.

There were eighteen prescribed cuts ranging in difficulty from the *ryo kuruma* ("pair of wheels") across the hips, to the *sodesuri* ("cutting the sleeve"), in which a hand was lopped off.

Lesser blades were tested on bundles of straw.

GALLERY

Stan Sakai's cover art for the issues collected in this volume.
Colors by Tom Luth, except on painted covers and where noted.

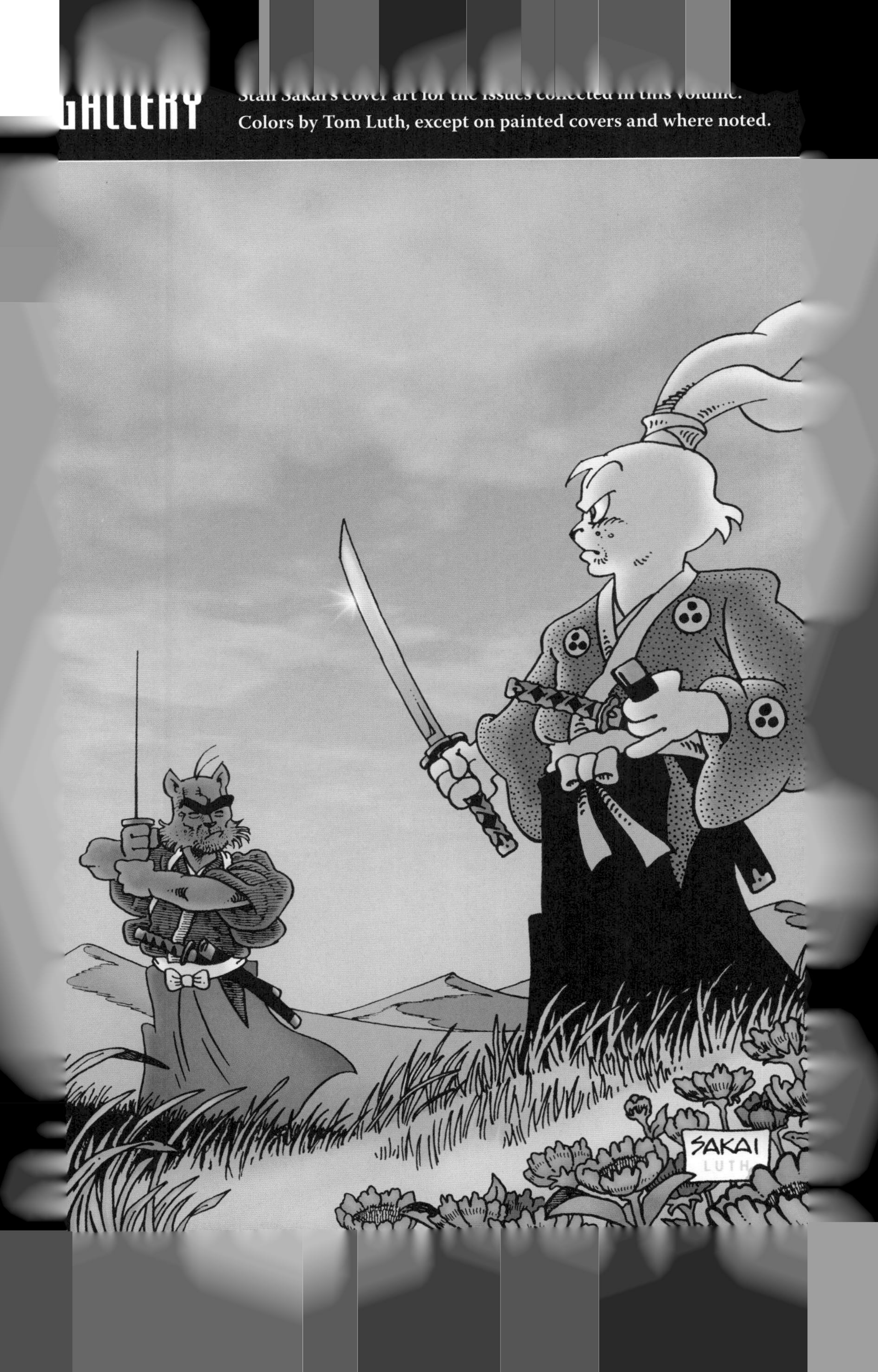
SAKAI
LUTH

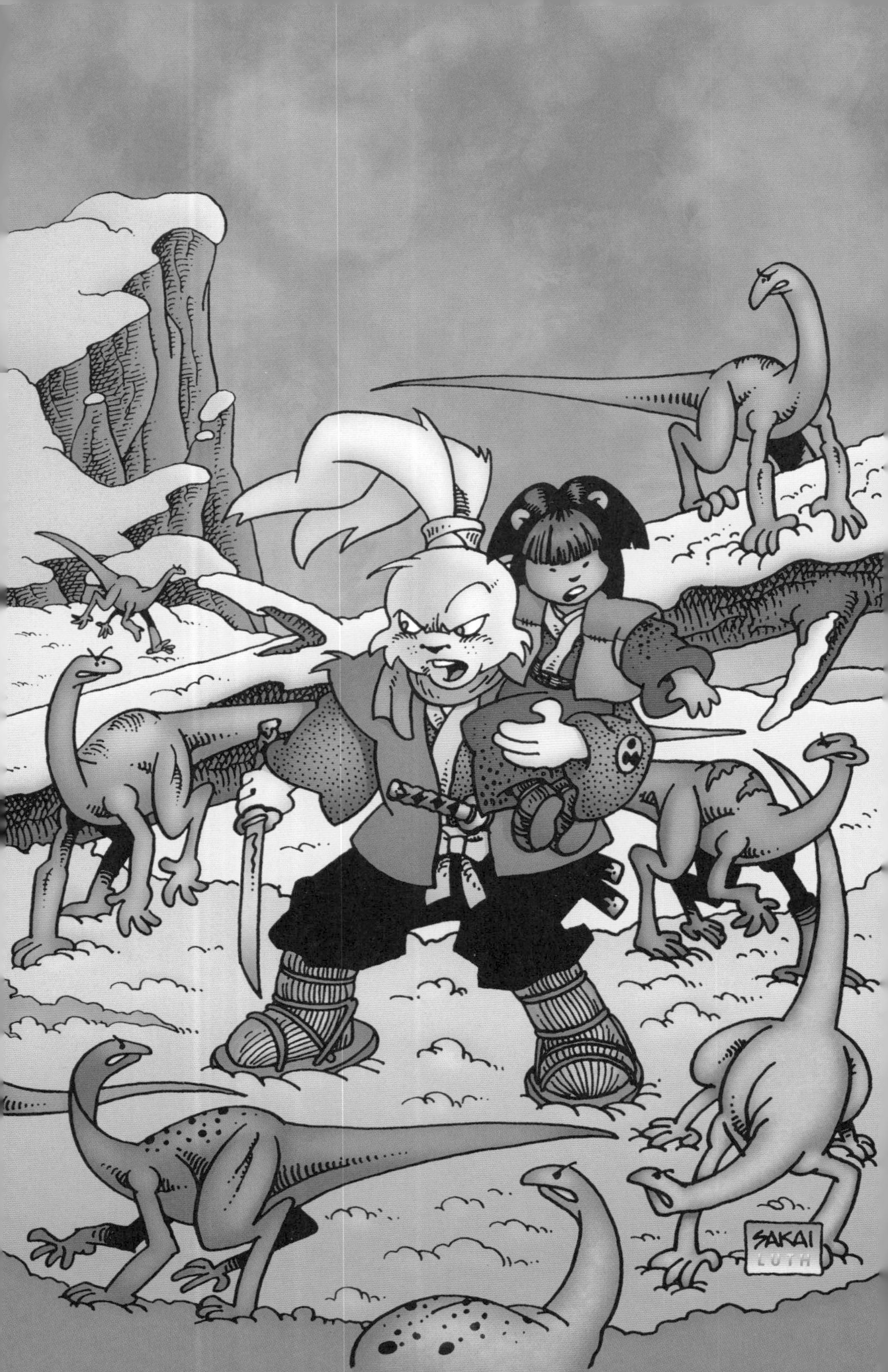
SAKAI
LUTH

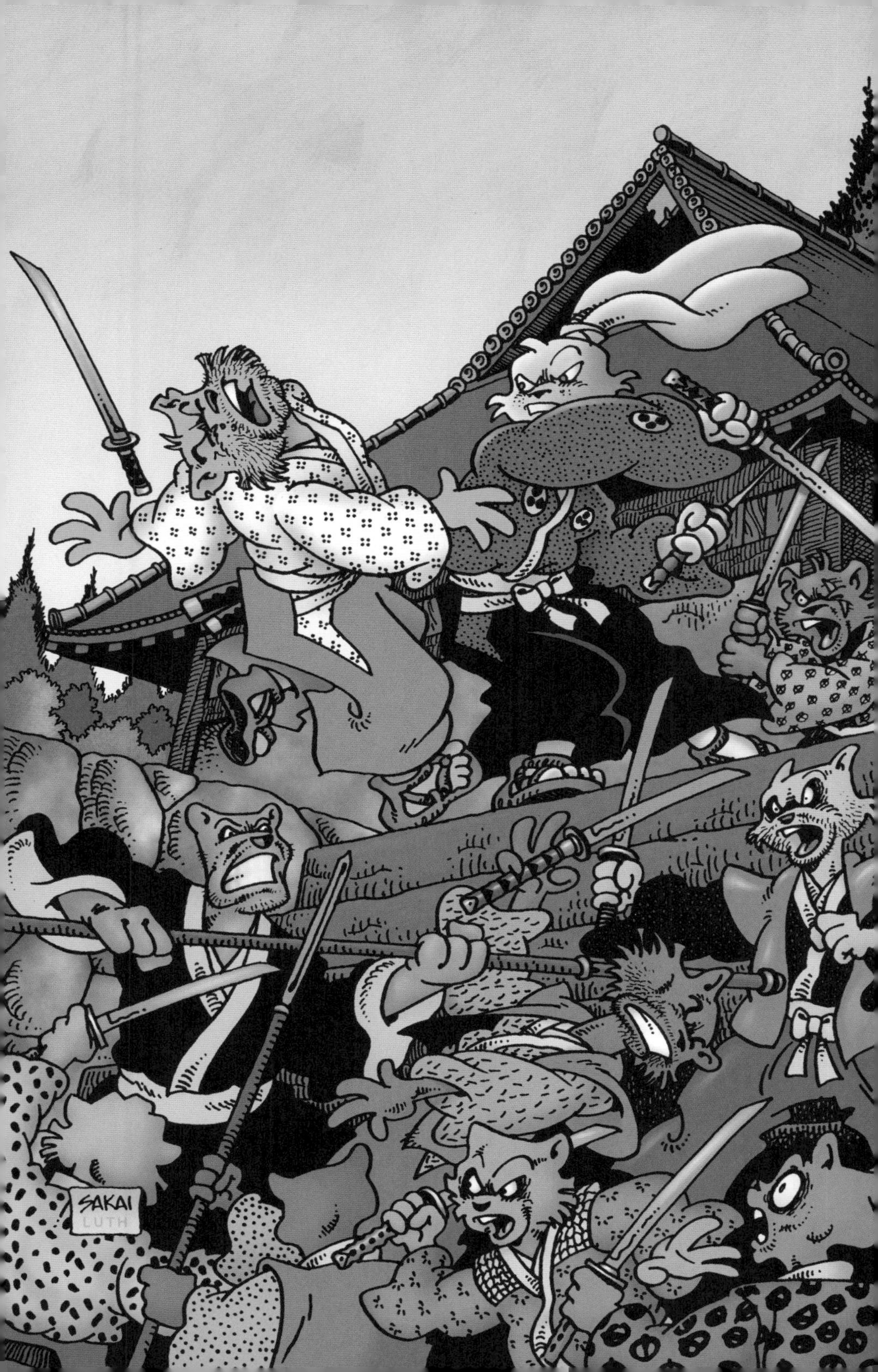
SAKAI
LUTH

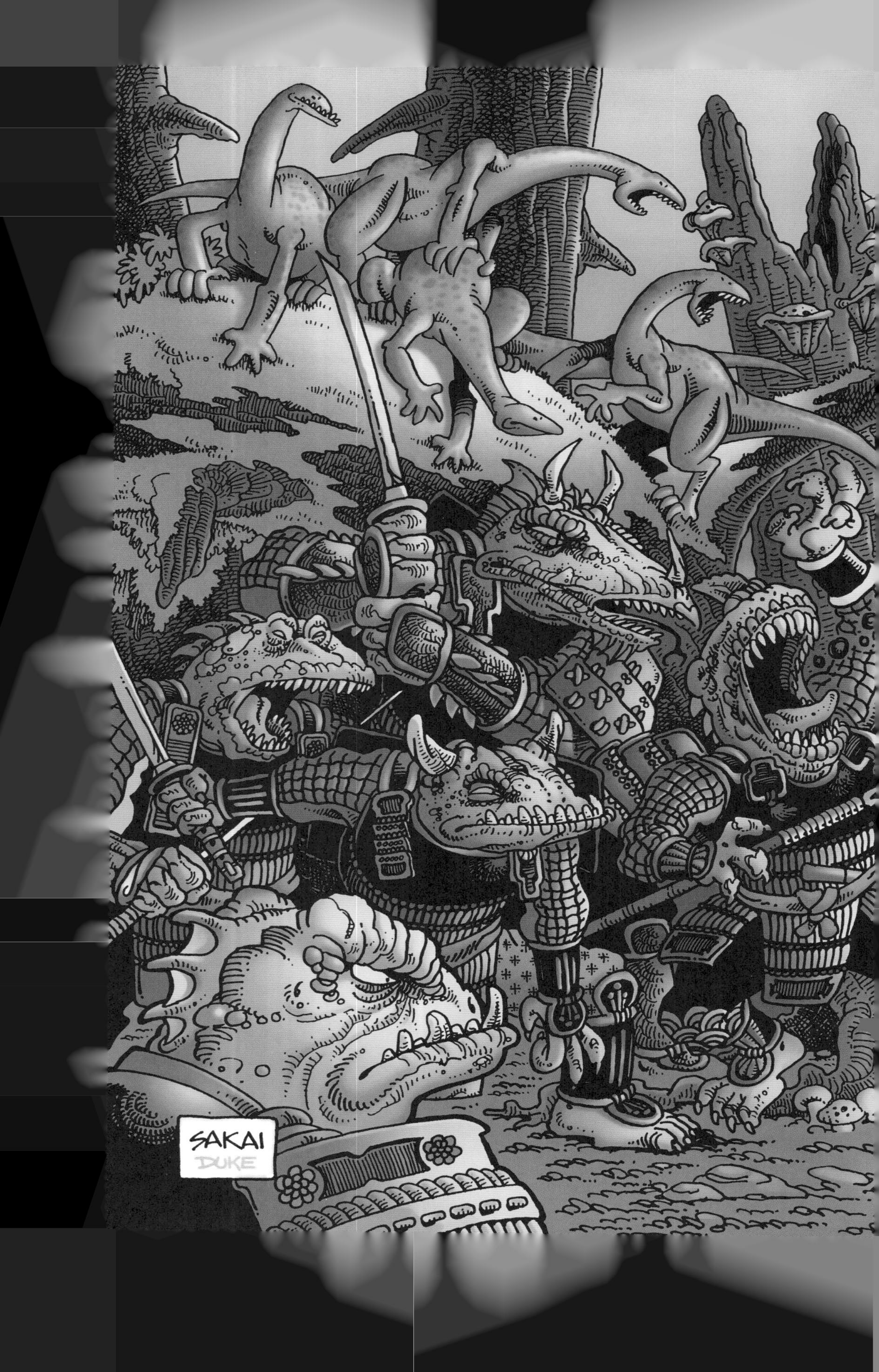
SAKAI
DUKE

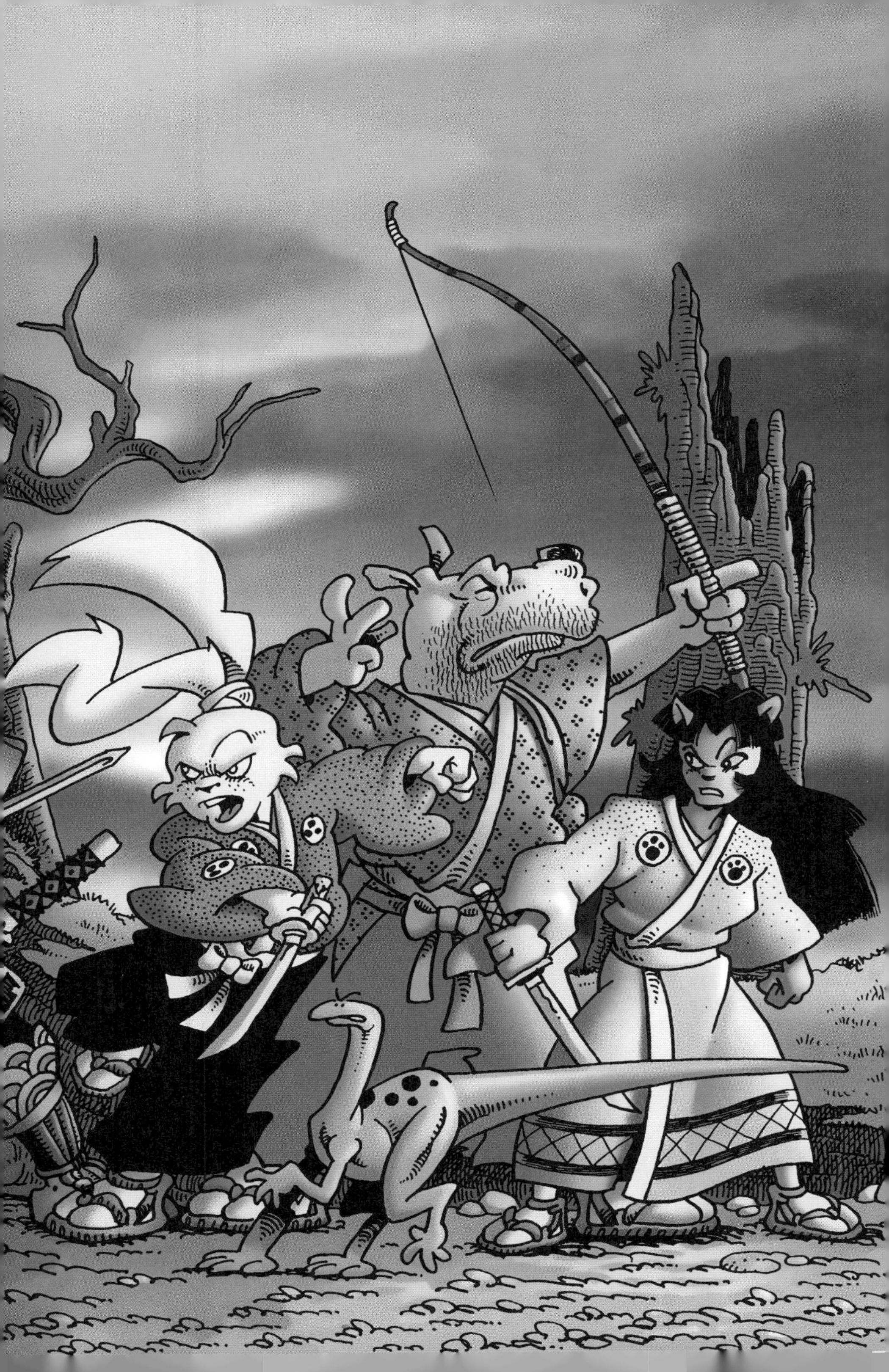

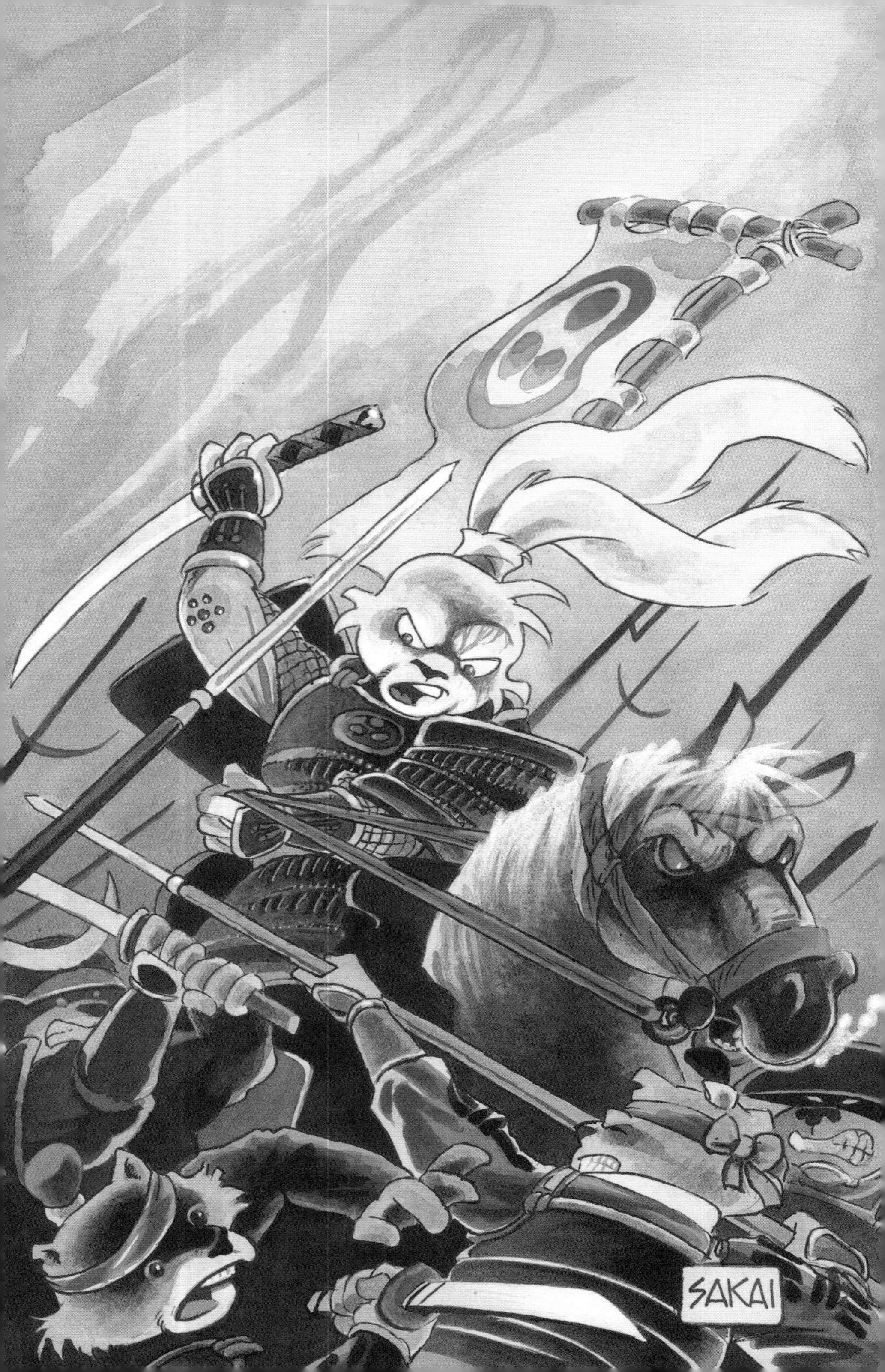
SAKAI

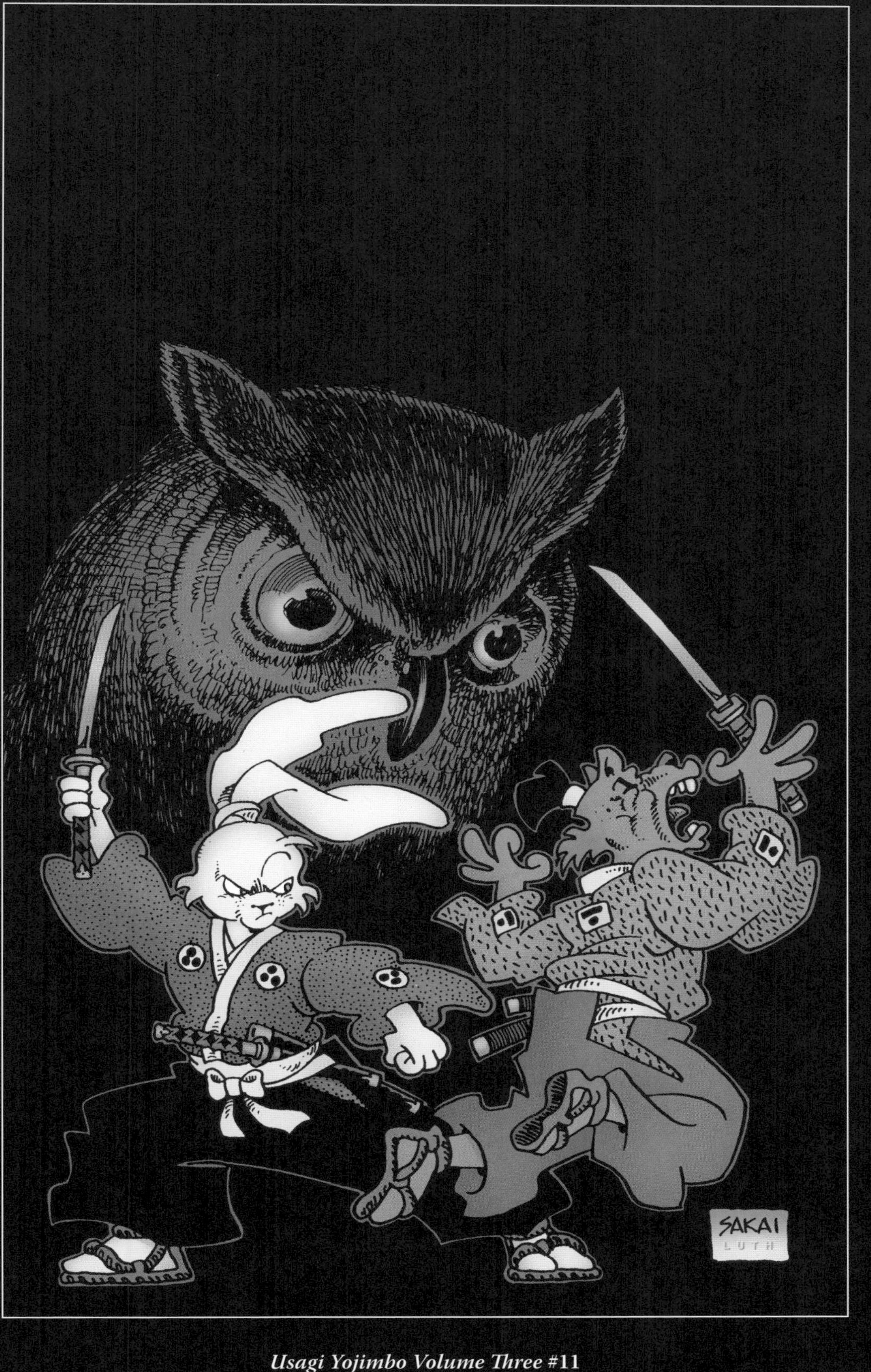
SAKAI
LUTH

Usagi Yojimbo Volume Three #11

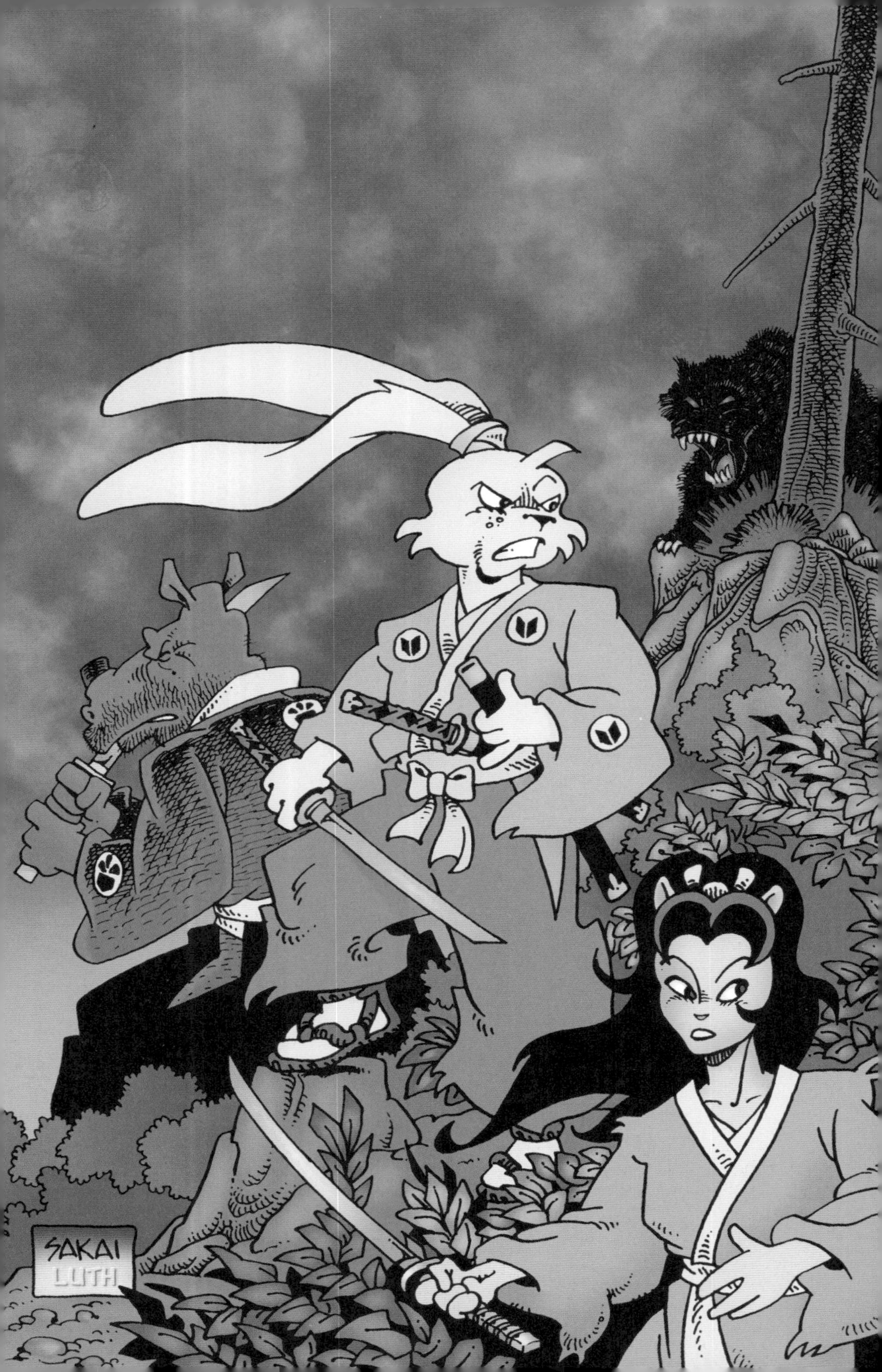
SAKAI
LUTH

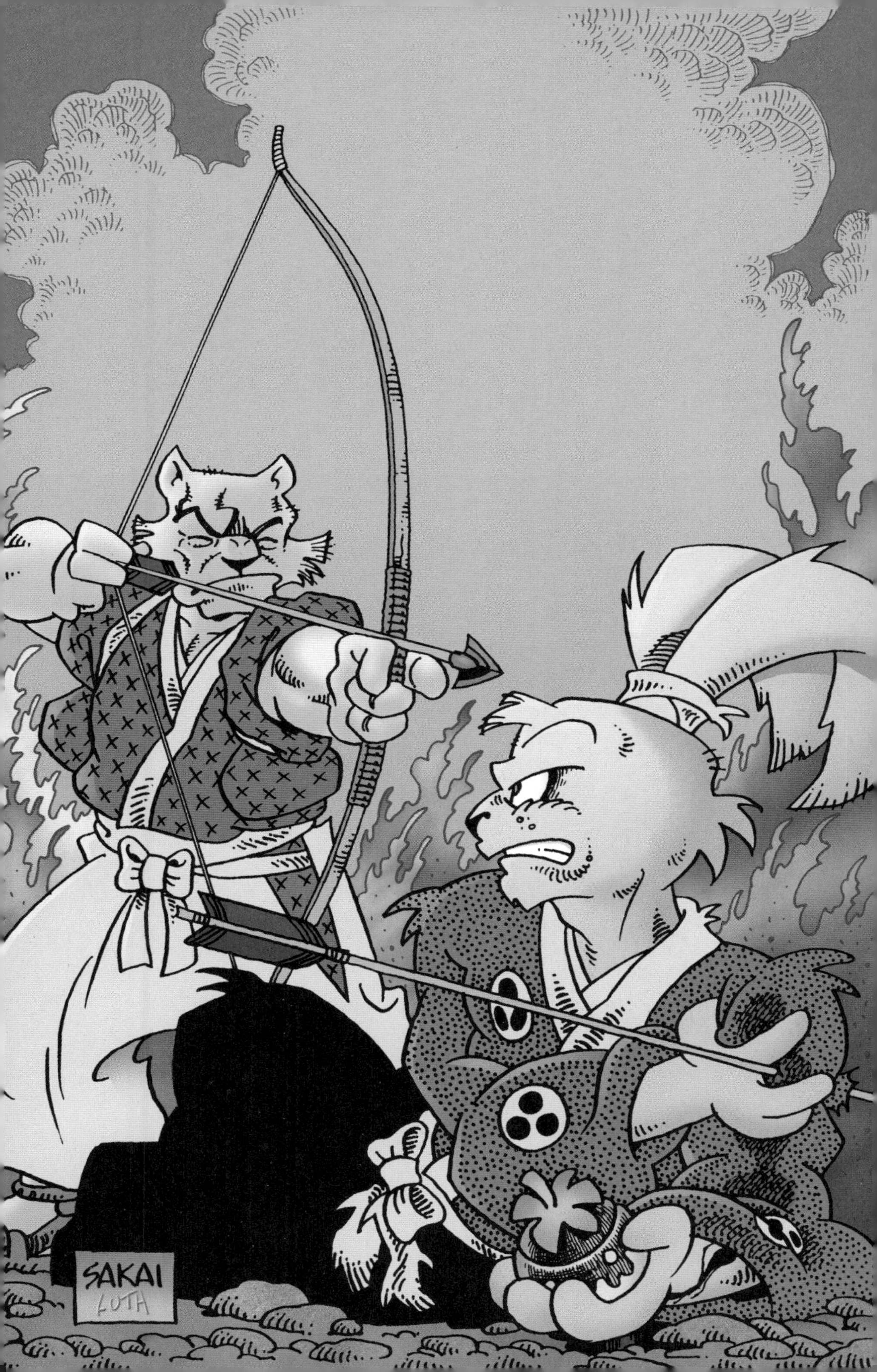
SAKAI
LOTH

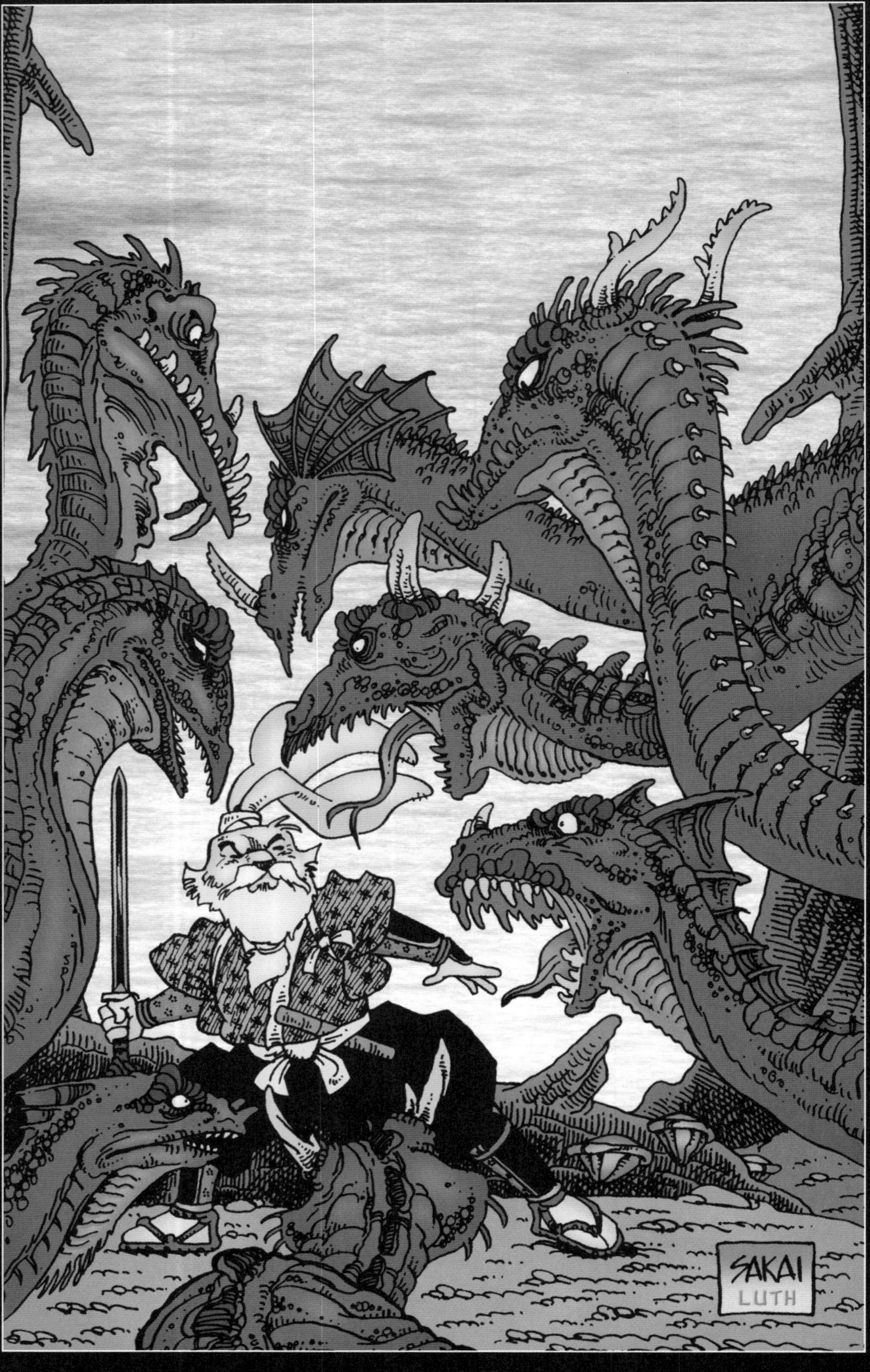
SAKAI
LUTH
Usagi Yojimbo Volume Three #13

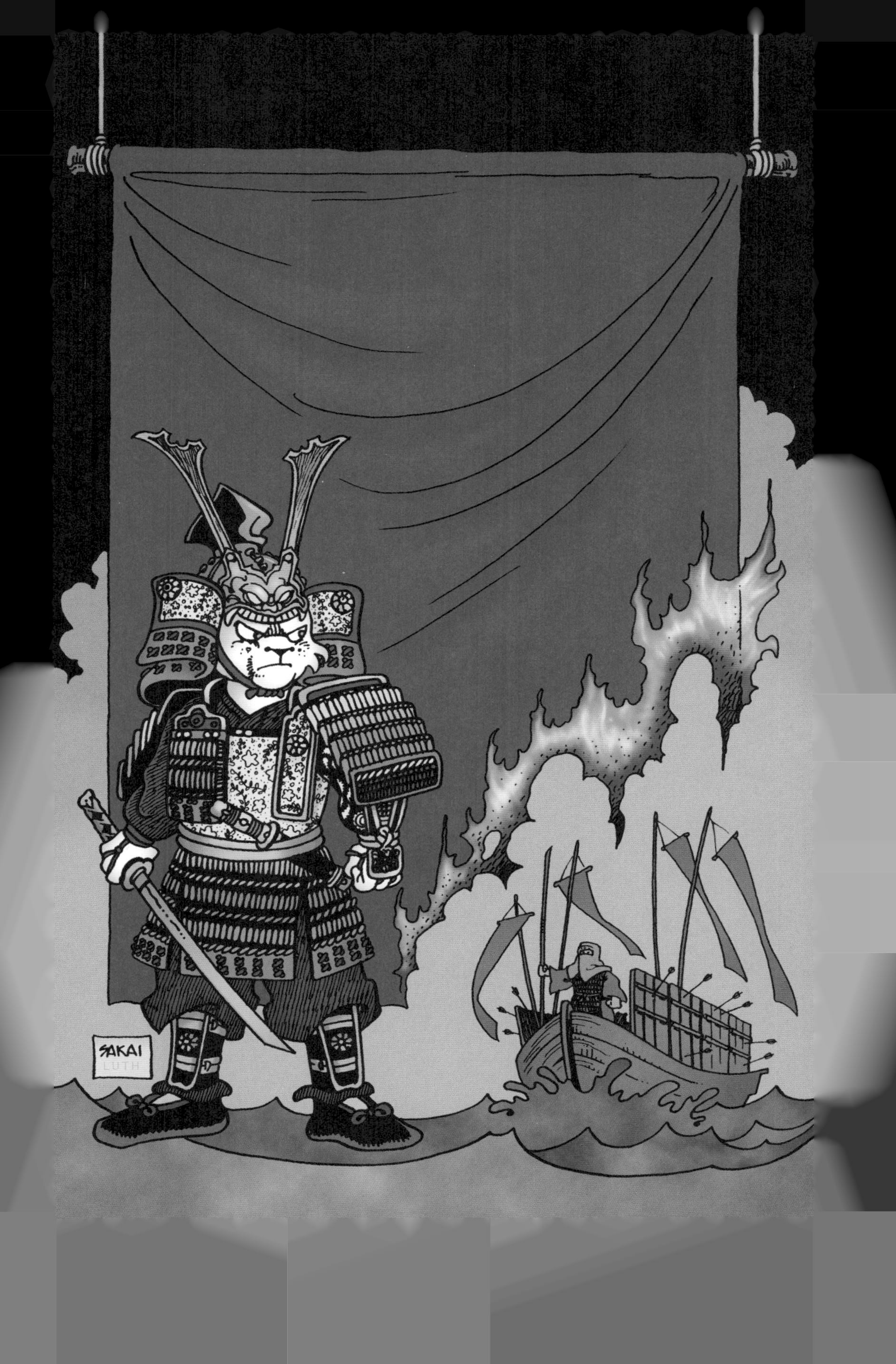
SAKAI
LUTH

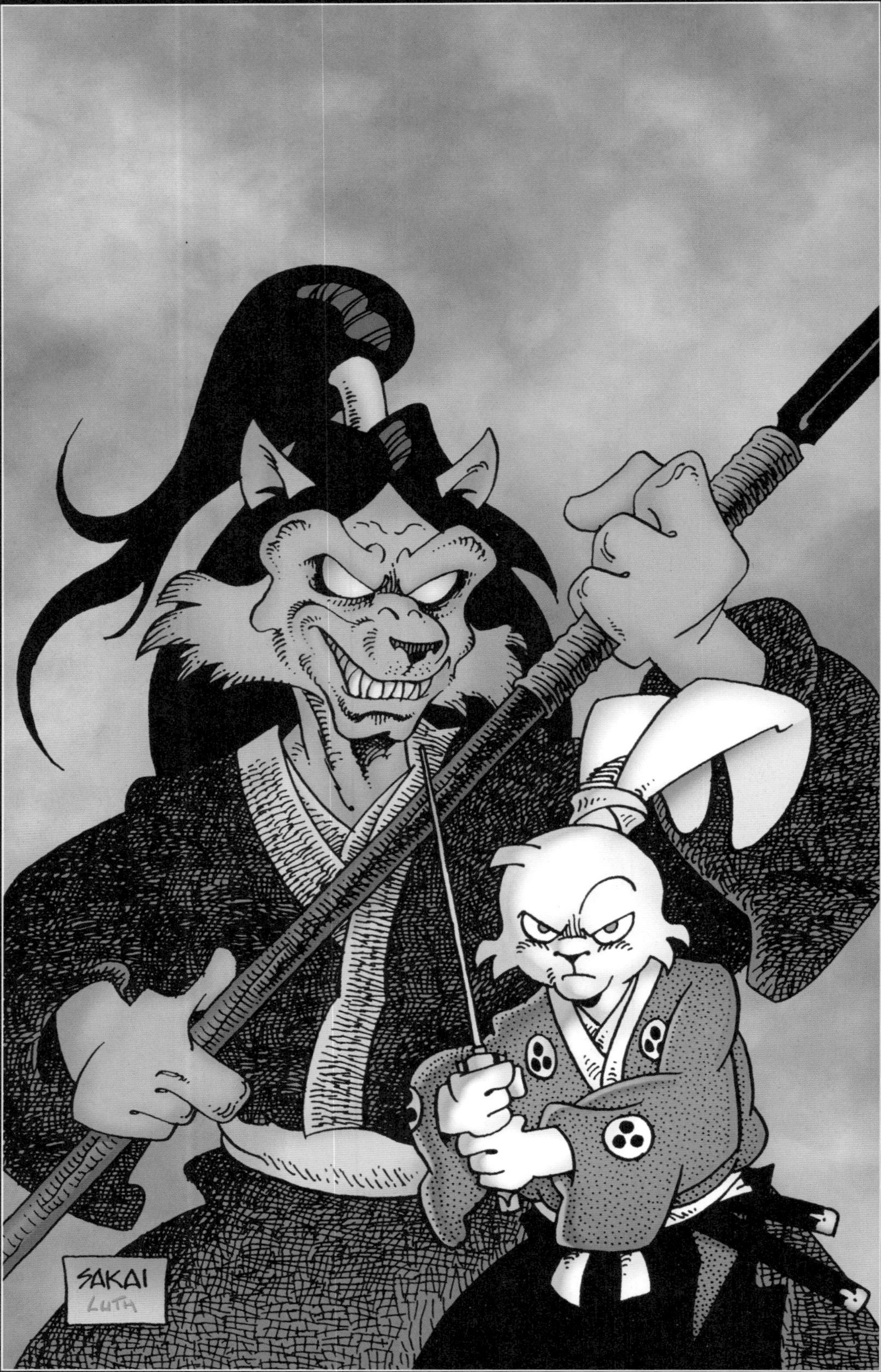
SAKAI
LUTH

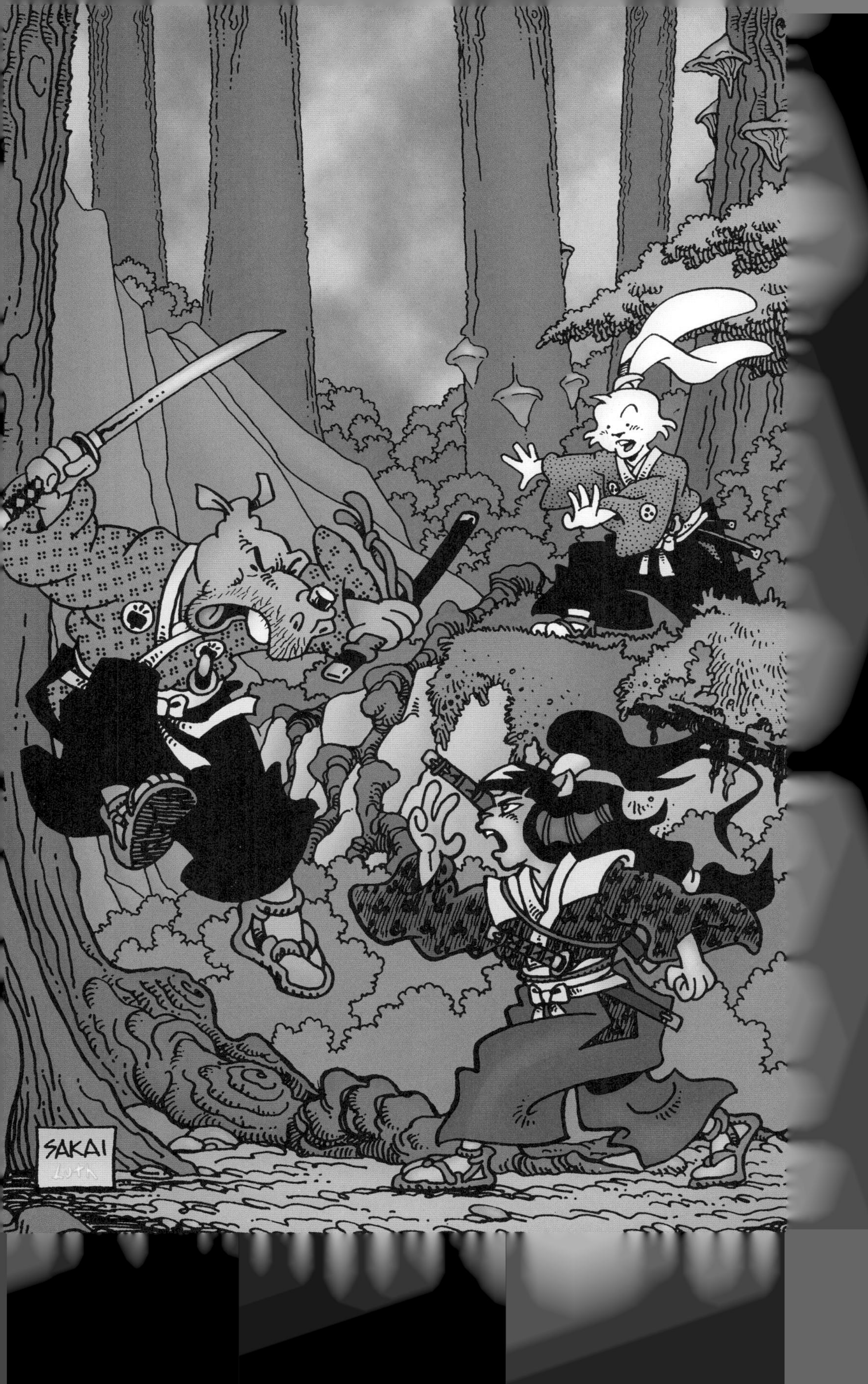
SAKAI

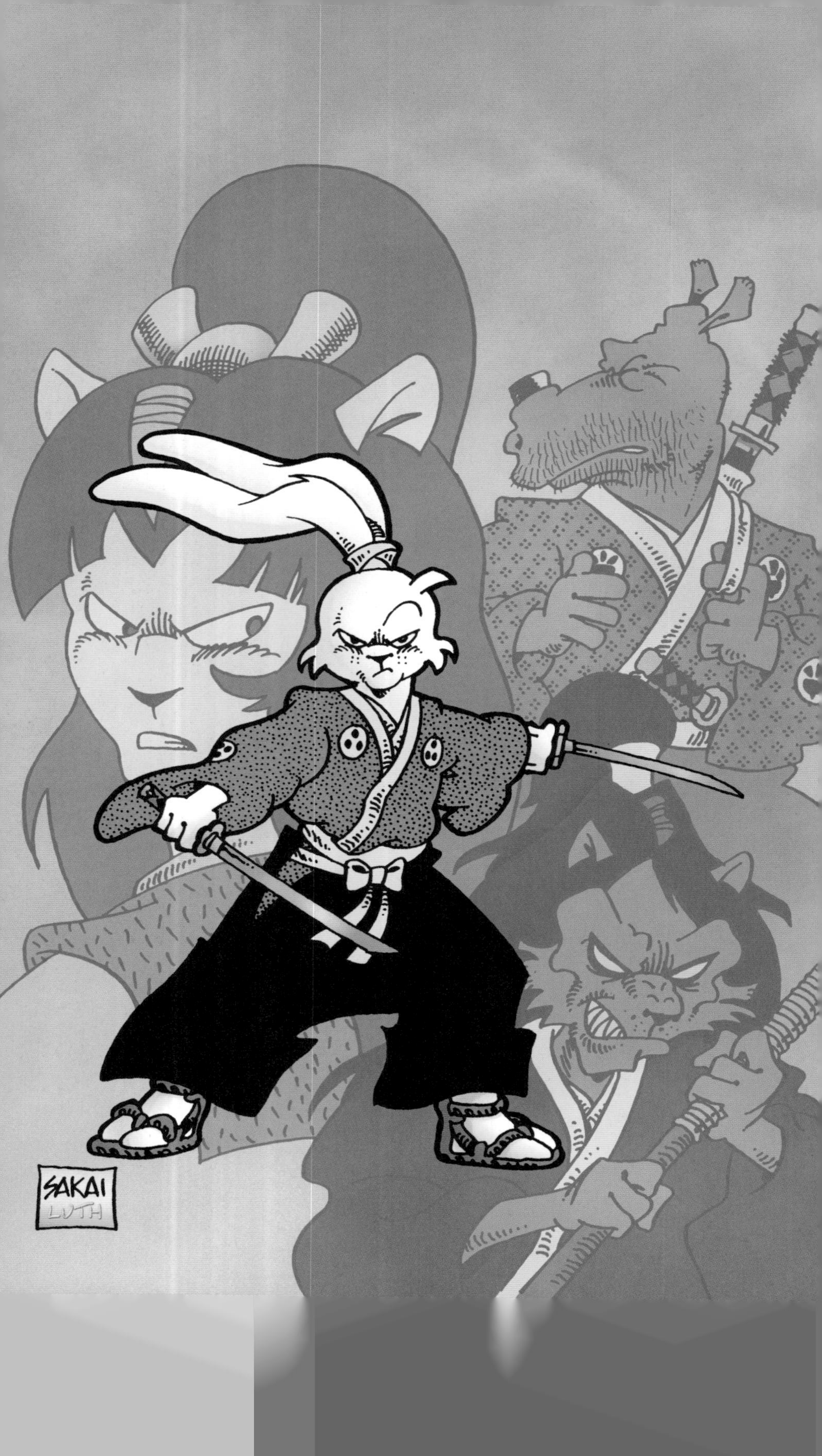
SAKAI
LUTH

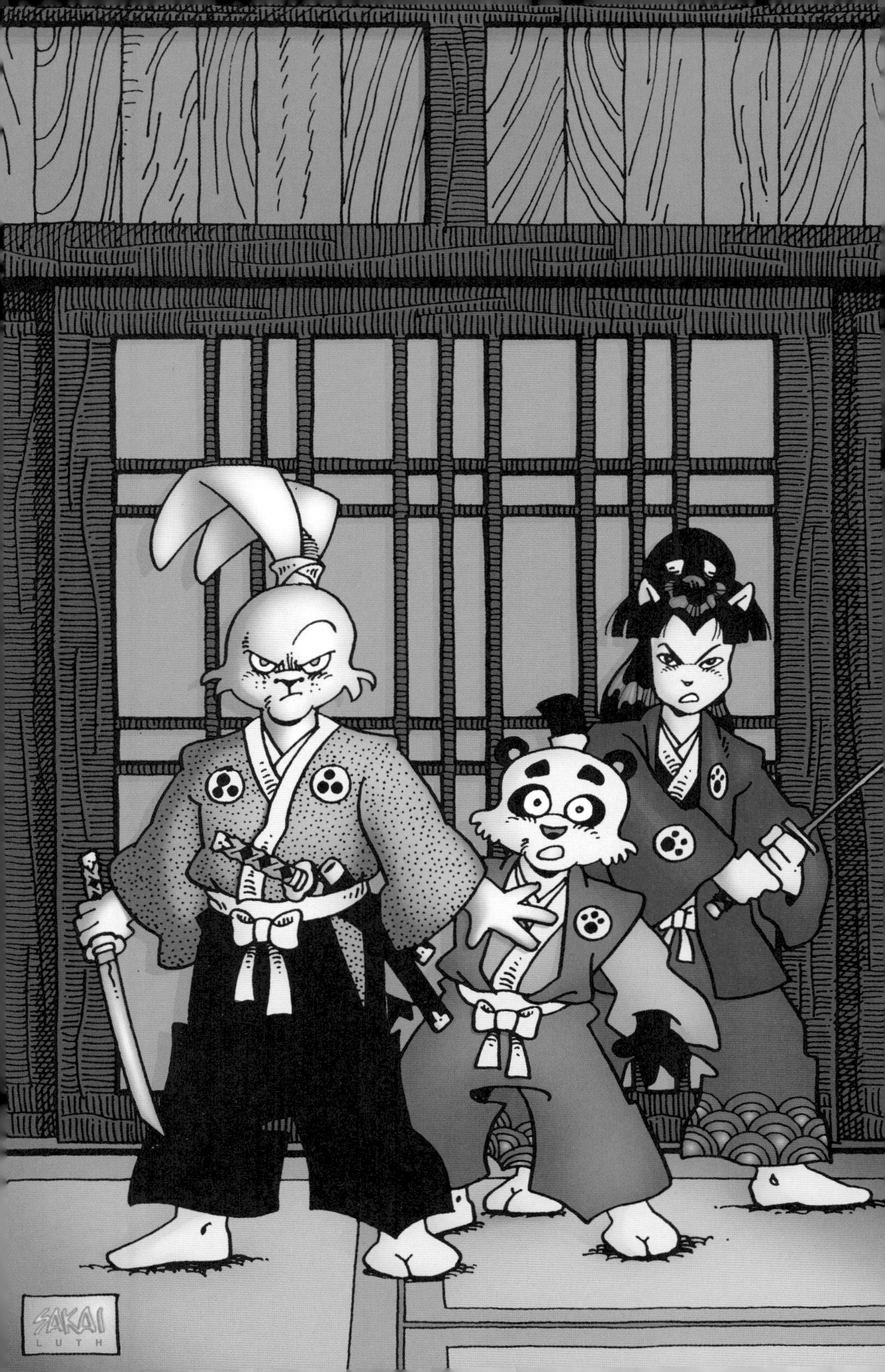
SAKAI
LUTH

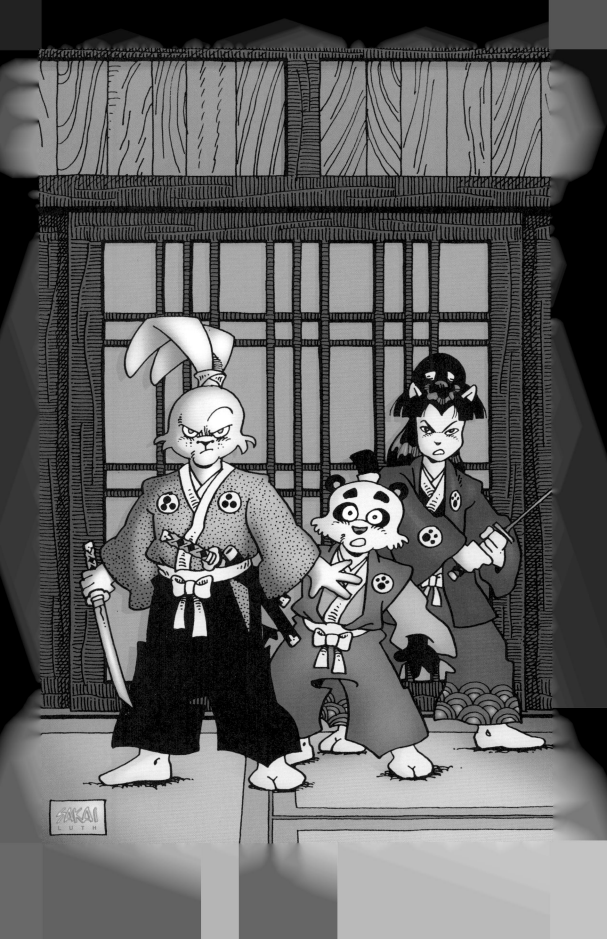

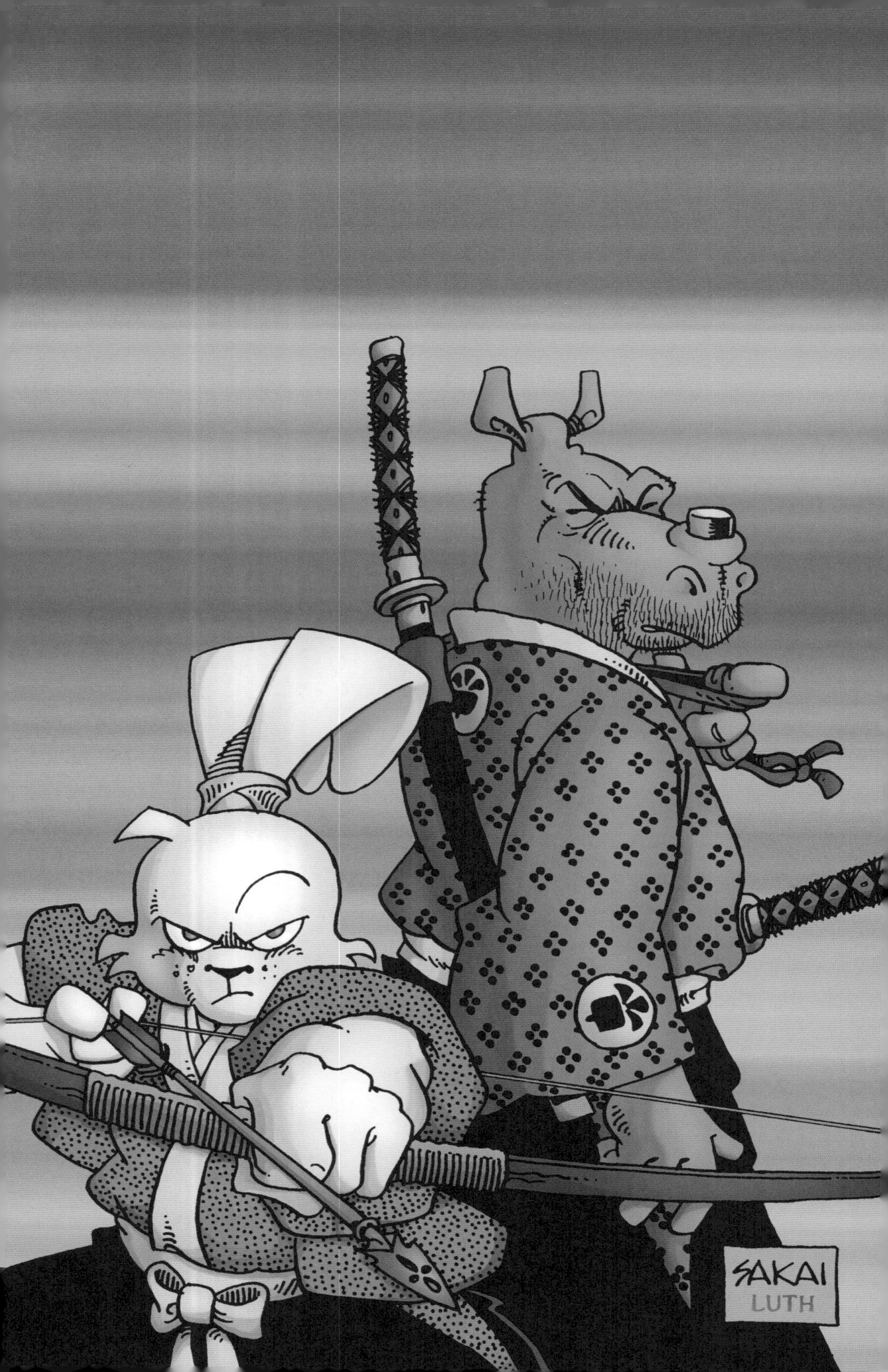
SAKAI
LUTH

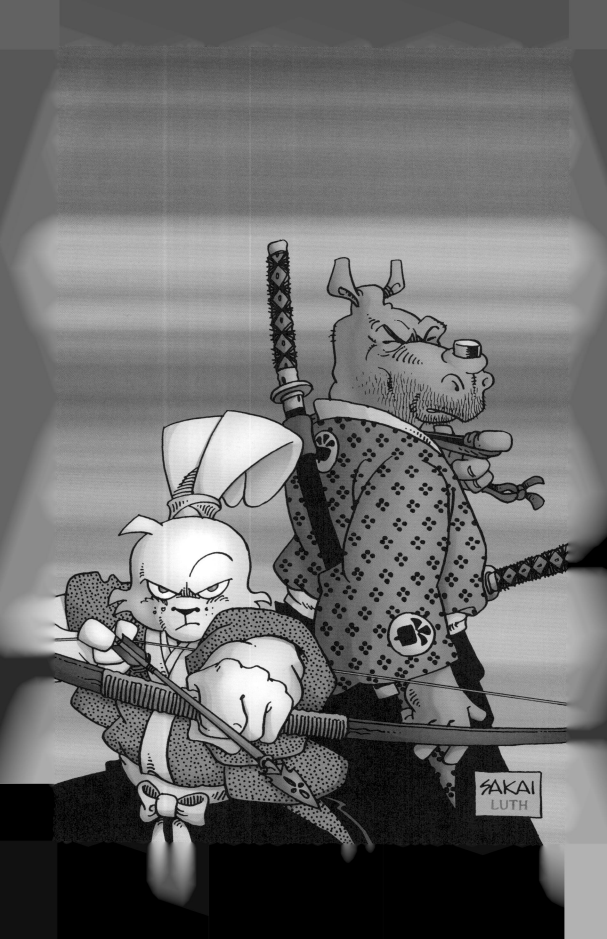

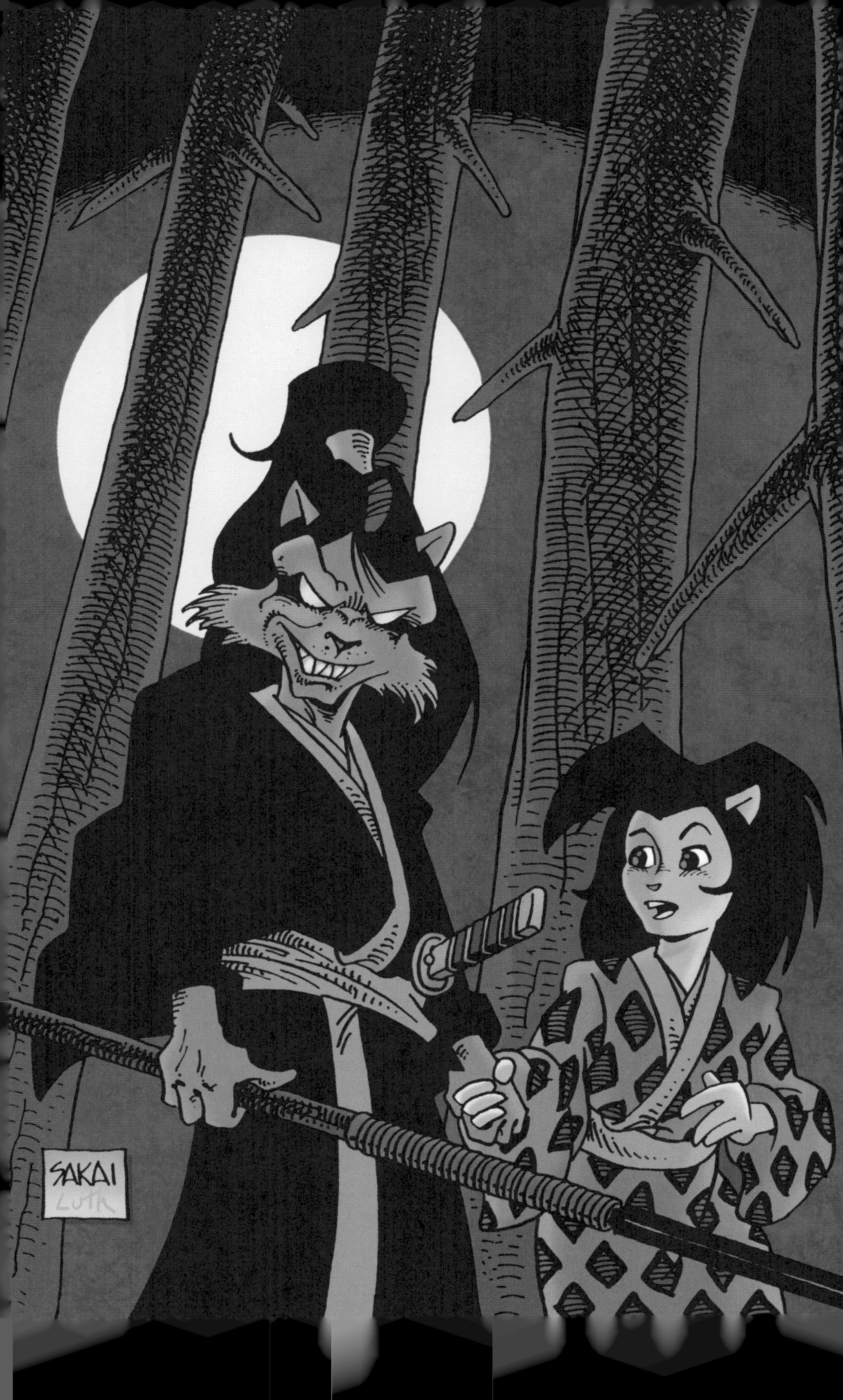
SAKAI
Luth

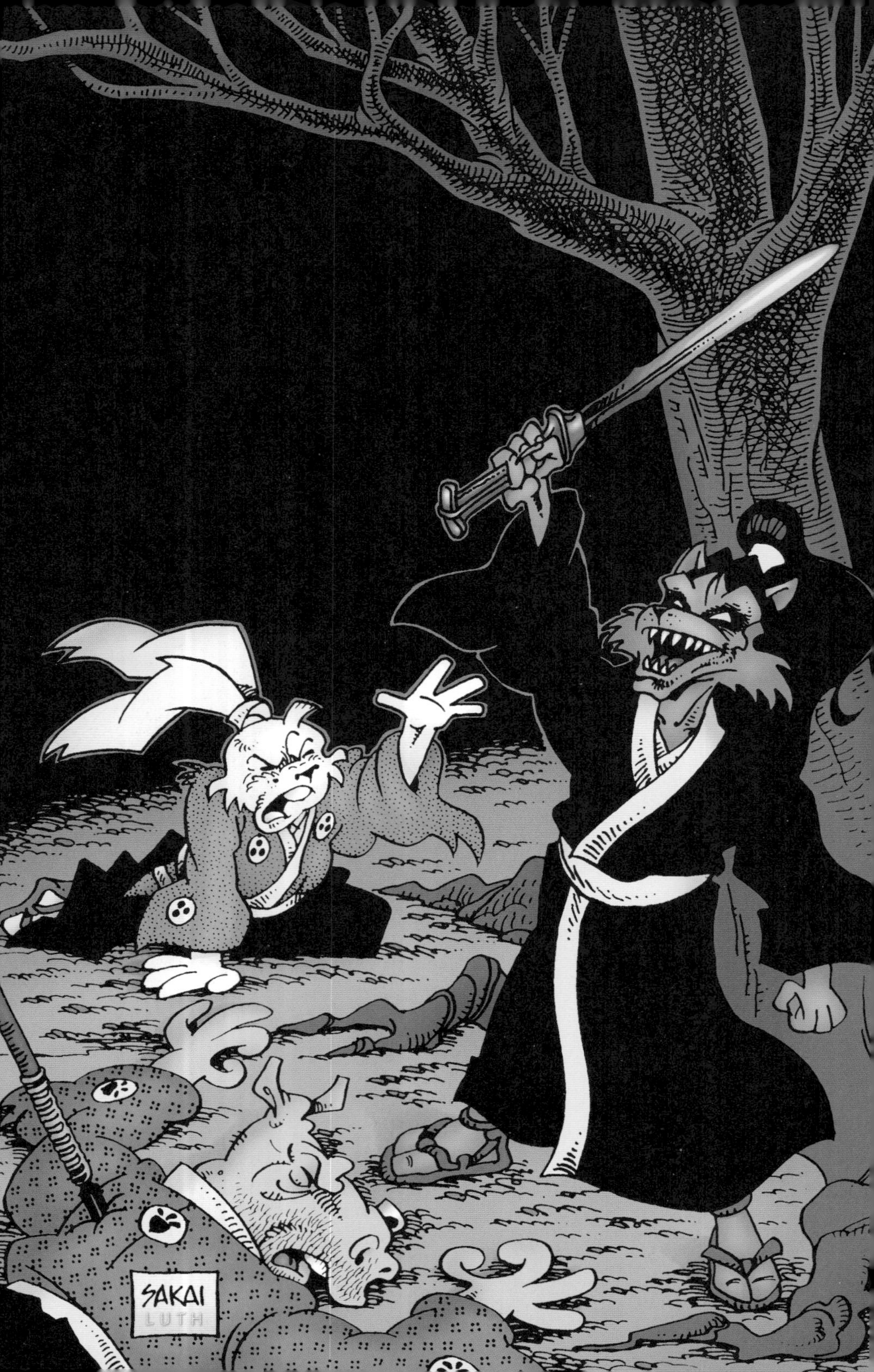
SAKAI
LUTH

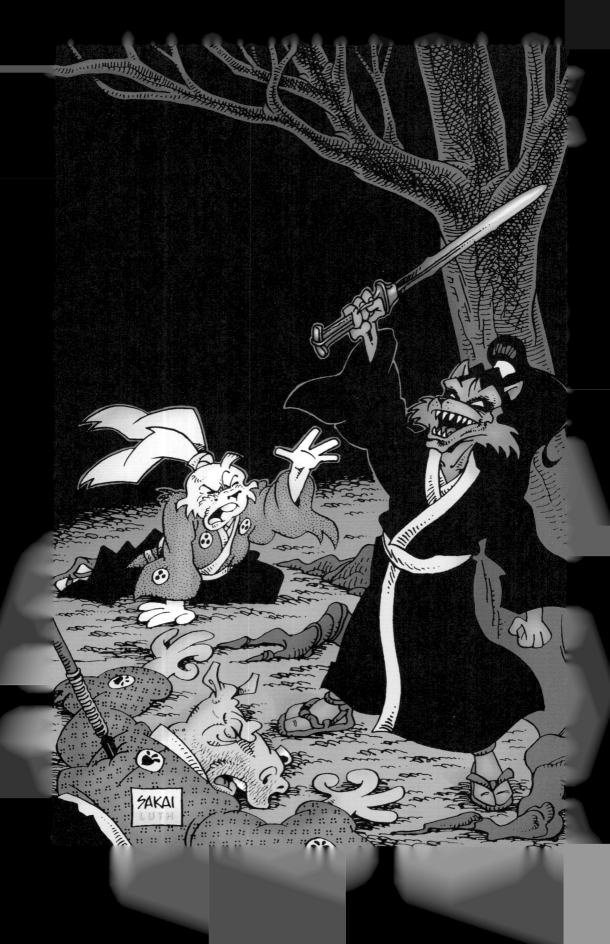

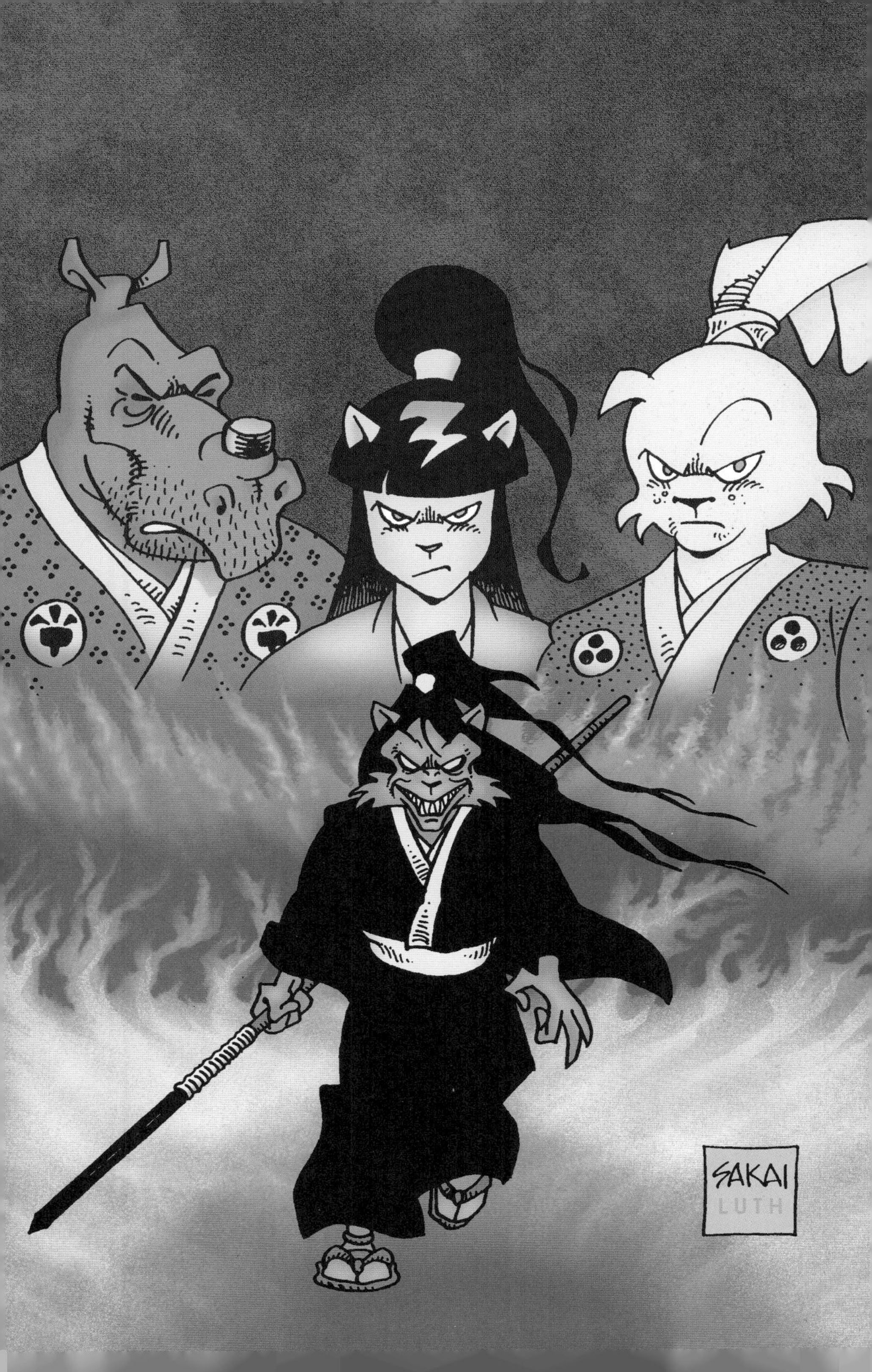
SAKAI
LUTH

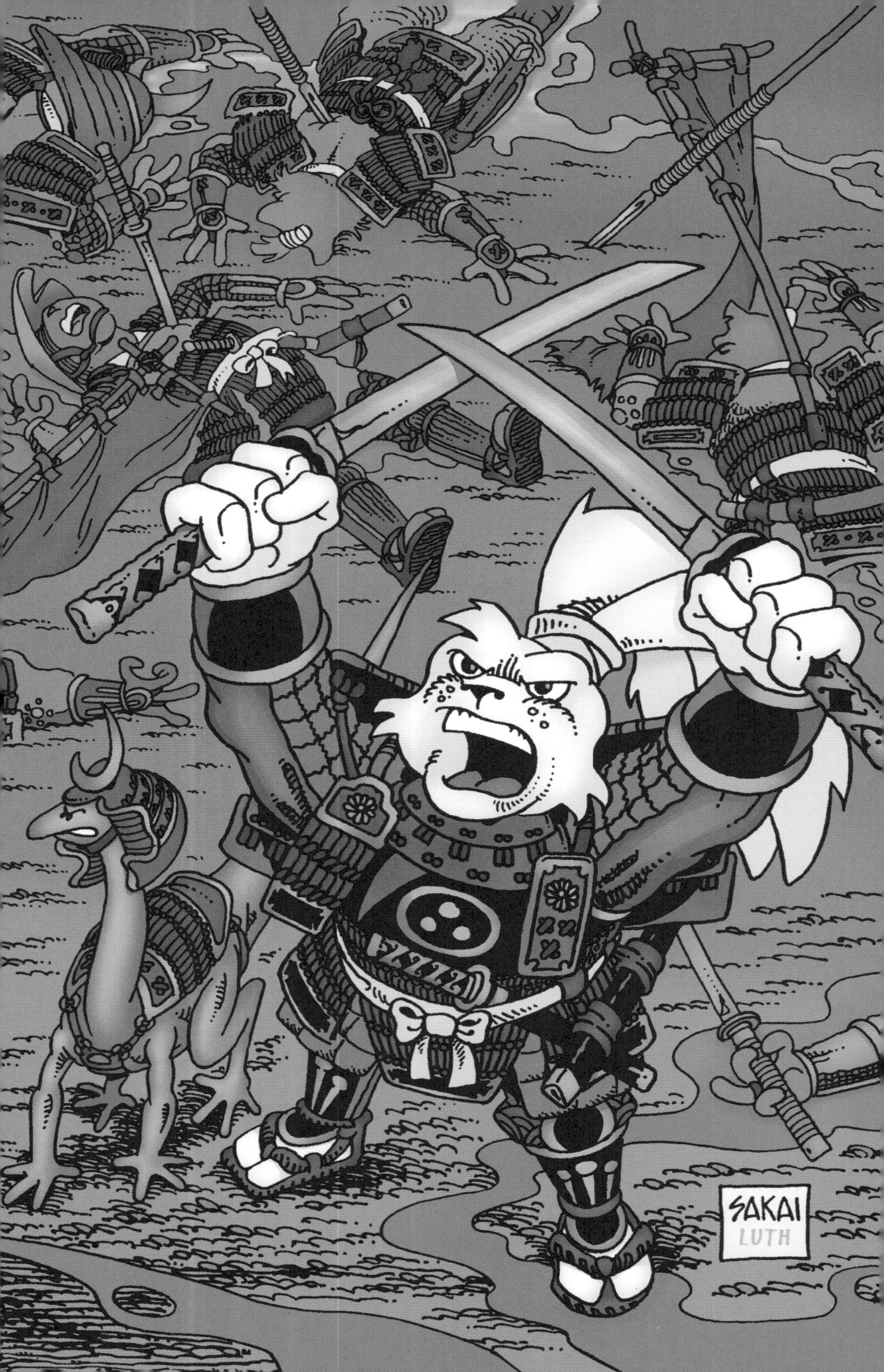
SAKAI
LUTH

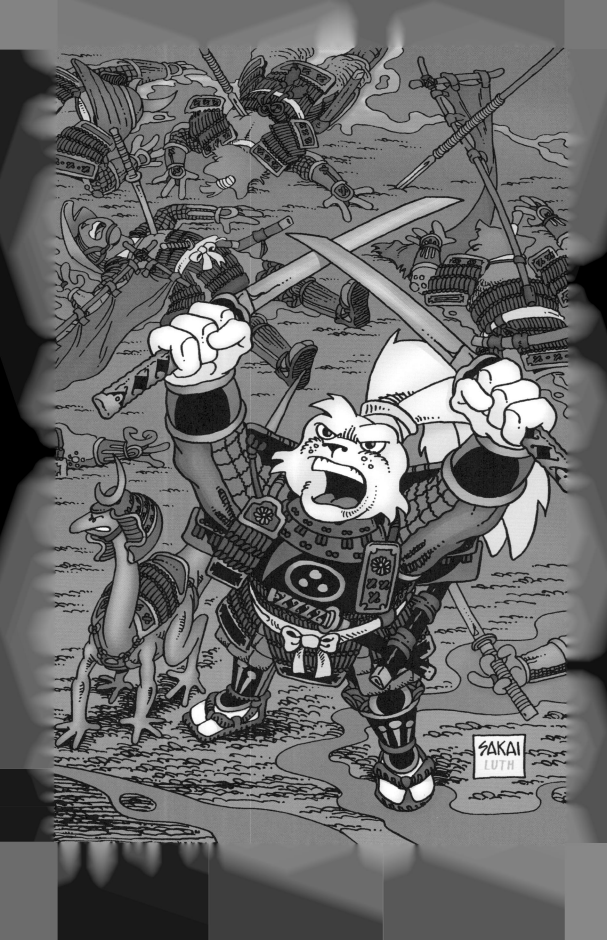

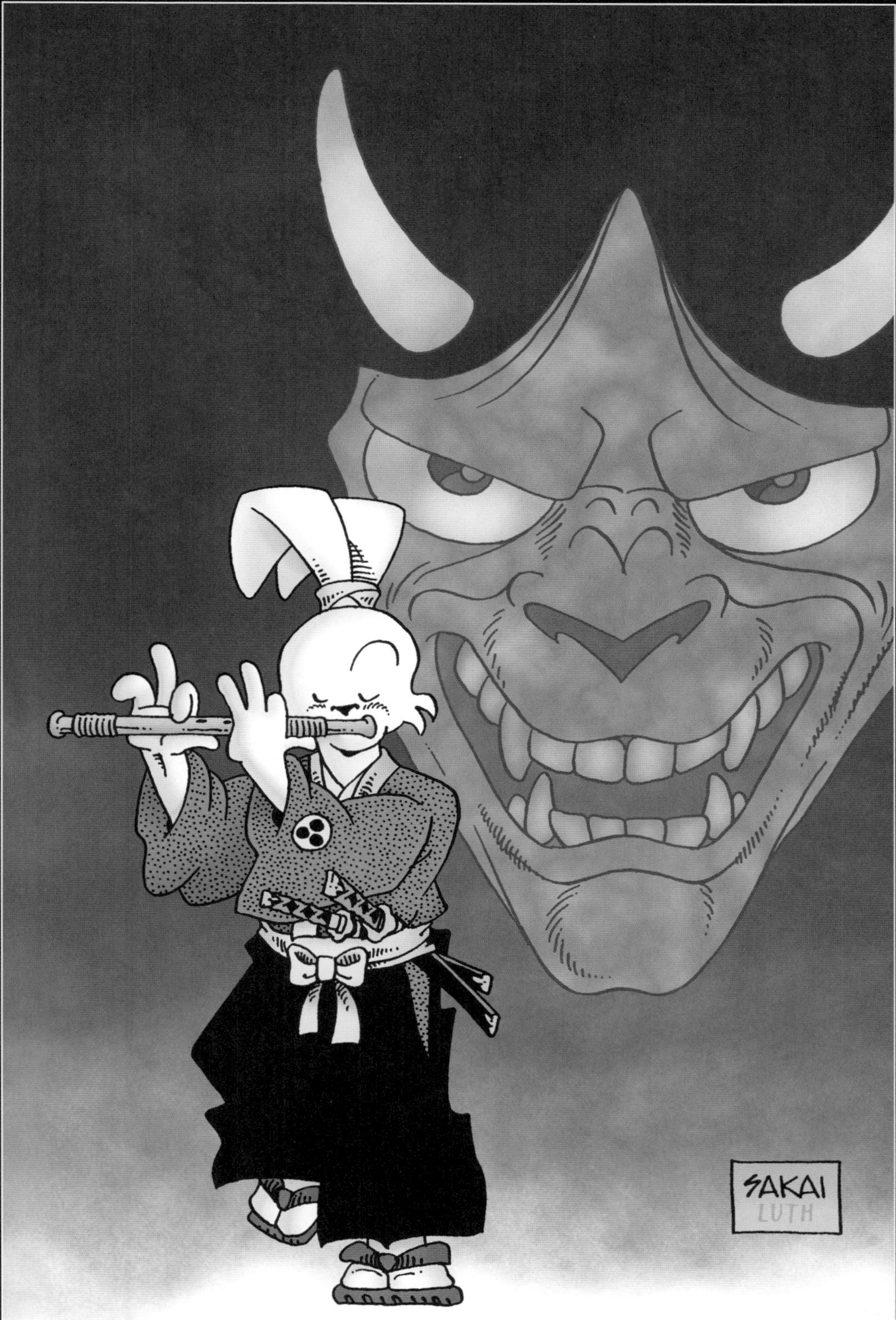
SAKAI
LUTH

Usagi Yojimbo Volume Three #24

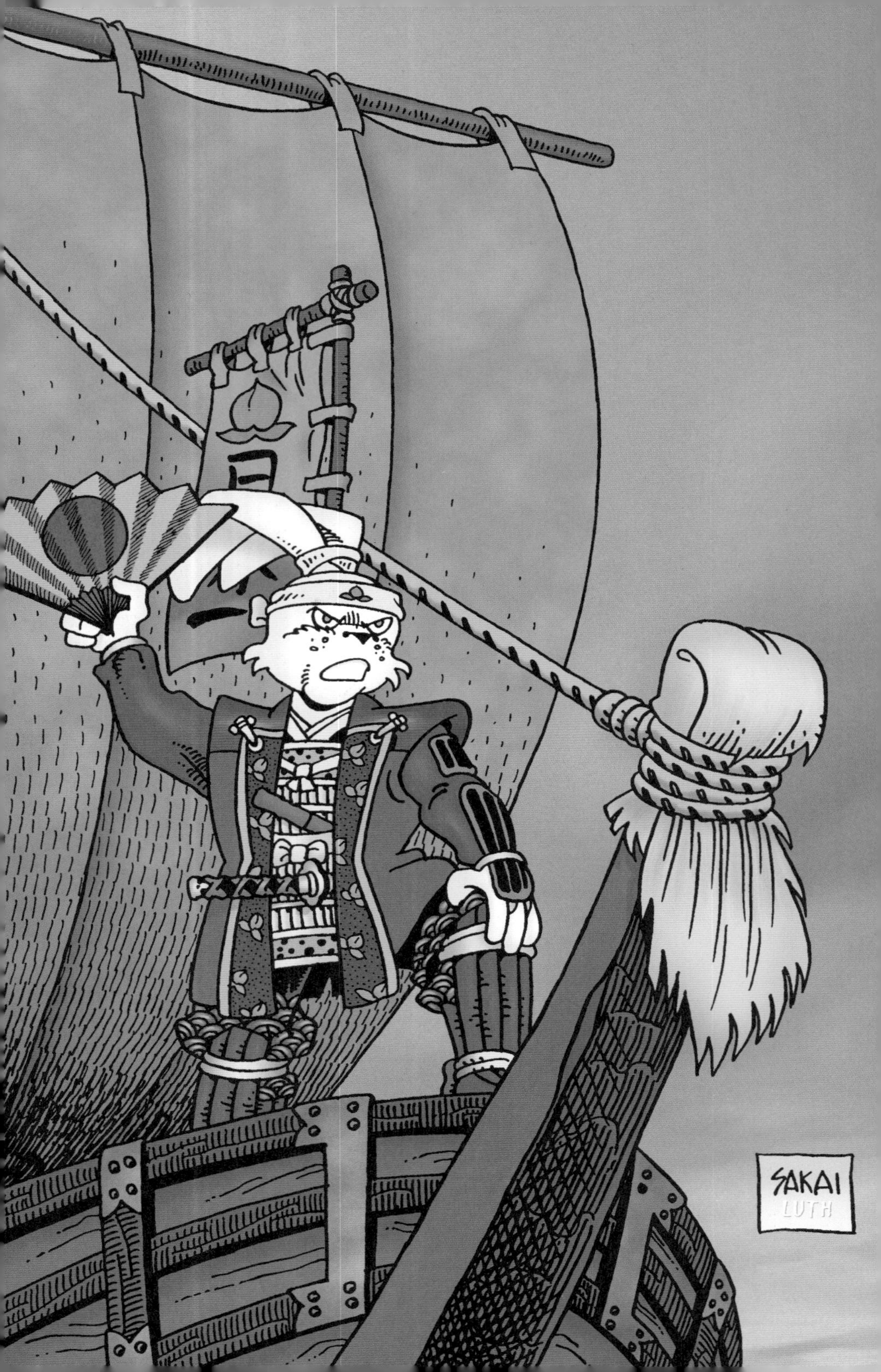
SAKAI
LUTH

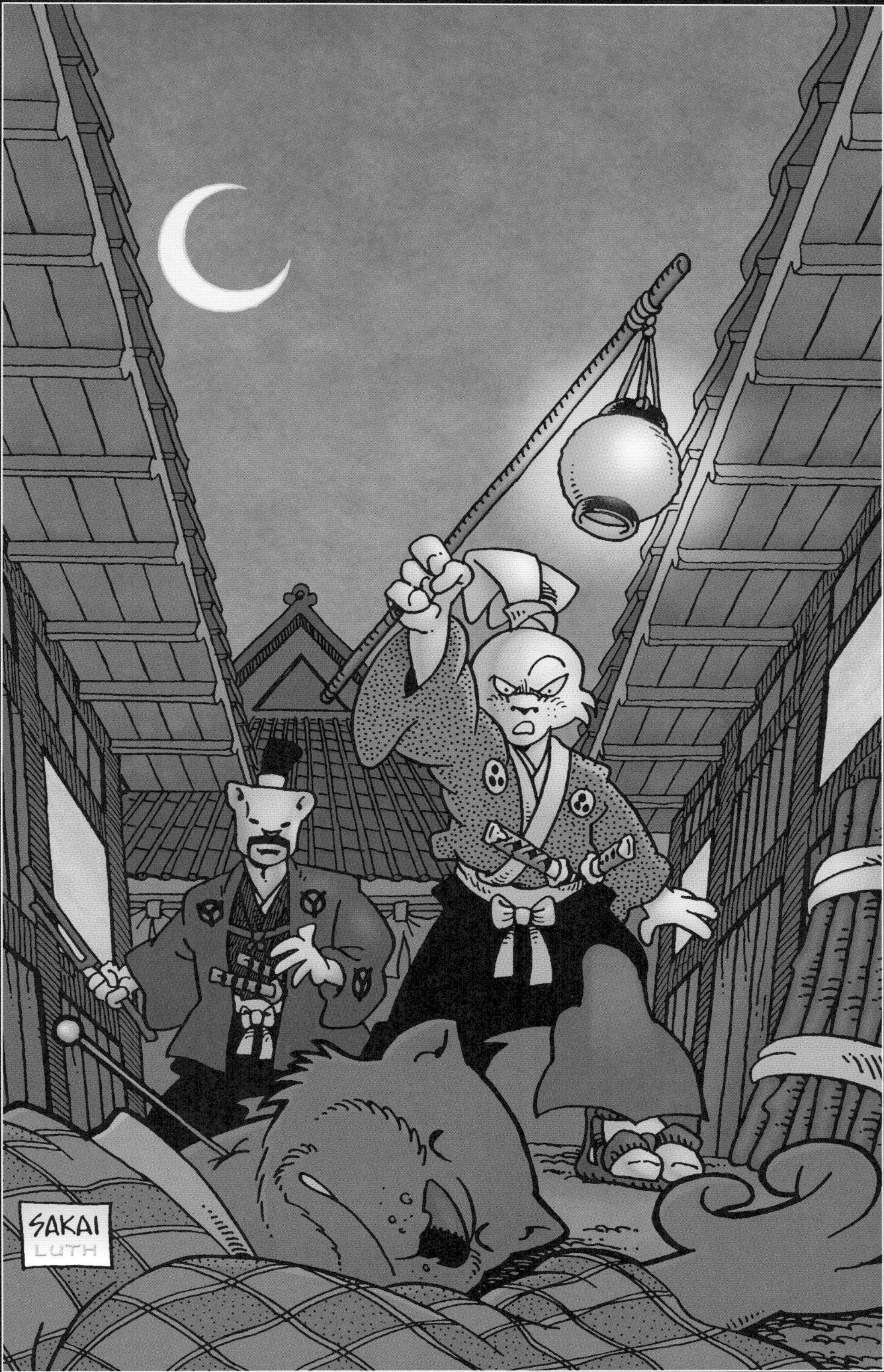
SAKAI
LUTH

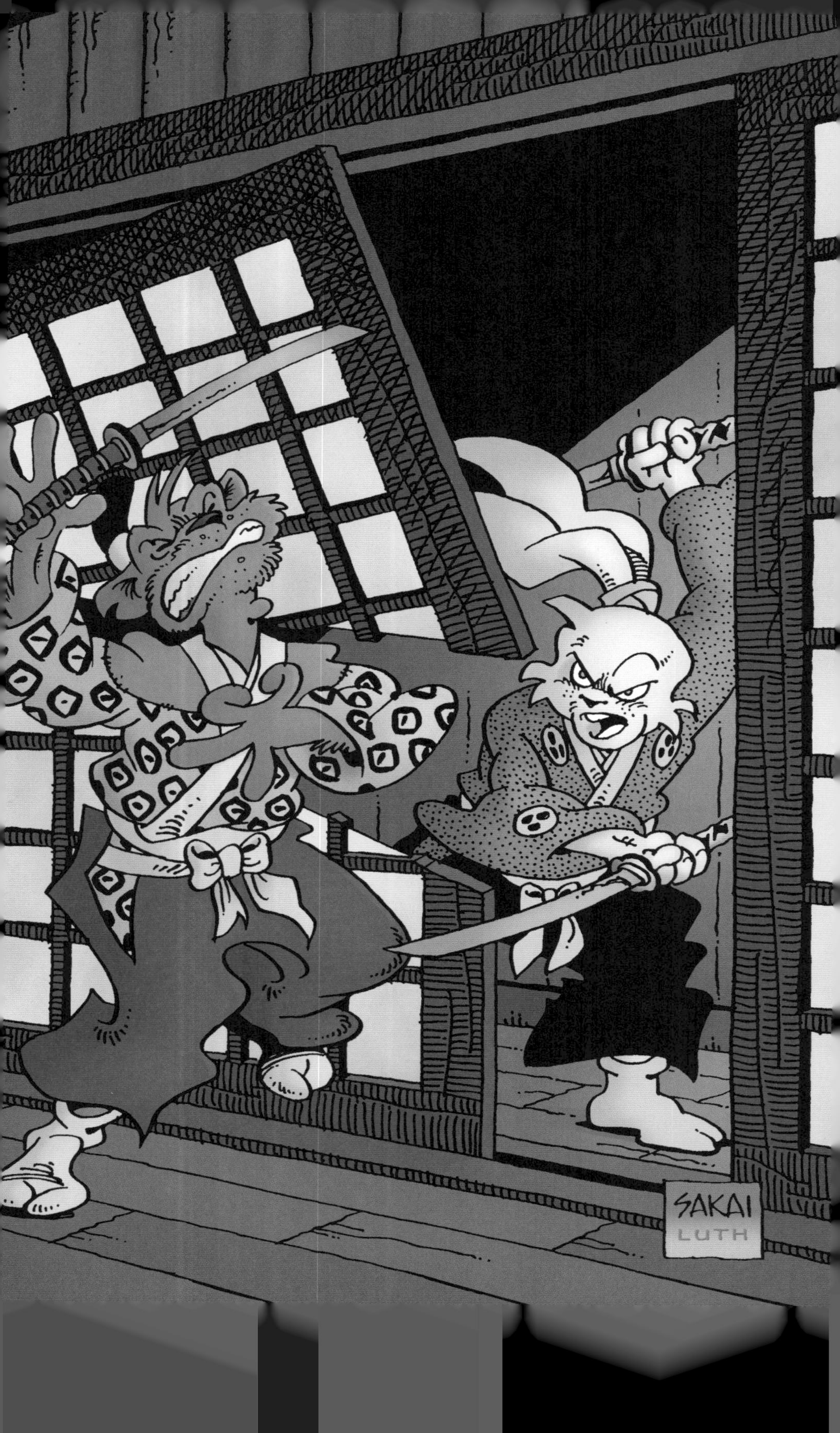
SAKAI
LUTH

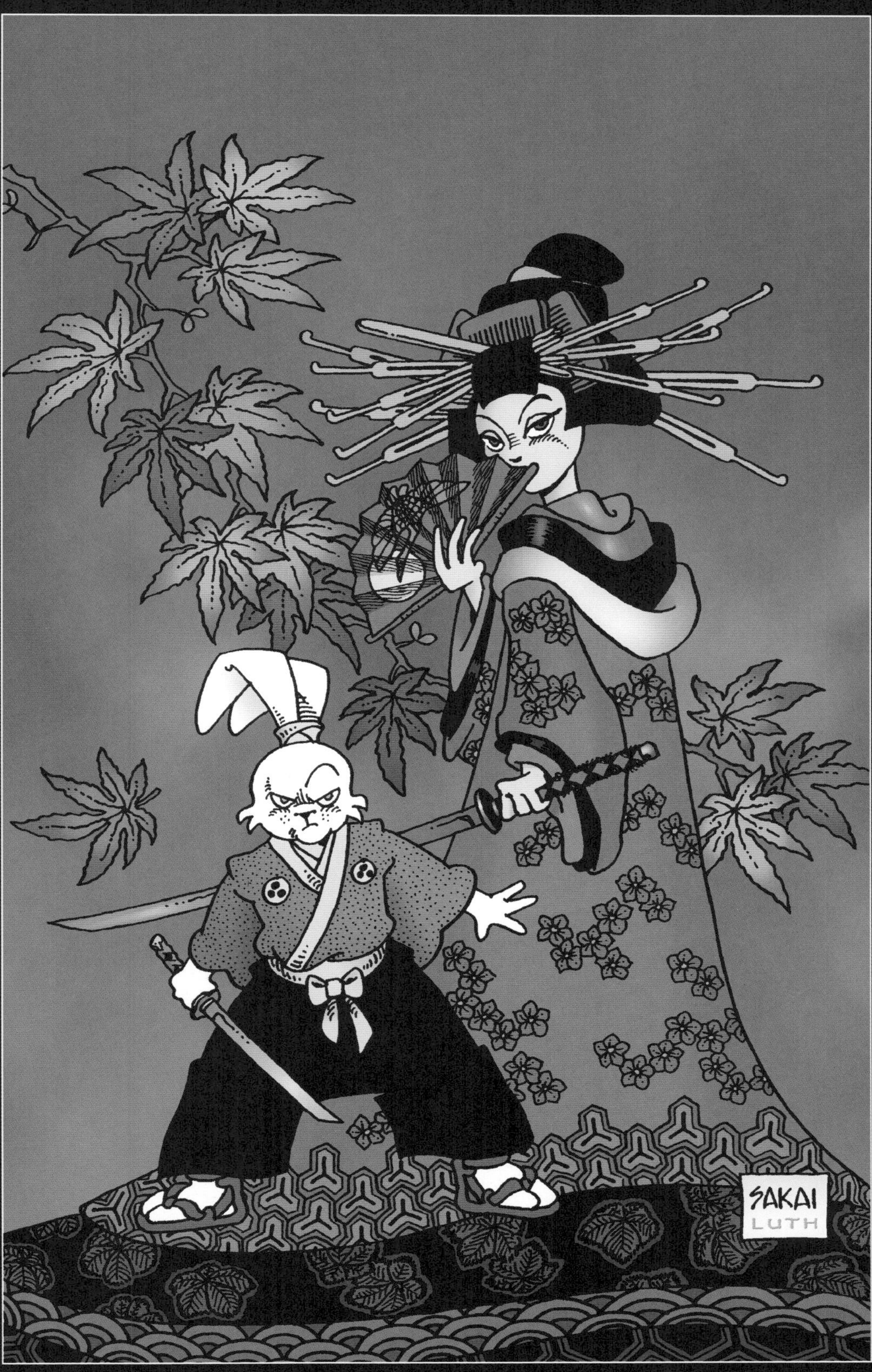
SAKAI
LUTH

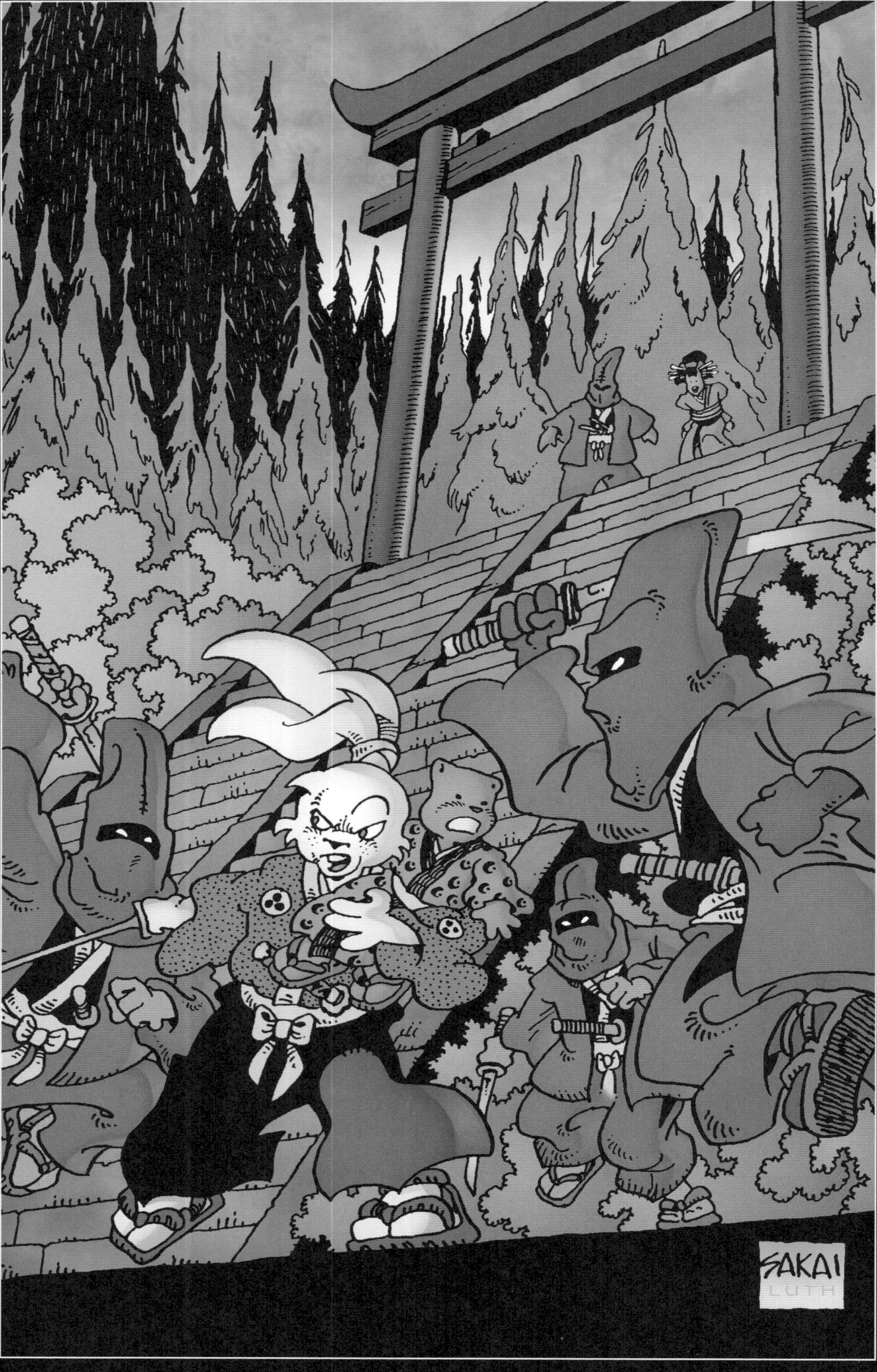
SAKAI
LUTH

Usagi Yojimbo Volume Three #29

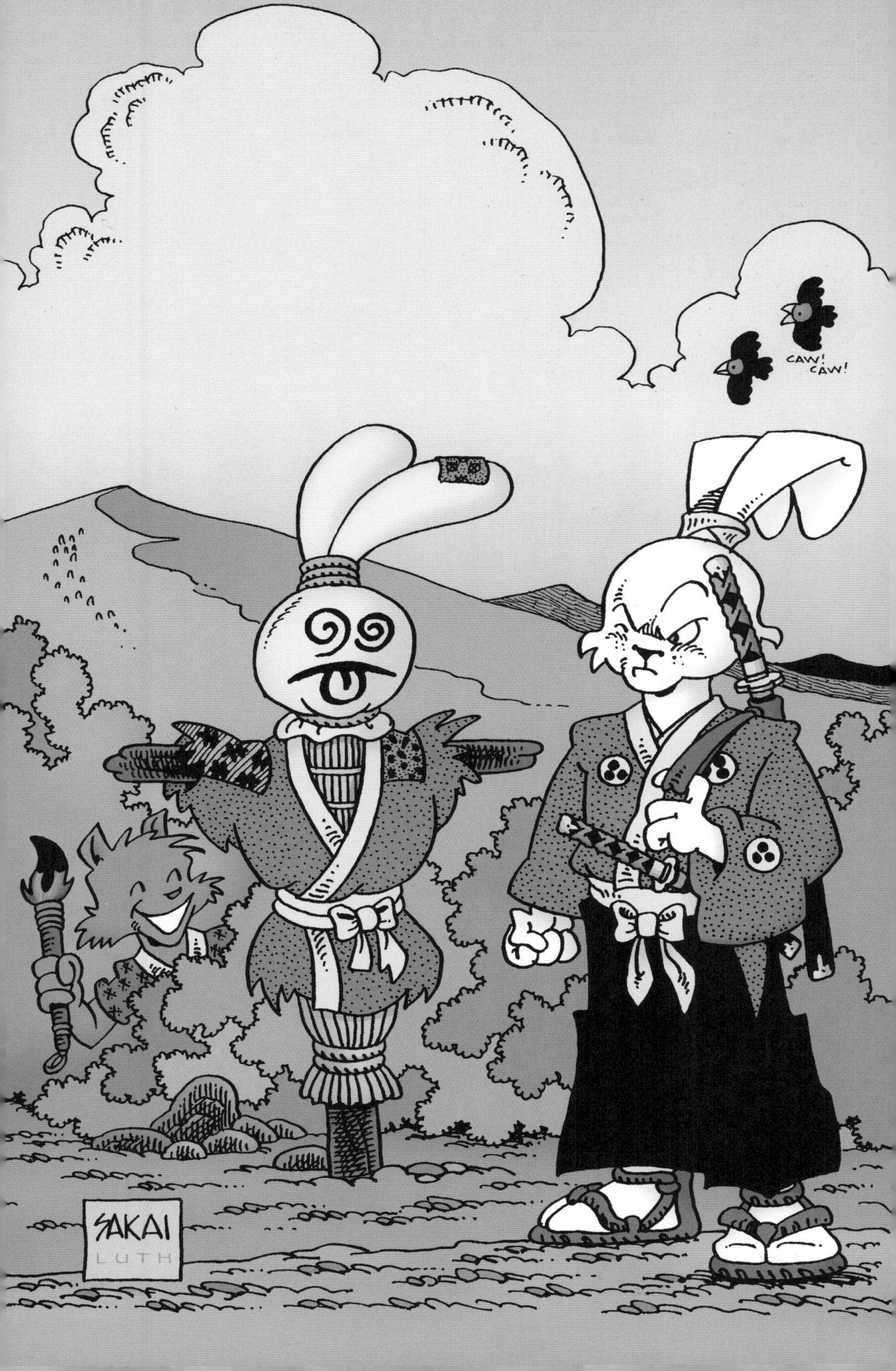
CAW! CAW!
SAKAI
LUTH

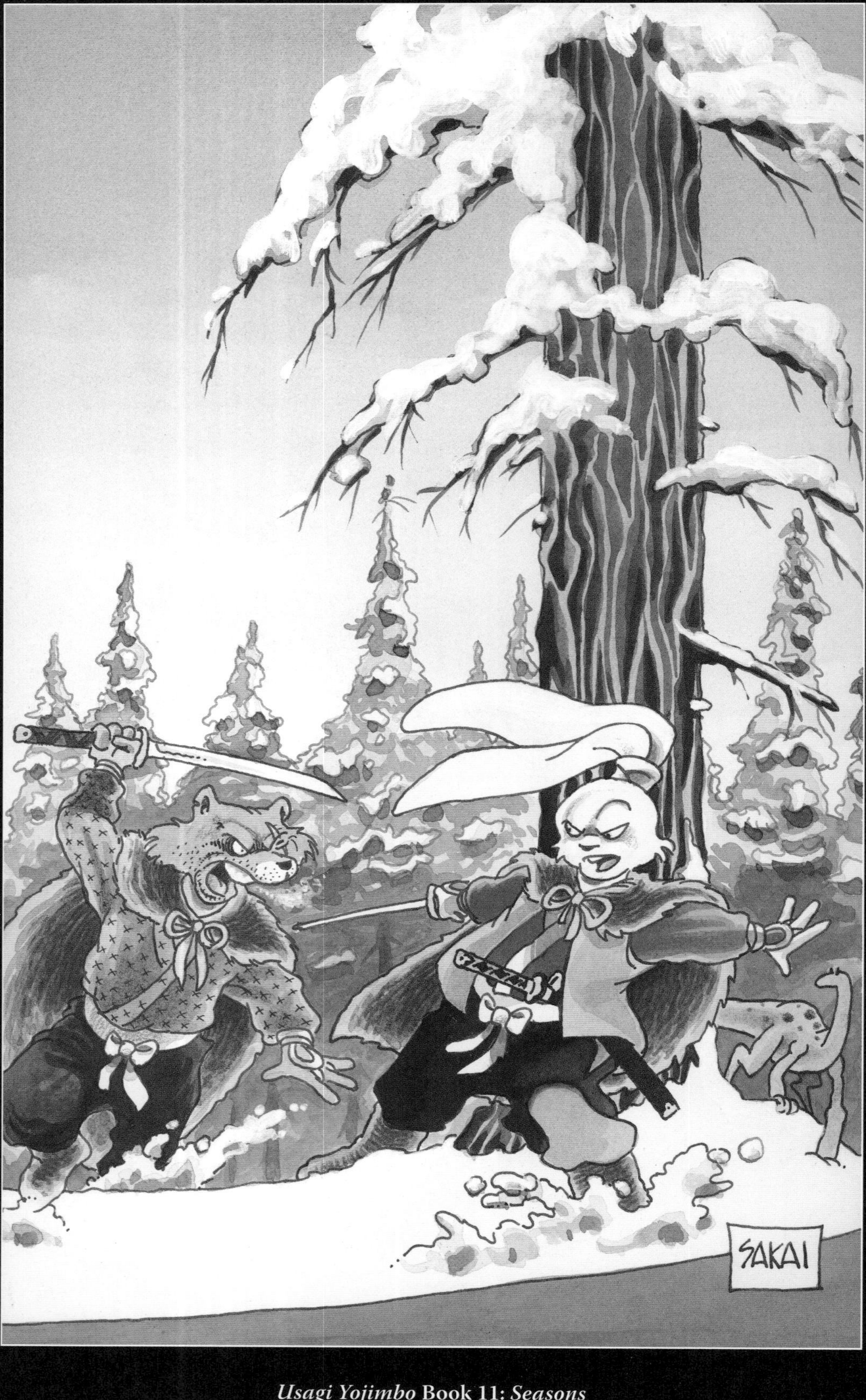
SAKAI

Usagi Yojimbo Book 11: *Seasons*

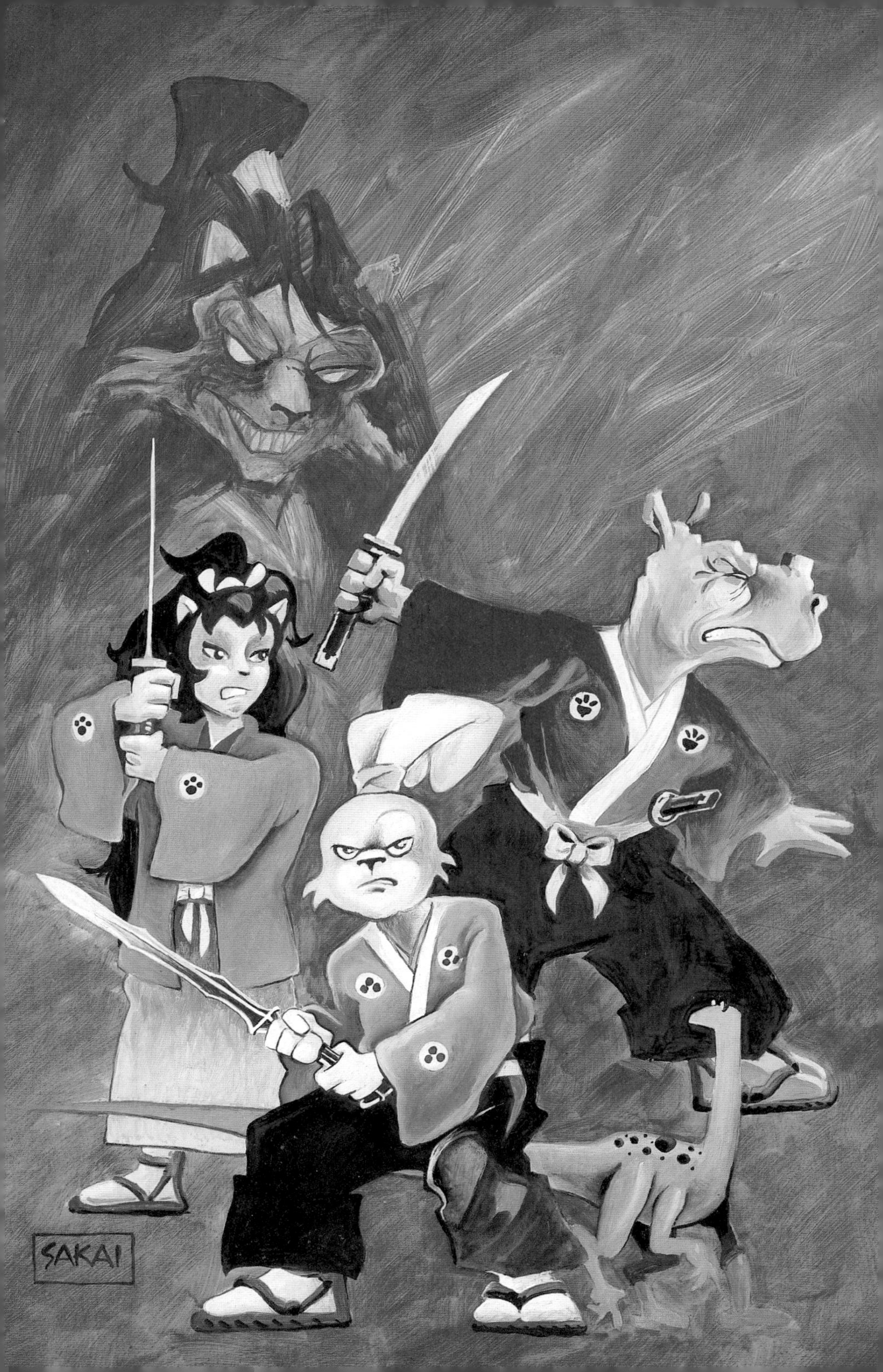
SAKAI

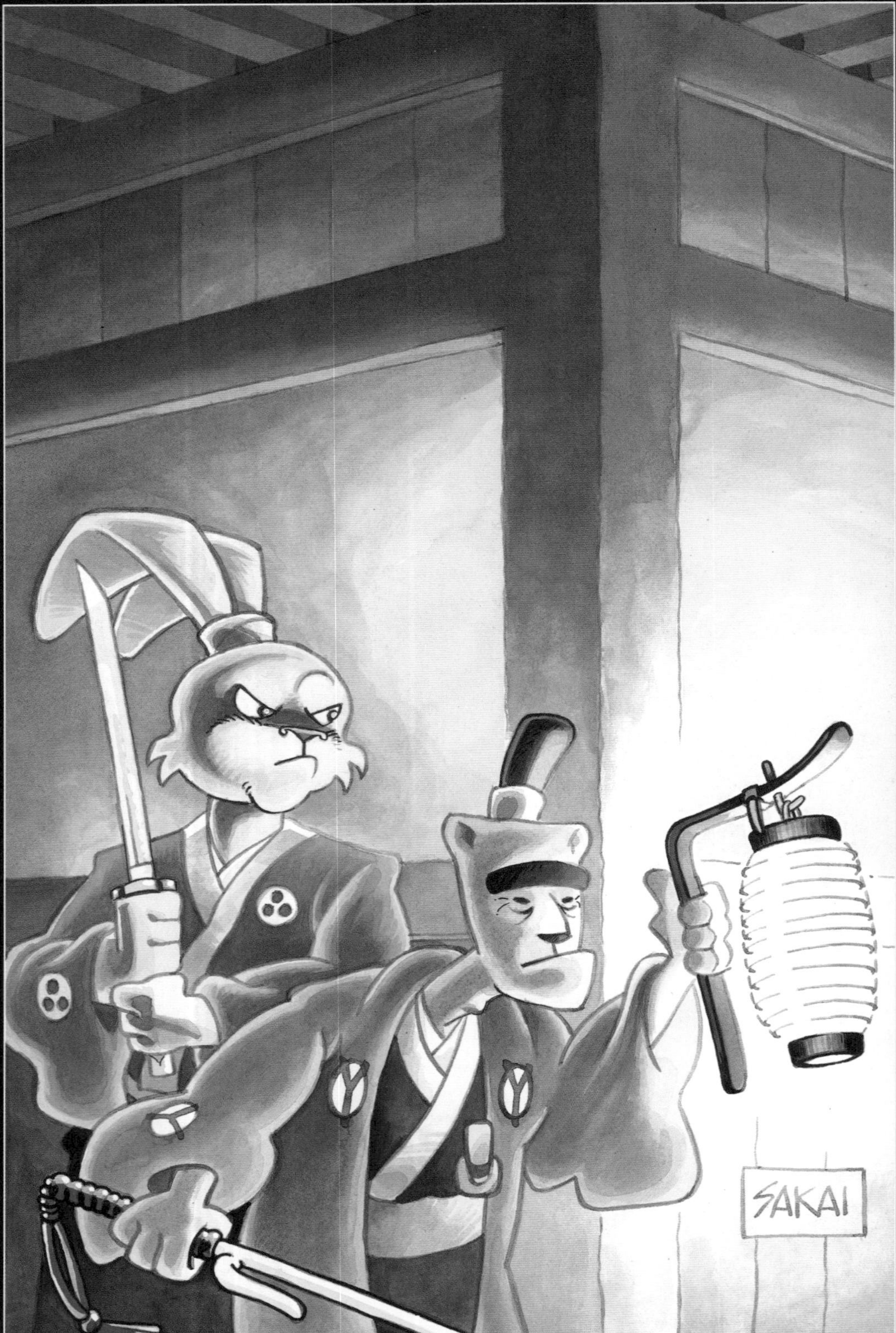
SAKAI

Usagi Yojimbo Book 13: *Grey Shadows*

Stan at the Pyramid of the Sun in Teotihuacán, Mexico. Photo by Sharon Sakai.

STAN SAKAI was born in Kyoto, Japan, grew up in Hawaii, and now lives in California with his wife, Sharon. They have two children, Hannah and Matthew. Stan received a fine arts degree from the University of Hawaii and furthered his studies at the Art Center College of Design in Pasadena, California.

Stan's creation *Usagi Yojimbo* first appeared in comics in 1984. Since then, Usagi has been on television as a guest of the Teenage Mutant Ninja Turtles and has been made into toys, seen on clothing, and featured in a series of graphic novel collections.

In 1991, Stan created *Space Usagi*, a series dealing with samurai in a futuristic setting, featuring the adventures of a descendant of the original Usagi.

Stan is also an award-winning letterer for his work on Sergio Aragonés's *Groo*, the *Spider-Man* Sunday newspaper strips, and *Usagi Yojimbo*.

Stan is the recipient of a Parents' Choice Award, an Inkpot Award, an American Library Association Award, a Harvey Award, four Spanish Haxtur Awards, several Eisner Awards, and most recently an Inkwell Award. In 2002 he won the prestigious National Cartoonists Society Award in the Comic Book division, and in 2011 Stan received the Cultural Ambassador Award from the Japanese American National Museum.

Dark Horse Comics, Inc.

President and Publisher **MIKE RICHARDSON**
Executive Vice President **NEIL HANKERSON**
Chief Financial Officer **TOM WEDDLE**
Vice President of Publishing **RANDY STRADLEY**
Vice President of Book Trade Sales **MICHAEL MARTENS**
Editor in Chief **SCOTT ALLIE**
Vice President of Marketing **MATT PARKINSON**
Vice President of Product Development **DAVID SCROGGY**
Vice President of Information Technology **DALE LAFOUNTAIN**
Senior Director of Print, Design, and Production **DARLENE VOGEL**
General Counsel **KEN LIZZI**
Editorial Director **DAVEY ESTRADA**
Senior Books Editor **CHRIS WARNER**
Executive Editor **DIANA SCHUTZ**
Director of Print and Development **CARY GRAZZINI**
Art Director **LIA RIBACCHI**
Director of Scheduling **CARA NIECE**
Director of Digital Publishing **MARK BERNARDI**

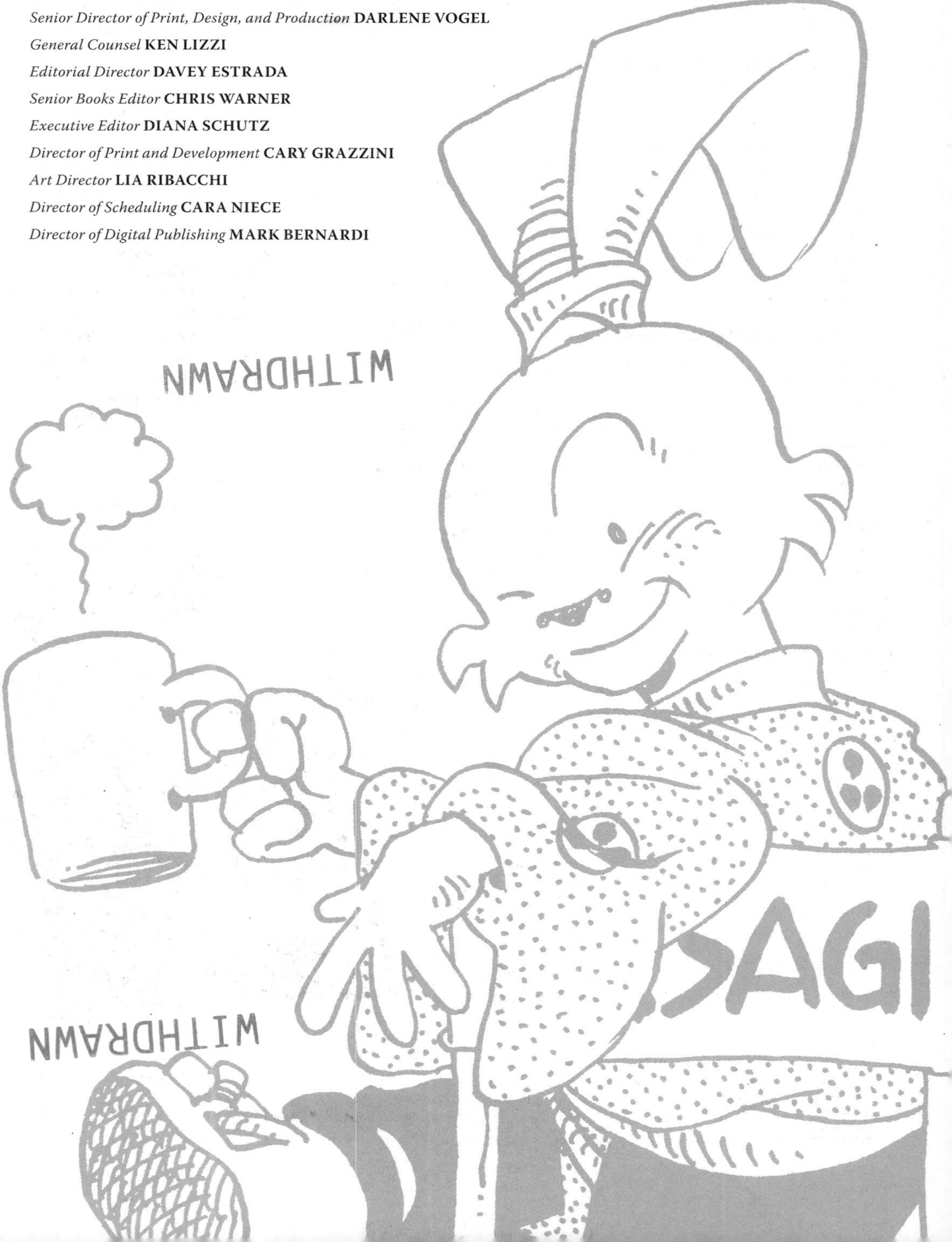
SAGI

WITHDRAWN
WITHDRAWN